THE OXFORD HANDBOOK OF

THE ETHIOPIAN ECONOMY

Dear Mark,

Arkebe

27 March 2019

THE OXFORD HANDBOOK OF THE ETHIOPIAN ECONOMY

Edited by
FANTU CHERU, CHRISTOPHER CRAMER,
and
ARKEBE OQUBAY

OXFORD
UNIVERSITY PRESS

OXFORD
UNIVERSITY PRESS

Great Clarendon Street, Oxford, OX2 6DP,
United Kingdom

Oxford University Press is a department of the University of Oxford.
It furthers the University's objective of excellence in research, scholarship,
and education by publishing worldwide. Oxford is a registered trade mark of
Oxford University Press in the UK and in certain other countries

First Edition published in 2019

Impression: 1

Published in the United States of America by Oxford University Press
198 Madison Avenue, New York, NY 10016, United States of America

British Library Cataloguing in Publication Data
Data available

Library of Congress Control Number: 2018954094

ISBN 978-0-19-881498-6

Printed and bound by
L.E.G.O. S.p.A., Lavis (TN), Italy

Acknowledgements

We set off on the journey of this *Oxford Handbook of the Ethiopian Economy* in 2015 and it has been quite an experience. We have all learned new things about Ethiopia and about editing through working on this project, and we have deepened our own friendships through the experience. We have relied on a great deal of enthusiasm and hard work from many people to produce this work and to do so within a tight timeframe.

In particular, the editors thank all seventy contributors to the *Handbook* for their commitment and tireless efforts to ensure the success of the first Oxford University Press economics handbook on an individual African economy, despite many other personal commitments. We also thank all those contributors, from Ethiopia and abroad, who attended one, two, and in some cases all three of our contributors' workshops in Addis Ababa, giving presentations and making extremely constructive comments that helped the chapters, and the *Handbook* overall, take shape and deepen in its quality.

The editors thank commissioning editor Adam Swallow of Oxford University Press and his team for their outstanding support, wisdom, and encouragement throughout the project, as well as the anonymous reviewers who helped us improve the initial proposal, and the OUP delegates who approved the final version of our proposal.

The draft chapters of the *Handbook* benefited immensely from the critical reviews and valuable comments received from many internal and external reviewers. The editors are particularly grateful to Professor Mohamed Salih, Erasmus University (Holland), and Professor Peter Lawrence, University of Keele, for their support. Among our 'internal' reviewers we received particularly dedicated help from Professor Christopher Clapham (University of Cambridge) and Professor John Sender (SOAS, University of London). We also had invaluable help from other external reviewers including Professor Ben Fine (SOAS) and Professor Vishnu Padayachee (University of the Witwatersrand). Special thanks also go to Keith Povey and his team for the copy-editing of the volume.

The editors also thank the following government offices for providing the necessary information and data, which has been a tremendous input for the volume: the Ministry of Finance and Economic Cooperation, the Ethiopian Revenue and Customs Authority, the National Bank of Ethiopia, the National Planning Commission, the Central Statistical Agency, the Ministry of Industry, the Ministry of Foreign Affairs and the Ethiopian Investment Commission.

Many thanks go to the various institutions that provided valuable operational and administrative support to the project. Of particular mention are: the Ethiopian Development Research Institute and the Ethiopian Economic Association. The editors are especially grateful for the generous financial assistance received from the Bill and Melinda Gates Foundation and the Swedish Embassy in Addis Ababa, as well as the New Venture Foundation in Washington, DC for funding that made it possible for Christopher Cramer to work on the *Handbook*.

We also want to extend sincere thanks to Ethiopian Airlines for providing continuing logistical support to international collaborating scholars throughout the process. We thank Dr Alemayehu Tafesse (IFPRI), Professor Akbar Noman (Columbia University), Dr Abraham Tekeste (MOFEC), and Mr. Haddis Tadesse (Bill and Melinda Gates Foundation) for their continued personal support for the project, and 251 Communications for the cover design.

And finally, our sincere appreciation goes to Deborah M. Kefale for her consistent support and management of the project over the last twenty-four months. Thanks also to our dedicated research assistants Meron Tilahun and Yohannes Ghebru, our admin assistant Sergut Abate and the following interns who contributed to the success of the three workshops held in Addis Ababa: Tsion Kifle, Koen Maaskant, Edom W. Haile, Mussie Tsegaye, and Emmanuel Merissa.

Contents

PART II ECONOMIC DEVELOPMENT

PART III SOCIAL POLICY AND DEVELOPMENT

PART IV AGRICULTURE AND RURAL TRANSFORMATION

PART V INDUSTRIALIZATION AND URBAN DEVELOPMENT

PART VI STRUCTURAL TRANSFORMATION AND THE AFRICAN CONTEXT

List of Figures and Maps

Figures

Maps

List of Tables

List of Acronyms

5DE	Five Dimension Endowment
AAAE	African Association of Agricultural Economists
AACCSA	Addis Ababa Chamber of Commerce and Sectoral Association
ACC	Agriculture Commercialization Cluster
ACCORD	African Centre for the Constructive Resolution of Disputes
ACET	African Center for Economic Transformation
ACIAR	Australian Centre for International Agricultural Research
ADF	African Development Forum
ADLI	Agricultural Development-Led Industrialization
AERC	African Economic Research Consortium
AfCFTA	African Continental Free Trade Area
AFD	Agence Française de Développement (French Development Agency)
AfDB	Africa Development Bank
AFP BP	African Program Briefing Paper
AFTES	Africa Technical Department, Environmentally Sustainable
AGOA	African Growth and Opportunity Act
AGP	Agricultural Growth Program
AgSS	Agricultural Sample Survey
AIDS	Acquired Immune Deficiency Syndrome
AKLDP	Agriculture Knowledge, Learning, Documentation and Policy Project
AMD	Agribusiness Marketing and Development Project
AMISOM	African Union Mission in Somalia
ANDM	Amhara National Democratic Movement
ANH-FEWG	Agriculture, Nutrition and Health Academy Food Environment Working Group
ASF	animal-sourced food
ATA	Agricultural Transformation Agency
AU	African Union
BBC	British Broadcasting Corporation
BIS	Bank for International Settlement
BITs	Bilateral Investment Treaties
BMC	BioMed Center
BMI	Body Mass Index
BoP	Bern open Publishing
BPR	business process re-engineering

CAADP	Comprehensive Africa Agriculture Development Programme
CAD	computer-aided design
CAE	Centre of African Economies
CAF	Charities Aid Foundation
CAFTA	Central America Free Trade Agreement
CAGR	Compound Annual Growth Rate
CALASIATIC	California Asiatic Oil Company
CBB	Construction and Business Bank
CBE	Commercial Bank of Ethiopia
CCI	Council of Constitutional Inquiry
CDE	Centre for Development and Environment
CDP	Committee for Development Policy
CDR	Center for Development Research
CFSVA	Comprehensive Food Security and Vulnerability Analysis
CGE	Computable General Equilibrium
CITI	Clothing Industry Training Institute
CMC	Coffee Marketing Corporation
CMO	Commodities
CMT	cut-make-trim
CODESERIA	Council for the Development of Social Science Research in Africa
COGD	Cost of Government Day
COI	Country of Origin Information
COMESA	Common Market for East and Southern Africa
COMPETE	Competitiveness Employing Information Communication Technologies
CPC	Civil Procedure Code
CPI	Consumer Price Index
CPRC	Chronic Poverty Research Centre
CRGE	Climate Resilient Green Economy
CSA	Central Statistical Agency
CTA	Commodity Trade
CTDMA	Coffee and Tea Development and Marketing Agency
CUD	Coalition for Unity and Democracy
DBE	Development Bank of Ethiopia
DD	Dire Dewa
Derg	Coordinating Committee of the Armed Forces, Police, and Territorial Army
DESA	Department of Economic and Social Affairs
DfID	Department for International Development
DHS	Demographic Health Survey
DIIS-GOVESA	Danish Institute of International Studies
DRC	Democratic Republic of Congo

DSA	debt sustainability analysis
EA	enumeration area
EAL	Ethiopian Airlines
EBA	Everything But Arms
ECR-3G2P	Ethiopian Resilient Cities, Green Growth and Governance Programs and Packages
ECCSA	Ethiopian Chamber of Commerce and Sectoral Association
ECEA	Ethiopian Commodity Exchange Authority
ECSU	Elizabeth City State University
ECX	Ethiopian Commodity Exchange
EDHS	Ethiopian Demographic and Health Survey
EDRI	Ethiopian Development Research Institute
EDRI–ESSP	Ethiopian Development Research Institute–Ethiopia Strategy Support Program
EEA	European Economic Area
EEPCo	Ethiopian Electric Power Corporation
EES	Ethiopian Electric Service
EEU	Ethiopian Electric Utility
EFFORT	Endowment Fund for the Rehabilitation of Tigray
EGRA	Early Grade Reading Assessment
EGS	Employment Generation Schemes
EGTE	Ethiopian Grain Trade Enterprise
EHDA	Ethiopian Horticulture Development Agency
EHPEA	Ethiopian Horticulture Producers and Exporters Association
EHRS	Electronic Health Records System
EIAR	Ethiopian Institute of Agricultural Research
EIC	Ethiopian Investment Commission
EIP	Eastern Industrial Park
EKI	Ethiopian Kaizen Institute
ELI	export-led industrialization
ELIA	Ethiopian Leather Industry Association
EPCC	Ethiopian Panel on Climate Change
EPLF	Eritrean People's Liberation Front
EPPCF	Ethiopian Public Private Consultative Forum
EPRDF	Ethiopian People's Revolutionary Democratic Front
EPZs	Export Process Zones
ERA	Ethiopian Roads Authority
ERC	Ethiopian Railways Corporation
ERCA	Ethiopian Revenue and Customs Authority
ERRP	Emergency Recovery and Reconstruction Program
ERSS	Ethiopia Rural Socio-economic Survey
ESDP I	Education Sector Development Program I

ESDP II	Education Sector Development Program II
ESDP III	Education Sector Development Program III
ESDP IV	Education Sector Development Program IV
ESDPs	Education Sector Development Programs
ESID	Effective States and Inclusive Development
ESLSE	Ethiopian Shipping and Logistics Service Enterprise
ESSP	Ethiopia Strategy Support Program
ESSP/IFPRI	Ethiopia Strategy Support Program/International Food Policy Research Institute
ESSP-II	Ethiopia Strategy Support Program-II
ET	Ethiopian
ETB	Ethiopian Birr
ETDZ	Economic and Technological Development Zones
ETGA	Ethiopia Garment
ETP	Education and Training Policy
EU	European Union
EUTF REF	European Trust Fund, The Research and Evidence Facility
EXPY	export-to-output Ratio
FAO	Food and Agriculture Organization of the United Nations
FDI	Foreign Direct Investment
FDRE	Federal Democratic Republic of Ethiopia
FET	Fair and Equitable Treatment
FGT	Foster, Greer, and Thorbecke
FHC	Federal High Court
FMoH	Federal Minister of Health
FOB	free on board
FPTP	first past the post
FSS	Forum for Social Studies
FSU	Former Soviet Union
FTAs	Free Trade Areas
FTEPR	Fair Trade, Employment, and Poverty Reduction
FY	fiscal year
GAMS	General Algebraic Modelling System
GCI	Global Competitiveness Index
GDP	gross domestic product
GEQUIP	General Education Quality Improvement Program III
GER	gross enrolment rate
GERD	Grand Ethiopian Renaissance Dam
GFCF	gross fixed capital formation
GFDRE	Government of the Federal Democratic Republic of Ethiopia
GGDC	Groningen Growth and Development Center
GGGI	Global Green Growth Institute
GHG	greenhouse gas

GIC	growth incidence curve
GIFF	Growth Identification and Facilitation Framework
GIGA	German Institute of Global and Area Studies
GIZ	*Deutsche Gesellschaft für Internationale Zusammenarbeit*
GMM	generalized method of moments
GMPI	Global Multidimensional Poverty Index
GNI	gross national income
GOE	Government of Ethiopia
GPA	grade point average
GPC	Quality Productivity and Competitiveness
GR	gratuitous relief
GRIPS	Graduate Institute for Policy Studies
GTP-I	Growth and Transformation Plan I
GTP-II	Growth and Transformation Plan II
GVA	gross value added
GVCs	global value chains
HABP	Household Asset Building Programme
HAZ	height-for-age Z-scores
HCEE	household consumption and expenditure
HEA	household economy analysis
HEP	Health Extension Programme
HH	household
HICEs	Household Income and Consumption Expenditure Surveys
HIID	Harvard Institute of International Development
HIPC	heavily indebted poor countries
HOF	House of the Federation
HPG	Humanitarian Policy Group
HPR	House of Peoples Representatives
HTSP	Health Sector Transformation Plan
IBTE	Imperial Board of Telecommunications of Ethiopia
ICF	International Classification of Functioning, Disability, and Health
ICO	International Coffee Organization
ICO/CFC	International Coffee Organization/Common Fund for Commodities
ICSID	International Center for Settlement of Investment Disputes
ICT	information communication technology
IDA	International Development Association
IDE-JETRO	Institute of Developing Economies-Japan External Trade Organisation
IDR	Institute of Development Research
IDS	Industrial Development Strategy
IDSE	Industrial Development Strategy of Ethiopia
IEA	International Energy Agency
IES	Industry Extension Service
IFAD	International Fund for Agricultural Development

IFPRI	International Food Policy Research Institute
IGAD	Intergovernmental Authority on Development
IGC	International Growth Centre
IGE	Institute for Global Ethics
IHA	Imperial Highways Authority
IHSN	International Household Survey Network
IIED	International Institute for Environment and Development
ILO	International Labour Organization
IMF	International Monetary Fund
IMF/WB	International Monetary Fund/World Bank
IMMANA	Innovation Methods and Metrics for Agriculture and Nutrition Actions
IMR	infant mortality rate
INDC	Intended Nationally Determined Contributions
INSE	Inspired Energy
INDSTAT	Industrial Statistics
INV	investment rate
IP	Identity Preserved
IPs	industrial parks
IPDC	Industrial Park Development Corporation
IPE	interprofessional education
IPR	import penetration rate
ISDS	Investor-State Dispute Settlement
ISEN	Institute for the Study of Ethiopian Nationalities
ISI	import-substitution industrialization
ITC	International Trade Center
JARC	Jimma Agricultural Research Centre
JBIC	Japan Bank for International Cooperation
JETRO	Japan External Trade Organization
JICA	Japan International Cooperation Agency
KDB	Korea Development Bank
KDI	Korea Development Institute
KIP	Kunshan Industrial Park
KKR	Kohlberg, Kravis Roberts & Co.
KMT	Kuomingtang
KSP	Knowledge Sharing Program
LDCs	Least Developed Countries
LEWIE	Local Economy-Wide Impact Evaluation
LFS	Labour Force Survey
LIDI	Leather Industry Development Institute
LIAMCO	Libya American Oil Co
LMSM	large- and medium-scale manufacturing
LOWES	locally weighted scatterplot smoothing
LSE	London School of Economics

LSMS-ISA	Living Standards Measurement Study-Integrated Surveys on Agriculture
M2 GDP	money supply gross domestic product
MBS	marginal budget share
MCB	Ministry of Capacity Building
MCSER	Mediterranean Center of Social and Educational Research
MDGs	Millennium Development Goals
MDDI	Meat and Dairy Industry Development Institute
MEFCC	Ministry of Environment, Forest, and Climate Change
MERIT	Maastricht Economic and Social Research Institute on Innovation and Technology
METEC	Metals and Engineering Corporation
METI	Ministry of Economy, Trade, and Industry
MFN	Most Favoured Nation
MIDI	Metals Industry Development Institute
MIDROC	Mohammed International Development Research and Organization Companies
MIGA	Multilateral Investment Guarantee Agency
MITI	Ministry of International Trade and Industry
MLRA	Ministry of Land Reform and Administration
MLSM	medium and large-scale manufacturing
MMR	maternal mortality rate
MoE	Ministry of Education
MoFA	Ministry of Foreign Affairs
MOFCOM	Ministry of Commerce of People's Republic of China
MoFEC	Ministry of Finance and Economic Cooperation
MoFED	Ministry of Finance and Economic Development
MoI	Ministry of Industry
MoLSA	Ministry of Labor and Social Affairs
MoPED	Ministry of Planning and Economic Development
MoST	Mobile Security Technologies
MoT	Ministry of Transport
MoT	Ministry of Trade
MoU	Memorandum of Understanding
MoWIE	Ministry of Water, Irrigation, and Electricity, Ethiopia
MPDC	Metal Products Development Center
MPI	Multidimensional Poverty Index
MSE	micro and small enterprises
MSIP	Multi-Sector Investment Plan
MTD	Mettler Toledo
MTT	Maria Theresa Thaler
MUDH	Ministry of Urban Development and Housing
MUDHCo	Ministry of Urban Development, Housing and Construction

NAP-GE	National Action Plan for Gender Equality
NBDC	Nile Basin Development Challenge
NBE	National Bank of Ethiopia
NBER	National Bureau of Economic Research
NCD	non-communicable disease
NCE	National Export Committee
NCOT	net commercial off-take
NECC	National Export Coordinating Council
NEPAD	New Partnership for Africa's Development
NER	net enrolment rate
NGO	non-governmental organization
NIR	net intake rate
NLA	National Learning Assessments
NLFS	National Labour Force Survey Program
NNP	National Nutrition Programme
NNP II	National Nutrition Programme II
NN&P	Nations, Nationalities and Peoples
NPC	National Planning Commission
NPL	non-performing loan
NPO	non-profit organization
NSE	New Structural Economics
NSOs	National Statistical Organizations
NT	National Treatment
NTBs	non-tariff barriers
OBM	original brand manufacturing
ODI	Overseas Development Institute
ODM	original design manufacturer
OECD	Organisation for Economic Co-operation and Development
ÖFSE	Austrian Foundation for Development Research
OFSP	Other Food Security Programme
OLF	Oromo Liberation Front
OPDO	Oromo Peoples' Democratic Organization
OPHC	Office of the Population and Housing Census
OPHI	Oxford Poverty and Human Development Initiative
OSS	Operational Support Services
OSSREA	Organization for Social Science Research in Eastern and Southern Africa
PA	Peasant Association
PADEP	Peasant Agricultural Development Extension Project
PASDEP	Plan for Accelerated and Sustained Development to End Poverty
PASDEP II	Plan for Accelerated and Sustained Development to End Poverty II
PCA	principal components analysis
PCP	Programme for Country Partnership

PDRE	People's Democratic Republic of Ethiopia
PEA	private employment agencies
PFFSPA	Policy Framework for Food Security in Pastoral Areas
PFP	Policy Framework Paper
PIDC	Program-for-Results Information Document Concept Stage
PMO	Prime Minister's Office
POSCO	Pohang Iron and Steel Company
PPG	public and publicly guaranteed
PPP	purchasing power parity
PPS	proportional to size
PR	public relations
PRSP	Poverty Reduction Strategy Papers
PSD	private sector development
PSL	parallel strand lumber
PSNP	Productive Safety Net Program
PSRC	Policy Study Research Centre
PW	public water
PWT	Penn World Tables
QEH	Queen Elizabeth House
QGRL	Quantum Global Research Lab
QPC	Quality, Productivity, and Competitiveness
R&D	research and development
RAI	Relative Autonomy Index
RCMs	Reciprocal Control Mechanisms
REDD+	Reducing Emissions from Deforestation and Forest Degradation
REST	Relief Society of Tigray
RMMS	Regional Mixed Migration Secretariat
ROE	returns on equity
ROW	rest of the world
RPK	Revenue Passenger Kilometre
RRC	Relief and Rehabilitation Commission
RSDP	Road Sector Development Program
RTC	Rural Transformation Centers
SAC	structural adjustment credit
SAF	structural adjustment facility
SAM	Social Accounting Matrix
SAP	Structural Adjustment Programme
SCRP	Social Conversation Research Program
SDI	Simple Deprivation Index
SDPRP	Sustainable Development and Poverty Reduction Program
SEPDM	Southern Ethiopian People's Democratic Movement
SEZs	Special Economic Zones
SLITA	Sri Lanka Institute of Textile and Apparel

SLM	Sustainable Land Management
SME	small and medium-sized enterprise
SNA	System of National Accounts
SNNP	Southern Nation Nationalities and Peoples
SNNPR	Southern Nation Nationalities and Peoples Region
SOAS	School of Oriental and African Studies, University of London
SOE	state-owned enterprises
SSA	sub-Saharan Africa
SSM	small-scale manufacturing
SSRN	Social Science Research Network.
STAARS	Structural Transformation of African Agriculture and Rural Spaces
STI	science, technology, and innovation
SWC	soil and water conservation
T & G	textile and garment
TEDA	Tianjin Economic Development Area
TFP	total factor productivity
TFR	total fertility rate
TGE	Transitional Government of Ethiopia
TICAD IV	Tokyo International Conference on African Development IV
TIDI	Textile Industry Development Institute
TLUS	tropical livestock units
TMD	temporomandibular disorders
TPLF	Tigray People's Liberation Front
TTSC	Textile Training and Services Centre
TWA	Trans World Airlines
TVET	Technical and Vocational Education and Training
U5MR	under-five and maternal mortality rates
UAE	United Arab Emirates
UCT/CCT	unconditional cash transfer/conditional cash transfer
UEUS	users and uses
UN	United Nations
UNECA	United Nations, Economic Commission of Africa
UN-ECA	United Nation Economic Commission for Africa
UN-Habitat	United Nations-Habitat
UN Women	United Nations Entity for Gender Equality and the Empowerment of Women
UNCITRAL	United Nations Commission on International Trade Law
UNCTAD	United Nations Conference on Trade and Development
UNDP	United Nations Development Program
UNDESA	United Nations Department of Economic and Social Affairs
UNEP	United Nations Environment Programme
UNESCO	United Nations Educational Scientific and Cultural Organization
UNFPA	United Nations Fund for Population

UNFCCC	United Nations Framework Convention on Climate Change
UNHCR	United Nations High Commissioner for Refugees
UNICEF	United Nations International Children's Emergency Fund
UNIDO	United Nations Industrial Development Organization
UNJP-RWEE	United Nations Joint Programme on Rural Women's Economic Empowerment
UN OCHA	United Nations Office for the Coordination of Humanitarian Affairs
UNRTSD	United Nations Research Institute for Social Development
UN–REDD	United Nations–Reducing Emissions from Deforestation and Forest Degradation
UNU	United Nations University
UNU-MERIT	United Nations University–Maastricht Economic and Social Research Institute on Innovation and Technology
UNU-WIDER	United Nations University–World Institute for Development Economics Research
USAID	United States Agency for International Development
USDA	United States Department of Agriculture
USMR	US Mounted Rifles
USSR	Union of Soviet Socialist Republics
VAT	value added tax
VSS	Voluntary Sustainability Standards
WDI	World Development Indicators
WDR	World Development Report
WEAI	Women's Empowerment in Agricultural Index
WFO	workforce optimization
WFP	World Food Programme
WIPO	World Intellectual Property Organization
WHO	World Health Organization
WMO	World Meteorological Organization
WPE	Workers' Party of Ethiopia
WTO	World Trade Organization

List of Contributors

Teferi Abate Adem, PhD, is a research anthropologist at HRAF (Yale University), specializing in the local agrarian and ecological impacts of expanding state powers, global market forces, and climate-change-induced environmental shocks. His publications explore these issues both ethnographically among smallholder households in Ethiopia and through cross-cultural comparison of agrarian societies from other societies and times.

Kibrom A. Abay, PhD, is a postdoctoral researcher at the International Livestock Research Institute (ILRI). Kibrom's research interest lies at the intersection of agricultural, behavioural, and development economics. Most of his research involves applied micro-econometrics and policy evaluation methods. He is an expert on impact evaluation methods and has recently worked on rural finance and rural credit markets. He holds MSc and PhD degrees in economics from the University of Copenhagen.

Edlam Abera Yemeru, PhD, heads the urbanization section in the Social Development Policy division of the UNECA where she leads the development of policy knowledge and tools to support African member states in leveraging the potential of urbanization for accelerated and inclusive growth and structural transformation. Previously, she held research, teaching, and programmatic positions in the field of urban development at UN-Habitat, and at academic and research institutes. Edlam holds a PhD in human geography from the University of London.

K. Y. Amoako began his career in 1974 at the World Bank, becoming the Bank's director for education and social policy from 1992 to 1995 before joining ECA as executive secretary from 1995 to 2005. In 2008, he founded the African Center for Economic Transformation, an economic policy institute headquartered in Accra and working across Africa with the mission of supporting the economic transformation of African countries. K. Y. Amoako holds a PhD in economics from the University of California, Berkeley.

Mesele W. Araya is an assistant professor of economics at Addis Ababa University. Before joining AAU, he worked as a quantitative researcher for Young Lives based at the Ethiopian Development Research Institute, and as a research associate for ADAPT Labour Studies in Italy. He also is a consultant and policy adviser to public and private institutes on issues related to poverty and inequality, the youth labour market, and the economics of education.

Berihu Assefa Gebrehiwot, PhD, is a research fellow at the Ethiopian Development Research Institute (EDRI). He specializes in development economics and his research more broadly features the application of microeconomics and microeconometrics to the policy analyses of economic development problems in developing countries in general and Ethiopia in particular. Berihu received his PhD in development economics from the National Graduate Institute for Policy Studies (GRIPS), Tokyo in 2013.

Yohannes Ayalew Birru, PhD, is the vice governor and chief economist of Ethiopia's central bank (National Bank of Ethiopia). He is a member of the board of directors of the National Bank of Ethiopia and chairman of the African Trade Insurance (ATI), among other responsibilities. He has over twenty-eight years of cumulative experience in the areas of finance, monetary policy, and economic growth. He holds a PhD in economics from the University of Sussex.

Fantu Bachewe, PhD, is a research coordinator at IFPRI-ESSP. He received his PhD from the University of Minnesota in 2009. Research topics he has investigated include: productivity and efficiency in crop production; rural labour markets and non-farm employment; livestock production and prices; and food prices and nutrition availability. His general research interests are development economics, efficiency and productivity analyses, household modelling, and monitoring and evaluation.

Shiferaw Bekele is professor emeritus at Addis Ababa University, where he has taught modern Ethiopian history, and colonial and contemporary African history for many years. His research interests cover the economic, social, and political history of modern and contemporary Ethiopia.

Guush Berhane, PhD, is a research fellow at the Development Strategy and Governance Division of the International Food Policy Research Institute (IFPRI), based at IFPRI's Ethiopia Strategy Support Programme (ESSP) in Addis Ababa, Ethiopia. His research interests include microeconomic analyses of smallholder household behaviour, livelihoods, food and nutrition security, and agricultural transformation.

Ha-Joon Chang teaches economics at the University of Cambridge. His main books include *Kicking away the Ladder*, *Bad Samaritans*, *23 Things They Don't Tell You about Capitalism*, and *Economics: The User's Guide*. By 2018, his writing has been translated into forty-one languages in forty-four countries. Worldwide, his books have sold around 2 million copies. He is the winner of the 2003 Gunnar Myrdal Prize and the 2005 Wassily Leontief Prize.

Fantu Cheru is emeritus professor of international relations, American University (Washington, DC) and a senior researcher at the African Studies Centre, Leiden University (The Netherlands). Between 1998 and 2001, Dr Cheru was the UN special rapporteur on foreign debt for the Human Rights Commission in Geneva. He was associate senior fellow at the Stockholm International Peace Research Institute (Sweden), and the North-South Institute (Ottawa, Canada). From 2007 to 2012, Cheru was research director at the Nordic Africa Institute in Uppsala, Sweden. Dr Cheru was a member of

UN Secretary-General Kofi Annan's Panel on Mobilizing International Support for the New Partnership for African Development (2005–7) as well as convener of the Global Economic Agenda Track of the Helsinki Process on Globalization and Democracy (Finland). Dr Cheru has served as both adviser and consultant to many governments and donor institutions and is on the editorial board of several scholarly journals. He has also authored several books including *The Rise of China and India in Africa* (Zed Books, 2012), with Obi; and *Africa and International Relations in the 21st Century* (Palgrave Macmillan, 2015), with Cornellison and Shaw.

Christopher Clapham is based at the Centre of African Studies, Cambridge University. Professor Clapham specializes in the politics of Ethiopia and the Horn of Africa, and his books include *Haile-Selassie's Government* (1969), *Transformation and Continuity in Revolutionary Ethiopia* (1988), *Africa and the International System* (1996), *African Guerrillas* (1998), and *The Horn of Africa: State Formation and Decay* (2017).

Ken Coutts is a senior research associate at the Centre for Business Research, Judge Business School, University of Cambridge and life fellow of Selwyn College, Cambridge. His main interests are in applied macroeconomics, monetary and fiscal policy, trade, capital flows, and balance of payments. He has published widely in these areas and has also written extensively on price setting in UK manufacturing industries.

Christopher Cramer is professor of the political economy of development at SOAS, University of London. He is a fellow of the Academy of Social Sciences, vice-chair of the Royal African Society, and a former chair of the Centre of African Studies in the University of London. He is chair of the International Scientific Committee of the African Programme on Rethinking Development Economics (APORDE). His publications include the prize-winning *Civil War Is Not a Stupid Thing: Accounting for Violence in Developing Countries* (Hurst, 2006), *African Economic Development: Evidence, Theory, and Policy* (forthcoming), with Oqubay and Sender; with co-authors the research report 'Fair-trade, Employment and Poverty Reduction in Ethiopia and Uganda' (2014), and related journal articles. He has undertaken commissioned work for international organizations. He has research and teaching experience in Ethiopia.

Stefan Dercon is professor of economic policy at the Blavatnik School of Government and the Economics Department at the University of Oxford. He is also director of the Centre for the Study of African Economics. Between 2011 and 2017, he was chief economist of the UK's Department for International Development (DFID). Previously, he taught at Addis Ababa University between 1992 and 1994. He has published extensively on various aspects of the Ethiopian economy.

Tadele Ferede is an assistant professor of economics at Addis Ababa University. He obtained his PhD in applied economics from the University of Antwerp, Belgium. He is the president of the Ethiopian Economics Association and a member of the Behavioural Research Insights Committee (Geneva). He previously also served as associate dean for graduate programmes, deputy center director and senior research fellow at the

Environment for Development Initiative, and editor-in-chief of the Ethiopian Economics Association's *Ethiopian Journal of Economics*.

Belay File is an assistant professor in urban and development economics at Ethiopian Civil Service University. He has immense experience in the urban development sector. His areas of research focus include the role of urbanization in economic growth, local economic development, sustainable cities, and urban–rural linkages. He is an economist by training. His education includes a PhD in economics from Erasmus University, Rotterdam.

Assefa Fiseha, PhD, is a researcher with fifteen years of extensive experience in the areas of governance, constitutional design, comparative federalism, developed systems, legislative–executive relations, role of legislative bodies, and role of the judiciary in the Horn of Africa (Ethiopia, Sudan, South Sudan, Malawi) and Yemen. Dr Assefa has published books, book chapters, and journal articles reputable journals, published both in Ethiopia and abroad.

Mulu Gebreeyesus, PhD, is currently a senior fellow at the Ethiopian Development Research Institute. He was a research fellow at the United Nations University (UNU-MERIT), Maastricht, the Netherlands. He has published widely in the field of development economics, particularly on trade opening and enterprise performance, industrial policy, small businesses dynamics, and the emergence of non-traditional exports. Gebreeyesus obtained his PhD in economics from the University of Gothenburg, Sweden in 2006.

Tegegne Gebre-Egziabher is a professor of urban and regional planning and development at Addis Ababa University. He received a PhD in city and regional planning from Ohio State University. His teaching and research interests lie in the field of urban and regional development and policy, decentralization and development, urban and rural linkages, micro and small enterprises, local economic development, and cluster development.

Jenna Golan is a PhD student in the Division of Nutritional Sciences at Cornell University. She holds a master's degree in human nutrition from Colombia and a master's degree in epidemiology from Harvard T.H. Chan School of Public Health. She has experience working in research studies focusing on maternal and child health in sub-Saharan Africa.

Douglas Gollin is professor of development economics in the Department of International Development at Oxford University and a fellow of St Antony's College. He holds research affiliations with the Centre for Economic Policy Research (CEPR) and the Bureau for Research and Economic Analysis of Development (BREAD). Professor Gollin also serves on the Research Advisory Group of the UK Department for International Development (DfID).

Fiseha Haftetsion Gebresilassie, PhD in federalism, MA in peace and security studies, LLB, is a lead researcher at the Policy Studies and Research Centre of the Federal Democratic Republic of Ethiopia. He has extensive research experience and has published in the areas of governance, federalism, justice, and conflict resolution and transformation. He previously worked as a community service provider, law lecturer, and leader mainly in higher education.

Sarah Hager is a senior project research specialist at the Institute of New Structural Economics at Peking University. Her focus is on field practice and in this capacity she has directed studies in more than five countries including Ethiopia, the Gambia, and Nepal. These studies mainly use semi-structured interview methodologies and investigate industrialization, special economic zones, and data creation in developing countries.

Assefa Hailemariam is the founder and associate professor at the Center for Population Studies, Addis Ababa University and principal researcher at Birhan Research and Development Consultancy, Ethiopia. He received his PhD in population studies from the London School of Economics. His research interest covers population dynamics, age structural transition, demographic dividend, and population policy. He has published several articles in peer-reviewed journals, book chapters, and two co-edited books.

Laura Hammond, PhD, is a reader in development studies at SOAS, University of London. She has been working in the Horn of Africa since 1993. Her research encompasses the themes of migration and displacement, food and livelihood security, and conflict and humanitarian response. She is currently the team leader of the Research and Evidence Facility for the EU Trust Fund for Africa (Horn of Africa Window), as part of a consortium between SOAS, the International Migration Institute at the University of Oxford, and Sahan Research based in Nairobi.

Jostein Hauge, PhD, is a research associate at the Institute for Manufacturing at the University of Cambridge. His research interests include economic development, the role of the state in economic change, technological paradigms, industrialization, international trade, and globalization.

Derek Headey, PhD, is a senior research fellow in the Poverty, Health, and Nutrition Division at the International Food Policy Research Institute (IFPRI), where he has worked since 2008. He is an economist who principally works on the linkages between food policies and nutrition. He received his PhD in economics in 2008 from the University of Queensland, Australia.

Kalle Hirvonen, PhD, is a development economist and a research fellow at the International Food Policy Research Institute (IFPRI). He is based in Addis Ababa in Ethiopia where he works in the Ethiopia Strategy Support Programme and IFPRI's Development Strategy and Governance division.

John Hoddinott is the H. E. Babcock Professor of food and nutrition economics and policy, professor of applied economics and management, and professor of nutritional sciences, Cornell University. Professor Hoddinott has worked in Ethiopia since 2003, publishing seventeen articles in refereed journals and six book chapters. Between 2006 and 2015, he led the independent evaluation of Ethiopia's Productive Safety Net Programme.

Deborah Johnston, PhD, is a professor in development economics and pro-director (learning and teaching) at SOAS, University of London. Her academic work focuses on the political economy of food and nutrition, the analysis and measurement of poverty, and the interrelationship between economics, labour markets, and health.

Won L. Kidane, PhD, is a tenured associate professor of law at the Seattle University School of Law, and a partner at the Addis Law Group in Washington. He specializes in international arbitration and litigation. Author of *The Culture of International Arbitration* (Oxford University Press, 2017) and *China-Africa Dispute Settlement* (Kluwer, 2012) and several more publications. He holds an SJD (Georgetown), JD (University of Illinois), LLM (University of Georgia), and LLB (Addis Ababa University).

Tadesse Kuma Worako, PhD, is a research fellow and Director of the Agriculture and Rural Development Research Centre at the Ethiopian Development Research Institute. His research focuses on agricultural commodity marketing in the emerging market economies: specifically, on coffee production and marketing, teff value chain, household food security, agricultural extension and productivity gains, CAADP initiatives, land certification and tenure security, private investment in commercial agriculture, and related works.

Christina Laskaridis is a PhD candidate in economics at the School of Oriental and African Studies (SOAS), University of London. Her research explores theory and practice of debt sustainability. She was a senior teaching fellow at SOAS and teaching assistant at UCL teaching macroeconomics, economic development of Africa, and history of economic thought. Christina is a research fellow at the Center for the History of Political Economy at Duke University, United States.

Carlos Lopes is a professor at the Graduate School for Development Policy and Practice, University of Cape Town and visiting professor at Sciences Po, Paris. He was visiting fellow at Oxford Martin School, University of Oxford in 2017 after serving as executive secretary of the Economic Commission for Africa. He is also an associate fellow at Chatham House. His latest book is *Africa in Transformation* (Palgrave Macmillan, 2018).

Mekonnen Manyazewal has held several leadership positions in key Ethiopian public institutions since 1992. He served as the vice minister for planning and economic development, and was part of the high-level leadership team that led the design and implementation of Ethiopia's series of economic reform programmes in the 1990s. He also served as state minister for finance and economic development, subsequently serving as minister of industry.

Haileselassie A. Medhin, PhD, is director of the Environment Climate Research Centre at the Ethiopian Development Research Institute. He is also a research fellow at the University of Gothenburg. Dr Medhin's research has been published in top scholarly journals such as the *Journal of Environmental Economics and Management, World Development*, and the *Oxford Journal of African Economies.*

Alemu Mekonnen is an associate professor at the Department of Economics, Addis Ababa University and a research fellow at the Environment and Climate Research Center of the Ethiopian Development Research Institute. He received his PhD in economics from the University of Gothenburg. He has over three decades of experience in teaching, research, academic/research administration, and consultancy. He has published more than twenty peer-reviewed articles in leading journals, and several book chapters.

Belachew Mekuria Fikre, PhD, is a commissioner at the Ethiopian Investment Commission. He previously served as the deputy commissioner for the Industrial Parks Division, mandated to attract, support, and regulate industrial park developers, enterprises, and operators. Prior to joining EIC, he worked at UNODC, and was the faculty dean of Bahir Dar University School of Law. He also taught at the Addis Ababa University Centre for Human Rights. He holds a PhD from the University of Surrey.

Kidane Mengisteab is professor of African studies and political science at Pennsylvania State University. The focus of his current research includes security in the Greater Horn of Africa; new approaches to democratization in Africa; relevance of 'traditional' institutions in Africa's governance; and the socio-economic implications of the expansion of extractive industries in Africa.

Bart Minten, PhD, has been senior research fellow at the International Food Policy Research Institute since December 2006 and works with the Development Strategy and Governance division. He is the programme leader of the Ethiopia Strategy Support Programme, which focuses on research, capacity building, and outreach and communication of research related to food and agricultural issues in Ethiopia.

Annet A. Mulema, PhD, is a sociologist currently working for the International Livestock Research Institute as a 'social scientist—gender'. Her research has focused on women's empowerment, gendered value-chain analysis, the environment, and agricultural innovation platforms. Dr Mulema obtained a PhD in sociology from Iowa State University, an MSc in management of agro-ecological knowledge and socio-technical change from Wageningen University, the Netherlands, and a BSc in agriculture from Makerere University, Uganda.

Likimyelesh Nigussie is a gender and development consultant working for the International Water Management Institute (IWMI) East Africa, based in Addis Ababa. She has a background in development economics and project management and her work focuses on gender studies in agriculture and natural resource management. Her key areas of research interest include: gender (pathways to women's empowerment, methodologies used to measure empowerment, unpaid care work, etc.), institutions, and governance.

Seid Nuru Ali, PhD, is a senior research fellow at the Ethiopian Economics Association/Ethiopian Economic Policy Research Institute, and leader of the Association's macro-economic unit. He is adjunct professor of economics at Bahir Dar University and Arba Minch Universities.

Izumi Ohno is a professor at the National Graduate Institute for Policy Studies (GRIPS), Tokyo, specializing in international development strategy, Japanese development cooperation policy, and development aid and business partnership. From 1981 to 2001, she worked at various development institutions including the Japan International Cooperation Agency (JICA), the World Bank, the Overseas Economic Cooperation Fund of Japan (OECF), and the Japan Bank for International Cooperation (JBIC).

Kenichi Ohno is a professor at the National Graduate Institute for Policy Studies, Tokyo, specializing in development economics and industrialization strategy. He has been advising the Japanese government on bilateral industrial cooperation since 1995. He also served as an economist at the International Monetary Fund (1987–91) and associate professor at the Institute of Socio-Economic Planning, Tsukuba University (1991–6) before taking up his current position. His publications include *Japanese Views on Economic Development* (1998), *Learning to Industrialize* (2013), *Eastern and Western Ideas for African Growth* (2013), and *History of Japanese Economic Development* (2017). He holds a PhD in economics from Stanford University, California.

Arkebe Oqubay, PhD, is a senior minister and Special Adviser to the Ethiopian Prime Minister, and has been at the centre of policymaking for over twenty-five years. He is a former Mayor of Addis Ababa, and was awarded the Best African Mayor of the Year 2005 by ABN, and finalist in the World Mayor Award 2005 for transforming the city. He is a recipient of the Order of the Rising Sun, Gold and Silver Star presented by the Emperor of Japan. He currently serves as board chair of several leading public organizations and international advisory boards. He is a research associate at the Centre of African Studies in the University of London, and holds a PhD in Development Studies from SOAS, University of London. His recent works include path-breaking *Made in Africa: Industrial Policy in Ethiopia* (OUP, 2015); *China-Africa and an Economic Transformation* (OUP, 2019); *How Nations Learn: Technological Learning, Industrial Policy, and Catch-up* (OUP, 2019); *African Economic Development: Evidence, Theory, and Policy* (OUP, forthcoming); and *The Oxford Handbook of Industrial Hubs and Economic Development* (OUP, forthcoming). He was recognized as one of the *100 Most Influential Africans* of 2016 and a 'leading thinker on Africa's strategic development' by the *New-African*, for his work, both theoretical and practical, on industrial policies. His research focus includes structural transformation, catch-up, industrial policy, and policy-making, with a special emphasis on Africa.

Carlos Oya, PhD, is reader (associate professor) in political economy of development at SOAS, University of London. His main research interests are: labour relations and employment, agrarian political economy, development policy, poverty, and research methodology. He is currently leading a project on structural transformations and employment dynamics in infrastructure construction and manufacturing sectors in Ethiopia and Angola.

Thomas Reardon has been professor of agricultural, food, and resource economics at Michigan State University since 1992 and was previously at the International Food Policy Research Institute since gaining his PhD from UC Berkeley in 1984. Tom is prominent in research on transformation of agri-food value chains in Africa and Asia, and among agricultural and food economists he is ranked second globally in Google Scholar citations.

Zinabu Samaro Rekiso is a PhD candidate in innovation and technology governance at Ragnar Nurkse School of Innovation and Governance, Tallinn University of Technology (Estonia). His research interests include late development, industrialization, structural transformation, and economic integration. He currently works for UN-HABITAT as a research and M&E consultant. Previously he has consulted for international organizations including UNCTAD, ITC, COMESA, and several international NGOs.

Florian T. Schäfer is a postdoctoral research fellow in development studies at SOAS, University of London, from where he also obtained his PhD. His main research interests are the political economy of industrialization and agrarian change, the development of entrepreneurship and labour markets, and empirical research methods. Much of his research focuses on Ethiopia, where Florian has lived and worked for several years.

John Sender is emeritus professor of economics, SOAS, University of London. Earlier appointments include: director of the African Studies Centre, University of Cambridge; adviser to Mandela's Presidential Commissions on Labour and on Rural Credit; economic consultant to Offices of the President and the Minister of Public Enterprises, South Africa and to the Federal Democratic Republic of Ethiopia.

Alemayehu Seyoum Taffesse, PhD, is currently a senior research fellow at the International Food Policy Research Institute (IFPRI). His most recent research covered aspirations and well-being, impact evaluation of large multi-year development programmes, productivity and change in smallholder agriculture, and performance of cooperatives. His research papers have been published in major peer-reviewed journals. He holds a DPhil in economics from the University of Oxford.

Admasu Shiferaw is associate professor of economics and Africana studies at the College of William and Mary in the United States. His research interests lie in understanding the behaviour and performance of African firms in terms of investment, productivity dynamics, product diversification, and competitiveness. His recent projects examine job creation and labour-market dynamics in Ethiopian manufacturing. Shiferaw has published in leading development journals including *World Development*, *Journal of Development Studies*, and *Economic Development and Cultural Change*.

Abebe Shimeles, PhD, is currently the manager of the Development Research Division, African Development Bank. Previously Dr Shimeles has worked for The World Bank, UNECA, ACTIONAID, and Addis Ababa University in different capacities. He holds a

PhD in economics from the University of Gothenburg, an MSc from Delhi School of Economics, and a BA in economics from Addis Ababa University.

Måns Söderbom is a professor of economics at the Department of Economics, School of Business, Economics and Law, University of Gothenburg. His research has been published by leading international journals and he has also contributed to several books on economic development. Industrial development is his main area of interest, and he specializes in development economics and applied econometrics. Most of his work focuses on the decisions and performance of firms.

Cornelia Staritz, PhD, is senior researcher at the Austrian Foundation for Development Research (ÖFSE) and a research associate at Policy Research in International Services and Manufacturing (PRISM) at the University of Cape Town. She holds a PhD in economics from the New School for Social Research. Her research focuses on economic development, international trade, global value chains, industrial policy, and commodity-based development. She is also part of the AfriCap research team.

John Sutton is the Sir John Hicks Professor Emeritus of Economics at the London School of Economics. His Enterprise Map series, which began in 2010 with the Enterprise Map of Ethiopia, written jointly with Nebil Kellow, provides the first uniform description of industrial capabilities and their origins across five sub-Saharan countries.

Fanaye Tadesse is a research officer at the Ethiopia Strategy Support Program (ESSP)—a collaborative programme of the International Food Policy Research Institute (IFPRI) and the Ethiopian Development Research Institute (EDRI). Her research focuses on agricultural productivity, women's empowerment, and nutritional outcomes and aspirations. Fanaye holds an MSc in economics from Addis Ababa University, specializing in economic policy analysis.

Menberetsehai Tadesse, PhD, is the former vice president of the Federal Supreme Court of Ethiopia (1996–2010) and served as a judge in the COMESA Court of Justice, first instance division (2005–15). He was also head of the Federal Judicial Training Institute and Justice and Legal Systems Research Institute. Dr Tadesse teaches on a part-time basis at Addis Ababa University and Adigrat University. He holds a PhD from the University of Birmingham.

Seneshaw Tamru is a PhD candidate at KU Leuven. He specializes in development economics and food security. He has been doing research in different areas including agricultural production, consumption behaviour, grain marketing, and price analyses in Ethiopia. His research interests include development economics and food security, value chain analysis, markets and price analysis, and agricultural economics. Seneshaw has already published several articles in peer-reviewed journals.

Taffere Tesfachew, PhD, is an international consultant on trade- and development-related issues. Until May 2016, he was director of the Division on Africa and Least Developed Countries, UNCTAD, where he led a team of economists who conducted research and analysis for two major annual reports, the 'Economic Development in

Africa Report' and the 'Least Developed Countries Report'. He has also authored and co-authored articles on a range of topics. Dr. Tesfachew holds a PhD in development economics from the Institute of Development Studies, University of Sussex.

Ayelech Tiruwha Melese is a PhD candidate in Roskilde University, Denmark. Her study examines the technological capabilities of Ethiopian-owned floriculture firms and their investment in learning. Ayelech studied business management at Jimma University in Ethiopia and gained her MA in development studies from the International Institute of Social Studies in the Netherlands. She has worked for international NGOs and research institutes and published academic and action research papers.

Helen Walls, PhD, is an assistant professor at the London School of Hygiene and Tropical Medicine. She is a public health researcher, with a research focus on the structural influences of population health, particularly relating to food systems and nutrition, and associated policy and governance. She currently leads a grant of the Drivers of Food Choice Competitive Grants Programme, investigating the impact of agricultural policy on food choice and nutrition.

Lindsay Whitfield is professor MSO in global studies and leader of the Centre of African Economies at the Department of Social Sciences and Business, Roskilde University, Denmark. She is the author of several books on African politics and economies, including *The Politics of African Industrial Policy: A Comparative Perspective* and *Economies after Colonialism: Ghana and the Struggle for Power*, and is co-editor of the journal *African Affairs*.

Tassew Woldehanna is professor of economics at the Department of Economics, Addis Ababa University and senior research fellow at the Ethiopian Development Research Institute. Currently, he is the principal investigator on several projects including Young Lives (an international study of childhood poverty), RISE Ethiopia (a six-year project on Assessing the Impact of General Education Quality Improvement Programme), and the Early Learning Partnership Research Programmes.

Jiajun Xu is an assistant professor and the executive deputy dean of the Institute of New Structural Economics at Peking University. Xu acts as the general secretary of the Global Research Consortium on Economic Structural Transformation. Previously Xu worked at the UN and the World Bank. Her monograph *Beyond US Hegemony in International Development* was published by Cambridge University Press. Xu holds a DPhil from the University of Oxford.

Justin Yifu Lin is director of the Institute of New Structural Economics, Dean of the Institute of South–South Cooperation and Development, and professor and honorary Dean of the National School of Development at Peking University. He was the senior vice president and chief economist of the World Bank from 2008 to 2012. Prior to this, Professor Lin served for fifteen years as founding director and professor of the China Centre for Economic Research (CCER) at Peking University. He is the author of twenty-three books.

PART I

CONTEXT, CONCEPTS, AND HISTORY

CHAPTER 1

INTRODUCTION

FANTU CHERU, CHRISTOPHER CRAMER, AND ARKEBE OQUBAY

From a country that by the early 1990s was devastated by famine and years of war, Ethiopia emerged to become one of the fastest-growing economies in the world between the early 2000s and 2018. Growth in Ethiopia has surpassed that of every other sub-Saharan country in the past decade and was forecast by the IMF to exceed 8 per cent over 2018–20. The government has set its sights on transforming Ethiopia into a middle-income country by 2025 and, at the heart of this agenda, into a leading manufacturing hub in Africa. Figure 1.1 gives some idea of the pace of economic growth and of sectoral expansion.

Confidence in these ambitions grew from rates of economic growth and of improvements in a range of social welfare indicators that were impressive by most standards of comparison. The ambitions arose from commitment to a particular model of development in which the state plays a central role in trying to guide economic activity and underlying patterns of structural change. And the ambitions also took shape as responses to the acute pressures faced by the government and the country: the pressures of a rapidly growing, very young population, of an often unstable regional geo-political environment, of the enduring tensions at the heart of the country's own political economy, and of often hostile climatic conditions.

Ethiopia's strategic approach to economic development has attracted intense research interest—both supportive and highly critical—from academics and the mainstream media.[1] More specifically, there has been increased interest in Ethiopia's successful industrialization drive, which has sought to challenge the assumption long held by many that industrial policy can never work in poor African countries (Oqubay 2015). Although there are debates to be had, and this *Handbook* contributes to them, at a very immediate level it is obvious to many Ethiopians living in the country or returning to it, as well as to *farengi* (foreigners) who have been going there over many years, that the country has changed dramatically. It is obvious when driving on numerous new and improved roads around much of the country. It is clear in the skyline of not just Addis

[1] See, for example, Lefort (2012), Goodfellow (2017), Vaughan (2011), and Zenawi (2012).

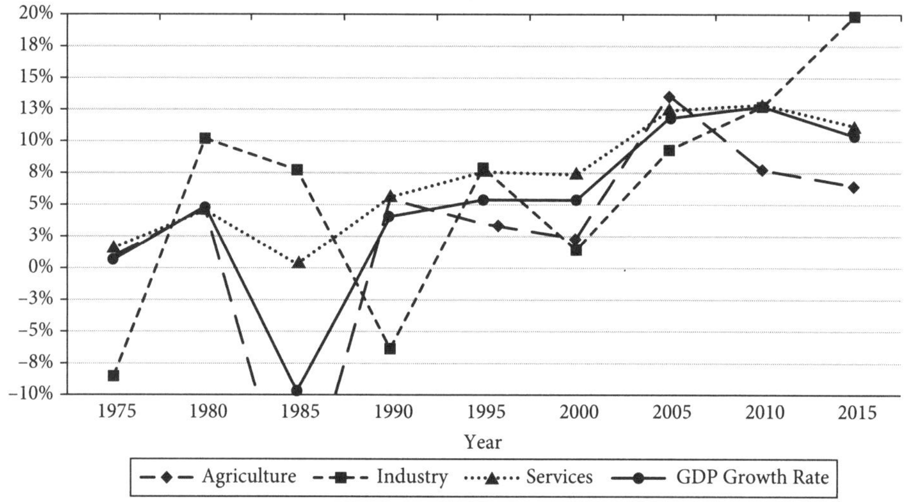

FIGURE 1.1 Economic growth in Ethiopia, 1975–2017

Source: National Planning Commission (2018) (unpublished).

Ababa but other major cities and towns (and it is even obvious from 'before and after' satellite images of towns like Ziway, in Oromia, which underwent spectacular expansion in the wake of the boom in floriculture). And it can clearly be seen in the change to the 'Balance of Payments Highway', the road running south-east from Addis to Bishoftu and Adama that then makes its way to the port in Djibouti. Around the millennium this road ran largely through countryside between Bishoftu and Addis and was unlit at night, but during the day a solid line of trucks crawled along its narrow lane uphill to Addis, loaded with imports. Now that stretch of road is built up with small stores, commercial offices, factories, private colleges, and industrial parks. And parallel to it there is a new three-lane toll road easing the bottleneck. Additionally, the old and long-abandoned Ethio-Djibouti railway was replaced by the new standard-gauge Addis Ababa–Djibouti Railway, inaugurated on 1 January 2018.

Notwithstanding Ethiopia's recent economic success, there is a significant gap in the literature and empirical evidence on the performance of the Ethiopian economy. *The Oxford Handbook of the Ethiopian Economy* is the first major reference work on the subject. Drawing on high-quality research by local and international scholars specializing in a wide range of issues, the *Handbook* will be an important contribution to the expanding field of study not only of Ethiopia itself but also of the wider African context and of structural transformation more broadly in the twenty-first century.

Among other issues, the chapters of the *Handbook* look closely at: economic performance and policymaking; macro-economic management; the government's insistence on a gradualist approach to financial sector reform (in the face of intense pressure to liberalize faster); manufacturing; agriculture; infrastructure; and social sectors. We have not striven for a false consensus: the *Handbook* contains varied and sometimes sharply conflicting views. While the chapters confirm that Ethiopia's recent economic history has been remarkable and that it has wider significance, at the same time they reveal the enormous strains on the economy and on policymakers; the profound level of under-nutrition endured by too many Ethiopians; the enormous weaknesses in the economy; and the manifold shortcomings of policies. We unashamedly underline many of the achievements of the Ethiopian economy, but there are no grounds for triumphalism. For every dramatic achievement, there are mistakes, failures, and disappointments. Developing an internationally competitive manufacturing sector has proved difficult. The country's extraordinary history and diversity of coffee production has not stopped the coffee sector performing well below the level that might be expected. The government's Growth and Transformation Plan has run up against a balance of payments crisis that threatens the whole strategy. Food price inflation has often been high by international standards, which not only threatens to undermine investment but has clearly already undermined efforts to raise the living standards of the poorest. Indeed, for all the remarkable achievements in reducing child and maternal mortality and reducing poverty rates, very large numbers of Ethiopians continue to live in conditions of extreme deprivation and many government interventions have failed to reach the very poorest.

Not surprisingly, these difficulties have encouraged many observers and advisers, within Ethiopia and outside, to dismiss the pretentions of the government's 'developmental state' strategy. All along there have been arguments that such a strategy could never work, or that (Moller and Wacker 2017) it might have achieved quite a lot but heterodox policies would prove unsustainable, or that things would have been even better had the government followed international advice. In 2018, as the country entered the latest in a series of periods of political crisis and uncertainty, these views reached fever pitch, with an overwhelming volume of advice being offered to the government assuming that rapid and full-scale liberalization would solve all the country's economic (and hence political) problems.[2]

This makes it especially important to take the measure of the country's recent economic history. And it is also important—as some of the contributions to the *Handbook* in particular try to do—to view Ethiopia's economic policies and performance in the context of wider international experiences. Whatever the shortcomings of these policies, the record is clear: Ethiopia, at least to some extent because of a policy mix that most acknowledge to have been 'heterodox', has grown rapidly and, despite rising inequality, has nonetheless improved welfare for millions of people.

Contrast that with the slow growth of many other African economies; with the combination of quite rapid growth with very disappointing rates of poverty reduction in countries like Mozambique; or with the IMF's forecast in mid-2018 that Nigeria's income per capita would fall every year for eight years up to 2023. More broadly, in our view (though not necessarily in the view of all our contributors), the international and historical experience also serves up many warnings against headlong economic liberalization. The evidence suggests, on the one hand, that all countries that have successfully 'caught up'

[2] And it appeared to be having some effect: see 'Ethiopia Signals Intent to Open Economy with Sale of Prized Assets' (*Financial Times*, 6 June 2018).

with income levels of advanced OECD economies have had a strong role for the state in intervening in markets to promote structural change (Storm 2015). That structural change has fundamentally meant an increasing share of the population becoming engaged in higher productivity economic activities, which historically meant manufacturing but may now increasingly involve high productivity agricultural and service activities as well, given the blurring of clear categorical boundaries between sectors.[3] On the other hand, the evidence suggests that rapid liberalization, especially of trade and the financial sector, exposes lower-income economies to unwarranted levels of volatility and risk (Griffith-Jones and Gottschalk 2016; UNECA 2016).

Against this background, the major focus of the *Handbook* is on the recent economic history, policies, and performance of the Ethiopian economy during a moment of ongoing and significant structural change. These recent experiences, however, are set against the deeper background of the long-run trajectories and features of Ethiopian economic history and state formation—from the Imperial period until the present—as well as against the background of wider sub-Saharan African political economy. The *Handbook* provides a background focusing on the context, concepts, history, and political economy of Ethiopia in the post-1991 period, with particular focus on agriculture and rural socio-economic differentiation, on industrialization, trade, infrastructural development, urbanization, and macroeconomic and fiscal policies, as well as important themes including private-sector development, gender, poverty and inequality, and climate change.

1.1 Preparing the *Handbook*: the Process and the Focus on Quality

This is the first ever *Oxford Handbook* on the economy of a single African country and it focuses on the theme of structural transformation. It is intended to serve as a major reference book on the Ethiopian economy for university students, researchers, and policymakers over the next decade. While much of the volume is focused on post-1991 economic development policy and strategy, the analysis is set against the background of the long history of Ethiopia: more specifically on the Imperial period which ended in 1974, the socialist development experiment of the Derg regime between 1974 and 1991, and the policies and strategies of the current EPRDF government that assumed power in 1991.

Among the critical factors for the *Handbook* have been the following: careful selection of a mix of Ethiopian and international contributors; identification of the key economic sectors to be covered; and the time frame that stretches from as far back as the period of Emperor Menelik to the present day. By encouraging contributors to consider a historical perspective, we have sought to elicit analysis of the continuities and discontinuities in economic policy across successive regimes.

[3] See Cramer, Di John, and Sender (2018).

As volume editors, we have relied on a great deal of enthusiasm and hard work from many people to produce this work and to do so to a very tight schedule. We have made considerable efforts to maintain high scholarly standards, with an emphasis on originality and evidence-based research—two key requirements for an *Oxford Handbook*. In conceptualizing the *Handbook* project, we sought to encourage different and conflicting theoretical views, but at the same time we insisted that alternative views be backed by strong empirical evidence, and accompanied by a consideration of the provenance and reliability of that evidence. With these goals in mind, the volume editors organized three writers' workshops in Addis Ababa where draft chapters were discussed, not only among contributors but also with invited external peer reviewers. After the third workshop, draft chapters were sent to readers (the editors and a small group of reviewers who included fellow contributors and external reviewers), leading to further revisions and re-writing. Thus, all chapters have been subjected to successive rounds of critical review and re-drafting within the guiding principles of Oxford University Press.

Conducting research on, and making claims about, developments in the Ethiopian economy involves dealing with empirical problems. Ethiopian officials have long prided themselves on the quality of statistics in the country. But there are very clearly major difficulties and gaps in official statistics, there has been under-investment in building the capacity of statistical services, and there have been at times quite heated debates on the provenance and veracity of data on the economy. As editors, we encouraged contributors to consider the evidence for their analysis and claims and to discuss, where possible, the quality of that evidence. In some cases contributors have made particular efforts to highlight statistical problems and to recommend statistical changes. Hopefully, the contributions in this *Handbook* will provoke further debate about the evidence and new investment in more and better data. That in turn will help to make possible stronger analysis and richer insights into the economy and the people in it.

1.2 Organization of the Book

The *Handbook* is organized in five sections. Part I, covering the period 1890–2017, deals with the transition from a traditional to a modern economy, particularly during the period of Imperial rule under Emperor Haile Selassie, followed by the Derg regime that ended imperial rule, and the post-1991 policies and strategies of the EPRDF. The contributors in this section address land tenure and land policy in the evolving development discourse in Ethiopia; the post-1995 experiment in ethnic federalism; and the constitutional framework and legal institutions for economic development. Part II deals with economic policies for structural transformation after 1991, covering such topics as trade policy, the development of the financial sector, infrastructure policies, poverty reduction strategies, and the focus on green and climate-resilient transformation. Part III focuses on social policy and development, with attention to growth, poverty, and inequality, and the shifting debates on demography, child nutrition, social protection, education, employment creation, and food security. Chapters in this section examine critically how pro-poor the policies of the government have been and what modifications might be needed to make them truly pro-poor. Part IV examines the progress made in transforming Ethiopian agriculture and the remaining constraints on harnessing the potential of the sector in value addition. Part V discusses the processes and policy adaptations undertaken by the government to put late-industrializing Ethiopia on an industrialization path, with special reference to the garment and textile industry. In addition, the section picks up on the topic of urbanization's impact on growth and transformation. Part VI situates the Ethiopian state-led development model in the wider debate on the significance of the East Asian development model for other developing countries such as Ethiopia.

1.2.1 Part I: Context, Concepts, and History

Part I examines the historical, political, and economic factors that have given rise to the resurgence of Ethiopia as a formidable economic and political power in the Horn of Africa. The dramatic economic and political transformations of the country since 1991 cannot be understood in isolation from Ethiopia's history, from the tensions between sources of political and economic power over the centuries (see Chapter 3), and from its geography. Due to the turbulent dynamics of its internal politics, successive Ethiopian rulers have never been able to fully build a strong and capable state and a vibrant economy. Centrifugal tendencies, and frequent alliances between internal opposition and external rivals, have characterized much of the political history of the modern Ethiopian state. Weakened statehood, endemic poverty, and contested borders have all shaped the capacity of successive regimes to put the country on the path of structural transformation and economic growth (see Chapter 2). These conditions, however, seem to have changed since 1991 under the leadership of the EPRDF, which presided over an economy that displayed double-digit GDP growth rates for almost a decade and more than doubled in size from the 1990s (see Chapter 9). In addition to growth in infrastructure and social services, other aspects of this development have been an increase in tax revenues and taxation capacity, as a consequence of which foreign aid now accounts for less than 30 per cent of the government budget.

On the political front, after 1991 the EPRDF engaged in a highly political state-building project, underpinned by a long-term 'emancipatory' vision of structural transformation on all fronts—social, economic, political, and cultural. As an example, the EPRDF dealt with the contentious issue of the 'national question' by adopting a national constitution in 1995 that grants self-determination in the form of ethnic federalism to the country's 90-plus nations and nationalities. Despite the federal structure of the current state, the EPRDF more than any of its predecessors succeeded in stabilizing political power and provided unprecedented security and administrative control of the state's population and territory (see Chapter 5). Although various opposition groups still draw attention to the centrifugal tendencies of the state, their capacity is considerably weakened, such that no insurgency faction has constituted a serious threat to the central government. Nonetheless, the actions of the EPRDF and the severe pressure on the country's political economy led to repeated and serious threats to the regime's survival, including in the 2005 elections, and the unrest and state of emergency in 2016–18.

To achieve its ambitious development vision, the EPRDF also redefined the country's foreign policy objectives. Having identified 'poverty' and 'undemocratic governance' as the greatest threats to Ethiopia's national security, the government has given primacy to economic diplomacy as a means of advancing the national interest. From 2002 the government centred its diplomatic activities on the promotion of trade, encouraging investment, tourism, and regional integration (see Chapter 7). Massive investment in dams and major transport infrastructure was designed not only to meet Ethiopia's development ambition, but also to improve regional connectivity and kick-start the process of regional integration. The economic diplomacy strategy has shown tangible results as the country was able to mobilize large amounts of external resources (Chapter 11). Political stability and economic growth in turn increased Ethiopia's appeal as a political ally and economic partner. The government's clear development vision, its ability to professionally utilize foreign funds to accelerate development, and the implications of its development for meeting several global targets, are some of the factors behind the value given to partnership with Ethiopia by both traditional and new development partners.

1.2.2 Part II: Economic Development

Part II is exclusively focused on economic development policies and strategies from 1991 onwards, covering several thematic areas including the macro-economy, trade, fiscal policy, and financial markets and policy. By and large, economic development strategy in the post-1991 period was incremental, and the assumptions and the strategies chosen changed over time, largely as a result of increased learning and a preference for pragmatism rather than a blind adherence to a particular ideological line. This pragmatism and adaptability sometimes gets lost under the cover of the late Prime Minister Meles Zenawi's catchy notion of a 'democratic developmental state'. The period following 2005 signalled a major turning point in economic development thinking in Ethiopia. The limits of smallholder-dependent agriculture-led industrialization were recognized. Henceforth the government consciously pursued structural economic transformation by improving the productivity and competitiveness of smallholder agriculture, as well as promoting industrialization, value addition, and export development. To unlock the country's productive potential, the government expanded its investment in critical infrastructure such as roads, rail, and energy (for example through hydro-power and wind farm schemes). In the past twenty years alone, the country's annual energy output has risen from 360 to 4,200 MW. Taking into account the projects that were still under construction as this *Handbook* was written, above all the Grand Ethiopian Renaissance Dam (GERD), the total renewable energy output from hydro, wind, geothermal, and solar sources was expected to reach 12,000 MW within the next few years.

Chapters in this section also detail the infrastructure projects that have played such a key part in leading and enabling growth and overcoming fundamental constraints on people's mobility, and their access to such fundamentals as electricity, schooling, and health services. Public spending on these projects has been at the heart of macro-economic policy and of debates about the sustainability of the government's strategy. Chapter 13, drawing inspiration from a form of financial balance analysis that has been used mainly in OECD economies, weighs up trends in the public sector, private, and foreign balances in Ethiopia and argues that despite some evidence of rising imbalances, there has as yet been no serious risk to the sustainability of the strategy. Other chapters broadly agree with this view. Chapters 11 and 12 elaborate on the highly particular financial policy and banking history of recent years, detailing the efforts to mobilize resources for structural change and the insistence on a policy stance of gradual financial opening, but also the many strains in the financial system. These strains have included, not least, desperately weak capacity in the state banking system to monitor loans directed to developmental, productive enterprises, which has increased the incidence of bad loans. The section also looks at trade policy experiences in Ethiopia, setting the issue within the context of a difficult debate on how far, and how quickly, low-income countries should open their foreign trade. The issue is especially relevant given signs that the government, in mid-2018, was looking to accelerate the process of joining the WTO.

1.2.3 Part III: Social Policy and Development

Progress in economic growth and social development in Ethiopia has been impressive over the past decade and a half. For over a decade, the country registered double-digit GDP growth and invested heavily in economic and social infrastructure. Growth was largely pro-poor but with major qualifications, as chapters in this and other sections make clear. Ethiopia deployed 70 per cent of its budget, the largest of its kind in Africa, on pro-poor activities such as education, health, agriculture, and food security. This was supplemented by the donor-funded Productive Safety Net Program (PSNP). Thanks to these interventions, progress in social development has also been impressive. School enrolments, health coverage, and the percentage of the population with access to drinking water more than doubled between 2002 and 2010, although there were increasing complaints about the quality of education and some other social services. The contributors in this section examine critically how pro-poor the policies of the government have been and what modifications they might need to make them truly pro-poor. Topics covered in the chapters include the growth–poverty–inequality nexus, the shifting debate on demography, child nutrition, social protection, education, employment creation, and food security. While there is unambiguous evidence that social progress has been made over the past fifteen years, these gains are being eroded by growing income and wealth inequality, exacerbated by endemic corruption and rent seeking.

1.2.4 Part IV: Agriculture and Rural Transformation

The contributors in Part IV examine the policies and strategies developed and implemented in the post-1991 period to transform Ethiopian agriculture and rural society in general. They analyse the patterns that emerge from the data and they engage with debates about agricultural and rural transformation in Ethiopia as well as with theories of agrarian change more broadly. To varying degrees they also touch on the significant issue of the credibility and limitations of the official data.

The evidence suggests that the majority of the poorest Ethiopians and the majority of new entrants to labour markets continue to live (and will continue to live at least till the middle of the century) in rural areas. Keeping in mind the broader macro-economic, fiscal, and structural policies covered in Part II (economic development), contributors in this section discuss the success and failure of agricultural transformation strategies during 1994–2016. Upon assuming power in 1991, the EPRDF embarked on an agricultural development-led industrialization (ADLI) strategy to transform peasant agriculture, along with a rural industrialization strategy to promote value addition to agricultural products. Support services in the form of rural roads, extension services, and irrigation were expanded to enable farmers to become productive. This was supplemented by the Productive Safety Net Program, which helped protect many people from exposure to risks and shocks, though some evaluations have pointed out that it failed to reach many of the very poorest. ADLI was, therefore, both a growth strategy and a redistributive vehicle to empower the millions of poor peasants who had suffered under feudal rule and the failed socialist experiment of the military regime in the 1970s and 1980s.

By 2005, the limitations of the ADLI strategy were widely recognized by the government.[4] The next development plan, the Plan for Accelerated and Sustained Development to End Poverty (PASDEP), aimed at moving away from dependence on subsistence agriculture and towards industrialization and value addition in agricultural products. PASDEP also put the role of a strong developmental state in economic growth and structural transformation centre stage. This was a paradigm shift that potentially set Ethiopia on a development path along the lines of the East Asian countries. Following this logic, the contributors in this section discuss the following topics: key drivers; institutional arrangements for pushing through the reforms; financing modality; specific approaches to smallholder farmers and commercial agriculture; the structure of incentives; the role of rural infrastructure in raising productivity; markets and marketing strategy for agriculture; and of course, the role of land ownership. Contributors to this section also address the key question of whether policies have devoted sufficient attention and resources to promoting agricultural exports. Given their significance for wage employment and foreign exchange, there is also particular emphasis on the coffee and floriculture sectors.

[4] Indeed, there had already been discussion between government and donors about the limitations of ADLI (Cramer et al. 2004).

1.2.5 Part V: Industrialization and Urban Development

Ethiopia's ambitious drive to become a middle-income country by 2025 and a manufacturing hub in selected sectors is relatively new and it is too early to pass judgement on whether the industrial policy strategy had a strong chance of producing the desired outcomes. The priority accorded to manufacturing (especially if a broad definition of manufacturing and industry is adopted, to account for the scope for higher-productivity, knowledge-intensive agricultural production) makes sense as it has the potential to provide demand stimulus for growth of the agricultural sector. Manufacturing has high forward and backward linkages, thereby contributing to domestic investment, employment, and output in the development process. But as several contributors point out, these linkages have not thus far taken shape automatically or to any significant degree. While there was relative success in the floriculture, textile and garment, and leather manufacturing sectors in a short period of time, several contributors emphasize a range of institutional and policy barriers that could undermine the effectiveness of the industrial policy.

One critical element addressed in this section is the role of urbanization in structural transformation and industrialization along the agricultural value chain. Cities are the most productive parts of Ethiopia and offer the greatest potential for accelerated growth, job creation, and strengthening rural–urban linkages. Their continued success is fundamental to the country's ability to participate effectively in a more open global economy. At present, however, Ethiopian cities are beset by bottlenecks in infrastructure, skill shortages, inefficient trade logistics, poor internal and external connectivity, an inefficient land distribution system, and a severe shortage of domestic credit. These constraints collectively act as a brake on growth and competitiveness. The role of the federal and local governments is, therefore, to guide urbanization in the right direction so that Ethiopian cities can become nodes of innovation, economic production, and accumulation in a globally integrated production chain.

1.2.6 Part VI: Structural Transformation and the African Context

The quest for structural transformation and inclusive growth in Ethiopia under the guidance of a strong developmental state dates from the early 1990s when the EPRDF embarked on ADLI to improve the productivity of peasant agriculture through the provision of technology and better farming practices, improved seeds, fertilizers, irrigation, rural roads, and marketing services.[5] The idea of ADLI found its expression first in the Sustainable Development and Poverty Reduction Program (SDPRP), covering the period 2002/3–2004/5, then later in the first five-year plan, the PASDEP (2005–2010),

[5] Ministry of Planning and Economic Development (1993), *An Economic Development Strategy for Ethiopia: A Comprehensive Guidance and a Development Strategy for the Future*, Government of Ethiopia, Addis Ababa.

and more recently in GTP-I and GTP-II. While the country experienced a marked increase in food production compared to past historical trends, overall productivity and crop diversification was not commensurate with the resources invested by the government in the peasant sector under the ADLI programme. There were also some doubts about the veracity of official claims about the rate of growth of agricultural output. The level of early improvements could not be sustained mainly because of policy and institutional constraints required for a dynamic agricultural intensification programme. As in so many areas of ambitious economic development plans in Ethiopia (and elsewhere), the experience suggests there are easy phases and then more difficult phases of development, as the requirements become more complex and the range of interest groups proliferates.

The government soon decided to change course and adopted a new development plan, the Program for Accelerated and Sustained Development to End Poverty (PASDEP), 2005–2010, which recognized the potential role of commercial farmers in agricultural transformation. Unlike the SDRP, PASDEP aimed at moving Ethiopia from dependence on subsistence agriculture towards industrialization and the export of value-added products under the guidance of a strong and development-oriented state (Zenawi 2012). This was a turning point in economic policy in Ethiopia. PASDEP made important adjustments by broadening the policy scope to include other sectors, especially industry and the urban sector. The new approach of 'state-led' systemic transformation drew its inspiration from the successful development experience of East Asia.

Indeed, in the first three years of PASDEP implementation, the agricultural and industrial sectors performed well, and export volumes increased significantly. Overall GDP growth during the planned period averaged 11.3 per cent, compared to a low of 1.5 per cent in 2001/2. Correspondingly, GDP per capita rose to US$357 in 2007/8 from a very low figure of US$127 in 2000/1. Physical infrastructure and human capital development expanded substantially. This was a dramatic achievement for a country that had been stuck with extremely low economic growth for a long time. Based on the lessons learned from implementing PASDEP, the government formulated the first Growth and Transformation Plan (2010–15) in 2010. The GTP once again drew its inspiration from the East Asian model of development.

Drawing from international experience, the contributors in this section attempt to contextualize Ethiopia's unique development approach in comparative perspectives based on a review of the historical experiences of the successfully industrializing countries of East Asia. They also attempt to identify the areas of convergence and divergence between the recent Ethiopian experience and broader historical patterns. The aim is to identify the key sources of growth and the key determinants and new institutional arrangements required to push through a comprehensive reform agenda; to assess the progress made thus far; to highlight the challenges faced by the government (financial, political, institutional); and to consider the implications of Ethiopia's recent economic history and policy for the coming years. Finally, contributors to this section of the *Handbook* assess the relevance of the Ethiopian experience for other African countries in terms of the design of policies and strategies to achieve rapid industrialization and structural transformation (See also Lin and Monga 2019, and Cramer, Oqubay, and Sender 2019).

1.3 Gaps in the Volume

This *Handbook* is large and covers many topics. But such a volume cannot cover all relevant or even all the important issues. Inevitably, there are gaps. We wish we had been able to provide more coverage of a number of issues in particular. The list is not exhaustive but it includes: gender; the role of donor countries and institutions, given the direct or indirect reliance on external borrowing for funding of major infrastructure investment-led development; employment and labour markets; and fiscal institutions and policy. Some of these issues are addressed but we would have liked more detail. For a host of reasons this was not possible. We have attempted to provide an overview of the scale of external borrowing, for example, but a complete breakdown of lending countries and institutions was difficult to come by due to the different reporting requirements of government institutions responsible for power, roads, and rail transport. In addition, there are sensitivities in the government regarding disclosures on foreign loans. In some other cases, the reasons were more prosaic and practical. And there are issues—very much including gender—where a number of different chapters address gendered dimensions of the topics they deal with.

1.4 Conclusion

As the work on this *Handbook* was drawing to a close in May 2018, Ethiopia was at a political crossroads. There had been, especially between 2016 and 2018, protests in a number of areas, especially in Oromia and Amhara states. Ethnic tensions within the framework of an ethnic-based constitutional federalism, demands for more governance reforms and political pluralism, and demands for more and better jobs, were among the sources of political tension. There were fears that the 'political marketplace', which De Waal (2015) argued dominated politics in the Horn of Africa but had not taken over in Ethiopia, might be creeping into the centre of Ethiopian political economy. Meanwhile, if part of the rationale for the adoption of an ambitious state-led development strategy had been one of political survival—the idea that the delivery of development would guarantee legitimacy—the reality seemed to involve the delivery of development calling forth new and more articulate political voices and new ('crisis of expectations') economic and political challenges. Some of the chapters in this *Handbook* touch on these and other issues, and as we pointed out above, there are clearly many strains and shortcomings in both policy and performance in recent years. But this is primarily a work of economic analysis and the origins and dynamics of the political situation are beyond its scope. It is of course clear that in the coming years further research will need to be done on the political economy, and on the links between the patterns of economic performance and structural change in Ethiopia and the voicing of political grievances and challenges. Meanwhile, with the appointment of a new Prime Minister in March 2018, the political upheavals across the country subsided and some quarters saw renewed optimism that the new leadership might start the process of democratization and put the country back together.[6]

By 2018, reconciling a coherent and ambitious 'heterodox' development strategy while giving greater respect to proliferating democratic demands was becoming increasingly difficult. The relationship between political and economic progress (Hirschman 1994) has never been as straightforward as many people have wished or claimed but many thoughtful people believed that some things had to 'give', both on the economy and in politics in Ethiopia. How political leaders would address these evolving problems remained, as we completed work on this *Handbook*, extremely unclear. It remained equally unclear whether policymakers would be able to continue designing and implementing a bespoke economic strategy that drew pragmatically on a range of international experiences, that adapted in the face of its own mistakes, and that held to its principles in the face of intense pressures from domestic and international interest groups.

Whatever the trajectory of politics, policy, and economics, we hope the evidence, analysis, and discussion in the chapters of this *Handbook* provide useful insights and reference for those who continue to take an interest in the Ethiopian economy. Scholars, donor agency staff, interested officials in other African countries, and perhaps above all Ethiopian policymakers, may want to heed the signals given across many chapters that more, and more reliable, data is fundamental to really understanding the Ethiopian economy and to designing effective policies. That implies a need for greater investment in and openness with data. It also implies a need for further research at all levels, from macro-economic management to local dynamics of labour markets, deprivation, and nutritional status.

Hopefully too, readers will note the value of a work that, we suggest, shows how limited are broad sweeping labels—'developmental state', 'industrial policy', 'institutional capacity', and so on. What the evidence in this *Handbook* shows is the unevenness of policy and the unevenness of performance, even within sectors. Seeing that unevenness more clearly and beginning to probe what accounts for the variation (over time and across sectors or enterprises or organizations) is a basis not just for future scholarship and research but also for future policy design by officials.

References

Cramer, Christopher, Mulat Demeke, Alemayehu Geda, et al. (2004). 'Concretization of ADLI and Analysis of Policy and Institutional Challenges for an Ethiopian Diversification Strategy.' MoFED Long-Term Strategy and Source of Growth Study. (Addis Ababa, Ethiopia: MoFED).

Cramer, Christopher, Jonathan Di John, and John Sender (2018). *Poinsettia Assembly and Selling Emotion: High Value Agricultural Exports in Ethiopia*. (Paris: Agence Française de Développement).

Cramer, Christopher, Arkebe Oqubay, and John Sender (2019). *African Economic Development: Theory, Policy, and Evidence* (Oxford: Oxford University Press).

[6] As one commentator put it: 'Ethiopia has never been this united and Ethiopia has never been this divided' ('A Last Ditch Gamble for Ethiopia's "Miracle on the Nile"', *Financial Times*, 6 June 2018).

De Waal, Alex (2015). *The Real Politics of the Horn of Africa: Money, War and the Business of Power* (Cambridge, UK; Malden, MA: Polity).

Goodfellow, Tom (2017). 'Taxing Property in a Neo-Developmental State: The Politics of Urban Land Value Capture in Rwanda and Ethiopia', *African Affairs* 116 (465): 549–72. https://doi.org/10.1093/afraf/adx020.

Griffith-Jones, Stephany, and Ricardo Gottschalk (eds) (2016). *Achieving Financial Stability and Growth in Africa* (London: Routledge Taylor & Francis Group).

Hirschman, Albert O. (1994). 'The On-and-off Connection between Political and Economic Progress', *The American Economic Review* 84 (2): 343–48.

Lefort, René (2012). 'Free Market Economy, "Developmental State" and Party-State Hegemony in Ethiopia: The Case of the "Model Farmers"', *Journal of Modern African Studies* 50 (4): 681–706. https://doi.org/10.1017/S0022278X12000389.

Lin, Justin, and Celestin Monga (2019). *Oxford Handbook of Structural Transformation* (Oxford: Oxford University Press).

Moller, Lars Christian, and Konstantin M. Wacker (2017). 'Explaining Ethiopia's Growth Acceleration: The Role of Infrastructure and Macroeconomic Policy', *World Development* 96 (August): 198–215. https://doi.org/10.1016/j.worlddev.2017.03.007.

Oqubay, Arkebe (2015). *Made in Africa: Industrial Policy in Ethiopia* (Oxford: Oxford University Press).

Storm, Servaas (2015). 'Debate: Structural Change', *Development and Change* 46 (4): 666–99. https://doi.org/10.1111/dech.12169.

UNECA (2016). *Transformative Industrial Policy for Africa* (Addis Ababa: United Nations Economic Commission for Africa).

Vaughan, Sarah (2011). 'Revolutionary Democratic State-Building: Party, State and People in the EPRDF's Ethiopia', *Journal of Eastern African Studies* 5 (4): 619–40. https://doi.org/10.1080/17531055.2011.642520.

Zenawi, Meles (2012). 'States and Markets: Neoliberal Limitations and the Case for a Developmental State', in *Good Growth and Governance in Africa: Rethinking Developmental Strategies*, ed. Akbar Noman et al. (Oxford: Oxford University Press): 140–74.

CHAPTER 2

ETHIOPIA'S TRANSITION FROM A TRADITIONAL TO A DEVELOPING ECONOMY, 1890S–1960S

SHIFERAW BEKELE

2.1 The Traditional Economy

As the nineteenth century wore on, the traditional economy was still intact in Ethiopia. Agriculture, which was dependent on the age-old plough-oxen technology, was the mainstay of the economy, supported by crafts and trade. Transactions were conducted mainly by barter and through crude media of exchange. *Amole*, a salt bar, was the most widely used primitive monetary unit. Other items, such as beads, bracelets, cartridges, and cloth served at times as medium of exchange. The Austrian coin, the Maria Theresa Thaler (or dollar) (hereafter MTT) found its way into the country at the turn of the nineteenth century. It was a unit of measurement and a means of payment. It weighed 28 grams, which was equal to one *weqet*, a unit used to measure gold. The MTT was a (pure) silver coin, which gave it intrinsic value. From time to time, it was withdrawn from circulation to be converted into jewellery. Its intrinsic value and its metallic nature also encouraged hoarding. People commonly put the coins in a clay pot to bury in the ground, another way of withdrawing the money from circulation and also an established way of saving. Merchants also took the coins out of the country to use for transactions or simply to sell them if the price of silver went up on the international market. This created the recurrent problem of exchange fluctuations at the coast or even within Ethiopia when people with other currencies sought change. A French merchant, Vanderheym, reported that an MTT was bought at the French coast for 5fr.50 in the late 1880s, for 3fr.60 in 1893, and for 2fr.35 at the beginning of 1894 (Vanderheym 1896: 53). As trade expanded and the economic transition continued in the 1920s and 1930s, currency fluctuation and coin flight posed great challenges to the Ethiopian government. The MTT was a rather heavy currency: 'a sack of 500 MTD weighed at least 14 kilograms'.[1] With the expansion of trade in the early twentieth century, foreign merchants complained of the weight, preferring to travel with the newly made bank notes than heavy sacks of MTT. Another disadvantage of this currency was that it did not have fractional coins. For this reason, the *amole* was used as a fraction (Soleillet 1886: 95).

Economic historians generally state that the MTT was used for transactions involving luxury or expensive goods or in import/export trade. This generalization does not always match the reality when we examine detailed descriptions of specific markets or transactions. For instance, Vanderheym, who came to work in 1893 at the Addis Ababa trading post of a French company, Compagnie Commerciale Franco-Africaine, states in his memoir that Ethiopian merchants came to his shop to barter their export items (gold, elephant tusks, civet) against the manufactured goods they got from the trading post. On the other hand, the elite of the town, including Menelik, paid in thalers for whatever they bought (Vanderheym 1896: 53–4). Paul Soleillet, a French explorer-cum-merchant who visited central and southern Ethiopia from 1881 to 1884, gives a description of a market in the town of Were Ilu, one of the residences of Menelik, then King of Shewa (Soleillet 1886: 95–6). The open market was made up of two parts—the area for manufactured items from abroad such as textiles and other cheap commodities, where the merchants displayed their goods, and the area where the peasants of the region brought their agricultural produce for sale.

Soleillet wished to buy barley for his mules. First, he changed thalers to *amoles*, at the rate of 14 for the Austrian coin. Then he went in search of a peasant who was selling barley and offered to buy in *amoles*. The peasant told him that he needed wheat rather than salt bars. He went in search of the wheat, which turned out to be time-consuming and tiresome. Finally, he found a wheat merchant whom he asked to sell in *amole*s. The desire of the wheat merchant was to exchange his wheat for *teff* rather than for salt bars, so Soleillet went to a *teff* merchant, who fortunately wanted to sell his good in *amole*s. They took the *teff* to the wheat merchant from whom they took the wheat to the barley peasant to barter it at the rate of two measures of barley against one of wheat, the price at the time (Soleillet 1886: 95–6; Pankhurst 1968: 460). The French explorer found this procedure a rather complicated one, but it was a simple transaction for the local people.

To understand how the political economy of the country functioned in the last decades of the nineteenth century, we need to ask how the rulers ran their state. The polity collected tributes from its subjects to raise its revenues. The tributes were of two types: payment in kind or in labour. The royal courts always kept large granaries for grains, and store rooms for honey, butter, varieties of spices, artefacts, and cloth, as well as large temporary corrals for cattle, horses, mules, sheep, and goats. (The animals would later be farmed out to peasants in the surrounding districts for safe-keeping.) One of the duties of provincial and district governors was to collect similar tributes, keep a part for

[1] Peter Symes, 'Banknotes and Banking in Abyssinia and Ethiopia: A Story of British and American Interests', on http://www.pjsymes.com.au/articles/Abyssinia.htm (downloaded on 9 December 2017). This otherwise useful article, written by an established expert on currency, is not paginated.

themselves and pass a given amount to the royal court. When Menelik accepted vassalage to Yohannes, he was required to give a huge tribute annually:

> In December 1880, for example, Menelik paid the emperor 50,000 talers in cash, 600 mules and horses with tack trimmed in silver and gold, and first quality shammas worth about 80,000 talers; and the following May, 10,000 talers, 30,000 duallas [*sic.*] of grain, 10,000 cows, 2,000 measures of flour, and 40 urns of butter, the last four items having an estimated net worth of 50,000 talers. (Marcus 1975: 64)

Menelik in turn collected big tributes from his vassals and lieutenants. The arrival of Abba Jifar, the vassal king of Jimma in Addis, for the annual payment of his tributes was something of an event in the town. The court also looked forward to another annual pilgrimage with some excitement—the arrival of the chiefs of Bela Shangul, a remote province in western Ethiopia bordering the Sudan. Among other things, they submitted alluvial gold whose amount varied from year to year depending on the availability of the precious mineral in the river beds. The palace would also collect tributes from areas that were under its direct administration. So did the other members of the establishment who were assigned extensive amounts of land to support them either in ownership or as rights holders for part of the produce. Apart from the revenue in kind, all the land in the kingdom belonged to the king. Scholars always hasten to point out that this 'ownership' was more theoretical than practical, that in actual fact the authority of the kings was restricted by many traditions. This was beside the point, because actual ownership was not needed for the task of managing the huge and elaborate state.

The state remunerated all the people who served it and the elites that depended on it, and supported the institutions that were integral to it, such as the Ethiopian Church, by drawing upon these two resources—arable land and tributes—that were two sides of the same coin. They are presented here separately only for analytical purposes. A large number of the people who served the state in one capacity or another (military service, court service, Church service) were given a parcel of land by the government, either to live and work on it or to take a part of the tributes that the peasants who farmed it owed the state. The complex and detailed arrangements of this allocation of land and the tributes derived from it have confused students and researchers for many years. Nevertheless, it can be generalized that the state gave out either the land or the tribute that was due from it. In short, rather than collecting the tributes itself, the government simply transferred its right to its servants who collected them, used a part for themselves and paid the other part to the polity.

An integral element of this tributary system was the pervasive tribute in labour that the people gave to the state, the Church, and the ruling elite. The application of the European term of '*corvée* labour' for this type of tribute has made it difficult to grasp the ubiquity of the Ethiopian institution. In the European feudal system, *corvée* labour was used for public works, agriculture, and other economic projects. It was essentially an economic institution. In the African case, the state drew upon the labour of all its people (not just the peasants as in Europe) to provide a wide range of services including, of course, economic.

For instance, numerous transportation duties in the army such as moving and erecting tents, or transporting food, were met by the people as a tributary obligation.

The second system involved paying out salaries, not in cash but in kind, on a regular basis from the state's own treasury. The word for salary, *demoz*, was used for well over two centuries. The term *dergo* (an Ethiopian equivalent to *per diem*) was also widely used. When people were travelling from one province to another on official business, the state ordered the people of the area through which they passed to support them by giving them food, drinks, and other essential items,[2] inns being unknown at that time. *Dergo* was allocated to traveller after traveller who came into the country and whom the government wanted to host. This payment was so common that references to it are found in any book by a traveller.

The two systems—giving out arable land or payment in kind from the tributes that were collected—essentially boiled down to different ways of administering tributes. Provincial administration was a replica of the royal court, with district governors using the tribute allocated to them to manage local administration. Rulers used tributes to run the state but this did not exclude the use of money—MTTs from the beginning of the nineteenth century, or gold before that. One established way for the government to obtain silver coins was by selling abroad tributes of ivory, gold, civet, and similar goods they had collected. Through the centuries slaves were a major export item, with sales going directly to the treasury of the king (or the state), lending a predatory character to the state.[3] Another, equally well-known, method was to engage in import/export trade through surrogate merchants. The last traditional king, Menelik, engaged extensively in import/export. Local chiefs, from the highest to the lowest, also took part in foreign trade if the tributes they collected were tradeable abroad. Yet, in spite of the circulation of currency, the part that money played in the distribution of goods and services was minimal; it was barter, crude medium of exchange, and above all tributes that ensured the functioning of polity and economy.

2.2 The Base Years, 1894–1907

From the 1880s onwards, questions of how Ethiopia could get its own currency, develop trade, and increase the revenues of the state were discussed at the highest level of government. The available evidence shows that these discussions took place in the court of Menelik (Rubenson et al. 2000). He could not introduce the national currency until he sat on the imperial throne following the death of Yohannes in 1889. Another very difficult challenge was access to the sea. For northern Ethiopia, this was hindered by

[2] There was another institution that also served Ethiopian nobles during their travel from place to place—*el'f*. In this case, the peasants were called upon to take the luggage and other goods of the lord from their area to the next stop, usually a district away.

[3] Slavery was also widespread, mainly for domestic services. This pervasive institution was found in all households from royal courts to peasant homesteads.

hostile foreign control of the major port of the region, Massawa. For central Ethiopia, the route across the arid, waterless region to the coast was long, exposing travellers to malaria and, worse, to attack. Moreover, Ethiopia did not have its own territory along the Afar and Somali coast. However much the governments of Yohannes and Menelik wished to have their own outlets to the sea, they lacked the necessary military strength for the task.

The chronic problem of a dangerous route to the sea was resolved after 1887 when Shewan forces conquered the Amirate of Harar and established Ethiopian rule up to the areas close to (but not on) the Somali coast. Merchants, diplomats, and other international travellers found the trajectory from the British-ruled Zeila and the French port of Djibouti to the Harar plateau a shorter and safer route than the old one crossing the length of Afar land to the Shewan plateau. In the 1890s, Harar emerged as a big regional market town with an estimated population of around 30,000, large by the standards of the time. It was the city of novelties, where new things first made their appearance. The Egyptians, who had ruled it for ten years (1875–85), had improved communications with the outside world. The incorporation of this medieval city into the Ethiopian empire offered great opportunities for the envisaged transition. Moreover, the enlargement of Ethiopia proved beneficial for commerce—very quickly trade in Harar flourished as never before, attracting Greeks, Indians, Arabs, a mixture of Europeans and Armenians to settle there. In the last decade of the old century and the first of the new, it became the biggest emporium in the Ethiopian empire, with the prospect of railway construction into the hinterland looming large.

Railway construction was discussed in government circles in Shewa from as far back as the late 1870s. However, like the issue of coin minting, the railway idea took many years to be implemented. The rulers were aware that railways were potent instruments that could impose foreign domination, and the country was surrounded by powerful colonial powers. Of these, the French were thought to be the least dangerous neighbour, and therefore their colony was selected to serve as the starting point of the line. Even then, the government decided that the railway company had to be a private firm with no close ties with the French government. Menelik signed the concession with Alfred Ilg, a trusted Swiss counsellor, who was allowed to partner with Chefneux, a long-time resident French merchant, in order to be in a stronger position to raise capital on the French market. A private company was set up in 1896 and construction work began in 1897. Construction took five years to reach the place that was later called Dire Dawa in 1902.

Dire Dawa, about 300 km from the coast, came to acquire the distinction of being the first modern planned town in the history of Ethiopia. The planners of the railway company divided it into two: the neighbourhood by the railway station, Kezira, was assigned to white settlers, railway workers, merchants, and members of the Ethiopian elite, while Megala located further away from the station and separated from Kezira by a dry river bed, Dechatu, was set aside for Ethiopians, Indians, and Arabs. Dire Dawa became second only to Harar as a town of novelties. Hotels, restaurants, cafés, and shops were opened for the first time. A big customs house by the railway station served as a modern and important customs office of the country until the railway line reached Addis Ababa in 1917. But by then much had happened in Addis and in other places.

When it was born in 1886, and for several years afterwards, Addis Ababa ('the new flower') was no more than a collection of villages around a noble residence made up of huts (*tukuls*) with thatched roofs. The biggest village was the one around the palace of the emperor, which was also the centre of government. Perhaps the first dramatic development in the modernization of Addis Ababa took place in 1904–5 when the palace decided to demolish all the wood and mud houses covered with thatched roofs and rebuild them in stone with corrugated iron roofs (De Coppet 1930–2). Menelik's chronicler regarded this change as a milestone of modernity in the narrative of his sovereign. The development was made possible by the arrival of the railway line in Dire Dawa and, following that, the introduction of ox-drawn carts to haul heavy cargo from Dire Dawa to the capital city. The administrators of the 'new flower' fixed the principal market in the town centre, which they called Arada, with merchants settling around it. In a few years' time, at about the time of the construction boom in the palace, durable one-storey or even two-storey buildings made of stone, cement, and iron began to go up in Arada. Foreign merchants engaged in import/export and retail trade opened shops—another novelty in the era of novelties!—and foreign companies based in Aden opened branches. The first modern roads were built to connect Arada and the palace. By the turn of the second decade of the twentieth century, Addis Ababa overtook Harar as the empire's major emporium. Yet another novelty in Addis was the opening of the first major hotel (the Taitu Hotel) by the government in 1907. The Taitu Hotel was the beginning of the end for the institution of *dergo*; the government lodged its guests in the hotel where they were expected to pay their costs. It would of course take a long time for the tributary system to die out fully but its decline can be regarded as beginning at this time.

The initiative that turned out to be a hard nut to crack was the policy of monetization. It took the state a long time to get the country's own coins (called the Menelik thaler) minted in Paris; the new coins reached Ethiopia in 1894. But the people were not willing to use the new currency, even though it was a silver coin like the MTT and had more or less the same weight. In the place of the effigy of the Austrian queen, Maria Theresa, it now bore the image of Menelik and, on the obverse, the Lion of Judah. The other challenge associated with the sovereignty of the country was the introduction of banks. The state wished to give the concession to a private company, and Ilg and Chefneux were thought to be the ideal agents to establish a banking company. But they were not successful. The government also considered a big French bank, Credit Lyonnais, but the negotiations broke down. After a long series of negotiations, the Bank of Egypt, itself under the Bank of England, was given the right to open a bank in 1905. This was a major landmark in the monetary and banking history of Ethiopia. The first bank, Bank of Abyssinia, opened its doors to clients a year later.

Ethiopia had thus taken huge steps in the direction of a fundamental transformation in the years 1894 to 1907. In addition to those already listed, a series of important measures were adopted by the government to introduce modern infrastructure that was decisive for the transition: the introduction of a postal system (1894); the installation of telegraph and telephone lines (1898); and the policy of enticing foreign merchants (Indians, Armenians, Greeks, Arabs, and Europeans) to settle in the country to conduct trade on modern lines. The Westernization of the state was inaugurated by the establishment of ministries for the first time in October 1907. The move was dismissed as window dressing by contemporary observers and later by historians. Yet the Council of Ministers and the ministries turned out to be resilient institutions that went on to grow, expand, and further modernize.

Collectively, the years 1894 to 1907 can be summed up as the period when the country's transformation along Western lines was launched. Borrowing from economists, I call this time 'the base years' in the economic history of Ethiopia. The base years show that Ethiopia was a late arrival in the global process of Westernization otherwise known as modernization or development.

2.3 The Fledgling Decades, 1906–36

The most successful foreign direct investment was the railway project, even if construction was disappointingly slow. The 780-km long line (of which 100 kms were in the Djibouti Republic) reached Addis Ababa in 1917, fifteen years after its arrival in Dire Dawa in 1902. The impact on trade was, however, immediate, as Figure 2.1 shows.

About 80 per cent of the total trade of the country passed through Djibouti. The remaining foreign trade passed through Zeila, Berbera, Massawa, Gambella, and other small outlets. Total import/export trade rose steadily over the years from under ten million thalers for 1905 to over 90 million for 1935, a nine-fold increase in three decades. The steady increase in foreign trade augmented the revenue of the state. Apart from the year 1925, the imbalance between exports and imports also steadily increased.

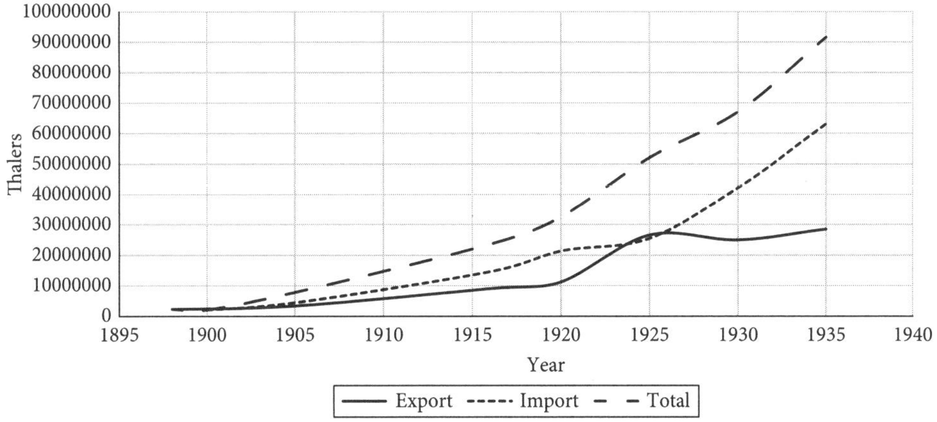

FIGURE 2.1 Import/export trade through Djibouti

Source: Pankhurst (1968: 412, 430).

But the railway was not the only factor that explains this development in foreign trade. A series of legislations, including a criminal code in 1930 and a constitution in 1931, regulated, among other things, the economic sphere. Customs administration was steadily modernized and centralized. The economic ministries (trade and finance) were steadily strengthened. Though historians have not been able to study it in depth due to shortage of sources, there was growth in the urban population of the country which expanded the market. The peace dividend was also a factor because there was no major war after 1917.

Manufacturing came onto the horizon in this period. Aside from the grain mills and saw mills constructed in increasing numbers in different parts of the country from the very beginning of the century, bona fide manufacturing plants were built in the 1920s and early 1930s.[4] A beer factory, a total of five printing presses, skin processing, shoe factories, and beverage factories all appeared, mainly in Addis Ababa with a few in Dire Dawa. Mining concessions were given to some foreigners and Ethiopians who searched for gold and other precious minerals in different parts of the country. The estimated labour population was a few thousand, not including railway workers. Labour, a newly born social group, was indeed a tiny force at the time of the country's invasion in 1935. There are no statistics for boutiques, restaurants, bars, and cafés that opened mainly in Addis Ababa and, to a certain extent, in towns such as Harar and Dire Dawa. A number of hotels opened in the capital city as well as in the railway town and its neighbour Harar. Infrastructure building was a big challenge, mainly due to shortage of finance.

Government revenue was contingent upon the degree of monetization of the economy. Monetization remained low throughout the years under study. A study by a one-time IMF economist on the degree of monetization of some Third-World countries reached the following conclusion: 'The ratio of money supply to national income serves as some guide to the extent of monetization achieved in the economies of different countries. The relevant data for 1954 . . . show that the ratio varies from 7 per cent in Ethiopia to 51 per cent in Lebanon.' (Ali 1957: 51). Even as late as the early 1950s, the ratio of money supply to national income was very low, which suggests that the extent of monetization in the 1920s and 1930s was even lower. The economic historian Richard Pankhurst cites MacGillivray, the first governor of the Bank of Abyssinia, who had access to the books of the palace between 1906 and 1910:

> MacGillivray indicated that there was a considerable accumulation of wealth in the palace. He tells of three treasuries: The Emperor's treasury, which contained 2,000,000 dollars, the public treasury with 60,000 dollars, and Menelik's private treasury with 1,000,000. Well satisfied with the accuracy of such figures, he observes: "the books of the various Treasuries were very neatly kept, though primitive. In Harar the custom-house books are written in Arabic, and also some of the books at the capital. Many of the government officials I interviewed spoke Arabic, and the custom-house at Addis Ababa is run by a Suakin Arab." (Pankhurst 1968: 539)

[4] A soda factory opened in the first decade of the century was thus the oldest (or one of the oldest) manufacturing plants in Ethiopia.

Dollar here means the MTT. The rounded figures cast doubt on the precision of the informant, MacGillivray. Neither Pankhurst nor the informant give the year in which the banker read these figures in the palace books. Nevertheless, the bank governor deserves to be taken seriously because, as he claims, his figures are based on what he observed. There was no neat separation of government money from the money of the emperor and, therefore, the figures here given can be taken as the amount of money that was at the disposal of the state at any given time. The quotation shows that the government did indeed have a small amount of money in its coffers. On the other hand, it is interesting to observe that the banker saw, in this sum, an accumulation of wealth in the palace. State revenues steadily increased many-fold over the years but hard facts that would enable analysis are lacking. Yet, however much the revenue grew, it could not finance development starting from such a low base. Moreover, the military took the lion's share of the available financial resources, leaving little for investment in infrastructure.

With a small budget, the government embarked on roadbuilding projects in the 1920s. In 1935, when the invasion was launched, all-weather gravel roads linked Addis Ababa with Dessie and Jimma, while the roads to Gojam and Wollega were built half way, to the edge of the Abay gorge and the town of Ambo respectively. The provincial administration built all-weather gravel roads from Harar to Jegjega, from Dire Dawa to Harar, and from Miesso to Asebe Teferi (present-day Chiro). A planned road to the then province of Sidamo had reached Modjo when the war broke out. The government asphalted some of the axis roads of Addis Ababa.

Education was regarded as a key to development. In speech after speech in the 1920s and 1930s, Haile Selassie hammered home this point. Leading figures in the regime also underlined the critical role of education. But education was a very expensive undertaking. Teachers, textbooks, and other teaching aides must be imported in addition to the buildings that had to be put up. Missionaries provided elementary education together with a big dose of their religions. The first public establishment, called Menelek II School, was opened in 1907; it took the government a decade and a half to open the next one in 1925, Teferi Makonnen School. The government took up seriously the task of expanding education in the years that followed. A 6 per cent education tax was levied on import/export trade in 1926. From 1926 to 1930, two schools were opened in Addis Ababa and four in the provinces (Dessie, Dire Dawa, Jigjiga, and Neqemt). The rate of expansion increased after the coronation of Haile Selassie in 1930. In the following five years, the major provincial capitals each acquired a school. A vocational school, a teacher training institute, and a girl's school were also opened in the capital city. From two in 1925, the number of schools grew to twenty-one ten years later, a ten-fold increase (Firesenbet 2006: 8–11). The student population, which was about three hundred in 1926, had grown to 4,200 by the time of the invasion in 1935—an over ten-fold increase in a space of ten years. The government was proud of this achievement, and the modern propaganda machine that Haile Selassie had put in place presented the narrative in glowing terms.

But all this was elementary education. For secondary education, the government sent students to Egypt, Lebanon, and the Sudan, because the cost in these countries was lower than in Europe. When the first big batch (20 students) was dispatched to a *lycée* in

Alexandria in 1926, it was the talk of the town. The heir apparent officially sent them off, and the newspaper presented the news as a major event. Successive waves went. When they completed their secondary education, some of the students moved on to universities in France or Belgium. The government paid in many cases also for university education, increasing the cost. In 1931, Ernest Work, an African American professor in the United States, was brought in to design a plan for an educational pyramid from kindergarten to university level. He quickly submitted a proposal that included giving a name to the university that would be established in the future—Haile Selassie I University. But progress was interrupted by the Italian invasion. The first secondary school would be opened much later (1943).

The government encouraged foreign direct investment even if very little came, and it also invested in partnership with foreigners. An interesting case was the company known in the sources and in the scholarly literature by its French name, La Société Nationale d'Ethiopie pour le Développement de l'Agriculture et du Commerce, which has come down to today as the Development Bank of Ethiopia. It was first set up in 1908 with a paid-up capital of 3,200,000 thalers in 40,000 shares of 80 thalers each; the shareholders were Menelik, Taitu, and the big chieftains of the country. Its objective was to be an alternative institution to the foreign-owned Bank of Abyssinia. But the shareholders did not get the requisite professional manpower to run it; and this quickly led to its hibernation. The government decided to revive it in 1928 in partnership with French firms who put up part of the capital with the Ethiopian government providing the rest. The board of directors was dominated by Ethiopian senior officials. This firm operated as both a commercial and 'development' bank and also engaged in import/export trade. Very soon, it emerged as one of the biggest companies in the country. The government also decided to buy out the Bank of Abyssinia because the British were willing to sell it. In 1931, it was converted into the Bank of Ethiopia, serving as the central bank and also as a commercial bank. Both banks opened branches in the provinces, issued new paper currency and carried out their other banking duties. The Bank of Abyssinia reported profits from 1924 to 1931. In spite of all the efforts of these banks, the populace refused to part with the MTT, which continued as a medium of exchange, store of value, and unit of measurement into the late 1940s.

2.4 The Italian Interlude, 1936–41

Road building was a major project undertaken even during the war by the victors. In five years of occupation, they upgraded the Ethiopian government's roads and built a new network of interprovincial highways that connected Addis Ababa, now the capital of Italian East Africa, with the regional capitals and with the economically important areas—Addis with Asmara, Harar, Jimma, Gondar (via Dessie), and Moqadishu. They constructed a total of 7,000 kms of which about half were asphalt. In the major towns, particularly in Addis Ababa, they built asphalt streets and rough roads (Gascon 2010: 394).

They opened new factories to support house building, including a cement factory and a brick factory, and also flour mills, oil presses, a macaroni factory, and bottling businesses to cater to their newly settled populations (Pankhurst 2014: 351). They invested heavily to expand the capital city, regional capitals, and towns which were targeted to become manufacturing hubs, such as Dire Dawa, Kombolcha, and Dessie. The regime's urban policy was informed by its race policy, with towns divided into white areas and native quarters. The city centre and the old quarters of Addis Ababa were allocated to whites, and the Ethiopians from these parts were resettled in the western outskirts, which was also made the central market for Africans. The vast new village came to be called MerKato. In the European quarter, a massive housebuilding project was undertaken for functionaries, workers, and Italians being encouraged to settle. No fewer than 35,000 Italians made their homes in Addis Ababa, an unprecedented number. Those who settled in provincial towns were smaller in number (Del Boca 1982: 170, 172). The cultural impact of this extensive Western presence must have been large, although it has not yet been studied. There was large-scale employment for the numerous construction projects.

The sum total of Italian activities expanded the process of monetization of the Ethiopian economy. The government's plan to replace the MTT with the Italian lira did not, however, succeed. The Ethiopian people still preferred the silver coins to the bank notes of the victors. Pragmatism prevailed and the authorities allowed the two currencies to operate side by side. The Bank of Ethiopia was replaced by Banca d'Italia. The commercial banks—Banco di Roma, Banco di Napoli, and Banca Nazionale del Lavoro—opened for business in the country. They also allowed La Société Nationale d'Ethiopie to continue to operate. Fully fledged insurance companies came over from Italy to offer their services—to Italians and other whites.

2.5 Planning Development

The Italian occupation was short-lived, lasting barely five years. The project of building a modern state—a central issue in development—was taken up with great vigour after liberation in 1941. The foundations of a modern civil service, a national army, a police force, a parliament, a judiciary, specialized departments of the state, monetary and banking institutions were laid very quickly. The government declared that it would abolish the tributary system in a short time, and took measures to that effect. The first measure, issued a few months after the liberation of Ethiopia, was the decision to pay civil servants, members of the armed forces, and the police force their salaries in cash. This policy included governors, ministers, and senior army officers, who were traditionally put in command of vast amounts of tributary resources when they were appointed to high offices. The vast army of palace servants was also put on the government payroll. To further strengthen the policy of abolishing the tributary system, the state proclaimed that taxes should be paid in cash to the government rather than in kind to an individual lord. These decrees did not immediately put an end to the age-old institution; nevertheless, the government had definitely tolled the bell for the tributary system.

A notable feature of the new status quo was that the leaders started to think systematically about development, as can be seen in the predilection for planning from the very beginning. There was awareness that the manpower resources of the country were still deficient and recourse to external technical assistance was felt to be unavoidable if planning had to be installed as an institution:

> In July 1943 the Ethiopian Government requested the United States of America to provide technical advice and assistance in connection with rebuilding and developing the country. They later asked that technical missions be sent to cover the important problems. Accordingly, a mission to cover technical, agricultural and geological fields was sent from America. This mission, which was formally designated the 'United States Technical Project in Ethiopia', operated here during 1944 and 1945.
> (*Guide Book of Ethiopia*, 1954: 353)

This plan was called, rather pompously, the Ten-Year Programme of Industrial Development. One of the merits of this exercise was that it brought systematic thinking to the complicated issue of development. Government departments were encouraged to articulate their own specific programmes, such as projects for port development, airport improvement, highway reconstruction and repair, telecommunications, and industrial development (*Guide Book of Ethiopia*, 1954: 353). A detailed ten-year plan for the expansion of education was also developed. This continued until the preparations for the First Five Year Plan, which was launched in 1957. Then the second (1963–7) and the third (1968–73) Development Plans were successively launched. An important event in this respect was the publication in 1962 of a twenty-year development strategy outlining the road map for national transformation, which would take Ethiopia out of its status as a Least Developed Country. Official development thinkers and international advisers loudly preached the wisdom of adopting the policy of import substitution and land reform as a means of speeding up growth. The philosophy that underlay all these plans, policies, road maps, and vision statements was the corpus of modernization theories that were called developmentalism. The government's policy was to play the role of a development agent by getting heavily involved in the economy and by building a mixed economy (Imperial Ethiopian Government 1957: 144; Imperial Ethiopian Government 1962: 35; Ferede forthcoming). Economic growth was seen as a source of political legitimacy for the ruling class, which was a major feature of developmentalist thinking. Hence, much energy and resources were allocated to the official propaganda machinery, which presented Haile Selassie and his government as the champions of 'civilization' and modernity. The emperor was routinely portrayed more as the Sun King than as the scion of the Solomonic dynasty. The fact that the economy started to undergo transformation after the World War II was used to undergird the official claims.

Another notable feature of the post-war years was the focus on institution building. The task of constructing a modern state entailed the establishment of numerous agencies and departments. The Economic Council was established in 1955, bringing together all the key economic ministries to deliberate on development issues and to prepare the national plan. In the same year the Council set up the Planning Board which elaborated the First and the Second Five Year Plans. The Board was upgraded to the Ministry of Planning in 1966 and was later (1969) made Planning Commission. In 1961, two technical agencies that were of crucial importance to state and economy were established—the Central Statistical Agency and the Central Personnel Agency. Instituting regular government budgeting turned out to be difficult for a state that had not shed all its premodern attributes. After trials and errors in the first half of the 1950s, budgets became a normal feature from the fiscal year 1956/7 onwards.

The government adopted a policy of establishing companies for some of the strategic sectors. The State Bank of Ethiopia (1943) took on the functions of a central bank and a commercial bank at the initial stage; in 1963, when the economy had expanded sufficiently, it was split into two—the National Bank of Ethiopia and the Commercial Bank of Ethiopia. The government resurrected the old Société Nationale d'Ethiopie and gave it a new name, the Agricultural Bank of Ethiopia (1945), which was then rechristened the Agricultural and Industrial Bank of Ethiopia (1949), to be further restructured into the Development Bank of Ethiopia (1951), the name it bears today. In the 1960s, other financial institutions were set up—the Imperial Savings and Home Ownership Association (1962), the Mortgage Company of Ethiopia (1965), and Commercial Nominees (1967). All these firms were state owned. Transportation was the other sector in which the state involved itself, starting with Ethiopian Airlines (1946), the Ethio-Djibouti Railway Company (jointly owned by the French and the Ethiopian governments as of 1952, ownership by Ethiopia and Djibouti since 1977), and Ethiopian Shipping Lines (1967). In 1951, the Imperial Highway Authority was also brought into existence. Utilities remained a government domain. Shewa Electric and Power (1948) which later became the Ethiopian Electric Light and Power Authority (1955) and the Imperial Board of Telecommunications (1953) enabled the state to retain monopoly over these sectors. In the sphere of construction, the government brought together the cement factories that had already been established during the Italian period into the Cement Corporation.

Manufacturing steadily expanded in the decades after World War II to constitute a sector in its own right. In the first half of the 1950s, the sector 'nearly doubled and a number of modern enterprises were created' ('Industry' 2014: 351) The upward trajectory continued at an even higher tempo in the second half of the 1950s and for the first half of the 1960s, registering an annual growth rate of 17 per cent. The surge in coffee exports helped the expansion of the sector. 'In 1972/73 the contribution of agriculture to the GDP declined to 54.6%, while that of the industrial sector increased to 15.4% and that of services to 30%' ('Industry' 2014: 352). In the years from 1960 to 1965, GDP grew at an average rate of 5 per cent, slightly declining in the next five years to 4 per cent (Shiferaw 1995: 17). The early 1970s saw a further decline to 3 per cent due to the global crises resulting from the oil embargo imposed by Arab countries and the drought in the country. 'Thus, the growth of the economy averaged about 3% in the 1950s, 4.5% in the 1960s, and 3% between 1970 and 1974' (Shiferaw 1995: 17). Foreign and domestic investment was growing, which naturally brought about an increase in the number of share companies, which in turn produced the need for a securities market. In 1965, the National Bank decided to lay the foundations for a future stock exchange by establishing the Share Dealing Group, which would enable the selling and buying of shares. Very soon, it became a very robust arrangement that led to a brisk trade in shares (Von Pischke 1968). The expansion of the modern economy and the concomitant growth of the business class called for new legislation to govern economic transactions, dealings, and contracts as well as the establishment of enterprises as share companies or as private limited companies and corporations. The Commercial Code, the Maritime Code, and the Civil Code were all promulgated in 1960, creating a suitable legislative environment.

Education, which as we have seen was regarded as a key to development, was given serious attention by the government. On the liberation of the country, the government immediately set about re-establishing the educational system. Elementary schools were opened in 1941–2 using available resources: more than one military barrack of the Italian armed forces was converted into a school. A commercial school (to train secretaries, bank clerks, and accountants), a technical school (the equivalent of a vocational school), and a teacher training school were opened only a year after the restoration of independence. The first secondary school in the country's history was opened in 1943 at Kotebe, then located in the suburbs of Addis. Each inauguration was a big occasion presided over personally by the emperor. The first secondary school received special attention because Haile Selassie frequently visited it, encouraged students and teachers whom he got to know personally, and looked into their administrative problems. Three years later, in 1946, the General Wingate secondary school opened at the western end of the city. It was again the monarch in person who followed the construction of the buildings and the provision of facilities, and who presided over the inauguration. Over the next few years, secondary schools rapidly opened in the provincial capitals and also in Addis. In the provinces the inauguration ceremony was attended (if possible) by Haile Selassie, if not by ministers, with the event providing the occasion for speech making and other festivities. In provincial towns, the director of the school was regarded as one of the top government officials, in much the same way as today's university presidents. Ten years after independence (1950) saw the opening of Ethiopia's first tertiary establishment, the University College of Addis Ababa—another occasion for a grand inauguration ceremony. In the 1950s, a degree-granting engineering college, a public health college, and an agricultural college were opened. The government combined all the tertiary institutions into Haile Selassie I University, which was formally opened in 1961. Its main campus was located in the imperial residential palace which was donated by the monarch. When the university started its first classes, its student body numbered 974. In the academic year 1973/4, this population rose to 6,474, registering a well over six-fold increase in twelve years (Wagaw 1990: 167). The government allocated about 20 per cent of the national budget to education during the 1940s, enabling an average annual expansion of 16 per cent. Private as well as public schools registered rapid growth. There were also mission schools. Ten years after independence, the number of elementary schools reached 400 and there were eleven secondary schools, while the total student population was about 60,000 (Vestal 2005: 235b). When the revolution broke out in 1974, the student population had reached 957,300 and schools numbered 3,196 (Vestal 2005: 236b).

2.6 Conclusion

The expansion was indeed impressive, but it reached only 12 per cent of primary school-age children (Vestal 2005: 236b). This disparity brings us to the methodological question of how to evaluate the performance of the imperial government. On the one hand, seen from a historical perspective, the figures for the manufacturing sector and for GDP as well as for education appear impressive. On the other hand, in absolute terms the figures show that the transformation of the country was still in its initial stages. Yet, it can be argued that the changes introduced up to the 1960s have indeed taken the Ethiopian economy from a traditional one in which goods and services circulated through barter, crude media of exchange and, to a very large extent, the tributary system to a developing economy where money was the main medium. Moreover, the economy underwent a fundamental mutation from plough-based agriculture and traditional crafts to one boasting several modern sectors—infrastructure, services, manufacturing, and finance. In short, in the seven decades or so that are surveyed, the system underwent a structural transformation from a traditional economy to a developing one. The focus of economists, politicians, and other observers globally has always been on the shortcomings of a developing country (its prevalent poverty, low per capita real income, high population growth, dependence on primary products, and high rates of unemployment), which has obscured the fact that being a developing country means standing one notch higher in the process of transformation from a traditional economy to an industrial economy. Ethiopia entered that stage several decades ago.

References

Ali, Anwar (1957). 'Banking in the Middle East', *Staff Papers*, Vol. 6, No. 1. International Monetary Fund.

Chandavarkar, Anand G. (1977). 'Monetization of Developing Economies', Staff Papers, Vol. 24, No. 3, International Monetary Fund, Washington, DC.

De Coppet, Maurice (ed.). (1930–2). *Chronique du regne de Ménélik II, roi des rois d'Ethiopie*, by Guebre Selassie. Tr. Tesfa Selassie, 2 vols. (Paris: Librairie orientale et americaine).

Del Boca, Angelo (1982). *Gli italiani in Africa Orientale Italiana: III. La caduta dell'impero* (Roma-Bari: Laterza).

Ferede, T. (forthcoming). 'Setting the Context: Economy and Policy Environment', in *The History of the Commercial Bank of Ethiopia*. Addis Ababa (forthcoming).

Firesenbet, Kebede. (2006). 'Modern Education in Pre-Revolution Ethiopia' [text in Amharic]. Paper presented at a workshop organized by the Forum for Social Studies, Addis Ababa (unpublished).

Gascon, A. 'Roads' (2010). *Encyclopaedia Aethiopica*, Vol. IV (Wiesbaden: Harrassowitz).

Guide Book of Ethiopia (1954). Addis Ababa: n.p.

Imperial Ethiopian Government (1957). 'Five-Year Development Plan, 1957–1961'. Ministry of Finance, Addis Ababa.

Imperial Ethiopian Government (1962). 'Second Five-Year Development Plan, 1963–1967', Ministry of Finance, Addis Ababa.

'Industry' (2014). *Encyclopaedia Aethiopica*, Vol. 5 (Wiesbaden: Harrassowitz).

Marcus, H. (1975). *The Life and Times of Menelik II: Ethiopia, 1844–1913* (Oxford: Clarendon Press).

Pankhurst, R. (1968). *Economic History of Ethiopia (1800 to 1935)* (Addis Ababa: Harrassowitz).

Pankhurst, R. (2014). 'Industry in Ethiopia until 1941', in *Encyclopaedia Aethiopica*, Vol. 5 (Wiesbaden: Harrassowitz).

Rubenson, Sven, et al. (eds) (2000). *Internal Rivalries and Foreign Threats, 1869–1879*, Acta Aethiopica, Vol. 3 (Addis Ababa: Addis Ababa University Press).

Shiferaw, Jamo (1995). 'An Overview of the Economy', in *An Economic History of Ethiopia*, ed. Shiferaw Bekele (Dakar: CODESRIA).

Soleillet, P. (1886). '*Voyage en Ethiopie: janvier 1882–Octobre 1884, Bulletin de la Société normande de géographie' (Notes, lettres et documents divers)* (Rouen: impr. de E. Cagniard).

Symes, Peter. 'Banknotes and Banking in Abyssinia and Ethiopia: A Story of British and American Interests'. http://www.pjsymes.com.au/articles/Abyssinia.htm (downloaded 9 December 2017).

Vanderheym, J. G. (1896). *Une expedition avec le negous Ménélik*. (Paris: Hachette Livre-BNF).

Vestal, T. (2005). 'Modern Education', in *Encyclopaedia Aethiopica*, Vol. 2 (Wiesbaden: Harrassowitz).

Von Pischke, J. D. (1968). *Shares and Share Trading in Addis Ababa* (Addis Ababa: College of Business Administration, Haile Selassie University).

Wagaw, Teshome (1990). *The Development of Higher Education and Social Change: An Ethiopian Experience* (East Lansing: Michigan State University Press).

CHAPTER 3

THE POLITICAL ECONOMY OF ETHIOPIA FROM THE IMPERIAL PERIOD TO THE PRESENT

CHRISTOPHER CLAPHAM

3.1 Introduction: The Legacies of Ethiopian Statehood

'Development is first of all a political process', as Meles Zenawi argued (Lefort 2015: 357–94). It is deeply concerned with identities, interests, cultures, institutions, aspirations, arguments, and the exercise of power. This chapter explores how these factors have affected Ethiopia's development both in the past, and during the period since the EPRDF government took power in 1991.

The starting point must be Ethiopia's position as the sole indigenous African state to maintain its independence through the period of colonial conquest. As well as being a justifiable source of national pride and self-confidence, this distinctive legacy continues to have an enormous impact on Ethiopia's political economy, and helps to account for some of the successes, and also some of the continuing problems, in its developmental trajectory. It is also a factor in the potential replicability of the Ethiopian model in other African states. Its two key features, which resonate throughout the country's recent history under very different regimes, are the political and economic geography of the country on the one hand, and the distinctive character of Ethiopian statehood on the other.

The first of these features concerns the historical divergence between the sources of political and economic power. Historically, political power in Ethiopia has been rooted in the 'core' area of the northern highlands, characterized economically by grain cultivation through ox-plough agriculture, and politically by hierarchical structures often characterized as 'feudal'. While this sustained relatively dense populations, and formed the basis for an ancient and impressive civilization capable of defending itself against European colonialism, it was very poorly equipped to participate in the global economy into which Africa was incorporated from the late nineteenth century onwards. The area was subject to progressive ecological degradation and was barely capable of sustaining its own population, while producing very little that could generate income from the global economy. The Ethiopian state compensated for this weakness by conquering vast areas of territory, especially to the south and west of the highland zone, which helped to provide it with a much more resilient economic base, including export crops of which the most important was coffee. This geographical shift was reflected in the creation of a permanent capital in Addis Ababa, in a region at the very south of the historic territory of the Ethiopian state, but well placed for access to the conquered lands. It was accompanied by the construction of a new outlet to the sea at Djibouti, which was linked to Addis Ababa by rail, and helped to open up the southern regions from which the economic resources of the state derived.

This shift in the location of economic power was not, however, accompanied by any corresponding shift in that of political power, which continued to derive from the northern highlands, and was represented in the imperial structure of government, the continuing role of the Ethiopian Orthodox Church, and the development of Amharic as a 'national' language. Instead, northern control over the most productive areas of the economy was imposed through a highly exploitative system in which land was alienated to those who held power in the government, and indigenous populations were reduced to the role of serfs, generating deep-seated resentments which to some extent replicated both ethnic and religious divisions.

The second enduring feature of Ethiopia's political economy was its ability to sustain a state whose power, reach, and durability were unequalled in sub-Saharan Africa. Led until recent times by an emperor or king of kings, it placed a very high emphasis on leadership, and its primary goal was to maintain imperial control over the large and disparate territory that it claimed. Even before its late nineteenth-century expansion, this was an extremely challenging task, since the northern highlands were themselves divided by deep ravines that impeded communication, and its different regions and provinces acquired identities and sustained local political authorities of their own. At times, notably in the late eighteenth and early nineteenth centuries, the country broke apart into what were effectively independent principalities. The power of the emperor was nonetheless in principle absolute, and both the revival of imperial leadership in the later nineteenth century, and the conquest of the southern territories that gave the central government a greatly strengthened economic base, reinforced a structure of control in which the development of autonomous institutions was very limited. This applied not least to the management of the economy, which until modern times was effectively restricted to the extraction of the resources needed to sustain the country's political and religious authorities, while such trading networks as existed were largely in the hands of Moslems, who were excluded from positions of political power. The hierarchy of statehood, reinforced by a strong sense of historic mission and a very restricted capacity for delegation, thus intensified the problems generated by the divergence between political and economic power, and created major challenges for economic governance. This chapter examines the attempts to meet these challenges under the imperial, revolutionary, and federal systems of government in place since 1941.

3.2 The Imperial Regime, 1941–74

Ethiopia's liberation from Italian occupation in May 1941 led to the restoration of the imperial government under Emperor Haile Selassie, within a markedly changed domestic and international political order. Domestically, the wars of conquest and liberation between 1935 and 1941 destroyed much of the autonomy of local authorities, and enabled the central government to exercise far greater control than previously over the territories that it ruled. This control was implemented through a uniform structure of provincial administration, backed by improved communications and a national army. Internationally, Ethiopia was able to take its place within a global order orchestrated by the United Nations, and allied itself with the United States—an alliance that was instrumental in enabling it to incorporate the former Italian colony of Eritrea in 1952. During this period, therefore, Ethiopia's foreign policy stance was closely aligned with the major trading powers in the international economy, in a way that encouraged external aid and investment. The independence of other African territories from colonial rule, and the formation in 1963 of the Organisation of African Unity headquartered in Addis Ababa, reinforced Ethiopia's diplomatic standing, while the emergence of 'development' as a key goal of global economic management helped the country to benefit from external aid funds and expertise.

The imperial government accepted the development agenda, because—and insofar as—this reinforced its own power. Notable in this respect was the formation of a number of state corporations, including the Imperial Highways Authority (IHA), the Imperial Board of Telecommunications of Ethiopia (IBTE), and Ethiopian Air Lines (EAL), the basic function of which was to create the infrastructure, centred on Addis Ababa, through which control could be exercised. The regime did not to any significant extent engage in productive activities, but provided a framework within which these could be conducted by the private sector, two aspects of which were particularly noteworthy. The first was the encouragement of foreign direct investment in commercial agriculture, for which the Awash valley running south and southeast of Addis Ababa was the key location, conveniently placed to take advantage of access to the sea through the port of Assab, which became Ethiopian territory following the federation with Eritrea in 1952. The two most important investors were the Dutch HVA company for sugar, and the British Mitchell Cotts for cotton. 'Virgin lands' schemes of this kind were to become a staple of the Ethiopian development enterprise, situated in politically peripheral parts of the country, and introduced with little concern for the interests of their indigenous inhabitants. The second was the appropriation by powerful individuals associated with the regime, of whom Ras Mesfin Sileshi, former governor of Sidamo region, was the most notorious, of lands in the southwest, which could be exploited, especially for coffee. Addis Ababa and a string of satellite towns along the line of rail to Djibouti hosted the country's still embryonic industry.

But while these initiatives could be presented as part of a modest but positive process of economic growth, any sustained development programme was incompatible with the very narrow political base of the regime. Attempts to project an appearance of developmental dynamism through the publication of a Five-Year Plan in 1957, or the establishment of a Ministry of Land Reform in 1966, could readily be dismissed as window-dressing. In the peripheries, the alienation of local populations gave rise to a number of peasant revolts, the most important of which took place in the Bale region, where the dispossession of land by northern settlers was particularly acute, between 1963 and 1970 (Tareke 1991). At the centre, the attempt to modernize the state involved the creation of a powerful government with the personnel needed to staff it, especially through a greatly expanded education system and a professional army. But neither students nor soldiers owed any loyalty to what they increasingly regarded as a corrupt, incompetent and outmoded imperial regime, and instead they became attracted to a still inchoate revolutionary nationalism in which they themselves would hold the central place, backed by an ideological commitment to Marxism-Leninism. Although the plight of the peasantry provided (under the slogan 'Land to the Tiller') a significant part of the moral and ideological justification for the revolution that was to sweep away the imperial government in 1974, the agents and beneficiaries of that revolution derived overwhelmingly from subaltern elites at the centre. Ethiopia differed sharply from those colonial African territories in which nationalist parties competed for rural votes, and in the process created political linkages to the countryside. In short, the imperial regime did not resolve—and more basically *could* not resolve—the contradiction between the two critical elements in Ethiopia's political economy: the existence of a powerful state tradition, which the development process ineluctably reinforced, and the deeply unequal relationship between those who controlled the state and the areas of the countryside in which this development process necessarily took place. The struggle to reconcile these elements was the legacy that the imperial system of government—and most basically of all, the way in which the Ethiopian state had been created in the first place—left to its successors.

3.3 The Derg Regime, 1974–91

The revolutionary military regime that overthrew the imperial government in 1974, and consolidated its control after a vicious struggle for power by 1977 (widely known as the Derg, from the Amharic name for the Provisional Military Administrative Council on whose behalf power was formally exercised until 1984), sought to resolve this contradiction through the wholesale adoption of a model borrowed from the Soviet Union. As its ideological origins indicate, this project placed an overwhelming emphasis on the projection of state power. Its central measure, the land reform of 1975, nationalized all land, rural and urban, and established a structure of peasants' associations in the countryside and urban dwellers' associations in the towns, known as *kebeles*, through which individual plots of land would be allocated to their users. Since peasants had rights to land only in their own home areas, they were locked into these areas in a way that inhibited emigration and led to intensified pressure on land, as part of a process that Dessalegn Rahmato has described as 'agrarian involution' (Rahmato 1984: 61–2). Control of peasants' associations thus became critical to local-level governance, and they were rapidly brought under the control of a hierarchy imposed from the centre, which for the first time provided the Ethiopian government with a mechanism through which power—hitherto dispersed between a myriad of local actors—could be concentrated in state hands. Other means of production, including the agricultural estates established by foreign corporations, were nationalized, and an apparatus of Soviet-style central planning was established. The crowning structure of the whole enterprise, the formation of a Leninist vanguard party, the Workers' Party of Ethiopia (WPE), was delayed until the tenth anniversary of the revolution in 1984, at which point the Derg formally gave way to the People's Democratic Republic of Ethiopia (PDRE), in which the members of the ruling Politburo, under its leader Mengistu Haile Mariam, largely replicated the previous military regime.

At the same time, the new system did indeed represent a revolutionary transformation of the imperial structures of government. The landowning class was destroyed, and many of its individual members were either killed or forced into exile, to the benefit of the formerly exploited peasantry, especially in the south of the country. And though local elites sometimes reappeared in the guise of *kebele* chairmen, the impact of revolution resonated down to the very lowest levels of a society much of which had hitherto been almost untouched by 'modernity' (Donham 1999). A massive expansion in access to education, along with less welcome innovations such as military conscription, brought Ethiopians within the grasp of the state in a way that had never previously been the case. But these changes only very partially bridged over the divergence already noted between the regions that exercised political power, and those that sustained economic development. Even though the regime was committed to the idea of an inclusive Ethiopian nationalism, and there was some increase in the number of powerful individuals coming from outlying areas, the over-representation of highlanders in both the military and the intelligentsia, from which most of the new leadership came, with the intensified emphasis on centralized state power and on national symbols that were inevitably drawn from the northern highlands, helped to perpetuate the existing divide. The new structures of state-centred economic management, moreover, applied disproportionately to those parts of the centre and south of the country that were already in some degree incorporated into the market economy. The former commercial estates like those in the Awash valley were converted into state farms, with inevitably disappointing (or indeed disastrous) effects. The pursuit of 'virgin lands' schemes in the periphery was intensified, and extended to areas such as Gambela on the Sudanese border in the southwest. And though the old settler class in the south had been swept away, a new form of northern immigration arrived in the form of the 'resettlement' schemes established in the wake of famine in the northern highlands in 1984–5; these new settlers were destitute peasants rather than conquerors, but nonetheless (in the eyes of indigenous populations) brought about the loss of local resources to incomers.

The political economy of the Derg regime failed most basically at the political level, because it did not establish any structure of participation through which to pass on the benefits that had ostensibly accrued to the 'broad masses' as a result of land reform and the removal of some of the most blatant forms of exploitation. At the local level, the *kebeles* rapidly emerged as instruments of state power, rather than of local empowerment. At the central level, a government engaged in bitter struggles in Eritrea, the Somali region, and Tigray and increasingly had nothing to offer beyond an Ethiopian nationalism that, despite some incorporation of individuals from the periphery, continued to rest essentially on the historic core, and was intensely reluctant to make any concessions to the country's ethnic and religious diversity. Not until very late in the day, when the need to recognize this diversity had become urgent and obvious, did it establish the Institute for the Study of Ethiopian Nationalities (ISEN), which just had time to conduct a basic mapping exercise of the country's ethnic composition, before the regime itself was swept away, and ISEN's map came to serve as the initial basis for the federal system established by its successor.

The regime failed equally basically at the economic level, because of the evident inability of a system of central planning derived from the Soviet Union (where its inadequacies were becoming increasingly obvious) to tackle the problems of one of the least developed countries in the world. Although trade with the Soviet bloc remained at a very low level, and both imports and exports continued to be oriented towards the Western capitalist states, external investment in the Ethiopian economy came to an abrupt halt. Though the regime stopped short of the full collectivization of agriculture on the Soviet model, it made determined but largely unsuccessful efforts to induce peasants to join together to form agricultural producers' cooperatives, the yields from which (insofar as government statistics can be trusted) were appreciably lower than for the individual peasant plots that they displaced (Clapham 1990: Ch. 7). In an attempt to encourage peasants to form cooperatives, and in the process to gain closer control over them, the government from 1985 promoted a programme of 'villagization', designed to group previously scattered homesteads into compact villages, with further negative impact on agricultural production. The impossibility of combining rural development with the demands of state control was most vividly illustrated by the Peasant Agricultural Development Extension Project (PADEP), proposed by the World Bank and other external funding agencies from the early 1980s. This sought to provide assistance and incentives to farmers in potentially surplus-producing areas, but was aborted as a result of the government's refusal to permit the higher producer prices and trading opportunities that the donors regarded as essential to the project. State control of agricultural marketing, as in many other African countries, served as a vital mechanism for transferring resources from the countryside to the towns, and in Ethiopia also for feeding the army, the size of which grew massively in an attempt to control the rebellions in Eritrea and Tigray, and which in the process also reduced agricultural manpower and drained the regime's political support. The state farms were even more disastrous. They were provided with impressive quantities of mechanical equipment, which soon stood rusting in the untilled fields, while the clearance of trees required to produce the fields in which this equipment was intended to operate had a devastating impact on fragile environments. This was 'socialist gigantism' at its most counter-productive.

Agricultural failure in turn affected the issue for which the political economy of Ethiopia was best known to the outside world during the Derg era, that of famine. Although the famine that imposed itself on global attention in 1984–5 was immediately prompted by the failure of rainfall in the northern highland areas especially of Wollo and Tigray, it more basically reflected the revolutionary regime's inability to promote agricultural production in those parts of the country that were capable of producing a surplus. The northern highlands were in any event carrying a population barely able to sustain itself even under normal conditions, which was therefore badly exposed in the event of natural disaster. The political effects of famine were extensive and complex. Internationally, it obliged a regime closely allied to the Soviet Union, which was essential as a source of the armaments needed to fight its civil wars, to turn to the North American and Western European states which were needed to provide the food aid that the USSR was quite incapable of producing. This aid in turn was provided not only by governments, but also by humanitarian civil society organizations that thus became deeply embedded in the international politics of the region. Domestically, famine reinforced the cleavage between the northern areas of the country where it took place, and the southern regions, leading to a government programme for the 'resettlement' of what were deemed to be 'surplus' people in the north to supposedly 'underpopulated' territories elsewhere, replicating a southward shift in population that had been taking place over a long period, but in a form that could only exacerbate tensions between the indigenous groups and the incomers.

But the most acute political effects of famine resulted from the fact that it took place in those parts of the country, notably Eritrea and Tigray, in which the government was fighting bitter civil wars against highly effective insurgencies, the EPLF in Eritrea and TPLF in Tigray, that were seeking either independence (in the Eritrean case) or greatly increased autonomy (in that of Tigray). These wars, which directly challenged the regime's commitment to a highly centralized nationalism, had by this time become its highest priority, and the politics of famine was subsumed in that of civil war. In some respects, famine could be used by the government as a mechanism of political control: a starving population is necessarily a dependent one, and the Relief and Rehabilitation Commission (RRC) established to co-ordinate famine relief rapidly became one of the primary instruments through which this control could be exercised. At the same time, what were then the 'rebel' movements against which the regime was fighting could also use famine relief as a means of reinforcing their own hold over local populations. And whereas 'official' food aid entered the country by what became known to aid agencies as the 'front door', through the then government-controlled ports of Massawa and Assab on the Red Sea, its opponents took advantage of food brought in through the 'back door' from Sudan. They formed their own equivalents to the RRC, the Relief Society of Tigray (REST) for the TPLF, and the Eritrean Relief Association (ERA) for the EPLF, through which to solicit aid from donors and then distribute it to their own populations.

One particularly damaging effect of this process was its impact on the relations between the two insurgent movements themselves. The famine cruelly coincided with a breakdown in relations, which—although expressed in terms of Marxist theory—most basically reflected their different goals (separate independence for the EPLF, federation within a radically reformed Ethiopia for the TPLF), and military strategies (conventional warfare for the EPLF, guerrilla war for the TPLF). The outcome was that the EPLF denied access to Sudan across its own territory to the TPLF, for the import of food and evacuation of refugees, and although the TPLF responded by building its own road to Sudan, south of the Eritrean border, the episode left a lasting bitterness on the part of the TPLF towards its northern neighbour that was at least a contributory factor in the conflict between what had by then become the separate governments of Ethiopia and Eritrea that erupted in 1998.

The collapse of the Derg regime in May 1991, rapidly followed by the de facto independence of Eritrea (formalized in 1993), and the installation of the EPRDF government in the remaining part of Ethiopia, is most basically explained in military terms. Underlying it, however, was the regime's failure to deliver the economic benefits of revolution that had been predicated on land reform, the destruction of the system of exploitation that had been built on the southward expansion of Ethiopian territory in the late nineteenth century, and its replacement by a development programme heavily directed from the centre under the aegis of 'scientific socialism'. Instead, the population were subjected to a no less onerous system of surplus expropriation through the state-run agricultural marketing corporation, accompanied by heavy-handed central planning, and a sharp reduction in opportunities for integration into the global economy that has fuelled rapid development in the most successful parts of the developing world. This in turn eroded the popular support that had been a striking feature of Ethiopia in the immediate aftermath of the revolution, and helps to account for the collapse of the regime's conscript army. It bequeathed to the incoming government the challenge of dealing with the twin problems of a highly centralized state and a structural imbalance between the sources of political power and economic development that the Derg had itself inherited from its imperial predecessor.

3.4 The Political Economy of Ethiopia under the EPRDF

The new government of the Ethiopian People's Revolutionary Democratic Front (EPRDF) was rapidly able to extend its control over the whole of the national territory, except for Eritrea, the independence of which was immediately acknowledged, and formalized in 1993. At the same time, it found itself confronted by a country whose economy and political structure had effectively collapsed, while its own core support derived disproportionately from the small northern region of Tigray, which—despite

Tigrayans' often truculent sense of difference from the historically dominant Amhara to the south—reinforced rather than rectifying the imbalance between the sources of economic and political power. The lessons that the EPRDF could draw from the experience of nearly two decades since the revolution in 1974 were basically ones about what *not* to do. At the political level, it recognized that Ethiopia could not be governed through the enforcement of top-down control in the way that the Derg had attempted; some new and far more participatory mechanism would be needed to fill the yawning gap between Ethiopians and the way in which they were ruled. At the economic level, it likewise recognized that state ownership and central planning were incapable of displacing the market as a means of achieving the level of development needed to transform the living standards of Ethiopians—a point reinforced by the collapse of the Soviet Union after 1989, and the apparent triumph of market economies throughout the world.

The attitudes that the EPRDF brought to the tasks that it faced were, however, mixed. At an ideological level, its leadership possessed the almost automatic orientation towards Marxism-Leninism that was common not only to the generation of Ethiopian students who had played a key role in bringing about the revolution, but also to rural guerrilla movements throughout the world. In some areas, and notably in its commitment to state ownership of land, the new government followed its predecessor. The *kebele* system was likewise retained and indeed strengthened. The belief in the need for a strong state, guided by a party constructed on democratic centralist lines, was equally part of its ideological inheritance. Nowhere, whether in Africa, Asia, or Latin America, have governments derived from insurgent movements sympathized with capitalist or market approaches to economic management, which they associated with corrupt ruling classes at home, and with historically dominant imperialist states in the global economy. Their instinct has almost invariably been to bring into government the command approaches through which they managed their victorious liberation wars. Nor have such movements shared the liberal democratic ethos that was at that time gaining a new lease of life in Africa, with the end of the Cold War and the overthrow of several of the continent's most notorious dictators. Ethiopia, in any case, had never experienced that period of open political party formation that accompanied the movement towards independence in colonial Africa, and its indigenous culture of governance, whether imperial or revolutionary, was hierarchical and authoritarian. It was, and indeed remains, extremely uncertain whether this culture could be reconciled with liberal democracy, or still more basically whether liberal democracy could itself provide a plausible basis for managing the country's underlying tensions and divisions.

At the same time, the EPRDF proved to be quite exceptional among post-insurgent governments in its willingness to consider new ideas, and adapt its own policies to experience and changing circumstances. Even before assuming power in Addis Ababa, the TPLF leadership had developed a far more open and participatory organizational structure than is normal in such movements, characterized by *gemgema*, a mechanism for discussing the successes and failures of military operations, and agreeing on changes in tactics and strategy when these were called for. Though much of the credit is commonly given to Meles Zenawi, who led the TPLF from 1989 onwards and became head of the provisional government in May 1991, this ethos was shared through the organization as a whole. It likewise gave far closer consideration than is common in such movements to the structural problems of governing Ethiopia, and was deeply aware that a radical reorientation of both the political system and the economy would be needed to overcome its inheritance both of famine and of civil war.

First among its priorities was the need to confront the inherent inequalities built into the Ethiopian state by the manner of its formation, and hence to give all its peoples a role in its management and thus an interest in its survival. The solution adopted—surprisingly, given that it coincided with the break-up of the USSR into its constituent union republics—was taken directly from Joseph Stalin's approach to the 'national question' in the Soviet Union. This involved the division of the country according to ethnicity or 'nationality', and establishing an autonomous administration within each of the territories thus defined, whose people were—quite exceptionally for a national constitution—guaranteed a right to self-determination, 'up to and including secession' (FDRE 1995). Ethiopia was indeed constitutionally defined as a free association of its constituent 'nations, nationalities and peoples', and it was these, rather than the boundaries of the state established in the late nineteenth and early twentieth centuries, that officially determined what Ethiopia *was*. This led to the formation of a political structure diametrically at variance from that followed in the great majority of post-colonial African states, in which the prime consideration was to foster a territorial nationalism that would bridge over the ethnic divisions that resulted from the often haphazard way in which these states had been formed by an external colonialism. At the same time, the new system gave the regime, whose origins disproportionately derived from the north of the country, a powerful source of political support among historically disadvantaged peoples especially in the south, who were for the first time offered an equal status in its government.

The assumption underlying this remarkable restructuring of the Ethiopian state was that ethnic divisions within the country were the result of the inherent inequalities created by the way in which that state had been established, and that once the basis for these inequalities had been removed, the resentments and hostilities to which they had given rise would likewise disappear, leading to the emergence of a national identity derived from equality rather than conquest. This in turn implied that Ethiopians already shared a more developed sense of an imagined community than the citizens of post-colonial African states, and that Ethiopia could therefore afford a very different approach to the common African problems of governing multi-ethnic territories. This assumption had nonetheless yet to be tested by exposure to the politics of identity and participation, of a kind that Ethiopia had never previously experienced.

The new dispensation entailed the establishment of new administrative units defined by the territories of each of the country's constituent peoples. Given that different groups within Ethiopia, as in other states both within Africa and worldwide, had been subject to complex processes of migration and integration, this was an extremely difficult task. The solution adopted was to take over, at least for the initial division, the territories ascribed to each group by the Institute for the Study of Ethiopian Nationalities established in its dying years by the Derg regime, though since this had not been accompanied by any demarcation on the ground, and raised politically very sensitive issues as to which group 'owned' any particular territory, the precise borders have been subject to constant dispute and frequent minor alterations. There is still no official map indicating precisely where the boundaries between regional states actually lie. Equally, while the larger groups, such as the Oromo, Amhara, Somali, Tigrayans, and Afar, inhabited areas that could be formed into relatively viable administrative units (albeit in the case of the Oromo with very awkward boundaries), Ethiopia also included a large number of smaller groups, which in many cases occupied tiny areas that were quite unable to sustain any full regional administration. Different solutions were adopted for different areas. The two cities of Addis Ababa and Dire Dawa had special multi-ethnic structures. The city of Harar became a region of its own, under the indigenous Adere group who constituted much less than half of its population. The two western frontier regions of Gambela and Benishangul-Gumuz were constituted as multi-ethnic states. And a very large number of groups in the southwest were formed into a federation under the cumbersome title of the Southern Nations, Nationalities and Peoples Regional State (SNNPRS).

The federal structure of Ethiopian government resulted in a complex and often obscure delimitation of the powers of the federal government on the one hand, and the individual states on the other. This applied not least to economic policy. The Preamble to the Federal Constitution of 1995 defined Ethiopia as a single economic community, while Article 51 gave the federal government responsibility for overall economic policy and for the currency. The individual states, however, were ascribed responsibility for the extremely important area of land administration, while both federal and state governments had taxation powers. Residual powers remained in the hands of the individual states. In practice, economic decision-making and implementation continued to be the almost exclusive domain of the federal government, and potential conflicts between federal and state administrations were averted because every state remained continuously under the control of the EPRDF and its constituent or allied political parties. The inherent tensions implicit in the federal arrangement were, however, unresolved, and were liable to be activated as a result either of the emergence of rival parties at the regional level, or of EPRDF-affiliated administrations looking to their own regional bases rather than to the central government as their key source of political support.

At the same time, the historic coincidence between the transfer of power in Ethiopia, and the collapse of the Soviet bloc and the end of the Cold War, enabled the regime to dissociate itself from the alliance with socialist states in the international order characteristic of post-insurgent governments, and to seek connections with the now dominant Western capitalist order. Ethiopia rapidly positioned itself among a group of 'new African' states, along with Uganda, Eritrea, and Rwanda, that were seen as leading a process of reform designed to rectify the all-too-evident political and economic failures of the first three decades of African post-colonial independence. This most evidently gave the country a favoured status as a recipient of foreign aid, but also accorded it a degree of policy space in resisting the 'structural adjustment' programmes that were at that time commonly imposed by donors on indebted and highly dependent African aid recipients. The renewed concern for security issues in the wake of the 9/11 attacks in the United

States also enabled Ethiopia to position itself as a leading actor in the 'global war on terror' in a strategically sensitive part of the world, and thus to regain some of the leverage with Western states that it had lost with the end of the Cold War. Linkages with the rapidly emerging economies of East Asia were relatively slight in the early years of the new regime, but were to assume a greatly increased importance after the start of the new millennium.

The EPRDF regime's first distinctive approach to economic policy, called agricultural development-led industrialization (or ADLI), drew directly on its origins. This sought to place the peasantry at the base of the whole development project, as producers of a surplus that would then be processed into goods for the international market, and in the process provide them with a means to escape the miseries of subsistence farming in a deeply impoverished environment. The central problem with this project was, however, that peasants—especially in the northern highland regions—simply could not produce the surplus on which the entire edifice rested. While the regime remained deeply committed to the welfare of the peasantry, on whose support its own triumph in the war against the Derg rested, and continued to invest heavily in areas such as agricultural extension services, the answers would have to be sought elsewhere.[1]

At this point, as has frequently happened in Ethiopia, development policy had to be subordinated to pressing security needs, as the result of the outbreak of war against Eritrea. This lasted from May 1998 until May 2000, when the Ethiopian forces succeeded in ousting the Eritreans from the territories that each state claimed as its own. The changed situation in the post-war period in turn established the conditions that guided subsequent development policy. The war, and the failure of the subsequent settlement to normalize relations between Ethiopia and Eritrea, denied Ethiopia access to the Red Sea ports of Assab and Massawa, and left the country heavily dependent on Djibouti. Alternative ports, including Port Sudan, Mombasa, Berbera in Somaliland, or the projected new Lamu port in northern Kenya, were distant, difficult of access, congested, or required very substantial investment to meet Ethiopia's needs. This combined with the need to contain Eritrean attempts to destabilize the country, and the ongoing security threats arising from civil war and state breakdown in Sudan and Somalia, to impose a strong regional dimension on subsequent development policy. Only by assuring good relations with its other neighbours could Ethiopia achieve its own ambitious plans. Ethiopia consequently played a leading role in the regional organization IGAD (Intergovernmental Authority on Development), helped to negotiate the separation of South Sudan from Sudan, and attempted (with very mixed results) to broker peace settlements in both South Sudan and Somalia. One key element in regional development policy was the Grand Ethiopian Renaissance Dam (GERD), situated on the Abbay or Blue Nile close to the Sudanese border, which was designed to provide electricity for

[1] I once asked Meles Zenawi, in the early 1990s, whether ADLI would actually work. He replied, with characteristic candour, 'I don't know. We thought we'd give it a go. If it doesn't work, we'll try something else.' Such openness on the part of national leaders is almost unknown, and provides an insight into the distinctive mindset that has driven Ethiopian development policy.

Sudan and other regional states as well as Ethiopia, in the process symbolizing a shift from territorial rivalry to economic integration as the key driver of Ethiopia's policies towards its neighbours.

The development imperative also underlay Ethiopia's domestic politics. Inheriting a country shattered by civil war and famine, the EPRDF regime had a pressing need to deliver benefits to its population. This was emphasized by the election in 2005, in which opposition parties achieved a far greater level of success than the ruling party had expected, triggering a search for the 'performance legitimacy' needed to assure popular support for the political settlement established after 1991. At the same time, by the early 2000s, changes in the global economic landscape had opened up opportunities for a fresh approach to development policy. On the one hand, the 'structural adjustment' policies imposed by the leading international financial institutions on deeply indebted states, especially in Africa since the 1980s, were widely seen as having failed to produce the expected economic turnaround. On the other, the rapid rise of newly industrializing East Asian states and especially China provided both an economic counterweight to the hitherto dominant industrial economies of North America and Europe, and an alternative model of how development could best be achieved.

The result was the formulation of the Ethiopian 'developmental state' as the overarching goal of the national government from the mid-2000s onwards. The economic implications and achievement of this project are examined in great detail elsewhere in this volume, but it is also important to emphasize its political elements. First of these was that the East Asian model predicated a heavy dependence on the state, and was particularly appropriate to Ethiopia in the light of its longstanding experience of statehood. One critical issue in the potential replicability of the Ethiopian quest for developmental statehood elsewhere in Africa is indeed whether many of the continent's post-colonial states (which themselves differ markedly in their own levels of state capacity) would be able to achieve the levels of control (especially over the distribution of rents) that this requires. The implications of the model for the second major issue in Ethiopia's political economy, the imbalance between the sources of political and economic power, were even more problematical. The dramatic levels of economic growth achieved in Ethiopia since the mid-2000s were, despite undoubted progress elsewhere, most evident in the regions incorporated into Ethiopia is the late nineteenth century, and especially in Oromiya and to some extent the southern region. Most of the critical development corridor from Addis Ababa to the coast at Djibouti lay in Oromiya. Marxist logic dictates that, in one way or another, this imbalance must eventually be resolved.

The developmental state project likewise highlighted the tensions between an economic policy that viewed Ethiopia as a single national unit, and a governmental structure that rested on the high level of autonomy granted to the constituent units in the federation. This was not only a matter of the formal distribution of powers, but also raised critical issues for economic integration. Economic development worldwide has been an essentially integrative process, not only between individual states and the global economy of which they increasingly form part, but within those states themselves. The massive infrastructural projects that provided one of the most visible achievements of the

Ethiopian developmental state had as their primary goal the creation of an economy in which goods, services, and people could flow with a minimal level of obstruction between one part of the country and another, as well as between Ethiopia and the outside world. A mobile labour force was a key part of this process, but risked turning internal immigrants into semi-citizens within the ethnically defined units among which the federal system was divided. Equally, however, a federal system tends to impose an imperative to distribute benefits between regions within the federation, in a way that corresponds to political rather than economic priorities, and increases unproductive government spending.

Nor was the strength of the Ethiopian state, central though this was to the developmental project, entirely unproblematic. The state in Ethiopia has historically been preoccupied with issues of control, and the social attitudes that underlie it, especially in the northern parts of the country, have been correspondingly hierarchical. Under the new dispensation, its role was to provide an overall framework of political stability, together with other key public goods, notably the social and communications infrastructure, and the regulatory framework within which the economy had to operate. It was recognized that the private sector had to provide the essential skills required for running the productive part of the economy, a lesson made all the more evident by the catastrophic economic failures of the previous regime. However, managing the interface between the state and the private sector raises complex and contested political issues in any market economy, and in Ethiopia, which historically lacked any strong and independent private sector, the emphasis was characteristically on the role of a state and a bureaucracy that regarded autonomous economic actors with suspicion, a legacy intensified by the appeal of Marxism to the country's intellectuals.

3.5 Conclusion

The political management of 'development' calls for a complex interaction between the application of principles of universal validity derived from successful and failed attempts to promote economic welfare throughout the world, and the often highly distinctive circumstances of particular states and societies, conditioned as these are by specific geographical endowments, social values and identities, and historical experiences. Ethiopia is in many ways an outlier among the world's developing states, possessing both elements in common with, but also very substantial differences from, the post-colonial states of sub-Saharan Africa with which it is most readily compared, as well as the rapidly developing (and largely non-colonial) states of eastern Asia from which it has recently sought its inspiration, and indeed other states such as the former Soviet Union that have guided its policies in the recent past. Crafting a response to the demands of development that draws on experiences elsewhere in the world, while also taking account of aspects of the country's situation that have been deeply problematic in some ways, but also very positive in others, has proved an extremely challenging task that in recent years has achieved far greater success than at any previous period in the country's history. The underlying issues that have historically shaped Ethiopia's political economy nonetheless remain unresolved, and may indeed well be regarded as unresolvable.

References

Clapham, Christopher (1990). *Transformation and Continuity in Revolutionary Ethiopia* (Cambridge: Cambridge University Press).

Donham, Donald (1999). *Marxist Modern: An Ethnographic History of the Ethiopian Revolution* (Oakland, CA: University of California Press).

Federal Democratic Republic of Ethiopia, Constitution 1995, online at: http://www.ethiopia.gov.et/constitution

Lefort, René (2015). 'The Ethiopian Economy: The Developmental State vs. the Free Market', in *Understanding Contemporary Ethiopia: Monarchy, Revolution and the Legacy of Meles Zenawi*, ed. Gérard Prunier and Ēloi Ficquet (London: Hurst): 357–94.

Rahmato, Dessalegn (1984). *Agrarian Reform in Ethiopia* (Uppsala: Scandinavian Institute of African Studies).

Tareke, Gebru (1991). *Ethiopia: Power and Protest* (Cambridge: Cambridge University Press).

CHAPTER 4

LAND TENURE AND LAND POLICY IN ETHIOPIA, 1950–2000

TEFERI ABATE ADEM

4.1 Introduction

LOCAL land-holding systems in many parts of Ethiopia were historically neither purely communal nor absolutely private. Instead, both systems existed, sometimes side by side on different parcels of land, at other times hierarchically on the same tract of land.[1] Three successive regimes, with widely contrasting ideologies and development approaches, viewed this complexity as an impediment to the modernization and intensification of agriculture to varying degrees, and pursued different land policies. Beginning in the 1950s, Emperor Haile Selassie introduced scope for the emergence of a Western-style freehold system in some parts of the country, while allowing communal ownership of land in others. The military regime that deposed Haile Selassie in 1974 launched a radical land reform programme and other socialist policies. The current ruling Ethiopian People's Revolutionary Democratic Front (EPRDF) implemented a comprehensive land registration and title certification programme, while upholding public ownership of land.

This chapter reviews some of the cultural and political difficulties each regime encountered in addressing what it diagnosed as 'development-impeding' land tenure issues. As Hoben (2002) noted in an earlier review, most of the difficulties have to do with the ways land policies have been embraced by political elites, and subsequently transformed and implemented through different government levels. This argument is updated here with new nuances while some generalizations are also ventured about the

[1] I thank Allan Hoben, my former professor and long-time mentor, for commenting on an earlier draft of this chapter.

local land tenure impacts of each regime. Focusing on Ethiopia's recent efforts to register all agricultural parcels and issue title certificates to all qualified holders, the analysis suggests significant progress in enhancing the tenure security of heads of established households and their designated heirs. Unfortunately, however, the tenure security of these groups tends to pose serious challenges to the land rights of others. This contradiction suggests that unresolved land issues continue, despite some improvements brought about by Ethiopia's comprehensive holding registration and title certification programme.

In some Highland Ethiopian communities, which provided ethnographic data for this chapter, one of the unresolved questions concerns the land rights of young men and women who came of age without receiving a government-allotted share of land. Regardless of wealth, employment, education, and family background, these young adults are culturally expected to build their own viable households by marrying, building a house, and acquiring productive assets including land and oxen. In the absence of opportunities for off-farm employment and decreasing agricultural land, accommodating this cultural aspiration has been the cause of painful land conflicts, often along the fault lines of age and gender, within households.

A second unaddressed issue concerns the tenure security of relatively better-off farmers who must rent, often in sharecropping, fixed cash payment, or a combination of these and other informal arrangements, the land of their less fortunate neighbours and relatives. With rising land value and continued prohibition of mortgages and sales, these farmers seek to establish long-term access to the land through arguably destructive strategies such as planting trees or building a house on prime agricultural plots. The net effect has been to diminish the potential incomes of both parties, and, arguably, the country.

4.2 Historical Context: Land and Power in the Traditional Ethiopian Governance System

By the turn of the twentieth century, which provides the historical context most relevant for understanding the three regimes under discussion, local land-holding systems in Ethiopia varied from region to region. The most important variation was between the older regions associated with the emergence and consolidation of the Ethiopian state, and those brought under control by Menelik II. For the most part, there were also contrasts in other political-economic features of these two broad regions, most notably in culturally preferred ways of life and aspects of traditional political organization (Markakis 2011).

In the primarily agricultural northern provinces—home of the core Tigray, Amhara, and Agaw peoples—a person's access to land depended on his or her changing social position in an indigenous feudal-like, patronage system (Pankhurst 2006 [1966]; Levine 1965;

Bauer 1973; McCann 1987). The majority of farmers held land-use rights, generically called *rist* in Amharic, by virtue of direct lineal ties, through any of the ancestors both in the mother's and father's line, with a person, real or imagined, believed to be the original owner of the land. In theory, *rist* rights were inalienable and partible, regardless of a person's gender, age, social standing, or wealth. In practice, however, a person's ability to actually acquire *rist* land greatly depended on establishing physical residence on it. It also depended on whether the person was influential in mediating disputes, winning court cases and invoking the support of authority figures both in the community and beyond (Hoben 1973; Bruce 1976).

Furthermore, *rist* land was simultaneously subjected to a class of land rights called *gult*, typically given to members of the ruling civilian and military elites, and by them to local notables, as a reward for loyal services, and to religious institutions as endowments. *Gult* holders had the right to demand free labour and collect taxes and tributes from those who farmed the land, and over whom they held judiciary and administrative authority (Hoben 1973). In theory, these rights were temporary, tied to the provision of specific services on behalf of the central government. In practice, however, some *gult* holders were powerful enough to turn them into hereditary rights (Crummey 2000; Weissleder 1965).

In the Marchlands brought under Menelik II, rights in land and other natural resources were obtained by membership and good standing in kinship-based groups, village communities, or a combination of both and other similar institutions (Hebo 2006; Bekele 2017). Along with the incorporation of these areas, a variant of the *rist* and *gult* model was imposed on their indigenous landholding systems (Wolde Mariam 1995). The historical outcome of this imposition varied across communities, often depending on local responses. Dynastic regional/ethnic chiefs and clan leaders who accepted peaceful incorporation into the empire were granted a degree of administrative autonomy over the land and people in their respective jurisdiction, provided that they also paid tributes to the central government (Donham 1986).

By contrast, militarily conquered ethnic groups were subjected to land alienation by a class of northern war leaders and farmer soldiers called *neftagna* (literally, one who bears a gun). In theory, the authority of these conquerors, like their *gult*-holding counterparts in the north, was limited to extracting tributes and free labour from people who lived on and used the localities they each governed. Over the years, however, most of the farmer-soldiers used their privileged position to own considerable land as private property, most likely relegating previous owners to the status of landless tenants (Tareke 1991; Donham 1999).

Meanwhile, many pastoral and agro-pastoral communities in Ethiopia's frontier areas pursued their culturally preferred way of life, which was (and arguably still is) the herding of different species of animals, by seasonally moving along designated range lands. The movement was influenced not just by availability of better grass and water, but also other considerations, most notably safety from raiders and other predators. These concerns were better addressed by staying in one's own designated territory, often associated with particular lineages, clans, or other ethnic-based sociological entities. The central government ruled most of these areas by recruiting clan leaders and other notables loyal to the reigning emperor, while they commanded significant respect and authority in their respective communities (Markakis 2011).

One long term agrarian and structural legacy of Ethiopia's dominant indigenous land tenure system, especially in the old northern provinces, was the complex link between land and wealth. Unlike in feudal Europe (Bloch 1989), or elsewhere in contemporary Africa, where preferential land access has reportedly led to variation in lifestyle and economic aspirations (e.g. Amanor 2001), the Ethiopian experience shows no clearly lineal link. Specifically, accumulating more land than others, whether among the ruling elites or ordinary farmers, did not necessarily translate into increased cultural aspirations for success through investment in agriculture, commerce, or entrepreneurship (Crummey 1980; Levine 2014).

Historically, this paradox was reflected in Amhara and Tigray communities in the notorious absence of labour-intensive soil conservation measures, irrigation schemes, rural roads, innovation in farming technologies, or other tangible production-enhancing agronomic practices. Members of the secular elite were primarily concerned with keeping themselves in power rather than improving their estates. This was best achieved through success in court politics, loyalty to superiors, and military prowess, especially in the conquest of new lands, rather than through the accumulation of wealth (Hoben 1970, 1995; Bauer 1985).

In the same way, ordinary *rist*-holding farmers also lacked strong incentives to make long-term investments in land management. First, production was intended primarily for subsistence, tax, and tribute. Intensification was constrained by lack of urban markets and transportation problems. Second, farmers lacked long-term tenure security in the particular fields they cultivated at any given time. Co-owners of a founding ancestor's land were often compelled to undertake some type of redistribution whenever they were faced with a new and powerful claimant (*balanta*; literally, one who demands a share). Besides, inheritance rules generally demanded that the fields of a deceased person (unless they were too small to allow division) be divided among his children regardless of their marital status, age, gender, and economic capabilities (Bruce 1976). As a consequence, the holdings of each household were (and arguably still are) viewed not as a 'family estate' to be passed down intact through generations. As Hoben (1995: 10) notes, they were instead viewed as 'a unique constellation of land parcels' brought together by the personal skills and efforts of individual household heads.

4.3 Land Tenure Change under Haile Selassie

During his long reign, spanning 1916–74, first as regent and then as emperor, Haile Selassie introduced a series of reforms in land tenure, rural administration, and taxation. Following a trend begun by Emperor Menelik II (1889–1913), the aim was to centralize power and modernize the country by dismantling the land-based, feudal-like system discussed in Section 4.2. To this effect, the emperor was highly successful in replacing regional lords and local notables with centrally appointed functionaries and government-employed experts. However, Haile Selassie owed much of his success not so much to the intended goal of the reforms but to his personal ability to redefine and creatively re-use long-standing royal prerogatives. Specifically, in the domain of land reform, this paradox was revealed in the continuity of the claim that the emperor ultimately owned all land, and could grant it, especially if deemed unused and unoccupied, as a reward to favoured persons and institutions (Zewde 1984).

Haile Selassie's success in turning customary royal prerogatives into critical assets for power building was best exemplified in a series of land grant orders he issued, especially at critical moments of consolidation and restoration.[2] Interestingly, the list of designated recipients of these grants, which were often bestowed on the emperor's birthdays and coronation anniversaries, was not limited to soldiers and war veterans who were traditionally considered worthy of royal favour, provided that they displayed exceptional military prowess and/or provided unreserved services to the country. It also included other categories such as salaried 'government employees', 'unemployed' city dwellers, and 'all other landless Ethiopians'.[3] The inclusion of these civilian categories was officially justified on the grounds of Haile Selassie's vision of modernizing and developing the economy by matching land and labour efficiently. Underlying this claim was the idea that there was unutilized land (*täf*; literally, waste land) in some parts of the country which could contribute to growth if granted to individuals who could put it under cultivation.[4]

As mentioned in Section 4.2, this assumption, regardless of its economic merit, provided scope for a revival of the claim that the emperor bestowed land rights to any man worth the name. Parallel to this, Haile Selassie also introduced a new tax reform that enabled him to strengthen the financial power of the central government at the expense of provincial rulers and local landed elites (Zewde 1984). Specifically, the reform required the payment of all taxes in cash, as opposed to in kind and labour, directly to the central government through newly employed tax collectors (Crummey 2000). As part of this reform, the tax collectors were also tasked to map out landholdings, including unclaimed and unused land, into a supposedly standard unit called *gasha* (a block of about 40 hectares of land). This reform involved measuring, in some cases re-measuring, the holdings of each person, or group of closely related families. This was done either by actually squaring the land with a rope (*qälad*) or by approximation (*äynä-gämäd*).

[2] According to one source, the emperor issued five major land grant orders in the years 1934–57 alone (MLRA, File No. 2075/1974, quoted in Wolde Mariam 1995).

[3] Wolde Mariam (1995) provides several interesting cases that show how these proclamations enabled many urbanites to accumulate prime agricultural land especially in Addis Ababa's hinterlands.

[4] What constituted *täf* (waste land) was not clear. Theoretically, it included all land that was not either cultivated or effectively claimed by an individual or a group of land users. Much of this land was located in the Lowlands and border areas of the country, and was used by local people for grazing and other uses (Bekele 2017).

Studies show that the measurement process enabled the central government to reclaim not only unclaimed land, but also excess land confiscated from individuals who held more land than they had legally reported. It also enabled the ruling elites to expand their own private holdings through purchase and the use of their political authority (Wolde Mariam 1995).

However, government reports and later studies show that Haile Selassie's land grant system was not successful in increasing food production and rural income. In retrospect, there were at least three main reasons for its failure. First, a sizeable portion of the land was already being used by local people in one form or another. The new recipients simply became new overlords who demanded a share of the harvest, as in the previous feudal-like system, rather than as new forces to be directly engaged in agriculture. Second, even when the land was not significantly used or claimed by locals, the new recipients lacked incentives for developing it.[5] Instead, these largely urban-based bureaucrats and soldiers kept the land mainly for prestige and speculative purposes. Third, the land grant procedure was too expensive, time-consuming and risky for poor farmers to benefit. Expensive and time-consuming because it involved costs of transportation, lawyer's fees, registration, and *däji tinant* (staying at the gate of a court to be heard by authorities). Risky because it involved disputes, since in most cases the land was either already being used for some purpose or previously granted to somebody else.

From the early 1960s through the mid-1970s Ethiopia's nascent educated elites, mainly urban-based government employees and university students, attacked Haile Selassie's land policy on different grounds (Pausewang 1983). In parts of the northern provinces where the *rist* system continued as status quo policy, these critics claimed that farmers suffered from tenure insecurity and corruption caused by competition over land rights and hopelessly outdated land governance practices. In the southern half of Ethiopia and elsewhere, critiques saw the increasing concentration of land in the hands of elites who used their political authority and privileged connection to the emperor to qualify for the receipt and/or purchase of land grants.

Influenced by Marxist ideology, critiques demanded that land be nationalized and redistributed to all farmers—a radical policy position which they articulated in the slogan 'Land to the Tiller!' (Zewde 2002). Haile Selassie's response to this demand was slow and unsatisfactory. The most important measure was the appointment of an inter-ministerial committee in 1962, which later became the Land Reform and Development Authority, and then, in 1966, the Ministry of Land Reform and Administration (MLRA). Drawing on survey data regarding land tenure issues in different provinces, experts at these agencies drafted a series of tenancy bills that were submitted to Parliament in the late 1960s and early 1970s (Bruce 1975). The proposed tenancy bills were repeatedly rejected by conservative parliamentarians who saw themselves as the targets of this legislation. A modest version of the bills was finally endorsed by the

[5] That the grant recipient lacked incentives to use the land was especially observed in arid and semi-arid areas where nomadic and semi-nomadic pastoralism was the culturally preferred, as well as economically viable, way of life (Bekele 2017).

parliament in 1972, only to be rejected by the emperor himself. The ministry would later (1975) design and implement a significant land reform programme under the military regime, calling itself the Derg, which had dethroned Haile Selassie in 1974 (Rahmato 1984).

4.4 Land Tenure under the Military Regime

In comparison to similar programmes elsewhere in Africa, it is widely recognized that Ethiopia's 1975 land reform was politically successful. It eradicated absentee land ownership and all other exploitative vestiges of traditional landed elites by nationalizing and redistributing rural land to all farmers on a fairly equal basis (Rahmato 1984). Yet, the reform did very little to improve the well-being of smallholder farmers and Ethiopia's food security. Its initial success and far-reaching implications were dwarfed by the negative effects of perverse socialist policies that the regime pursued over the ensuing years (e.g. Clapham 1988; Poluha 2002). It embraced a broad programme of promoting large-scale state farmers and collective farms, wrongly portraying them as more efficient and progressive than ostensibly inefficient and backward smallholder farmers (Rahmato 1993).

Section 4.4.1 nuances and extends this state-centred analysis to argue that this mixed outcome can also be linked to other factors beyond state action. Our principal concern is with the agency of farmers from different age, gender, and economic groups, who had to struggle, with varying degree of success, to qualify for more land while also coping with tenure insecurity and unwanted intervention by party cadres.

4.4.1 Adopting a Popular Land Reform

On 4 March 1975, the military regime of Ethiopia launched a radical land reform programme of the kind previously undertaken by communist parties in Vietnam and Chile (Rahmato 2009). Over the next few months, the regime forcibly eradicated absentee ownership, large holdings, and landlessness with astonishing success. Two broad historical and political economic conditions contributed to this success.

First, the Ethiopian political landscape was ripe for radical land reform because of pressures generated by the 1974 revolution. This was exemplified by the 'Land to the Tiller' slogan long espoused by highly vocal urban-based political activists (Zewde 2014). In the face of this political pressure, the military regime was forced to adopt a more radical option than it would have liked (Rahmato 2009). Furthermore, the reform also appealed to the aspirations of millions of tenants, serfs, and sharecroppers, especially in the southern and western part of the country. These farmers hoped that the reform would extricate them from the burdens of exorbitant rents, unpaid labour, and other arbitrary services they used to provide for absentee landlords (Rahmato 1984). The reform was also well received in the northern highlands because the idea of taking land from those who had more and allocating it to those who had none appealed conceptually and was morally plausible (Hoben 2002).[6]

Second, as part of the land reform, the military regime remapped rural communities into roughly equivalent units called peasant associations (PA). These units, which later became the local administrative units, enabled the regime to mobilize farmers politically in defence of the reform. For their part, farmers used these associations to claim substantial discretionary power in redistributing land. As Rahmato (1984: 42) notes, the regime was forced to allow greater farmer participation 'by default rather than by design' as it lacked its own trained agents.

4.4.2 Redistributing Land

With the overnight eradication of absentee land ownership, the land reform freed sharecroppers and landless tenants from the heavy burdens of the past. They could now take the next harvest home without giving up a share or paying rent and other land-related dues previously owed to landlords. For the most part, this component of the land reform was 'self-implemented' by the beneficiary farmers themselves (Ege 1990). When farmers displayed some hesitation about doing so, often from moral economic considerations, the provision was implemented by militant students and teachers who were stationed locally as participants in a programme called National Campaign for Development through Cooperation (Rahmato 1984; Donham 1999).

This revolutionary change was followed by the much harder task of equalizing the holdings of households in each *kebele* by measuring and redistributing land uniformly. As mentioned in Section 4.4.1, the implementation processes was entrusted to the local Land Distribution Committee elected by farmers (hereafter Committee). The wide discretionary power these committees exercised led to significant variations from community to community, as well as within each community, in 'method of land distribution' and 'criteria used' (Rahmato 1984: 41). Yet, local-level accounts of the implementation processes in selected highland Ethiopian communities show a striking similarity both in methods and criteria (see, e.g., Ege 1990; Aspen 1993; Amare 2000; Adem 1998).

First, the idea of equalizing holdings was interpreted very pragmatically and gradually in ways that show astute understanding of both difficulties and possibilities. Early on in the years 1975–7, rural communities variously underwent political uncertainty and insecurity. As a consequence, the equalizing of holdings was operationalized lightly to mean confiscating land selectively from large and absentee landowners and allocating it to qualified landless tenants and land-short sharecroppers (Rahmato 1984). This interpretation left a majority of smallholders unaffected by bestowing use rights on the plots they held within the *kebele* territory (Admassie 2000). From 1977 onwards, however, the military regime increased its efforts to enhance control with the use of repressive tactics. It supervised the election of Land Distribution Committees in every community.

[6] To be sure, the reform in the north had met pockets of armed resistance by former government functionaries and traditional elites who lost their power and land. None of the resistance reversed the land reform as they were all crushed early on (Rahmato 2009).

With some guidance from above, these committees undertook a more comprehensive distribution that involved detailed inventories of landholdings and redistributions using family size and land quality as key criteria in allocating land equally (Ege 1990).

In one community studied, the comprehensive land redistribution was carried out as a three-part act. First, using a 25-metre-long rope (locally translated as 50 arms' lengths), Committee members divided the total arable land of each community into roughly equivalent units locally called *dereja* (standard). Second, the Committee also surveyed the family size of each household to determine the size of land it qualified for. Finally, the Committee allocated land to households, often by physically standing on the plot and showing the boundaries to recipients. As to the size of the newly allocated land, a household with no children received half a hectare of land, and an additional quarter of a hectare was allocated for each qualifying child. Childless widows and dependent elderly persons also received their own share of land in the amount of half of the size allocated to a married couple. To account for variations in soil fertility, topography, and other micro-ecological features, a household's share of land consisted of plots vertically scattered across three locally recognized micro-agro-ecological niches. These were foothills where the homestead is located, prime farmland encircling villages, and distant plots in low-lying plains and along river banks. To guarantee fairness, distant plots were allocated using the lottery system (Adem 1995).

Second, even when such comprehensive redistributions were undertaken, as happened in many communities, equalizing holdings was easier said than done. To begin with, communities varied both in demography and their total land fund. For this reason, the equality of holdings was only relative to households living in the same community, sometimes even specific villages within the larger community (Rahmato 1984). Even when communities tend to be roughly equivalent in demography and topography, land redistribution involved social relationships and processes, differentially affecting the ability of individuals and households to receive land. When measuring plots, for example, it is alleged that Committee members found room to favour some at the expense of others. When they want to favour a person, the allegation goes, the Committee used their own judgment (*äynä-gämäd*, 'eye rope') instead of the actual rope.

Even when measuring with real rope, nepotism and favouritism reportedly occurred. Sometimes, Committee members used non-standard rope. At other times, the rope was either loosely stretched to enlarge plot size or tightly held to reduce it. Committee members also reportedly displayed favouritism when assessing land quality and enumerating family size. Sometimes they gave more land to relatives and friends by mislabelling fertile plots located in highly desirable locations as less fertile and more precipitous. At other times, they permitted relatives and friends to receive more land by allowing them to include non-qualifying family members (Amare 2000; Adem 1995).

4.4.3 Unresolved Land Issues and Emerging Challenges

As became evident later on, farmers' sense of equality and fair access to a share of land could not be effectively addressed by a one-time land distribution alone, whether comprehensive or restricted to targeted households. With subsequent demographic changes in the size and composition of households, such a system led to increasing inequalities in holdings. Established household heads who happened to have more children when land was redistributed continued to have more land, while young farmers who were minors back then lacked enough land to start their own viable households (Adem 1995, 1998).

In the absence of other income-generating options, this tension was reinforced by culturally expected household developmental cycles. Young men and women of every generation are expected to marry and start their own household, regardless of wealth, employment, or education. In the past, this aspiration was met by asking parents or other members of the extended family for a personal share (*gulma*), often in return for anticipated help in old age. With the military regime's emphasis on equalizing holdings, however, both parents and youngsters were led to consider this generational tension as a land policy issue, as opposed to an informal family matter.

There are good reasons to assume that the periodic redistribution the military regime enforced in the years leading to 1989 were responses to this tension. If land was to be redistributed once again, it would weaken fathers' holdings and authority by enabling sons and daughters to establish their own household independent of parental blessings and benevolence. If not, however, the young who came of age after the last land distribution had to remain landless and subordinates to their elders (Adem 1995, 1998). As Ege (2017) noted in North Shewa, it is also possible that some, or most, of the periodic redistribution was primarily induced by the regime's socialist projects and perverse policies, as opposed to demographic increases. The most important of these political causes were the remapping of PA boundaries, the establishment of producer cooperatives, the forced relocation of farmers to government-designated villages and resettlement schemes, the establishment of villages, and the closure of hillsides.

Regardless of their real causes, periodic land redistributions were more frequent than might be assumed. The frequency varied spatially, with the smallest number near the capital, Addis Ababa. In Gojjam, for example, Adal (2001) reported that seven rounds of redistribution occurred in the years 1976–88. Similarly, a survey in Wollo, spanning 1975–92, found several rounds of redistribution including 7 in Ambasäl, 6.7 in Yäju and 5 in Däsé Zuriya Awrajas (Admassie 2000: 194). The net effect of all this frequency of redistributions undermined the tenure security of household holdings. By 1988, the regime issued a national directive which put a stop to land redistribution.

4.5 Land Policy Since 1991

Coming to power after winning a long and difficult insurgency war, the Ethiopian People's Revolutionary Democratic Front (EPRDF) has offered its own responses to the land policy debates of the 1960s and 1970s. During the civil war, the Tigray People's Liberation Front (TPLF)—one of the forces in the EPRDF coalition—redistributed land to farmers (Chiari 1996). With the expansion of the war into the south of the country, EPRDF forces refined and replicated this experience in areas under their control. From the outset, EPRDF was committed to a radical land reform programme aimed at eradicating exploitative agrarian relations once and for all by equalizing household holdings. This goal was also what the military regime promised to accomplish through the 1975 land reform.

However, EPRDF's land allocation criteria were different in at least one major way. Unmarried young women and men who were aged 18 and 21, respectively, at the time of land distribution were entitled to receive their own share of land. This provision, which was probably reinforced by the exigency of recruiting young fighters to win the war, had far-reaching implications for inter-generational relations within households. It enabled young men and women to acquire land, and in most cases establish their own viable households, without being allocated land by parents. As became evident later, however, this led to increased inter-generational and intra-household tension between those who received land when it was last redistributed and those who came of age over after that.

Early on during the first years of transition towards democracy and market economy, EPRDF leaders sought to resolve this tension by finding 'extra land' whenever it was deemed available. Along the Awash valley and some parts of Oromia, the much-needed land was acquired by downsizing, and in some cases confiscating, state farms (Kassa 2001). In other areas, EPRDF leaders redistributed tracts of land previously held by collective farms, community woodlots, and other local government projects (Admassie 2000). In still other areas, significant amounts of land were obtained by reducing the holdings of former peasant association leaders and local notables who had reportedly used their political position to acquire more land than others (Ege 1997; Adal 1997; Adem 2000).

After 1998, however, EPRDF officially stopped land redistribution. It has instead embraced the new global policy shift towards enhancing the tenure security and transferability of land rights through a comprehensive programme of land registration, title certification, and investment promotion (Hagos and Holden 2013). However, unlike in other developing countries where these new waves of land reform are primarily mediated by market forces, the key actor in Ethiopia remains the state. Specifically, land in Ethiopia is held and governed variously by federal, regional, district, and local governments. Drawing on information from selected communities, Section 4.5.1 reviews what changed or remained unsolved because of EPRDF's deep commitment to addressing a range of land questions while upholding public ownership of land as a constitutionally enshrined law.

4.5.1 Land Registration: Land Redistribution by Other Means?

Over the past ten or so years, EPRDF has carried out a comprehensive land-holding registration and title certification programme. The initial aim of this programme was to enumerate household heads by the location and size of plots they each hold. This information was collected mainly with the active participation of residents of village communities who held adjacent plots, while also co-managing common pool resources such as grazing grounds, burial sites, and water sources. By the end of the registration process, each household head was issued a landholding book which listed all his/her parcels, described by location within the village landscape, boundary, size, and other distinct features. Although not yet completed, a second round of registration was piloted in selected districts. The aim was to formalize the qualitatively described spatial information from existing paper title certificates with parcel-level cadastral data and geo-referenced maps (Menberu, Lecki, and Smith 2017). The information would then be digitized and managed by the district government. Meanwhile, a paper copy of certificates would be issued and handed over to each approved land-holder.

The comprehensive paper-based land registration and title certification programme was implemented with great vigour, often ahead of schedule, cost-effectively and with farmer participation (Deininger et al. 2011; Rahmato 2009). Ethiopia has been increasingly mentioned in the development literature as a 'promising' model to emulate for other countries wanting to implement large-scale land registration and titling programmes (Quisumbing and Pandolfelli 2010). Curiously, the last time Ethiopia stood out for undertaking an exemplary land reform was in 1975. And, as Hoben (1995) showed retrospectively, that programme primarily owed its success to the political, as opposed to legal, nature of land access, especially in the northern highlands. More specifically, farmers found the programme 'morally plausible' and technically enforceable because it sought to take land from households which happened to have larger holdings and allocate it to those with little or no land (Hoben 1995: 20).

Along the same lines, it can be argued that the timely completion of land registration was made possible, at least in part, by deep-seated struggles over land between farmers who received land when it was land redistributed and those who, coming of age afterwards, received no allocation. This generational tension was starkly reflected in, for example, one particular meeting in which the land register of a study village was presented for verification (*ticheta*) by residents. The time was late March 2016[7] when the programme of digitizing title certificates was being piloted in the district. As recounted to me, the meeting was co-chaired by the chief local administrator. Next to him stood an elected Land Administration officer, holding the village's land register in his hand. Following the verification guideline, the meeting proceeded with the Officer calling one household head at a time and reading aloud the list of parcels they held. Before continuing with the next household, the chairman asked those at the meeting to verify whether or not the list was correct. The meeting continued in this manner until the land of each household head was read and verified.

Rivalry between farmers who feared that some of their parcels might be taken away and those who hoped to receive land came to life as the meeting continued. For the most part, the contours of this rivalry followed the ever-changing fault lines between the generations. Despite the land registration programme's goal of enhancing the tenure security of holders, landless young men used the verification process as an opportunity to find

[7] This particular fieldwork was in part supported by Human Relations Area Files (HRAF) at Yale University.

illegally held land. They did so in anticipation that the 'extra-land' would be redistributed to the landless. Not surprisingly, this claim was not an empty charge. Many of the accused had held some parcels, or a portion of a given parcel, on contestable terms. In some cases, land users had illegally encroached on uncultivated land and this created a discrepancy between the official plot size in the register and the actual size known to villagers. In other cases, household heads illegally held parcels on which they only had secondary rights as sharecroppers or caretakers. In still other cases, the contest was over parcels on prime land encircling homesteads that had been registered as part of the homestead itself.

In accordance with the holding verification guideline, the chairman's immediate response to these charges was to flag all the parcels under question as 'unverified'. Interestingly, the presence of many such cases created more incentives for farmers to have all the other uncontested plots registered as fast as possible. Follow-up ethnographic work in the summer of 2017 showed that some of the accused were forced to give up their claim to the disputed parcel or a portion of it. In some cases, the claim was belatedly verified. Regardless of the outcome, the registration process, which was supposed to be a politically neutral and largely technical act, did not change the expectation on the part of farmers that local officials can expropriate parcels if deemed unlawfully held and apportion them to landless youth. Understanding this context-specific nuance is essential for capturing farmers' sense of how and why land title certificates, whether issued as handwritten papers or computerized hard copies, were extremely important (Adem 2004; Cochrane and Adem 2017).

4.5.2 What Title Certification Changes (or Doesn't)

Although undertaken within a public ownership of land framework, Ethiopia's paper-based land titling programmes sought to improve rural livelihoods and economic growth by facilitating the accelerated intensification and commercialization of smallholder subsistence agriculture. It sought to introduce these changes by addressing three critical issues. One was to reduce tenure insecurity by enabling household heads to enjoy long-term, inheritable and, to some extent, transferable use rights over the parcels they hold. The second was to guarantee the land access of women and other vulnerable groups through improved land governance and formal enforcement mechanisms. Related to the above, the third issue was mitigating the many causes of social conflict over land by fostering transparency in land transactions, whether by inheritance, informal social arrangements, lease, plot sub-division, or government allocation.

The tenure security outcome as yet appears inconclusive, with mixed results emerging. Farmers' own self-evaluation and willingness to pay for land titles suggested increased tenure security which is needed for encouraging investment in land (Deininger et al. 2011). The newly enhanced tenure security has also led to a greater degree of trust and flexibility in local land-sharing arrangements (Gray and Mueller 2012). Ambitious men and women seeking off-farm entrepreneurial activities can now leave home without the fear of losing their land. Options for doing so include not just informal sharecropping arrangements, but also formally enforceable fixed rentals (Tsegaye, Adgo, and Selassie 2012). Yet, government involvement in enforcing contracts seems to have increased the tenure insecurity of well-off farmers who want to increase their income by renting and sharecropping the land of less fortunate neighbours and relatives (Gebrehaweria and Holden 2011). With continued restrictions on other market-based options for acquiring land, this insecurity undermined the production capacity of hard-working farmers (Ege 2017). Furthermore, studies also show that land titling did not stop government intervention in the land rights of households and communities (Chinigo 2015). Not surprisingly, some of the strongest evidence in support of this concern comes from peri-urban communities where local officials have to accommodate the land demands of investors and home-builders (Megersa and Mammo 2010; Beka 2016).

As to guaranteeing the land access of women and other vulnerable groups, results so far appear equally mixed. The title certificate of each married couple clearly attests that the wife is a co-holder. However, this recognition alone is not a profoundly new provision. Under the military regime, as discussed in Section 4.4.1, women held officially recognized rights to a share of government-allocated land either as wives in male-headed households or independently as divorcees or widows. EPRDF broadened this right significantly by allowing young women, as well as men, who came of age at the time of land redistribution to receive their own share of land, regardless of marriage or family status. Too often, however, the potentials of all progressive reforms have been dwarfed by micro-political processes at implementation.

Although the second round is not yet completed, the land-titling programme represents a significant advance towards addressing implementation issues in two major ways. First, it provides enforceable evidence by minimizing ambiguities related to plot boundaries and legal rights. Second, it decentralized land administration down to the community and district levels, entrusting the critical task of information verification and updating to a body of elected farmers. However, having land titles at hand has not as yet given women new mechanisms for defending their land rights against male-biased cultural expectations especially within their own households and kinship groups. Specifically, some households and individuals cannot manage to plough the land allocated to them alone, while others do. The former may have to rely on others for a host of reasons. As in the pre-land titling times, most female-headed households also lacked sufficient male labour and traction power to plough the land, as well as weed, watch over, harvest, and thresh crops, all at the optimal times. They had to resolve this problem by giving the land, or a portion of it, to others in informal sharecropping arrangements.

Finally, the least satisfactory outcome of land titling so far is the failure to reduce conflicts over land. Insightful evidence on this includes Svein Ege's recent article poignantly entitled 'Land Tenure Insecurity in Post-Certification Amhara, Ethiopia'. Drawing on multi-year ethnographic and historical information from Wäyr Amba, a village in North Shewa, Ege (2017: 2) observed 'a land conflict or worries about potential conflict' going on 'in more or less every house'. Ironically, much of the conflict related to tensions between the newly increased land tenure security of parents, on one hand, and the more deeply rooted customary rights of children, on the other. The availability of land titles and village-level elected Land Administration officers have enabled farmers to enter into complex land transactions. Short of mortgages and sales, parents can, for example, rent out to anyone on terms they want. More importantly, parents can designate anyone, including a non-household member, as future heir(s). Parents can also invoke their certified land holding rights over prior customary rights and remove anyone, including adult household members who live on the land or use a portion of it (Adem 2004). As Ege (2017) shows, the resulting conflict can be extremely bitter and painful, because the dispossessed have no other legal option for long-term access to land. These difficulties, which are reinforced by rising land values, suggest that the certification programme, while solving some problems, has created new ones.

4.6 Conclusion

In debates on the land tenure legacy of Ethiopia's transition from an old feudal-like monarchial system, through nearly two decades of socialism, to the current broadly decentralized, federal system, most analysts tend to focus on what each regime achieved or failed to achieve. While acknowledging the centrality of state action in agrarian change, the focus of this chapter has been on the question of whether the land policies of each regime were based on a thoughtful understanding of what farmers themselves were trying to do, or needed to do, to make a living and improve their status. The review shows that, unfortunately, policymakers at each juncture tended to overlook the real concerns of some farmers while addressing those of others. Under each regime, this omission was variously revealed by the continued existence of certain contradictions and unresolved land issues.

Under Haile Selassie, for example, the drive towards Western-style private ownership was at odds with customary royal prerogatives related to land grants and the elite role in influencing large-estate transactions, whether by inheritance or concession. During the military regime, the most important contradiction was the regime's increasing concern with staying in power by exerting central control over land and fostering the intensification, modernization, and commercialization of agriculture, instead of addressing the dilemma of growing population pressure and decreasing land resources. The EPRDF government has shown unprecedented commitment to pursuing pro-poor policies aimed at addressing landholding inequalities while also simultaneously enhancing the tenure security and transferability of smallholdings. While successful in some ways, these policies have generated new problems, most notably increased conflict over land both within households and along the ever-changing fault lines between the generations.

Acknowledgements

I thank Allan Hoben, my former professor and long-time mentor, for commenting on an earlier draft of this chapter.

References

Adal, Yigremew (1997). 'Rural Land Holding Readjustment in West Gojjam, Amhara Region', *Ethiopian Journal of Development Research* 19 (2): 57–89.

Adal, Yigremew (2001). 'Land Redistribution and Female-headed Households: A Study in Two Rural Communities in Northwest Ethiopia'. FSS, Discussion Paper No. 5, Forum for Social Studies, Addis Ababa.

Adem, Teferi Abate (1995). 'Land Redistribution and Intra-household Relations: The Case of Two Northern Ethiopian Farming Communities', *Ethiopian Journal of Development Research* 17 (1): 17–29.

Adem, Teferi Abate (1998). *Land, Labour and Capital in the Social Organization of Farmers: A Study of Local-level Dynamics in Southwestern Wollo*. Monographs in Social Anthropology. (Addis Ababa: Addis Ababa University Press).

Adem, Teferi Abate (2000). 'Government Intervention and Socio-economic Change in a Northeast Ethiopian Community: An Anthropological Study', PhD dissertation, Boston University.

Adem, Teferi Abate (2004). 'Decentralized There, Centralized Here: Local Governance and the Paradox of Household and Autonomy and Control in North-east Ethiopia, 1991–2001', *Africa* 74 (4): 611–32.

Admassie, Yeraswork (2000). *Twenty Years to Nowhere: Property Rights, Land Management, and Conservation in Ethiopia* (Lawrenceville, NJ: Red Sea Press).

Amanor, Kojo (2001). 'Land, Labour and the Family in Southern Ghana: A Critique of Land Policy under Neo-Liberalisation', Research Report No. 116, Nordiska Afrikainstitutet, Uppsala.

Amare, Yared (2000). 'Household Resources, Strategies and Food Security in Ethiopia: A Study of Amhara Households in Wogda, Northern Shewa (Vol. 1)', published jointly by the Dept. of Sociology and Social Administration and the Addis Ababa University Press.

Aspen, Harald (1993). *Competition and Co-operation: North Ethiopian Peasant Households and their Resource Base* (Trondheim: Trondheim University).

Bauer, Dan (1973). 'Land, Leadership and Legitimacy among the Enderta Tigray of Ethiopia', PhD dissertation, University of Rochester.

Bauer, Dan (1985). *Household and Society in Ethiopia* (East Lansing, MI: Michigan University Press).

Beka, Girma (2016). 'Urban Expansion and its Socio-economic Impacts on the Livelihood of the Farming Community in Sululta', MA Thesis in Social Anthropology, Addis Ababa University.

Bekele, Getnet (2017). *Ploughing New Ground: Food, Farming and Environmental Change in Ethiopia* (Rochester, NY: Boydell & Brewer).

Bloch, Marc (1989). *Feudal Society, Vol. 1: The Growth and Ties of Dependence* (London: Routledge).

Bruce, John (1975). 'Ethiopia: Nationalization of Rural Lands Proclamation', *Land Tenure Center Newsletter* 47 (Jan–Mar): 1–15.

Bruce, John (1976). 'Land Reform and Indigenous Communal Tenures: The Case of Chiguraf-Gwoses in Tigray, Ethiopia', SJD Dissertation, Law, Madison: University of Wisconsin.

Chiari, Gian Paolo (1996). 'Land and Democracy in Tigray.' Unpublished paper.

Chinigò, Davide (2015). 'The Politics of Land Registration in Ethiopia: Territorialising State Power in the Rural Milieu', *Review of African Political Economy* 42 (144): 174–89.

Clapham, Christopher (1988). *Transformation and Continuity in Revolutionary Ethiopia* (Cambridge: Cambridge University Press).

Cochrane, Logan and Teferi Abate Adem (2017). 'Knowledge Gaps and Opportunities for Future Research on Ethiopian Food Security and Agriculture', *Ethiopian Journal of Applied Science and Technology* 8 (2): 33–41.

Crummey, Donald (1980). 'Abyssinian Feudalism', *Past & Present* 89: 115–38.

Crummey, Donald (2000). *Land and Society in the Christian Kingdom of Ethiopia, 1200–1900* (Urbana, IL: Illinois University Press).

Deininger, K., et al. (2011). 'Impacts of Land Certification on Tenure Security, Investment, and Land Market Participation: Evidence from Ethiopia', *Land Economics* 87 (2): 312–34.

Donham, Donald (1986). 'Old Abyssinia and the New Ethiopian Empire: Themes in Social History', in *The Southern Marches of Imperial Ethiopia: Essays in History and Social Anthropology*, ed. D. Donham and W. James (Cambridge: Cambridge University Press): 3–48.

Donham, Donald (1999). *Marxist Modern: An Ethnographic History of the Ethiopian Revolution* (Oxford: James Currey Ltd).

Ege, Svein (1990). 'Changing patterns of land tenure in Ayne, Mafud Warada', Working Papers on Ethiopian Development, Ethiopia Research Programme, College of Arts and Science, University of Trondheim, (5): 225–36.

Ege, Svein (1997). 'The Promised Land: The Amhara Land Redistribution of 1997', Working Papers on Ethiopian Development No. 12, Norwegian University of Technology and Science.

Ege, Svein (2017). 'Land Tenure Insecurity in Post-certification Amhara, Ethiopia', *Land Use Policy* 64: 56–63.

Ethiopian People's Revolutionary Democratic Front (EPRDF) (1995). 'EPRDF's Program for Development, Peace, and Democracy' (in Amharic), EPRDF, Addis Ababa.

Gebrehaweria, Gebregziabher, and Stein T. Holden (2011). 'Distress Rentals and the Land Rental Market as a Safety Net: Contract Choice Evidence from Tigray, Ethiopia', *Agricultural Economics* 42 (1): 45–60.

Gray, Clark L., and Valerie Mueller (2012). 'Natural Disasters and Population Mobility in Bangladesh', *Proceedings of the National Academy of Sciences* 109 (16): 6000–5.

Hagos, Hosaena Ghebru and Stein Holden (2013). 'Links between Tenure Security and Food Security: Evidence from Ethiopia', Vol. 1288. International Food Policy Research Institute.

Hebo, Mamo (2006). *Land, Local Custom and State Policies: Land Tenure, Land Disputes and Disputes Settlement among the Arsii Oromo of Southern Ethiopia* (Keyoto: Shoukadan Book Sellers).

Hoben, Allan (1970). 'Social Stratification in Traditional Amhara Society', in *Social Stratification in Africa*, ed. A. Tuden and L. Plotnicov (New York: Free Press): 187–224.

Hoben, Allan (1973). *Land Tenure among the Amhara of Ethiopia: The Dynamics of Cognatic Descent* (Chicago, IL: University of Chicago Press).

Hoben, Allan (1995). 'Paradigms and Politics: The Cultural Construction of Environmental Policy in Ethiopia', *World Development* 23 (6): 1007–21.

Hoben, Allan (2002). 'Ethiopian Land Tenure Revisited: Continuity, Change and Contradictions', Working Paper No. 236, MA: African Studies Center, Boston University, MA.

Kassa, Getachew (2001). 'Resource Conflicts among the Afar of North-east Ethiopia', in *African Pastoralism: Conflict, Institutions and Government* (Addis Ababa: Organization for Social Science Research in Eastern Africa): 145–67.

Levine, Donald (1965). 'Ethiopia: Identity, Authority, and Realism', in *Political Culture and Political Development*, ed. L. Pye and S. Verba (Princeton, NJ: Princeton University Press): 245–81.

Levine, Donald (2014). *Interpreting Ethiopia: Observations of Five Decades* (Los Angeles, CA: Tsehai Publishers).

Markakis, John (2011). *Ethiopia: The Last Two Frontiers* (Rochester, NY: Boydell & Brewer).

McCann, James (1987). *From Poverty to Famine in Northeast Ethiopia: A Rural History 1900–1935* (Madison, WI: University of Wisconsin Press).

Megersa, Birhanu, and Mamo Hebo (2010). *Exploring the Dynamic Linkages: Land Tenure Systems, Agricultural Investment and Food Security among Smallholder Farmers in Sululta, Oromia Regional State* (Saarbrücken: VDM Verlag Dr. Müller).

Menberu, Allebachew, John Lecki, and Andrew Smith (2017). 'Large-scale Rural Land Certification and Administration in Ethiopia: The Challenges of a Decentralized Approach.' Paper prepared for presentation at the 2017 World Bank Conference on Land and Poverty, 20–24 March 2017 (Washington, DC: The World Bank).

Pankhurst, Richard (2006 [1966]). *State and Land in Ethiopian History*. No. 3. Institute of Ethiopian Studies (Los Angeles, CA: Tsehai Publishers).

Pausewang, Siegfried (1983). *Peasants, Land and Society: A Social History of Land Reform in Ethiopia*. Afrika-Studien (Munich: Weltforum Verlag).

Poluha, Eva (2002). 'Learning Political Behaviour: Peasant–State Relations in Ethiopia', in *Contesting 'Good' Governance: Crosscultural Perspectives on Representation, Accountability and Public Space*, ed. Eva Poluha and Mona Rosendahl (New York: RoutledgeCurzon): 101–36.

Quisumbing, Agnes R., and Lauren Pandolfelli (2010). 'Promising Approaches to Address the Needs of Poor Female Farmers: Resources, Constraints, and Interventions', *World Development* 38 (4): 581–92.

Rahmato, Dessalegn (1984). *Agrarian Reform in Ethiopia* (Uppsala: Scandinavian Institute for African Studies).

Rahmato, Dessalegn (1993). 'Land, Peasants and the Drive for Collectivization in Ethiopia', in *Land in African Agrarian Systems*, ed. T. Bassett and D. Crummey (Madison, WI: University of Wisconsin Press): 274–97.

Rahmato, Dessalegn (2009). *The Peasant and the State: Studies in Agrarian Change in Ethiopia 1950s–2000s* (Addis Ababa: Addis Ababa University Press).

Rahmato, Dessalegn (2011). 'Land to Investors: Large-Scale Land Transfers in Ethiopia'. FSS Policy Debate Series No. 1, Forum for Social Studies, Addis Ababa.

Tareke, Gebru (1991). *Ethiopia: Power and Protest: Peasant Revolts in the Twentieth Century* (Cambridge: Cambridge University Press).

Tsegaye, Abate, Enyew Adgo, and Yihenew G. Selassie (2012). 'Impact of Land Certification on Sustainable Land Resource Management in Dryland Areas of Eastern Amhara Region, Ethiopia', *Journal of Agricultural Science* 4 (12): 261.

Weissleder, Wolfgang (1965). 'The Political Ecology of Amhara Domination', PhD dissertation, University of Chicago.

Wolde Mariam, Tekalign (1995). 'A City and its Hinterlands: The Political Economy of Land Tenure, Agriculture and Food Supply for Addis Ababa, Ethiopia (1887–1974)'. PhD dissertation, Boston University.

Zewde, Bahru, (1984). 'Economic Origins of the Absolutist State in Ethiopia (1916–1935)', *Journal of Ethiopian Studies* 17: 1–29.

Zewde, Bahru, (2002). *Pioneers of Change in Ethiopia: The Reformist Intellectuals of the Early Twentieth Century* (Athens, OH: James Currey).

Zewde, Bahru (2014). *The Quest for Socialist Utopia: The Ethiopian Student Movement, c.1960–1974* (Rochester, NY: Boydell & Brewer).

CHAPTER 5

FEDERALISM IN ETHIOPIA'S TRANSFORMATION

KIDANE MENGISTEAB

5.1 Introduction

AFTER taking power in 1991, the Ethiopian People's Revolutionary Democratic Front (EPRDF) transformed Ethiopia's governance structure from a unitary to a federal system. The immediate goal of the new ruling party in undertaking such a measure was to arrest the country's pandemic ethnic conflicts by replacing the highly centralized rule that was widely regarded as oppressive, especially by marginalized ethnic identities. A federal system that devolves power to the regional states, along with a sustainable democratization process, can engender a peaceful process of nation building by ensuring the advancement of the political, social, economic, and cultural rights of all segments of the population, especially those of formerly marginalized ethnic groups.

Under the federal system, Ethiopia has registered rapid economic growth. It has also created the governance infrastructure that would allow the country's diverse cultures to flourish. Yet forging a peaceful process of nation building remains a major challenge and the country is still highly unstable, as underscored by its score of 101.1 on state fragility in 2017 (The Fund for Peace 2017).[1] The central issue this chapter grapples with is why a peaceful process of nation building remains one of the country's major challenges, despite notable progress in a number of other areas under the federal arrangement. More specifically, the chapter has the following four objectives. One is to explain how historical legacies and the socioeconomic contexts that existed at the time shaped the characteristics of the country's federal arrangement, which has provoked intense criticism

[1] The only African countries scoring higher than Ethiopia on fragility in 2017 are the DRC (110) Guinea (102.4) and Nigeria (101.6).

in some circles. The second highlights the areas of notable achievement of the federal arrangement so far. The third objective is to explain why the federal arrangement, despite its many achievements, has not yet overcome the challenges of nation building. The last objective is to explore if the recent protests in two of the largest regional states, Oromia and Amhara, and the appointment of a new prime minister create opportunities for further devolution of political power, giving new impetus to the federal arrangement.

The chapter has four parts corresponding to the four objectives. Section 5.2 briefly examines how the country's historical legacy of state formation and state–society relations under the centralized structures of the previous two regimes shaped the nature of state–identity relations in the country and the rather unique characteristics of Ethiopia's federal arrangement. Section 5.3 examines the most important areas of socioeconomic change the country has witnessed under the federal arrangement. Section 5.4 examines the critical factors hindering the federal arrangement from achieving its principal goal of a peaceful process of nation building. Section 5.5 recaps the major challenges of nation building and suggests that a substantive democratization process would be required to overcome the centrifugal forces undermining the nation-building project.

5.2 Characteristics of Ethiopia's Federal Arrangement

The Ethiopian federal system has two characteristics that have drawn incessant criticism from opponents. One is that the regional states of the federal system are drawn mostly along the lines of ethnic (language) boundaries. Six of the regional states (Afar, Amhara, Harari, Oromia, Somali, and Tigray) are named after ethnic identities, while the remaining three states (Benishangul-Gumuz, Gambela, and Southern Nations, Nationalities, and Peoples) are multi-ethnic regional entities that are not identified with a single ethnic identity (Engedayehu 1993; Fiseha 2012). The two cities, Addis Ababa and Dire Dawa, are also multi-ethnic. Although named after ethnic identities, the Amhara, Harari, Oromia, and Tigray states host minority groups who often demand some form of local autonomy or special governance arrangement. Ethiopia's federal entities, therefore, are formed essentially along ethnic and regional lines and the phrase 'ethno-regional' might be a more accurate description (Brietzke 1995; Mengisteab 1997).

Some scholars oppose the use of 'ethnic' to refer to Ethiopia's federal arrangement (Gebrehiwot and Haftetsion 2015). The Constitution uses the terms 'nation' and 'nationalities' instead of 'ethnic'. However, the meaning of nation and nationalities, as used in the Constitution, is not different from the term ethnic. According to the Constitution, nation, nationality or people 'is a group of people who have or share large measure of a common culture or similar customs, mutual intelligibility of language, belief in a common or related identities, a common psychological make-up, and who inhabit an identifiable, predominantly contiguous territory' (Article 39 no.4). Article 46 also explains that the regional states are 'delimited on the basis of the settlement patterns, language, identity and consent of the peoples concerned' (FDRE 1995; Minasse 1996; Clapham 2004).

The second controversial, and rather unique, characteristic is that the arrangement extends to the nations and nationalities (the regional states) the right of self-determination up to secession (Article 39 of the 1995 Ethiopian Constitution) (FDRE 1995). The conditions that need to be met for exercising this right to secession are difficult, however. There is also ambiguity as to whether the right to secession is granted to nations and nationalities or to the regional states. If it applies to the former, the right to secession would be hard to actualize. Opponents contend that the ethnic composition of the federal states politicizes ethnicity, promotes ethno-nationalism, fosters ethnic conflicts, and along with the right of secession risks the break-up of the country (Gebre-Selassie 2003; Abbink 2006; Aalen 2006; Fiseha 2012). Contrary to the contention of critics in this regard, the core goal of the Ethiopian federal system is to prevent state–identity conflicts by giving identity groups that had been mobilized on claims of marginalization the right of secession. The right to secession is essentially a protection that identity groups can invoke if they face oppressive marginalization within the country.

At the theoretical level, it is not certain that a federal system with ethno-regional boundaries inherently creates more conflicts than a unitary state system if it is less oppressive (more liberating) than the unitary system. It is also unclear why the right of secession necessarily encourages secession if the regional states can exercise genuine self-rule and if being part of the country proves more beneficial than secession. Ethnically based arrangements in countries such as Switzerland and Belgium have not been prone to ethnic conflicts or demands for secession. In any case, despite the passionate criticism of the ethno-regional arrangement, hardly any viable alternative proposal has emerged on how best to draw the regional states and what level of rights to grant them. The unitary state system, which was rife with ethnic conflicts, was, however, hardly an option, given the experience of the country. Support for a unitary state system has also waned in the country. However, there have been cases of illegal discriminatory practices against members of other ethnic groups in some of the ethnic-based regional states.

More importantly, political programmes and arrangements often are adopted not because they constitute optimum solutions to problems such as state–identity conflicts, but because they are pragmatic in the sense that they are acceptable to the contending or dominant political forces. The reason why ethnicity features prominently in the demarcation of the boundaries of the regional states in Ethiopia's federal arrangement is also that it reflected the political realities and political views of the predominant political actors at the time they were established. The country's historical context is also important since it shaped state–society relations (political conditions) and the diverse visions on strategies of nation building of the political forces involved in designing the arrangement (see Chapter 2).

The formation of the modern Ethiopian state in the mid-nineteenth century came about through forceful unification of many of the components of the Abyssinian Empire, which had fragmented into regional kingdoms during that period of the country's history known as the Era of Princes (1769–1855) (Abir 1970). Soon after its formation, the new state built an empire by conquering territories in competition with European powers, which at the time were engaged in the scramble for Africa. The expansion brought about the incorporation in the last three decades of the nineteenth century and the first decade of the twentieth of over half the country's current regional states, including Benishangul Gumuz, Oromiya, Gambela, the Southern Nations, Nationalities, and Peoples, Somali, Harari, and Dire Dawa (see Chapter 2).

The expansion, which often involved brute force and a great deal of looting, also produced lasting socio-economic conditions. It, of course, defined present-day Ethiopia's physical map and shaped its political, economic, and cultural landscape for decades to come. It also established parallel state–society relations in the country with the state establishing more oppressive political, economic, and cultural relations with the populations in the newly incorporated territories than it did with the populations in Abyssinia proper. The imperial state reduced large numbers of the population in the incorporated territories to landless tenant status, as the monarch granted their land to the occupying troops and administrators in lieu of wages (Pankhurst 1968). With their subjugation, the communities in the newly incorporated areas also suffered subordination of their culture (language and religion) to those of the identities that spearheaded the expansion.[2]

Simultaneous to the expansion of the empire southwards, notable changes occurred in the northern part of the country, including the Italian colonization of Eritrea. Tigray, which at different periods of the country's history was the centre of the empire, also suffered political and economic marginalization. The formation of the modern Ethiopian state, thus, brought about the subjugation of the populations in the southern parts of the country, the marginalization of Tigray in the north, and concentration of state power in the hands of the Amhara elite, especially those in the former central province of Shoa. It also coincided with the loss of the parts of Eritrea that were under the Abyssinian Empire during the reign of Emperor Yohannes IV (Erlich 1996). The political and economic systems and cultural hierarchy established by the new empire fostered sporadic rebellions by various ethnic, social, and religious identities against the empire, which largely failed to address the grievances of various groups through programmes of diversity management and equitable allocation of citizenship rights and public services.

The overthrow of the monarchy by the military regime (the Derg) in 1974 led to some changes, the most significant of which was the land reform of 1975. The land reform did not give the landless tenants in the southern parts of the country ownership rights. Rather, it gave them use rights, while vesting ownership in the state (Land Proclamation, 4 March 1975; see Mengisteab 1990). The land reform modified the level of deprivation of the populations in the newly incorporated parts of the empire, but it did not eliminate it altogether. Beyond the land reform, the Derg failed to bring about political changes that would grant equitable citizenship rights to all identities in the country or to facilitate a peaceful process of nation building. The governance structure remained highly centralized with few political or cultural rights extended to the population. In the

[2] Indigenous property owners who provided service to the monarchy were also allowed to become landlords. However, in most cases these people facilitated the subjugation of their societies.

absence of fundamental changes addressing the plight of the oppressed ethnic identities and marginalized areas, the country continued to witness a proliferation of ethnic-based liberation movements, especially in the northern and southern parts of the country. In the 1980s over a dozen armed groups of different levels of strength operated in the country, some of them demanding socioeconomic reforms, others fighting for independence. The groups that were successful in changing the country's political landscape were, however, the Eritrean People's Liberation Front (EPLF), the Tigray People's Liberation Front (TPLF), and to a lesser extent the Oromo Liberation Front (OLF).

Immediately after driving the Derg out of power in 1991, the EPLF established a provisional government in Eritrea while the TPLF, along with its coalition partners who formed the Ethiopian People's Revolutionary Democratic Front (EPRDF), organized a national conference, at which around four hundred delegates from twelve political groups deliberated on a transitional government (Vaughan 1994). The participants represented a wide spectrum of positions, ranging from a continued unitary state system to the independence of some ethnic groups, which would result in the break-up of the country. The conference adopted the ethno-regional federal arrangement, with the right of self-determination up to secession to the nations and nationalities, as a compromise solution (Vaughan 2011).

The two rather controversial characteristics of the Ethiopian federal arrangement (largely ethnic-based regional states and the right to secession) were, thus, products of the political context and the different visions of how to deal with the context held by the most powerful political forces in the country at the time. Whether the new arrangement proves a formula that saved the country from disintegration and unifies it under a new political system or paves a slow path to fragmentation of the country remains uncertain. However, the latter outcome is much less likely, since no identity group has demanded independence in the twenty-seven years since the institution of the federal system. In Section 5.3 we examine the achievements of the federal arrangement as well as the political conditions that may undermine the federal formula (Abbink 2011).

5.3 Progress under the Federal Arrangement

Since its institution, Ethiopia's federal arrangement has fostered notable progress in a number of areas. The most visible achievements are in the areas of infrastructure development and economic growth. Road and rail construction and hydroelectric power generation have seen significant development (MoFED 2014). The country has also been among the fastest-growing economies in the world for over a decade. According to the World Bank (2018), Ethiopia's economy experienced strong broad-based growth averaging about 10.5 per cent a year from 2005/6 to 2015/16. Higher economic growth has also brought with it positive trends in the reduction of income poverty both in urban and rural areas. In the year 2000, 55.3 per cent of Ethiopians lived in extreme poverty, but that figure had shrunk to about 30 per cent by 2014 (MoFED 2014; World Bank 2017, 2018).

There is some scepticism about such impressive growth, or at least some qualifications, one of which is that a portion of the growth is due to recovery. Ethiopia's GDP in 2004, when the rapid growth started, was US$10 billion, while 13 years earlier in 1991 the GDP stood at US$13.4 billion. This recovery is estimated to account for about 6 per cent of the growth (MoFED 2005). Another qualification is that Ethiopia's growth is in large part due to unprecedented public investment in infrastructural schemes and public enterprises, driven by a combination of foreign aid, foreign borrowing, especially from China, and non-transferable services, such as construction and transport. Ethiopia's public investment rate is the third highest in the world, while the private investment rate is the sixth lowest. A third qualifier is that Ethiopia's growth has not yet brought about significant change in the structure of the economy. Agriculture and services dominate the economy, while the contribution of manufacturing to GDP remains low at 4.34 per cent in 2016, despite its notable growth rate (World Bank 2017).

An Oxford Poverty and Human Development Initiative (OPHI) report also shows progress in reducing the country's poverty rates, although the number of the poor remains rather high in contrast to those confirmed by the World Bank, IMF, and the African Development Bank.[3] The percentage of the country's population in severe poverty stood at 63 per cent in 2016, while the ratio of the destitute was 45.4 per cent in the same year (see Table 5.1). The OPHI Global Multidimensional Poverty Index (MPI) data also shows that there is significant variation in poverty rates among the regional states, although the most recent data for this index dates from 2011 (see Table 5.2). The absence of the MPI for earlier and more recent years makes it difficult to compare progress, or the lack of it, in narrowing the unevenness of poverty rates among the regional states.

Despite the qualifications and the stark difference between the MPI index and the data from the World Bank, IMF, and African Development Bank, Ethiopia's economic growth has been impressive. Even the MPI data, where the poverty rates are higher, show that progress in reducing the poverty rate is notable. Over the past two decades,

Table 5.1 MPI for Ethiopia, selected years

Year	% of population in severe poverty	% of population that are destitute
2000	72.3	82.1
2011	67.2	65.4
2016	63.0	45.4

Source: Oxford Poverty and Human Development Initiative, Global Multidimensional Poverty Index, 2017.

[3] The MPI is a composite measure of poverty that includes standard of living, education, and health, while those of the World Bank, IMF, and the African Development Bank only consider income poverty.

Table 5.2 GMPI by region in 2011

Country/region	% of population in severe poverty	% of population that is destitute	Population share %
Addis Ababa	4.8	2.5	3.8
Harari	36.6	28.2	0.3
Dire Dawa	38.5	35.0	0.4
Gambela	57.5	54.3	0.4
Tigray	66.2	57.1	6.6
SNNPR	73.2	54.2	20.6
Benishangul-Gumuz	74.3	62.3	1.0
Amhara	74.6	65.7	25.2
Oromiya	74.9	59.8	38.7
Somali	81.9	74.6	2.3
Afar	79.2	77.6	0.9

Source: Oxford Poverty and Human Development Initiative, Global Multidimensional Poverty Index, 2017.

Table 5.3 Number of students in government and non-government schools

Academic year	Number of students in primary and secondary schools (millions)	Students enrolled in universities (thousands)
1994/5	Under 3.5	–
2000/1	8.3	48.1
2002/3	8.8	77.9
2003/4	9.6	77.7
2004/5	11.8	91.7
2005/6	11.9	91.7
2006/7	12.6	104.6
2007/8	15.5	104.6
2008/9	15.6	135.8
2009/10	15.9	370.6
2010/11	16.9	–
2011/12	17.4	–

Source: Ethiopia Statistical Abstracts, various years.

the country has also attained significant progress in key human development indicators. The child mortality rate has shrunk by half, and the number of people with access to clean water has more than doubled (World Bank 2017). Despite this notable progress, poverty remains rampant in the country because the situation before the institution of the federal system was poor. There has also been an impressive increase in the number of student enrollments in primary and secondary schools and in university education (see Table 5.3). There are, however, notable differences among the regional states in terms of student enrollments at different levels, with the regional states of Afar, Somali and Beni Shangul Gumuz lagging behind (Ethiopia Statistical Abstracts). The differences in poverty rates among the regional states also are significant with the Somali and Afar states lagging behind.

The country, however, faces the challenge of youth unemployment. The urban youth unemployment rate (23.3 per cent) was higher than the total urban unemployment rate of 16.5 per cent (Africa Development Bank 2018). The country's debt has also grown rapidly, causing concern to the IMF. In June 2016 public and publicly guaranteed debt rose to about 54.2 per cent of GDP, of which 30.2 per cent of GDP corresponds to external debt. The gap between the rich and the poor has also risen rapidly.

5.4 Management of Cultural Diversity

Another area of major progress under the federal arrangement is the extension to ethnic groups of the infrastructure for developing their own culture. The strategy of nation building during the unitary state system of the previous two regimes was essentially assimilation to the country's dominant Amhara culture, which represented the elite who had spearheaded the expansion of the empire and occupied a dominant position in its governance. The strategy no doubt allowed individuals and groups from various ethnic groups to assimilate and even join the ranks of the political and economic elite. A freely evolving mutual assimilation of cultures can foster the development of a community of citizens sharing a common (hybrid) culture, along with common institutions of governance. By contrast, an unequal assimilation imposed by political authority over politically marginalized identities amounts to imperialistic domination that is likely to be resisted. Similarly, an assimilation which marginalized groups accept in an attempt to gain access to the citizenship rights enjoyed by those of the dominant culture, can be detrimental to peaceful nation building by deepening the frustration of those who have to assimilate (Clapham 2004). The cost of assimilation during the unitary state system was self-denial. As eloquently stated by Mohamed Hassen (1994), those who assimilated or Amharized 'ceased to be themselves'. It was common during the unitary state system for various ethnic groups to adopt Amharic names to hide their identity in an effort to escape discrimination in the economic and political life of the country. The country has now witnessed conspicuous reversal of this trend. Ethnic identities are reverting to adopting their ethnic names. Different ethnic groups are also developing literature in their own languages. Several ethnic groups in the southern parts of the country, including the Oromo, have even adopted the Latin alphabet for writing their languages instead of the Geez alphabet.

There is, of course, the risk that in the euphoria of cultural liberation and aspirations to develop formerly oppressed cultures, some identities or authors of identity narratives may impede the development of a common culture through cultural sub-nationalism. This is likely to occur, especially if the hierarchical political and economic relations are perpetuated, provoking ethnic-based resistance. Under equitable citizenship rights, however, inter-identity socioeconomic interaction is likely to point towards the emergence of common culture in the longer run. The federal arrangement has already created the political structure that enables different ethnic groups to develop their own culture even if the devolution of power is incomplete and self-rule faces limitations.

5.5 Reduction in Political Violence

Another area of notable progress under the federal arrangement has been the reduction of armed conflicts in the country. As already noted, at the time of the institution of the federal arrangement, Ethiopia was on the verge of disintegration under the weight of over a dozen armed rebel groups. Since then, the number of armed groups fighting the state as well as the intensity of the fighting have declined considerably. The devolution of power to the states and the political liberalization extended to citizens, although measured, have contributed to transforming the nature of political struggle in the country. The mushrooming of opposition political parties has largely replaced the proliferation of armed liberation movements of the 1970s and 1980s. The effectiveness of the central state in suppressing rebellion is another factor in reducing the magnitude of armed opposition.

The federal arrangement has also made progress in localizing ethnic politics. The regional states now have more responsibility for dealing with issues raised by their minority group and with boundary issues with other regional states. While the federal state cannot entirely steer clear of such problems, it can remain above the fray and intervene only when necessary.

Although it is by no means free of armed political violence, the country endures fewer civil wars now than it did before the federal arrangement. The reduction in the level of violence has also reduced the level of disruption of economic activity. The protests which started in November 2015 in Oromia state and later spread to the Amhara state have raised the level of instability. The government declared a state of emergency on 9 October 2016 to quell the protests. However, the protests restarted after the lifting of the state of emergency on 4 August 2017 and a second six-month state of emergency was imposed on 18 February 2018. The protests, triggered by both general and specific factors, including land grabbing by the state, especially for the expansion of Addis Ababa, indicate that the federal system has yet to achieve its core objective of a peaceful nation-building process.

5.6 Factors undermining the Process of Nation Building

Despite the progress it has achieved in a number of areas, the federal system has yet to register comparable progress in advancing effective diversity management and a peaceful process of nation building (Mengisteab 2007). The many factors that have hindered success in this area have evolved over time. One overriding problem is the contesting visions of the characteristics of the federal arrangement and the level of devolution of power necessary to satisfy the different nations and nationalities or the key regional states. There are three competing visions. One vision, which can be referred to as 'maximalist', contends that a genuine federal system requires much greater devolution of power than has taken place. A widespread allegation by adherents of the maximalist vision is that the federal government, in contravention of the constitutional provisions that grant self-determination to the regional states, has not devolved real power to the states (Abbink 2011).

A second vision—and one that risks the disintegration of the country—opposes a federal system based on ethnic boundaries and opposes extending the right of secession to the nations and nationalities (Mehretu 2012). A widespread claim among the adherents of this vision is that the ethnic-based federal arrangement is a ploy by the TPLF, which dominates the EPRDF, to extend its control of power by dividing Ethiopia along ethnic lines (Temesgen 2015). The third vision, to which the government adheres, favours a managed devolution of power while in principle accepting extensive devolution of power, as warranted by the Constitution. From this point of view, practical implementation of extensive devolution of power is hindered by many technical problems, including human resource limitations, although the elite in power is hardly likely to champion devolution of power, regardless of the constitutional provisions.

It is difficult to define the scope and timing of the decentralization necessary for the federal arrangement to satisfy the different identity groups while advancing nation building, especially given that granting greater self-determination to ethnic groups can be manipulated to discriminate against ethnic identities residing outside their ethnic homes or to advance the cause of secession. Reconciling these different visions is likely to be challenging and time-consuming and they are hard to overcome without advancing democratic governance that can peacefully manage the contestations among the different visions. This means that developing a successful federal arrangement and building a democratic system are intricately intertwined and both face formidable challenges in the country.

5.7 Challenges of Democratization

As noted already, since embarking on the federal system, Ethiopia has made some progress in liberalizing its political process. It has established a multi-party system, despite many alleged restrictions on opposition parties, and has conducted several rounds of elections, although these have often been marred by boycotts and irregularities. Notwithstanding the periodic clampdowns on journalists, Ethiopia has also made progress in liberalizing the press and has taken steps to extend civil liberties to the population, although human rights violations remain widespread, according to human rights organizations. Despite these positive initial steps, a sustainable democratization process in the country faces formidable structural obstacles, in particular in relation to the structures of the state, where the executive branch dominates the other constituent parts of the state, such as the judiciary, the legislature, the bureaucracy, the military, the central bank, and the electoral commission. The dominance of the executive branch, which is common to most African states, precludes genuine checks and balances and horizontal accountability within the state and fosters corruption. Additionally, the weak structure of checks and balances produces concentration of power on the executive branch, a major hindrance to democratization at federal level and to devolution of power to the regional states, as well as the source of autocratic rule. Without strong mechanisms of checks and balances, elections, even if conducted cleanly, are unlikely to lead to democratization. At best, they would simply lead to a rotation of autocratic rulers among the elite.

5.8 The 'Double Whammy' of the Nature of the Ruling Party

The ruling party, which is the architect of the federal arrangement, has played a critical role in registering the country's economic progress and in reducing the political violence that characterized the country in the 1970s and 1980s. However, the nature of the party also poses a 'double whammy' for both democratization and the success of the federal arrangement. The EPRDF has established itself as a dominant party with little challenge to its hegemonic power from contending parties. Like a single-party system, a dominant-party system, both at the federal level and at the level of regional states, implies that any devolution of power occurs essentially at the pleasure of the ruling party. Even if the infrastructure for devolution of power were in place, a dominant ruling party would ensure concentration of power since the policies of the regional states are unlikely to diverge from those of the central government, as they all emanate from the same party. This has no doubt created tensions between the federal state and the regional states as well as driving a wedge between the coalition partners of the EPRDF.

The fragmentation of opposition parties has contributed to the perpetuation of the hegemony of the EPRDF, while the EPRDF's interference has kept opposition parties weak. Ethiopia has seen the formation of a large number of political parties, most of which are ethnically based. Some of these parties are in opposition to the ruling party while others have some level of affiliation with it. The opposition parties have remained of little significance, as they have not been able to transform themselves into a national party capable of offering an alternative vision to that of the ruling party. Strong opposition parties that capture power in some of the regional states could put pressure on the ruling party to extend the devolution of power in earnest. They could also enhance the democratization process by acting as checks on the ruling party. Their inability to capture power in any of the states or even to serve as a national loyal opposition enables the ruling party to perpetuate its hegemonic grip on power.

A second factor is that the ruling party is a coalition of four ethnic-based parties, including:

- the Oromo Peoples' Democratic Organization [https://en.wikipedia.org/wiki/Oromo_Peoples%27_Democratic_Organization] (OPDO)
- the Amhara National Democratic Movement [https://en.wikipedia.org/wiki/Amhara_National_Democratic_Movement] (ANDM)
- the Southern Ethiopian People's Democratic Movement [https://en.wikipedia.org/wiki/Southern_Ethiopian_People%27s_Democratic_Movement] (SEPDM)
- the Tigray People's Liberation Front [https://en.wikipedia.org/wiki/Tigrayan_People%27s_Liberation_Front] (TPLF).

These four parties represent four of the most dominant regional states, and rivalry between them and differences over policy issues within the ruling party are likely to make it difficult to maintain the cohesion of the EPRDF indefinitely. If the cohesion of the coalition breaks down before the emergence of a national party capable of taking power, national unity could also be at risk. Under the present ruling party, therefore, the federal arrangement and national unity remain rather unstable. Progress in the democratization process is also curtailed.

5.9 Corruption and the Rise of the Rent-Seeking Class

Another factor undermining the federal arrangement is the ruling party's loss of legitimacy. As noted already, the absence of strong mechanisms of checks and balances, along with a dominant party, creates fertile ground for corruption. With little challenge to its power, the EPRDF has come to be surrounded by a growing class of rent seekers. Perhaps facilitated by the dominance of public investment in the country's economy, the ruling party has come to be seen as a dispenser of wealth. Affiliation with the ruling party has allegedly become a source of access to capital. The land tenure system, particularly in urban and peri-urban areas, has also facilitated corruption by people affiliated or connected to the ruling party. There is also the perception, real or imagined, that affiliation and loyalty to the ruling party have become criteria for access to privilege, including jobs. Unsurprisingly, these conditions have damaged the image of the ruling party. The poor image of the party, in turn, has become a drag on the federal system.

5.10 Conclusion: No Quick Fixes

As we have seen, the federal arrangement in Ethiopia has registered notable success in a number of areas, including in reducing violent conflicts, in promoting rapid economic growth, and in granting identity groups cultural autonomy and self-rule, though of limited scope. The federal system is also widely accepted, and it is, indeed, difficult to envision a stable Ethiopia without the federal system. Yet, the federal arrangement continues to face some formidable challenges (Kefale 2013). The popular protests in Oromia and Amhara regional states over the last two years or so have shown the fragility of the cohesion of the ruling coalition and the vulnerability of the country's nation-building process. Restoring strong cohesion within the ruling party is one challenge. Forging a shared vision of nation building among the regional states, devolution of power to the states, and advancing democratic governance are others. Boundary disputes between some of the regional states and land ownership issues are other challenges. The image of the ruling party, which has been tarnished by corruption and by the mushrooming of a class of rent seekers around it, is also a significant challenge.

The appointment of a new prime minister, Abiy Ahmed, seems to have quieted the two-year-long popular protests and generated widespread goodwill towards the new government. Unfortunately, there are no quick fixes to many of the challenges of peaceful nation building the federal arrangement faces. Mending the cohesion within the ruling party, forging a shared vision of nation building among the regional states, and democratizing the county's political system are likely to be difficult and time-consuming undertakings.

References

Aalen, Lovise (2006). 'Ethnic Federalism and Self-Determination for Nationalities in a Semi-Authoritarian State: The Case of Ethiopia', *International Journal on Minority and Group Rights* 13: 243, 261.

Abbink, Jon (2011). 'Ethnic-Based Federalism and Ethnicity in Ethiopia: Reassessing the Experiment after 20 Years', *Journal of Eastern African Studies* 5: 4.

Abbink, J. G. (2006). 'Ethnicity and Conflict Generation in Ethiopia: Some Problems and Prospects of Ethno-Regional Federalism', *Journal of Contemporary African Studies* 24 (3): 389–413.

Abir, Mordechai (1970). *Ethiopia: The Era of The Princes: The Challenge of Islam and the Re-Unification of the Christian Empire 1769–1885*, 2nd edition (New York: Praeger).

Africa Development Bank (2018). *Ethiopia Economic Outlook 2018* (AfDB: Abidjan).

Bekele, Yeshtila Wondemeneh, Darley Jose Kjosavik, and Nadarajah Shanmugaratnam (2016). 'State–Society Relations in Ethiopia: A Political-Economy Perspective of the Post-1991 Order', *Social Sciences* 5 (3): 1–19.

Brietzke, Paul (1995). 'Ethiopia's Leap into the Dark: Federalism and Self-determination in the New Constitution', *Journal of African Law* 39 (1): 19–38.

Clapham, Christopher (2004). 'Ethiopia and the Challenge of Diversity', *Africa Insight* 34 (1): 50–5.

Engedayehu, Walle (1993). 'Ethiopia: Democracy and the Politics of Ethnicity', *Africa Today*, 2nd Quarter 40 (2): 29–52.

Erlich, Haggai (1996). *Ras Alula and the Scramble for Africa: A Political Biography: Ethiopia and Eritrea 1875–1897* (Trenton, NJ: Red Sea Press).

FDRE (1995). 'Constitution of the Federal Democratic Republic of Ethiopia', *Negarit Gazeta.*' Proclamation No. 1, FDRE, Addis Ababa.

Fiseha, Assefa (2012). 'Ethiopia's Experiment in Accommodating Diversity: 20 Years' Balance Sheet', *Journal of Regional and Federal Studies* 22 (4): 435–73.

Gebre-Selassie, Alemante (2003). 'Ethnic Federalism: Its Promise and Pitfalls for Africa', *Yale Journal of International Law* 28: 51, 88.

Gebrehiwot, Mulugeta and Fiseha Haftetsion (2015). 'The Politics of Naming Ethiopian Federation', *Journal of Ethiopian Studies* 48: 89–117.

Hassen, Mohammed (1994). 'Ethiopia Missed Opportunities for Peaceful Democratization Process'. Paper presented at the 37th annual meeting of the African Studies Association, Toronto.

Kefale, Asnake (2013). *Federalism and Ethnic Conflict in Ethiopia* (Abingdon: Routledge).

Mehretu, Assefa (2012). 'Ethnic Federalism and its Potential to Dismember the Ethiopian State', *Progress in Development Studies* 12 (2–3): 113–33.

Mengisteab, Kidane (1990). *Ethiopia: Failure of Land Reform and Agricultural Crisis* (New York: Greenwood Press).

Mengisteab, Kidane (1997). 'New Approaches to State Building in Africa: The Case of Ethiopia's Ethnic-Based Federalism', *African Studies Review* 40 (3): 111–32.

Mengisteab, Kidane (2007). 'Identity Politics, Democratisation and State Building in Ethiopia's Federal Arrangement', *African Journal of Conflict Resolution* 7 (2): 63–92.

Minasse, Haile (1996). 'The New Ethiopian Constitution: Its Impact upon Unity, Human Rights and Development,' *Suffolk Transnational Law Review* 20 (1): 1–84.

MoFED (2005). *A Plan for Accelerated and Sustained Development to End Poverty* (PASDEP), 2005/6-2009/10, Federal Democratic Republic of Ethiopia, Addis Ababa.

MoFED (2014). *Growth and Transformation Plan Annual Progress Report for F.Y. 2012/13*, Ministry of Finance and Economic Development, Addis Ababa: February 2014.

Pankhurst, Richard (1968). *Economic History of Ethiopia: 1800–1935* (Addis Ababa: Haile Selassie I University Press).

Pausewang, Siegfried, Kjetil Tronvoll, and Lovise Aalen (eds) (2002). 'Ethiopia since the Derg: A Decade of Democratic Pretension and Performance', *The International Journal of African Historical Studies* 36 (1): 246.

Temesgen, Siraw Megibaru (2015). 'Weaknesses of Ethnic Federalism in Ethiopia', *International Journal of Humanities and Social Science Invention* 4 (11): 49–54.

The Fund for Peace (2017). 'Fragile States Index', The Fund For Peace, Washington, DC.

Vaughan, Sarah (1994). *The Addis Ababa Transitional Conference of July 1991: Its Origins, History and Significance* (Edinburgh: Centre of African Studies, Edinburgh University).

Vaughan, Sarah (2011). 'Revolutionary Democratic State-Building: Party, State and People in the EPRDF's Ethiopia', *Journal of Eastern African Studies* 5 (4): 619–40.

World Bank (2017). 'The World Bank in Ethiopia'. http://www.worldbank.org/en/country/ethiopia/overview.

World Bank (2018). *Ethiopia Economic Update: The Inescapable Manufacturing–Services Nexus* (Washington, DC: World Bank).

CHAPTER 6

THE INTERFACE BETWEEN FEDERALISM AND DEVELOPMENT IN ETHIOPIA

ASSEFA FISEHA AND
FISEHA HAFTETSION GEBRESILASSIE

6.1 Introduction

Federalism and devolution were often unpopular political projects in post-colonial Africa. Most countries in the continent were associated with 'imperial presidency', one-party rule in which federalism was viewed as a colonial tool for 'divide and rule' that could facilitate state fragmentation in the context of artificially drawn borders. Most of these countries transplanted the European 'nation state' along with its myth that each state must serve a single nation and the normative assumptions of a centralized and homogenizing political system, despite the enormous diversity on the ground. The result was a concentration of power and resources in the hands of the ruling elite that also promoted its own language and culture to be the state's language and culture, and imposed it on ethno-national minorities while marginalizing them from power, leading to various conflicts (see Kymlicka 2007: 61–2). The nation state did not aim to provide political and cultural space to diversity. The pursuit of unity and territorial integrity at the expense of ethno-national minorities remained a leading priority for African states.

In Ethiopia, it was not until the twentieth century that political mobilization was transformed from a regional/provincial to an ethno-national form, largely in reaction to extreme centralization of power in the hands of the centrist elite. It was in this context that, following the collapse of the military junta in 1991, Ethiopia adopted a federal system of governance with a view to accommodating politically mobilized ethno-national groups. The initial signs of this political dispensation were remarkable.

The federal design has played a positive role as it has opened political space for hitherto marginalized ethno-nationalist forces, particularly in the area of language, culture, local self-government, and the promotion of their own histories. This, combined with the impressive economic growth, has ensured relative peace and stability in an otherwise troubled region.

Ethiopia's political and economic transformation in the last two decades is widely recognized (Monteiro and Thukwana 2018). The country registered double-digit GDP growth rates for more than a decade. Initially led by agriculture, economic growth has become more broad based, with mining, services, and manufacturing sectors generating an increasing share of output (IMF 2017). Several hydroelectric dams are boosting its economy and it plans to be the energy giant of the Horn region, exporting electricity to neighbouring countries. Federal government spends nearly 50 per cent of its budget on capital and mega development projects such as massive expansion of higher education and of road, rail, airport, and telecommunications infrastructure distributed fairly across the different regional states (MoFED 2010). Access to basic services such as education and health has also increased throughout the country to an unprecedented degree (see Chapters 9, 19, and 24).

What is remarkable in the evolution of the Ethiopian federal system is the political will and commitment of the political leadership to enhance the political and administrative institutions of the constituent units and improve the life of the ordinary people through anti-poverty policies and programmes. When the federal process began formally in 1995, the regional states had hardly any expertise owing to centuries of centralization and lack of political will from the centrist elite. Realizing this key challenge, the new leaders established new institutional mechanisms specifically geared to upgrading the capacity of the existing and newly recruited civil servants and political figures in the states. Impressed by the ability of the state to use limited resources for effective transformation, Lefort (2015: 367) wrote: 'with a mixture of resolve, efficiency, integrity and clear sightedness [this trend] had no equivalence anywhere else in Africa'. This development was instrumental in realizing the goals of the new Constitution's promise of self-rule.

6.2 Accommodating Ethno-National Diversity Through Federalism

Four divergent views on how to deal with diversity emerged following the fall of the military junta in 1991 and during the making of the Constitution. Centrist political elites (Ethiopia first)[1] insisted on absolute loyalty to the overarching state and aimed to

[1] This was the view of the late surgeon Dr Asrat Woldeyesus and Major Admasu Zeleke. See also programmes of the Coalition for Unity and Democracy (CUD) that emerged as one of the major opposition political parties in the 2005 election.

entrench the unity and territorial integrity of the country. According to this elite, it was hardly possible to combine self-rule with Ethiopian statehood. Some ethno-nationalist groups reacted by insisting one should demonstrate absolute loyalty to sub-state identity.[2] The moderates, who could be described as instrumentalists,[3] did not fully rule out federal divisions based on geographical or historical lines rather than ethnicity. Some moderate opposition parties propose geographic or territorial-based federalism, the ideological roots of which are often linked to American federalism. Yet these parties do not realize that in such federations the same majority at federal level also enjoys a majority at state level, the resulting nation-state federation having little to offer to strongly mobilized ethno-national groups (see McGarry and O'Leary 2004).

It is vital to note that federalism or devolved forms of government often have a space for both identities (overarching and sub-state identity) and do not insist that one should eliminate the other. On the contrary, both identities are preconditions that manifest themselves in the form of *unity in diversity*. Unity is one's loyalty to the overarching state, one's positive identification with the institutions, common citizenship, and symbols of the state, while diversity is a manifestation of sub-state identity that people enjoy at state or local government level. The most crucial point is the ability of the political elite at various levels to maintain a fair balance. As the recent protests (late 2015 and early 2016) in Oromia demonstrate, unregulated ethno-nationalism focusing on building sub-national identity at the expense of overarching symbols of the state and common citizenship, and nurtured over the years, generates a weak 'we belong' feeling and sows fertile soil for conflict and fragmentation (Stepan, Linz, and Yadiv 2011).

The fourth view is represented by the EPRDF—the main architect of the transition (1991–4) and the 1995 Constitution—which considers itself the successor to the Ethiopian Student Movement of the 1970s and has long advocated for 'nationalities' right to self-determination up to and including secession' (see Vaughan 1994). As a result, the key features of the federal Constitution are designed to ensure self-rule for politically mobilized ethno-national groups, which is not necessarily always respected owing to the party system and centrally designed development policies. States have responded quite differently to demands by mobilized ethno-national groups (see Simeon 2008). For countries with deep divisions where ethno-national groups are politically mobilized, and identity is politically salient, the two well recognized alternatives are power sharing and federalism or a combination of both (Horowitz 2002).

The works of Lijphart (1979) and McGarry and O'Leary (2004) have articulated the various elements of consociational as opposed to majoritarian democracy. The inclusion of the major political actors in political institutions through a proportional electoral system along with representation of the different groups in public institutions is one of the vital elements. Power sharing, unlike federalism, often takes non-territorial form (McGarry and O'Leary 2004: 10–12; Simeon 2008: 64). In other words, it is often

[2] The Oromo Liberation Front was once a champion of this view.

[3] See *The Third Way (2010)* by Lidetu Ayalew, a vocal opposition figure, which prescribes federalism but not on an ethnic basis.

recommended for societies that are deeply divided by identity differences but where groups are found to be geographically intermixed. Through a combination of power sharing at the centre, which enables them to influence policymaking at the centre, and autonomy that entitles them to decide issues related to language, education, and culture, groups are thought to contribute to political stability.

Power sharing is significant in the Ethiopian context, given the fact that none of the ethno-national groups on its own constitutes a '50 plus 1' majority. O'Leary has argued that in a context where there is no *Staatsvolk* (a dominant group that enjoys an absolute majority and hence has the demographic advantage), political instability will prevail unless there is an inclusive political system that brings the major political actors to power (O'Leary 2001: 273–96). The solution he proposed is executive power sharing among the major political actors. Since the establishment of the Ethiopian federation, both as a result of constitutional principle (Art. 39(3)) and practice, there has been every attempt to reflect the country's diversity in the establishment of the executive, which is the central element of integrating diversity politically. The federal executive power, a key institution in the African political context, is fairly shared among the four coalitions of the ruling party and its affiliates. Of the 31 federal executive positions appointed in October 2015, the SNNPRS and Oromia each had eight ministers, the Amhara nine, Tigray four, and Afar and Somali one each.[4] The ruling party in Ethiopia claims to be a coalition but it is only so in the limited (ethnic) sense. It is not a coalition in the true sense as members of the ruling party are ideologically united and the coalition does not include major political actors from the opposition that do not share its ideology. Apart from the crucial element of power sharing, the proportional electoral system is missing in Ethiopia, as the Constitution's Art. 54 provides for a first-past-the-post (FPTP) electoral system.

Thus, designing a more inclusive electoral system than FPTP to accommodate the diverse votes of the electorate remains a critical question (Lijphart 1977). Dr Mulatu Teshome, Ethiopia's President, in his annual state-of-the-nation address in September 2016, rightly stated:

> In the last two elections, the ruling party, and its allies, won 99.9% and 100% of the seats in the House of Peoples' Representatives. Although all those seats were won through free and fair, periodic elections, the result left the substantial number of votes given to opposition parties unrepresented in the House of Peoples' Representatives. The electoral system in effect left out demands that might have been represented by parties other than the ruling party.[5]

The President further indicated that the electoral system would be reviewed.[6] Whether the review process will result in the adoption of a proportional electoral system is too

[4] See Ethiopia: Hailemariam Forms New Administration at http://allafrica.com/stories/201510070627.html (accessed 17 October 2016).

[5] Quoted in Solomon Goshu 'Electoral Reform on Horizon', The *Reporter* 22 October 2016.

[6] Solomon Goshu, 'Electoral Reform on Horizon', The *Reporter* 22 October 2016.

early to tell, but the need to design a more inclusive electoral system has rightly been pointed out. It is vital to mention that successful federations that are diverse often combine federalism with power sharing. Groups are often found to be intermixed at times and in other places geographically concentrated. It is for this reason that as Elazar (1994: 57) argued, consociational federations are the best fit for divided societies. It is here that one finds a major loophole for further refining the Ethiopian federal system.

The highest form of accommodating ethno-nationalist groups, particularly when they are territorially concentrated and politically mobilized, as in Ethiopia, is through federalism (McGarry and O'Leary 2004). As Livingston long since articulated, the essence of federalism is not in the Constitution or the institutions alone but in the social and political diversity that necessitates its adoption (Livingston 1952: 81–95). The geographic distribution of diversity remains a vital factor. If mobilized ethno-national groups are found concentrated in a certain defined area, federalism remains a relevant alternative. Through its combination of constitutionally entrenched division of power as well as the principles of shared rule and self-rule (Elazar 1994: 12), it allows mobilized groups to enjoy political autonomy at sub-unit level while ensuring representation at federal level. Through the institutions of shared rule and representation in federal institutions, ethno-nationalist groups are given the opportunity to influence decision-making at the centre. The logic of this form of federalism is that ethno-nationalist groups can only respect the institutions of governance and thus contribute to a stable federation when they are granted a satisfactory combination of *influence* at the centre and *meaningful autonomy* at sub-state level with regard to their own affairs (Lijphart 1979: 500). This somehow determines whether ethno-nationalist groups will remain loyal to the overarching federation or prefer to fight or walk away from it. As it recognizes more than one public identity (at the federal and sub-state levels) and aims to secure co-existence among them, it remains a key instrument for polity building and managing diversity. The sharing of executive power, albeit in the limited sense mentioned in Section 6.2, and the second chamber (HoF), which currently has 153 members representing seventy-six nationalities indirectly elected by the states and plays a critical role in the allocation of subsidies, the main source of revenue for the states, and resolution of disputes are examples (Fiseha 2017: 295–313).

The federal system in Ethiopia shares some of the basic features of federal polities but it also has distinct elements which, however, are not entirely explained in the elaborate description of the division of powers between the federal government and the states that appears in the Constitution. Beyond serving as another centre of power, the states have the additional and critical role of empowering ethno-national groups who are considered as founders of the new federal dispensation. The Constitution is viewed as a political contract and the result of the 'free will of nations, nationalities and peoples' that are politically mobilized, territorially grouped and declared as sovereign (Article 8). It insists on the need for some congruence between the nation and nationalities and the territory of their regional states in order to ensure self-rule. Moreover, Article 39 ensures three principal group rights. First: 'every nation, nationality and people in Ethiopia has an unconditional right to self determination, including the right to secession'. This right, often overshadowed by the right to secede, confers on ethno-national groups the more important right to internal self-determination. Second, it grants each nationality 'the right to speak, to write and to develop its own language; to express, to develop and to promote its culture and to preserve its history'. In sharp contrast to centrist regimes that aimed at assimilating diversity, since the adoption of the federation, Ethiopian nationalities have publicly celebrated their diversity, so much so that 8 December, the date the current Constitution was adopted in 1994, has been designated by the government 'Nations, Nationalities and Peoples' Day'. Third, nationalities also have 'the right to full measure of self-government, which includes the right to establish institutions of government in the territory that they inhabit and to *equitable representation* in the state and federal governments'.

Thus, the Ethiopian federal system accommodates and empowers the nations, nationalities, and peoples primarily through the provision of territorial and political autonomy to geographically concentrated ethno-national groups (Article 46(2) of the Constitution). While each nationality taken alone is a minority at federal level, relatively larger ethno-national groups become a majority at regional state- and local-level governments and thus dominate the political institutions of self-rule. The Constitution dictates organization of regional states on 'the basis of settlement patterns, language, identity and consent of the people concerned'. Language has played a key role in redrawing the boundary of the constituent units. The major ethno-national groups have established their own regional states with their own constitutions and mandates. Six of the nine regions (Afar, Oromo, Tigray, Somali, Amhara, and Harari) directly represent empowerment of specific ethno-national groups. In the Southern Nations, Nationalities and Peoples Regional State (SNNPRS), a state with extraordinary heterogeneity, it is *local* governments, not the regional state as in other states, that are designed to ensure self-rule to the various groups. Each of these six regional states and some twenty local governments in the SNNPRS are, in short, a motherland to a particular ethno-national group that accounts for the majority of their respective population, allowing the group to control the regional and local political institutions.

Critics have argued that in empowering ethno-national groups to self-rule and putting resources and the media at their disposal, the Constitution emphasizes the politics of difference and may weaken common ties, and that ethno-national groups and their elites may have independent nationhood as their ultimate objective. It is thus a high-risk strategy that may eventually bring about the country's disintegration (see Minasse 1996). Some of the above symptoms were clearly manifested in the pre-election debates in 2005, when some leaders from the opposition fomented ethnic hatred.[7] The signs were also visible in the 2016 protests, in which in some remote districts carrying

[7] A key figure from the opposition, Bedru Adem, in a widely televised speech on the eve of the 2005 election, read to his audience 'let them go to where they came from', widely understood to imply to the Tigrayan community associated with the ruling party as if they came from another continent. See *Asqual* 10 May 2015.

the federal flag was considered by hardliner ethno-national elites as a crime.[8] Intra-unit minorities have been widely discriminated against in the states by dominant ethno-national groups as well. While the status of intra-unit minorities in the regional states has long been a thorny issue, it has recently taken an ugly turn with evictions and mass expulsions occurring more frequently. The nature of the conflicts has also changed. What used to be local conflicts over water and grazing land between different communities on the border between regional states have now become regional state conflicts, which neither level of government is able to arrest, with the local media, elites, and local security officers taking sides, and deaths and mass displacements occurring. While the federal education policy required states to promote the federal working language in schools, in some parts of the Oromia regional state this was largely seen as a continuation of the old regime and was resisted. Despite its defects and the scope for improvement, however, the achievements of the federal system in terms of accommodating diversity remain impressive.

6.3 Aligning Federalism and Development: Results and Emerging Issues

The introduction of a federal system of governance that gives due recognition to previously marginalized ethno-national groups and popular demands enabled Ethiopia to withstand the threat of a break-up in the early 1990s. Predictions regarding the fate of the country during the inception of the federal system were at best gloomy. Nonetheless, Ethiopia has continued to register impressive economic performance since the early 2000s (World Bank 2016: 3; MoFED 2013). The economic success story of the country has largely been driven by an interventionist government policy that focused on mass mobilization of the poor, capital investment, and infrastructure. The real Gross Domestic Product (GDP) of the country has shown growth above 10 per cent annually in the last fifteen years (World Bank 2016: 3). Vital infrastructure including roads of all types, electric power generation and access, and telecoms services have expanded tremendously. The distribution of the newly created wealth is also fair: Ethiopia is among the most equal countries according to the Gini coefficient measurement (UNDP 2014; MoFED 2013).

The government's investment in social services including health and education has multiplied since the adoption of the federal system. As a result, primary health coverage and elementary school enrolment have tripled (World Bank 2016: 24; MoFED 2013). The tremendous economic changes are evidenced by the high rate of reduction of absolute poverty, slashed by more than half in the last decade. The country has also met almost

[8] Interview conducted in Dire Dawa with participants of a focus group discussion from Oromia, November 2016.

all the Millennium Development Goals (MDGs). Improved access to health care, improvements in income and hence improved nutrition have raised the life expectancy of Ethiopians from about 45 years in the 1990s to above 63 in 2015. Although still low in absolute terms, human development in Ethiopia ranks among the leading countries in terms of absolute gains in the last couple of decades (UNDP 2014: 1).

A thorough investigation of the role of federalism in bringing about the positive changes witnessed so far may call for a separate work of its own. Yet, it should be obvious that the federal system of governance has addressed many pressing issues that once led the country into a civil war, including ethno-cultural, linguistic, religious, and economic injustices. The federal system has decentralized decision-making and spending powers, which has helped build the capacity of local governments. This has had a decisive impact on the successes registered in all sectors, particularly in primary health services and education (see Chapters 23 and 25). The relative peace ensured by accommodating ethno-national diversity through federalism, in the otherwise troubled region of the Horn of Africa, has created a favourable environment for socio-economic progress. The decentralization of resources and the subsidy regional states obtain from the federal government have been the main sources of progress in the socio-economic sector.

Notwithstanding the above developments, federalism is an evolving process and there are bound to be tensions and new challenges on the way as both society and the economy undergo significant transitions. In an open and competitive democratic system, some of these contradictions and tensions can be brought to the fore by interest groups negatively affected by government decisions. This is not the case in countries such as Ethiopia where a vanguard party dominates policy decisions.

Rapid economic growth always brings with it unintended consequences. In the case of Ethiopia, this has manifested itself in the form of jurisdiction and decision-making powers over the use of land for large-scale investments and geographical extension of the federal capital, which is also an autonomous administration. This is the first contentious issue to test the current federal-regional arrangement, and it will have to be resolved through consultation and the effective use of the mechanisms provided by the Constitution. The issue of land use is not going to be the last problem to challenge the federal government and regional states. There may be many more to come as the Ethiopian economy and Ethiopian society in general undergo massive transformation.

In the initial phase of the federal process there was certainly much focus on addressing the demands of politically mobilized ethno-national groups through self-rule. Yet the system slowly began to evolve differently with the ethno-national elite controlling state power, leading to central government's hegemony over the states. This was particularly visible with the emergence of the political ideology of the developmental state nearly a decade after the adoption of the federal system. As illustrated in the following sections, this development brought its own dynamics that at times clashed with the values and institutions of federalism and the autonomy of the states. Further fuelling the tension is the monopoly of power exercised by a hegemonic party.

Three interrelated issues (the Addis Ababa–Oromia Integrated Development Plan and the main land and investment-related laws and policies) are examined to show that federalism and developmentalism, although each is individually subject to the law of evolution and is a vital commitment of the government, have not necessarily always been in harmony with each other in the Ethiopian context.

6.3.1 Addis Ababa–Oromia Integrated Development Plan

The Addis Ababa and the Surrounding Oromia Integrated Development Plan (2014) provided for 'a megacity of between 8 and 10 million in the coming 25 years'. The plan aimed to integrate (its critics argue, to *expand*) the current size of the federal capital by a factor of twenty. Decades back the focus was, as provided in the Constitution's Article 49(5), to address the concerns of ethno-national groups. Addis Ababa is situated within Oromia National Regional State, one of the largest geographically and in terms of population, and thus '[t]he special interest of the State of Oromia in Addis Ababa, regarding the provision of social services or the utilization of natural resources and other similar matters, as well as joint administrative matters arising from the location of Addis Ababa within the State of Oromia shall be respected'. Lately, the focus has been on 'integration and development'. Yet the city is facing challenges as the seat of three governments: the city government, the federal government, and the government of Oromia National Regional State.

The plan was designed by the political leadership with the help of technocrats but contains little detail about the political, legal, and economic implications of integration. Ethiopia's government routinely adopts this kind of top-down approach to policymaking with little genuine public consultation before implementation. Crucial development plans are designed behind closed doors without necessarily consulting stakeholders. Such policies are often made public at the implementation stage (Lefort 2015: 361). The three relevant legislative bodies (the federal parliament, Addis Ababa City Council, and Oromia regional state) have not debated and agreed on the Integrated Development Plan. The three governments, though controlled by the same ruling party, represent three different interests. The federal government has a constitutional duty to make sure that the federal capital is managed in such a way as to conform to international standards.

Addis Ababa is a cosmopolitan city of no less than four million people. Its residents expect an efficient urban governance system and an administration that is elected and accountable to its voters. The city is also the seat of the Oromia National Regional State which has a special interest in the city. Growing Oromo ethno-nationalism coupled with poorly managed urban expansion to the outskirts of the federal capital has produced tension. Legal and illegal occupation of land by the urban elite and the subsequent eviction of Oromo farmers from the surroundings were a key mobilizing factor for both Oromo elites and Oromo opposition parties in June 2014 and in the widespread protests in Oromia regional state in early 2016 (Muradu 2014: 157). Lack of transparency and the failure to consider all major stakeholders in the process of designing the Integrated Development Plan were also critical factors. The plan was subsequently abandoned by the government.

6.3.2 Powers Related to Land and Large-Scale Agricultural Investments

The Ethiopian Constitution stipulates a peculiar type of concurrent power that separates legislative and administrative powers between the federal and the state governments. This feature of concurrency is provided for in Article 51(5) and Article 52(2) (d) of the Constitution. Article 51(5) authorizes the federal government to *enact laws* regarding the utilization and conservation of land and other natural resources, historical sites, and objects. Article 52(2) (d) provides the states with the power to *administer* land and other natural resources in accordance with federal laws. This would seem to imply that setting the norms related to utilization and conservation of land and other natural resources is the responsibility of the federal government, while implementing these norms and laws belongs to the states. Hence, the Constitution separates the legislative and administrative aspects of the use of land and natural resources. But this should be seen against the background of Article 40(3) which stipulates 'the right to ownership of rural and urban land, as well as of all-natural resources, is exclusively vested in the *state and in the peoples* of Ethiopia. *Land is a common property of the nations, nationalities and peoples of Ethiopia* and shall not be subject to sale or to other means of exchange.'[9]

With a view to enforcing its mandate over land, the federal government has issued several proclamations relating to the use of land, invoking Article 51(5) of the Constitution as its source of authority. These include Proclamations 818 (2014),[10] 721(2011), 574 (2008), 455 (2005), Proclamation 89 (1997), Council of Minsters Regulation Number 283/2013[11] and Proclamation number 886(2015).[12] The first proclamation regulates all urban centres in the country including those falling within the mandate of urban local governments. The second proclamation deals with allocation of urban land on lease for 'developmental activities'. The proclamation broadly defines the developmental activities and sets the maximum lease period for a specific developmental activity. It further regulates the manner in which the land lease rate is determined and evictions of illegal landholders are undertaken. The third proclamation regulates urban planning, while the fourth deals with matters relating to rural and urban land expropriation. Regulation Number 283/2013 establishes a federal government

[9] Italics added by the author.

[10] Art. 3 of Proclamation No. 818/2014 deals with registration of urban land holding in all urban areas across the country. Not only the mandate of states but also that of urban local governments have been expropriated by this proclamation.

[11] Regulation Number 283/2013 establishes the (federal) Ethiopian Agricultural Investment Land Administration Agency that has the mandate to administer and allocate land exceeding 5,000 hectares in the regional states to investors.

[12] Federal *Negarit Gazeta* of the Federal Democratic Republic Ethiopia: Re-Enactment of Urban Lands Lease Holding Proclamation No 272 (2002); Federal *Negarit Gazeta* of the Federal Democratic Republic Ethiopia: A Proclamation to Provide for Urban Plans No. 574 (2008); Federal *Negarit Gazeta* of the Federal Democratic Republic Ethiopia: Expropriation of Landholdings for Public Purposes and Payment of Compensation Proclamation No. 455 (2005).

agency to *administer* (defined in the regulation as identify, demarcate, take possession, supervise, and control—an express mandate of the states) land allocated for large-scale agricultural investment in the states; it has also the power to establish agricultural investment zones.

The final proclamation establishes federal industrial parks in the regional states and the federal investment board, chaired by the Prime Minister and other senior government officers, which allocates land (which may be under the administration of the regional states) to industrial parks (Articles 22 and 25). Based on these federal proclamations, the regional states, more specifically the cities in the regional states, allocate urban and rural land for development, undertake town planning, evict illegal landholders, expropriate lands for development purposes, and allocate land for large-scale agricultural investment and industrial parks. The new laws do not clarify where the legislative power of the federal government ends and the administrative power of the states begins with respect to land and natural resources. The issue here is whether the power of the federal government to enact laws related to urban and rural land also extends to imply the administration of land, expressly stipulated by the federal Constitution as mandated to the states.

In 2010 a decision by the top leadership of the ruling party, which has never been given legal status in the form of a proclamation or regulation, required the states to delegate the power to administer large-scale agricultural investment land. Article 50(9) of the Constitution does not, however, allow upward delegation by the states to the federal government. The alleged justification for this move was that foreign and domestic large-scale agricultural investment needed to be centrally managed because regional states, particularly those in the periphery, did not have the capacity to manage it. An assessment conducted after some time revealed that centrally managing large-scale agricultural commercial farming was highly inefficient, and it was finally suspended by the federal government in March 2016.[13] This indicates that in the absence of a holistic approach involving careful design and proper consultation between tiers of government, a well-intentioned development project or plan could end up clashing with the overarching federal system or may fail to produce the desired outcomes.

6.3.3 Powers of Investment

According to the Constitution, the federal government formulates and executes the country's financial, monetary, and *foreign investment policies* and strategies (italics added) (Article 51(4)).[14] The Constitution provides no further details about investment. The investment proclamation (Art. 4) states that the federal government is empowered to administer investments that involve foreign components. The power of the federal

[13] See 'Ethiopia: Agency Suspends Giving Land for Investors' at http://www.2merkato.com/news/alerts/4522-ethiopia-agency-suspends-giving-land-for-investors, accessed 2 May 2016.

[14] The authors would like to acknowledge the research assistance of Meron Tilahun for this section.

government, through its investment commission, extends to administering investments by domestic investors if the investment is eligible for incentives, and it should be licensed by the federal government (Art. 4(1)(d) of the investment proclamation).

The Constitution is clear only to the extent that the federal government is empowered to make policies on foreign investment. This looks compatible with the overall theoretical foundations of federations and distribution of powers thereof (Anderson 2008: 24; Watts 1998: 117–37). Nevertheless, it is unclear whether empowering the federal government to administer all sorts of investments that involve foreign elements or investments in preferred areas that should be licensed by the federal government is coherent with the overall division of mandates as per the Constitution.

Developmentalism, which is among the top priorities of the contemporary Ethiopian state and which focuses on bringing about state-led development (Zenawi 2012: 167), it could be argued, requires foreign investment to be administered centrally and quickly. However, the Indian experience suggests that foreign direct investment could increase when the constituent units are directly involved in mobilizing and administering foreign investments (Sharma 2017: 7). Of course, legislating on policy-related issues including priority areas, reserved areas, incentives, setting standards, and the like should be conveniently left to the federal government, as empowering the constituent units to deal with such issues could lead to negative competition and inefficiency.

In the Ethiopian case, although the federal government is empowered to license and administer investments with foreign components, it must depend on the states to supply some vital inputs for investment including land, which they administer. It has recently been observed that even if the federal government issues a licence to an investor, there seems to be no guarantee that the required land will be obtained.[15] Failure to procure such a vital input as land (within a reasonable time) hampers investment and eventually development. Exploring the reasons why some of the states hesitate to provide land to federally licensed investors suggests that the states claim it is they who should have the first say regarding investments in their territory, which challenges the investment proclamation. If the states are engaged in mobilizing and administering foreign investments, since they will be involved in the process from the very beginning, it could be argued that not only are jurisdiction-induced conflicts less likely to arise but there is also a high chance of success. Thus, assigning investment-related mandates, a key component of developmentalism, to any tier of government calls for a well thought-out design and proper consultation, lest it contradicts the overarching constitutional framework.

A recent significant phenomenon in the area of investment is the construction of huge industrial parks by the federal government and the states. In terms of attracting and expanding investment, this is a huge step forward. In terms of clarifying the mandates or roles of the federal and the state governments and continuity, however, there are questions that need to be addressed. What is the legal basis for the federal government to build such huge and capital-intensive parks in the states, apart from the industrial parks proclamation (FDRE 2015), which is a law enacted by the federal government

[15] Interview with an official in the sector, Addis Ababa, 8 December 2017.

itself? What are the criteria for allocating such parks? Could the federal government force the states to provide land for constructing parks? Who bears the environmental costs? Although the interviewees from the federal investment commission confirmed that complaints regarding industrial parks are rare, the situation seems different in the case of Oromia.[16] There is a possibility that industrial parks could be perceived as expanding the administrative powers of the federal government in relation to investments. This happens because of the blanket stipulation that the federal government, regardless of the origin or status of the investor, administers any investment within the parks. As indicated in Section 6.3.2, there are emerging issues that need negotiation, discussion, and cooperation between the two levels of government to avoid tension and facilitate the smooth operation of investments in the country.

6.4 Conclusion

Federalism and development are two major pillars of the Ethiopian government. Federalism is meant to address Ethiopia's political ills while development is a means to transform Ethiopia's economy. Yet how these two major government projects align themselves in practice remains an issue. There seems to be a shift from the earlier focus on the 'rights of nations, nationalities and peoples' to a new vocabulary of 'building one political and economic community' where the developmental state and the focus on delivery in the economy and the services is being used as a new source of legitimacy. As the lack of transparency and consultation during the making and abandoning of the Addis Ababa–Oromia Integrated Development Plan, and laws and policies issued by the federal government regulating land and large-scale agricultural investment projects and investments in general demonstrate, the idea of 'creating one political and economic community' and the developmental state are used as a means to design mega development policies while sometimes not giving enough attention to the federal principle of a constituent unit's mandate to self-rule.

The idea that development is *centrally* designed and managed along with the identification of poverty as an existential threat against which all resources must be mobilized means that development may take on a central role as an over-riding priority. Federalism, nations and nationalities' right to self-rule, and associated rights to land are occasionally sidelined for the sake of development. The outcome, as witnessed in the protest against the Integrated Development Plan and the widespread protests in 2016, is becoming a source of discontent and a new source of mobilization and conflict. This tension is further aggravated by weak institutions that are overshadowed by the vanguard party. A political system dominated by a single party that marginalizes the political opposition fails to

[16] Interview with officials from the Ethiopian Investment Commission, Addis Ababa, 8 December 2018; interview with Belay Dufera and Berhanu Yadesa, Oromia Investment Commission, Addis Ababa, 12 January 2018.

provide space for peaceful political dissent while emboldening hardliners, leading to political instability. Discontent on this scale would not otherwise normally be manifested immediately after a '100 per cent' electoral success. The way out is a more inclusive political system that brings the major political actors to power through electoral reform, strict enforcement of and respect for the political autonomy of the states, and a comprehensive policy for promoting shared values that cross-cut ethno-national boundaries.

References

Anderson, George (2008). *Federalism: An Introduction* (Oxford: Oxford University Press).

Davison, William (2016). 'Twitter, WhatsApp Down in Ethiopia Oromia Area after Unrest', *Bloomberg News*, 12 April. https://www.bloomberg.com/news/articles/2016-04-12/twitter-whatsapp-offline-in-ethiopia-s-oromia-area-after-unrest

Elazar, Daniel (1994). *Federalism and the Way to Peace* (Ontario: Kingston, Institute of Intergovernmental Relations).

FDRE (1995). '*Negarit Gazeta* of the Federal Democratic Republic Ethiopia: Constitution of the Federal Democratic Republic of Ethiopia, *Negarit Gazeta*.' Proclamation No. 1 (1995).

FDRE (2002). '*Negarit Gazeta* of the Federal Democratic Republic Ethiopia: Re-Enactment of Urban Lands Lease Holding.' Proclamation No. 272 (2002).

FDRE (2005). '*Negarit Gazeta* of the Federal Democratic Republic Ethiopia: Expropriation of Landholdings for Public Purposes and Payment of Compensation'. Proclamation No. 455 (2005).

FDRE (2008). '*Negarit Gazeta* of the Federal Democratic Republic Ethiopia: A Proclamation to Provide for Urban Plans'. Proclamation No. 574 (2008).

FDRE (2012). '*Negarit Gazeta* of the Federal Democratic Republic Ethiopia: Investment Proclamation of the Federal Democratic Republic of Ethiopia, *Negarit Gazeta*.' Proclamation No. 769 (2012).

FDRE (2015). '*Negarit Gazeta* of the Federal Democratic Republic Ethiopia: Industrial Park Proclamation of the Federal Democratic Republic of Ethiopia, *Negarit Gazeta*.' Proclamation No. 886 (2015).

Fiseha, Assefa (2017). 'Constitutional Adjudication through Second Chamber in Ethiopia', *Ethnopolitics* 16 (3): 295–313.

Horowitz, Donald (2002). 'Constitutional Design: Proposals, Process,' in *The Architecture of Democracy: Constitutional Design, Conflict Management and Democracy*, ed. Andrew Reynolds (Oxford: Oxford University Press): 15–37.

IMF (2017). 'The Federal Democratic Republic of Ethiopia; Staff Report for the 2017 Article IV Consultation—Press Release', IMF, Washington, DC.

Imperial Government of Ethiopia (1955). 'Revised Constitution of the Empire of Ethiopia', (1955) *Negarit Gazeta* 15 (2), Addis Ababa.

Kymlicka, Will (2007). *Multicultural Odysseys: Navigating the New International Politics of Diversity* (Oxford: Oxford University Press).

Lefort, Rene (2015). 'The Ethiopian Economy: Developmental State vs. The Free Market', in *Understanding Contemporary Ethiopia: Monarchy, Revolution and the Legacy of Meles Zenawi*, ed. Gerard Prunier and Eloi Fiequet (London: Hurst and Company): 357–94.

Lefort, Rene (2016). 'Unrest in Ethiopia: The Ultimate Warning Shot?' Open Democracy, February 2, 2016. https://www.opendemocracy.net/ren-lefort/unrest-in-ethiopia-ultimate-warning-shot (accessed 18 April 2016).

Lijphart, Arend (1977). *Democracy in Plural Societies* (New Haven, CT: Yale University Press).

Lijphart, Arend (1979). 'Consociationalism and Federalism: Conceptual and Empirical Links', *Canadian Journal of Politics* 12 (3): 499–515.

Livingston, William (1952). 'A Note on the Nature of Federalism', *Political Science Quarterly* 67 (1): 81–95.

McGarry, John and Brendan O'Leary (2004). *The Northern Ireland Conflict: Consociational Elements* (Oxford: Oxford University Press).

Minasse, Haile (1996). 'The New Ethiopian Constitution: Its Impact upon Unity, Human Rights and Development', *Suffolk Transitional Law Review* 2 (1): 1–84.

MoFED (2010). *Growth and Transformation Plan, 2010/2015*, 2 vols, Federal Democratic Republic of Ethiopia, Addis Ababa.

MoFED (2013). *Growth and Transformation Plan: Annual Progress Report for FY.2011/12*. Federal Democratic Republic of Ethiopia, Addis Ababa.

Monteiro, Ana and Ntando Thukwana (2018). 'IMF Sees Ethiopia Beating Ghana as Fastest Growing African Economy', *Bloomberg News*. https://www.bloomberg.com/news/article

Muradu, Abdo (2014). 'State Policy and Law in Relation to Land Alienation in Ethiopia', PhD thesis, University of Warwick.

O'Leary, Brendan (2001). 'An Iron Law of Nationalism and Federation? A Neo-Diceyian Theory of the Necessity of a Federal Statsvolk, and of Consociational Rescue', *Nations and Nationalism* 7 (3): 273–96.

Sharma, Chanchal Kumar (2017). 'Federalism and Foreign Direct Investment: How Political Affiliation Determines the Spatial Distribution of FDI–Evidence from India', GIGA Working Paper.

Simeon, Richard (2008). 'Managing Conflicts of Diversity', in *Building on and Accommodating Diversities*, ed. Ronald Watts and Rupak Chattopadhyay (New Delhi: Viva Books): 54–70.

Stepan, Alfred, Juan Linz, and Yogendra Yadiv (2011). *Crafting State Nations: India and Other Multinational Democracies* (Baltimore, MD: Johns Hopkins University Press).

UNDP (2014). 'Ethiopia National Human Development Report 2014: Accelerating Inclusive Growth for Sustainable Human Development in Ethiopia', UNDP, Addis Ababa.

Vaughan, Sarah (1994). 'The Addis Ababa Transitional Conference of July 1991: Its Origins, History and Significance', Centre of African Studies, Edinburgh University.

Verhoeven, Harry (2015). 'Africa's Next Hegemon: Behind Ethiopia's Power Plays', *Foreign Affairs*, April 12. (https://www.foreignaffairs.com/articles/ethiopia/2015-04-12/africas-next-hegemon) (accessed 23 July 2015).

Watts, Ronald (1998). 'Federalism, Federal Political Systems, and Federations', *Annual Review of Political Science* 1: 117–37.

World Bank (2016). 'Federal Democratic Republic of Ethiopia Evaluation of MDGs Specific Purpose Grant to Regions', Report No: ACS17500, World Bank, Washington, DC.

Zenawi, Meles (2012). 'States and Markets: Neoliberal Limitations and the Case for a Developmental State', in *Good Growth and Governance in Africa: Rethinking Development Strategies*, ed. Akbar Noman, Kwesi Botchwey, Howard Stein, and Joseph E. Stiglitz (Oxford: Oxford University Press): 140–73.

CHAPTER 7

ETHIOPIA'S CONSTITUTIONAL FRAMEWORK AND LEGAL INSTITUTIONS FOR DEVELOPMENT

MENBERETSEHAI TADESSE AND
BELACHEW MEKURIA FIKRE

7.1 Introduction

The government in power since 1991 has adopted various policies and enacted different laws to implement its developmental orientation. The task of achieving economic progress is undertaken within the framework of a federal constitution that reflects homegrown legal concepts in addition to the accepted constitutional norms commonly found in other constitutions. The defining feature of the constitution is its recognition of the nations, nationalities, and peoples as the basic building block of the whole constitutional framework. As recent legal instruments are overlaid on previously transplanted substantive and procedural laws, tensions are bound to arise when law is used as an instrument to achieve economic development.

This chapter examines how the government navigates through the legal system, which is an amalgam of Western, socialist, development-oriented, and traditional systems, to achieve economic development. The chapter will also discuss the fundamental features of the constitution on matters that are pertinent for economic development, such as distribution of powers, land ownership, dispute resolution systems, and constitutional interpretation. It will also assess the basic features of the legal institutions and how they function within the overall goal of attaining economic development.

The authors argue that the injection of homegrown values into the law-making process and the landscape of litigation has contributed to the economic progress Ethiopia has registered over the past decade.

7.2 General Background

The legal experiments that are being engineered in Ethiopia are animated by the instrumental approach that law is an instrument for economic growth (Trubek and Santos 2006). This line of thinking is apparent in the constitution of the Democratic Republic of Ethiopia and can be gathered, for example, from the constitutional preamble, which links advancing economic and social development on the one hand with the rule of law and protection of fundamental individual and group rights on the other (FDRE 1995).

The constitution adopts liberal values such as human rights, separation of powers, and the independence of the judiciary. It also recognizes international human rights treaties ratified by Ethiopia (Article 9, Constitution). On the other hand, it adopts new principles, arguably dictated by the need to respond to local challenges and ensure economic development. Some of the principles are significantly different from Western legal postulates. The recognition of Nations, Nationalities and Peoples (NN&P) as subjects of rights including the right to secede, public ownership of land, the composition and function of the House of the Federation (HoF),and the model of constitutional interpretation are some of the homegrown features crafted as part of an endeavour to enhance economic performance.

7.3 Division of Powers

The preamble of the Constitution of the Federal Democratic Republic of Ethiopia, unusually, starts with the statement 'We, the Nations, Nationalities and Peoples of Ethiopia', indicating the nature of its organizing principles and its defining features. These groups are recognized as subjects of rights (Article 39, Constitution), as owners of sovereign power (Article 8), and as basic building blocks of the overall federal framework (Article 46, Constitution). The constitutional design is predicated on the premise that protection of the *individual and people's* fundamental freedoms and rights is required to advance economic and social development and to build one economic and political community. The fundamental principles, division of powers, the human rights regime, and the federal state structure envisaged are heavily influenced by the peculiar position assigned to these groups.

As a federal system, powers are shared between the federal government and the constituent member states. The federal and the states have legislative, executive, and judicial powers on matters attributed to each of them (Article 50(2), Constitution).While the constitution enumerates the powers attributed to the federal government (Article 51), it grants the residual powers to the states by providing that 'all powers not given expressly to the Federal Government alone, or concurrently to the Federal Government and the States are reserved to the states' (Article 52(1)). The federal and state governments share concurrent powers; however, such powers are not listed in a single provision but scattered through different parts of the constitution. In this chapter we will examine some aspects of this division of power and show their relevance to economic development.

7.3.1 Policymaking and Enactment of Civil Laws

Policymaking in economic and social matters is one of the powers concurrently attributed to both the federal and state governments. While the federal government is empowered to formulate and implement the country's policies, strategies, and plans in respect of overall economic social, and development policy (Article 51(2), Constitution),the states have the power to formulate and execute economic, social, and development policies, strategies, and plans for their respective states (Article 52(2(c)), Constitution). The concurrence of powers in formulating and implementing economic policies at the federal and state level may be problematic when the two levels follow different approaches to basic policy matters. In light of the difficulty of drawing a line between federal and state powers, the formulation of the legal framework on policymaking areas is arguably within the federal powers (Fiseha 2006: 304).

Many of the powers of the federal government that are enumerated have a bearing on the direction and regulation of the economy, including the power to formulate and execute the country's financial, monetary, and foreign investment policies and strategies; and development, administration, and regulation of air, rail, waterway, and sea transport. Enactment of branches of law that play a pivotal role in the legal relationships between economic agents, such as labour law and commercial law, are also under federal competence (Article 55, Constitution). The federal government enjoys wide powers to shape the overall direction of the country's economic development.

The federal government's competence to regulate matters of economic significance is enumerated in the constitution, giving the states significant powers in all other areas that influence the direction of economic development. A closer reading of the constitution, however, reveals that there are inbuilt mechanisms to redistribute powers of great economic significance anew when the need to do so arises. In some cases, the federal government has the authority to reclaim powers that fall within state competence. In other cases, the power holders are determined on a piece meal basis. Two instances will be discussed briefly later to show how the constitutional framework responds to economic demands and that the power-sharing scheme is not frozen.

The first scenario relates to powers of taxation. While the powers of the federal government and those of the states to levy and collect taxes are enumerated under Articles 96 and 97 respectively, the concurrent powers are provided under Article 98. If one follows the general formula for power distribution, any residual power on taxation matters should fall within state competence. The constitution, however, follows a different approach when taxation powers are not specifically provided for. Instead of vesting such powers in the states—following the residual power formula—the constitution empowers the HoF to decide on a piecemeal basis whether the power to levy and collect such taxes should be a federal or state competence. The parameters for the redistribution of such powers by the HoF are not clearly articulated in the constitution. This may become a source of tension between the federal and state governments. There is, however, a general direction that revenue should be shared between the federal and state governments, 'taking the federal arrangement into account' (Article 95, Constitution). The HoF is also the primary institution empowered to handle tensions that arise between the federal and state governments (Article 62(6)) and is likely to take such matters into account in making its decision.

The second example shows the federal government's power to reclaim some matters that ordinarily fall within the competence of the states. The federal government's constitutional powers to enact laws on inter-state commerce, foreign trade, patents, copyright, labour, and commercial law allow it to regulate matters that have an impact on economic performance. In addition, the federal law-making organ may enact civil law on matters that fall under state competence when this is found 'necessary to establish and sustain one economic community' (Article 55 and 62(8), Constitution). The decision to reclaim such powers affects the constitutional power of the states to regulate economic activities. The constitution sacrifices some aspects of self-determination in the interest of overall economic development needs. The decision to shift such powers from the states to the federal government is made by the HoF. This legal arrangement allows the constitution to continuously manage the tension between the right to self-determination and the mandate to build one economic community.

The HoF has, in one instance, directed the Federal House of Peoples Representatives (HPPR) to enact law based on this scheme. The HPPR passed Proclamation 334/2003 on the authentication and registration of documents. The proclamation regulates the duties of the notary, lays down the procedures for authentication, enumerates notarial activities, and defines the powers and responsibilities of the authority it established. The essence of this law falls within administrative law. One may therefore argue that civil law was interpreted by the HoF to include areas not envisaged by the constitution.

7.4 Land Ownership and Administration

Land, both urban and rural, was nationalized in 1975 (Proclamation 31/75), long before the adoption of the FDRE constitution. Nonetheless, the ownership and administration of land was one of the contentious issues in the drafting process.

The FDRE constitution embraces the right to private ownership of private property, including the right to acquire, use, and transfer property as one deems fit (Article 40,

Constitution). The basic powers of the right to use *(usus)*, enjoy the fruits *(fructus)* and dispose the property *(abusus)* on private property are thus recognized under the constitution. However, it takes a different stand regarding ownership and administration of land. The constitution declares that:

> right to ownership of rural and urban land, as well as of all natural resources is exclusively vested in the state and the peoples of Ethiopia. Land is a common property of the Nations, Nationalities and Peoples of Ethiopia and shall not be subject to sale or to any other means of exchange. (Article 40(3), Constitution)

The legal regime regarding ownership and administration of land may be summarized according to the following features:

1. The right to ownership over land is attributed both to the state and the NN&P of Ethiopia. The legal framework recognizes NN&P as legal entities having their own rights including the right to own land and natural resources. The state being a legal entity of its own, the extent to which these two legal entities share the right to ownership over land may have far-reaching implications for economic activities. Consideration of the other parts of the constitution seems to indicate that ownership is vested in the NN&P. Article 89(5) of the constitution, for example, imposes on the government the duty to hold land and other natural resources on behalf of the people and to deploy them for their common benefit and development, hinting that the state acts as an agent of the NN&P who arguably are the real owners of land and natural resources.
2. Land is a *common property* of the NN&P of Ethiopia. A question that is likely to arise in this connection is which piece of land each NN&P owns. The answer to this question is significant for economic decision-making. It should be noted that states are 'delimited on the basis of the settlement patterns, language, identity and consent of the people concerned' ((2), Constitution) and NN&P have the right to establish institutions in the territory they inhabit (Article 39(3)). Given such an arrangement, some argue that each NN&P should be considered an owner of the land it inhabits, implying that self-administration would be meaningless without such right. The authors of the present chapter, however, contend that this argument is not consistent with the wording and spirit of the constitution. First, the constitution clearly states that land is a *common* property of the NN&P. It does not single out one NN&P as an exclusive owner of any piece of land. Second, although states are delimited based on settlement patterns, states are not the owners of land and the basis for their demarcation should not affect land ownership rights. Land should thus be considered a shared property of all the peoples in Ethiopia. This is consistent with the constitution's objective of building one economic and political community and the duty of the government to deploy land for the 'common benefit and development of the people' (Article 98, Constitution). It is also consistent with the government's duty to formulate policies which ensure that Ethiopians benefit from the country's material resources (Article 89, Constitution).

3. While land is owned by the peoples of Ethiopia, this needs to be distinguished from the tasks of administration. Land administration, for instance in the context of rural land holdings, is a process whereby rural land-holding security is provided, land-use planning is implemented, disputes between rural landholders are resolved, the rights and obligations of rural landholders are enforced, and information on farm plots and grazing landholders are gathered, analysed and made available to users (Proc. 456/2005 Article 2(2)). Similarly, urban land is managed through the lease-holding system for which detailed legislation has been issued by both the federal and regional governments (Proc. 272/2002, as amended by 721/2011).
4. The constitution has listed some core functions that the states shall assume, which Fiseha calls 'framework powers' (Fiseha 2006: 303). All these powers and functions operate within framework legislation to be issued by the federal parliament, which is 'subject to strict conditions because it has to leave substantial room for the states to issue their own legislation within the limits by the federation'. One of these functions specifically relates to land administration, stipulating that 'States shall have the power... to administer land and other natural resources in accordance with Federal laws' (Article 52(1), Constitution). The federal parliament is to 'enact laws for the utilization and conservation of land and other natural resources, historical sites and objects' (Article 51(5), Constitution), while states are empowered to administer land and natural resources. In other words, the federal parliament is to issue framework legislation based on which the states' councils shall come up with enabling legislation for direct implementation within their respective territories. The expectation is therefore that the federal law shall remain, as far as possible, general and lay down only the principles relevant for land administration. Recognizing that ownership is neither centralized nor peripheralized, the emphasis is on how its administration should be contextualized within the ambits of the framework legislation of the central government.
5. Although the federal government has the power to issue laws regarding the utilization of land, there are important limitations on this power. These limits relate to the rights of Ethiopian peasants and pastoralists on the one hand, and the right of private investors on the other. Peasants and pastoralists have the right to obtain land for free. They also have the right not be evicted from the land (in the case of peasants) and not to be displaced (in the case of pastoralists) (Article 40(4 and 5), Constitution). The legal regime for investors' use of land is slightly different. First, use of land by investors is not limited to Ethiopians. Second, the use of land by investors is subject to payment arrangements. Third, while peasants and pastoralists have the constitutional right to use land, an investor's use of land is contingent on the decision of government which, of course, has the duty to 'ensure the right of private investors to the use of land' (Article 40(6), Constitution).
6. The particulars regarding the utilization of land by Ethiopian peasants, pastoralists, and investors are determined by law. As stated earlier, law-making power concerning the utilization of land is vested in the federal government. The federal

government has issued proclamations to regulate the utilization of land, such as Proclamations 818/2014 on lease, 721/2011 and 574/2008 on urban planning, 455/2005 and 456/2003 on rural land, and 886/2015 on industrial parks. The regulatory environment needs to strike a balance between the federal government's power to regulate, the state's powers to administer, and the people's right to own land.

7. The Industrial Parks Proclamation, together with the regulation establishing the Industrial Parks Development Corporation, stipulates that land for industrial park development purposes shall be made available by the regional governments for which the Industrial Parks Development Corporation is mandated to serve as an administrator by holding it as a land bank (Regulation 326/2014). This is consistent with the constitutional provision whereby the regional government may legitimately delegate its power to administer the land that is commonly owned by the state and the people of Ethiopia through specific agreement for an efficient and effective utilization of the industrial park land.
8. Finally, land is not subject to sale or other means of exchange. This limits the power of individuals over land to *usus* and *fructus* as the power of *abusus* is not allowed. Thus although land has a market value, it is not a marketable commodity (Nahum 1997).

7.5 Legal Institutions

The task of harnessing economic development is undertaken within the context of a legal system that is an amalgam of state and no-state systems that compete for hegemony to govern legal relationships. Development of legal institutions in Ethiopia is characterized by an incremental shift from traditional and customary norms and institutions to transplanted ones (Beckstrom 1973; Brietzke 1974). The state law consists of layers of Western values at the bottom, socialist features in the middle, and developmental state-oriented laws at the top, in parallel with traditional systems for governing social and economic relations that remain vibrant in many parts of the country.

The government in power since 1991 is using law as an instrument to both establish judicial institutions and achieve economic development. In this process, the government uses laws following a Western paradigm that were enacted during previous regimes (David 1963; Vanderlinden 1966). At the same time it manipulates the legal system to inject new values to enhance its developmental orientation.

Within the Ethiopian legal system, competition may be observed between normative values that are embedded in laws adopted in different eras. The legal institutions of contract, property, company law, and trade are primarily influenced by liberal Western values such as freedom of contract, private ownership of property (including land), and such other rules as allow private companies to operate with maximum freedom (David 1963; Escarra 1972). It was believed that this path would help Ethiopia catch up with the others in terms of economic development (Seidman 1973). On the other hand, the behaviour of the government in power since 1991 provides sufficient evidence of its reluctance to fully adhere to this experience. This is particularly evident in areas the government considers crucial for economic empowerment and progress. As stated earlier, the prohibition of private ownership of land and recognition of multinational groups as an organizing principle for statehood are good examples of this phenomenon. The legal framework that limits some economic activities only to Ethiopians, such as banking, insurance, and power distribution (Regulation No. 270/2012) demonstrate how the government in power uses legal schemes to implement its developmental policies within the context of laws adopted in previous regimes.

7.6 Developments in Investment Laws

While Ethiopia has a long history of handicrafts and productive skills, modern Ethiopia, more specifically over the past decade, has focused on developing the structures and infrastructure conducive to attracting foreign direct investment (FDI), largely in the manufacturing sector, to drive its structural economic transformation agenda. Recent legal developments related to investment, and early positive achievements, demonstrate the importance attached to attracting FDI rather than creating an 'organic domestic base' (Chole 2004: 154). The Growth and Transformation Plan (GTP) II notes domestic investors' limited participation in the productive sectors and concentration instead on the service sector, primarily 'driven by short-term profit maximization through taking advantage of market failures and government incentive schemes rather than through enhancing their productivity, quality and competitiveness' (National Planning Commission 2016: 22). A strong FDI promotion institution that has managed to develop strong value propositions in favour of investing in Ethiopia has been in the making over the past few years. The restructure has placed the institution directly under the Prime Minister's Office, which has boosted investors' confidence. The creation of the Industrial Parks Development Corporation, the restructuring of the Ethiopian Investment Commission, and an overhaul of the incentive packages were instigated over the past few years to expand investment in the productive sectors which it is believed will drive the country's economic transformation.

Legal developments, therefore, have to constantly adjust to the demands of highly sophisticated, largely capital-intensive FDI that comes as a result of the comparative advantages that the country provides. The focus on FDI is not a recent phenomenon and even in 1940s Ethiopia, 'the industrial structure that evolved was characterized by substantial foreign ownership [and] technological dependence' (Chole 2004: 155).

With a proper regulatory framework, there is no doubt that FDI has positive technological spillover effects, and contributes to human capital formation, the integration of international trade, and the development of enterprise. Ethiopia's present legal structure has moved towards complete deregulation, apart from the setting of minimum capital requirements. There are no value-added requirements concerning the use of locally sourced inputs for manufactured goods for export or the number of expatriate staff. Foreign capital, like foreign law, lacks strong long-term impact and weakens the economy. This is largely due to the full repatriation of profits and dividends, the pure drive for profit, and the tendency to be highly sensitive to any form of insecurity. The absence of a clear national policy to enhance cross-fertilization between foreign and domestic capabilities leaves them passing by as 'perfect strangers'. The agency (Regulation 373/2016) established to serve as a catalyst for local capabilities development has two broad objectives but there is no reference to linking these with inward investment:

1. The acceleration and the expansion of small and medium manufacturing industry in order to lay a broad base for the development of large-scale industry, maintain equitable distribution of wealth and accelerate the transformation of agricultural-led economy to industrial-led economy; and
2. Strengthening, assisting, and coordinating institutions that provide support to small and medium manufacturing industry sector with a view to making the sector competitive and sustainable and thereby create a strong base for industrial development (Article 5 of the Ethiopian Constitution).

Even though these homegrown small and medium industries are to be responsible for accelerating the transition to industrialization and serve as a firm foundation for industrial development, investment-related laws encouraging the FDI-led growth of manufacturing for export as a key driver for industry development have been in place for a long time. A high standard of infrastructure to enable the growth of manufacturing is being developed in the form of industrial parks targeting largely FDI. It is the need to forge links between these homegrown small and medium industries that lies behind the recent creation of sectoral institutes—such as TIDI, LIDI, and MIDI—to facilitate the development and transfer of technologies specific to their sector and enhance the rapid development and competitiveness of their industries (Regulations 181 and 182, 2010).Local capacity to participate actively in the international market is stunted by the absence of a level playing field in terms of management skills, sector-specific technology and, above all, access to finance for local and foreign investments.

A stark parallel in terms of industrial development policy could be drawn, with only minor adjustments, between present-day Ethiopia and the pre-Derg period, as both periods saw an emphasis on private foreign investment, with the former focusing on manufacturing for import substitution and the other on manufacturing for export (Chole 2004: 61). The pre-revolution period also saw an extensive transplantation of laws in matters concerning civic life, business operations, and criminal law. Little literature exists on those early attempts to transact modern legal development together with industrial policymaking. However, a continuous adjustment of investment rules and regulations to suit the complex features of private foreign investment, rather than to support development of the organic industries and local capabilities ultimately needed to drive the industrialization agenda, can be clearly seen. Laws in the areas of contract administration and enforcement, together with the institutions and local expertise required, remain largely neglected.

7.7 Dispute Resolution

For an economy to thrive, the legal framework must provide institutions that ensure enforcement of contracts, adequate protection of property rights, including guarantees against arbitrary alienation, and a substantial freedom for the formation of companies and their orderly dissolution (Sherwood, Marcos, and Shepherd 1994). The extent to which the Ethiopian legal system provides such protection in its substantive and procedural laws, and the functioning of dispute resolution institutions, will be discussed in the following sections.

Ethiopia's ability to attract long-term and highly specialized investments partly depends on the ability of its legal and judicial system to protect the rights and enforce the contracts inherent in such economic activities. Specialized investments need assets that are specific to a particular production and cannot be salvaged for other purposes, narrowing the parties' options to exit from contracts linked to the investment. Besides, all the contingencies that may arise during the lifetime of such investments are difficult to fully foresee (Menkel-Meadow 1996: 6). As a result, a well-functioning judiciary is needed to reduce the contractual hazards and risks of long-term investments. Studies conducted in other countries show that a strong and independent judiciary is a necessary condition for sectors with specific investment (Levy and Spiller 1994). The proper functioning of the courts enlarges markets, brings technological spillovers and diffusion of knowledge through the transmission of sound marketing, financing, and managing practices, and creates an environment conducive to economic development (Levy and Spiller 1994; Pinheiro 1996).

In addition to the economic rationale, the need for an impartial body that umpires federal disputes and interprets the constitution is necessary in federal arrangements. There are, however, variations in the organization and function of the courts within the federal framework. While some consider the state courts sufficient to protect the interests of the federal government, subject to review by the federal courts, others contend that effective implementation of the powers of the federal government requires the establishment of federal courts at all levels. This view takes the federal principle of division of power seriously and insists that judicial authority be divided between the federal and the member states, just like legislative and executive powers (Fiseha 2006: 415).

The Ethiopian constitution divides judicial power between the federal and the state courts according to the subject matter. The federal judiciary has jurisdiction over federal matters, whereas the state courts have jurisdiction over state matters (Article 80, Constitution).

The federal judiciary, like its counterpart at state level, has a three-tier system, with the Supreme Court at the apex, the High Court in the middle, and the First Instance Court at the bottom (Article 78, Constitution). The Federal Supreme Court is a court of appeal with power to review errors of fact and law on matters decided by lower courts. The legal interpretation provided by the cassation division of the Federal Supreme Court sets a precedent for all other courts in the country, federal as well as regional (Proclamation No. 454/2005, Article 2(1)).

The Ethiopian constitution in principle accepts the existence of parallel federal and state courts. The full implementation of the principle is, however, postponed pending decision of the House of Peoples Representatives, which requires a two-thirds majority vote. As a result, federal jurisdiction has been delegated by the constitution to state courts, making them the main forum for dispute resolution on federal as well as state matters (Article 80, Constitution).

At present the federal courts operate only in limited parts of the country, namely Addis Ababa, Dire Dawa, SNNPR, Gambella, Benshangul Gumuz, and Afar. In the remaining states of Tigray, Amhara, Oromiya, and Harar, the state courts adjudicate federal as well as state matters. This judicial federalism design addresses a number of interests at the same time. In principle, it accepts the dual court system. But it has also considered the practical difficulties of immediately putting this into practice and has come up with the solution of delegating the federal powers to the state courts until the federal parliament decides otherwise.

7.8 Civil Litigation

Civil proceedings in federal and state courts in Ethiopia are governed by the Civil Procedure Code (CPC) enacted in 1965. Some states have made amendments, but these changes mainly concern the organizational and jurisdictional aspects of the process. Under Ethiopian law, civil litigation includes any proceeding in the ordinary courts other than criminal cases. Disputes concerning commercial matters, labour relations, contracts, property, and so on are treated as civil proceedings even in cases where state or other government institutions are party to the dispute, unless an administrative act excludes their jurisdiction (Article 4, CPC).

The design of the CPC was heavily influenced by the adversarial model of civil litigation transplanted from the common-law tradition. This system gives the parties to the dispute extensive powers in the preparation of their pleas, and the gathering and presentation of facts and evidence (Zuckerman 2006). The parties determine the nature of their claim or defence, the nature of the evidence they adduce, and the type of remedies they are seeking from the court. By using this power, they manipulate the pace of litigation, the framing of issues, and the outcomes of the whole process. Studies have shown that excesses of such adversarial combat increase complexity, duration, and cost to the litigants and to the system and compromise the accuracy of judicial outcomes (Woolf 1997).

The CPC limits such adversarial excesses by transplanting yet more mechanisms from the European continental tradition. The power of judges to control the unfolding of litigation, impose sanctions when parties fail to comply with procedural requirements, examine witnesses called by the parties, call additional evidence when the interests of justice require, and become actively involved in the process are some examples of the judges' role in ensuring fairness of process and accuracy of outcomes (Articles 264 and 266, CPC). In either case, the organizing principles of the CPC are not compatible with local perceptions and systems of justice in the traditional dispute resolution mechanisms that remain alive and well in many parts of the country. The differences between the imported and the local procedures can be seen in the way claims are initiated and processed, the roles of the parties, the community, the state and the fact finders, and the remedies they provide. Procedural justice is thus an amalgam of common- and civil-law traditions, leaving no room for local perceptions. Disputes that may arise during economic interactions, acts, and decisions are adjudicated within this hybrid system of civil litigation.

The complex, imported procedural system adopted in 1965 requires highly educated legal professionals to fully understand and enforce it. Ethiopia's first law school was established in 1963 and its first cohort had not even graduated when the CPC was enacted. This partly explains the poor performance in the civil administration of justice which is regarded as one of the drawbacks in attracting investment (Ministry of Capacity Building 2005).

The mismatch of expectations between civil justice and human capital is great indeed. Available data shows that of the total number of judges in 1990, 7.8 per cent had LLB degrees or above, 7.9 per cent had a diploma in law, and 5.7 per cent acquired their certificates through crash programmes. The remaining 78.6 per cent had no training in law at all, and 47 per cent of the judges were only church educated (Tadesse 2010).

After the adoption of the constitution in 1994, the civil justice system was trapped in a triple dilemma. First, it was expected to implement transplanted substantive and procedural concepts of justice. Second, it was expected to meet the emerging demands of the new federal arrangement and adjudicate disputes based on laws inspired by new concepts that negate the transplanted ones. Third, the system lacked the ability to discharge its basic responsibilities because of the weak institutional capacity and availability of trained manpower. For instance Ethiopia had only 2,649 judges in 2007, with a ratio of 3.6 judges per 100,000 people. The only law school, established in 1963, produces forty to fifty graduates a year and can hardly meet the growing demand for trained lawyers. As a result, an acute shortage of trained professionals, inaccessibility, delays, long backlogs, and repeated adjournments have become hallmarks of the judicial process, creating negative perceptions of the court's role in economic development endeavours (Belay 2002).

The government introduced a comprehensive programme of justice reforms aiming, among other things, to accelerate social and economic development (Belay 2002; Ministry of Capacity Building 2005). The available data indicate that since implementation of this programme, federal courts have begun to recover from some of the major challenges.

The demand for judicial services, measured in new claims brought before federal courts, has increased by 273 per cent in thirteen years (Table 7.1). One likely explanation

Table 7.1 Performance of federal courts

Year	2005	2006	2007	2008	2009	2010	2011	2012	2013	2014	2015	2016	2017
Beginning inventory									**27,459**	**27,651**	**33,366**	**45,851**	**77,737**
Filed	55,474	56,903	66,737	85,916	98,521	97,108	90,647	86,493	87,912	118,226	128,571	146,713	151,833
Disposed	71,161	67,834	74,383	99,957	121,852	114,328	100,094	97,043	105,760	104,633	138,011	163,631	179,743
Clearance rate %	128	119	111	116	124	117.6	112.22	104.73	99.62	94.33	91.7	94.6	100.5
Amount in a Statement of Claim, millions birr (for Federal High Court only)	756	101	1,386	950	909	810	1,163	3,282	209	118	5,215	4,667	3,889

Source: Federal High Court.

is economic growth. The value of claims filed in the Federal High Court increased from 756 million birr in 2005 to 38 billion birr in 2016–17. In the first six months of the fiscal year beginning June 2017, civil claims worth 75 billion birr were filed in the Federal High Court. In December 2017 alone, the total value in the 2,300 first-instance civil cases that were pending in the same court was 105.1 billion birr, one-third the annual budget of the federal government for 2017–18.

The nature of the parties involved in litigation also shows the link between economic performance and civil litigation. The data collected from the federal high courts shows that 54 per cent of the litigants appearing either as defendants or plaintiffs in civil suits are private and government-owned companies.

The rising demand in terms of number, value, and complexity of cases requires a proper response from the judiciary. Table 7.1 shows that the number of cases disposed by federal courts has been greater than the number of incoming cases, making the clearance rate higher than 100 per cent for many years and resulting in a proportionate reduction in backlog. Since 2013, however, the performance has been slowing down, resulting in a 283 per cent increase in the ending inventory in five years.

The processing time for cases has also gone down to some extent: 66.3 per cent of the cases pending on 30 December 2017 were less than twelve months old, 27.1 per cent between one and three years and 6.6 per cent were more than three years old. Likewise, in 2016–17, 53.1 per cent of the total cases were disposed within a year, 40.3 per cent in one to three years, and 6.6 per cent in more than three years (Federal Supreme Court 2017).

The optimum duration for cases depends on many factors and may vary from one case to another. Nor is it the only yardstick to measure court performance. However, the figures indicated above show that the performance of the courts seems to improve as the overall economic dynamics improve. The courts, however, face many more challenges that affect their independence, effective delivery of justice, and accessibility (Assessment Report of the Justice Sector, 2014).

7.8.1 Administrative Justice

Administrative law regulates the relationship between public authorities and individuals, and between authorities themselves. Administrative justice plays an important role in ensuring the government's accountability in its interaction with economic agents. Ethiopia does not have a comprehensive and codified system of administrative justice. It follows a piecemeal approach to the regulation of administrative justice, making dispute resolution between administrative bodies and economic agents a very uncertain process.

Unlike many civil-law systems, Ethiopia does not have a unified system of administrative courts. There is a significant number of tribunals administering justice within the ambit of the executive arm of government. Such agencies include the Tax Appeal Commission, the Labour Board, and the Investment Commission. Tribunals involved in administrative justice do not share any common features. These institutions adjudicate complaints by economic agents but there is no procedure to provide minimum guarantees during the process. The composition of the tribunals, the remedies they provide, and the routes for error correction by the ordinary courts vary from one tribunal to another. The relationship between administrative tribunals and the regular courts is not well defined. In some cases appeal to the ordinary courts is allowed and in other cases their decision is final. In still others, appeal may not even be available. Thus there is no uniform review system for administrative decisions.

A recent decision by the HoF has introduced a possible review by judicial organs. It decided that administrative decisions may be reviewed by the cassation division if there is a fundamental error of law (HoF decision, 2017).

7.9 Constitutional Interpretation

Adjudication of constitutional disputes is a crucial area for all federations. However, no uniform system across the federations has yet been developed. The main differences are between the centralized and decentralized models of constitutional interpretation. In both models, the power to adjudicate constitutional disputes and interpret the constitution is vested in the courts—the ordinary courts in decentralized systems and specially established courts in centralized systems. The system of constitutional adjudication in Ethiopia differs from these models. The Ethiopian model involves two constitutional organs outside the ordinary courts in constitutional adjudication and interpretation: the HoF and the Council of Constitutional Inquiry (CCI) (Articles 63 and 84, Constitution). While the ultimate power to adjudicate constitutional disputes and interpret the constitution is vested in the HoF, one chamber of the bicameral parliament, the CCI provides recommendations to the HoF. The CCI is chaired by the Chief Justice and is composed of eleven members, at least eight of whom are lawyers (Articles 63 and 84, Constitution).

Some authors have found two related reasons for such an arrangement. The first concerns how the framers of the constitution perceived its nature and the importance attached to the nations and nationalities. It is argued that the constitution is an outcome of the 'coming together' of the nations and nationalities, the constitution being an embodiment of their free will and consent. It is also argued that as a political contract, the constitution can only be interpreted by its authors—the nations, nationalities, and peoples. The second argument concerns the fear of judicial adventurism and activism. It is argued that this may prompt judges to put forward their own personal preferences and philosophies in the name of constitutional interpretation, hijacking the compact between the authors of the constitution (Fiseha 2001).

Others criticize this model, arguing that it denies the ordinary courts the power to adjudicate constitutional matters and enforce human rights, which adversely affects economic performance (Haile 1996).

It should be noted, however, that the courts have the power to adjudicate justiciable matters as well as a duty to implement the constitution (Articles 9 and 13, Constitution).

The ordinary courts cannot discharge these responsibilities without interpreting the constitution. The judicial experience also indicates that courts do indeed adjudicate matters of constitutional significance such as the right to bail, the right to appeal, the right to be represented by counsel, presumption of innocence, and the rights of arrested and detained persons. The authors argue that what the ordinary courts are not allowed to do is nullify acts of parliament on grounds of constitutionality.

Data collected from the CCI indicate that more than 2,800 complaints have been filed by citizens claiming that their constitutional rights have been violated, and that the number of complaints is increasing. While the number of complaints filed in 2008 was fifty-eight, it rose to 388 and 572 in 2016 and 2017 respectively. The workload is likely to rise following a recent decision of the HoF. In its decision the HoF held that complaints regarding violation of constitutional rights should not be subject to any period of limitation.

The economic significance of the HoF and CCI is apparent in the nature of the cases they have picked for constitutional interpretation. Out of the total number of complaints lodged, forty-five have been upheld by the HoF on grounds of violation of constitutional rights. Two patterns emerge from these decisions. The first relates to the subject matter of the complaints, while the second concerns the state organ against which complaints are lodged.

The sample decisions reviewed by the authors reveal that the CCI's recommendations and the HoF's decisions are mainly focused on constitutional provisions concerning ownership of private property and use rights over land (Article 40, Constitution). In 67 per cent of the cases reviewed by the authors, the HoF reversed decisions of state organs on the grounds that they were in violation of one or another part of the right to property articulated in the constitution. This can be considered an indication of the interest in guaranteeing the right to property and avoiding arbitrary deprivation of property which are crucial for economic development. It also indicates that land remains an important source of dispute and litigation despite the nature of ownership envisaged in the constitution. It is also important to note that almost all the cases reviewed by the authors involved disputes between individuals. Decisions challenging the constitutionality of laws and acts of the executive are rare. The HoF has, however, in one instance nullified law passed by the federal government, vesting first-instance jurisdiction to hear criminal charges against government officials in the Federal Supreme Court as unconstitutional.[1]

An additional pattern that clearly emerges from the HoF's decisions is its focus on judicial decisions rather than decisions by any other government organ. The authors found that 86 per cent of the HoF decisions reversed final judgements of the Federal Supreme Court or Supreme Courts of the member states. The HoF reversed the decisions or acts of other government organs in only 16 per cent of the sample cases reviewed. The authors were also informed by the head of the CCI secretariat that a majority of the pending complaints challenge the constitutionality of the final decisions of the ordinary courts.

[1] Melaku Fanta vs Anti-corruption Commission

The tendency of litigants to treat constitutional review as a continuation of the judicial process may potentially damage the integrity of the ordinary courts. This may require the demarcation between the jurisdiction of the ordinary courts on the one hand, and the CCI and HoF on the other, to be further refined.

The model for constitutional interpretation in Ethiopia is different from those practised elsewhere. Experience so far indicates that the decisions it provides focus on areas that have far-reaching implications for economic development.

7.10 Conclusions

Ethiopia has followed a different path in its efforts to achieve economic development since 1991. Instead of subscribing to the previous experiences of legal engineering which were animated by transplantation of the values, laws, and institutions of the West, it has relied on homegrown values to achieve economic progress by implementing its developmental orientation. Although the resolve to use law as an instrument to achieve economic development is a common feature, its departure from accepted Western legal concepts of legal relationships make the Ethiopian experience of legal engineering an area worth exploring. Some authors, for example, have argued that the legal regime on land ownership would have a negative impact on economic development. The economic progress Ethiopia has registered, on the other hand, shows that a country can catch up in spite of its rejection of such established wisdom. This, however, invites tension between the legal arrangements inspired by different ideological premises.

Ethiopia's economic performance has coincided by and large with its determination to regulate fundamental legal relationships based on homegrown values. Ethiopia's experience thus proves that catching up does not necessarily require verbatim copying of Western laws and legal institutions by developing countries.

References

Assessment Report of the Justice Sector (2014). Addis Ababa, Ethiopia (Unpublished, in Amharic).

Beckstrom, John H. (1973). 'Transplantation of Legal Systems: An Early Report on the Reception of Western Laws in Ethiopia', *American Journal of Comparative Law* 21 (3): 557–83.

Belay, Mandefrot (2002). 'Justice System Reform Program: Preliminary Reform Profile, Program and Objectives in *Justice System Reform in Ethiopia*', Ministry of Capacity Building, Addis Ababa: 35–45.

Brietzke, Paul H. (1974). 'Private Law in Ethiopia', *Journal of African Law* 18 (2): 149–67.

Chole, E. (2004). *Underdevelopment in Ethiopia*. Organisation for Social Science Research in Eastern and Southern Africa, Addis Ababa.

David, Rene (1963). 'Civil Code for Ethiopia: Considerations on the Codification of the Civil Law in African Countries', *Tulsa Law Review* 37 (187): 204.

Escarra, Jaques (1972). 'Expose des motifs' in *Background Documents of the Ethiopian Commercial Code of 1960*, (Addis Ababa: Faculty of Law, Haile Selassie University): 185–220.
FDRE (1995). 'The Constitution of the Federal Democratic Republic of Ethiopia', Addis Ababa.
Federal Supreme Court (2017). Annual Report (unpublished).
Fiseha, A. (2001). 'Constitutional Interpretation: The Respective Role of the Courts and the House of Federation', in *Proceedings of the Symposium on the Role of Courts in the Enforcement of the Constitution* (Addis Ababa: Birhanina Selam Press): 6–26.
Fiseha, Assefa (2006). 'Theory versus Practice in the Implementation of Ethiopia's Ethnic Federalism', in *Ethnic Federalism: The Ethiopian Experience in Comparative Perspective*, ed. David Turton (Addis Ababa: Addis Ababa University Press): 131–64.
Haile, M. (1996). 'The New Ethiopian Constitution: Its Impact upon Unity, Human Rights and Development', *Suffolk Transnational Law Review* 20: 1–84.
Levy, B. and P. T. Spiller (1994). 'Institutional Foundations of Regulatory Commitment: A Comparative Analysis of Telecommunications Regulation', *Journal of Law, Economics and Organization* 10 (2): 201–46.
Menkel-Meadow, C. (1996). 'The Trouble with the Adversary System in a Postmodern, Multicultural World', *William and Mary Law Review* 38: 5–45.
Ministry of Capacity Building (2005). 'Comprehensive Justice Reform Program'. Consultant's report, Center for International Legal Cooperation, Leiden, The Netherlands.
Nahum, Fasil (1997). *Constitution for a Nation of Nations: The Ethiopian Prospect* (Trenton, NJ: Red Sea Press).
National Planning Commission (2016). *Growth and Transformation Plan II (GTP II)—(2015/16–2019/20)* (Addis Ababa: Federal Republic of Ethiopia).
Pinheiro, A. C. (1996). 'Judicial System Performance and Economic Development'. Paper prepared for the seminar Economic Growth. Institutional Quality and The Role of Judicial Institutions, IRIS, University of Maryland. Washington, DC, December 5–6.
Seidman, R. B. (1973). 'Contract Law, the Free Market, and State Intervention: A Jurisprudential Perspective', *Journal of Economic Issues* 7 (4): 553–75.
Sherwood, Robert M., Celso Marcos, and Geoffrey Shepherd (1994). 'Judicial Systems and Economic Performance', *Quarterly Review of Economics and Finance* 34 (1): 101–16.
Tadesse, Menberetsehai (2010). '*Judicial Reform in Ethiopia*', PhD thesis, University of Birmingham.
Trubek, David and Alvaro Santos (2006). *The New Law and Economic Development: A Critical Appraisal* (Cambridge: Cambridge University Press).
Vanderlinden, Jacques (1966). 'An Introduction to the Sources of Ethiopian Law from the 13th to the 20th Century', *Journal of Ethiopian Law* 3 (1): 227–55.
Woolf, Lord Harry (1997). 'Civil Justice in the United Kingdom', *The American Journal of Comparative Law* 45 (4): 709–36.
Zewde, Bahru (2002). *The History of Modern Ethiopia: 1955–1991* (Athens, OH: Ohio University Press).
Zuckerman, Adrian A. S. (2006). *Civil Procedure: Principles and Practice*, 2nd edition (London: Sweet & Maxwell).

CHAPTER 8

ETHIOPIA'S 'ECONOMIC DIPLOMACY' AND REGIONAL INTEGRATION

FANTU CHERU
AND ZINABU SAMARO REKISO

8.1 Introduction

Until the early 1990s, weakened statehood, endemic poverty, and contested borders all negatively affected the capacity of successive Ethiopian regimes to engage the outside world strategically to advance Ethiopia's national interests. Specifically, the country's neighbours in the Horn of Africa were viewed with great suspicion and as a threat to Ethiopia's integrity. With the coming to power of the Ethiopian People's Revolutionary Democratic Front (EPRDF) in 1991, however, the determinants and decision-making processes behind Ethiopia's foreign and economic policy changed dramatically, largely due to the changing political economy context at both domestic and global levels.

While the foreign policies of previous Ethiopian regimes were based on a 'siege mentality' and were exclusively focused on external threats to the detriment of domestic ones, the EPRDF, by contrast, identified 'poverty and undemocratic rule' as the greatest threats to Ethiopia's national security (FDRE 2002). The EPRDF sought to address these twin threats by embarking on a highly political state-building project aimed at transforming the economy and democratizing Ethiopia's political order. It adopted a new constitution in 1995 that granted—at least on paper—the right to self-determination to Ethiopia's 90-plus nations and nationalities (MoFED 1993; Vaughan 2015; FDRE Constitution 1995).

In terms of its foreign policy, the EPRDF-led government gave primacy to 'economic diplomacy' aimed at attracting foreign direct investment and external aid inflows to realize its radical economic transformation agenda (FDRE 2002; Tewelde and Prasad 2015). Indeed, Ethiopia since 2001 has emerged as one of the 'super-powers' of Africa—playing an important role in global and regional affairs and positioning itself as the best investment destination in Africa (Verhoeven 2015). The EPRDF has presided over an economy that has displayed double-digit GDP growth rates for more than a decade. The economic growth has largely been pro-poor, lifting millions of people out of poverty. The number of households with improved living standards as measured by electricity, piped water, and infrastructure doubled from 2000 to 2011 (MoFED 2013).

The EPRDF has also succeeded in providing unprecedented security and administrative control of the state's population and territory while playing a critical role in regional peace and security in the Horn of Africa. Economic growth and political stability have in turn increased Ethiopia's appeal as a political ally and economic partner to both emerging partners, such as China, Turkey, and India, and traditional Western development partners (Cheru 2016). In 2015, for example, Ethiopia received US$3.2 billion in investment from the total US$7.8 billion received by East Africa (UNCTAD 2017: 35).

8.2 Ethiopian Foreign and Economic Policy Under the EPRDF: Context and Objectives

In the early 2000s, the Ethiopian government undertook a major review of the country's foreign and security policies and strategies against the background of dramatic changes that were taking place in the country, the region, and the world at large. This major internal rethinking resulted in the publication of a comprehensive document, 'Foreign Affairs and National Security Policy and Strategy of Ethiopia' in 2002 (FDRE 2002).

The shift in foreign and development policy was an outcome of a confluence of internal and external factors. The first factor had to do with the regime's dissatisfaction with the poor track record of the neoliberal policies that it reluctantly followed between 1991 and 2005 due to pressures from key development partners. The second factor involved deep disagreement within the EPRDF over the conduct of the 1998 war with Eritrea and the political crisis this generated within the Tigray People's Liberation Front (TPLF)—the influential component of the EPRDF coalition—when the leadership of Prime Minister Meles was challenged (Clapham 2017).Once he and his allies had survived the leadership challenge and consolidated their power base, Meles was able to push through radical economic and foreign policy reforms unopposed.

The political crisis following the 2005 disputed national elections, when the opposition gained a significant number of parliamentary seats, provided the EPRDF with a third impetus for introducing far-reaching economic reforms to appease a population opposed to its rule. The EPRDF was forced to acknowledge that its socialist-oriented economic policy was not working and that a new course of action was needed to reorient the Ethiopian economy away from agriculture and towards industrialization and value addition in agriculture. Subsequently, the first Growth and Transformation Plan (GTP1) put heavy emphasis on large-scale infrastructure investments (from roads, rail, and power generation) and investment in education, health, and other services to raise the productivity of the economy and in the process, improve the quality of life of citizens (MoFED 2010).

At the same time, the government reoriented Ethiopian foreign and security policy and aligned them to the overall development strategy of the country. The EPRDF redefined the concept of 'security threat' as 'poverty and undemocratic trends'. To address these twin threats, the 2002 Foreign Affairs and National Security Strategy emphasized 'economic diplomacy' to attract badly needed foreign investment and loans to transform the economy and to create jobs (FDRE 2002). The government particularly focused its economic diplomacy towards emerging countries, such as China, India, and Turkey. The strategy has paid off, as the government has been able to mobilize huge amounts of infrastructure finance and to attract a sizeable number of manufacturing firms to locate in Ethiopia (Cheru 2016; MoFEC 2017).

8.3 Ethiopia and the Horn of Africa

Ethiopia's relations with its neighbours have been shaped not only by its internal social, economic, and political dynamics but also by the dynamics of the region which is fraught with conflicts and political instability (Clapham 2017; Keller 1987). This vast area—comprising Sudan, South Sudan, Ethiopia, Eritrea, Djibouti, Somalia, Kenya, and Uganda, home to about 240 million people—is linked not only by a shared history of conflict but also by a complex web of economic, social, and cultural ties. The incongruence between the legacy of colonial boundaries, ecological zones, ethnic overlap across borders, and cultural affinities peculiar to the region often means that disputes in any one country can have political and economic significance beyond their own local sphere (Cliff 1999; Healy 2007; Bereketeab 2013).

Moreover, the security challenges of terrorism and armed militias are intertwined in a web of various actors that have both regional and global dimensions (IGAD 2016: 14; Healy 2007). China is the latest country to open a naval base in Djibouti. Turkey and the United Arab Emirates are also vying to have a foothold on the Red Sea Coast, highlighting the strategic importance of the Horn of Africa to competing global and regional powers (Hussein 2018). Cognizant of these complex geopolitical dynamics and domestic political instability, the Ethiopian government has been working tirelessly to strengthen regional integration and ensure peace and stability in the Horn of Africa. Towards this end, the country has deployed thousands of Ethiopian UN peacekeepers to the Abyi border region between Sudan and South Sudan, the African Union-led peacekeeping mission in Somalia (AMISOM), and the UN peacekeeping mission in South Sudan. The Ethiopian government believes that the task of tackling poverty and underdevelopment at home is intricately linked to the maintenance of peace and stability in the Horn of Africa region (Mehari 2017; IGAD 2016: 46).

In the long-term, however, Ethiopia's strategy for the Horn of Africa revolves around regional integration through energy, road, rail, and water infrastructure, connectivity, and trade, but very much on Ethiopian terms. The plan is to tie the region to Ethiopia by exporting electricity generated by dams on Ethiopian rivers and to facilitate cross-border trade by improving logistics, rail, and road transport connectivity. Besides mutual economic benefits, regional economic integration is expected to provide a climate conducive to the maintenance of peace and stability in the region (Mulugeta 2016: 63–87; Mehari 2017; Verhoeven 2015). Despite these ambitious goals by the Ethiopian government, neighbouring countries do not see Ethiopia in a positive light, and lingering historical animosities cannot be overcome overnight.

8.4 Regional Economic Integration as an Economic and Political Imperative

Ethiopia is one of the few African countries that has taken a radical approach to strengthening economic integration with its neighbours by investing heavily in transport infrastructure, energy connectivity, and improved logistics to help unleash productive potential at the national and regional levels and create a larger regional market and trade interactions (MoFED 2010). Several studies have shown that high logistic and infrastructure costs are the key impediments to productive integration on the continent, disrupting supply- and value-chain linkages at the national, regional, and global levels (Foster and Briceno-Garmendia 2010; Ndulu 2006).

Infrastructure affects growth through two channels: directly through physical capital accumulation and indirectly through improvement in productivity. At a micro-level, investment in infrastructure enhances private-sector activities by lowering the cost of production and opening new markets, presenting new production opportunities and trade. At the same time, infrastructure investment in power generation, water, sanitation, and housing improves the social well-being of citizens (Foster and Briceno-Garmendia 2010).

The first Growth and Transformation Plan (GTP1) accorded top priority to massive investment in critical infrastructure, such as roads, rail networks, telecommunications, hydroelectric power, wind and thermal energy, and irrigation projects (Figure 8.1). The key targets included the building of 10,000 miles of roads and a 1,500-mile rail network; the quadrupling of power generation coupled with 82,000 miles of power lines; increasing the number of mobile telephone users from 7 million to 40 million and internet service subscribers from 200,000 to 3.7 million; and the establishment of four industrial cluster zones. The cost of these investments was estimated at US$57 billion over the planned period (MoFED 2010: 33–46). In 2013 budget year alone, the government planned to spend US$7.8 billion dollars on mega projects such as electric power, roads, rail, and public housing.

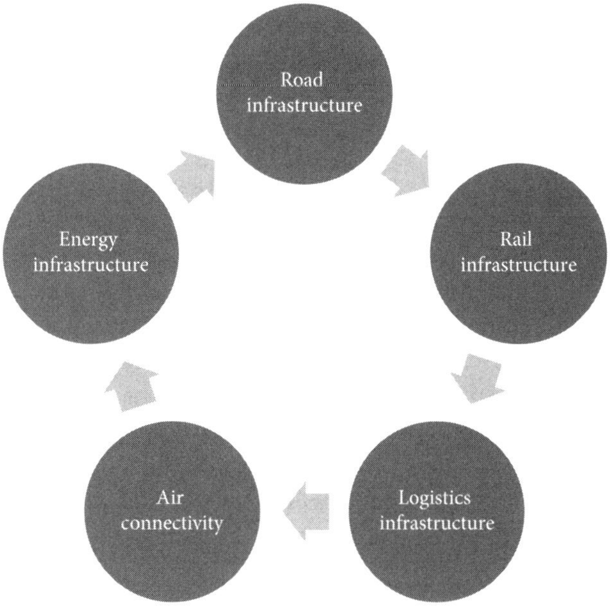

FIGURE 8.1 Transformation enablers in the GTP
Source: Author's own diagram.

Moreover, the government has made great efforts to build an efficient logistic service sector for the country's importers, exporters, and investors by reducing bottlenecks in the shipment of goods and cutting transit time and costs. It has invested heavily to enhance the capacity of the Ethiopian Shipping and Logistics Service Enterprise (ESLSE) through the purchase of additional ships and heavy trucks, and by improving sea and dry dock facilities to reduce transit time and costs to private investors (MoFEC 2017: 8).

The massive investments in critical infrastructure are expected to facilitate intra-African trade and regional value chains, leading to Africa's eventual entry into global value chains. The value-chain linkage would then facilitate accelerated industrial development among the IGAD member countries, namely Djibouti, Sudan, South Sudan, Somalia, and Kenya.

For a landlocked country such as Ethiopia, the issue of infrastructure connectivity involves a different dimension above and beyond the concern for economic growth. Ensuring Ethiopia's access to the sea is a matter of national security. With the independence of Eritrea in 1993, Ethiopia lost the use of the ports of Assab and Massawa and effectively became the largest and most populous landlocked country in the world. Currently, almost 95 per cent of Ethiopia's export–import trade is handled through the ports of Djibouti, a situation that Ethiopia hopes to change by seeking additional alternative access routes in the neighbouring countries. The need to diversify its access to the sea is one of the major motivating factors for the Ethiopian government to invest heavily in infrastructure and energy connectivity and to develop friendly relations with Sudan, Somalia, and Kenya.

8.5 Ethiopia's Proactive 'Economic Diplomacy': Results and Performance

Economic diplomacy is the process by which countries engage with the outside world, to maximize their national gain in all fields of activity, including trade, investment, and other forms of economically beneficial exchanges (Rose 2007: 22–38; Rana, 2004). With the adoption of the Foreign Affairs and National Security Policy in 2002, the Ministry of Foreign Affairs (MoFA) prepared a five-year strategic plan and conducted an extensive business process re-engineering (BPR) study of most of the ministry's core functions. Among the core functions of the MoFA that have undergone re-engineering are investment, trade, and tourism promotion services (FDRE 2012). The exercise resulted in the publication of the 'Foreign Trade Promotion Manual for Ethiopian Diplomatic Missions', with the aim of providing practical guidelines to embassy staff on how to carry out trade promotion activities (MoFA 2007). Accordingly, the focus of Ethiopia's economic diplomacy is on the following:

- attracting direct foreign investment to the country using different communication methods;
- lobbying for facilitating the expansion of the market horizons of the nation's export products globally;
- luring as many foreign tourists as possible to visit the country;
- soliciting development assistance consisting of financial and technical support through bilateral and multilateral cooperation.

The economic diplomacy and strategy focuses on attracting labour-intensive rather than capital-intensive investments capable of generating as many jobs as possible, particularly given the high level of youth unemployment. In addition, foreign investments which use agricultural resources as raw materials, and process and produce industrial products by adding value are given prime attention (FDRE 2012: 25).

As shown in Table 8.1, Ethiopian missions abroad, in collaboration with the Ethiopian Investment Commission (EIC), have been very active since 2007 in promoting Ethiopia as the best investment destination in Africa (MoFA 2015: 11). These intense economic diplomatic activities have enhanced the country's role in regional and international fora. Moreover, Ethiopia's efforts to attract FDI have been strengthened by a favourable external environment for FDI, the availability of cheap labour in the country, Ethiopia's improved access to US and EU markets, growing domestic demand, and improved economic infrastructure.

In terms of the regional distribution of investment flow to Ethiopia (Table 8.2), Europe and Asia remain the most important source of FDI, followed by the Middle East and North America. Africa plays a marginal role although the number of investors that have made pre-investment visits to Ethiopia is increasing.

Table 8.1 Performance overview of MoFA and Ethiopian diplomatic missions in attracting FDI, 2010/11–14/15

Budget year	FDI recruitment plan	Actual number of investors recruited	Performance (%)
2010/11	250	324	129.60
2011/12	326	360	110.43
2012/13	355	368	103.66
2013/14	1005	1001	99.60
2014/15	1227	1347	109.78
Total	3163	3400	107.49

Source: Ministry of Foreign Affairs (2015: 11).

Table 8.2 Performance of pre-investment facilitation by MoFA and Ethiopian diplomatic missions, 2014/15

Region	Investment recruitment plan	Investors conducting pre-investment visits	Performance (%)
Europe	470	470	100
North & South America	102	82	80.39
Africa	156	197	126.28
Asia & Oceania	349	436	124.93
Middle East	150	162	108
Total	1227	1347	

Source: Ministry of Foreign Affairs (2015: 9).

Table 8.3 shows that the foreign companies recruited by Ethiopian diplomatic missions represent almost all sectors. Manufacturing, agriculture, energy and power, and construction have attracted the most investors.

Figure 8.2 shows that most of the companies recruited by Ethiopian diplomatic missions are from East Asia, Europe, and the Middle East. China, Turkey, and India are the three most important investors in Ethiopia. This not only reflects the focus of Ethiopia's economic diplomacy efforts but also how these economies have globally become important sources of cheap labour-seeking FDI. There is a clear recognition within the government of the increasing trend for labour-intensive manufacturing to try to move to countries with abundant supply of cheap labour and a conducive business environment. It is not, therefore, surprising that the Ethiopian government has focused its strategy on attracting FDI from China, India, and Turkey where labour costs are rising. This is a positive trend but its effect on regional integration is mixed (MoFA 2015: 9).

In addition to the efforts of the Ministry of Foreign Affairs, the Ethiopian Chamber of Commerce and Sectoral Association have been active in organizing business-to-business meetings with their foreign counterparts and providing information about the

Table 8.3 Sectoral composition of companies recruited and conducted pre-investment visits, 2014–15

Sectors	Number of companies recruited
Manufacturing industry	477
Agriculture	135
Agro-processing	74
Construction	130
Infrastructure and logistics	25
Mining	50
Energy and power	114
Hotels and tourism	25
Education	8
Investment project financing	5
Consultancy and engineering	19
Health	14
Information and communications technology (ICT)	45
Multi-sectors investors	226
Total	1347

Source: Ministry of Foreign Affairs (2015: 7).

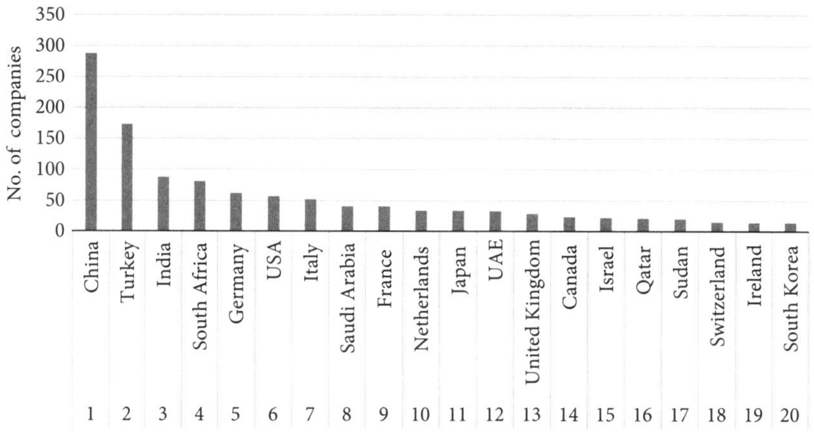

FIGURE 8.2 Number of companies recruited by Ethiopian diplomatic missions conducted pre-investment visit to Ethiopia, 2014/15

Source: MoFA (Ministry of Foreign Affairs) (2015).

considerable business opportunities that Ethiopia offers. In the fiscal year 2016–17, seven business fora took place with investors from Spain, Saudi Arabia, China, Poland, Morocco, the United States, and Germany (MoFEC 2017: 11–12). It is thought that business fora like these arranged by the private-sector associations reinforce government efforts to build confidence and change the negative perceptions created following the recent unrest in some parts of the country.

In sum, the efforts of the government of Ethiopia to promote economic diplomacy and business-to-business conclaves have been shown to produce tangible results. Renowned textile and garment companies from the United States, Hong Kong, India, China, and Sri Lanka have already launched operations in the Hawassa Industrial Park. Ethiopia's proximity to the Middle East, European, and Asian markets, its large population, and its preferential trade access to the United States under AGOA and to Europe under the EU's 'Everything but Arms' arrangements, are important reasons why foreign investors are flocking to the country (MoFEC 2017). To remain ahead of the game, however, the government must continue to improve the business environment by reducing bureaucracy and red tape, ensuring policy stability and predictability, and developing upstream supply chains, such as cotton for textiles.

8.6 Economic Integration with IGAD Countries

This section analyses the trends, performance, and current state of Ethiopia's economic integration with the countries of the IGAD sub-region and evaluates the overall effectiveness of the economic diplomacy strategy vis-à-vis Ethiopia's neighbours. This is done using trade, investment, transport infrastructure, and energy as vectors of integration.

8.6.1 Trade Relations

Ethiopia's external trade is very much dominated by unprocessed primary commodities, while its imports are predominantly manufactured products. Until recent years, a policy of export-led agriculture was encouraged to generate the foreign exchange that the country needs to cover the cost of its essential imports (MoFA 2007: 12). For example, during the period 2009/10–2015/16, the country obtained on average 89 per cent of its export earnings from unprocessed primary products.[1]

Table 8.4 shows that almost 83 per cent of Ethiopia's exports are to Europe, North America, the Middle East, and Asia. About 20.8 per cent of Ethiopia's export went to Africa, mainly Somalia (55.8 per cent), Djibouti (21.5 per cent), Sudan (12 per cent), Kenya (4.9 per cent) and Egypt (3.6 per cent), which altogether accounted for 97.8 per cent of the total exports to Africa during 2015–16. By 2016, the value of Ethiopian exports to these countries had increased substantially in comparison to the early 2000s: in current US$ Kenya (30.8 million), Djibouti (109.2 million), Uganda (290,000), Somalia (271.2 million), Sudan (44.5 million) (National Bank of Ethiopia 2017: 63). Given the similarities in the structure of African economies, with heavy dependence on unprocessed primary

[1] Computed based on *Annual Report of National Bank of Ethiopia*, various years.

Table 8.4 Ethiopia's top ten export and import destinations, 2016

Country	Exports (US$)	Export (%)	Country	Imports (US$)	Import (%)
United States	169,446,868	9.83	China	609,598,745	31.6
Saudi Arabia	167,111,227	9.69	United States		8.8
		8.6	India	1,681,886,324	7.45
Germany		7.5	Kuwait		5.56
Switzerland	148,318,495	5.14	Japan	1,425,330,717	4.17
China		4.99	Italy		4.0
UAE	130,810,096	4.41	Turkey	1,062,332,437	3.58
Pakistan		3.47	Sweden		2.66
Japan	88,693,600	3.41	UAE	797,179,318	2.47
Italy	86,025,777	3.1	Bahrain	764,671,935	2.25
Belgium	75,996,657			684,801,787	
	59,842,063			508,846,480	
	58,828,850			473,132,883	
	53,425,172			430,231,011	

Source: UN COMTRADE data (2016).

Table 8.5 Import/export trade with the IGAD, 2016

Partner	Exports(US$)	Imports (US$)	Balance
Sudan	48,835,378	94,069,143	-45,230
Djibouti	44,123,031	707	44,120
Kenya	32,464,539	37,715,211	-5,250,672
Uganda	865,209	371,492	493,267
Somalia	7,678,024	2,416,341	5,261,683

Source: UN COMTRADE data (2016).

products and a low level of industrialization, it is not surprising that Ethiopia's trade with Africa remains low.

Table 8.5 shows Ethiopia's import and export trade with the IGAD. While Ethiopia's exports to Djibouti, Sudan, and Somalia have shown very dramatic increases in recent years, they consist predominantly of a single commodity, *chat*, which is widely consumed as part of cultural practices in the region. Meanwhile, Kenya and Uganda have not been prominent destinations for Ethiopia's exports since the two countries are also primary commodity exporters, and their external trade is more oriented towards the developed economies and the East African Community.

On the import side, the most important source of Ethiopian imports is the Middle East and Asia. During the budget year 2015–16, for example, about 62.7 per cent of Ethiopian merchandise imports originated from Asia, 25.1 per cent from Europe, 8.3 per cent America (National Bank of Ethiopia 2017: 64). The major import origins in Asia were China (53.0 per cent), India (12.0 per cent), Japan (6.7 per cent), Kuwait (5.3 per cent),

United Arab Emirates (4.4 per cent), Saudi Arabia (3.6 per cent), Indonesia (3.4 per cent), Malaysia (2.4 per cent), and South Korea (2.1 per cent) (National Bank of Ethiopia 2017: 64). Africa accounted for a mere 3.9 per cent of Ethiopia's total imports during the same period and the major countries of origin were Egypt (28.5 per cent), South Africa (27.6 per cent), Morocco (26.7 per cent), Sudan (6.5 per cent), and Kenya (5.2 per cent) (National Bank of Ethiopia 2017: 65). These five African countries have relatively better manufacturing bases from which Ethiopia can source its imports. On the other hand, countries such as Djibouti, Somalia, and Uganda have been insignificant suppliers of Ethiopia's import needs.[2]

8.6.2 Investment Relations

The EPRDF-led government of Ethiopia has been following a mixed approach to foreign direct investment (FDI) in general. On the one hand it has been relentlessly pursuing policies, strategies, and incentive schemes that are aimed at attracting foreign investment with a view to complementing the domestic private sector and state-owned enterprises, and to securing technology, know-how, capital, and access to markets of advanced economies which it believes can help to achieve its export-driven foreign trade objectives. In this sense, it can be said the government has been one of the most liberal to FDI inflows into the country. However, on the other hand, it has been pursuing one of the most illiberal investment policies in Africa; most of the service sector in Ethiopia (such as retail and merchandise trade, telecoms, banking, and finance) is off limits to foreign investors despite intense pressure from the Bretton Woods institutions and bilateral donors.

Despite the government's mixed policy on FDI, Ethiopia has become increasingly attractive for market- and resource-seeking FDI from advanced and emerging economies. For instance, FDI stock, which amounted to US$941 million in 2000, increased to US$4.206 billion in 2010 and to US$13.7 billion in 2016 (UNCTAD 2017: 227). According to Figure 8.3, FDI inflows have been rising constantly since 2012, even when FDI was declining in many other least developed countries (LDCs). To put this in perspective, East Africa received US$7.1 billion in FDI in 2016, of which Ethiopia alone received US$3.2 billion (45 per cent), propelled by investments in infrastructure and manufacturing which helped it become the second-largest LDC host economy, up from the fifth position in 2015 (UNCTAD 2017: 46, 81). According to data from the Ethiopian Investment Commission, Ethiopia attracted FDI worth $4.17 billion in the 2016–17 fiscal year despite heightened political tensions in the country since August 2015 (MoFEC 2017: 13).

On the other hand, FDI inflows into Ethiopia from the IGAD member countries have been minuscule both in terms of the total capital invested and the number of licensed projects. For instance, data from the Ethiopian Investment Commission show a total of 564 licensed projects in 2017: Kenya (114), Sudan (423), Djibouti (18), and Somalia (9).

[2] Average value of imports between 2002 and 2016 (thousands of US$): Djibouti 430, Uganda 570, and Somalia 212.

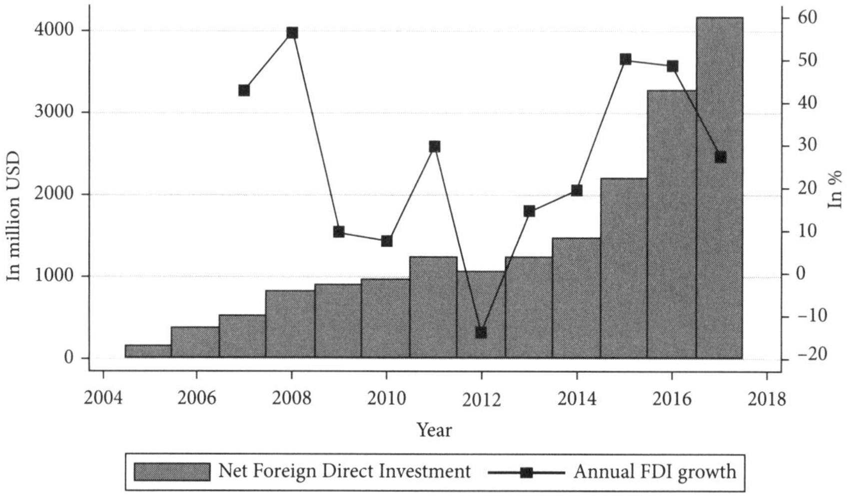

FIGURE 8.3 Net FDI, US$ millions, and annual FDI growth rate (per cent)

Source: National Bank of Ethiopia (2018) (unpublished).

Table 8.6 Investment in Ethiopia from selected IGAD countries

	Kenya	Sudan	Djibouti	Somalia
Total projects	114	423	18	9
Manufacturing	68	150	8	2
Real estate	22	91	1	2
Pre-implementation	17	160	9	1
Under implementation	28	104	5	1
Operating	69	159	4	7
Capital in birr, thousands	2,719,886	1,281,213	154,400	324,250

Source: Ethiopian Investment Commission.

Table 8.6 shows that, while 187 projects are in pre-implementation stage, another 138 projects are under implementation. Of the four countries studied, Djibouti and Somalia have the lowest level of investment in Ethiopia. The database contains no FDI projects from Uganda at all.[3]

Of the four IGAD countries, Sudan is emerging as an important investor in the Ethiopian economy. Out of a total of 423 licensed projects in 2017 from Sudan, 150 are in the manufacturing sector while another 91 are in real estate. Moreover, 159 projects are in operation, 104 under implementation, and 160 projects in pre-implementation

[3] Ethiopian Investment Commission (2017); investment data on Somalia, Sudan, Kenya, Uganda, and Djibouti provided by the commission in November 2017.

stage. In fact, based on information from the Sudanese Investors Society in Addis Ababa, the Economist Intelligence Unit reported in 2014 that Sudanese capital investment in Ethiopia totalled US$2.4bn, making Sudan the second-largest investor in Ethiopia after China.

The large influx of Sudanese investment in Ethiopia had to do with the loss of Sudan's traditional source of income from oil which ended with the independence of South Sudan in 2011. To offset this loss, the government of Sudan began to cultivate closer relations with Ethiopia, which has embarked on huge hydropower and infrastructure projects to expand its own economic relations with the neighbouring countries in line with the tenets and objectives of the Foreign Affairs and Security Policy. This commitment has been further strengthened by the long-standing no-war, no-peace situation with Eritrea which has severely restricted Ethiopia's accesses to sea ports, and by the increasingly visible tendency of Sudan to distance itself from its 'big brother' in the north (Egypt) and incline towards the main source of the Nile waters (Ethiopia) over the hydro-politics of the Nile.

In the case of investment flow from Kenya to Ethiopia, there exists complementarity between the two economies given the relative advancement and size of the Kenyan economy and its well-developed manufacturing sector. Data from Ethiopian Investment Agency indicate that a total of 114 Kenyan investment projects were registered between 1994 and 2017, with a registered capital of around 2.719 billion birr (~US$100.332 million at exchange rate of November 2017). Of these, only twenty-eight had become operational by September 2017. An interesting feature of Ethiopia's investment relations with Kenya is that, due to the comparative advantage Kenya has developed in service sectors such as banking, finance, telecoms, and wholesale and retail trade, there has been sustained interest from the Kenyan side in entering these sectors in Ethiopia.[4] However, the Ethiopian government has had justifiable reasons for its reluctance to allow Kenyan investment in these sectors to date.

It is safe to conclude that economic exchanges between Ethiopia and its neighbours are growing, albeit slowly. This is bound to change with increased road and electricity connectivity. While Ethiopia's efforts to promote economic integration in the Horn of Africa are commendable, a similar level of commitment is required from the other members of IGAD if regional economic integration is to materialize in the long term.

8.6.3 Transport Infrastructure and Services

Given colonial and post-colonial legacies, transport infrastructure in Africa has not only been underdeveloped but also has not been geared towards linking African economies with each other; rather, it is oriented towards export of primary commodities to and import of manufactured products from developed countries (Zinabu 2017: 96–7).

[4] See for instance 'Ethiopia, Kenya Integration: Together, But with Misaligned Priorities', in *Addis Fortune* 14(724), 16 March 2014.

Therefore, any efforts to genuinely integrate African economies requires this outward orientation to be reversed through development of good-quality, efficient transport infrastructure networks and services in such a way as to link production centres and distribution hubs across the continent.

As a landlocked country, Ethiopia has invested heavily over the past decade in transport infrastructure connectivity across the country and with its immediate neighbours to improve economic productivity and raise living standards. Since the launch of the Road Sector Development Programme I in 1997, the Ethiopian Roads Authority has consistently enjoyed the largest allocation of the national budget (Ethiopian Roads Authority 2014: 9). Between 2010 and 2015, for example, total road network increased from 50,000km to more than 110,000km and is planned to double to 220,000km by 2019–20 during the Growth and Transformation Plan II implementation period (MoFEC 2017: 5). As of now, the country has good road linkages with Sudan, Kenya, and Somaliland, whereas the road linking it with South Sudan is complete on the Ethiopian side but not developed on the South Sudanese side of the border (Mehari 2017: 28).

In addition to road linkages, the government has been investing heavily in the development of railways aimed at linking the country to the world market by ensuring seamless access to one or several sea ports in the Horn and East Africa. The primary port for Ethiopia is Djibouti although there are plans to connect to the port of Berbera (Somalia), Port Sudan to the north, and with the ports of Lamu and Mombasa in Kenya. For instance, the Growth and Transformation Plan II (2015/16–2019/20) includes railway infrastructure development as one of its top priorities with a plan to complete development of 2,782km of rail network which would reach the borders with Djibouti, Kenya (Moyale), and South Sudan (Dima). It also includes preliminary plans that would extend the rail links with Sudan (Metema) and Somalia (MoFEC 2015: 136). So far, only the Ethio-Djibouti railway project, extending for 758km at a cost of around US$4.5 billion (70 per cent over the original estimated cost), has been completed.

The success of regional integration efforts through rail linkages largely depends on Ethiopia's ability to secure the necessary project financing. Several auxiliary railway extensions into neighbouring countries, namely Kenya, South Sudan, and Sudan, have been planned, but securing the necessary financing has been difficult. With the mounting debt of the Ethiopian Railways Corporation (ERC), which in 2016 stood at US$4.7 billion (or 6 per cent of Ethiopia's GDP), creditors are unwilling to enter project financing, particularly in the face of declining export earnings. Consequently, the government announced in July 2017 the cancellation of any new railway project until new ways of financing, such as public–private partnerships, are found. The effectiveness of this strategy also depends on the willingness and ability of the neighbouring countries to extend, maintain, and efficiently run the rail and road networks within their borders.

Air transport is one of the areas where Ethiopia has recorded outstanding success, particularly in recent years. For consecutive years since 2001, Ethiopian Airlines, which was founded in 1945 and is a state-owned enterprise, has been registering rapid growth averaging 25 per cent annually. The airline has distinguished itself as the largest and most profitable airline group in Africa, commanding the lion's share of pan-African passenger and cargo network and now serving more than ninety international destinations. As part of its 2025 vision, the airline intends to provide extensive intra-Africa networks, and extensive and reliable air linkages for African economies with the rest of the world (Ethiopian Airlines 2016).

Two points are worth raising with respect to Ethiopia's relentless efforts to achieve economic integration with neighbouring countries through transport networks and services. First, the effectiveness of these investments largely depends on the political, economic, and security situation in those countries. For instance, the continued political instability in South Sudan and Somalia significantly reduces the economic usefulness and effectiveness of any road and rail linkages with these countries. Second, Ethiopia's efforts to build economic infrastructure linking it with neighbouring countries have a lot to do with attempts to find alternative access to seaports. Ethiopia's over-reliance on Djibouti is costly. Ethiopia reportedly spends as much as US$1.2 billion a year for the use of the ports of Djibouti (Mehari 2017: 28). Besides the high cost, the country faces frequent and serious uncertainties, administrative tussles, and disagreements over costs, fees, and taxation from the Djiboutian side (Styan 2013: 3,7).In the long run, however, finding amicable solutions to the Ethio-Eritrean conflict could pave the way for Ethiopia to have access to the Eritrean ports of Massawa and Assab that are natural and convenient alternative outlets to the sea.

8.6.4 Energy and Trans-Boundary Water Resources

Ethiopia has substantial potential for generation of renewable energy, with its hydroelectric potential of 45,000MW sufficient to meet most of sub-Saharan Africa's current demand. Within Africa, Ethiopia's green energy potential is surpassed only by that of Democratic Republic of Congo (Verhoeven 2015: 5). However, this potential remained untapped until recently: power generation capacity in the national grid stood at 4,254MW in 2017.

In recent years, however, the government has been heavily investing in energy projects including in three hydro-dam projects on the Gilgel Gibe (fourth and fifth dams are in the works) and the Grand Ethiopian Renaissance Dam (with the capacity to generate more than 6,000MW) on the main tributary of the Nile planned to begin power generation in 2018. While the primary focus of these investments has been on meeting domestic demand, since 2014, however, the government has turned its focus towards the sale of excess electricity to neighbouring countries to generate badly needed foreign exchange (Table 8.7). Projections show that Ethiopia's electricity generation potential is such that even if current consumption levels were to triple or quadruple, there would still be ample scope to export power (Verhoeven 2011: 6).

Table 8.7 Export of energy to neighbouring countries (in GWh)

Country	2012–13	2013–14	2014–15	2015–16	2016–17
Djibouti	386.14	267.39	379.15	271.53	492.05
Sudan	175.31	340.41	381.27	427.02	–

Source: Ethiopian Electric Power.

The demand for Ethiopia's electricity is very high and growing fast, both domestically and among neighbouring countries. If we consider domestic demand, between 2002 and 2008 demand for electricity grew on average by 17 per cent annually and this growth is projected to rise to almost 25 per cent annually (Verhoeven 2011: 5). With respect to international demand, Ethiopia has cross-border electricity connection with Sudan and Djibouti at 230kV level, and there is power flow of up to 250MW to Sudan and up to 90MW with Djibouti (Ministry of Water, Irrigation and Electricity 2017: 11). The Ethiopian government also has standing agreements to export electricity to Uganda, Tanzania, Burundi, and Rwanda with Ethiopia–Kenya interconnection of 500kV capacity and flow of up to 2,000MW expected to be completed by 2019 (Verhoeven 2011: 6). The existence of a lucrative demand for electricity in the neighbouring countries, therefore, offers a good opportunity for Ethiopia to capitalize on its ample energy generation potential.

Beyond this obvious economic logic, one can mention three other strategic motivating factors for the ambitious investment of the Ethiopian government in the export of electricity. The first is the need for closer and friendly ties with strategically important neighbours to ease the economic costs associated with being a landlocked country. The second strategic motive is to create an additional source of precious hard currency which Ethiopia needs and to ease its balance-of-payment problems. The third strategic motive is related to Ethiopia's desire to develop and maintain a strong alliance with Nile basin countries to counter the dominance of Egypt in the hydro-politics of the Nile and ensure fair and equitable utilization of the Nile water resources. In other words, Ethiopia wants to entice and commit these countries into supporting its position with respect to the Nile waters by offering them cheap and affordable electricity.

Overall, Ethiopia's performance in the African Regional Integration Index has been mixed. Table 8.8 shows that, within the IGAD sub-regional block, Ethiopia ranked fifth out of six member countries that were included in the calculation of the overall index. Out of the five integration dimensions, Ethiopia has scored above the IGAD average only with respect to free movement of people and productive integration. The same cannot be said when it comes to Ethiopia's role in the Common Market for East and Southern Africa (COMESA). Within the COMESA regional economic community, Ethiopia is ranked 19th out of 19 members, indicating that it is the least integrated country within the block with respect to the five dimensions of integration index (AU/AfDB/UNECA 2016). These results suggest that Ethiopia has a long way to go before it becomes a key driver of regional integration in the Horn and Eastern Africa.

Table 8.8 Ethiopia's performance in the Africa Regional Integration Index, 2016

	Integration dimension	Ethiopia's score vs. COMESA members	COMESA average integration score	Ethiopia's integration rank in COMESA	Ethiopia's score vs. IGAD members	IGAD average integration score	Ethiopia's rank in IGAD
1	Trade integration score	0.185	0.572	18/19	0.277	0.505	6/7
2	Regional infrastructure integration score	0.402	0.439	14/19	0.577	0.630	6/8
3	Productive integration	0.344	0.452	16/19	0.400	0.434	4/8
4	Free movement of people	0.074	0.268	16/19	0.700	0.454	4/8
5	Financial and macroeconomic integration	0.162	0.343	17/19	0.168	0.221	5/7
	Overall regional integration score	**0.233**	**0.542**	**19/19**	**0.424**	**0.531**	**5/6**

Source: Compiled based on 'Africa Regional Integration Index Report 2016' (AU, AfDB, and UNECA 2016).

8.7 Conclusions

In this chapter, we have examined Ethiopia's 'economic diplomacy' to promote investment and trade with the rest of the world and with its IGAD neighbours. The empirical evidence shows that, by investing heavily in infrastructure and energy, Ethiopia has successfully positioned itself as an attractive investment destination to companies from China, Turkey, India, and other emerging economies. Three important factors play in Ethiopia's favour: the availability of cheap labour; potential for cheap energy; and Ethiopia's preferential access to the EU and US markets, which foreign investors want to take advantage of (MoFEC 2017).

On the other hand, economic diplomacy towards the neighbours, apart from Djibouti and Sudan, has not produced substantial results. Part of the reason for the low level of economic exchange with the neighbouring countries has to do with the similarities in the structure of their economies. While success in developing the manufacturing sector in Ethiopia can potentially lead to increased intra-Africa trade in the future, the fact remains that most of the FDI projects in Ethiopia aim to produce products destined for advanced economies, with little spill-over effect to the region.

The government's current approach to trade and investment promotion could be significantly enhanced by systematically involving many relevant government and non-government actors who might possess critical knowledge and information on trade and investment promotion. While export promotion can include activities such as visits by business delegations, arranging buyers-and-sellers meets, FDI mobilization involves sensitizing potential foreign investors to the opportunities in the home country, and thereafter taking targeted promotions. This means that institutions assigned for export promotion must work side by side with the agency charged with the mobilization of foreign direct investment. Such promotions must also be done in consultation with domestic business associations and individual enterprises.

Moreover, economic diplomacy efforts on their own are meaningless unless the necessary macroeconomic policy conditions to promote trade and investment are already in place (Kruger 1990). Policy misalignment on many fronts—such as tariff and non-tariff barriers; investment protection; shipping and transport-related challenges; taxation and repatriation of profits—can cause the best-thought economic diplomacy efforts to become undone (Lederman, Olarreaga, and Payton 2006). In addition, entry into foreign markets requires a good knowledge of foreign legislation, cultural differences, and local preferences. This will inevitably involve the need to strengthen knowledge and capacity in trade and investment promotion within the Ministry of Foreign Affairs.

In the final analysis, however, Ethiopia's success in attracting investments and promoting regional economic integration with its neighbours will largely depend on the government's ability to find a lasting solution to the internal political crisis and long-standing political conflicts with those neighbours. These problems are compounded by increasing meddling from the Middle East and the Gulf States, particularly from Egypt, Saudi Arabia, and the United Arab Emirates (UAE) in the regional politics of the Horn of Africa. These Middle Eastern actors are joined by the United States, China, and Russia, who are increasing their already active presence in the sub-region (Clapham 2017; Hussein 2018). While the background to the conflicts with Sudan, Somalia, and Eritrea are different from one another, trying to address them requires Ethiopia to take a broader perspective for the region and avoid being perceived by the neighbours as a rising regional hegemon. In terms of priority, resolving the political stalemate with Eritrea and Somalia should be top on the list of Ethiopia's regional agenda. The status quo of 'no-war, no-peace' with Eritrea has not produced tangible results. The Ethiopian government must seek an alternative approach that will produce permanent peace between the two countries. This will pave the way for a much closer economic relationship between Eritrea and Ethiopia, with the current idle ports of Assab and Massawa potentially becoming Ethiopia's main gateway to the world.

With respect to Somalia, a more cautious approach will be needed given the historical animosity of Somalis towards Ethiopia. Ethiopia's desire to have access to the port of Berbera in the breakaway republic of Somaliland is unlikely to be received positively by the Somalia Federal Government in Mogadishu. In fact, in early March 2018, Somalia's lower house of parliament voted to nullify a port investment deal between DP World, Ethiopia, and the autonomous region of Somaliland with a landslide 168 vote out of 170.

The agreement, announced on 1 March 2018, would have given landlocked Ethiopia a 19 per cent stake in the port of Berbera, which is being developed by Dubai's DP World under a thirty-year concession agreement.[5] The port deal, which was concluded without consultation with the federal government in Mogadishu, was viewed as a deliberate violation of the sovereignty of Somalia by the government of Ethiopia.

On the other hand, Ethiopia's relation with Sudan and South Sudan is less problematic. While Ethiopia has been able to draw Sudan onto its side in the conflict with Egypt over the use of the Nile waters, the South Sudanese political crisis has placed a new burden on Ethiopia, with the latter now hosting over one million refugees inside its borders. Plans to export electricity and increase cross-border trade between the two countries will remain constrained if the political crisis in South Sudan continues. In short, the overall political situation in the Horn of Africa is not conducive for the development of a viable regional integration despite Ethiopia's effort to the contrary.

References

AU/AfDB/UNECA (2016). *Africa Regional Integration Index Report 2016* (Addis Ababa: AU/AfDB/UNECA).

Bereketeab, R. (2013). *The Horn of Africa: Intra-State and Inter-State Conflicts and Security* (London: Pluto Press).

Cheru, Fantu (2016). 'Emerging Southern Powers and New Forms of South–South Cooperation: Ethiopia's Strategic Engagement with China and India', *Third World Quarterly* 37 (4): 592–610.

Clapham, Christopher (2017). *The Horn of Africa: State Formation and Decay* (London: Hurst Publishers).

Cliff, Lionel (1999).'Regional Dimensions of Conflict in the Horn of Africa', *Third World Quarterly*, 20 (1): 89–111.

Ethiopian Airlines (2016). *Annual Report 2015/2016* (Addis Ababa: Ethiopian Airlines).

Ethiopian Roads Authority (2014). *Road Sector Development Program 17 Years Assessment* (Addis Ababa: ERA).

Federal Democratic Republic of Ethiopia (1995). *Constitution of the Federal Democratic Republic of Ethiopia* (Addis Ababa: Ministry of Information Press).

Federal Democratic Republic of Ethiopia (2002). *Foreign Affairs and National Security Policy* (Addis Ababa: Ministry of Information Press).

Federal Democratic Republic of Ethiopia (2012). 'Ethiopian Foreign Policy and its Achievements' Government Communication Affairs Office, Addis Ababa.

Foster, Vivien and Cecilia Briceno-Garmendia (2010). *Africa's Infrastructure: A Time for Transformation* (Washington, DC: World Bank).

Healy, Sally (2007). 'Conflict in the Ogaden and its Regional Dimension', Chatham House Seminar Report.

Hussein, Hassan (2018). 'Storm on Ethiopia's Doorsteps: Tackling Convulsions in the Greater Middle East and Northeastern Africa', *Addis Standard*, 21 March 2018.

[5] https://www.middleeastmonitor.com/20180305-somalia-rejects-uaes-port-deal

IGAD (2016). *IGAD State of the Region Report 2016* (Djibouti: IGAD Secretariat).

Keller, Edmond (1987). 'The Politics of State Survival: Continuity and Change in Ethiopia', *The Annals of the American Academy of Political and Social Sciences* 489 (1): 76–87.

Kruger, Anne O. (1990). 'Government Failures in Development', *Journal of Economic Perspectives* 4 (3): 9–23.

Lederman, Daniel, Marcelo Olarreaga, and Lucy Payton (2006). 'Export Promotion Agencies: What Works and What Doesn't', Working Paper No. 4044, World Bank Policy Research.

Mehari, Taddele Maru (2017). 'A Regional Power in the Making: Ethiopian Foreign Diplomacy in the Horn of Africa', Occasional paper 261, South African Institute of International Affairs, Johannesburg, p. 28.

Ministry of Finance and Economic Cooperation (2015). *Growth and Transformation Plan (GTP II)* (Addis Ababa: National Planning Commission).

Ministry of Finance and Economic Cooperation (2017). 'A Note on Developments of Foreign Direct Investment in Ethiopia', Fiscal Report Series No. 001/2017, Fiscal Policy Directorate, (April).

Ministry of Finance and Economic Development (1993). *An Economic Development Strategy for Ethiopia: A Comprehensive Guidance and a Development Strategy for the Future* (Addis Ababa: Government of Ethiopia).

Ministry of Finance and Economic Development (2010). *Growth and Transformation Plan, 2010/2015* (Addis Ababa: MOFED).

Ministry of Finance and Economic Development (2013). *Growth and Transformation Plan: Annual Progress Report for FY 2011/12* (Addis Ababa: MOFED).

Ministry of Foreign Affairs (2007). 'Foreign Trade Promotion Manual for Ethiopian Diplomatic Missions', Economic and Business Affairs General-Directorate, Addis Ababa.

Ministry of Foreign Affairs (2015). 'Performance Report on Economic Diplomacy for the Budget Year 2014/15', Addis Ababa (in Amharic).

Ministry of Water, Irrigation and Electricity of Ethiopia (2017). 'The Ethiopian Power Sector: Renewable Future'. Berlin Energy Transition Dialogue Conference 2017.

Mulugeta, Geberehiowt Berhe (2016). 'Economic Integration as a Peacebuilding Strategy in the Horn of Africa', *African Solutions Journal* 1 (1): 63–87.

National Bank of Ethiopia (2017). *Annual Report* (Addis Ababa: NBE).

Ndulu, Ben (2006). 'Infrastructure, Regional Integration and Growth in Sub-Saharan Africa: Dealing with the Disadvantages of Geography and Sovereign Fragmentation', *Journal of African Economics* 15 (2): 212–44.

Rana, Kishan S. (2004). 'Economic Diplomacy in India: A Practitioner's Perspective', *International Studies Perspectives* 5: 66–70.

Rose, Andrew K. (2007). 'The Foreign Service and Foreign Trade: Embassies as Export Promotion', *The World Economy* 30 (1): 22–38.

Styan, David (2013). 'Djibouti: Changing Influence in the Horn's Strategic Hub', Briefing Paper AFB BP 2013/01, Chatham House Africa Programme, London.

Tewelde, Gebresselase and R. Durga Prasad (2015). 'Analysis of Foreign Affairs and National Security Policy with Special Reference to Strategy of FDR of Ethiopia', *International Research Journal of Business and Management* 8 (13): 86–94.

UNCTAD (2017). *World Investment Report 2017* (Geneva: United Nations Conference on Trade and Development).

Vaughan, Sarah (2015). 'Federalism, Revolutionary Democracy and the Developmental State', in *Understanding Contemporary Ethiopia: Monarchy, Revolution and the Legacy Meles Zenawi*, ed. Gerard Prunier and Eloi Ficquet (London: C. Hurst & Co.): 283–312.
Verhoeven, Harry (2011). 'Black Gold for Blue Gold? Sudan's Oil, Ethiopia's Water and Regional Integration', *Chatham House Briefing Paper*, AFP BP 2011/03, June: 1–24.
Verhoeven, Harry (2015). 'Africa's Next Hegemon: Behind Ethiopia's Power Plays', *Foreign Affairs*, 12 April.
Zinabu Samaro (2017). 'Rethinking Regional Economic Integration as if Industrialization Mattered', *Structural Change and Economic Dynamics* 43: 87–98.

PART II

ECONOMIC DEVELOPMENT

CHAPTER 9

ECONOMIC POLICY AND STRUCTURAL TRANSFORMATION IN ETHIOPIA

MEKONNEN MANYAZEWAL
AND ADMASU SHIFERAW

9.1 Introduction

Reduction of mass poverty and economic transformation in developing countries remain quintessential topics in development economics. Conventional growth theories built around the one-sector model have been widely used to understand sources of macroeconomic growth by focusing on the rates of factor accumulation and technological change. Such growth models and their empirical counterparts have contributed to policy discussions where some consensus has emerged on broad policy directions such as ensuring macroeconomic stability, trade openness, deregulation of domestic markets including those for capital and labour, and intensifying investment in human capital and infrastructure (COGD 2008). However, because of a lack of sensitivity to country contexts, this approach hardly informs policymakers on the mix and sequence of policy reforms that may work best in a given country. Some economists go a step further and argue that the one-sector growth model is inadequate for understanding the processes of economic diversification, which are crucial to building economies that are resilient to shocks and capable of sustaining a high-growth path (Rodrik 2015; Chang 1994; Kuznets 1971).

Earlier contributions to development economics specifically focused on industrialization as the only way to achieve sustainable growth and structural transformation in developing countries (Chenery 1960; Kaldor 1967). The underlying assumption is that manufacturing not only exhibits higher productivity but also generates dynamic spillover effects on the rest of the economy more effectively than other activities. The focus on industrialization is particularly relevant for African economies, many of which continue to rely heavily on natural resource rents and have a very narrow industrial base while facing stiff competition globally as very late industrializers (Newman et al. 2016; Abegaz 2018). Carefully designed industrial policy and strategy are expected to play a critical role in this context as market mechanisms are deemed inadequate to bring about structural change driven by industrial expansion (Chang 1994; Newman et al. 2016). Over the last two decades, the Ethiopian economy has emerged as one of Africa's economic success stories with rapid GDP growth and significant poverty reduction. And yet, change in the structure of the Ethiopian economy has been relatively slow. The 2014 African Transformation Report, which uses five indicators of structural transformation (economic diversification, export competitiveness, productivity gain, technology upgrading, and human economic well-being) ranks Ethiopia among the least transformed of the fifteen African countries measured for the report (ACET 2014).

As shown in Figure 9.1, structural change, in the simple but widely used sense of a shift in the relative shares of sectoral activity in the Ethiopian economy, has been modest, with agriculture's share in GDP remaining at about 55 per cent on average during the 1980s and 1990s, while value added in services and industry contributed on average 35 per cent and 10 per cent of GDP, respectively. Towards the end of the 1990s, the share of agriculture started to drop below 50 per cent for the first time while that of services increased by 10 percentage points to a 45 per cent share. In the meantime, industry's share—including manufacturing—remained at about 10 per cent except for 2015 and 2016 where its share rose to 15 per cent and 17 per cent of GDP, respectively. Whether the latter marks a permanent shift in economic structure remains to be seen, as manufacturing's share remained at 5 per cent. The direction of structural change in Ethiopia since 2000 has largely been the result of rapid expansion of services rather than industrial activities where historical evidence suggests dynamic spillover effects pertain. This faster expansion of services has been observed in many African countries and has raised concerns about the sustainability of rapid growth in the continent (Rodrik 2014). This suggests that the nature of economic opportunities available to broader sections of the Ethiopian society may not have changed much despite rapid growth in average income. This would have been a promising development had growth in services been driven by high-productivity sub-sectors that improve overall economic efficiency. Unfortunately, service-sector productivity in African countries does not seem to be significantly different from that of traditional agriculture (Rodrik 2014).

Understanding the nature and challenges of structural transformation is thus crucial to overcoming underlying economic rigidities, some of which may require policy interventions. Accordingly, this chapter closely investigates the trajectory of economic structure in Ethiopia since the mid-1970s. We examine the implications for structural change of government policies during the Derg regime that lasted from 1974 to 1991, and under EPRDF's rule since 1991, focusing mainly on the latter. The analysis goes beyond simple comparison of sectoral composition of output, and examines changes in economic

FIGURE 9.1 Sectoral composition of Ethiopia's GDP

Source: World Bank's World Development Indicators.

relationships that ultimately bring about economic transformation. We consider structural transformation as a process that involves the re-allocation of resources across and within sectors in such a way as to raise overall productivity. While the possibility of achieving structural transformation in Africa through high-productivity agricultural and service activities has not been ruled out (Rodrik 2014), there is very little historical precedent for this strategy, implying that the focus still remains on industrialization. In fact, the African Mining Vision put forward by the African Union (AU 2009) and a recent publication by the UN Economic Commission for Africa (UN-ECA 2016) highlight industrialization as a shared vision of African economic development. The second Growth and Transformation Plan (GTP-II) of the Ethiopian government echoes this sentiment and aims to raise the GDP share of manufacturing by at least 10 percentage points during 2015 to 2020.

9.2 Conceptualizing Structural Change

To better understand structural transformation, or the lack thereof, it is imperative to go beyond examining outcome variables that only capture contributions to GDP and employment by broad economic sectors. Structural transformation is actually a dynamic process involving fundamental shifts over time in both the demand and supply sides of an economy (Chenery 1960). Rosenstien-Rodan's (1943) 'big push' hypothesis, for instance, is based on the assumption that firm-level investment in a given industry would remain weak as firms anticipate lacklustre domestic demand for their products. Overcoming this challenge requires large investment in multiple industries simultaneously, through direct state intervention and/or coordination, in order to boost investor confidence across the economy. The unbalanced growth theory suggested by Hirschman (1958), on the other hand, recommends large initial investment only in selected key industries to bring the entire economy to a high-growth path through forward and backward linkages. Hirschman's focus is thus on production linkages among domestic firms through the production of intermediate inputs. While Rosenstien-Rodan emphasized the change in consumer demand as a driver of structural transformation, Hirschman underscored the change in firms' demand for intermediate inputs. While some economists treat the balanced and unbalanced growth models as two alternative policy directions, in fact they strongly complement each other.

A focus on demand-driven structural change is not confined to development economists. According to the conventional wisdom of neoclassical economics, industrialization and structural change can be achieved through market mechanisms. Specifically, this approach asserts that as per capita income increases, the structure of domestic demand shifts in favour of manufactured goods of increasingly high quality—consistent with Engel's law. Such shifts in demand would also be accompanied by more investment in education, both by the state and the private sector, increasing the supply of skilled labour demanded by manufacturing firms. This implies that conventional macroeconomic policy reforms that promote growth, i.e. stabilization, deregulation, and trade openness, would in the long run bring about structural transformation without the need for articulated industrial policy. The latter is actually perceived by neoclassical theory as inefficient and potentially self-defeating for the industrial agenda as it often involves ill-informed efforts by policymakers to pick winners and influence resource allocation to selected industries against the dictates of market fundamentals. Conventional wisdom also asserts that a country's specialization patterns do not affect its long-term growth prospects and hence there are no special gains from manufacturing.

Recent studies challenge the passive neoclassical approach to structural change on a number of grounds. To begin with, specialization patterns could remain static despite rising income if demand for manufactures is met by imports, a point made early on by Chenery (1960). Second, structural change requires the introduction of new and better-quality products, which in turn involves risk taking and upfront spending on product discovery by entrepreneurs (Hausmann, Hwang, and Rodrik 2007; Imbs and Wacziarg 2003). Since the cost of introducing new products is fully internalized by innovative firms while the benefits often spill over to other firms, the intensity of product discovery in a country could be suboptimal both in terms of the number of entrepreneurs engaged in discovery and how much they spend on it. Third, while developing-country firms introducing new and sophisticated products may not manufacture them as efficiently as developed-country firms, there is evidence of faster convergence in productivity between technology leaders and laggards within narrowly defined industries (Rodrik 2004). Fourth, structural transformation is a dynamic process with a certain degree of path dependence (Kaldor 1967). As such, certain sectors—particularly manufacturing—allow firms to introduce new products at a faster pace relative to the non-manufacturing sector where degrees of asset and knowledge specificity are high (Hausmann and Klinger 2007). The upshot of this discussion is that a country's initial levels of industrialization affect the pace of structural transformation, and that industrial policy may have a self-reinforcing effect on industrialization rather than a self-defeating effect as the conventional wisdom suggests.

Other scholars have recently re-evaluated the role of agriculture in structural transformation. Efforts to enhance the productivity of agriculture can contribute to poverty reduction directly while facilitating growth and poverty reduction in the non-agricultural sector (Christiaensen, Demery, and Kuhl 2011). There are at least three important considerations from the perspective of structural transformation that are all linked to productivity in agriculture (see also Chapter 26). To begin with, productivity growth in agriculture would release labour on a permanent basis for potential employment in the non-agriculture sector. This is very important given the seasonality of agricultural production, which tends to keep labour tied to farming although underemployment remains high throughout the non-peak season. Second, improved agricultural productivity would boost food supply allowing food prices, and consequently wage growth, to remain under control, which in turn contributes to the competitiveness of manufacturing. Keeping food inflation under control would also allow households to increase spending on non-food items most of which is likely to fall on manufactured goods. Third, improved efficiency in agriculture would contribute to capacity utilization and productivity in manufacturing directly through the supply of inputs for agro-processing industries and indirectly through agricultural exports that allow import of intermediate inputs. Finally, agricultural employment and rising farm income boost the domestic market for manufactures.

In Section 9.3 we use both micro- and meso-level data to capture the underlying economic processes and linkages that have shaped structural transformation in Ethiopia over the last four decades. We first examine productivity growth in Ethiopia's agriculture and its implications for structural transformation. Firm-level data will be used to analyse the investment behaviour of Ethiopian manufacturing firms and to measure changes in the import intensity of intermediate inputs to capture backward linkages of manufacturers with domestic suppliers. Sector/industry-level data will be used to measure the import penetration rate across manufacturing industries and how this might affect industry-level output growth. Highly disaggregated trade data at the product level provide us with insights into the country's export diversification which is an important indicator of productivity growth. Finally, we rely on household surveys to assess the structure of consumption expenditure among rural and urban households as a proxy for domestic demand for manufactures. Throughout the chapter, we discuss the policy context in which the selected microeconomic and sectoral processes have taken place in an effort to shed light on structural transformation in Ethiopia under two different political regimes with distinct economic visions.

9.3 The Ethiopian Experience

9.3.1 Slow Growth and Static Economic Structure under the Derg (1974–91)

Understanding why Ethiopia's economic structure remained static throughout the Derg era of 1974–91 is relatively straightforward. Just as structural change is important for long-term growth, so growth is essential for structural change (Kuznets 1966). Unfortunately, economic growth was very slow under the Derg due to misguided policies, poor provision of public goods, and protracted civil war. The nationalization of private enterprises and the proliferation of government restrictions on the private sector (such as investment caps, credit constraints, price controls, and shortage of imported intermediated inputs) constituted major disincentives for entrepreneurship, productivity growth, and introduction of new products. Dire conditions in the quantity and quality of infrastructure also contributed to high production and marketing costs across sectors but particularly for transaction-intensive activities like manufacturing. The slow and at times negative growth in per capita income also implies weak domestic demand for manufactured goods despite a large and growing population. Although a number of state-owned manufacturing firms were established during the Derg especially in the food and textile industries, partly to meet the demands of the armed forces, performance was poor because of mismanagement. The protracted civil war in northern Ethiopia and frequent droughts exacerbated economic uncertainty, which in turn choked investment and innovation in the modern sector.

It is thus unsurprising that the country failed to attract meaningful foreign direct investment during the Derg era, while accumulating substantial amounts of external debt mainly from the communist bloc, to build the largest military force in sub-Saharan Africa. Performance in the agricultural sector was even worse partly because of errors of omission including weak provision of modern agricultural inputs and basic infrastructure, and partly because of errors of commission such as the introduction of an agricultural marketing board that extracted resources from the rural economy by denying farmers direct access to product markets (Chole 2004). There was thus neither productivity growth that would push labour out of agriculture, nor a growing industrial sector that would lure labour towards high-productivity activities as in the Lewis model.

The Derg's economic policy direction was clearly guided by a Marxist-Leninist ideology that allowed no room for pragmatism and context specific approaches that take into account social and cultural norms and existing economic relationships. Although signs of troubled times ahead were detected from the outset and potential solutions were proposed, concerted action was not taken in time to avert crisis. Attempts to introduce a mixed economy in the last days of the Derg were too late and deemed inadequate to accommodate the demand for change.

9.3.2 Faster Growth and Slow Structural Transformation under EPRDF (1991–2017)

The dramatic conclusion of the civil war in May 1991 allowed the country to reorganize its investment priorities and development strategies. Resources previously spent on financing the war were redirected towards addressing formidable development challenges: agriculture and food security, environmental degradation, human resource development, employment, industrialization, etc. The Transitional Government of Ethiopia (TGE) implemented a series of economic reforms in collaboration with its development partners to restore macroeconomic stability, rationalize the role of the state, and boost private-sector participation. The Emergency Recovery and Reconstruction Program coordinated by the World Bank helped to rehabilitate war-damaged infrastructure including roads, schools, and health centres. It also provided foreign exchange to finance essential imports.

The Ethiopian economy, thus, escaped from the stagnation of the Derg era, achieving strong recovery in the 1990s and rapid growth from the early 2000s. The lack of substantial structural change since 1991 is thus intriguing in view of the strong economic growth that has been sustained for at least two decades—conditions often considered necessary for structural transformation. Part of the concern about the long-run sustainability of Ethiopia's recent growth emanates from this lack of transformation. It is, therefore, important to examine the prevailing macroeconomic and sector policy environments to better understand the nature of growth during this period, why the country's economic structure exhibited rigidities, and why such rigidities have not apparently, at least until now, stymied growth.

As already indicated, initial policy reforms under the EPRDF aimed at reviving the economy by lifting egregious restrictions on the private sector, reinstating market forces, reducing tariffs, and devaluing the currency. These conventional macroeconomic and microeconomic reforms coupled with the peace dividend after the civil war succeeded in reducing major inefficiencies and triggered economic recovery during the first half of the 1990s. By maintaining and further deepening this progressive policy stance, the government solidified the recovery in the second half of the 1990s. With increased development aid support from the international community, the government launched a series of sector development programmes in the second half of the 1990s that aimed at expanding education, health, and economic infrastructure. Public investment in infrastructure intensified in the late 1990s with substantial expenditure on hydro-electric power plants, roads, and airports. There is some evidence that the Road Sector Development Program (RSDP), for instance, has significantly increased the rate of entry of manufacturing firms in cities that previously were not important centres of manufacturing (Shiferaw et al. 2015). The 1992 investment law and its subsequent iterations offered incentives to domestic and foreign private investors in the form of tax holidays, duty-free imports of capital goods, duty drawbacks for exporters, etc. The combined effect of growth-enhancing policies, policy consistency, and macroeconomic stability, as well as rising public expenditure on human capital and infrastructure are regarded as major reasons for the rapid economic growth in Ethiopia (Moller and Wacker 2017). While the government's reform agenda is broadly conventional, the Ethiopian financial sector remains highly regulated, dominated by state-owned banks, and protected from foreign competition despite pressure from the World Bank and IMF since the early 1990s. While this policy stance allowed the government to increase public investment on infrastructure and human capital, it has reduced external credit to the private sector (World Bank 2015). Moller and Wacker (2017) argue that the positive effects on infrastructure of such heterodox financial policies appear to have outweighed their negative effects on economic growth.

Beyond the macroeconomic environment highlighted earlier, the government actively followed the Agricultural Development Led Industrialization (ADLI) strategy from 1993. ADLI aimed at enhancing productivity growth in smallholder agriculture through better access to modern agricultural inputs, extension services, and road connectivity, with the ultimate objective of industrial expansion (see Chapter 28). While ADLI includes a major poverty reduction component, given the prevalence of poverty in rural areas, it is inherently a strategy for structural transformation. The underlying premise is exploiting the country's comparative advantage in agro-processing industries. These efforts to increase value addition domestically were backed by trade policies that restricted the export of raw hides and skins through high export taxes imposed in 2008. Increased agricultural income was, in turn, expected to raise demand for manufactured consumer goods. Although asserting causality is difficult, growth in agricultural value added increased from 1.9 per cent per annum during the 1980s to 2.5 per cent during the 1990s. Agricultural growth intensified after 2000 with an average growth rate of 6.5 per cent during 2000–9 and 5.8 per cent during 2010–16. While the agricultural sector did manage to grow faster than before, with some evidence of increased export orientation and diversification (Bachewe et al. 2018), there is no evidence that it served as a basis for industrial expansion (Dorosh, Schmidt, and Shiferaw 2012). The expected linkages between smallholder agriculture and manufacturing turned out to be elusive. As the first decade of the twenty-first century drew to a close, it became clear that ADLI had not achieved economic transformation in Ethiopia.

Here it is important to state that economic policies and institutions are informed and shaped by the prevailing political context. The 1974–2016 review period has seen contrasting political systems with critical consequences for growth and transformation. The political implications for the effectiveness of economic policies and institutions are examined in greater detail elsewhere in this volume (see specifically Chapters 2, 3, and 7 in Part I as well as Chapter 46 in Part VI).

9.3.3 Agriculture Remains Important but Hard to Transform

Agriculture features prominently in the Ethiopian economy, and developments in this sector have ramifications for the structure of the entire economy. Of particular importance is productivity growth in agriculture, which affects the supply of inputs for agro-processing and other downstream industries as well as generating demand for upstream producers. It is thus crucial to re-examine salient features of Ethiopian agriculture, the sectoral policies that shaped the trajectory of productivity in this sector, and its role in structural transformation.

Ethiopian agriculture has long been characterized as a rain-fed production system operated predominantly by smallholder farmers using traditional techniques (see Chapter 27). The lack of international research and innovation on African staples notwithstanding, adoption of existing technologies is hampered by the smallholder nature of farming coupled with credit constraints and the risk of adverse shocks; smallholder farmers would be reluctant to apply fertilizers or improved seeds if the risk of crop failure is quite high (Dercon and Christiaensen 2011). The Derg regime attempted to address this problem partly by introducing large-scale state-owned commercial farms primarily for cash crops. This intervention failed disastrously principally because of poor management. During the Derg, attempts were made to mitigate exposure to weather shocks through forced resettlement and villagization programmes that failed for lack of social support. The Derg also introduced an agricultural marketing corporation as the sole buyer of agricultural products from farmers with the stated objective of price stabilization. Marketing boards have been widely criticized for disincentivizing agricultural productivity around the world and the Ethiopian experience is no exception. Poorly designed disaster relief efforts and inadequate infrastructure under the Derg also meant that relief support to drought-affected areas was often too late if not too little as well. The loss of farm assets during drought undermined productivity even when weather conditions returned to normal. It is, therefore, unsurprising that agricultural productivity remained very low throughout the Derg era. The left panel of Figure 9.2 shows the very low and volatile yield per hectare during the 1980s.

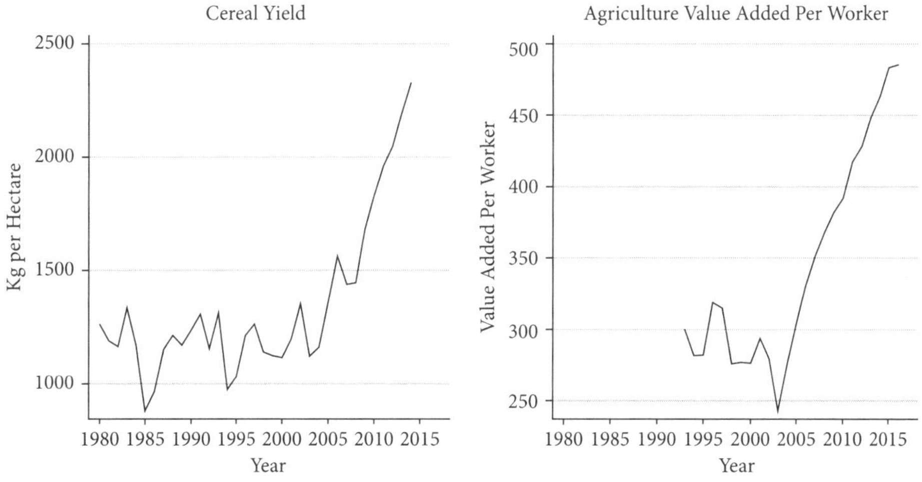

FIGURE 9.2 Trends in agricultural productivity

Source: World Bank's World Development Indicators.

The post-1991 period has seen encouraging developments in agricultural output and productivity. To begin with, there has been some reduction in the frequency and intensity of drought since the early 1990s, relative to the 1980s, except for the drought in 2003 and the El Niño-induced drought episodes in 2016/17 (Bachewe et al. 2018). Most importantly, efforts were made to increase the supply of modern agricultural inputs to smallholder farmers often combined with access to credit as well as extension services under the ADLI rubric. Removing the marketing corporation while expanding road infrastructure has significantly reduced frictions in agricultural markets, benefiting farmers substantially. Better roads and well-designed systems for disaster prevention, early warning, and response also mitigated the adverse effects of drought with limited effect on productivity. The government also introduced a Productive Safety Net Program (PSNP) for poor households in drought-prone areas to prevent depletion of productive assets and achieve consumption smoothing. Figure 9.2 shows the rapid increase in agricultural productivity since the late 1990s in terms of cereal yield per hectare as well as agricultural value added per workers. Agricultural output, therefore, started to grow strongly from the mid-1990s, achieving growth rates of 3.2 per cent, 5.6 per cent, 7.9 per cent, and 6.6 per cent during 1996–2000, 2001–5, 2006–10, and 2011–16, respectively. This is believed to have accounted for major reductions in poverty in the second half of the 1990s and in the 2000s.

However, there remain important challenges to achieving radical improvements in agricultural productivity. As shown in Figure 9.2, yield per hectare increased significantly only after 2005. Productivity was stagnant in the preceding decade despite concerted efforts to boost agricultural productivity under ADLI. While cereal yield per hectare has grown sharply since 2005, it still remains well below productivity levels in other developing countries. According to World Bank data, average cereal yield per hectare in Ethiopia in 2015 stood at 60 per cent of that of Latin America and at 49 per cent of that of East Asia. The combined use of fertilizers, improved seeds, and irrigation is absent in the Ethiopian context as the share of irrigated agricultural land still remains less than 1 per cent and as most farmers use chemical fertilizers without at the same time using improved seeds (Bachewe et al. 2018). Per capita arable land holding in the more productive highlands of Ethiopia has long been very low relative to other developing countries and continues to drop over time. Headey, Dereje, and Taffesse (2014) show a positive relationship between average landholding and age of household head in rural areas, suggesting declining farm size for younger generations while also showing that about 40 per cent of households had less than 0.5 hectares of land in 2012. It is also well documented that food prices have continued to rise in Ethiopia especially since 2007, and the country has not reached a point where food can be considered relatively cheap—although conditions have improved from the high inflation of 2007–9. Durevall, Loening, and Birru (2013) show that inflation in Ethiopia is largely related to food inflation and that short-term price movements are explained to a significant degree by supply shocks in cereal production. The Productive Safety Net Program (PSNP), which was intended as a short- to-medium-term intervention to shore up productive assets, is still operational, suggesting that there remain potent underlying factors that make rural households vulnerable to adverse shocks. This seems consistent with the study by Andersson, Mekonnen, and Stage (2011) that shows that participation in PSNP did not prevent reduction of livestock at times of adverse shocks, nor did it increase livestock holdings, although there has been some increase in trees. While agricultural productivity is rising in Ethiopia, it has not been fast enough to achieve reliable food security and reduce the cost of food. The effect of food prices on low-income urban households has been shown to be substantial (Alem and Söderbom 2012). These developments have important implications for household demand for manufactured goods.

This is not surprising given the relatively low, albeit increasing, application of modern farm inputs, limited irrigation and very traditional farming practices in most parts of Ethiopia (Bachewe et al. 2018). Also important is the country's large population, which continues to grow on average by about 2.5 per cent per annum. In recognition of the lack of success with the ADLI strategy that initially focused on smallholder agriculture, efforts were made after 2007/8 to expand commercial agriculture, primarily but not exclusively through foreign direct investment. Large parcels of agricultural land were leased to private investors in sparsely populated and low-lying areas of the country as farmland is already scarce in the well-established highlands of Ethiopia. The main reason for this approach was to increase agricultural exports, which would generate desperately needed foreign exchange, facilitating import of capital goods and intermediate inputs for manufacturing firms, while also augmenting food security through import of food items. By 2018 the large-scale farming strategy in Ethiopia had achieved only limited success, as most agricultural investment projects under this arrangement had not become fully operational,[1] and the government repossessed land from a large number of commercial farms because of failure to meet expectations several years after the land was leased. Nonetheless, there were major successes in attracting foreign investors in horticulture which contributed to export earnings. Food production still remains rain fed and small-farm based.

It is clear that while efforts to boost agricultural productivity have started to bear fruit, a lot more needs to be done to raise productivity well above population growth. Innovative approaches to increase access to modern farm inputs, credit, and farm equipment should be considered in addition to exploring avenues to ensure the effectiveness of access to land, widely considered to be long overdue.

Nevertheless, it is important to recognize the strong growth in agricultural exports since 2000 as well as a shift in the composition of agricultural exports. The share of coffee, historically Ethiopia's top export earner, has declined from two-thirds of total export earnings in 1995 to 20 per cent in 2015. In the meantime, the share of non-coffee agricultural exports increased sharply. Data from the UN-COMTRADE database show that the strong growth in Ethiopia's export earnings since 2005 is driven by growth in non-traditional agricultural exports (see Figure 9.3). Key among the latter are the export of cut flowers, mainly to Europe, which experienced a 49 per cent annual growth during 1995–2014 followed by a 29 per cent growth in dairy products and eggs. The rest of the

[1] See *Financial Times* report of March 2016.

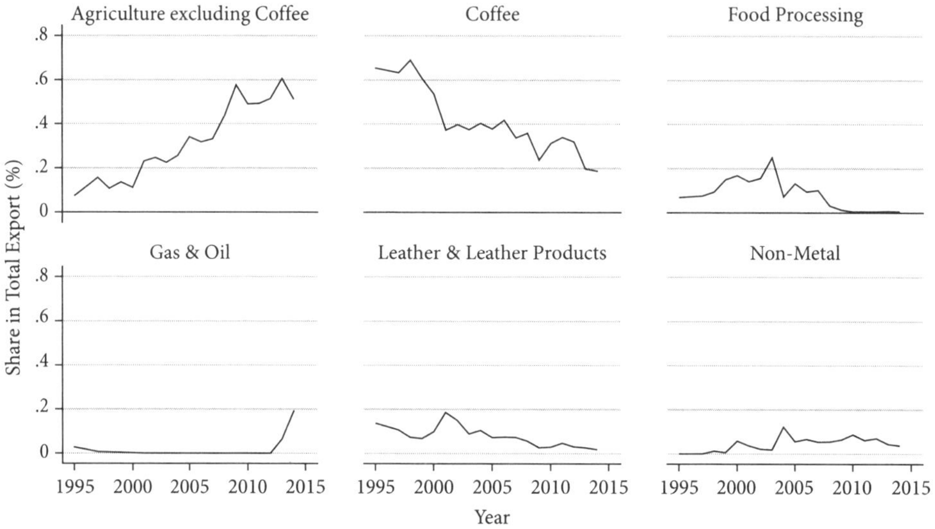

FIGURE 9.3 Composition of Ethiopian exports: percentage share

Source: UN-COMTRADE Database.

increase in non-coffee agricultural exports comes from traditional items that have experienced faster growth since 2005: 29 per cent growth in live animals, 22 per cent growth in vegetables, 18 per cent growth in meat and fish, 18 per cent growth in oilseeds, and a 10 per cent growth in fruit. Coffee exports grew by 6 per cent, explaining the secular decline in its share during the study period. This rapid growth of agricultural exports and diversification within the agricultural export basket is to a large extent driven by an increase in global commodity prices rather than an increase in productivity which explains why maintaining a high growth rate in such export items has become difficult in recent years. As shown in Bachewe et al. (2018), the bulk of modern agricultural inputs are applied for cereal production, which is primarily destined for domestic markets.

9.4 Manufacturing and Economic Transformation

The second Growth and Transformation Plan (GTP-II) for the period 2015–19 has high hopes of a robust performance in manufacturing to meet its ambitious goals. This is partly in recognition of strong but less than expected attainments in manufacturing during GTP-I and under ADLI. The obvious question in this respect is why the share of manufacturing remained at 5 per cent of GDP for so long. In countries like Ethiopia with a very low manufacturing base, the first order of business is intensifying capital formation at the firm level. However, the firm-level gross investment rate in Ethiopian manufacturing remains about 12 per cent of capital stock on average among firms that employ at least ten workers (Shiferaw 2009, 2016). This implies a lacklustre net investment rate of about 2 per cent assuming a depreciation rate of 10 per cent per annum. The average gross investment rate masks substantial variation across firms. Data from the Central Statistical Agency of Ethiopia show that more than 50 per cent of manufacturing firms have a zero investment rate at any given point in time and this fraction rises to about 70 per cent among small firms that employ less than fifty workers. Evidence shows that the investment rate among privately owned manufacturing firms has not increased significantly over the years although the number of manufacturing firms has been rising substantially. This is quite disconcerting given the massive public investment in infrastructure, which presumably should crowd in more private investment.

As shown in Shiferaw (2016), a major factor that explains weak overall investment among incumbent firms is lack of access to credit. Recent studies by the World Bank (2015) and Zewdu (2014) show that credit to the private sector as a percentage of GDP declined during 2004–12 with a modest increase in more recent years. Part of the problem was excessive collateral requirements by banks and burdensome regulation on the private banking sector (World Bank 2015). These problems disproportionately affect small firms (employing at least ten but less than fifty workers) as they do not meet the very high collateral requirements and also because they often lack long-term relationships with banks (Shiferaw 2016). Large firms are thus in a better position to take advantage of investment opportunities and the financial sector policies seem to reinforce this dichotomy. The investment proclamations that have been issued also provide incentives geared towards large firms, foreign or private. Exemptions from profit taxes, duty-free importation of capital goods, and preferential credit are all biased in favour of large firms. While the overwhelming majority of manufacturers are small firms, the policy environment is not particularly designed to promote their growth. It is thus not surprising that the graduation rate of small manufacturing firms into medium and large firms is extremely slow, suggesting the difficulty they face in expanding their businesses (Shiferaw and Bedi 2013). This feature is observable across the manufacturing industries of many African countries.

Another important challenge for Ethiopian manufacturing is the high level of import penetration rate at the industry level (calculated as value of imports divided by the sum of domestic output and imports less exports). As shown in Table 9.1, import penetration has been rising even in those industries in which Ethiopia is considered to have a comparative advantage. To examine the extent to which import competition is posing a challenge for growth in manufacturing, we run a simple regression model of growth in manufacturing output at the industry level on a number of control variables including investment rate, import penetration rate, export orientation, industry fixed effects and time fixed effects. The industry fixed effects control for time-invariant factors that make some industries grow faster than others while the time fixed effects control for global and nation shocks that affect output growth in all industries. The results, based on industry-level panel data from UNIDO and trade statistics from UN-COMTRADE for the period 1990–2009, are as follows:

$$\underset{(0.18)}{Yg = 0.04} + \underset{(0.22)}{0.38\,INV} - \underset{(0.16)}{0.35\,IPR} - \underset{(0.15)}{0.21\,EXPY} + \underset{(0.18)}{0.08\,PRIORITY} + i + t$$

where Yg is annual growth in industry-level output, INV is investment rate, EXPY is export-to-output ratio, PRIORITY is a dummy for industries prioritized by government's industrial policy, i controls for industry fixed effects, and t controls for time fixed effects. The numbers in parenthesis are robust standard errors.

The regression results indicate a positive and statistically significant effect of investment on output growth, consistent with the firm-level evidence provided earlier. We also find that the import penetration rate significantly reduces the rate of growth of manufacturing output in Ethiopia. Specifically, a one percentage point increase in the IPR reduces industry level output growth by 0.0038 percentage points. Therefore, an industry with 50 per cent import penetration rate will grow 14 per cent less than an industry with only 10 per cent import penetration rate. It is interesting to note that, although the coefficient on export orientation of manufacturing is statistically insignificant, the negative sign on the coefficient suggests that the benefits of export orientation are not very strong at least in the current context. This finding is similar to the study by Hailu and Shiferaw (2016) which found that the employment benefits of export orientation are very weak in most developing countries.

These regression results and trends in Table 9.1 suggest a sector that is struggling to compete with imports and hence is largely focused on domestic rather than export markets.

Table 9.1 Import penetration and export orientation in Ethiopian manufacturing, per cent

	Import penetration rate			Export orientation		
Industry	1990–9	2000–8	Total	1990–9	2000–8	Total
Tobacco	2.13	8.06	6.36	0.00	0.08	0.04
Beverage	10.01	10.81	10.58	0.10	0.37	0.24
Food	30.25	35.21	33.81	0.46	2.95	1.71
Garments	32.28	61.24	53.47	0.33	2.99	1.28
Leather & footwear	42.01	47.31	45.79	9.19	32.18	19.64
Metal	49.26	49.10	49.14	0.00	0.01	0.00
Textile	59.54	61.33	60.81	0.00	0.08	0.03
Chemical	65.24	68.97	67.89	0.17	0.38	0.27
Non-metal	65.27	73.49	71.25	0.02	0.00	0.01
Transport equipment	80.05	80.39	80.29	0.00	0.00	0.00
Printing	85.44	85.52	85.50	0.00	0.00	0.00
Wood & furniture	100.00	100.00	100.00	0.00	0.00	0.00
Machinery	100.00	100.00	100.00	0.00	0.00	0.00

Source: Author's computation based on UNIDO Indstat database and UN-COMTRADE database.

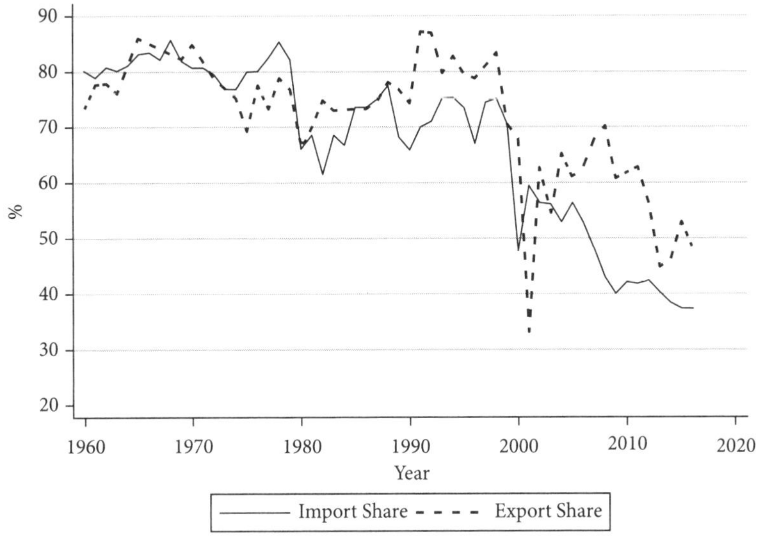

FIGURE 9.4 Percentage shares of Ethiopian exports to and imports from high-income countries

Source: World Bank's World Development Indicators.

The only industry with a substantial degree of export orientation is the leather sector where the export-to-output ratio increased from 9.2 per cent during the 1990s to nearly a third during 2000–8. This is believed to be a direct result of the tariff hikes on the export of raw hides and skins since 2008, as well as the growing number of multinational companies investing in this sector. This is distantly followed by garments and processed food industries where exports accounted for about 3 per cent of output during 2000–8, up from a less than 1 per cent share during the 1990s. This indicates on the one hand the large potential for export orientation, while also revealing the massive efforts needed to make Ethiopian manufacturing internationally competitive. Closer investigation is needed, for instance, of why Ethiopian firms have not taken advantage of their preferential access to European and US markets. Instead, Figure 9.4 shows that Ethiopia's trade is increasingly oriented away from high-income countries and towards other developing countries. For instance, only 50 per cent of exports are destined for high-income countries in 2014 and 2015, down from an 80 per cent share in the early 1990s. While the shift in import partners presumably reflects the rising competitiveness of East Asian manufacturing, it is not clear what explains the shift in Ethiopia's export destinations. It could be because of the growing demand for Ethiopian exports from emerging economies or the difficulty of meeting quality standards in high-income countries. Nonetheless, this shift may have important implications in view of recent evidence that exporting to high-income countries contributes more to quality upgrading and skill utilization than exporting to middle- and low-income countries, underscoring that where you export matters (Brambilla, Lederman, and Porto 2012; Verhoogen 2008).

As discussed in the analytical framework, an important avenue through which growth in manufacturing contributes to structural transformation is backward and forward

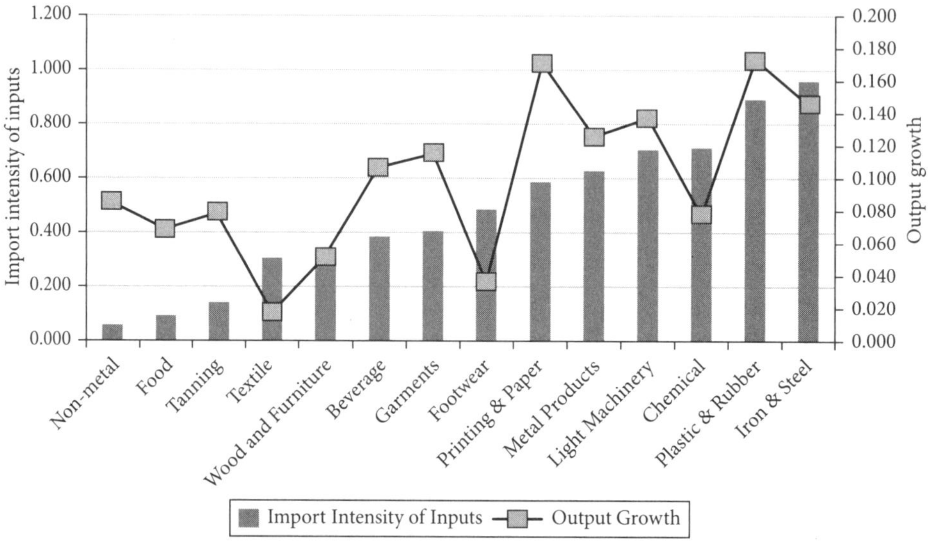

FIGURE 9.5 Import intensity of intermediate input consumption and output growth

Source: CSA, 'Large and Medium-Scale Manufacturing Survey Report' (2017).

linkages. In an effort to assess the extent of such domestic production linkages, we examined the import intensity of intermediate input consumption by manufacturing firms. Figure 9.5 shows substantial heterogeneity in the percentage of intermediate inputs sourced from domestic and foreign suppliers. The sectors that depend heavily on domestic inputs are the non-metal industries that use bulky inputs such as cement and other construction materials, as well as the food, leather, and textile industries which rely on agricultural raw materials. Although not indicated in Figure 9.5, there is very little change over time in the ranking of industries based on their dependence on imported inputs. It is interesting to note that the industries with faster output growth are the ones that rely heavily on imported intermediate inputs, suggesting that these industries have weak backward linkages with domestic suppliers. A panel fixed effects regression of output growth on import intensity of inputs shows a positive coefficient of 0.056 that is significant at 18 per cent after controlling for time, industry, and firm fixed effects. While the bulk of manufacturing output is indeed accounted for by industries with high domestic input content, growth in these industries seems to be substantially slower than in others. Our own calculation based on firm-level data from the CSA indicate that intermediate inputs account for about 75 per cent of total variable production costs, which has important implications for competitiveness. Input costs in African countries are estimated to be about 25 per cent higher than those in China, offsetting Africa's competitive edge in low-wage manufacturing (Abegaz 2018: 248).

These are industry-level averages over 1996–2007 based on firm-level data from the Central Statistical Agency (CSA). Import intensity of intermediate inputs is calculated as expenditure on imported inputs divided by total spending on intermediate inputs.

There has been very little attempt in industrial policy to promote exploitation of potential production linkages between manufacturing firms and their suppliers. This clearly requires more refined information about backward and forward linkages as well as close collaboration between industrial policymakers and private enterprises. A more detailed examination of Ethiopia's industrial policy and institutional dynamics can be found in Chapters 35, 36, 37, and 39.

9.4.1 Domestic Demand for Manufactures

Since Ethiopian manufacturing is overwhelmingly domestic market oriented, it is important to gauge the change in the structure of domestic demand. Ideally, one would like to measure the share of non-food expenditure, excluding services, assuming that non-food expenditure would largely fall on manufactured goods in a monotonic fashion. We proxy household expenditure on non-food items using ownership of specific assets such as TV, radio, and bicycles, etc., that are captured by household surveys. We have such data for the 2004 and 2015 household surveys. However, the list of assets is different in the two rounds of surveys as there are more assets in the 2015 round. To make these surveys comparable and measure change over time, we construct a simple index of asset ownership at the household level by taking the mean of a series of dummy variables that indicate whether a household owns a particular asset or not. This index would obviously range between zero (for a household that does not own any of the assets) and one (for a household that owns all the assets listed in a given survey). We construct this asset index for rural and urban dwellers for both the 2004 and 2015 rounds of the household survey. We then plot this asset index against percentiles of per capita consumption expenditure to see how asset ownership rises with income.

Figure 9.6 shows that asset ownership is substantially higher in urban areas at any given level of per capita expenditure relative to rural households, and that household asset ownership increases with per capita consumption expenditure, particularly in urban areas. This suggests that inequality in asset ownership is higher across urban households and less so in rural areas. The graph also shows that asset ownership has increased in 2015 relative to 2004 particularly among rural households.

Figure 9.7 shows the growth rate of asset ownership between 2004 and 2015 for rural and urban areas at different percentiles in a manner that also shows inequality in asset accumulation. Figure 9.7 is essentially a growth incidence curve (GIC) for asset ownership. Asset ownership grew faster among rural households across all expenditure percentiles than urban households reflecting partly the very low asset position of rural households in 2004. Moreover, the steep slope of the urban asset GIC in Figure 9.7 indicates that asset growth was higher among high-income households than low-income households in urban areas. This suggests rising inequality in urban asset ownership while asset ownership grew proportionately across income percentiles in rural areas (for a basic non-food consumption good index providing information on some of the very poorest rural Ethiopians see Chapters 18 and 19).

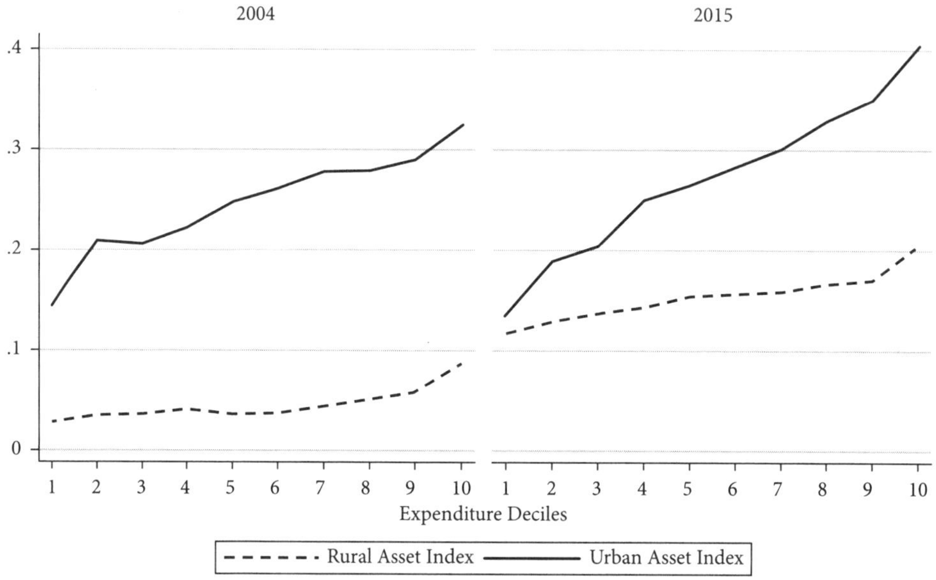

FIGURE 9.6 Asset ownership index in rural and urban areas, 2004 and 2015

Source: CSA, 'Household Income Consumption and Expenditure Report' (2017).

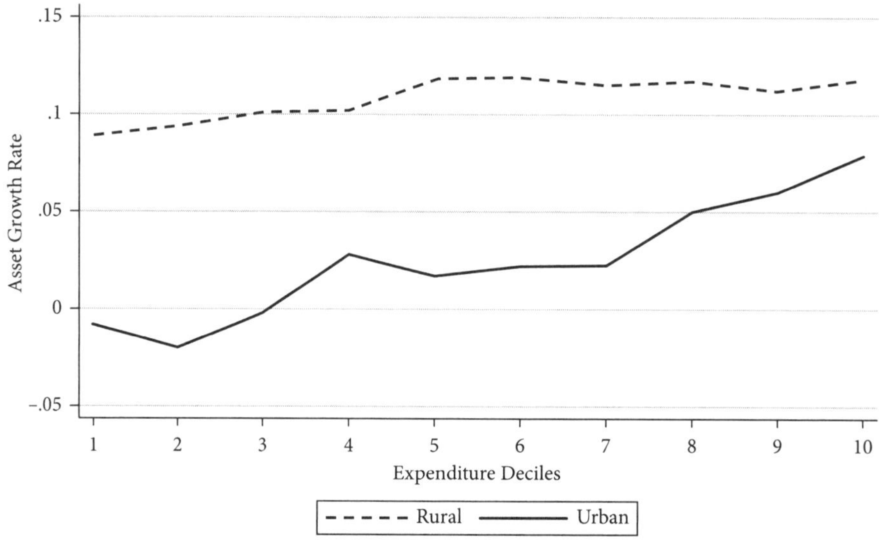

FIGURE 9.7 Asset growth incidence curve in rural and urban Ethiopia

Note: The asset GICs are calculated using household asset and consumption expenditure data from the 2004 and 2015 household surveys.

Source: CSA, 'Household Income Consumption and Expenditure Report' (2004 and 2015).

What does all this mean for demand for manufactured goods? It is very difficult to draw strong inferences from these graphs, as the asset index is just a proxy for non-food expenditure. However, Figures 9.6 and 9.7 seem to suggest that the demand for non-food consumer goods is higher in urban areas. However, the slow rate of urbanization in Ethiopia implies that overall demand for non-food consumption items, and by implication for manufactured goods, is somehow restricted by this constraint. The fact that asset inequality is rising in urban areas also suggests urban demand for non-food consumption items is driven largely by the top 20 per cent of households. It is quite encouraging that demand for non-food consumer goods increased faster in rural areas where nearly 80 per cent of the population resides. However, even in 2015 the asset position of the average rural household is half that of the average urban household. It appears that the elasticity of asset ownership with respect to income is stronger in urban areas than rural areas. For instance, moving a rural household from the bottom 10 per cent consumption basket to the top 10 per cent would increase the asset index by 9 percentage points while the same movement in urban areas will increase the asset index by 22 percentage points. While more investigation would be needed to explore this point, the simple analysis in Figures 9.6 and 9.7 suggests that the increase in rural income has not translated into substantial growth in the effective demand for non-food consumption items—at least not to the extent that would result in a major increase in consumption of manufactured goods. In other words, while growth in agriculture has helped reduce poverty in rural areas substantially, income levels remain too low to change the composition of household demand in favour of manufactured goods. Given that our asset index does not take into account differences in quality and prices, which are presumed to be higher in urban areas, the rural–urban divide in asset ownership and by implication demand for manufactures is likely to be underestimated.

9.5 Conclusions

The Ethiopian economy has come a long way to become one of the fastest-growing economies in the world. The growth experience has lifted millions out of poverty, especially in rural areas where growth in agricultural output has been strong. A big push in public investment in infrastructure (road, rail, telecommunications, and energy) as well as human capital accumulation has greatly contributed to the accelerated growth of the economy. However, the strong growth performance has not been accompanied by substantial structural transformation. The economy continues to rely heavily on smallholder agriculture while the shares of the industrial sector and manufacturing remain extremely low.

The main challenge for the Ethiopian economy, therefore, is structural transformation through diversification towards more dynamic economic activities that may have positive externalities. In this chapter, we examined the performance of agriculture and manufacturing, as these were the sectors that were targeted by direct and indirect government policies and interventions.

A major growth in agricultural productivity has to be achieved if the Ethiopian economy is to transform structurally. While application of chemical fertilizers has expanded rapidly since 1991, only half of the arable land is treated with chemical fertilizers and unlike Asian countries, most Ethiopian farmers do not practise the combined application of fertilizers, improved seeds, and irrigation. Moreover, the application of modern agricultural inputs has so far been restricted to cereals, above all maize, with limited application on agricultural items destined for export markets and for agro-processing industries. Recent efforts to increase agricultural output through private investment in commercial farms has encountered serious setbacks and needs to be revisited if it is to maximize its role in productivity growth. The combined effect of agricultural intensification and commercialization, as stated in Section 9.3, might lead to rapid growth in agriculture which in the short to medium term may keep the GDP share of agriculture at its current level, but the resulting increase in rural household income, food security, agricultural exports, and industrial raw materials will spur industrial progress in the long run.

Efforts in agriculture should also be matched by private investment in manufacturing if structural transformation is to be achieved. Efforts so far to improve economic infrastructure have not yet seen a rise in private investment in manufacturing, as discussed earlier. While the number of manufacturing firms has increased substantially since 1991, average firm size has been declining and the graduation of small firms into medium- and large-size categories has been extremely slow. A major constraint remains access to external finance as witnessed by the decline in credit to the private sector as a percentage of GDP. The investment law still seems to favour large start-ups and export-oriented firms as the incentives packages require a minimum capital threshold. However, most firms start as small ventures, as in most other countries, and it takes time for them to enter export markets. In fact, the probability of exporting increases with firm size.

References

Abegaz, B. (2018). *Industrial Development in Africa: Mapping Industrial Pathways for a Leaping Leopard* (London: Routledge).

African Union (2009). *The African Mining Vision* (Addis Ababa: African Union).

Alem, Y. and M. Söderbom (2012). 'Household-Level Consumption in Urban Ethiopia: The Effects of Food Price Shock', *World Development* 40: 146–62.

African Center for Economic Transformation (ACET) (2014). 'Growth with Depth', 2014 African Transformation Report.

Andersson, C., A. Mekonnen, and J. Stage (2011). 'Impacts of the Productive Safety Net Program in Ethiopia on Livestock and Tree Holdings of Rural Households', *Journal of Development Economics* 94 (1): 119–26.

Bachewe, F., G. Berhane, B. Minten, and A. S. Taffesse (2018). 'Agricultural Transformation in Africa? Assessing the Evidence in Ethiopia', *World Development* 105: 286–98.

Brambilla, I., D. Lederman, and G. Porto (2012). 'Exports, Export Destinations, and Skills' *American Economic Review* 102 (7): 3406–38.

Chang, H. (1994). 'State, Institutions and Structural Change', *Structural Change and Economic Dynamics* 5 (2): 293–313.

Chenery, H. (1960). 'Patterns of Industrial Growth', *American Economic Review* 50 (4): 624–53.

Chole, Eshetu (2004). *Underdevelopment in Ethiopia* (Addis Ababa: Organisation for Social Research in Eastern and Southern Africa (OSSREA)).

Christiaensen, L., L. Demery, and J. Kuhl (2011). 'The (Evolving) Role of Agriculture in Poverty Reduction: An Empirical Perspective', *Journal of Development Economics* 96 (2): 239–54.

Commission on Growth and Development (COGD) (2008). *The Growth Report: Strategies for Sustained Growth and Development* (Washington, DC: World Bank).

Dercon, S. and L. Christiaensen (2011). 'Consumption Risk, Technology Adoption and Poverty Traps: Evidence from Ethiopia', *Journal of Development Economics* 96 (2): 159–73.

Dorosh, P., E. Schmidt, and A. Shiferaw (2012). 'Economic Growth without Structural Transformation: The Case of Ethiopia', *Journal of African Development* 14: 7–40.

Durevall, D., J. L. Loening, and Y. A. Birru (2013). 'Inflation Dynamics and Food Prices in Ethiopia', *Journal of Development Economics* 104 (C): 89–106.

Financial Times (2016). 'The Great Land Rush, Ethiopia: The Billionaire's Farm', a report by Tom Burgis. https://ig.ft.com/sites/land-rush-investment/ethiopia/.

Hailu, D. and A. Shiferaw (2016). 'Job Creation and Trade in Manufactures: Industry-Level Analysis across Countries', *IZA Journal of Labor and Development* 5 (1): 1–36.

Hausmann, R., J. Hwang, and D. Rodrik (2007). 'What You Export Matters', *Journal of Economic Growth* 12: 1–25.

Hausmann, R. and B. Klinger (2007). 'The Structure of the Product Space and the Evolution of Comparative Advantage.' CID Working Paper No. 146, Kennedy School, Harvard.

Headey, D., M. Dereje, and A. S. Taffesse (2014). 'Land Constraints and Agricultural Intensification in Ethiopia: A Village-Level Analysis of High-Potential Areas', *Food Policy* 48: 129–141.

Hirschman, A. (1958). *The Strategy of Economic Development* (New Haven, CT: Yale University Press).

Imbs, J. and R. Wacziarg (2003). 'Stages of Diversification', *American Economic Review* 93: 63–86.

Kaldor, N. (1967). *Strategic Factors in Economic Development* (Ithaca, NY: Cornell University Press).

Kuznets, S. (1966). *Modern Economic Growth: Rate, Structure, and Spread* (New Haven, CT: Yale University Press).

Kuznets, S. (1971). *Economic Growth of Nations: Total Output and Production Structure* (Cambridge, MA: Harvard University Press).

Lavers, T. (2012). '"Land Grab" as Development Strategy? The Political Economy of Agricultural Investment in Ethiopia', *Journal of Peasant Studies* 39 (1): 105–32.

Moller, L. C. and K. M. Wacker (2017). 'Explaining Ethiopia's Growth Acceleration: The Role of Infrastructure and Macroeconomic Policy', *World Development* 96: 198–215.

Newman, C., J. Page, J. Rand, A. Shimeles, M. Soderbom, and F. Tarp (eds) (2016). *Manufacturing Transformation: Comparative Studies of Industrial Development in Africa and Emerging Asia* (Oxford: Oxford University Press).

Rodrik, D. (2004). 'Industrial Policy for the Twenty-First Century', mimeo, Harvard University, JFK School of Government.

Rodrik, D. (2014). 'An African Growth Miracle?' NBER Working Paper No. 20188, Cambridge, MA.

Rodrik, D. (2015). 'Premature Deindustrialization', NBER Working Paper 20935, February.

Rosenstien-Rodan, P. (1943). 'Problems of Industrialization of Eastern and South-Eastern Europe', *Economic Journal* 53: 210/211, 202–11.

Shiferaw, A. (2009). 'Which Firms Invest Less under Uncertainty? Evidence from Ethiopian Manufacturing', Working Paper No. 2, Courant Research Center-PEG, University of Goettingen.

Shiferaw, A. (2016). 'Constraints to Private Investment in a High-growth Environment: Firm-Level Evidence from Ethiopia', Working Paper 168, Economics Department, The College of William and Mary.

Shiferaw, A. and A. S. Bedi (2013). 'The Dynamic of Job Creation and Job Destruction in Sub-Saharan Africa: Evidence from Ethiopia', *Journal of African Economies* 22: 651–92.

Shiferaw, A., M. Söderbom, E. Siba, and G. Alemu (2015). 'Road Infrastructure and Enterprise Dynamics in Ethiopia', *Journal of Development Studies* 51: 1541–58.

United Nations Economic Commission for Africa (ECA) (2016). 'Transformative Industrial Policy for Africa', United Nations Economic Commission for Africa, Addis Ababa.

Verhoogen, E. (2008). 'Trade, Quality Upgrading, and Wage Inequality in the Mexican Manufacturing Sector', *Quarterly Journal of Economics* 123: 489–530.

World Bank (2015). 'SME Finance in Ethiopia: Addressing the Missing-Middle Challenge', Working Paper 96365, Washington, DC: World Bank.

Zewdu, G. (2014). 'Financial Inclusion, Regulation and Inclusive Growth in Ethiopia', ODI Working Paper 408, London: Overseas Development Institute.

CHAPTER 10

ETHIOPIAN FINANCIAL SECTOR DEVELOPMENT

YOHANNES AYALEW BIRRU

10.1 Introduction

Ethiopia has become one of the few countries in Africa that has built resilience to both internal and external headwinds and has been able to sustain a high-growth high-investment scenario. Even after the 2013 international commodity prices collapse and the 2016 drought, the country managed to sustain economic growth at near pre-commodity-price-collapse levels despite experiencing unprecedented declines in almost all prices of its major export goods and a major drought that affected about 14 million people nationwide (IMF 2017). Such resilience could partly be attributable to the financial sector, which played a key role in making the country's transition to a high-investment high-growth trajectory possible, without letting the hard-won macroeconomic stability be sacrificed.[1] For instance, as investment demand surged from 24.3 per cent of GDP in 2003 to 39.0 per cent in 2017, domestic banks expanded total outstanding credit as a percentage of GDP from 20.8 to 31.0 per cent in the same period, which was largely financed by deposits mobilization. Banks managed to expand their deposit mobilization capacity from 27.8 per cent of GDP in 2003 to 31.4 per cent in 2017.

Nonetheless, by the standards of East and South-east Asian countries during their heyday of growth, Ethiopia lags behind in terms of financial deepening and addressing the challenges of domestic savings mobilization. For instance, between 1970 and 1984, Malaysia managed to increase its M2/GDP ratio from 40.9 per cent to 102.1 per cent and its savings-to-GDP ratio from 26.9 per cent to 32.6 per cent, while in South Korea, domestic savings surged from 16.6 per cent in 1970 to 33.1 per cent in 1984. On the other

[1] With the collapse of the commodity prices and the consequent widening of the current account of the balance-of-payments deficit and the rising external debt service ratio, the economy has experienced increased pressure on the foreign exchange market since 2015.

hand, Ethiopia suffered from demonetization between 2004 and 2010, as commercial banks continued to shed non-performing loans that were mounting up in the pre-2003 period and the tight monetary policy pursued between 2006 and 2008 following the international food price crises. As a result, the broad money-to-GDP ratio declined by more than 12 percentage points in just six years, between 2004 and 2009, from 37.5 per cent to 25.4 per cent. During this period, the domestic savings-to-GDP ratio remained at its lowest level, hovering around 9 per cent on average. The trend was reversed with the launching of the first Growth and Transformation Plan (2011–15) in 2011 and the government started to play an active role in financial sector development. Consequently, the broad money-to-GDP ratio and domestic savings-to-GDP ratio surged to 31.4 per cent and 24.1 per cent in 2017, respectively.

Performance in the Eastern Africa region has been mixed. Kenya, which managed to increase its broad money-to-GDP ratio from 38.2 per cent in 2002 to 42.2 per cent in 2017, failed to translate its achievement in financial deepening into domestic savings, unlike its East Asian counterparts. Kenya's gross domestic savings-to-GDP ratio remained one of the lowest in the region, hovering around 8 per cent in the last twenty years, between 1996 and 2016. In contrast, Tanzania registered significant improvements both in financial deepening and in translating the latter into domestic savings. Between 2000 and 2015, the broad money-to-GDP ratio increased from 17.1 per cent to 24.3 per cent while the gross domestic savings-to-GDP ratio surged from 10.1 per cent to 23.2 per cent (World Bank 2017).

Against this background, this chapter analyses the recent development of the financial sector in Ethiopia, particularly the banking sector, and its contributions to macroeconomic stability and growth. The chapter focuses on the post-2003 period, the landmark year when Ethiopia embarked on a rapid economic growth trajectory. Section 10.2 presents a brief historical background of the financial sector, followed by an outline of the theoretical underpinning behind the Ethiopian financial sector reform strategy. Developments of the financial sector in the last twenty-six years since the initial reform in 1992 are explored in Sections 10.3–10.6, which also present an analysis of the financial sector's contribution to macroeconomic stability and economic growth. Section 10.7 offers conclusions.

10.2 Historical Background

Prior to 1992, the financial sector was part of a command economy system. Zeidy (1993) noted that monetary and exchange rate policies were relegated to secondary importance. The National Bank of Ethiopia directly determined the level and structure of the interest rate and exchange rate. Credits were allocated according to the central plan. The financial sector was closed to the private sector until 1994. Before the partial opening of the sector there were only three government banks, one commercial and two specialized banks—the Housing and Saving Bank and Agricultural and Industrial Bank of Ethiopia (now the Development Bank of Ethiopia). Outside the banking system, the financial sector included only one government-owned insurance company and a post office[2] until 1995.

Unlike most other sectors, after the overthrow of the Derg and the formation of the EPRDF-led transitional government in 1991, government adopted a gradual approach in the financial sector. The sector's reform began with the streamlining of monetary and exchange rate policies. Between 1992 and 1995, the NBE took a series of measures reforming the interest rate policy. The Bank transited from a sector-by-sector discriminatory interest rate structure to setting only a minimum deposit rate and a maximum lending rate. In 1995 the cap on the lending rate was lifted, and the Bank began to set only the minimum deposit rate. As noted in Ayalew (1993), in the foreign exchange market, the birr was initially devalued from 2.07 to 5 birr per US$ in October 1992 to correct the exchange rate misalignment. Then, in a move to allow the market determination of the value of the birr, a wholesale auction system was introduced in May 1993 which served for the next five years until it was finally replaced by an interbank foreign exchange market in 1999. A harmonized system of import tariffs was introduced in 1993 (Ayalew 1993).

In a move to strengthen the private sector and invigorate the market system, the financial sector was opened to Ethiopian nationals in 1994 and the remaining restrictions on the current account of the balance of payments, such as ex ante import and export price controls and import quotas, were removed. Nonetheless, in line with its gradualist approach, the government keeps the capital account of the balance of payments closed and has restricted ownership in the financial sector to Ethiopian nationals, except in the case of investment in lease financing.

10.3 Gradual Financial Sector Reform Strategies and Policies

The Ethiopian government's gradualist approach towards financial sector reform emanated from its beliefs that, first, in developing countries markets are subject to widespread failures because of underdevelopment and sometimes complete absence and, second, finance is only the means and not the end in economic development, so that government should do whatever it takes to make sure that the necessary finance is available for development projects or what are called priority sectors, such as public physical infrastructure, health, and education. The government's thoughts about financial sector reform are clearly outlined in its industrial development strategy paper (Ethiopian Federal Democratic Republic 2001). The government has continued to resist mounting

[2] The post office is the only institution that is allowed to render financial services such as money transfer on its own. Other institutions that give similar services serve must attach themselves to banks. In other words, they are allowed only to serve as agents of banks.

pressure from the International Monetary Fund and the World Bank to open up the financial sector to foreign competition. Even after more than twenty years of financial sector reform experience since 1995, and after a significant transformation in terms of assets, profitability, and prudence,[3] discussion about any form of financial sector liberalization[4] was still taboo in government circles, at least till mid-2018.

Although Ethiopia's development strategy has unique features in terms of focus and details of implementation, which are designed to fit the country's level of development and sophistication of the markets, it is clear that the strategy draws heavily on the East Asian developmental state experiences. For instance, the thought behind the gradual, managed, and limited liberalization of the capital account of the balance of payments and the resistance to opening up the financial sector to foreign investors draws on the East Asian countries' development strategies and experiences, including those of China. First, these countries focused on industrial upgrading along with a pro-investment macroeconomic policy, which did not necessarily mean low inflation and which in many cases involved state interventions that 'got prices wrong' (Öniş 1991; Chang 2006; Rodrik 2004; Addison and Ndikumana 2001). Second, as Chang (2006: 115) argues, the East Asian countries 'were more open in the areas like trade, technology and debt, but less open to foreign direct investment, and almost completely closed in relation to the capital market'. They followed a gradual liberalization approach in opening the financial sector and the capital market (Chang 2006; Stiglitz 2008). In a contribution for the African Development Bank, Lee (2017) noted: 'For an effective state activism or industrial policy, state ability for financial control was critical... In the Korean experience, the banking sector had always been expected to "serve" the real sectors by providing a stable supply of the so-called "growth money" at affordable rates, whereas manufacturing or production sectors had always been given priority.' This was possible because of the establishment of development banks and because of the strong state control of commercial banks.

Moreover, rightly or wrongly, the aftermath of the 1997–8 East Asian crisis has also influenced Ethiopia's very cautious approach.

10.4 Gradual Opening Up of the Financial Sector

There is also a rich history of theoretical and empirical debate on the role of finance in capitalism and in growth and development. The debates on whether finance leads economic growth or growth leads financial development are at least as old as the seminal papers of the two prominent economists Schumpeter (1911) and Robinson (1952). While

[3] The second five-year Growth and Transformation Plan (2016–20), which was launched in 2016, did not mention financial sector liberalization (Ethiopian Federal Democratic Government 2016).

[4] The only exception is lease financing, which is now open to foreign investors.

Schumpeter argues for indiscriminate opening of the sector, Robinson (1952) argues for guided and gradual opening. Schumpeter (1911) claims that financial development is strongly associated with real per capita GDP growth, the rate and efficiency of physical capital accumulation. McKinnon and Shaw (1973) argue that repressing the monetary system by imposing restrictions on interest rates, heavy reserve requirements on bank deposits and compulsory credit allocations 'fragments the domestic capital market with high adverse consequences for the quality and quantity of real capital accumulation' (McKinnon 1989: 206). A robust capital market requires an adequately liquid financial system and a stable monetary system (McKinnon 1989). Moreover, economists such as King and Levine (1993) argue that in a market economy, development of the financial sector determines the efficiency and proper functioning of the incentive system,[5] be it prices, interest rate, credit, or exchange rate. When the financial sector is stable and efficient,[6] economic actors gain confidence in government policies and the market, and investors are willing to take risks today trusting that the system is capable of rewarding their venture tomorrow, while, on the other hand, consumers are willing to postpone current consumption in favour of savings, fully relying on the system that they will be able to maximize consumption tomorrow. It is this coincidence of willingness of investors and consumers that enables an economy to achieve faster and sustainable economic growth, and the macro-economy to maintain a sustainable resource balance.

On the other hand, the Robinson camp argues that financial development follows economic growth. They argue that higher economic growth boosts the demand for financial services. Consequently, financial institutions and financial services expand in all dimensions, i.e. in type, quantity, and quality. Ang and McKibbin (2005: 22) argue that 'financial liberalization is unlikely to result in higher economic growth without an efficient and well-functioning financial system. To accelerate growth, the financial system must be properly shaped before undertaking any liberalization program.' De Aghion (1999) and Öniş (1991) also contend that, in developing countries, markets are not ready to provide finance to long-term development projects, which calls for these countries' governments to intervene in the market to ensure that there is adequate finance for industrial growth and that resources are directed to long-term projects by creating the necessary price distortion: the state has to 'socialize' the risk and high capital requirements of large-scale projects that may take years to generate returns, many of which are social rather than purely private returns. Therefore, unlike McKinnon and Shaw (1973), the Robinson camp favours a careful and phased approach towards financial liberalization.[7] According to the latter, the debate must not be whether to open or not to

[5] Through monetary policy and credit and exchange-rate markets.

[6] However, Ismail and Smith (1994: 457) argue that sometimes these two conditions seem to be incompatible because 'stability may come to mean over-cautiousness, whereas efficiency may entail higher risk-taking and lead to financial fragility. It then becomes important for the authorities to tread a careful path between ensuring the integrity of the financial system and enabling entrepreneurial risk.'

[7] However, Ang and McKibbin (2005) warn policymakers not to indulge in inflationary financing and provision of sub-standard loans in the name of development financing, which are equally detrimental to economic growth in the long run by creating negative externalities in the process.

open. Rather, when to open and which necessary conditions must be fulfilled before resorting to full liberalization of the sector.

A further set of arguments have emphasized the inherent instability of financial markets and the tendency for financial innovation to outstrip regulatory efforts and to aggravate cyclical tendencies to instability. Economists working in this vein draw perhaps above all on Minksy (1986), and many have argued that their ideas were validated by the global financial crisis of 2007/8, whose effects rippled out beyond the United States and other advanced economies to affect many African and other low- and middle-income economies. Recent work—especially in the wake of the financial crisis—clearly reinforces the need for caution with respect to the size and rate of growth of finance and underlines the argument for 'strong and counter-cyclical regulation of finance' (Griffith-Jones, Karwowski, and Dafe 2016).

Empirical research on this area is also divided along the lines of the above two groups. Although a growing number of empirical researchers, including King and Levine (1993) and Calderon and Liu (2003), seem to support Schumpeter's view, studies such as Atje and Jovanovic (1993), Demetriades and Hussein (1996), and Ang and McKibbin (2005), claim to disprove Schumpeter's line of argument. Using data on eighty countries over the 1960–89 period, King and Levine (1993: 717) claimed to prove Schumpeter's view that 'financial development is strongly (and causally) associated with real per capita GDP growth, the rate of physical accumulation, and improvements in the efficiency with which economies employ physical capital'. On the other hand, Ang and McKibbin (2005) challenge King and Levine's finding by arguing that there is a bias in the cross-country analysis caused by the lack of adequate time series data and that this tilts the regression findings in favour of Schumpeter's camp. Applying co-integration analysis on the Malaysian time series data between 1960 and 2001, Ang and McKibbin (2005) claim to find that, in the long run, output growth causes financial depth.

The Ethiopian government has tended to agree with the Robinson camp. The debate is not on whether to open the sector or not, rather on how and when to open it. Although markets may be relatively efficient in allocating resources, this is only the case under certain demanding conditions (Ang and McKibbin 2005). Perhaps particularly in developing countries, where markets are even more fragmented and less developed than in advanced capitalist economies, market failures are believed to be widespread. Thus, it is feared that letting 'the market' make resource allocation decisions completely freely might produce a sub-optimal allocation of very scarce resources.

In addition, as markets tend to direct resources to sectors whose benefits can be appropriated privately in full, critical sectors for long-run growth, i.e. sectors that help to expand the long-run capacity of the economy, such as public infrastructure, education, and health, will fall short of finance. In other words, if the economy does not redirect resources to development sectors, the economy will remain trapped in a vicious circle of poverty. Hence, to break the circle of poverty and turn it into a virtuous circle of growth, government must intervene to create the necessary conditions to increase the rate of domestic investment and savings and deposit mobilization. Plus, government should also make sure that mobilized resources are redirected to development projects by providing the necessary incentives and, when necessary, through direct allocation, for example, through the budget.

10.5 Gradual Liberalization of the Capital Account of the Balance of Payments

The financial sector, particularly the banking system, is one of the most sensitive sectors in developing countries, whose success or failure could have wider ramifications for the economy. Didier, Hevia, and Schmukler (2011) and Radelet and Sachs (1998) argue that financial crises can easily end up as full-blown domestic crises if they are not properly managed.[8] Countries that have been able to secure a stable and healthy financial sector, particularly the banking sector, for a relatively long period have enjoyed faster and more sustainable investment and economic growth. The East Asian experience was one of the most widely cited examples in this regard. Until the onset of the 1997–8 crises, East Asian countries enjoyed one of the fastest and most sustained growth episodes in the history of the modern world over more than three decades. Until the beginning of the 1990s, the capital accounts of many of the East Asian Tigers were well protected (Radelet and Sachs 1998).

Moreover, many of these countries continued to offer preferential treatment to their strategic sectors such as the export and infrastructure sectors, including using intentional undervaluation of their exchange rates and providing low-cost credit. The foreign exchange market was tightly regulated and effectively protected from domestic and external speculative attacks. This makes it possible for the government to intervene in the credit and foreign exchange market to redirect resources to the productive sectors, using either subsidized interest rate, undervalued exchange rate, or direct credit.

Some studies published after the 1997 crises argue that liberalization of the capital account was the main culprit for the onset of the most debilitating economic crisis in the region's modern history. Stiglitz (2008) argues that immediately after the opening up of the capital account, East Asian countries experienced unprecedented inflows of short-term private capital, attracted by high returns and a booming economy. According to the estimates by Radelet and Sachs (1998: 9), 'total foreign bank lending to the five East Asian countries expanded from \$210 billion at end-1995, to \$261 billion at the end-1996, an increase of 24 per cent in a single year'.[9] Consequently, on the one hand, banks began to feel over-liquid, put strong downward pressure on domestic interest rates, and

[8] Many of the major international economic crises that happened in the second half of the twentieth century and the twenty-first century could be, in one way or another, attributable to crises in the financial sector, including the 1929–33 Great Depression, the 1980s debt crisis in Latin America, the 1987 US stock market crash, the 1997–8 East Asian crisis, and the 2007 international financial crisis.

[9] The five East Asian countries are Indonesia, Korea, Malaysia, the Philippines, and Thailand.

pushed real-estate prices artificially high while, on the other hand, central banks were unable to apply counter-cyclical policies due to unprecedented private capital inflow.[10] For instance, the sudden and unprecedented inflow of private portfolios led local currencies to appreciate against the US dollar, prices of goods and services to increase, return to capital of banks to surge, and prices of money to go down.

Then, when investors feel that there is a problem in the fundamentals of the economy, the pressure to withdraw their capital starts to mount to avoid sudden losses as a result of depreciation of the domestic currency or collapse of the economy. Sudden withdrawal of capital by foreign investors causes economies to fall into a liquidity crunch and a rise in interest rates, which, in turn, leaves many firms unable to repay loans. For instance, in 1996, the non-performing loans (NPLs) ratio surged to between 8 per cent in South Korea and 14 per cent in the Philippines.[11] In just a little more than three years of capital account liberalization, it became evident that the new system had significant shortcomings. Returns on investment began to falter, causing investors to worry about the stability of the macro-economy. Consequently, those worried domestic and foreign investors began to short-sell their asset holdings and withdraw, catching the East Asian economies, whose fundamentals had stayed sound for about three decades uninterrupted, off guard. For instance, more than US$100 billion were withdrawn from the ASEAN countries and Korea in the space of the eighteen months after the Thai baht devaluation. Finally, those proud East Asian countries found themselves suddenly forced to go cap in hand to the IMF for major bail-outs (Radelet and Sachs 1998).[12] The rationale for the restriction of the capital account in Ethiopia has, therefore, emanated from its interventionist approach to addressing market failure. Accordingly, foreign residents are neither allowed to invest in the financial sector nor to purchase domestic financial securities, such as treasury bills or bonds. Domestic residents, except banks, are also not allowed to buy foreign financial securities or to deposit their assets in foreign banks.

10.6 Financial Sector Performance and Implications for Economic Growth and Stability

10.6.1 Financial Sector Performance

Ethiopia has achieved significant progress in terms of financial sector growth, adopting a gradualist approach and government intervention in the credit and foreign exchange

[10] For Radelet and Sachs (1998) the 1997–8 crisis bears witness to the shortcomings of the international capital market and its vulnerability to sudden reversal of confidence.

[11] In Thailand and Indonesia, NPLs reached 13 per cent each in the same period.

[12] The bailout money requested reached US$50 billion.

market. On the other hand, in terms of financial market development, Ethiopia still lags behind many of its African peers such as Kenya, Tanzania, Ghana, and Nigeria. The money market is underdeveloped, and there is neither a debt nor an equity market. It is highly likely that the absence of these markets might negatively affect the economy through lack of market-based price discovery or availability of alternative financing mechanisms. However, from the deposit mobilization and credit allocation perspectives, Ethiopia has achieved impressive results compared to its peers.

Figure 10.1 shows that, in the last seven years, between 2010 and 2017, total banking sector assets as a share of GDP registered significant growth only in Ethiopia and Ghana. Moreover, the increase in the ratio implies that the sector was growing faster than other sectors of the economy. On the other hand, Kenya and Nigeria experienced a marginal decline in total banking sector assets. Figure 10.2 indicates that Ethiopia lags behind Kenya in terms of financial deepening, as measured by broad money-to-GDP ratio.

Ethiopia's financial sector growth has been uneven. Based on the government's policy focus and the sector's performance, the development process can be divided into three distinct phases since the initial year of the reform in 1992: Phase I (1992–2003), Phase II (2004–10), and Phase III (2011–17).

During the first phase, government policy focused on macroeconomic stabilization and restoring growth after seventeen years of negative annual average per capita growth of 1.9 per cent. Supported by the IMF and World Bank, in this period, the country adopted successive three-year structural adjustment and economic stabilization programmes. The main focus of macroeconomic policies was eliminating monetary overhang, which was believed to be one of the main reasons for the build-up of inflationary pressure (inflation rising to 22 per cent in 1992). Measures were taken to shrink the central bank balance sheet through a government domestic debt repayment programme and by raising the minimum deposit interest rate to 12 per cent. By contrast with the situation in the second and third phases, the average real interest rate for the period reached positive 5 per cent (see Figure 10.2). On the other hand, as the financial sector

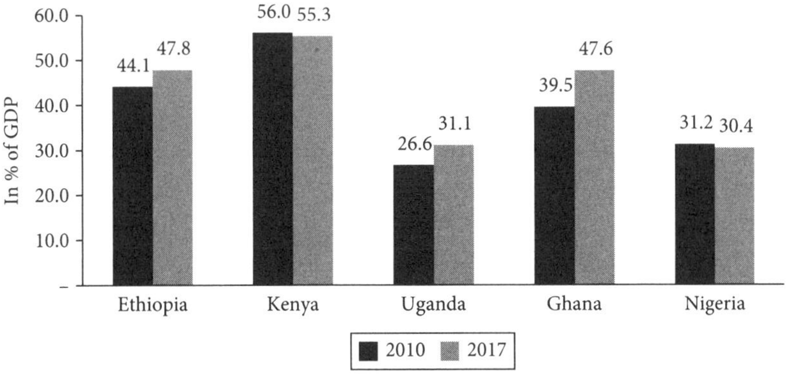

FIGURE 10.1 Total banking sector assets
Source: NBE and IMF-SSA Regional Economic Outlook.

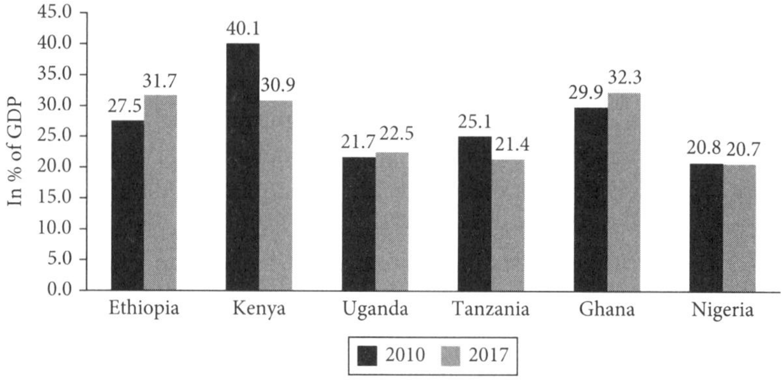

FIGURE 10.2 Broad money, per cent of GDP

Source: NBE and IMF-SSA Regional Economic Outlook.

was now open to the private sector, new private banks joined the market. However, as shown in Figure 10.3, lack of experience in project analysis and absence of information on the quality of customers led to a historically high non-performing loans ratio of 38.3 per cent. Another significant development in this period was that government secured IMF/World Bank-initiated external debt relief, which widened the fiscal space, further lowering the demand for central bank financing.

In Phase II (2004–10), as the consolidation of the monetary and fiscal balance sheets had been completed, government began to reorient the economy towards growth. Monetary and fiscal policies were relaxed. Therefore, as depicted in Figure 10.2, the base money bar, central bank's balance sheet expanded significantly. On the other hand, claims on the private sector began to shrink as banks continued to shed non-performing loans from their balance sheet. While the central bank balance sheet saw rapid expansion, with a growth rate of 20.8 per cent, compared to the other two periods this was the only period when commercial banks' balance sheet expansion fell below the central bank's balance sheet growth. Consequently, NPL ratios fell significantly (Figures 10.3 and 10.4).

Phase III (2011–17) was the period when government launched the first and second five-year Growth and Transformation Plans: GTP-I (2011–15) and GTP-II (2016–20). Unlike the first two phases, in Phase III the financial sector was assigned a special role in addressing the huge financing gap identified in the plan. In 2010, a year before the first five-year plan was launched, the domestic savings-to-GDP ratio was less than 10 per cent; but government planned to raise the investment-to-GDP ratio from 24 to 28 per cent, further widening the financing gap to 18 per cent. Hence, the financial sector needed to intensify its deposit mobilization efforts. Additionally, the government planned to undertake huge infrastructure projects and was determined to meet the Millennium Development Goals in health and education. As depicted in Figures 10.3 and 10.4, this was the period when commercial banks registered a significant growth in deposit and loan expansion while, on the other hand, banks' soundness indicators improved dramatically.

Moreover, the government has made substantial progresses in terms of bank branch expansion and financial inclusion. As depicted in Figure 10.5, the number of commercial

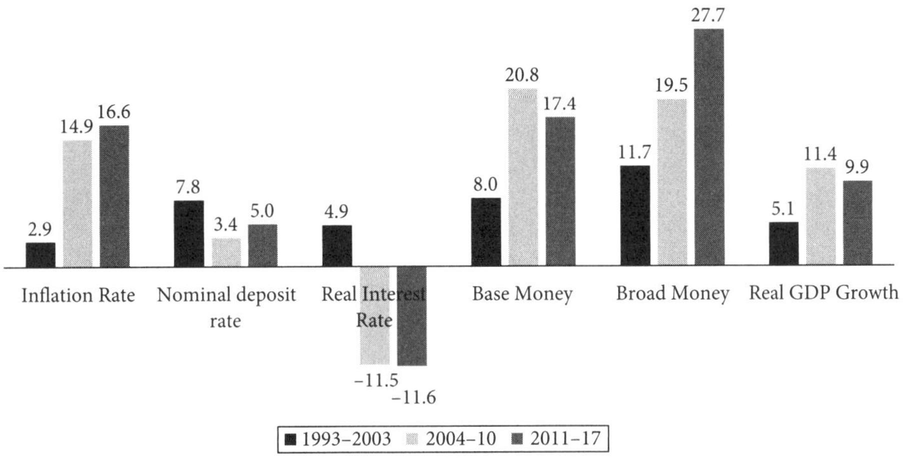

FIGURE 10.3 Selected macro indicators

Source: National Bank of Ethiopia (2017) (unpublished).

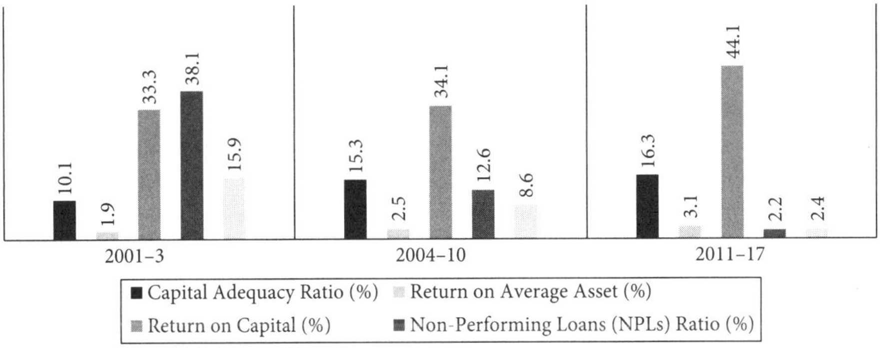

FIGURE 10.4 Banks' soundness indicators (annual average)

Source: National Bank of Ethiopia (2017) (unpublished).

bank branches increased by more than five fold, between 2010 and 2017, from 681 to 4257. As a result, population per bank branch dropped from 115,712 to 21,940 in the same period. These were made possible through the following ways. First, the NBE advised the Commercial Bank of Ethiopia (CBE), the largest government owned bank, to take the lead in opening more branches outside Addis Ababa and pave the way for private banks to follow. Accordingly, in 2011, CBE managed to open more than 100 branches and the private banks immediately followed. Second, the NBE introduced a financial security called the 'NBE Bill', an instrument, which demands each private commercial bank to allocate every 27 per cent of its total loans disbursed a every month for the purchase of the Bill.[13] The outstanding amount of NBE-Bills held by private banks reached

[13] The Bill has a five-year maturity and the NBE pays 3 per cent interest per annum on it. Then, the NBE automatically transfers the fund to the Development Bank of Ethiopia at 3 per cent interest. The latter uses the fund to finance medium and long-term private-sector investment projects.

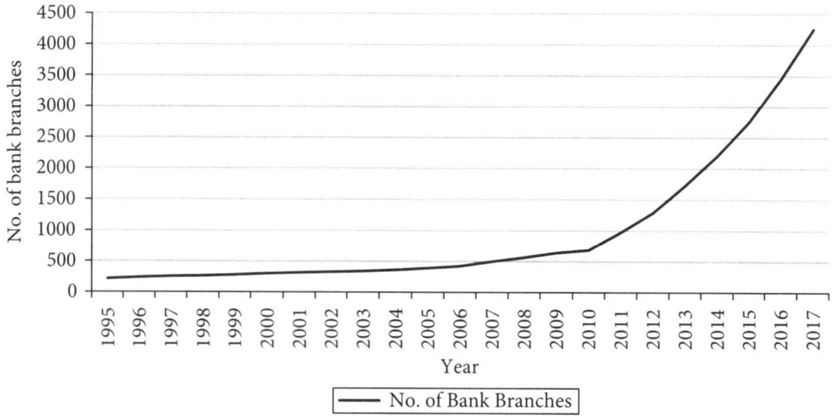

FIGURE 10.5 Bank branch expansion

Source: National Bank of Ethiopia (2017) (unpublished).

68.9 billion birr in 2017. Practically, this left private banks in need of more liquidity to protect their share of loan disbursement to the rest of the economy and remain as profitable as before. Hence, in search of more deposits, they began to aggressively open new branches including in areas which had never seen any bank branch before.

In terms of development banking, all was not so rosy. With the launching of GTP-I, the role of the Development Bank of Ethiopia in financing development projects intensified. The total assets increased by more than 470 per cent between 2010 and 2017 from 9.2 billion birr to 53.1 billion birr, and its branches numbered 110 in 2017 from just thirty-two in 2010. On the other hand, DBE's non-performing loans ratio surged to 20.5 per cent in 2017 from 9.1 per cent in 2013. This suggests the government needs to think deeply and strategically about its current development banking model (De Aghion 1999; Di John 2016).

However, relative to Ethiopia's regional peers, the domestic capital market is absent, the money market is less developed, and the foreign exchange market is less flexible. The current impressive growth is not sustainable as Ethiopia transitions from investment-led growth to productivity- and efficiency-led expansion. As the economy becomes more complex and the country's integration into international markets intensifies, the importance of price discoveries and efficient use of resources will increase significantly if the country is to remain competitive in the international market.

10.6.2 Implications for Macroeconomic Stability and Growth

Ethiopia's financial sector development is found to have a significant positive impact on macroeconomic stability and growth. In terms of efficiency and allocation of resources to economic sectors, banks continue to show strong improvement from one phase to the next, despite the shift in the government's focus from stabilization to growth. As is clearly evident from Figure 10.6, interest rate spreads continue to decline. On the other hand, the inflation rate experiences surges in both Phase II and Phase III, partly reflecting the effect of government policy reorientation towards growth and partly thanks to imported inflation resulting from international food price rises in 2006–7 and 2012 (Durevall, Loening, and Birru 2013).

The financial sector has also made an unprecedented contribution to domestic savings mobilization to finance the surge in investment demand as per the GTP. As depicted in Figure 10.7, the bank deposit-to-GDP ratio climbed from 25.9 per cent in 2010 to 31.4 per cent in 2017.

As shown in Figure 10.8, the composition of loans has shifted in favour of public sector credit. The government's increased demand for finance for infrastructure projects is reflected in the sharp rise of public sector outstanding credit since 2010, coinciding with the launch of GTP-I.

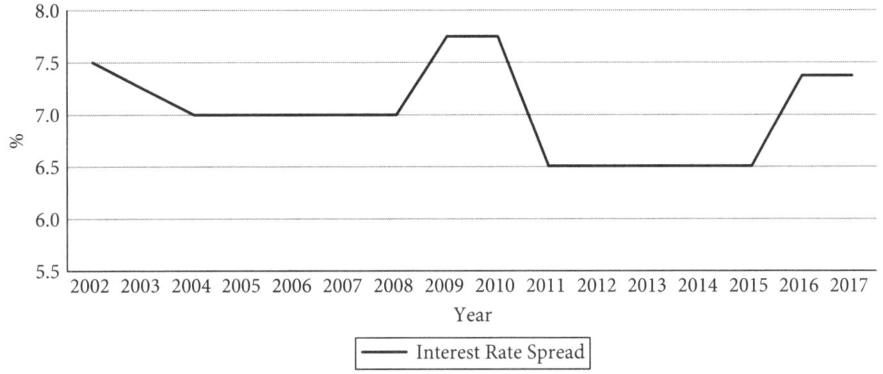

FIGURE 10.6 Interest rate spread

Source: National Bank of Ethiopia (2017) (unpublished).

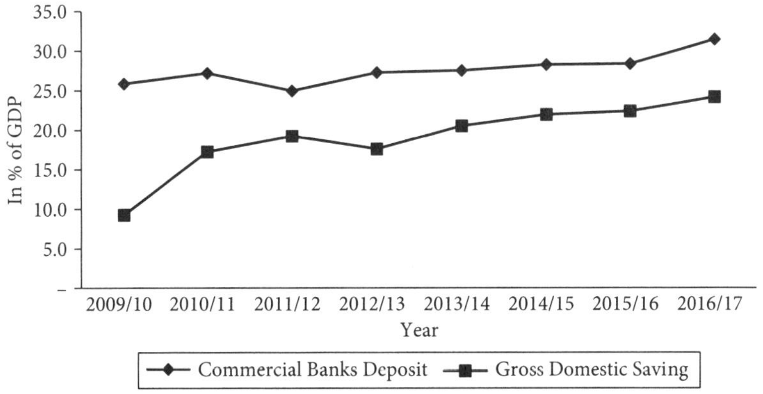

FIGURE 10.7 Banks' deposit and gross domestic savings

Source: NBE and MoFEC.

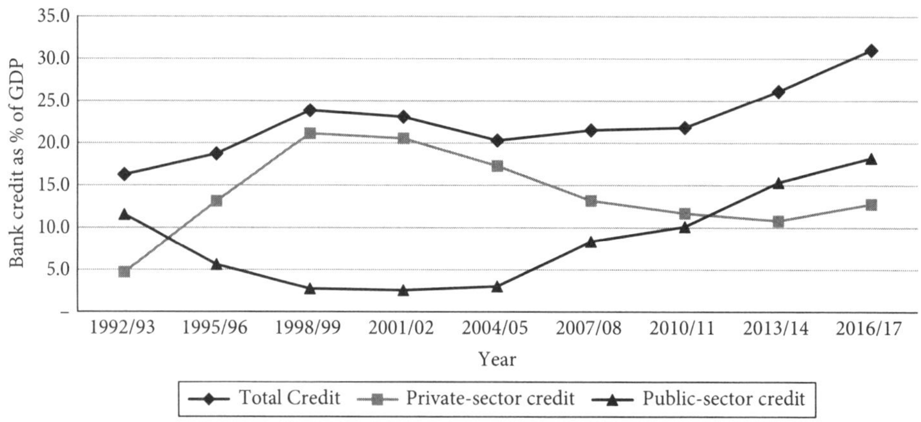

FIGURE 10.8 Bank credit

Source: National Bank of Ethiopia.

As the economy grows more complex while financial sector policy has remained more or less where it was in 2000, the challenges on the macroeconomic front have intensified. The balance-of-payments crisis that intensified after 2015 was a reflection partly of the less flexible foreign exchange market and partly of the collapse in international commodity prices. In terms of the foreign exchange market, the exchange rate remained overvalued for the last six years to 2017 despite the sharp decline in exports and the widening gap between the official and parallel market exchange rates. The wedge between the official and the parallel market exchange rates reached about 30 per cent in May 2018 from less than 5 per cent in May 2014.

10.7 Conclusion

The financial sector has played a key role in Ethiopia's economic development, particularly since the launching of the first Growth and Transformation Plan. Although Ethiopia's financial sector growth generally followed output growth in the first two phases, government has started to play a key role in accelerating the sector's growth through active interventions. Consequently, the number of bank branches expanded from 681 to 4,257 in just seven years between 2010 and 2017 while the deposit-to-GDP ratio rose from 25.9 per cent to 31.4 per cent in the same period.

However, as the economy has been expanding very rapidly and shifting from volume (investment)-based growth to price- and market-led growth, price discovery and efficient allocation of financial resources have become increasingly important. In this context, there may be a case for rethinking policy. Whether a strategy could be developed that allowed for faster change in the finance sector and capital markets without exposing Ethiopia to the full force of liberalization and the very evident risks that accompany this remained, at the pivotal moment of 2018, to be seen. Clearly, there was by 2018 a case for financial sector reform, but the government needed still to heed the multiple warnings about the risks of unbridled financial liberalization.

There is growing evidence that inflexibility in the foreign exchange market has been negatively affecting the long-term growth prospects of the country. The country remains less competitive in international markets and the foreign exchange market imbalance loomed large. Again this signalled a need perhaps to inject some form of flexibility in the foreign exchange market or at least to push for a major export earnings drive of the kind the Korean government adopted in the late 1970s that effectively prevented its debt problem becoming a debt crisis.

Finally, development banking is one of the most important sectors for the government to realize its long-term growth vision. However, the mounting non-performing loans ratio sends a message to the government that the current model is unsustainable. So, there is a need to reconsider a more moderate development banking strategy that involves the participation of more diversified actors, including the private sector, and/or a more effective and selective approach to development banking.

References

Addison, T. and L. Ndikumana (2001). 'Overcoming the Fiscal Crisis of the African State', WIDER Discussion Papers No. 2001/12, World Institute for Development Economics (UNU-WIDER).

Ang, J. B. and W. J. McKibbin (2005). 'Financial Liberalization, Financial Sector Development and Growth: Evidence from Malaysia', Centre for Applied Macroeconomic Analysis Working Paper Series.

Atje, R. and B. Jovanovic (1993). 'Stock Markets and Development', *European Economic Review* 37 (2–3): 632–40.

Ayalew, Y. (1993). 'Trade Liberalization Policy and the Prospects of the Private Sector in Export Promotion: The Case of Ethiopia.' in *The Ethiopian Economy: Problems and Prospects of Private Sector Development*, ed. Getachew Yoseph and Abdulhamid B. Kello, Third Annual Conference on the Ethiopian Economy (Addis Ababa): 177–90.

Calderón, C. and L. Liu (2003). 'The Direction of Causality between Financial Development and Economic Growth', *Journal of Development Economics* 72 (1): 321–34.

Chang, H.-J. (ed.) (2006). *Rethinking Development Economics* (London: Anthem Press).

De Aghion, B. A. (1999). 'Development Banking', *Journal of Development Economics* 58 (1): 83–100.

Demetriades, P. O. and K. A. Hussein (1996). 'Does Financial Development Cause Economic Growth? Time-Series Evidence from 16 Countries', *Journal of Development Economics* 51 (2): 387–411.

Didier, T., C. Hevia, and S. L. Schmukler (2011). 'How Resilient Were Emerging Economies to the Global Crisis?' Policy Research Working Paper 5637, World Bank, Washington, DC.

Di John, Jonathan (2016). 'What Is the Role of National Development Banks in Late Industrialization?' Issues Papers on Structural Transformation and Industrial Policy No. 010–2016, EDRI, SOAS, and AFD.

Durevall, D., J. L. Loening, and Y. A. Birru (2013). 'Inflation Dynamics and Food Prices in Ethiopia', *Journal of Development Economics* 104: 89–106.

Ethiopian Federal Democratic Republic (2001). 'Ethiopian Federal Democratic Republic Government Industrial Development Strategy' (Amharic version), Government Communication Affairs Office, Addis Ababa.

Ethiopian Federal Democratic Government (2016). 'The Second Growth and Transformation Plan (2016–2020)', National Planning Commission, Addis Ababa.

Griffith-Jones, S., E. Karwowski, and F. Dafe (2016). 'A Financial Sector to Support Development in Low Income Countries', in *Achieving Financial Stability and Growth in Africa*, ed. S. Griffith-Jones and R. Gottschalk (Oxford: Routledge): 1–20.

International Monetary Fund (2017). 'The Federal Republic of Ethiopia: Staff Concluding Statement of the 2017 Article IV Mission', IMF, Washington, DC.

Ismail, A. G. and P. Smith (1994). 'Financial Deregulation in Malaysian Banking', *Savings and Development* 18 (4): 457–72.

King, R. G. and R. Levine (1993). 'Finance and Growth: Schumpeter Might Be Right', *The Quarterly Journal of Economics* 108 (3): 717–37.

Lee, Keun (2017). 'Financing Industrial Development in Korea and Implications for Africa', How they did it (HDI) series, African Development Bank.

McKinnon, Ronald (1989). 'Case against Financial Repression', in *Leading Issues in Economic Development*, ed. Gerald M. Meier (Oxford: Oxford University Press): 205–11.

McKinnon, R. and E. Shaw (1973). *Financial Deepening in Economic Development* (Washington, DC: Brookings Institution).

Minksy, H. (1986). *Stabilizing an Unstable Economy* (New Haven, CT: Yale University Press; 2nd edition 2008, New York: McGraw-Hill).

Önis, Z. (1991). 'The Logic of the Developmental State', *Comparative Politics* 24 (1): 109–126.

Radelet, S. and J. Sachs (1998). 'The Onset of the East Asian Financial Crisis', NBER Working Paper No. w6680, National Bureau of Economic Research.

Robinson, Joan (1952). 'The Generalization of the General Theory', in *The Rate of Interest and Other Essays* (London: Macmillan): 67–142.

Rodrik, D. (2004). 'Industrial Policy for the Twenty-First Century' CEPR Discussion Paper No. 4767, Centre for Economic Policy Research, London.

Schumpeter, J. A. (1911). *The Theory of Economic Development*, reprinted 1969 (Oxford: Oxford University Press).

Stiglitz, J. E. (2008). 'Capital Market Liberalization, Globalization, and the IMF', in *Capital Market Liberalization and Development*, ed. Jose Antonio Ocampo and Joseph E. Stiglitz (Oxford: Oxford University Press): 76–100.

World Bank (2017). World Development Indicators.

Zeidy, I. A. (1993). 'The Impact of Monetary Control and Fiscal Contraction on Private Sector Development in Ethiopia's Stabilization and Adjustment Program', in *The Ethiopian Economy: Problems and Prospects of Private Sector Development*, ed. Getachew Yoseph and Abdulhamid B. Kello, Third Annual Conference on the Ethiopian Economy (Addis Ababa): 143–60.

CHAPTER 11

FINANCING ETHIOPIA'S DEVELOPMENT

MEKONNEN MANYAZEWAL

11.1 Introduction

After the overthrow of the Derg regime in May 1991, the incoming EPRDF-led government introduced new development policies and strategies to transform the Ethiopian economy and to tackle the widespread poverty and marginalization in the country. From 1992/3 onwards, a series of economic reform programmes were implemented, with assistance from the IMF, World Bank, and bilateral donors. These short-term programmes (ESAF 1 and 2) implemented as part of SDRP and PASDEP helped to stabilize the economy and engender economic recovery (MoFED 2007). However, it was not until the adoption of the first Growth and Transformation Plan (GTP-I) in 2010 that the foundations for accelerated growth, industrialization, and structural transformation of the Ethiopian economy were laid down. Central to the whole industrialization agenda has been the massive investment in critical infrastructure, such as roads, rail networks, power generation, and irrigation. The ambitious plan articulated in the GTP required huge resources. Accordingly, Ethiopia took measures to mobilize both domestic and external resources—with resource flows showing a significant increase, thereby enhancing Ethiopia's capacity to finance huge investment in infrastructure including power, railways, roads, and telecommunications as well as investment in human capital.

But as the implementation of GTP picked up momentum, achieving structural change through industrialization and export diversification became steadily more challenging as a result of a severe foreign exchange constraint in the face of poor export performance. This was compounded by the reluctance of key lenders such as China to keep their cheque books open for Ethiopia. The resolution of this financing constraint is fundamental if Ethiopia is to realize its 'Renaissance' vision. Meanwhile, tax revenue remained very low, despite rising in recent years.

The objective of this chapter is, therefore, to examine the state of Ethiopia's' development finance—its evolution, policies, financing sources, and instruments employed. It also identifies emerging financing constraints and possible options to adequately and sustainably finance the unfinished agenda of growth and economic transformation through rapid industrialization.

11.2 The Development Policy Context

The central development agenda for the Ethiopian government is to eradicate poverty and improve the living standards of the Ethiopian people. Overall development strategies and sectoral policies adopted since 1992/3 are informed by these overriding objectives. The choice of an Agricultural Development-Led Industrialization Strategy (ADLI) points to this fact. ADLI was designed to serve as a springboard for rapid and broad-based growth and structural transformation and was accompanied by a big push in investment in infrastructure and human capital (MoFED 2006; MoFED 2010; see also Chapter 26). By the early 2000s, however, the limitations of an agricultural-led industrialization strategy exclusively focused on raising the productivity of peasant farming were recognized. ADLI interventions could not create opportunities for smallholders working in different agro-ecology and farming systems to exploit the comparative advantage of their specific area. The strategy underestimated the limitation of technology-oriented intervention to solve the complex and many-faceted problems in low-potential areas, particularly in the north.

In 2010, the government adopted the Growth and Transformation Plan (GTP)—an ambitious development strategy aimed at promoting industrialization to create employment and income on a sustained basis to reduce poverty (MoFED 2010). The effort made by the government to accelerate growth and diversify the economy through the implementation of a series of development plans, including the GTP, helped lead to double-digit GDP growth for more than a decade. From 2000/1 the economy grew on average by 10 per cent per annum with per capita income growing rapidly. The national poverty level steadily declined from 45.5 per cent in 1995/6 to 38.7 per cent in 2004/5, subsequently declining to 23.5 per cent in 2015/16 (NPC 2017). Despite impressive growth, however, poverty is still a major development challenge.

Economic growth and addressing the complex development needs of Ethiopia obviously requires scaled-up and sustained investment in the priority areas identified in the development plans. During GTP-II, gross fixed capital formation is expected to reach 41.3 per cent of GDP in 2019/20 while the share of domestic saving in GDP is expected to be 29.6 per cent by the end of the GTP-II period (NPC 2016). Looking at GTP-II's demand for foreign exchange, it is projected to be US$119.5 million while supply of foreign exchange is expected to reach US$115.3 billion leaving a gap of US$3.8 billion. Supply of foreign exchange is planned to be mobilized from exports of goods and services, official transfers, foreign direct investment (FDI), and external borrowing. Given the reality of foreign exchange constraints and weak export performance, financing is bound to affect the attainment of the GTP-II planned targets. This inevitably calls for an aggressive and innovative approach to address the financing gap.

Investment is a key driver of the rapid economic growth on the demand side. In Ethiopia, the investment rate, which stood at 40 per cent during the GTP-I period, has been a key driver of economic growth thus far. Domestic saving has increased significantly, particularly in recent years, reaching about 22 per cent of GDP in 2015/16. While the effort of increasing the rate of domestic saving from a mere 9.5 per cent in 2009/10 to about 22 per cent in 2014/15 through various instruments is commendable, the large resource gap—of the order of 18 per cent—clearly shows that foreign savings play an important role in financing investment in Ethiopia (MoFED 2010).

The gap between savings and investment in Ethiopia has been filled by additional resources from foreign savings in the form of aid, foreign direct investment, and external loans. For a developing country like Ethiopia with limited resources, relying on foreign savings to jump-start and drive economic growth is not unusual. The reason is that it is generally difficult to mobilize sufficient resources through taxation where the tax base is narrow. Growth theories and the experience of other countries, however, demonstrate that heavy and increasing dependence on foreign finance is unsustainable, though the key issue is not the level of foreign financing but what the financing is used for by the recipient country. There are observations, however, that foreign financing shows more volatility compared to domestic revenue (Lane and Bulir 2002). More often than not, foreign financing is influenced by political considerations affecting its predictability (Alesina and Dollar 2000). Moreover, global economic downturns affect the economic performance of donors. This, in turn, affects their decisions about aid (Dang, Knack, and Halsey Rogers 2013).

Considering the unpredictability of donor funding, besides the desire by countries to maintain policy space, it is imperative that Ethiopia gradually shift its reliance on foreign sources of finance towards domestic resource mobilization to meet its development ambitions. This will entail a host of domestic policies on tax administration, investment, and spending. Effective mobilization of domestic resources through taxation is meaningless if there is inefficiency in investment and project management. These are particularly significant for Ethiopia, which considers itself a developmental state that views policy space, autonomy, and ownership among its key defining characteristics.

Paradoxically, Ethiopia seems to have been able to protect a considerable degree of policy independence despite relying rather heavily on external finance. How is this possible? One explanation often advanced is that this has been possible because of the coherence of domestic policy, combined with judicious exploitation of geo-strategic significance (Cheru 2016). In this way, Ethiopia has been a modern-day example of what the East Asian Tiger economies achieved during what Amsden (in *Escape from Empire*) called the 'first American Empire', when the motto of that empire was 'you do it your way'—rather than 'do it our way', which has been the motto of the second American Empire.

11.3 Financing Growth and Development

11.3.1 Fiscal Policy as an Instrument of Macroeconomic Stability for Growth

It is axiomatic to say that macroeconomic stability is a necessary condition for sustained long-term economic growth. Fiscal policy is key to that stability. Overall, Ethiopia has managed to maintain a stable macroeconomic environment, though there has been a period of inflationary pressures partly induced by external economic factors. This in turn is made possible through a judicious combination of fiscal, monetary, and financial sector policies.

The tool being used to ensure a supportive role for fiscal and monetary policy is the Macroeconomic and Fiscal Framework (MEFF). The MEFF provides a medium-term resource envelope and indicative allocation to priority sectors identified as critical for accelerated growth and poverty reduction. It carefully takes an inventory of available resources (both internal and external) and sets the medium-term envelope. It also sets a feasible level of deficit financing over the medium term.

The strategy is to include priority projects even if there is no apparent budgetary source allocated for these projects. Resource mobilizations are set in motion as the implementation of the plan proceeds. This was the experience during GTP-I for key infrastructure projects including railway projects now completed and those under construction. One instrument used when bids are issued for the construction of the projects is a requirement for prospective contractors to come up with a financing package with acceptable terms and conditions. This gives potential contractors a signal not to expect financing from the government. This strategy ensures that priority projects are not left out due to shortage of finance.

There is a lot of preparatory work before financing. Planned projects will only be ready for implementation when finance is made available. The second strategy requires that the plans are implemented through annual plans and budgets. These are subjected to close examination and vetting to ensure that planned implementation is based on reasonably available domestic and external resources. The strength and discipline of this vetting process underlie the supportive role of fiscal and monetary policies in financing growth and transformation in an overall stable macroeconomic environment. Nevertheless, despite the attempt by the authorities to ensure a stable macroeconomic environment, Ethiopia has experienced periods of high inflation with serious welfare loss for people on low incomes. It also created pressure on the birr to appreciate, affecting export competitiveness. This was particularly the case during 2006/7–2008/9 and 2010/11–2012/13. The inflationary pressure was largely driven by food inflation, averaging 32.2 per cent during 2006/7–2008/9 and 23.7 per cent during the 2010/11–2012/13 period (NBE 2017a).

During periods of inflationary pressure three approaches are used by policymakers to reduce inflation to single digit. The first addresses supply-side constraints, particularly supply of basic commodities, primarily through imports (applicable taxes are waived) to arrest inflationary expectations. The second employs tight fiscal and monetary policies. And, in the third, the budget deficit is limited with no deficit financing from the National Bank and the start of new projects is postponed. The financing of the budget is limited to the available level of domestic revenue and to disbursing external loans and assistance (Figure 11.1). The disbursement from the Treasury is very much aligned with the cash flow prevailing at any given point in time. These and other accompanying measures helped to tame inflation and restore macroeconomic stability in recent years. After a period of inflationary pressure, inflation quickly fell to single digit. During 2010/11–2012/13, for example, average inflation was 23.7 per cent; in subsequent years ending in 2016/17 inflation fell to an average of 8.1 per cent (NBE 2017a).

There are debates about how sustainable over time the development model and macroeconomic management really are. The World Bank and the IMF have often been uncomfortable with the unorthodox development approach of Ethiopia and they still raise significant questions of sustainability (Moller and Wacker 2017), but others (see, for example, Chapter 13), argue that fears for sustainability are exaggerated. With the beginning of the implementation of GTP-II, increasingly officials and observers acknowledged a serious balance-of-payments problem owing primarily to continued poor performance of exports, including manufacturing exports as envisaged in GTP-I. Cognizant of these dangers, in June 2018 the government announced a major economic reform programme, including the privatization of key state-owned enterprises and a gradual liberalization of the economy. Time will tell if these new measures will reverse the poor performance of exports and relieve the severe foreign exchange shortages.

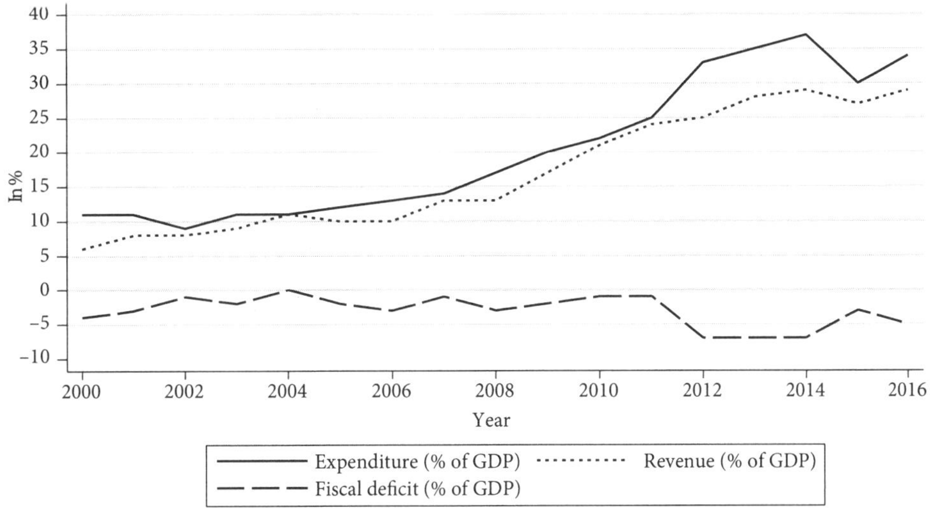

FIGURE 11.1 Government revenue and expenditure (per cent of GDP), 2000–16

Source: MoFEC (2017) (unpublished).

11.3.2 Mobilizing Domestic Resources

One of the early reform areas focused on by the economic reform programme was to reorient fiscal policy towards supporting resource mobilization and restructuring public expenditure to focus on productive sectors, infrastructure, and human development. The first phase of the programme, covering 1992/3–1994/5, focused primarily on stabilizing and jump-starting the economy after decades of command-economy management. The second phase of the reform programme—1995/6–1997/8—was designed to continue to strengthen the macroeconomic environment and promote more private-sector investment. The third phase covered the Enhanced Structural Adjustment Facility (ESAF)—1996/7–1998/9. The objective was to deepen the reform that had begun earlier so as to achieve rapid economic growth and reduce poverty in a stable macroeconomic environment. This programme did not continue after the first year due to differences with the IMF on the policy package to be implemented.

The government felt the policy package envisaged by the IMF undermined policy ownership and the sovereign right to set national development policy and priorities. This controversy is discussed in Stiglitz (2002). Central to the differences in policy was the IMF's insistence on the break-up of the Commercial Bank of Ethiopia, the opening of the banking sector to foreign banks, the liberalization of financial markets so as to allow free market determination of interest rates, and using the grants that Ethiopia was to receive during the programme to build reserves as a cushion. As can be imagined, the donors want to see what they are giving, and government wants to build the schools, health centres, and so on that are essential for communities. The controversy signalled the ever-present fiscal risk that Ethiopia lives with as an aid-dependent country. It underlines the significance of enhancing domestic resource mobilization, which Ethiopia embarked upon as a matter of strategic importance—including the diversified exports growth which is central to its vulnerabilities.

Accordingly, tax reforms were implemented to widen the tax base and to increase efficiency. These reforms included benchmarking and adapting working systems, automating the system, and organizational innovation such as the creation of a Large Taxpayers Unit. Tax administration was overhauled, and an institutional capacity-building programme was designed and implemented. New taxes were introduced, including VAT. As a result of these actions, over the years, tax revenue has been steadily increasing, with average growth of 31 per cent during the first GTP. Combined with restraint on recurrent expenditure, public finances were able to make a partial contribution to the capital budget. However, in recent years revenue has been losing dynamism (Figure 11.2). As a share of GDP, total revenue showed a decline from 16.2 per cent in 2003/4 to 14.2 per cent in 2016/17 (NBE 2017a). This is also reflected in the tax-to-GDP ratio, which amounted to 11.6 per cent in 2016/17—lower than the sub-Saharan average of 17 per cent. Despite the progress made in establishing a strong foundation for an efficient and effective tax system, Ethiopia still faces capacity deficiencies in collecting

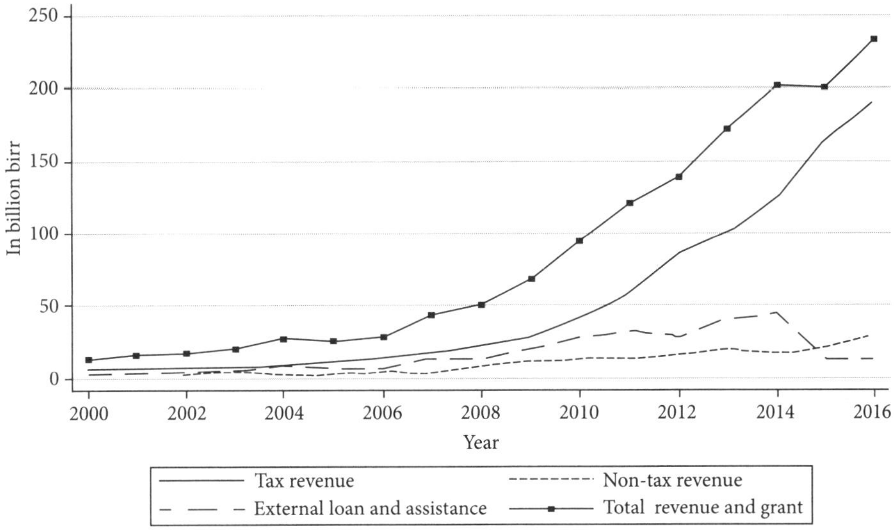

FIGURE 11.2 Revenue trends: general government revenue by component

Source: MoFEC (2017) (unpublished).

taxes and ensuring compliance. Further, as in other African countries, Ethiopia also experiences illicit financial flows (UNECA 2015).

11.4 Restructuring Public Expenditure

In the 1980s public spending was dominated by defence spending. The end of the war created the environment for reorienting public expenditure towards addressing problems of growth and development. Government expenditure has not only grown in size but has also seen a qualitative change in composition. There is a clear shift from recurrent to capital expenditure and increased spending on infrastructure, human development, and productive sectors.

Recurrent expenditure showed a steady decline, as a share of GDP, from 15.6 per cent in 2002/3 to 9.8 per cent in 2016/17. On the other hand, capital expenditure continued to grow steadily, averaging 10 per cent of GDP (Figure 11.3).

Besides the size and composition of public expenditure, ensuring the efficiency and effectiveness of the use of public resources is equally important. This realization led to the preparation of a comprehensive Expenditure Management and Control Reform Program. This programme has been under implementation over the last decade. The objectives of the programme are to enhance transparency, effectiveness, and the linking of rcsources to development outcomes.

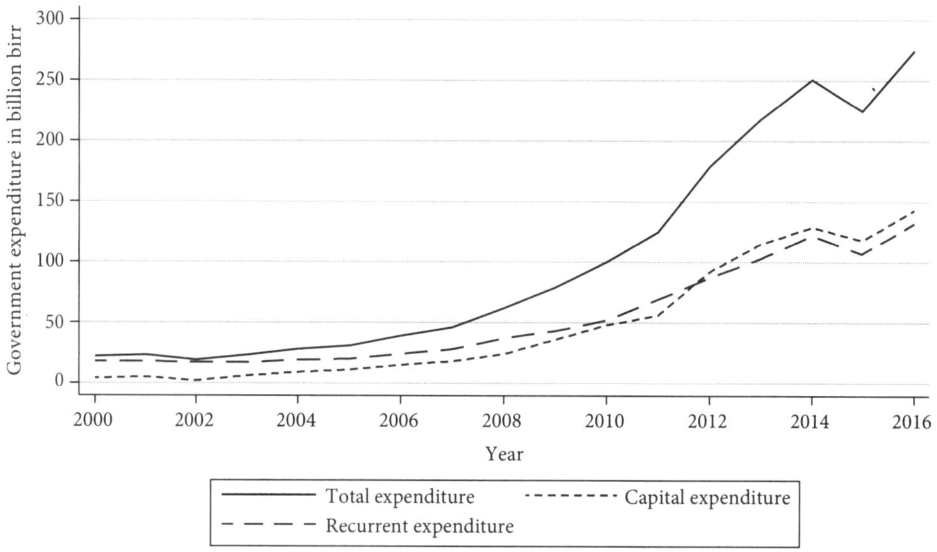

FIGURE 11.3 General government spending

Source: MoFEC (2017) (unpublished).

11.5 Domestic Savings have been Growing but Remain Low

The rapid economic growth Ethiopia has achieved has contributed to domestic resource mobilization. Domestic savings, as a share of GDP, increased from 9.3 per cent in 2001/2 to 17.2 per cent in 2010/11, subsequently reaching 21.9 per cent at the end of the first GTP (in 2014/15). By the end of the second year of GTP-II (2016/17) domestic savings had reached 24.1 per cent of GDP (NBE 2017b).

Reflecting a string of very large projects (dams, roads, railways, etc.), the share of gross capital formation in GDP increased from 26.4 per cent in 2001/2 to 39 per cent by the end of GTP-I. Clearly, domestic savings are not large enough to cover Ethiopia's big investment undertaking. The resource gap averaged 18 per cent of GDP during the period 2001/2–2016/17.

Many developing countries face this kind of growing resource gap. Ethiopia's experience of a big push in investment in the face of a savings constraint appears to confirm the expectations of economists like Kalecki and the post-Keynesians (such as King) that growth will generate savings, rather than insisting on generating savings first. The important question is the source of finance and instruments used to fill the gap in a predictable and sustainable manner.

Ethiopia has made concerted efforts to mobilize non-public sector finance to fund the resource gap. Mobilizing external loans and assistance has been by far the most important source for financing development. Total external flows amounted to US$19.7 billion over the five-year period of GTP-I. The external loan component amounted to US$16 billion (NPC 2016).

11.6 Mobilizing External Resources

Ethiopia's strategy for external resource mobilization has focused on maximizing grants followed by highly concessional loans, preferably through budget support and related modes of resource flow that are channelled through the public finances. Over the years, many development partners have provided and continue to provide sizeable amounts in the form of loans and development assistance. The World Bank, African Development Bank, the EU, United States, United Kingdom, Germany, Sweden, Japan, and the United Nations system, to name just a few, have been Ethiopia's key development partners. In more recent years, China and India have emerged as important sources of infrastructure finance. This development has helped Ethiopia to diversify its sources of loans and assistance.

In this regard Ethiopia's relationship with China and India was critically examined by Cheru (2016) through the lenses of trade, foreign direct investment, and concessional financing, as well as details of their sectoral and projects engagement. Ethiopia's long-term development vision, committed political leadership, and capacity to engage new development partners strategically has, on balance, helped produce a mutually beneficial relationship. This is contrary to various contending views, particularly on the role of China in Africa.

Here the terms and conditions of loans from China and India are of interest. Though detailed data are difficult to come by, Cheru (2016) was able to draw on MoFEC's Public Sector Debt Statistical Bulletin. It is clear from the outset that the loan terms and conditions cannot compare to those of World Bank's IDA window. According to Cheru's reconstructed table of terms and conditions for Chinese loans, interest rates are Libor+3 per cent, +2.6 per cent, and in some cases fixed at about 2 per cent. The grace period ranges from three to eight years while maturity periods range from ten to twenty years (MoFED 2012). The loans are committed for power, telecommunications, railway infrastructure, and the sugar industry—all important pillars of the GTP priorities for sustained growth and transformation. Compared to its peers (Figure 11.4) Ethiopia receives a lower official development assistance per capita.

The Ethiopian government has put in place a coordinating framework for dialogue with development partners. The main development partners are represented by the Development Assistance Group (DAG). Regular consultations have been conducted between the government and the donors under the framework. The launch of the Protection of Basic Services (PBS) has introduced the Joint Aid and Budget Review (JBAR). This platform has helped to build confidence by showing the partners that their money is being put to good use in terms of producing development results. This

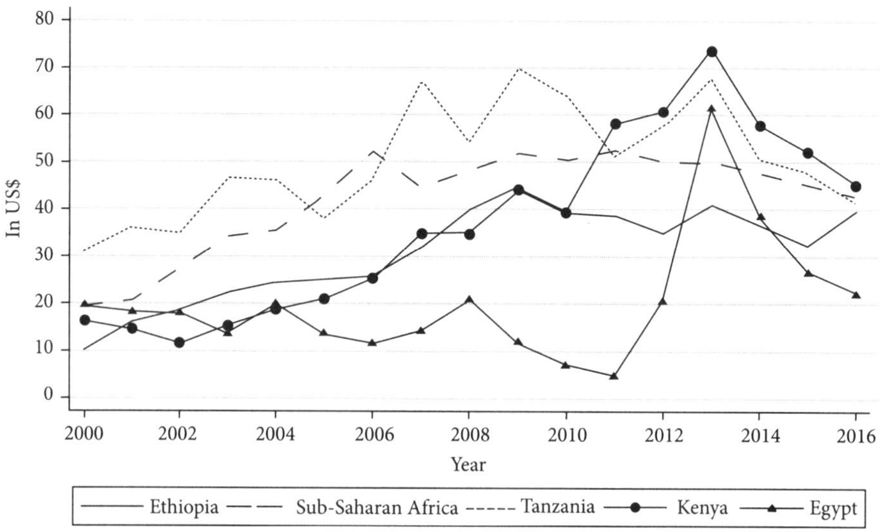

FIGURE 11.4 Official development assistance per capita
Source: World Bank, Economic Indicators Database.

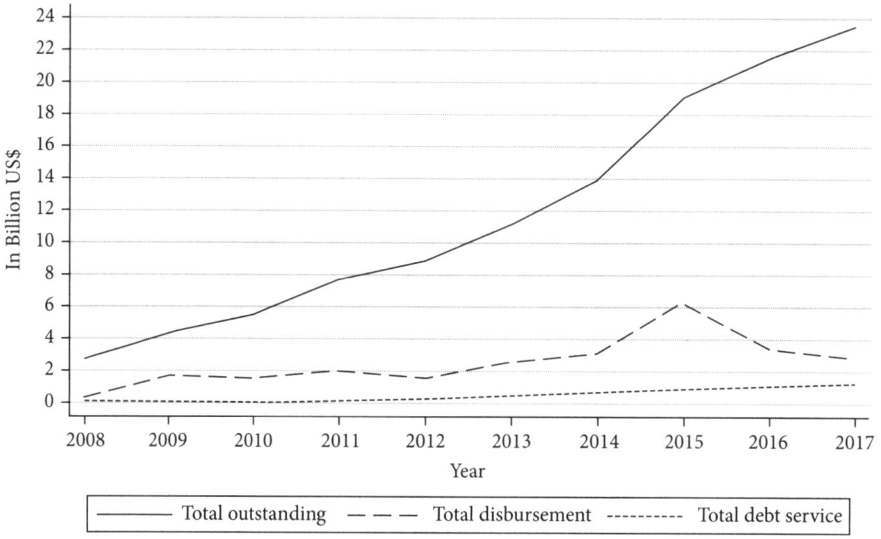

FIGURE 11.5 External debt
Source: MoFEC, *Public Debt Statistical Bulletin* No. 9 and No. 23.

has helped the continuity of external resource flows, improved predictability, and reduced transaction costs. That being said, the well-known risks associated with external resources remain potent.

Ethiopia's outstanding external debt has been increasing since 2010/11, which was the beginning of the implementation of GTP-I (Figure 11.5). In 2007/8 the share of multilateral

Table 11.1 Public-sector external debt disbursement by sector (US$ millions), 2007/8–16/17

	2007/8		2013/14		2016/17	
Economic sector	US$	%	US$	%	US$	%
TOTAL	**395.06**	**100**	**3,153.45**	**100**	**2,874.99**	**100**
Agriculture	21.64	5.48	290.97	9.23	519.76	18.08
Financial sector	20.33	5.15	6.95	0.22	–	–
Transport and communications	1.76	0.45	1,402.18	44.46	202.21	7.03
Highways transport infrastructure	105.29	26.65	319.88	10.14	822.37	28.6
Electricity, gas, and steam	165.1	41.79	452.75	14.36	504.47	17.55
Industry and tourism	0.5	0.13	159.26	5.05	422.99	14.71
Education and capacity building	39.34	9.96	58.13	1.84	106.93	3.72
Health	7.43	1.88	6.87	0.22	6.55	0.23
Public and social admin.	–	–	90.96	2.88	104.39	3.63
Water works and supply	33.67	8.52	80.96	2.57	94.09	3.27
PBS	–	–	284.54	9.02	91.25	3.17

Source: MoFEC Statistical Bulletin 9 and 23.

debt was 56 per cent compared to private creditors' share of 10 per cent. By 2016/17 the multilaterals' share had declined to 39 per cent compared to the jump in private creditors' share to 27 per cent (MoFEC 2017). Loans have predominantly been channelled towards key strategies of the GTP: infrastructure, agriculture, human development, and manufacturing (Table 11.1). With declining export receipts in recent years, however, debt repayment has become a big problem and the performance of key sectors of the economy is hampered by foreign exchange shortages (see Chapter 13). Ethiopia also benefited from the Highly Indebted Poor Countries (HIPC) debt relief programme. This opened up fiscal space allowing for an increased allocation to growth-enhancing priority sectors.

Besides mobilizing external loans, Ethiopia has also mobilized domestic borrowing and utilized it for priority projects. Just like external loans, domestic borrowing has shown growth over time, with the share of domestic debt increasing from 26.8 per cent in 2010/11—at the beginning of GTP-I—to 35 per cent in 2016/17 (MoFEC 2017).

One of the earliest policies Ethiopia put in place was the issuing of an Investment Proclamation to attract foreign direct investment (FDI). The investment law has gone through a series of changes informed by experience and policy learning (see Chapter 7 and Chapter 42). As a result of rapid economic growth and relative improvement in service provision, FDI flows to Ethiopia have been growing. In 2017 FDI flows to Ethiopia amounted to US$4.2 billion and the country was recognized as a top performer in attracting FDI (UNCTAD 2017), with major brands investing. Moreover, Ethiopia has received global recognition for excellence in investment promotion in the form of the United Nations Award for Promoting Investment in the Sustainable Development Goals (2017), as well as the World Bank Group's Star Reformer Award for its performance in investment policy reform and promotion (EIC 2017).

11.7 Mobilizing Private-Sector Savings

Private-sector savings are an important complement to public savings. In this respect, financial institutions serve to mobilize and allocate savings. At the beginning of the implementation of GTP-I in 2010/11, a new DBE financing instrument was introduced to strengthen its capacity to fund projects that require medium- and long-term financing. The policy directive of NBE required private commercial banks to allocate 27 per cent of their monthly disbursement to buy NBE-Bills. The resources mobilized through NBE-Bills are channelled to DBE to finance private sector industrial and agricultural projects, clearly priority sectors of GTP-I.

In the Ethiopian context banks are the main instrument. Banks are complemented by insurance companies and micro-finance institutions. The total number of branches reached 4,257, with the Commercial Bank of Ethiopia (CBE) making the major contribution to branch expansion (NBE 2017a, b). This growth in the branch network has facilitated deposit mobilization and the ability of banks, particularly the CBE, to lend to priority sectors. The financial sector has expanded following the opening of the sector to nationals. There are eighteen banks, of which sixteen are private; seventeen insurance companies; thirty-five micro-finance institutions; and five that provide capital goods finance (NBE 2017b). Capital markets are in the early stage of development, limited to Treasury bills and government bond operation. Leasing is just starting with support from the government. In Ethiopia, access to financial services is limited, leaving a large section of the population underserved and potential saving untapped. According to the National Financial Inclusion Strategy (NBE 2017b) there are four key barriers to financial inclusion: (i) underdeveloped financial infrastructure; (ii) limited availability of suitable financial products and access; (iii) limited consumer protection; and (iv) low level of financial capability awareness (see Chapter 28). The implementation of the National Financial Inclusion Strategy was expected to go a long way towards addressing the barriers to inclusion, broadening the banks' deposit base and thus contributing to GTP-II's goal of enhanced mobilization of domestic savings.

Ethiopia also has a policy bank—the Development Bank of Ethiopia (DBE)—which focuses on financing industrial and agricultural projects. As a policy bank the DBE is also entrusted with providing lease financing to micro, small, and medium enterprises and as a result the DBE is expanding its branches. But the DBE has faced difficulties as its non-performing loans (NPL) have increased above the legal limits. This has forced suspension of its lending for commercial agriculture, though lately the bank has resumed its lending to the sector. This reflects problems with the bank loan application appraisal and supervision and the commercial borrowers themselves.

It is important to note here that the launch of the Grand Ethiopian Renaissance Dam (GERD) at the beginning of the first GTP meant a search for innovative financing mechanisms to meet the huge financing requirement. One of these was the issue of a government GERD Bond. There has been extensive purchase of this bond by citizens.

Given the size of the financing need and the fact that no willing external financing partner came forward, the Ethiopian government has had to finance the whole project itself—to the tune of an estimated US$5 billion at the outset of the project.

It is important to highlight another policy instrument referred to by a number of studies (World Bank 2016; Bienen, Ciuriak, and Ferede 2013) as an unconventional instrument of financing. This refers to the prevalence of negative interest rates that have supported investment financing.

Ethiopian policy does not allow foreign banks to invest in the financial sector, a firmly held position going back to the beginning of the economic reforms in 1992/3. This policy position has always been at the centre of policy debate and differences. For a comprehensive examination of the state of Ethiopia's financial sector and its regulation, see Chapter 10.

11.8 Big Ambitions but a Growing Financial Constraint

Over the past decade Ethiopia has managed to generate rapid growth that translated into declining poverty and increased provision of basic services in both urban and rural areas. The second Growth and Transformation Plan set even higher goals of accelerating growth and structural transformation. It has set the goal of making Ethiopia a manufacturing hub through accelerated construction of industrial parks (see Chapter 35) combined with other institutional and policy support.

But the push to follow through on the GTP-II plans has run up against increasingly serious financing constraints. To protect the development gains achieved so far and to attain the GTP goals, the government actively set out in search of new financing sources. Underlying the growing financing constraint is the sluggish performance of exports, which began during the first Growth and Transformation Plan, and the limited tax base of the economy. Export earnings were expected to grow from US$2 billion in 2009/10 to US$6.5 billion in 2014/15. But export revenue managed on average only US$3 billion over the GTP period (GTP-II 2016)—less than 50 per cent of planned earnings. The growth and diversification of exports through rapid manufacturing exports did not materialize (see Chapter 36). With GTP-II in its third year of implementation, there was still no significant improvement in export earnings, leading to severe foreign exchange shortages affecting not only planned investment projects but also normal economic operations. Under these circumstances there was no choice but to look for other sources to finance growth and transformation.

In 2014 the government took the landmark measure of issuing a ten-year Eurobond. The finance obtained was directed towards financing accelerated industrial parks construction to house carefully selected export-oriented foreign investment (see Chapters 35 and 36). This increased manufacturing investment was expected to expand exports and relieve the foreign exchange constraints. The government also signed a loan agreement with Credit Suisse to finance the railway and infrastructure projects that were to contribute to transport efficiency and export competitiveness.

Ethiopia's access to these commercial loans reflected emerging confidence in the performance of the economy, though there was clearly rising anxiety within and outside Ethiopia about the strength of the economy during 2017/18. And the tight terms and conditions of these loans imply serious debt financing risks—a real possibility if the underlying assumptions of dynamic export growth, particularly manufacturing exports, are not realized. The IMF as part of its 2017 Article IV consultation conducted an update of its Debt Sustainability Analysis (DSA). The DSA indicated that Ethiopia's debt risk has increased and advised caution. Meanwhile, another review of the financial balances and the dynamics of the Ethiopian economy and the risks to sustained growth noted that public investment-led growth has the potential to continue to push growth provided the macroeconomic measures taken since October 2017 contribute to relieving the foreign exchange constraint (see Chapter 13). The government has already instituted measures restricting non-concessional borrowing to contain the build-up of debt distress.

The government, meanwhile, was also preparing the way in 2018 to engage in public–private partnerships (PPPs) to finance critical infrastructure projects envisaged in the GTP. Given the complexity of the PPP instrument, it was not clear at that stage how long it would take before any such schemes were implemented. Moreover, there is clear evidence that experiences with such instruments have not shown the expected results, suggesting that the government may be taking on fresh risks by engaging in PPPs (Loxley 2013; Bayliss and Van Waeyenberge 2017).

Given Ethiopia's adoption of a Climate Resilience and Green Economy (CRGE) strategy and the global community's commitment, underscored by the Paris Agreement, climate financing holds great potential for Ethiopia. The establishment of a CRGE Facility Fund under MOFED in cooperation with bilateral assistance to the CRGE strategy is a good beginning to bring new finance to Ethiopia.

The current financing constraint underlines the urgency of enhancing domestic resource mobilization, particularly through tax revenues, by effective implementation of the measures envisaged in the GTP. Strategically addressing a political economy that gives rise to rent-seeking practices, tax evasion, leakages and illegal trade practices, and broadening the tax base are urgent issues of the day (Geda and Yimer 2016: 34–49). A contributory factor is weakness in the domestic trade sector, which occupies a lowly place in the development discourse of Ethiopia. It is traditional, lacks transparency and efficiency, and has serious consequences for the productivity and competitiveness of the productive sectors, particularly the manufacturing and export sector.

It is possible for Ethiopia to explore new taxes and more effectively collect existing ones. This is particularly true of rental income tax, which is usually avoided or under-reported. The agricultural income tax and land-use fees, which are administered at regional state levels, have not yielded a strong revenue stream, despite rapid agricultural growth expansion (Chapters 26 and 27). Given the predominance of smallholder farmers, land tax is a sensitive matter. Moreover, Ethiopia could carefully consider the introduction of a property tax given the booming real-estate market.

11.9 Conclusion

Ethiopia has recorded impressive economic growth at a level unseen in its economic history. The government managed to stimulate growth in resource mobilization from both domestic and external sources, and channelled these resources to large-scale infrastructure, human capital, and productive-sector investments. But it has not been enough. Domestic revenue as a share of GDP increased but was still far below potential. External loans and assistance are used to complement and cover part of the resource gap. But Ethiopia was, by 2018, facing a serious financing constraint. The twin sources of the problem are the weak tax revenue and the desperately weak performance of exports, while the structural transformation expected from the Growth and Transformation Plan was not happening at anything like the pace that had been hoped for. Going forward, committed strategic measures are required: (a) to effectively mobilize domestic resources; (b) to maximize the use of potentially available external concessional loans and assistance while minimizing the uncertainty associated with this source by improved engagement and coordination with development partners; (c) to search for new non-debt-creating instruments that Ethiopia has not utilized so far to diversify the sources of finance; and (d) to continue to push hard on the drive to industrialize and significantly diversify and increase export earnings to successfully and sustainably resolve the prevailing foreign exchange constraint threatening to halt economic growth and the attainment of Ethiopia's vision (IMF 2018).

Capital formation during Ethiopia's period of dramatic growth up to 2018 was financed largely by foreign savings and imports. Notably, the elasticity of tax revenue with respect to GDP growth has been low and this has presented a major challenge. If tax revenue were to grow more rapidly as the economy expands, this would among other things reinforce the conditions for sustained and stable foreign capital inflows. Thus, the tax problem and the balance-of-payments problem are twinned, and their solutions complementary.

References

Alesina, A. and D. Dollar (2000). 'Who Gives Foreign Aid to Whom and Why?' *Journal of Economic Growth* 5 (1): 33–63.

Bayliss, Kate and Elisa Van Waeyenberge (2017). 'Unpacking the Public Private Partnership Revival', *Journal of Development Studies* 54 (2): 1–17.

Bienen, Derk, Dan Ciuriak, and Tadele Ferede (2013). 'Financing Ethiopia's; Development: Confronting the Gap between Ambition and Means', *Ethiopian Journal of Economics* 22 (2): 21–62.

Cheru, Fantu (2016). 'Emerging Southern Powers and New Forms of South-South Cooperation: Ethiopia's Strategic Engagement with China and India', *Third World Quarterly* 37 (4): 592–610.

Dang, H.-A., S. Knack, and F. Halsey Rogers (2013). 'International Aid and Financial Crises in Donor Countries', *European Journal of Political Economy* 32 (December): 232–50.

EIC, Ethiopian Investment Commission (2017). 'Ethiopian Investment Report', EIC, Addis Ababa.

Geda, Alemayehu and Addis Yimer (2016). 'Capital Flight and its Determinants: The Case of Ethiopia', *African Development Review* 28 (51): 39–49.

IMF (2018). 'Ethiopia Staff Report for the 2017 Article IV Consultation', January, International Monetary Fund, Washington, DC.

Lane, Timothy and Ales Bulir (2004). 'Aid and Fiscal Management', IMF Working Papers 02/112, Washington, DC.

Loxley, John (2013). 'Are Public Private Partnerships (PPPs) the Answer to Africa's Infrastructure Needs?' *The Review of African Political Economy* 40 (137): 485–95.

MoFEC (2017). 'Public Sector Debt—Statistical Bulletin No. 23, (2013–2017)', Debt Management Unit, Addis Ababa.

MoFED (2006). 'Ethiopia: Building on Progress A Plan for Accelerated and Sustained Development to End Poverty (PASDEP)', Vol. I (main text), September, Federal Democratic Republic of Ethiopia, Addis Ababa.

MoFED (2007). 'A Plan for Accelerated and Sustained Development to End Poverty (PASDEP): Annual MoFED Progress Report 2005/6', Federal Democratic Republic of Ethiopia, Addis Ababa.

MoFED (2010). 'Growth and Transformation Plan, 2010/11–2014/15', Vol. I (main text), November, Federal Democratic Republic of Ethiopia, Addis Ababa.

MoFED (2012). 'Public Sector Debt Statistical Bulletin No. 9, (2007/08–2011/12)', Debt Management Directorate, Ministry of Finance & Economic Development, Addis Ababa, October 2012.

MoFED (2014). 'Growth and Transformation Plan: Annual Progress Report FY. 2012/13', Ministry of Finance and Economic Development, Addis Ababa.

Moller, L. and K. M. Wacker (2017). 'Explaining Ethiopia's Growth Acceleration: The Role of Infrastructure and Macroeconomic Policy', *World Development* 96 (C): 198–215.

National Bank of Ethiopia (2017a). 'Annual Report 2016/17', NBE, Addis Ababa.

National Bank of Ethiopia (2017b). 'Ethiopia: National Financial Inclusion Strategy.' April, NBE, Addis Ababa.

National Planning Commission (2016). 'Growth & Transformation Plan II (GTP II), (2015/16–2019/20)', Vol. I, (main text), Addis Ababa.

National Planning Commission (2017). 'Ethiopia's Progress towards Eradicating Poverty: An Interim Report on 2015/16', Poverty Analysis Study, Sept., Addis Ababa.

Stiglitz, J. E. (2002). *Globalization and its Discontents* (New York: W. W. Norton).

UNCTAD (2017). *World Investment Report* (Geneva: United Nations).

UNECA (2015). 'Illicit Financial Flows, Report of the High-Level Panel on Illicit Financial Flows from Africa', Addis Ababa.

World Bank (2016). 'Ethiopia Public Expenditure Review', Report No. ACS14541, World Bank, Washington, DC.

CHAPTER 12

INFRASTRUCTURE AND ECONOMIC TRANSFORMATION IN ETHIOPIA

SEID NURU ALI

12.1 Introduction

Infrastructure has been important, of course, throughout Ethiopia's long history, especially given the difficulties in access to the sea for long stretches of that history. During the heyday of international trade in the early civilization of the country, ports such as Adulis were important.[1] In modern history, Ethiopians began to understand the role of infrastructure as a fundamental prerequisite for economic development from the time of Emperor Menelik II in the nineteenth century (Zewde 1991; Gnogno 1992). One of the grand infrastructure projects during his reign was the construction of a railway line linking Addis Ababa and Djibouti (see Chapter 2). The project was eventually completed in collaboration with the French government. At about the same time, rulers began to emphasize other types of infrastructure such as a telephone network, electricity, water supply, and roads. Individuals and households were compelled to contribute towards these public projects through their respective traditional chiefs or nobility. According to Paulos Gnogno (2010), Emperor Menelik instructed all governors to impose levies per head of cattle owned by a household to finance the railway project. No one was exempted from the levy.

[1] 'Early in the sixth century, Cosmas Indicopleustes recorded that Axumite ships penetrated as far as Sri Lanka, furthermore, when a fleet was being assembled for the invasion of southern Arabia, a significant number of the available vessels were Aksumite ones built at Adulis itself' (Phillipson 2012: 200).

During the reign of Emperor Haile Selassie, the Imperial Government of Ethiopia also emphasized social infrastructure, such as schools and hospitals. The foundations for today's successful aviation industry in Ethiopia were laid during that period.[2] The first five-year development plan of the Imperial regime, launched in 1957, gave priority to infrastructure development along with a strategy for resource mobilization to kick-start the country's economic development (Imperial Ethiopian Government, (IEG 1957) First Five Year Development Plan, 1957). The trend continued in subsequent development plans that lasted until the end of Imperial rule in 1974 (IEG 1962; IEG 1968).

The Derg regime that came to power in 1974 continued the policies of the previous regime and expanded infrastructure development. Despite being consumed by escalating wars with its neighbours—Somalia in particular—and by various liberation fronts challenging its rule, the Derg built hydroelectric power dams, road, and irrigation infrastructure, though on a limited scale. After the drought in 1985 that threatened the lives of millions of peasants, the government increased resource spending on irrigation infrastructure. The Alwero dam in Gambella regional state was the result of that strategy. Another massive multipurpose infrastructure project was the Tana–Beles project. Generation of hydroelectric power and integrated agro-processing industry constituted the core components of the project. The project was interrupted in 1991 and was only revived in 2006 to generate electricity.

Upon taking power in 1991, the Ethiopian People's Revolutionary Democratic Front (EPRDF) prioritized the development of infrastructure as a key element of its development strategy. Since the mid-1990s, road infrastructure and education have been the top two sectors attracting the highest share of the government budget (MoFEC, various issues). Between 1997 and 2017, the road network more than quadrupled. Of the 120,171km total road network the country had until 2017, about 59 per cent was built during the first seven years of the Growth and Transformation Plan (GTP), that is, from 2011 to 2017 (NBE 2017; ERA 2016). The recent massive expansion in economic and social infrastructure is believed to have triggered the rapid economic growth the county has registered since 2003. Based on empirical data from 2000 to 2013, Moller and Wacker (2017) concluded that Ethiopia's 'accelerated growth was driven by public infrastructure investment and restrained government consumption and supported by a conducive external environment'.

This chapter documents and analyses the contributions of infrastructure development in Ethiopia to economic growth, poverty reduction, and improved social welfare. Investment in infrastructure augments demand with potential impact on short-term growth. In the medium to long run, infrastructure affects growth through two channels: directly through physical capital accumulation, and indirectly through improvement in productivity. At a micro level, investment in infrastructure enhances private sector

[2] Ethiopian Airlines (EAL) Inc. was established in 1945 as a joint venture between the Ethiopian government and Transcontinental and Western Airlines (TWA) (Zewde 1991: 196). The first scheduled flight was made to Cairo via Asmara using a Douglas C-47 Skytrain on 8April 1946. Ethiopian Airlines is a success story in Africa's aviation industry with modern aircraft including 13 Boeing Dreamliners, 15 Boeing 777s, 19 B737, and an Airbus A350XWB fleet. https://www.ethiopianairlines.com

activities by lowering the cost of production and opening new markets, presenting new production opportunities and trade. At the same time, infrastructure investment in power generation, water, sanitation, and housing improves the social well-being of citizens.

The empirical analysis in the chapter is based on the national income accounts data from the National Planning Commission, government expenditure data from the Ministry of Finance and Economic Cooperation, and data on public investment in the energy sector from the Ethiopian Electric Power Corporation.

12.2 Infrastructure Policy and Infrastructure Development in Ethiopia

12.2.1 Infrastructure Policy

Motivations for infrastructural investment in Ethiopia over the last quarter of a century can be grouped into three main episodes. Infrastructure development during the period 1997 to 2005 was designed to reverse the perceived concentration of infrastructure in major urban centres at the expense of rural areas where the majority of Ethiopians reside, thus undermining the productivity of agriculture. The second episode of infrastructural investment took place during 2005–10 and it was aimed at urban renewal and improving the quality of housing and social infrastructure in cities. The third phase, which started with the adoption of GTP in 2010, was dictated by the need to improve infrastructure connectivity to support the government's ambitious industrialization strategy. Investment projects in major hydroelectric dams such as Gibe III and the GERD, in the Addis Ababa Light Rail project, the railway system, and express roads were meant to foster the transformation of the country under the GTP.

12.2.2 Infrastructure Development, 1995–2010

In the early 1990s, Ethiopia was characterized by a low level of infrastructure. After three decades of civil war, the infrastructure already available was either obsolete or dysfunctional. The first official document released by EPRDF on its vision of economic development recognized the relevance and urgency of rehabilitating and expanding infrastructure (EPRDF 1995).[3] The strategy is known as Agricultural Development-Led Industrialization (ADLI), and it recognized that infrastructure development in the areas of electric power, roads, railways, telecommunications, and water supply were critical to

[3] The first document that introduced the ADLI strategy was the EPRDF's 'Development, Peace, and Democracy Strategy' published in 1995.

trigger economic growth through the active participation of the private sector. The document recommended an energy strategy that would double electric power within five to seven years based on the country's comparative advantage, above all through hydroelectric power (EPRDF 1995).

The other economic infrastructure that attracted the attention of government was the expansion and rehabilitation of rural roads. As the overall strategy was anchored in rural development in the spirit of ADLI, the major mode of infrastructure targeted for rural development was roads. Upgrading and rehabilitating major roads linking urban nodes and highways connecting the country to ports were emphasized. Roads connecting major urban centres were at the same time expected to benefit rural farmers (EPRDF 1995).

Over the five-year period after the launch of the ADLI strategy in 1995, investments were made in electric power generation with an expected capacity of 329.3MW. The new projects had already begun generating 39.3MW. Upon completion of these projects, the overall power capacity of the country would reach 715MW (EPRDF 2000). During the five-year plan period, the government constructed about 7,499km of rural roads. The population with access to potable water increased from 23 per cent in 1995 to 32 per cent in 1999 (EPRDF 2000).

Policies and strategies that were launched during the following years, such as the second EPRDF five-year strategy on development, peace, and democracy (2000) and the Sustainable Development and Poverty Reduction Program (SDPRP) in 2003 gave due emphasis to infrastructural development. However, a more aggressive approach to planning and implementing infrastructure projects took shape during the Plan for Accelerated Development to End Poverty (PASDEP) (2006–10) (MoFED 2002; MoFED 2006).

Under SDPRP, the Ethiopian government planned provision of infrastructure that targeted expansion of the road network, and increasing access to clean water, irrigation schemes, electricity, and telecommunications services. The three years of effort by the Ethiopian government resulted in the expansion of road networks from 33,297km in 2002 to 37,018km in 2005, improving road density from 32.3km to 33.6km per 1,000 km^2. The road density was, however, still very low compared to the African average of more than 50km/1000km^2 (MoFED 2006). Moreover, the power-generating capacity of the country improved from 473MW in 2002 to 791MW in 2005 (see Table 12.1).

PASDEP envisaged the construction of about 20,000km of new roads under the roads network programme by the end of the plan period (2010). About 90 per cent of the new roads were planned to be constructed in rural areas. A sub-programme under the Road Sector Development Program known as the Ethiopian Rural Travel and Transport Sub-Program (ERTTP) constituted a key part of the PASDEP and focused on increasing road access to the rural population and supporting agricultural and other commercial activities of the communities (MoFED 2006).

Another major infrastructure that attracted the government's attention during PASDEP was a rural electrification programme called the Universal Electrification Access

Program (UEAP). Over 6,000 rural towns and villages were identified for electrification throughout the country, with about 24 million people expected to benefit. To achieve such goals, the wider power-sector programme during the PASDEP period planned to harness some of the country's water resources by constructing eleven power generation stations with a total capacity of 4,091MW. The broader plan would see the increase of the total power capacity of the country from 791 in 2005 to 2,218 through the construction of five major new dams (MoFED 2006). By the end of the plan period, the country had a power capacity of 2,000MW (MoFED 2010; see also Table 12.1).

Similarly, the Ethiopian government planned to expand telecommunications infrastructure under PASDEP. A successful accomplishment of the plan would see an increase in fixed telephone subscribers from 620,000 to over 3.23 million, in mobile phone subscribers from about 410,000 to over 6.76 million, and in internet connections from 17,000 to 0.193 million between 2005 and 2010 (MoFED 2010). Achievements in expanding mobile phone and internet coverage were encouraging (see Table 12.1).

By the end of PASDEP implementation, many of the targets established in 2005 had been met. As shown in Table 12.1, there were noticeable improvements in the road and energy infrastructure, particularly when compared to the situation in 2002.

Table 12.1 Selected indicators of infrastructural development in Ethiopia (performance under SDPRP and PASDEP)

		End of SDPRP	End of PASDEP
Infrastructure	2002	2005	2010
Roads			
Total road network, km	33,297	37,018	48,800
Average time taken to all-weather road (hours)		5.0	3.7
Road density (km/1,000 km^2)	32.3	33.6	44.5
Road density (km/1,000 people)	0.49	0.51	0.64
Energy			
Power generation capacity (MW)	473	791	2,000
Electricity service coverage (%)		16	41
Telecommunications			
Fixed line telephone density (%)		0.85	1.36
Distribution of mobile telephones (%)		0.56	8.7
Fixed telephone subscriptions (millions)	0.546	0.62	1.0
Mobile telephone subscriptions (millions)		0.411	6.52
Internet service subscriptions (millions)		0.0175	0.187
Water			
Overall population coverage of potable water (%)			68.5
Land under medium- and large-scale irrigation (%)			2.5

Sources: MoFED (2002, 2006); NBE.

12.2.3 Infrastructure Development under the GTP

The GTP has had the target not only of maintaining high growth at 11 per cent per annum to claim middle-income status by 2025, but also of laying the foundations for the transformation of the economy under which manufacturing becomes the main driver of growth. Such an ambitious plan can only be realized with better infrastructure capabilities. At the launch of GTP, the country could produce no more than 2,000MW of electric power, which was not even enough to meet household demand for electricity, and there was no railway system. As a result, the Ethiopian government identified key infrastructural investment projects in parallel with investments in strategic industrial projects (MoFED 2010).

In the total planned outlay of US$11.4 billion to be invested under GTP-I, 66 per cent was allocated for infrastructure development in the country. Energy took the lion's share of the budget as it accounted for 31.2 per cent of the total investment (see Table 12.2). The GTP planned investment of about US$10.4 billion in the major hydroelectric dams, including the GERD, which was to have an installed capacity of 6,750MW on completion[4] (MoFED 2010: 42).[5] The aim was to go beyond expected domestic energy needs and to generate foreign exchange by exporting electricity to the neighbouring countries. Needless to say, successful completion of the plan in the energy sector would curb a major bottleneck in the industrialization Ethiopia is envisaging by increasing the supply of electric power from about 2,000MW per annum at the launch of the project to more than 10,000MW per annum. A recent study by UNDP showed that major manufacturing industries in Ethiopia ranked power interruption, foreign exchange constraint, limited access to electric power, shortage of domestic raw material, and poor internet services as the top five major constraints among forty-two identified potential constraints (UNDP 2018).

In addition, other sources of energy such as geothermal and wind farms have been established as the country embraces a green approach to the economy. The Ethiopian government stressed in the GTP-II (second phase of the Growth and Transformation Plan) document that addressing environmental issues is critical in the process of transformation. It sets out plans to implement the Climate Resilient Green Economy (CRGE) strategy at all levels of engagement to ensure environmental safety. Implementation of CGRE under GTP-II targets mitigation measures to limit environmental pollution, including safe removal of about 200 tons of dangerous chemicals, clearing fifty identified polluted areas, creating a clean and green environment in 150 towns, and expanding conservation efforts (NPC 2016). To this end, the projected energy sources of the country are not fossil-based. The country has immense potential for hydroelectric power, geothermal energy, and wind power.

[4] The initial expected capacity from GERD was 6,000MW. It was later revised to a capacity of 6,750MW.

[5] Figures in the MoFED document are in the local currency, the birr.

Table 12.2 Major investment projects of the GTP and the emphasis given to infrastructure

	US$, millions	Share, per cent
Industry	**11,386**	**34.0**
Sugar	4,446	12.9
Chemicals, pharmaceuticals, cement	2,035	6.1
Metals and engineering	1,204	3.6
Textiles	938	2.8
Fertilizer complex	777	2.3
Energy	**10,455**	**31.2**
Transport	**9,512**	**28.4**
Railways	6,517	19.5
Telecommunications	**1,275**	**3.8**
Addis Ababa housing project	**880**	**2.6**
Total	**33,508**	**100**

Source: Federal Democratic Republic of Ethiopia, Ministry of Finance and Economic Development, 'Growth and Transformation Plan, 2010/11–2014/15', November 2010, Addis Ababa.

Consistent with the requirement of mass transportation to foster industrialization, investment in transport including railway infrastructure worth US$9.5 billion, or 28 per cent of the total investment budget, was planned (Table 12.2). The Addis Ababa–Djibouti railway project has been successfully completed. The construction of the Awash–Woldia–Mekele railway began in the second phase of GTP. The plan to extend the railway system to the western, southern, south-western, and north-western parts of the country during the second phase did not materialize due to financial constraints.

Road infrastructure improved significantly over the period of the first phase of GTP. Road density increased from 44.5km per 1,000km^2 in 2010 to 100.4 per 1,000km^2 in 2015 (Table 12.3). While this is still far below the African average of 204km per 1,000 km^2, GTP-II targets to reach the African average.

As shown in Table 12.3, most of the GTP targets in infrastructure have been achieved, particularly in the expansion of the road network in the country. Targets in the energy sector are progressing slowly, but will be finally met when the GERD is completed.

12.2.4 Urban Infrastructure

The boom in the construction sector in the urban centres such as Addis Ababa attracted migrant workers from various regional states, putting a strain on the already limited capacity of residential housing and public utilities such as transport. In 2005, about 11.7 million people (16 per cent of the country's total population) lived in urban areas. The urban population was projected to reach 22 million by 2020 as it was growing at an annual average rate of 4.4 per cent. Thus, apart from the projected increase in the volume

Table 12.3 Selected indicators of infrastructural development in Ethiopia (performance under GTP)

Infrastructure	Base year 2010	GTP-I 2015 Target	GTP-I 2015 Actual	GTP-II 2020 (Target)
Roads:				
Total road network, km	48,800	64,500	110,414	220,000
Average time taken to all-weather road (hours)	3.7	1.4	1.7	0.8
Road density (km/1,000 km2)	44.5	123.7	100.4	200
Road density (km/1,000 people)	0.64	1.54		
Railways (km)	–	2,395	*	**
Energy				
Power-generating capacity (MW)	2,000	8,000	4,180	17,208
Electricity service coverage (%)	41	75		
Transmission line power losses (%)	11.5	5.6	23	11
Telecommunications				
Fixed line telephone density (%)	1.36	3.4	10.5	54
Distribution of mobile telephones (%)	8.7	45	43.9	100
Fixed telephone subscriptions (millions)	1.0	3.05	0.386	10.4
Mobile telephone subscriptions (millions)	6.52	40	38.8	103
Internet service subscriptions (millions)	0.187	3.69	9.14	56
Internet data density (%)			3.3	10
Water				
Overall population coverage of potable water (%)	68.5	98.5	84	100
Land under medium- and large-scale irrigation (%)	2.5	15.6		
Postal services traffic (millions)			28.7	657.4
Number of postal service centres			1,000	16,475

Notes: *Construction in progress. **The Addis Ababa Light Rail project and the Addis Ababa–Djibouti railway were completed in the first year of the GTP-II period.
Sources: MoFED (2006, 2002); NBE; NPC.

of international trade, which required a railway system (and dramatic expansion of freight-handling facilities at Bole International Airport), the rapid growth in urbanization following the high rate of rural-to-urban migration necessitated a modern transport system. To curb the transport problem in the capital (in 2005 Addis Ababa had a population fourteen times higher than the second-largest city in Ethiopia, Dire Dawa) (MoFED 2006), and in an attempt to introduce a new mass transport system to the country, the Addis Ababa Light Rail project was launched in the first year of the implementation of GTP. The 34km light train project criss-crossing Addis Ababa from east to west and from north to south was successfully completed and became operational.

Addis Ababa was poorly planned in the past and given the large tract of land in the city under slum housing, sustainable urban development was a challenge. Slum houses had to give way for developers in the prime locations. At the same time, households being evacuated needed to be relocated to better housing. Partly to accommodate such displaced residents, but mainly to meet the housing demand of the increasing population of Addis Ababa, the Ethiopian government launched a massive condominium housing project. Under this scheme, beneficiaries are required to save 10 per cent, 20 per cent, and 40 per cent of the estimated cost of the house at the disposal of the Commercial Bank of Ethiopia, based on different size and quality arrangements. The balances in each category are covered by the government with a loan that is to be settled over time once the houses are completed and delivered to the beneficiaries. During the first phase of GTP, 174,190 houses were built in Addis Ababa under various programmes (NPC 2016).

Both the GERD and the Addis Ababa condominium housing projects have played a significant role in mobilizing domestic resources and creating jobs, as well as creating an important avenue to transfer technical know-how in construction and hydro-power engineering. Besides motivating citizens to save to purchase their own apartment units, the Addis Ababa housing development and related projects created 845,900 jobs (NPC 2016). In the case of the GERD, Ethiopians bought Grand Renaissance Dam Bonds worth more than half a billion US$. This and other related schemes helped increase the rate of gross domestic saving of the country from 9.5 per cent in 2010 to 21.8 per cent in 2015 (NPC 2016). Further GERD financing is provided by investments by the Ethiopian Electric Power Corporation and diaspora bonds.

12.3 Infrastructure Stocks

12.3.1 Energy

In 2015, the electric power supply reached 4,180kWh per annum. The GERD, which is regarded as an iconic infrastructural investment project, will have an installed capacity of 6,750MW on completion, and will have important inspirational and demonstration effects in addition to the huge economic return of relieving major bottlenecks in the industrialization process to which the country aspires.

12.3.2 Roads

Following the ADLI strategy, the Ethiopian government launched the Road Sector Development Program (RSDP) in 1997. Under the RSDP, the total road network in the country more than quadrupled in nineteen years, increasing from 26,550km in 1997 to 113,066km in 2016. This resulted in the improvement of the nation's road density from 24km per 1,000km^2 in 1997 to 102.8km per 1,000km^2 in 2016. Over the same period, average distance to all-weather roads decreased from 21km to 4.9km (ERA 2016).

There are three implementation levels for RSDP: federal roads, regional roads, and district or *woreda* roads. The latter is formally known as the Universal Rural Road Access Program (URRAP). About 83 per cent of the total new road network constructed over the nineteen-year RSDP programme was accomplished during 2010–16, with about 81 per cent of URRAP construction and about 48 per cent of the total federal and regional programme road network completed (ERA 2016).

12.3.3 Telecommunications and IT

The number of fixed line and mobile subscribers stood at 1.2 million and 58.2 million, respectively, in 2017. This translates into a telecommunications density of 63 per 100 users. In the same year, the number of recorded internet subscribers stood at 16.5 million. In terms of coverage, internet and data density was limited to 17.5 per 100 users.

12.3.4 Other Sectors

In other sectors of infrastructure, the Addis Ababa–Djibouti railway and the Addis Ababa Light Rail project have been completed. Moreover, in the aviation industry in which Ethiopia is considered to have a comparative advantage, new airports have been constructed in various regions of the country.

Although there has been a high level of infrastructure investment, as shown in Section 12.3, Ethiopia still ranks only 50th among 54 African countries in the Africa

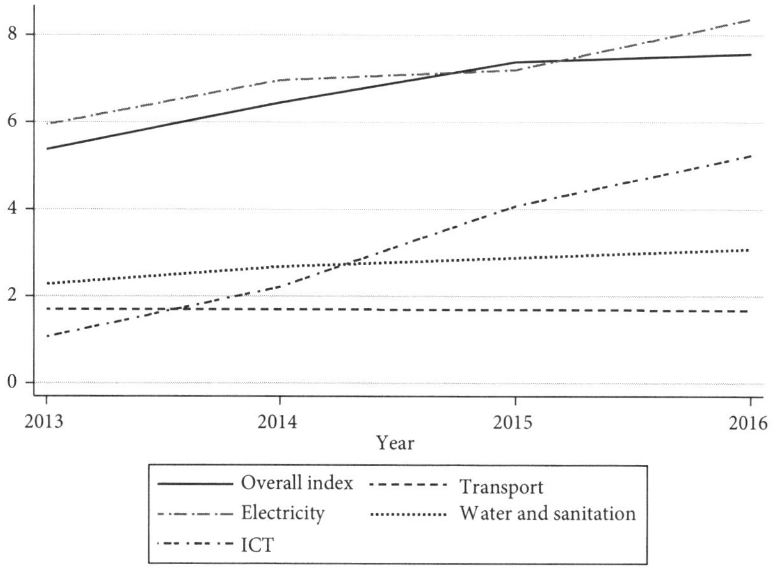

FIGURE 12.1 Trends in Ethiopia's infrastructure development index

Source: AfDB, The African Infrastructure Development Index 2016.

Development Bank's (AfDB) infrastructure development index in 2016. As shown in Figure 12.1, between 2013 and 2016 Ethiopia improved on its overall infrastructure development index, ICT composite index, and electricity infrastructure composite index. This improvement shifts the rank of the country in the ICT index from 52nd in 2013 to 48th in 2016, and the rank in the electricity index from 40th in 2013 to 36th in 2016. The county's rankings in the transport, and water and sanitation indices remained low.

12.4 Financing Infrastructure

The road sector attracted the largest share of government capital expenditure, followed by education. Between 1994 and 2014, the shares of roads and education in total government capital expenditure were 25.2 per cent and 13.3 per cent, respectively. During the same period, energy, and transport and telecommunications accounted for 4.8 and 3.6 per cent, respectively, of the total government capital budget (Figure 12.2). The seemingly low share of the latter two sectors was due to the fact that investments in these sectors were made by Ethiopian Electric Corporation and Ethio Telecom which emerged as public enterprises after 2001. Over the seven years before 2001, the shares of road, energy, and telecommunications sectors in the total government budget were, respectively, 21.6, 10.4, and 6.8 per cent.

During the period 1994–2014, domestic sources accounted for 69.3 per cent of total capital expenditure. Loans and grants covered the balance (20.3 per cent, and 10.2 per cent, respectively). In 1994, 66 per cent of the capital expenditure on infrastructure was financed by domestic sources. The share of domestic financing of infrastructure investment increased to 75 per cent in 2014. In general, road, energy, and health infrastructure were largely (more than 82 per cent) financed by domestic sources, while loans and grants were equally important (more than 50 per cent) in financing infrastructure investment in education, and transport and communications (MoFEC).

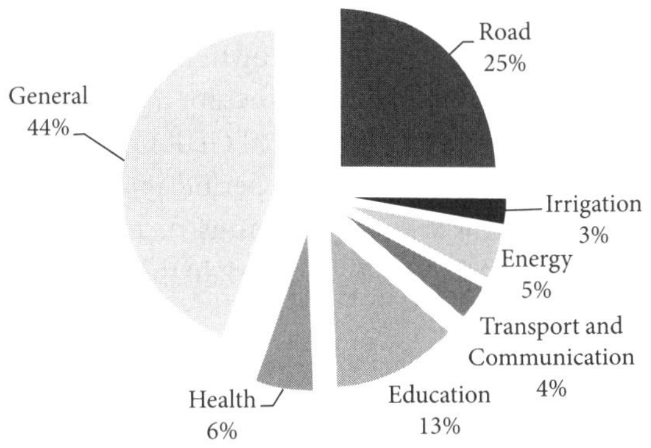

FIGURE 12.2 Share of major infrastructure sectors in the government capital budget, 1994–2014

Source: GTP 2010–2014/15.

12.5 Contribution of Infrastructure to Growth in the Ethiopian Economy

There are three major avenues through which infrastructure can contribute to economic growth. The first is investment. Wages and salaries earned in the process of expansion of infrastructure are parts of income counted in the national economy. In the typical Keynesian framework, this investment also has a multiplier effect on income and output. Through the second channel, investment contributes directly to output as an additional input. Investment in infrastructure increases the production capacity of the economy and may be considered part of the overall conventional capital stock. Third, infrastructure may spur growth by raising total factor productivity as it enhances the efficiency of more conventional inputs by reducing transaction costs. Investment in improved infrastructure may thus, by raising the profitability of firms and generating employment income, lead to rising savings (see Chapter 13).

In this chapter, the contribution of infrastructure to the Ethiopian economy is demonstrated at aggregate and micro levels. The analysis of the role of infrastructure in growth at an aggregate level is limited to growth decomposition exercises on the demand and supply sides. I present two case studies to demonstrate the role of road infrastructure in the urban and rural economies in Ethiopia.

12.6 Contribution of Economic Infrastructure Investment to Growth: The Demand Side

Between 1994 and 2000, private consumption and government consumption (mainly dominated by recurrent expenditure) dominated the pace of aggregate demand as they jointly accounted for about 74 per cent of the growth in the nominal GDP.[6] Gross fixed investment in general and in economic infrastructure in particular made a very small contribution to the overall growth in the nominal GDP. Out of the 10.4 per cent rate of growth of nominal GDP recorded during the period 1994–2000, overall gross fixed capital formation and investment in economic infrastructure contributed shares of 0.7 and 0.04 percentage points, respectively (Table 12.4). In the following five years (2001–5),

[6] Figures used in the computation of the contribution of infrastructure consider only economic infrastructure. These include investments in roads, irrigation, energy, and transport and telecommunications. Investment data were not available for aviation infrastructure. It should be noted that the Ethiopian government allotted a significant amount of the capital budget to social infrastructure, in particular education. With the inclusion of social infrastructure in the growth decomposition exercise, the share of infrastructure in growth would increase significantly.

the overall contribution of gross fixed capital formation including investments in infrastructure was even negative. In fact, during the period 1992–2005, the government gave more emphasis to rural development through extension services and rural education under the ADLI strategy. An important critique of the then policy was that the Ethiopian government exerted much effort on the supply side of the rural economy without due consideration to the demand side in the urban economy. A particular case in point was the price of grains during the bumper harvests of the mid-1990s; it plummeted significantly to the extent that farmers were discouraged from producing surplus output. The Ethiopian government attempted to persuade farmers not to sell their produce until the price rose. The government also offered purchases by government agencies at pre-set high prices, and credit facilities (EEA 2011).

The year 2005 was a turning point in terms of policy shift for the Ethiopian government, following the 2005 election in which the ruling party lost to the opposition in major towns including Addis Ababa. The government shifted the emphasis to the development of the urban sector. Investment in infrastructure such as roads, telecommunications, and urban housing in the urban centres is believed to have boosted the overall economy as it triggered the much-needed demand from the urban centres. As intervention in the infrastructure development by the government has intensified during the period of the GTP, since 2011 the contribution of economic infrastructure to aggregate demand as measured by nominal GDP has risen to 9.3 per cent.

Overall, expansion in infrastructure generated employment primarily in urban centres. While the primary objective of investing in infrastructure is to foster long-term growth and tackle poverty, investments in infrastructure have helped generate growth episodes by augmenting demand.

12.7 Contribution of Economic Infrastructure Capital to Growth: The Supply Side

In this section, I estimate the real values of investments in economic infrastructure to economic growth, using the standard Cobb–Douglas production function and Solow's growth accounting technique.[7] I estimated the initial capital stock (in 1961) by multiplying the capital–output ratio by the level of real GDP. I used the relation between growth,

[7] Letting Y = real GDP, K_{NI} = non-infrastructure capital stock, K_I = infrastructural capital (economic), L = labour, and A = a shifter such as technical change, the production function can be given by $Y = AL^{\alpha}K_{NI}^{\beta}K_I^{\gamma}$ where $\alpha + \beta + \gamma = 1$ and each parameter represents the share of each input. Growth in GDP is decomposed according to:

$$g \equiv \frac{\dot{Y}}{Y} = \alpha\frac{\dot{L}}{L} + \beta\frac{\dot{K}_{NI}}{K_{NI}} + \gamma\frac{\dot{K}_I}{K} + \frac{\dot{A}}{A}$$

Table 12.4 Contribution of infrastructure to growth: demand side

			Gross Fixed Investment				
	Private consumption	Government consumption	All investments	Non-infrastructure	Economic infrastructure	Export	Growth in nominal GDP
1994–2000	5.14	2.55	0.70	0.67	0.04	2.04	10.44
	49.28	**24.45**	**6.74**	**6.38**	**0.36**	**19.53**	
2001–5	8.04	0.05	−0.14	−0.01	−0.13	2.27	10.22
	78.7	**0.5**	**−1.3**	**−0.1**	**−1.3**	**22.2**	
2006–10	21.97	1.95	2.27	1.61	0.7	3.40	29.58
	74.3	**6.6**	**7.7**	**5.5**	**2.2**	**11.5**	
2011–17	12.65	2.23	7.49	5.22	2.27	2.16	24.52
	51.6	**9.1**	**30.5**	**21.3**	**9.3**	**8.8**	

Source: Author's computations using data from National Planning Commission and Ministry of Finance and Economic Cooperation.

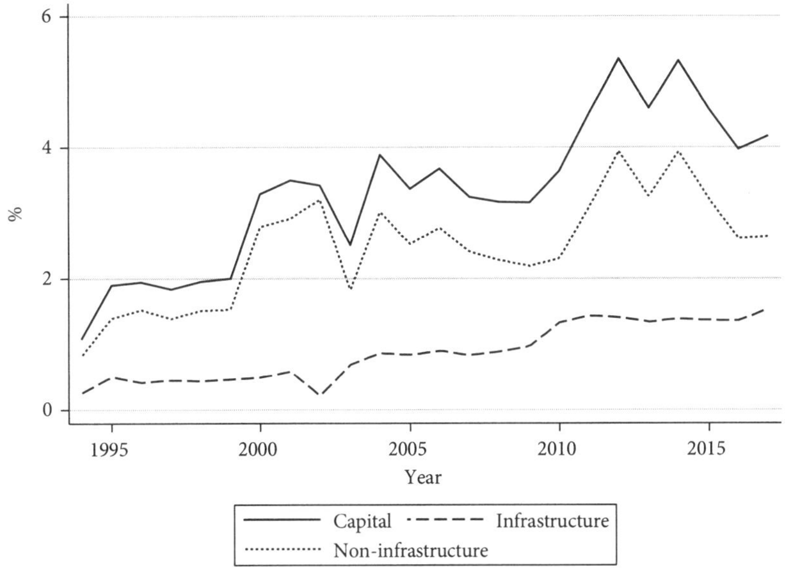

FIGURE 12.3 Trends in the contribution of capital to growth, 1994–2017

Sources: National Planning Commission, and Ministry of Finance and Economic Cooperation.

the saving rate, and the capital–output ratio to estimate the latter as proposed by the Harrod–Domar model.[8] While there are appropriate methods to estimate capital stock more precisely when data allows (Pritchett 2000), this method can still give a fair approximation of the level of capital stock.

An important issue in such exercises is the relative share of infrastructure in output growth. Some empirical studies estimate the average output elasticity of physical infrastructure for developed countries at about 0.15 per cent (Bom and Ligthart 2009). Other empirical studies on developing economies show that a 1 per cent increase in physical infrastructure induces a 1–2 per cent growth in output in the short run (Loayza and Odawara 2010). In this particular case, infrastructure is assumed to have a similar share to conventional physical capital (i.e. $\gamma = 0.33$). Results are presented in Figure 12.3 and Table 12.5.

Figure 12.3 depicts three major episodes in terms of the contribution of economic infrastructure to growth. During the period 1994–2005, the contribution of economic infrastructure was small in magnitude and flat in absolute terms. Economic growth in general was not robust. Real GDP grew at an average rate of 4.8 and 5.9 per cent during the periods 1994–2000 and 2001–5, respectively. Economic infrastructure is estimated to have had a 0.44 percentage-point contribution to the 4.8 per cent growth recorded between 1994 and 2000 (equivalent to a 9.1 per cent contribution to growth). The contribution of economic infrastructure to growth marginally increased to 0.64 percentage

[8] The Harrod–Domar model relates growth with rate of saving and capital–output ratio according to $g + \delta = s/k$, where g = growth rate in real GDP, δ = rate of depreciation, s = investment rate, κ = capital–output ratio.

Table 12.5 Contribution of economic infrastructure to growth: supply side

Period	Labour	Capital		Total factor productivity	Growth in real GDP
		All capital	Infrastructure r = 0.33		
	2.67	2.00	0.44	0.12	4.79
1994–2000	55.7%	41.8%	9.1%	2.5%	
	3.01	3.34	0.64	-0.49	5.87
2001–5	51.4%	56.9%	10.9%	-8.3%	
	2.80	3.38	0.99	4.67	10.86
2006–10	25.8%	31.1%	10.9%	43.1%	
	2.45	4.65	1.40	2.64	9.73
2011–17	25.1%	47.7%	14.4%	27.1%	

Source: Author's computations using data from the National Planning Commission and Ministry of Finance and Economic Cooperation.

points (10.9 per cent of the 5.9 per cent growth in real GDP). The deep trough of the contribution of capital and infrastructure to growth in 2003 was due to the severe drought which occurred in that year.

The second episode was observed between 2006 and 2010 when robust growth was recorded. This period saw the implementation of PASDEP. Real GDP grew at an annual average rate of 10.9 per cent. Absolute contributions of economic infrastructure to economic growth increased. Economic infrastructure had a contribution of 0.99 percentage points to the 10.9 per cent growth in GDP. That means that economic infrastructure accounted for about 9 per cent of the total growth in real GDP recorded in the country under PASDEP.

The third episode was observed during GTP, which began in 2011. Ethiopia's economy measured by real GDP continued to grow at a robust rate of 9.7 per cent for the period between 2011 and 2017 under GTP. Capital deepening dominated the high growth episode recorded in this period. Capital accounted for about 48 per cent of the growth. In other words, 4.7 percentage points of the 9.7 per cent growth in real GDP were contributed by growth in physical capital. About 1.4 percentage points (14.4 per cent) of the total growth was contributed by economic infrastructure. The rate of gross fixed investment increased from 28.6 per cent of GDP in 2006 to 39 per cent in 2017. Estimates showed that investment in economic infrastructure accounted for about 36.1 per cent of total government capital expenditure (78 per cent of capital expenditure on economic and social sectors) over the period 1994 to 2014. The share of investment in economic infrastructure in the total gross fixed investment during the same period was 25.6 per cent.

The direct contribution of infrastructure to growth as capital input and its indirect contribution through making other conventional capital more productive are not disentangled in this exercise. The notion that infrastructure contributes to growth indirectly by making conventional capital more productive in addition to its role as a conventional capital stock implies that the share of infrastructure in growth should be greater than that of conventional capital. This needs to be empirically determined. The bottom line is that the estimated contribution of infrastructure to growth in Ethiopia in this exercise is the minimum possible contribution.

The high share of total factor productivity (TFP) observed under PASDEP (2001–5) (4.7 percentage points) tempted researchers and international partners such as the IMF to doubt the accuracy of the data. Nevertheless, TFP needs to be interpreted in such a way that it represents factors such as restoration of the good weather after two serious droughts during the preceding years, improvements in the capacity utilization of firms in the industrial sector, and of course technical changes.

12.8 Case Studies

More fine-grained evidence and analysis from case studies of the local significance of access to roads complements the aggregate growth analysis in Sections 12.5 and 12.6. The two case studies very briefly summarized here, in turn, may be combined with other relevant evidence. Thus, for example, Cramer, Sender, and Di John (2018) draw on primary research in the Upper Awash Valley to show how serious a constraint the lack of a properly graded and surfaced road is on the profitability of firms producing high-value agricultural exports in the valley and on the scope for further linkages and agglomeration. ODI (2016) show that the economic, social, and environmental costs of 'unconstrained and uncoordinated water development are increasing rapidly'. One example is, again, the Upper Awash Valley, where water scarcity (and increasingly competing interests) has been a constraint on commercial, export-oriented (and domestic market-oriented) agriculture. Poor 'upstream planning and successive below average rainfall in the Awash Basin during 2014 and 2015 meant that even large-scale producers of export commodities experienced water shortages, forcing them to cut back irrigation and curtail planned investment' (ODI 2016: 15). Moreover, water and energy are closely related. For example, in November 2015 the 300MW Tekeze hydro-power scheme in Tigray had to be shut down for days in the wake of poor rains, with a knock-on effect on agriculture, industry, and household energy consumption (ODI 2016: 15). And Shiferaw et al. (2015) draw on firm-level census panel data, combined with town-level panel data on road accessibility, to argue that 'better road accessibility is associated with a town's desirability for manufacturing firms' (i.e. that more firms enter the market in a town that is better connected), and that better road links between a town and major economic destinations is linked to a stronger presence of large firms.

Two local case studies help to show how access to asphalt roads affects, in one case, land values on the outskirts of Addis Ababa and, in the other, patterns of crop choice and incomes among rural farmers. In the first case study, a town on the outskirts of Addis Ababa with a single asphalt road was selected to control for the impact of access to multiple roads. The town of Legetafo is located in the Oromia national regional state adjacent to the north-eastern suburbs of Addis Ababa. Plots of land were selected based on their distances from the single asphalt road passing through it. The plots on either side of the road are located within a 0–2km distance from the road. A regression analysis of the relationship between the price of plots of land and their distance from the asphalt road took into account other likely variables affecting land values. It also looked at how accessibility of a plot of land by vehicle (on a gravel track) affected land values.

The analysis showed that for every increase in distance of 1km from the asphalt road, the price per square metre of land decreased by 1,785 birr (equivalent to US$64 per m^2). Accessibility of the plot by vehicle (for example, on a gravel track) increased the price of the plot by another 415 birr per square metre (US$15 per m^2). In general, prices of plots for business purposes were higher by 3,840 birr per square metre (US$137 per m^2) at zero distance from the asphalt road, while the price of a plot of land allotted to business purposes dropped faster than the price of plots of land allotted for residential purposes as distance from the asphalt road increases.

The second case study[9] investigates the impact of access to a road linking smallholder farms to urban markets, and of access to irrigation infrastructure, on crop choice and levels of rural income in several districts of the Amhara National Regional State. Six villages were selected from two districts with different agro-ecologies, based mainly on distance from urban centres and access to a road linking them to the nearest town. The villages are not necessarily linked by the same road. The village with the nearest distance from a road is 1km away from that road and the furthest village from a road is 10km away from the road. The main premise of this study was that cash crops such as vegetables and fruits fetch higher prices than staple crops and thus can make households better off in terms of income, but that investments in cash crops are riskier in the absence of irrigation and access to markets, which may be made easier and cheaper with better road infrastructure.

Regression analysis showed that both infrastructural facilities—roads and irrigation—significantly affect crop choice in favour of cash crops and raise per capita income. More specifically, the results showed that, at the margin, a 1km increase in distance from the road tended to reduce the proportion of land allocated to the production of cash crops by 12.5 per cent. Distance from urban centres, access to an irrigation scheme, and access to primary and junior schools had significant positive effects on the proportion of land allocated to cash crops.

In addition, other things being equal, an increase in distance from roads of 1km was predicted to reduce per capita income by about 32 per cent. Similarly, farmers operating plots with access to irrigation infrastructure are 36 per cent better off in per capita income compared to those farmers operating plots of land with no access to irrigation schemes.

[9] This case study is adapted from my dissertation 'Rural Livelihood, Migration and Human Capital Formation: The Ethiopian Case', (2007). The theme of the study in the dissertation was, however, different as the focus was on the impact of proximity to urban centres on crop choice and level of rural income.

Clearly, the sample sizes for these studies are far too small to be able to make generalizations about national patterns. But the findings from the case studies do shed some light on the micro-level economic significance of infrastructure. Given the very low levels of infrastructure provision in Ethiopia, this evidence, along with that from other research, suggests an immense scope for further gains from infrastructure investment.

12.9 Infrastructure and Long-Term Growth

Expansion in infrastructure has undoubtedly made a significant contribution to the high growth rates registered in Ethiopia over the twelve years from 2006. The sustainability of the contribution of infrastructure to growth heavily depends on the quality and the kind of sectors that make use of the infrastructure developed. Infrastructure may trigger growth in the short run either by augmenting demand or by serving as a conventional capital input. As capital expansion replaces capital deepening due to diminishing returns, the role of infrastructure in growth will be limited to its capacity to make other conventional capital more productive. It is, therefore, the type and quality of infrastructure in terms of technological content, and the level and direction of structural change, that determine the extent to which infrastructure contributes to long-term growth.

There are cases where infrastructure was expected to play a significant role in triggering long-term growth in developing countries. William Easterly (2001) in his book *The Elusive Quest for Growth* discussed the case of Ghana. In the early 1950s, with the advice of some of the best minds in development economics such as Arthur Lewis, Nicholas Kaldor, Dudley Seers, Albert Hirschman, and Tony Killick, Ghana's President Nkrumah was convinced that investment in roads and even more importantly in a hydroelectric dam on the Volta river with financial support from development partners, notably the United States, the United Kingdom, and the World Bank, would trigger high growth. The Akosombo dam was expected to generate electricity that would be used to smelt and process aluminium, and provide the necessary conditions for a caustic soda plant, water transportation scheme, major new fishing industry, and large-scale farming. A railway system was also planned as an integral part of the project. After more than half a century, only the core component of the project—electricity generation and aluminium smelting—is functional. Most importantly, Ghanaians were no better off as the Ghanaian economy was plunged into stagnation for half a century (Easterly 2001). This implies that infrastructure development is a necessary but not sufficient condition for sustainable economic growth.

Similar projects arose in Ethiopia in the late 1980s. The most notable was the Tana–Beles project. The project aimed at establishing an integrated scheme with components of hydroelectric power generation, urban water supply, mechanized agriculture, agro-industry, and urban infrastructure. The well-planned town of Pawe was one part of that project. Unfortunately, the Tana–Beles project was stalled for about sixteen years until 2006. A stripped-down version of the project is currently operational and generates hydroelectric power.

A third case that shows the importance of the quality and type of infrastructural capital is the different trajectories of growth followed by Botswana and South Korea. When both countries began to lay the foundations for structural transformation in the early 1960s, Botswana was accumulating capital at a rate of more than 50 per cent of GDP, and exhibiting a 12 per cent annual average growth rate in real GDP. South Korea's rate of investment was 30 per cent, and its economy was expanding at an annual rate of 10 per cent. After half a century, the difference in income between the two countries is stark: South Korea is an industrialized high-income country, while Botswana is struggling to maintain its middle-income status. The explanation for the different trajectories of income growth in the two countries may be found not in the size of the initial capital they accumulated but in the quality and type of sector it helped to lead the economy. South Korea's investment in conventional and infrastructural capital fostered a globally competitive manufacturing sector, while capital in Botswana was limited to the extraction of mineral resources (and diamonds in particular).

The contribution of infrastructure to augmenting demand in Ethiopia by creating employment appears to have been already exhausted in the face of supply-side rigidities. Signs include the high cost of living following episodes of high inflation and the recent foreign exchange constraint. Another round of growth can be generated from infrastructural investment if it is accompanied by responses from the supply side, mainly the manufacturing and agriculture sectors, in the form of high productivity. Infrastructure investment in Ethiopia needs to solve strategically critical structural supply bottlenecks in manufacturing and agriculture, such as inefficiency, the technology gap, competitiveness in international markets, and institutional stagnation. However, investment in infrastructure also needs to be accompanied by structural change and institutional transformation.

12.10 Conclusions

In recent years the Ethiopian government has increasingly recognized the indispensable role of infrastructure in fostering economic development. Consecutive development strategies, plans, and overall policy directions since 1995 have stressed infrastructure development. Nevertheless, serious investment by the government in economic infrastructure, in an effort to lay the foundations of structural transformation, only began after 2006, during the PASDEP and GTP periods. From then on, investment in economic infrastructure contributed to growth by inducing aggregate demand and as an important capital input in the production process. Small-scale case studies summarized in this chapter also illustrate how access to road infrastructure significantly and positively affects urban and rural livelihoods. Nevertheless, the stabilization role of infrastructural investment should give way to the more sustainable role of infrastructure: there should be more conventional capital in the productive sectors that make use of the infrastructure already available.

Future research needs to focus on domestic capacity to complete infrastructural projects on time, on ways of improving efficiency in the construction of infrastructure, and on the quality of infrastructure acquired through hard-won financial resources.

References

Bom, P. and J. Ligthart (2009). 'How Productive Is Public Capital? A Meta-Regression Analysis', Working Paper 09–12, Andrew Young School International Studies Program.

Cramer, Christopher, John Sender, and Jonathan Di John (2018). 'Poinsettia Assembly and Selling Emotion: High Value Agricultural Exports in Ethiopia', AFD Research Paper Series, No. 2018–78, August, Paris.

Easterly, William (2001). *The Illusive Quest for Growth: Economists' Adventures and Misadventures in the Tropics* (Cambridge, MA: MIT Press).

Ethiopian Economics Association (2011). 'Report on the Performance of the Ethiopian Economy', EEA, Addis Ababa.

EPRDF (1995). *Development, Peace, and Democracy Plan of Ethiopian People's Democratic Front* (in Amharic). Addis Ababa.

EPRDF (2000). 'Evaluation of the Performance of EPRDF's Development, Peace, and Democracy, and the Second Five-Year Plan of Development, Peace, and Democracy' (in Amharic), Addis Ababa.

ERA (2016). 'Road Sector Development Program: 19 Years Performance Assessment', Ethiopian Road Authority.

Gnogno, Paulos (1992). *Emperor Menilik II* (in Amharic). Ayinalem Book Store (distributor), Addia Ababa, Ethiopia.

Gnogno, Paulos (2010). *Domestic Communications of Emperor Menelik II* (in Amharic) (Addis Ababa: Bole Printing Press).

IEG, Imperial Ethiopian Government (1957). 'First Five-Year Development Plan (1957–1961)', National Economic Council, Office of the Prime Minister, Addis Ababa.

IEG, Imperial Ethiopian Government (1962). 'Second Five-Year Development Plan (1963–1967)', National Economic Council, Office of the Prime Minister, Addis Ababa.

IEG, Imperial Ethiopian Government (1968). 'Third Five-Year Development Plan (1968–1973)', National Economic Council, Office of the Prime Minister, Addis Ababa.

Loayza, N. and R. Odawara (2010). 'Infrastructure and Economic Growth in Egypt', Policy Research Working Paper 5177, World Bank, Washington, DC.

MoFED. National Income Accounts, various issues. Addis Ababa

MoFED (2002). 'Ethiopia: Sustainable Development and Poverty Reduction Program', Addis Ababa.

MoFED (2006). 'Ethiopia: Building on Progress: A Plan for Accelerated and Sustained Development to End Poverty (PASDEP), 2005/06–2009/10', Addis Ababa.

MoFED (2010). 'Growth and Transformation Plan: 2010/11–2014/15', Addis Ababa.

Moller, Lars Christian, and Konstantin M. Wacker (2017). 'Ethiopia's Growth Acceleration and How to Sustain It: Insights from a Cross-Country Regression Model', Policy Research Working Paper 7292, World Bank, Washington, DC.

National Bank of Ethiopia (2017). National Bank of Ethiopia Annual Report, 2016/17.

NPC (2016). 'Growth and Transformation Plan II (GTP II) (2015/16–2019/20)', Vol I (main text), National Planning Commission of the Federal Democratic Republic of Ethiopia, Addis Ababa.

ODI (2016). 'A Thirsty Future? Water Strategies for Ethiopia's New Development Era', ODI, London.

Phillipson, David W. (2012). *Foundations of an African Civilization: Aksum and Northern Horn 1000 BC–AD 1300* (Addis Ababa: Addis Ababa University Press).

Pritchett, L. (2000). 'The Tyranny of Concepts: CUDIE (Cumulated, Depreciated, Investment Effort) Is Not Capital', *Journal of Economic Growth* 5 (4): 361–84.

Shiferaw, Admasu, Måns Söderbom, Eyerusalem Siba, and Getnet Alemu (2015). 'Road Infrastructure and Enterprise Dynamics in Ethiopia', *Journal of Development Studies* 51 (11): 1541–58.

UNDP (2018). 'Understanding African Experiences in Formulating and Implementing Plans for Emergence, Growing Manufacturing in Ethiopia, A Case Study', UNDP, New York.

Zewde, Bahru (1991). *A History of Modern Ethiopia, 1855–1991* (Addis Ababa: Addis Ababa University Press).

CHAPTER 13

FINANCIAL BALANCES AND THE DEVELOPMENT OF THE ETHIOPIAN ECONOMY

KEN COUTTS AND CHRISTINA LASKARIDIS

13.1 Introduction

The Ethiopian economy has shown an impressive growth of GDP over the past decade, averaging over 10 per cent per annum. With population growth of about 2.5 per cent per annum, real GDP per head increased by nearly 8 per cent per annum over the period. Unusually among African countries, growth has been led by substantial infrastructure investment by the public sector, as part of a deliberate strategy not only to secure rapid growth but also to stimulate structural change (see Chapters 12 and 35). The strategy is set in the Growth and Transformation Plan (GTP), whose design embodies the aspirations to developmentalism and which drew on a significant consultation effort within Ethiopia (see Chapter 50). Möller and Wacker (2015) applaud the success of this public investment-led growth performance but question whether this strategy is sustainable without hitting macroeconomic constraints that would bring the growth strategy to a halt.

In this chapter we explore recent trends in the macroeconomic balance of the economy to see whether the stance of fiscal and monetary policy can sustain further large-scale public-sector investment as part of Ethiopia's continuing economic development. We use the available national accounts data to obtain estimates of the financial balances between disposable income and expenditure of the public sector, private sector, and external sector to see what inferences may be drawn about the macroeconomic sustainability of Ethiopia's development. We adopt an analytical framework that has not been applied previously to Ethiopia; we draw on official data and on data that has not previously been made publicly available; and, on the basis of the evidence and analysis, argue that claims that the macroeconomic strategy of the government is unsustainable are exaggerated.

Section 31.2 introduces the macroeconomic framework used to derive financial balances, and this framework is then applied using national accounts data. Finally the implications of the trends in assessing macroeconomic sustainability are discussed.

13.2 Financial Balances

To get a sense of the interrelationships between government fiscal decisions, external trade, and the savings and investment decisions of domestic firms and individuals, it is useful to construct a consistent set of financial balances between the private sector, the public sector, and the balance of payments on current account. The size of the financial balances should indicate aspects of the growth of the economy and the sustainability of its trajectory. The balance for each sector is the difference between the disposable income of that sector and the spending on both consumption and investment. If the balance is positive, it implies that the sector is acquiring *financial* assets (or reducing financial liabilities) from other sectors. This emphasizes the interdependencies of the sectors, such that the spending decisions of the 'real' economy are reflected in the financial transactions between the sectors.[1] This approach to macroeconomic analysis is based on stock-flow consistent macroeconomic modelling, which is particularly associated with the work of Wynne Godley, who in a series of papers and books developed the ideas from the late 1970s onwards (see Godley and Lavoie 2007). The approach integrates the flows of income and expenditure, which are the traditional concern of Keynesian macroeconomics, with the level and changes in financial assets, which have mainly been the focus of monetary economics. A key insight is that persistent surpluses or deficits in the balances imply that assets are accumulating relative to flows of income (or in the case of deficits, liabilities are increasing). Such a process cannot continue indefinitely; at some point the flow imbalances will be corrected. Households will eventually prefer to spend rather than to save, stabilizing the wealth-to-income ratio. Debt can only accumulate until the actual or future expected capacity to service interest payments and repayment of principal is reached. Godley (1999) used this framework for the US economy to predict that rapid growth of GDP over the previous eight years, based on borrowing by the private sector to finance spending, could not be sustained. He was one of the few economists to predict that a financial crisis was imminent around 2008.

We set out below a simple re-arrangement of the basic national income identity to illustrate the approach:

$$Y = C + I + G + X - M \tag{13.1}$$

[1] For example, it implies that if the external sector (the balance of payments on current account) is persistently in deficit, the stock of external debt is increasing over time. If the deficits are large enough, the stock of debt is rising relative to the flow of national income. For further detail, see Equation (13.5) and its discussion.

where Y is the value of GDP (the net output of all goods and services produced annually)
C is consumers' expenditure
I is gross fixed capital formation (investment)
G is government expenditure of current goods and services
X is exports of goods and services
M is imports of goods and services

By deducting total taxation from both sides of Equation (13.1) we re-arrange it as:

$$Y-T=C+I+G-T+X-M \tag{13.2}$$

where T is total taxation. This can be re-expressed in the following form:

$$(S-I)=(G-T)+(X-M) \tag{13.3}$$

where $S=(Y-T)-C$ is saving by the private sector. Equation (13.3) is a much-simplified presentation of the financial balances of the national accounts. In practice we can separate the investment spending of the public and private sectors. There are also various current transfers of income between sectors that may be included. The national income, Y, can be measured to include any net property income and foreign remittances of wages, i.e. the gross national income (GNI), so that the term $X–M$ becomes the current account of the balance of payments.

The Ethiopian national accounts use two independent estimates of GDP. The first is based on final expenditures as set out in Equation (13.1). The second is based on the aggregation of value added by each sector of agriculture, manufacturing, and services. There is as yet no independent income estimate of the GDP based on the wages, rents, and profits earned.[2] Nevertheless, we can infer the scale of the private-sector balance, $S-I$, based on estimates of the current account of the balance of payments and the budget balance of general government (local and central government combined). A significant amount of investment is carried out by state-owned enterprises (SOEs), amounting in recent years to about 15 per cent of GDP. Although we lack information on the retained earnings of the SOEs, as a first approximation we include the investment of the public enterprises with the general government balance, so that we can infer the balance between private saving and private investment.

Our basic financial balance (Equation (13.3)) is just an identity derived from the system of national accounts, reminding us that the financial balances are all inter-related.

Another expression for (13.3) is:

$$(S-I)+(T-G)=(X-M) \tag{13.4}$$

[2] Authorities at the National Accounts Directorate informed us that the latest rebasing of GDP took place in 2015/16, and that under the five-year improvement plan for National Accounts the income approach would soon be available from that year on. This will enable much-improved estimates of the financial balances presented in this chapter. All data in this chapter are based on 2010/11 base year data.

In this form the left-hand side, being the sum of private and public net savings, is equal to national savings less investment. The identity reminds us that national savings less investment equals the current account balance. If the public sector is running a budget deficit of 2 per cent and the current account is also in deficit by 5 per cent, it is a matter of logic that the private sector must be investing 3 per cent more than private saving, i.e. it is borrowing. The government and public enterprise sectors are collectively borrowing from abroad. The counterpart to the current account deficit is an inflow of capital to 'finance' the deficits of the other two sectors.[3]

This is illustrated in the following identity showing the transactions in assets and liabilities that are implied by the sectoral imbalances of income and spending in Equation (13.4):

$$(\Delta A_P - \Delta L_P) + (\Delta A_G - \Delta L_G) = (\Delta A_F - \Delta L_F) \tag{13.5}$$

> A are assets, L are liabilities, Δ is the symbol meaning a change in stock and the subscripts refer to the private (P), government (G), and external sectors (F) respectively. This identity says in conjunction with Equation (13.4) that, for example, if the private sector has a surplus of saving compared with investment, it must be increasing its net *financial* assets (which could imply adding to its gross assets or reducing its gross liabilities). These financial transactions are claims on the public sector or external sector. Equation (13.5) introduces an important distinction between the flows of income less spending and the finance of the imbalances between income and spending for each sector.[4]

The identities (13.4) and (13.5) hold irrespective of the level of GDP. Thus, for any given size of deficit, the financing occurs whether the economy is at a low or high level of activity. It is one of the aims of fiscal and monetary policy that an appropriate set of balances occurs at a high level of demand, relative to the productive capacity of the economy.

[3] It is important to distinguish net saving (income not spent on consumption and investment), which equals the net acquisition of financial assets, from 'financing', which is concerned with the gross flows of assets and liabilities of sectors. On this distinction, see Borio and Disyatat (2015). As an illustration, consider the rapid growth in inward FDI to Ethiopia, which had increased from negligible rates in 2005 to over 2.7 per cent of GDP by 2016. It represents a foreign source of financing of domestic private-sector gross capital formation. The FDI may finance the installation of foreign-sourced machinery in factories, in which case the FDI will be linked with greater imports of machinery. During this phase, although the current account deteriorates, it does not put pressure on the central bank reserves because the FDI 'finances' the imports. If the factories using imported machinery are producing products for export, the current account will subsequently improve, but profits from FDI remitted abroad will worsen the current account.

[4] The identities (4) and (5) indicate that we can attempt to estimate the financial imbalances in two equivalent ways. The first, which we have adopted, is to use the annual time series on the national accounts to measure the flow of saving and investment. A second approach is to use a flow of funds analysis, by measuring directly the transactions in financial assets and liabilities. Such data is much more limited in scope and availability. A third approach is to use social accounting matrices (SAMs), which can be aggregated to give the balance of saving and investment. The SAMs constructed for Ethiopia have so far covered only a few years. We therefore rely on the annual national accounts data for our estimates.

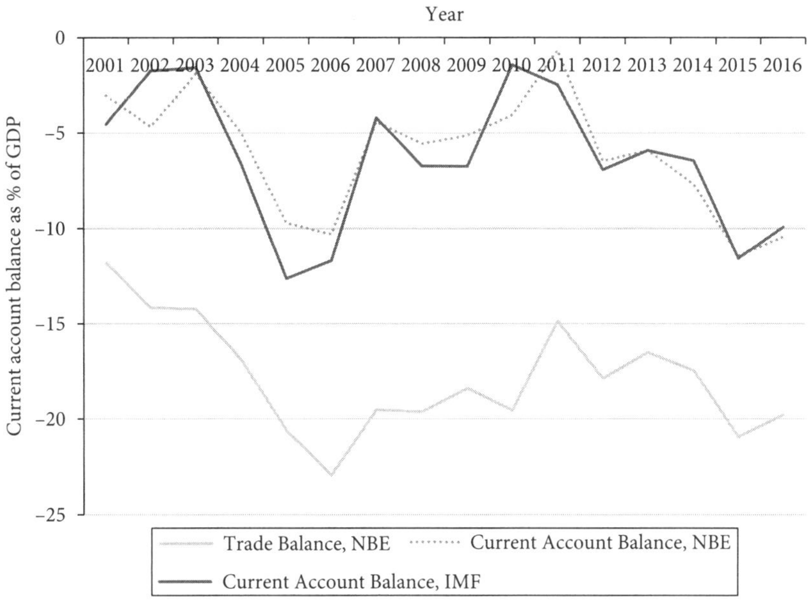

FIGURE 13.1 Current account balances, per cent of GDP

Source: National Bank of Ethiopia (NBE) and IMF.

Before we look at the available macroeconomic data, it is important to be cautious on interpreting the accuracy of the underlying data. Jerven (2016) reminds us of the considerable difficulties of producing reliable data on GDP in African countries.[5] We will be working with data potentially subject to significant degrees of error (on debates about data see also Chapter 18).

13.2.1 The Current Account of the Balance of Payments

Figure 13.1 shows the current account of the balance of payments between 2001 and 2016 and, separately, the balance of goods and services.[6] There are two sources of data on the current account. The first is published by the World Economic Outlook, while the

[5] Geda and Yimer (2016) argue that the growth rates of output measured from the national accounts appear overstated compared with other data on poverty rates in various sectors of the economy and claim that the growth achieved is about half that of the official figures, pointing out that IMF growth rates have been lower than national accounts estimates. Whatever the disagreements on past data, official and IMF calculations of GDP are now in complete alignment and the Fund uses the national accounts data generated by the Ethiopian statistical authorities. Our view is that the data are of sufficient quality to give us confidence in calculating the financial balances presented in this chapter.

[6] Data published by the national authorities are typically based on the Ethiopian fiscal year, which runs from July to the following July. There is a seven-year gap between the Gregorian and the Ethiopian calendars. The latest data we work with are for 2016/17 in the Gregorian calendar, which is 2009 in the Ethiopian calendar.

second comes from the National Bank of Ethiopia, the central bank. The data show some divergences and there is a structural break in the data in 2012, after which the two series move closely together. Prior to 2012, there are large discrepancies in 2002 and 2005. The current account deficit averaged around 5 per cent of GDP between 2001 and 2014 but deteriorated sharply in the last two years reported. The other feature of Figure 13.1 is the large deficit on the balance of goods and services, which has averaged around 17 per cent of GDP since 2005. This has been offset by large income inflows, which are remittances from Ethiopian citizens working abroad and funds from international cooperation (aid). Part of the deterioration in the last two years in Figure 13.1 is in the deficit on goods and services. If this were to continue, with the current account deficit averaging 10 per cent of GDP, this would raise concerns about the sustainability of the domestic development programme with rapid growth of GDP and high investment.

13.2.2 General Government Balance

We have the same two sources of data for the general government balance of taxation and other income less current and capital expenditure: the World Economic Outlook and National Bank of Ethiopia (see Figure 13.2). The two series are broadly consistent but with larger deficits in 2002 and 2006 according to the central bank data. The main feature of the data is the major reduction in the size of the deficit between 2001 and 2009

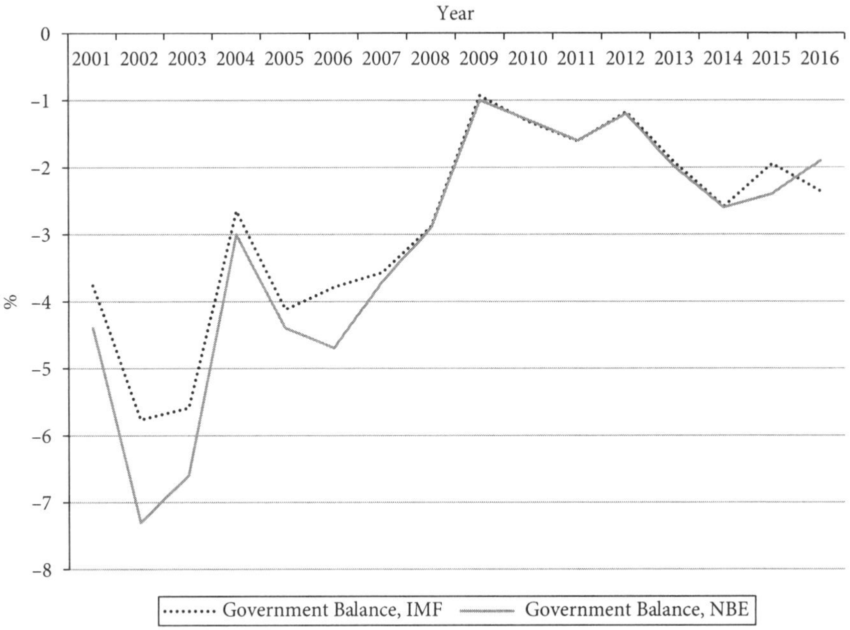

FIGURE 13.2 Government balance, per cent of GDP

Note: Government revenue includes grants.
Source: National Bank of Ethiopia and IMF.

according to both sources. Thereafter, the deficit has been maintained at 1–2.5 per cent of GDP. This trend was also noted by Möller and Wacker (2015) who point out that the government current expenditure was kept constrained, enabling substantial capital expenditure without requiring large budget deficits. Since 2010 the government's balance on current expenditure has averaged a surplus of 8 per cent of GDP.

13.2.3 Fixed Investment

Figure 13.3 shows the trend in public- and private-sector investment. The key features are the high rates of investment of both sectors, with the public sector averaging around 15 per cent of GDP for most of the period (combining general government and state-owned enterprises). Between 2001 and 2011, public-sector investment was the leading contribution to total Ethiopian investment. After 2012, private-sector investment overtook the public sector, averaging about 23 per cent of GDP, although public-sector investment has remained at about 15 per cent of GDP. Within the public sector, general government investment was stable at about 8 per cent of GDP. The investment of public enterprises increased from under 4 per cent to about 10 per cent of GDP in fifteen years. This is a substantial rate of investment and a significant contribution to the overall growth in GDP. The other feature is the sharp rise in private-sector investment after 2011 (Figure 13.4).[7]

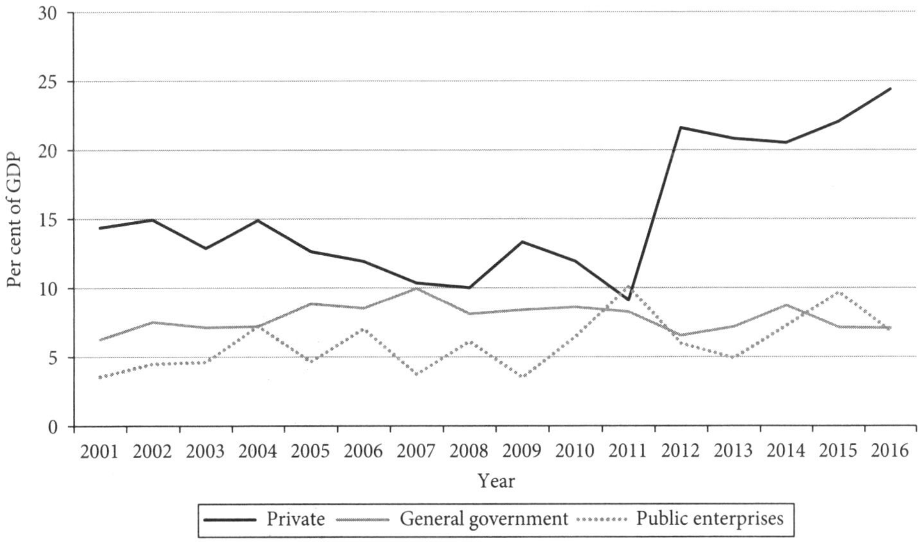

FIGURE 13.3 Gross fixed capital formation by sector, per cent of GDP
Source: National Account Directorate, National Planning Commission.

[7] The structural break in the data occurs in Ethiopian fiscal year 2003 (2010/11) and may be related to the improvement in private investment.

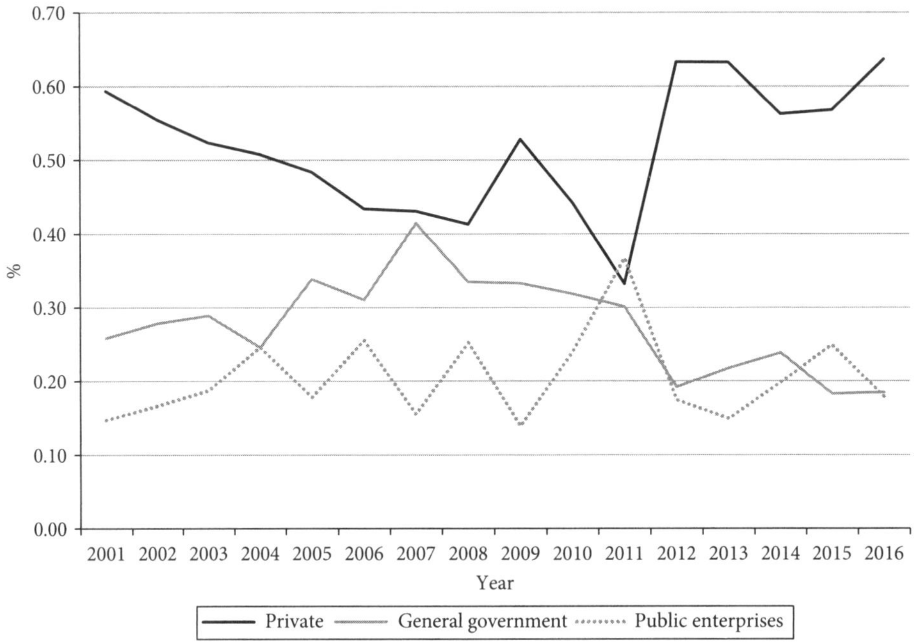

FIGURE 13.4 Composition of investment, share of total

Source: National Account Directorate, National Planning Commission.

Total investment in the past three years has averaged 36 per cent of GDP, peaking at nearly 40 per cent of GDP devoted to gross domestic investment. Together, these figures show the high rate of investment as a leading driver of Ethiopia's economic growth in this period. They also suggest that anxieties that high public investment 'crowds out' private investment are in the Ethiopian case misplaced (see below, Section 13.4).

The structure of investment when separating the public sector into the public enterprises and general government reveals that as a proportion of total investment, the state-owned enterprises have consistently invested around 20 per cent of total investment in the period. Investment by general government, having been substantially higher than the SOEs, has declined since 2011, while the private sector has become the dominant component of total investment since 2012.

13.3 The Financial Balances of the Three Sectors of the Economy

Our derivation of financial balances for the private, public, and the external sector relies on the available published national accounts and balance-of-payments data, supplemented by detailed data provided on request by the national statistical authorities.

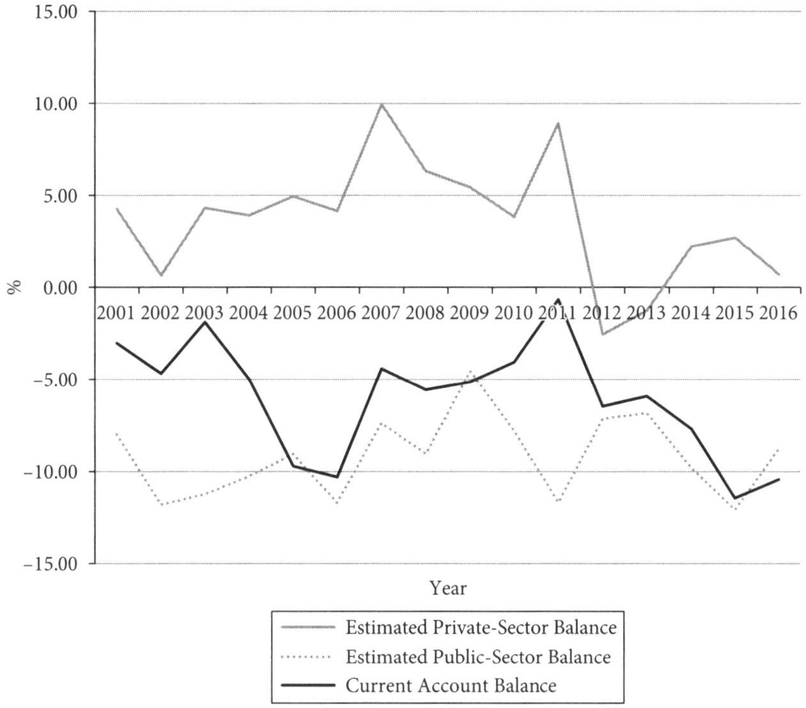

FIGURE 13.5 Three balances, per cent of GDP

Source: National Sources: Central Bank and National Account Directorate.

Our method is to begin with data for gross national savings, which comes from published national accounts sources. We estimate general government savings as revenue less current government expenditure and deduct this from national savings to obtain an estimate of private-sector saving. Total investment is divided into the public sector (general government and public enterprises) and the private sector. The private-sector financial balance is obtained as the difference between private saving and private investment. The public-sector financial balance is the general government balance including the investment of the public enterprises. We do not have a fully consolidated account for the financial balance of the public sector, as the main element of income we lack is the retained profits of the public enterprises.[8]

Our best estimate of the three financial balances is shown in Figure 13.5.

To our knowledge, this is the first presentation of the financial balances of the Ethiopian economy using annual data in this form.[9] As noted earlier, the balance of

[8] After several experiments using international as well as domestic sources of data, we settled on the derivation of the private-sector financial balance as described in the main text. Data on national savings and on the general government balance, as defined in the Government Finance Statistics Manual, comes from the National Bank of Ethiopia. Data on the sectoral composition of investment is from the National Planning Commission.

[9] The IMF publishes regular data on financial balances in its annual reports under Article IV. The data are provided by the Central Statistical Agency and the National Bank of Ethiopia. There is no attempt to

payments has been in deficit with a sharp deterioration in 2015 and 2016. While the general government deficit has remained relatively small since 2009, the addition of the investment spending of SOEs to the public-sector balance increases the deficit to about 9 per cent of GDP on average since 2009. We emphasize that the public-sector deficit is overstated because we lack data on the disposable income of the SOEs. Equivalently, the saving of the private sector is overstated as it includes any retained profits of the SOEs. Despite this lacuna the statistical residual of the financial balances is relatively small for the most recent and, we believe more reliable, years. The average residual for the period shown is just 1 per cent of GDP and since 2010 has been in the range of −3 per cent to +2 per cent of GDP.[10]

The main feature of Figure 13.5 is a deterioration in the private-sector balance from a surplus of about 10 per cent of GDP in 2007, to a surplus of less than 1 per cent by 2016. Given that the current account deteriorated to a 10 per cent deficit in 2016 and that the public-sector deficit was 9 per cent, the private-sector deficit implied by Equation (13.4) would have deteriorated to 1 per cent of GDP:[11]

$$(S-I)+(T-G)=(X-M)$$
$$(-1)+(-9)=-10$$

In the face of the deterioration in the current account deficit, the National Bank of Ethiopia devalued the birr by 15 per cent relative to the US dollar in October 2017. The government hoped that the improvement in the price competitiveness of Ethiopian exports and the effects of past infrastructure investment, increased agricultural export products, and manufacturing projects such as the industrial parks would gradually improve the current account deficit. As an illustration, an improvement in the current account to a small deficit of 3 per cent of GDP, with the public sector limiting its deficit to 9 per cent, would imply that the private-sector surplus increases to 6 per cent of GDP, which was the average surplus achieved between 2001 and 2012. If the improvement were to come from strong growth in net exports, economic growth could be maintained and, by increasing domestic income, would also improve private-sector savings. If net exports were to stagnate, then to reduce the current account deficit to 3 per cent would require restrictive fiscal and monetary policies that reduce the budget deficit, but with

reconcile the balance-of-payments current account with the financial balances for the private and public sectors. The item referred to as the 'resource gap' should in principle be equal to the current account of the balance of payments. It has also been pointed out to us that estimates of private saving less private investment have been published, based on SAMs for 1999/2000, 2005/6 and 2010/11. In their treatment, the SOEs are part of the non-government sector, whereas we have included SOE investment as part of the public sector.

[10] The residual error between the expenditure and production estimate of GDP ranges from −2.9 per cent of GDP to +7.6, averaging around 2 per cent.

[11] Figure 13.5 shows a small surplus for the private sector in 2016 because of a 2 per cent positive residual.

adverse effects on the growth rate of GDP and employment (see Thirlwall (2011) on the balance of payments as a constraint on economic growth).

13.3.1 Debt Implications of the Financial Balances and the Risks to Sustained Growth

Ethiopia is one of many low-income countries that were beneficiaries of the debt relief initiatives of recent decades. External debt stocks were significantly reduced to their lowest level in 2007; so recent rises start from a low level. UNCTAD has warned of the dangers of a new debt trap across the continent, placing Ethiopia among the twelve sub-Saharan African heavily indebted poor countries whose indicators have recently deteriorated (UNCTAD 2015, 2016). Both the head of the African Development Bank and the Managing Director of the IMF have warned of the potential of a new debt crisis in sub-Saharan Africa (Aglionbi 2016). One of the characteristics of this recent trend is the change in borrowing patterns brought about by the increasing importance of private actors among sub-Saharan Africa's debtors and creditors (Bonizzi and Laskaridis 2018). Although historically excluded from capital markets, access to international borrowing has eased, with one reason identified being expansionary US monetary policy and abundant global liquidity (Akyüz 2017).

Ethiopia's external and domestic debts have risen in recent years; total foreign borrowing stands at approximately 30 per cent of GDP, with state-owned enterprises comprising close to two-thirds of it. Debt indicators, although far from perfect, show the trajectories in the burden and ability to service debts. In Figure 13.6 a set of relevant indicators shows the deterioration over the past decade. By 2016, close to 20 per cent of exports of goods, services, and primary income were in the service of repaying external public and publicly guaranteed debt (PPG), approaching the threshold set by the IMF and World Bank as representing danger levels. With respect to government revenue, this external debt service takes up over 10 per cent of general government revenue excluding grants. As indicated in IMF (2018a), the PPG debt-to-exports ratio breaches the threshold for consecutive years and, as such, according to the most recent classification in the IMF and World Bank's Sustainability Framework, Ethiopia is at high risk of debt distress alongside ten other countries in sub-Saharan Africa. It was only fairly recently, in 2013 and 2014, that Ethiopia was classified as low risk.[12]

Although the absolute level of international reserves has risen almost four-fold from 2007 to a peak in 2015, as a share of GDP and as a share of external debt, reserves have declined substantially. The ratio of reserves to external debt has declined from a high of around 30 per cent to a recent low of just over 10 per cent. In terms of months of imports,

[12] A recent IMF policy paper (IMF 2018b) on macroeconomic developments in low-income developing countries noted that Ethiopia was assessed as at high risk of debt distress in the latest debt sustainability analysis of January 2018. Commenting on the IMF policy paper, UNCTAD officials were even more cautious about debt prospects (UNCTAD 2018), arguing that IMF forecasts have had an optimistic bias.

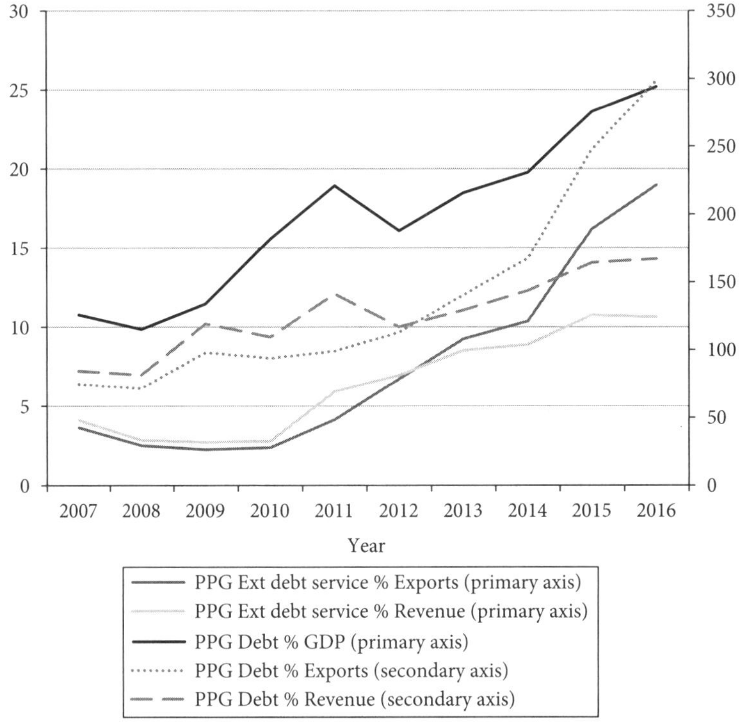

FIGURE 13.6 Debt indicators

Source: National Accounts Directorate, World Bank International Debt Statistics and National Bank of Ethiopia.

the traditional rule-of-thumb measure of reserve adequacy, which is three months of imports, was last reached in 2010–11. Currently reserves amount to one and a half months of imports.

The composition of Ethiopia's external creditors has changed over the last decade. Ethiopia's public sector has borrowed from previously absent private foreign sources. Since 2009 the public sector has borrowed from foreign commercial banks and since 2014 from international capital markets.

The composition of Ethiopia's official external creditors has also shifted; since 2014, the largest official lenders are non-Paris Club bilateral lenders, overwhelmingly China, followed by IDA (World Bank) and the African Development Bank. Another characteristic of this change in composition of Ethiopia's foreign creditors is the decline in the incidence of concessional debt as a share of total external debt. Averaging over 85 per cent between 1981 and 2005, this declined to an average of 66 per cent in the period 2006–16. This indicates that a larger share of foreign loans is on market terms. There is also a concomitant rise in the share of total external debt that is under a variable rate, increasing the risks to debt servicing, should global interest rates rise as is likely to occur after such a prolonged period of low rates in developed countries. In 2016 the proportion of total external debt that was variable rate was 37 per cent. Although in a number of cases the rise in variable rates has not yet been charged to borrowers, this is likely to occur eventually. The main currency of Ethiopia's external public and publicly guaranteed debt is the US dollar. With the global financial crisis, the share of the dollar in external debt declined from the peak of 77 per cent in 2001 to 54 per cent in 2008 but has since returned to its previous peak. However, although close to 80 per cent of foreign loans are in US dollars, the United States represents one of *several* important trading partners, making Ethiopia particularly vulnerable to dollar–euro and dollar–renminbi exchange rate fluctuations.

Does the continued current account deficit and the risks raised by increased foreign borrowing warrant a change of macroeconomic policy at this stage? Our judgement is that the debt and servicing ratios are not excessive by historical standards. The factors discussed earlier as a consequence of the investment programme and the recent devaluation of the currency could provide the conditions for export-led growth at a time when world trade is growing strongly. In some sectors of agriculture which trade at prices set in international markets, the main improvement is a rise in profitability of exporting, but supply responses may be small. For other commodities such as Ethiopian coffee, prices can be lower, leading to more coffee exports. Manufacturing may also benefit from lower prices leading to greater production. While supply responses may be slow, the birr value of exports can be expected to increase more rapidly.[13] Despite our concerns regarding the debt position, our view is that the best way of managing the reduction in the current account is by more net exports rather than slow growth induced by restrictive fiscal and monetary policy.

13.4 Prospects for Macroeconomic Stability

There has been considerable debate about whether the strategy pursued by the Ethiopian government remains sustainable. Drawing on our analysis of macroeconomic balances and the interactions between public, private, and external balances, we contribute to this debate. In particular we relate our analysis to three recent studies. The first is a World Bank report that concentrates on the aggregate savings ratio and policies that might be taken to raise it. The second is a paper by World Bank economists using cross-country evidence to assess the effects of continuing policies and alternatives on

[13] There is a considerable literature on the role of the real exchange rate in promoting economic growth. Rodrik (2008) argues in favour of a maintained undervalued exchange rate to promote growth in developing countries. Guzman, Ocampo, and Stiglitz (2017) argue that a managed and stable real exchange rate provides a means of reallocating factors of production to sectors with learning spillovers that promote development.

economic growth. The third is the annual IMF report (IMF 2018a), which focuses on conjunctural and policy factors to assess prospects for continuing growth without a financial crisis.

The World Bank (World Bank 2013) argues that given the high rates of domestic investment, the savings rate from domestic sources is inadequate and risks relying on external financing in circumstances that could make the economy vulnerable to changes in capital markets and interest rates. The report considers the determinants of saving according to economic theory. The report accepts that there may be two-way causation between income growth and the savings rate in aggregate. The direction of causation makes a great difference to the type of policy adopted which aims to raise the savings rate. Economic theory is not conclusive on the direction of causation. However, the main evidence put forward in the report is based on a panel data analysis for nearly twenty countries over approximately twenty-five years. There are positive and significant relationships between the savings rate and economic growth for sub-Saharan African countries but not for Asian countries in the sample. There is a significant negative and non-linear relation between real interest rates and the savings rate. A quadratic term is used to specify the non-linear relation, implying that at low real interest rates (positive or negative) there is a positive relation with saving, but at high real interest rates the relation is negative. If the data points are on the positive arm of the quadratic, the relation is positive but at a declining rate. If the data points include the negatively sloped arm, raising real interest rates reduces savings. With this type of panel data analysis, the difficulty is in disentangling macroeconomic effects that interest rates have on the rate of growth. Restrictive monetary policy, by raising real interest rates, may reduce aggregate demand, lowering the rate of economic growth and therefore ultimately lowering overall domestic savings. Disentangling episodes of restrictive policy by various countries to reduce inflation or improve current account deficits from the factors that are affecting the rate of saving achieved as the economy grows is extremely difficult. While reforms at the microeconomic level to extend pension provision, widen access to savings banks, and so on, are welcome and while a move to positive real returns is necessary, there is a risk that if restrictive monetary policy is the main way of raising interest rates, the resulting impact on aggregate demand may result in lower economic growth and savings.

Möller and Wacker (2015) praised the successful economic development of the past decade, led by public-sector investments while maintaining macroeconomic stability. They noted that the public sector-led structure of development included heterodox financing policies such as direct borrowing from the central bank in contrast to that of other African countries, in which reforms to promote private-sector development were more prominent. They questioned whether, despite this phase of success, the strategy was sustainable without hitting macroeconomic constraints that would bring the rapid growth to a halt. The authors use panel data from 125 or more countries and four time period averages (to reduce the influence of business-cycle factors) to explain growth in GDP per head. The explanatory variables include a range of economic and development indicators. In particular, the explanatory variable for government size is government consumption relative to GDP. The specific role of public-sector investment by Ethiopia is only captured indirectly if, as has been the case, current government expenditure has been tightly controlled. The role of this variable is to indicate whether investment is 'crowded out' by excessive government spending.

The results of the analysis are used to examine three scenarios. The first is *business as usual*, i.e. a continuation of the public sector-led investment strategy. The second is *private-sector reform*, with greater prominence given to market incentives for the private sector to develop. The third is *accelerated public investment*, which they argue might risk the private sector being crowded out and higher inflation. Their results show that the outcomes for growth are not sensitive to the assumptions underlying each scenario, with average growth rates of around 4 per cent per annum for each scenario. This lack of sensitivity is probably a limitation of the underlying panel data analysis. The growth projections are, however, likely to be too low, whatever strategy for the future is adopted by the Ethiopian authorities. Even if the 10 per cent per annum over the past decade is not maintained, it is more likely to remain in the 6–8 per cent range. The IMF expects growth to be closer to 8 per cent per annum.

The annual report from the IMF on economic developments in Ethiopia, agreed with the Ethiopian government in January 2018, is generally positive (IMF 2018a). The combination of past investments in infrastructure, the development of manufacturing by domestic and foreign companies, the strong growth in private investment, and the boost to price competitiveness given by the devaluation of the birr in 2017 are likely to help maintain rapid growth of GDP over the next five years. The Fund's main caveat is concern about current account imbalances with only a slow improvement in the deficit projected, increasing debt ratios, and weak central bank reserves. The IMF approves the measures taken in conjunction with the devaluation to adopt a more restrictive fiscal stance and tighter monetary policy to contain the inflation effect of the devaluation. IMF staff expect continued growth of about 8 per cent per annum, not far short of the 10 per cent rates achieved over the past decade.

Drawing on the financial balance approach, this chapter puts forward a view that highlights the interconnectedness of the three macroeconomic sectors: the private, the public, and the external. A reconstruction of the three balances for the Ethiopian economy shows that a positive private-sector balance is most effectively maintained by closing the current account deficit, which may materialize given recent government policy. Contrary to the concern that high public-sector investment may 'crowd out' private-sector investment, the figures confirm that the private sector is the lead investing sector alongside high levels of public-sector investment.

There are some grounds for the view that Ethiopia's high rate of infrastructure investment and recent currency depreciation will improve the balance of payments. The re-opened rail link to the port at Djibouti, the Modjo dry port southeast of Addis Ababa, improved road links such as the toll road to Adama, and the expansion of Bole International Airport passenger and freight facilities all contribute to easier and quicker flow of trade. The industrial parks, such as Hawassa, are designed to promote more exports. Although much remains to be done to link areas of high value agricultural exports to improved roads, the infrastructure will enhance the capacity to raise export earnings.

The main caveat is that if the benefits of past infrastructure and development investment, supplemented by the macroeconomic policies put in place following the devaluation of the currency, fail to make a significant reduction in the current account deficit, then there are real risks of exposure to external debt with consequences for the impressive growth achieved to date. The crux of the issue may lie in other policy areas and institutions and whether these can relax constraints on the growth of exports and productivity throughout the economy. Other chapters in this *Handbook* address this issue (see Chapters 15, 39, 35, and 36).

Acknowledgements

We are very grateful to officials of the national statistical authorities of Ethiopia and the Ethiopian Development Research Institute (EDRI) for their help and cooperation in providing detailed data and in answering our many questions about data sources. We are particularly indebted to Yohannes Ghebru at EDRI and Mr Leluseged at the National Accounts Directorate. We are also grateful to participants of the OUP *Handbook* authors' workshop held in Addis Ababa on 9–11 February 2018, for helpful comments on a preliminary outline of this chapter. Finally, we are grateful to the editors of this volume for their help and advice. All errors are our own.

References

Aglionbi, J. (2016). 'African Development Bank Chief Warns Africa on International Debt', *Financial Times*, 30 August.

Akyüz, Y. (2017). *Playing with Fire: Deepened Financial Integration and Changing Vulnerabilities of the Global South* (Oxford: Oxford University Press).

Bonizzi, B. and C. Laskaridis (2018). 'Global Liquidity, Private Actors and Debt Sustainability in Sub-Saharan Africa', unpublished working paper.

Borio, C. and P. Disyatat (2015). 'Capital Flows and the Current Account: Taking Financing (More) Seriously', BIS Working Papers No 525, Bank for International Settlements.

Geda, A. and A. Yimer (2016). 'Growth, Poverty and Inequality in Ethiopia, 2000–2013: A Macroeconomic Appraisal', <https://www.researchgate.net/profile/Alemayehu_Geda/publication/264004552_Growth_Poverty_and_Inequality_in_Ethiopia_2000-2013_A_Macroeconomic_Appraisal/links/00b7d53c88d4ed0f9e000000.pdf> (15 January 2016).

Godley, W. (1999). 'Seven Unsustainable Processes: Medium-Term Prospects and Policies for the United States and the World', reprinted in *The Stock-Flow Consistent Approach: Selected Writings of Wynne Godley*, ed. M. Lavoie and G. Zezza (Basingstoke: Palgrave Macmillan): 216–54.

Godley, W. and M. Lavoie (2007). *Monetary Economics: An Integrated Approach to Credit, Money, Income, Production and Wealth* (Basingstoke: Palgrave Macmillan).

Guzman, M., J. A. Ocampo, and J. E. Stiglitz (2017). 'Real Exchange Rate Policies for Economic Development', NBER Working Paper 23868.

IMF (2018a). 'IMF Report for the 2017 Article IV Consultation', IMF Country Report 18/18, January, IMF, Washington, DC.

IMF (2018b). 'Macroeconomic Developments and Prospects in Low-income Developing Countries—2018', IMF Policy Paper, Washington, DC.

Jerven, M. (2016). 'Africa by Numbers: Reviewing the Database Approach to Studying African Economies', *African Affairs* 115 (459): 342–58.
Möller, L. C. and K. M. Wacker (2015). 'Ethiopia's Growth Acceleration and How to Sustain It', Policy Research Working Paper 7292, World Bank, Washington, DC.
Rodrik, D. (2008). 'The Real Exchange Rate and Economic Growth', Brookings Papers in Economic Activity No. 2.
Thirlwall, A. P. (2011). 'Balance of Payments Constrained Growth Models: History and Overview', *Economia civile* 64 (259): 307–51.
UNCTAD (2015). 'Revisiting Debt Sustainability in Africa', Note by the UNCTAD Secretariat, Trade and Development Board, 61st Executive Session, United Nations, Geneva.
UNCTAD (2016). 'Economic Development in Africa Report: Debt Dynamics and Development Finance in Africa', United Nations, Geneva.
UNCTAD (2018). 'Debt Warning Lights Flash for Poorest Countries, Experts Say', 3 May 2018, News report on IMF paper presented in Geneva (Geneva: United Nations). Available at: http://unctad.org/en/pages/newsdetails.aspx?OriginalVersionID=1742
World Bank (2013). 'Ethiopia Economic Update II: Laying the Foundation for Middle Income Status', Report 78501, June, World Bank, Washington, DC.

CHAPTER 14

TRADE POLICY IN ETHIOPIA, 1991–2016

BERIHU ASSEFA GEBREHIWOT

14.1 Introduction

Trade is a critical part of Ethiopia's recent economic experiences and its prospects for sustained structural transformation. The overarching aim of trade policy in the country has been to support an acceleration of this transformation by exploiting the dynamic advantages of trade, which include productivity gains, technological learning, and scale advantages. In order to understand Ethiopia's trade policy and examine its place in the overall development process, it is critical to first analyse the overall development context within which trade policy has been designed and framed. We suggest that at least the following three elements of that context help provide a background to subsequent sections.

First, Ethiopia has pursued a 'developmental state' model since the early 2000s, largely inspired by the development experience of East Asian countries, including the more recent remarkable growth of China. In developmental state thinking, the state plays a crucial and irreplaceable role in development (see Chapter 46). The implications for trade policy are immense. Under the developmental state framework, trade policy emerges as a key instrument to be used in tandem with other development policies such as investment to revamp and increase efficiency of economic activities, and to achieve competitiveness in international markets.[1] Trade policy designed in isolation does not serve much purpose in development. The state defines the overall policy objectives first,

[1] There is no single 'developmental state' framework on which all commentators agree and the concept itself is varied and contested but for the sake of clarity we draw on a simple summary idea of the developmental state as a state whose policies are organized primarily around securing accelerated structural change and economic 'catch-up' with advanced economies; this typically involves a state that 'gets prices wrong' and intervenes in the interests of long-run economic development.

and trade synchronized with other complementary policies simply serves to realize this objective. This is the reason why Ethiopia's trade policy does not exist as one unified document; rather, it is integrated with other policies, strategies and programmes. For example, it exists as the 'Trade and Industry' chapter in the Growth and Transformation Plans (GTP) I and II.

Second, Ethiopia's development strategy, as described in GTP-II (NPC 2016) has been to promote an agricultural-based, manufacturing sector-driven and export-led development strategy. Ethiopia has invested heavily in infrastructure, industrial skills development and agricultural productivity, all of which contribute critically to industrial development by reducing production costs and creating a conductive business environment. This has entailed a distinctive emphasis on public (capital) expenditure (Moller and Wacker 2017). Much of the infrastructural investment has been directed along what the government calls 'development corridors or development hubs', which include industrial and integrated agro-parks. While most of the industrial parks were initially inhabited by FDI firms, the government expected most of the investment linkages with the local economy to happen along these development corridors and around the industrial parks. The urgent need was for trade policy, linked to these infrastructure investments and supported by them, to promote faster growth of Ethiopian exports by augmenting their global competitiveness, made all the more important by the pressing balance-of-payments constraint and the frequent foreign exchange shortages with which Ethiopia is grappling.

Third, a key feature of the globalizing world in recent years has been the emergence of global value chains (GVCs) and the increasing concentration of organizational power within them, in what Nolan, Zhang, and Liu (2007) call the 'global business revolution'. It has become a global reality that production is increasingly organized within these GVCs. Any country that tried to stay outside these production networks would simply lose its competitiveness. A more realistic approach would be to position oneself to exploit opportunities that such enhanced involvement in GVCs might bring and to try to minimize the scope for getting stuck on the bottom rung of value chains. GVCs have grown complex, interlinking networks of trade in goods and services as well as capital and ideas globally. This global reality has great implications for Ethiopia's trade development. Ethiopia's trade policy, which guides the country's trade negotiations, agreements, and accessions, needs to factor in this quickly spreading global phenomenon. Its relevance for Ethiopia is even more direct because the sectors that Ethiopia prioritizes—textile and apparel, and agri-business—now come under international production networks with a range of countries involved.

Against the backdrop of these policy and global contexts, the government's development ambition has been to become Africa's leading manufacturing hub by 2025. In order to achieve this, Ethiopia has to achieve and sustain accelerated growth. GTP-II identifies that at the heart of accelerated growth are increasing agricultural productivity and building manufacturing capability. Central to this are the investments that Ethiopia has been making in skill development, infrastructure, and institutional and regulatory reforms. These investments have created a favourable investment climate for both domestic and foreign firms (ECA 2016). Some of these investments and reforms have already started to pay off. For example, in the past five years the FDI flow to Ethiopia has increased more than four-fold from a little over 1 billion US$ in 2012/13 to more than 4.2 billion in 2016/17.[2] The fact that most of these FDI firms are investing in the manufacturing sector shows that the quality of investments is improving and this is expected to catalyse industrial linkages, learning, and upgrading, which will eventually speed up Ethiopia's structural transformation. The other indicator that may show the quality of investments is improving is the arrival of top brand groups such as PVH and TAL in the textile and apparel sector in Ethiopia.

However, Ethiopia's ambition of becoming Africa's leading manufacturing hub will be realized when the manufacturing firms are able to find and consolidate regional and global markets. As the productive sector swells, Ethiopia will need to be more aggressive in both finding and consolidating markets bilaterally, regionally, and internationally. Beyond securing market access for its products in international markets, there has been a growing recognition that if Ethiopia is to achieve its vision and GTP targets, it will have to significantly improve the efficiency of its domestic industries. Exporting is regarded as the most important avenue to increase quality and efficiency through international learning.

To this end, the government is already making efforts to improve its trade integration. As Ethiopia proceeds to greater trade integration (through negotiations, agreements, and accessions) to secure and consolidate markets for its growing manufactured goods, the key questions are:

(a) What should Ethiopia's approach be towards these trade negotiations at the regional, extra-regional and multilateral levels?
(b) How does Ethiopia exploit the opportunities and minimize the risks from the trade integrations?

Our goal in this chapter is to provide some answers to these questions. We take these to be the central questions of policy relevance. To the extent that the empirical literature demonstrates that the size of the benefit from trade integration depends on how well thought through and coherent a country's trade policy is in relation to its overall development policies, discussions on what Ethiopia could do to improve its trade regime, institutions, and facilitations are relevant. To generate forward-looking suggestions for better trade integration, it would be useful to critically scrutinize the trade policy reforms of the past two decades and a half.

The rest of the chapter is organized as follows. We first discuss Ethiopia's trade policy regimes and reforms of the past two decades and their implications for the country's trade integration plans. We next look at Ethiopia's ambitions, plans, and efforts in trade integration so far before considering how the country can improve its trade regime, trade institutions, and trade facilitation and minimize political economy constraints,

[2] https://www.ethioembassy.org.uk/wp-content/uploads/2018/02/January-2018-Newsletter.pdf (see page 9)

exploiting the opportunities of trade integration to sustain its growth and transform its economy. Finally we offer some conclusions.

14.2 Review of Ethiopia's Trade Policy Regimes and Reforms

The wave of trade liberalization that has been engulfing sub-Saharan African (SSA) countries since the 1980s (Milner and Morrissey 1999) has also lately struck Ethiopia, which had been pursuing a protective trade regime for several decades. This section critically reviews Ethiopia's trade regime and the trade policy reforms that have been implemented since 1991.

Since the change in government in 1991, the Ethiopian economy has undergone major transformation, moving away from central planning towards a market-based economy. The socialist government's (1974–91) economic restructuring, based on massive regulation and nationalization, led the country to become one of the most heavily regulated and closed economies in the world. The outcome, especially when combined with protracted civil war, was severe macroeconomic instability, dismal economic outcomes, and social crisis.

Since 1992, the new government has implemented a series of extensive economic reforms.[3] The economic liberalization processes were supported by, and strongly encouraged by, the IMF and World Bank as part of the Structural Adjustment Programme implemented in transition economies during that time. The key elements of the reform programme included:

- import liberalization through rationalization of the tariff structure;
- reduction of quantitative restrictions and simplification of licensing procedures on imports;
- liberalization of the foreign exchange market (such as the removal of restrictions and the substantial devaluation of the birr);[4]
- removal of subsidies and export tax rebate;
- liberalization of input and output prices (except for petroleum); and
- introduction of a new investment code, labour and public enterprise laws, and privatization agency.

[3] See Gebreeyesus (2013).

[4] The Ethiopian birr remained at the rate of 2.07 between 1973 and 1992. The exchange rate was one of the reform areas the new government embarked on. Consequently, the first devaluation wave slashed the birr by about 142 per cent (i.e. from 2.07 to 5 birr per dollar) in 1992. Since 1992, Ethiopia has followed an exchange-rate arrangement which the IMF would classify as crawl-like exchange rate. In the recent past, the National Bank of Ethiopia conducted two devaluations, in September 2010 (17 per cent) and in October 2017 (15 per cent), in an attempt to boost exports and alleviate the foreign exchange shortage.

Although supported by the IMF and the Bank, most of these were unilateral, home-driven reforms in response to market failures or policy demands. The immediate objective was to stabilize, restructure, and rehabilitate a very weak economy inherited from the socialist government. The longer-term objective of implementing trade liberalization was to increase the efficiency of national industries through competition with the outside world (Milner and Morrissey 1999). Below we analyse more closely some of the major trade reforms, focusing on tariff and non-tariff reforms.

14.2.1 Tariffs

The pre-1991 period was characterized by high tariffs and excessive quantitative restrictions. Before reform, the tariff structure was complex with highly variable rates, many exemptions, and high average tariff rates. Pre-1991, there were about twenty-five ad valorem tariff bands ranging from zero to 230 per cent, and covering about 91 per cent of all importable items. While a 230 per cent tariff rate was levied on luxury consumer goods, many intermediate and investment goods were imported with zero duty. By 2018 the maximum tariff rate was only 35 per cent, which is 85 per cent less than the rates in the pre-reform period. The number of tariff bands was reduced from the pre-reform twenty-five to six in 2003. And the simple average tariff rate was also slashed substantially over the reform period, contracting to 17.5 per cent in 2018 from about 41.96 per cent prior to 1993 (see Table 14.1).

14.2.2 Non-Tariff Barriers

The key element under this is foreign exchange pegging and rationing. The birr remained strictly pegged to the US dollar for most of the pre-reform period. Parallel to this, stringent foreign exchange rationing was introduced. Before the reform, importers were classified under four categories for the purpose of foreign exchange allocations: state-owned enterprises, government departments such as ministries, private sector

Table 14.1 Maximum tariffs and weighted averages by year

	Year				
	Prior to 1993	1993	1996	2000	2002
Maxim tariff rates	230%	80%	60%	40%	35%
Weighted average rate	41.96%	29.96%	25%	19.5%	17.5%

Source: Gudissa and Mishra (2014).

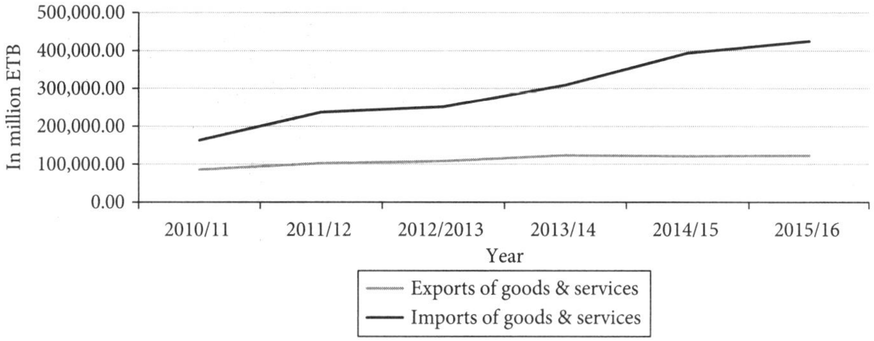

FIGURE 14.1 Current account deficit
Source: National Planning Commission (2016).

producers, and commercial traders. State-owned firms and government departments enjoyed preferential treatment in the allocation of foreign exchange compared to their private counterparts (World Bank 2002). These preferential treatments have been abolished. The negative list, which lists consumer goods that are not entitled to obtain foreign exchange from the official channel, was revised several times before being eliminated altogether in 1997. All import items except second-hand clothing and those prohibited for health and safety reasons are now entitled to obtain foreign exchange from the official channel without any restrictions (IMF 1999).

Despite the tariff and non-tariff liberalization efforts, trade reform outcomes have not been impressive. As indicated in Figure 14.1, Ethiopia has not only sustained a large trade balance gap but also faced a widening trade balance.

The key question is why, despite the significant trade reforms that have moved the country towards a more market-oriented economy in line with international advice, the balance of payments problem has worsened over the last fifteen years, with the gap increasing recently to reach nearly 20 per cent of GDP in 2015/16 (see Table 14.2).

What is even more worrying is the finding revealed in Table 14.3, which presents merchandise trade by broad sector categories: agriculture, government-targeted sectors, and major net importing sectors. Column 6 presents the amount of net trade for these sector categories. Not surprisingly, agriculture shows a positive net trade. On the other hand, sectors targeted for government support (such as textiles and apparel, leather and leather products, food and beverages, metals and metal products, and chemicals) show a large trade deficit. Of the government-targeted sectors, only leather and leather products show a slight positive net trade. All the rest have a negative net trade. This is not good news for Ethiopia given that these sectors have been strongly supported by the government and are expected to be major generators of foreign currency for the country.

There are several explanations for the widening current account deficit. The first is the weak performance of the government-targeted (or priority) sectors. This can be further explained by the existence of an anti-export bias. Gebreeyesus, Abebe, and Berhanu (2017)

Table 14.2 Ethiopia's current account deficit

Description	2010/11	2011/12	2012/2013	2013/14	2014/15	2015/16
Exports of goods & services (in million ETB)	85,950.40	102,886.60	108,227.10	123,496.00	121,532.20	122,365.70
Imports of goods & services (in million ETB)	162,487.10	236,383.90	251,300.60	308,691.30	393,188.50	424,525.30
Trade deficit (in million ETB)	−76,536.70	−133,497.30	−143,073.50	−185,195.30	−271,656.30	-302,159.60
GDP at market prices (in million ETB)	515,078.50	747,326.50	866,921.10	1,060,825.40	1,297,961.40	1,528,044.20
Deficit as % of GDP	−14.9	−17.9	−16.5	−17.5	−20.9	−19.8

Source: National Planning Commission.

Table 14.3 Ethiopian merchandise trade by broad categories, 2017

	Imports	Share of total imports	Exports	Share of total exports	Net trade	Ratio of imports to export
Traditional agricultural products	**106617**	**0.248410791**	**2243553**	**78.37416658**	**2136936**	**0.047521498**
Coffee, tea, mate, and spices	4656	0.010848182	963031	33.64161757	958375	0.004834735
Oil seeds and oleaginous fruits	9791	0.022812404	446273	15.5896805	436482	0.021939485
Live trees and other plants; bulbs, roots and the like; cut flowers and ornamental foliage	2567	0.005980946	221928	7.752623647	219361	0.011566814
Edible vegetables and certain roots and tubers	74913	0.174542499	538365	18.80673565	463452	0.13914909
Live animals	8864	0.020652553	61918	2.162985072	53054	0.143157079
Lac; gums, resins and other vegetable saps and extracts	5826	0.013574207	12038	0.42052415	6212	0.483967436
Sectors targeted for government support	**1986510**	**4.628441254**	**164022**	**5.729790003**	**−1822488**	**12.11124117**
Textiles and apparel	331409	0.772161775	68080	2.378242574	-263329	4.867934783
Leather and leather products	20437	0.047616903	82483	2.881383405	62046	0.247772268
Processed agricultural products	113702	0.264918388	12747	0.445291688	−100955	8.919902722
Metals and metal products	1368778	3.189165201	92	0.003213841	−1368686	14878.02174
Chemicals	152184	0.354578987	620	0.021658496	−151564	245.4580645
Major net import sectors	**17931831**	**41.78001941**	**58221**	**2.033837557**	**−17873610**	**307.9959293**
Commodities not elsewhere specified	0	0	NA	0	0	0
Boilers, machinery, etc.	14692143	34.23175357	379	0.013239629	−14691764	38765.54881
Electrical and electronic equipment	1297245	3.022497886	56202	1.963307713	−1241043	23.08182983
Pharmaceutical products	536110	1.249102014	1616	0.056451821	-534494	331.7512376
Vehicles other than rail and tram	1406333	3.276665949	24	0.000838393	−1406309	58597.20833
All other sectors	**22894675**	**53.34312854**	**396822**	**13.86220585**	**−22497853**	**57.69507487**
Total	**42,919,633**	**100**	**2,862,618**	**100**	**−40057015**	**14.9931402**

Source: https://www.trademap.org/Product_SelCountry_TS.aspx?nvpm=1|231||||TOTAL|||2|1|1|2|2|1|1|1|1

and World Bank (2014) found that the majority of manufacturing firms are increasingly interested in the domestic market. The studies showed that the average nominal rate of protection for Ethiopia is 25.3 per cent and the nominal rates of protection in agriculture, foodstuffs, textiles and clothing, and footwear are all over 30 per cent. Logistics inefficiency, insufficient and less effective export incentives, weak export institutions, and exchange-rate overvaluation generate a significant anti-export bias that constitutes a disincentive for exporters.

The second explanation relates to lack of policy focus. Ethiopia's driving policy has been export-led industrialization. But recently increasing attention has been paid to import substitution due to Ethiopia's shortage of foreign currency. Policy discussions on import substitution are anchored in the notion that substituting imports should be part of the efforts to ease foreign currency shortages. Ethiopia might promote import substitution in some strategic sectors. But the purpose should not and cannot be to solve foreign currency shortages. The problem of foreign currency shortage can only be adequately addressed over the longer run by increasing Ethiopia's ability to generate foreign currency through export activities. But it must be clear that the role of exports goes beyond generating foreign currency. It generates rapid and sustained economic growth through productivity gains, international learning, and technological upgrading (Spence 2007). Empirical literature shows that export sectors have consistently higher productivity gains than non-exporting sectors; and within sectors exporting firms tend to be more productive than non-exporters (Brenton, Newfarmer, and Walkenhorst 2009). Moreover, as Thirlwall (2002) shows, exporting allows a country to benefit from 'autonomous' demand, unconstrained by the small size or possible volatility of demand in the domestic market. Therefore, Ethiopia's overarching theme for industrialization and trade must be to promote its export activities more effectively. Selective and strategic blending of import-substituting activities with export-oriented activities might help, but the primary focus should remain on promoting export activities. It is important to build policy consensus to avoid confusion and lack of focus.

The third explanation relates to Ethiopia's export vulnerability. Most of Ethiopia's exports (about 78 per cent) come from agriculture (column 5 in Table 14.3). Despite significant reforms to speed up structural transformation, Ethiopia's transition away from traditional commodity exports into higher-value sectors and sectors that are not heavily affected by external price and demand shocks has been quite slow (Assefa and Gedefe 2016). Its exports are still prone to demand shocks and price swings in overseas markets.

In summary, Ethiopia began serious development efforts slightly more than a decade ago. Starting from a very low base, Ethiopia has made major economic reforms and infrastructural investments to reverse the previous dismal economic outcomes. Some of these reforms and investments have started to pay off—for example, investments are quickly increasing in quantity and quality. However, trade outcomes (as discussed in Section 14.2) have not been that impressive. In Section 14.3 we argue that greater integration into global markets would allow the Ethiopian economy to reap larger benefits from its investments and its other reforms.

14.3 Ethiopia's Trade Integration: Opportunities and Constraints

Ethiopia has only gradually been integrating into the global economy, with the external trade sector still accounting for a relatively low share of GDP (see Figure 14.2). A similar finding is presented in the World Bank (2014) Ethiopia economic update. Given its size and level of development and compared to other countries of comparable size, Ethiopia appears to under-trade goods and services by about 10 percentage points of GDP. The figure is even lower (about 13 percentage points) when inland trade costs are controlled for.

14.3.1 Opportunities

As part of its overall strategy to deliver on its medium- and long-term development objectives and to reverse the dismal trade outcomes, Ethiopia has engaged in many trade negotiations at the regional, continental, and multilateral levels. The government has aspired to join the World Trade Organization (WTO) and has taken concrete steps towards its accession. Ethiopia has become well acquainted with the workings of the WTO system through participating in its forums as an observer. Ethiopia is also part of continental and regional integration efforts such as the African Union's continental free trade area initiative, the COMESA free trade area, and so on.

GTP-II identified that Ethiopia now considers trade integration an urgent requirement. For the past few years Ethiopia has been allowed access to some established markets through preferential treatment arrangements such as the African Growth and Opportunity Act (AGOA) and the European Everything but Arms (EBA). However, we

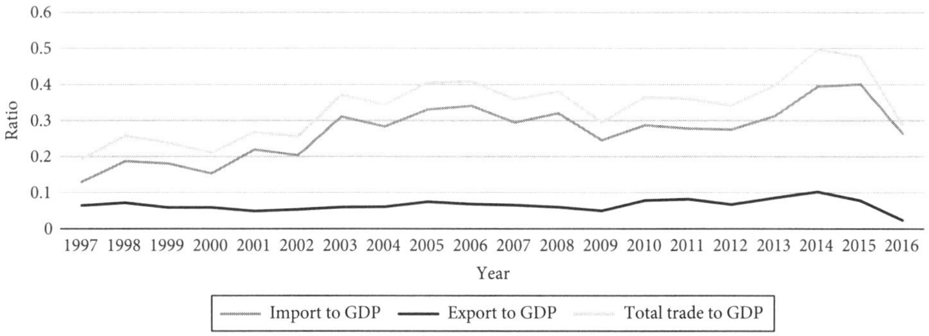

FIGURE 14.2 Import-to-GDP ratio, export-to-GDP ratio, and total trade-to-GDP ratio, 1997–2016

Source: The World Bank 2017, World Development Indicators: https://data.worldbank.org/

argue that Ethiopia's trade integration efforts and plans should go beyond these preferential treatments for the following reasons.

First, tariff rates are already low across the preferential treatments (AGOA, EBA, etc). But significant non-tariff barriers (NTBs) have still been imposed on non-member countries. Developed countries have significant non-tariff barriers in place. The NTBs represent serious barriers to Ethiopia's exports both in the United States and the European Union. A series of studies by UNCTAD strongly support the view that NTBs are far more important than tariffs in restricting access to markets (UNCTAD 2013). These studies show that although existing preferential treatments grant low-income countries a relatively low tariff (about 5 per cent on average) for their agricultural exports, once the ad valorem equivalent effect of NTBs is taken into consideration the total trade barrier becomes much larger, at about 27 per cent. Moreover, preferential treatments are, by their very nature, unilateral concessions and they can be annulled any time by the granting country. Trade integration cannot be genuine and lasting in the presence of preferential treatment arrangements.

Second, Ethiopia can join the WTO and other trade agreements with no (less) further commitments on tariff reductions. Ethiopia's current weighted average tariff rate falls within the range that is allowed for least developed countries. Because of the significant trade reforms that have lowered trade barriers, trade integration at the bilateral, regional, or multilateral levels would likely entail no (or less) additional tariff reduction commitments. Without further commitments, genuine trade integration such as acceding to the WTO will help Ethiopia exploit larger benefits. A major concern raised by some is whether developing countries like Ethiopia would be able to use industrial policies under such an environment. There is a large body of literature showing that the recent changes in the global industrial policy environment, such as the WTO system, have not made industrial policies irrelevant (e.g. see Wade 2003; Dicaprio and Gallagher 2006; ECA 2016). In fact, industrial policies will continue to be even more important for late industrializers to manage the process (e.g. the distributional effects) and effectively make use of global integration (e.g. technology learning). The instruments of industrial policies are vast—for example, see ECA (2016) for the list of industrial policy measures that are not directly covered by WTO agreements, and Rodrik (2004) for the list of industrial policy instruments that can be utilized by developing countries in the twenty-first century. Even the most conventional instruments of industrial policies—tariffs and non-tariffs—are still available for developing countries. For example, tariffs and import quotas are still possible under the closure of balance of payments for developing countries. So, the real question is not whether industrial policies will continue to be relevant. The real question is whether policymakers have high-level industrial policymaking capability. It is important for policymakers to understand not only what industrial policy instruments are possible under the new global economic rules but also which of them are likely to be transformative and accelerate growth.

Third, recent data show that investment (especially FDI) is increasing. To sustain a higher level of growth, Ethiopia needs more investment flows. One way (perhaps the best way) to do this is to attract FDI on a massive scale. FDI will encourage domestic investment. Domestic and foreign direct investments reinforce each other. These investment dynamics would require better market access. Market access not only allows existing firms to sell their products in wider and established markets but it also attracts new investments into the productive sector. Ethiopia's policymakers seem to have learned from their frequent engagements with investors that regional and global market access beyond preferential treatment is a key instrument for attracting giant and established investors. One of the questions investors ask governments in developing countries is whether they have wider market access through bilateral and multilateral systems. Consequently, in addition to labour and a good business environment, access to better and wider markets is a key competitive advantage for countries that would like to attract critical mass and quality FDI investments. Even more important than market access is that WTO membership provides a strong signal for investors. Once a country is a member of the WTO, it has to pursue policy certainty and stability, but this has the added value of increasing investment flow.

Fourth, Ethiopia should consider the trade integration process itself as a learning tool to improve its standing and extend reform of some of the remaining barriers to trade. No country finishes its homework before entering into any trade integration schemes, and this includes WTO accession. Our review of Ethiopia's trade negotiation experience quickly reveals that Ethiopia is not yet a member of the Common Market for Eastern and Southern Africa Free Trade Area (COMESA FTA) but does partially implement the COMESA Preferential Trade Agreement, providing a reciprocal 10 per cent duty reduction on imports that originate from the COMESA Region. But the COMESA FTA is regarded as the most important trade negotiations Ethiopia is currently engaged in, mainly because it has the most economic potential and because it is the most advanced of the negotiations Ethiopia is involved in (COMESA 2013). Likewise, Ethiopia applied to join the WTO in 2003 and is currently in the process of accession, with a Working Party having been established. Ethiopia has submitted her Memorandum of Foreign Trade to the WTO for examination by WTO members and is working on its services offer. Ethiopia has also signed up to the African Continental Free Trade Area (AfCFTA) which aims to create a single market for goods and services with free movement of business people and investments. Although Ethiopia has not concluded any of the above negotiations, it has acquired some experience through the few rounds of negotiations it has participated in. And some of the remaining issues will be better addressed after integration. A good example is the opening of some sectors for foreign investments.

14.3.2 Key Constraints

Our discussion in this section so far has focused on the opportunities of trade integration for Ethiopia. However, these opportunities do not happen automatically. This section addresses this important question: what are the key constraints to Ethiopia taking fuller advantage of integration into bilateral, regional, and multilateral trading systems? Understanding and solving the key constraints would unleash the maximum benefits of trade. In the context of Ethiopia, there are three main types of constraint: (a) political economy; (b) institutional capacity; and (c) policy.

While political economy constraints have not presented an obstacle to the massive trade reforms of the past two decades and a half, they are likely to be one from now on. Until now there have been no major political constraints simply because the private sector was non-existent, the previous socialist government having nationalized almost all private firms. The nationalization legacy has endured and the private sector has been weak until recently. So if political constraints did not exist until recently, what motivated the massive trade reforms of the past two decades?

Following the fall of the socialist government in 1991, the country was already in deep crisis, with severe macroeconomic instability and social crisis. The new government started to implement reforms, most of which were initially designed to first stabilize, then restructure and rehabilitate the economy. Since then a great deal has changed. Ethiopia has registered impressive growth records and the private sector has started to emerge. It would therefore be naïve to assume that political economy constraints would remain as minimal as they were before. Arguably, the state was previously more 'autonomous' vis-à-vis domestic interest groups than it has become in the course of nearly twenty years of profound social and economic change.

The source of political economy constraints on trade is distributional issues (Grossman and Helpman 1993). Even if trade integration is beneficial to the country, there are gainers and losers, so the decision-making process will unavoidably be influenced by various stakeholders. The major ones include: government (both federal and regional); enterprises (both private and state owned); foreign firms; external multilateral actors such as the WB and IMF; and farm and consumer communities.

The domestic private sector (and the remaining state-owned business sector), which has grown over the last twenty years, has become active in promoting and protecting its own interests and influences trade negotiations individually and through its associations. The main formal venue through which the domestic private sector influences trade policy formation and negotiation is the private–public dialogue forum, where the government and the industry associations meet to discuss issues of interest, including trade accession issues. Other formal venues include policy consultancy conferences, hearings, working meetings, and so on. However, most trade lobbying activities are likely to happen behind the scenes in informal, private settings. Since interest-group lobbying is not officially legitimized in Ethiopia, enterprises usually use their affiliations with governmental entities in various forms to lobby and influence the negotiating authority informally. Prominent among these are import-substituting private and state-owned manufacturers.

FDI firms are another source of interest-group constraint on trade liberalization. In view of the wide range of incentives these firms enjoy, the Ethiopian government expects FDI to contribute to economic development—increasing employment, upgrading technology and skills, and promoting competition and efficiency in the domestic market to raise local manufacturing capability. However, FDI firms might lobby government officials in favour of protections and more incentives to take full advantage before trade liberalization sets in, especially when the domestic market is attractive to FDI products. Gebreeyesus and Demile (2017) found that that a good number of FDI firms want to sell in the relatively protected Ethiopian domestic market due to the significant anti-export bias.

Urban consumers constitute another political economy constraint. Urban consumers can benefit either from subsidized consumer goods or from a completely liberalized market that offers access to lower prices, higher quality, and better choices. While urban groups tend to be politically organized and vocal, farmers, who constitute another major interest group, do not seem to play a significant role in trade policy decision-making through collective action: despite their huge number they are geographically scattered and hardly organized.[5] However, farmers indirectly affect trade policies through the ruling EPRDF party, which has historically considered farmers as its main constituency. This emanates from the party's background and the need to accelerate rural transformation and agricultural productivity to stir industrialization.

The second key constraint is institutional coordination and capacity. Institutional coordination is usually a binding constraint to taking fuller advantage of trade integration because many government institutions are involved in trade-related decision-making. While foreign trade policy falls under the jurisdiction of the federal government, many other institutions are involved in its implementation and regulation. While the Ministry of Trade (MoT) is mandated with overall trade policy formulation and implementation activities, and the Ministry of Foreign Affairs is responsible for signing trade agreements, other ministries such as the Ministry of Health (on pharmaceuticals and related), the Ministry of Agriculture (on veterinary drugs), the Ministry of Economic Development and Cooperation (on fiscal issues), and the National Bank (on foreign exchange) are also involved as regulatory bodies. For better outcomes, intra-governmental policy coordination mechanisms need to be developed.

The second aspect of the institutional constraint is analytical capacity. Several studies indicate that Ethiopia's ability to understand and analyse trade-related issues and conduct high-level trade negotiations is quite inadequate (UNDP 2012). Limited access to trade-related information and a lack of skilled and experienced trade experts and analysts at the Ministry of Trade are among the reasons. The relatively strong and well-organized National Export Committee (NEC) focuses on export performance review and solving key binding constraints, not on evaluating Ethiopia's efforts and plans to join regional and multilateral agreements. A National Steering Committee has been assembled to conduct trade negotiations, including the WTO accession, on behalf of the government, but its members are senior government officials who require support from a strong institution that has adequate trade-related information and skilled personnel. The lack of strong trade institutions will negatively impact Ethiopia's negotiation process and outcomes. Ethiopia's representatives should have not only high-level understanding

[5] This has begun to change with the emergence of a group of larger export-oriented horticulture firms (both domestic and foreign owned) and with the resurgence of a group of relatively large coffee producer-exporters (see Chapter 30, this volume).

and negotiation skills but also the capacity and will to articulate Ethiopia's interests and concerns in global trade forums.

The third key constraint concerns policy issues. Trade alone will not induce economic growth and structural transformation (Rodrik 1999). In the context of Ethiopia, trade should be considered part of the industrial policies and the limitations and opportunities of advancing trade policies need to be examined in this context. At the heart of Ethiopia's industrialization agenda is the promotion of exports and penetration of the world market. However, the capability of domestic manufacturing firms is still weak. Instead of waiting for local firms to build capability, Ethiopia's strategy has been to expedite the creation of domestic capability and attract FDI through establishing industrial parks and export-processing zones that produce for the world market but also catalyse local firms' capability. However, there is more competition for FDI among developing countries. Skilled labour, good infrastructure services, and good policy environment alone are no longer enough to attract FDI. Trade integration needs to be part and parcel of industrial policy. Late industrializers like Ethiopia have the advantage of exploiting global FDI dynamics and trade integration. The policy constraint arises when late industrializers fail to take the initiative in defining and owning their own national industrialization processes. Governments must learn from their own and others' experience that they cannot afford to be passive recipients of foreign influences through trade and FDI flow. Historically, trade has affected how development policies were determined. For example, there has been massive and sustained support for free trade policy to determine development policy for developing countries, an impetus that comes from advanced countries both at bilateral and multilateral levels under the cover of trade. The state needs to be active in its national industrialization process.

14.4 Benefiting from Trade Integration: Maximizing Opportunities and Addressing the Binding Constraints

Ethiopia is involved in a number of trade agreements and negotiations. This shows that the country is keen to transition from industrialization under protectionism to industrialization under integration. However, this does not imply that Ethiopia should move from one extreme to the other. Ethiopia should reject both full control and full liberalization. We believe that economic integration should combine the following strategies:

i) building a long-term comprehensive plan for regional and global integration;
ii) exploiting FDI dynamics for efficiency gain, structural transformation, and trade integration;
iii) upgrading the business environment;

iv) mainstreaming trade in development policies and plans; and
v) taking cautious, targeted trade-related liberalization measures to further deepen trade reforms to promote investment.

To maximize the benefits of trade and alleviate the key constraints to trade integration discussed in Section 14.3.2, action is required in the following two broad areas.

14.4.1 Strengthening Trade Institutions

The Ministry of Trade should have a dedicated department or unit staffed by highly capable people experienced in trade analysis and trade negotiation strategies. With this capacity it can coordinate the other trade-related institutions such as the MoFA, MoA, MoFEC, and ERCA. The suggested department at the MoT needs to: (i) organize and catalogue trade-related information relevant to Ethiopia and make it accessible; (ii) have core staff who are highly specialized in trade analytics and negotiation; (iii) provide training and other capacity-building programmes to other trade-related institutions; (iv) serve as a coordinating unit between trade-related institutions; (v) conduct awareness-raising programmes among different stakeholders about bilateral, regional, and multilateral trading systems; and (vi) commission or conduct targeted studies to assess the implications of bilateral, regional, and multilateral agreements for the Ethiopian economy.

At a higher level, progress and setbacks in key trade negotiations such as COMESA, AfCFTA, and WTO should be discussed and evaluated at the National Export Committee (NEC). Reviewing the process at a higher level will provide the appropriate policy direction and ensure the negotiation processes address Ethiopia's interests and concerns.

14.4.2 Alleviating Political Economy Constraints

It would be wrong to assume that political economy constraints will remain as weak as before. Political economy constraints will arise as Ethiopia tries to engage in the planned trade negotiations, and the outcome largely depends on the nature and capability of the state. The literature distinguishes between a developmental state and a subordinate state (Rodrik 1995). A key question is: how can both parties exploit the public–private forum, where industry associations representing the collective interests of their members engage with the government? Oqubay (2015) argues that industrial policies can work better in low-income countries where industry associations ('intermediary institutions') are encouraged to engage with the government, both benefiting by eliciting information. The government will use the information to refine its industrial policies and the private sector will use it to make better investment decisions. Depending on the nature of the state, the forum might also be used for lobbying and other rent-seeking activities.

The implication of this discussion is that if the state makes decisions autonomously based on its development agenda, the private sector lacks the mechanism to influence those decisions. Knowing that it is unable to influence decisions, the private sector will decide to behave productively, i.e. to use the intermediary institutions as information institutions, and not lobbying forums.

We have seen that in order to benefit society, trade needs to be combined with other policies. A major concern is the possible political economy constraint that may emanate from the recent changes in the global industrial policy environment. With the coming of WTO, it may seem that late industrializers have little policy space to experiment with industrial policies. However, this is not the case. Within the existing global environment, there is significant freedom for industrial policies, but the capability to understand what industrial policy instruments are possible and which are likely to be transformative is the key.

14.5 Conclusions

Several issues and arguments have emerged from our analysis. First, the fact that Ethiopia has undergone major economic reforms in the post-1991 period shows that reforms and liberalization can be home driven in response to certain policy demands. The current government inherited a degenerating economy. Consequently, most of these liberalization reforms were initially designed to stabilize, restructure, and rehabilitate the economy. Since then much has changed. Ethiopia has registered impressive growth and the private sector has started to emerge, with a lot of foreign direct investment flowing to the country. However, trade reform outcomes have been disappointing based on two measures: current account deficit and trade integration (trade-to-GDP ratio). Disaggregating by sector, we find that the current account deficit is even worse in Ethiopia's priority sectors. Anti-export bias, export vulnerability, and limited trade integration are some of the major explanations.

The GTP-II identifies trade integration as an urgent requirement. In connection with this, two important facts must be highlighted. One, the preferential treatment markets (notably AGOA and EBA) should not sidetrack Ethiopia from its main agenda—negotiating and joining the COMESA, AfCFTA, and WTO. Two, Ethiopia must realize that in view of its significant unilateral liberalization, the country may be in a position to join the WTO and other trade agreements with no (or less) additional commitments in terms of tariff reductions, enabling it to reap overdue trade benefits.

Second, as Ethiopia's investments in infrastructure, skills development, and industrial parks have started to pay off, investment (especially FDI) flow is rapidly increasing. Ethiopia can use trade integration to further attract investment as membership in regional and multilateral agreements sends a strong signal to investors; and as a market access for its exporting firms to further expand. It will also increase efficiency for domestic firms through international learning as global markets provide the requisite discipline to learn and engage in technological and production upgrading.

Finally, lack of institutional capacity, policy coherence, and political economy constraints may reduce or even obscure the benefits of trade integration. Indeed, trade-related institutions must have the capacity to understand and analyse trade-related data and information and Ethiopia's representatives at trade negotiations must have an appropriate understanding of Ethiopia's interests, intentions, and concerns, as well as negotiating skills. In terms of policy coherence, trade as an instrument of industrial policy needs to be complemented with other policies. In relation to political economy constraints, there are a number of interest groups seeking to influence trade policies and negotiations. Autonomous decision-making by the state, based on its development agenda, may alleviate political economy constraints, sending strong signals to the private sector to engage with the state productively, and relinquish rent-seeking activities such as lobbying.

References

Assefa, B. and K. Gedefe (2016). 'An Economic Inquiry into Ethiopian Exports: Pattern, Characteristics, Dynamics and Survival', No. 014, Ethiopian Development Research Institute, Addis Ababa.

Brenton, P., R. Newfarmer, and P. Walkenhorst (2009). 'Avenues for Export Diversification', World Bank Publications, Washington, DC.

COMESA (2013). 'The Competitiveness of Ethiopian Firms for Participation in the COMESA Free Trade Area (FTA).' Mimeo. Addis Ababa.

Dicaprio, A. and K. P. Gallagher (2006). 'The WTO and the Shrinking of Development Space: How Big is the Bite?', *Journal of World Investment & Trade* 7: 781.

ECA (2016). 'Transformative Industrial Policy for Africa', Addis Ababa.

Gebreeyesus, M. (2013). 'Industrial Policy and Development in Ethiopia: Evolution and Present Experimentation', WIDER Working Paper No. 2013/125.

Gebreeyesus M., G. Abebe, and T. Berhanu (2017). 'Foreign Direct Investment in Ethiopia: Challenges, Opportunities and Policy Options.' Mimeo. Ethiopian Development Research Institute, Addis Ababa.

Gebreeyesus, M. and A. Demile (2017). 'Why Export Promotion Efforts Failed to Deliver? Assessment of the Export Incentives and their Implementation in Ethiopia', No. 017, Ethiopian Development Research Institute, Addis Ababa.

Grossman, G. M. and E. Helpman (1993). 'The Politics of Free Trade Agreements', NBER Working Paper No. 4597, National Bureau of Economic Research, Cambridge, MA.

Gudissa, L. and D. K. Mishra (2014). 'The Role of Customs Tariff: A Historical, Theoretical and Empirical Review', *Journal of Economics and Sustainable Development* 5(11): 99.

IMF (1999). Ethiopia: Recent Economic Developments', Staff Country Report 99/98, IMF, Washington, DC.

Milner, C. and O. Morrissey (1999). 'Measuring Trade Liberalization in Africa', in *Evaluating Economic Liberalization*, ed. M. McGillivary and O. Morrissey (London: Palgrave Macmillan): 60–82.

Moller, L. C. and K. M. Wacker (2017). 'Explaining Ethiopia's Growth Acceleration: The Role of Infrastructure and Macroeconomic Policy', *World Development* 96: 198–215.

NPC (2016). 'Growth and Transformation Plan II (GTP II)—(2015/16–2019/20)', National Planning Commission, Federal Democratic Republic of Ethiopia, Addis Ababa.

Nolan, P., J. Zhang, and C. Liu (2007). 'The Global Business Revolution, the Cascade Effect, and the Challenge for Firms from Developing Countries', *Cambridge Journal of Economics* 32 (1): 29–47.

Oqubay, A. (2015). *Made in Africa: Industrial Policy in Ethiopia* (New York: Oxford University Press).

Rodrik, D. (1999). *The New Global Economy and Developing Countries: Making Openness Work*, Vol. 24. (Washington, DC: Overseas Development Council).

Rodrik, D. (2004). 'Industrial Policy for the Twenty-First Century', CEPR Discussion Paper No. 4767. Available at SSRN: https://ssrn.com/abstract=666808.

Rodrik, R. (1995). 'Trade and Industrial Policy Reform', *Handbook of Development Economics* 3: 2925–82.

Spence, M. (2007). *Wealth of Nations: How Poor Countries Get Richer* (New York: Dow Jones).

Thirlwall, A. P. (2002). *The Nature of Economic Growth: An Alternative Framework for Understanding the Performance of Nations.* (Cheltenham: Edward Elgar Publishing).

UNCTAD (2013). 'Non-Tariff Measures to Trade: Economic and Policy Issues for Developing Countries', Developing Countries in International Trade Studies.

UNDP (2012). 'Impact of Trade Related Issues in the Economic Partnership (EPA) Agreement on Ethiopia', UNDP Ethiopia No. 2/2012.

Wade, R. H. (2003). 'What Strategies Are Viable for Developing Countries Today? The World Trade Organization and the Shrinking of "Development Space"', *Review of International Political Economy* 10 (4): 621–44.

World Bank (2002). "The Federal Democratic Republic of Ethiopia: Developing Exports to Promote Growth', Report No. 23294-ET, World Bank, Washington, DC.

World Bank (2014). "Ethiopia 3rd Economic Update: Strengthening Export Performance through Improved Competitiveness', World Bank, Addis Ababa.

CHAPTER 15

POLICY, POLITICAL ECONOMY, AND PERFORMANCE IN ETHIOPIA'S COFFEE SECTOR

CHRISTOPHER CRAMER AND JOHN SENDER

15.1 Introduction

Coffee exports have played a key role in experiences of rapid growth and change in Brazil, Colombia, Costa Rica, and to some extent in growth episodes in Kenya and Cote d'Ivoire.[1] First, coffee exports help to relax the balance-of-payments constraint on growth. As economies like Ethiopia's grow, they develop a structural thirst for imports. Export earnings are a more reliable way of addressing the balance-of-payments constraint than relying on foreign aid or the whims of global capital flows. A rapid increase in foreign exchange earnings also allows a low-income economy to exploit global demand (Thirlwall 2011): the growing global demand for coffee acts as a stimulant to Ethiopian economic activity.

Second, increased coffee production may provoke changes and dynamic linkages throughout the economy, including technical and institutional changes and the development of a class of productive Ethiopian capitalists. And because coffee in Ethiopia involves millions of people in production, harvesting, processing, marketing, and trade, this sector can also raise standards of living, especially for many extremely poor rural

[1] For example: 'Coffee and development are synonymous in Colombia ... as the coffee industry has been the principal motor of Colombia's economic and social development for the past 100 years' (García-Cardona 2016).

people. Third, coffee may not only contribute to wider structural change but also embody that structural change in rising productivity and technical improvement within the sector. Structural change (Lewis 1954) involves a growing (private and state) capitalist class in a low-income economy drawing in rising numbers of people from the 'subsistence' sector and, in the process, generating savings out of the high rates of profit made possible by low wages paid to a readily available flow of unskilled workers. This is a shift from lower- to higher-productivity activities, which can take place within agriculture just as much as from agriculture to urban manufacturing.

That there are frequent crises in the global coffee market, especially since the collapse of the International Coffee Agreement in 1989, often leads to pessimism about prospects for the sector. Coffee trading is characterized by dramatic mood swings. Price volatility may be amplified by speculative activity in commodity derivative markets and is difficult for policymakers to manage. But it is no reason not to support investment in coffee. There is a simple, deeper fact about the global trade that should guide strategic thinking: everything suggests that the long-term global expansion in demand for coffee will only continue. As incomes rise, people usually consume more coffee. In China coffee consumption has been expanding at more than 16 per cent a year for the past ten years; given that per capita coffee consumption is still very low, it will continue to rise for a long time to come (ICO 2015).

Despite frequently unstable prices, there is a structurally strong global aggregate demand pull from which Ethiopia can benefit (see Figure 15.1). Despite rising market interest in Robusta coffees, Ethiopia is still well placed to take advantage of global demand trends, given the wide variation in taste profiles and the scope for distinctive high quality coffees from the country (Davis et al. 2017).

A further source of potential growth is climate change. Despite considerable uncertainty and risks, careful research (Moat et al. 2017) projects a range of negative and positive scenarios: with carefully timed and designed interventions to support a shift in the geographical area under coffee, there is potential for a more than four-fold expansion in the area cultivated with coffee compared to the 'do nothing' scenario.[2]

Against this background, this chapter highlights the commonly identified problems of the Ethiopian coffee sector. We then analyse the types of policy recommendation most common in the recent literature on Ethiopian coffee, before concluding that there are significant shortcomings in much of this literature. We set out what these are and why they matter and briefly make the case for a new set of urgent priorities for the sector. This chapter complements others in this volume (Chapter 29 provides a historical overview of the sector; Chapter 30 expands on the specific history of large-scale coffee plantations; Chapter 39 provides a critique of policies towards the private sector; and others address other dimensions of structural change). We suggest that the recent

[2] The main areas where coffee is likely to become more suitable are in higher-lying parts of the southwest though there are likely to be opportunities elsewhere too and in all cases considerable efforts would be needed to assess agronomic suitability, possible land-use contradictions or opportunity costs, and logistics.

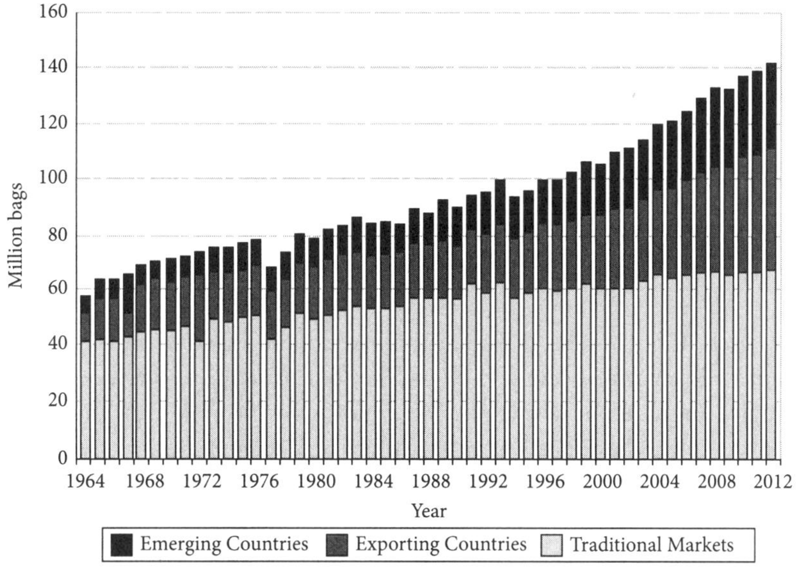

FIGURE 15.1 World coffee consumption, 1964–2012

Source: ICO (2014).

history of coffee policy is given pride of place in a policy 'error museum' where it may be studied for clues to more effective policy design.[3] We conclude by highlighting recent policy initiatives.

Given the strategic significance of coffee, it is astonishing how little reliable detailed knowledge there is about coffee production in Ethiopia. One report noted: 'Nobody is really in a position to provide accurate data on the actual annual production of coffee in Ethiopia' (EU 2014: 25). Another concludes: 'The lack of updated representative information is a constraint for evaluations of projects, programs, and policies. This hampers the design of appropriate policies and investments that would lead towards a better performing coffee sector' (Minten et al. 2015: 26). While it is often stated semi-officially that the domestic market is absorbing roughly half of total output, seasoned coffee buyers in Ethiopia believed (in 2017) that the domestic market more likely accounted for 60 per cent of output. (Behind the common guesstimate of a 50:50 domestic/export split are vague and possibly outdated ICO estimates of per capita coffee consumption in Ethiopia, combined with trade data.)

While USDA estimates that the area cultivated with coffee has remained static at about 525,000 hectares between 2012 and 2018 (Table 15.1), other sources (the CSA and regional Agriculture Bureaus in SNNPR and Oromia) suggest that the area under coffee

[3] Enzo Ferrari would often hold company strategy meetings in his 'error museum', with its cabinets displaying motor parts that had failed in races and that were used to inspire engineers to develop improvements.

Table 15.1 Ethiopia's coffee production

	2012	2013	2014	2015	2016	2017
Production (1000 MR 60-kg bags)	6,500	6,345	6,475	6,510	6,520	6,545
Area (1000 ha)	518	519	525	528	529	532

Source: USDA 2017: 2.

may be as great as 715,000 ha.[4] By some estimates of the area under coffee, the average yield would be something like 800–900kg/ha; but prevailing conditions in Ethiopia (technologies used, input availability) 'do not warrant yields of this magnitude' (EU 2014: x). Collated estimates of a range of experts suggest average yields of roughly 400kg/ha (or lower); these estimates suggest that Arabica yields in Ethiopia are among the lowest in the world, as shown in Figure 15.3.

15.2 Widely Accepted Failures in the Ethiopian Coffee Sector

It is widely accepted that Ethiopia has not fully taken advantage of the enormous potential coffee production and trade offers. By 2014/15 the volume of exports was only 30 per cent of what had been targeted for that year in the first Growth and Transformation Plan (GTP-I) and the volume of total production was estimated to be just 54 per cent of targeted output. GTP-II proclaimed an ambitious commitment to raising coffee output, productivity, and export earnings (with a target of becoming the number two exporter in the world by 2020), a commitment that implied an unprecedented annual increase in output of 20 per cent (EIAR 2017). But Ethiopia's recent production trends suggest that these commitments were unlikely to be achieved unless a number of problems could be overcome.

15.2.1 Poor Export Performance

What success there has been in recent years in increasing foreign exchange earnings from coffee has been mainly a function of global coffee price trends. These have masked the failure to achieve a sustained and significant increase in export volumes (see Figure 15.2). This is especially clear when we compare Ethiopian exports with other

[4] Additional data on the area under coffee that is in forest-like habitats and the area cultivated on small plots in only partial shade or in full sun are provided in Davis et al. (2017).

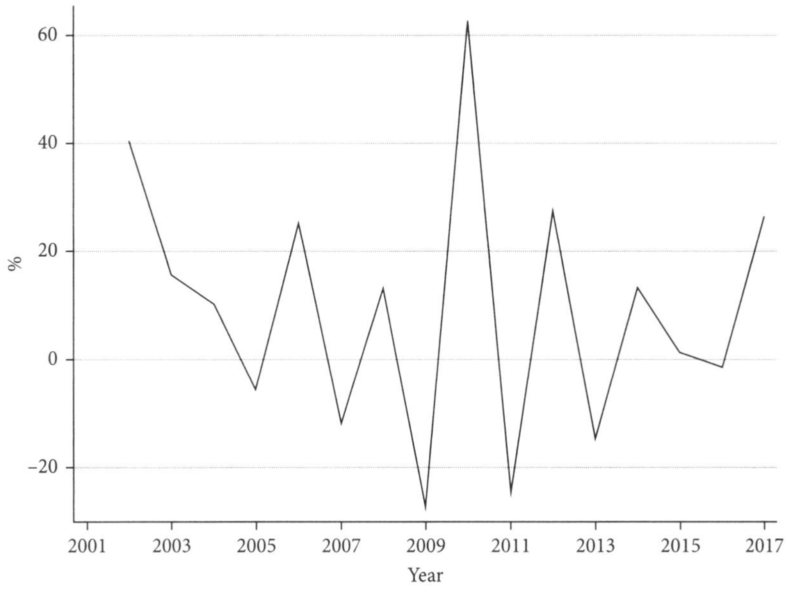

FIGURE 15.2 Annual rate of growth of coffee export quantities from Ethiopia, 2002–17

Source: ITC (2018).

producers and when we consider recent missed opportunities. For example, Colombia (also a producer of washed Arabica coffees) suffered a drastic fall in coffee export volume after 2007/8 when its production was hit by disease, leading to sharply rising international prices for washed Arabica beans. Other producers moved in to fill the gap in supply and reaped the gains from high prices; Ethiopia floundered. Ethiopia's export volumes shrank precisely when prices rose and after recovering recorded only a modest increase. Coffee in Colombia is marked by a relatively rapid rise in export values (largely a function of substantial investments in adding value) and the ability to recover from huge challenges such as leaf rust disease.

15.2.2 The False Trade-Off between Domestic Consumption and Exports

In recent years the Ethiopian government has tried to prevent coffee traders from making allegedly 'excessive' profits by concentrating on supplying the domestic market. The assumption appears to be that there is a trade-off between domestic production and exports. Ethiopia is one of a small number of leading coffee exporters that have a sizeable domestic market for coffee. Brazil and Colombia also consume a large proportion of their production domestically. But these countries have sought to expand, not restrict, domestic consumption (as a useful hedge against international price drops and because

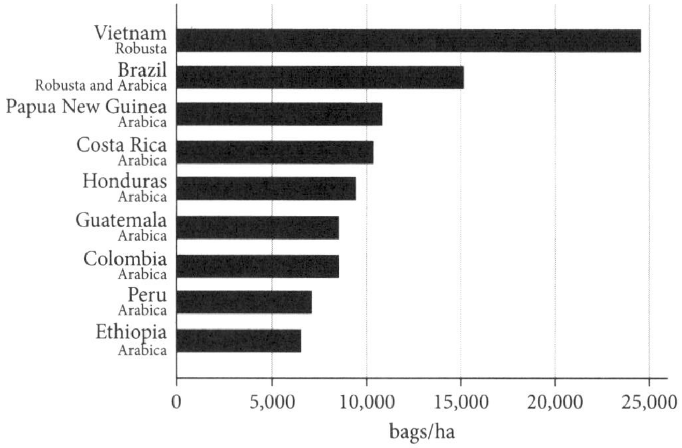

FIGURE 15.3 Coffee yields in nine selected producing countries (bags/ha)

Source: FAOSTAT 2018.

greater overall demand for coffee stimulates investment, incomes and multiplier effects, and employment). Ethiopia is unique in recent years in failing to expand domestic consumption and exports simultaneously.

15.2.3 Extremely Low Yields

There has been a failure to increase yields in Ethiopia and a failure to renew the stock of coffee trees. Ethiopia's ageing coffee trees are losing productivity and typically achieve lower yields than the newer, high-yield and more disease-resistant varieties that are available (see Figure 15.3). The huge number of scattered, often very small coffee farms in Ethiopia may make it difficult to achieve a rapid overhaul of the stock of trees.

Evidence shows that straightforward changes in the density of planting, in mulching, fertilization, weeding, and in how beans are harvested and cared for after picking can quickly improve yields in Ethiopia, although smaller farmers are likely to believe that the costs of introducing these changes are prohibitive.[5] Most Ethiopian coffee farmers do not use or are prevented by regulations from using inorganic fertilizers and key pesticides (USDA 2014: 4). Those that do acquire these fertilizers apply them at significantly below the recommended rates, although it has been shown that proper coffee nutrition improves not only yield but also bean quality and size (Melke and Ittana 2014). International market experts consider that there are important areas of Ethiopia (e.g. around Jimma) where the growing conditions (climate and slopes) are more similar to some parts of Brazil than, say, Colombian production. This means that there are

[5] Most farmers are very small: one survey estimated that more than 60 per cent of coffee farmers produced coffee on less than half a hectare and 40 per cent cultivated less than a quarter of a hectare of coffee (see Chapter 29).

unexploited opportunities on some medium and slightly larger-scale coffee farms to take advantage of scale economies, achieving productivity gains by adopting improved tree spacing, irrigation, and high input use (FAO 2004: 35).

15.2.4 Too Low a Share of High Quality Coffee in Total Output

The next failure is the costly lack of success in meeting international demand for specialty coffees—high quality coffees clearly traceable to specific growers—that command price premiums internationally. A host of reasons explains this. Some have to do with the relatively low share of Ethiopian output that is of sufficiently high quality, which in turn may be traced to farming practices and post-harvest care, but also to the ageing coffee tree stock. Others are tied together in a knot of policy and institutional control that many argue has encouraged corruption, the adulteration of better quality coffee, and stagnant export revenues. Even where there clearly is good quality coffee produced in Ethiopia it has not achieved premium prices because of the lack of full traceability to specific growers. The specialty coffee market derives value from judgements of quality and from narratives of origin: saying that a bag of coffee comes from Yirgacheffe is not enough—roasters and retailers need to be able to link the coffee to a particular farm that practises approved methods of cultivation and then processes in a particular way. For these reasons, the unit prices achieved by Ethiopian coffee exports between 2005 and 2014 were considerably below prices achieved by Colombia, Costa Rica, and Kenya (ATA 2016).

15.2.5 A Failing Institutional and Policy Framework

At the heart of the traceability problem in the 2000s was the Ethiopian Commodity Exchange (ECX) and the set of rules concerning marketing, warehousing, and trading in coffee, which after the ECX took on responsibility for the bulk of Ethiopian coffee sales broke the chain of traceability connecting consumer and producer.[6] This broken vertical chain of production and trade is something that many critics, from individual roasters and buyers internationally to the European Commission (EC) and other organizations, emphasized. A clear vertical chain is important not just to narratives of origin but also to developing coffee quality. For example, one international coffee business used to have very close links, sustained over many years, with a large private washing station and coffee buyer in southern Ethiopia, with whom the firm worked to spread best practice among many small and medium-sized coffee farmers in the area. Prices paid to farmers were consistently higher than prevailing market prices because of the

[6] A brief description of these rules and regulations is provided in Belete (2015: 40–1).

superior quality of output achieved. ECX rules cut the ties and the international firm could no longer buy a reliable supply (at high prices) from the area.[7]

There have been many efforts to improve the functioning of the ECX and to address complaints about the system. Limited traceability was introduced. Cooperatives and some larger farmers were permitted to sell directly to international buyers. A bar-coding system was introduced.[8] There was talk of new three-day windows for batches of coffee to be sold direct before it has to be traded through the ECX. None of these limited reforms fundamentally changed the system, which relied on attempts to enforce controls rather than on a set of incentives. On the initiative of the Prime Minister's Office, it became possible towards the end of 2017 for coffee exporters to sell identity-preserved (IP) coffee without passing through the ECX, but it is too early to assess the impact of this radical change on the value of exports (USDA 2017: 5).

Efforts to control the coffee market were probably introduced and reinforced because of the desperately tight foreign exchange constraint facing the government and because of popular ideas about how to improve the lot of poor farmers by reducing the scope for 'rent' accumulation by scapegoated intermediaries or middlemen (Abbink 2017: 119; see also Chapter 29). However, the evidence suggests that these controls failed. The policy regime did not relax the foreign exchange constraint. It did not lead to an increase in incomes for smaller, poorer coffee farmers who are not well served by the cooperatives: in Ethiopia, these institutions have been shown to benefit only a handful of members, not the smallest farmers (Cramer et al. 2014). The Cooperative Unions especially, but also the Primary Societies, have a long and undistinguished record of corruption and inefficiency. New brokers have also become active, buying from *akrabi*s (traders; see Chapter 29) and earning a commission on volumes, meaning that they have an incentive to prioritize quantity over quality. And what populist slogans ignore is how important market intermediaries are: 'As much as it is justified to protect the smallholder producer from unscrupulous brokers, it must also be recognized that these value chain actors fulfil a certain role and carry a considerable risk, justifying their existence for which they must be compensated. Besides, they represent the link between the farmer and the exporter in the context of the local market value chain' (EU 2014: 16).

Meanwhile, the control system itself probably fostered the very rent seeking it was meant to eliminate. It raised costs, introduced double handling of coffee in storage and transport, undermined the competitiveness of Ethiopian coffee, and in what must be the clearest indication of an outcome against the aims of government policy it contributed to a situation where sellers command higher prices in the domestic coffee market than they can obtain by exporting, exacerbating the effect on the relative prices of traded goods of the over-valuation of the birr.[9] Restrictions on selling domestically led to a situation where there was no incentive to offer higher quality coffee to exporters.

[7] Personal communication to the authors.

[8] The new tagging system linked bags of coffee traded through the ECX to one of over 2,500 geo-referenced washing, hulling, and cleaning stations.

[9] The government devalued the birr by 15 per cent in late 2017.

Key exporters and buyers who were tied into the ECX struggled to secure access to reliable supplies of high quality coffee. Further, the institutional and policy framework has led to widespread malpractice. Traders were fiddling coffee grades to be able to sell domestically. As one coffee buyer put it, 'phony exporters' are damaging the Ethiopian brand by selling poor quality coffee internationally under licence just so they can get access to scarce foreign exchange to use in importing consumer goods, which, given shortages, is far more profitable than coffee trading itself under current rules (see also Belete 2015: 53). 'This not only ruins the business reputation but also deprives the public coffers of taxes, only due if the balance sheet of the respective exporter shows profits' (EU 2014: 67).

15.2.6 Weak Technical Research and Development

The last major weakness of the Ethiopian coffee sector, on which all observers agree, is the striking limitation of research and development. Spending on coffee R&D is extremely low by any comparative standard. When asked about the sources of Colombia's recent impressive coffee tree restocking programme, which helped the country to recover from a disease outbreak in a very short time, one observer simply said: forty years of R&D lies behind that. The Colombian government spent US$8.5 million on coffee R&D in 2011; and the Brazilian government spent US$9.4 million (Diaz Rios, nd). The annual coffee research budget for the Jimma Agricultural Research Centre (JARC) has been between US$273,000 and US$318,000 in recent years (EIAR 2017).[10] Meanwhile, fearful of a loss of biological competitive advantage, Ethiopian research and plant stock material is relatively cut off from the rest of the world. Observers argue that Ethiopia could gain by sharing some of its plant stock material in exchange for productively vital information (e.g. from Brazil), and that in the longer run it is in all producers' interests to stabilize coffee output by spreading genetic diversity.

15.3 How to Improve Coffee Performance: Recent Proposals

15.3.1 The Contribution of Smallholder Producers

A large number of development economists agree that small farmers should play the major role in expanding Africa's agricultural commodity exports. They use two main arguments to justify policy support for smallholders: first, larger-scale production is

[10] Appropriate planting material has not been developed for all agro-ecologies, a failure that may limit future opportunities in the face of climate change (EIAR 2017).

less efficient, less likely to achieve a high yield per hectare than small producers; and, second, an increase in small farmer output is more likely to reduce poverty and improve macroeconomic performance. A great deal of effort has been devoted to convincing policymakers that these arguments are conceptually and empirically valid (Larson, Muraoka, and Otsuka 2016; Savastano and Scandizzo 2017).

The key agricultural technologies required to increase output (e.g. the application of irrigation and agrochemicals to modern varieties) are said to be 'scale neutral'. If small producers nevertheless fail to achieve higher yields than large-scale farms or if they fail rapidly to increase their contribution to marketed output, then removing price distortions and intervening to compensate for asymmetric information and missing markets will, policy officials are often told, remedy these failures. For example, if smaller farmers face artificially low/high market prices for their output/inputs (discriminatory prices that reflect the collusion and dominant power of traders and larger enterprises), then smallholder cooperatives can be provided with more accurate price information and with training to compete more effectively in these markets, subsidies to large farmers can be eliminated, and monopolistic suppliers of fertilizer and seeds can be replaced by creating competitive input markets. If existing markets for financial products such as credit are not supplying smaller farms, then new providers of relevant products (e.g. micro-credit, savings accounts, and crop insurance) need to be encouraged, disrupting the discriminatory practices of banks and the oligopolistic formal financial institutions.

Recent policy recommendations to reverse disappointing trends in the value and volume of Ethiopian coffee exports are underpinned by this belief in the huge potential of smallholder production: 'major changes in production and productivity in long-term planning can only be expected from this [smallholder, unorganized] producer group' (EU 2014: 23). To overcome any possible diseconomies of scale faced by smallholders (in wet processing, transport, and finance, for example) many recommend additional state support for cooperatives (Tamru and Minten 2016: 25; EU 2014: 36; USAID 2015: 22; ATA 2012). Their argument is that collective action through producers' organizations will allow groups of small farmers to achieve the necessary scale in processing and marketing and to increase their bargaining power with larger-scale buyers (Shumeta, D'Haese, and Verbeke 2017). To overcome information deficits the same experts propose improved extension services, using demonstration plots to train smallholders 'intensively' in good agricultural practices. It is argued that farmers not only require training to adopt these techniques, but they also need access to credit, which the market is unlikely to provide because of high transaction costs (on rural finance in Ethiopia see Chapter 28).[11]

Small farmers are also said to suffer from a lack of access to other important information, particularly about the prices that coffee (and different qualities of coffee) achieve at auction. If the price transmission mechanism to the farm gate (and to sellers of red coffee cherries as opposed to green beans) could be more efficient and transparent, small-

[11] The credit requirement has been estimated at about US$200 per smallholder with a payback period of seven to ten years at an interest rate that should be subsidized by the state or international donors (TechnoServe 2014).

holders would receive clearer signals and perhaps have a greater incentive to invest in production improvements.

Although the ECX introduced detailed real-time price information for standardized green beans—through mobile SMS, electronic price display boards, the internet, and a freephone service—these prices are not relevant for the 1.2 million small farmers who usually sell unstandardized sun-dried cherries to local traders in thin, segmented, and personalized markets.[12] These local markets are said to be insufficiently competitive because prices are distorted by the oligopsonistic power of purchasers of cherries; legal rules prohibit free mobility of traders across districts; and rural infrastructure is too thinly spread, especially for transport and storage (Gelaw, Speelman, and van Huylenbroeck 2017). The policy proposed to reduce these price distortions is, once again, to provide subsidized credit to cooperatives—to enable them to invest in additional washing/wet-processing facilities that offer more convenient and locally competing sales outlets for smallholders' red cherries (Tamru and Minten 2016: 25). It is also proposed that small groups of coffee farmers who feel exploited by the margins currently gained by the Cooperative Unions,[13] as well as other private sector enterprises such as coffee roasters and traders, should be encouraged to invest in their own wet processing and in upgraded dry-processing/hulling mills—again through the provision of subsidized credit (Monitor 2011).

Recommendations to encourage private investment in coffee processing, to remove legislative restrictions on coffee trading, and to encourage private sector participation in the marketing of agro-chemicals and new varieties of planting material are consistent with the broader policy advice of almost all the bilateral donors, marshalled by the World Bank, the IMF, and IFPRI. A recurring theme in their recommendations is that financial services, both savings instruments and credit facilities for coffee farmers, processors, and traders, would be improved by deregulating the banking sector and reducing the market dominance of the Commercial Bank of Ethiopia. They also recommend a general reduction in the dominant role of state-owned enterprises and in the role of the public sector in infrastructure provision, especially in telecommunications, but also in transport and marketing (World Bank 2016: chapter 7). In addition, they argue that greater exchange rate flexibility would encourage private sector investment in the coffee sector; an extremely large devaluation of the birr was recommended, so that prices in the domestic market provide an incentive to increase export production (IMF 2016: Annex III).

To summarize, the mainstream argument is that Ethiopia's farmers could build on the intrinsic advantages of small-scale production to achieve a breakthrough in coffee exports, *if* they had access to reliable information and advice, *if* all markets were more competitive and prices were higher and less distorted, *if* cooperatives and the private sector

[12] The contracts with these traders, who also supply consumption credit and hire labourers, are often inter-linked. Vulnerable and dependent small farmers have to sell red cherries at low prices because they are indebted to traders, and/or have to provide labour at below the prevailing wage rate. The implicit interest rates for these widespread forms of consumption credit are very high.

[13] Supply chain costs in Ethiopia are said to be much higher than in other Arabica-exporting countries (and rising), reducing the farmer's share of the export price (TechnoServe 2014: 26).

were encouraged to invest, and *if* many other areas of state intervention (especially in banking, but also in resisting a massive devaluation of the birr) were reduced. We argue that this list of ifs is unlikely to be satisfied. Meanwhile, there are other relevant and, in the Ethiopian context, more realistic proposals that might be considered.

15.4 Critical Comments on Recent Proposals to Increase Coffee Export Revenues

15.4.1 Weak Evidence

The evidence base to support these proposals is remarkably weak. There is a dearth of reliable statistical information on the yields achieved by farms of different sizes; the area planted with coffee and the age of coffee bushes on farms of different sizes; the proportion of output geared to the domestic and to the export market; prices received for cherries by farms of different sizes selling through legal and illegal channels, and so on. There is good evidence that Ethiopian coffee plantations are achieving much greater yields per hectare than smallholders (Schäfer 2016: 195). There is no evidence to suggest that the most efficient and highest yielding coffee farms in Ethiopia are small or that cooperatives are an important, or even a significant, channel for marketing smallholder coffee (Savastano and Scandizzo 2017; Minot and Sawyer 2013: Tables 27–8). Colombia's success in increasing revenues from Arabica exporting has *not* been achieved by 'micro' coffee farmers; farms growing less than one hectare account for only about 6 per cent of the total area producing coffee in Colombia. Although the institutional basis for supporting agronomic improvements on small farms is far stronger in Colombia than in Ethiopia, the prospects for Colombian coffee farms smaller than one hectare have been assessed as 'bleak' (García-Cardona 2016: 183, 120).

The main proposals for specialized extension advice to smallholders have been developed on the basis of TechnoServe and USAID projects. These projects have only had an impact on a tiny percentage of Ethiopia's total coffee exports and, after almost a decade, TechnoServe has trained an even smaller percentage of the country's coffee farmers. Evaluation of these projects has not been able to establish a causal link between training and the adoption of improved practices: analysis of the impact of extension almost invariably finds that wealthier and larger farmers are the earliest and most consistent adopters and cannot rule out the probability that their wealth and political connections, rather than any advice offered by extension staff, provide a good explanation of their use of modern inputs (IPE 2017: 11, 38; Minten et al. 2015: 9; Planel 2014: 424). A recent analysis of the Ethiopian Rural Household Survey (ERHS) concludes that, 'access to extension services does not appear to be effective in generating positive economic returns for rural households' (Bowser 2015: 17). Further, the bulk of Ethiopian extension services are provided for a bundle of crops and there is next to no specialization in coffee growing practices.

Meanwhile, the effects of a nominal currency devaluation on the medium-term volume of coffee exports are uncertain. Among other things this would depend on the supply response of coffee output. Yet the empirical evidence on the price elasticity of supply of coffee exports is also not encouraging; it has been shown, paradoxically for neoclassical economic theory, that 'low prices seem to spur exports more than high ones' (Mold and Prizzon 2009: 23).

15.4.2 The Role of Public-Sector Investment

Recent mainstream proposals do not accept the theory and evidence showing the importance of getting prices 'wrong', of intervening deliberately to distort prices and to 'crowd in' as well as to subsidize private sector investment (Amsden 2001). Some World Bank economists now grudgingly accept the extraordinary success of Ethiopia's drive to increase public-sector investment over the last decade, but continue to insist that while 'rapid and inclusive growth' was achieved, it could have been faster, because this investment 'led to a crowding out of many private investment projects' (Moller and Wacker 2017: 2; but see also Chapter 13). On this logic, Ethiopia's floricultural exports would also have grown faster without state subsidies to input prices and tax exemptions.

Recent literature and policy proposals place a high priority on recurrent state expenditure to finance the salary bill of the huge number of extension staff and to subsidize credit allocated by cooperatives to favoured smallholders. But there is very little emphasis on capital expenditure to invest in, for example, improved roads and electricity supply in coffee growing areas.

15.5 How to Increase Revenue from Coffee Exports

One of the shortcomings of many studies of Ethiopian coffee is that they fail to help policymakers to *prioritize* interventions; instead, and not surprisingly given the complexity of the challenges, these reports set out long lists of things that may help revive the sector, but without identifying the most binding constraints and the most pressing priorities. We have distilled a short and, in some respects, different set of priorities.

It is often thought that there is a binary contrast between an 'unsustainable' Ethiopian policy approach (Moller and Wacker 2017) depending on high levels of public expenditure and a leading role for the state, on the one hand, and, on the other hand, the blanket market deregulation and liberalization that many recommend both for the economy overall and for the coffee sector in particular. Framing debate in terms of this stark choice does not contribute to the urgent task of identifying a small number of key investments and initiatives to expand coffee exports.

15.5.1 Priority 1: A Major Programme of Public Investment in Restocking

A programme of large-scale public investment would reduce the costs to private sector actors of production and exports of high yielding, more disease resistant, 'sustainable', and high quality coffee. Yields are horribly low, the stock of coffee trees is woefully old, and knowledge of best practices is restricted to a tiny area. Overcoming these and other constraints on producing, marketing, and exporting coffee is costly and without major public investment will be poorly coordinated, slow, and inadequate.

A public investment programme needs to be combined with selective, carefully monitored incentives. The first major objective for such a programme should be to promote a massive and carefully designed restocking scheme, learning from what Colombians were able to do, for example, to achieve widespread coffee replanting in the wake of a devastating disease outbreak. The need is to ensure the rapid planting of new coffee seedlings on productive farms and to take advantage of the opportunities this presents to combine seedling distribution with incentives to adopt improved spacing, mulching, weeding, picking, and caring for berries after harvest. Seedling distribution can obviously be combined with subsidized input supply—above all, fertilizer. But there also needs to be support for farmers foregoing income while waiting for new trees to mature. A replanting programme would also have to be sensitive to the need to preserve *terroir* (the unique combination of environmental factors shaping the characteristics of crops like wine, coffee, chocolate, cheese, etc.), which is considered critical to the high value of Ethiopian coffee.

Bearing in mind the urgency of stimulating a rapid expansion of high quality coffee output, the wide dispersion of large numbers of (very) smallholder coffee growers (breadline producers), the low level of effectiveness of extension services geared to coffee, and the experience from other countries suggesting that small size is typically a constraint on maximizing productivity, the priority should be to target medium and larger coffee farmers. There is growing evidence that success in high value agricultural commodity export markets depends upon nurturing larger-scale 'export superstars' who make a disproportionate contribution to total export revenues (Moran 2018; Cramer and Sender 2015). This has an added benefit in that it is more likely to generate additional demand for labour for the very poorest rural people who will find wage employment on the larger farms.

Small farmers are unlikely to be able to lead a concerted effort to improve the resilience of Ethiopian coffee in the face of extreme weather, to develop rapidly the combination of practices necessary for increases in productivity compatible with evolving agro-ecological conditions, or to lead the push into new areas for cultivation. Observers of Ethiopian coffee production already see examples of medium- and larger-scale producers (10 ha and above) applying improved practices and disseminating knowledge to other local producers. These are the nodes around which change is most likely and they need targeted support.

At the same time, a great deal of very different targeted support is needed for those micro coffee farmers unlikely to survive in competition with emerging capitalist farmers. This support should *not* provide huge numbers of marginal smallholders with incentives to continue to struggle to market tiny quantities of low quality beans; rather, their future and the probable future of their children as off-farm wageworkers needs to be taken very seriously indeed. The need is for public sector investment to dramatically improve the quality of rural schooling available—with new resources targeted specifically to benefit the children of micro- and non-viable coffee farmers.

15.5.2 Priority 2: Major Public Investment in Infrastructure

Restocking needs to be combined with public investment in infrastructure. This should include the upgrading of roads to facilitate all-weather access for vehicles, which will reduce the cost of securing modern inputs and of getting coffee beans to wet processing facilities and to trading posts. And it may include expansion of the electricity grid in major coffee growing areas, again to lower costs, for example, on washing stations.

The Ethiopian government has a proven record of delivering improvements in public infrastructure. It should draw on the capabilities acquired in the course of its major infrastructure projects to target road and electricity investments specifically to those areas with the greatest potential for generating a rapid expansion of high quality coffee output. Rolling out the same level of road upgrading and power grid extension everywhere at once is impossible, economically and technically. It makes most sense to do so precisely where the export revenue gains are greatest and quickest.

A targeted infrastructure programme would need to take account of the best research on the implications of climate change. Some well-known coffee producing regions—most notably around Harar—are already suffering climate related constraints. Some of the most careful research suggests that it is already increasingly difficult to produce a reliable supply of high quality coffee in some areas of Ethiopia (Moat et al. 2017; Davis et al. 2017). But there are also areas that are currently not used for coffee growing that are very likely to become especially well suited to this within the coming years. Indeed, if the government intervenes to support a shift of coffee production, and commits resources to a major tree-planting programme to secure forest cover in some areas, Moat et al. (2017) estimate potential coffee output gains of more than 400 per cent. The possible outcomes of climate change for coffee in Ethiopia range from a dramatic shrinkage, in the absence of state intervention, to an even more dramatic increase in potential output, including of excellent quality coffee, if there are interventions to make that possible.

15.5.3 Priority 3: Shifting from Controls to Targeted Incentives

Incentives for producers in existing and selected new areas of high potential may be built on a principle of pledging large increases in subsidies on proof of performance. The evidence of satisfactory performance should include the rate of growth of coffee output, share of output that is high quality, and detailed evidence of new jobs provided. Overall, a rigorously monitored and targeted incentive system needs to replace an excessively regulated system policed by legislative controls, which many coffee traders and millions of smallholders continuously struggle to evade. This does not mean blanket or rapid liberalization of all areas of coffee production and trade. The purpose of incentives will be to subsidize costs—making it less costly for selected producers to expand output, improve yield, and raise quality; for these producers to apply chemical and organic fertilizers and replace existing with new trees and to plant in new areas; for washing stations to generate a greater output of high quality coffee;[14] and for exporters to sell internationally at high prices. Only some 30 per cent of Ethiopian coffee is currently wet processed; there is still a low presence of washing stations in rural communities; and an added advantage of wet processing is that the careful harvesting, the post-harvest demands, and the processing itself together generate higher demand for labour, which has important implications for addressing extreme poverty in coffee growing areas (Tamru and Minten 2016: 19).

Ethiopia could also introduce a package of conditional support to a small group of roasters who could be considered potential national champions. Not only would they be expected to expand sales to a growing tourist, urban, and middle -class domestic market (following the model of Rift Valley Wine, but in this case Ethiopian owned), but they would also compete for opportunities to sell packaged branded specialty coffees on all Ethiopian Airlines flights.

15.5.4 Priority 4: Investing in Data and R&D Capabilities

Government targets for a dramatic expansion of coffee output, whether sold domestically or internationally, and a new emphasis on the high quality and 'sustainable' coffees most likely to fetch high export prices, cannot succeed without two further forms of support: for a radical improvement in reliable data and for a sustained improvement in research and development capabilities. A first investment could be in a properly designed and conducted sample survey of coffee producers farming anything less than five hectares, together with a complete and regularly updated census of all producers farming more than five hectares. These middle- and larger-scale producers are likely to

[14] Tamru and Minten (2016: 14) show that the average accessibility of washing stations, despite a recent increase particularly in some regions, remains low, with a low number of washing stations per community. Their survey results show that farmers who are closer to washing stations sell a higher share of their crop in red berry form, which through the washing stations produces the wet processed coffee that on average commands higher international prices.

be the lead actors in any successful coffee strategy and yet they are perhaps the group (a very differentiated group) about which least is known.

Meanwhile, the knowledge economy is just as much a feature of high value global trade and competitiveness in agricultural commodities as it is of manufacturing and services. This, along with branding and marketing, is one facet of the 'servicification' of non-service sector activities, in which a rising share of the value of output is accounted for by services (Baldwin, Forslid, and Ito 2015). And a fundamental factor is research and development capabilities. There is a particular need to build a core body of specialists in coffee agronomy capable of selecting the combination of interventions (irrigation, mulching, shade management, terracing, pruning, etc.) that can best develop the resilience of Ethiopian coffee growing areas (Moat et al. 2017: 31). To develop the knowledge foundations of the sector, the government, with donor support, will need to spend very large amounts on building up facilities at the Jimma Agricultural Research Centre and increasing the number of PhD-qualified research staff specializing in coffee.

15.5.5 Priority 5: Institutional Reforms

It is difficult to imagine a large increase in coffee exports unless the commitment to controlling whether coffee is sold domestically or for export is abandoned. The strategic aim has to be to raise overall coffee output, quality, and sustainability. Foreign exchange access for traders could be skewed towards a target group, i.e. those processors and traders who can prove they have a strong track record of regularly supplying overseas buyers with substantial quantities of highly priced coffee. And new public sector investments could be made to establish inspection offices using near-infrared spectroscopy to confirm coffee origin and the spectral print of beans before they can be exported.

These sectoral investments and reforms could be combined with macroeconomic policy efforts to ensure a competitive exchange rate for the birr. The evidence on the effects of devaluation on growth is mixed. Two mechanisms might account for disappointing outcomes: first, the inflationary impact on the price of imported intermediate inputs, which raises the costs of firms and farms, undermining partially or totally their price competitiveness and incentives to invest; and, second, a redistribution of income from wages to profits, which reduces domestic aggregate demand (Ribeiro, McCombie, and Lima 2017). Nonetheless, sustained rates of growth of exports—especially of manufactured exports—have frequently been associated with currency undervaluation (Rodrik 2008).

15.6 Conclusion

This chapter has focused on the major constraints on expansion of the coffee sector in Ethiopia. It has put Ethiopian coffee production in an international, comparative framework, the better to engage in the debates about policy that have developed in recent years. We have argued that effective policy has been undermined by the accumulation of long to-do lists that fail to distinguish the highest priorities and by pervasive and questionable assumptions. We then identify a small number of policy priorities.

In 2017–18, the Ethiopian government completed a review of coffee sector policies. This has involved wide consultation with domestic and foreign coffee market actors. And, as with the development of policy towards industrial parks, for example, it has involved a process of intensive learning from other countries' experiences, the results of which have been fed into the National Export Coordinating Committee (NECC). One presentation to this committee highlighted two main constraints on Ethiopian coffee: the proliferation of 'non value adding middlemen' and the non-traceability of coffee exports. Although the coffee marketing chain within Ethiopia is complex and costly by comparison with most other producer countries, we do not think it is sensible to regard all middlemen as 'non value adding'. And it is notable that the presentation largely drew on the very set of existing consultancy reports that this chapter has critically discussed. In parallel, a set of recommended interventions was submitted to the NECC, running to eight pages of detailed recommendations. Some of these align clearly with our own arguments for policy priorities—including reforms to facilitate traceable 'identity preserved trading', to encourage greater vertical integration between producers and exporters, to invest in infrastructure in particular clusters of coffee production, and to reduce from 300 ha to 30 ha the minimum land size threshold for access to low-cost finance for investors, as well as to improve the number and quality of coffee research specialists. A recommendation to set up a Coffee Sector Advisory Council to ensure consistent public/private engagement in the sector complements our suggestion that the government, or the Coffee and Tea Development Authority, should set up an 'error museum' to maintain a focus on constraints and policy mistakes.

By 2018 it remained to be seen whether these recommendations and others would be adopted in full and whether this, together with the reforms already underway at the ECX, would be enough to lead to a positive supply response and an increase in the unit price of coffee exports. The hope is that the learning process, in general such an important feature of the policy process in recent years in Ethiopia, will lead to a rejection of inherited assumptions underpinning so much policy advice and the 'list' syndrome that has made it difficult to isolate and act on the very highest priorities.

References

Abbink, J. (2017). 'Paradoxes of Electoral Authoritarianism: The 2015 Ethiopian Elections as Hegemonic Performance', *Journal of Contemporary African Studies* 35 (3): 303–23.

Agricultural Development Transformation Agency (ATA) (2012). *Agricultural Cooperatives Sector Development Strategy 2012–2016* (Addis Ababa: Federal Democratic Republic Ministry of Agriculture).

Agricultural Transformation Agency (ATA) (2016). *Smallholder Access to Specialty Coffee Markets via Cooperatives and Commercial Farm Outgrower Schemes, Diagnostic and Program Planning* (Addis Ababa: Federal Democratic Republic Ministry of Agriculture).

Amsden, A. H. (2001). *The Rise of 'the Rest': Challenges to the West from Late-Industrialization Economies* (Oxford: Oxford University Press).

Baldwin, Richard, Rikard Forslid, and Tadashi Ito (2015). 'Unveiling the Evolving Sources of Value Added in Exports', draft, http://www.ide.go.jp/library/English/Publish/Download/Jrp/pdf/161.pdf [accessed 4 April 2017]

Belete, K. M. (2015). 'The State of Competition and the Competition Regime of Ethiopia: Potential Gaps and Enforcement Challenges', Organization for Social Science Research in Eastern and Southern Africa (OSSREA).

Bowser, W. H. (2015). 'The Long and Short of Returns to Public Investments in Fifteen Ethiopian Villages', 3ie Replication Series Paper 4.

Cramer, C., D. Johnston, C. Oya, and J. Sender (2014). 'Fairtrade Cooperatives in Ethiopia and Uganda: Uncensored', *Review of African Political Economy* 41(sup1): S115–S12.

Cramer, C. and J. Sender (2015). 'Agro-Processing, Wage Employment and Export Revenue: Opportunities for Strategic Intervention', TIPS Working paper for the Department of Trade and Industry.

Davis, A. P., T. Wilkinson, Z. K. Challa, J. Williams, S. Baena, T. W. Gole, and J. Moat (2017). *Coffee Atlas of Ethiopia* (London: Royal Botanic Gardens).

Diaz Rios, Luz (nd). 'Coffee Sector in Figures: benchmarking Vietnam's performance against leading global coffee players.' PowerPoint presentation.

EIAR (Ethiopian Institute of Agricultural Research) (2017). 'National Coffee Commodity Research Strategy, Fifteen Years (2016–2030)', EIAR, Addis Ababa.

EU (2014). 'Coffee Sector Development Strategy for Ethiopia, Final Report Vol. 1', European Union's External Cooperation Programme in Ethiopia, Addis Ababa.

FAO (2004). *Fertilizer Use by Crop in Brazil* (FAO, Rome: Land and Plant Nutrition Management Service Land and Water Development Division).

García-Cardona, J. (2016). 'Value-Added Initiatives: Distributional Impacts on the Global Value Chain for Colombia's Coffee', PhD dissertation, University of Sussex.

Gelaw, F., S. Speelman, and G. van Huylenbroeck (2017). 'Impacts of Institutional Intervention on Price Transmissions: The Case of the Ethiopian Commodity Exchange', *Review of Development Economics* 21 (4): e88–e106.

ICO (International Coffee Organization) (2014). *World Coffee Trade (1963–2013): A Review of the Markets, Challenges and Opportunities Facing the Sector* (London: ICO).

ICO (International Coffee Organization) (2015). *Coffee in China* (London: ICO).

IMF (2016). 'Article IV Consultation', in *Country Report: Federal Democratic Republic of Ethiopia*, No. 16/322, IMF, Washington.

IPE (2017). 'Evaluation of the TechnoServe East Africa Coffee Initiative (Final Report)', London.

ITC, International Trade Centre (2018). Trade Map. Trade Statistics for International Business Development. https://www.trademap.org/Index.aspx [last access 25.05.2018]

Larson, D. F., R. Muraoka, and K. Otsuka (2016). 'On the Central Role of Small Farms in African Rural Development Strategies.' Policy Research Working Paper No. 7710, World Bank, Washington, DC.

Lewis, A. (1954). 'Economic Development with Unlimited Supplies of Labour', *The Manchester School* 22 (2): 139–191.

Melke, A. and F. Ittana (2014). 'Nutritional Requirement and Management of Arabica Coffee (Coffea arabica L.) in Ethiopia: National and Global Perspectives', *American Journal of Experimental Agriculture* 5 (5): 400–18.

Minot, N. and B. Sawyer (2013). *Agricultural Production in Ethiopia: Results of the 2012 ATA Baseline Survey* (Washington, DC: IFPRI).

Minten, B., M. Dereje, E. Engeda, and S. Tamru (2015). 'Who Benefits from the Rapidly Increasing Voluntary Sustainability Standards? Evidence from Fairtrade and Organic

Certified Coffee in Ethiopia', Ethiopia Strategy Support Program, Working Paper 71, EDRI/ IFPRI, Addis Ababa.

Moat, J., J. Williams, S. Baena, T. Wilkinson, T. W. Gole, Z. K. Chassa, S. Demissew, and A. P. Davis (2017). 'Coffee Farming and Climate Change in Ethiopia: Impacts, Forecasts, Resilience and Opportunities—Summary', The Strategic Climate Institutions Programme (SCIP), Royal Botanic Gardens, Kew.

Mold, A. and A. Prizzon (2009). 'Explaining Africa's Recent Export Performance and the Limited Gains from the Commodity Boom', (mimeo) OECD Development Centre, Paris.

Moller, L.C. and K. Wacker (2017). 'Explaining Ethiopia's Growth Acceleration: The Role of Infrastructure and Macroeconomic Policy', *World Development* 96: 198–215.

Monitor (2011). 'East Africa Coffee Value Chain Partnership Opportunity', PowerPoint presented for the Bill and Melinda Gates Foundation, May.

Moran, T. (2018). 'FDI and Supply Chains in Horticulture (Vegetables, Fruits, and Flowers, Raw, Packaged, Cut, and Processed): Diversifying Exports and Reducing Poverty in Africa, Latin America and Other Developing Economies', Centre for Global Development, Washington, DC.

Planel, S. (2014). 'A View of a *Bureaucratic* Developmental State: Local Governance and Agricultural Extension in Rural Ethiopia', *Journal of Eastern African Studies* 8 (3): 420–37.

Ribeiro, R. S. M., J. S. McCombie, and G. T. Lima (2017). 'Some Unpleasant Currency-Devaluation Arithmetic in a Post Keynesian Macromodel', *Journal of Post Keynesian Economics* 40 (2): 1–23.

Rodrik, D. (2008). 'The Real Exchange Rate and Economic Growth', *Brookings Papers on Economic Activity*, Fall: 365–412.

Savastano, S. and P. L. Scandizzo (2017). 'Farm Size and Productivity: A "Direct-Inverse-Direct" Relationship', Policy Research Working Paper No. 8127, World Bank, Washington, DC.

Schäfer, F. (2016). 'Revisiting the Agrarian Question: Coffee, Flowers and Ethiopia's New Capitalists', PhD thesis, SOAS, University of London.

Shumeta, Z., M. D'Haese, and W. Verbeke (2017). 'A Two-Step Econometric Estimation of Covariates of Side Selling: The Case of Coffee Cooperatives in Southwest Ethiopia', *Journal of Development Studies* https://doi.org/10.1080/00220388.2017.1324146.

Tamru, S. and B. Minten (2016). 'Value Addition and Processing by Farmers in Developing Countries: Evidence from the Coffee Sector in Ethiopia', in *2016 AAAE Fifth International Conference, September 23–26, 2016, Addis Ababa, Ethiopia*. African Association of Agricultural Economists (AAAE).

TechnoServe. (2014). 'Ethiopia: A Business Case for Sustainable Coffee Production', PowerPoint presentation, January, Addis Ababa.

Thirlwall, A. P. (2011). 'Balance of Payments Constrained Growth Models: A History and Overview', Studies in Economics 1111, School of Economics, 2011/05. University of Kent.

USAID (2015). 'Agricultural Growth Programme: Agribusiness Marketing and Development Project (AMDe), Ethiopia (External Mid-Term Performance Evaluation Report)', Agriculture Knowledge, Learning, Documentation and Policy Project (AKLDP), Addis Ababa.

USDA (2014). 'Ethiopia Coffee Annual', GAIN Report No. ET1402, Foreign Agricultural Service, Addis Ababa.

USDA (2017). 'Ethiopia Coffee Annual', GAIN Report No. ET1710, Foreign Agricultural Service, Addis Ababa.

World Bank (2016). 'Ethiopia's Great Run: The Growth Acceleration and How To Pace It', No. 99399, World Bank, Washington, DC.

CHAPTER 16

LIVELIHOODS AND MOBILITY IN THE BORDER REGIONS OF ETHIOPIA

LAURA HAMMOND

16.1 Introduction

Ethiopia's borderlands are key sites of population mobility and migration. Not only do these areas host most of the 800,000 refugees from neighbouring countries who in 2018 were being hosted in Ethiopia (USAID 2018), they also are home to populations whose livelihoods and movements are influenced by regional dynamics. As a landlocked nation, Ethiopia shares borders with six countries (Djibouti, Eritrea, Kenya, Somalia, South Sudan, and Sudan), and its ties with its neighbours provide a range of particular economic and social opportunities for those living near the borders.

Communities living near or spanning both sides of the Ethiopian border are influenced by trade and labour market opportunities. They are also affected by restrictions on movements of people and goods, availability of natural resources, the advantages of social networks that transcend borders, and the levels of social services available on one side or the other. In addition to migration and displacement within and across borderlands, mobility—regular seasonal or annual movements—is an important feature of the Ethiopian borderlands. The borderlands are sites of some of the region's most important rangelands, and Somali, Borena, Afar, and other pastoralists regularly move back and forth across the border to take advantage of pasture, water, and market resources, as well as to access education, health, and other services.

This chapter considers the factors that influence decision-making about migration and mobility in Ethiopia's border regions. The aim is to analyse the particularities of border regions in social, economic, and political terms which give rise to displacement, environmental-induced migration, economic migration, and urbanization, and the ways in which borders facilitate or restrict both necessary and safe movement as well as that which is unsafe or risky.

The chapter is guided by the basic premise that not all forms of migration and mobility from, within, and through borderlands are inherently problematic. Indeed, a great deal of human mobility is essential to the sustainability of livelihood systems, and much migration reflects the strong desire of people to improve their lives and to seize opportunity. Where migration becomes problematic, however, is when it is undertaken under duress, in the absence of other options. Movement made under such conditions is very often unsafe, as people become vulnerable to exploitation at the hands of a wide range of characters including employers, agents, landholders, and police.

In practice, distinguishing movement that is chosen from that which is involuntary is often difficult. As will be discussed, people's reasons for moving are often multiple, and may be influenced both by the desire to take advantage of opportunities near to, or away from, the borders, and by a need to escape from an unsafe situation or to minimize risks. Migration decisions are often highly politicized and reflect people's positions vis-à-vis power structures and authorities in areas of origin, transit, and destination.

Just as lack of ability to make safe choices about movement can lead to displacement, it can also lead to a kind of 'forced immobility' (Lubkemann 2008) where people are unable to afford to move or to continue pursuing livelihood activities that feature mobility (such as pastoralism). Such immobility can further deepen destitution and place people in danger. Thus an analysis that considers the risks that mobility and immobility entail provides a lens through which to better understand political, economic, and social processes in the borderlands.

The chapter builds on available data and research on borderlands, mobility, livelihoods, and resilience and vulnerability in Ethiopia's peripheries. Much of the data used are qualitative. Where statistics exist and are cited they must be understood to be rough estimates. A great deal of cross-border movement of both humans and goods, not to mention livestock, is not recorded due to weak governmental capacity, the desire of borderland residents to evade formal taxation or registration, and the historical practices of crossing borders that have gone on since long before the establishment of international boundaries. Statistics available are generally informed guesses or minimum figures at best. For instance, Little estimates that the volume of informally traded livestock in the Horn of Africa region is more than 95 per cent of total production; while much of this trade is never recorded, some of it does get recorded at wholesale and retail markets (2007: 2–4). Golub discusses the difficulties of estimating flows of cross-border trade and smuggling throughout Africa given the clandestine nature of many of the transactions; he advocates triangulating data through a range of qualitative and quantitative methods and by extrapolation from case study data (2015: 183–4).

16.2 Mobility and Livelihoods in the Borderlands

Borderland areas in Ethiopia, as in many other countries around the world, are often the visible manifestation of economic, social, and political marginality (Pankhurst 2003; Markakis 2011). They are spaces where vulnerability and insecurity are greatest. With the exception of the militarized and formally closed northern border with Eritrea, governance at the borders is commonly at its weakest or least evident. Where it is present it often takes the form of security or immigration control rather than service provision or protection of personal or economic freedoms. Yet it is these latter elements of governance that arguably represent the most significant factors in terms of convincing people to support and give their allegiance to the state (see Markakis (2011: 15) who applies this thinking from Crawford Young (1982) in his references to the Ethiopian lowland peripheries as the 'last frontier' in the process of nation-state building). This form of engagement has historically been a major challenge for the Ethiopian state, as it is for the wider region. Development actors (donors, international organizations, and nongovernmental organizations) also very often do not engage as much in borderland development as they do in the hinterland or at the central level. This makes promoting economic inclusion more difficult, and complicates addressing the root causes of involuntary mobility and migration.

While there is a growing body of literature and analysis of the political economy and livelihoods conditions in borderland areas (Goodhand 2014; Hagmann and Stepputat 2016), this work has not so far focused much on the role of mobility and migration—within borderlands as well as across borders—as a source of both vulnerability and resilience. In Ethiopia, the mobility of resident populations, and of those who may not be normally resident in these zones but at times rely on border regions (the internally displaced, refugees, etc.) are major features of the socio-economic landscape of border regions rather than aberrations of the status quo.

The chapter considers the socio-economics of border regions in which population mobility and migration are major features. It considers border regions that transect international boundaries as livelihood zones, in which common livelihood activities and access to shared or complementary resources are central in organizing people's lives. In many of Ethiopia's trans-border livelihood zones, particularly the pastoralist Somali, Borana, and Afar on both sides of the border practise the same activities, rely on the same resources, and belong to the same social and economic networks. They rely on shared livestock management practices, use of grassland and water resources, mobility patterns that respond to seasonal variations in resource use, trade links, and spread of information about weather, prices, and water availability (Pavanello 2009). Many agricultural communities, such as those along Ethiopia's western border with Sudan, seek to take advantage of borders by marketing their produce in towns and cities across the border, or by attracting seasonal labour from across borders. These cross-border ties are often stronger than the ties between Ethiopia's centre and periphery. The intertwined lives of people within the borderland livelihood zones determine the degree of economic integration and resilience to shocks that they are able to achieve. Mobility can be an important manifestation of resilience, or conversely when it occurs involuntarily, it can be an indicator of stress and vulnerability.

Borders can generate what Goodhand calls a 'spatial discount' where buyers, sellers, and employers can take advantage of differences between different state regulatory regimes and the disparity in economic conditions that they create, otherwise known as arbitrage. In this way, 'fields of opportunity' are created. Goodhand observes, 'These dynamics take place not just in the border but because of the border. The intensity of economic flows and relations may be greater across the border than with the metropolitan centre within the state' (Goodhand 2014: 19).

Borderland opportunities may include differing prices, wage rates, levels of security, degree of regulation and enforcement, availability of natural resources, quality of health or education systems, or access to markets further from the border. All of these considerations come into play when people are navigating their way in borderlands and ultimately when they make decisions about mobility. For states, borderlands become the focus of political and economic interest when they provide trade corridors for landlocked countries, available manpower for seasonal agricultural activities, and increased qualitative animal production for exports.

Ethiopia's border regions are not particularly well understood and the arm of development policy has a weaker reach to the peripheries of the state. Weak communication, service provision, and market integration both within Ethiopian border areas and between those areas and their corresponding areas in Kenya, Somalia, or Sudan creates an unevenness of opportunity and can impact negatively on the livelihood outcomes of communities on both sides of the border. Closure of the border with Eritrea since 2008 has brought cross-border communication and official trade to a standstill. Only the smallest amounts of contraband trade items make it across the border or transit through a third country (Sudan, Djibouti, or the Gulf countries).

Marginalization of areas in Ethiopia's peripheries is associated with development deficiencies, higher rates of violence, and sub-national conflict (OECD 2015; Markakis 2011). Marginalization and violence have a cyclical relationship: heightened insecurity complicates development work just as it disrupts trade links, mobility within and through border regions, and labour markets. Communities that feel they have not felt any positive effects of state governance systems may see no reason to engage with those systems. They may prefer to be left to manage their own affairs, or may seek alternative support from non-state actors or even engage with political and militant activity aimed at undermining the state. Livelihood vulnerability can thus translate into further physical insecurity.

Insecurity in Ethiopia's border areas provides opportunities for infiltration by actors—whether from inside Ethiopia or from its neighbours. To contain this threat, borders are dealt with through national security policies aimed at hardening them, creating a military presence to stop infiltration of all kinds, which may in turn encourage further insecurity (Goodhand 2014). Ethiopia's policy towards Somali region has long been one of securitization and counter-insurgency operations that also impacted trade and mobility in and across border regions. This stance has shifted somewhat in recent years (as will be discussed later in this chapter), partly in response to the limited gains that the policy brought.

Many of Ethiopia's borderlands are affected by conflicts in neighbouring countries—particularly Somalia and South Sudan—that spill across borders and affect dynamics inside the country, contributing to instability, economic decline, and population displacement. The northern border with Eritrea suffers from the closed border that has been in place since the border war broke out in 1998. As Goodhand argues, 'borderland blindness' and 'methodological nationalism' prevent a complete understanding of conflict dynamics, and impede engaging with both the drivers of conflict and the implications (Goodhand 2014). This focus on national as opposed to regional processes can be seen in national development planning as well as international engagement with individual countries within the Horn of Africa. Increasingly, however, more notice is being taken of borderlands in terms of their potential economic benefits as well as the security implications of regional conflict dynamics (see for example Hagmann and Stepputat 2016; Little 2010, 2013).

Displacement can be both a cause and effect of development challenges, conflict, political violence, and political persecution. As can be seen in Map 16.1, Ethiopia's refugee camps are located in its borderlands, along the borders with Eritrea, South Sudan, and Somalia. Most of the camps have been in place for more than five years, and Gambella and Somali regions have been hosting refugees for decades. Pugnido, the oldest of the refugee camps in Gambella region, was opened in 1993, and hosts both longer established and newly arrived refugees. The camps for Somali refugees near the town of Dolo Ado first opened in 2009 (Jesuit Refugee Service 2011). Camps are effectively urban settlements, and as such they shape the local economy of the border regions in significant ways, creating market opportunities as well as competition for resources with local host populations (Agier, Nice, and Wacquant 2002; Stevenson and Sutton 2011; Oka 2011).

16.3 Environmentally Induced Displacement and Urbanization

Displacement in the region is the result of food insecurity and conflict; these dynamics are interrelated. In 2017, it was estimated that 8.5 million people in Ethiopia were in need of emergency food assistance (WFP 2017). While droughts in 2015, 2016, and 2017 were cited as the cause of these food shortages, the most acute needs were in Somali and southern Oromiya regions, where localized conflict also impeded humanitarian and market access. Faced with both drought and insecurity, those affected are rendered destitute, and generally move across as short a distance as they can afford to—often to the nearest town or city—for relief and protection.

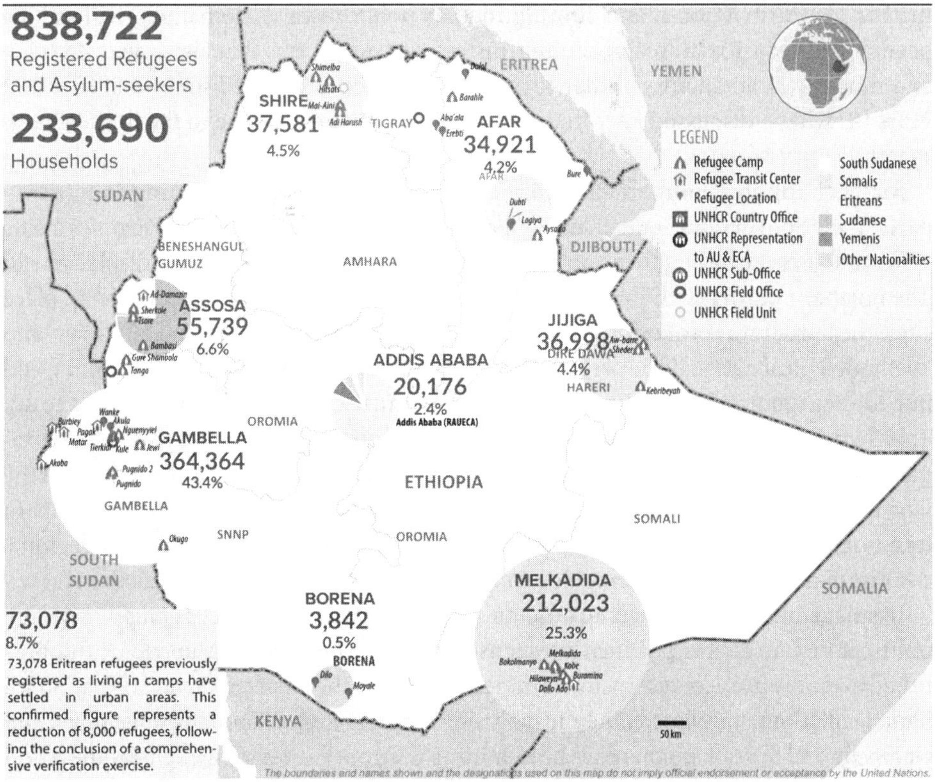

MAP 16.1 Refugees and asylum seekers, Ethiopia 2018

Source: UNHCR 31 May 2017.

Rural–urban migration comes with a host of other challenges. Urbanization can lead to greater productivity in cities with an adequate industrial base. However, Ethiopia does not yet have a sufficiently industrialized base—in terms of either exports or domestic markets—to fully benefit from increasing urban populations (Henderson, Storeygard, and Deichman 2014, cited in AfDB 2016: 170). Ethiopia's recent shift to promotion of industrial-led growth may change this, by opening up new employment opportunities for people in urban areas. Some of the industrial hubs being constructed are close to borders and thus may influence mobility in those areas. In some of the large industrial parks being constructed provision is also being made to designate up to 30 per cent of jobs for refugee or displaced workers. The impact of such employment schemes on the ethnic balance, and on community relations between local and displaced people, will need to be followed closely to ensure that the initiative does not lead to tensions and conflict.

A great deal of rural–urban migration in the Horn of Africa is related to the declining viability of rural livelihoods due to environmental stress (Iazzolino 2018). Yet urban areas are not always places to seek relief—they may also themselves be negatively impacted by environmental factors. Urban residents may be affected by declining availability of drinking water, declining conditions for urban agriculture, and the increasing vulnerability of some settlements due to floods or other weather events. It is therefore important not to associate climate change vulnerability only with those pursuing rural livelihoods.

Urbanization affects not only the capital, Addis Ababa, but Ethiopia's secondary cities as well, many of them located in or near the borderlands. Ethiopia's urban population is expected to increase from 19 million in 2015 to 51 million in 2050 (AfDB 2016). Ethiopia's cities are seeing rapid expansion not only of population, but of infrastructure and general construction with Addis Ababa embodying what Goodfellow calls the 'city as construction site' (2018). Yet much of the trend towards urbanization in Ethiopia involves people moving into secondary cities such as Dire Dawa, Hawassa, or Mekelle rather than the capital. This mirrors a global trend: the UN Department of Economic and Social Affairs reports that 'the fastest-growing agglomerations are medium-sized cities and cities with 500,000 to 1 million inhabitants located in Asia and Africa' (UNDESA 2014: 2). Large cities—cities of 5 to 10 million inhabitants—accounted for only 6 per cent of the world's urban population in 2014, and this proportion is expected to grow to 9 per cent by 2030 (UNDESA 2014: 2).

Ethiopia is responding to increasing pressure on its secondary cities with investment in infrastructure and labour markets. It is embarking on an ambitious plan to develop industrial parks in several cities to provide employment for people in and around the urban areas while increasing opportunities for foreign direct investment. Some of these parks will, when completed, include jobs reserved for refugee labour as well, which will be the first time such a scheme has been extended to refugees. However, Ethiopia will also need to respond to demands being placed on housing, transport, public utility, and social service sectors in secondary cities.

16.4 Pastoralism, Changing Resource Use, and Urbanization

Pastoralism, a major feature of livelihood systems in many border regions of Ethiopia, particularly in the southwest, south, and east of the country, depends on access to grazing and markets across borders as well as a stable natural resource base. Feyissa estimates the total pastoral population of the Horn of Africa region to be more than 155 million (Feyissa 2016: 4). Pastoral livelihood systems in the border regions have been undergoing changes in the context of increasing livestock populations, declining water and vegetation levels, and enclosure of rangelands reducing the available common land available for grazing. These constraints on pastoralist movement and use have been shown to lead to overgrazing, further depletion of the surface water table, loss of biodiversity, long-term degradation of rangeland resources, and in some cases an increase in conflict (Makki 2014). In Borena society, for example, the *gada* system prohibits private land enclosures known as *kalo* on the basis that if individuals divide up communal land then there will be less land available for pastoralist grazing and a potential increase in conflict

(McPeak and Little 2018).[1] Ethiopia's strategy for dealing with pastoral populations includes encouraging sedentarization through villagization, increased agricultural activity, and engagement with local labour markets to generate employment in large commercial enterprises (both agricultural and manufacturing) (Belayneh 2016; Catley 2017). While some agropastoralism and irrigated agriculture is possible—with significant investment in agricultural technology—in Ethiopia's border areas (particularly in the south, southwest, and west of the country), most of Afar and Somali regions, and parts of Oromiya region, are not suitable for sedentary agriculture and thus more transhumant or diversified livelihood practices are necessary if people are to remain in rural areas. In Western Ethiopia, along the border with Sudan, commercial agricultural production of sesame, sorghum, and cotton depends on the mobility of agricultural labour both domestically and across borders. Asfaw, Tolossa, and Zeleke report that more than 200,000 workers move to the northwestern border area near Humera in Tigray Region each year, and 100,000 move to the area around Metemma in Amhara Region on the western border with Sudan (2010: 62, citing 2007 figures from the Regional Bureaus of Agriculture in Amhara and Tigray Regions). A study by the EU Trust Fund's Research and Evidence Facility (2017) describes the movement of Ethiopian workers into Sudan:

> The Guba exit in Metekel is dominated by labour migration. Most of the farm workers recruited and employed by investors in commercial farms in Ethiopia migrate irregularly to Sudan when weeding is over in the Ethiopian side, which ends mostly in the middle of September. This season coincides with the ripening of corn farms in the Sudanese side of the border. (2017: 25)

For many pastoralists, increasing population and the challenges to the natural resource base brought by environmental change, development interventions such as large-scale infrastructure projects, and restrictions on cross-border mobility have necessitated finding ways of diversifying their livelihoods. Often diversification involves pastoralists moving into urban areas either temporarily or permanently, or, if conditions permit, engaging in agricultural activities to replace lost income from pastoral activities. Where such diversification is not possible, people may 'fall out of pastoralism [and] use various and potentially damaging livelihood strategies, including non-sustainable use of natural resources, such as cutting trees for charcoal production and sale, sending daughters to work as house servants in towns, thereby exposing them to risk of abuse; engaging in illegal contraband trade; and criminal activity such as "organised livestock raiding" or banditry' (ibid, 4). The movement of people out of pastoralist livelihoods through urbanization and livelihood diversification is also noted by Catley (2017).

Movement of pastoralists—notably Borana and Somalis—into urban and peri-urban areas to take advantage of non-livestock-based livelihood opportunities is increasing

[1] In areas where land enclosures have been created in order to protect or regenerate land, evidence suggests that within enclosures land may enjoy better quality as compared to land outside the enclosures, but that for those who are not able to access enclosed land the results in terms of quality and quantity of rangelands were poorer (Feyisa et al. 2017).

(Aberra 2003). In Ethiopia's Somali region, for instance, the annual rate of urban growth between 2006 and 2008 was 4.69 per cent, compared to the rural growth rate in Somali region of 2.25 per cent and to an average national urban growth rate of 4.4 per cent, according to national census figures (Government of Ethiopia 2007, cited in HPG 2010: 18). Similar rates are reported for Oromiya and SNNPR (Scott-Villiers 2015: 2).

16.5 Borderland Trade

Official trade relations between Ethiopia and the rest of the region vary widely, from officially non-existent (e.g. Eritrea) to close and better integrated (e.g. Kenya). Ethiopia is pursuing stronger trade links with Somalia and Somaliland, including a joint venture with the latter to develop the port of Berbera with the private company DP World. Unofficial small-scale trade is widely credited with being more significant in terms of value and numbers of people involved than formal trade, and exists even where formal trade links are weak or non-existent.

Borderland ethnic groups have variable relations with their neighbours on the other side of the border. Somali and Afar pastoralists cross borders regularly with their livestock and share social ties with people across the border. Borana rely on cross-border livestock trade, particularly through the town of Moyale between Ethiopia and Kenya. In the more agricultural west of Ethiopia, ethnic groups tend not to have as much social interaction and are more circumscribed by the border, despite using it for economic resources.

The impact of increasing regional integration can be directly felt in many of Ethiopia's border regions. Improving road and telecommunications infrastructure between Ethiopia and its neighbours provides opportunities for traders operating at all levels in the border regions. Efforts to improve management of shared water resources and common management of pastoral rangelands, and to promote free movement of people, also bears dividends in increasing cross-border trade. Informal and small-scale trade far outweighs the significance of formal trade through most corridors of the region. Trade in livestock, khat, cereals, second-hand clothing, and consumer goods either produced in the region or imported from outside the region (particularly the Gulf States) and then moved further inland constitute important sources of income for people living in border communities. Cross-border trade is particularly important for women. IGAD claims that more than half of the region's informal cross-border traders are women (IGAD 2018).

Women engaged in informal cross-border trade have low profit margins, face security risks, and are often unable to protect themselves against exploitation. A USAID Policy Brief, 'Women in Cross-Border Agricultural Trade', notes that 'while men tend to dominate the trucking sector carrying large cargo loads over long distances, women are more likely to face time, mobility, and asset constraints that limit their trade participation to the transport of small cargo loads via foot, bicycle, cart, or small vehicle'. Women traders are often also at a disadvantage when it comes to negotiating with men. However, they may also have an advantage in negotiating with kin if they come from patrilineal societies in which women form the links between clans or ethnic groups.

Mobility also plays an important role in the circulation of goods through regional trade. Work done by Little (2013), Mahmoud (2010), Hagmann and Stepputat (2016), and others highlights the importance of cross-border trade for regional distribution of food and other essential resources, as well as for export of cash crops, livestock, and other commodities. The value of cattle, goats, sheep, and camels from Ethiopia sold across the border in Somalia, Kenya, and Djibouti was estimated at US$250 to 300 million in 2009 (COMESA 2009, cited in Pavanello 2009). Where borders are more restrictively managed, the circulation of key economic resources can be endangered, to the disadvantage not only of those living within the border zones but also those who depend on the goods further down the market chain. Vegetables grown in the agro-pastoral zones of Ethiopia, for instance, are traded at markets within border areas for onward distribution to Southern Somalia. Blockages of borders can result in severing of the market chains that deliver goods to markets as far away as Mogadishu.

Cross-border trade is hampered by states' efforts to block avenues for informal trade in order to boost the formal sector revenue. Feyissa discusses the efforts of the Ethiopian government to clamp down on unofficial trade in livestock, which was estimated to be 'up to ten times the value of officially recorded trade'. This has been done through securitization of the borders, seizure of tradable goods and livestock, and other controls (Feyissa 2016: 17).

Recently, Ethiopia has been introducing measures to convert informal trade to more formal trade. Ethiopia and Sudan have signed an agreement allowing traders to make forty-eight trips a year with goods up to US$117 in value on each trip. Ethiopia has also taken steps to allow small-scale cross-border trade with Djibouti, Kenya, and Somalia by specifying an upper limit for some goods, as well as limiting the number of crossings and the distance from border posts that trade is permitted. Ethiopia has also made strengthening cross-border trade a major part of its second Growth and Transformation Plan (2015–20). These steps benefit traders who are able to obtain licences, but they may squeeze out those who are not, particularly women. Scott-Villiers notes that women on the Ethiopia–Kenya border are disproportionately affected by government efforts to formalize trade routes, as they are not able to operate at sufficient scale to take advantage of the formalization and their profit margins are too small to be able to accommodate the costs of working through formal channels (Scott-Villiers 2015: 6).

The significance of trade for borderland livelihoods is highly dependent upon security conditions and the extent to which the state regulates border crossings. Along the Ethiopia–Somali border:

> Tougher restrictions on unlicensed cross-border trade in recent years, the volatile security situation in Somalia with the growth of Al-Shabaab, and the development of an asphalt road between Jigjiga and Gode town have changed the trade routes for imported food and non-food items in the southern zones. Five years ago, most goods were coming across what was - at the time - a highly porous border with Somalia; but today most goods come through a single route (Wajale-Jigjiga) via

> licensed traders and associations. From Gode market goods are distributed onward throughout the southern livelihood zones. On the Somalia side, products which used to flow smoothly across the border to markets like Beletweyne and Mogadishu are now less likely to be transported due to the changing security situation at the border. Trade routes for livestock have shifted to Gode-Degahbur, from which most are exported to Somaliland through Wajale or taken directly to Hargeisa.
> (Boudreau 2015: 5)

As Feyissa notes, 'a critical indicator for food security in the border areas is the terms of trade between what herders receive for their products (livestock) and what they must pay to purchase needed grains (such as maize flour and sorghum)' (2016: 16). Widening gaps in terms of trade such as those seen in 2017, particularly between livestock and cereals, is a reliable indicator of increased risk of food insecurity.

Local trade relations are also dependent upon wider regional dynamics. Following the devastating drought of 2011, demand for livestock increased in Kenya, creating opportunities for Ethiopian stock to be sold. At the same time, the development of meat-processing facilities in Ethiopia for export to the Middle East has produced a demand for Kenyan livestock to be sold inside Ethiopia (Little, Debsu, and Tiki 2014: 392).

Cross-border trade networks involve complex networks of kin, clan, and occupational specialists within border zones. Scott-Villiers, citing work by Umar and Baulch, notes that 'most trade links cover relatively short spans, after which the stock or goods are handed over to another actor in the marketing chain. This, they explain, is because local relations are essential in handling dealings with officials, warlords and other authorities, which might otherwise disrupt the passage of goods' (Scott-Villiers 2015: 5, citing Umar and Baulch 2005).

Such localized trade links create a web of what Scott-Villiers calls 'low-paid but vital opportunities for informal employment and profit in the facilitation, brokerage and arbitrage of transactions' (Scott-Villiers 2015: 5).

16.6 Decision-Making about Mobility

Key to understanding the role of mobility in border regions is the role that it plays in everyday livelihood practices and in adaptations to shocks. In the pastoral livelihood zones of Ethiopia's Somali region close to the Kenya border, households derive 60–70 per cent of their incomes from milk and ghee sales, and 20–40 per cent from livestock sales. All of these activities depend on favourable rains and the ability to move in order to bring livestock to available pasture and to be able to bring animals to market (milk is sold more locally). Among agro-pastoral groups, for example, milk sales are less significant, but still make up approximately 10 per cent of total incomes, and livestock sales account for up to 40 per cent of incomes. Mobility is more localized than with purely pastoral Somalis, but is still needed for grazing and marketing purposes. However, agro-pastoral groups depend more on casual labour and self-employment, for which they require access to markets and towns, often across borders (Boudreau 2015). For each of these groups, mobility features differently as a livelihood strategy.

This information can be useful assessing the likely impact of drought, the tightening or opening of borders for trade and transport, and the impact of future development projects such as the proposed oil pipeline through Somali region or, when applied to groups in South Omo Region, the development of geothermal power across the border in Kenya's Lake Turkana.

Different forms of mobility also interact with each other. The scale and direction of labour migration may be influenced by the existence of large numbers of refugees in a given border area, just as displacement may be directed towards available centres of employment. Ethiopia's introduction of Special Economic Zones—large industrial parks in cities including Hawassa, Dire Dawa, and Mekele—some of which plan to employ refugee labour in addition to recruiting locally, may become significant attractions for people, which influence their mobility decisions.

16.7 Gendered Aspects of Migration and Mobility Decision-Making

Migration and mobility are highly gendered, as are the livelihood strategies that influence them. Where women and men move to, what factors tend to lead to their decisions to move or to stay in place, what the differing experiences of displaced men and women or male and female labour migrants are—all are influenced by the underlying dynamics that lead to their movement, including the levels of vulnerability and resilience that men and women face in both 'normal' times and periods of shock. During times of food insecurity and economic hardship, Somali and Borana move into cities or to stay with relatives, while men move further afield for labour migration, to graze larger animals such as camels, or to find work in other countries. Refugee populations also typically have a higher proportion of women than in society more generally, as women take their children and seek assistance while men are engaged in employment, business, military activity, or maintaining the family's property in the area of origin.

Another major form of gendered migration is in the move of young women to Gulf countries to find employment as domestic workers. In 2013, the Ethiopian Ministry of Foreign Affairs' Consular Monitoring and Support Directorate estimated that 1,500 Ethiopian women were leaving the country every day (Woldemichael 2013: 1). Unlike men who leave the country for the Gulf, most women travel through the assistance of private employment agencies (PEAs), who have (or who claim to have) secured an offer of employment for them prior to departure. The Regional Mixed Migration Secretariat (RMMS) reported that in the first half of 2012, 160,000 Ethiopian women travelled to Saudi Arabia using PEAs. Between November 2013 and April 2014, 52,119 Ethiopian women were deported from Saudi Arabia, yet the flows continue. The conditions under which many women are working are precarious, and there are frequently reports of physical, sexual, and emotional abuse by employers and women working in conditions of slavery (Woldemichael 2013; Austrian Red Cross 2016; RMMS 2014: 19). Despite these clear risks, many women claim that the opportunities to earn money to remit to relatives or to save are significant and they (sometimes with considerable pressure from their families) continue to choose to move despite the dangers. Women who migrate to Gulf countries report average monthly wages of US$120–180, between three and five times more than they could expect to earn in Ethiopia. Despite this, there are also frequent reports of partial, delayed, or entirely withheld payments (Jones, Presler-Marshall, and Tefera 2014: 37).

While some Ethiopian women travel to the Gulf countries by air, many travel overland to one of the many ports that dot the coast of the Horn of Africa (the Obock port in Djibouti and the Bossaso port of Somalia being the largest exit points for Ethiopian migrants). Women must pass through the borderlands to get to the ports. Such crossings involve security risks; if women lack the necessary documentation and permission to cross the border, or if they are travelling using smuggling networks, they are at risk of extortion, trafficking, and sexual assault (RMMS 2014). Many run out of money along the way and remain in the border areas, trying to earn enough money in Djibouti, for instance, to continue their journeys (Zeleke 2018).

16.8 Youth Mobility in the Borderlands

Just as mobility is highly gendered, it is also generational. Many of those who are on the move are youth between the ages of 15 and 24.[2] It is difficult to know precisely how many migrant youth are living in border regions of Ethiopia given that they tend to be undocumented and to move using irregular channels. However, RMMS estimates that almost half of international migrants in the Horn of Africa are under the age of 20, and that the proportion of children and youth on the move is rising (RMMS 2016: 10). It is estimated that 20 per cent of migrants moving to Yemen are children or youth (RMMS 2016: 10–11).

Migration can be an indicator of resilience and bring opportunity to young people, opening up access to education, providing access to new or better-paying employment, or paving the way for greater professional and personal development (UNESA 2016). However, economic vulnerability and the search for greater opportunities are encouraging increasing numbers of poor young men and women to leave their rural livelihoods and seek employment in nearby as well as remote cities of the region, or make plans for further

[2] Youth are defined in different ways by different sources, but the United Nations defines youth as being between the ages of 15 and 24.

onward migration. Those who are most vulnerable are likely to move over short distances; they cannot afford to move further. Very often they settle close to the borders, taking advantage of the economic opportunities created by the movement of goods and people across borders. Those with more economic and social capital (for example, with relatives living abroad) may aspire and be able to travel further. If they have access to cash themselves or through their families, they may attempt to move. Sometimes, however, young people are able to begin their migration journeys with a small portion of the cash that they will ultimately require to reach their destinations (EUTF REF 2017). The agents or smugglers who facilitate their travel may wait until they are en route to contact the youth's family to demand larger payments in exchange for the safety of their son or daughter. In such cases, the risks to young people are often enormous. Even where trafficking and predatory smuggling networks are not in operation, vulnerable youths may be subject to discrimination or exploitation in the workplace or in accessing services, and they may lack the power to be able to protect themselves, given their age and the fact that they may be far from their social support networks (EUTF REF 2017).

16.9 Linking Decision-Making Processes to Wider Borderland Dynamics

Considering the dynamics behind how and why people decide to move towards borderlands, within borderlands, and across borders, can reveal a great deal about the wider social, cultural, economic, and political conditions that they are living with. For refugees, the influence of political factors (persecution, discrimination, direct coercion, or violation of civic and political rights) may have more of an impact on the decision-making process than economic or social conditions, although importantly all of these variables may play a role in determining where the person, once displaced, chooses to go. Even with regular mobility, such as pastoral transhumance, the framework can be used to explain how people maximize environmental resources to protect their livelihoods. Pastoral mobility is affected by such factors as the ease with which people can cross borders, the restrictions that may be placed on their marketing activities, and clan or ethnic ties. Factors influencing individuals', families', and communities' decisions to move include:

- political persecution[3] or conflict (as in the case of internally displaced persons or refugees fleeing generalized or specific security threats)
- economic shocks or opportunities (due to shifting employment or trade opportunities or dramatic changes in economic conditions caused by local or global factors)

[3] 'Persecution' is here used in the sense that it is used in international refugee law, whereby a person suffers threat due to race, religion, nationality, membership in a particular social group, or political opinion (see the 1951 Geneva Convention on the Status of Refugees, Article 2).

- environmental threats (in particular related to drought and flood in the regional context, but possibly also due to severe weather events or other environmental factors)
- demographic transitions (for instance related to the burgeoning number of unemployed youth or population pressure on a given area).

In practice, mobility decisions are not likely to be framed in reaction to a single factor. Some factors may be more determining and others less so, but are still contributing factors.

In thinking about how migration decisions are made, it is useful to look at whose livelihoods or decisions are being considered—over what geographical area is a particular livelihood picture prevalent? And within a particular geographical area, how do the strategies of different groups vary? How do border dynamics at local, meso, and macro levels influence different decisions within the same border area?

These questions can be unpacked, and ultimately assistance can be targeted, by considering the distribution of livelihood zones and wealth groups in border areas, available in household economy analysis (HEA) on the region.[4] HEA analyses livelihoods-defined geographic areas and provides detailed analysis of the income, expenditure, and consumption patterns of people living within those areas to arrive at an approach to better understand livelihoods in border areas and how people respond to one or more shocks (from environmental, political, or economic drivers) which threaten their access to cash and food.

Within livelihood zones, different wealth groups (the very poor, poor, better off, etc.) approach decision-making about mobility and migration in different ways depending on their levels of vulnerability and resilience, livelihood practices, and social networks. Poorer households are more reliant on cash than better-off ones, in part because those who are wealthier are able to produce more milk for consumption. Milk amounts to 50 per cent of the income of the middle-income and better-off groups, while poorer households produce less milk. The better off are more mobile, moving to the furthest and best grazing areas to maintain the productivity of their milk-producing animals (Scott-Villiers 2015: 7, citing Little, Debsu, and Tiki 2014). The mobility of the poorer groups is influenced more by a need to access cash through waged labour; people move towards towns and cities or commercial farming areas for these opportunities. They also sometimes move towards refugee camps in the border areas to engage with the aid-fuelled economy through trade.

Mobility of people through this border zone is influenced by the permeability of the border. Horwood reports that as many as 7,000 Ethiopian migrants were passing through the Moyale border crossing each day in 2009, constituting at least 60 per cent of the town's overall economy (Horwood 2009: 119, cited in Scott-Villiers 2015: 6). When the border is closed, communities in border regions experience a significant loss of income.

[4] HEA is used widely by (among others) the Famine Early Warning System, Save the Children, and the Ethiopian Livelihoods Integration Unit.

16.10 Conclusion

Mobility and migration in, from, and through borderlands is a central feature of the political economy and social organization of these areas. The decisions that people make about whether or not to move reflect the conditions of life in border zones, just as they may also affect them. Border crossing points become thriving business centres that attract people, and struggling border economic zones are often places that people opt to move out of. By integrating the study of mobility into an analysis of how border zones function in Ethiopia, and by seeing mobility as a central feature of border systems, we can bring the dynamics of borderland livelihood systems and their relationships to wider national and regional processes more sharply into focus.

Acknowledgements

This chapter is based on work commissioned by the World Bank Group. The author would like to thank Anton Baare and Andrew Roberts of the World Bank for their support. In addition, the chapter has benefited from discussions with Jonathan Goodhand, Richard Black, and Christopher Cramer, Pencho Garrido-Ruiz of the European Union's Development Cooperation section, and Vincent Chordi of the Research and Evidence Facility for the Horn of Africa.

References

Aberra, Edlam (2003). 'Pastoral Livelihoods in Urban and Peri-Urban Spaces of Ethiopia: The Case of Yabello, Borana Zone,' Paper given to the International Conference on African Development, https://scholarworks.wmich.edu/cgi/viewcontent.cgi?article=1052&context=africancenter_icad_archive.

AfDB (African Development Bank), OECD, and United Nations Development Programme (2016). *African Economic Outlook 2016 Sustainable Cities and Structural Transformation: Sustainable Cities and Structural Transformation*. OECD Publishing. https://www.afdb.org/fileadmin/uploads/afdb/Documents/Publications/AEO_2016_Report_Full_English.pdf

Agier, Michel, Richard Nice, and Loïc Wacquant (2002). 'Between War and City: Towards an Urban Anthropology of Refugee Camps,' *Ethnography* 3 (3): 317–41.

Asfaw, Woldie, Degefa Tolossa, and Gete Zeleke (2010). 'Causes and Impacts of Seasonal Migration on Rural Livelihoods: Case Studies from Amhara Region in Ethiopia,' *Norsk Geografisk Tidsskrift—Norwegian Journal of Geography* 64 (1): 58–70.

Austrian Red Cross (2016). 'Ethiopian Female Domestic Workers inside Ethiopia and Abroad (Household Slavery, Trafficking): COI Compilation,' Austrian Red Cross/Austrian Centre for Country of Origin Research and Documentation (ACCORD), Vienna, Austria. https://www.ecoi.net/en/file/local/1258385/1930_1454414233_56aa450f4.pdf

Belayneh, Demissie (2016). 'State Development Interventions versus Indigenous Resource Management Institutions: Whose Reality Counts? Evidence from Borana Pastoral System of Southern Ethiopia,' *Munich Personal RePEc Archive* https://mpra.ub.uni-muenchen.de/70780/1/MPRA_paper_70780.pdf

Boudreau, Tanya (2015). 'Regional Overview and Summary of the Results of the 2015 Household Economy Analysis Baseline Update: Somali Region, Ethiopia', The Food Economy Group. https://www.prime-ethiopia.org/wp-content/uploads/2015/10/SOMALI%20REGION%20OVERVIEW%20HEA%20UPDATE%202015%20FINAL.pdf

Catley, Andy (2017). 'Pathways to Resilience in Pastoralist Areas: A Synthesis of Research in the Horn of Africa', Tufts University Feinstein International Centre, Medford, MA. http://fic.tufts.edu/publication-item/pathways-to-resilience-in-pastoralist-areas-a-synthesis-of-research-in-the-horn-of-africa/

COMESA (Common Market for Eastern and Southern Africa) (2009). 'Policy Framework for Food Security in Pastoral Areas (PFFSPA): Comprehensive African Agriculture Development Programme (CAADP) Pillar III', Consultative Draft, COMESA. http://fic.tufts.edu/pacaps-project/Pastoralism%20&%20Policy/PFFSPA%20Consultative%20Draft%20Dec%2009%20final.pdf

EUTF REF (2017). 'Migration between the Horn of Africa and Yemen', SOAS University of London. https://www.soas.ac.uk/ref-hornresearch/research-papers/file122639.pdf

Feyisa, Kenea, Sheleme Beyene, Ayana Angassa, Aster Abebe, Mohammed Y. Said, Bekele Megersa, and Jan de Leeuw (2017). 'Effects of Enclosure Management on Carbon Sequestration, Soil Properties and Vegetation Attributes in East African Rangelands', *CATENA* 159: 9–19.

Feyissa, Dereje (2016). 'Background Note on Resilience and Development Assistance in the Horn of Africa's Borderlands and Lagging Regions', International Law and Policy Institute, Addis Ababa.

Golub, Stephen (2015). 'Informal Cross-Border Trade and Smuggling in Africa', in *Handbook on Trade and Development*, ed. O. Morrissey, R. A. Lopez, and K. Sharma (Cheltenham: Edward Elgar Publishing): 179–209.

Goodfellow, Tom (2018). 'Seeing Political Settlements through the City: A Framework for Comparative Analysis of Urban Transformation', *Development and Change* 49 (1): 199–222.

Goodhand, Jonathan (2014). 'Fragility and Resilience Analysis Background Note: The Political Economy of Development in Borderlands', Draft report written for the World Bank Group.

Government of Ethiopia (Central Statistical Authority) (2007). 'Population and Housing Census'. http://unstats.un.org/unsd/censuskb20/Attachment489.aspx?AttachmentType=1

Hagmann, Tobias and Finn Stepputat (2016). 'Corridors of Trade and Power: Economy and State in Formation in Somali East Africa', DIIS-GOVSEA Working Chapter, Danish Institute of International Studies (DIIS), Copenhagen. http://pure.diis.dk/ws/files/624676/DIIS_WP_2016_8.pdf

Henderson, J. Vernon, Adam Storeygard, and Uwe Deichmann (2014). '50 Years of Urbanization in Africa: Examining the Role of Climate Change', Policy Research Working Chapter, World Bank, Washington, DC. https://openknowledge.worldbank.org/handle/10986/18757

Horwood, C. (2009). 'In Pursuit of the Southern Dream: Victims of Necessity: Assessment of the Irregular Movement of Men from East Africa and the Horn to South Africa', International Organization for Migration, Geneva. http://publications.iom.int/system/files/pdf/iomresearchassessment.pdf

Humanitarian Policy Group (HPG) (2010). 'Pastoralism Demographics, Settlement and Service Provision in the Horn and East Africa: Transformation and Opportunities', Overseas Development Institute, London. http://www.oxfamblogs.org/eastafrica/wp-content/uploads/2010/09/REGLAP-REPORTv2-fina-Demographic-trends-settlement-patterns-and-service-provision.pdf

Iazzolino, Gianluca (2018). 'The Lure of the City: Synthesis Report on Rural to Urban Migration in Ethiopia, Kenya and Uganda', EU Trust Fund Research and Evidence Facility, SOAS University of London and Rift Valley Institute, Nairobi. https://www.soas.ac.uk/ref-hornresearch/research-papers/file128760.pdf

IGAD (2018). 'About Us: The IGAD Region'. https://igad.int/about-us/the-igad-region

Jesuit Refugee Service (2011). 'Situation Report: Dollo Ado, Ethiopia', Addis Ababa, 17 August 2011. http://www.jesuits-chgdet.org/wp-content/uploads/2011/08/august-17-2011-jrs-situation-report-ethiopia.pdf

Jones, Nicola, Elizabeth Presler-Marshall, and Bekele Tefera (2014). 'Rethinking Girls on the Move: The Intersection of Poverty, Exploitation and Violence Experienced by Ethiopian Adolescents Involved in the Middle East "Maid Trade"', Overseas Development Institute, London. https://www.odi.org/sites/odi.org.uk/files/odi-assets/publications-opinion-files/9307.pdf

Little, Peter D. (2007). 'Unofficial Cross-Border Trade in Eastern Africa', Paper presented to the FAO Workshop on 'Staple Food and Market Policy Options for Promoting Development in Eastern and Southern Africa', 1–2 March 2007, Food and Agricultural Organisation, Rome.

Little, Peter D. (2010). 'Unofficial Cross-Border Trade in Eastern Africa', in *Food Security in Africa*, ed. Alexander Sarris and Jamie Morrison (Edward Elgar Publishing): 158–81. http://www.elgaronline.com/view/9781848448513.00012.xml

Little, Peter D. (2013). 'Reflections on the Future of Pastoralism in the Horn of Africa', in *Pastoralism and Development in Africa: Dynamic Change at the Margins*, ed. A. Catley, I. Scoons, and J. Lind (London: Routledge): 243–9.

Little, Peter D., Dejene Negassa Debsu, and Waktole Tiki (2014). 'How Pastoralists Perceive and Respond to Market Opportunities: The Case of the Horn of Africa', *Food Policy* 49: 390.

Lubkemann, S. (2008). 'Involuntary Immobility: On a Theoretical Invisibility in Forced Migration Studies', *Journal of Refugee Studies* 21 (4): 454–75.

Mahmoud, Hussein A. (2010). 'Livestock Trade in the Kenyan, Somali, and Ethiopian Borderlands', Africa Programme, Chatham House, London.

Makki, Fouad. (2014). 'Development by Dispossession: Terra Nullius and the Social-Ecology of New Enclosures in Ethiopia', *Rural Sociology* 79 (1): 79–103.

Markakis, John (2011). *Ethiopia: The Last Two Frontiers* (Oxford: James Currey Press).

McPeak, John G., and Peter D. Little (2018). 'Mobile Peoples, Contested Borders: Land-Use Conflicts and Resolution Mechanisms among Borana and Guji Communities, Southern Ethiopia', *World Development* 103: 119–32.

OECD (Organisation for Economic Cooperation and Development) (2015). 'Secretary General's Report to Ministers', OECD, Paris. http://www.oecd.org/about/secretary-general/SG-Annual-Report-to-Ministers-2015.pdf

Oka, Rahul (2011). 'Unlikely Cities in the Desert: The Informal Economy as Causal Agent for Permanent "Urban" Sustainability in Kakuma Refugee Camp, Kenya', *Urban Anthropology and Studies of Cultural Systems and World Economic Development* 40 (3/4): 223–62.

Pankhurst, Alula (2003). 'Dimensions and Conceptions of Marginalisation', in *Peripheral People: The Excluded Minorities of Ethiopia*, ed. Dena Freeman and Alula Pankhurst (Trenton, NJ: Red Sea Press): 1–26.

Pavanello, Sarah (2009). 'Working across Borders: Harnessing the Potential of Cross-Border Activities to Improve Livelihood Security in the Horn of Africa Drylands', Humanitarian Policy Group/Overseas Development Institute, London. https://www.odi.org/publications/4997-working-across-borders-harnessing-potential-cross-border-activities-improve-livelihood-security-horn

Regional Mixed Migration Secretariat (RMMS) (2016). 'Young and on the Move: Children and Youth in Mixed Migration Flows within and from the Horn of Africa', Regional Mixed Migration Secretariat, Nairobi. http://www.regionalmms.org/images/ResearchInitiatives/Young%20and%20on%20the%20Move%20Sep%202016.pdf

RMMS (2014). 'Abused and Abducted: The Plight of Female Migrants from the Horn of Africa in Yemen', RMMS, Nairobi. http://regionalmms.org/images/ResearchInitiatives/Abused___Abducted_RMMS.pdf

Scott-Villiers, Patta (2015). 'Background Note: IGAD Borderlands Cluster 2', Institute of Development Studies, Sussex.

Stevenson, Anne and Rebecca Sutton (2011). 'There's No Place Like a Refugee Camp? Urban Planning and Participation in the Camp Context', *Refuge* 28 (1): 137–48.

Umar, A. and B. Baulch (2005). 'Risk-Taking for a Living: Trade and Marketing in the Somali Region of Ethiopia', UN OCHA, Addis Ababa. http://www.pastoralists.org/wp-content/uploads/2012/02/Risk-Taking.pdf

UNDESA (2014). 'World Urbanization Prospects, the 2014 Revision: Highlights', UN Dept. of Economic and Social Affairs, New York. https://esa.un.org/unpd/wup/Publications/Files/WUP2014-Highlights.pdf

UN Dept of Economic and Social Affairs (UNDESA) (2016). 'Youth and Migration', Youth Issue Briefs, UN Dept. of Economic and Social Affairs, New York. http://www.un.org/esa/socdev/documents/youth/fact-sheets/youth-migration.pdf

USAID (2018). 'Complex Emergency Fact Sheet #2, 8 March 2018', United States Agency for International Development. https://www.usaid.gov/sites/default/files/documents/1860/03.08.18_-_USAID-DCHA_Ethiopia_Complex_Emergency_Fact_Sheet_2.pdf

Woldemichael, Selamawit Bekele (2013). 'The Vulnerability of Ethiopian Women and Girls: The Case of Domestic Workers in Saudi Arabia and Kuwait', Master's thesis, Dept. of Sociology, Uppsala University. http://www.diva-portal.org/smash/record.jsf?pid=diva2%3A624613&dswid=-293

WFP (2017). 'WFP Ethiopia 2017 Emergency Situation Report No.6', World Food Programme, Addis Ababa. https://docs.wfp.org/api/documents/WFP-0000050315/download/

Young, Crawford (1982). 'Nationalising the Third World State: Categorical Imperative or Mission Impossible', *Polity* 15 (2): 161–81.

Zeleke, Meron (2018). 'Close and Yet Far: Lived Experiences of Ethiopian Maids in Djibouti', EU Trust Fund Research and Evidence Facility Working Papers, EU Trust Fund for Africa Research and Evidence Facility, London and Nairobi. https://www.soas.ac.uk/ref-hornresearch/working-papers/file128685.pdf

CHAPTER 17

GREEN AND CLIMATE-RESILIENT TRANSFORMATION IN ETHIOPIA

HAILESELASSIE A. MEDHIN AND
ALEMU MEKONNEN

17.1 Introduction

Climate change is expected to affect society and ecosystems in various ways ranging from extreme weather events such as heat waves, cold waves, tropical cyclones, and erratic precipitation to sea-level rise, high risk of extinction of biodiversity, and declining agricultural yield. Among the regions that are highly vulnerable to such effects is sub-Saharan Africa. For poor countries like Ethiopia, climate change poses a greater challenge, as mitigation and adaptation strategies will need to be coherent with the need to foster economic growth and improve the livelihood of citizens.

Ethiopia is increasingly being cited as the country that is committed to take on this multifaceted challenge: the country has started implementing an ambitious Climate-Resilient Green Economy (CRGE) strategy since 2011. In a nutshell, the CRGE strategy envisions transforming Ethiopia into a middle-income economy by 2025 while keeping greenhouse gas emissions at the level that they were in 2010. The strategy has been incorporated in the country's Growth and Transformation Plan (GTP-II) and also served as a basis for the country's Paris Agreement commitments. Ethiopia's Nationally Determined Contributions promise to reduce GHG emissions by 64 per cent in 2030 compared with the business as usual (BAU) scenario (FDRE 2011). This is to be done while maintaining two-digit growth in the economy which is a huge task. Added to this is the aim of building climate resilience as detailed in sectoral strategies for agriculture and forestry, water and energy, urban development, and housing and transport

(FDRE 2015b, 2015c; MoT 2017; FDRE 2017b). If successful, this may make Ethiopia the first country to achieve a rapid, green and climate-resilient structural transformation, setting an example for other least-developed countries.

But is the CRGE strategy necessary? Is it possible for Ethiopia to maintain fast growth while meeting the emission targets in the strategy? What are the sectoral challenges and implications of the strategy? This chapter attempts to answer these questions with the objective of providing perspectives on the economic rationale of Ethiopia's ambitious green transformation agenda and identifying issues for further consideration.

17.2 Putting Ethiopia's Green Transformation Agenda into Perspective

To follow a green and climate-resilient development pathway Ethiopia needs to address the adverse local impacts of climate change. Ethiopia has been exposed to different climate change hazards and natural disasters for the past several decades. The country's varied topography has caused complex and varied climates. There are areas of hot arid desert, cool wet highlands, and wet humid lowlands, all within few a hundred kilometres. Land degradation, drought, extreme heat events, floods, increased precipitation, and environment-related diseases are the most common climate-related risks in Ethiopia. The country has also been exposed to unpredictable rains as well as complete absence of rains and seasonal shifts in patterns. This uncertainty is expected to increase with climate change (FDRE 2017a).

The general observed trends include continued increase in temperature and rainfall variability. Mean annual temperature has been increasing by 1°C, which is an average rate of 0.25°C per decade (USAID 2016). The average number of hot nights increased by 37.5 per cent between 1960 and 2003 while the average number of hot days per year increased by 20 per cent. Future projections of temperature show a 1°–2° C increase in mean annual temperature by 2050 while rainfall is expected to change from −25 per cent to +30 per cent by 2050 (USAID 2016). These trends are expected to have severe economic and social impacts for Ethiopia. The impact of climate change in Ethiopia is projected to cause a 10 per cent or more reduction in GDP by 2050 (World Bank 2010; FDRE 2015b).

17.2.1 Ethiopia's CRGE Vision

Ethiopia's drive for resilient and green development—as articulated in the CRGE strategy and a number of sectoral adaptation/resilience strategies[1]—is often lauded as a model

[1] There are currently adaptation/resilience strategies for agriculture and forestry, water and energy, urban development and housing, and transport.

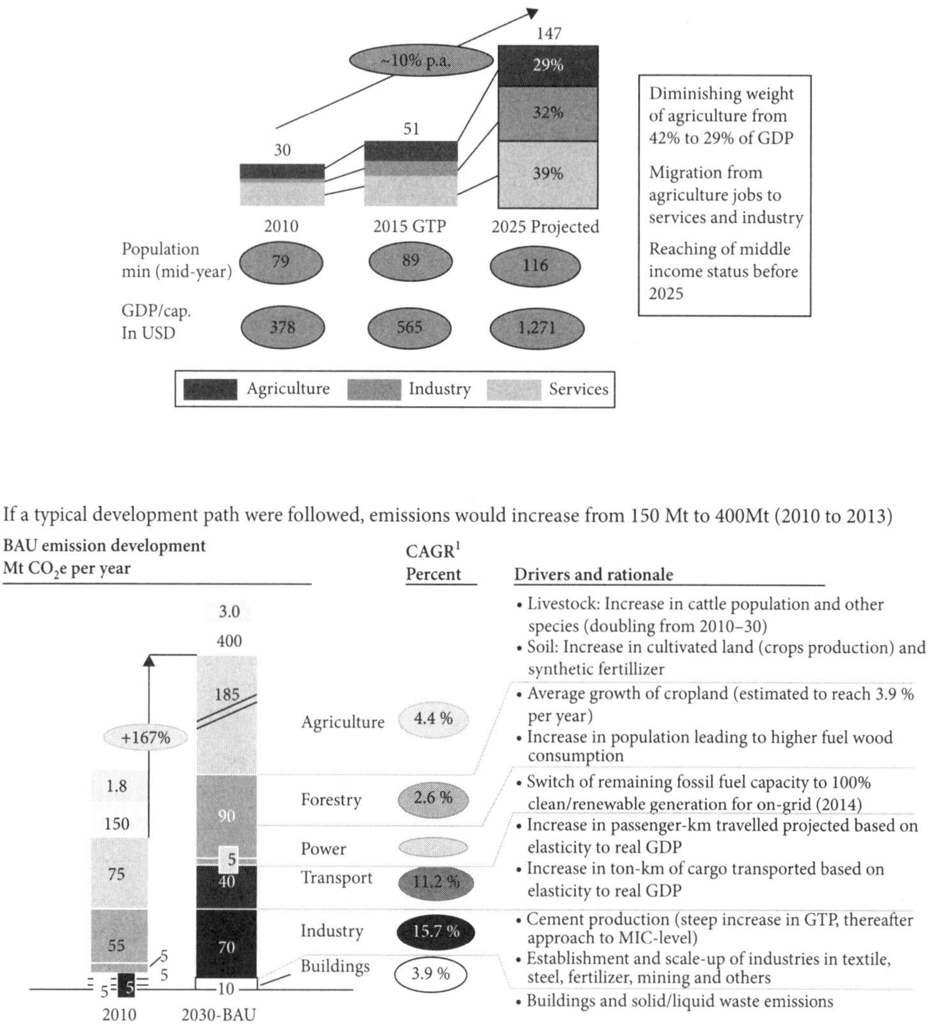

FIGURE 17.1 The CRGE strategy's assumptions, rationale, and targets

Source: FDRE (2011) Climate-Resilient Green Economy Strategy Document, pp. 10, 15, 21, and 29.

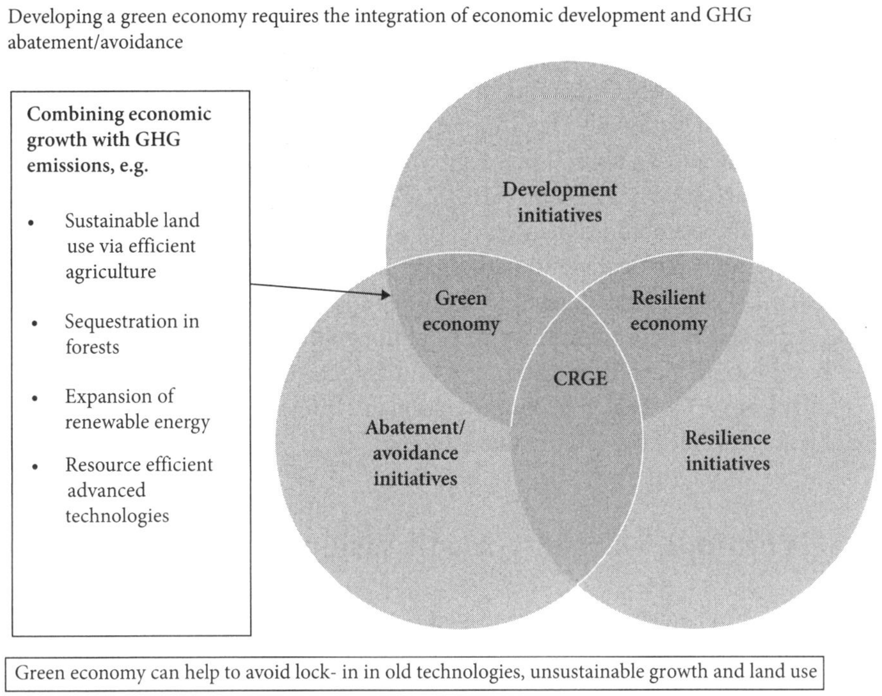

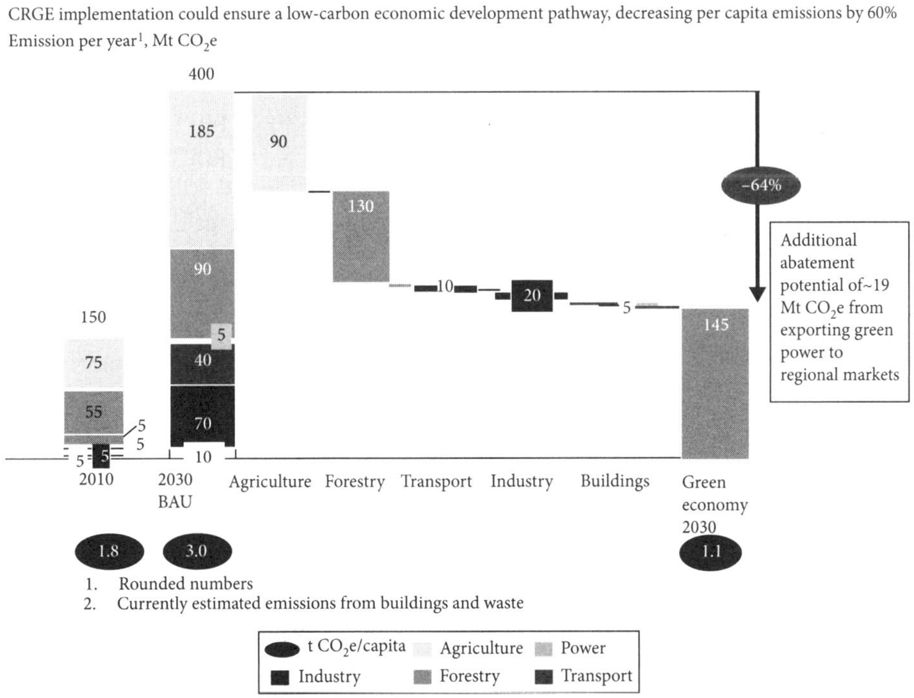

FIGURE 17.1 Continued

that other countries should follow. For example, out of eighty countries, Ethiopia ranks fourteenth overall in the Global Green Economy Index, and first in leadership and climate change performance (Tamanini 2016). Ethiopia was also one of only five countries to present Intended Nationally Determined Contributions (INDCs) commitments sufficient to reach the most ambitious 1.5-degree target during the milestone global climate agreement in Paris in 2015 (FDRE 2015d).

But, despite these ambitious plans, Ethiopia also faces enormous challenges of environmental and resource degradation and management. For example, Yale University's Environmental Performance Index puts Ethiopia 163rd out of 180 countries, a ranking that has improved by 15 per cent since 2006, although this also represents performance worse than Ethiopia's peers in the region.[2] A fundamental question, therefore, is whether the country's ambition has an economic rationale. Is a green development paradigm preferable and feasible for a country like Ethiopia?

17.2.2 Is Ethiopia's Green-Growth Vision Well Founded?

Green growth can be defined as growth that is *efficient* in the use of natural resources, *clean* in that it minimizes pollution and environmental impacts, and *resilient* in that it accounts for natural hazards and the role of environmental management and natural resources in preventing disasters (World Bank 2012). Despite the ever-increasing enthusiasm for such a development paradigm,[3] concerns are often raised as to whether green growth is a viable pathway for low-income countries. The primary concern is whether a focus on green growth risks sidelining objectives of poverty reduction, equity, and rapid economic development. The higher cost of pursuing a green growth pathway—for example switching to cleaner sources of energy—is also cited as a potential impediment (OECD 2012). Indeed, rapid and equitable development should still be the primary objective of developing countries like Ethiopia, and it is important that green growth passes this stress test.

Ethiopia's commitment to green growth appears to be founded on a belief that green and climate-resilient growth is compatible with a rapid exit from poverty. A vivid illustration of this belief is the mainstreaming of the CRGE strategy into the country's second Growth and Transformation Plan (GTP-II), which targets very high rates of economic expansion and reduction in poverty. As can be seen from Figure 17.1, the emissions projections under BAU as well as the emission reduction targets of the CRGE strategy assume an annual economic growth rate of about 10 per cent. It is therefore safe to conclude that Ethiopia's vision is based on the notion that green growth is an opportunity, not a constraint, for low-income countries. Indeed, such a notion is also gaining

[2] Yale University's Environmental Performance Index (EPI) is a method of quantifying and numerically marking the environmental performance of a state's policies (Archive.epi.yale.edu).

[3] Many countries are also making visible strides in green growth, partly supported by the ever-declining costs of green technologies. An example is China's progress in solar energy.

traction across sub-Saharan Africa in general. For example, the African Economic Commission's flagship annual economic report for 2015 focused on green industrialization. There are a number of reasons why a green and climate-resilient development paradigm could be preferable for Ethiopia, and indeed other developing countries.

17.2.2.1 *The Need for a New Development Paradigm in the Anthropocene*

The earth has now entered the Anthropocene age, where human activities are the dominant driver of changes in the earth's systems. This unprecedented increase in human activity has posed the challenge of crossing critical planetary boundaries, putting the future of the entire world (and its economy) at severe risk (Rockström et al. 2009; Omilola 2014; Steffen et al. 2015). This is mainly the result of the conventional growth pattern that has been followed by today's developed and emerging economies, which has been characterized by unsustainable production and consumption, and poor natural resource management (World Bank 2012). Population and income growth have resulted in increased demand for natural resources (land, water, energy) which, given the traditional growth path, in turn result in inefficient resource use and unsustainable production. The conventional growth path is particularly challenging for developing countries where the natural resource base is getting lower due to continued degradation, severe threat from climate change, rapid population growth, and economic growth.

Reversing this trend requires a new development paradigm that focuses on the principles of sustainable production and consumption (OECD 2013). Green growth fits this bill as it integrates sustainable development, climate change resilience, and sustainable natural resource management. This implies that a green growth pathway is perhaps the only pathway remaining for today's low-income countries to catch up, if the world is to avoid a disaster. That is, even if a green development pathway were not the preferred option for individual countries, it is the preferred option collectively. This argument would of course imply that the world should take collective action to include a mechanism for filling green growth financing gaps in developing countries, such as a global carbon taxation scheme.

But there are strong arguments and evidence to show that a green development path is also preferable for low-income countries like Ethiopia, even without considering the global externalities. Despite the gains from growth in the last twenty years, 1.3 billion people do not have access to electricity, 2.6 billion people have no access to sanitation, and 900 million people lack safe and clean drinking water (World Bank 2012; IEA 2014), bringing the conventional economic growth path into question, and putting the case for more sustainable and inclusive growth. For example, Freire (2013) argues that green growth is a superior policy approach for African countries in the provision of sustainable and inclusive growth, given the continent's demographic and urbanization patterns. Similarly, Hallegate et al. (2011) argue that green growth best reconciles the short- and long-term objectives by maximizing synergies and mitigating trade-offs across space and time, increasing social and political acceptability of the policies. Most green policies have an economic cost in the short term and better environmental and natural capital in the long term. A green growth path adequately responds to the opportunities and challenges posed by climate change and the pressure on natural resources and ecosystem services resulting from economic and population growth (Reilly 2012; UNECA 2015; Saufi, Daud, and Hassan 2016). Recent emerging evidence also suggests that green growth leads to poverty reduction, reduced vulnerability to climate change, greater energy security, and more secure livelihoods for those who depend on natural resources (World Bank 2012; ADB 2012; OECD 2013; Lukas 2015; Carfora et al. 2018). For example, according to OECD (2012), for developing countries whose natural capital accounts for 26 per cent (which is 2 per cent for developed countries) of their total wealth, following the conventional growth path will significantly deteriorate their natural capital. A green development paradigm that values natural capital and their ecosystem services can therefore be preferable.

17.2.2.2 *Impacts of Climate Change*

Ethiopia is heavily dependent on rain-fed agriculture, so the sector is highly vulnerable to climate change impacts. Around 95 per cent of smallholder farmers produce cereal crops (mainly teff, wheat, maize, sorghum, and barley), which constitute more than 77 per cent of the cereal production, and these crops account for about three-quarters of total area cultivated and 29 per cent of agricultural GDP in 2005/6 (14 per cent of total GDP) (ATA 2016; Taffesse, Dorosh, and Gemessa 2012). Increase in spells and intensity of drought as a result of climate change would therefore have severe impacts on the economy. For example, the 2002/3 drought is estimated to have led to a 4 per cent decline in GDP and a 12 per cent reduction in agricultural output (FDRE 2015b). According to USAID (2016), if the current decline in average annual rainfall continues, Ethiopia could forego more than 6 per cent of each year's agricultural output.

According to the Ethiopian Panel on Climate Change (EPCC 2015), by 2020 the major cereal crops of Ethiopia such as maize, teff, sorghum, and barley will lose over 14, 11, 7, and 31 per cent of their current suitable area of production, respectively. For maize, teff, and barley the loss will be expected to increase to over 18, 11, and 37 per cent by 2050, respectively. EPCC (2015) also shows impacts of different climate change scenarios on the revenue from different sectors (see Table 17.1). Climate change could also cause loss of arable land due to shifting agro-ecological zones and alter growing cycles. An increase in the incidence of floods and landslides will damage crops and exacerbate soil erosion. (EPCC 2015: 18).

The livestock sector also relies heavily on climate-sensitive resources. According to Gashaw, Bantider, and Silassie (2014), all pastoral regions in Ethiopia are highly prone to the adverse impacts of climate change, and the problem is more prevalent in the north-eastern lowlands. Problems of feed shortage, water shortage, reduced productivity, and decreased mature weight and/or longer time to reach mature weight could be exacerbated by climate change. Most pastoralists in the country are dependent on limited water. Projected increase in evaporation and changes in rainfall pattern may further reduce availability of water in these areas. Limited resources and higher temperatures directly impact livestock's health and productivity. For example, USAID (2016) projects a

Table 17.1 Climate change impact on revenue from crops, livestock, and agriculture

	Change in net revenue (in ETB/ha)		
Climate change scenarios	Crops	Livestock	Agriculture
+ 2.5°C increase in temperature	-1812.4	-274.0	-1035.5
+ 5°C increase in temperature	-3039.7	368.5	363.8
-7% in precipitation	-1609.0	-1112.5	-645.1
-14% in precipitation	-2676.7	-1833.4	-1141.6

Source: Ethiopian Panel on Climate Change (2015: 29).

30 per cent decrease in flow volume on several Nile tributaries by 2050, leading to crop failure and livestock mortality that could reduce incomes by as much as 19–30 per cent.

17.3 Implementation: Challenges and Progress

17.3.1 Maintaining Rapid Growth while Achieving Ambitious Emission Targets

While we assume that the emissions estimations and targets in the CRGE strategy are outcomes of some kind of macro-economic model of Ethiopia, there is limited information about the model, data, and assumptions in the strategy document. We have therefore conducted our own macro-economic analysis of the Ethiopian economy. Specifically, we conducted a Computable General Equilibrium (CGE) analysis using Ethiopia's Social Accounting Matrix (SAM) for 2011,[4] for the period 2011–30. The model assumes that the economy will maintain an annual growth rate equal to that of the first two years of GTP-II. The basic results of the analysis are presented in Figures 17.2–17.4.

As can be seen from Figure 17.2, if the economy grows as per the GTP-II targets, emissions will steadily rise to a level that is about 190 per cent higher than what is targeted in CRGE by 2030. This is consistent with the gap between the BAU scenario and the target emissions in the CRGE strategy. But more importantly, our results show that

[4] The CGE model is developed by the Ethiopian Development Research Institute (EDRI) in collaboration with researchers from the International Food Policy Research Institute (IFPRI). The model is formulated as a set of simultaneous linear and non-linear equations that define the behaviour of economic agents and the economic environment in which these agents operate. For detailed description of the model see e.g. Thurlow (2008).

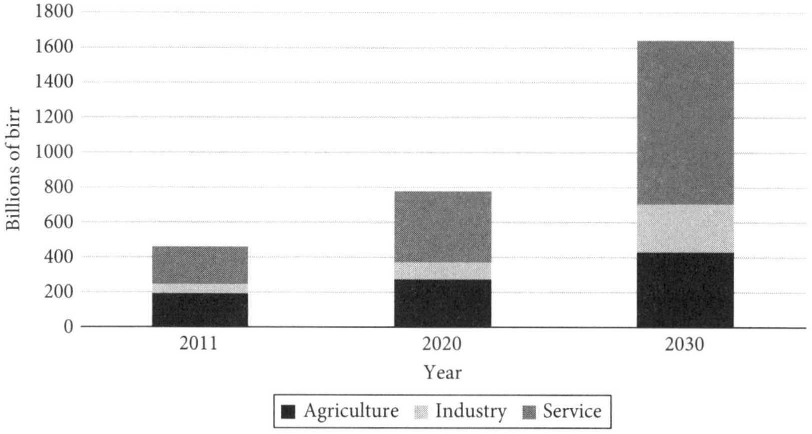

FIGURE 17.2 Evolution of GDP and sectoral composition, 2011–30

Source: Author's computations from EDRI's CGE model of the Ethiopian economy.

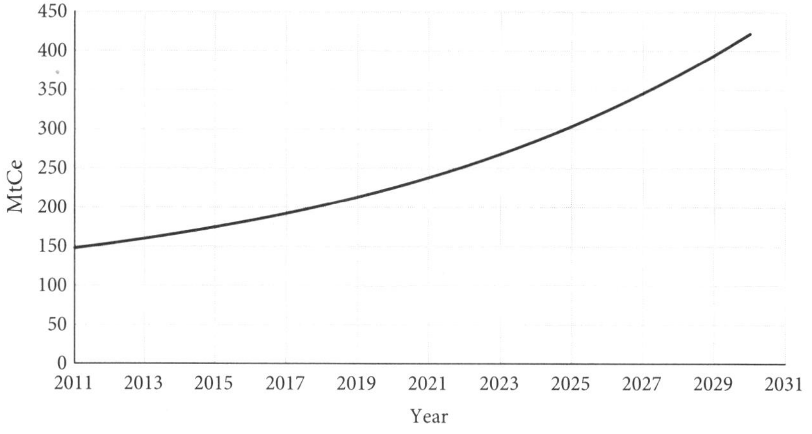

FIGURE 17.3 GHG emissions growth, 2011–30: a GTP-II trajectory

Source: Author's computations from EDRI's CGE model of the Ethiopian economy.

Ethiopia is currently not in the emissions trajectory to meet the CRGE targets by 2030. For example, emissions in 2018 are already 37 per cent higher than the target emissions for 2030. Simply put, Ethiopia is not achieving the expected reductions in emissions from the agriculture and forestry sectors as envisioned in the CRGE strategy, as illustrated in Figure 17.4. The closer we get to the target year, the more challenging it will become to achieve a sharp reversal in emissions unless drastic changes happen in cutting emissions from agriculture, forestry, and firewood burning (e.g. rapid electrification of rural areas with green energy). It is noteworthy that the growth of the industrial sector will have a lower impact on emissions. This is primarily because the sector is already based on green electricity.

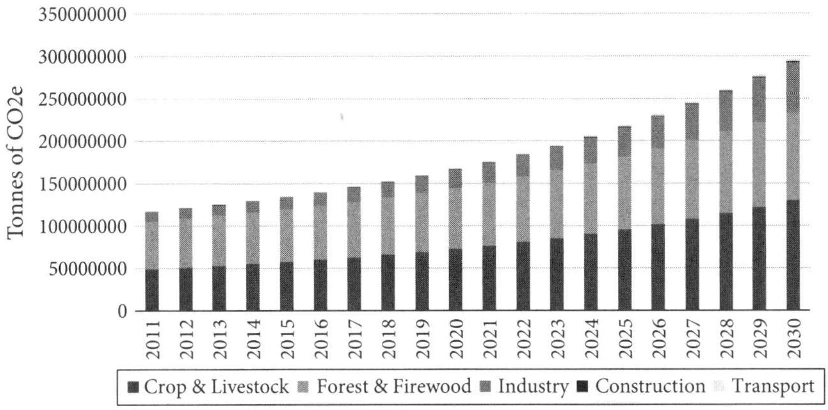

FIGURE 17.4 Major sources of GHG emissions, 2011–30

Source: Author's computations from EDRI's CGE model of the Ethiopian economy.

17.3.2 Towards Achieving a Green and Climate-Resilient Transformation

Despite the rapid economic growth since the turn of the millennium, Ethiopia is still at the early stage of structural transformation. For example, the share of industry valued added in GDP is lower than the average for sub-Saharan Africa (World Bank 2017). Similarly, despite a rapid rate of urbanization over the past decade, more than 80 per cent of the country's population still resides in rural areas (Godfrey and Zhao 2015). And despite the huge potential for renewable energy, the energy sector in Ethiopia is dominated by wood, charcoal, crop residues, and animal dung, which constitute more than 90 per cent of the total energy consumption (Samuel 2014). Given this, achieving Ethiopia's green and climate-resilient transformation necessitates simultaneous multiple transformations in the economy (Danyo et al. 2017). Rural landscapes need to be productive and sustainable. There is also a need to promote sustainable urbanization, mobility, and living conditions and to green the country's industrialization. And all this will require sustainable production and distribution of cleaner energy (Danyo et al. 2017). Achieving these multiple transformations simultaneously is a tall order, but the fact that Ethiopia's structural transformation is only just warming up means that it has the opportunity to get it right—a golden opportunity, for example, to steer its fledging industrial sector along a sustainable pathway.

17.3.3 Building Productive and Resilient Rural Landscapes

This section focuses on sustainable management of agriculture and land, water, and forests, which are critical for building productive and resilient rural landscapes in Ethiopia.

17.3.3.1 *Sustainable Agriculture and Land Management*

The impacts of climate change on agriculture have been noted. Moreover, due to the terrain and a long history of cultivation as well as other factors, land degradation in Ethiopia is a key environmental problem that is estimated to contribute towards a 3 per cent reduction in agricultural GDP (Bojo and Cassells 1995; Sonneveld 2002). Two components of land degradation are soil erosion and depletion of soil nutrients. For areas lying 1,000 metres above sea level, recent estimates of annual net erosion are about 18 tons/ha; the rates for cropland are higher, at about 20 tons/ha (Hurni et al. 2015). There are also large differences in land degradation across regions (FDRE 2015a; Gashaw, Bantider, and Silassie 2014). Soil nutrient depletion is mainly caused by use of crop residues and cattle dung that could have been used as fertilizer and fuel sources.

Sustainable land management (SLM) and climate-smart agricultural (CSA) practices which help address land degradation and impacts of climate change have improved the welfare of Ethiopian rural households through increased incomes as well as improved nutrition (Teklewold, Kassie, and Shiferaw 2013; Kassie et al. 2015; Manda et al. 2016). In the Blue Nile basin, Schmidt and Tadesse (2014) found a 24 per cent increase in value of production due to investment in sustainable land and watershed management between 1992 and 2002. Effects of SLM and CSA practices also differ across regions and agro-ecological conditions (Hurni et al. 2015; Kato et al. 2011). Tesfaye et al. (2016) found positive net present values from soil conservation measures but results differed across conservation type.

Studies have also found that the first-level land-user rights registration and certification that has taken place over the last couple of decades in Ethiopia has improved land tenure with positive effects on tree growing and land management, participation (of women) in land rental markets, off-farm employment, and agricultural productivity (Holden, Deininger, and Ghebru 2009, 2011; Bezabih, Holden, and Mannberg 2016). Ethiopia's first-level land-user right registration and certification is low cost (at US$1 per farm plot or US$3.5 per household) with comparatively high benefits (Deininger et al. 2008). The net benefits of the more expensive ongoing second-level land rights certification (at about US$6 or more) requires further evaluation (Bezu and Holden 2014; Ghebru and Holden 2016).

Benefits of SLM and CSA practices have been achieved through restoration of over 11 million ha of degraded lands by 2015, with a plan to increase this to over 22 million by the end of GTP-II (in 2020). Such practices contribute towards adaptation to and mitigation of climate change. Over one million farm plots have also been granted secondary land-holding certificates by 2015 with a plan to increase this to 30 million by the end of GTP-II (FDRE 2016b).

Studies show that farmers and pastoralists are already taking steps to adapt to climate change in various ways. The government is also supporting farmers and pastoralists through measures such as providing climate and weather information, and early warning, safety net, and insurance services. The government uses drought early warning tools and hotspots assessments to provide early warning services during the onset of drought (Drechsler and Soer 2016). The benefits of providing early warning services outweigh the costs even under conservative scenarios (Law 2012 cited in WMO 2015). However, the service is limited partly due to the low density of observation networks which is well below WMO standards. The National Meteorology Agency plans to expand automatic weather stations with about 700 planned during GTP-II, but more is needed to increase coverage. The Productive Safety Net Program has also contributed a lot towards supporting farmers and pastoralists by reducing their vulnerability to climate shocks such as drought while also improving the environment. Weather index insurance is another important activity that helps protect farmers and pastoralists in the aftermath of a climate-related disaster; progress is, however, more limited.

GHG emissions from the agriculture sector are estimated to increase from 75 MtCO2e in 2010 to 185 MtCO2e in 2030 under a business as usual scenario. The CRGE strategy envisages that the sector will reduce GHG emissions by 90 MtCO2e in 2030. While we do not have data to assess progress on this, maintaining and increasing existing sustainable livestock and land management efforts will help achieve these goals.

17.3.3.2 *Sustainable Agricultural Water Management*

Water availability and quality as well as use is a critical issue given the uneven distribution of water across regions. While there is a considerable quantity of surface water and an uncertain amount of ground water, projections suggest that per capita water availability in Ethiopia could be below 1000 m^3 per year, which would be classed as physically water scarce (Stacey et al. 2008). Only about half of the small-scale irrigation potential of the country has been exploited for various reasons including limited expansion of irrigation infrastructure, institutional issues, and inefficiencies (Awulachew, Erkossa, and Namara 2010).

Irrigation is an important adaptation measure in the face of variable and extreme weather exacerbated by climate change. Irrigation has helped boost agricultural productivity and incomes. For example, in the Lake Tana basin, mean household income of households using small-scale irrigation increased by 3,350 ETB per year, compared with non-irrigating households, a 27 per cent increase (Ayele et al. 2013). Benefits of irrigation also include reduced deforestation and land degradation made possible by agricultural intensification, and hence the consequent reduction in possible agricultural land expansion; this contributes towards reduction in GHG emissions.

Over 2 million ha of small-scale irrigation development increasing agricultural productivity and household income had taken place by 2015; the plan is to increase this to over 4 million ha by the end of GTP-II. Medium- and large-scale irrigation development is also planned to increase from over 400,000 ha in 2015 to over 900,000 ha in 2020 (FDRE 2016b). Water-level monitoring is another important activity, the benefits of which include improved hydropower production, irrigation downstream, and flood early warning.

17.3.3.3 *Sustainable Forest Management*

Deforestation and forest degradation are key environmental challenges for Ethiopia. A recent Forest Reference Level study put the net forest loss at about 70,000 ha per year for the period 2000–13 (FDRE 2016c). Earlier estimates of deforestation are higher: reusing (1998) put it at 141,000 ha/year. In 2013, MEFCC-WB (2015) estimated that well over 90 per cent of the 124 million m^3 of wood consumed was extracted illegally and unsustainably. Causes of deforestation and forest degradation include agricultural expansion, livestock grazing, and use of biomass for energy and construction (FDRE 2016c).

Official reports on the contribution of the forest sector to GDP put it at about 4 per cent (FDRE 2016b). UNEP's (2016) estimates are as high as 12.9 per cent of GDP. This difference of about 9 per cent is mainly explained by attribution of the following services of forests to other sectors in official reports: forest pollination services, forest-derived fodder and fuel wood, soil erosion control services, and tourism in protected areas. Non-timber forest products are important to the livelihoods of rural people and the economy at large with a total value of close to a billion dollars per year, over half of which is contributed by forest and semi-forest coffee (MEFCC-WB 2015). Bamboo is also very important for Ethiopia with one million ha of bamboo forest, representing about two-thirds of the bamboo reserves of Africa. Domestic demand for forest products outstrips domestic supply and forest products are imported (MEFCC-WB 2015).

Forest management in Ethiopia has taken place in various forms including natural forest, plantations, participatory forest management, exclosures, and agro-forestry. Using a new definition of forest,[5] Ethiopia's forest cover in 2015 is estimated at 15.5 per cent. Ethiopia aims to reverse deforestation and forest degradation and even increase forest cover from 15.5 per cent to 20 per cent in 2020; this implies an increase of over 4 million ha of forest cover during the five-year period (FDRE 2016b). Reducing emissions from deforestation and forest degradation (REDD+) is one of the strategies used to address the problem of deforestation and forest degradation. During GTP-II Ethiopia also plans to preserve and utilize 0.7 million ha of bamboo.

By providing different types of benefits, forest resources contribute to adaptation to and mitigation of climate change in a number of ways: as sources of food, feed, fuel, construction, industrial wood, gums, resins, and medicine: sequestering carbon; soil and water conservation; ensuring a healthy hydrological cycle; and minimizing the silting up of hydroelectric dams. In terms of GHG emissions from forests, recent estimates show net emissions of over 9.2 million CO_2/year for the period 2000–13 (FDRE 2016a, 2016c). This underlines the challenge of reducing emissions from the forestry sector, with about half of GHG emission reduction in Ethiopia by 2030 (130 Mt CO2e) expected to come from this sector, including reductions due to use of improved stoves (FDRE 2011).

17.3.4 Enabling Green Modernization

This section discusses sustainable urbanization, mobility, and living conditions, and green industrialization, all of which are key for green modernization.

17.3.4.1 *Sustainable Urbanization, Mobility, and Living Conditions*

Currently Ethiopia is among the least urbanized countries but has one of the highest rates of urbanization in the world, increasing at 5.4 per cent per annum. With Ethiopia's population

[5] The following is the new definition of forest: 'Land spanning at least 0.5 ha covered by trees and bamboo, attaining a height of at least 2m and a canopy cover of at least 20 per cent, or trees with the potential to reach thresholds *in situ* in due course' (MEFCC 2016).

expected to be more than 170 million by 2050, sustainable urbanization is expected to contribute to the goals of a climate-resilient and green Ethiopia. Rapid urbanization is presenting social and environmental risks such as pollution (water, air, and noise), urban sprawl, solid and liquid waste management problems, illegal settlements, and loss of open green areas, and climate change is likely to exacerbate this challenge. For example, WHO (2016) estimates that the third leading cause of under-five mortality in Ethiopia is diarrhoeal disease due to exposure to unsafe water, sanitation, and hygiene accounting for 20 per cent of all deaths. A large proportion of the increasing stock of vehicles are old and therefore more polluting. Urban areas are also likely to suffer from flooding which also damages infrastructure in addition to its effects on lives and livelihoods.

The Ethiopian government stresses the importance of building green, resilient, and well-governed cities to achieve its vision of middle-income country status by 2025 and a green and climate-resilient economy. As part of the mainstreaming of CRGE into GTP-II, the plan is to improve living conditions through an increase in green areas, sustainable mobility, improved access to potable water, and improved stoves and lighting. Establishing solid waste collection and disposal system in urban areas and increasing their coverage is also an important part of the plan. Potable water supply coverage is projected to increase from 58 per cent in 2015 to 83 per cent by the end of GTP-II (FDRE 2016b). By 2030 efficient lighting and waste gas management are projected to reduce GHG emissions by 5.1 and 1.8 MtCO2e respectively. While the projected reduction in GHG emissions due to transport moving from roads to the electric rail network is 9 MtCO2e, changing the fuel mix through the use of biodiesel and bioethanol, and promoting the adoption of hybrid and plug-in electric vehicles has a combined abatement potential of about 1.0 MtCO2e (FDRE 2011). While these are projections for 2030, the following are important developments that contribute to GHG emissions reduction: 15 per cent blending of ethanol with gasoline that started a few years ago; efficient lighting; conversion of solid waste to energy which is about to start; and the electric rail network (both light rail in Addis Ababa and electric trains from Addis Ababa to Djibouti which have started operation).

17.3.4.2 *Sustainable Industrialization*

Green industrial development can be an important means to improve urban livelihoods through the creation of green and productive jobs. It also facilitates economic transformation because it absorbs labour from agriculture and other primary sectors. To accommodate the increasing rural–urban migrants with jobs, the government is facilitating micro and small enterprise (MSE) development and industry expansion. GTP-II also targets a continued average industrial growth rate of 20 per cent and plans to increase industry's share of value added in GDP from about 15 per cent in 2015 to 22 per cent by 2020.

If such industrial expansion follows a traditional path it would result in high dependency on carbon-intensive materials, expensive infrastructure, and energy- and material-intensive solutions. A green industrialization trajectory that addresses emerging problems of pollution while reducing costs and increasing productivity is important to achieve the CRGE vision.

Under a BAU scenario, industrial GHG emissions in Ethiopia are projected to grow by 16 per cent per year and reach 71 $MtCO_2e$ in 2030, compared to 4 $MtCO_2e$ in 2010

(FDRE 2011). This is the largest GHG emissions growth rate of all economic sectors. The CRGE strategy for the industry sector aims to reduce the sector's annual GHG emissions to 50 $MtCO_2e$ in 2030, representing a reduction of about 30 per cent compared to the BAU scenario.

The CRGE strategy mainly targets greening the cement, mining, and textile and leather industries due to their larger contribution to industrial GHG emissions. Cement production is the largest contributor to Ethiopia's industrial CO_2e emissions (50 per cent) and it constitutes around 70 per cent of the identified industrial abatement potential. A main greening activity in the cement industry is substitution of clinker—a product produced because of energy-intensive heating and cooling of a homogenized raw materials mixture during the first stage of cement production—which provides 5 $MtCO_2e$ of abatement. Displacement of fossil fuels in cement production through the use of biomass as a source of energy is also projected to provide a 4.2 MtCO2e reduction.

Ethiopia has formulated an Industrial Development Roadmap (2013–25) that envisions building a diversified and globally competitive environmentally friendly industrial sector with the highest manufacturing capability in Africa. Ethiopia's vision for green industrialization is in line with the global promotion of inclusive and sustainable industrialization as part of the 2030 Sustainable Development Goals.

GTP-II also states specific targets for the development of eco-industrial parks with waste treatment technologies and energy efficiency in factories—activities that safeguard the environment while boosting manufacturing. The government has plans to build about fourteen industrial parks with a total area of 5,025 ha (www.ipdc.gov.et) and green existing industries through measures such as building industrial zones with a common waste disposal system and moving existing industries to 'eco-industrial villages'.

17.3.5 Accelerating Sustainable Energy Transition

Sustainable energy production and access is the golden ticket of climate-resilient green transformation. Accelerating the sustainable energy transition in Ethiopia requires expansion of improved technologies using different types of energy source and expansion of electricity.

Over 90 per cent of energy used in Ethiopia comes from biomass fuels (Johanson and Mengistu 2013). Electricity contributes only about 2 per cent while oil products (mainly consumed in the transport sector) contribute about 6 per cent (IEA 2014). Most of the biomass fuel is consumed by rural people who not only constitute over 80 per cent of the population but also rely on biomass fuel more heavily than the urban population, the latter using other options such as kerosene and electricity more heavily in per capita terms. Heavy reliance on biomass fuels contributes to deforestation and forest degradation, indoor air pollution causing about 75,000 deaths per year (WHO 2009), and reduced welfare of households due to time spent collecting biomass fuel which could have been spent on activities such as education and other productive activities.

Ethiopia is moving towards cleaner energy consumption with electricity generation capacity more than quadrupling over a decade to reach over 4,000MW by 2015; but this represents less than 6 per cent of the potential. About 96 per cent of the electricity is generated from hydropower with an increasing role for wind (currently contributing about 4 per cent, which could increase given the country's huge potential) (IEA 2014). By the end of GTP-I, the electricity network reached 60 per cent of towns with only about 2.58 million households connected to electricity. Most of the households connected to electricity use it for lighting, with most of the cooking using other energy sources, mostly biomass fuels in rural areas. To help reduce forest degradation and indoor air pollution, about 8.87 million improved cooking stoves have been distributed during GTP-I (FDRE 2016b; Beyene et al. 2015). The existing energy mix calls for an increase in the share of cleaner and more sustainable renewable energy sources.

By the end of GTP-II, the plan is to increase electricity generation capacity to over 17,000MW. In addition to satisfying the increasing domestic demand, this increased generation capacity is expected to increase foreign exchange earnings from export of electricity. The plan also includes increasing the coverage of towns to 90 per cent and the length of distribution lines from 13,000km to 22,000km, reaching 6.955 million customers. The government also plans to distribute 11.45 million improved cooking stoves and increase home solar energy systems from 41,000 to 400,000 during GTP-II (to reach remote areas which may not have access to the grid) (MoWIE 2015; FDRE 2016b). Improving the energy mix by reducing the share of hydropower in electricity generation is an important priority in the face of climate change. Use of biofuels is also expanding; bioethanol for cooking reduces not only GHG emissions but also demand for foreign exchange, as it replaces kerosene which is imported. Biogas is another option that is also expanding. In addition to reduction in GHG emissions from use of improved stoves (which is considered under forestry in the CRGE strategy), an abatement potential of 19 MtCO2e is estimated from the export of green power to regional markets (FDRE 2011).

17.4 Issues for Consideration

Ethiopia has one of the most ambitious green and climate-resilient structural transformation visions in the developing world, and has made strong commitments in its NDCs as part of the Paris Agreement on climate change action. This chapter set out to examine the efficacy of the vision, and provide perspectives on its implications in the context of the Ethiopian economy. The vision has strong foundations in the discourse on the nature of economic development in the twenty-first century, especially in the emerging evidence that shows that climate-friendly growth might be the only option remaining for latecomers like Ethiopia. The targets of Ethiopia's green and climate-resilient development vision, as illustrated in the CRGE strategy, are also consistent with the economic realities of the country. For example, the core avenue for achieving emissions targets is reversing deforestation trends. Similarly, the strategy seeks to leverage the country's huge potential for renewable energy to build a green industrial sector. Achieving Ethiopia's green and climate-resilient transformation agenda requires multiple transformations across different sectors of the economy. Coordinated efforts are required to build resilient and productive rural landscapes, promote sustainable urbanization, develop green industrialization, and support all these efforts with a sustainable and green energy system.

There are, however, a number of issues that require due consideration in the effort to implement Ethiopia's climate-resilient green transformation vision. First, the finance gap needs to be addressed. The CRGE strategy indicates that abatement costs are less than US$15 per ton of CO_2e for more than 80 per cent of the abatement potential, and a number of these offer positive returns on investment (FDRE 2011). While this suggests that the initiatives identified are mostly relatively low cost and involve 'no or low regret options', the total expenditure required to achieve the emissions reduction over 2010–30 is about US$120 billion (FDRE 2011). The costs would be much higher if we also include expenditure on implementation of sectoral climate resilience strategies. Considering that climate change is a global problem and that Ethiopia is a low-income country with limited capacity to address climate change issues, a good part of the financing requirement may have to come from the international community. Thus, there is a significant challenge of meeting the financing needs. In this respect, Ethiopia should explore innovative sources of finance, including carbon pricing.

Another issue that should be considered is institutional coordination and resource-use planning. Achieving the multiple transformations demanded by the CRGE vision requires vertical and horizontal coordination of institutions from planning to implementation. These include inter-sectoral coordination for efficient management and use of land, water, forest, and energy resources. Such coordination and informed decisions about the use of resources is important given the fact that key resources like land and water have competing uses for agriculture/food production, forestry, urban development, and industry. The role and effectiveness of environmental policies and regulations also needs some consideration, including incentives such as water and energy pricing, and payment for ecosystem services. There is also a need to put coordinated institutional processes in place for continuous monitoring and evaluation as Ethiopia needs to learn from its own experimentation.

References

ADB (2012). 'Green Growth, Resources and Resilience: Environmental Sustainability in Asia and the Pacific', Asian Development Bank, Bangkok.

ATA (2016). 'Agricultural Transformation Agenda: Annual Report', ATA, Addis Ababa.

Awulachew, S. B., T. Erkossa, and R. E. Namara (2010). 'Irrigation Potential in Ethiopia: Constraints and Opportunities for Enhancing the System', unpublished report to the Bill and Melinda Gates Foundation, Addis Ababa.

Ayele, G. K., C. F. Nicholson, A. S. Collick, et al. (2013). 'Impact of Small-Scale Irrigation Schemes on Household Income and the Likelihood of Poverty in the Lake Tana Basin of Ethiopia', in 'Rainwater Management for Resilient Livelihoods in Ethiopia: Proceedings of the Nile Basin Development Challenge Science Meeting, Addis Ababa, 9–10 July 2013', ed. Wolde Mekuria, NBDC Technical Report 5, International Livestock Research Institute, Nairobi: 14–19.

Beyene, A. D., R. Bluffstone, Z. Gebreegziabher, et al. (2015). 'Do Improved Biomass Cookstoves Reduce Fuelwood Consumption and Carbon Emissions? Evidence from Rural Ethiopia Using a Randomized Treatment Trial with Electronic Monitoring', World Bank Policy Research Working Paper No. 7324, Washington, DC.

Bezabih, M., S. Holden, and A. Mannberg (2016). 'The Role of Land Certification in Reducing Gaps in Productivity between Male- and Female-Owned Farms in Rural Ethiopia', *Journal of Development Studies* 52 (3): 360–76.

Bezu, S. and S. Holden (2014). 'Demand for Second-Stage Land Certification in Ethiopia: Evidence from Household Panel Data', *Land Use Policy* 41: 93–205.

Bojo, J. and D. Cassells (1995). 'Land Degradation and Rehabilitation in Ethiopia: A Reassessment', AFTES Working Paper No. 17, World Bank, Washington, DC.

Carfora, A., V. Pansini, A. Romano, and G. Scandura (2018). 'Renewable Energy Policies and Green Public Policies Complementarities: The Case of Developed and Developing Countries', *Renewable Energy* 115: 741–9.

Danyo, Stephen, Abate, Asferachew, Bekhechi, Mohammed, et al. (2017). 'Realizing Ethiopia's Green Transformation: Country Environmental Analysis, Environment and Natural Resources Global Practice', World Bank, Washington, DC.

Deininger, K., D. A. Ali, S. Holden, and J. Zevenbergen (2008). 'Rural Land Certification in Ethiopia: Process, Initial Impact, and Implications for Other African Countries', *World Development* 36 (10): 1786–812.

Drechsler, M. and W. Soer (2016). 'Early Warning, Early Action: The Use of Predictive Tools in Drought Response through Ethiopia's Productive Safety Net Programme', Policy Research Working Paper, Finance and Markets Global Practice Group, World Bank, Washington, DC.

EPCC (Ethiopian Panel on Climate Change) (2015). 'First Assessment Report, Working Group II, Agriculture and Food Security, Ethiopian Academy of Sciences', EPCC, Addis Ababa.

FDRE (2011). 'Ethiopia's Climate-Resilient Green Economy: Green Economy Strategy', FDRE, Addis Ababa.

FDRE (2015a). 'Ethiopia: Land Degradation Neutrality National Report', FDRE, Addis Ababa.

FDRE (2015b). 'Ethiopia's Climate-Resilient Green Economy Climate Resilience Strategy: Agriculture and Forestry', FDRE, Addis Ababa.

FDRE (2015c). 'Ethiopia's Climate-Resilient Green Economy Climate Resilience Strategy: Water and Energy', FDRE, Addis Ababa.

FDRE (2015d). 'Intended Nationally Determined Contribution (INDC) of the Federal Democratic Republic of Ethiopia', FDRE, Addis Ababa.

FDRE (2016a). 'MSIP (Multi-Sector Investment Plan) for Climate Resilient Agriculture and Forest 2017–2030.' Final document presented to and approved by the Climate Investment Funds' Pilot Program for Climate Resilience, MoFEC, Addis Ababa, June 2017.

FDRE (2016b). 'Growth and Transformation Plan II (GTP II): 2015/16–2019/20', National Planning Commission, Addis Ababa.

FDRE (2016c). 'Ethiopia's Forest Reference Level Submission to the UNFCCC', FDRE, Addis Ababa, December.

FDRE (2017a). 'National Adaptation Plan: Ethiopia's Climate Resilient Green Economy' FDRE, Addis Ababa.

FDRE (2017b). 'Climate-Resilient Strategy: Urban Development and Housing, Final Report', FDRE, Addis Ababa.

Freire, M. E. (2013). 'Urbanization and Green Growth in Africa', The Growth Dialogue: http://www.greengrowthknowledge.org/sites/default/files/downloads/resource/Urbanization_and_GG_in_Africa_The_Growth_Dialogue.pdf

Gashaw, T., A. Bantider, and H. G. Silassie (2014). 'Land Degradation in Ethiopia: Causes, Impacts and Rehabilitation Techniques', *Journal of Environmental and Earth Science* 4 (9): 98–104.

Ghebru, H. and S. T. Holden (2016). 'Land Tenure Reforms, Tenure Security and Food Security in Poor Agrarian Economies: Causal Linkages and Research Gaps', *Global Food Security* 10: 21–8.

Godfrey, N. and X. Zhao (2015). 'The Contribution of African Cities to the Economy and Climate', New Climate Economy Working Paper Series, The Global Commission on the Economy and Climate.

Hallegate, S., G. Heal, M. Fay, and T. Treguer (2011). 'From Growth to Green Growth: A Framework', Policy Research Working Paper No. 5872, World Bank, Washington, DC.

Holden, S. T., K. Deininger, and H. Ghebru (2011). 'Tenure Insecurity, Gender, Low-Cost Land Certification and Land Rental Market Participation in Ethiopia', *Journal of Development Studies* 47 (1): 31–47.

Holden, S.T., K. Deininger, and H. Ghebru (2009). 'Impacts of Low-Cost Land Certification on Investment and Productivity', *American Journal of Agricultural Economics* 91(2): 359–73.

Hurni, K., G. Zeleke, M. Kassie, et al. (2015). 'Economics of Land Degradation (ELD): Ethiopia Case Study. Soil Degradation and Sustainable Land Management in the Rain-Fed Agricultural Areas of Ethiopia: An Assessment of the Economic Implications', Report for the Economics of Land Degradation Initiative 104.

IEA (2014). 'International Energy Agency Statistics: Share of Ethiopia's Total Primary Energy Supply in 2014',International Energy Agency. https://www.iea.org/statistics/statisticssearch/report/?year=2014andcountry=Ethiopiaandproduct=Balances

Johanson, F. X. and A. T. Mengistu (2013). 'Alternative Future Pathways for Household Biomass Use in Ethiopia', Discussion Brief Series, Stockholm Environment Institute, Stockholm.

Kassie, M., H. Teklewold, M. Jaleta, et al. (2015). 'Understanding the Adoption of a Portfolio of Sustainable Intensification Practices in Eastern and Southern Africa', *Land Use Policy* 42: 400–11.

Kato, E., C. Ringler, M. Yesuf, and E. Bryan (2011). 'Soil and Water Conservation Technologies: A Buffer against Production Risk in the Face of Climate Change? Insights from the Nile Basin in Ethiopia', *Agricultural Economics* 42: 593–604.

Lukas, N. (2015). 'Green Economy for Sustainable Development and Poverty Eradication', *Mediterranean Journal of Social Sciences* 6: 655.

Manda, J., A. D. Alene, C. Gardebroek, M. Kassie, and G. Tembo (2016). 'Adoption and Impacts of Sustainable Agricultural Practices on Maize Yields and Incomes: Evidence from Rural Zambia', *Journal of Agricultural Economics* 67 (1): 130–53.

MEFCC (2015). 'Study of Causes of Deforestation and Forest Degradation in Ethiopia and the Identification and Prioritization of Strategic Options to Address Those', Final Report, Ministry of Environment, Forest and Climate Change, Addis Ababa.

MEFCC (2016). 'National Tree-Based Landscape Restoration Potential Priority Maps. Version 1', Ministry of Environment, Forest and Climate Change, Addis Ababa.

MEFCC-WB (2015). 'Ethiopia Forest Sector Review—Focus on Commercial Forestry in Industrialization', Ministry of Environment, Forest and Climate Change, Addis Ababa and World Bank, Washington, DC.

MoT (2017). 'Ethiopia's Climate-Resilient Transport Sector Strategy', Ministry of Transport, Addis Ababa.

MoWIE (2015). 'Growth and Transformation Plan II', Ministry of Water, Irrigation and Electricity, Addis Ababa.

OECD (2012). 'Green Growth and Developing Countries: A Summary for Policy Makers', June, OECD, Paris.

OECD (2013). 'Putting Green Growth at the Heart of Development', OECD Green Growth Studies, OECD Publishing, Paris.

Omilola B. (2014). 'Inclusive Green Growth in Africa: Rationale, Challenges and Opportunities', Policy brief, United Nations Development Program (UNDP), South Africa.

Reilly, M. (2012). 'Green Growth and Efficient Use of Natural Resources', *Energy Economics* 34: 585–93.

Reusing, M. (1998). 'Monitoring of Natural High Forests in Ethiopia', GTZ, Addis Ababa.
Rockström et al. (2009). 'Planetary Boundaries: Exploring the Safe Operating Space for Humanity', *Ecology and Scoiety* 14 (2): 32.
Samuel, S. (2014). 'Evaluating the Economic Impact of Energy Efficiency Improvement in Ethiopia: A Recursive Dynamic Computable General Equilibrium Analysis', MSC thesis, University of Gondar.
Saufi, A., S. Daud, and H. Hassan (2016). 'Green Growth and Corporate Sustainability Performance', *Procedia Economics and Finance* 35: 374–8.
Schmidt, E. and F. Tadesse (2014). 'Sustainable Agriculture in the Blue Nile Basin: Land and Watershed Management Practices in Ethiopia', *Environment and Development Economics* 19 (5): 648–67.
Sonneveld, B. (2002). *Land under Pressure: The Impact of Water Erosion on Food Production in Ethiopia* (Netherlands: Shaker Publishing).
Stacey, N., A. Alemu, S. Gedion, B. Jennie, and S. John (2008). 'Water and Poverty Linkages in Africa: Ethiopia Case Study', Stockholm Environment Institute.
Steffen et al. (2015). 'Planetary Boundaries: Guiding Human Development on a Changing Planet', *Science* 347: 6223.
Tamanini, J. (2016). 'The Global Green Economy Index: Measuring National Performance in the Green Economy', 5th edition, Dual Citizen LLC.
Taffesse, A. S., P. Dorosh, and S. A. Gemessa (2012). 'Crop Production in Ethiopia: Regional Patterns and Trends, in *Food and Agriculture in Ethiopia: Progress and Policy Challenges*, ed. P. Dorosh and S. Rashid (Philadelphia: University of Pennsylvania): Ch. 3.
Teklewold, H., M. Kassie, and B. Shiferaw (2013). 'Adoption of Multiple Sustainable Agricultural Practices in Rural Ethiopia', *Journal of Agricultural Economics* 64 (3): 597–623.
Tesfaye, A., R. Brouwer, P. van der Zaag, and W. Negatu (2016). 'Assessing the Costs and Benefits of Improved Land Management Practices in Three Watershed Areas in Ethiopia', *International Soil and Water Conservation Research* 4 (1): 20–9.
Thurlow, J. (2008). 'A Recursive Dynamic CGE Model and Microsimulation Poverty Module for South Africa', International Food Policy Research Institute, Washington, DC.
UNECA (2015). 'Inclusive Green Growth in Ethiopia: Selected Case Studies', United Nations Economic Commission for Africa.
UNEP (2016). 'The Contribution of Forests to National Income in Ethiopia and Linkages with REDD+.' UN-REDD Programme report, UNEP, Nairobi, (draft).
USAID (2016). 'Climate Change Information Fact Sheet of Ethiopia'.
WHO (2009). 'Country Profile of Environmental Burden of Disease: Ethiopia', Public Health and Environment, World Health Organization, Geneva.
WHO (2016). 'World Health Statistics 2016: Monitoring Health for the SDGs (Sustainable Development Goals)', World Health Organization, Geneva.
WMO (2015). *Valuing Weather and Climate: Economic Assessment of Meteorological and Hydrological Services*. WMO No. 1153 (Geneva: World Meteorological Organization).
World Bank (2010). 'Economics of Adaptation to Climate Change: Ethiopian Case Study', World Bank, Washington, DC.
World Bank (2012). 'Inclusive Green Growth: the Pathway to Sustainable Development', World Bank, Washington, DC.
World Bank (2017). Atlas of Sustainable Development Goals 2017. From World Development Indicators. World Bank Atlas. World Bank,Washington, DC. https://openknowledge.worldbank.org/handle/10986/26306 License: CC BY 3.0 IGO.

CHAPTER 18

ASSESSING POVERTY TRENDS IN ETHIOPIA, 1990–2015

JOHN SENDER

18.1 Introduction and Context

Reliable evidence is fundamental to effective policy. This chapter's discussion of statistics on poverty is not an attempt to belittle the achievements of the staff of the Ethiopian Central Statistics Authority (CSA). Rather, its aim is to locate some of the problems they face in a wider historical and geographical context. General comments about the political economy of collecting and publishing data on poverty are followed by a few remarks on African statistics in general and Ethiopian rural statistics in particular. The second part of this chapter provides a short overview of the evidence concerning the impact of policy interventions on the poorest people in Africa, especially in Ethiopia. Finally, a case will be made for using a simple and cost-effective method of assessing anti-poverty policies. The arguments to support this method are based on primary data collected from several Ethiopian sites producing coffee and flowers.

Many policymakers pay a great deal of attention to demographic surveys and to statistics measuring the incidence of poverty. Political leaders may be unsettled by these statistics, but few are prepared to execute the nation's most senior statisticians if the data in the population census fail to support implausible claims about the rate of growth of output (Merridale 1996). Unlike Stalin, Mussolini did not murder his statistical officials in the 1930s, but he did ensure that a fascist ideological ally was appointed to lead the national statistical organization. Mussolini was in daily contact with the President of the Istituto Centrale di Statistica (Giorgi 2011: 6). More recently, it was reported that Donald Trump planned to nominate a Republican ally as Deputy Director of the United States Census Bureau, raising fears that the 2020 Population Census would over- or under-count certain populations (Tracy 2017).

Other political leaders have been willing to punish government statisticians. For example, in 2017 the former head of the Greek national statistics agency was criticized by the country's president and received a two-year (suspended) prison sentence for publishing revised estimates of Greece's debt-to-GDP ratio (Langkjær-Bain 2017); a former head of China's statistics bureau was sentenced to life imprisonment; while the current director of China's National Bureau of Statistics admits that local statistics continue to be falsified and demands 'serious punishment' for statistical fraud (Wildau 2016).

Direct and punitive interventions are not the only threats faced by official statisticians. In Africa, political leaders allocate fluctuating and very limited resources to national statistical organizations (NSOs), leaving the funding and much of the design of statistical investigations to external donors (Hoogeveen and Nguyen 2017). Most NSOs in Africa are said to be 'constrained by budget instability and a lack of autonomy that leave them vulnerable to political and interest group pressures' (Glassman and Ezeh 2014: xii). It is also reported that 'ad hoc donor-funded projects generate significant revenue for statistics offices and individual NSO staff. Increasing take home pay by chasing donor-funded per diems via workshop attendance, training, and survey fieldwork is the order of the day. As a result, NSOs lack incentives to improve national statistical capacity' (Glassman and Ezeh 2014: xii). In Ethiopia, vacancy rates for statistical staff are high, especially at headquarters, 'due to high staff turnover owing mainly to low salaries and poor conditions of service compared to similar agencies in government' (Multi-Agency Mission 2015: 6–7).

The World Bank publishes an index of national statistical capacity for sub-Saharan African countries, including Ethiopia.[1] Ethiopia's overall statistical capacity score declined between 2009 and 2017, while the scores in Rwanda and Malawi increased—overtaking Ethiopia's score as well as the latest score recorded for South Africa. Another and more recently developed index aims to measure the degree to which the websites of African NSOs follow best international practice in terms of coverage, accessibility, and quality of publicly accessible data (Hoogeveen and Nguyen 2017: Appendix). In 2014, Ethiopia's score on this Statistics Access Indicator was 0.52—a score matched by Senegal, Burkina Faso, and Zambia but overshadowed again by superior scores in Rwanda (0.78), Malawi (0.64) and South Africa (0.67).[2]

These scores and, in particular, the apparent superiority of Statistics South Africa—so fiercely defended against academic critics by its recently retired leader—need to be examined alongside other evidence.[3] In five major South African surveys, interviewer cheating (and other sources of error) were widespread (Finn and Ranchhod 2017). The most politically embarrassing statistics—the trends in South African inequality and real wages—are difficult to analyse because of serious data quality issues and because

[1] http://datatopics.worldbank.org/statisticalcapacity/

[2] The Final Evaluation Report of Ethiopia's National Strategy for the Development of Statistics also commented on the deficiencies of CSA's website (Multi-Agency Mission 2015: 12).

[3] Allison (2013) describes the extremely defensive response to criticism by South Africa's Statistician-General.

the officially published series has been interrupted by breaks in the measurement process (Wittenberg 2017).

In Ethiopia, the CSA reported that when conducting the Large and Medium Scale Commercial Farms Sample Survey (2014/15), serious problems were encountered: enumerators 'forged' information if farms were hard to reach; sampling targets were not achieved; and selected farmers refused to provide accurate responses or to be interviewed (Habekiristos Beyene 2016: 21). There is also evidence of inadequate enumerator effort, weak supervision of enumerators, and poor fieldwork design in a survey carried out collaboratively by the CSA and the World Bank (Himelein, Eckman, and Murray 2014: 210). Perhaps even more seriously, questions have been raised about the CSA's Agricultural Sample Surveys, which provide time series data on food crops that should underpin all poverty analysis. In addition to the 'puzzling inconsistencies' in these data that Gollin observed (2011: 27), a more recent examination of this series highlights sudden, massive, and unexplained jumps in the yields of crops that play a particularly important role in the diets of the rural poor. For example, the series suggests that yield per hectare for the root crops taro and sweet potato tripled in the 2012/13 season (Cochrane and Bekele 2018: 1026).[4]

Apart from the need accurately to assess trends in the supply of the types of food eaten by the poorest rural people, it is also important to monitor their ability to acquire this food. There is growing evidence to suggest that the most vulnerable and deprived people in rural Ethiopia depend on low-paid wage work for their survival, i.e. they must use the income they derive from wages, usually casual, temporary, or seasonal wages, to *purchase* much of the food they consume. Data collected through the Agricultural Growth Program (AGP) indicate that the poorest income quintile of households derive a relatively *small* percentage of their total income from crop production and a much larger percentage from wage labour compared to richer households; this survey also shows that less educated (and probably poorer) household heads are much more dependent on agricultural wage income (Bachewe et al. 2016: 4 and 6).

But these authors also believe that rural real wages have been rising in Ethiopia (Bachewe et al. 2016: 16; Worku et al. 2017: 73) and this claim may be questioned: first, their survey covers a purposively selected ninety-three of Ethiopia's 800 *woredas* and is not representative of *all* rural households or of regional labour markets in Ethiopia (Berhane et al. 2012: 57–8); second, the many seasonal agricultural workers employed by large-scale floricultural and coffee enterprises in Ethiopia are excluded from this survey; third, some of the CSA nominal wage data underpinning this claim also cannot be considered representative of wages in rural labour markets, because they were only collected in 119 *urban* areas—the CSA casual labour data series does not provide reliable information about rural wage rates.

It is important to emphasize this third point, which has also been stressed in earlier IFPRI publications: 'we believe that the wage series... are a good proxy for the income of

[4] On the role of root crops in Ethiopian rural diets see Worku et al. (2017: 77), who also describe changes in survey methods that make it difficult to use the series of Ethiopian Household Consumption Surveys (completed between 1995/6 and 2010/11) to identify trends.

a substantial section of the urban poor... A limitation is that we can say nothing about the rural poor, who still make up the bulk of Ethiopia's total poor' (Headey et al. 2012: 3). While there is little doubt that 'daily' wage labourers do make up a large number of the urban poor, the earnings of many other poor urban workers, for example, landfill garbage reclaimers, or young women working in restaurants, cafes, and as sex workers, may well be lower, and are not captured in the CSA series (Tarekegn and Tefera 2016; Erulkar, Medhin, and Negeri 2017; Lucci, Bhatkal, and Khan 2018). Besides, the CSA enumerators appear to collect the wage series for casual labour by questioning only the same three employers every month in each urban location (Headey et al. 2012: 4). More reliable data about the wide range of nominal wages being paid in highly segmented casual labour markets can usually be obtained if the workers themselves are questioned (Cramer et al. 2014a). Besides, many of those paid to do casual agricultural labour are *not* paid on a daily basis; piece rates and task rates are common, as is part-payment with varying types of food and drink rather than cash, making it challenging to obtain reliable estimates of average monthly nominal wage earnings (Cramer et al. 2017: 841–56).

If more reliable data on heterogeneous nominal wages in rural Ethiopia were to become available, it might still be difficult to be confident about trends in *real* rural wages, because the prices of consumer goods collected in 119 urban areas might be very different from the prices paid by the poor in the hundreds of thousands of rural markets and *kebeles* where they actually purchase their food. Even within one urban area well served by transport links, huge variations have been recorded in consumer credit availability and in the retail price of maize, which is so important a component of the diet of the poor (Woldu et al. 2013: 9).

It is possible to monitor long-term rural poverty by focusing research efforts on trends in real wages.[5] But, in Ethiopia, a consistently reliable investigation of these trends would require the investment of substantial resources. These new resources could be devoted to producing and distributing the sort of data contained in the Indian quinquennial Rural Labour Reports and in the Indian Consumer Price Index for Agricultural Labour. This investment would add to the limited information on the poorest available in Ethiopia's official Household Consumption Surveys, because these typically exclude the tails of the distribution of households, hard-to-reach populations, and the poorest of the poor (Carr-Hill 2017).

18.2 Policy Interventions and the Poorest People

Aid officials often champion anti-poverty policies (Ravallion 2015: 7). But in sub-Saharan Africa, over the period 1998–2012, most of the poorest 20 per cent of the population

[5] As shown by economic historians such as Humphries and Weisdorf (2016) and economists such as Himanshu and Kundu (2016).

failed to benefit from any of these anti-poverty programmes (Ravallion 2015: 23). A more recent analysis covers African Development Bank and World Bank project aid to seventeen African countries (including Ethiopia) and 'reveals that aid does not favor the poorest. Rather, aid disproportionately flows to regions that hold more of a country's richest people' (Briggs 2017: 203).

The Ethiopian government is publicly committed to targeting the most vulnerable, for example by improving their access to nutritional services and ending hunger (Federal Democratic Republic of Ethiopia 2016: 50 and 3). Nevertheless, Ethiopia's distribution of resources to reduce malnutrition provides a good example of the skewed impact of anti-poverty programmes observed in other African countries: the beneficiaries of major interventions to reduce malnutrition have been concentrated in selected *woreda*s, but 'Ethiopia's malnutrition rate could likely be substantially reduced by shifting some of the programmes from the *woreda*s with a high concentration of major programs into those with high malnutrition rates but no major programs' (Rajkumar, Gaukler, and Tilahun 2011: 134).

In Ethiopia, the bottom 10 per cent of rural households has actually suffered from declining consumption since 2005—at an annual average rate of close to 2 per cent in real terms robust to the choice of deflator, while inequality as measured by a Theil Index, a measure sensitive to the share of the poorest, increased over the period 2000 to 2011 (World Bank 2015: 12–14). But the flagship anti-poverty intervention, the 'Productive Safety Net Program (PSNP), excludes—by design—at least 52 per cent of vulnerable Ethiopian households' (World Bank 2015: 12 and 49). Econometric evidence suggests that the PSNP has had no effect on household dietary diversity or children's height for age in participating households (Gebrehiwot and Castilla 2017). Perhaps this is because the people benefiting from Ethiopia's PSNP (about one-tenth of Ethiopia's population) were *not* selected by applying simple anthropometric rules or quantitative criteria; in practice, it proved 'both technically and socially difficult to divide beneficiaries from non-beneficiaries' (Sharp, Devereux, and Amare 2003: 21). People have been excluded (graduated) from the PSNP for not supporting the political elite and also because 'the criteria were subjective and no household data existed to support decision making' (Cochrane and Tamiru 2016: 657; Roelen, Devereux, and Kebede 2017: 22).

This type of outcome is predictable whenever local officials beholden to politically appointed leaders are required to distribute scarce resources. The political imperatives underlying resource allocation in rural Ethiopia have been described by Lefort (2012) and have also been illustrated by ethnographic research in seven different *kebele*s, which concludes that the 'social protection programme is being implemented in a way to eliminate opposition and…entrench power of the existing elite' (Cochrane and Tamiru 2016: 655). Research in East Gojjam Zone has also shown that agricultural inputs and extension services have been concentrated on the wealthiest households with the strongest connections to the *kebele* adminstration (Elias et al. 2013: 177).[6] In these rural

[6] Similarly, in Uganda, donor-funded technical reports on 'how to select' the beneficiaries of antipoverty programmes have been brushed aside to pursue 'vote-buying clientelism' (Hickey and Bukenya 2016: 18).

contexts, unreliable self-reported measures of 'food insecurity' and complex multidimensional indicators of poverty may be useful to less scrupulous elite administrators, creating opportunities to ignore errors of inclusion and exclusion in targeting. The rest of this chapter not only argues for a more transparent indicator—the Simple Deprivation Index (SDI)—but also applies this SDI to provide some insights into the lives of the poorest people in Ethiopia.

18.3 The Case for an Sdi

Policymakers who have to deal with an excessive and mystifying array of poverty indicators may find the SDI useful. A bewildering *smörgåsbord* of indices and definitions of poverty has been set out before policymakers in Africa. Apart from household per capita expenditure data, often prescribed as the 'gold standard' for defining poverty and ultra-poverty, the buffet table is also laden with a variety of new, non-monetary indices of poverty: some of these make brave attempts to quantify levels of 'empowered decision-making'.[7] These novel indices may then be used in combination with the increasingly fashionable Multidimensional Poverty Index or other 'mash-up indices' (Ravallion 2012) to report, for example, the percentage of women 'deprived in at least three dimensions' (Beegle et al. 2016: 108). Almost every international agency has begun to publish its own multidimensional index. For example, the International Food Policy Research Institute (IFPRI) publishes the Global Hunger Index, with four arbitrarily weighted components—each derived from unreliable data—to track and rank every nation's progress in decreasing hunger (von Grebmer et al. 2015).

The simple index proposed here is neither a multidimensional nor a comprehensive indicator of the quality of life. It does not include attitudinal responses or measures of deprivation of non-marketed goods, and it certainly could not be used to count the number of 'the poor', to track changes over time, or to be applied by aid bureaucrats at the national level. It cannot be used to rank households in terms of *wealth*, because the selected items included in our simple index are not defined as 'assets', i.e. as investment goods purchased in the hope of generating a flow of income over time. Consequently, these items cannot be aggregated to provide a measure of the total monetary value of the sum of the assets owned by a respondent, or a proxy indicator of wealth.

What this index can do is to focus attention on extreme deprivation. The SDI provides a new type of measure based on a context-specific selection of *the most basic of non-food wage goods*, a very small bundle of consumer goods, each of which can make a huge difference to rural life in certain areas of Ethiopia. The focus here is on private consumption; those goods that may have been provided by the public sector, such as water and

[7] For example, the Relative Autonomy Index (RAI), aims to provide a direct measure of women's motivational autonomy (Vaz, Pratley, and Alkire 2016). Another, less fashionable, index has been proposed to track the quality of governance in public institutions—the Gross Toilet Index (Mahajan 2014).

sanitation, are *not* included in this index. The practical relevance of the SDI is that it allows a quick, reliable and cost-effective way of identifying people who are extremely poor and of assessing the impact of policy interventions.

18.3.1 Constructing the SDI

We begin with a very brief discussion of the method used to analyse the Ethiopian data collected for a research project (the FTEPR) in Ethiopia and Uganda. This project asked questions about a very wide range of the basic consumer goods owned by more than 1,700 rural respondents.[8] Principal Components Analysis (PCA) together with a theoretical argument combined with qualitative fieldwork were used to select a very small number of key consumer durables to be included in the SDI. The selection process clearly distinguishes our work from many other studies because, when discussing the selection of items to be included in indices of socio-economic status, most studies are content to follow conventions established by earlier social scientists, admitting that 'there remains a paucity of underlying theory to support the choice of variables for PCA' (Tusting et al. 2016: 651), and, in making their choices, they do not focus on the most basic of consumer durables as defined in this chapter.

PCA enabled us to derive a short list of consumer goods: thermos, cupboard, metal or wooden bed, table, sofa set, stove or cooker, torch, mattress, bicycle, and radio. These ten items have a particularly high income-elasticity of demand at low levels of income in rural areas. This conclusion was reached after spending many hours in respondents' homes; our fieldwork confirmed that access to these consumer goods would result in an absolute improvement in the quality of rural life. Without reliable access to electricity, a torch makes the night safer; sleeping on earthen floors cannot be compared to sleeping on a bed; a radio can expand intellectual horizons, reduce isolation and even help in searching for casual wage employment. Respondents may also be able to benefit in less obvious ways if they own 'honorific' or 'prestige-based' consumer goods, such as a sofa set (Kaiser, Hruschka, and Hadley 2017: 3).[9]

Our fieldwork made it clear that even the most deprived and poverty-stricken respondents might reasonably expect to benefit from access to at least some of these items. Nonetheless, there were respondents so deprived that, like one particular young woman in rural Ethiopia, they lived in an utterly bare room and had to borrow a rudimentary bench from a neighbour to offer to interviewers.

[8] The wide range of consumer goods examined, as well as details concerning the project's methods, can be examined at: http://ftepr.org/

[9] A ranking of consumer goods—from basics to luxuries—has been used in other research to investigate welfare levels: households in Uganda have to pass above a certain threshold level of income before being able to afford durables from the more expensive categories, such as a sofa, a radio, or a kerosene lamp (Pouw and Elbers 2012: 1367). On the very large expenditure elasticity for furniture in rural Kenya—'beds, chairs, tables, etc.'—see Haushofer and Shapiro (2013: 30).

We also used PCA to construct a weighted index from the ten selected variables. But it was discovered that a simpler, un-weighted index identified *the same* respondents as 'most deprived', i.e. falling into the lowest 20 per cent of the dataset because they own none (or only one or two) of the consumer goods listed.[10] As with all poverty lines, choosing a cut-off point to demarcate the most deprived from the less deprived is arbitrary (Deaton 2006). Here the cut-off is the bottom quintile of the distribution of scores on the SDI.

18.4 Describing Deprivation in Ethiopia

Using the SDI, it is easy to show that the people identified in the research project as 'most deprived' share some characteristics with the poorest rural populations captured by larger surveys designed to estimate household expenditure or wealth including those surveys claiming to be 'representative' of the national populations of Ethiopia. This suggests that SDI results are broadly consistent with the results of much more expensive surveys. But there are three important differences: first, FTEPR respondents appear, on average, to be *more* deprived and vulnerable than respondents covered in many other rural surveys; second, unlike most household expenditure surveys, the SDI does *not* suggest that larger households are more likely to suffer from deprivation, but identifies small and 'female dominated' households as more vulnerable; finally, the SDI shows very clearly how deprivation is linked to different types of employment, something that many other surveys, especially if they do not make determined efforts to capture rural wage workers, cannot do.

The SDI is also used to highlight very large gaps between the experiences of the 'most deprived' and 'less deprived', confirming that inequality is a central feature of rural African life (Jayne et al. 2015). The dramatic contrasts between the most and less deprived (shown in Table 18.1) raise important questions about the processes, dynamics, and trends that could account for the extreme deprivation of Ethiopian adults and children in the bottom quintile. Regressions may help in highlighting some potential determinants, but they may be less helpful in explaining the *causal mechanisms and processes* that lead to a given condition, such as being very deprived, or working for very low wages.[11]

Educational attainment is closely correlated with poverty in sub-Saharan Africa; extremely poor adults (conventionally defined as living in households with per capita

[10] Similarly, research on household material deprivation in Latin America and in rural South Africa has found no significant difference when comparing results based on an asset index weighted using PCA and a simple, un-weighted index (Liu, Esteve, and Treviño 2017; Kabudula et al. 2017).

[11] Oya and Sender (2009) showed the limited ability of logistic regression to explain female vulnerability in rural Mozambique.

Table 18.1 Most deprived and less deprived households: contrasting education, diet, and demography

Education	Percentage among most deprived	Percentage among less deprived
Principal respondent illiterate	63.1%	50.3%
Principal respondent (aged 20–40) no schooling or incomplete primary	76.9%	54.2%
Principal respondent (female) attended secondary school	2.8%	17.3%
HH Roster contains individual who completed secondary school (Ethiopia)	3.8%	6.8%
HH Roster contains child school drop-out (Ethiopia Flowers)	47.8%	33.3%
Regular consumption (consumed 1x or >1x per Week)	**Percentage among most deprived**	**Percentage among less deprived**
A. Beef/meat	7.1%	23.7%
B. Eggs	3.9%	17.0%
C. Milk/yoghurt	8.5%	32.7%
High-value foods (A, B, or C)	13.8%	45.3%
Demography	**Percentage among most deprived**	**Percentage among less deprived**
Female dominated: >75% of adults on HH Roster female (Ethiopia)	8.3%	4.7%
No male support (entire sample)	38.1%	29.8%
No male support (Ethiopia Coffee)	61.5%	42.2%
Larger household size (> 6 members)	20.4%	79.6%
Largest household size (>10 members)	13.3%	32.7%
Smaller household size (<5 members)	16.7%	5.3%
Husband/wife average age gap (Ethiopian Flowers)	11.87 years	7.67 years
Husband/wife average age gap (entire sample)	9.46 years	8.04 years

Note: Pearson Chi Square test suggests that all differences in proportions are significant ($p < 0.001$)
Source: Fairtrade, Employment and Poverty Reduction in Ethiopia and Uganda Dataset (www.ftepr.org).

income/consumption below US$1.90 in PPP terms) are much more likely to have no education than moderately poor adults, who are in turn much more likely to have no education than the non-poor (Castaneda et al. 2016: 21). In Ethiopia, the national Demographic and Health Surveys show that low levels of adult female education are associated with household poverty as measured by a wealth index.[12] A low level of female educational attainment is widely believed to be a useful marker of poverty and of the adverse longer-term consequences of deprivation, because a woman's lack of

[12] STATcompiler, The DHS Program (http://www.statcompiler.com).

education is likely to be transmitted inter-generationally, negatively affecting the health, productivity, and lifetime earnings of her children.[13]

In our survey female respondents were much more likely to be functionally illiterate (62.3 per cent) than male respondents (47.7 per cent), and the SDI consistently predicted differences between the educational attainment of the 'most deprived' and 'less deprived' individuals. The majority of the FTEPR respondents are functionally illiterate, claiming that they *never* read newspapers, emails, text messages, books, or any other written documents; but a higher proportion—63.1 per cent—of those respondents classified by the SDI as 'most deprived' are functionally illiterate, compared to only 50.3 per cent of the 'less deprived' respondents (Table 18.1).

In our survey about 60 per cent of respondents aged between 20 and 40 years did not complete primary school. Again, the SDI identifies the individuals in this prime age group who are *least* likely to have completed primary school: 77 per cent of the 'most deprived' fall into this category, compared to 54 per cent of the 'less deprived' (Table 18.1). The 'less deprived' households were more likely to contain at least one secondary school graduate; and female respondents in the 'less deprived' households were significantly more likely to have attended secondary school. Almost half of the relevant households in the Ethiopian Coffee sample include at least one child who has dropped out of school; the Flower sample provides a good example of the contrast between the proportion of 'most deprived' households with a child school dropout (47.8 per cent) and the proportion of 'less deprived' households with a school dropout (33.3 per cent).

The typical links between parental educational attainment and the nutritional status of children cannot be estimated directly, because the FTEPR survey did not have the resources to collect anthropometric data. However, data on dietary diversity and on the frequency of consumption of different food types may be used as a proxy for nutritional status/vulnerability (Hernández 2012; Herrador et al. 2015; Hirvonen et al. 2017: 305). Our survey asked questions about how frequently different types of food were eaten by anyone in the household, for example if any high-value food item (such as beef, milk/yoghurt, or eggs) was consumed once or more per week. The answers to these questions (Table 18.1) suggest that the SDI is surprisingly useful in predicting dietary diversity (and nutritional status) as well as educational attainment: only 13.8 per cent of the 'most deprived' claimed to eat any high value food items regularly, compared to 45.3 per cent of the 'less deprived'.

There have been many attempts to link deprivation with female-headed households in sub-Saharan Africa and in Latin America, but these typically reach ambiguous conclusions (Milazzo and van de Walle 2015; Liu, Esteve, and Treviño 2017). The FTEPR survey took a different approach to analysing the relationship between the gender composition of households and deprivation; we refused to identify a household 'head' and carefully trained enumerators to look beyond relatives and permanent residents when adding *all*

[13] In rural Ethiopia, it has been argued that an increase in each level of maternal education reduces the relative probability of stunting by almost 20 per cent (Alemayehu Azeze and Huang 2014). See also Ambel et al. (2015: 14).

individuals economically linked to the principal respondent to the household roster.[14] We believed that the 'most deprived' households might contain relatively few adult males, because in rural Ethiopia (and Uganda) women are known to suffer from relatively extreme forms of deprivation and discrimination compared to men (Marshall, Lyytikainen, and Jones 2016; Semahegn and Mengistie 2015).

Households where women account for more than 75 per cent of adults were defined as 'female dominated'; these households are likely to fall into the 'most deprived' category (Table 18.1). Not only were the 'most deprived' households more likely to be female dominated, but also they were more likely to lack regular access to any financial support from an adult male.[15] In the Ethiopian Coffee sample there was a large difference between the proportion of households *without* regular male support falling into the 'most deprived' category (61.5 per cent) compared to the proportion of unsupported households that fell into the 'less deprived' category (42.2 per cent).

Household size has also often been linked to poverty—larger households are usually believed to be more vulnerable to poverty. For example, the national Household Income Expenditure and Consumption Surveys (HIECS) in Ethiopia have been used in an analysis of the correlates of household poverty, concluding that: 'Larger households were more likely to be ultra-poor than smaller households *ceteris paribus*' (Abebaw and Admassie 2014: 127). HIECS surveys are regarded as the World Bank's 'gold standard' for measuring poverty: using these surveys and a poverty line, analysts measure household expenditure *per capita* by dividing survey estimates of household expenditure by the size of the household. If the denominator (i.e. the size of the household) is large, it is not a surprising arithmetic result that the incidence of poverty is higher in larger households: analyses of poverty based on the 'gold standard' surveys usually agree on this result.[16] By contrast, when using the SDI the 'most deprived' household size was considerably *smaller* (mean = 7.35 and median = 7) than the size of the 'less deprived' households (mean = 9.75 and median = 9). Large households with more than 10 members were rare among the 'most deprived', but more common among the 'less deprived' (Table 18.1). National surveys in Ethiopia confirm that household size in the poorer *wealth* (not expenditure) quintiles is *smaller* than in the richer quintiles (Central Statistical Agency and ICF International 2012: author's calculations).

Partly because many of the 'most deprived' households are small with limited access to adult male labour (and to agricultural inputs and credit), they face serious difficulties when attempting to survive through farming on their own account (Siyoum 2012: 50 et seq.). The implication—that their main or most reliable source of income may be seasonal wage labour—is rarely emphasized. It is still widely believed that very few rural

[14] These innovative methodological choices are described in detail in http://ftepr.org/ and in Cramer et al. (2014a).

[15] Access to adult male labour (or to seasonal remittances from male migrants) has been identified as a determinant of lower household deprivation elsewhere in rural Ethiopia (Sharp, Devereux, and Amare 2003: 56).

[16] In Vietnam, results linking poverty with large households have been criticized in detail by Dinh Vu Trang Ngan, Pincus, and Sender (2012).

African households depend on wage labour. The importance of family labour in rural Africa (and the irrelevance of wage labour) is emphasized: 'adult household members contributed at least 90 percent of all labor devoted to crops (including child and hired labor) and 97 percent of all adult labor' (Palacios-Lopez, Christiaensen, and Kilic 2015: 7). This result stems directly and tautologically from the sampling strategy of the World Bank surveys (LSMS-ISA) that underpin these conclusions: these surveys excluded large-scale labour-hiring agricultural enterprises; capitalist farms and estates were *not* included in any of the samples, because they aimed to be representative of 'Agricultural Households' (Lowder et al. 2016). Of course, rural households that do not 'own or cultivate land', i.e. proleterianized or semi-proleterianized rural households, were also excluded. The conclusion that income derived from wage labour only makes a minor contribution to rural household income is reinforced, again tautologically, because analyses of LSMS assume that incomes from remittances or transfers should *not* be considered part of rural households' wage-income stream, i.e. if an Ethiopian household member migrates in a desperate attempt to obtain seasonal agricultural employment and transfers some of her wages to her mother, these remittances should not be classified as contributing to total household *wage* income. Despite these confusing assumptions, almost a quarter of the rural households surveyed in Ethiopia were found to be engaged in agricultural wage labour, and 'poorer rural households tend to have a higher rate of participation in agricultural wage employment... the share of income from agricultural wage labor is more important for poorer households' (Davis, Di Giuseppe, and Zezza 2017: 161 and Table A2).

The households captured in the FTEPR survey are, on average, more deprived (in terms of educational attainment, for instance) than other rural households in Ethiopia.[17] Our survey was specifically designed to ensure that wage labourers were captured: more than two-thirds of respondents in the coffee-growing areas had, during the three years preceding the survey, been employed as manual agricultural wage labourers and, unsurprisingly, they live in households that appear to suffer from more acute deprivation than the average rural household captured in nationally representative surveys. A respondent living in one of the 'most deprived' FTEPR households is particularly likely to have worked as a manual agricultural wage labourer. For example, in the Ethiopian Coffee sample, while about 65 per cent of all respondents had worked as manual agricultural wageworkers, a higher proportion of respondents living in the 'most deprived' households (73 per cent) had done this type of work, compared to the proportion living in 'less deprived' households (58 per cent).

FTEPR investigated the labour market experiences not only of the principal respondent, but also of all the many other people recorded on the Household Roster.

[17] There are other examples of the relative deprivation of respondents in the FTEPR sample compared, for instance, to more 'official' samples in coffee-producing areas in Ethiopia: only about 13 per cent of respondents in the Ferro and Kochere smallholder coffee research sites owned a mobile phone, compared to 53 per cent of coffee growers in the ESSP/IFPRI survey, which over-sampled large farmers (Tamru and Minten 2016: 8). In our other coffee research sites the prevalence of mobile phone ownership was about half the national prevalence in rural Ethiopia as recorded by the contemporaneous Ethiopia Rural Socioeconomic Survey (Central Statistical Agency and the World Bank 2013: 31).

Enumerators provided a qualitative description of the 'the most important single job done in the last year', using the length of time employed to assess importance. These descriptions allowed us to identify two crude categories of job: the 'worst' and the 'less bad'. The worst is a large category covering all the lowest paid and least desirable types of rural wage work, especially manual labour performed in the open air. Other menial jobs in this category include working as a domestic servant for a rural private household(s), and shining shoes. The 'less bad' jobs ranged over many different types of (mainly) non-agricultural wage employment in peri-urban as well as rural areas, including: nursing, teaching, police, supervisory work both in the field and inside processing plants and pack-houses, bricklaying, carpentry, electrical and construction work, mechanics, drivers, hairdressers, cooks, security guards. The two largest groups of workers in this category were 'guards' and construction workers.

Unsurprisingly, in all the research sites female respondents are much less likely than male respondents to have found employment in a 'less bad' job.[18] In the coffee sample only 5 per cent of female respondents had a 'less bad' job, compared to almost 20 per cent of male respondents; and in the flower sample, twice as many male as female respondents had a 'less bad' job. If not a single person listed on the household roster had managed to secure a 'less bad' job, the household was likely to be 'most deprived' according to the SDI. For example, in the Ethiopian Coffee sample a relatively small proportion of the 'most deprived' households (about 14 per cent) included a household member who succeeded in obtaining a 'less bad' job, compared to about 22 per cent of all households. Escapes from poverty are conceivable if at least one household member can obtain decent employment. Unfortunately, if a respondent works as a manual agricultural wage labourer, she is unlikely to live in a household where *anyone* listed on the Household Roster has managed to secure a decent job in the last twelve months. This suggests that the consequences of deprivation can be cumulative; it may never be easy to escape from poverty by building on the success in the labour market of your parents or another household member.[19]

18.5 Conclusion

At extremely low levels of income, deprived rural Africans devote most of their expenditure to low-cost calories. But even when food intake is inadequate and child stunting remains common, they will also attempt to acquire a few non-food consumer goods,

[18] Recent migrants also appear to be excluded from 'less bad' jobs. For example, in those research sites containing the largest numbers of recent migrants (Ziway, Jimma and Mubende) only about 7 per cent of migrants have 'less bad' jobs, compared to about 20 per cent of those who did not migrate to obtain their current job.

[19] In the United States after 1945, a surprisingly similar story of cumulative disadvantage—rooted in a labour market that provided inadequate job opportunities for people with low education—is discussed in Case and Deaton (2017: 29 et seq.).

because owning these basic wage goods makes a real difference to the quality of their lives. It was easy to identify a few basic wage goods that ordinary rural people in a variety of Ethiopian (and Ugandan) rural contexts wanted to own. A small proportion of people in our research sites were defined as the 'most deprived' on the basis that they owned none, or only one or two, of these basic wage goods.

The 'most deprived' people had very low scores on the SDI and were similar to, if a little more desperate than, the bottom quintile of households ranked by per capita expenditure captured by far more expensive and extremely complex survey instruments, such as the LSMS (which asks respondents more than 150 questions about their expenditures on basic goods). The 'most deprived' respondents identified so easily by the SDI were consistently and significantly *more* deprived than other respondents in our own survey in terms of their education and nutrition; the gender composition and size of their households; their vulnerability to domination by much older husbands; their dependence on manual agricultural wage labour; and their limited access to decent jobs.

The SDI might play a progressive role in policymaking designed to reduce poverty. If easily and cheaply collected data expose the fact that current interventions offer few or no benefits to the poorest rural people, then pressures to introduce new policies may intensify, or at least become less easy to ignore. For example, if the SDI makes it increasingly obvious that vulnerable rural women depend on the number of days of wage employment they are offered (and the real daily wage rate), then there is a strong case for a new focus on relevant interventions: for example, a massive increase in expenditure to monitor and publish the real wage rates of poorly educated seasonal workers; and a surge in investments to expand the demand (direct and indirect) for their labour in rural areas. Or, if donors are funding rural co-operatives but the SDI shows that the most deprived people working for or living near these co-operatives have not benefited from these subsidies (Cramer et al. 2014b), then it is possible that some aid agencies may react to adverse publicity by re-examining their policies.

The great advantage of the SDI is the ease and low cost with which it can be constructed. A context-specific SDI can be used for any rural site as an instrument for identifying the most deprived and for assessing the effectiveness of interventions designed to address deprivation. We suggest that such an index may come to be an effective instrument in the governance of anti-poverty policy.

References

Abebaw, Degnet and Assefa Admassie (2014). 'Correlates of Extreme Poverty in Rural Ethiopia', in *Marginality: Addressing the Nexus of Poverty, Exclusion and Ecology*, ed. J. von Braun and F. W. Gatzweiler (Dordrecht: Springer): 117–31.

Alemayehu Azeze, A., and W. Huang (2014). 'Maternal Education, Linkages and Child Nutrition in the Long and Short Run: Evidence from the Ethiopia Demographic and Health Surveys', *International Journal of African Development* 1 (2): 5–28.

Allison, Simon (2013). 'Don't Touch Me on my Statistics—Pali Lehohla Pulls the Plug on UNECA Speaker', *Daily Maverick*, Kenilworth.

Ambel, A. A., C. Andrews, A. M. Bakilana, et al. (2015). 'Maternal and Child Health Inequalities in Ethiopia', Social Protection and Labor Global Practice Group No. 7508, Policy Research Working Paper, World Bank, Washington, DC.

Bachewe, F. N., G. Berhane, B. Minten, and A. S. Taffesse (2016). 'Non-Farm Income and Labor Markets in Rural Ethiopia' Vol. 90, International Food Policy Research Institute, Addis Ababa.

Berhane, G., M. Dereje, J. Hoddinott, et al. (2012). 'Agricultural Growth Program (AGP) of Ethiopia–Baseline Report 2011', International Food Policy Research Institute, Addis Ababa.

Briggs, R. C. (2017). 'Does Foreign Aid Target the Poorest?', *International Organization* 71 (1): 187–206.

Case, A. and A. Deaton (2017). 'Mortality and Morbidity in the 21st Century', Presented at the Brookings Panel on Economic Activity, March 17, Draft Version.

Castaneda Aguilar, Raul Andres, Dung Doan, et al. (2016). 'Who Are the Poor in the Developing World?' Policy Research Working Paper No. 7844, World Bank, Washington, DC.

Carr-Hill, R. (2017). 'Improving Population and Poverty Estimates with Citizen Surveys: Evidence from East Africa', *World Development* 93: 249–59.

Central Statistical Agency [Ethiopia] and ICF International (2012). *Ethiopia Demographic and Health Survey 2011*. Addis Ababa and Calverton, MD: Central Statistical Agency and ICF International.

Central Statistical Agency and World Bank (2013). *Ethiopia Rural Socioeconomic Survey (ERSS) Survey Report*. Addis Ababa.

Cochrane, L. and Y. W. Bekele (2018). 'Average Crop Yield (2001–2017) in Ethiopia: Trends at National, Regional and Zonal Levels', *Data in Brief* 16: 1025–33.

Cochrane, L. and Y. Tamiru (2016). 'Ethiopia's Productive Safety Net Program: Power, Politics and Practice', *Journal of International Development* 28 (5): 649–65.

Cramer, C., D. Johnston, B. Mueller, C. Oya, and J. Sender (2014a). 'How to Do (and How Not to Do) Fieldwork on Fair Trade and Rural Poverty', *Canadian Journal of Development Studies/Revue canadienne d'études du développement*, 35 (1): 170–85.

Cramer, C., D. Johnston, B. Mueller, C. Oya, and J. Sender (2017). 'Fairtrade and Labour Markets in Ethiopia and Uganda', *Journal of Development Studies* 53 (6): 841–56.

Cramer, C., D. Johnston, C. Oya, and J. Sender (2014b). 'Fairtrade Cooperatives in Ethiopia and Uganda: Uncensored', *Review of African Political Economy* 41 (sup1): S115–S127.

Davis, B., S. Di Giuseppe, and A. Zezza (2017). 'Are African Households (Not) Leaving Agriculture? Patterns of Households' Income Sources in Rural Sub-Saharan Africa', *Food Policy* 67: 153–74.

Deaton, A. (2006). 'Measuring Poverty' in *Understanding Poverty*, ed. A. V. Banerjee, R. Benabou, and D. Mookherjee (Oxford: Oxford University Press): 3–15.

Dinh Vu Trang Ngan, Jonathan Pincus, and John Sender (2012). 'Migration, Employment and Child Welfare in Ho Chi Minh City and the Surrounding Provinces', Working Paper No. 2, Fulbright Economics Teaching Program, HCMC, Vietnam. <http://www.fetp.edu.vn/en/working-paper-series/migration-employment-and-child-welfare-in-ho-chi-minh-city-and-the-surrounding-provinces/>

Elias, Asres, Makoto Nohmi, Kumi Yasunobu, and Akira Ishida (2013). 'Effect of Agricultural Extension Program on Smallholders' Farm Productivity: Evidence from Three Peasant Associations in the Highlands of Ethiopia', *Journal of Agricultural Science* 5 (8): 163–81.

Erulkar, Annabel, Girmay Medhin, and Lemi Negeri (2017). 'The Journey of Out-of-School Girls in Ethiopia: Examining Migration, Livelihoods and HIV', Report, Population Council, Addis Ababa.

Federal Democratic Republic Ethiopia (2016). 'National Nutrition Program, 2016–2020', Addis Ababa.

Finn, A., and Vimal Ranchhod, V. (2017). 'Genuine Fakes: The Prevalence and Implications of Data Fabrication in a Large South African Survey', *The World Bank Economic Review* 31 (1): 129–57.

Gebrehiwot, T. and C. Castilla (2017). 'Do Safety Net Transfers Improve Household Diets and Reduce Undernutrition? Evidence from Rural Ethiopia', Working Paper, PEP-Structural Transformation of African Agriculture and Rural Spaces 'STAARS' Project-06.

Giorgi, G. M. (2011). 'Corrado Gini: The Man and the Scientist', *Metron: International Journal of Statistics* 69 (1): 1–28.

Glassman, A. and A. Ezeh (2014). 'Delivering on the Data Revolution in Sub-Saharan Africa', Center for Global Development, Washington, DC.

Gollin, Douglas (2011). 'Crop Production in Ethiopia: Assessing the Evidence for a Green Revolution.' (Mimeo with Rebecca Lee Funk, Irene Scher, and Claire Schlemme). Department of Economics, Williams College and Yale School of Forestry and Environmental Studies.

Habekiristos Beyene (2016). 'Large and Medium Scale Commercial Farms Annual Survey, The Domino Effect of World Bank Intervention, Challenges and Innovative Approaches: The Experience of Ethiopia', Agriculture, Natural Resource and Environment Statistics, CSA, Washington, DC.

Haushofer, J. and J. Shapiro (2013). 'Household Response to Income Changes: Evidence from an Unconditional Cash Transfer Program in Kenya', Working Paper, Poverty Action Lab.

Headey, Derek, Fantu Bachewe Nisrane, Ibrahim Worku, et al. (2012). 'Urban Wage Behavior and Food Price Inflation: The Case of Ethiopia', Ethiopia Strategy Support Program II Working Paper 41, International Food Policy Research Centre (IFPRI), Addis Ababa.

Hernández, Valeria Morúa (2012). 'Are Wealth Indices Good Predictors of Diet Quality? Using Alternative Socio-Economic Measures to Determine Welfare in Ethiopia', MSc development economics dissertation, SOAS, University of London.

Herrador, Z., J. Perez-Formigo, L. Sordo, et al. (2015). 'Low Dietary Diversity and Intake of Animal Source Foods among School-Aged Children in Libo Kemkem and Fogera Districts, Ethiopia', ed. J. van Wouwe *PLOS ONE* 10 (7): e0133435.

Hickey, S. and B. Bukenya (2016). 'The Politics of Promoting Social Cash Transfers in Uganda', ESID Working Paper No. 69, Effective States and Inclusive Development Research Centre, University of Manchester.

Himanshu, and S. Kundu (2016). 'Rural wages in India: Recent trends and determinants', *The Indian Journal of Labour Economics* 59 (2): 217–44.

Himelein, K., S. Eckman, and S. Murray (2014). 'Sampling Nomads: A New Technique for Remote, Hard-to-Reach, and Mobile Populations', *Journal of Official Statistics* 30 (2): 191–213.

Hirvonen, K., J. Hoddinott, B. Minten, and D. Stifel (2017). 'Children's Diets, Nutrition Knowledge, and Access to Markets', *World Development* 95: 303–15.

Hoogeveen, J. and N. T. V. Nguyen (2017). 'Statistics Reform in Africa: Aligning Incentives with Results', *Journal of Development Studies* 1–18. https://doi.org/10.1080/00220388.2017.1417583

Humphries, Jane and Jacob Weisdorf (2016). 'Unreal Wages? A New Empirical Foundation for the Study of Living Standards and Economic Growth in England, 1260–1860', No. 310, Competitive Advantage in the Global Economy (CAGE).

Jayne, T., J. Chamberlin, L. Traub, et al. (2015). 'Africa's Changing Farmland Ownership: Causes and Consequences', Department of Agricultural, Food, and Resource Economics, Michigan State University.

Kabudula, C. W., B. Houle, M. A. Collinson, et al. (2017). 'Assessing Changes in Household Socioeconomic Status in Rural South Africa, 2001–2013: A Distributional Analysis Using Household Asset Indicators', *Social Indicators Research* 133 (3): 1047–73.
Kaiser, Bonnie N., Daniel Hruschka, and Craig Hadley (2017). 'Measuring Material Wealth in Low-Income Settings: A Conceptual and How-to Guide', *American Journal of Human Biology* 29 (4): 1–8.
Langkjær-Bain, R. (2017). 'Trials of a Statistician', *Significance* 14 (4): 14–19.
Lefort, R. (2012). 'Free Market Economy, "Developmental State" and Party-State Hegemony in Ethiopia: The Case of the "Model Farmers"', *Journal of Modern African Studies* 50 (4): 681–706.
Liu, C., A. Esteve, and R. Treviño (2017). 'Female-Headed Households and Living Conditions in Latin America', *World Development* 90: 311–28.
Lowder, Sarah K., Raffaele Bertini, Panagiotos Karfakis, and Andre Croppenstedt (2016). 'Transformation in the Size and Distribution of Farmland Operated by Household and Other Farms in Select Countries of Sub-Saharan Africa', in *2016 AAAE Fifth International Conference, September 23–26*, Addis Ababa: African Association of Agricultural Economists (AAAE).
Lucci, P., T. Bhatkal, and A. Khan (2018). 'Are We Underestimating Urban Poverty?', *World Development* 103: 297–310.
Mahajan, S. (2014). 'The Gross Toilet Index', *Economic and Political Weekly* 49 (12): 74–5.
Marshall, E. P., M. Lyytikainen, and N. Jones (2016). *Child Marriage in Ethiopia* (Addis Ababa and London: UNICEF and ODI).
Merridale, C. (1996). 'The 1937 Census and the Limits of Stalinist Rule', *The Historical Journal* 39 (1): 225.
Milazzo, A. and D. P. van de Walle (2015). 'Women Left Behind? Poverty and Headship in Africa', World Bank Policy Research Working Paper No. 7331.
Multi-Agency Mission (2015). 'Ethiopia National Strategy for the Development of Statistics (2009/10–2014/15) Final Evaluation Report' (No. 26, January–4 February, 2015). www.paris21.org/sites/default/files/Ethiopia_NSDS_Evaluationreport_cover.pdf
Oya, C. and J. Sender (2009). 'Divorced, Separated, and Widowed Women Workers in Rural Mozambique', *Feminist Economics* 15 (2): 1–31.
Palacios-Lopez, A., L. Christiaensen, and T. Kilic (2015). 'How Much of the Labor in African Agriculture is Provided by Women?' Policy Research Working Paper No. 7282, World Bank, Washington, DC.
Pouw, N. and C. Elbers (2012). 'Modelling Priority Patterns in Asset Acquisition: The Case of Smallholder Farmers in Three Rural Districts in Uganda', *Journal of Development Studies* 48 (9): 1360–74.
Rajkumar, A. S., C. Gaukler, and J. Tilahun (2011). 'Combating Malnutrition in Ethiopia: An Evidence-Based Approach for Sustained Results', World Bank, Washington, DC. doi: 10.1596/978-0-8213-8765-8
Ravallion, Martin (2012). 'Mashup Indices of Development', *World Bank Research Observer* 27 (1): 1–32.
Ravallion, Martin (2015). *The Economics of Poverty: History, Measurement, and Policy* (Oxford: Oxford University Press).
Roelen, K., S. Devereux, and D. Kebede (2017). 'Evaluation of the UNICEF Social Cash Transfer Pilot Programme in SNNPR, Ethiopia. Midline Report (Final).' Centre for Social

Protection, Institute of Development Studies, United Kingdom; REBRET Business and Consultancy, Ethiopia.

Semahegn, A. and B. Mengistie (2015). 'Domestic Violence against Women and Associated Factors in Ethiopia: Systematic Review', *Reproductive Health* 12 (1).

Sharp, K., Stephen Devereux, and Yared Amare (2003). 'Destitution in Ethiopia's Northeastern Highlands (Amhara National Regional State), Final Report', Institute of Development Studies and SC-UK Ethiopia.

Siyoum, A. D. (2012). 'Broken Promises: Food Security Interventions and Rural Livelihoods in Ethiopia', PhD thesis, Wageningen University.

Tamru, S. and B. Minten (2016). 'Value Addition and Processing by Farmers in Developing Countries: Evidence from the Coffee Sector in Ethiopia', 2016 AAAE Fifth International Conference, 23–26 September 2016, Addis Ababa, Ethiopia. African Association of Agricultural Economists (AAAE).

Tarekegn, M. M. and N. F. S. Tefera (2016). 'Practices of Informal Resource Recovery from a Solid Waste Stream; Case Study: Addis Ababa, Ethiopia', *International Journal of Scientific & Engineering Research* 7 (9): 1061–8.

Tracy, Abigail (2017). 'How Trump's New Census Nominee Could Rig Future Elections', *Vanity Fair*, 21 September.

Tusting, Lucy, John, Rek, Emmanuel Arinaitwe, et al. (2016). 'Measuring Socioeconomic Inequalities in Relation to Malaria Risk: A Comparison of Metrics in Rural Uganda', *The American Journal of Tropical Medicine and Hygiene* 94 (3): 650–8.

Vaz, A., P. Pratley, and S. Alkire (2016). 'Measuring Women's Autonomy in Chad Using the Relative Autonomy Index', *Feminist Economics* 22 (1): 264–94.

von Grebmer, K., J. Bernstein, A. de Waal, et al. (2015). *2015 Global Hunger Index: Armed Conflict and the Challenge of Hunger* (Washington, DC: International Food Policy Research Institute).

Wildau, Gabriel (2016). 'China's Statistics Chief Admits Some Economic Data Are False', *Financial Times*, 8 December, London.

Wittenberg, Martin (2017). 'Wages and Wage Inequality in South Africa 1994–2011: Part I—Wage Measurement and Trends', *South African Journal of Economics* 85 (2): 279–97.

Woldu, T., G. Abebe, I. Lamoot, and B. Minten (2013). 'Urban Food Retail in Africa: The Case of Addis Ababa, Ethiopia', ESSP Working Paper No. 50, Ethiopian Development Research Institute and International Food Policy Research Institute.

Worku, I. H., M. Dereje, B. Minten, and K. Hirvonen (2017). 'Diet Transformation in Africa: The Case of Ethiopia', *Agricultural Economics* 48 (S1): 73–86.

World Bank (2015). *Ethiopia Poverty Assessment* (No. ACS12005). Poverty Global Practice Africa Region, Washington DC.

PART III

SOCIAL POLICY AND DEVELOPMENT

CHAPTER 19

POVERTY AND INEQUALITY IN ETHIOPIA, 1995/6–2015/16

TASSEW WOLDEHANNA AND
MESELE W. ARAYA

19.1 Introduction

In a marked departure from its historical past as recently as the early 1990s, Ethiopia has been registering strong economic growth and remarkable human development over the past two decades. In particular, the country has shown a rate of economic growth that is higher than that of most African countries, and it overtook Kenya as East Africa's largest economy in 2017 (IMF 2017). With an estimated real GDP growth rate of 8.5 per cent, Ethiopia also became Africa's fastest-growing economy in 2018, beating Ghana, Ivory Coast, Rwanda, and Senegal (IMF 2018). Ethiopia has been following a holistic approach to boosting the economy by designing a series of poverty reduction strategies since the beginning of the 2000s. These include the Sustainable Development and Poverty Reduction Programme (2001/2–2005/6); the Plan for Accelerated and Sustained Development to End Poverty (2005/6–2009/10) and the Growth and Transformation Plan (2010/11–2019/20). The Growth and Transformation Plan features huge public investment in large-scale infrastructure projects, including the Grand Renaissance Dam and a railway network.

The purpose of this chapter is, therefore, to examine whether the growth experienced over the last two decades has been translated into poverty reduction at household level using national representative Household Income Consumption and Expenditure (HICE) surveys conducted in the years 1995/6, 1999/2000, 2004/5, 2010/11, and 2015/16. These high-quality surveys are appropriate for discussion of poverty trends, as the sample size of each survey grew over time in proportion to the population growth of the country. These are also the surveys that have been used as the main official instruments for tracking poverty and informing a series of poverty reduction strategies being designed by Ethiopia's policymaking body (MoFED 2008).

In Section 19.2 we review the country's recent macroeconomic performance, including economic growth trends, per capita GDP change over time, levels of public investment, pro-poor expenditure, and emergency relief aid redistributed in times of economic shocks. The nature of the HICE surveys and the measurement of poverty is then explained. Poverty and inequality trends over time and space (national and regional distribution) are then presented before the concluding remarks.

19.2 Macroeconomic Conditions

19.2.1 Economic Growth

The government of Ethiopia has been implementing a series of poverty-focused development strategies since the beginning of the 2000s. In 2001/2 an economic plan called the Sustainable Development and Poverty Reduction Programme (SDPRP) was introduced. During the early phase of this economic plan, the GDP per capita of the country was very low (US$125) but rose to about US$205 by the end of the economic plan in 2005/6.

Upon completion of the SDPRP, the government adopted the Plan for Accelerated and Sustained Development to End Poverty (PASDEP: 2005/6–2009/10) throughout which the country enjoyed remarkable economic growth rates (World Bank 2013). A growth rate of 11 per cent recorded between 2005 and 2008 was particularly well above the planned target and as the result the per capita GDP of the country further rose to about 373 US$ in 2009/10. The growth achieved during this economic plan was backed by improvements in all three main sectors of the economy, albeit with some degree of variability. The services sector saw very strong growth, with an average rate of 14.6 per cent over 2005/6–2009/10, while growth rates from the industry and agricultural sectors respectively were 10 per cent and 8.4 per cent (MoFED 2010/11).

In 2009/10 with the need to transform the economy structurally to an advanced level, the government introduced a third economic plan, called Growth and Transformation Plan (GTP-I). This ambitious development plan was characterized by huge public investment in infrastructural facilities throughout the country. During this plan the per capita GDP doubled from US$373 in 2009/10 to US$725 in 2014/15. An extension to GTP-II from 2015/16–2019/20 emphasized industrialization and structural transformation of the economy (NPC 2015/16).

Overall, despite the fact that Ethiopia is still among the world's low-income countries, with GDP per capita of US$1,608 in PPP in 2017 and a rank of 164 out of 187 countries (World Bank 2017), its economy has been on an upward trajectory over the past decade or so. The government under GTP-II particularly underlines the importance of a sustainable and green economy and creating a skilled and competitive workforce to accelerate and sustain the economic growth of the country so that it may become a lower-middle income nation by 2025 (World Bank 2013).

19.2.2 Public Expenditure

Ethiopia has been investing heavily in public infrastructure and mega projects such as roads, railways, and power plants in the hope that this investment will help reduce poverty in a sustainable manner. As a result, total public expenditure has increased continuously with an average annual growth rate of 10 per cent between 2007/8 and 2015/16 (Table 19.1). Disaggregating by type of expenditure shows that the capital component is larger than the recurrent component. The difference between the two categories of public expenditure was 2 billion birr in 2007/8, widening in the subsequent periods to reach a maximum value of 19 billion birr in 2012/13. Even though increments in real public expenditure have been observed in absolute terms, its share as a percentage of GDP has been decreasing. It was 19.08 per cent of GDP in 2007/8, reaching its lowest point in 2012/13 with 16.65 per cent. The average total public expenditure-to-GDP ratio was 17.94 per cent which is 1.14 percentage points short of the total expenditure-to-GDP ratio in 2007/8. According to World Bank (2014), the decrease is due to the government's prudent fiscal stance matching the total spending to total revenues and grants. But the decrease did not occur in both expenditure components of GDP. While the average of recurrent expenditures share of GDP decreased to 8.1 per cent from its 9.2 per cent of GDP, the average capital expenditure share of GDP slightly increased to 9.9 per cent from its 9.8 per cent share in 2007/8. The fact that the share of capital expenditures in GDP has increased while that of recurrent expenditure has decreased is due to the government's reorientation of expenditure from recurrent to capital spending in order to finance social and infrastructural developments (World Bank 2014).

19.2.3 Pro-poor Expenditure, Productive Safety Net, and Emergency Relief Aid

In addition to the huge public capital investment on social infrastructure and mega projects, Ethiopia has also been allocating a significant amount of funds to pro-poor sectors over recent years. Table 19.2 presents pro-poor expenditure in five sectors: education, health, agriculture, roads, and water. It appears that the share of the five pro-poor sectors in GDP rose from 10.9 per cent in 2008/9 to 12.1 per cent in 2015/16. In absolute real terms this pro-poor spending amounts to 97.1 billion birr or 65.7 per cent of total public expenditure in 2015/16. The share of pro-poor spending was as high as 70.4 per cent in 2011/12. Such a high pro-poor share in terms of both GDP share and total government spending serves to demonstrate the government's commitment to lifting millions out of absolute poverty during the Growth and Transformation Plans.

Table 19.1 Public expenditure, revenue, and GDP between 2007/8 and 2015/16

	2007/8	2008/9	2009/10	2010/11	2011/12	2012/13	2013/14	2014/15	2015/16	Average	Average growth
Total public expenditure	70.92	70.41	87.23	93.90	92.70	110.00	123.6	136.3	148.62	103.74	9.98
Recurrent expenditure	34.48	33.13	39.05	40.70	38.30	44.79	52.07	64.97	72.33	46.65	10.20
Capital expenditure	36.44	37.28	48.18	53.30	54.40	65.21	71.60	71.33	76.30	57.12	10.06
Total public expenditure (% GDP)	19.08	17.41	19.15	18.23	16.65	17.76	17.49	17.33	18.38	17.94	
Recurrent (% GDP)	9.27	8.19	8.57	7.90	6.88	7.23	7.36	8.26	8.95	8.07	
Capital (% GDP)	9.80	9.22	10.58	10.35	9.77	10.53	10.12	9.07	9.44	9.88	
Total government revenue	60.03	66.51	79.54	85.60	86.22	98.00	105.4	120.9	129.52	92.42	10.22
Revenue	45.06	48.97	64.76	69.10	76.68	88.64	97.47	113.1	122.65	80.71	13.58
Tax revenue	35.99	35.33	52.03	59.00	63.86	76.43	88.73	100.2	100.79	68.04	14.55
o/w: capital gains tax	0.05	0.02	0.05	0.04	0.07	0.07	0.08	0.12	0.12	0.07	26.16
Non-tax revenue	9.07	13.64	12.62	10.10	12.74	12.21	8.73	12.91	21.85	12.65	16.69
Grants	14.97	17.66	14.90	16.50	9.54	9.36	7.93	7.88	6.88	11.74	-7.45
Real GDP	371.7	404.5	455.5	515.08	556.9	619.23	707.2	786.6	808.49	580.59	10.26
Total government revenue (% GDP)	16.15	16.44	17.46	16.62	15.48	15.83	14.90	15.38	16.02	16.03	
Tax revenue (% GDP)	9.68	8.73	11.42	11.45	11.47	12.34	12.55	12.74	12.47	11.43	
Non-tax revenue (% GDP)	2.44	3.37	2.77	1.96	2.29	1.97	1.23	1.64	2.70	2.26	
Grant revenue (% GDP)	4.03	4.37	3.27	3.20	1.71	1.51	1.12	1.00	0.85	2.34	

Source: Computed based on MoFEC (2016/17).

Table 19.2 Total real poverty-targeted expenditure at 2010/11 prices

Real expenditure	2008/9	2009/10	2010/11	2011/12	2012/13	2013/14	2014/15	2015/16
Education	15.5	20.7	23.4	22.2	24.7	26.6	32.2	35.7
Health	4.7	5.6	6.3	5.7	8.1	8.5	10.7	11.5
Agriculture	9.1	8.4	8.3	8.2	10.5	11.1	10.7	16.5
Roads	11.9	16.8	18.5	21.5	24.6	24.1	24.9	22.1
Water	2.8	5.9	5.9	7.6	9.0	8.9	8.7	11.3
Total	44.1	57.4	62.4	65.3	77.0	79.2	87.3	97.1
Total public expenditure	70.4	87.2	93.9	92.7	110.0	115.9	132.3	147.8
Share of pro-poor expenditure (%)	62.7	65.8	66.5	70.4	70.0	68.4	66.0	65.7
Share of pro-poor in GDP (%)	10.9	12.6	12.3	11.9	12.4	12.0	11.4	12.1
Total public expense in GDP (%)	17.4	19.1	18.6	16.9	17.8	17.5	17.3	18.4

Source: MoFEC (2016/17).

Besides the sizeable pro-poor public investment, Ethiopia has also been heavily involved with emergency relief aid and Productive Safety Net expenses to provide support to households and individuals in situations adversely affecting their welfare. Figure 19.1 shows the trends in the number of public work and direct (unconditional) recipients of the rural Productive Safety Net (hereafter called RPSNP) programmes between 2004/5 and 2016/17. The number of direct RPSNP recipients is close to one million and it varies very little. The number of public work beneficiaries, on the other hand, is much larger, at about 4 million in 2004/5, increasing to 6 million in 2005/6 and slightly more until 2011/12. The number of public work beneficiaries decreased after 2011/12, reaching its lowest level in 2014/15 at about 4 million beneficiaries, though it increased again after 2014/15 after the El Niño-driven drought that hit many parts of the country.

Expenditure on the several emergency relief programmes from 2009/10 to 2016/17 are presented in Table 19.3. Emergency assistance includes food, targeted supplementary feeding especially to infants and pregnant women, health and nutrition, water and sanitation services, agriculture and livestock services, school feeding, protection, and emergency shelter (when there are displacements during natural and man-made disasters). The total expenditure increased from 9.3 billion to 9.7 billion birr between 2009/10 and 2010/11. It reached its highest level at over 13.1 billion in 2015/16 and over 16.8 billion birr in 2016/17 due to the rapid increase in emergency relief recipients following the severe drought of 2015/16. Of the various components of emergency relief expenditure, food assistance accounts for the major share with an average annual share of over 78 per cent between 2009/10 and 2016/17 followed by health and nutrition support and targeted supplementary feeding (Table 19.3).

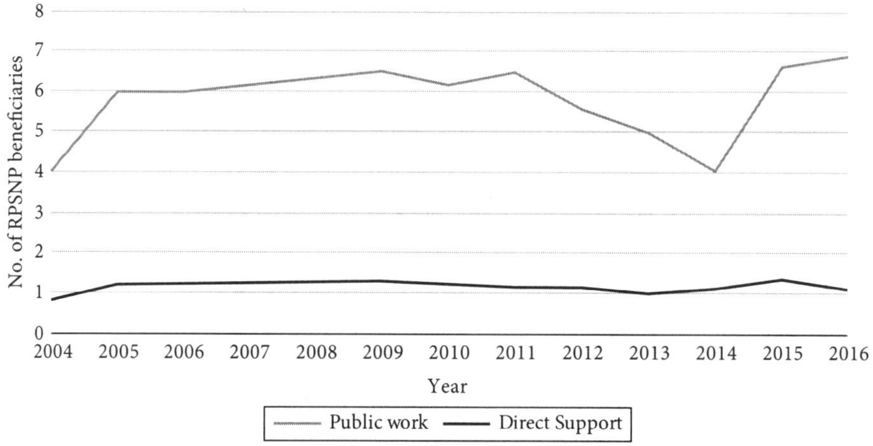

FIGURE 19.1 Number of RPSNP beneficiaries between 2004/5 and 2016/17

Source: Computed based on MoANRS (2017).

Table 19.3 Expenditure on emergency relief programmes by donors and federal government

Type of assistance	2009/10	2010/11	2011/12	2012/13	2013/14	2014/15	2015/16	2016/17
Food	7,937.36	7,886.60	3,697.57	3,398.66	4,912.21	3,943.41	10,194.5	15,126.3
TSF (targeted supplementary feeding)	793.42	854.24	588.43	182.58	414.14	276.57	274.62	0.00
Health and nutrition	375.45	516.37	362.38	322.71	311.59	451.69	1,225.52	757.61
Water and sanitation	95.82	270.13	251.57	243.31	158.26	309.77	655.81	430.74
Agriculture and live stock	148.05	170.95	102.18	210.80	163.74	191.32	543.3	271.71
School feeding	0.00	65.14	53.76	68.13	66.66	33.10	120.27	98.00
Protection	0.00	0.00	0.00	0.00	0.00	0.00	66.44	69.83
Emergency shelter (IDPS)	0.00	0.00	0.00	0.00	0.00	0.00	45.79	48.12
Total emergency relief expenditure	9,350.10	9,763.43	5,055.88	4,426.20	6,026.61	5,205.86	13,126.3	16,802.4
Contributions by GoE to NDRMC							1,136.17	4,107.25
% GoE contribution in total emergency relief expenditure through NDRMC							8.66	24.44

Source: MoFEC (2016/17).

19.3 Data, Measurement, and Method

19.3.1 Data

This study makes use of data from a national representative Households, Income, and Consumption Expenditure Survey (HICE) conducted by the Central Statistical Agency (CSA) every five years since 1995/6. Using consumption expenditure as proxy to income, the survey provides empirical evidence to assess poverty situations and to analyse changes in the households' living standard over time. It monitors and evaluates impact of socio-economic policies and programmes on welfare and is also an important source of information for establishing databases from which household accounts in the System of National Accounts (SNA) are compiled, and for construction and/or rebasing of consumer price indices in the country (NPC 2010/11).

The surveys covered all regions of Ethiopia. In each round a stratified random sampling technique was used to draw a representative sample. The country was first stratified into nine regional states and two city administrations; and each regional state was further stratified into rural and urban areas except Addis Ababa which has only the urban category, but a sub-city. So far the HICS survey has been conducted five times—in the years 1995/6, 1999/2000, 2004/5, 2010/11, and 2015/16. In keeping with the annual population growth rate of the country, the household sample size grew from 12,342 in 1995/6 to 30,229 in 2015/16 (Table 19.4).

19.3.2 Method for Measuring and Aggregating Poverty

Poverty in this study is measured by household consumption expenditure. Consumption is conventionally viewed as a preferred welfare indicator, for practical reasons of reliability and because it is thought to better capture long-run welfare levels than current income (Ravallion 1996, 1998; World Bank 2000). This is particularly true in developing countries like Ethiopia where income is so erratic and seasonal that it may be very difficult for respondents to recall, although there is still widespread argument in the literature that recalled food expenditure data is also believed to suffer from considerable measurement errors compared to diary records (see Brzozowski, Crossley, and Winter 2017). In this

Table 19.4 Trends in households' sample size of HICE survey in Ethiopia

Year	1995/6	1999/2000	2004/5	2010/11	2015/16
Sample size	12,342	17,332	21,596	27,830	30,229

Source: HICES 1995/6, 1999/2000, 2004/5, 2010/11, and 2015/16.

way, to be an indicator of household's welfare, consumption has to be adjusted for difference in the calorie requirements of different household members (for age and gender of adult members). The adjustment can be made by dividing real household consumption expenditure by an adult equivalent scale that depends on the nutritional requirement of each family member, so that it will be different for different age groups and according to the gender of adult members (Deaton and Zaidi 2002).

Establishing poverty lines is the first task when analysing trends in poverty and inequality. The most widely used method of estimating the poverty line is the 'cost of basic needs' method, because the indicators will be more representative and the threshold will be consistent with real expenditure across time, space, and groups. The food poverty line is first defined by choosing a bundle of food items typically consumed by the poor. The quantity of the bundle is determined in such a way that the bundle supplies the predetermined level of minimum calorific requirement (2,200 kilocalories). This bundle is valued at local prices or at national average prices if the objective is to get a consistent poverty line across regions and groups. A specific allowance for non-food goods consistent with the spending of the poor is then added to the food poverty line. To account for the non-food expenditure, the food poverty line is divided by the food share of the poorest quartile or quintile.

Based on the cost of 2,200 kcal per day per-adult food consumption with an allowance for essential non-food items, a poverty line is established for each survey year. The absolute poverty line was set at 1,075 birr at national average prices for 1995/6; 1999/2000 and 2004/5; and at 3,781 birr for 2010/11. The 2015/16 national poverty line was similarly set by applying the GDP deflator to the poverty line figures set for the other years. In this manner, the absolute poverty line for 2015/16 is 7,184 birr per year per adult person (Table 19.5).

Setting the poverty lines this way, we used the Foster, Greer, and Thorbecke (1984) class of poverty measures to aggregate poverty in which the real per-adult (per capita) household expenditure, Y_i, is ranked as:

$$Y_1 \leq Y_2 \leq ....Y_q \leq Z <_{q+1} .... \leq Y_n,$$

where Z is poverty line, n is the total population, and q is the number of poor, then $P\alpha$ is given by:

Table 19.5 Total (absolute) poverty lines in calories and birr

	1995/6	2010/11	2015/16
Kilocalorie per day per adult	2,200	2,200	2,200
Food poverty line (birr)	648	1,985	3,772
Absolute poverty line (birr)	1,075	3,781	7,184

Source: Computed using HICE survey 1995/6, 2010/11, and 2015/16 and MoFEC (2015).

$$P_\alpha = \frac{1}{N}\sum_{i=1}^{q}\left(\frac{Z-Y_i}{Z}\right)^\alpha ; \alpha \geq 0, \text{ for } Y< Z.$$

Here the parameter α reflects the policymaker's degree of aversion to inequality among the poor. If $\alpha = 0$, there is no concern about the depth of poverty and the corresponding poverty index is called the *headcount index* (P_0). Hence P_0 corresponds to the fraction of individuals falling below the poverty line. The headcount index is easily understood and communicated, but it is insensitive to differences in the depth of poverty. If $\alpha = 1$, the poverty index is called the *poverty gap index* (P_1) and it measures the aggregate poverty deficit of the poor relative to the poverty line. This index is generally interpreted as an indicator of the potential for eliminating poverty by targeting transfers to the poor. The minimum cost of eliminating poverty using targeted transfer is the sum of all poverty gaps in a population: $(Z-\bar{Y}_0)\times q$. The drawback of this measure is that it does not capture the differences in the severity of poverty among the poor. That is, it does not capture the transfer of income among the poor. If income is transferred from the poor to the least poor, the poverty gap index will be unaffected. When $\alpha > 1$, the P_α calculation gives more weight to the average income shortfall of the poorest of the poor. Thus P_2 (where $\alpha = 2$) measures the squared proportional shortfalls from the poverty line, which is commonly known as an index of the severity of poverty. The measures of depth and severity of poverty are important complements of the incidence of poverty. It might be the case that some groups have a high poverty incidence but low poverty gap (when numerous members are just below the poverty line), while other groups have a low poverty incidence but a high poverty gap for those who are poor (when relatively few members are below the poverty line but with extremely low levels of consumption or income). With this in mind, this chapter uses all three poverty indices in an effort to examine the nature of poverty over time.

19.3.3. Growth–Inequality Poverty Decomposition

The incidence of poverty can be affected by economic growth as well as by the relative size distribution of wealth (Datt and Ravallion 1992; Kakwani and Subbarao 1990; Jain and Tendulkar 1990). In this way the change in headcount poverty over two periods is decomposed into growth and redistribution components. While the growth component represents the change in headcount poverty attributable to changes in mean consumption expenditure (holding the distribution of the base year constant), the redistribution component represents the change in headcount poverty attributable to changes in the distribution, holding the mean consumption expenditure constant (see Datt and Ravallion 1992).

Put it differently, let us define P_t as the rate of poverty incidence at time t; μ_t as mean consumption at time t; z as the poverty line; and π_t as the parameters of the inequality at time t. For time periods 1 and 2, headcount poverty can be written as

$P\left(\frac{\mu_1}{z}, \pi_1\right)$ and $P\left(\frac{\mu_2}{z}, \pi_2\right)$, respectively. If the inequality is unchanged over time, then $\pi_1 = \pi_2$ and therefore a change in poverty is a function solely of the change in mean consumption, $\left(\frac{\mu_1}{z} - \frac{\mu_2}{z}\right)$. It is however true that both mean consumption and inequality can change at the same time. Let P_{11} equals $P\left(\frac{\mu_1}{z}, \pi_1\right)$; i.e. the first subscript refers to the time period in which we measure average consumption, and the second refers to the time period in which we measure the inequality. Given that the interest is in determining the relative roles of changes in growth and inequality in the change in poverty, this could be written as:

$$P_{22} - P_{11} = P\left(\frac{\mu_2}{z}, \pi_2\right) - P\left(\frac{\mu_1}{z}, \pi_1\right)$$

The term on the right hand side represents the change in poverty brought about by the change in mean consumption between periods 1 and 2, holding inequality constant at period 1, while the second term shows the change in poverty resulting from changes in inequality with consumption remaining constant at period 1. The problem with this equation is that if we change the base year, we would most likely get a slightly different result. So, the usual way of resolving this is to take a simple average of the two 'base' period calculations:

$$P_{22} - P_{11} = \left[(P_{21} - P_{11}) + (P_{22} - P_{21})\right]/2 + \left[(P_{22} - P_{12}) + (P_{12} - P_{11})\right]/2$$

19.4 Results

19.4.1 Poverty and Welfare Trends

Table 19.6 reports the trends of national absolute poverty and average welfare in Ethiopia for the years 1995/6, 1999/2000, 2004/5, 2010/11, and 2015/16. It appears that, on average, real per-adult total consumption expenditure rose substantially from 7,885 birr in 1995/6 (at 2015/16 prices) to 10,777 birr in 2010/11 (at 2015/16 prices); and further to about 12,391 birr in 2015/16 (at 2016 prices). The increase in average welfare is also evidenced by substantial poverty reduction over the same time.

As there have been dynamic changes in the Ethiopian economy over the last decade and a half, the national absolute poverty lines vary in each of the five survey years. Each poverty line was set by applying the GDP deflator provided by the Ministry of Finance and Economic Cooperation (MoFEC). Using this inflation information, the poverty line was set at 1,075 birr for the years 1995/6, 1999/2000, and 2004/5 per-adult equivalent per year at 1995 prices; at 3,781 birr per-adult equivalent per year at 2011 prices and at 7,184 birr per-adult equivalent per year at 2016 prices.

Table 19.6 Trends in national poverty and average welfare

	Average real per-adult total consumption expenditure at 2015/16 constant prices (birr)	Headcount index	Poverty gap index	Poverty severity index
1995/6	7,885	45.5	12.9	5.1
1999/2000	8,054	44.2	11.9	4.5
2004/5	8,972	38.7	8.3	2.7
2010/11	10,777	29.6	7.8	3.1
2015/16	12,391	23.5	6.7	2.8

Source: Computed from HICE survey of 1995/6, 1999/2000, 2004/5, 2010/11, and 2015/16.

The percentage of Ethiopians living under this line fell from almost one in every two Ethiopians (45.5 per cent) in 1995/6 to less than one in every four (23.5 per cent) in 2015/16. The decline in poverty incidence has been particularly evident since 2004/5, with the 2010/11 incidence of poverty 9.1 percentage points lower than the index for 2004/5. A similar pattern occurs when we look at the poverty gap, which declined from 13 per cent in 1995/6 to about 7 per cent in 2015/16. However, despite the overall poverty decline as measured by the headcount and poverty gap ratio over 1995/6–2015/16, there was no continuous decline in the squared poverty gap. In fact, this poverty severity declined from 5.1 per cent in 1995/6 to 2.7 per cent in 2004/5, but rose again to 3 per cent in 2010/11. The increase in poverty severity index over this time shows that households who were poorer in 2004/5 became much poorer in 2010/11, perhaps as they were much further from the poverty lines and did not equally benefit from economic gains, though there seem to be some improvements in the last survey, with poverty severity declining to 2.8 per cent in 2015/16.

In terms of rural and urban areas, urban household real per-adult total consumption expenditure appears to be higher than for rural households throughout the five surveys, which may imply clear differences in the amount of welfare. In other words, the level of urban poverty is lower than rural poverty. In line with the national level both rural and urban poverty substantially declined over time, but with the rate of decline differed between the survey times (Table 19.7). Over 2010/11–2015/16 the decline in urban poverty indices (incidence by 42 per cent, depth by 47 per cent, and severity by 47 per cent) was generally much higher than rural poverty, while the opposite was the case over 2004/5–2010/11 (in which the decline of rural poverty indices exceeded the decline of urban poverty). Although the percentage fall in rural poverty indices are small compared to urban poverty, all measures of rural poverty also declined: the 2015/16 rural poverty headcount, poverty gap, and severity are lower than those of 2010/11 by 16 per cent, 7 per cent, and 3 per cent, respectively. The decline in rural poverty can also be explained by the pro-poor programmes in place, including extension of improved agricultural technologies and farming practices, commercialization of smallholder farming agriculture, rural infrastructural development, and a range of food security programmes

Table 19.7 **Trends in rural/urban poverty and average welfare**

	Rural				Urban			
	Average real per-adult total consumption expenditure at 2015/16 constant prices (birr)	Head count index	Poverty gap index	Poverty severity index	Average real per-adult total consumption expenditure at 2015/16 constant prices (birr)	Head count index	Poverty gap index	Poverty severity index
1995/6	7,516	47.5	13.4	5.3	10,152	33.2	9.9	4.1
1999/2000	7,731	45.4	12.2	4.6	10,119	36.9	10.1	3.9
2004/5	8,364	39.3	8.5	2.7	12,656	35.1	7.7	2.6
2010/11	9,454	30.4	8	3.2	17,434	25.7	6.9	2.7
2015/16	10,946	25.6	7.4	3.1	18,518	14.8	3.7	1.4

Source: Computed from HICE survey of 1995/6, 1999/2C00, 2004/5, 2010/11, and 2015/16.

(Productive Safety Net Programs, provision of credit, etc.) and emergency aid during the drought years as illustrated in Table 19.3.

19.4.2 Regional Poverty Trends

Looking at the regional poverty situation may contribute further insights to the design and implementation of more equitable development policy across regional states. Although there is evidence that poverty has declined over the years, the estimated level of poverty and the rate of poverty decline vary considerably across regions. In 2015/16, the poverty headcount index was the highest in Tigray (27 per cent) followed by Benshangul Gumuz (26.5 per cent) and Amhara (26.1 per cent), while Harari (7 per cent), Dire Dawa (15.4 per cent), and Addis Ababa (16.8 per cent) experienced much lower poverty incidence than the national average of 23.5 per cent. The difference in poverty incidence among the regional states in 2015/16 has narrowed substantially compared with the first four surveys, indicating balanced growth among regional states. Poverty reduction has also been more rapid in regions where poverty was higher a decade and a half ago such as Tigray, Afar, and Benshangul Gumuz, where more than half of the population in each region was living in poverty in 1990/2000. The reason for this convergence is the fact that poverty is still geographic in nature, but it is geographical characteristics such as remoteness rather than regional location that strongly correlates with poverty (for geographic poverty traps, see Jalan and Ravallion 2002; Bird et al. 2002).

All in all, despite severe economic shocks such as drought and inflation over recent years, a marked regional poverty reduction is recorded across all regional states (see Table 19.8). This suggests that much has been done in Ethiopia to protect vulnerable section of society from economic shocks through various means such as Productive Safety Net Program (PSNP), emergency relief aid, and the increasing resilience that comes from broad-based economic growth. By way of example, the Productive Safety Net Program (PSNP) in Ethiopia has helped 1.5 million people move out of poverty since 2005 (World Bank 2014).

19.4.3 Inequality

The trends in consumption inequality as measured by the Gini coefficient over the period 1995/6–2015/16 are reported in Table 19.9. Despite the decline in all measures of national poverty (incidence, depth, and severity), inequality at national level appeared to increase over time. The Gini coefficient inequality at national level was about 0.29 in 1995/6, rising to 0.3 in 2010/11 and to 0.33 in 2015/16, indicating there is relatively less shift of economic gains from higher income households to lower income households. The ever-increasing national inequality over time warrants further attention as rising inequality of this kind could result in the rolling back of poverty reduction.

Table 19.8 Trends in regional poverty headcount indices

	1999/2000			2004/5			2010/11			2015/16		
Region	Rural	Urban	Total	Rural	Urban	Total	Rural	Urban	Total	Rural	Urban	Total
Tigray	61.6	60.7	61.4	51	36.7	48.5	36.5	13.7	31.8	31.1	14.2	27.0
Afar	68	26.8	56	42.9	27.9	36.6	41.1	23.7	36.1	26.5	10.6	23.6
Amhara	42.9	31.1	41.8	40.4	37.8	40.1	30.7	29.2	30.5	28.8	11.6	26.1
Oromia	40.4	35.9	39.9	37.2	34.6	37	29.3	24.8	28.7	25.3	15.3	23.9
Somali	44.1	26.1	37.9	45.2	35.3	41.9	35.1	23.1	32.8	22.3	22.9	22.4
B.G	55.8	28.9	54	45.8	34.5	44.5	30.1	21.3	28.9	28.7	17.7	26.5
SNNP	51.7	40.2	50.9	38.2	38.3	38.2	30	25.8	29.6	21.9	14.4	20.7
Gamb.	54.6	38.4	50.5	–	–	–	32.5	30.7	32	26.4	16.6	23.0
Harari	14.9	35	25.8	20.6	32.6	27	10.5	11.7	11.1	8.5	6.0	7.1
AA	27.1	36.2	36.1	29.9	32.6	32.5	–	28.1	28.1	–	16.8	16.8
DD	33.2	33.1	33.1	39.8	32.9	35.2	14.2	34.9	28.3	23.3	11.1	15.4
Total	45.4	36.9	44.2	39.3	35.1	38.7	30.4	25.7	29.6	25.6	14.8	23.5

Source: Computed from HICE surveys of 1995/6, 1999/2000, 2004/5, 2010/11, and 2015/16.

Table 19.9 Trends in national, rural, and urban Gini coefficients

	1995/6	1999/2000	2004/5	2010/11	2015/16
National	0.29	0.28	0.30	0.30	0.33
Rural	0.27	0.26	0.26	0.27	0.28
Urban	0.34	0.38	0.44	0.37	0.38

Source: Computed from HICE surveys of 1995/6, 1999/2000, 2004/5, 2010/11, and 2015/16.

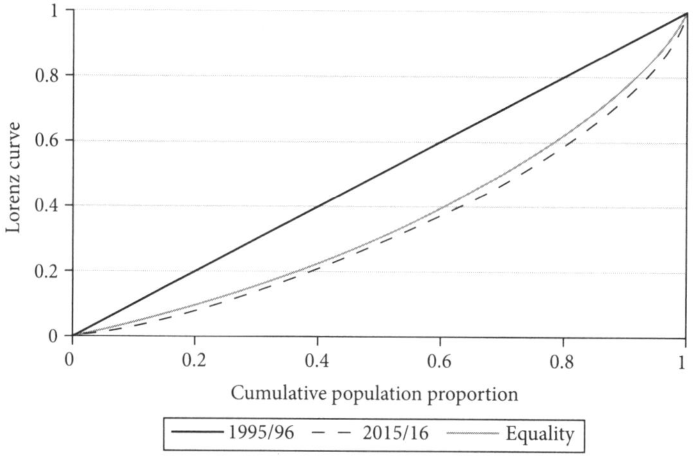

FIGURE 19.2 Lorenz curve for national consumption over time, 1995/6–2015/16

Source: CSA, 'Household Income, Consumption, and Expenditure Survey Report' (2017).

Inequality is much worse in urban areas, where it stood above the national average throughout the HICE surveys from 1995/6 to 2015/16. In 2010/11 the Gini coefficient was 0.37 in urban areas, increasing to 0.38 in 2015/16, while it was respectively 0.27 and 0.28 in rural areas over the same period. In fact, urban inequality reached historically high levels in 2004/5 with a Gini coefficient of 0.44, up from 0.34 in 1995/6, so the rise in inequality between 2010/11 and 2015/16 is marginal relative to the increase seen from 1995/6 to 2004/5 (see Figures 19.2 and 19.3).

We also decomposed the Gini coefficient inequality into two by rural versus urban or among regions (Table 19.10). The total within-group inequality from the rural and urban area indicates that the coefficient slightly declined from 20 per cent in 1995/6 to 18.5 per cent, while the between-group inequality increased from 4.1 per cent in 1995/6 to 9.4 per cent in 2015/16. The increase in between-group inequality suggests that rural–urban society is becoming polarized in terms of welfare. The overlap term for rural and urban areas remained flat between 1995/6 and 2004/5 at 4.8 per cent, rising to 6 per cent in 2010/11 but declining again to 5 per cent by the latest survey. The decomposition by geographic region, however, seems to have a slightly different pattern. While within-group inequality did not show significant variation over time and stood at about 7.5 per cent,

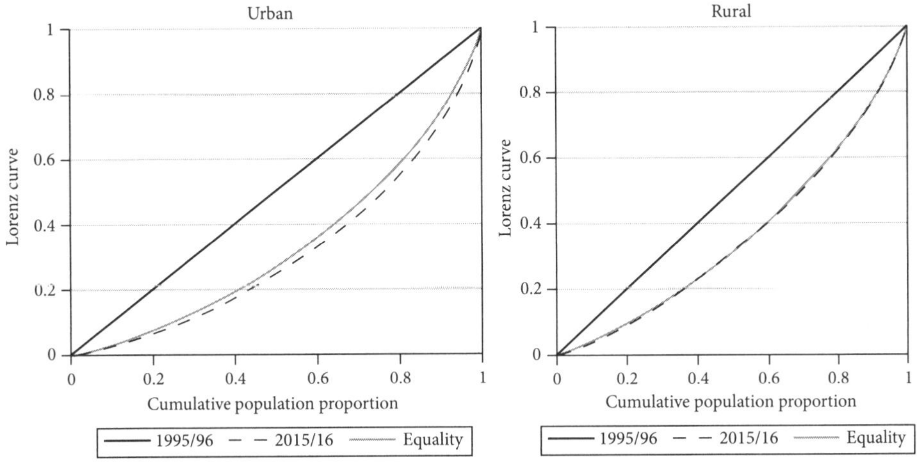

FIGURE 19.3 Lorenz curve for consumption over time by area, 1995/6–2015/16

Source: CSA, 'Household Income, Consumption, and Expenditure Survey Report' (1995/6–2015/16).

Table 19.10 Geographic breakdown of Gini coefficient

	1995/6	1999/2000	2004/5	2010/11	2015/16
Urban/rural					
Within-group inequality	20.0	19.3	19.0	19.4	18.5
Between-group inequality	4.1	4.3	6.6	4.4	9.4
Overlap	4.8	4.8	4.8	6.0	4.9
Region					
Within-group inequality	7.5	7.1	7.5	7.7	7.6
Between-group inequality	7.4	4.8	5.3	1.6	3.6
Overlap	14.0	16.4	17.6	20.5	21.6

Source: Computed from HICE surveys of 1995/6, 1999/2000, 2004/5, 2010/11, and 2015/16.

the between-group inequality significantly declined from 7.4 per cent in 1995/6 to 3.6 per cent in 2015/16. The continuous decline in between-group inequality may be a sign of the economic convergence of the regions. The overlap term for regional geography registers a significant increase over time from 14 per cent to 22 per cent. The overlap term is much larger for the decomposition across the geographic regions than across rural and urban areas. This could be because the probability of overlap increases when the number of groups increases (Foster et al. 2013).

19.4.4 Growth–Inequality Poverty Decomposition

To examine the factors that contributed most to the decrease of poverty over time, we decompose poverty change into growth and inequality components over 2010/11–2015/16;

Table 19.11 Growth and redistribution decomposition of poverty changes

	20010/11–2015/16				
	Headcount poverty ratio 2010/11	Headcount poverty ratio 2015/16	Total percentage change in poverty	Growth Component	Redistribution component
All households	0.296	0.235	-0.061	-0.087	0.027
Rural households	0.304	0.256	-0.048	-0.045	-0.003
Urban households	0.257	0.148	-0.108	-0.132	0.024
	1995/6–2015/16				
	Headcount poverty ratio 1995/6	Headcount poverty ratio 2015/16	Total change in poverty	Growth Component	Redistribution component
All households	0.455	0.235	-0.219	-0.361	0.142
Rural households	0.475	0.256	-0.219	-0.307	0.088
Urban households	0.332	0.148	-0.183	-0.294	0.110

Source: Computed from HICE survey of 1995/6, 1999/2000, 2004/5, 2010/11 and 2015/16.

and 1995/6–2015/16. Table 19.11 reports the results of the basic growth-inequality decomposition analysis. The results indicate that poverty substantially declined across all periods of the study. The headcount poverty index fell by 6 percentage points from 2010/11 to 2015/16, and by 22 percentage points over 1995/6–2015/16. If we have a close look at the growth and redistribution components of the decomposition process, it appears that growth has played a more important role than redistribution in achieving the change in poverty. The redistribution component is positive for all poverty measures, suggesting that overall inequality has been on the rise and is undermining the contribution of economic growth to poverty reduction. For example, over the period 2010/11–2015/16, if inequality had remained constant as observed in 2010/11, the headcount index would have decreased by 9 percentage points in 2015/16. On the opposite side, if average consumption had remained constant as observed in 2010/11, the rise in inequality would have increased poverty by 3 percentage points. That is, a rise in inequality offsets gains from the reduction of headcount poverty. According to this, in our case, as the growth component of the decomposition (9 percentage points) exceeds the redistribution component (3 percentage points) in absolute value, the marginal effect was a decline of the poverty rate by 6 percentage points over 2010/11–2015/16. This means that the decrease in poverty observed over the period is entirely due to high positive growth. The same is also true during 1995/6–2015/16, where growth accounted for the reduction in poverty while changes in distribution drown out the growth of mean consumption.

19.4.5 Elasticity of FGT Family Indices

In addition to the growth–inequality decomposition discussed earlier, it is important to explain the decomposition process using an elasticity approach. Elasticity of poverty in this case refers to the percentage change in poverty resulting from a 1 per cent change in the average real per-adult total consumption expenditure. This approach would help to obtain an approximation of the components based on the slope of the distribution function around the poverty line, because poverty alleviation depends on where the poor are in relation to the poverty line. If a large proportion of the poor are close to the poverty line, an increase in consumption expenditure will have a bigger effect on poverty than if they are far below the absolute poverty line.

Table 19.12 provides the elasticity of the FGT family of indices across five years: 1995/6; 1999/2000; 2004/5; 2010/11, and 2015/16. If we look at the poverty headcount rate, the elasticity with respect to the mean consumption expenditure is –1.54 in 1995/6. Negative elasticities mean a fall in poverty caused by an increase in consumption expenditure; and hence a higher magnitude implies a higher elasticity even though the sign is negative (Foster et al. 2013). This means that the average real per-adult total

Table 19.12 Elasticity of FGT indices to real per-adult total consumption expenditure

	1995/6	1999/2000	2004/5	2010/11	2015/16	Change 1995/6–2015/16
Poverty headcount rate						
Urban	-1.61	-1.69	-2.69	-1.98	-2.13	-0.53
Rural	-1.53	-1.60	-2.67	-2.10	-1.86	-0.33
Total	-1.54	-1.61	-2.68	-2.08	-1.90	-0.36
Poverty gap						
Urban	-2.10	-2.36	-2.95	-2.34	-2.59	-0.49
Rural	-2.25	-2.41	-3.02	-2.37	-2.13	0.12
Total	-2.24	-2.40	-3.01	-2.37	-2.18	0.06
Squared poverty gap						
Urban	-2.40	-2.76	-3.27	-2.60	-2.74	-0.34
Rural	-2.66	-2.83	-3.41	-2.60	-2.41	0.25
Total	-2.63	-2.83	-3.39	-2.60	-2.44	0.19

Source: HICE surveys of 1995/6, 1999/2000, 2004/5, 2010/11, and 2015/16.

consumption expenditure increases by 1 per cent and the headcount ratio falls by −1.54 per cent. To put it another way, 1.54 per cent of the population who were living under the poverty line of 1,075 birr in 1995/6 will be out of poverty if real per-adult total consumption expenditure increases by 1 per cent. The response of poverty to a change of consumption expenditure appears to be higher over the other years compared to 1995/6, rising to −2.68 in 2004/5 and about −2 in 2015/16. This means that poverty has been more elastic since 2000 than in the mid-1990s.

The overall change in the responsiveness of poverty to consumption growth is −0.36 between 1995/6 and 2015/16, but it varies by geographic area. Throughout the period 1995/6–2015/16 the urban headcount elasticity ratio is more sensitive to consumption growth than in rural areas. Likewise, the elasticity of poverty gap to consumption in 1995/6 is −2.24, but declined by 0.06 to −2.18 in 2015/16. The elasticity of squared gap measure in 1995/6 is −2.63 and it declined by 0.19 to −2.44 in 2015/16. Generally, over the twenty-year period the poverty gap measure and the squared gap measure are more sensitive to consumption expenditure than the headcount ratio.

19.5 Sensitivity Analyses

As the setting of the poverty line is open to debate, it is vital to perform a sensitivity analysis of the choice of poverty line. If a change in the poverty line results in a radical change in any of the poverty measures discussed earlier, then a cautious policy conclusion should be drawn from the analysis based on that particular poverty line, whereas if a poverty measure does not differ much because of a change in the poverty line, then a more robust conclusion can be drawn. To do this, we follow the work of Foster et al. (2013), who checked the sensitivity of the poverty measure by changing the poverty line in more than one direction, and we ask how the actual poverty measure changes from its initial value for a given percentage change on the poverty lines, say for example, −10 per cent, −5 per cent or +5 per cent, +10 per cent . . . In this case −5 per cent means the poverty line is reduced by 5 per cent while +5 denotes an increase in the poverty line by 5 per cent.

Table 19.13 presents the change for the headcount ratio, the poverty gap measure, and the squared gap measure, and their change from their initial values. If we take the headcount ratio for the year 1995/6, a 5 per cent increase in the poverty line causes the headcount ratio to rise by 4.3 percentage points from its actual level of 45.5 per cent to 49.8 per cent. The same is true with other years: changing the poverty line by 5 per cent results in a moderate change of the three poverty measures. It is, however, important to note that the change in the poverty gap and poverty severity seems to be more sensitive to a given percentage change in the poverty line across all the five years (see Table 19.13 for more details).

Table 19.13 Sensitivity of poverty measures to the choice of poverty line

	Poverty headcount rate	Change from actual (%)	Poverty gap	Change from actual (%)	Squared poverty gap	Change from actual (%)
1995/6						
Actual	45.5	0.0	12.9	0.0	5.1	0.0
+5%	49.8	9.6	14.6	12.8	5.9	15.8
+10%	53.6	18.0	16.3	25.9	6.8	32.3
-5%	41.4	-8.9	11.3	-12.4	4.3	-14.9
-10%	37.7	-17.1	9.8	-24.5	3.6	-28.7
1999/2000						
Actual	44.2	0.0	11.9	0.0	4.5	0.0
+5%	49.1	11.0	13.6	13.9	5.3	17.2
+10%	53.4	20.8	15.3	28.3	6.1	35.4
-5%	40.3	-8.8	10.3	-13.3	3.8	-16.1
-10%	36.4	-17.7	8.8	-26.4	3.1	-30.8
2004/5						
Actual	38.7	0.0	8.3	0.0	2.7	0.0
+5%	40.7	5.0	9.8	17.9	3.3	22.1
+10%	43.0	11.0	11.3	35.2	3.9	46.0
-5%	32.2	-17.0	6.9	-17.5	2.2	-19.6
-10%	27.6	-28.7	5.6	-32.8	1.7	-36.9
2010/11						
Actual	29.6	0.0	7.8	0.0	3.1	0.0
+5%	33.3	12.4	9.0	14.3	3.6	16.0
+10%	36.8	24.5	10.2	29.4	4.1	33.2
-5%	26.0	-12.3	6.8	-13.4	2.6	-14.8
-10%	22.8	-22.8	5.8	-25.9	2.2	-28.4
2015/16						
Actual	23.5	0.0	6.7	0.0	2.8	0.0
+5%	26.1	11.0	7.6	12.8	3.2	14.7
+10%	28.9	23.0	8.5	26.2	3.6	30.3
-5%	21.3	-9.7	5.9	-12.3	2.4	-13.8
-10%	18.7	-20.5	5.1	-23.8	2.0	-26.7

Source: HICE surveys of 1995/6, 1999/2000, 2004/5, 2010/11, and 2015/16.

19.6 Concluding Remarks

The aim of this chapter is to provide detailed evidence about poverty trends and inequality in Ethiopia over the period 1995/6–2015/16. Using five rounds of HICE surveys, we analyse the trends in national, rural, urban, and regional poverty incidence, depth and severity, and inequality. The results indicate that the national poverty incidence has declined markedly over the last two decades, with the proportion of population living under the national absolute poverty line declining from one in every two Ethiopians (45.5 per cent) in 1995/6 to one in every four (23.5 per cent) in 2015/16. The decline in poverty incidence was also experienced in both rural and urban areas. The rural poverty headcount index declined from 47.5 per cent in 1995/6 to 25.6 per cent in 2015/16, while that of urban poverty incidence declined from 33.2 per cent to 14.8 per cent over the same period. Despite the decline of poverty incidence in both rural and urban areas, the rural poverty incidence is still almost twice as high as that of urban poverty, which warrants further attention. Over the same period, the regional poverty headcount index has also declined across all regional states.

But despite the substantial declining trend in the headcount ratio, poverty gap, and poverty severity, overall inequality—as measured by the Gini coefficient of consumption expenditure—has been rising over time from 0.29 in 1995/6 to 0.33 in 2015/16, with a higher increase in urban areas to 0.38 in 2015/16.

In an attempt to understand whether the poverty reduction that has been achieved was caused by growth and/or by a change in inequality, we further conducted a growth–inequality decomposition analysis. Results from this decomposition process show that declines in poverty are primarily attributable to growth rather than redistribution, suggesting that the redistribution policy appears to play only a minor role over the period of study. In other words, although policies and interventions that increase growth will reduce poverty, the upward trend in the Gini inequality coefficient from 0.29 in 1995/6 to 0.33 in 2015/16 might limit the scope for further poverty reduction. Thus, it may be imperative to design economic/social policies that consider both growth and inequality at the same time.

References

Bird, K., D. Hulme, A. Shepherd, and K. Moore (2002). 'Chronic Poverty and Remote Rural Areas', CPRC Working Paper No. 13, Chronic Poverty Research Centre.

Brzozowski, M., T. F. Crossley, and J. K. Winter (2017). 'A Comparison of Recall and Diary Food Expenditure Data', *Food Policy* 72: 53–61.

Datt, G. and M. Ravallion (1992). 'Growth and Redistribution Components of Changes in Poverty Measures: A Decomposition with Applications to Brazil and India in the 1980s', *Journal of Development Economics* 38 (2): 275–95.

Deaton, A. and S. Zaidi (2002). 'Guidelines for Constructing Consumption Aggregates for Welfare Analysis', Living Standards Measurement Study Working Paper No. 135, World Bank, Washington, DC.

Foster, J., J. Greer, and E. Thorbecke (1984). 'A Class of Decomposable Poverty Measures', *Econometrica* 52: 761–66.

Foster, J., S. Seth, M. Lokshin, and Z. Sajaia (2013). 'A Unified Approach to Measuring Poverty and Inequality—Theory and Practice: Streamlined Analysis with ADePT Software', World Bank, Washington, DC.

HICES (1995/6, 1999/2000, 2004/5, 2010/11 and 2015/16). 'Household Income, Consumption and Expenditure (HICE) Surveys Central Statistical Agency of Ethiopia, Addis Ababa.

IMF (2018). http://www.imf.org/en/Countries/ETH
IMF (2017). 'World GDP per Capita Ranking'. http://ethiopia.opendataforafrica.org/sijweyg/world-gdp-per-capita-ranking-2017-data-and-charts-forecast; last accessed 2 September 2017.
Jain, L. R. and S. D. Tendulkar (1990). 'Role of growth and distribution in the observed change in headcount ratio measure of poverty: a decomposition exercise for India', *Indian Economic Review* 25 (2): 165–205.
Jalan, J. and M. Ravallion (2002). 'Geographic Poverty Traps? A Micro Model of Consumption Growth in Rural China', *Journal of Applied Econometrics* 17 (4): 329–46.
Kakwani, N. and K. Subbarao (1990). 'Rural poverty and its alleviation in India', *Economic and Political Weekly* 25 (13) (Mar. 31): A2–A16.
MoFED (2008). 'Dynamics of Growth and Poverty in Ethiopia (1995/96–2004/05)', Development Planning and Research Department, Ministry of Finance and Economic Development, Addis Ababa.
MoFED (2010/11). 'Growth and Transformation Plan (GTP) 2010/11–2014/15 Draft', Ministry of Finance and Economic Development, Addis Ababa.
MoFEC (2016/17) 'EMIS data', Ministry of Finance and Economic Cooperation, Addis Ababa.
NPC (2010/11). 'Interim Report on 2010/11 Poverty Analysis Study', National Planning Commission, Addis Ababa.
NPC (2015/16). 'Interim Report on 2015/16 Poverty Analysis Study', National Planning Commission, Addis Ababa.
Ravallion, M. (1996). 'Issues in Measuring and Modelling Poverty', *The Economic Journal* 106 (438): 1328–43.
Ravallion, M. (1998). 'Poverty Lines in Theory and Practice (Vol. 133)', World Bank Publications, Washington, DC.
World Bank (2000). *World Development Report 2000/2001: Attacking Poverty* (Oxford: Oxford University Press).
World Bank (2013). 'Ethiopia Economic Update II: Laying the Foundation for Achieving Middle-Income Status', World Bank, Washington, DC.
World Bank (2014). 'Ethiopia Poverty Assessment', Poverty Global Practice Africa Region, Ethiopia.
World Bank (2017). 'Ethiopia GDP per Capita PPP'. https://tradingeconomics.com/ethiopia/gdp-per-capita-ppp (accessed 2 September 2017).

CHAPTER 20

GROWTH, POVERTY, AND DISTRIBUTION IN ETHIOPIA

ABEBE SHIMELES

20.1 Introduction

The Ethiopian economy has been growing at a respectable rate of 6 per cent since 1996, the year the first national household survey was conducted to monitor poverty and well-being. According to results from household surveys, the poverty rate declined from 45.4 per cent in 1996 to 29.6 per cent in 2011. In recent years in particular, GDP has been growing at around 9 per cent per annum. A recent poverty assessment by the World Bank (2017) suggests that Ethiopia has recorded one of the fastest rates of reduction in poverty in Africa through rapid and relatively inclusive growth. Given that the country started with high initial poverty, and an agrarian economic base characterized chiefly by subsistence farming, the fight against poverty is still a formidable challenge and is likely to remain important to Ethiopian policymaking for decades to come. This chapter examines three important aspects of the poverty–growth–inequality nexus. First, it considers the long-term characteristics of Ethiopia's economic growth by decomposing annual changes in labour productivity into within-sector productivity and movement of labour between sectors. This exercise brings into sharp focus the link between economic growth and employment, which is an important factor in determining the path of poverty and inequality. Second, the chapter looks at poverty dynamics in the forty-six regions of Ethiopia for which the data may be representative. The main focus is to model change in poverty as a function of initial per capita GDP, inequality, and poverty drawing basically from the neo-classical theory of income convergence. That is, we examine whether or not poor regions were growing at a faster rate than initially less poor regions so that poverty convergence has been achieved within and across regions. In this exercise, we also use available longitudinal data to explore the persistence of poverty at the household level and gain insights into the transient and permanent attributes of poverty dynamics. The third objective is to provide key characteristics of the Ethiopian labour market and its potential impact in accelerating the pace of poverty and inequality reduction.

Some of the preliminary findings suggest that growth in per capita consumption tended to be pro-poor in Ethiopia in the first fifteen years of the twenty-first century. But only two-thirds of the growth achieved during 2005–11 translated into consumption growth, a critical component when it comes to short-term poverty reduction. The other one-third of growth has been mainly due to growth predominantly in public and to a certain extent also in private investment, which may be expected to lay the foundations for continued growth, employment, and poverty reduction. During these years, the elasticity of poverty with respect to growth in GDP has been respectable. Furthermore it was possible to document that initially poor regions of Ethiopia performed very well in the last fifteen years, leading to accelerated convergence with regions that had relatively higher initial per capita consumption. However, we also found evidence that high initial inequality impeded the pace of poverty reduction. Ethiopia also exhibited high persistence of poverty at the household level. The chance that poverty propagates itself once a household experiences it is very significant. This could be due to several factors, including lack of sufficient safety net and insurance schemes as well as access to credit to smooth consumption. We have also documented that the pace of poverty propagation declined in the last decade compared with the situation in the 1990s, indicating improvements in several areas of social protection and other forms of risk-mitigation possibilities, including migration.

Most importantly, the link between structure of the labour market and poverty reduction remains the least understood of economic dynamics (see Chapter 18). This study attempts to shed light on how flexibility in the labour market, particularly towards the formal sector, could be an important pathway for Ethiopia to reduce poverty and inequality on a sustained and rapid basis. Preliminary results suggest that despite faster GDP growth, wage employment in the formal sector has been rising only very slowly. For every 1 per cent increase in GDP, the country registered a 0.25 per cent increase in employment. This weak relationship between employment creation and growth is very worrying. The rule of thumb is that employment should be expanding at a rate of at least 0.75 per cent for every 1 per cent increase in GDP. In a country where the labour force expands every year at a rate of 3 per cent or more, employment expansion at an average rate of 2 per cent is not sufficient to address the unemployment and underemployment problem. Thus, the focus of the Ethiopian government will have to be how to make growth efficient in generating productive employment. In this context, the role of structural change in accelerating poverty reduction cannot be underestimated. In a cross-country study undertaken recently across Africa (African Development Bank 2018), poverty and inequality reduction were strongly correlated with growth acceleration even after controlling for per capita GDP levels, signalling the importance of sustaining high growth for an extended period of time. Often the growth acceleration is stronger in countries where labour productivity was achieved through the movement of labour from low- to high-productive sectors, instead of productivity growth within sectors.

The rest of the chapter is organized as follows. Section 20.2 provides highlights of the pattern of per capita GDP growth in the last fifty years to understand the intrinsic problem of sustained and accelerated growth. We then offer an overview of the evolution of poverty and inequality based on nationally representative surveys conducted in 1996, 2000, 2005, and 2011. Poverty dynamics are analysed using regional-level disaggregation to simulate the potential impact of structural change on poverty and inequality. Section 20.5 briefly addresses the state of the Ethiopian labour market in relation to poverty and inequality, before Section 20.6 concludes with some reflections on policy implications.

20.2 Brief Characteristics of Ethiopia's GDP Growth

Ethiopia's long-term pattern of GDP growth reflects its tumultuous history but also its recent spectacular success. As Figure 20.1 shows, Ethiopia's output per worker increased from around an estimated 357 US$ in purchasing power parity (PPP) in 1951 to around 1,242 US$ in PPP in 2014, which is a 3.5-fold growth in about sixty years. This translates roughly into a 2 per cent compounded annual growth rate in output per worker. We also note the high level of growth volatility during the past sixty years underpinning the major instabilities the country experienced (Jerven 2011).[1] The main message of Figure 20.1 is that Ethiopia's growth narrative changed significantly after 2000. The question therefore is whether the country can sustain the rapid growth it has registered in recent decades and avoid the volatility that typified its historical growth trends (see also Chapter 13).

Following the definition of growth acceleration by Hausmann, Pritchett, and Rodrik (2005)[2] and borrowing the mapping of growth episodes from Berthelemy (2006), we can now combine the trend in per capita GDP levels and growth rates to understand the character of growth in Ethiopia. What we can infer from this and analytical work on growth episodes[3] is that Ethiopia managed to complete one growth episode that enabled the country to move from a low steady-state per capita GDP to a new and higher steady-state per capita GDP in almost sixty years. Although this is encouraging, it is also worrying given the rapidly growing population and still high level of poverty.

[1] Caution is required regarding the data on per capita GDP given the limitations on statistical capacity of Ethiopia especially in the 1950s and 1960s and the way the PPP is computed. Earlier population and GDP figures may have been overstated and understated, respectively, leading to lower per capita GDP in early years (see Jerven 2011).

[2] A country is said to have experienced an episode of growth acceleration if the following three conditions are met: a) per capita GDP has grown at a rate of at least 3.5 per cent or more; b) the growth acceleration (the rate of growth in per capita GDP growth during the same period) is at least 2 per cent; and c) per capita GDP in the initial period is higher than in the last period in the growth episode. See also Berthelemy (2006).

[3] See African Development Bank (2018) for more details.

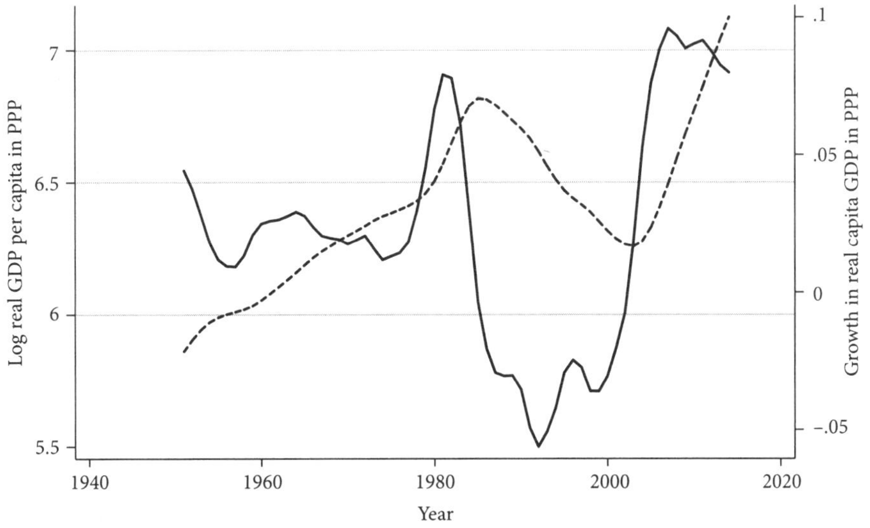

FIGURE 20.1 Real per-capita GDP levels in PPP and growth per capita, 1950–2014

Note: Locally weighted scatterplot smoothing (LOWES or Lowess).

Source: Computations based on Penn World Tables.

In its recently released *African Economic Outlook*, the African Development Bank (AfDB) (2018) showed that the number of completed growth episodes is a much more powerful source of accelerated poverty and inequality reduction than average growth rate in per capita GDP. The findings of the AfDB report suggest also that the most important source of growth acceleration is rapid growth in labour productivity, particularly through structural transformation. This sends a strong signal to policymakers that they should have a laser-focused strategy to initiate a process of structural transformation that facilitates rapid and sustained growth. In this connection, a decomposition of labour productivity growth in Ethiopia shows a story of very limited structural transformation (see also Chapter 36).

The standard approach to measuring the rate of structural transformation is to decompose economy-wide labour productivity growth into two components: 'within-sector' labour productivity growth and 'between-sector' labour productivity growth caused by the movement of labour from low-productivity to high-productivity sectors. The latter is referred to as labour productivity growth due to structural transformation. Following McMillan and Rodrik (2011),[4] economy-wide labour productivity growth can be decomposed as:

$$\Delta y^{t} = \Sigma_{i}\, \theta_{i}^{t-k}\, \Delta y_{i}^{t} + \Sigma_{i}\, y_{i}^{t}\, \Delta\theta_{i}^{t}, \tag{20.1}$$

[4] See also Diao, McMillan, and Rodrik (2017), de Vries, Timmer, and de Vries (2013), and McMillan and Rodrik (2011) for further discussion.

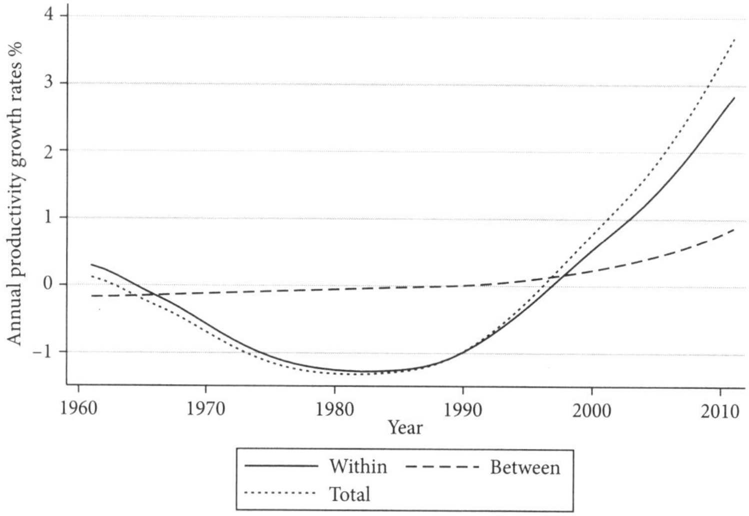

FIGURE 20.2 Lowest estimate of decomposition of labour productivity growth in Ethiopia, 1960–2014

Source: Author's computations based on data provided by Groningen Growth and Development Center.

where y^t denotes economy-wide productivity, y_i^t denotes sectoral productivity levels, θ_i^t is the share of employment in sector *i*. The first term in the RHS of the equation represents the 'within-sector' component, while the second term measures the productivity effect of reallocating labour between different sectors, i.e. structural change. Using the Groningen Growth and Development Center (GGDC) 10-Sector Database, we perform the decomposition exercise given in Equation (20.1). The database has historical information for eleven African countries on output and employment across ten sectors which are internationally comparable. Ethiopia is one of these countries. Figure 20.2 provides the trend in the decomposition of labour productivity growth into between- and within-sector productivities.

Here the picture we get is very different from the overall trend in GDP growth, which was more or less rosy and told a story of accelerated growth in some years. For the labour productivity growth trend shows that between 1960 and 1995, it was in negative territory and started to register positive growth only more recently. In the 2000s, there was significant acceleration in total labour productivity growth. But it is easy to see that for much of the last fifty years, between-sector labour productivity growth has been near zero. That means literally no sign of movement of labour from low- to high-productivity sectors. In the context of Ethiopia this would mean we did not see improvements in modern sectors creating employment opportunities either for those in traditional farming or for informal-sector employees in urban areas. Rather, within-sector productivity perfectly traced total labour productivity. Only after 2000 did the pace of between-sector productivity growth start to pick up, suggesting the stirrings of structural change. Sustaining this sign of a quickening of structural change would therefore be a policy priority.

Overall the picture we get is that Ethiopia has remained an agrarian economy with still over 75 per cent of its labour force engaged in agriculture and only 25 per cent in services and industry. The obvious question to ask is: what happened to poverty and inequality in Ethiopia during this period of rapid economic expansion and positive structural change?

20.3 Poverty and Inequality in Ethiopia

20.3.1 Evolution of Poverty and Inequality

The first nationally representative household survey that collected information on household consumption expenditure was conducted in 1995/6. Since then four waves have been carried out by the Central Statistical Agency of Ethiopia (CSA), including histories of over 70,000 households. The consumption expenditure computed from these surveys suggests that consumption grew at a modest annual rate of 3 per cent between 2005 and 2011 (Table 20.1).

What is evident is that the efficiency of per capita consumption growth in reducing poverty has also improved significantly, particularly during the period 2005–11. As a result, we see that the elasticity of poverty with respect to growth remained above 1 in the last decade and a half, peaking at −1.8 (1 per cent growth leads to a reduction of poverty by 1.8 per cent) in 2000. This basically means that a 1 per cent growth in per capita consumption would yield a more than proportional decline in absolute poverty. In essence, the pro-poorness of growth has improved significantly. Section 20.3.2 provides a measure of pro-poor growth between different survey waves to understand how poverty reduction evolved in Ethiopia during 1996–2011.

Table 20.1 Trends in poverty and inequality, 1996–2011

	1996	2000	2005	2011
Headcount (absolute poverty) %	45.4	44.2	38.7	29.6
Gini coefficient %	26.3	26.7	26.9	28.8
Per capita consumption growth in adult equivalent annual (%)	NA	0.3	3.0	3.1
Elasticity of poverty with respect to growth	NA	-1.8	-0.8	-1.3

Source: Computations based on Ethiopian Household Consumption and Income Surveys.

20.3.2 How Pro-Poor Have Been Growth Episodes in Ethiopia.

As can be inferred from Table 20.2 and Figures 20.3a–3c, the pace of pro-poor growth has been remarkably positive for Ethiopia.[5] In all periods, the consumption expenditure of the poorest decile increased either close to the rate of growth of or higher than the growth of the median household's consumption expenditure. Again, the remarkable trend in the growth of the poorest decile, as captured in these surveys, should have led to significant reductions in poverty.

Table 20.2 Measure of pro-poor growth in Ethiopia, 1996–2011

Percentiles	2005 to 2011	2000 to 2005	1996 to 2000
10	7.16	23.74	4.43
15	10.73	21.85	4.12
20	13.61	20.3	3.88
25	15.97	18.92	3.77
30	17.7	17.88	3.69
Median growth rate	18.14	22.56	7.16

Source: Author's computation based on Ethiopian Rural Household Survey data.

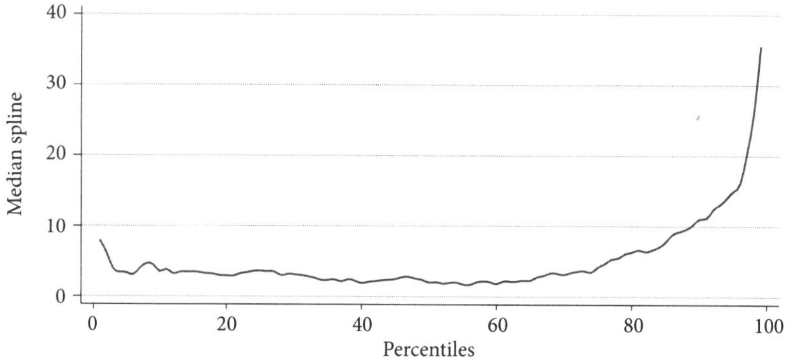

FIGURE 20.3a Growth incidence curve, 1996–2005

Source: Household Income Consumption Expenditure Survey (HICES); Central Statistical Agency (CSA) 1996–2005.

[5] The chapter uses the pro-poor growth index developed by Ravallion and Chen (2003). The graphs depict the growth-incidence curve, summarizing for each percentile the growth rate attained between two periods. Growth is called pro-poor if the growth rates in the bottom deciles are at least positive and higher than the upper decile or the mean income.

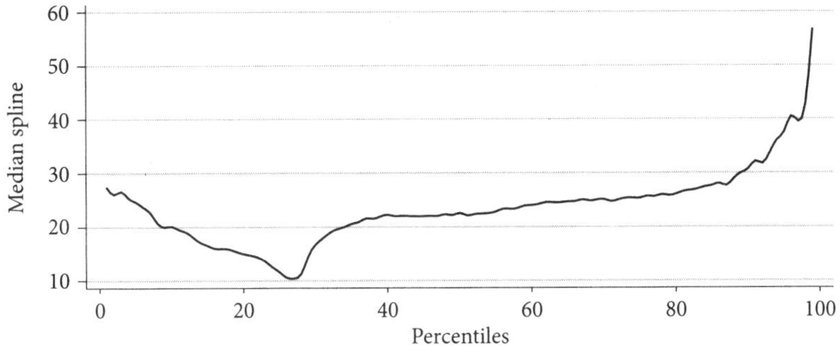

FIGURE 20.3b Growth incidence curve, 2000–5

Source: Household Income Consumption Expenditure Survey (HICES); Central Statistical Agency (CSA) 2000–5.

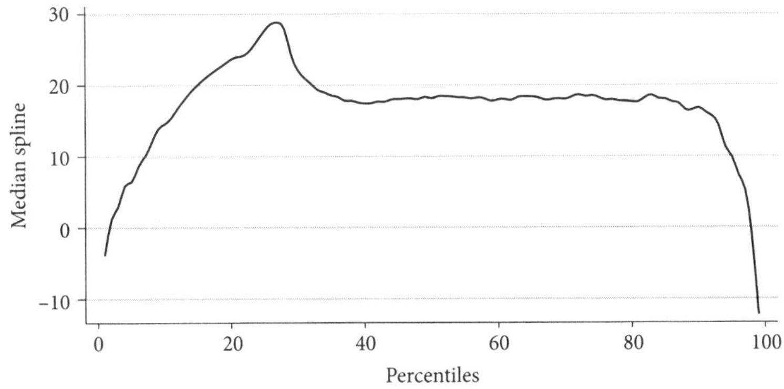

FIGURE 20.3c Growth incidence curve, 2005–11

Note: The growth rate for each percentile indicates a significant (dramatic) shift in consumption expenditure of almost more than 40 per cent a year.

Source: Household Income Consumption Expenditure Survey (HICES); Central Statistical Agency (CSA) 2005–11.

20.4 Poverty Convergence: Does it Exist in Ethiopia?

One of the most relevant policy questions to preoccupy policymakers in countries such as Ethiopia is the possibility that poverty is so widespread and deeply entrenched that it tends to behave like a trap from which it is extremely difficult to escape.[6] This section examines

[6] This section draws heavily from the forthcoming paper by Ouyang, Shimeles, and Thorbecke (2018), particularly the empirical model specification and the results thereof.

whether or not a high level of initial poverty has impeded the pace of poverty reduction directly and indirectly by reducing the pace of subsequent growth. To explore these possibilities we use two approaches. One is a simple model of poverty dynamics that attempts to capture the existence of true-state dependence on the path of poverty status of an individual or the persistence of poverty over time. For the purpose of identifying the underlying causes of poverty persistence, we specify a general model of poverty as follows:

$$P_{it} = \phi\left(P_{it-1}, X_{it}, \alpha_i\right) \tag{20.2}$$

($i=1,\dots,$ N; $t=2,\dots,$T), where P_{it} is equal to 1 if the ith household is poor at time t and zero otherwise. The vector X_{it} captures covariates of poverty and α_i controls for the unobserved heterogeneity of each household. True-state dependence in poverty dynamics exists if current poverty is significantly correlated with lagged poverty. Equation (20.2) can be easily implemented if there is real panel data where individual households are observed in repeated surveys with limited attrition over time. The advantage of this approach is that it can easily capture the possibility of persistence over an extended period of time and provide a formal test of poverty traps. (This does, however, demand that surveys are strictly comparable, which may be questionable in practice.) Previous work on this (e.g. Dercon 2004; Bigsten and Shimeles 2008) has shown that short-lived shocks, such as illness, drought, or other factors that lead to significant income losses, could have a much longer and lasting effect on households' poverty. Such a possibility can be better illustrated by taking a typical case of poor smallholder farmers in Ethiopia. Suppose a farm household faces severe drought in a particular season leading to low consumption. Depending on the severity of the shock, and the cushioning opportunities, the household may be trapped in poverty for an extended period of time. Households may sell off assets and/or significantly reduce food intake (see Chapter 22), both of which could lead to degrading of the physical and human capital needed for the next farming season. Thus starts the cycle of poverty from which it may become difficult to escape. Therefore, for policymakers, the immediate concern should not only be to help the existing poor exit poverty, but also to protect the current non-poor from entering poverty.

The second approach is proposed in a seminal paper by Ravallion (2012) using cross-country data where he shows that countries with a high level of initial poverty may a face double problem in reducing future poverty and that there may be a possibility of being stuck in poverty for a long period of time. We adopt Ravallion's (2012) empirical model which is within the class of Barro regressions motivated by the Solow-Swan model when augmented to allow initial distribution to affect the growth rate. Specifically, Equation (20.3) explores the existence (or absence) of convergence in mean welfare as measured by either per capita income or consumption expenditure:

$$g_i\left(\mu_{it}\right) = \alpha_i + \beta_i \ln \mu_{it-\tau} + \varepsilon_{it}, \dots \tag{20.3}$$

where the annual average rate of growth in mean welfare for country i between year t and year $(t-\tau)$—which approximately equals the annualized change in natural log mean $(g_i(\mu_{it}) \equiv (\ln\mu_{it} - \ln\mu_{it-\tau})/\tau)$—is regressed on the country's initial mean level—also in natural logarithm $(ln\mu_{it-\tau})$. If the regression returns a negative and statistically significant estimate of β, then we have evidence for a strong, unconditional mean convergence. Adding controls to this specification gives an estimate of conditional mean convergence rate.

Assuming a log-linear relationship between poverty (H_{it}) and mean income or consumption (μ_{it}) as specified in Equation (20.4) one could then combine Equations (20.3) and (20.4) to derive Equation (20.5) for the identification of poverty convergence:

$$\ln H_{it} = \delta_i + \eta_i \ln \mu_{it} + v_{it} \ldots \text{ and hence} \tag{20.4}$$

$$g_i(H_{it}) = \alpha_i^* + \beta_i^* \ln H_{it-\tau} + \varepsilon_{it}^* \ldots \tag{20.5}$$

In Equation (20.5), the annual average rate of poverty reduction for country *i* between year *t* and year $(t-\tau)$—which approximately equals the annualized change in log headcount index $g_i(H_{it}) \equiv (\ln H_{it} - \ln H_{it-\tau})/\tau$ —is regressed on its initial poverty level (also in natural logarithm $\ln H_{it-\tau}$). The parameters in Equation (19.4), of course, are related to those in Equations (20.3) and (20.4): $\alpha_i^* = \alpha_i \eta_i - \beta_i \delta_i$, $\beta_i^* = \beta_i$ and $\varepsilon_{it}^* = \varepsilon_{it}\eta_i + v_{it} - (1+\beta_i)v_{it-1}$. We would need a negative and statistically significant estimate of β^* to argue that there exists a strong unconditional poverty convergence. Adding controls to this specification gives an estimate of conditional poverty convergence rate. To explore the direct link between initial poverty and subsequent poverty, we augment Equation (20.2) into the following (20.6):

$$g_i(\mu_{it}) = \alpha + \beta ln\mu_{it-\tau} + \gamma lnH_{it-\tau} + \varepsilon_{it} \ldots \tag{20.6}$$

where a significantly negative estimate of γ would be interpreted as suggesting a strong direct poverty effect, whereby high initial poverty directly retards subsequent growth in mean welfare and hence poverty reduction.

We present briefly the results based on two data sets. One is a true panel data for limited parts of rural Ethiopia collected during the period 1994–2009 and covering sixteen Ethiopian villages and around 1,400 rural households.[7] The data consist of, among other things, detailed consumption expenditure, demographic and other characteristics of the household, ownership of land, etc. Our results focus on the period 1994–2009 and provide first some descriptive statistics on the dynamics of poverty in Table 20.3. As can be seen, in these parts of rural Ethiopia, the percentage of households that escaped extreme poverty[8] was less than 10 per cent, signifying the scourge of poverty. Close to 90 per cent of households experienced poverty at least once in the fifteen years the survey was conducted and more than 70 per cent of households had been in poverty at least

[7] Details of the data are also available on IFPRI's website (http://www.ifpri.org/publication/ethiopian-rural-household-surveys-erhs-1989-2009).

[8] See Bigsten and Shimeles (2008) for the methods of computing the poverty line and definition of poverty adopted in the table.

Table 20.3 Poverty spells experienced by (some) rural households in Ethiopia, 1994–2009

Number of times in poverty	%
Never	9.79
Once	20.3
Twice	19.85
Thrice	17.59
Four times	15.75
Five times	11.76
Always	4.97

Source: Author's computation based on household survey data 1995–2011.

Table 20.4 Poverty convergence in Ethiopian regions: system GMM estimation

Dependent variable: rate of reduction in poverty	coefficient	z-statistics
Initial poverty	-0.35***	-3.98
Initial inequality	0.27***	4.01
Time dummies	Yes	
Wald statistics	35.5	
N	106	

Note: *** denotes the severity of inequality.
Source: Author's computation based on household survey data 1995–2011.

twice during this period. The picture we get from Table 20.3 is of persistent, deeply entrenched poverty, with limited mobility.

Finally we examine whether the findings from the panel data set on the effect of initial poverty on subsequent poverty are evident for initially poor regions as well. As can be seen from Table 20.4, initially poor regions were able to rapidly reduce poverty, suggesting strong evidence of poverty convergence even within each region itself as implied by the generalized method of moments (GMM) result. We can therefore infer safely that the poverty trap at the regional level may not be evident, unlike the observation at the household level in rural areas. Part of the explanation lies in the fact that there has been strong policy emphasis by the federal government in the last two and a half decades on helping lagging regions gain better public services and opportunities. As a result, we are able to document that these regions have been able to reduce poverty rather rapidly compared with relatively richer regions. On the other hand, we also note that initial inequality has been too bad for subsequent poverty reduction. High initial inequality impacted strongly and negatively the pace of poverty reduction. Regions of high inequality were basically experiencing an increase in poverty for a given level of initial poverty.

20.5 Job Creation and Poverty Reduction

Section 20.4 documented that poverty conditions in Ethiopia have seen both better and more difficult days. The better days indicate that at the national level, poverty reduction has been faster for a unit increase in per capita GDP, followed by a steady decline in inequality. However, we have also seen evidence of the persistence of poverty, particularly in rural areas, at the household level, while initially poorer regions experienced faster reduction in poverty. In addition, the last decade has seen a growth rate unprecedented in Ethiopian history. GDP growth has been above 7 per cent during 2000–16. However, per capita consumption growth of 3 per cent has been the most the Ethiopian economy has achieved in the last few decades, which also translated into better outcomes in terms of poverty reduction. It has also not seen a worsening of inequality. By those standards, Ethiopia's growth has been pro-poor. However, there is still considerable poverty in the country and a rapidly growing population that also continues to demand better jobs and opportunities. Most notably, the speed at which the economy was generating jobs was not proportional to the rate of GDP growth achieved. The elasticity of employment with respect to growth has been one of the lowest in Africa at around 0.25 (AfDB 2018). This means that Ethiopia would need a minimum of 10 per cent growth in GDP to be able to expand employment generation at 2.5 per cent per year. This is incompatible with an estimated 3 per cent growth in the labour force. Thus, despite its stellar performance, Ethiopia, like most low-income countries in Africa, needs to shift towards more inclusive growth whereby employment elasticity reaches at least the minimum rate of 0.75 and that can only be done by raising the employment share of the modern sector as well as improving the functioning of the labour market.

20.6 Conclusions

Ethiopia has achieved remarkable per capita GDP growth in recent years. When seen from a long-term perspective, there are still areas of concern that required the attention of policymakers. The country has had its own share of tumultuous history, which produced growth decelerations in some years and stagnation in others. It has also had a remarkable period of economic renaissance. Combined, this makes for a mixed picture of hope and caution. Hope in the sense that the double-digit growth attained particularly after 2005 has enabled the country to rise to a steady-state per capita GDP level that is higher and more stable than in the past. In other words, the country was able to register a per capita income growth higher than 3.5 per cent without interruption for at least eight years. This in itself is remarkable and implies per capita incomes have increased significantly and may stay higher unless significant shocks occur. On the other hand, there is a history of growth reversals that led to deep recessions lasting almost a decade. This exploration of growth episodes brings to light the areas of focus for policymakers, particularly when we decompose the labour productivity into components of structural change (between-sector movements) and within-sector productivity growth. The evidence for Ethiopia suggests that the country is on the right track in both cases. There has been a clear trend of positive structural change in the last six to seven years that also helped fuel overall labour productivity. But, compared with other countries such as Kenya that started structural change in the 1980s, Ethiopia is just starting and without acceleration it may also risk stagnation.

Section 20.5 also highlighted that the pace of poverty reduction in Ethiopia has been quite impressive for the level of growth achieved. The overall growth trend has been inclusive in that it has benefited households in the bottom percentile as much as those in the upper decile. This is encouraging. However, we also noted that high GDP growth did not translate into comparable growth in household consumption expenditure. This large disconnect between GDP growth and household income (consumption growth) is an important area for policy focus in Ethiopia.

Well-intentioned policies aimed at facilitating growth and poverty reduction in initially poor and backward areas has paid off. There is clear evidence of poverty convergence that has not often been found in cross-country regressions. In Ethiopia, high initial poverty in poor regions did not impede the pace of growth and poverty reduction in these regions. This is very encouraging from a policy perspective. No matter how dire initial conditions might be, it is not a reason to lose hope. On the other hand, high inequality and persistence of poverty at the household level is a cause for concern. We documented the presence of poverty traps, particularly in rural areas, and the negative role of income inequality in undermining the pace of poverty reduction.

References

African Development Bank (2018). *African Economic Outlook 2018*. Abidjan: African Development Bank.

Berthelemy, J. (2006). 'Convergence and Development Traps: How Did Emerging Economies Escape the Under-development Trap?', Growth and Integration—Annual World Bank Conference on Development Economics, ed. François Bourguignon and Boris Pleskovic (Washington, DC: World Bank): 127–157.

Bigsten, A. and A. Shimeles (2008). 'Poverty Transition and Persistence in Ethiopia', *World Development* 36 (9): 1559–84.

Dercon, S. (2004). 'Growth and Shocks: Evidence from Rural Ethiopia', *Journal of Development Economics* 74 (2): 309–29.

de Vries, Gaaitzen, Marcel Timmer, and Klaas de Vries (2013). 'Structural Transformation in Africa: Static Gains, Dynamic Losses', GGDC, Working Papers, Vol. GD 136, Groningen, The Netherlands.

Diao, Xinshen, Margaret McMillan, and Dani Rodrik (2017). 'The Recent Growth Boom in Developing Economies: A Structural-Change Perspective', NBER Working Paper No. 23132.

Hausmann, R., L. Pritchett, and D. Rodrik (2005). 'Growth Accelerations', *Journal of Economic Growth* 10 (4): 303–29.

Jerven, M. (2011). 'The Quest for the African Dummy: Explaining African Post-colonial Economic Performance Revisited', *Journal of International Development* 23 (2): 288–307.

McMillan, Margaret and Dani Rodrik (2011). 'Globalization, Structural Change, and Productivity Growth', NBER Working Paper 17143.

Ouyang, Y., A. Shimeles, and E. Thorbecke (2018). 'Revisiting Poverty Convergence in the Developing World with Special Focus on Sub-Saharan Africa', IZA DP No. 11388.

Ravallion, M. (2012). 'Why Don't We See Poverty Convergence?' *American Economic Review* 102 (1): 504–23.

Ravallion, Martin and Shaohua Chen (2003). 'Measuring Pro-poor Growth', *Economics Letters* 78 (1): 93–9.

World Bank (2017). 'Ethiopia: Poverty Assessment'. http://www.worldbank.org/en/topic/poverty/publication/ethiopia-poverty-assessment.

CHAPTER 21

ETHIOPIA'S CHANGING DEMOGRAPHY

ASSEFA HAILEMARIAM

21.1 Introduction

Ethiopia, covering an area of 1,127,127 square kilometres (Nations Encyclopedia 2018), is the tenth largest country in Africa. In terms of population size, it is the second most populous country in Africa and the twelfth in the world with a population of 102.4 million in 2017 (United Nations 2018). Ethiopia is known as one of the poorest countries in the world with a per capita GDP of US$660. However, it has been experiencing vigorous and broad-based double-digit growth between 2005/6 and 2015/16 and has emerged as one of the fastest-growing economies in the world (see Chapters 9 and 36, this volume). It has also been undergoing demographic changes of historic proportions since the early 1990s. It has seen remarkable declines in infant and under-five mortality, modest decline in fertility, and a significant increase in life expectancy. Furthermore, the country is undergoing a demographic transition from high fertility and high mortality to low fertility and low mortality. At an early stage of the transition, the declining fertility rates result in fewer young mouths to feed and a temporary increase in the working-age population greater than that of the population dependent on it, freeing up resources for investment in economic development and family welfare. This may result in a more rapid growth in per capita income and the first demographic dividend (Lee and Mason 2006). Understanding these changes within both their historical and current settings is vital as Ethiopia plans the pathway for its future development.

The chapter starts with a brief discussion of the data sources and the approach used in the data analysis. This is followed by an examination of key demographic patterns and trends over the past six decades, with emphasis on population size, growth, and distribution. We then examine the main demographic drivers of change in population size and growth—mortality and fertility—and how they have been changing in recent decades.

The latter part of the chapter focuses on changes in the age structure and the prospects for seizing the demographic window of opportunity.

21.2 Data and Methods

The absence of accurate time series of population data limits the estimation of past population size and growth rates. Although figures on the size of the population started appearing as early as the mid-nineteenth century, these were based on guesses made by travellers and visitors (Wolde Mariam 1965). Moreover, these figures did not include the most densely populated southern and south-western regions. Consequently, until about the mid-1960s, no population data existed for the whole country. The first national sample survey was conducted in 1964/5 by the then Central Statistical Office (now Central Statistical Agency, CSA) and since then various sample surveys have been undertaken providing estimates of population data for the country. However, these data had their own limitations and they permit only a crude approximation of the actual size of the Ethiopian population (Hailemariam 1991). The first population and housing census was conducted in 1984, the second in 1994, and the third in 2007.

The main data sources used in this chapter are the three population and housing censuses (1984, 1994, and 2007) and the four rounds of the demographic and health surveys that provide crucial records of the major changes in the country's population dynamics. In addition, data from the United Nations Population Division were used and recent studies relating to the country's population dynamics were reviewed. Data from national sources were analysed to show past population trends and current population, while data from UN sources were explored to show future trends. Our approach is essentially descriptive and involves the examination of levels and trends.

21.3 Trends in Population Size, Growth, and Distribution

21.3.1 Population Size and Growth

The first population and housing census, conducted in 1984, resulted in a population of 39.5 million (CSA 1988). Based on the census enumeration and earlier surveys, the CSA made a projected reconstruction of the population back to 1900, which showed that at the turn of the last century, Ethiopia had a population of about 12 million (CSA 1988).

The modern expansion of the population of Ethiopia started in the early decades of the twentieth century with the onset of a long-term decline in the death rate. By 1950, the population had increased to 19 million, growing at the rate of 2.1 per cent. Since then, however, the growth rate has accelerated sharply due to a further decline in mortality resulting from lower incidence of epidemics as well as improvements in public health and standards of living. In 1960, Ethiopia had a population of about 23 million that was growing by 2.4 per cent per annum, and by 1970, the population had increased to 28 million and was growing at 2.7 per cent (Figure 21.1).

A sharp decline in population growth rate occurred between 1970 and 1975 (Figure 21.1). The annual growth rate declined to 1.6 per cent during this period, mainly due to the 1973–4 famine and the political repression that killed hundreds of thousands of Ethiopians and drove many more out of the country (Bariagaber 1997). In spite of the decline in the rate of growth, due to the inherent effect of population momentum, the population increased to reach 39 million at the time of the first census in 1984 and at the time of the second population and housing census in 1994, the country's population was 53 million and in 2007, it reached 73.9 million (CSA 1999, 2010).

The annual rate of population growth increased sharply from the mid-1970s onwards. Concerns about the rapid rate of population growth led to the roll-out of a national population policy in 1993, with the major objective of harmonizing the rate of population growth with that of the economy (TGE 1993). Since then, the population growth rate has been declining. At present, the estimated annual rate of growth of the population stands at about 2.0 per cent implying a doubling time of almost thirty-five years (CSA 2014).

Ethiopia ranks second only to Nigeria in Africa with a population of 102.4 million (United Nations 2018). While the population growth rate has been declining and is expected to continue declining further (Figure 21.1), the population will continue increasing in size because as the high proportion of children under 15 years grow and enter their reproductive years, the cohort of childbearing age will continuously increase in size and produce more children overall, even though the number of children per woman is declining. Therefore, the population of Ethiopia may reach 138 million in 2037

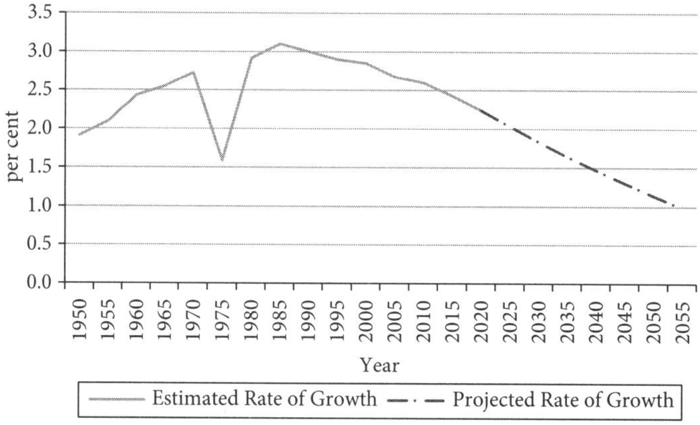

FIGURE 21.1 Population growth rates: estimated and projected

Source: Own presentation, based on data from United Nations, Department of Economic and Social Affairs, Population Division (2017).

according to the 2012 CSA median variant projection or 148.6 million according to the UN median variant projection.

21.3.2 Population Distribution

The distribution of Ethiopia's population, that is, how the population numbers are spread over the country's geographical area, is generally related to altitude, climate, and soil. These physical factors explain the concentration of population in the highlands, which are endowed with moderate temperatures, rich soil, and adequate rainfall.

Nearly 14 per cent of the country's population lives in areas above 2,400 metres (temperate zone), about 75 per cent between 1,500 and 2,400 metres (moderate climate), and the rest below 1,500 metres above sea level (Bekele and Hailemariam 2010). Areas below 1,500 metres are classified as hot climate zones. The hot climate zones bordering Sudan, Kenya, and Somalia encompass more than half of Ethiopia's land area but contain only 11 per cent of its population. Localities above 3,000 metres and below 1,000 metres are sparsely populated, the former because of cold temperatures and rugged terrain, which limit agricultural activity, and the latter because of high temperatures and low rainfall.

21.4 Urbanization

In spite of its long history of settled population, Ethiopia did not witness sustained growth of urban centres and urban population before the twentieth century. The process of modern urbanization started under Emperor Menelik II with the formation of a centralized state, through which Addis Ababa was established as the state capital in 1887 (Wolde Mariam 1965). The following years saw the creation of towns that served as administrative garrisons, but also attracted other activities such as trade and services. The construction of the Ethio-Djibouti railway at the turn of the twentieth century further stimulated the construction of several towns as transport outposts. Likewise, the construction of roads linking Addis Ababa with different parts of the country during the five-year Italian invasion and since then further contributed to the formation of new urban centres in different regions of the country. The establishment of commercial agriculture and associated agro-industries in the 1960s enhanced the growth of urban centres within the Rift Valley and other parts of the country (Wolde Mariam 1965). Moreover, the formation of regional planning commissions and the advancement of state-led industrial development under the socialist regime of the 1980s also contributed to the expansion of towns.

Nevertheless, the level of urbanization in the country remained low (see Figure 21.2). It was only 8.5 per cent in 1967 (CSO 1971), increased to 10.4 per cent in 1984, and further increased to 13.7 per cent in 1994 (CSO 1984, 1999). In 2007, the level of urbanization in Ethiopia was 16.1 per cent (CSA 2010). According to the medium variant UN projection,

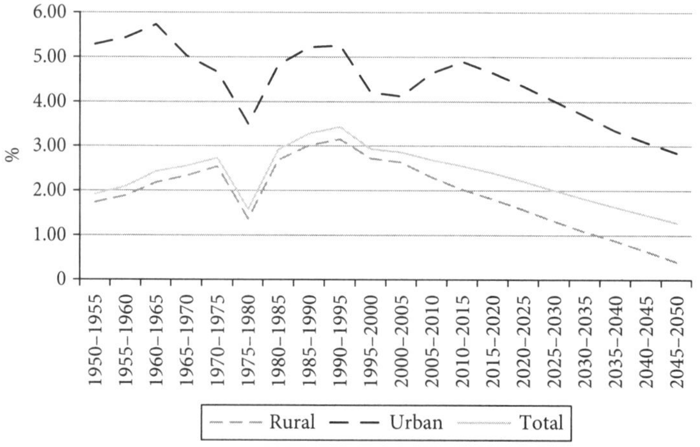

FIGURE 21.2 Growth rate of population by residence

Source: Own presentation, based on data from United Nations, Department of Economic and Social Affairs, Population Division (2014).

it was 20.4 per cent in 2017, whereas for Africa as a whole, it was 40.3 per cent and for Eastern Africa, 26.3 per cent (United Nations 2017). This shows that compared to other countries in Africa, Ethiopia is the least urbanized.

Ethiopia's relative lack of urbanization is the result of the country's history of agricultural self-sufficiency, which has reinforced rural peasant life. However, currently, as a response to shortage of farmland and the absence of any off-farm employment opportunities in the rural areas as well as the socio-economic developments taking place in the country and the resulting rural–urban migration, the number of urban localities as well as urban population is increasing rapidly. In 1984, there were 325 localities with a population of 2,000 or more but within ten years, it increased by two-thirds to reach 530 in 1994, and in 2007, there were 812 urban localities (CSA 2010). Similarly, urban population increased from about 2 million in 1967 to 4.7 million in 1984. Between 1984 and 2007, it increased more than two and half times to reach 11.9 million in 2007.

The distribution of population by size class in urban localities (Table 21.1) shows that small towns with a population of less than 20,000 constitute the majority of urban centres in Ethiopia. In 1967, 91.2 per cent of urban centres had a population less than 20,000, a figure that increased to 96 per cent in 1984, but declined to 94.4 per cent in 1994 and further declined to about 88 per cent in 2007. On the other hand, large cities (with a population of 100,000 or more) constituted less than half a per cent in 1984 and 1994 but in 2007, 1.6 per cent of the total urban population. Addis Ababa, with an estimated population of 3.5 million in 2017, is the only primate city. Including Addis Ababa, Ethiopia has a total of ten cities, each with a population of at least 100,000 in 2017. These cities constituted 40 per cent of the country's urban population.

In spite of the low level of urbanization, homelessness, overcrowded living arrangements, poor sanitation, and shortage of health services and employment opportunities are

Table 21.1 Distribution of population by size-class of urban localities

Size-class	1984		1994		2007	
	Number	%	Number	%	Number	%
< 5,000	511	78.9	683	74.1	395	40.6
5,000–19,999	111	17.1	187	20.3	457	47.0
20,000–99,999	24	3.7	48	5.2	104	10.7
100,000–2,499,999	1	0.2	3	0.3	12	1.2
≥2,500,000	1	0.2	1	0.1	4	0.4
Total	648	100.0	922	100.0	972	100.0

Source: Own presentation, based on data from CSA (1988, 1999, 2010).

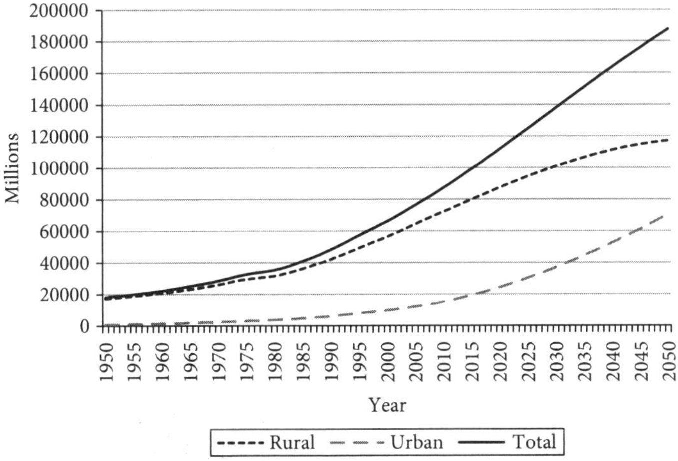

FIGURE 21.3 Trends in population size: total, urban, and rural

Source: Own presentation, based on data from: United Nations, Department of Economic and Social Affairs, Population Division (2017).

common features of most urban centres in Ethiopia. About 28 per cent of urban housing units have no toilet facility, 27 per cent are without kitchens and only 27 per cent of urban dwellers had access to improved sanitation facilities in 2015 (CSA and ICF 2016).

Urban population is likely to increase more rapidly given the shift in emphasis from agricultural to industrial-led development. According to the projection made by the Ministry of Urban Development and Housing, by 2025, the country's urban population is expected to account for 27–30 per cent of the country's total population, and by 2037, it will contribute about 40 per cent of the total population. This means that the urban population of Ethiopia will increase to about 39 million, and that the urban population expansion accounts for around 75 per cent of the total population increase of over 50 million between 2015 and 2037 (MUDHo, 2015) (see Figure 21.3).

21.5 Drivers of Change in Population Size and Growth

From a demographic perspective, fertility, mortality, and migration are the drivers of change in population size and structures. A population increases or decreases in number and growth rate due to changes in these factors. In the absence of technological intervention, one might say these variables are almost the sole drivers of change in population size and structure. However, changes in marriage and reproductive behaviour (improvements in contraceptive uptake, increasing acceptance of abortion) and loosening of some religious and cultural norms and values have in many parts of the world reduced the role of fertility (Atoh 2001). The effect of mortality on population size and structure, on the other hand, is to reduce the component of the population in which the mortality occurs. The role migration plays in shaping population structures is rather limited and conditional. Its effect is more pronounced at times when natural disasters or political unrest and military concerns lead to populations being displaced. Opportunistic migration tends to occur mostly among younger adults, and may be permanent or temporary. It has the effect of depleting the size and structure of the population of the sending area in the young adult groups and augmenting this group in the receiving areas. However, its effect at national level may be felt if the volume of international migration is significant (United Nations 2018).

21.6 Trends in Mortality and Fertility

There are two major difficulties in studying past fertility and mortality trends in Ethiopia. The first is the lack of detailed data on fertility and mortality. Until 1990, when the first comprehensive demographic survey was conducted, there was no large-scale nationally representative survey that could be used for studying levels and trends of fertility and mortality. The second difficulty is that the available demographic data from previous surveys are plagued by reporting errors typical of developing countries (Hailemariam 1991). Furthermore, it is difficult to assess how differences in coverage and in quality of data collection and tabulation affect the estimated rates. Despite these difficulties, this study has pulled together data from a variety of sources to show levels and trends in fertility and mortality until 1990 when data from the Family and Fertility Survey became available.

21.6.1 Trends in Infant and Child Mortality

During the period 1950–2000, Ethiopia had the highest mortality of all countries in sub-Saharan Africa. Mortality indices such as infant, under-five, and maternal mortality

Table 21.2 Infant and under-five mortality rates in Ethiopia and sub-Saharan Africa

	IMR		% Change		U5MR		% Change	
	Ethiopia	SSA	Ethiopia	SSA	Ethiopia	SSA	Ethiopia	SSA
1950–5	199	185			333	310		
1990–5	114	111	42.7	40	190	184	42.9	40.6
1995–2000	78	87	31.6	21.6	123	141	35.3	23.4
2010–15	48	58	38.5	3.3	67	82	45.5	41.8

Source: Own presentation, based on data from: United Nations, Department of Economic and Social Affairs, Population Division (2017); CSA (1993); CSA and ICF (2016).

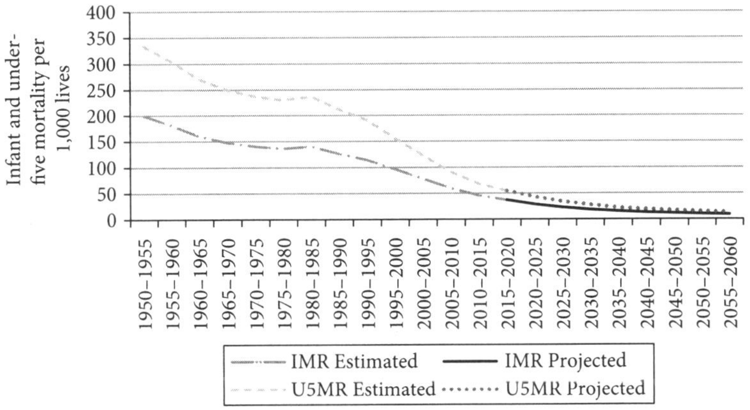

FIGURE 21.4 Infant and under-five mortality

Source: Own presentation, based on data from United Nations, Department of Economic and Social Affairs, Population Division (2017).

rates were considerably higher and life expectancy was much lower in Ethiopia compared to the levels that prevailed in sub-Saharan Africa during the period.

In Ethiopia in 1950, infant mortality rate (IMR) was 199 and under-five mortality rate (U5MR) was 333 per 1,000 births, whereas in sub-Saharan Africa, it was 185 and 310 deaths per 1,000 live births, respectively (Table 21.2). Though there has been an accelerated decline in both IMR and U5MR in both Ethiopia and sub-Saharan Africa as a whole, mortality decline has been much faster in Ethiopia than in sub-Saharan Africa. During the forty years from 1955 to 1995, IMR declined from 199 to 114 (by 42.7 per cent) in Ethiopia and in sub-Saharan Africa, it declined from 185 to 111 (40 per cent). IMR further declined to 78 per 1,000 (31.6 per cent) in Ethiopia and to 87 (21.6 per cent) in sub-Saharan Africa between 1990 and 2005. During the period 2005–15, IMR declined to 48 per 1,000 (38.5 per cent) in Ethiopia and to 82 (41.8 per cent) in sub-Saharan Africa (Table 21.2; Figure 21.4).

As Figure 21.4 shows, during the last sixty years or so, the country has registered unprecedented declines in infant and under-five mortality with a more pronounced reduction occurring over the last ten years with a faster pace of the decline in infant mortality. Following the decline in infant and under-five mortality, Ethiopia has also registered significant increases in life expectancy. Life expectancy at birth increased from about 34.1 years for both sexes during 1950–5 to 63.7 in 2015 (United Nations 2017).

Mortality has been declining in both urban and rural areas. However, urban mortality has been much lower than rural mortality due to improved lifestyles and access to health services. For instance, in 2016, IMR and U5MR were 42 and 66 per 1,000 live births in urban Ethiopia, while these values were 54 and 83 per 1,000 live births, respectively, in rural areas (CSA and ICF 2016). Similarly, there is considerable variation in mortality by region. Afar regional state has the highest infant and under-five mortality rates (81 and 125 per 1,000) followed by Somali (67/1000 and 94/1000, respectively), while Addis Ababa has the lowest IMR and U5MR (29/1000 and 39/1000, respectively) (CSA and ICF 2016).

21.6.2 Maternal Mortality

Maternal mortality as measured by maternal mortality ratio (MMR) was the highest in Ethiopia during the 1980s and 1990s. It was estimated at about 1,250 maternal deaths per 100,000 live births in 1990, and at about 1,080 deaths per 100,000 live births in 1995 (Berhan and Berhan 2014; World Health Organization 2015). Since then, however, it has been declining steadily, and in 2000, it was estimated at 871, in 2005 at 673, and in 2011 at 676 per 100,000 live births (CSA and ICF 2016). This indicates that MMR decreased between 2000 and 2005 by 22.7 per cent, but slightly increased between 2005 and 2011 by 0.44 per cent. In 2016, it declined to 412 per 100,000, a decline of 39.5 per cent between 2011 and 2016. Though MMR has been declining throughout the period 1990 to 2016, a relatively faster decline was observed after 2000. Between 1990 and 2000, MMR declined by 3 per cent per year, but between 2000 and 2016, it declined by 3.3 per cent per year.

In general, there has been a faster decline in mortality in Ethiopia since 2000. Improvement in public health measures such as malaria control, access to safe drinking water, and improved personal and environmental hygiene have contributed to the decline in overall mortality, while maternal education and improvements in access to and use of maternal and child health services are among the factors behind the decline in maternal, infant, and childhood mortality.

21.6.3 Trends in Fertility

The main feature of fertility in Ethiopia is that it has been at a high level. During the period 1970–95, total fertility rate (TFR)—the average number of children that would be born to a woman if all women lived to the end of their childbearing years and bore children according to the age-specific fertility rates for that area and period)—remained well above seven children per woman (Teller, Hailemariam, and Gebreselassie 2011). The country recorded its peak TFR in 1990, with an average of 7.7 live births per woman of childbearing age (CSA 1993). Since then, however, TFR has been declining. It fell from 7.7 children per woman of childbearing age in 1990, to 5.5 in 2000, 5.4 in 2005, 4.8 in 2011, and in 2016, it further declined to 4.6 children per woman (CSA and ICF 2016). During the ten years from 1990 to 2000, TFR declined by 28.6 per cent (2.6 per cent per year), but between 2000 and 2011, it declined by 12.7 per cent (1.3 per cent per year) and between 2011 and 2016 by 4.2 per cent only (0.8 per cent per year).

Although fertility has been declining in the whole of sub-Saharan Africa, the decline in Ethiopia since 2000 has been much faster. Between 1950 and 2000, TFR in Ethiopia declined by 22.5 per cent whereas in sub-Saharan Africa, it declined by only 9.7 per cent and between 2005 and 2015, it declined by 14.5 per cent in Ethiopia whereas in sub-Saharan Africa, it declined by 8.9 per cent. Moreover, TFR in Ethiopia is lower than that in sub-Saharan Africa (Table 21.3).

There is a significant regional as well as rural–urban differential in fertility in Ethiopia. Addis Ababa city administration has the lowest fertility of 1.8 children per woman followed by Dire Dawa with 3.1. Somali region has the highest fertility of 7.2 children per woman followed by Afar (5.5 children per woman), Oromia (5.4 children per woman), and Tigray (4.7 children per woman). In the remaining regions, total fertility rate ranges between 3.5 and 4.4 children per woman in 2016 (CSA and ICF 2016).

Fertility has been much lower in urban areas compared to rural areas. Urban fertility has been half that of the national fertility since 2000. In 2016, urban fertility was 2.3 children per woman, which is close to replacement-level fertility, whereas rural fertility was 5.2 children per woman (CSA and ICF 2016). The low fertility in urban Ethiopia may be explained by the fact that urban woman are better educated, marry at a slightly older age, and have better access to contraceptives compared to rural women.

Table 21.3 Total fertility rate in Ethiopia and in sub-Saharan Africa

Period	Total fertility		% change	
	Ethiopia	SSA	Ethiopia	SSA
1950–5	7.2	6.6		
1990–5	7.1	6.2	1.4	6.1
2000–5	5.5	5.6	22.5	9.7
2005–15	4.7	5.1	14.5	8.9

Source: Own presentation based on data from CSA (1988, 1993); United Nations, Department of Economic and Social Affairs, Population Division (2017); custom data acquired via website.

The rapid declines in fertility and mortality that have taken place in the country are the outcomes of the progress the country has been making in the areas of health, education, and urbanization as well as in the economy. The Health Extension Programme (HEP), an innovative community-based programme introduced in 2003 with the aim of creating healthy environments and healthy living, has almost certainly contributed to the decline in infant, child, and maternal mortality in the country. The HEP has also contributed to the decline in fertility through increased access to and use of family planning services (Hailemariam 2016).

21.7 Changing Age Structure

The age structure of a population shows the distribution of a country's population in different age groups at a given point in time. It is both the determinant and the consequence of population growth. The distribution of a population between the young (< 15), working age (15–64) and the elderly (65 and over) determines the social and economic structure of the population and influences the priority issues in a country and allocation of resources for its development.

The Ethiopian population is characterized by its young age structure with a median age of 18.6 years in 2017—a feature of rapidly growing populations. Figure 21.5 presents the size of total population as well as that of children under the age of 15, the working-age population, and the elderly (65 years and above) over a period of 100 years from 1950 to 2050, while Figure 21.6 presents the share of the population under 15, those in the working-age population, and the elderly population. The change in the size of the population was very slow until the 1970s and then the total and working-age populations increased sharply. The child population (under 15 years of age) and the elderly (those aged 65 and above) showed slower increase even after the 1970s.

The population of children (0–14 years of age) was 8 million in 1950, constituting 44.1 per cent of the total population of the country. It increased to 24.1 million, accounting for 45.1 per cent of total population in 1994. At the time of the 2007 census, 32.5 million or 44 per cent of the country's total population was aged 0–14 years. According to the CSA median variant projection, it is expected to increase to about 41 million in 2037. However, its share of the total population has been declining as of 2015 (Figure 21.6).

The working-age population, that is, the population aged 15–64 years which is the productive age group, on the other hand, was 9.5 million (accounting for 50.8 per cent of the total population) in 1950 and increased three-fold to 27.3 million in 1994, constituting 51.1 per cent. This increased to 38.2 million (which accounts for 51.8 per cent of the country's total population) in 2007. According to the 2012 Inter-censual Population Survey, the population belonging to this age group increased to 46.4 million, accounting for 55.4 per cent of the country's population. Between 1994 and 2000, it increased by 0.7 percentage points but between 2007 and 2012 it was projected to increase by 3.6 percentage points. It is expected to continue increasing until 2050 but at a slower pace.

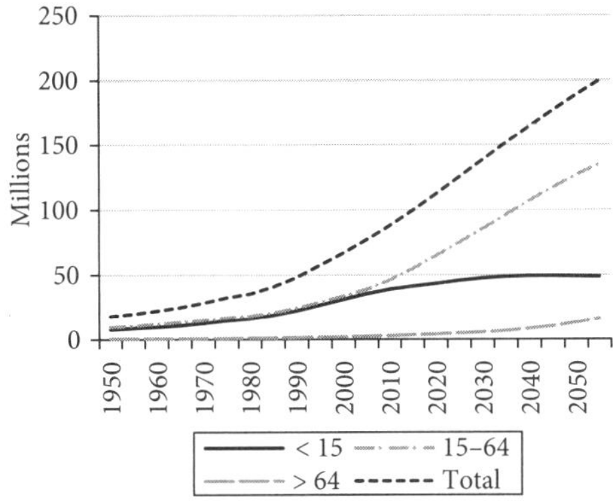

FIGURE 21.5 Population size by broad age groups

Source: UNDESA (2017).

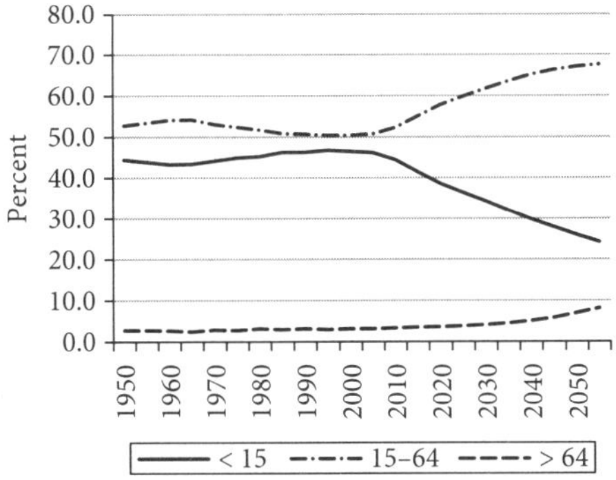

FIGURE 21.6 Percentage of total population by broad age groups

Source: Own presentation based on data from United Nations, Department of Economic and Social Affairs, Population Division (2017).

The elderly population, i.e. the population aged 65 and over, is a much smaller proportion of the total population. In terms of size, this age group was about half a million in 1950, and increased to 1.7, 2.3, and 2.6 million in 1994, 2007, and 2012, respectively. It accounted for 2.8 per cent of the total population in 1950, 3.2 per cent in 1994 and 2007, and 3.1 per cent in 2012. It is expected to increase to 5 per cent in 2037 and to 6.9 per cent in 2050 (Figure 21.6).

21.7.1 Population Age Pyramids: 1980, 2010, 2030, and 2050

Population age pyramids show the distribution of a population by sex and age group as a percentage of the total population. The population pyramids presented in Figure 21.7 show the expected course of the population distribution for Ethiopia from 1980 to 2050.

The 1980 pyramid shows Ethiopia with a young and growing population—large proportions of young people and smaller proportions in older age groups. The shape of the population age pyramid is similar to that of a typical developing country with high fertility and mortality in which the youngest segment of the population is also its largest segment. The 2010 population pyramid is not very different from that of the 1980 except that it shows that the population structure has started to experience some change. The population pyramid shows that it is still young, with the largest segment between the ages of 10 and 14.

The 2030 population pyramid shows that the country will experience significant change in the age structure of its population. By 2050, Ethiopia will have transitioned to an ageing population with a relatively large proportion of the age group 65-plus (about 7 per cent). The two largest segments of the Ethiopian population in 2050 will be in the 50–54 and 55–59 age groups. Ethiopia will have made this dramatic transition in just thirty-three years from now. The population age structure changes that the country is expected to make are similar to the changes experienced in other countries like those in South-east Asia during their demographic transition.

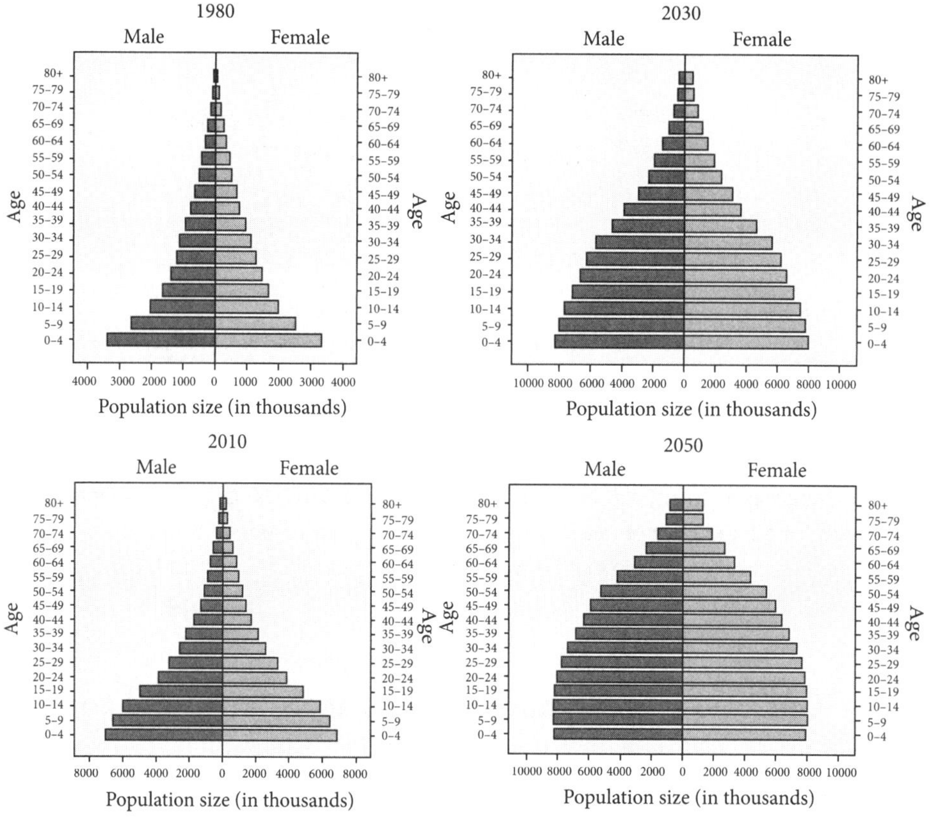

FIGURE 21.7 Age pyramids: 1980, 2010, 2030, and 2050

Source: Own presentation based on data from United Nations, Department of Economic and Social Affairs, Population Division (2017).

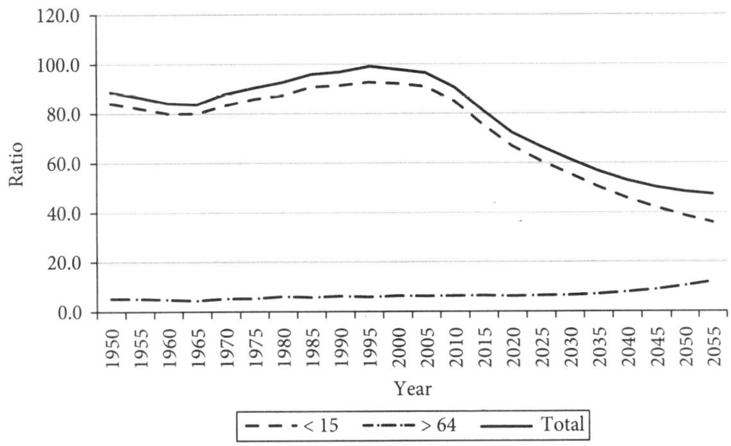

FIGURE 21.8 Dependency ratios

Source: Own presentation based on data from United Nations, Department of Economic and Social Affairs, Population Division (2017).

21.7.2 Age Dependency Ratio

Age dependency ratio is the ratio of persons in the ages defined as dependent (under 15 and over 64 years) to persons in the ages defined as economically active or of working age (15–64 years) in a population. In 1950, the youth dependency ratio was 83.3 and the old-age dependency ratio was 5.7, giving a total dependency ratio of 89 persons for every one hundred persons of working age. The youth dependency ratio increased to about 86 in 1975 and to 93 in 1995 while the old-age dependency ratio increased to 6 in 1975 and remained unchanged until 1995. The increase in the youth dependency ratio was due to the high fertility and declining infant and under-five mortality, while that of the old-age dependency was due to the increasing life expectancy. Since 1995, youth dependency has been progressively declining, whereas old-age dependency, which had remained at six persons per hundred persons of working age, started increasing gradually after 2005 (Figure 21.8).

21.8 Demographic Windows of Opportunity

The preceding sections have summarized the remarkable changes in population structures as the country goes through the process of demographic transition. The share of the working-age population is growing and that of the young cohort decreasing, while the old cohort is still small. A rising share of the working-age population can be seen as an indication for opening the *demographic window of opportunity*—the period of time

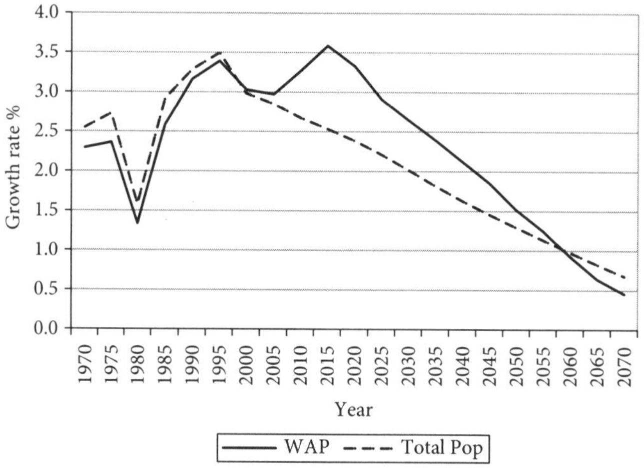

FIGURE 21.9 Demographic window of opportunity

Source: Own presentation based on data from United Nations, Department of Economic and Social Affairs, Population Division (2017).

in a country's demographic development when the proportion of the working-age population is particularly prominent. The demographic window of opportunity for harnessing the demographic dividend occurs when the growth rate of the working-age population exceeds the growth rate of the total population.

For a precise determination of the length of Ethiopia's demographic window of opportunity, we take into account population growth rates for the total population and the working-age population. As Figure 21.9 shows, the growth rate of the working-age population started to exceed that of the total population around 2005. Thus, it appears that Ethiopia's demographic window of opportunity began in 2005 when the growth rate of the working-age population first exceeded that of the overall total population growth rate. It is predicted to end in 2060 when the growth rate of the working-age population will, for the first time since 2005, drop below that of the total population. Thus, it is important to note that, according to these calculations, 'demographically' the window of opportunity is open for Ethiopia and will remain open until 2060. However, this is not in itself a sufficient condition for harnessing the demographic dividend. The key features contributing to reaping the demographic dividend include, among others, sound economic, social, and health policies, and good governance (Lee and Mason 2006).

Ethiopia is in the third stage of the demographic transition where falling fertility is leading to a temporary rapid growth of the labour force. Its demographic image is not very different from that of China in the 1980s and of South-East Asian countries in the 1950s. These countries went through remarkable economic growth during the second half of the twentieth century partly because of the demographic transition that supplied the economies with a young workforce (Lee and Mason 2006).

In Ethiopia, the key to reaping this demographic dividend is that there are adequate jobs for the close to one million youth entering the workforce every year. While a young population can be a positive economic factor, it can also be a political risk in an economy that does not create enough job opportunities.

21.9 Conclusion

This chapter has attempted to provide a demographic sketch of Ethiopia. It has disclosed the position of the country regarding its changing population structure. It has shown that fertility and mortality rates are falling and that the country's population is growing but at a slower rate. Declining fertility and increasing longevity are bringing about a shift in the age structure. The proportion of children under the age of 15 years is declining, while that of the working-age population (15–64) is increasing and the proportion of the elderly population is also increasing. The age structure of the population is still broad based but changing. Age-structural change leads to the opening of the demographic window of opportunity, which may bring accelerated socio-economic development to the country. In order to exploit the benefits of the changing age structure, as reflected by shifts in both the size and internal demographic composition of the working-age population, the county must accelerate its ongoing investment efforts in physical and human capital, and in economic and governance policies, sooner rather than later. Failure to exploit the window of opportunity may retard the progress in socio-economic development the country is making and could result in severe economic and social problems. Reforms in the health and education sector, financial inclusion, and adequate employment opportunities are essential prerequisites to ensure that Ethiopia's young population is truly an asset. Moreover, if steps are not taken to develop and implement sound social security plans, the increasing number of the elderly is likely to be a serious challenge for the not-too-distant future.

References

Atoh, M. (2001). 'Very Low Fertility in Japan and Value Change Hypotheses', *Review of Population and Social Policy* 10: 1–21.

Bariagaber, A. (1997). 'Political Violence and the Uprooted in the Horn of Africa: A Study of Refugee Flows from Ethiopia', *Journal of Black Studies* 28: 26.

Bekele, S. and A. Hailemariam (2010). 'Population Dynamics and Environment in Ethiopia', *Ethiopian Environment Review* 1: 23.

Berhan, Y. and A. Berhan (2014). 'Review of Maternal Mortality in Ethiopia: A Story of the Past Thirty Years', *Ethiopian Journal of Health Sciences* Special Issue, September 2014.

CSA (1988). 'Population Situation in Ethiopia: Past, Present and Future', Population Studies Series No. 1, Central Statistical Authority, Addis Ababa.

CSA (1993). 'The 1990 Family and Fertility Survey Report', Central Statistical Agency, Addis Ababa.

CSA (1999). *The 1994 Population and Housing Census of Ethiopia: Results at Country Level, Vol. I, Analytical Report*. (Addis Ababa: Central Statistical Agency).

CSA (2010). *The 2007 Population and Housing Census of Ethiopia*. National Statistical Report (Addis Ababa: Office of the Population Census Commission).

CSA (2014). 'Intercensal Survey Report', Central Statistical Office, Addis Ababa.

CSA and ICF (2012). *Ethiopia Demographic and Health Survey 2011* (Addis Ababa and Rockville, MD: CSA and ICF).

CSA and ICF (2016). *Ethiopia Demographic and Health Survey 2016* (Addis Ababa and Rockville, MD: CSA and ICF).

CSO (1971). *Population of Ethiopia*, Central Statistical Office, Addis Ababa.

CSO (1984). 'Ethiopia 1984: Population and Housing Census Preliminary Report', Office of the Population and Housing Census, Addis Ababa.

CSO (1999). 'Population and Housing Census for Ethiopia', Addis Ababa.

Hailemariam, A. (1991). 'Fertility Levels and Trends in Arsi and Shoa Regions of Central Ethiopia', *Journal of Biosocial Science* 23: 387–400.

Hailemariam. A. (2016). 'Implementation of the Population Policy of Ethiopia: Achievements and Challenges', *Population Horizons* 13 (1): 1–14.

Lee, R. and A. Mason (2006). 'What Is the Demographic Dividend?' *Finance & Development* 43. A quarterly magazine of the IMF.

MUDHo (2015). 'Urban Development Spatial Planning', Ministry of Urban Development and Housing, Addis Ababa.

Nations Encyclopedia, 'Ethiopia'. http://www.nationsencyclopedia.com (accessed 20 March 2018).

Teller, C., A. Hailemariam, and T. Gebreselassie (2011). 'The Nature, Pace and Determinants of the Incipient Fertility Transition in Ethiopia, 1984–2007: Can the 4.0 TFR Target for 2015 be Met?' in *Demographic Transition and Development in Africa: The Unique Case of Ethiopia*, ed. C. Teller and A. Hailemariam (Dordrecht: Springer): 45–68.

Transitional Government of Ethiopia (TGE) (1993). 'The National Population Policy of Ethiopia', Office of the Prime Minister, Transitional Government of Ethiopia, Addis Ababa.

United Nations, Department of Economic and Social Affairs, Population Division (2017). 'World Population Prospects: The 2017 Revision', DVD edition (median variant). https://esa.un.org/unpd/wpp/Download/Standard/Population/ (accessed 15 February 2018).

United Nations (2018). 'Migration and Population Change: Drivers and Impacts', Population Facts. http://www.un.org/en/development/desa/population/migration/publications/population-facts/docs/MigrationPopFacts20178.pdf (accessed 20 March 2018).

Wolde Mariam, M. (1965). 'Some Aspects of Urbanization in the Pre-Twentieth Century Ethiopia', *Ethiopian Geographical Journal* 3 (2): 13–19.

World Health Organization (2015). 'Trends in Maternal Mortality: 1990 to 2015', estimates by WHO, UNICEF, UNFPA, World Bank Group, and the United Nations Population Division www.who.int (accessed 15 March 2018). http://www.who.int/reproductivehealth/publications/monitoring/maternal-mortality-2015/en/

CHAPTER 22

ECONOMIC POLICY AND FOOD SECURITY IN ETHIOPIA

DEBORAH JOHNSTON AND HELEN WALLS

22.1 Introduction

Ethiopia has an integrated approach to addressing nutrition; however, there is little clarity about the wider impact of government policy on food and nutrition. In this chapter we focus on the interrelationship in Ethiopia between economic policy broadly conceptualized and nutrition policy (defined as including all food- and nutrition-relevant policy). Overall, there have been notable successes in nutrition policy in Ethiopia, but significant challenges remain. If these challenges are to be met successfully, greater consideration of how to address rapidly changing food systems in Ethiopia is needed at national policy level. We argue that the focus of government policy needs to shift from food availability to broader issues of food acquisition and particularly food affordability, which is mediated through food prices and waged employment.

Historically, food and nutrition security in Ethiopia have arguably been addressed by national policy, predominantly in relation to improving food production and emergency food aid responses. This reflects the extent of drought and famine that Ethiopia has faced, including devastating events such as the 1983–5 famine, which is estimated to have led to up to a million deaths and received attention globally (Devereux 1988). Today, despite improvements in child stunting and wasting, undernutrition remains a significant challenge in Ethiopia (see Chapter 23). Furthermore, recent studies describe how Ethiopia is also facing an increasing prevalence of overweight, obesity, and related non-communicable diseases (NCDs) in urban settings (Zello 2015; Tebekaw, Teller, and Colon-Ramos 2014). Thus, Ethiopia is now beginning to experience what is referred to as the 'double burden' of malnutrition: the co-existence of underweight and micronutrient deficiencies, as well as overweight, obesity, and NCDs (Baker et al. 2018; Malik, Willet, and Hu 2013; Walls, Kadiyala, and Smith 2016).

Official data point to substantial improvements in nutrition between approximately 2000 and 2015, but with some exceptions (FDRE 2016b). We interrogate this data in more detail in Section 22.2, and find three areas of particular concern. First, high levels of malnutrition do remain. Worst affected by malnutrition and food insecurity are the close to 30 per cent of Ethiopia's population living below the poverty line of US$1.25 a day (USAID 2016). Recent USAID figures indicate that 10 million more people are in need of emergency food assistance in 2016 (USAID 2016). Second, some indicators such as childhood anaemia worsened significantly after 2015. Third, where the data can be disaggregated, there is evidence that the poorest have not benefited as substantially in those indicators which have improved.

Furthermore, Ethiopia has in recent years, in 2008 and 2011, experienced 'spikes' in food prices (Admassie 2014: 138; Headey et al. 2012). In 2008, Ethiopia had the highest rate of month-on-month inflation in key food groups among low- and middle-income countries, at 3.5 per cent per month (Headey et al. 2012). This food price inflation was driven by higher prices of staple foods such as maize, wheat, and teff. Admassie (2014: 140) reviewed a range of studies that suggest that after the 2008 price spike, poverty levels in Ethiopia rose, and consumption fell, particularly among the poorest households.

This mixed picture suggests a need to understand better the relationship between economic growth, food, and nutrition security in Ethiopia. In the following, we draw on analytical approaches in key academic texts to assist our examination of the relationship between economic growth and the achievement of food and nutrition security, drawing on several key national policy documents.

22.2 Establishing a Conceptual Approach for Policy Examination

The UNICEF conceptual framework (Smith and Haddad 2015), of which caring practices and changes to the wider health environment form a key part, is a commonly used approach to understand nutrition outcomes. This framework outlines the factors leading to malnutrition, including the factors that shape and mediate the effects of dietary intake: adequacy of access to food; adequacy of care practices, particularly for women and children; and adequacy of health services and wider environments affecting health. However, the UNICEF approach does not provide for an understanding of how dietary intake and adequacy of access to food are determined. This is particularly important as 'nutrition-sensitive' interventions are considered to be key to improving nutritional outcomes—'nutrition-sensitive' interventions being interventions for which the primary objective is not nutrition, but that have nonetheless been designed to achieve nutritional objectives and address the underlying causes of malnutrition (as opposed to 'nutrition-specific' interventions, the primary objective of which is to address nutrition) (Ruel, Alderman, and Maternal and Child Nutrition Study Group 2013; Girard et al. 2012).

To assist our examination of nutrition in Ethiopia, we develop a new conceptual framework for examining the determinants of food environments and how they shape food acquisition and nutrition outcomes. Ultimately, people's food acquisition is a result of their interaction with local food environments. Swinburn et al. (2013) defined the food environment as the 'collective physical, economic, policy and sociocultural surroundings, opportunities and conditions that influence people's food and beverage choices and nutritional status' (Swinburn et al. 2013: 2). Furthermore, Turner et al. (2017) have defined a set of measurable dimensions of food environments, and a conceptualization that provides for two inter-related aspects of food environments, distinguishing between:

- the 'external food environment', relating to: food availability, food price, vendor and product characteristics, and food marketing and regulation; and
- the 'personal food environment', relating to: accessibility (for example, physical distance to food sources, time, and transport), food affordability, convenience, and desirability.

Both notional and effective demands are thus a function of characteristics of the food environment—both the 'external' and 'personal' characteristics (Turner et al. 2017). To understand the factors that influence these various aspects of the food environment, we draw on the work of Sen (1981), who described a framework for understanding effective demand, and Fine (1997) who provides a theoretical challenge to the framework of Sen.

In his entitlement approach to famine, Sen identifies four key factors influencing the effective demand for food—and, essentially, food environments. These are: production-based entitlements (i.e. consumption of food produced from one's own garden or field); trade-based entitlements (i.e. food purchase funded by the income from sales of another product, such as a cash crop); own-labour entitlements (i.e. food purchase funded by waged income); and transfer-based entitlements (i.e. food access through gifts, food aid, etc.). Importantly, Sen's approach shifts attention away from food availability per se, focusing attention instead on those factors affecting effective food demand.

Fine (1997) has argued that much of the dissent over Sen's work stems from disagreements over underlying implicit theoretical propositions that themselves are not readily apparent in the entitlement framework. Specifically, Fine argues that a focus on effective demand for food needs to be combined with an understanding of how various kinds of demand emerge in a political economy context, including:

(i) how own production is related to land access and production;
(ii) how wages and employment are determined;
(iii) how, and at what prices, food is produced, processed, and distributed through national and international processes;
(iv) how the state provides food aid, transfers, and generally responds to food crises;
(v) how international agencies operate.

Also important to this discussion is the work of the various political economists who have described the role agriculture plays in the process of industrialization. Eschewing the comparative static approach to sectoral growth of mainstream economics, many political economy writers have focused on the long-term synergies between agrarian transformations and capitalist development (see also Chapters 26 and 49). On the interaction of the agricultural and industrial sectors, Kay (2009) has concluded: 'In a dynamic understanding of poverty and development, the key aspect is... attainment of a dynamic interaction and synergies between both sectors.' There are a range of interactions between these two sectors, such as transfers of labour, raw materials, and finance. However, agriculture is seen as having a key impact on industrial growth through its role in producing affordable food (Kay 2009). The impact of cheap food is mediated through two pathways: the effect on real wages (and therefore on the potential for accumulation in industry); and through the creation of domestic demand for non-food products (through the impact on disposable income). In the early stages of industrialization, agriculture's contribution to this industrialization is thus crucial (Kalecki 1993).

The frameworks described earlier help with understanding how food environments, and food and nutrition security, may be affected by a wide range of social, economic, and political changes. Therefore, to examine how state policy influences the determinants of local food environments (and thus food and nutrition security), we focus on four areas that the work of both Turner and Fine suggest affect both the structure of effective demand and the nature of the food environment:

- Own production
- Wages and employment
- Food processing and market distribution
- Food transfers through government and international agency operation.

We will use these domains to examine how state policy influences the various aspects of food environments in Ethiopia, and thus the interrelationship between economic and nutrition policy in Ethiopia.

22.3 Trends in Food and Nutrition Outcomes in Ethiopia

Several key nutrition indicators improved in Ethiopia from 2008 onwards, the most significant being the improvement in child stunting (see also Chapter 23). Table 22.1 also shows declines in the prevalence of wasting, underweight, and anaemia in children aged under five years.

Table 22.1 Comparison of changes for average children and bottom asset quintile

		2005	2011	2016	Percentage change (2005–16)
Stunting	all children	47	44	38	-19%
	bottom quintile	*48*	*49*	*45*	*-7%*
Underweight	all children	38	29	24	-37%
	bottom quintile	*43*	*36*	*31*	*-28%*
Wasting	all children	11	10	10	-10%
	bottom quintile	*13*	*12*	*14*	*+8%*
Childhood anaemia	all children	54	44	57	+6%
	bottom quintile	*60*	*48*	*68*	*+13%*

Sources: DHS data 2005 (CSA); DHS data 2011 (CSA/ICF 2012); DHS data 2016 (CSA/ICF 2016).

While Table 22.1 describes a positive picture for some indicators, there are two key concerns. First, data collected in 2016 suggest that childhood anaemia began to rise again rapidly (CSA/ICF 2016). Second, where the data can be disaggregated by asset quintile, there is evidence that overall, the bottom quintile experience a much smaller improvement than the population average (see Table 22.1).

Chapter 23 of this volume argues that exclusive breastfeeding, latterly as an outcome of Ethiopia's National Nutrition Programme (NNP), the first version of which covered the period 2008–13 (Ministry of Health 2015), has been a key driver of improvements in child stunting, while further improvements are challenged by poor dietary diversity in complementary feeding for infants. Their research, using a dietary diversity score compiled from DHS data, confirms the findings of other studies that suggest a range of nutrition problems in Ethiopia are due to reliance on a diet dominated by carbohydrates. The low intake of other macro- and micro-nutrients has been documented (FMoH/UNICEF/EU 2016), with data showing a concentration of food consumption on cereals, tubers, and pulses, with iron deficiencies driven by low intake of animal-source protein. Alongside a mixed record on nutrition outcomes, there has also been a volatile dependence on food imports over the period (2005–13).

As shown in Table 22.2, the data on food imports suggest a significant rise in food imports around the time of the food price spikes of 2008 and 2011. The relationship between imports and agricultural performance is complex. In Ethiopia, agricultural imports have been rising while agricultural exports have also risen, partially reflecting an expansion of non-traditional agricultural exports, such as cut flowers and teff (Mulugeta 2010).

UNCTAD (2003) argues that three factors have been increasing the rate of growth of food demand in Africa: rapid population growth, rapid urbanization, and rising income. Hassen et al. (2016) note that high recent urbanization rates in Ethiopia suggest 30 per cent of Ethiopia's population are expected to be living in cities in 2028. Using household

Table 22.2 Cereal import dependency ratio and value of food imports over total merchandise exports

Years	Cereal import dependency ratio (%) (3-year average)	Value of food imports over total merchandise exports (%) (3-year average)
2005–7	6.1	27
2006–8	7.2	30
2007–9	9.8	51
2008–10	11.9	60
2009–11	11.8	61
2010–12	9.3	55
2011–13	7	50

Source: FAO Stat.

expenditure data, Hassen et al. (2016) suggest that more affluent consumers demand more variety and choice, consume more processed and ready-to-eat foods, and pay more attention to food quality and safety. They conclude that urban dwellers allocate a much larger share of their food budget to animal products than rural dwellers (14.3 per cent versus 9.8 per cent). Similarly, the average household in an urban area consumed 11 kg of oils and fats per adult equivalent, while the corresponding figure for the average rural household was 4 kg. The consumption of fruit and vegetables is also considerably higher in urban areas.

These trends are reflected in changing patterns of food imports (USDA 2016). Palm oil, sugar and sweeteners, and wheat were the three largest agricultural imports by value in Ethiopia in 2015. The USDA (2016) finds that from 2010 to 2015, imports of palm oil doubled to nearly US$425 million, wheat imports climbed 20 per cent to over US$360 million, while imports of sugar and sweeteners grew 65 per cent to almost US$180 million. In addition, imports of rice, prepared foods, distilled spirits, pasta, and vegetable oil showed significant growth (USDA 2016). Over the six-year period from 2010 to 2015, rice imports increased six-fold, prepared food imports quadrupled, distilled spirit imports doubled, and pasta imports increased seven-fold.

22.4 Changing Nutrition Policy in Ethiopia

Ethiopia's political administrative structures to address nutrition policy have been shaped by the cycle of drought and famines that the country has historically experienced (Keller 1992; de Waal 1996; Webb and von Braun 1994). Thus, nutrition policy responses in Ethiopia have historically focused on acute or emergency food shortages. Examples of such policies include the establishment of a surveillance system for food security and acute malnutrition through the Disaster Prevention and Preparedness Commission (FDRE 2016b), and the 1996 National Food Security Strategy (FDRE 1996). However, there have been efforts in recent years to establish broader, more systematic policy responses to nutrition in the country. For example, in 2005 a study of the underlying causes of malnutrition was conducted by the MoH and Ministry of Agriculture (MoA) in collaboration with UNICEF (Benson 2005), and this formed the basis for the National Nutrition Programme (NNP).

22.5 The Evolution of the National Nutrition Programme

This progression of the policy landscape for nutrition is reflected in Ethiopia's first National Nutrition Programme (NNP) (FDRE 1996), which acknowledged the role of multiple sectors including health, agriculture, education, and social affairs, in addressing nutrition (Ministry of Health 2015). With its focus on multisectoral coordination, this more comprehensive nutrition policy thus includes greater clarity regarding the role of economic growth and development in improving nutrition.

The evolution of policy appears to have been influenced by greater recognition internationally of the way that economic policy influences food and nutrition security, with nutrition policy now widely considered to involve, at a minimum, collaboration between the agriculture, health, and environment sectors (Gillespie et al. 2013; Mendis 2010; Reinhardt and Fanzo 2014; Hawkesworth et al. 2010). Thus, 'nutrition-sensitive' interventions are considered to be key to improving nutritional outcomes (Ruel, Alderman, and Maternal and Child Nutrition Study Group 2013).

Despite this recognition of the need for coordinated policy, the first version of the NNP was judged to have been unsuccessful in developing multisectoral strategies (FDRE 2013). As a result, the NNP was revised (resulting in NNP-I, covering 2013–15) to give a greater focus on 'the multisectoral and multidimensional nature of nutrition' with the recognition that broad economic policy is key (FDRE 2013: 15). Three high-level indicators were set: i) reduce the prevalence of stunting from 44.4 per cent to 30 per cent by 2015; ii) reduce the prevalence of wasting from 9.7 per cent to 3 per cent by 2015; and iii) reduce the prevalence of chronic undernutrition in women of reproductive age from 27 per cent to 19 per cent. These were to be achieved through:

- agricultural policy: increases in production and improvements in seeds and technology; biofortification of staple foods (such as maize and sweet potato) (FDRE 2013: 26–7);
- industrial policy: the support of food production generally, and fortified food in particular; and ensuring local food quality and safety (FDRE 2013: 27–8);

- trade policy: better regulation of imported food items, and encouraging the importation of fortified food; and improving awareness of the benefits of fortified food (FDRE 2013: 1–28);
- social protection policy: implementing gender-sensitive safety net and credit programmes (FDRE 2013: 1–29); and
- finally, a group of disaster-preparedness interventions were designed to strengthen early warning systems and improve community participatory risk assessments (FDRE 2013: 1–29).

The government of Ethiopia sought to integrate NNP (and NNP-I) with the overarching national strategic framework, the Growth and Transformation Plan 2010/11–2014/15 (GTP-I) (FDRE 2011). Overall, the GTP provides a coherent set of mandates for sectoral action, and establishes targets within a five-year timeframe for each sector. GTP-I (2010–15) did not, however, explicitly reference nutrition, instead focusing on food-related targets, including cereal production targets, food reserve targets, and the number of people assisted by the Productive Safety Net Programme (FDRE 2011, Table 19).

Section 22.6 evaluates the success of these initiatives using our conceptual approach, and introduces critical literature. However, at this stage, it can be concluded that this period between 2010/11 and 2014/15 focused on the ability both to respond to acute nutrition crises through disaster preparedness (and enhanced food reserves) and to deal with chronic food security issues through agricultural productivity enhancement. Social protection support and other interventions to address food acquisition played a more limited role, with reductions planned in the percentage of households enrolled in the productive safety net scheme. These characterizations will be examined further in Section 22.6 using the conceptual framework.

22.6 Evaluating the Interrelationship between Economic Policy and Nutrition Policy in Ethiopia

This section describes the effectiveness of Ethiopian national policy in terms of the interrelationship between wider economic policy and nutrition outcomes. It should be read in conjunction with Chapter 23, which focuses on the evolution of nutrition-specific interventions to improve nutritional outcomes.

22.6.1 Own Production

Although the agricultural sector as a whole achieved a rapid rate of growth between 2010/11 and 2014/15—a 6.6 per cent annual average growth rate—this fell short of the 8 per cent annual average growth target (FDRE 2016a). Generally, GTP-II suggests that agricultural productivity did not rise as much as planned due to lower increases in the applications of agricultural inputs, such as fertilizer and improved seeds (FDRE 2016a: 25).

Given this growth, however, some of the improvements in nutrition and food outcomes shown in Table 22.1 are likely to have resulted from improvements in own production of food. There are two caveats about the limited impact of these improvements on overall nutrition: that this domain is one of five that affect food environments; and that own production alone is limited in its ability to address dietary diversity.

First, the data described in Section 22.3 show that food consumption is increasingly influenced by food purchased. From the trends in food imports, we can see a picture of a growing role for new and processed food in Ethiopian diets, especially to meet the demand from growing urban and middle-class populations. However, it is important that we do not ignore the role of purchased food more generally in Ethiopian food provisioning, including in rural areas. Using rural household survey data from 2004–6, Klugman (2007) estimated that about half the rural population are net buyers of food. Alternatively we can use data on household consumption to calculate the share met by own-food production. Hassen et al. (2016) have undertaken this exercise for data from the 2011 household survey and found that for an average rural household, only about 40 per cent of rural food consumption comes from own production. Neither Klugman (2007) nor Hassen et al. (2016) have disaggregated their results for the poorest rural households, who may be landless or have limited agricultural output or access to agricultural extension or improved inputs and so are likely to source even less of their food needs from own production (see Chapter 18).

Second, the diversity of own production will be important to improve diet quality. While the majority of farmers focus on staple production, own-food entitlements are unlikely to provide the dietary diversity necessary for improved nutritional outcomes (Hassen et al. 2016). More emphasis is needed on diversification for those rural households that are dependent on own consumption of food. Alternatively, marketed production of staples must rise, allowing households to purchase other more nutritious foods in order to achieve more diverse diets.

The analysis by Hassen et al. (2016) of 2011 household food expenditure data suggests that for average rural households, 34 per cent of food purchases were funded by the sales of agricultural output. This finding is complemented by that from other studies, such as Kuma et al. (2018) which provides evidence on the role of coffee sales for food security. Data on rising exports of agricultural products (discussed in Section 22.3) suggests that there have been increasing marketing opportunities for agricultural products in rural Ethiopia. For some staple products, export bans were introduced during food price spikes and then lifted. For other products, new 'non-traditional' markets have emerged although these are likely to have been less important for smaller-scale farmers, and high-value crops did not meet their growth targets in GTP-I (FDRE 2016a).

Complex dynamics do exist where these export crops are also domestic food crops, with the potential for increased income for net sellers being offset by the potential for income losses by net buyers. Teff, the major staple of Ethiopia, is a case in point. Its status as a new 'superfood' had led to concerns that the lucrative teff export market has been the cause of sharp price rises on local markets. Despite its success in earning scarce foreign exchange, there have been some criticisms of the partial lifting of the export ban on teff, with a concern that, however sensitive the policy was to nutrition concerns, its impact will be to reduce food security (Secorun 2016; Reda 2015).

22.6.2 Wages and Employment

We have seen in Section 22.3 evidence of changing food provision trends in Ethiopia, with a shift towards processed and purchased food. Using 2011 household expenditure data, Hassen et al. (2016) find that approximately 25 per cent of all food in average rural households is paid for by remittances, sales of non-agricultural products, and wage income.[1] This figure is higher in urban areas, where 40 per cent of food expenditures were paid for by wage income in the same survey.

These data show the importance of charting trends in real food prices and understanding the reasons for food price spikes. Headey et al. (2012) suggest particularly high food price rises in Ethiopia compared to other developing countries. Using household expenditure data, Hassen et al. (2016) suggest that the average price paid per calorie increased by 8 per cent between 1996 and 2011 in real terms. However, there were sharp differences in the trends for different food items. Hassen et al. (2016) suggest that the real prices paid for calories from cereals were 20 per cent lower in 2011 than the price paid in 1996, while the real prices of other food categories have mostly risen. Importantly, Hassen et al.'s (2016) data suggested that the prices per calorie of food commonly consumed by the poorest rural households, such as cassava, enset, and sorghum, showed a real price decline overall, with the important exception being pulses, and, given the importance of this food group for micronutrient adequacy, this again suggests the potential for deterioration in diet quality for the poorest.

While these data are somewhat problematic as they do not distinguish in a detailed way between the different prices paid by poorer and richer households in the same location (instead relying on price collection in a limited number of different locations), they do suggest that compiling nutritious food baskets with an appropriate balance of macro- and micro-nutrients has become more expensive over time.

Within the longer-run trends discussed in the Hassen et al. (2016) data, there have been two major periods of price spike, in 2008 and 2011. The causes of these food price spikes are debated. While the government (FDRE 2016a) suggests that the rise in global food prices and fuel prices was at the heart of domestic price rises in the GTP-I period (as do Durevall, Loening, and Birru 2013), Admassie (2014) argues that domestic factors were more salient. Admassie (2014) suggests the domestic food prices are relatively insulated from rises in world markets as more than 75 per cent of food consumption in Ethiopia is

[1] The source of remittances is unclear in this survey and these are likely to come from the waged employment of family members in other parts of Ethiopia or internationally. Also these shares are likely to be higher for the poorest rural households, where the importance of wage and remittance income is often underestimated (Cramer et al. 2017).

comprised of local staples (such as sorghum and teff) that are little traded internationally. Instead, Admassie (2014) points to currency devaluation and import restrictions as causing food price spikes. However, this ignores the greater role of food purchases in food provisioning (see also Section 22.6.3 on the monetization of food aid), and the importance of maize and wheat in household consumption, as well as the increased costs of fuel, fertilizer, and transportation. FAO (2014) in particular suggest that price rises in imported fertilizer have had a direct impact on food prices due to the high share of imported fertilizer in farm inputs in Ethiopia, despite the low use of fertilizer.

The food and fuel price rises of 2008 and 2011 caused significant balance of payments problems, and Table 22.2 shows the growing share of merchandise export revenue required to cover cereal imports, with the 3-year cereal import dependency ratio rising above 10 per cent in 2008–10 and 2009–11. Admassie (2014) notes the policy responses to stabilize food prices, including an export ban on cereals; attempts to reduce the money supply by raising the minimum deposit requirements for domestic banks; price controls; and action against speculative hording. FAO (2014) also note the distribution of subsidized food products (oil, wheat flour, and sugar) and the release of the strategic grain reserve—and we can see this as a key reason why GTP-I failed in its target to increase the national grain reserve. Indeed, FAO (2014) provide evidence that grain withdrawals from the national food reserve have substantially changed in character. Withdrawals for emergency operations reduced from 74 per cent (averaged over the period 1994–2009) to 28 per cent (averaged over the period 2005–9), whereas those intended for the safety net rose from 21 per cent (1994–2009) to 57 per cent (2005–9) and those for price stabilization increased from 5 per cent (averaged over the period 1994–2009) to 15 per cent (2005–9). Admassie (2014) argues that this release of wheat and maize helped to reduce the price of wheat in the domestic market.

However, this argument is weakened by the lack of data on the food prices paid by the poorest. What is clear from other evidence is that the bottom 10 per cent of rural households have actually suffered from declining consumption since 2005 and that inequality increased between 2000 and 2011 (see Chapter 18).

Thus in the GTP-I period, there were significant increases in the real prices of some foods that seem to have eroded real consumer purchasing power, thereby challenging food security. In GTP-II, however, specific attention is given to food prices and the purchasing power of consumers. This is achieved through a focus on job creation and the establishment of foreign currency and physical food reserves to withstand international shocks (FDRE 2016a). It will be important to evaluate whether these strategies are successful in stabilizing food prices and consequently purchasing power, especially for the poorest.

22.6.3 Food Processing and Market Distribution

The National Nutrition Policy (NNP/NNP-I) particularly envisaged that industrial and trade policies would increase the affordability and attractiveness of a diverse set of food goods. There was a particular focus on fortified food, both domestically produced and imported, with the NNP-I intending that the domestic food and retail industry would encourage greater consumption of fortified products by consumers. However, these multisectoral elements of the NNP-I were found to be the most challenging.

The obstacles to integration of nutrition-sensitive policy across sectors were outlined in the National Nutrition Policy for the subsequent period (NNP-II) (FDRE 2016b: 20–1), which describes how 'Although multisectoral nutrition coordination and integration had been advocated on every forum and seemed to have improved over the last 5 years, most line ministries have lagged in mainstreaming nutrition into their sectoral strategic plans. This was especially true of efforts to cascade nutrition down to the implementation level.' The NNP-II describes why this may have happened: sectoral departments lacked effective organizational structures to mainstream nutrition; sectoral plans were not always reshaped to include nutrition goals; sectoral nutrition plans were not allocated a budget; responsibilities and accountabilities were not clearly defined around shared goals; and, finally, the mechanisms to capture nutrition-relevant data from all sectors were not developed (FDRE 2016b: 20–1).

The structure for multisectoral working was strengthened in the third iteration of the NNP, NNP-II (2016–20) (FDRE 2016b). NNP-II aimed to improve multisectoral working via three broad sets of actions: strengthening the NNCB and local coordination bodies; requiring ministries to establish new nutrition capacity; and establishing both new evidence and new evidence-based decision-making systems (FDRE 2016b: 22–3).

22.6.4 Food Transfers

Using household expenditure data for 2011, Hassen et al. (2016) suggest that government donations and social security (mostly through the Productive Safety Net Programme (PSNP) and food aid) were relatively unimportant in both rural and urban areas in terms of funding food consumption, making up 2.3 per cent and 1.6 per cent of total food expenditures in urban and rural areas, respectively (Hassen et al. 2016). However, there is evidence that during this period, both direct transfers (through participation in social protection schemes) and indirect transfers (through the provision of subsidized products, discussed earlier) are likely to have increased.

The number of households in the PSNP did not fall as substantially as planned in the GTP-I, with 3.4 million enrolled in 2014/15 compared to the planned target of 1.3 million. As can be seen from the FAO (2014) and Admassie (2014), the PSNP has grown immensely since its inception in 2005, when it covered 5 million beneficiaries. In particular, there was rapid growth during the food price spike of 2008, when PSNP beneficiary numbers increased to 8 million and donors also expanded non-PSNP food aid schemes (Admassie 2014). Between 45 and 65 per cent of PSNP beneficiaries (Klugman 2007) receive cash through cash-for-work and direct cash transfers. This shift from food provision to cash provision has led to several changes. First, the share of food aid has fallen in food imports, with direct food aid seen previously as a depressing influence on domestic food prices (Klugman 2007). While cash transfers are seen as stimulating local demand, Klugman (2007) raises concerns about their potential for creating price inflation (Tadesse and Gerald 2009).

While the PSNP is envisaged to expand over time in the latest version of the GTP (and thereby improve effective food demand) (FDRE 2016a: 24), there are critical voices. Sender (Chapter 18) reviews the evidence on the PSNP, concluding that there is clear evidence that the PSNP targeting has been poor, with significant use of it to bolster the political elite. Moreover, Gebrehiwot and Castilla's (2018) evaluation of the impact of the PSNP suggests several reasons for caution. Overall, while they found that the receipt of PSNP support increased calorie intake, there was no impact on child anthropometrics nor on dietary diversity. Gebrehiwot and Castilla (2018) suggest that one reason may be that the price of higher-quality food may have risen, particularly for animal-sourced foods, over the two years of their study. They were also concerned that the PSNP had not been paired with nutrition education messages about food quality and child feeding.

22.7 Conclusions

Our analysis suggests that there have been important changes in the effective demand for food in Ethiopia over recent years. Own production of food may be important for some rural households, but overall the data suggest that rural and urban households purchase a significant proportion of their food. Policy during the period 2010–15 focused on own-production access, and somewhat on food transfers and reducing food emergencies. The data suggest that direct food production may have risen for some rural households, but this was more likely to be the middle- and high-income rural households, while the real price of particular foods, particularly animal products and non-staple foods, rose sharply. This is worrying given the evidence of the impact of low dietary diversity on nutrition outcomes for adults and children. Food and cash transfers in this period increased as a result of government response to the food price spikes. This partly occurred through the increased numbers enrolled in the PSNP, and partly through the transfer of food aid and subsidized food products. The distribution of subsidized products will likely have helped improve calorie intake and, somewhat, dietary diversity (as wheat flour, oil, and sugar were distributed). However, it would not have aided in the consumption of animal-source protein, nor of fruit and vegetables, and there are reasons to be concerned that these transfers were poorly targeted and had little impact on the poorest.

These sharply rising prices were only partly caused by international food price spikes; other contributory causes were currency devaluation, monetization of food aid, and rapid shifts in urbanization. New policy (particularly as described in GTP-II) recognizes that stabilizing food prices is of crucial significance, not only to achieve inflation targets but also for food security. To stabilize food prices, two components of policy must be effective. First, there needs to be greater effective demand for food, not only for staples but also for a variety of products that provide essential micro-nutrients, and this will require either real price falls or greater productivity of own production. While agricultural policies will be relevant, so too will be industrial and trade policy. Improvements in the capacity to produce and import both fortified and non-fortified food are essential. To deal with instability in international markets, the government must build up both foreign exchange and a physical food reserve. At the same time, the domestic production of fertilizer and other agricultural inputs will also reduce the impact of international price peaks on final food prices. A second component of a broad policy around food affordability would focus on the creation of 'decent' work, i.e. the growth of employment opportunities associated with higher wages.

A final issue to raise is the implications if the government of Ethiopia finds it difficult to maintain cheap food, for either urban or rural households. Our discussion has focused on the implications for food and nutrition security. However, there are clearly implications for the dynamics of economic development. When real food prices rise, there are two likely outcomes. First, there may be pressures to increase real wages and in this way accumulation can be constrained. Headey et al. (2012) have argued that there is no empirical evidence that this has yet occurred in Ethiopia. This may well be due to the actions by the government of Ethiopia to dampen down the food price spikes. However, if continued action were needed, both foreign exchange and food reserves may not be sufficient, and greater wage pressures may emerge. Second, if the real price of food rises, it can reduce the disposable income available for non-food consumption, and in a domestic market as large as that of Ethiopia, this could have significant impacts on the potential market for nascent industrial sectors.

References

Admassie, A. (2014). 'Food Price Policy in an Era of Market Instability: A Political Economy Analysis', in *The Political Economy of Food Price Policy in Ethiopia*, ed. Per Pinstrup-Andersen (Oxford: Oxford University Press): 133–53.

Baker, P., C. Hawkes, K. Wingrove, A. Demaio, J. Parkhurst, A. M. Thow, and H. L. Walls (2018). 'What Drives Political Commitment for Nutrition? A Review and Framework Synthesis to Inform the United Nations Decade of Action on Nutrition', *BMJ Global Health* 3 (1): e000485.

Benson, T. (2005). *Improving Nutrition as a Development Priority: Addressing Undernutrition within National Policy Processes in sub-Saharan Africa* (Washington, DC: International Food Policy Research Institute).

Cramer, C., D. Johnston, D,. C, Oya, and J. Sender (2017). 'Fairtrade and Labour Markets in Ethiopia and Uganda', *Journal of Development Studies* 53 (6): 841–56.

CSA/ICF (2011). 'Ethiopia Demographic and Health Survey: Key Findings', Addis Ababa, Central Statistical Agency and ICF International), Calverton, MD.

CSA/ICF (2012). 'Ethiopia Demographic and Health Survey 2011', Addis Ababa, Central Statistical Agency and ICF International, Rockville, MD.

CSA/ICF (2016). 'Ethiopia Demographic and Health Survey 2016', Addis Ababa, Central Statistical Agency and ICF International, Rockville, MD.

CSA/ORC Macro (2006). 'Ethiopia Demographic and Health Survey 2005', Central Statistical Agency, Addis Ababa and ORC Macro, Calverton, MD.

Devereux, S. (1988). 'Entitlements, Availability and Famine: A Revisionist View of Wollo, 1972–1974', *Food Policy* 13 (3): 270–82.
de Waal, A. (1996). *Famine Crimes: Politics and the Disaster Relief Industry in Africa* (Oxford: James Currey).
Durevall, D., J. L. Loening, and Y. A. Birru (2013). 'Inflation Dynamics and Food Prices in Ethiopia', *Journal of Development Economics* 104: 89–106.
Federal Ministry of Health (2008). 'National Nutrition Strategy', FDRE, Addis Ababa.
FDRE (1996). 'National Food Security Strategy', Ministry of Health, Addis Ababa.
FDRE (2011). 'Growth and Transformation Plan (2010/11–2014/15)', Addis Ababa.
FDRE (2013). 'National Nutrition Programme: June 2013–June 2015', Addis Ababa.
FDRE (2016a). 'Growth and Transformation Plan II (GTP II) (2015/16–2019/20)', Addis Ababa.
FDRE (2016b). 'National Nutrition Programme II: 2016–20', Addis Ababa.
Fine, B. (1997). 'Entitlement Failure?', *Development and Change* 28 (4): 617–47.
FMoH/UNICEF/EU (2016). 'Situation Analysis of the Nutrition Sector in Ethiopia: 2000–2015', Ethiopian Federal Ministry of Health, UNICEF and European Commission Delegation.
Food and Agriculture Organisation (FAO) (2014). 'Country Fact Sheet on Food and Agriculture Policy Trends', FAO.
Gebrehiwot, T. and C. Castilla (2018). 'Do Safety Net Transfers Improve Household Diets and Reduce Undernutrition? Evidence from Rural Ethiopia', Working Paper, Partnership for Economic Policy: Structural Transformation of African Agriculture and Rural Spaces.
Gillespie, S., L. Haddad, V. Mannar, N. Nisbett, and P. Menon (2013). 'The Politics of Reducing Malnutrition: Building Commitment and Accelerating Progress', *Lancet* 382: 552–69.
Girard, A. W., J. L. Self, C. McAuliffe, and O. Olude (2012). 'The Effects of Household Food Production Strategies on the Health and Nutrition Outcomes of Women and Young Children: A Systematic Review', *Paediatric and Perinatal Epidemiology* 26 (s1): 205–22.
Hassen, I. W., M. Dereje, B. Minten, and K. Hirvonen, (2016). 'Diet Transformation in Africa: The Case of Ethiopia.' Working Paper 87, International Food Policy Research Institute—Ethiopia Strategy Support Program (ESSP).
Hawkesworth, S., A. D. Dangour, D. Johnston, et al. (2010). 'Feeding the World Healthily: The Challenge of Measuring the Effects of Agriculture on Health', *Philosophical Transactions of the Royal Society B: Biological Sciences* 1554 (365): 3083–97.
Headey, D., F. B. Nisrane, I. Worku, M. Dereje, and A. S. Taffesse (2012). Urban Wage Behavior and Food Price Inflation: The Case of Ethiopia', Working Paper 41, Development Strategy and Governance Division, International Food Policy Research Institute—Ethiopia Strategy Support Program II.
Kalecki, M. (1993). 'The Problem of Financing Economic Development', in *The Collected Works of Michal Kalecki: Volume 5, Developing Economies*, ed. Jerzy Osiatynski, (Oxford: Clarendon Press): 23–44.
Kay, C. (2009). 'Development Strategies and Rural Development: Exploring Synergies, Eradicating Poverty', *Journal of Peasant Studies* 36 (1): 103–37.
Keller, E. J. (1992). 'Drought, War and the Politics of Famine in Ethiopia and Eritrea', *Journal of Modern African Studies* 30 (4): 609–24.
Klugman, J. (2007). 'Ethiopia: Explaining Food Price Inflation', Discussion Paper No. 72898, World Bank, Washington, DC.
Kuma T., M. Dereje, K. Hirvonen, and B. Minten (2018). 'Cash Crops and Food Security: Evidence from Ethiopian Smallholder Coffee Producers', *Journal of Development Studies* 54 DOI: 10.1080/00220388.2018.1425396.

Malik, V. S., W. C. Willet, and F. B. Hu (2013). 'Global Obesity: Trends, Risk Factors and Policy Implications', *National Review of Endocrinology* 9: 13–27.

Mendis, S. (2010). 'The Policy Agenda for Prevention and Control of Non-Communicable Diseases', *British Medical Bulletin* 96: 23–43.

Ministry of Health (2015). 'Health Sector Transformation Plan (HSTP)', Ministry of Health, Federal Democratic Republic of Ethiopia.

Mulugeta, F. Z. (2010). 'The Contribution of Major Export Commodities of Ethiopia to the Instability of the Country's Export Earnings', Working Paper, (TWP 1009), Trade Policy Training Centre in Africa.

Reda, A. (2015). 'Achieving Food Security in Ethiopia by Promoting Productivity of Future World Food Tef: A Review', *Advances in Plants & Agriculture Research* 2 (2): 1–10.

Reinhardt, K. and J. Fanzo (2014). 'Addressing Chronic Malnutrition through Multi-Sectoral, Sustainable Approaches: A Review of the Causes and Consequences', *Frontiers in Nutrition* 1: 13.

Ruel, M. T., H. Alderman, and Maternal and Child Nutrition Study Group (2013). 'Nutrition-Sensitive Interventions and Programmes: How Can They Help to Accelerate Progress in Improving Maternal and Child Nutrition?' *Lancet* 382 (9891): 536–51.

Secorun, L. (2016). 'Teff Could Be the Next Quinoa as Ethiopia Boosts Exports'. https://www.theguardian.com/sustainable-business/2016/oct/14/teff-quinoa-ethiopia-boosts-exports-food-africa

Sen, A. (1981). *Poverty and Famines: An Essay on Entitlement and Deprivation* (1st edition) (Oxford: Clarendon Press).

Smith, L. C. and L. Haddad (2015). 'Reducing Child Under-Nutrition: Past Drivers and Priorities for the Post-MDG Era', *Science Direct* 11 (68): 180–204.

Swinburn et al. (2013). 'Monitoring and Benchmarking Government Policies and Actions', *Obesity Reviews* (Suppl 1): 24–37.

Tadesse, G. and S. Gerald (2009). 'Food Aid, Food Prices, and Producer Disincentives in Ethiopia', *American Journal of Agricultural Economics* 91 (4): 942–55.

Tebekaw, Y., C. Teller, and U. Colon-Ramos (2014). 'The Burden of Underweight and Overweight among Women in Addis Ababa, Ethiopia', *BMC Public Health* 14: 1126.

Turner, C., S. Kadiyala, A. Aggarwal, J. Coates, et al. (2017). 'Concepts and Methods for Food Environment Research in Low- and Middle-Income Countries', Agriculture, Nutrition and Health Academy Food Environments Working Group (ANH-FEWG). Innovative Methods and Metrics for Agriculture and Nutrition Actions (IMMANA) programme, London.

UNCTAD (United Nations Conference on Trade and Development) (2003). 'Economic Development in Africa: Trade Performance and Commodity Dependence', UNCTAD, Geneva. http://www.unctad.org

USAID (2016). 'Ethiopia'. https://www.usaid.gov/ethiopia

USDA (United States Department of Agriculture) (2016). 'Ethiopia's Agriculture Imports Continue Growing', Global Agricultural Information Network, Addis Ababa.

Walls, H. L., S. Kadiyala, and R. D. Smith (2016). 'Research and Policy for Addressing Malnutrition in All its Forms', *Obesity* 24 (10): 2032.

Webb, P. and J. von Braun (1994). *Famine and Food Security in Ethiopia: Lessons for Africa* (Chichester: John Wiley & Sons).

Zello, G. A. (2015). 'National Nutrition Programs in Emerging Countries: Coping with the Double Burden of Malnutrition and Obesity in Ethiopia', *Canadian Journal of Diabetes* 39: 4.

CHAPTER 23

CHANGES IN CHILD UNDER-NUTRITION IN ETHIOPIA, 2000–16

JENNA GOLAN, DEREK HEADEY, KALLE HIRVONEN, AND JOHN HODDINOTT

23.1 INTRODUCTION

SINCE the early 2000s, the Ethiopian economy has recorded high rates of growth in per capita GDP (see Chapters 19 and 20). Poverty rates, while still high, have fallen, but are these improvements in well-being also seen when we consider non-monetary measures of welfare? In this chapter, we consider one such measure, the nutritional status of children.[1] Nutrition can be thought of as the outcome of a production function with three broad sets of inputs: food (or nutrients), health (particularly early childhood infections, chronic and acute) and care (decisions and behaviours of caregivers). Changes in these inputs are partly influenced by economic growth and thus nutritional status provides a lens through which we can assess how changes in income translate into changes into a non-monetary measure of welfare. It is also of interest given the high level of political commitment given to reducing child under-nutrition through the National Nutrition Program (GFDRE 2013; GFDRE 2016a). With the Seqota Declaration of 2015, Ethiopia further announced its ambitious goal of ending child malnutrition by 2030 (GFDRE 2016b).

We find that since 2000, the prevalence of chronic under-nutrition in children aged 0–5 years has fallen substantially, from 58 per cent in 2000 to 38 per cent in 2016. This translates into an annual reduction of 2.5 per cent a year. Compared to the international evidence on

[1] The chapter focuses on under-nutrition—a condition in which an individual is not receiving an adequate amount of macro or micro nutrients—either because of poor food intake/availability or because of increased nutrient requirements due to illnesses. Over-nutrition represents another form of malnutrition. In 2016, only 1 per cent of Ethiopian children less than 5 years of age were overweight—too heavy for their height (CSA and ICF 2016). Consequently, this form of malnutrition is not discussed here.

changes in stunting rates reported in Park, Heady, and Hoddinott (2016), this rate is one of the fastest reductions anywhere in the developing world. After documenting how chronic under-nutrition among young children has changed over time and space, and by wealth strata and gender, we use insights from the age dynamics of stunting to understand the possible underlying drivers of this rapid improvement in chronic under-nutrition rates.

23.2 Data

We use four rounds of nationally representative Demographic and Health Survey (DHS) data for Ethiopia. The first survey was administered in 2000 and the latest in 2016. In each round, heights and weights of children were measured and near-identical survey instruments were administered on the participating households in all rounds. The DHS also contains rich information on key inputs to child growth outcomes such as breastfeeding and complementary feeding practices and the prevalence of illnesses.

Stunting, or low height for a child's age, is considered a measure of chronic under-nutrition. This is measured through height-for-age Z-scores (HAZ) that capture the distance in height to the median child of a healthy and well-nourished reference population. The World Health Organization (WHO 1995) uses a cut-off of −2 standard deviation as an indicator of severe chronic under-nutrition, or stunting. In a healthy and well-nourished population this is rare: approximately 2 per cent of the population have a height-for-age Z-score that is two standard deviations below the international growth standard. Higher stunting prevalence rates imply that the population suffers from chronic under-nutrition.

Stunting manifests itself in the first 1,000 days of life, i.e. from conception to approximately 24 months of age (Victora et al. 2010; Shrimpton et al. 2001). The typical prognosis is the following. First, in many poor countries like Ethiopia, a sizeable fraction of the children is born stunted as a result of maternal malnutrition. In the first few months of life, most children are partially protected from infections and low-nutrient diets by intensive breastfeeding. Rapid growth faltering begins at around 6 months of age when children are: (i) introduced to complementary foods that often lack sufficient macro and micro nutrients to support growth; and (ii) exposed to diarrhoeal or other infections that sap growth. After this age, further growth faltering is less likely to occur as immune systems strengthen, but there is also little evidence of systematic catch-up growth in the first five years of life (Leroy et al. 2014). As in the UNICEF (1990) framework, inadequate dietary intake and exposure to infections can be regarded as immediate causes of under-nutrition. These immediate causes are further shaped by household food security (or incomes), maternal and child care, and access to health services, as well as hygiene conditions at home. Previous research has shown how various underlying causes, such as household assets, parental education levels, access to antenatal care, and access to safe water and proper sanitation, are associated with lower stunting prevalence in Ethiopia (Headey 2014; Woodruff et al. 2016; Endris, Asefa, and Dube 2017; Tadesse and Alemu 2015; Headey, Hoddinott, and Park 2017).

23.3 Trends in Stunting Rates

Table 23.1 reports the stunting prevalence for each year and by child gender. In 2000, nearly 58 per cent of Ethiopian children 0–5 years of age were stunted, indicating very high malnutrition severity. By 2016, the stunting rate had dropped to 38 per cent. Annualizing, the prevalence of stunting has fallen by 2.5 per cent per year. Despite this, stunting remains high. As has been documented elsewhere in sub-Saharan Africa (Wamani et al. 2007), boys are slightly more likely to be stunted than girls.

Table 23.2 provides an overview of the spatial distribution of stunting. Stunting rates are considerably higher in rural areas. In 2016, 26 per cent of children in urban areas were categorized compared to 39.9 per cent in rural areas. Moreover, urban areas have witnessed a considerably faster reduction in stunting prevalence; 3.6 per cent per year compared to 2.4 per year in rural areas. A regional disaggregation shows that stunting rates have decreased in all regions, except in Dire Dawa. Out of the four most populous Highland regions, stunting reduction was fastest in Tigray (−2.9 per cent per annum) and slowest in Amhara (−1.8 per cent per annum).

In Table 23.3 we look at stunting prevalence by wealth quintiles.[2] As has been documented elsewhere in sub-Saharan Africa (Moradi and Hirvonen 2016), wealth is strongly correlated with children's heights in Ethiopia. In 2016, 46 per cent of the children residing in the poorest households were categorized as stunted while the corresponding figure in the richest households was 26 per cent. Moreover, the reduction in stunting prevalence was fastest in the top wealth quintiles, averaging more than 3 per cent per annum compared to less than 2 per cent at the bottom quintiles.

Table 23.1 Trends in prevalence of stunted children in Ethiopia, 2000–16, by child gender

	All	Girls	Boys
2000	57.6	56.1	59.1
2005	50.9	49.4	52.3
2011	44.2	42.5	45.9
2016	38.4	35.4	41.4
CAGR	**−2.5**	**−2.8**	**−2.2**

Note: Based on survey weights. CAGR = compound annual growth rate.
Source: Demographic Health Surveys for Ethiopia.

[2] It is worth noting that these wealth quintiles are *rankings*, not absolute measures of wealth. For example, an average household in the richest quintile in 2000 is probably much poorer than the average household in the richest quintile in 2016.

Table 23.2 Trends in prevalence of stunted children in Ethiopia, 2000–16, by residence

Region	2000	2005	2011	2016	CAGR
Rural	58.8	52.1	46.1	39.9	**−2.4**
Urban	46.8	35.4	30.9	26.0	**−3.6**
Addis Ababa	33.8	24.2	22.4	14.7	**−5.1**
Afar	53.6	41.0	50.2	40.8	**−1.7**
Amhara	63.1	63.9	51.3	47.2	**−1.8**
Benishangul-Gumuz	50.6	44.1	48.1	42.9	**−1.0**
Dire Dawa	33.8	33.5	35.1	40.7	**1.2**
Gambella	41.1	39.0	28.1	23.2	**−3.5**
Harari	42.0	44.7	29.4	31.7	**−1.7**
Oromia	54.1	44.2	41.6	36.4	**−2.5**
SNNP	59.4	54.7	43.7	39.3	**−2.6**
Somali	50.9	50.2	32.5	26.8	**−3.9**
Tigray	61.3	47.0	50.8	38.6	**−2.9**

Note: Based on survey weights. CAGR = compound annual growth rate.
Source: Demographic Health Surveys for Ethiopia.

Table 23.3 Trends in prevalence of stunted children in Ethiopia, 2000–16, by asset quintile

	Poorest quintile	Second quintile	Middle quintile	Fourth quintile	Richest quintile
2000	62.9	55.1	59.9	55.2	48.2
2005	54.9	53.4	50.5	51.6	40.9
2011	49.1	48.3	46.5	44.5	28.6
2016	46.4	41.7	40.7	32.9	26.3
CAGR	**−1.9**	**−1.7**	**−2.4**	**−3.2**	**−3.7**

Note: Based on survey weights. CAGR = compound annual growth rate.
Source: Demographic Health Surveys for Ethiopia.

23.4 Changes in Stunting Age Dynamics

Building on Shrimpton et al. (2001) and Victora et al. (2010), we assess how stunting age dynamics have changed over time. In Figures 23.1 and 23.2 we use local polynomial regression methods to regress stunting prevalence on children's age in months in rural and urban areas, respectively. The solid regression line represents the estimated relationship in 2000 and the dashed the corresponding relationship in 2016. Interestingly, we see no improvements in stunting prevalence at birth: about 20 per cent of the rural children

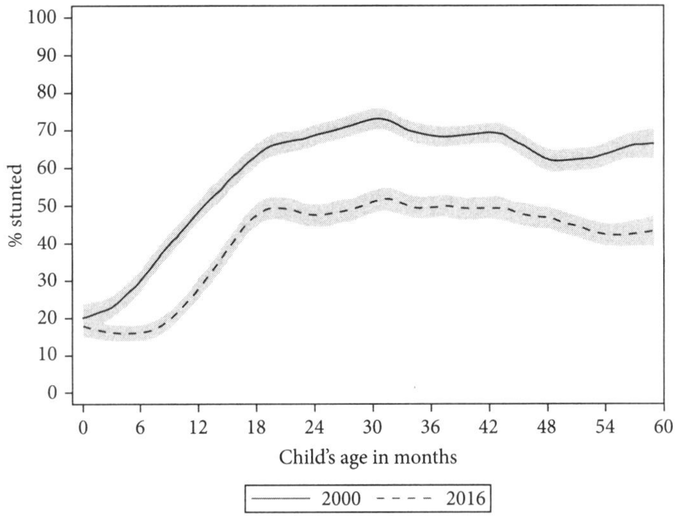

FIGURE 23.1 Trends in stunting rates in rural areas by children's age, 2000 and 2016

Note: Local polynomial regression. Vertical axis measures the (latent) probability that the child is stunted. Shaded area represents 95 per cent confidence interval.

Source: The Demographic Health Surveys for Ethiopia.

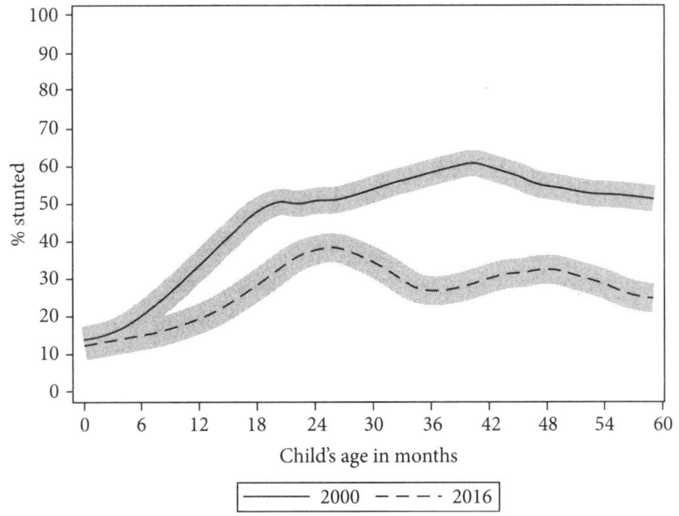

FIGURE 23.2 Trends in stunting rates in urban areas by children's age, 2000 and 2016

Note: Local polynomial regression. Vertical axis measures the (latent) probability that the child is stunted. Shaded area represents 95 per cent confidence interval.

Source: The Demographic Health Surveys for Ethiopia.

and 10 per cent of the urban children are born stunted both in 2000 and 2016. However, growth faltering now begins later in 2016. In 2000, stunting rates shoot up after birth, while in 2016 this 'growth collapse' occurs later, at around six months of age. After that, stunting prevalence increases at the same rate as observed sixteen years ago.

These age dynamics suggest three hypotheses. First, comparison of the intercept of the two regression lines in Figure 23.1 (rural areas) and Figure 23.2 (urban areas) suggests that there has not been a marked increase in birth sizes over the fifteen-year period. Second, for both rural and urban areas, we see that growth faltering occurs later in 2016, suggesting improvements in breastfeeding practices in the first six months of life, or postnatal health conditions. Third, the slopes of the curves after six months of age are similar, implying that there have been limited improvements in complementary feeding practices or in the health environment. The remainder of the chapter explores these hypotheses.

23.5 Possible Drivers of Stunting Reduction

23.5.1 Maternal Health

Most Ethiopian babies are not born at health facilities (CSA and ICF 2016) and as a result, reliable data on birth sizes do not exist. Maternal weight before pregnancy is associated with greater intrauterine growth (Kramer 1987), and thus is one of the main determinants of birth size. Guided by this, we consider how women's body masses have changed since 2000. We use the body mass index (BMI) which is computed by dividing weight in kilograms by the square of body height in metres. BMI is a measure of net current nutrition and considered a reasonable proxy for adult health risks (Fogel 1994). We restrict the analysis to women who are of reproductive age (15–49 years of age), who are not pregnant, and who have not given birth in the two months prior to the survey. Using the standard cut-off values, we categorized a woman as thin if her BMI is less than 18.5, normal weight if between 18.5 and 25, and overweight or obese if above 25.

There are two striking features in these data. First, while women's BMI is gradually increasing, on average, in both rural and urban areas (Figure 23.2), thinness remains widespread, especially in rural areas (Figure 23.3). This slow reduction in the prevalence of thinness stands in contrast to the rapid rates of economic growth observed over this period and the more rapid reduction in chronic under-nutrition described in Section 23.4. They are also consistent with the limited improvements in birth size shown in Figures 23.1 and 23.2. Second, there is a shift in the distribution of women's BMI in urban areas (Figures 23.3–23.5). As of 2016, 21 per cent of urban women aged 15–49 are overweight or obese (Figure 23.5). This high and increasing rate of overweight/obesity in urban areas is juxtaposed with continued high (though declining) rates of stunting, 26 per cent (see Table 23.2). Since a major driver of overweight/obesity is excess consumption of calories, this suggests that chronic under-nutrition is not simply a problem of there being too little food.

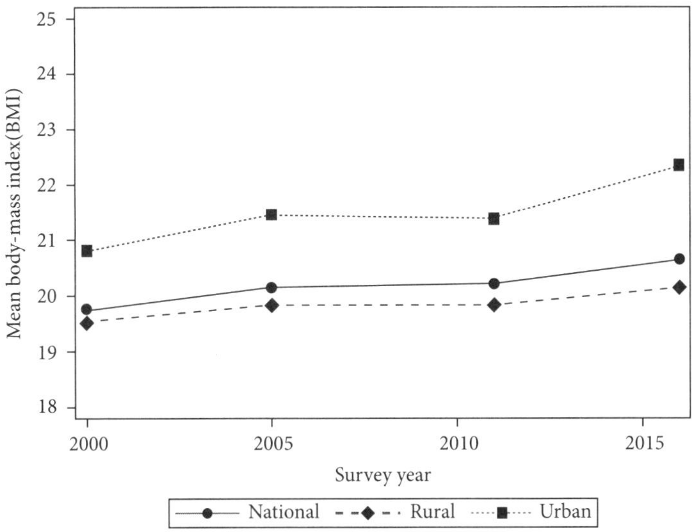

FIGURE 23.3 Mean BMI of women by survey year and location

Note: Sample 15–49 rural women in 2000, 2005, 2011, and 2016 DHS-Ethiopia. Survey weights used.

Source: The Demographic Health Surveys for Ethiopia.

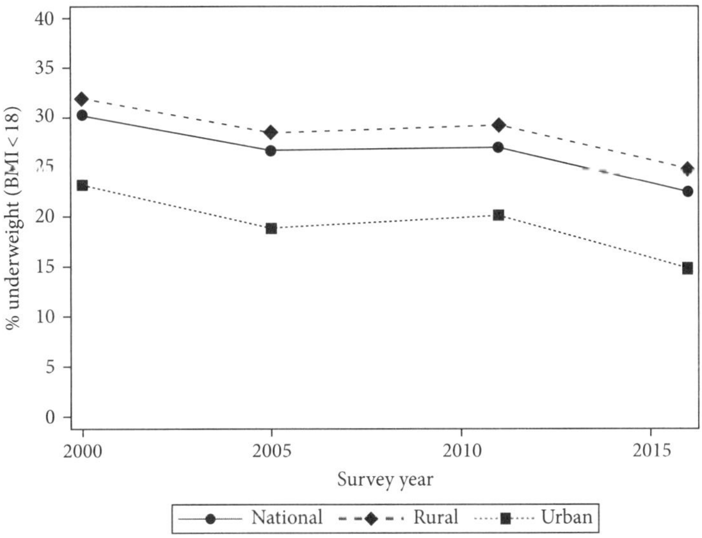

FIGURE 23.4 Percentage of women underweight by survey year and location

Note: Sample: rural women aged 15–49 in 2000, 2005, 2011, and 2016 DHS-Ethiopia. Survey weights used.

Source: The Demographic Health Surveys for Ethiopia.

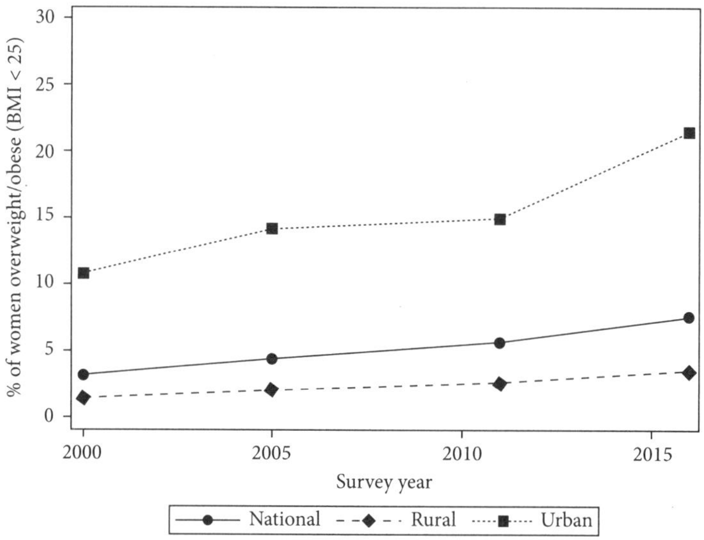

FIGURE 23.5 Percentage of women overweight/obese by survey year and location

Note: Sample: rural women aged 15–49 in 2000, 2005, 2011, and 2016 DHS-Ethiopia. Survey weights used.

Source: The Demographic Health Surveys for Ethiopia.

23.5.2 Breastfeeding

The World Health Organization recommends that babies are exclusively breastfed for the first six months of their life (WHO 2013). Breast milk contains all key ingredients—macro and micro nutrients—for the child's growth during this period. Moreover, exclusive breastfeeding during the first six months of life is associated with reduced risks of a child contracting gastrointestinal and respiratory infections (Kramer and Kakuma 2012). These risks are especially pronounced in countries with poor environmental conditions, such as contaminated water supplies.

Figures 23.6 and 23.7 provide an overview of the age-specific breastfeeding practices in 2000 and 2016, respectively.[3] Nearly all children are breastfed in the first two months of their life in 2000. However, the exclusive breastfeeding rate declines sharply as children turn three months, with just over 40 per cent of them being exclusively breastfed. By 2016, exclusive breastfeeding begins to decline when children are 4 months or older, confirming the second hypothesis: exclusive breastfeeding rates have improved since 2000. This is consistent with the observation that growth faltering occurs when children are somewhat older in 2016 compared to 2000.

23.5.3 Complementary Feeding

The WHO (2013) recommends that children are introduced to complementary feeding of solid or semi-solid foods at six months of age. During this period, children should be

[3] Due to the limited number of observations in this age range (0–5mo), especially in urban areas, we are not able to disaggregate these data across the rural–urban dimension.

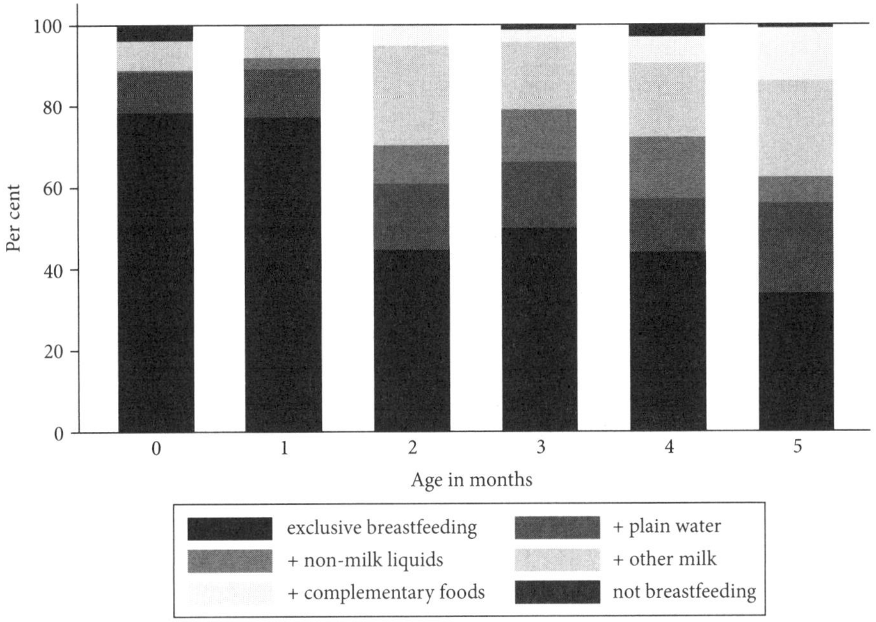

FIGURE 23.6 Breastfeeding practices by age, 2000

Note: Sample: 0–5mo children in 2000 DHS-Ethiopia. Survey weights used.

Source: The Demographic Health Surveys for Ethiopia.

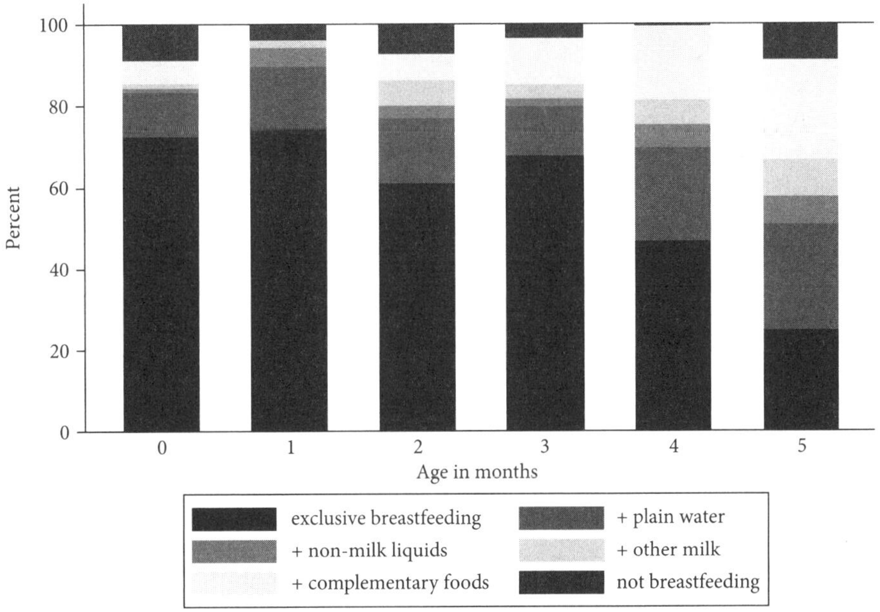

FIGURE 23.7 Breastfeeding practices by age, 2016

Note: Sample: 0–5mo children in 2000 DHS-Ethiopia. Survey weights used.

Source: The Demographic Health Surveys for Ethiopia.

fed frequently (so as to ensure adequate energy intake) with a diet that is of sufficient diversity (so as to ensure sufficient intake of key macro and micro nutrients).

The minimal meal frequency for breastfed children is two or more feedings of solid, semi-solid, or soft food for 6–8-month-old children and three or more for 9–23-month-old children. For non-breastfed children minimal meal frequency is defined as four or more feedings of solid, semi-solid, soft food, or milk feeds for children 6–23 months with at least two of these feedings consisting of milk. The minimum dietary diversity in this age group is defined as four or more food groups out of the following food groups: (i) grains, roots, and tubers; (ii) legumes and nuts; (iii) dairy products (milk, yogurt, cheese); (iv) flesh foods (meat, fish, poultry, and liver/organ meats); (v) eggs; (vi) Vitamin-A-rich fruits and vegetables; and (vii) other fruits and vegetables.

Table 23.4 shows the share of children aged 6–23 months achieving minimum meal frequency and minimum dietary diversity in 2011 and 2016.[4] About 43 per cent of the children achieved minimum meal frequency in 2016, down from 48 per cent in 2011. Compared to rural children, urban children are more likely to meet minimum meal frequency. The dietary diversity indicator shows that Ethiopian children consume extremely monotonous diets. Despite the impressive growth in national income, only 14 per cent of children consumed from four or more food groups in 2016, up from 4.8 per cent in 2011. There is also a large difference in dietary diversity between rural and urban areas, largely driven by differences in wealth and education levels (Hirvonen 2016).

Table 23.4 Dietary outcomes, children 6–23mo, 2011 and 2016, by residence

	2011	2016	Difference
Minimum meal frequency (%)			
National	47.9	42.5	-5.4
Rural	47.7	40.4	-7.3
Urban	48.9	57.8	8.9
Minimum dietary diversity (%)			
National	4.5	13.2	8.7
Rural	3.5	10.9	7.4
Urban	11.3	30.9	19.6

Note: Based on survey weights.
Source: Demographic Health Surveys for Ethiopia.

23.5.4 Infection Risks

Recurring infections sap growth and therefore increase the likelihood of stunting. Figures 23.8 and 23.9 show the diarrhoea and fever prevalence by child's age, respectively.

[4] The DHS did not collect 24-hour dietary recall data in 2000 and 2005. It is for this reason we focus on 2011 and 2016 here.

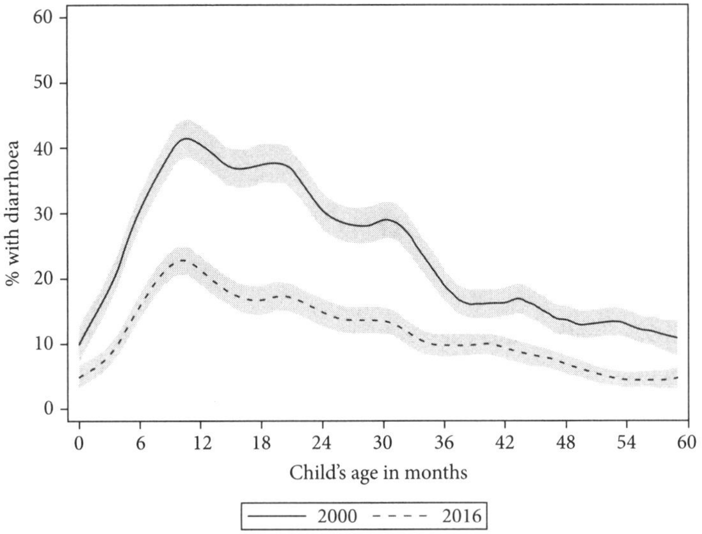

FIGURE 23.8 Diarrhoea prevalence by age

Note: Local polynomial regression. Vertical axis measures the (latent) probability that the child had diarrhoea in the past two weeks. Shaded area represents 95 per cent confidence interval.

Source: The Demographic Health Surveys for Ethiopia.

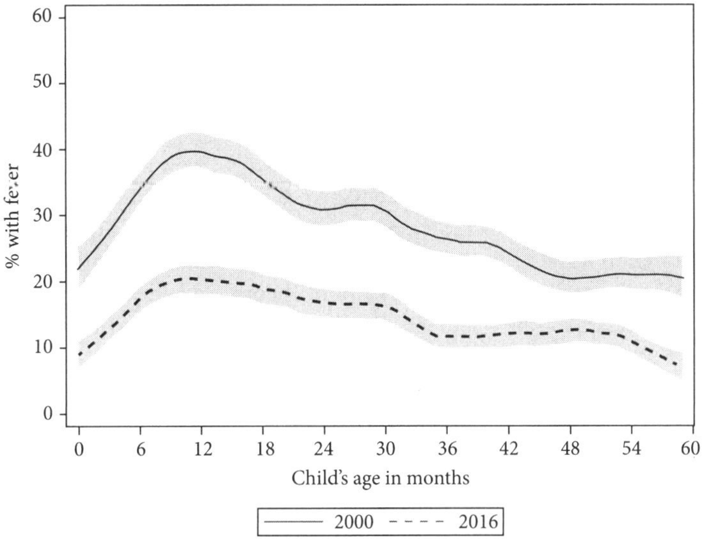

FIGURE 23.9 Fever prevalence by age

Note: Local polynomial regression. Vertical axis measures the (latent) probability that the child had a fever in the past two weeks. Shaded area represents 95 per cent confidence interval.

Source: The Demographic Health Surveys for Ethiopia.

We see that diarrhoea and fever prevalence have both drastically reduced in the last fifteen years. Age-specific trends show that infection risks are highest between 6 and 18 months, i.e. during the period when complementary foods are introduced, possibly linked to food contamination, or increased exploratory behaviour during this age.

23.6 Conclusions

Along with rapid growth in incomes (see Chapters 19 and 20), Ethiopia has experienced considerable reductions in an important non-monetary measure of welfare, chronic under-nutrition, with stunting rates falling from 58 per cent in 2000 to 38 per cent in 2016. Comparison of age dynamics of stunting over time suggests that there has been little improvement in average birth sizes—a hypothesis supported by limited increases in women's BMI, especially in rural areas. In 2016, growth faltering starts somewhat later. This is likely due to improvements in breastfeeding practices which may have led to reduction in infection rates among young children. Median duration of exclusive breastfeeding increased from 2.5 to 3.6 months between 2000 and 2016. Despite the remarkable increase in incomes in Ethiopia, child growth still 'collapses' around the time when complementary foods are introduced (~ 6 mo). In Ethiopia, these complementary foods are of extremely low nutrient density suggesting that this is the primary factor maintaining high stunting rates in the country.

References

CSA and ICF (2016). *Ethiopia Demographic and Health Survey 2016* (Addis Ababa and Rockville, MD: Central Statistical Agency (CSA) of Ethiopia and ICF).

Endris, N., H. Asefa, and L. Dube (2017). 'Prevalence of Malnutrition and Associated Factors among Children in Rural Ethiopia', *BioMed Research International* (2017): 1–6.

Fogel, R. (1994). 'Economic Growth, Population Theory, and Physiology: The Bearing of Long-Term Processes on the Making of Economic Policy', *The American Economic Review* 84: 369–95.

GFDRE (2013). *National Nutrition Programme 2008–2015* (Addis Ababa: Government of the Federal Democratic Republic of Ethiopia).

GFDRE (2016a). *National Nutrition Programme 2016–2020* (Addis Ababa: Government of the Federal Democratic Republic of Ethiopia).

GFDRE (2016b). 'Seqota Declaration Implementation Plan (2016–2030): Summary Programme Approach Document', Government of the Federal Democratic Republic of Ethiopia, Addis Ababa.

Headey, D. (2014). 'An Analysis of Trends and Determinants of Child Undernutrition in Ethiopia, 2000–2011', ESSP Working Paper, International Food Policy Research Institute, Washington, DC.

Headey, D., J. Hoddinott, and S. Park (2017). 'Accounting for Nutritional Changes in Six Success Stories: A Regression-Decomposition Approach', *Global Food Security* 13: 12–20.

Hirvonen, K. (2016). 'Rural–Urban Differences in Children's Dietary Diversity in Ethiopia: A Poisson Decomposition Analysis', *Economics Letters* 147: 12–15.

Kramer, M. S. (1987). 'Determinants of Low Birth Weight: Methodological Assessment and Meta-Analysis', *Bulletin of the World Health Organization* 65: 663.

Kramer, M. S. and R. Kakuma (2012). 'Optimal Duration of Exclusive Breastfeeding', *Cochrane Database of Systematic Reviews*, Issue 8.

Leroy, J. L., M. Ruel, J.-P. Habicht, and E. A. Frongillo (2014). 'Linear Growth Deficit Continues to Accumulate beyond the First 1000 Days in Low- and Middle-Income Countries: Global Evidence from 51 National Surveys', *Journal of Nutrition* 144: 1460–66.

Moradi, A. and K. Hirvonen (2016). 'The African Enigma: The Mystery of Tall African Adults despite Low National Incomes Revisited', in *The Oxford Handbook of Economics and Human Biology*, ed. J. Komlos and I. R. Kelly (Oxford: Oxford University Press): 669–92.

Park, S., D. Headey and J. Hoddinott (2016). 'Drivers of Nutritional Change among Children: Evidence from 47 Developing Countries', Presentation at Cornell University, November.

Shrimpton, R., C. G. Victora, M. De Onis, et al. (2001). 'Worldwide Timing of Growth Faltering: Implications for Nutritional Interventions', *Pediatrics* 107 (5): e75.

Tadesse, S. and Y. Alemu (2015). 'Urban–Rural Differentials in Child Undernutrition in Ethiopia', *International Journal of Nutrition and Metabolism* 7: 15–23.

UNICEF (1990). 'Strategy for Improved Nutrition of Children and Women in Developing Countries', UNICEF Policy Review, New York.

Victora, C. G., M. De Onis, P. C. Hallal, et al. (2010). 'Worldwide Timing of Growth Faltering: Revisiting Implications for Interventions', *Pediatrics* 125 (3): e473–80.

Wamani, H., A. N. Åstrøm, S. Peterson, et al. (2007). 'Boys Are More Stunted than Girls in Sub-Saharan Africa: A Meta-Analysis of 16 Demographic and Health Surveys', *BMC Pediatrics* 10 (7): 17.

WHO (1995). 'The Use and Interpretation of Anthropometry Report of a WHO Expert', Committee Technical Report Series, World Health Organisation, Geneva.

WHO (2013). 'Essential Nutrition Actions: Improving Maternal, Newborn, Infant and Young Child Health and Nutrition', World Health Organization, Geneva.

Woodruff, B. A., J. P. Wirth, A. Bailes, et al. (2016). 'Determinants of Stunting Reduction in Ethiopia 2000–2011', *Maternal & Child Nutrition* 13: 1–17.

CHAPTER 24

SOCIAL PROTECTION IN ETHIOPIA

JOHN HODDINOTT AND ALEMAYEHU SEYOUM TAFFESSE

24.1 Introduction

A handbook of the economics of a given country understandably contains chapters on different economic sectors (agriculture, industry), different markets (labour, capital) and policies (exchange rates, trade, fiscal, and monetary). These are the 'big' topics associated with an analysis of an economy. Why then have a chapter on social protection? Just over 25 years ago, social protection policies and interventions were seen as something of an afterthought in discussions about poverty reduction (World Bank 1990). Today, they are seen as central, reaching nearly one billion people globally and preventing 150 million from falling into poverty (Fiszbein, Kanbur, and Yemtsov 2014). In addition to their direct effect on recipient food security, consumption, and poverty, social protection interventions are seen as a means of facilitating asset accumulation, encouraging entry into higher-value economic activities, and generating spillover effects to the wider economy. But there are also persistent concerns that social protection interventions might have distortionary or disincentive effects, thus blunting the potential benefits. These issues, the potential food security, consumption, and growth impacts, are germane to Ethiopia because, as of 2016, the country was spending approximately 1.4 per cent of GDP (FDRE 2016) on a series of social protection interventions reaching nearly 10 million, or approximately 10 per cent of the population.

Mindful of this, in this chapter we do the following: we begin with a brief sketch of what is meant by social protection and which components of it are most relevant to our discussions. As social protection implementation has occurred in two distinct phases, it makes sense to discuss these separately. Accordingly, we begin with a review of the economic impacts of the social protection interventions that took place in the first thirteen years (1991–2004) following the downfall of the Derg before discussing the economic impacts of social protection since the introduction of the Productive Safety Net Programme (PSNP) in 2005. By so doing, we assess how social protection interventions have contributed to Ethiopia's economic growth and to the well-being of Ethiopians, a topic we consider in our summary section, Section 24.5.

24.2 Social Protection

Social protection encompasses three broad sets of public action (Figure 24.1). One, the focal point of this chapter, is social safety nets. These are targeted non-contributory programmes that transfer resources to poor households. In other developing and developed countries, they take many forms: transfers of cash through welfare payments; conditional cash transfers (popular in Latin America); child allowances or pensions; in-kind transfers such as food aid or school meal programmes; subsidies to goods purchased by the poor; and public works or workfare schemes. Social safety nets—primarily public works, and to a lesser extent, unconditional transfers—are the largest component of social protection in Ethiopia. Spending on the rural safety net currently runs to approximately 12 billion birr (US$600 million) with an addition 2 billion birr (US$100 million) spent on safety nets in urban areas; this 14 billion birr is equivalent to approximately 1.2 per cent of GDP (FRDE 2016). Approximately 10 million people benefit from these safety nets with an additional 600,000 school children benefitting from school meals (FRDE 2016). A second component is publicly provided state contingent (or social) insurance. Here, financial assistance is triggered by an event such as illness, disability, or unemployment. Eligibility and benefit levels are typically based on employment and contribution history, rather than, say, current poverty status. Ethiopia has a long history of such schemes dating back to the introduction, in 1963, of social insurance for civil servants and members of the military. However, coverage levels are low—less than one per cent of the population receives payments from contributory social insurance—and government expenditures on these amount to approximately 2 billion birr, or 0.25 per cent of GDP (FDRE 2016).[1] For this reason, these are not considered further in this chapter. More recently, there has been pilot work on another form of state contingent insurance, weather-based index insurance for agriculture, but this is too recent (and too small scale) to have effects that can be sensibly reported here.

The third component is elements of social-sector policies. For example, fee waivers for the use of primary health care facilities, interventions to prevent malnutrition in pre-school children living in poor households, and free primary education form part of policies in the health and education sectors respectively, while also complementing social safety net interventions. As some of these topics are too far removed from the central focus of this chapter and others are covered elsewhere in this volume, we do not discuss these further.

[1] There are efforts to expand contributory social insurance through schemes such as Community Based Health Insurance. At the time of writing (early 2018), this is being scaled up. No evidence is available on its economic consequences.

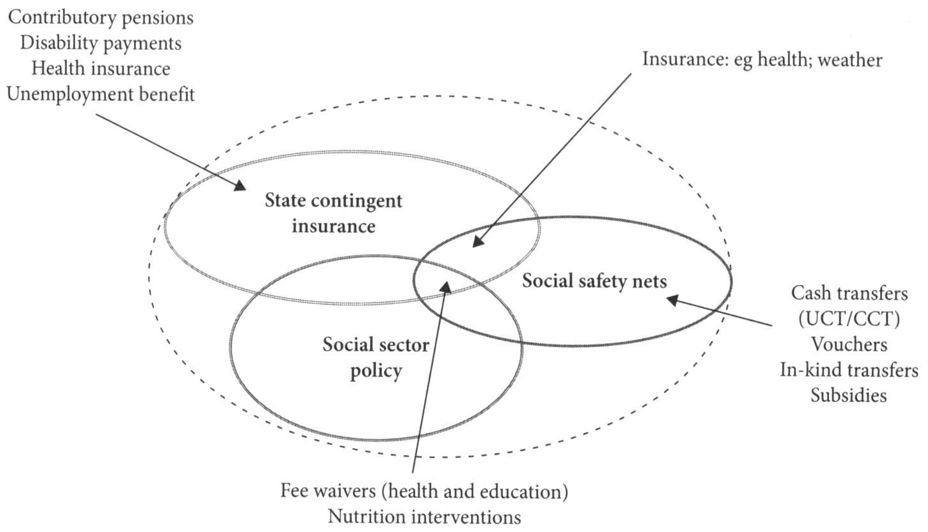

FIGURE 24.1 Components of social protection
Source: Adapted from Gentili and Omano (2009).

24.3 Social Protection and its Economic Consequences: 1994–2004

Limited social safety net programmes—largely food for work—existed under the Derg. These were expanded following the ascent of the EPRDF to power. Termed Employment Generation Schemes (EGSs), payments were made in food grains for work on soil and water conservation, roads, and other community assets. Individuals unable to work, for example because of age or disability or in the case of women, pregnancy, received Gratuitous Relief (GR) (Woldehanna 2010). There are only a handful of studies that assess the economic impact of these early social safety net interventions.

Using data from fifteen Ethiopian villages and propensity score matching estimators, Gilligan and Hoddinott (2007) found large significant average treatment effects of EGS participation on growth of both food and total consumption per adult equivalent 18 months after the ending of the 2002 drought. However, consistent with evidence that the work requirements of the EGS made the poor less likely to participate (Barrett and Clay 2003), results disaggregated by tertiles of pre-drought consumption showed that these benefits were skewed towards households in the middle and upper tail of the distribution. While GR showed fewer and smaller effects than the EGS—partly because it had narrower coverage and lower transfer levels—it had significant average impacts on growth in food consumption per adult equivalent, and these benefits were better targeted towards poor households. Gilligan and Hoddinott (2007) also looked at impacts on livestock holdings, finding that once measurement was taken into account, there was no evidence of impacts from either EGS or GR.

Using nationally representative data, Yamano, Alderman, and Christiaensen (2005) looked at the impact of EGS and GR on a measure of human capital, the nutritional status of pre-school children, specifically the height of children aged 6–24 months. After accounting for the endogeneity of receipt of these transfers, they found no evidence that separately, these programmes affected child height. However, when they combined food transfers received from either EGS or GR, they found a positive impact on child height.

Finally, using data from the same villages as Gilligan and Hoddinott (2007), Abdulai, Barrett, and Hoddinott (2005) assessed whether EGS and GR have disincentive effects. They found that with controls for household and locality characteristics and the potential endogeneity of food aid, there was no evidence of disincentive effects on labour supply. If anything, receipt of food aid appears to increase labour supply, particularly by males. There is a disincentive effect on days contributed to traditional labour-sharing groups, but this was small in magnitude. Further, Abdulai, Barrett, and Hoddinott (2005) found no evidence that these food transfers crowd out private transfers.

24.4 Social Protection and its Economic Consequences: 2005–16

Throughout the 1990s, the EGS and GR were the only real social safety nets operating in Ethiopia. However, they were not permanently funded programmes. Rather, they expanded and contracted in response to drought shocks and the need for emergency food aid to prevent famine. While, as Section 24.3 makes clear, they had some success in safeguarding food consumption and nutrition outcomes, as time passed, it became increasingly clear that these ad hoc responses were inadequate. The number of persons requiring assistance had risen steadily from 1996 onwards, from 2.1 million people to approximately 7.5 million by 2002. A severe drought shock in 2003 increased the numbers needing assistance to 13 million (Wiseman, Van Domelen, and Coll-Black 2010; World Bank 2004). The ad hoc nature of emergency response meant that organizations providing this assistance had no meaningful way of planning assistance, nor did prospective beneficiaries have any real expectation that assistance would be forthcoming. The severe 2002 drought and the subsequent near-escape from famine in the year that followed prompted considerable discussion within the government of Ethiopia, among its development partners, and between government and donors. The outcome was the Productive Safety Net Programme, a social safety net intervention funded by a consortium of donors who pooled their resources but managed and implemented by the government of Ethiopia. The PSNP was established as a multi-year intervention, initially for three years (2005–7) but subsequently extended to operate until at least 2020. The objective of the PSNP is to provide transfers to the food-insecure population in chronically food-insecure *woredas* so as to improve their food security. Further, the PSNP aims to prevent asset depletion at the household level while creating assets at the community level (FRDE 2004). There have been fluctuations in PSNP coverage and budget over time; for much of the period covered by this chapter, the PSNP reached approximately seven million beneficiaries annually with a budget of around US$500 million per year. The following are the core features of the PSNP:

1. It is a targeted intervention, operating in chronically food-insecure rural localities, primarily in the Highlands. Within these localities, community-based targeting is used to identify chronically food-insecure households.[2]
2. Most participants (~85 per cent) do labour-intensive public work, building assets of benefit to their communities. A small number of beneficiaries (~15 per cent) who lack able-bodied labour receive unconditional transfers, called Direct Support. Payments are made in food and in cash.
3. The PSNP was nested into broader efforts aimed at increasing household incomes through enhanced agricultural production and diversification of income sources.

While there were smaller pilot safety net interventions operating in different parts of the country, between 2005 and 2016 the PSNP was Ethiopia's primary social protection intervention. It has also been the subject of several large, systematic evaluations as well as smaller studies that focus on specific outcomes and specific localities. The principal source of data for much of this evaluation work[3] has been a longitudinal bi-annual evaluation survey beginning in 2006. For this work, *woredas* were randomly sampled proportional to size (PPS) from a list of 153 chronically food-insecure *woredas* selected for inclusion in the PSNP. Within each *woreda*, sample *kebeles* serving as Enumeration Areas (EAs) were randomly selected from a list of *kebeles* with active Productive Safety Net Programmes (PSNPs). Within each EA, fifteen beneficiary and ten non-beneficiary households were sampled from separate lists for each group, yielding a sample of twenty-five households per EA. This procedure yielded a sample of 146 EAs in sixty-eight *woredas* and, because a few sampled households were not interviewed, a sample of 3,688 households: approximately 900 in Tigray and SNNP, and 950 in Amhara and Oromia. These households were then re-surveyed in 2008, 2010, 2012, and 2014. Each round took place at approximately the same time of year (June–August) so as to minimize seasonality effects. The attrition rate across the five survey rounds is 15.2 per cent or 1.9 per cent per year, a rate comparable to (or better than) attrition rates in large-scale household surveys in developed countries.

[2] We note the following. Several assessments of the PSNP have shown that in the highlands, the programme is well targeted; see Coll-Black et al. (2012) and Berhane et al. (2015). Since 2010, and on a smaller scale and with less success, the PSNP has also operated in Afar and Somali; in particular, programme targeting has been poor (Sabates-Wheeler, Lind, and Hoddinott 2013).

[3] Specifically, the papers listed in the references by Berhane and co-authors (2014, 2015, 2016), Coll-Black et al. (2012), Gilligan, Hoddinott, and Taffesse (2009), and Hoddinott and co-authors (2010, 2012).

24.4.1 Food Security

Given, as noted earlier, that the primary objective of the PSNP is to improve food security, we begin with this outcome. In the documentation underpinning the PSNP, (FDRE 2009), this is defined as follows: 'Households have sufficient food for all 12 months, including the support of PSNP transfers.' Progress towards this objective is measured in terms of the number of months in a year that a household can satisfy its food needs. Alternatively, it is defined as eliminating the food gap, the number of months the household cannot satisfy its food needs.

These surveys included questions on the food gap. Figure 24.2 shows trends in the food gap by beneficiary status and year. Beginning with the period 2006–10, there is little change in the food security status of PSNP beneficiaries who average between 2.67 and 3.09 months of food gap. However, non-beneficiaries see, on average, their food insecurity rising from 2.30 to 2.85 months over this period, a consequence in part of the food price spike in 2008 and a drought in 2009. So while the PSNP was not necessarily improving food security, it appears to have been protecting further deteriorations in an unhelpful environment. After 2010, food security among PSNP beneficiaries improves markedly with the food gap falling by nearly half, from 3.04 to 1.75 months. These evaluation data also show that in 2006, around 25 per cent of beneficiaries were suffering from very severe food insecurity, reporting a food gap of five months or more. By 2014, this had fallen to 8.5 per cent. However, Figure 24.2 also shows that the food gap improves for non-beneficiaries between 2010 and 2014. This raises the question as to whether gains in food security among beneficiaries are directly attributable to the PSNP or to economic trends benefiting beneficiaries and non-beneficiaries alike.

Mindful of this concern, Gilligan, Hoddinott, and Taffesse (2009), Berhane et al. (2014), and Berhane, Hirvonen, and Hoddinott (2016) use a variety of econometric methods—principally matching methods and instrumental variables estimation—to assess the impact of the PSNP on the food gap. The consistent finding across all three studies is that the PSNP has a causal effect on the food gap but that this effect is dose responsive. Participation in the PSNP, but with low receipt of transfers, has no effect on the food gap but participation with a high level of transfers does. Using data from all five rounds, Berhane, Hirvonen, and Hoddinott (2016) find that a 100 (real) birr annual increase in payments for public works leads to a 0.2 month reduction in the food gap. The average real value of public works payments was 549 birr per household per year and so at mean transfer levels, the PSNP reduces the food gap by just over one month.[4]

Other studies also report positive effects on food security. Using OLS regressions, Sabates-Wheeler and Devereux (2010) look at the impact of PSNP payments on changes in the food gap between 2006 and 2008, finding that these reduce the food gap by 0.4–1.2 months, depending on the type of transfer (food or cash).

[4] We note, however, that these results are specific to the highlands. Evaluations of the food security impacts in the lowland regions of Afar and Somali have not found evidence of positive impacts, partly—as noted in Section 24.4.1 above—because programme targeting is poorer.

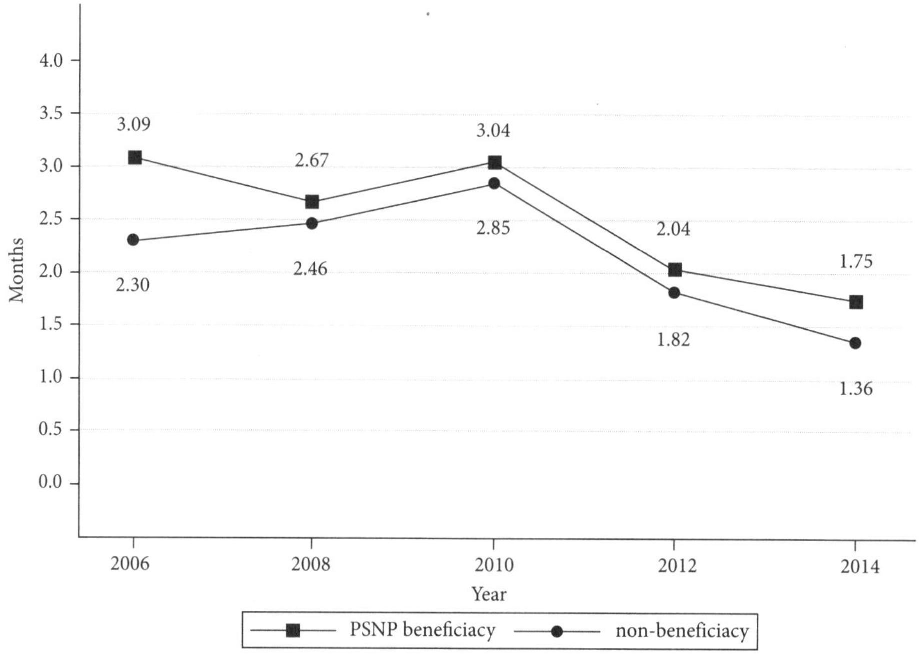

FIGURE 24.2 Mean food gap, by beneficiary status and year

Note: Sample consists of 2,862 households interviewed in all rounds 2006–14.

Source: Household surveys: 2006, 2008, 2010, 2012, 2014.

24.4.2 Income and Livelihoods

The PSNP evaluation surveys have also assessed whether PSNP participation has generated increases in income beyond the value of the payments themselves, for example by increasing yields, entry into new activities, or investments in agriculture. A series of studies address this question, including Gilligan, Hoddinott, and Taffesse (2009), Hoddinott et al. (2012) and Weldegebriel and Prowse (2013). A fairly uniform finding across these studies is limited evidence of impacts on incomes or livelihoods.[5] However, Gilligan, Hoddinott, and Taffesse (2009) and Hoddinott et al. (2012) make the important observation that alongside the PSNP were a series of government programmes (initially called the Other Food Security Programme (OFSP) before being revised and re-launched as the Household Asset Building Programme (HABP)) aimed at complementing the PSNP through the provision of extension services, advice on accessing inputs and on marketing and in some cases, through assisting participants in getting access to credit. Hoddinott et al. (2012) find that when looking at the combined effects of these programmes along with the high levels of PSNP payments, there was greater investment in

[5] We note that Adimassu and Kessler (2015) report negative effects of PSNP participation on household efforts to invest in soil fertility. However, we are cautious about generalizing from this assessment as it is based on a small-scale study in one locality using a single round of cross-sectional data.

land management practices (terracing and fencing), greater use of fertilizer, and thus higher yields. These results were derived from a generalized propensity score dose-response model, comparing households who had received PSNP transfers for five years (and who had relatively high levels of transfers) and OFSP services to a matched comparison group of households that received only one year of transfers. However, this treated group (high levels of transfers and received OFSP services) comprises a small fraction, perhaps 15 per cent, of all PSNP beneficiaries. This low coverage is consistent with other evidence suggesting that these complementary interventions have failed to attain the coverage of the PSNP. FRDE (2016) reports, for example, that only 9 per cent of PSNP public works participants and only 4 per cent of Direct Support beneficiaries received both extension services and credit.

24.4.3 Physical Assets

A series of studies have assessed the impact of PSNP participation on asset accumulation. Findings are mixed. Sabates-Wheeler and Devereux (2010) report that PSNP participation is associated with a rise in the value of livestock holdings, but the impact on assets more broadly is insignificant or negative. Andersson, Mekonnen, and Stage (2011) report, using a least-squares specification that treats PSNP participation as exogenous, no impact of PSNP participation in 2005 on livestock holdings observed in subsequent years but they do find some evidence of investment in trees and reforestation.

Asset accumulation is also addressed in studies that use the PSNP evaluation surveys. Gilligan, Hoddinott, and Taffesse (2009), Berhane et al. (2014), and Berhane, Hirvonen, and Hoddinott (2016) use matching methods and instrumental variables estimation to assess the impact of the PSNP on livestock and other assets. Gilligan, Hoddinott, and Taffesse (2009) and Berhane et al. (2014) find, as they did for the food gap, evidence of a dose-response relationship with positive impacts only found when payments were relatively large. Berhane, Hirvonen, and Hoddinott (2016) do not find such positive effects across the nine-year period covered by these surveys, though they do note that there are positive impacts on the livestock asset holdings of the poorest 20 per cent households.

24.4.4 Human Capital Formation: Schooling and Nutritional Status

It is widely understood that human capital formation—schooling, nutrition—is an important contributor to economic growth. For this reason, a number of studies have looked at the impact of PSNP participation on children's schooling and nutritional status.

We begin with schooling. As both Hoddinott, Gilligan, and Taffesse (2010) and Woldehanna (2010) note, public works programmes such as the PSNP affect children's schooling through two channels. First, there is an income effect. If child schooling is a normal good, the increased income will result in increased levels of school participation.

Second, public works programmes directly increase demand for household labour and may alter the intra-household division of labour between adults and children; if the PSNP results in an increase in children's work (for example, on domestic tasks, or in looking after livestock), these increased labour demands could adversely affect children's schooling.

There are three studies that assess the impact of the PSNP on children's schooling and, relatedly, child labour: Hoddinott, Gilligan, and Taffesse (2010); Woldehanna (2010); and Berhane et al. (2016). All use some variant of matching methods to generate their results. Taken in aggregate, results are inconclusive. Using the PSNP evaluation surveys described in Sections 24.4.1 and 24.4.2, Hoddinott, Gilligan, and Taffesse (2010) find no impact of PSNP participation on children's schooling in 2006 and Woldehanna (2010) finds no impact in his data obtained around the same time. Berhane et al. (2016) find no impacts in 2010. However, Berhane et al. (2016) also find that in 2012, the PSNP increased girls' grade attainment between 6 and 14 per cent (depending on the age of the child), improved schooling efficiency by 10 to 20 per cent, reduced boys' labour, but had no effect on boys' schooling. Hoddinott, Gilligan, and Taffesse (2010) find that in households receiving high levels of transfers, younger boys' and older girls' attendance increased. Finally, Berhane et al. (2016) report that in 2008, when PSNP payments were low relative to work requirements, participation in the PSNP lowered boys' and girls' grade attainments. It caused increased child labour on the family farm, although in the case of boys this was offset by reductions in domestic labour.

As with the education results, studies looking at the impact of the PSNP on children's nutritional status find mixed results. Using multiple rounds of the PSNP evaluation surveys and matching methods, Berhane et al. (2016) find no evidence that the PSNP reduces either chronic under-nutrition (height-for-age Z-scores, stunting) or acute undernutrition (weight-for-height, wasting) in children aged 6–24 months during the period 2008–12.[6] Debela, Shively, and Holden (2015) find that in sixteen villages in Tigray, participation in the PSNP increased the weight-for-height of children between 0 and 5 years of age. However, it is unclear how well their switching model accounts for the endogeneity of programme participation. Porter and Goyal (2016) report large positive effects of PSNP participation on older children, those between eight and fifteen. While Porter and Goyal are carefully to address the endogeneity of PSNP participation, their results are somewhat surprising. They find no evidence of improvements in dietary diversity, a potential pathway which could lead to these results, and their improvements are found in children outside the usual age where interventions are expected to affect height.

24.4.5 Disincentive Effects

As noted in our introduction, the issue of disincentive effects has long been a concern in discourse over the impact of social safety nets. These take two forms: reductions in

[6] This age range is considered to be a critical period, particularly for height growth.

labour supply; and the crowding out of private transfers. Several studies have assessed the impact on dimensions of household labour supply. Gilligan, Hoddinott, and Taffesse (2009) find no effect on wage labour in the 2006 evaluation survey. They find some evidence that PSNP participation increased the likelihood of entry into non-farm own-business activities, though Berhane et al. (2014), using data from the 2010 evaluation survey, did not confirm this result. Dillon, Brummund, and Mwabu (2017) using LSMS-ISA data find no impact on farm labour supply. Berhane et al. (2014) revisit the issue of crowding out of private transfers first explored by Abdulai, Barrett, and Hoddinott (2005), also finding no evidence of crowding out of private transfers; in fact, there is a small—but not statistically significant—increase.

24.4.6 Impacts of the Construction of PSNP Public Works

There is relatively little work on the impact of the public works constructed as part of the PSNP. One source of information is perceptual data from the evaluation surveys described earlier. In each survey round, PSNP beneficiaries (households receiving either public works payments or Direct Support transfers) as well as non-beneficiaries were asked if they had benefited from PSNP public works activities such as: road construction and improvements; the building of water harvesting structures; soil and water conservation on communal land; soil and water conservation on private lands; the building or rehabilitation of schools and health posts; and well construction. Table 24.1, taken from Berhane et al. (2016) shows large percentages of households indicating that they believed that they had benefited from these activities. This was true across a wide range of activities and across all highland regions where the PSNP operates. Road construction and road improvements were seen as being particularly valuable, not only because it improved access to markets, but also because it made it easier for children to attend school and women to travel to health clinics (Berhane et al. 2015: Table 10.3).

Yimer et al. (2016) investigate the cumulative impact of PSNP soil and water conservation (SWC) activities on crop yield growth. They find that every additional year in which SWC activities take place increases crop yield growth by 2.8 per cent. While they cannot precisely identify the mechanism underpinning this result, they note that SWC includes the building of bunds and terracing, tree planting, and irrigation, all of which helps rehabilitate soil and water resources within the community. Communities that have implemented SWC projects may have lower levels of flooding and erosion hazards, which in turn may have led to higher yields.

24.4.7 Economy-Wide Effects

The discussion so far has focused on the direct effects of the PSNP on beneficiaries. But these may understate the impacts of the programme. First, apart from Yimer et al. (2016), they do not account for the fact that the PSNP builds community assets that benefit all members of the locality within which they are created, not just PSNP beneficiaries.

Table 24.1 Percentage of households reporting that have ever benefited from PSNP public works activities, by activity and region

	Road construction and improvements	Water harvesting structure	Soil and water conservation on communal land	Soil and water conservation on private land	Schools	Health posts	Wells
Tigray	69.7	57.0	66.9	50.3	50.3	68.3	41.8
Amhara	80.2	51.0	60.6	55.8	62.4	57.2	64.5
Oromia	85.3	71.5	60.1	34.5	61.0	62.2	66.7
SNNP	96.9	54.4	64.6	44.4	74.1	61.5	68.1

Source: Berhane et al. (2016), Table 10.4.

Second, PSNP transfers can lead to significant income gains in these localities and beyond through consumption and other local linkages. The overall impact of the programme can thus be greater than the direct effects of transfers on immediate beneficiaries.

Filipski et al. (2016) consider these possibilities. In addition to the PSNP evaluation surveys (2006–12) described earlier, they draw on an enterprise survey focusing on non-farm activities that create linkages within a community as conducted in eight selected PSNP *woredas*. In parallel, in-depth case studies of the selected *kebeles* were conducted to generate a wealth of information in dimensions not covered by the PSNP and enterprise surveys, including detailed agro-ecological characteristics and administrative quality. Filipski et al. (2016) then apply three methods: econometric analysis, local economy-wide impact evaluation (LEWIE) modelling, and country-wide computable general equilibrium (CGE) modelling. The econometric analysis used the panel PSNP dataset to link community assets created by PWs to crop yield growth. The results thus obtained not only provide empirical evidence of impacts of these assets on crop productivity, but also serve as inputs in subsequent modelling and simulation. LEWIE modelling extends the analysis to the meso level by simulating the manner in which the PSNP interventions affect all actors in a local economy, beyond direct beneficiaries. In other words, the LEWIE model helps in getting at the corresponding second-order, or 'general equilibrium' impacts that arise through market linkages. Finally, the CGE modelling further broadens the analysis to the national scale using a CGE model of the Ethiopian economy.

The LEWIE models were constructed for eight *kebeles* located in four *woredas* in four regions—Tigray, Amhara, Oromia, and Southern Nations, Nationalities, and People's (SNNP)—to simulate PSNP impacts in the local *kebele*-level economy. The *kebeles* studied are in diverse agro-ecological settings, from well-watered tropical to highly drought-prone zones facing severe ecological constraints. The mix of PSNP projects

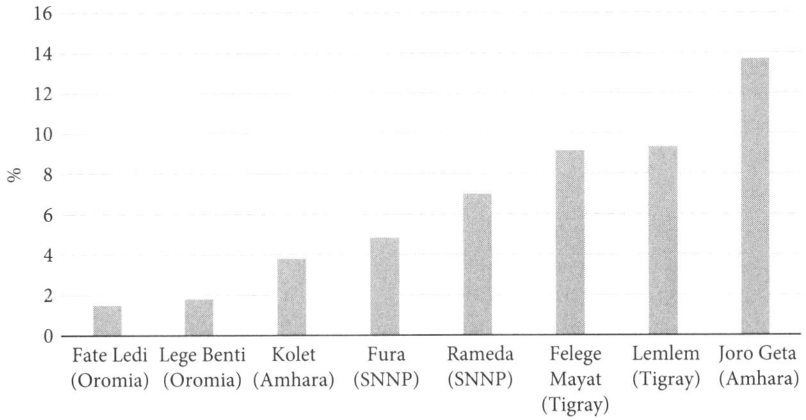

FIGURE 24.3 Impacts of PSNP on value of total production in the eight study *kebeles*, per cent increase in total output

Source: LEWIE simulations of PSNP at local scale.

varies among these *kebeles* with soil and water conservation projects implemented in all. Total impacts on local economic production range from less than 2 per cent to nearly 14 per cent (Figure 24.3). Agriculture's share of these impacts ranged from 0 to 80 per cent.

Higher production, together with income spillovers, creates *local income multipliers*, the increase in income per birr transferred to a poor household. It is equal to one if PSNP does not create additional income, and greater than one if PSNP public works projects plus spillovers create additional income in the local economy. PSNP local income multipliers are one or close to one in three of the *kebeles*, but they are considerably higher in the other five *kebeles*. In one of the *kebeles* (Joro Geta), local income increases by nearly 2.5 birr for each birr transferred to PSNP beneficiaries (Figure 24.4). Differences in local income multipliers are due mostly to differences in the mix of PSNP projects and how they affect local production, to agro-climatic constraints, and to integration of *kebeles* with outside markets. Trade with outside markets shifts PSNP benefits to other parts of Ethiopia, which is why our national analysis shows that PSNP increases income outside PSNP regions.

Lastly, Filipski et al. (2016) look at the economy-wide effects. Using a nationwide CGE model, they find that the PSNP raises the national gross domestic product by about 1 per cent. It does this by stimulating agricultural and non-agricultural production as well as demand inside and outside the *kebeles* that participate in PSNP. National agricultural production increases by 1.33 per cent, and total production by 0.76 per cent. The economy-wide analysis reveals that these productivity impacts, together with PSNP transfers themselves, raise household income by nearly 6 per cent in PSNP areas and by nearly 2 per cent in non-PSNP areas.

These findings highlight the positive income spillovers created by PSNP in Ethiopia's national economy. They demonstrate that the total economic benefits exceed the total

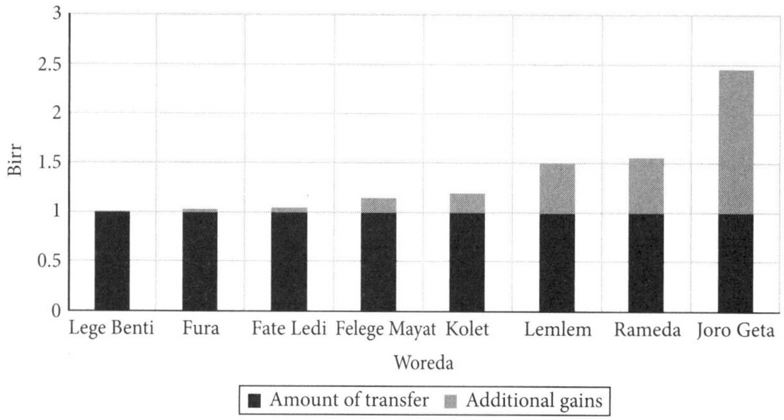

FIGURE 24.4 Local income multipliers of PSNP transfers, increase in income per birr transferred

Source: LEWIE simulations of PSNP at local scale.

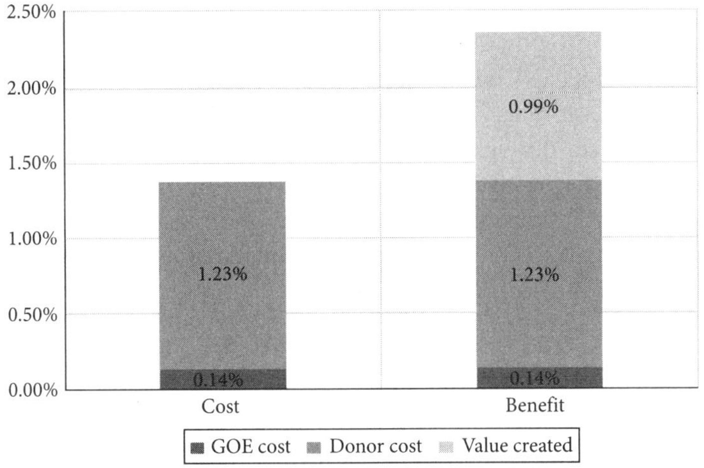

FIGURE 24.5 National benefits and costs of PSNP, as a percentage of Ethiopia's GDP

Source: CGE simulations of PSNP at national scale.

cost of PSNP (Figure 24.5). PSNP transfers were equivalent to 1.37 per cent of Ethiopia's GDP in the base year of our 2006 model (left bar in Figure 24.5). In our assessment, these funds are both a cost and a benefit, because they add to the income of poor and vulnerable households targeted by the programme. Productivity increases and income spillovers add the equivalent of 0.99 per cent of Ethiopia's GDP to the benefits of PSNP (top of right bar in Figure 24.5).

At a national level, PSNP creates more than 1.7 birr of benefits per birr transferred to a beneficiary household. Because most of the cost of PSNP currently is covered by foreign donors, there is a 16.9 birr return per birr that the Ethiopian government spends on PSNP. Government could increase its share of PSNP costs considerably while still reaping a large economic return.

24.5 Summary

We began this chapter by asking whether social protection interventions have contributed to Ethiopia's economic growth and to the well-being of Ethiopians. Having reviewed an extensive set of studies across a wide range of outcomes, we are now well placed to answer this question. The answer is largely, but not entirely, positive.

One consistent finding, across a range of studies, interventions, and time periods, is that social safety net programmes in Ethiopia improve food security in the Highlands as measured by the food gap. There is evidence of a dose-response relationship here, with larger transfers associated with larger impacts. A second consistent finding is the absence of evidence of disincentive effects. Safety net participation does not reduce labour supply, nor does it appear to crowd out private transfers. The evidence on livelihoods and asset creation is more mixed. Some studies find positive effects but others do not, or do not find these consistently. On an economy-wide basis, the benefits of PSNP significantly exceed the cost of PSNP transfers. New income created by PSNP benefits households that do not receive cash transfers; these non-beneficiaries benefit as markets transmit PSNP impacts to them through local and national markets. Taken collectively, these results point to both the positive effects of the PSNP on Ethiopia's economic growth and to the well-being of Ethiopians and the need to continue to strengthen these programmes, in particular to complement them with interventions which will lead to more rapid accumulation of physical and human capital.

References

Abdulai, A., C. Barrett, and J. Hoddinott (2005). 'Does Food Aid *Really* Have Disincentive Effects? New Evidence from Sub-Saharan Africa', *World Development* 33 (10): 1689–704.

Adimassu, Z. and A. Kessler (2015). 'Impact of the Productive Safety Net Program on Farmers' Investments in Sustainable Land Management in the Central Rift Valley of Ethiopia', *Environmental Development* 16: 54–62.

Andersson, C., A. Mekonnen, and J. Stage (2011). 'Impacts of the Productive Safety Net Program in Ethiopia on Livestock and Tree Holdings of Rural Households', *Journal of Development Economics* 94: 119–26.

Barrett, C. and D. Clay (2003). 'How Accurate Is Food-for-Work Self-Targeting in the Presence of Imperfect Factor Markets? Evidence from Ethiopia', *Journal of Development Studies* 39 (5): 152–81.

Berhane, G., D. Gilligan, J. Hoddinott, et al. (2014). 'Can Social Protection Work in Africa? Evidence on the Impact of Ethiopia's Productive Safety Net Programme on Food Security and Assets', *Economic Development and Cultural Change* 63 (1): 1–26.

Berhane, G. et al. (2015). *The Implementation of the Productive Safety Nets Programme and the Household Asset Building Programme in the Ethiopian Highlands, 2014: Program Performance Report* (Washington DC: International Food Policy Research Institute).

Berhane, G., K. Hirvonen, and J. Hoddinott (2016). *The Implementation of the Productive Safety Nets Programme, 2014: Highlands Outcomes Report* (Addis Ababa: Ethiopia Strategy Support Program, International Food Policy Research Institute).

Berhane, G., J. Hoddinott, N. Kumar, and A. Margolies (2016). *The Impact of the Productive Safety Net Programmme on Schooling, Child Labor, and the Nutritional Status of Children* (Addis Ababa: -IFPRI).

Coll-Black, S. et al. (2012). 'Targeting Food Security Interventions in Ethiopia: The Productive Safety Net Programme', in *Food and Agriculture in Ethiopia: Progress and Policy Challenges*, ed. P. Dorosh and S. Rashid (Philadelphia, PA: University of Pennsylvania Press).

Debela, B. L., G. Shively, and S. Holden (2015). 'Does Ethiopia's Productive Safety Net Program Improve Child Nutrition?' *Food Security* 7: 1273–89.

Dillon, B., P. Brummund, and G. Mwabu (2017). 'Asymmetric Non-Separation and Rural Labor Markets', mimeo (Seattle: University of Washington).

Federal Democratic Republic of Ethiopia (FDRE) (2004). *Productive Safety Net Programme: Programme Implementation Manual* (Addis Ababa: Ministry of Agriculture and Rural Development).

Federal Democratic Republic of Ethiopia (FDRE) (2016). *National Social Protection Strategy of Ethiopia* (Addis Ababa: Ministry of Labour and Social Affairs).

Filipski, M., J. E. Taylor, G. A. Abegaz, et al. (2016). *General Equilibrium Impact Assessment of the Productive Safety Net Program in Ethiopia* (Washington, DC: International Food Policy Research Institute).

Fiszbein, A., R. Kanbur, and R. Yemtsov (2014). 'Social Protection and Poverty Reduction: Global Patterns and Some Targets', *World Development* 61: 167–77.

Gentilini, U., and S. W. Omamo (2009). 'Unveiling Social Safety Nets', WFP Occasional Paper, No 20., World Food Programme, Rome.

Gilligan, D. and J. Hoddinott (2007). 'Is There Persistence in the Impact of Emergency Food Aid? Evidence on Consumption, Food Security and Assets in Rural Ethiopia', *American Journal of Agricultural Economics* 89 (2): 225–42.

Gilligan, D., J. Hoddinott, and A. S. Taffesse (2009). 'An Analysis of Ethiopia's Productive Safety Net Programme and its Linkages', *Journal of Development Studies* 45 (10): 1684–706.

Hoddinott, J., G. Berhane, D. Gilligan, N. Kumar, and A. Seyoum Taffesse (2012). 'The Impact of Ethiopia's Productive Safety Net Programme and Related Transfers on Agricultural Productivity', *Journal of African Economies* 21 (5): 761–86.

Hoddinott, J., D. Gilligan, and A. S. Taffesse (2010). 'The Impact of Ethiopia's Productive Safety Net Program on Schooling and Child Labor', in *Social Protection for Africa's Children*, ed. S. Handa, S. Devereux, and D. Webb (London: Routledge): 71–95.

Porter, C. and R. Goyal (2016). 'Social Protection for All Ages? Impacts of Ethiopia's Productive Safety Net Program on Child Nutrition', *Social Science and Medicine* 159: 92–9.

Sabates-Wheeler, R. and S. Devereux (2010). 'Cash Transfers and High Food Prices: Explaining Outcomes on Ethiopia's Productive Safety Net Programme', *Food Policy* 35: 274–85.

Sabates-Wheeler, R., J. Lind, and J. Hoddinott (2013). 'Implementing Social Protection in Pastoralist Areas: How Local Distribution Structures Moderate PSNP Outcomes in Ethiopia', *World Development* 50 (1): 1–12.

Weldegebriel, Z. and M. Prowse (2013). 'Climate-Change Adaptation in Ethiopia: To What Extent Does Social Protection Influence Livelihood Diversification?' *Development Policy Review* 31 (S2): 35–56.

Wiseman, W., J. van Domelen, and S. Coll-Black (2010). 'Designing and Implementing a Rural Safety Net in a Low-Income Setting: Lessons Learned from Ethiopia's Productive Safety Net Program 2005–2009', World Bank, Washington, DC.

Woldehanna, T. (2010). 'Productive Safety Net Program and Children's Time Use Between Work and Schooling in Ethiopia', in *Child Welfare in Developing Countries*, ed. J. Cockburn and J. Kabubo-Mariara (New York: Springer): 157–210.

World Bank (1990). *World Development Report 1990: Poverty* (New York: Oxford University Press).

World Bank (2004). 'Ethiopia: Public Expenditure Review', Report 29338-ET, World Bank, Washington, DC.

Yamano, T., H. Alderman, and L. Christiaensen (2005). 'Child Growth, Shocks, and Food Aid in Rural Ethiopia', *American Journal of Agricultural Economics* 87 (2): 273–88.

Yimer, F. et al. (2016). 'The Impact of the Productive Safety Net Program-Created Community Assets on Crop Yield Growth', mimeo (Addis Ababa: International Food Policy Research Institute).

CHAPTER 25

EDUCATION AND ECONOMIC DEVELOPMENT IN ETHIOPIA, 1991–2017

ZINABU SAMARO REKISO

25.1 Introduction

There is a long-standing consensus on the importance of education for economic development among scholars and within development policy circles. For instance, according to human capital theory, there is a strong link between investment in education and higher productivity and wages for individuals at the micro level and a country's economic growth at the macro level. Consequently, there has been strong emphasis on the importance of investment in human capital, particularly education (Krasniqi and Topxhiu 2016). However, there is hardly any literature that looks at the effect of the productive structure of the economy on the quality, effectiveness, and external efficiency of education in a developing economy.

This chapter critically examines the achievements and challenges of the education sector in Ethiopia from the perspective of long-term economic development and structural transformation. Specifically, the chapter critically examines two systemic challenges that have faced the education sector in the country since 1991: education quality and its external efficiency. The analysis points out that the exclusive focus on investment in education without sufficient attention to changing the productive structure of the economy has resulted in a vicious cycle of low-quality education, persistently high levels of unemployment, underemployment and brain drain of the better-educated human resources of the country.

The chapter is organized as follows. First, the theoretical literature and approach that will be employed are reviewed. Policies, strategies, programmes and the performance of the education sectors of Ethiopia over the past quarter century are reviewed. The chapter analyses the persistent cycle of low-quality education in Ethiopia, and an attempt to establish the linkages between productive structure of the economy, quality of education, and its external efficiency and effectiveness. Section 25.5 presents concluding remarks.

25.2 Education and Economic Development: Conceptual and Theoretical Framework

In the standard economics literature, emphasis on the role of education and human development in economic growth started with Theodore Schultz's inaugural speech at the 1960 Annual Meeting of the American Economic Association (Schultz 1961). Schultz pointed out that human capital comprises skills, knowledge, and abilities and argues that maximizing it enables individuals to maximize earnings, companies to maximize profits, and nations to maximize wealth. He also argued that differences in investment in human capital formation are a major explanation for the differences in national outputs of various countries. Therefore, he recommended that assistance to 'underdeveloped' countries should redirect attention from the formation of nonhuman to human capital to achieve economic growth (Schultz 1961: 15–16). Another major contributor to the human capital theory, Gary Becker, explains that the main motivating factor for the increased attention given to human capital was the realization that the growth of physical capital explains a relatively small part of the growth of income in most countries (Becker 1964, 1994: 11).

Becker's overall focus is on micro-level issues related to education such as how the amount invested by individuals is determined by optimization behaviour so that the individual maximizes economic welfare (Becker 1994). Later developments offered theoretical justifications for the central role of human capital in the growth process and demonstrated that inclusion of human capital in the aggregate production function can explain differences in cross-country income per capita (Savvides and Stengos 2009: 6).

Overall, the standard theoretical approach to human development is inappropriate to study education and economic development in Ethiopia for several reasons. One reason is the fact that it is based on the assumption of full employment of all resources (including labour), which clearly does not reflect the context of developing countries like Ethiopia. Second, it assumes perfectly competitive product and labour markets (see, e.g., Becker 1994: 304)—an assumption that is again clearly at variance with the reality in countries like Ethiopia. Third, the standard growth theories and human development theories consider economic development as a process largely driven by accumulation of investments in physical and human capital (Nelson 2016). This is what Schumpeter called 'the pedestrian view that it is capital per se that propels the capitalist engine' when in fact capital per se is sterile (Reinert 2006: 7). Fourth and a related weakness is the implicit but core assumption of standard economics that economic structure is irrelevant, i.e. accumulation of physical and human capital per se will lead to economic development regardless of the economic structure within which investment is made (Reinert 2006: 7).

Given these major weaknesses in the standard approach to human development and education, this chapter employs an alternative theoretical framework drawn from an economics tradition that may be broadly called evolutionary, historical, and pragmatic. The tradition can be traced back to at least the works of Antonio Serra (1613), Friedrich List (1827, 1909[1841]), the nineteenth-century American System of Political Economy (e.g. Carey 1888), and Ethiopia's early modern intellectual, Gebrahiwot Baykedagn (1924).[1] The framework considers capitalism as a system of production where the main elements of capitalist dynamics and drivers of development are not capital, labour, or markets but new knowledge, entrepreneurship, innovations, and organizational ability (Reinert and Kattel 2004: 2–3; Gebrehiwot Baykedagn 1924: 42, 53, 61). Thus, the core aspect of development is transforming productive structures based on superior technology, skill, knowledge, and organizational capability embodied in institutions (Chang 2011).

Based on historical evidence, this theoretical tradition posits that economic development requires transferring and mastering skills and, above all, creating a viable market for activities with increasing returns to scale where the absence of purchasing power and massive unemployment tend to go hand in hand (Reinert 2006: 7). Thus, in sharp contrast to the mainstream approach where full employment is routinely assumed, in this approach, creation of productive formal employment *is* a key policy objective. This is because massive unemployment, underemployment, and the lack of purchasing power are the key impediments to the formation and expansion of businesses in developing countries. In contrast to the standard approach, development is seen as 'activity specific': different economic activities and different professions have very different capacities to profitably absorb capital (human or other) and knowledge; different professions have different 'windows of opportunity' for creating welfare since 'one cannot profitably add as much human capital to the job of washing dishes as to the job of being a lawyer' (Reinert 1999: 313).

In this tradition of development economics, human development and education occupy important positions because economic development relies heavily on accumulation and use of knowledge, which together with innovation, helps build more knowledge and technical innovation in a circular and cumulative manner further strengthening virtuous cycles of economic development and improving living standards (see, e.g. Gebrehiwot Baykedagn 1924: 24–9). To be effective, however, investments in education and human capital development need to be nested and managed in a coordinated and synergistic manner with other components of an industrialization and structural transformation strategy.

Moreover, even though development requires heavy investment in formation of human and physical capital, the key driving force of catch-up with advanced economies 'is assimilation, learning to do effectively what countries at the frontier have been doing' (Nelson 2016: 330). To a considerable extent, innovation and effective learning tend

[1] See Zinabu (2018) for genealogy of this tradition and its relevance today.

to draw supplies of physical and human capital by enabling their rates of return to be high (Nelson 2016: 330). Therefore, scholars of this intellectual tradition argue that sustainable economic development requires a deliberate and comprehensive set of state-directed, synergistic complementary interventions in infrastructure development, human development and education, technology adoption and innovation, internal market development, financial sector development that favours long-term and strategic investments, and selective and dynamic industrial policy (including export promotion *and* import substitution)—all aimed at achieving structural transformation.[2]

The intended form of structural transformation is away from specialization in 'nature-intensive', low-skill, low-knowledge, low-technology economic activities towards 'knowledge-intensive', higher-skill, and technology-intensive economic activities. Otherwise, higher investments in education and human development in the absence of long-term development vision for economic diversification and structural transformation would only lead to unemployment, underemployment, and outmigration of the most educated elements of a society to more advanced economies. This is because an undiversified economy with low productivity and low technology cannot afford to hold onto the best, brightest, and most capable of its human resources, and counter the pull of much higher wages and better working and living conditions in the more advanced economies (UNCTAD 2012: 88). The implication in terms of policies and strategies aimed at job creation is to focus on higher-skill, knowledge- and technology-intensive jobs because growth of employment opportunities of this nature in an economy tends to increase the real wages rates and welfare of the low-skilled segments of the workforce in that economy as well.[3]

25.3 Education Sector Development in Ethiopia from 1991 to 2017

25.3.1 Education Policies, Strategies, and Programmes

The Derg military regime in Ethiopia was overthrown in May 1991 by a coalition of armed groups led by the Ethiopian People's Revolutionary Democratic Front (EPRDF). From the very beginning, the EPRDF government identified education as one of its priorities (Woldegiyorgis 2015). The government issued its comprehensive education and training policy (ETP) in 1994. The ETP aimed at improving the state of education at all levels and ensuring that education makes the required contribution to the country's development

[2] See Zinabu (2018) for details on this.

[3] In fact, real wage rates of the unskilled labour in an economy is largely determined by the real wage rates of those of high-skill, technology-intensive, increasing returns-to-scale sectors that operate in the economy. See Reinert (1999) and Chang (2010: Ch. 15) for details on this.

(Woldegiyorgis 2015: 2). The policy identified access, quality, equity, and relevance as the main challenges of the education system of the nation. In practice, however, expanding access and equity have been given priority over quality and relevance. Consequently, there has been a rapid quantitative expansion of education, partly motivated by the need to meet the globally agreed target of Universal Primary Education by 2015 (MoE 2006: 6).

The ETP has been operationalized and implemented through a series of five-year Education Sector Development Programmes (ESDPs) the first of which was introduced during the 1997/8 budget year; and currently ESDP V (2015/16–2019/20) is under implementation. Each of the ESDPs derives its goals and strategies from the ETP and identifies specific time-bound objectives for each level of education along with the resource and organizational requirements (MoE 2006: 5). ESDP I had the long-term goal of achieving primary education by the year 2015 (MoFED 2002: 89). ESDP II spanned three years from 2002/3 to 2004/5 and focused on 'ensuring access to elementary education for all citizens along with improving quality and relevance to socioeconomic development' (MoFED 2002: 44). Similarly, ESDP III, which was part of the Plan for Accelerated and Sustainable Development to End Poverty (PASDEP) (2005/6–2009/10), was focused on achieving the Millennium Development Goals (MDGs) and supplying qualified trained work force with the necessary quantity and quality at all levels (MoFED 2006: 109).

Until 2010 when the government introduced the Growth and Transformation Plan (GTP-I) (MoFED 2010), the goals, objectives and strategies of the policies and plans of the government were not aimed at structural transformation and industrialization. For instance, both the interim and full PRSP as well as PASDEP documents issued in 2000, 2002, and 2006, respectively, emphasize poverty reduction as the core agenda of the country's development (MoFED 2002: i, 2002: 8, 2006: 1). Consequently, there was deliberate defocus on changing the productive structure of the economy and an overriding focus on traditional, smallholder agriculture (MoFED 2002: i).

With the adoption of the GTP, however, priority shifted away from traditional smallholder agriculture towards industrialization and structural transformation. Following this shift in development policy, the objectives and targets of the education sector also show a marked shift towards producing the human resources required to achieve industrialization and structural transformation. For instance, ESDP IV, which was included in GTP-I, stresses as its goal the production of 'efficient and effective, knowledge based, inspired and innovative citizens who can contribute to the realization of the long-term vision of making Ethiopia into a Middle-Income Economy' (MoFED 2010: 49). The shift is more pronounced in GTP-II (2015/16–2019/20) which states: 'Sustainable economic growth and transformation demands a healthy workforce equipped with the knowledge and skills to be highly productive and to generate innovations in technologies, processes, products, and services... The development of human resource capabilities will be interlinked with proper technological development and utilization... Thus, ensuring quality and accessible education and health services and augmenting the innovation skills through encouraging Research and Development (R&D) activities in the public and private sectors are needed to develop the human resource capabilities' (MoFEC 2016: 88).

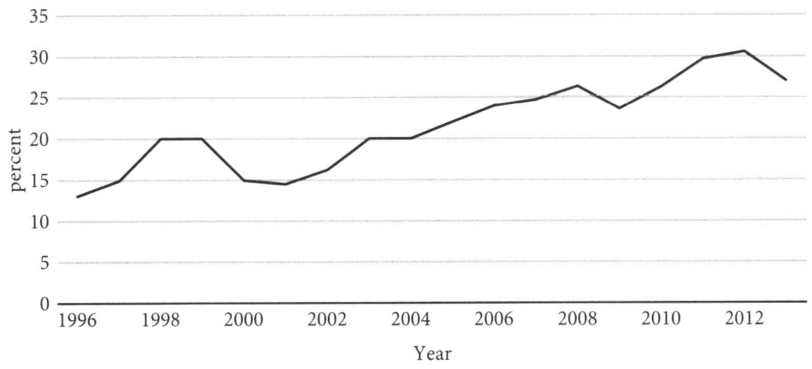

FIGURE 25.1 Total education sector expenditure as per cent of total government expenditure, 1996–2013

Source: World Development Indicators of World Bank and World Bank (2016: 92).

As can be seen from Figure 25.1, the government's consistent commitment to the education sector has been demonstrated through resource allocation as well: the national budget allocated to the sector has been one of the highest throughout the past quarter century. If we consider total government expenditure (including local, regional, and central government), the share spent on education for the years 2006–13 averaged 26 per cent; this share almost doubled from 15 per cent in 2000 to 27 per cent in 2013; in comparison, the sub-Saharan average, which stood at 15.26 per cent in 1998, increased only to 16.62 per cent in 2013 (source: World Development Indicators of World Bank). As a result, Ethiopia has been consistently ranking top in Africa with respect to the share of education sector in government expenditure for more than a decade. In addition, over the past quarter century, the education sector policies, strategies, and programmes have largely been aligned and closely linked with the overarching development priorities of the government. However, until recently, these priorities were not aimed at achieving structural transformation but poverty reduction and international targets such as the Universal Primary Education. As we shall see, this has had significant bearing on the quality of education and its external efficiency.

25.3.2 Organization and Management of the Education System

The educational system in Ethiopia follows the decentralized administrative structure of the government: it is divided into nine national regional states and two city administrations (MoE 2006: 5). Each regional state/city administration has its own Bureau of Education, various *woreda* [district] Education Offices and *kebele*s with their Education and Training Boards responsible for administering and managing the educational system. In some of the larger regions, the Zonal Educational Departments bridge administratively all educational activities between *woreda*s and regional bureaus.

Except for tertiary educational institutions, each Regional State Education Bureau is both administratively and financially responsible for general education, and technical and vocational education and training (TVET) as well as teacher training and other diploma-level institutions that operate in their respective regional states.

With respect to structure, the present educational system comprises primary, secondary, TVET, and tertiary education. Primary education is conducted from Grades 1 to 8, and is implemented in two cycles: primary first cycle (Grades 1–4) and primary second cycle (Grades 5–8). Secondary education has two cycles: Grades 9–10 and Grades 11–12. At the end of the first cycle of secondary education students take a national examination, which is used to select students that qualify for the next higher level of education called the preparatory level. The preparatory level (Grades 11 and 12) aims at preparing students for university education. Those who do not fulfil the criteria for the preparatory level can be enrolled in teacher education colleges and TVET schools. The achievements and performance of the post-1991 period are highlighted in Section 25.3.3 using selected indicators for each level of education. Given space limitations, the descriptions and discussion are brief. Discussion of the major challenges of the performance of the sector is deferred to Section 25.4.

25.3.3 Primary Education

As noted earlier, the driving force behind the government's investment in primary education has been equity of access; and attainment of quantitative targets has been seen as paramount so that the country can meet international commitments (such as Universal Primary Education by 2015). To this end, between 1996 and 2014, the number of primary schools increased from 11,000 to 32,048, allowing for full intake of students into Grade 1 when they reach the age of seven (MoE 2015: 13). By the academic year 2015/16, the net intake rate (NIR) (the proportion of 7-year-olds who enrol in Grade 1 at the national level) was 115.8 per cent (though there are significant regional variations) (MoE 2017: 24).[4]

Similarly, as can be seen from Table 25.1, the gross enrolment rate (GER)[5] for Grades 1–8 was 108.7 per cent in 2015/16, again with substantial regional variation.[6,7] This is a substantial improvement compared to as late as the 1999/2000 academic year when the GER at national level was 51 per cent. Net enrolment rate (NER), which only looks at the 7–14-year-olds enrolled in primary education, and which had stood at just 21.6 per cent

[4] NIR above 100 per cent is technically impossible as it indicates that there are more 7-year-olds in Grade 1 than there are in the population. This reflects the problems with the population projection and the fact that many children do not have accurate birth dates and are unsure of their age.

[5] GER shows the total number of children that have enrolled in Grades 1–8, irrespective of their age, as a proportion of the school-age population.

[6] This shows that there are more children in primary grades than there are children between 7 and 14 indicating that children younger than 7 and older than 14 are enrolling into primary schools.

[7] Dire Dawa and Afar had the lowest GER at 70 per cent and 66 per cent, respectively; Gambella and Addis Ababa had very high GERs both over 140 per cent.

Table 25.1 **Key performance indicators and trends for primary education (Grades 1–8), 1995/6–2015/16**

Year	GER Males	GER Females	GER Total	NER Male	NER Females	NER Total	Grade 8 completion rate (males)	Grade 8 completion rate (females)	Grade 8 completion rate (total)
1995/6	36.6	22.7	30.1	17.425.7	17.4	21.6			
1996/7	43	26	34.7	29.5	20	24.9			
1997/8	52	31.2	41.8	43	28	36			
1998/9	55.9	35.3	45.8	46.9	31.9	39.5			
1999/2000	60.9	40.7	51	51.2	36.6	44			
2000/1	67.3	47	57.4	55.7	41.7	48.8			
2001/2	71.7	51	61.6	59	45.2	52.2			
2002/3	74.6	53.8	64.4	60.6	47.2	54			
2003/4	77.4	59.1	68.4	62.9	51.8	57.4	34.9	19.1	27.1
2004/5	88	71.5	79.8	73.2	63.6	68.5	42.1	26.3	34.3
2005/6	98.6	83.9	91.3	81.7	73.2	77.5	50.1	32.9	41.7
2006/7	98	85.1	91.7	82.6	75.5	79.1	51.3	36.9	44.2
2007/8	100.5	90.5	95.6	86	80.7	83.4	49.4	39.9	44.7
2008/9	97.6	90.7	94.2	84.6	81.3	83	48.4	40.5	43.6
2009/10	96.6	90.1	93.4	83.7	80.5	82.1	51.0	44.5	44.5
2010/11	99.5	93.2	96.4	87	83.5	85.3	52.5	46.2	49.4
2011/12	99.5	92.9	95.4	86.8	83.9	85.4	52.4	51.9	52.1
2012/13	97.9	93	95.5	87.5	83.9	85.7	53.3	52.2	52.8
2013/14	104.8	97.8	101.3	95.1	90.1	92.6	46.7	46.7	46.7
2014/15	108.5	99.5	104	96.9	90.5	93.7	51.8	50.9	50.95
2015/16	113.71	113.7	108.67	104.2	96.2	100.3	55.3	53.3	54.3

Source: Compiled from MoE, 'Educational Statistics Annual Abstract' (various years).

in 1995/6, increased to 100.25 per cent in 2015/16, quadrupling over a twenty-year period. Overall, the Ethiopian primary education system enrolled and served 18.43 million children, employing 424,560 teachers in 34,867 primary schools located across the country (MoE 2017). Both gender and regional equity aspects have been showing consistent improvement over the years.

25.3.4 Secondary Education

In 1999/2000, 571,719 students were enrolled in 410 Ethiopian secondary schools, and the national GER for secondary education (9–12) was 10.3 per cent (MoE 2000). In contrast, in 2015/16, there were 3,156 secondary schools which enrolled 1,982,185 students where the GER for Grades 9–12 was 29.04 per cent (MoE 2017). In other words, both the intake capacity and GER at secondary education level more or less tripled over this period, but many children are either not completing primary education or are not proceeding into secondary education. When secondary education is split into first (Grades 9–10) and second (Grades 11–12) cycles, the GER drops significantly between the two cycles: national GER for the first cycle stood at 44.83 per cent but just 12.56 per cent for the second cycle in 2015/16 (MoE 2017: 53). There are wide regional variations, with a GER in Addis Ababa of 82.27 per cent and Afar (8.62 per cent) and Somali regional (11.2 per cent) states achieving the lowest GERs at this level (MoE 2017: 52). The disaggregation into the two cycles also shows high enrolment in Addis Ababa with GER over 100 per cent (112.91 per cent) and very low GER for Afar (12.63 per cent) and Somali (13.94 per cent) regions for Grades 9–10 (ibid.).[8] The national NER for the first cycle for the academic year 2015/16 was still a paltry 23.78 per cent (ibid.: 56). However, this is at least three times what it was in the 1999/2000 academic year (MoE 2000: 23). The data show that equity aspects of access to education have generally been improving across time, but they get progressively worse the higher the level of education.

25.3.5 Technical and Vocational Education and Training (TVET)

In Ethiopia, TVET is institutionally somewhat separate from the rest of the education system, and forms a parallel track where students entering TVET stream after completing Grade 10 have three options, depending on the score received in the national exam: one year of training (10+1); 2 years' training (10+2), or three years' training (10+3). Students who complete three years of training are considered to have completed the first year of college-level education and can join universities to complete their undergraduate degree. Students that attain level 4 in TVET can continue to higher education. TVET

[8] GER above 100 per cent for Addis means that many of the students in secondary schools in the city are not in the official age range and are under 15 or over 16.

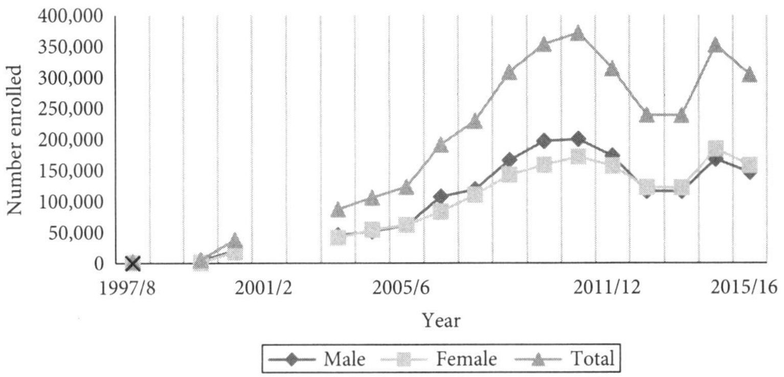

FIGURE 25.2 Enrolment trends in TVET by gender, 1997/8–2015/16

Source: Compiled from MoE, 'Educational Statistics Annual Abstract' (various years).

graduates have the option to go through official assessment of their skills for key competencies. The government plans to establish TVET institutes in all *woreda*s of the country by 2020 (MoE 2015: 10).

As can be seen from Figure 25.2, there has been substantial increase in enrolment in TVET between 1997/8 and 2015/16. During the academic year 2001/2 there were 123 government and eighteen non-government TVET schools in the country enrolling a total of 38,176 students (MoE 2000: 8). In addition, there were twenty-eight TVET centres under the Ministry of Agriculture that enrolled 12,494 students during that year. In contrast, during 2015/16, there were 582 TVET institutions across the country that enrolled 304,139 students (MoE 2017). In other words, the enrolment increased six-fold over the period while the number of institutions expanded close to four-fold. During the same year, 131,097 students graduated in TVET levels I–IV (MoE 2017: 117).

25.3.6 Higher Education

When the EPRDF government assumed power in 1991, there were only two universities (Addis Ababa and Haromaya), and the gross enrolment rate in higher education was 0.7 per cent in 1995 (Woldegiyorgis 2015: 2). However, by the turn of the century, the government had launched five new universities—by upgrading junior-level institutions—marking the beginning of an aggressive expansion programme (Woldegiyorgis 2015: 2). Because of the massive public investment programme implemented ever since, by 2016 the country had thirty-eight accredited universities (thirty-six of which are government owned).

As can be seen from Figure 25.3, due to this massive expansion, total undergraduate level enrolment expanded from 56,072 in 2003/4 to 778,766 in 2015/16 (MoE 2017: 123)—showing an annual growth rate of 25.5 per cent and a close to fourteen-fold increment. In addition to undergraduate programmes, enrolment in graduate programmes has also expanded rapidly during recent years with gross enrolment increasing from 2,560 in

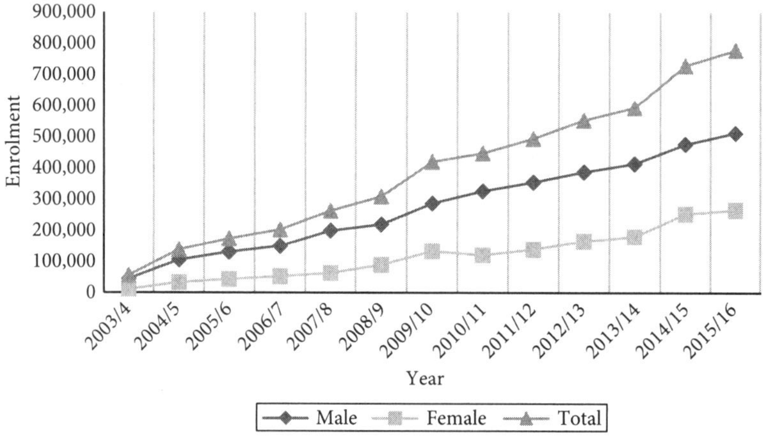

FIGURE 25.3 Trends in undergraduate enrolment in government and non-government institutions, all programmes

Source: Compiled from MoE, 'Educational Statistics Annual Abstract' (various years).

2003/4 to 51,521 in 2015/16 (MoE 2017: 127)—a twenty-fold increment in thirteen years. As pointed out earlier, the gender gap in access/enrolment progressively widens when moving from lower to higher levels of education (the highest gap being at the PhD level); nevertheless, the massive expansion and targeted affirmative action measures have partially reduced gender disparities in access to higher education.

Data compiled from MoE[9] shows that, in terms of graduation also, growth rates have been consistently high over recent years; for instance, 127,275 students obtained first degrees in 2015/16 compared to 75,348 in 2010/11. Since the introduction of ESDP IV in 2010, which for the first time admitted a need for economic transformation and that it would require a 'conscious application of science, technology and innovation as the major instruments to create wealth' (Woldegiyorgis 2015: 24), there has been a deliberate shift in undergraduate enrolment away from social sciences and towards natural sciences, with the target for the ratio of enrolment in natural science to that of social science set at 70:30. As of 2015/16, the ratio was 62:38 (MoE 2017: 127).

25.4 Major Shortcomings in the Ethiopian Education System

Despite the clear quantitative improvement in access to and provision of education at all levels, there have been major shortcomings in Ethiopian education in recent years. This section highlights two of the most important problems: poor quality education at all

[9] MoE, *Educational Statistics Annual Abstract* (various years).

levels, and low external efficiency due to the failure to achieve any meaningful level of transformation of the productive structure of the Ethiopian economy.

25.4.1 A Vicious Cycle of Low-Quality Education

At the primary level, National Learning Assessments (NLA) have been conducted since 2010. The results show that education quality is very low. For instance, an Early Grade Reading Assessment (EGRA) conducted in 2010 found that 33.9 per cent of children in Grade 2 and 20 per cent in Grade 3 read zero words correctly (Girma and Raysarkar 2017: 1–2). Moreover, according to World Bank (2017) between a third and over a half of 4th-grade and 8th-grade students tested in 2015 at the proficiency level were rated as 'below basic' in all subjects, except English for Grade 8. The 'below basic' proficiency level means that the student has minimal understanding of the subject and lacks the skills to solve simple problems appropriate for that grade level. Reading scores at Grade 4 were of particular concern, as 44 per cent of students nationally tested at the below basic level in reading in 2015 (World Bank 2017). NLA data also show that the proportion of students performing at advanced levels is very low—in most cases below 10 per cent—in Grades 4 and 8 (World Bank 2017). The situation of internal efficiency of the primary sub-sector is also not encouraging: the dropout rates are high (~18.1 per cent in 2015/16 for Grade 1) and completion rates are low (55.5 per cent for Grade 8 in 2015/16) (MoE 2017: 4).

At secondary level also, the 2010 NLA results show mean scores for Grade 10 (36 per cent) and Grade 12 (47.8 per cent) were both below the minimum standard of 50 per cent set by the 1994 Education and Training Policy. The main findings of the NLA that was conducted for Grade 12 in 2013 also indicated that the overall test performance of the students was far below the minimum standard. According to MoE (2015), 'In grade ten, the share of students that achieved an average score of 50 per cent across the five core subjects (mathematics, English, physics, chemistry, biology) stood at 23 per cent in the 2014 assessment. In the same assessment, only 3 per cent achieved 75 per cent or above in their average score' (MoE 2015: 17). The performance at Grade 12 was slightly better (possibly due to selection of better-performing students following Grade 10) in the latest assessment (2014): 34 per cent of students achieved an average score of 50 per cent across the five core subjects and 4 per cent of students achieved an average score of 75 per cent (MoE 2015). The situation of the TVET sub-sector is also not good. For instance, of the TVET graduates in Addis Ababa that took competence tests in 2012, only 10 per cent were found competent in their area of core competence (Shaorshadze and Krishnan 2012: 19).

With respect to higher education, MoE (2015) admits that many students join higher education institutions with results below the 50 per cent threshold in the higher education entrance examinations; in physics, a basis for engineering studies, students' results are extremely low; the graduation rate of regular undergraduate students is as low as 79 per cent; and this 'implies a low quality of instruction or perceived low relevance of the higher education courses being offered. It could also be a reflection of the low quality of students introduced to higher education, who, irrespective of teaching quality, have not been prepared for learning at this level' (MoE 2015: 22). Moreover, with a view to having sufficient numbers of qualified teaching staff for new universities, MoE invited students graduating from bachelor's programmes to sit for a qualifying examination at the end of the 2014/15 academic year (Woldegiyorgis 2017: 18). Close to 10,000 graduates from thirty-two universities across the country took the examination where eligibility requirements included a minimum cumulative grade point average (GPA) of 2.75 for men and 2.5 for women. The test results were such that, out of the possible 100 marks, only one person scored 81 followed by 28 candidates who scored between 70 and 79; and the overall average score was 57.8. (Woldegiyorgis 2017: 18). Ultimately, 716 candidates were selected and offered a job; but this is unfortunate because 'A score of 57.8 in one's major must be viewed at best as a mediocre result. Disturbingly, 127 of the selected candidates (or close to one-fifth) scored a failing result (less than 50 per cent)' (Woldegiyorgis 2017: 18).

We consider only two important factors that have undermined the quality of education in the country for lack of space: quality of schools and quality/motivation of teaching staff. The Ministry has instituted school quality standards where schools are assessed against twenty-six standards for school inputs, processes, and outcomes. According to World Bank (2017), inspections conducted between 2013 and 2016 found that about 90 per cent of primary schools and 83 per cent of secondary schools did not meet national standards; about 26 per cent of the primary schools and 16 per cent of the secondary schools are rated at the lowest level (level 1); almost two-thirds of each type, at level 2. Thus, one cannot expect sub-standard schools to be venues for high-quality education. One cannot also expect to achieve high-quality general education when it is those who fail to qualify for preparatory level (second cycle high school) who are enrolled in teachers' education colleges.

With respect to teaching staff in institutions of higher education in Ethiopia, the MoE has set a standard of 0:70:30 (Bachelor: Masters': Doctorate degree holders, respectively) (MoE 2015: 23). However, it admits, 'The supply of teaching staff with postgraduate qualifications has not kept pace with the increase in student enrolment. As a result, a large share of undergraduate students is taught by staff with a bachelor's degree', since the current ratio is 27:58:15 (MoE 2015: 22–3). However, the problem is not only about the supply of PhDs but also about skewed geographical distribution: in 2012, among teachers and researchers working in Ethiopian universities, only 6.4 per cent held a doctoral degree; and half of them worked at Addis Ababa University (UNCTAD 2012: 99). Moreover, the education system in Ethiopia is filled with teaching staff who are not motivated to teach or stay in the profession: 'A 2014 study conducted by the MoE, however, suggested that 70 per cent of teachers would, if given an equivalently paid option, leave the profession' (MoE 2015: 55–6).

25.4.2 Economic Structure, Equality, and External Efficiency of Education in Ethiopia

It is very clear that Ethiopia has achieved enormous success in terms of increasing access to all levels of education throughout the country. However, this success has been achieved at the expense of education quality at all levels in the form of a vicious cycle where low-quality inputs (e.g. teachers, schools) from the lowest level to the highest generate second- and third- round effects continually eroding the quality of education. However, even if there is consensus on the challenges of improving the quality of education, there does not exist the understanding that the low-quality inputs that are negatively and persistently affecting the quality of education are intimately tied to the level and structure of the Ethiopian economy.

For instance, there is ample evidence within the country that the income levels of the parents are directly related to the success of children in primary education: 'there are large disparities in learning levels between children from different socio-economic groups'; 'children from the poorest households and those from rural sites are making the slowest progress through grades' and 'children from better-off households, with care-givers who have completed primary school, and those living in urban sites, perform better in tests of maths and vocabulary' (Young Lives 2017). In addition, the dearth and skewed distribution of highly qualified staff at higher education institutions is—to a large extent—not due to lack of qualified Ethiopians but because the economy and the education system could not afford to keep them in the country/academic institutions. In fact, according to UNCTAD (2012), the number of PhD-holding teachers and researchers active in the country's universities is much lower than the members of the Ethiopian diaspora just in the United States and Canada who hold PhDs. 'The case study on the Ethiopian academic diaspora prepared for this Report identified 200 Ethiopian professors currently working in foreign universities, of whom 148 are active in the United States. Among these, 72 are full professors. In Ethiopia, by contrast, only 65 persons hold an equivalent position. In other words, there are more Ethiopian full professors working in the United States than in Ethiopia itself, in spite of the strong need of Ethiopian universities for very highly skilled people' (UNCTAD 2012: 101).

One of the main reasons why the Ethiopian economy cannot keep the best, brightest, and the most qualified within its boundaries is because it is poor, undiversified, and technologically backward where low-productivity, low-technology, low-skill and low value-added agriculture provides employment for more than 80 per cent of the population. For instance, modern manufacturing is historically well known for being the engine of economic development, the 'learning centre' of the economy, centre of technical change, innovation, technology diffusion, and the key driver of productivity growth in an economy.[10] However, the performance of the sector in Ethiopia has been dismal: 'its contribution to GDP not only remained low but also contracted slightly from about 6 per cent of GDP during 2000–4 to about 4 per cent during the first GTP [i.e. 2010–15]' (Admasu 2017: 4).

Meanwhile, the lack of structural transformation of the Ethiopian economy is intimately related to the economic policies and strategies that have been adopted and implemented by the Ethiopian government since it came to power in 1991. There was

[10] Consequently, historically, the terms industrialized country and developed country are used interchangeably. See Zinabu (2017) Section 3.1 for details and associated literature on this point.

deliberate and conscious focus on poverty reduction at the expense of structural transformation at least until 2010. This was in line with the prevailing orthodoxy in the international development discourse such as the poverty reduction and MDG agenda, which focus on treating the symptoms of underdevelopment rather than its causes (Reinert 2006; Chang 2011). The orthodoxy overlooked or ignored the fact that economic development requires structural transformation and industrialization, and pushed governments of developing countries including that of Ethiopia to focus their attention and resources on social sectors such as health and education (particularly at the primary and secondary levels) at the expense of changing the productive structure of the economy (UNCTAD 2011: 11–13).

Changing the productive structure of the economy could have created a virtuous and sustainable circle in the economies and enabled them to eventually afford the provision of high-quality social services such as education and health. Thus, the success achieved by Ethiopia in terms of expansion of access to education is not an unqualified blessing because the substantial policy attention and resources that were invested in the sector—averaging 27 per cent of the government's budget—have not been matched by policies and efforts to change the productive structure of the economy. For instance, while the government invested heavily in social sectors (such as education and health) as well as transport infrastructure, it ignored the other elements required for changing the productive structure of the economy, such as selective, dynamic, and context-specific industrial policy (since its main aim was addressing poverty rather than economic transformation). Moreover, as discussed earlier, it is only since 2010 that the government began explicitly emphasizing the links between economic transformation and (science- and technology-focused) education. Whether intentionally or not, the adherence of the Ethiopian government to the prevailing development orthodoxy may also have had a significant bearing on the external efficiency of education in the country.

The failure to achieve any meaningful structural transformation means that the private sector is not able to create enough well-paying jobs that require higher skills and academic qualification.[11] Small-scale, rain-fed, low-technology agriculture is the employer of approximately 83.5 per cent of the country's population; and this kind of economic activity cannot generate substantial skilled employment. Second, the focus of the government's employment creation initiatives is skewed towards unskilled and low-skilled jobs by default and design. Urban development was an ignored area in Ethiopia until the government issued the Urban Development Policy in 2005; and even when urban development got the necessary policy attention, the focus of creation of urban employment has been through micro and small enterprises (MSE). Even GTP-II argues that youth employment is best addressed by organizing young people in MSEs and sets a goal of organizing 7.43 million people in MSEs (MoFEC 2016: 127). It is no wonder that in Ethiopia, as late as 2012, MSEs comprised 99 per cent of all enterprises and over 60 per

[11] According to Broussar and Tsegay (2012: 28), in Ethiopia, individuals with higher education are more likely to work for the government and roughly 50 per cent of individuals with higher education are employed by the government.

cent of private employment (Broussar and Tsegay 2012: 30). Unfortunately, MSEs tend to create predominantly informal, unskilled, low-skilled, low-paying, non-permanent jobs under poor working conditions (Hampel-Milagrosa and Reeg 2016).

Therefore, it is not surprising that there has been a positive relationship between educational attainment and unemployment in Ethiopia since 1999 (since the first national labour survey was conducted). That is, since then, the share of the unemployed who were educated has increased (Broussar and Tsegay 2012: 26) despite the robust GDP growth rates that were registered during the same period. Moreover, urban youth unemployment across the country stood at 21.6 per cent; and in 2013, among the unemployed, the highest rate of unemployment (24 per cent) was recorded for those who attained preparatory education; the lowest unemployment rate was registered for persons who attained non-formal education (1.6 per cent); throughout the three national labour force surveys (1999, 2011, and 2013), the unemployment rate of literate persons is higher than illiterate persons; and the overall unemployment rate for twenty-six major urban centres is 21.3 per cent (CSA 2014). In short, even if the education system is producing very large working-age population, the economy has not been generating a sufficient number of well-paying, skill/knowledge-intensive jobs but jobs that require little or no education even when the job creation is through deliberate government intervention. The unbalanced focus on the supply side of the labour market while ignoring the demand side would just exacerbate the problem of unemployment. This is because, in the presence of high unemployment at all levels, improving the capabilities of job seekers will only lead to more unemployment and not to more paid employment or self-employment above the subsistence level (Amsden 2010: 57).

In summary, expansion of education in Ethiopia since 1991 without simultaneous and equivalent focus on and achievement of structural transformation and creation of high-skilled and well-paying jobs has resulted in the country being one of the worst affected Least Developed Countries (LDCs) in the world with respect to brain drain (UNCTAD 2012: 95, 96, 101). Thus, besides the large number of academicians and PhD-holders, the UNCTAD report estimates that, out of all Ethiopian medical doctors, between a third and a half work abroad (UNCTAD 2012: 101). Furthermore, it estimates the opportunity cost of training and then losing a medical doctor by the country to brain drain to be at least US$364,000 (UNCTAD 2012: 101).

25.5 Concluding Remarks

From the description and analyses presented in this chapter, it is clear that the achievement of massive expansion of access to education has resulted not only in a vicious cycle of low quality but also in increased unemployment and underemployment of the educated human resources, the loss of the best and the brightest human resources to the developed world, and substantial financial opportunity cost per the skilled/educated out-migrant. This failure to effectively and productively put the potential of the skilled and educated human resources to maximum use negatively affects the prospects for industrialization and structural transformation. Industrialization and structural transformation would not only have led to improved economic welfare/living standards for Ethiopian society but also would have enabled the public sector—through increased domestic resource mobilization—to afford further expansion and quality improvement of basic social services such as education.

Breaking these two mutually reinforcing vicious cycles of unbalanced focus on achieving social goals (of education) at the expense of changing the productive and technological/skill structure of the economy, and loss and wastage of precious human resources to brain drain, unemployment, and underemployment requires well-crafted, synergistic, dynamic, context-specific, and comprehensive policies and strategies aimed at deliberately and progressively moving the Ethiopian economy away from its current specialization in nature-intensive, low-skill, low-knowledge, low-technology economic activities towards 'mind-intensive', higher-skill and technology-intensive economic activities. Among other things, this will also require the government to move its focus away from creation and promotion of employment in low-skill economic activities and towards higher-skill activities. This is because creation of high-skill, well-paying jobs would tend to automatically lead to increased real wages for the low-skilled segment of the workforce as well.

References

Admasu, Shiferaw (2017). 'Productive Capacity and Economic Growth in Ethiopia', CDP Background Paper No. 34, Department of Economic and Social Affairs.

Amsden, Alice H. (2010). 'Say's Law, Poverty Persistence, and Employment Neglect', *Journal of Human Development and Capabilities* 11 (1): 57–66.

Becker, Gary (1964). *Human Capital: A Theoretical and Empirical Analysis, with Special Reference to Education* (New York: Columbia University Press).

Becker, Gary (1994). *Human Capital: A Theoretical and Empirical Analysis, with Special Reference to Education*, 3rd edition (Chicago, IL: University of Chicago Press).

Broussar, Nzinga H. and Tsegay Gebrekidan Tekleselassie (2012). 'Youth Unemployment Ethiopia Country Study', International Growth Center Working Paper.

Carey, Henry Charles (1888). *Principles of Social Sciences in Three Volumes, Vol. I.* (Philadelphia, PA: J. B. Lippincott Company).

Chang, Ha-Joon (2010). *23 Things They Don't Tell You about Capitalism* (London: Allan Lane).

Chang, Ha-Joon (2011). '*Hamlet* without the Prince of Denmark: How Development Has Disappeared from Today's 'Development' Discourse', in *Towards New Developmentalism: Market as Means rather than Master*, ed. S. Khan and J. Christiansen (Abingdon: Routledge): 47–58.

CSA (Central Statistical Agency) (2014). *Analytical Report on the 2013 National Labor Force Survey* (Addis Ababa: CSA).

Gebrehiwot Baykedagn (1924). *Mengistina YeHizb Astedader (Government and Public Administration).* (Addis Ababa: Berhaneena Selam Printing Press).

Girma, Woldetsadek and Cgandranani Raysarkar (2017). *Textbook Provision for All in Ethiopia: Lessons Learned from the General Education Quality Improvement Project (GEQIP).* (Washington: World Bank).

Hampel-Milagrosa, Aimee and Caroline Reeg (2016). 'Micro, Small and Medium Enterprises as Drivers for Job Creation and Decent Work', Paper presented to Inter-Agency Group Meeting on 'Employment and Decent Work for Poverty Eradication in Support of the Second UN Decade for the Eradication of Poverty (2008–2017)', UN Conference Centre, Bangkok, 4–6 May.

Krasniqi, F. X. and R. Topxhiu (2016). 'The Importance of Investment in Human Capital: Becker, Schultz and Heckman', *Journal of Knowledge Management, Economics and Information Technology* 6 (4).

List, F. (1827). *Outlines of the American System of Political Economy*. Philadelphia (National Gazette).

List, F. (1909[1841]). *The National System of Political Economy*. Translated from the German by Sampson S. Lloyd (London: Longmans, Green & Co).

MoE (2000). 'Education Statistics Annual Abstract, 1992 E.C. (1999/00)', Ministry of Education, Addis Ababa.

MoE (2006). 'Five Year Education Sector Capacity Development Strategic Plan', Ministry of Education, Addis Ababa.

MoE (2015). 'Education Sector Development Programme V (ESDP V) 2008–2012 E.C. (2015/16–2019/20 G.C. Programme Action Plan', Ministry of Education, Addis Ababa.

MoE (2017). 'Education Statistics Annual Abstract, 2008 E.C. (2015/16)', Ministry of Education, Addis Ababa.

MoFED (2000). 'Ethiopia: Interim Poverty Reduction Strategy Paper 2000/01–2002/03', Ministry of Finance and Economic Development, Addis Ababa.

MoFED (2002). 'Ethiopia: Sustainable Development and Poverty Reduction Program', Ministry of Finance and Economic Development, Addis Ababa.

MoFED (2006). 'Ethiopia: Building on Progress: A Plan for Accelerated and Sustained Development to End Poverty (PASDEP) (2005/06–2009/10) Vol. I: Main Text', Ministry of Finance and Economic Development, Addis Ababa.

MoFED (2010). 'Growth and Transformation Plan (GTP) (2010/11–2014/15), Vol. 1', National Planning Commission, Addis Ababa.

MoFEC (2016). 'Growth and Transformation Plan (GTP II), 2016–2020', National Planning Commission, Addis Ababa.

Nelson, Richard (2016). 'Economic Development from the Perspective of Evolutionary Economic Theory', in *Handbook of Alternative Theories of Economic Development*, ed. Erik S. Reinert, Jayati Ghosh, and Rainer Kattel (Cheltenham: Edward Elgar): 323–35.

Reinert, Erik (1999). 'The Role of the State in Economic Growth', *Journal of Economic Studies* 26 (4/5): 268–326.

Reinert, Erik (2006). 'Development and Social Goals: Balancing Aid and Development to Prevent "Welfare Colonialism"', DESA Working Paper 14, Economic and Social Affairs, UN-DESA, New York ESA.

Reinert, Erik and Rainer Kattel (2004). 'Qualitative Shift in European Integration: Towards Permanent Wage Pressures and "Latin Americanization" of Europe?' PRAXIS Working Paper No. 17, Tallinn University of Technology and Praxis Foundation, Tallinn, Estonia.

Savvides, Andreas and Thanasis Stengos (2009). *Human Capital and Economic Growth* (Stanford, CA: Stanford University Press).

Schultz, Theodore W. (1961). 'Investment in Human Capital (American Economic Association Presidential Address)', *American Economic Review* 51 (1): 1–17.

Serra, Antonio (1613). *A Brief Treatise on the Causes which can make Gold and Silver Plentiful in Kingdoms where there are no Mines (Breve trattato delle cause che possono far abbondare li regni d'oro e argento dove non sono miniere)* (Naples: Lazzaro Scoriggio).

Shaorshadze, Irina and Pramila Krishnan (2012). 'Technical and Vocational Education and Training in Ethiopia', Paper for the International Growth Centre—Ethiopia Country Programme.

UNCTAD (2011). *Economic Development in Africa Report 2011: Fostering Industrial Development in Africa in the New Global Environment* (NY and Geneva: UN).

UNCTAD (2012). *The Least Developed Countries Report 2012* (Geneva: UNCTAD).

Woldegiyorgis, Ayenachew A. (2015). 'A Glance at the Ethiopian Higher Education from the Developmental State Perspective', *Bahir Dar Journal Education* 15 (2): 1–37.

Woldegiyorgis, Ayenachew A. (2017). 'The Vicious Circle of Quality in Ethiopian Higher Education', *International Higher Education* 90 (Summer): 18–19.

World Bank (2016). 'Ethiopia Public Expenditure Review', Report No. ACS14541, World Bank, Washington, DC.

World Bank (2017). 'Program for Results Information Document on Education for Growth and Transformation (GEQUIP III)', Report No. PIDC0110495, World Bank, Washington, DC.

Young Lives (2017). 'Education and Learning: Preliminary Findings from the 2016 Young Lives Survey' (Round 5) (Ethiopia; Oxford: Young Lives).

Zinabu, Samaro Rekiso (2017). 'Rethinking Regional Economic Integration in Africa as if Industrialization Mattered', *Structural Change and Economic Dynamics* 43: 87–98.

Zinabu, Samaro Rekiso (2018). 'Economics of Late Development and Industrialization: Putting Gebrehiwot Baykedagn (1886–1919) in Context', *Cambridge Journal of Economics*. DOI: 10.1093/cje/bey001.

PART IV

AGRICULTURE AND RURAL TRANSFORMATION

CHAPTER 26

AGRICULTURE'S CHANGING ROLE IN ETHIOPIA'S ECONOMIC TRANSFORMATION

STEFAN DERCON AND DOUGLAS GOLLIN

26.1 Introduction

Agriculture remains a crucial sector in Ethiopia's economy, accounting for large shares of the country's employment—though making up a diminishing fraction of output. In this chapter, we trace the past role of agriculture in the Ethiopian economy and consider the new challenges faced by the sector as the economy grows and transforms. We approach the topic from a simple theoretical perspective, drawing heavily on dual-economy models of the linkages between agricultural and non-agricultural sectors, and their typical geographical counterparts, rural and urban areas. We focus in particular on the lessons from these models concerning agriculture's role in the economy at different stages of the growth process. The dual-economy models posit relationships between agriculture and other sectors of the economy.

In the simplest versions of the model, as in Lewis (1954), there is no productivity growth within either sector, and aggregate growth occurs simply from shifting resources from the subsistence sector into the capitalist sector. The driving force for Lewis was the accumulation of capital, which took place primarily through the profits earned in the modern sector. For Lewis, capital accumulation in the modern sector generated a strong pull that would eventually induce labour and other resources to leave the subsistence sector. Although Lewis was careful not to identify the subsistence sector directly with agriculture, it was clear that he saw a significant overlap between traditional agriculture and the subsistence sector.

Later formulations of dual-economy models looked to productivity growth as a driver of structural change. In some models, such as Johnston and Mellor (1961), productivity growth in agriculture stimulates growth in the non-agricultural sector. A similar view was articulated by Schultz (1964), who envisioned agriculture as a dynamic sector in developing countries, if the entrepreneurial potential of farmers could be unleashed. In general, dual-economy models all focused on a process by which investments or productivity growth in one sector would drive a process of structural change and transformation that would ultimately lead to growth across the entire economy. Contemporary literature on dual economies has generally supported this approach to conceptualizing the growth process (Gollin, Parente, and Rogerson 2002, 2007).

Against this theoretical backdrop, the Ethiopian growth strategy, based on Agricultural Development-Led Industrialization (ADLI), initially articulated a deliberate attempt to drive growth in such a dual-economy setting. In this chapter, we argue that ADLI offered a plausible and seemingly successful strategy for Ethiopia at an earlier stage of its growth and transformation. Twenty years later, however, Ethiopia sits at a different point in its development trajectory, and the ADLI strategy is ripe for revisiting. A particular question arises from the assumption of the ADLI strategy—consistent with Johnston and Mellor (1961)—that growth in rural demand would succeed in stimulating urban and non-agricultural growth relatively quickly. We argue that the current strategy, which appears to emphasize urban and industrial growth, may also have the potential to boost value added and labour productivity in agriculture, reversing the sectoral dynamics of the ADLI approach and, in some ways, adhering more closely to the original Lewis model. However, the links between sectors are relatively weak in Ethiopia, as in many other sub-Saharan economies, and the backward linkages from industrial growth to rural transformation will not be automatic.

Moreover, this chapter argues that the usual interpretation of the dual-economy models may need to be reconsidered for an economy such as that of Ethiopia. The standard view is that a dual economy grows by releasing labour from the traditional sector into a higher-productivity modern sector. To the extent that the traditional sector is identified with agriculture and rural areas, and the modern sector is identified with urban and industrial activity, the dual-economy model seems to envision a massive movement of labour out of rural areas into cities. For a country like Ethiopia, with a very large rural population, it is difficult to imagine that large fractions of the rural labour force can be easily absorbed into urban economies and industrial activities.

An alternative approach, bringing together the two views of structural change, is to transform the agricultural sector itself from a part of the subsistence economy into a part of the modern economy. We argue in this chapter that one of the ways in which the agricultural sector can transform is by moving beyond its current overwhelming emphasis on staple crop production. Although staple food productivity will always remain a critical area of concern for Ethiopia, there are also opportunities to boost the agricultural sector by recognizing and encouraging its links to the rest of the economy. In particular, there is a need to acknowledge and facilitate the transmission of urban and international demand, thereby encouraging higher-value crops and higher value addition. The emergence of a stronger agro-processing sector will also be an important part of the story (see also Chapters 15, 30, and 31).

26.2 Ethiopia's Agricultural Growth in Retrospective

Twenty-five years ago, one could have been forgiven for regarding Ethiopia as a 'basket case'. Not only had violent conflict been raging across many parts of the country, but in addition the economy was in a pitiable state. By 1992, GDP per capita (in constant 2010 US dollars) stood at US$162,[1] and it would stay below US$200 throughout the 1990s. Poverty was not measured until 1995/6, when the first representative household income and expenditure surveys were conducted. Throughout the 1990s, the vast majority of the population would have been below the global poverty line of US$1.90 in PPP; World Bank estimates in 1995 put the poverty rate at two-thirds of the population. Using a national poverty line on the same data suggested poverty rates of 46 per cent in 1995 and 44 per cent in 1999.

Throughout this period, and continuing today, the vast majority of the population were involved in farming, mainly crop agriculture (see Chapter 27). Throughout the 1990s, more than 85 per cent of the population lived in rural areas. Poverty rates were higher in rural areas than in urban areas. Other indicators of living standards also showed rural areas to be worse off, as is typical across the world across population densities (Gollin, Kirchberger, and Lagakos 2017). National poverty estimates suggested that in 1999 poverty was about a fifth higher in rural areas than in urban areas (45 per cent versus 37 per cent). The dual-economy model certainly seemed to apply in Ethiopia, with large pools of relatively unproductive rural labour. Land and labour productivity seemed very low—for example, by 1995/6 yields for wheat were about 1,300 kg/ha, which put it below yields of the United Kingdom in the eighteenth century (Allen 2009).[2]

In the 1990s, little sign could be detected of strong growth in the Ethiopian economy. Overall growth fluctuated widely (in a range of +13 per cent in 1993 to −3.5 per cent in 1998); agricultural growth fluctuated between −17 per cent in 1998 and +10 per cent in 1996. The fluctuations led to a relatively modest average growth over the period; average annual per capita growth was barely above 0.5 per cent per year (in constant prices); in agriculture, it even slightly declined. The share of agriculture in GDP declined, but this was hardly a sign of structural transformation.

These patterns make the last fifteen years in Ethiopia even more remarkable. Overall growth has been strong: between 2003 and 2016, overall GDP in constant prices grew by

[1] All data in this paragraph from World Bank, World Development Indicators, https://data.worldbank.org/

[2] These levels of yields were a large increase since the 1960s, when yields were around 500 kg/ha—less than medieval England.

7.7 per cent per year in real terms (or more than 5 per cent per capita). Extreme poverty using national poverty lines declined by a third to about 30 per cent[3] by 2010/11. GDP per capita in 2010 US$ is now well above US$500.

Agricultural growth has been central to this overall growth, especially in the first few years of this period—11.6 per cent growth between 2003 and 2008, slowing down in more recent years to 5.2 per cent between 2011 and 2016.[4] Even these lower growth rates clearly outpaced current population growth of 2.5 per cent. The rate of agricultural growth also outpaced most low-income or African economies.

The key driver of this growth in agricultural value added has been a considerable growth in value added from traditional food staples. This in turn came both from expansion in areas planted (and the number of holders; see Chapter 27) and (especially in more recent years) from yield increases. Production of cereals was in 2015/16 three times greater than the levels recorded in 1995/6. Area cultivated had increased in that period by 70 per cent (an annual growth of 2.8 per cent, above population growth) while yields increased by 86 per cent.[5] The fastest-growing crops were wheat and maize. Wheat saw a four-fold increase in output, based on a doubling of area cultivated and a doubling of yields to 2,530 kg/ha. Maize output rose by a multiple of 3.7 times over the twenty-year period, with a doubling of yield (to 3,390 kg/ha) and 80 per cent more area under cultivation. In the first part of this period, growth in area cultivated dominated overall production growth; in the more recent decade, yields increased more rapidly, with fertilizer and other modern input use increasing.

Some care has to be taken with these overall trends, especially in the earlier parts of this period. The agricultural growth data at least for the first decade of this century are not easily squared with evidence on input use or use of land and capital. Dercon and Zeitlin (2009) suggest that there may be overestimation, for example in cultivated land area growth. But even that study suggests that the presence of substantial agricultural growth, and its leading part in overall growth, is beyond question, even if the scale of it may not be properly measured. See also Dorosh and Rashid (2013) and Gollin (2010).

The relative decline of agricultural growth in GDP in recent years is nevertheless striking. Services, accounting for the largest share of GDP (around 45 per cent at present) sustained high growth rates of about 12.7 per cent between 2005 and 2013. And in the most recent years, industrial (including manufacturing) growth strongly outpaced agricultural and services growth, albeit from a very low base. Manufacturing still accounts for less than 5 per cent of GDP.

The data point to a process of structural transformation—not primarily between sectors, but mostly reflecting significant shifts in productivity within sectors. Some non-manufacturing components of industrial growth (especially construction) have

[3] Or 31 per cent in rural areas. At the time of writing, results for 2015/16 have not been published. The Central Statistical Agency published temporary estimates of around 24 per cent for that year (Central Statistical Agency 2018).

[4] The agricultural year 2015/16 was a drought year but even ignoring that year and calculating agricultural growth between 2010 and 2015 still shows a slower growth to 5.2 per cent.

[5] All data in this paragraph are from Central Statistical Agency (2018) and Dercon and Zeitlin (2009).

been important sources of growth; but what is clear is that urbanization has proceeded, drawing significantly on the ability of the agricultural sector to produce surpluses. Other evidence is consistent with this. Martins (2014) attempts a decomposition of overall per capita growth between population, within-sector productivity, and structural change between sectors. He finds that about a quarter of overall GDP growth per capita in the last decade can be associated with between-sector movements (largely towards services, given its dominant share in GDP), suggesting the dominance of within-sector productivity growth but nevertheless a substantial share of between-sector growth. This is also consistent with increased migration, with the share of the rural population having decreased from about 85 per cent to 80 per cent in the last fifteen years (or 5 million new rural–urban migrants in this period), but still a relatively modest decline given overall growth.[6]

The patterns of economic growth in the last fifteen years have been broadly consistent with the government's policy goals and development plans. In 2002, the first (three-year) Sustainable Development and Poverty Reduction Plan (SDPRP) was started, to run to 2005. A more ambitiously developed PASDEP (Plan for Accelerated and Sustained Development to End Poverty) covered 2005–10, followed by the GTP-I and GTP-II (Growth and Transformation Plans, covering 2010–15 and 2015–20). The underlying ideas for these plans, especially SDPRP and PASDEP, were captured in ADLI, the Agricultural Development-Led Industrialization, for which the earliest reference is a 1993 government document (Ministry of Planning and Economic Development 1993).[7] In Section 26.3, we discuss the content of these plans and how they drew on theories concerning the role of agriculture in development and its links with dual-development models. We then discuss the relative success of this model but also why it may offer less relevant guidance in recent years. We present elements of the kind of changes that can be observed at present in the Ethiopian economy and what it may mean for future strategies towards agriculture.

26.3 ADLI AND THE DUAL ECONOMY

Under ADLI, the government set out a specific development strategy: first, to improve agricultural technologies, particularly seeds; second, to expand irrigation, infrastructure, and the use of modern inputs, including fertilizers and pesticides; and, third, to expand rural non-agricultural opportunities (Ministry of Planning and Economic Development 1993: 19). As such it is resolutely an agriculture-led development process:

[6] Data on migration and urban–rural composition during rapid growth and change are always difficult to collect. Changing administrative boundaries, long lags in census data collection, *kebele* registration rules and land tenure policies may lead to underestimation of migration, but the extent is hard to assess.

[7] During the 1990s, there were also Plans, but only published in Amharic, and seemingly less strictly implemented or adhered to, even though they were also building on ADLI.

'agriculture should be the starting point for the structural transformation of the economy' (p. 5). A key assertion is that the primary driver of demand for industrial output will be domestic demand, rather than foreign demand, based on first initiating growth in agriculture and purchasing power in rural areas. Incomes should be a focus, with income growth providing a way to keep domestic demand from acting as a constraint on the industrial sector. The role of industry is evidently quite secondary: it is relegated to creating employment for 'redundant' rural labour, and to providing an 'expanding market for other sectors of the economy'. It was at least a decade before this policy became definitively established at the centre of government action, before being determinedly implemented during PASDEP from 2005.[8]

Conceptually, this model has intellectual roots in models such as Johnston and Mellor (1961) and much other subsequent work by Mellor that argued persistently that 'agriculture first' is always the right approach. In Dercon and Gollin (2014), the conceptual, theoretical, and empirical limitations of these models are discussed in further detail. Johnston and Mellor (1961) themselves saw their paper as linked to Lewis's work, offering a narrative framework for thinking about consumption and production linkages from agriculture. The basic premise, never shown either formally or empirically, was that agricultural productivity growth would, in a closed economy, simultaneously lead to (a) higher rural incomes, (b) lower food prices in urban areas, (c) increased savings in rural areas, allowing for mobilization of capital for domestic industry, and (d) expanded domestic markets for non-agricultural goods. Via (c) and (d) it provided an engine of growth that would lift non-agricultural sectors in a way not present in Lewis's formulation. Even though it did not refer to any literature, the earliest formulation of ADLI (see Ministry of Planning and Economic Development 1993) can be seen as fundamentally consistent with this view.

Subsequent versions became stronger and firmer in interpreting the necessity of starting all development from agriculture, appealing to at times contested historical evidence from Europe and Asia (for a discussion see Dercon and Gollin 2014). Nevertheless, an argument that growth in agriculture is a key engine for growth, not least to start a growth process in pre-industrial economies, has solid theoretical grounds (Eswaran and Kotwal 1993; Echevarria 1997; Gollin, Parente, and Rogerson 2002, 2007). Models in this spirit tend to be linked to a set of key assumptions, however, including critically that these are closed economies that must meet their own food needs through domestic production. Many of these models also assume that food consumption is subject to a minimum consumption requirement. Together, these two assumptions guarantee that a

[8] In the earlier phase, in the 1990s, ADLI was already official policy, but with a much less well articulated implementation strategy. No doubt there was much learning in this period, even though it would appear that ADLI had a much more narrow technology focus (seeds and fertilizer) and a one-size-fits-all approach. By the time of PASDEP, there was more recognition of agro-ecological diversity and the presence of chronically food-insecure low-potential areas, as well as the need for complementary investments such as in infrastructure or extension. Indeed, it could be said that it matured into a broadly coherent implementation plan.

large fraction of resources will be tied to food production when countries have low agricultural productivity.

Another strand of research developed more empirically detailed macro models at the country level, including those based on computable general equilibrium (CGE) models. In Ethiopia, these have been influential as well as a means of articulating how ADLI is to work. The prototype model of this kind is Dervis, de Milo, and Robinson (1982), updated by Lofgren, Harris, and Robinson (2002). A recent version for Ethiopia is described by Dorosh and Thurlow (2013).[9] Some of these models offer suggestive evidence of the large overall gains in value added that can be obtained from investing in agricultural productivity.[10]

These models provide a bridge between theory and empirics, but rely on calibration using data that are typically silent on many key parameters or functional relationships. The output of these models is very attractive for policy questions, as they appear to give 'exact' answers to policy simulations. The problem is nevertheless that the theoretical constructs as well as the assumptions underlying these models are hard to assess, leaving the robustness of results unclear. A more empirical literature seems to have offered better foundations for the conjectures of the growth linkages from agriculture, focusing on the presence of 'agricultural multipliers' that assess the overall growth impact from growth in agriculture (e.g. Block and Timmer 1994 and much subsequent literature) to estimate the effects of agricultural growth on the overall economy, focusing on forward and backward linkages. Their conclusion has often been that these linkages are strong, offering a further justification for an 'agriculture first' approach to development. The empirical methods used in the multiplier literature to establish this, however, are very much open to question (see Dercon and Gollin 2014).

Even if boosting agricultural growth has high positive growth and development benefits for the rest of the economy, one set of questions, strikingly, does not seem to be answered in this literature: how effective are policy tools in stimulating agricultural growth? Are they more or less effective than the tools available for boosting growth in other sectors? Indeed, much of the literature on boosting agriculture for growth focuses on the size of the benefits, but not on the cost—essential for any policy assessment. For example, given the low relative productivity of agriculture in many economies (as in Dercon and Gollin 2014), it would be surprising if in all circumstances it is strategically optimal to invest scarce public resources in the low-productivity sector to stimulate growth. It is beyond the scope of this chapter to assess whether the focus on agriculture as the engine of overall growth was the most cost-effective policy choice a few decades ago. We can nevertheless assess ADLI as having succeeded to some extent in what it had set out to do. In Section 26.4, we assess ADLI against what it initially set out to do, as well as the challenges it started to face.

[9] Chapter 8 in Dorosh and Rashid (2013).

[10] A notable recent example is McArthur and Sachs (2013), who use a CGE model for Uganda to argue for an aid-financed boost to agricultural productivity as an engine of growth and development.

26.4 Assessing ADLI and its Challenges

Ethiopia in the early 1990s clearly satisfied many of the stylized facts characterizing Mellor and Johnston (1961) or other agriculture-first models. There was only a small modern/non-agriculture/urban sector, with the vast majority of the population involved in agriculture.[11] Agriculture was characterized by low land and labour productivity, and deep poverty, seemingly shared. The urban population also faced considerable poverty. Across the population, food consumption still constituted about 60 per cent of consumer budgets, and diets were still predominantly based on staples.[12] Connectivity was poor, due to limited transport infrastructure, and the country became landlocked with the independence of Eritrea in 1993. While the economy was not formally closed, it had many features of a de facto closed economy—certainly with respect to food. Neither exports nor imports of staple foods were generally profitable for traders. Crop yields were nevertheless low, with modern fertilizer used on only a third of cropped area and virtually no use of improved seeds in the 1990s (see also Dercon and Zeitlin 2009).[13]

These conditions suggested that if a concerted effort could be made to boost agricultural productivity, it would have beneficial impacts across the entire economy. The political economy was clearly favourable to such pro-agriculture policies too: the leading coalition, the EPRDF, and its powerful member, the TPLF, traditionally had a considerable rural support base to which it needed to deliver as well as an ideology putting the rural population at its core (see, for example, Young 1997, or Bekele, Kjosavik, and Shanmugaratnam 2016). Alternatives were also not easily seen: then, and largely now as well, there is limited information on natural resource availability, even though there may be potential for gold, copper, potash, gemstones, oil, and gas. Poor connectivity and the lack of a port made a more manufacturing-oriented strategy also more challenging to pursue, requiring substantial logistics investments.

While government policy even pre-SDPRP had embraced ADLI, it took until PASDEP in 2005 for concerted efforts across a variety of areas to take place, including new extension efforts, boosting modern input use, accompanied by a fast and major expansion of the road network into rural areas. The data show patterns of growth consistent with ADLI, especially post 2010. The evidence quoted earlier shows that land productivity increases (i.e. yields) were not the most important factor in driving production growth in agriculture in the period 1995 up to 2010 or at least for the years shown, with area expansion playing a greater role (see Table 26.1). Only in GTP-I (post 2010) can large

[11] 85–90 per cent of the rural population is engaged in crop agriculture; pastoralism with various degrees of non-sedentary patterns constitutes the rest.

[12] In particular, in the 1995/6 Household Budget and Expenditure Survey, food consumption was both in rural and urban areas still close to 60 per cent and 56 per cent respectively, using a rather wide definition of non-food consumption.

[13] Fertilizer use in Ethiopia was by then higher on certain crops than in other neighbouring countries, but still well below potential. Improved seeds were available for wheat and maize, and to some extent teff—together the most important cereals.

Table 26.1 Yield, area, and production growth for the main cereals

	Yield kg/ha 1996/7	Yield kg/ha 2007/8	Yield kg/ha 2015/16	Annual yield growth 1996–2007	Annual growth area planted 1996–2007	Annual production growth 1996–2007	Annual yield growth 2007–15	Annual growth area planted 2007–15	Annual production growth 2007–15	Annual yield growth 1996–2015	Annual growth area planted 1996–2015	Annual production growth 1996–2015
Barley	1,390	1,380	2,010	−0.1%	1.3%	1.2%	4.8%	5.2%	10.3%	1.9%	2.9%	4.9%
Maize	1,650	2,120	3,390	2.3%	3.9%	6.3%	6.0%	2.2%	8.4%	3.9%	3.2%	7.2%
Sorghum	1,490	1,730	2,330	1.4%	4.1%	5.5%	3.8%	2.4%	6.3%	2.4%	3.4%	5.8%
Teff	850	1,170	1,560	2.9%	1.8%	4.8%	3.7%	1.4%	5.1%	3.2%	1.7%	5.0%
Wheat	1,300	1,620	2,530	2.0%	5.2%	7.3%	5.8%	2.0%	7.8%	3.6%	3.8%	7.5%
All Cereals	1,250	1,580	2,320	2.2%	3.1%	5.3%	4.9%	2.4%	7.4%	3.3%	2.8%	6.2%

Source: Data from Central Statistical Agency, (various years), Agricultural Sample Survey Private Holdings main season.

Table 26.2 Fertilizer, improved seeds, and extension coverage (all cereals)

	Per cent area with modern fertilizer	Quantity kg/ha on fertilized land	Per cent area with improved seed	Per cent of area covered by extension
1996/7	33	18	2.3	
1999/2000	38	11	4.5	
2005/6	40	43	5.3	22
2010/11	44	47	7.3	21
2014/15	58	130	11.7	39

Source: Data from Central Statistical Agency (various years), Agricultural Sample Survey Private Holdings main season.

yield increases be seen to drive cereal production growth. This is consistent with a gradual intensification of agriculture seen in Table 26.2. Up to 2010, there were only relatively small increases in the area covered by fertilizer or improved seeds compared to the 1990s even during PASDEP. Subsequently, fertilizer usage and application rates, as well as the proportion of area covered by improved seeds and extension services, increased substantially, according to these data from the Central Statistical Agency.

Beyond agricultural growth leading overall growth, other benefits were there for all to see: rural incomes increased and poverty started to come down gradually across large parts of the country. Indeed, analysis by Hill and Tsehaye (2014)[14] shows that growth in cereal production can be seen not just as the main driver of overall increases in rural incomes, but also of observed poverty declines.

A closer look reveals a somewhat more mixed picture of this undoubted success story. First, there has been a spatial dimension to progress. While agricultural growth has been widespread, significant impacts on poverty were confined to areas with reasonable proximity to urban centres (Hill and Tsehaye 2014).[15] Furthermore, intensification via fertilizer and modern inputs requires investment. Considerable populations live in low-potential areas, and as seen during the 2015 drought and its aftermath, their resilience remains relatively limited. Furthermore, the profitability of modern inputs is not always self-evident, but dependent on good weather and high prices (and therefore proximity to urban centres for demand), conditions often not met for many farmers (Minten, Koro, and Stifel 2014; Kedir, Schmidt, and Tilahun 2015; see also Dercon and Christiaensen 2011).

[14] Background paper prepared for the World Bank Ethiopia Poverty Assessment, World Bank (2015). The paper is essentially published as Chapter 4 of that report.

[15] Note that this also helps to square other evidence on growth in this period. Moller and Wacker (2017) argue that growth in Ethiopia can be 'explained' in an imputation from a cross-country growth regression as stemming largely from high infrastructure spending, of which a large part was road expenditure. However, they do not consider any sectoral mix or policies in their framework. The evidence quoted in the text suggests nevertheless that connecting rural areas to cities has played a crucial role in delivering impact from the overall strategy. In other words, the highest returns to the strategy will have been where infrastructure was present or improved. Dercon and Christiaenson (2011) has micro-evidence for this as well.

Assessing other aspects of ADLI's model or the Johnston-Mellor-style linkages is harder given the evidence available (and the lack of a counterfactual). Rising production would have been expected to keep food prices lower, but this impact has been offset by rising urban demand, which has put upward pressure on prices. For example, Headey et al. (2012) showed that from 2005 to 2011 consumption growth was negative for many households in Addis Ababa, as wages did not immediately increase to compensate households for the rising food prices that they faced, not least among unskilled workers. Next, while there is evidence of increased savings in rural areas, this is more reflective of more households holding livestock and in larger numbers, rather than resources that could be mobilized as savings for growth in industrial output. For example, Dercon et al. (2009) and Dercon, Hoddinott, and Woldehanna (2012) report that between 1994 and 2009, in the longitudinal data from the Ethiopian Rural Household Survey, the percentage of households owning oxen (the most valuable asset) increased from 13 to 49 per cent. Finally, despite evidence of rural income growth between 1996 and 2011,[16] demand for non-agricultural goods from domestic production remains quite limited in rural areas.[17]

As seen from a dual-economy perspective, a crucial factor for further labour productivity and income improvements is, typically, releasing labour from agriculture into non-agriculture or the urban sector. Ethiopia remains a country with limited urbanization (10 percentage points below the average urbanization percentage for low-income countries), even though this is increasing. (During the last 15 years, about 5 million people have moved to urban centres.) Beyond migration, Ethiopia's rural economy remains characterized by limited engagement in non-agricultural activities: a survey in seven African countries found that in Ethiopia only 23 per cent of households have a non-farm enterprise, low by regional standards (Naude and Nagler 2014). In short, if release of labour from crop agriculture is one key part of boosting labour productivity, it is not quite taking place at the rate to be expected.

One part of the explanation is likely to be the relative lack of opportunities in urban centres. Indeed, the lack of an urban growth engine with substantial job creation means that urban opportunities remain limited. The relatively high poverty levels observed in the two largest cities, Addis Ababa and Dire Dawa, reflect this fact. Unlike most countries in the developing world, poverty here was higher than poverty in secondary towns, and in 2011, at 28 per cent, close to average rural poverty (30 per cent).

Especially in GTP-II, this appears to have been acknowledged with an increased focus on creating job opportunities in urban areas. Unlike in previous plans, growth in agriculture, and specifically in crop agriculture, is not getting most focus, but more attention

[16] Data from various rounds of the nationally representative household expenditure surveys analysed in World Bank (2015) suggest that rural expenditure increased between 1996 and 2000 and between 2000 and 2005 across all deciles of the income distribution, while between 2005 and 2011 there were increases for all but the 15 per cent poorest rural consumers. The latter spending actually went down.

[17] Gunning, Krishnan, and Mengistu (2018) find in their survey that a typical rural town has 95 non-agricultural items for sale—but a village two hours away only has half these items, with each further hour reducing items available by a further nine items. Limited purchasing power and transportation costs are driving these findings.

has been paid to urban growth engines, such as via industrialization, combined with a strong focus on export earnings from labour-intensive manufacturing, Asia style. While a focus has remained on backward linkages to agriculture (in terms of trying to focus on industries in which inputs could be supplied domestically), rising agricultural incomes are not expected to drive demand for these goods; instead, industrialization is expected to be driven by export demand to international markets.

In sum, ADLI made considerable sense as an early source of growth in this pre-industrial society. The strategy was consistent with particular theories and with the conditions that Ethiopia faced at the start of the period. The strategy succeeded in delivering overall growth, as well as substantial improvement in living conditions in large parts of rural Ethiopia.[18] However, as a growth strategy to sustain progress into industrialization, it was bound to become deficient for further growth. As observed in other contexts, crop agriculture as an engine of growth tends to run out of steam before it can deliver the transformation required—whether in terms of offering a key demand driver for domestically produced industrial goods (as in Mellor and Johnston 1961) or generating surplus that can drive capital accumulation (as in MoPED 1993). Releasing labour from agriculture to boost average economy-wide labour productivity requires that there be sufficient demand for labour outside agriculture. Other sources of growth are required to boost this, as government strategies have now recognized.

While further productivity growth for staple food crops will continue to be needed to keep urban food prices in check, staple food productivity increases will not in themselves be sufficient to create transformation. Further productivity increases in these crops will also become harder to obtain, as intensification will become more and more costly. Growing urban demand can function as a source of returns to agriculture, with a gradual increase in urban labour demand, which will in turn create an impetus for increases in agricultural productivity through a shift in urban demand towards higher-value outputs. Indeed, to some extent this is already happening. In Section 26.5, this will be discussed and some suggestions will be made to ensure agricultural producers can benefit further through appropriate policy settings.

26.5 Emerging Urban Demand and a New Strategy for Transformation

Growth in urban areas could offer new opportunities for agriculture. In fact, we think urban growth will be essential for bringing further income growth and poverty reduction to rural areas. One route will be the classic structural transformation route: by

[18] Moller and Wacker (2017) argue that growth in Ethiopia can be 'explained' in an imputation from a cross-country growth regression as stemming largely from high infrastructure spending. However, they do not consider any sectoral mix or policies in their framework.

releasing labour to urban areas, output per worker in agriculture will increase simply by bringing down the denominator (given any kind of diminishing returns to labour), or more indirectly, by offering new sources of remittances to rural areas. Especially in more marginal production areas, exit from agriculture will be essential: there is little scope for any other route to continue or intensify poverty reduction and, more generally, growth in incomes. However, another route is through a shift in the sector's production towards higher-value products, creating new opportunities for higher returns. This process will offer new growth opportunities for agriculture, which it increasingly needs. This is effectively a transformation *within* agriculture, from low-value production to higher-value production. This transformation will depend heavily on the ability of the economy to connect agriculture with urban economic growth. Our view is that this kind of transformation within the smallholder agricultural sector is now essential to deliver growth for the largest part of the population still in the rural sector. This section is forward looking, and therefore by its nature to some extent speculative; nevertheless it builds on emerging evidence supportive of such changes and implied policy direction.

The key driver for this further transformation within agriculture will be that, as urban growth takes hold, consumer demand will shift away from staple foods and relatively unprocessed agricultural goods. Urban consumers in Ethiopia, as in other countries, begin to demand new foods and different characteristics in the foods that they do eat. They value a new set of traits: convenience of preparation and cooking (which in turn may imply processing, if only of the simplest kind, e.g. cleaning, milling, and packaging of grain); dietary diversity; food safety; food quality and nutritional quality; and standardization of food types. In particular, as the value of time (proxied by wages) increases in cities, and especially as women are pulled into the labour force, the demand grows for processed and prepared foods.

To a large extent, Ethiopia's growing urban demands for high-income diets will mirror the kind of dietary convergence that has taken place across the developing world. Hassan et al. (2016) report on the changing consumption patterns in Ethiopia and especially in urban areas. Comparing the Household Consumption/Expenditure Surveys between 1996 and 2011, they find that over time, improving living standards have implied reductions in budget shares going to cereals (within food spending, the expenditure share going down by a third), while spending shares on animal products and fruit and vegetables increased by a third and a half (albeit from a low base).[19] Spending on processed cereals (especially *injera*) also increased considerably. Comparing rural and urban areas shows that all these are much higher in the latter: urban households spend twice as much on animal products, and fruit and vegetables, and four times as much on processed cereals.

Animal products, fruit and vegetables, and processed foods all require value chains that are more sophisticated than those for unmilled or milled staple foods, with a clear premium on quality produce as well as opportunities for higher value added through investment in food processing. These products tend to demand higher prices, providing further

[19] About half of animal products spending is on dairy, and a third is on beef.

impetus for investment in these value chains. For example, Bachewe, Minten, and Yimer (2017) report on the rising prices of animal products in Ethiopia, reflecting rising demand.

The economic implications of the growth of food-processing industries should not be underestimated. Overall, it is estimated that this sector now employs about 1 million people, with commercial *injera* markets employing 100,000 people, mostly women, many in the kind of low-skilled jobs required for rapid absorption of a growing labour force (Minten et al. 2016). They find that larger *injera*-making companies innovate through higher quality, new technologies, and higher value added—and providing via different procurement of inputs, including teff flour, new impetus for quality improvements in agriculture.

The changes in urban diets have already led to a dramatic shift in the sources of supply for urban food. As is true of other cities in sub-Saharan Africa, Addis and other Ethiopian cities are increasingly turning to food imports to supply their demands for processed and prepared foods of various kinds. Ethiopia has seen large and rapid increases in food imports, from approximately US$1.0 billion in 2010 to US$1.8 billion in 2015, not including food aid. The imports are primarily of high-income elasticity foods: vegetable oil, sugar, rice, and wheat, reflecting the growing consumption of foods prepared with cooking oil and of prepared foods based on wheat (e.g. pasta and noodles, cookies, and biscuits), but also substitutes for staple commodities. For example, Minten et al. (2016) show that commercial ready-made *injera* producers use a mixture of local teff and imported rice, absorbing a significant part of the US$200 million imports of this commodity.

Importing these foods is not necessarily bad, even if it does create significant pressures on foreign exchange earnings. Provided Ethiopia's export earnings are sufficient, however, there is no reason for the country to seek self-sufficiency in food production. Moreover, although the agro-ecology of Ethiopia is sufficiently diverse to produce many different crops and commodities, there is certainly no reason for the country to seek self-sufficiency in each and every food item. For example, it almost certainly makes sense, from the perspective of comparative advantage, for Ethiopia to continue to export coffee but also perhaps teff, which commands a high price on international markets, and to import rice.

But beyond the question of self-sufficiency, the trade data point to a more fundamental issue related to the role of agriculture in the country's development strategy. As Ethiopia grows into middle-income status, and as the country pursues a more ambitious strategy of industrial development, agriculture's contribution to the economy will necessarily shift—and agricultural development strategies must also evolve. There remains some scope to drive the development process through the intensification of staple food production, but increasingly the opportunities in agriculture will lie further along value chains.

The importance of staple food crops will not diminish immediately; these crops are simply too important to rural livelihoods and to the consumption needs of the rural poor. But to increase the income of farmers—and to meet the food demand of urban areas—what will be needed is a gradual transformation of the food system. In the new system, staple food production will be accompanied by the emergence of value chains that connect rural areas to urban markets for high-value foods. To the extent that farmers can connect to these value chains, they can earn higher incomes by producing more valuable commodities; a 10 per cent increase in the value of a crop is equivalent from the farmer's perspective to a 10 per cent yield increase.

The next stage in Ethiopia's agricultural strategy must therefore involve a transition away from an almost exclusive focus on productivity in staple foods for domestic consumption and unprocessed commodities (such as low-quality coffee) for export markets. In its place, a new agricultural strategy will need to support the development of the value chains that will connect farmers to emerging domestic markets, while continuing to take advantage of export demand for commodities, but preferably driving up the quality of these commodities as well as boosting both yields and quality of this produce.[20]

In some countries, governments have sought to develop these value chains by directly promoting agro-processing industries with subsidized credit or with trade protection. But the challenge here is that the processing industries cannot develop by themselves. Sub-Saharan Africa is full of examples of failed processing industries, such as fruit-juice factories and canning factories. The problem typically is that there is limited demand for the output of these factories. Even where there is demand, it is not simple to connect sources of supply with consumer demand. Processed agricultural goods require distribution systems, with effective marketing networks. The processors themselves are not well equipped to develop these distribution systems.[21] Instead, many of the most effective processing industries have been those associated with export markets, where the end demand is well defined and reasonably assured, and where the exporting firms have been able to specify fully the product characteristics that are desired, based on quality and desirability benchmarks received from consumers in external markets.

For domestic markets, the development of these value chains is more complex. Some minimally processed goods (e.g. packages of milled rice or wheat, or vegetable oil) are already in high demand from better-off urban consumers, who do not have the time to clean and process bulk grain from the market. For these products, a producer can find ready markets. But for more complicated processed foods, such as biscuits, juices, or processed dairy foods, the challenge for processors is to build distribution networks and to keep up with rapid shifts in consumer tastes and market demand. Producers are not necessarily well positioned to do this work themselves, especially in an environment where wholesale trade and retailing are fragmented. There are few processors who have effective reach into consumer markets.

[20] This applies to traditional exports such as coffee—where scope for quality and value added is no doubt present. But it also applies to some non-traditional exports, such as various types of horticulture. Moreover, some of the discussion later in this chapter would also apply to finding international markets as well. Such steps are usually best taken by firms focusing both on domestic and international markets, including building on local demand from discriminating consumers who have the purchasing power and who value quality.

[21] Building these up takes time and effort, and quality is often lacking, while import distribution systems of higher-quality products tend to be more easily established, especially in capitals or main cities.

What may be needed, then, is a new agricultural strategy that begins with the demand side rather than the supply side. The goal is no longer simply to supply urban centres with raw staple foods, but instead to meet the growing urban demand for higher-value products. And the goal is no longer simply to supply basic food needs—although that imperative will not soon disappear in Ethiopia—but also to take advantage of the emerging growth opportunities for the agricultural sector. This new agenda for agricultural transformation will lead to several positive outcomes for the economy: an increase in agricultural incomes, substitution for imports of high-value foods (with concomitant savings of foreign exchange), and the democratization of high-quality diets in urban areas (by substituting lower-cost domestic supply of urban foodstuffs for imported items).

There are important caveats to this process. A first challenge is to ensure that support for farmers is appropriately geared to allow a variety of crops to be produced and supplied to markets. At present, the entire agricultural support eco-system, not least extension, is geared towards staple food production. A gradual rethinking towards more flexible support to production and markets is no doubt required to ensure that opportunities are taken. A second challenge is to avoid outright trade protection that would make domestic production high priced relative to imports. The domestic firms in this market must be able to compete with international brands on price and quality terms. Subsidizing or protecting domestic firms is likely to be a more expensive and less effective approach in this context than liberalizing markets. The goal is not necessarily to develop new domestic firms that can produce breakfast cereal. There is a subtle difference, but the goal is rather to have domestic agricultural commodities converted into breakfast cereals for the domestic market. In some cases, in fact, foreign producers may be precisely the ones to supply the market; the goal is to have them produce breakfast cereals or other goods from domestically sourced ingredients. The government's policy should be to support any firms, domestic or foreign, that want to participate in this value chain; experience has taught us that government efforts to promote such linkages often lead to failure.[22]

In this sector, sophisticated retail firms, including global supermarket chains, can play a valuable role. These firms bring expertise in market research, market development, advertising, and retail technologies. They are also adept at sourcing the products with strong consumer demand. There are precedents for allowing international supermarket chains to enter the market of a developing country subject to negotiated restrictions on the domestic content of their sales (Reardon, Timmer, and Minten 2012). This might become an attractive option in due course for a country like Ethiopia, which currently lacks international supermarket chains. These firms could be allowed to enter the market subject to requirements that they source a significant fraction of their fresh produce and

[22] The experience with cotton for the garments industry, and with hides and skins for leather, has suggested that production in itself is not enough, but the quality of the produce will matter for such firms—and this has been causing problems for these sectors. Vertically integrated firms or well-integrated value chains do not just emerge in such sectors, but tend to be driven by investor commitment first, at best complemented by supportive policies.

processed foods from domestic markets. The fear in many countries would be that these firms will then displace small and local supermarkets, although studies have argued that the overall impact on dynamics of the retail industry, overall employment, and the rural poor may well be positive (Reardon 2015).[23]

26.6 Conclusion

In this chapter, we assessed Ethiopia's agriculture-first growth strategy in recent decades. Its foundation was ADLI, Agricultural Development-Led Industrialization, which posited that economic growth should start from agriculture, which in turn would lead to low urban food prices, higher savings and demand for domestic industrial production. Its conceptual, theoretical, and empirical foundations are well established in the economic literature. Moreover, conditions in the Ethiopia of the 1990s suggest that even though we cannot say that it was the best alternative, it had a good chance of delivering. Not least post 2005, ADLI delivered high output growth, led by agriculture, and over time more intensification of staple food production.

In itself, it could only deliver an early phase of Ethiopia's transformation, and the more recent focus on boosting urban economic growth (partly driven by the need for more export earnings) was not only essential to keep growth sustained. We argue that it has also become essential to offer further opportunities to boost returns and labour productivity in agriculture, and in turn essential to keep incomes there growing and poverty decreasing further. Changing urban demand patterns give a sense of what is possible. Policies can assist these opportunities, such as by making sure that increasingly, agricultural support is not just targeting staple crop production, by creating an investment climate that is favourable to domestic investment in agro- and food-processing, and by creating conditions favourable for deepening value chains, for example via supermarkets.

References

Allen, R. C. (2009). 'Ethiopian Agriculture in a World-Historical Content', Background paper, DFID-funded study on Agriculture and Growth in Ethiopia.

Bachewe, F., B. Minten, and F. Yimer (2017). 'The Rising Cost of Animal-Source Foods: Evidence and Implications', ESSP working paper 107, IFPRI, Addis Ababa.

Bekele, Y., D. Kjosavik, and N. Shanmugaratnam (2016). 'State-Society Relations in the Post 1991 Political Economy', *Social Science* 48 (5): 19.

Block, S. and C. P. Timmer (1994). 'Agriculture and Economic Growth: Conceptual Issues and the Kenyan Experience', Development Discussion Paper No. 498, Harvard Institute for International Development, Cambridge, MA.

[23] For a case study from Kenya discussing these various effects, see Neven et al. (2009).

Central Statistical Agency (2018). 'The 2015/16 Household Consumption–Expenditure Survey', Statistical Report 585, Addis Ababa.

Dercon, S. and L. Christiaensen (2011). 'Consumption Risk, Technology Adoption, and Poverty Traps: Evidence from Ethiopia', *Journal of Development Economics* 96 (2): 159–73.

Dercon, S., D. O. Gilligan, J. Hoddinott, and T. Woldehanna (2009). 'The Impact of Agricultural Extension and Roads on Poverty and Consumption Growth in Fifteen Ethiopian Villages', *American Journal of Agricultural Economics* 91 (4): 1007–21.

Dercon, S. and G. Gollin (2014). 'Agriculture in African Development: Theories and Strategies', *Annual Review of Resource Economics* 6 (1): 471–92.

Dercon, S., J. Hoddinott, and T. Woldehanna (2012). 'Growth and Chronic Poverty: Evidence from Rural Communities in Ethiopia', *Journal of Development Studies* 48 (2): 238–53.

Dercon, S. and A. Zeitlin (2009). Rethinking Agriculture and Growth in Ethiopia: A Conceptual Discussion', Paper 2 for DFID-funded study on Agriculture and Growth in Ethiopia.

Dervis, K., J. de Melo, and S. Robinson (1982). *General Equilibrium Models for Development Policy* (Cambridge: Cambridge University Press).

Dorosh, P. and S. Rashid (2013). *Food and Agriculture in Ethiopia* (Washington, DC: IFPRI).

Dorosh, P. and J. Thurlow (2013). 'Implications of Accelerated Agricultural Growth for Household Income and Poverty in Ethiopia', in *Food and Agriculture in Ethiopia*, ed. P. Dorosh and S. Rashid (Washington, DC: IFPRI): Ch. 8.

Echevarria, C. (1997). 'Changes in Sectoral Composition Associated with Economic Growth', *International Economic Review* 38 (2): 431–52.

Eswaran, M. and A. Kotwal (1993). 'A Theory of Real Wage Growth in LDCs', *Journal of Development Economics* 42 (2): 243–69.

Gollin, D. (2010). 'Crop Yields in East Africa: a Review of Recent Data', Manuscript, Department of Economics, Williams College.

Gollin, D., M. Kirchberger, and D. Lagakos (2017). 'In Search of a Spatial Equilibrium in the Developing World', National Bureau of Economic Research Working Paper 23916, NBER, Cambridge, MA.

Gollin, D., S. L. Parente, and R. Rogerson (2002). 'The Role of Agriculture in Development', *American Economic Review Papers and Proceedings* 92.

Gollin, D., S. L. Parente, and R. Rogerson (2007). 'The Food Problem and the Evolution of International Income Levels', *Journal of Monetary Economics* 54: 1230–55.

Gunning, J.-W., P. Krishnan, and A. Mengistu (2018). 'Consumer Welfare Impact of High Transportation Costs in Ethiopia', International Growth Centre, LSE–Oxford, mimeo.

Hassan, I. W., M. Dereje, B. Minten, and K. Hirvonen (2016). 'Diet Transformation in Africa: The Case of Ethiopia', ESSP Working Paper 87, IFPRI, Addis Ababa.

Headey, D., F. Bachewe Nisrane, I. Worku, et al. (2012). 'Urban Wage Behavior and Food Price Inflation: The Case of Ethiopia', ESSP Working Paper 41, IFPRI, Addis Ababa.

Hill, R. and E. Tsehaye (2014). 'Growth, Safety Nets and Poverty: Assessing Progress in Ethiopia from 1996 to 2011', Background Paper prepared for the World Bank Ethiopia Poverty Assessment, World Bank, 2015.

Johnston, B. F. and J. W. Mellor (1961). 'The Role of Agriculture in Economic Development', *American Economic Review* 51: 566–93.

Kedir, M., E. Schmidt, and H. Tilahun (2015). 'Production Patterns and Fertilizer Use', mimeo, IFPRI, Washington, DC.

Lewis, W. A. (1954). 'Economic Development with Unlimited Supplies of Labour', *The Manchester School* 22: 139–91.

Lofgren, H., T. L. Harris, and S. Robinson (2002). 'A Standard Computable General Equilibrium (CGE) Model in GAMS', TMD Discussion Paper, IFPRI, Washington, DC.

Martins, P. (2014). 'Structural Change in Ethiopia: An Employment Perspective', World Bank Policy Research Working Paper 6749, World Bank, Washington, DC.

McArthur, J. W. and J. D. Sachs (2013). 'A General Equilibrium Model for Analyzing African Rural Subsistence Economies and an African Green Revolution', Brookings Institution Africa Growth Initiative Working Paper 12. http://dx.doi.org/10.2139/ssrn.2450842.

Mellor, J. and B. Johnson (1961). 'The Role of Agriculture in Economic Development', *The American Economic Review* 51 (4): 566–93.

Ministry of Planning and Economic Development (1993). 'An Economic Development Strategy for Ethiopia: A Comprehensive Guidance and Development Strategy for the Future', September, Addis Ababa.

Minten, B., T. Assefa, G. Abebe, et al. (2016). 'Food Processing, Transformation and Job Creation: The Case of Ethiopia's Enjera Markets', ESSP Working Paper 96, IFPRI, Addis Ababa.

Minten, B., B. Koro, and D. Stifel (2014). 'The Last Mile(s) in Modern Input Distribution: Evidence from Northwestern Ethiopia', ESSP 2 Working Paper 51, IFPRI, Addis Ababa.

Moller, L. C. and K. M. Wacker (2017). 'Explaining Ethiopia's Growth Acceleration: The Role of Infrastructure and Macroeconomic Policy', *World Development* 96: 198–215.

Naude, P. and W. Nagler (2014). 'Farm Entrepreneurship in Rural Africa: Patterns and Determinants', World Bank Working Paper Series, World Bank, Washington, DC.

Neven, D., M. M. Odera, T. Reardon, and H. Wang (2009). 'Kenyan Supermarkets, Emerging Middle-Class Horticultural Farmers, and Employment Impacts on the Rural Poor', *World Development* 37 (11): 1802–11.

Reardon, T. (2015). 'The Hidden Middle: The Quiet Revolution in the Midstream Agrifood Value Chains in Developing Countries', *Oxford Review of Economic Policy* 31 (1): 45–63.

Reardon, T., P. Timmer, and B. Minten (2012). 'Supermarket Revolution in Asia and Emerging Development Strategies to Include Small Farmers', *Proceedings of the National Academy of Sciences* 109 (31): 12332–37.

Schultz, T. W. (1964). *Transforming Traditional Agriculture* (New Haven, CT : Yale University Press).

Young, J. (1997). 'Development and Change in Post-Revolutionary Tigray', *Journal of Modern African Studies* 31 (1): 81–99.

World Bank (2015). 'Ethiopia Poverty Assessment 2014', World Bank, Washington, DC.

CHAPTER 27

THE TRANSFORMATION OF SMALLHOLDER CROP PRODUCTION IN ETHIOPIA, 1994–2016

ALEMAYEHU SEYOUM TAFFESSE

27.1 INTRODUCTION

ETHIOPIA'S smallholder agriculture has changed in major ways over the last twenty-five years. Productivity has increased significantly, albeit starting from a low base. Combined with an expansion of the cultivated area, this has led to growing total output and rising marketed surplus. This chapter aims to capture the key features of smallholder grain production and producers (circa 2014) in the context of these trends. Early sections locate grain production in a broader context of Ethiopian geography, recent history, institutional setting, and the ongoing overall growth episode. Subsequent sections describe the structure of grain production in terms of farm size, factors of production, output and productivity, and commercialization (both in terms of levels and changes). These are emphasized because they are basic features of a production system and as such lie at the heart of its transformation. The chapter highlights the heterogeneity within smallholder grain production using farm size as the denominator. It also summarizes what is known about proximate drivers of change during the two decades spanning 1994–2016 (the most significant period in terms of rapid growth and signs of transition began in 2004/5). The chapter ends with a brief mention of some of the major challenges and opportunities currently facing smallholder crop agriculture.

It is helpful to put both smallholder crop production and the period covered in perspective. That agriculture is a major economic sector in Ethiopia is well known. Its employment and GDP shares started at 96 per cent and 84 per cent in 1962, respectively.

By 2012, these shares had fallen to a still considerable 73 per cent and 40 per cent.[1,2] Crop production accounted for a large fraction of agriculture's overall shares. Between 2003 and 2016, crop production on average contributed 28 per cent of overall GDP and 67 per cent of agricultural GDP.[3,4] The bulk of these contributions, in turn, was associated with smallholders. Large farms—cooperatives, state farms, and private commercial farms—played a limited role (except in specific cases such as tea, sugarcane, and flowers). Even as recently as 2014/15, commercial farms (including state-owned ones) accounted for around 4 per cent of crop area and output.[5]

Unprecedented economic growth in the country has been an important feature of the period in question. Figure 27.1 clearly marks three distinct periods in terms of GDP growth. The first, spanning 1950–70 and coinciding with most of the Imperial period, was a period of moderate but sustained growth. A period of decline followed under the Derg ending in 1992 with real output per person employed slightly lower than that of

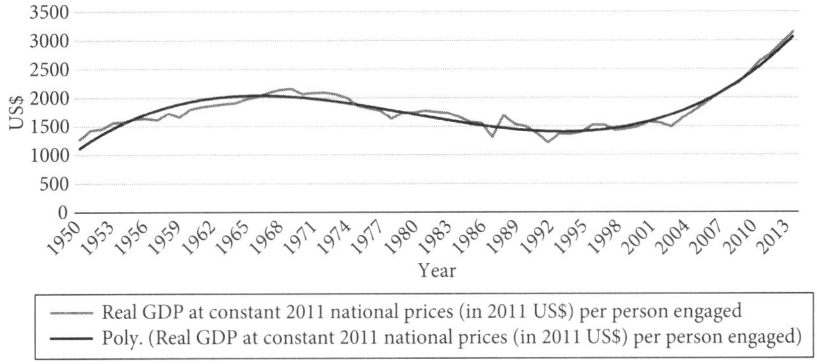

FIGURE 27.1 Real gross domestic product (GDP) per person engaged, 1950–2014

Note: 'Persons engaged' is the sum of employees and the self-employed (Feenstra, Inklaar, and Timmer 2015).

Source: Author's computation using the Penn World Tables 9.0 (PWT 9.0) available for download at www.ggdc.net/pwt. See Feenstra, Inklaar, and Timmer (2015).

[1] These shares are computed using the 'GGDC 10-sector Africa database' of the Groningen Growth and Development Centre (GGDC) at https://www.rug.nl/ggdc/productivity/10-sector/other-releases/africa-sector-database. See de Vries, Timmer, and de Vries (2015).

[2] A major trend in the fifty-year period 1960–2012 was thus the considerable decline in the importance of the sector. Importantly, the decline in agriculture's share in employment has accelerated since 2003 reflecting the faster growth in non-agricultural sectors.

[3] Author's computation from the National Accounts data prepared by MoFED/NPC and compiled by the Ethiopian Economic Association (EEA).

[4] Most of Ethiopia's exports originated and continue to originate in agriculture (see Chapters 14 and 29).

[5] Unless explicitly specified otherwise statistics reported in the text are the author's computation using CSA's Annual Agricultural Sample Survey (AgSS) data (see CSA, various years).

1950. The third period, 1993–2014, was initially a time of recovery and later of rapid growth. During 2003–14, real GDP per person employed doubled.

27.1.1 Conceptual Issues

The chapter adopts the broad approach that productivity is a critical feature of an economic activity and that its level and growth reflect the size and allocation of resources (physical, natural, human, infrastructural—including technology); the effectiveness of the relevant institutions (including markets, property rights, government policy, agencies of public service delivery, farmers' organizations, and early-warning systems); and the incidence and magnitude of shocks (such as climatic, market, and other non-market shocks). In broad terms, and data permitting, this approach is followed below.

'Who is a smallholder?' is a conceptual issue that needs to be briefly addressed from the outset. As emphasized by Gollin (2014), it is hard to characterize smallholder agricultural producers, in part because of their economic and geographic heterogeneity. Nevertheless, several features have been associated with developing-country smallholders in terms of farm size, labour supply, and economic objective, among others. These are producers who operate small farms, largely rely on family labour, employ little manufactured physical capital in production, produce primarily for their own consumption, have relatively low labour productivity for the most part, and are likely to additionally engage in non-farm economic activities (Gollin 2014; Rapsomanikis 2015). This smallness has also been linked with advantages and disadvantages conditional on specific circumstances.[6] The chapter empirically identifies smallholders in Ethiopia based on this broad characterization.

27.1.2 Coverage

A number of chapters in this *Handbook* also address dimensions of smallholder agriculture in Ethiopia: Chapter 33 on the livestock sub-sector, Chapter 29 on coffee, Chapter 32 on market development, Chapter 28 on the role of credit, Chapter 24 on social protection, and Chapter 9 on post-1991 agricultural policy. This chapter thus focuses primarily on smallholder crop production and productivity in the country. Note also that *meher* production is the focus because comparable data is lacking for the *belg* season.[7] Moreover, available data implies that *belg* accounts for less than 10 per cent of cultivated area and about 4 per cent of crop output. Similarly, data paucity limits the analysis to grain (cereals, pulses, and oil seeds) production. This may not be a significant limitation since grains

[6] Gollin (2014) and Rapsomanikis (2015) review aspects of the complex task of characterizing small agricultural producers across space and time.

[7] These are named after the two main rainy seasons in the country. *Meher* is the main rainy season (June–September) for most grain producers, while *belg* refers to the shorter rainy season (February–May) and is the major source of rain in some parts of the country. Only some parts of the country experience both.

on average contribute more than 80 per cent of crop output from around 90 per cent of the crop-cultivated area.

The chapter uses the Annual Agricultural Sample Survey (AgSS) of the Ethiopian Central Statistical Agency (CSA) as its main data source.[8] Complementary information collected via smaller and targeted sample surveys is also used as appropriate. See Bachewe et al. (2018) for a look at data-related issues using alternative sources to compare and contrast with CSA data.

27.2 Smallholder Crop Production in Ethiopia

27.2.1 Context

This section briefly describes the key elements of the natural and institutional context within which smallholder crop producers operate during the period under study.[9,10]

27.2.1.1 *Geography*

Crop production is highly diverse in Ethiopia. A major cause, in that regard, is the considerable agro-ecological diversity in the country. Perhaps the best known agro-ecological classification system was first proposed by Hans Hurni in 1986 (reprinted and discussed in Hurni 1998).[11,12] It is based on traditional altitude-temperature categories and classifies the country into fifteen zones combining altitude and rainfall levels. Dry *berha* (altitude below 500m and annual rainfall less than 900ml) and wet *wurch* (altitude above 3,700m and annual rainfall more than 1,400ml) represent the two extremes of this classification. The country's surface area is divided among *berha* (48 per cent), *weyna dega* (31 per cent), *kolla* (16 per cent), and *dega* (4 per cent). The system also maps sixteen main crops, of which ten are grains, onto these zones. The bulk of crop production occurs within the nine elevation-rainfall zones of the *weyna dega* and *dega* belts spanning the elevation range of 1,500–3,200m (see Hurni 1998).[13]

[8] A brief description of the AgSS is included in the Annex.

[9] The CSA currently considers all farmers with 5 hectares or less as smallholders. The chapter adopts that cut-off. Other defining features of smallholders will be examined below.

[10] Unsurprisingly, there is a large literature on Ethiopian agriculture. McCann (1995) provides an extensive historical account of agriculture in Ethiopia. Rahmato (2008) chronicles the complex relationship between farmers and the state since the middle of the last century. Dejene (1987), Pickett (1991), and Taffesse (1997) explore the state of affairs during the Derg period. Dorosh and Rashid (2012) cover the recent period until around 2010.

[11] Hurni (1998) also reviews other attempts at agro-ecological classification of Ethiopia.

[12] Note also that this classification is used by the latest Ministry of Agriculture's guidelines for soil and water conservation (see Hurni et al. 2016).

[13] A related approach with the same aim of capturing geographic diversity uses farming systems. Westphal (1975) is a pioneer in this tradition. The latest such effort is Amede et al. (2017), which identify

As both approaches make apparent, diverse geographies, combined with still thin markets, lead to a multiplicity of crops and farming practices. There is in fact no single nationwide staple crop analogous to rice or maize in many other countries. Indeed, the potential for productivity growth reflects this diversity and its realization demands correspondingly aligned policies and research and development efforts. It is important to keep in mind that the actual pattern of change described below captures an average picture that spans multiple agro-ecologies.

27.2.1.2 *Institutional Setting*

The 1990s began with the fall of the Derg, followed by significant changes in the policy regime that had prevailed in the country. The Derg period was characterized by widespread direct government controls in the economic sphere, including state ownership of all major enterprises in industry, services, and large-scale farming. For smallholders, it involved a complete ban on renting land and the sale and purchase of labour; the compulsory grain delivery (or quota) system under which farm households were forced to sell a part of their produce to the government at prices fixed below those ruling in the free market; the administrative distribution (or rationing) of manufactured consumer goods and fertilizers at subsidized prices, and involuntary cooperative membership. In part because of these policies, crop productivity stagnated.[14]

In contrast, the EPRDF period is associated with a radical shift in overall government policy. Both the Transitional Government (1991–4) and the EPRDF government that followed initiated extensive economic reforms including significant market liberalization and privatization of state-owned enterprises. In particular, both the quota system and subsidized rationing of manufactured consumer goods and fertilizers were discontinued. The Agricultural Development-Led Industrialization (ADLI) strategy was also adopted (see Chapters 9 and 26). More broadly, a federal system with considerable devolution of power to regional states was instituted. The subsequently introduced fiscal decentralization enabled substantial *woreda*-level decision-making. Still, the government has a wide-ranging role within smallholder production including land tenure, agricultural extension, and provision of modern inputs, and public services.

27.2.1.2.1 LAND TENURE

The Rural Land Reform Proclamation of 1975 nationalized all rural lands and brought about a radical change in land tenure in one fell swoop.[15] The Proclamation banned the sale or renting of land. It stipulated that all farm households access land in the form of

sixteen farming systems in the country, eleven of which are dominated by grain crops. Also, IFPRI's 'development domains' approach can be viewed as another example, albeit broader and more focused on growth potential (see Chamberlin and Schmidt 2012).

[14] Taffesse (1997) systematically explores the impact of these policies on crop production.

[15] The question of land tenure is complex, and the chapter briefly notes some key features and developments. See Chapter 4, this volume, for further exploration of land tenure issues.

holdings allotted to them on a usufructuary basis. The public ownership of all rural land remains the core feature of the land tenure system in the EPRDF period. Indeed, it has been enshrined in the country's constitution with the regional states assuming significant powers of land administration. Nevertheless, a variety of reforms have been implemented to modify this basic feature. It is now possible for landholders to bequeath land to their children or rent it out for a period of time. There has also been a significant effort to enhance tenure security through land certification and that process has been deepening in recent years with the gradual introduction of what is called second-stage certification, which involves cadastral map-based deeds.

27.2.1.2.2 ORGANIZATIONS

Currently, two key organizations figure prominently in the socio-economic life of Ethiopian farm households: *kebeles* and cooperatives.

The Kebele Peasants' (Farmers') Association (PA) was introduced by the 1975 Rural Land Proclamation. A PA was established as a permanent association of farm household heads living within an area not exceeding 800 hectares. Initially, the primary roles of a PA were to implement the provisions of the Proclamation, and land redistribution among its members, in particular. Subsequently, however, it turned into the lowest administrative unit of the state, and its name shortened to just *kebele* from the 1980s. The *kebele* has been significantly revamped during the EPRDF period and now functions as the key interface between the government and farm households in terms of policy implementation and public service provision. By 2017, more than 20,000 *kebeles* served as the focal point for the extensive interaction between the government and smallholders.

Cooperatives are the other organization important to smallholders. The significant push towards the formation of service and producers' cooperatives of the Derg period was halted during the early years of the EPRDF period. This initial hesitancy was partly explained by the widespread dislike of cooperatives due to their forced formation and their role in enforcing unpopular policies of the Derg such as the quota system. Gradually, the EPRDF government started to encourage cooperative development, with its effort intensifying considerably since the early 2000s. The establishment of the Federal Cooperative Agency contributed to that fast pace. Currently, a range of cooperative types, from multipurpose marketing cooperatives through to crop-specific ones, operate in rural Ethiopia. They engage in output marketing, input distribution, agro-processing, saving and credit, and public service provision. They are central to the distribution of chemical fertilizers and improved seeds to farmers. There were around 71,000 such primary cooperatives by 2014.[16,17]

[16] The Ethiopian Federal Cooperative Agency: at http://www.fca.gov.et/webapp/php/documents/Wednesday%208th%20of%20March%202017%2002_58_15%20PM%20Document_111.pdf

[17] See Bernard et al. (2010, 2013) for discussions on the effectiveness of cooperatives.

27.3 Evolution and Current State, 1996–2015

27.3.1 Broad Pattern

Three key measures of the size of smallholder grain production can be identified: area cultivated, output produced, and number of holders engaged.[18,19] All experienced an upward trend during 1996–2014. Output grew at annual average rate of 9.5 per cent. This has been faster than the other two indicators due to rising productivity (see Section 27.3.3). Cultivated area and number of holders grew at the same annual rate, though the latter had a brisker pace during the second half of the period.

The pattern is clearly discernible in Figure 27.2. The early dips or low levels were partly due to drought (1997 and 2002) and war (1998–9). Both output per hectare (yield or land productivity) and output per holder (an indicator of labour productivity) grew consistently from 2003. Area per holder, on the other hand remained more or less the same for most of the period, showing a decline towards the end of the period. Thus, as noted before, the period is one of growth and the beginnings of transition towards a more modern production system. As will be discussed later in this chapter, there is much heterogeneity behind this overall pattern.

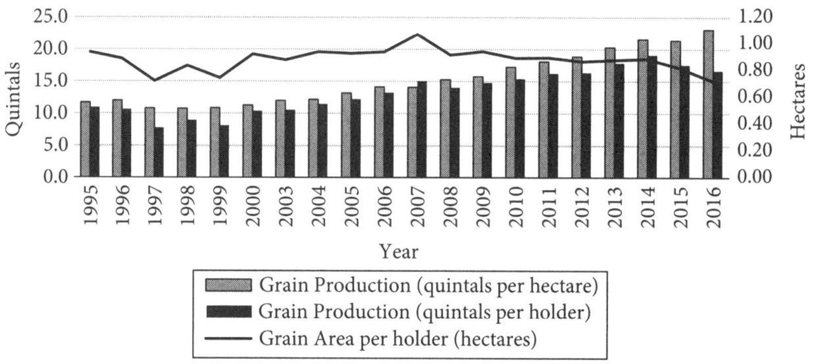

FIGURE 27.2 Smallholder grain production, 1995–2015

Source: Author's computation using CSA's AgSS data (CSA, various years).

[18] Most of the analysis is restricted to up to 2014 to avoid the potential complications caused by the 2015/16 major drought. These complications cannot be meaningfully discussed in this short chapter.

[19] The CSA defines a holder as 'a person who exercises management control over the operation of the agricultural holding and makes the major decision regarding the utilization of the available resources. He/she has primary technical and economic responsibility for the holding. He/she may operate the holding directly as an owner or a manager' (CSA, various years).

27.3.2 Factors of Production

27.3.2.1 *Farm size*

Though the absolute level is context specific, relatively small farm size is a defining feature of smallholders.[20] As Table 27.1 shows, the same applies in Ethiopia. During 2003–16, the average farm size was slightly less than a hectare. Half of these smallholders operated less than 0.65 hectares of crop land, while the bottom tenth of the distribution manage less than 0.13 hectares. Only the top 10 per cent of holders operated more than 2 hectares and 0.75 per cent had more than 5 hectares.

In short, crop production in Ethiopia is populated by a lot of very small farms.

27.3.2.2 *Other Capital*

Apart from oxen as a source of traction power, little physical capital is used by smallholders. A third of these producers own two or more oxen (Table 27.2). Since the traditional ox-plough technology requires a pair of oxen, the rest use different ways of meeting their demand including pairing up or hiring. It is noteworthy that, given their farm size, a significant fraction of smallholders may find owning a pair of oxen neither economically feasible nor efficient. Traditional farm implements related to

Table 27.1 Farm size distribution, 2003–16

Per centile	Number of Holders	Farm size in hectares		
		Mean	Minimum	Maximum
1	50,767	0.09	0.05	0.13
2	50,766	0.18	0.13	0.23
3	50,767	0.29	0.23	0.35
4	50,766	0.42	0.35	0.49
5	50,767	0.57	0.49	0.65
6	50,766	0.74	0.65	0.84
7	50,767	0.96	0.84	1.09
8	50,766	1.26	1.09	1.44
9	50,767	1.71	1.44	2.04
10	50,766	2.81	2.04	5.00
All	507,665	0.92	0.05	5.00

Source: Author's calculation using CSA's AgSS Data (CSA, various years).

[20] Farm size is total cropped area operated by a holder. It is thus a bit smaller than total land holdings because it excludes fallow land, grazing land, woodland, and other land use. On average, total crop area amounted to about 83 per cent of total land holdings. Also note that rented land is unlikely to create a big wedge between operated and 'owned' land. Land rental markets, though developing, are still nascent. For instance, only 8 per cent of plots were reported as rented or leased in 2014.

Table 27.2 Ox ownership and strategies used by non-owners, 2009–16

		Average 2009–16 (%)
Ox ownership—Holders owning:	No ox	43.6
	One ox	24.3
	Two or more oxen	32.2
Strategies to cope with not owning enough oxen—Holders:	Hiring oxen	8.7
	Pairing with someone's ox	30.2
	Borrowing oxen	27.3
	Digging by hand	29.4

Source: Author's computation using CSA's AgSS Data (CSA, various years).

ploughing and harvesting represent the majority of physical capital deployed by farm households. Tractors, combine-harvesters, threshers, and water pumps are still very rare. Nevertheless, a growing proportion of farmers, particularly in some parts of the country (Western Tigray, South Gondar, West Gojjam, East Shewa, Arsi, Bale, and Jigjiga zones), are utilizing agricultural machinery rental services for land preparation and harvesting (Berhane et al. 2017).

27.3.2.3 *Labour*

Smallholders' own families supply the bulk of labour used in their grain production. The average family size is around five (Table 27.3) and almost all participate to varying degrees. Men provide the bulk of the labour used in production, while women contribute around 25 per cent (Palacios-Lopez, Christiaensen, and Kilic 2017). The use of hired labour is widespread, though its share in total labour deployed in grain production is low. For instance, about a quarter of surveyed households claim to have hired labour during the *meher* season—mostly for weeding and harvesting (Feed the Future 2015). Moreover, traditional labour-sharing arrangements are common. Finally, educational levels are rising but from a very low base, with average years of schooling being around two in 2014 (Table 27.3).

27.3.2.4 *Improved Inputs and Practices*

Modern farming practices and use of inputs are expanding within smallholder agriculture, again from low initial levels. Chemical fertilizers were applied on half of the grain-cropped area in 2014 (Table 27.3). Ten per cent of the same area was planted with improved seeds. Farmers are also increasingly deploying pesticides and herbicides (Tamru et al. 2016). In contrast, irrigation coverage was strikingly low at about 1 per cent of cultivated area in the same year. Adoption of modern inputs, particularly chemical fertilizers, and improvements in farming practices were promoted by an enlarged extension system. By 2014, about a third of grain acreage benefited from this system.

27.3.3 Output and Productivity

27.3.3.1 *Crop Mix*

In 2014, 14 million smallholders cultivated close to 13 million hectares and produced 270 million quintals of grains. This total output was made up of cereals (87 per cent), pulses (10 per cent), and oilseeds (3 per cent). As noted in Section 27.3.1, grains dominate smallholder crop production. Their share of area cultivated has been around 90 per cent. In value terms, they accounted for 78 per cent of crop output value (Figure 27.3). Again, cereals are the largest subset of grains with more than 60 per cent of output. Pulses are a distant second, followed by oilseeds. This distribution of crop output typified the period covered. As to individual crops, teff tops the list when ranked by share of acreage and value of output. Maize is second, though it accounted for the largest fraction of the output. Wheat, sorghum, and barley are, in that order, the other major grain crops.

At the farm level, Ethiopian smallholders cultivate diversified crop portfolios to meet their subsistence needs and cope with market and yield risks. In 2014, an average small farmer produced nine crops. This lack of specialization is likely to lower productivity relative to what is potentially achievable. The diverse crop mix also poses challenges to the design of new technologies and their subsequent promotion.

27.3.3.2 *Productivity*

Grains are a diverse mix with differing productivity.[21] The following brief discussion focuses on the whole set using two measures: grain output per hectare (or yield), and grain output per holder (as an indicator of labour productivity).

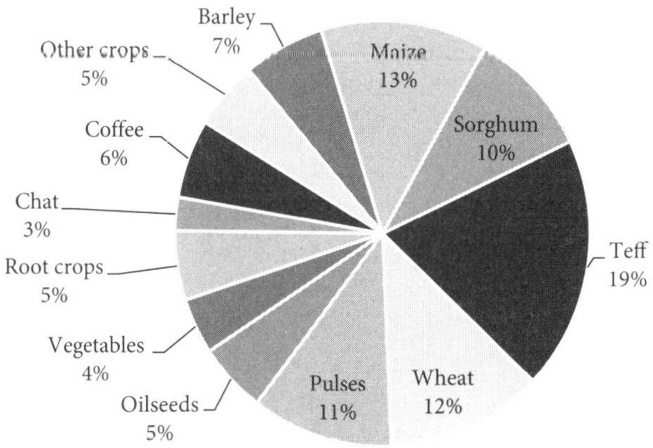

FIGURE 27.3 Average composition of the real value of crop output, 2004–13 (per cent)

Source: Figure 3.2 in Bachewe et al. (2015).

21 Cereals have higher yields than most pulses and oilseeds. For example, in 2015/16 maize production recorded the highest yield at 34 quintals per hectare. Yield in teff production for the same year was about 16 quintals per hectare—the lowest for a cereal, but still higher than the level for most pulses and oilseeds.

Table 27.3 Smallholder crop producers: basic characteristics and trends by farm-size terciles, 2003–14

	2003				2014				Average (2003–14)				Average annual growth rates (2003–14) (%)				Ratio of 2014 and 2003 levels (2003–14) (%)[2]			
	All	T-I[1]	T-II	T-III	All	T-I	T-II	T-III	All	T-I	T-II	T-III	All	T-I	T-II	T-III	All	T-I	T-II	T-III
Grain area per holder	**0.87**	0.15	0.6	1.73	**0.87**	0.14	0.63	1.81	**0.89**	0.15	0.63	1.82	**0.1**	0.2	0.8	0.5	**100**	97	105	105
Grain output per holder (kg)	**1,064**	192	760	2077	**1,966**	311	1,385	4102	**1,520**	255	1,046	3,082	**6.4**	5.5	6.5	7.2	**165**	121	162	190
Grain output per hectare or yield (kg)	**1,240**	1,293	1,271	1,169	**2,135**	2,072	2,197	2,138	**1,669**	1,713	1,684	1,616	**5.6**	4.9	5.7	6.3	**172**	160	173	183
Gender of the household head (Male=1) (%)	**83.9**	73.5	86.6	91.8	**83.5**	73.9	85	90.8	**83.5**	73.7	84.7	90.9								
Household size (number)	**5.3**	4.7	5.3	5.9	**5.2**	4.6	5.1	5.7	**5.3**	4.7	5.2	5.9	**−0.3**	−0.2	−0.3	−0.4	**97**	97	96	96
Schooling (years)	**1.2**	1.2	1.2	1.1	**1.9**	1.9	1.9	1.9	**1.5**	1.5	1.5	1.6	**5.3**	4.9	5.3	5.8	**185**	178	186	196
Chemical fertilizer application: share in crop area (%)	**24.2**	20.3	22.2	29.5	**49.6**	47.5	49.9	51.2	**33.7**	30.6	33.1	37.4	**8.5**	9.8	9.7	6.9	**105**	134	125	74
Extension incidence: share in crop area (%)	**11.2**	7.5	11.5	14.2	**33**	29.2	33.6	35.6	**18.8**	15.2	19.3	21.8	**13.2**	18.0	13.6	10.8	**194**	290	192	150

Improved seed application: share in crop area (%)	**4.2**	4.4	4.2	4.1	**10**	11	10	9.2	**6.3**	6.5	6.3	6.2	**16.0**	17.3	16.3	16.5	**136**	149	136	124
Irrigated area: share in crop area (%)	**1.2**	2	1	0.6	**1.1**	1.8	1.1	0.6	**1.2**	2	1.1	0.6	**2.5**	4.8	3.6	1.1	**-3**	-11	16	-6
Own-consumption share of grain production (%)[3]					**61.6**	68.8	63.4	58.3	**62.1**	68.9	64.2	58.7	**−0.5**	−0.3	−0.6	−0.5	**98.9**	99.5	98.8	99.1
Marketed output share of grain production (%)[3]					**21.1**	17.9	20.2	22.6	**20.4**	16.9	18.8	22.5	**2.1**	5.8	4.8	−0.2	**104**	112	109	99

Notes: [1]T-I, T-II, and T-III stand for 'bottom tercile', 'middle tercile', and 'top tercile' of the farm size distribution.[2] The last four columns report the ratio of 2014 to 2003 levels such that the difference between these numbers and 100 provides a measure of the total change between the two years.[3] Only for 2009, 2012, and 2015.

Source: Author's calculation using CSA's AgSS Data (CSA, various years).

Table 27.3 reports on the levels of these measures for 2003–14. For that period, overall grain yield averaged 1,669kg, while it reached 2,135kg in 2014. Grain output per holder was 1,966kg in 2014 with a period average level of 1,520kg. Both measures indicate relatively low productivity. In terms of yields, it is comparable to cereal yields in Kenya and Tanzania but is much lower than Egypt's, which was 7,231kg in 2014.[22] The gap with Egyptian yield levels indicates what is possible.

27.3.3.3 *Commercialization*

As expected, small-scale grain producers in Ethiopia utilize the bulk of their output themselves. During 2003–14, on average they consumed 62 per cent of their output and sold 20 per cent (Table 27.3).[23] There is significant diversity across crops, however. Almost half of oilseed and a fifth of pulse output were marketed. Teff is the most commercialized cereal with nearly a third of output supplied to the market.

27.3.3.4 *Heterogeneity*

A striking feature of smallholders is their considerable heterogeneity. One way of capturing this is to categorize these producers into groups by farm size and compare their other attributes. In what follows we therefore use three brackets (or terciles) to classify holders by their farm size.[24]

Table 27.3 summarizes the diversity of grain producers across several indicators over 2003–14. In terms of acreage, on average, farms in the top tercile are three-fold and twelve-fold bigger than those in the middle and bottom terciles, respectively. Comparable gaps exist in output per holder across these farms. On average, top-tercile farms produced 3,082kg per holder, which is much higher than that attained by those in the middle (1,046kg) and bottom (255kg) terciles. Labour availability, technology, and market orientation may cause these differences. Indeed, families in the top tercile are 26 per cent larger (or have an additional 1.2 persons) than those in the bottom tercile. More of the former have male heads with a 7-percentage point advantage. Modern input use also favours the larger farms. Compared to bottom-tercile farmers, top-tercile ones have respectively 22 per cent and 43 per cent more of their crop area covered by chemical fertilizer application and extension service provision. Also, the marketed share of the top-tercile farmers' output is 18 per cent higher than that of their bottom-tercile counterparts. In contrast, differences in schooling, improved seed adoption, and irrigation use are negligible because they are small, and levels are still low in all cases. Moreover, the gap in output per holder remains even with the faster growth of fertilizer adoption and extension coverage found in the bottom tercile. Finally, average grain yield in the bottom tercile is higher than that in the top tercile, with the latter amounting to 94 per cent

[22] World Development Indicators (2018): at https://data.worldbank.org/indicator.

[23] About 13 per cent of output is saved as seed for the next production cycle.

[24] These differences are recorded with little attempt to explain their causes or deeply consider their implications. Headey, Dereje, and Taffesse (2014) explore some pertinent causes and implications in greater detail.

of the former. It is not clear whether this is a case of the widely debated inverse farm size–productivity relationship.[25]

In short, small grain producers in Ethiopia are highly heterogeneous. A large proportion of them appear to be too small to produce significantly higher levels of output under the existing crop mix and farming technology.[26] In part reflecting these constrained opportunities, farm households seek alternative income-generating activities. Off-farm and non-farm wage labour as well as non-farm enterprise are important sources of income, particularly to those at the bottom of the landholding distribution (see Bachewe et al. 2016).

27.3.4 Growth and its Drivers

As noted earlier, rapid economic growth has been occurring in the country, particularly since 2003 (Figure 27.2). Smallholder crop production has experienced the same growth spurt. Average grain output per holder grew by 6.4 per cent per annum during 2003–14, while grain yield rose by 5.6 per cent per year in the same period (Table 27.3). Consequently, 66 per cent and 72 per cent more grain was produced respectively per holder and per hectare by the end of that period than was achieved at the beginning. Importantly, these changes were experienced by farms of all sizes albeit from a low base and at differential rates. Yield and output per holder of farmers in the bottom farm-size tercile grew by around 5 per cent. Those in the higher terciles had slightly faster growth.

Adoption of improved inputs has been going on in parallel during the period, implying a strong association with the growth outcomes reported in the paragraph above. Chemical fertilizer use rose by 8.5 per cent per year such that, by 2014, these fertilizers were used on 50 per cent of grain acreage. In other words, chemical fertilizer application doubled over the period. Similarly, improved seed adoption increased at an annual rate of 16 per cent, though from a low starting level. By 2014, 10 per cent of grain area was planted with improved seeds. Expansion of extension coverage (at the rate of 13 per cent per year) more than likely encouraged improvements in farm management practices including the adoption of modern inputs.[27]

A systematic exploration of the factors that underlie these changes is beyond the scope of this chapter. Instead it highlights the key findings of a recent comprehensive

[25] A large literature has grown around this issue. Multiple explanations (imperfect factor and insurance markets, soil quality differences) have been put forward over the years (see Barrett, Bellemare, and Hou (2010) for a review and some tests). More recently, the focus has shifted to measurement error and, to a lesser extent, econometric specification (see respectively Desiere and Jolliffe (2018) and Savastano and Scandizzo (2017) for these analyses using Ethiopian data).

[26] The incidence of holders in the bottom tercile is highest in the SNNP region and least in the Oromiya region.

[27] The case of irrigation is complicated with much uncertainty about what is known and measured. Given the data in Table 27.3, it can only be stated that irrigation use during the *meher* season appears to be quite limited and does not seem to have changed much during the period covered.

study of agricultural transformation in Ethiopia by Bachewe et al. (2018) that identifies, with empirical evidence, the following as important ingredients of the circumstances that have led to rapid growth:

- expansion of the agricultural extension system and the resultant considerable increase in farmers' access to information on new and improved farming practices;[28]
- deepening of input and output markets, with the concomitant decline in transaction costs, largely driven by big public investments in roads and telecommunications;
- accelerated human capital accumulation with both education levels and life expectancy rising, again strongly linked to public investments in significantly expanding the education and health systems; and
- reduced exposure to shocks and their negative consequences through the implementation of the extensive Productivity Safety Net Program (PSNP) and a widespread land certification programme.

The pattern of growth observed in output and productivity reflects the responses of smallholder farmers to the circumstances created by these and related drivers[29] in the form of, among others, adoption of modern inputs and farming practices.

It should also be noted that many of these policy actions reflect the adoption of the Agricultural Development-Led Industrialization (ADLI) strategy by the Ethiopian government in the late 1990s. Undergirding ADLI was the belief that agricultural growth is vital during the early stages of development. Accordingly, the government prioritized investments linked to the above-mentioned drivers of agricultural change. This prioritization found expression in the sequence of development plans since the late 1990s, particularly the Plan for Accelerated and Sustained Development to End Poverty (PASDEP, 2006–10) and the Growth and Transformation Plans I and II (2011–15 and 2016–20).[30]

27.4 Conclusion

Smallholder grain production provides a livelihood for the majority of Ethiopians and generates the bulk of the country's crop output. The sector has been undergoing considerable change in recent years (particularly since 2003). Its total output and productivity have grown at a brisk pace, though starting from a low base. These changes are correlated with greater intensification through the adoption of chemical fertilizers, improved seeds, and other better farm management practices. Public investments in extension, education, health, roads, and telecommunications have promoted this intensification.

[28] See also Berhane et al. (2018).

[29] Population pressure and environmental degradation are noteworthy, in this regard.

[30] See Chapter 9 for more on policies.

These changes strongly suggest that smallholder farming is in transition. Nevertheless, its transformation into a modern, highly productive, and commercialized sector closely integrated with the rest of the economy is yet to happen.[31] Average productivity, particularly labour productivity, is still relatively low. Moreover, the task of moving up the productivity ladder will be harder since it starts from a higher base due to the considerable achievements so far from a low base. Indeed, a significant fraction of holders seem to have farms that are too small for them to meaningfully rise above subsistence without radical changes in what they produce and how they produce.

Strong interlinkages with other economic sectors is another important dimension of transformation that has yet to emerge for grain production. Twenty per cent of grain output in value terms serves as input in cattle and milk production (the share is twice as high for barley and wheat).[32] Industry's and services' intermediate demand for grain amount to 10 per cent and 1.6 per cent of the value of grain output, respectively. The former largely originates in animal feed processing and grain milling, while the latter comes from hotels. On the other hand, grain production demands an equivalent of about 6 per cent of its output as intermediate goods from industry. These are entirely inorganic fertilizers (by far the largest) and other chemical inputs (herbicides and pesticides). Also, maize, teff, and wheat production have demand levels 2 to 6 percentage points higher than this average. In short, both backward and forward production linkages of the smallholder grain sub-sector are still weak.

The sector has significant potential, however. As a simple illustration, consider the gain in productivity and output if all farmers adopted chemical fertilizers and improved seeds, and benefited from extension advice. Given production outcomes in 2014, this would raise yields by 29 per cent above actual levels—an equivalent of 73.6 million quintals of additional output per year. Moreover, rising incomes and accelerating urbanization and industrialization would create huge opportunities. On the other hand, the difficulty of the task is compounded by climate change, water scarcity, environmental degradation, and fast (though decelerating) population growth. Sustainable accommodation of these challenges would require greater specialization and substantial resource reallocation at the farm level and across agro-ecologies, combined with appropriate technological and institutional innovations.

Acknowledgements

The author thanks the editors for the opportunity and sustained encouragement as well as four reviewers for valuable comments. The Central Statistical Agency (CSA) generously shared the data from its Annual Agricultural Sample Survey for multiple years. Fanaye Tadesse and Feiruz Yimer provided invaluable research assistance.

[31] Timmer (1988) comprehensively discusses the nature, phases, and policy implications of agricultural transformation broadly, while Delgado (1995) explores the specific case of sub-Saharan Africa.

[32] These estimates are based on the 2011 Ethiopian Social Accounting Matrix (SAM).

Annex

The Annual Agricultural Sample Survey (AgSS)

The AgSS is a nationally representative annual sample survey conducted by the CSA, which appears to be the longest-running regular survey of its kind in sub-Saharan Africa.[33] It commonly covers all rural areas in the country except nine zones with non-sedentary populations (three in Afar and six in Somali regional states). Each round involves the selection of enumeration areas (EAs) from a list of EAs in the latest census frame. Subsequently, a specified number of holders (currently 20) are randomly selected per EA from a complete listing of all holders in the EA, newly conducted by the CSA for the purpose in each round. On average, the AgSS was conducted in about 2,100 EAs and covered more than 51,000 holders each year during 2003–15. The survey collects data on crop area, farming practices, holder characteristics, and yield levels using the crop-cut method.

References

Amede T., C. Auricht, J.-M. Boffa, et al. (2017). 'A Farming System Framework for Investment Planning and Priority Setting in Ethiopia', ACIAR Technical Reports Series No. 90, Australian Centre for International Agricultural Research, Canberra.

Bachewe, Fantu, Guush Berhane, Bart Minten, and Alemayehu Seyoum Taffesse (2016). 'Non-Farm Income and Labour Markets in Rural Ethiopia', ESSP Working Paper 90, Ethiopian Strategy Support Programme, IFPRI.

Bachewe, Fantu N., Guush Berhane, Bart Minten, and Alemayehu S. Taffesse (2018). 'Agricultural Transformation in Africa? Assessing the Evidence in Ethiopia', *World Development* 105: 286–98.

Barrett, Christopher B., Marc F. Bellemare, and Janet Y. Hou (2010). 'Reconsidering Conventional Explanations of the Inverse Productivity–Size Relationship', *World Development* 38 (1): 88–97.

Berhane, Guush, Mekdim Dereje, Bart Minten, and Seneshaw Tamru (2017). 'The Rapid—But from a Low Base—Uptake of Agricultural Mechanization in Ethiopia: Patterns, Implications and Challenges', ESSP Working Paper 105, Ethiopian Strategy Support Programme, IFPRI.

Berhane, Guush, C. Ragasa, Gashaw T. Abate, and T. W. Assefa (2018). 'The State of Agricultural Extension Services in Ethiopia and their Contribution to Agricultural Productivity', ESSP Working Paper No. 118, Ethiopian Strategy Support Programme, IFPRI.

Bernard, Tanguy, David J. Spielman, Alemayehu Seyoum Taffesse, and Eleni Gabre-Madhin (2010). 'Cooperatives for Staple Crop Marketing: Evidence from Ethiopia', Research Monograph, 164, International Food Policy Research Institute (IFPRI).

Bernard, Tanguy, Gashaw T. Abate, and Solomon Lemma (2013). 'Agricultural Cooperatives in Ethiopia: Results of the 2012 ATA Baseline Survey, International Food Policy Research Institute, Washington, DC.

Chamberlin, Jordan and Emily Schmidt (2012). 'Ethiopian Agriculture: A Dynamic Geographic Perspective', in *Food and Agriculture in Ethiopia: Progress and Policy Challenges*,

[33] See CSA (various years) for further details.

ed. Paul Dorosh and Shahidur Rashid (Philadelphia, PA: University of Pennsylvania Press (in collaboration with IFPRI)): Chapter 2.

CSA (various years). 'Annual Agricultural Sample Survey (AgSS) 1996–2017', Central Statistical Agency (CSA), Addis Ababa, Ethiopia.

Dejene, Alemneh (1987). *Peasants, Agrarian Socialism and Rural Development in Ethiopia* (Boulder, CO: Westview Press).

Delgado, C. L. (1995). 'Agricultural Transformation: The Key to Broad-based Growth and Poverty Alleviation in Sub-Saharan Africa', MSSD Discussion Paper No. 7, Markets and Structural Studies Division, International Food Policy Research Institute.

Desiere, Sam and Dean Jolliffe (2018). 'Land Productivity and Plot Size: Is Measurement Error Driving the Inverse Relationship?' *Journal of Development Economics* 130: 84–98.

de Vries, G. J., M. P. Timmer, and K. de Vries (2015). 'Structural Transformation in Africa: Static Gains, Dynamic Losses', *Journal of Development Studies* 51 (6): 674–88. http://dx.doi.org/10.1080/00220388.2014.997222.

Dorosh, Paul and Shahidur Rashid (eds) (2012). *Food and Agriculture in Ethiopia: Progress and Policy Challenges* (Philadelphia, PA: University of Pennsylvania Press on behalf of International Food Policy Research Institute (IFPRI)).

Feed the Future (FtF) of Ethiopia (2015). 'Midline Report 2015', Ethiopia Strategy Support Program (USAID) and International Food Policy Research (IFPRI), October.

Feenstra, Robert C., Robert Inklaar, and Marcel P. Timmer (2015). 'The next generation of the Penn World Tables.' *American Economic Review* 105 (10): 3150–82.

Gollin, Douglas (2014). 'Smallholder Agriculture in Africa: An Overview and Implications for Policy', IIED Working Paper, IIED, London. http://pubs.iied.org/14640IIED.

Headey, Derek, Mekdim Dereje, and Alemayehu Seyoum Taffesse (2014). 'Land Constraints and Agricultural Intensification in Ethiopia: A Village-Level Analysis of High-Potential Areas', *Food Policy* 48: 129–41.

Hurni, Hans (1998). 'Agroecological Belts of Ethiopia: Explanatory Notes on Three Maps at a Scale of 1:1,000,000', Soil Conservation Research Programme (SCRP) and Centre for Development and Environment (CDE), Addis Ababa and University of Bern.

Hurni, Hans, Berhe Wolde-Aregay, Punjab Chadhokar, Daniel Dannano, Gete Zeleke, Martin Grunder, Kassaye Goshu (2016). *Soil and Water Conservation in Ethiopia: Guidelines for Development Agents*, 2nd revised edition (Bern, Switzerland: Centre for Development and Environment (CDE), University of Bern, with Bern Open Publishing (BOP)).

McCann, James (1995). *People of the Plow: A Modern History of Highland Agriculture in Ethiopia* (Madison, WI: University of Wisconsin Press).

Palacios-Lopez, Amparo, Luc Christiaensen, and Talip Kilic (2017). 'How Much of the Labor in African Agriculture Is Provided by Women?' *Food Policy* 67: 52–63.

Pickett, J. (1991). *Economic Development in Ethiopia: Agriculture, the Market, and the State* (Paris: OECD).

Rahmato, Dessalegn (2008). *The Peasant and the State: Studies in Agrarian Change in Ethiopia 1950s—2000s* (CreateSpace, ISBN 978-1438266534).

Rapsomanikis, George (2015). *The Economic Lives of Smallholder Farmers: An Analysis Based on Household Data from Nine Countries* (Rome: Food and Agriculture Organization of the United Nations).

Savastano, Sara, and Pasquale L. Scandizzo (2017). 'Farm Size and Productivity A "Direct-Inverse-Direct" Relationship', Policy Research Working Paper No. WPS 8127, World Bank, Washington, DC.

Taffesse, Alemayehu Seyoum (1997). 'Three Essays on Ethiopian Farm Households', DPhil thesis, Sub-faculty of Economics, University of Oxford.
Tamru, Seneshaw, Bart Minten, Dawit Alemu, and Fantu Bachewe (2016). 'The Rapid Expansion of Herbicide Use in Smallholder Agriculture in Ethiopia: Patterns, Drivers, and Implications', ESSP Working Paper No. 94, Ethiopian Strategy Support Programme, IFPRI.
Timmer, C. Peter (1988). 'The Agricultural Transformation', in *Handbook of Development Economics, Vol. I*, ed. H. Chenery and T. N. Srinivasan (Amsterdam: Elsevier Science Publishers): Chapter 8.
Westphal, E. (1975). 'Agricultural Systems in Ethiopia', Agricultural Research Reports 826, Centre for Agricultural Publishing and Documentation, Wageningen.
World Bank (2018). 'World Development Indicators'. https://data.worldbank.org/indicator.

CHAPTER 28

RURAL FINANCE AND SMALLHOLDER FARMING IN ETHIOPIA

GUUSH BERHANE AND KIBROM A. ABAY

28.1 Introduction

SUSTAINED access to rural financial markets remains crucial to income-enhancing opportunities and hence to the improvement of rural livelihoods in developing countries. This transformative role has generated renewed interest in the development of rural financial markets, which has become known as the 'microfinance revolution' in the last four decades. The long-list of hopes that rural finance is thought to deliver are conceptually well founded and intuitive—that small loans can, among other things, transform the poor's economic activities, increase incomes, and enable their children to go to school (Yunus 2006). These arguments find their origins in the common assumption that the marginal return to capital is larger when capital is scarce, and by implication, finance should flow from richer areas to poorer areas, enabling the poor to reap sizeable returns from access to finance (Conning and Udry 2007; Morduch and Karlan 2009).[1] The focus on access to credit has, over time, moved to embrace the provision of broad-based financial services (such as credit, savings, and insurance) to all, rather than just delivering credit to small businesses (Morduch and Karlan 2009). Given the importance placed on the transformative power of access to broader financial services, microfinance institutions (MFIs) have flourished across the developing world—including in Ethiopia—in the last few decades.

Following the global movement, rural financial markets (RFMs) in Ethiopia have received substantial policy attention in recent years, which has led MFIs and member-based financial cooperatives to flourish. Ethiopia's rural financial markets have seen

[1] Some studies have shown that marginal returns to capital investments in developing countries are large enough (De Mel, McKenzie, and Woodruff 2008; Duflo, Kramer, and Robinson 2008) and unparalleled in current investments.

unprecedented growth in the last few decades and the outreach of rural cooperatives to rural households is expanding over time.[2] However, despite the significant progress and the enormous resources mobilized in the form of micro-credits, the vast majority of households in Ethiopia remain underserved (Amha and Peck 2010). According to the World Bank's Global Financial Inclusion data (Demirguc-Kunt et al. 2014), only 22 per cent of adults (aged 15 and above) had an account in Ethiopia in any financial institution in 2014 (as compared to 29 per cent for SSA and about 62 per cent globally). A significant proportion of rural households in Ethiopia still rely on informal finances even if costs are substantially lower in the formal than in the informal sector and both coexist in the same market.[3] Recent country-wide representative surveys from the Central Statistical Agency (CSA) show that only about 23 per cent of smallholders in Ethiopia have access to credit and less than 10 per cent participate in formal financial institutions. Moreover, those households with limited access to these financial markets participate in these financial transactions irregularly and sporadically, coupled with poor financial performance involving significant non-repayment during drought years. Against the estimated huge potential unmet demand (80 per cent according to Wiedmaier-Pfister et al. 2008, for example) and the relatively wider coverage of MFIs and financial cooperatives in recent years, the fact that only a small proportion of households take up loans remains a paradox. A substantial proportion of these non-participants provide reasons that range from the unsuitability of existing financial products to contract designs and the legal provisions governing the MFIs.

A critical question facing policymakers in Ethiopia, given the substantial expansion of rural financial services in recent years (mainly through MFIs and rural financial cooperatives), is therefore why the majority of rural households remain unbanked (Bernard, Tafesse, and Gebre-Medhin 2008). In other words, what explains the continuing low uptake of financial services, mainly credit and savings, despite improvements in the physical access to these services? This relates to the generic intriguing question of why rural microfinances are not fully achieving their hopes of transforming rural livelihoods (Morduch and Karlan 2009; Banerjee 2013). These questions are likely to remain important in the context of Ethiopia as well as globally in the years to come.

At the centre of these debates is the question of whether it is the nature of participants or the nature of financial products offered by rural microfinances that is inhibiting participation in these markets. For instance, Karlan and Mullainathan (2007) argue that the existing requirements and one-size-fits-all nature of microfinance might be one reason why it fails to satisfy the financial needs of the poor in developing countries. In addition, offering financial services to rural households operating in risky contexts where agriculture is predominantly rain fed involves additional costs and challenges.

[2] For example, the number of MFIs in Ethiopia jumped from 26 in 2004 to 35 in 2015/16. Similarly, member-based rural cooperatives grew from 7,057 in 2010/11 to 18,959 in 2015/16; reaching out to about 3.4 million clients (see Abay et al. 2018).

[3] Indigenous social networks in Ethiopia, such as *iddir* and *equib* are well suited to facilitate credit and related financial transactions among members of these networks (e.g. Abay Kahsay, and Berhane 2017).

In this chapter, we aim to assess and document the development of rural financial markets in Ethiopia in view of their role in transforming[4] smallholder agriculture. We do this, first, by providing a brief overview of recent developments in rural financial markets in Ethiopia. These markets include credit, savings, and to a limited extent, insurance markets. Given that the latter remains in its infancy, the focus remains on the former two markets. Second, we use large datasets covering most parts of the country to explore why rural financial markets in Ethiopia fail to satisfy the financial needs of rural households, examining the most important demand- and supply-side bottlenecks preventing households from taking advantage of the financial products offered. We combine nationally representative datasets collected by the CSA and other large surveys collected by the International Food Policy Research Institute (IFPRI) in collaboration with the CSA. Despite recent theoretical explanations, empirical evidence on why RFMs fail in contexts like Ethiopia is largely missing. This chapter contributes to this important gap in the empirical literature for Ethiopia and beyond.

28.2 The Transformative Role of Rural Finance and Why it Fails

28.2.1 The Transformative Role of Rural Finance

Well-functioning financial markets that provide broad-based financial services (e.g. loans, deposits, insurance, etc.) have long been recognized as critical to reducing poverty and achieving inclusive economic growth and transformation. This is more so in rural areas where substantial time lags exist between use of inputs and realization of outputs in the organization of agricultural production and rural economic activities. Rural households need inclusive financial services—defined as accessible and usable services—for a variety of purposes, mainly credit to purchase critical farm inputs and undertake non-farm activities as well as for bridging periodical consumption gaps.

In addition, being poor is not just about having too little income, or not being able to satisfy financial needs per se. Rather, it is about insecure incomes and uncertain livelihoods. In other words, in the absence of access to inclusive financial markets that can bridge the time lag between production and consumption, poor households are subject to enormous production and livelihood uncertainties. Lack of appropriate financial services to overcome these uncertainties, as is often the case in rural areas of Ethiopia, forces households to forego profitable but risky investment opportunities to avoid subsequent volatility in consumption. In contexts where agriculture is rain fed, uninsured

[4] Agricultural transformation can be defined as a process in which farm households shift their production system from a highly diversified and subsistence-oriented to a more specialized and market-oriented one characterized by sustained increase in labour productivity (Jayne, Minde, and Argwings-Kodhek 2002: 3).

weather risk exacerbates the effect of lack of credit. A number of studies have shown that in the absence of inclusive financial services and when production is subject to the vagaries of nature, rural households are forced to choose low-risk but low-return undertakings (Dercon and Christiaensen 2011), leading to substantial welfare losses that contribute to persistent poverty or poverty trap (Morduch 1990; Dercon 1996, 2004).

In the Ethiopian context, lack of access to credit coupled with weather shocks has been shown to discourage farm households from adopting yield-improving technologies such as fertilizers and improved seed, limiting agricultural productivity and transformation (Dercon and Christiaensen 2011). Sustainable access to credit can also prevent distressing sales of assets by bridging consumption gaps that arise when shocks hit. More importantly, recent insights from behavioural economics suggest that having access to financial services can have far-reaching implications for poverty reduction by reducing the psychological cost of not having enough—relaxing the poor's mental 'bandwidth' in their everyday lives (Mullainathan and Shafir 2013). At the household level, all these factors contribute to the role of inclusive rural finance in transforming small farming in poor rural communities such as in Ethiopia. At the macro level, widening financial access to individuals and households contributes to reducing income inequality and reducing poverty (Beck, Demirguc-Kunt, and Peria 2007; Burgess , Pande, and Wong 2005).

Compared with the rest of the world, financial penetration is, however, very limited in Africa and Ethiopia stands out as one of the lowest in Africa (Demirguc-Kunt et al. 2015). According to the World Bank's Global Financial Inclusion data (Demirguc-Kunt et al. 2015), 62 per cent of global adults (aged 15 and above) had an account in 2014—about 2 billion adults were left unbanked globally. Only 22 per cent of adult Ethiopians had an account in any financial institution in the same year (as compared to 29 per cent for the sub-Saharan African (SSA) average), and 7 per cent borrowed from formal financial institutions. In the same year, while about 48 per cent of adult Ethiopians saved some money, only 14 per cent saved at a financial institution (the SSA average was 16 per cent). The rest was saved informally, including in the form of cash at home—known as 'under-the-mattress' savings. Mobile accounts have recently helped narrow the gap in account ownership in some parts of SSA. While the SSA (12 per cent) region led the world (2 per cent) in mobile accounts, Ethiopia stands out as one of the lowest in the region (negligible percentage).

28.2.2 Evidence on Access to and Impact of Rural Finance

The evidence on the transformative role of access to finance has remained mixed, partly due to the methodological challenges of identifying impacts. Some studies have shown that access to rural finance improves livelihoods and boosts agricultural investments, including use of modern agricultural inputs (e.g. Giné and Yang 2009; Zerfu and Larson 2010; Abate et al. 2016); facilitates start-up of new enterprises (e.g. de Mel, McKenzie, and Woodruff 2008); and reduces poverty (Berhane and Gardebroek 2011).

Other studies find no or negligible impacts. Using the randomized control trial method on Indian MFI borrowers, Duflo et al. (2013) find no effect on consumption expenditures and related outcomes while documenting some impact on durable goods. They report that their results are largely consistent with four similar studies in different contexts. Others have argued that rural households may lack consumer education, training, and other complementary interventions to exploit existing financial products (Karlan and Valdivia 2011; Giné and Mansuri 2011; Karlan, Knight, and Udry 2012). For the case of Ethiopia, Amha and Peck (2010) argue that such skill gaps are contributing to the limited access to financial services. More broadly, despite the long-list of hopes, several empirical studies are not able to support such claims and the potential of MFIs to transform rural livelihood remains debatable. Rooyen, Stewart, and Wet (2012) provide a systematic review of the impact of microfinance in sub-Saharan Africa. They particularly review the impact of microfinance on various outcomes and conclude that 'microfinance does harm, as well as good, to the livelihoods of the poor' (Tarozzi, Desai, and Johnson 2015). Based on their systematic review, Rooyen, Stewart, and Wet (2012) highlight that the microfinance industry continues to grow in sub-Saharan Africa despite the 'deepening crisis'.

These findings highlight the lack of conclusive evidence on when and how microfinance can improve the livelihoods of poor rural households (Banerjee 2013). Banerjee (2013) notes that while we have some evolving evidence on the potential of microcredit, 'We still do not know why microcredit does not do more to transform the lives of its participants'. The discussion on rural financial markets has moved from access to finance to financial inclusion—the latter focusing on use of financial instruments rather than just access (Demirguc-Kunt et al. 2015).

In terms of access and financial inclusion, figures from the World Bank's global measure of financial inclusion are strikingly consistent with the results from household surveys and datasets considered in this study. First, CSA's nationally representative data show that about 23 per cent of households have reported having accessed financial services, mainly credit, in about the same year as shown by the World Bank data. Second, the figures from the household-level analysis show that about 6–10 per cent of households have actually used credit services each year in the period 2013–16 (covered by the surveys). As such, informal finance remains the most prevalent in rural Ethiopia: about 30 per cent of adults borrowed from family or friends (the SSA average for the latter was 42 per cent) in 2014. In the same year, about 48 per cent of adult Ethiopians saved in some form (formal and informal), but only about 14 per cent saved at a financial institution (the SSA average was 16 per cent). The rest was informal saving, including in 'under-the-mattress' savings. Mobile accounts have recently helped narrow the gap in account ownership in some parts of SSA.

28.2.3 Why Rural Financial Markets Can Fail

Providing financial services to poor rural households, as in the context of Ethiopia, is extremely difficult. A large literature points to rural financial market failures due to the imperfect information problem that prevents rural households from accessing these services (Stiglitz and Weiss 1981; Hoff and Stiglitz 1990). In the case of credit, for example, the information problem arises because lenders lack the critical information needed to screen the creditworthiness of potential borrowers and monitor them after loans are granted (Stiglitz and Weiss 1981).

Information asymmetry thus leads to the well-known problems of: (i) adverse selection, where lenders cannot discriminate against bad borrowers and thus simply raise interest rates to compensate for the risk they assume, which in turn drives deserving borrowers out of the credit market; and (ii) moral hazard, where lenders cannot observe the efforts and actions taken by the borrower once the loan is granted. Lenders thus have to incur high costs to determine the default risk for each borrower and ensure that borrowers take actions that make repayment most likely. In addition, transaction costs are high when working with poor rural communities dispersed over a large geographic area (higher than, for example, a single large transaction for a richer borrower) (Adams and Nehman 1979; Armendáriz and Morduch 2010), making lending costly. In response to these information and cost problems, lenders resort to requiring collateral providing borrowers with incentives to reduce the risk of failure to repay, which can theoretically address both adverse selection and moral hazard problems.

Collateral provides a guarantee to lenders without the lenders having to directly screen or monitor borrowers. Unfortunately, borrowers such as those in rural Ethiopia lack the collateral required by lenders. Since insurance markets also fail for the same reasons as credit markets fail, lenders are obliged either to set interest rates high, or simply restrict (exclude) potential borrowers who cannot pledge sufficient collateral (Conning and Udry 2007; Guirkinger and Boucher 2008). The coexistence of these two hurdles in rural financial markets—the information asymmetry among lenders and borrowers, and the poor's lack of collateral to pledge—leads to credit market failures often referred to as credit rationing (Conning and Udry 2007; Guirkinger and Boucher 2008; Boucher, Carter, and Guirkinger 2008; Armendáriz and Morduch 2010).

The literature identifies households not participating in the credit market as facing one or more of the three types of credit rationing at work in these contexts: quantity rationing, transaction cost rationing, and risk rationing. Quantity-rationed households are those that have a positive demand for credit but are unable to offer the required collateral to access supplied loans and are restricted by the credit limits set out by the lender or are totally excluded from the credit market for similar reasons. The transaction cost rationed are those for whom participation in the credit market has been made expensive due to the hassle of processing loans, or for whom costs related to screening, monitoring, and enforcement are high relative to the amount of loan required. Households are risk rationed when the risks involved in participation in the credit market are prohibitive in terms of indebtedness or potential loss of collateral in case of default.[5]

The arrival in recent years of MFIs that use the innovative method of group lending as a means to overcome these informational and collateral problems has been seen as a

[5] Unlike the first group, quantity rationed, which is involuntarily excluded, the latter two groups voluntarily refrain from participating in the credit market even if they have feasible projects that can be profitable in the absence of the information asymmetry problem.

beacon of hope for credit-constrained poor borrowers around the world (Armendáriz and Morduch 2010), including in Ethiopia.[6] A number of theoretical studies have proved that group lending does indeed address these problems by making group members jointly liable for each others' loans, which induces them to take advantage of the information they have about fellow members and use it to screen, monitor, and sanction each other to the lender's advantage. In the last four decades MFIs using group lending have flourished around the world, including in Ethiopia, with enormous support from donors and governments. However, given the covariance of production risk in rain-fed agriculture, where group members fail altogether when droughts hit, group lending introduces an additional layer of risk of having to bail out fellow group members (Berhane and Gardebroek 2008). In these contexts, group lending is very unpopular with borrowers (Berhane and Gardebroek 2008; Giné and Karlan 2009). This is a key challenge limiting the expansion of credible financial services to farm households in Ethiopia, as almost all MFIs in Ethiopia use group lending to extend credit in rural areas (Berhane and Gardebroek 2008).

In theory, this is not a problem as theoretical studies assume the presence of limited liability—borrowers are not liable beyond the project for which loans are taken. In practice, for example in Ethiopia, this is rarely the case, particularly in MFIs serving smallholders where identifying the project for which loans are used is difficult, and lenders, scared of setting bad precedents, force everyone to repay including when droughts hit. Clearly, this adds up to the risk-rationing problem discussed earlier, stifling demand for group-based credit. We return to this discussion later, highlighting the role of this additional layer of risk brought about by the inherent nature of agricultural production in Ethiopia, which potentially limits households from accessing loans available for agriculture. This has also posed a serious existential threat to MFIs, challenging their financial sustainability, given their mandate to serve the poorest of the poor. Recent anecdotal evidence indicates that MFIs are increasingly shifting their attention away from agriculture where they also require collateral.

Besides the above product-related bottlenecks, other demand-related attributes of rural households may contribute to the failure of rural financial markets. Some studies, for example, argue that rural households may lack the consumer education, training, and other complementary interventions to exploit existing financial products (Karlan and Valdivia 2011; Giné and Mansuri 2011; Karlan, Knight, and Udry 2012). These constraints and imperfections imply that the physical availability of rural finance may not mean it is used and several other factors may limit access to it. Consequently, the discussion on rural financial markets has moved from access to finance to financial inclusion—the latter focusing on the use of finance rather than just access to it (Demirguc-Kunt et al. 2015).

[6] Group lending refers to the formation of credit groups by individuals for the purpose of obtaining credit from lenders without collateral. An important feature of group lending is that loans are distributed to individual group members but that all group members are jointly liable for the total credit received by the group.

28.3 The Evolution of Rural Financial Markets in Ethiopia

The rural financial sector is dominated by microfinance institutions and rural savings and credit cooperatives, with commercial banks mostly serving urban populations. Ethiopia's rural financial markets have gone through turbulent trajectories—ranging from complete state control prior to the EPRDF to partial liberalization during the EPRDF period. Since the change of government in 1991, a number of steps have been taken to liberalize these markets in Ethiopia, ranging from creating enabling environments and designing legal provisions that allow microfinance institutions and member-based cooperatives to flourish, to the roles played to establish them. The development of the microfinance industry in Ethiopia has been largely state led, viewed solely as a tool to support other development programmes, with a strong focus on the very poor. To that extent, it can be argued that there is an Ethiopian model of microfinance that works and remains unique in terms of the operations and roles played by the state. For example, loans are small, with relatively longer terms—a minimum of one year—covering an agricultural season. Legal threats keep the default rate low—crucial to keep lending rates relatively lower (Berhane and Gardebroek 2012).

Unlike in many other countries with similar contexts, the Ethiopian microfinance industry is highly regulated (given also that most of the big MFIs are state affiliated). A major law was introduced in 1996 to regulate and supervise the behaviour of MFIs in Ethiopia. The National Bank of Ethiopia (NBE) is mandated to oversee the activities of MFIs, which are routinely checked for consumer protection and other transparency issues often considered sources of 'mission drift' in similar contexts. Regulation has also transformed the previously donor-funded, NGO-run, micro-credit programmes to business-oriented but regulated institutions, paving the way for profit-oriented, but smallholder-focused MFIs to flourish in rural Ethiopia. Currently, there are about 35 MFIs formally registered by the NBE, reaching several million borrowers and active clients. They provide conventional financial services, mainly credit and savings and, in some cases, credit-life insurance. The most common loan products offered include agricultural, micro-enterprise, equipment leasing, and housing loans. Agricultural loans account for more than 90 per cent of all loans (though they have declined in recent years), as almost all MFIs in the country are tasked with expanding credit access geared towards poverty reduction and agricultural transformation.

Figure 28.1, panels a–d, shows recent developments in the client base, loans, and savings of these MFIs. Between 2006 and 2016, the number of active borrowers increased from 1.3 to 3.7 million. The majority of these are smallholder agriculture borrowers. The size of the average loan per borrower grew nearly four-fold in the same period. Similarly, the level of savings mobilized from rural areas of Ethiopia grew twenty-fold (from about 600 million birr in 2006 to about 16.5 billion birr in 2016) with a substantial increase in savings per person, suggesting the enormous savings mobilization potential in these areas.

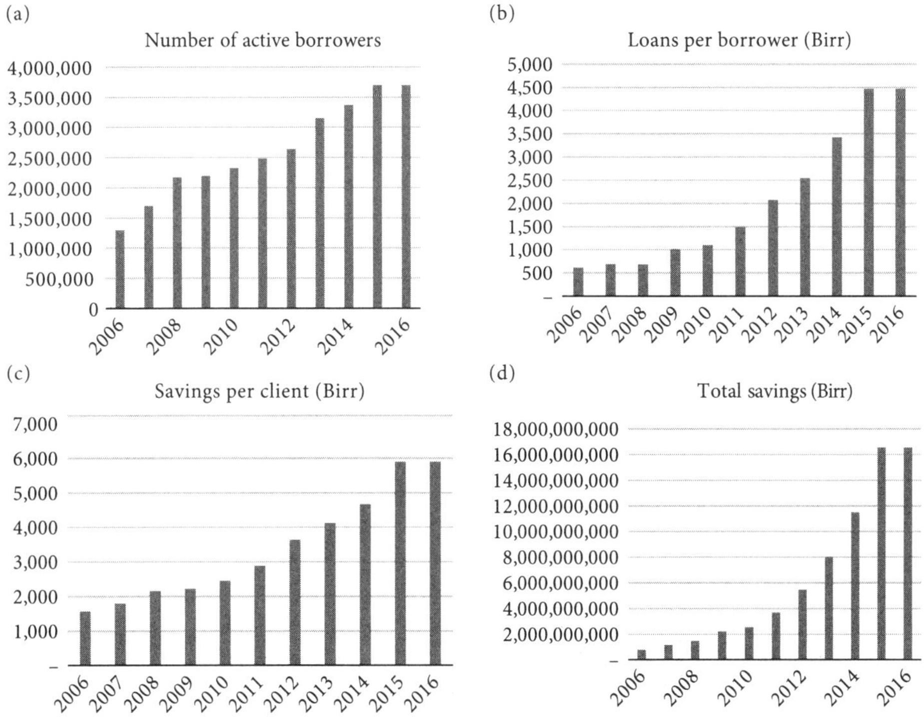

FIGURE 28.1 Number of borrowers, loans and savings per borrower, and total savings, 2006–16

Source: Compiled from AEMFI database accessed in 2017. http://www.aemfi-ethiopia.org

Considering these growth rates, many argue that in the last two to three decades Ethiopia has experienced a similar revolution in microfinance to the rest of the world. In fact, Ethiopia is now home to two of the largest MFIs in Africa, ACSI (Amhara Credit and Savings Institution) and DECSI (Dedebit Credit and Savings Institution), specializing in serving rural populations. In terms of lending approach, MFIs in Ethiopia focus on group-based lending and promote compulsory and voluntary savings. They use joint liability, social pressure, and compulsory savings as alternatives to conventional forms of collateral (Berhane 2009).

Other key players in the rural financial sector in Ethiopia are rural saving and credit cooperatives (RUSACCOs). Unlike other formal financial institutions (banks and MFIs), most saving and credit cooperatives are owned, controlled, and capitalized by their members. However, these savings and credit cooperatives provide conventional financial services, including credit, savings, and in some cases credit-life insurance services, to the poor in rural areas of Ethiopia. The Federal Cooperatives Agency (FCA) is mandated to oversee and supervise their functioning. RUSACCOs in Ethiopia cover a relatively smaller client base than MFIs and they deal with rural households and a clientele that most microfinances cannot reach.[7] As for MFIs, RUSACCOs in Ethiopia

[7] *Kebele* is the smallest administrative unit in Ethiopia, which may correspond to a group of villages.

have enjoyed a succession of unprecedented growth, both in numbers and membership base (see Abay et al. 2018). Currently, there are about 14,000 registered RUSACCOs serving more than 2.5 million rural households. In addition to deposit taking and credit service provision to their members, RUSACCOs sometimes serve as fertilizer distribution channels and are often subject to the heavy hand of government limiting their efficiency and innovation.

28.4 The Demand for and Supply of Rural Financial Services in Ethiopia

This section provides an overview of the current state of demand for and supply of rural financial markets in Ethiopia, with particular reference to credit markets and related financial products. Several household- and community-level datasets collected in the last few years will be used.

28.4.1 Data and Data Sources

We use three large household surveys to explore the functioning of rural financial markets in Ethiopia. These datasets contain interesting and complementary features. The first dataset has been collected to evaluate the Agricultural Growth Program (AGP)—a national growth programme implemented in 2011. Operating in the four main regions in Ethiopia (Tigray, Amhara, Oromia, and SNNP), it aims at improving agricultural productivity and commercialization of agricultural products in areas of Ethiopia with high potential. The second dataset comes from a survey evaluating the USAID's Feed the Future (FtF) programme in Ethiopia. FtF aims to address the root causes of global hunger by sustainably increasing agricultural productivity and facilitating rural households' access to market. FtF covers five regional states of Ethiopia, including Oromiya, Amhara, Tigray, SNNPR, and Somali. The third dataset comes from a large survey evaluating the Productive Safety Net Program (PSNP)—a flagship food security programme in Ethiopia. It covers food-insecure districts (*woredas*) and households in the four major regions: Tigray, Amhara, Oromia, and SNNP. All three large datasets were collected by the CSA in collaboration with the International Food Policy Research Institute (IFPRI). AGP covered about 7,500 households in 282 communities; FtF covered 7,000 households in 252 communities, and PSNP covered about 7,300 households in 252 communities. Community-level surveys formed part of each survey. With the AGP and FtF covering areas of high potential while the PSNP covers food-insecure and drought-prone areas, our data cover the two sides of Ethiopia, enabling us to assess a broader national picture.

28.4.2 Low Uptake of (Demand for) Credit Products

To assess the current demand for formal credit, Table 28.1 presents interesting evidence on the share of households who have been given credit by formal financial institutions in the last 12 months of the given survey years. The descriptive figures in Table 28.1 clearly show that a very small proportion of rural households (6–10 per cent) are participating in formal rural credit markets—in the form of borrowing. This implies that a vast majority of rural households in Ethiopia remain underserved by existing credit markets. Table 28.1 also suggests that there are substantial gender differences in households' access to financial services. Importantly, female-headed households have lesser access to formal credit. Clearly, these figures are in sharp contrast to the flourishing of MFIs in recent years and the enormous resources they mobilize to rural areas in the form of micro-loans. These figures are also in contrast to the commonly held view of a large potential demand remaining unmet (e.g. Wiedmaier-Pfister et al. 2008), and not consistent with the much-touted potential of rural finance to boost agricultural investments (e.g. Giné and Yang 2009; Zerfu and Larson 2010; Abate et al. 2016) and smooth consumption during drought (e.g. Berhane and Gardebroek 2011).

In what follows, we examine both the demand and supply sides of the credit market to assess potential explanations for such low credit market participation and empirical regularities that may contribute to this. From a supply point of view, we assess the availability of credit and savings institutions in individual villages (*kebeles*). Results from the community-level datasets confirm the existence of one or more MFIs in these communities. The figures in Table 28.2 suggest that lack of physical access to financial markets may not necessarily explain the low credit market participation.

The quest to explain the low demand for credit products therefore extends to the demand side of the credit market. Table 28.3 presents the disaggregated reasons for not participating in existing rural credit markets obtained from the three datasets. Four striking insights can be deduced from this descriptive evidence.

Table 28.1 Households' demand for credit from formal sources

	AGP (2013)			FtF (2013)			PSNP (2016)		
Data source	Full sample	Male headed	Female headed	Full sample	Male headed	Female Headed	Full sample	Male headed	Female headed
Households who took credit (%)	9.7	11.0	7.0	5.7	6.0	5.0	5.8	7.0	4.0
No. of observations	7512	5209	2303	6992	5039	1953	7287	5236	2051

Source: Authors' computation from AGP (2013), FtF (2013), and PSNP (2016) datasets.

Table 28.2 Availability of rural financial institutions in the community

Data source	AGP	FtF	PSNP
How many RUSACCOs operate in this *kebele*? (average)	2	3	1
How many microfinance institutions operate in this *kebele*? (average)	1	1	–
Is there a RUSACCO operating in this *kebele?* (% yes)	40	38	52
Is a microfinance institution operating in this *kebele?* (% yes)	17	18	–
Number of *kebeles* visited (a *kebele* per *woreda*)	282	252	252

Source: Authors' computation from AGP (2013), FtF (2013), and PSNP (2016) datasets.

Table 28.3 Reasons for not applying for loans from financial institutions

Data source	AGP	FtF	PSNP
Survey year	2013	2013	2016
Afraid of losing collateral/fear not able to pay back (%)	33.2	25.9	3.5
Afraid that I cannot pay back/don't like to be in debt (%)	25.3	27.9	26.5
No need for a loan/have adequate farm or business (%)	4.6	4.1	30.7
Tried to get loan but was refused/too much trouble (%)	9.4	10.9	5.6
No one available to get a loan from (%)	7.3	9.3	11.8
Expected to be rejected/assumed not to get loan	5.0	6.4	3.0
I have no asset/capacity for collateral (%)	4.2	4.7	9.2
Interest rates too high/too expensive (%)	5.0	3.5	4.9
Others (religious prohibition, has outstanding loan) (%)	5.3	7.3	4.8
I do not have farm or other business (%)	2.0	3.3	–
No. of observations	6,472	5,749	5,816

Source: Authors' computation from AGP (2013), FtF (2013), and PSNP (2016).

The most visible and consistent pattern in Table 28.3 is what can be summarized as households' risk aversion, and this appears to be the most important reason limiting households' participation in credit markets. In all datasets, large shares of households are not borrowing due to fear either of being in debt or of losing assets in case of default. More than half the households in the FtF and AGP data reported that credit risk and related risk of default are the major constraining factors. Intuitively, we can relate this type of credit rationing to three sources and market failures. First, information markets in developing countries are incomplete, leading to information asymmetry between lenders and borrowers (Stiglitz and Weiss 1981; Hoff and Stiglitz 1990). Lenders, lacking critical information needed to screen the creditworthiness of potential borrowers and monitor them after issuing loans (Stiglitz and Weiss 1981), usually resort to requiring collateral that can provide borrowers with an incentive to reduce default. Second, in contexts like rural Ethiopia, borrowers either lack the collateral required by lenders or operate in rain-fed agriculture involving covariance production risk that may endanger their collateral.[8] Third, insurance markets to deal with covariance production risk are not present in rural economies of the Ethiopian type. These multiple layers and market failures clearly introduce a problem of risk rationing that effectively limits households' participation in rural credit markets. The coexistence of these three hurdles in rural financial markets, therefore, leads to credit market failures often referred to as risk-related rationing.

The next insight is that, according to the PSNP data, about 30 per cent of households have no interest in credit products from financial institutions. This is a large fraction, especially given that this dataset covers poor rural households that are expected to be food insecure and prone to idiosyncratic shocks. Although more rigorous investigations are needed to explain these empirical patterns, we may speculate that there are at least three plausible explanations. First, the sample came from drought-prone areas with limited potential and returns to agricultural investments. However, given that these areas are drought prone, the demand for consumption smoothing and hence credit may be higher there. This is particularly plausible given the potential of microfinance to smooth consumption in the Ethiopian context (Berhane and Gardebroek 2011). Second, in contrast, the environment in which rural farmers in Ethiopia operate and associated market failures may effectively limit households' demand for credit. Third, rural households in these areas may lack the consumer education to exploit existing financial products (Karlan and Valdivia 2011; Giné and Mansuri 2011; Karlan, Knight, and Udry 2012). Amha and Peck (2010) argue that such skill gaps are contributing to the limited access to financial services in Ethiopia.

In addition to these two 'behavioural' and demand-related constraints, rural farmers in Ethiopia seem to face additional supply-related constraints. Around 20–25 per cent of households have no (or limited) access to financial institutions or other sources of credit. These households have been refused credit (or expected to be), or could not find potential lenders. Finally—an acknowledged and much-studied source of credit market failures—there are constraints related to the credit product itself, with some financial products requiring collateral and some involving high interest rates. In the Ethiopian context, rural households lack the collateral required by lenders, leading to the type of credit rationing we observe in our data (effective demand being less than potential demand for credit).

To sum up, while access to credit is supply driven, actual usage is determined by the interaction between demand and supply. The overall interaction between the supply and demand for credit defines the actual take-up of products. In our datasets, a large number of households do not have access to credit while another substantial share of households faces additional constraints that inhibit their credit market participation. As shown in Table 28.3, more than 70 per cent of the households from all datasets were credit

[8] To confirm this, we ran a simple regression to understand the effect of drought risk (rainfall variability) on demand for credit. Results (available on request) show that this variable significantly and negatively affects credit demand. This is consistent with the descriptive results, suggesting that the available group credit product is not attractive to borrowers, given the drought risk.

Table 28.4 Purposes for which credit is taken up

Purpose of loan	PSNP	AGP	FtF
Survey year	2016	2013	2015
To buy inputs: fertilizer/seed (%)	15.6	82	65
To buy livestock (%)	33.4	–	–
To start business/expand business (%)	23.7	4.5	7
To buy farm and other tools (%)	18.2	–	–
To pay off debt (%)	4.4	–	–
Other temporary purpose (build house, household expense) (%)	4.8	13	28
No. of observations	611	948	1,067

Source: Authors' computation from AGP (2013), FtF (2013), and PSNP (2016) datasets.

constrained, partly attributable to risk rationing, while some of it may be driven by transaction costs or price-related rationing.

In fact, the demand for loans depends on the self-financing potential, access to credit facilities and risk-taking ability of borrowers. Thus, it is worth assessing what households do with the loans and hence the sources of their demand for credit. Despite some variations across datasets, Table 28.4 indicates that a substantial share of households use credit to buy farm inputs. This is more the case for the datasets from the areas of high potential. This is consistent with the Ethiopian government's priority of providing credit for input use, partly to facilitate the adoption of agricultural technologies. Another significant share of households reported that they took out loans to finance non-farm activity and start/expand their business.

28.5 Concluding Remarks

The role of rural finance in transforming smallholder agriculture and livelihoods has recently received considerable attention globally. Providing financial access to the poorest is challenging as it requires small and fragmented loan transactions to be managed involving high monitoring and transaction costs.

To address the above informational and transaction costs, most MFIs and rural cooperatives have embraced group-based financial transactions. MFIs channel their financial services through groups to mitigate the informational and collateral challenges. This approach has been hailed as a breakthrough in the goal of transforming rural livelihoods and has been commonly applied all over the developing world in the last few decades.

Ethiopia has followed the same route since the early 1990s and 2000s, which has led to substantial expansion in its rural financial markets. This chapter has attempted to document Ethiopia's progress and the challenges of realizing the potential of this sector for transforming smallholders in rural Ethiopia. A notable phenomenon is that a number of MFIs and rural financial cooperatives have been established to serve rural areas of Ethiopia in the last three decades. Important to note is that these institutions were tasked with providing appropriate financial services to smallholders and hence supporting Ethiopia's ambitious agricultural development-led industrialization. The hope was that the age-old challenge of providing financial services to the majority of rural households in Ethiopia would be addressed once and for all. This in itself, together with political will, has substantially changed the rural financial market landscape and brought with it important opportunities.

However, despite the progress that has been made, the majority of rural households remain unbanked and beyond the reach of these services. The most recent evidence suggests that only about 22 per cent of adult Ethiopians held an account with any financial institution in 2014 (as compared to 29 per cent for SSA average) and that only 7 per cent borrowed from formal financial institutions. Out of these, only 12 per cent borrowed for a farm or business (the SSA average was 13 per cent). These findings are consistent with those obtained from household-level surveys. Despite recent initiatives, Ethiopia lags far behind the rest of Africa in mobile banking services; however, as most Ethiopians, even in remote rural areas, are now connected to mobile networks—thanks to the massive telecoms investment of recent years—this is an area in which the country could excel. Anecdotal evidence suggests that efforts to exploit this potential are already under way. Until then, informal finance continues to play an important role in rural Ethiopia.

A number of demand- and supply-side factors explain low credit market participation in Ethiopia. First, not all remote areas have closer access to any of these financial services: 7–12 per cent of households reported 'there was no one available to get a loan from'. Second is the credit product itself. Although innovative in some respects, the group lending approach simply transfers credit risk from the lender to the borrower, given that rain-fed agriculture fails for everybody when rain fails, creating an additional layer of risk associated with partners that they will have to assume. In fact, the majority of respondents that wanted to apply for loans but did not apply consistently mention 'fear of being indebted or losing own assets as collateral in case of default' as a main reason for not applying for loans.

Third, there are transaction costs, paperwork, and other intangible criteria used to screen applicants. Around 35–40 per cent of respondents stated, 'there was no need for a loan', explaining loans were expensive, limiting the pool of opportunities which otherwise would have been profitable. Fourth, products are inflexible—limited loan term and no flexibility for the borrower to negotiate defaults when faced with real challenges such as droughts. Most MFIs in Ethiopia have one-year agricultural loans running from planting season to the harvest season. Agricultural commodities are cheaper during harvest season, making production loans that mature in this period ex ante unattractive. Fifth, the loans offered by most MFIs are, in terms of size, meant for agricultural inputs, making them not only short maturing but also small. New start-ups, however, might require medium-sized loans for other transformational purposes. Such loans are available from formal banks, but they require collateral, which most medium-sized smallholders lack. This important group of emerging successful model farmers—which we can call the 'missing middle' of rural finance—is increasing in number given the progress in agriculture of recent years, and it is this group that is expected to transform small farming now and in the years to come.

In sum, despite the significant developments of recent years, rural finance in Ethiopia is lagging far behind, given the important roles it is expected to play in the transformation process. Further detailed studies are warranted to understand many of the issues outlined here as well as other issues limiting the sector's performance.

References

Abate, G. T., S. Rashid, C. Borzaga, and K. Getnet (2016). 'Rural Finance and Agricultural Technology Adoption in Ethiopia: Does the Institutional Design of Lending Organizations Matter?' *World Development* 84: 235–53.

Abay, K. A., G. A. Kahsay, and G. Berhane (2017). 'Social Networks and Factor Markets: Panel Data Evidence from Ethiopia', *Journal of Development Studies* DOI: http://dx.doi.org/10.1080/00220388.2017.1288224

Abay, K. A., B. Koru, G. A. Abate, and G. Berhane (2018). 'How Should Rural Financial Cooperatives Be Best Organized? Evidence from Ethiopia', ESSP Working Paper 100, IFPRI.

Adams, D. W. and G. I. Nehman (1979). 'Borrowing Costs and the Demand for Rural Credit', *Journal of Development Studies* 15 (2): 165–76.

Amha, W. and D. Peck (2010). 'Agricultural Finance Potential in Ethiopia: Constraints and Opportunities for Enhancing the System', AEMFI, Addis Ababa.

Armendáriz, B. and J. Morduch (2010). *The Economics of Microfinance* (Cambridge, MA: MIT Press).

Banerjee, A. (2013). 'Microcredit under the Microscope: What Have We Learnt in the Last Two Decades, What Do We Need to Know?' *Annual Review of Economics* 5: 487–519.

Beck, T., A. Demirguc-Kunt, and M. S. M. Peria (2007). 'Reaching out: Access to and Use of Banking Services across Countries', *Journal of Financial Economics* 85 (1): 234–66.

Berhane, G. (2009). 'Econometric Analyses of Microfinance Credit Group Formation, Contractual Risks and Welfare Impacts in Northern Ethiopia', PhD thesis, Wageningen University.

Berhane, G. and C. Gardebroek (2008). 'Joint-Liability Borrowing Decisions under Risk: Empirical Evidence from Rural Microfinance in Ethiopia', 2008 International Congress, European Association of Agricultural Economists, 26–29 August, Ghent, Belgium.

Berhane, G. and C. Gardebroek (2011). 'Does Microfinance Reduce Rural Poverty? Evidence Based on Household Panel Data from Northern Ethiopia', *American Journal of Agricultural Economics* 93 (1): 43–55.

Berhane, G. and C. Gardebroek (2012). 'Assessing the Long-Term Impact of Microcredit on Rural Poverty: Does the Timing and Length of Participation Matter?' ESSP Working Paper No. 43, International Food Policy Research Institute (IFPRI).

Bernard, T., A. S. Taffesse, and E. Z. Gebre-Medhin (2008). 'Impact of Cooperatives on Smallholders' Commercialization Behavior: Evidence from Ethiopia', *Agricultural Economics* 39: 147–61.

Boucher, S. R., M. R. Carter, and C. Guirkinger (2008). 'Risk Rationing and Wealth Effects in Credit Markets: Theory and Implications for Agricultural Development', *American Journal of Agricultural Economics* 90 (2): 409–23.

Burgess, R., R. Pande, and G. Wong (2005). 'Banking for the Poor: Evidence from India', *Journal of the European Economic Association* 3 (2–3): 268–78.

Conning, J. and C. Udry (2007). 'Rural Financial Markets in Developing Countries', *Handbook of Agricultural Economics* 3: 2857–908.

De Mel, S., D. McKenzie, and C. Woodruff (2008). 'Returns to Capital in Microenterprises: Evidence from a Field Experiment', *Quarterly Journal of Economics* 123 (4): 1329–72.

Demirguc-Kunt, A., Leora Klapper, Dorothe Singer, and Peter Van Oudheusden (2015). 'The Global Findex Database 2014: Measuring Financial Inclusion around the World', World Bank Policy Research Working Paper, Washington, DC.

Dercon, S. (1996). 'Risk, Crop Choice, and Savings: Evidence from Tanzania', *Economic Development and Cultural Change* 44 (3): 485–513.

Dercon, S. (2004). 'Growth and Shocks: Evidence from Rural Ethiopia', *Journal of Development Economics* 74 (2): 309–29.

Dercon, S. and L. Christiaensen (2011). 'Consumption Risk, Technology Adoption and Poverty Traps: Evidence from Ethiopia', *Journal of Development Economics* 96 (2): 159–73.

Duflo, E., A. Banerjee, R. Glennerster, and C. Kinnan (2013). 'The Miracle of Microfinance? Evidence from a Randomized Evaluation', NBER Working Paper 18950, NBER, Cambridge, MA.

Duflo, E., M. Kremer, and J. Robinson (2008). 'How High Are Rates of Return to Fertilizer? Evidence from Field Experiments in Kenya', *American Economic Review Papers and Proceedings* 98 (2): 482–8.

Giné, X. and D. S. Karlan (2009). 'Group versus Individual Liability: Long-Term Evidence from Philippine Microcredit Lending Groups', *Journal of Development Economics* 107: 65–83.

Giné, X. and G. Mansuri (2011). 'Money or Ideas? A field Experiment on Constraints to Entrepreneurship in Rural Pakistan', manuscript, World Bank, Washington, DC.

Giné, X. and D. Yang (2009). 'Insurance, Credit and Technology Adoption: Field Experimental Evidence from Malawi', *Journal of Development Economics* 89 (1):1–11.

Guirkinger, C. and S. R. Boucher (2008). 'Credit Constraints and Productivity in Peruvian Agriculture', *Agricultural Economics* 39 (3): 295–308.

Hoff, K. and J. E. Stiglitz (1990). 'Introduction: Imperfect Information and Rural Credit Markets: Puzzles and Policy Perspectives', *World Bank Economic Review* 4: 235–50.

Jayne, T. S., I. J. Minde, and J. Argwings-Kodhek (2002). *Perspectives on Agricultural Transformation: A View from Africa* (New York: Nova Science Publishers).

Karlan, D. and M. Valdivia (2011). 'Teaching Entrepreneurship: Impact of Business Training on Microfinance Clients and Institutions', *Review of Economics and Statistics* 93 (2): 510–27.

Karlan, D., R. Knight and C. Udry (2012). 'Hoping to Win, Expected to Lose: Theory and Lessons on Micro Enterprise Development', *NBER* Working Paper 18325, Cambridge, MA.

Karlan, D. and S. Mullainathan (2007). 'Rigidity in Microfinancing: Can One Size Fit All?' Qfinance.http://www.qfinance.com/financing-best-practice/rigidity-in-microfinancing-can-one-size-fitall?page=1

Morduch, J. (1990). 'Risk, Production and Saving: Theory and Evidence from Indian Households', manuscript, Harvard University.

Morduch, Jonathan and Dean S. Karlan (2009). 'Access to Finance', NYU Wagner Research Paper No. 2011-03. https://ssrn.com/abstract=1871922

Mullainathan, S. and E. Shafir (2013). *Scarcity: Why Having Too Little Means So Much* (New York: Times Books).

Rooyen, C. V., R. Stewart, and T. D. Wet (2012). 'The Impact of Microfinance in Sub-Saharan Africa: A Systematic Review of the Evidence', *World Development* 40 (11): 2249–62.

Stiglitz, J. and A. Weiss (1981). 'Credit Rationing in Markets with Imperfect Information', *American Economic Review* 71 (3): 393–410.

Tarozzi, A., J. Desai, and K. Johnson (2015). 'The Impacts of Microcredit: Evidence from Ethiopia', *American Economic Journal: Applied Economics* 7: 54–89.

Wiedmaier-Pfister, M., D. Gesesse, W. Amha, et al. (2008). 'Access to Finance in Ethiopia', *Sector Assessment Study* 2, German Organisation for Technical Cooperation (GTZ).

Yunus, M. (2006). Nobel Lecture. Oslo, Norway.

Zerfu, D. and D. F. Larson (2010). 'Incomplete Markets and Fertilizer Use: Evidence from Ethiopia', Policy Research Working Paper No. 5235, World Bank, Washington, DC.

CHAPTER 29

PERFORMANCE AND INSTITUTIONS OF THE ETHIOPIAN COFFEE SECTOR

BART MINTEN, FLORIAN T. SCHÄFER,
AND TADESSE KUMA WORAKO

29.1 Introduction

The people of Ethiopia have enjoyed a long and storied relationship with coffee, and the production and consumption of coffee continues to hold great economic, social, and cultural significance. Although the share of coffee in total exports has dropped in the last decade, it is still the largest single contributor to export earnings, accounting for 30 per cent of total exports in 2016/17 (NBE 2018). This chapter provides an overview of the Ethiopian coffee sector, with a particular emphasis on the organization of production and trade. Our central argument is that, despite the importance of coffee to both the Ethiopian macro-economy and the livelihoods of many Ethiopians, the coffee sector has received only inconsistent attention from successive governments. Most regimes have been more interested in imposing control over the coffee trade and attendant revenues than in sustainably raising the productive capacity of the sector, both in terms of quality and of quantity. As a result the coffee sector has suffered from both policy neglect and reform efforts that were ill suited to the needs of Ethiopian coffee producers.

29.2 Ethiopia's Place in the World Market

To understand the coffee sector in Ethiopia, it is useful to take a brief look at the world market for coffee. Ethiopia is a comparatively small exporter. Ethiopian coffees are nonetheless accorded a special place in the global coffee trade, due to their high potential quality and their genetic variety. As the likely origin of the *Coffea Arabica* plant (Wellman 1961; Wrighley 1988), the remnants of Ethiopia's coffee forests contain a treasure trove of natural coffee varieties that can provide a vital diversification of the genetic base the global coffee industry relies upon (Aerts et al. 2013; Laboussie et al. 2008). Arabica coffee is the backbone of the global coffee trade, typically accounting for around 60 per cent of global production (ICO 2016).

Global coffee production in 2016 was worth around US$29bn.[1] The coffee sector in producing countries alone was estimated to be employing around 26 million people.[2] Coffee is grown mostly by smallholder farmers, but also on large-scale plantations. Both smallholder farms and plantations vary widely in size both across and within countries. Coffee cherries are picked and the beans are processed into green (i.e. unroasted) coffee, before being graded and packed either by producing-country exporters or by consuming-country importers, depending on the country in question. In Ethiopia, all coffee is by law exported by domestically owned firms. After the green bean stage, the other steps in creating the final product bought by consumers (notably blending, roasting, packaging, and distribution) predominantly occur in consuming countries (ITC 2011).

The contemporary global coffee market is highly concentrated, both in terms of market actors and in terms of the spatial distribution of consumption. A few large multinational enterprises control much of the import and roasting stages of the value chain. Panhuysen and Pierrot (2014) estimated the market share of the ten largest roasters at 40 per cent of all coffee consumed worldwide, and more than half of global coffee exports go to the European Union and the United States (USDA 2017). On the supply side, coffee production is dominated by Brazil. In 2016/17 Brazil produced 56 million 60kg bags of coffee, of which it exported 34.3 million, which in 2016 accounted for about 35 per cent of global production and around 28 per cent of global exports. Ethiopia's production in the market year 2016/17 was estimated at around 6.6 million bags (ICO 2016). The sizeable domestic consumption of coffee in Ethiopia means that only part of the production is exported, making Ethiopia only the ninth largest exporter in the world, while Uganda is seventh (USDA 2017).

[1] Estimated using production data from ICO (2016) and price data from the World Bank (2016).

[2] http://www.thecoffeeguide.org/coffee-guide/world-coffee-trade/world-coffee-exports—basic-figures/ (accessed 28 October 2018)

29.3 Coffee Production Systems in Ethiopia

Ethiopia is home to a number of unique coffee varieties. The country is endowed with a good production environment for growing coffee with a combination of appropriate altitude, temperature, rainfall, soil type, and pH characteristics. Ethiopia produces a range of distinctive Arabica coffees and has considerable potential to sell a large number of specialty coffees (Nure 2008).[3] Wild Arabica coffee forests still occur in eight demarcated areas: Kaffa (Boginda Yeba), Illubabor-yayo (Geba-Dogi), Bench Maji (Harena), Bench Maji (Kontir Berrhan), Sheka (Amora Gedel), Kellem Wollega (Dawo tobi), Jimma (Belete-Gera), and Kaffa (Mankira) on the southern Ethiopian highland plateau, four of which have been registered by UNESCO. At the turn of the millennium about 95,400 ha of wild coffee forests still remained in Ethiopia (Feyera and Denich 2006). The major commercial coffee cultivation areas are located in the southern, southwestern, and eastern parts of the country (Map 29.1). The southwestern coffee-producing regions cover Illubabor, Wollega, Jimma, Kaffa, Sheka, and Bench Maji. The southern coffee-growing regions include Sidama, Gedeo, Borena, Wolayta, Gamo Goffa, Kambata Alaba Tambaro, Gurage, and others. The eastern coffee-growing region comprises Hararghe, Arsi, and Bale. These three major coffee-producing areas account for the lion's share of national commercial coffee production. Thus most coffee production in Ethiopia is concentrated in two regions—Oromia and the Southern Nations, Nationalities, and People Regions. Apart from these main coffee-growing regions there are small patches of coffee production to the west (Gambella and Benishangul Gumuz) and the north (Amhara and Tigray) that grow coffee mainly for own consumption.

While the origins of coffee consumption in Ethiopia are shrouded in myths, the country has exported wild coffee, gathered from naturally occurring coffee trees in its Afromontane forests, since at least the sixteenth century (Aregay 1988). Commercial coffee farms in the modern sense are much younger, though. The first experiments with large-scale coffee farms were undertaken by quasi-feudal landlords in the mid-nineteenth century (Gemeda 1994; see also Chapter 30).[4] After World War II, both large-scale plantations and share-cropping by tenant farmers became more widely established in the south, often at the behest of imperial landlords. They were aided by Emperor Haile Selassie's policy of opening and modernizing the economy, which brought inflows of

[3] High-quality coffees are called specialty. The Specialty Coffee Association of America (SCAA) defines specialty coffee in its green stage as coffee that is free of primary defects, contains no unripe beans, is properly sized and dried, is free of faults and taints, and has distinctive attributes (Rhinehart 2017). Such coffees can command premium prices in the global market.

[4] Ellis (1976) argues convincingly that the feudal paradigm fails to provide a good description of imperial Ethiopia.

capital and technical assistance. These large-scale coffee plantations were important pioneers in the use of agricultural wage labour in Ethiopia (Negash 2017).

Today coffee is produced under several types of production systems, including forest, semi-forest, garden, and plantation coffee. Forest coffee is grown in the wild under natural forest cover and is gathered by farmers from trees that receive only minor maintenance. Semi-forest coffee is also grown in forest conditions, but there is some maintenance by farmers, mostly annual weeding. This type of coffee has clearly delineated boundaries of ownership, although the trees are usually located away from agricultural plots. Garden coffee is defined as coffee from trees planted by farmers in the vicinity of their residences. It is often intercropped with other crops or trees. Plantation coffee is grown on large commercial farms. Modern production practices—such as irrigation, modern input use, mulching, stumping, and pruning—are often applied in this case. While the Derg had established large state-owned plantations, these have slowly been privatized since the end of 2009. Minten et al. (2014) estimate that by 2013 the private sector was responsible for almost 90 per cent of coffee exports and by 2014 the last state farms had been transferred into private hands.

The vast majority of Ethiopian coffee is produced by smallholder farmers. The gathering of wild coffee goes back to prehistoric times (Stellmacher 2007), though in contemporary times purposive growing methods predominate. Reliable statistics on the shares of different production, and in particular the shares of small-scale and large-scale farms,

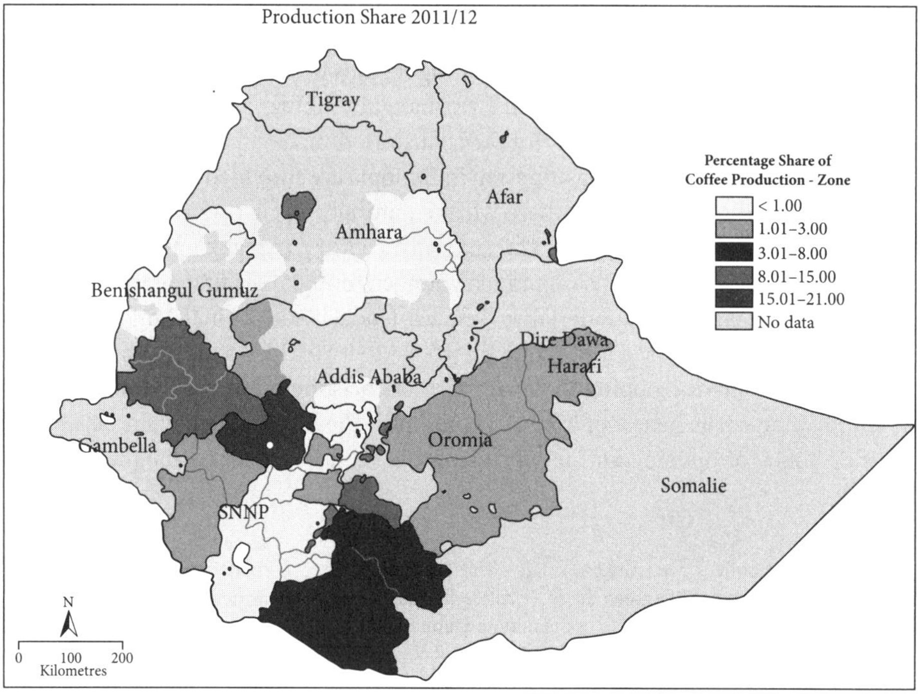

MAP 29.1 Location of coffee production in Ethiopia

Source: Authors' calculations based on data from the Central Statistical Agency (CSA).

are lacking, but Schäfer (see Chapter 30) uses CSA data to estimate smallholders' land share at around 85 per cent.

According to data from the Central Statistical Authority (2017), 5.3 million farm households produce most of Ethiopia's coffee. Land holdings within the smallholder category vary greatly in size, albeit within relatively narrow confines, and there is substantial inequality among farmers. A census in 80 coffee-producing villages conducted by Minten et al. (2014) found that 63 per cent of farmers hold coffee land of less than half a hectare and around 40 per cent hold less than a quarter hectare. However, these holdings account for less than 25 per cent of the coffee land in the area, and the remaining 75 per cent of land is held by just 37 per cent of the farmers. The 15 per cent of farmers who hold more than one hectare each control 47 per cent of the coffee land, while the richest 0.3 per cent of farmers, those who hold between 5 and 10 hectares each, collectively farm 3.4 per cent of the land. In short, most farmers hold only very small quantities of land but most of the land is held by relatively large farmers.

Smallholder farmers in major coffee-producing areas rely on coffee income as an important source of their livelihood, though the degree of reliance is highly variable, with estimates for the share of coffee income in total household incomes ranging from 37 per cent (Worako, Dejene, and Minten 2015) to 73 per cent (Jena et al. 2012) across different areas. Moreover, coffee production is labour intensive during harvesting and processing and provides an important source of income from casual labour for many poor rural households (Cramer et al. 2014; Rizzo 2011). Any fluctuation in earnings due to price or production shocks therefore affects the welfare of large numbers of smallholders, agricultural wage labourers, and their families, who face substantial price risks and have limited ability to mitigate these (Tröster and Staritz 2015).

29.4 Overview of Production, Consumption, and Export

Figure 29.1 illustrates how coffee exports from Ethiopia have performed over the last decade. In real 2016 US$, the value of coffee exports in 2016 was 107 per cent higher than in 2004, having increased from US$425m to US$882m (Figure 29.1). Part of that increase is explained by a significant rise in international prices of coffee but quantities exported from Ethiopia did also increase during the same period from 148 to 225 thousand tons, a 53 per cent increase. Figure 29.1 further shows a large increase in national coffee production, based on official national statistics. This has been a result mostly of increasing expansion of the coffee area, rather than through yield increases, as illustrated by the similar developments in production and area expansion over the last decade. Taken together, the production and export figures indicate high levels of coffee consumption within Ethiopia, usually about half of the production.

The official data on the Ethiopian coffee sector, however, should be treated with caution as they show large and unexplained fluctuations. For instance, the CSA data on

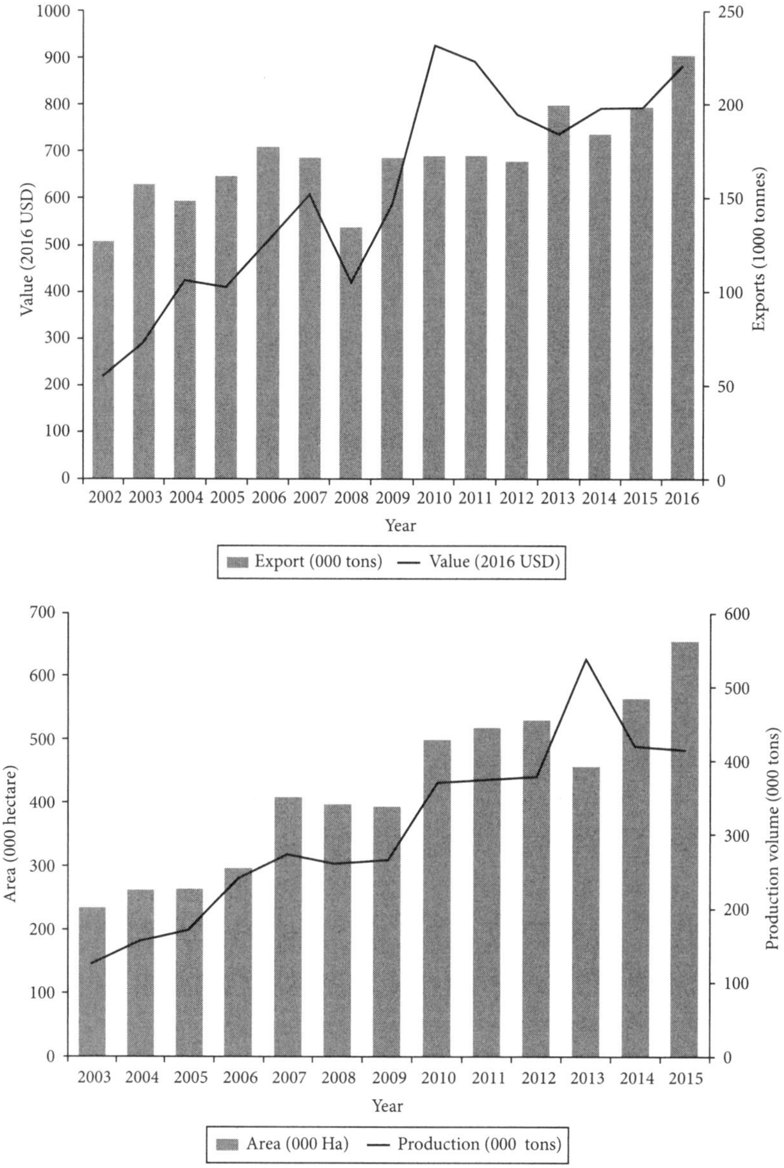

FIGURE 29.1 National coffee export and production performance of Ethiopian smallholder coffee producers

Source: Authors' calculations from NBE (2018) and CSA (2016).

coffee area shown in Figure 29.1 indicate that the total coffee-growing area expanded by almost a third from 2006 to 2007 and then by over a quarter from 2009 to 2010 and production data record an increase of almost a third from 2012 to 2013, while the total coffee area apparently contracted that same year. It is not immediately clear what could have caused such changes.

While quantities matter, coffee quality is a key determinant of prices in coffee markets. Quality is partly intrinsic to variety and microclimate, but can be improved in a number of ways. First, there are two methods for harvesting coffee, selective and strip harvesting. Selective harvesting reduces the number of unripe green berries in the harvested coffee, leading to a more homogeneous and higher-quality product. By contrast, strip harvesting—where coffee branches are grabbed and pulled outward—produces lots with various levels of matured coffee, leading to mixed bean batches and a lower-quality product. Strip harvesting appears to no longer be much practised in Ethiopia (Minten et al. forthcoming).

Second, two different procedures can be used to process coffee cherries into beans: wet and dry processing. The quality of coffee can generally be increased by washing, i.e. processing red cherries immediately after harvest in 'wet mills', instead of sun-drying the cherries (Nure 2008). Washed coffee preserves the intrinsic quality of the bean better than unwashed beans, and the process leads to homogeneous coffee with fewer defective beans. Coffee that is processed in this way is sold at significantly higher prices in international markets.[5] Over time, there has been an increasing shift from unwashed to washed coffee in Ethiopia. For example, Petit (2007) showed that washed coffee made up only 9 per cent of total coffee exports in 1980, but by 2005 this share had increased to 33 per cent. However, the share has stabilized over the last decade.

Third, the geographic origin of coffee is an important quality consideration, as it is strongly related to taste. Kufa (2012) associates tastes and regions across the five major coffee types that are exported from Ethiopia as follows: spicy for Sidama, fruity for Wollega (Nekempt), floral for Yirgacheffe, winey for Limu and Jimma, and mocha for Harar.

Fourth, and of particular importance for the coffee sector of Ethiopia, is the international market for high-quality, or specialty, coffee. In the specialty coffee trade, coffees generally have to be traceable back to the processing station at which they were produced, as premium prices are charged for these coffees by retailers both for the intrinsic quality of the coffee and on the 'symbolic value' attributed to specialty coffees (Ponte 2002; Daviron and Ponte 2005). Plantations mostly possess their own processing stations, while smaller farms either deliver their cherries to processing stations owned by local traders or cooperatives, or process the coffee themselves by sun-drying. Without such traceability, specialty roasters find it more difficult to charge premium prices for their coffee. Knowing where a coffee was produced also enables exporters and foreign buyers to establish direct business relations with producers. Through these they can provide the incentives for producers to increase or maintain the quality of their product, in particular with regard to harvesting and processing practices. Careful processing is vital to producing high-quality coffees and in the specialty market premium prices can be fetched for both washed and sundried coffee varieties.

[5] Although there are exceptions to this in the specialty market, see later in the chapter.

29.5 The Institutions of the Ethiopian Coffee Sector

The institutions that govern economic interactions in the Ethiopian coffee sector, internally as well as externally, are a key determinant both of its overall performance and of the distribution of gains across the different sector actors. In modern times the Ethiopian state has taken an increasingly active role in shaping these institutions. Since the imperial era, coffee has constituted an important pillar of the Ethiopian fiscal state and the regulation of the coffee sector has been a key concern of every Ethiopian regime since the late nineteenth century. The important contribution of coffee to foreign exchange generation, and thereby to the state- and war-making abilities of Ethiopian political elites, meant that coffee-sector institutions have generally been oriented towards guaranteeing these revenues by facilitating exports and enabling taxation. In practice this has meant a focus on controlling the flow of coffee from producing areas to auctions, controlling the quality assessment systems to make sure exportable coffee is actually exported, and controlling the taxation of sales. Much less effort has generally been put into increasing the productivity of coffee farmers, increasing the quality of Ethiopian coffees, and marketing Ethiopian coffee abroad through building domestic skills and targeted advertisement campaigns.

The first national-level coffee-sector institutions were founded in the late imperial era. In imperial times, coffee exports peaked at 65 per cent of total export revenues in 1964 (CTDMA 1978) and by 1969, coffee was generating 6 per cent of all tax revenue of the Ethiopian state (Love 2001). In the late nineteenth and early twentieth century the imperial centre came to increasingly rely on revenues generated by coffee plantations established after the military conquest of the southern highland periphery (McCann 1995; McClellan 1986). The imperial government in 1957 founded a National Coffee Board and established official coffee auctions at Addis Ababa and Dire Dawa (Berhe 2010). The government also instituted a licencing system for all actors in the coffee sector, elements of which continued to exist even into the twenty-first century (Petit 2007). In this period, coffee marketing, including exports, was completely in private hands. Suppliers processed coffee up to export standard and directly delivered their coffee to exporters' warehouses. Thus, coffee origin was easily traceable.

The state-socialist military dictatorship of the Derg imposed direct government control over the sector and transferred the exclusive right to store and trade coffee to the state in 1975. Private coffee-processing stations and the large-scale coffee farms were nationalized or given to newly formed peasant associations (*kebeles*). Washing stations became the property of rural service cooperatives. In 1978 the government created the Coffee Marketing Corporation (CMC), which dominated the entire coffee marketing chain and bought most of the country's coffee. By the end of the Derg regime, only fourteen private exporters remained active (ICO 2000a). The Derg taxed both production and sale of coffee, both through direct taxation and the manipulation of prices. By 1978 coffee taxes constituted around 30 per cent of all government revenue, but productivity had fallen and the large state farms were operating at a loss (Griffin 1992).

In 1991 the incoming transitional government, and later the EPRDF regime, inherited the institutional framework put in place by the Derg. In 1992 the EPRDF began what has been called a 'tightly regulated liberalization' of the coffee sector, which lasted until 2008 (Schäfer 2016). Direct government control over much of the sector was relinquished in favour of a market system dominated by private actors. While the state farms were initially kept in public ownership, these produced less than 5 per cent of Ethiopia's coffee during the 1990s and early 2000s (USAID 2010). Private capital was allowed to flourish in all parts of the value chain, including processing, trading, export, and the production of coffee.

The vacuum left by the withdrawal of the CMC's purchasing privileges drew new participants into the market. By 2008 there were 104 active private exporters (Berhe 2010) and private capital soon handled 85 per cent of all coffee at the country's coffee auction (ICO 2000b). The government retained control over the sector by maintaining a strict licencing system and setting minimum export prices (Love 2001). While the reforms were successful in raising producer prices (ICO 2000b), the marketing system was beset with problems, from finance through grading credibility to logistics (ECEA 2008), and price volatility increased, posing a risk especially for smaller and more vulnerable producers (Gemech and Struthers 2007).

Ethiopia's regulatory landscape changed dramatically in August 2008, when a new government proclamation meant that all of the country's coffee had to be graded by, and sold through, the Ethiopian Commodity Exchange (ECX). The ECX was based on the notion that the fundamental problems in Ethiopian agricultural markets were a lack of information available to participants and high transaction costs that inhibited the spread of enforceable contracts. These ideas draw on an intellectual tradition that goes back to von Mises and von Hayek's ideas about prices as transmission mechanisms for information, and the work of Coase and the new institutional economists about economic order (Gebre-Madhin and Goggin 2005). The introduction of the ECX was supposed to be the institutional fix necessary to bring about an efficient and self-regulating market for coffee in Ethiopia (Gebre-Madhin 2012). The old coffee auctions in Addis Ababa and Dire Dawa were abolished. The ECX had been set up earlier that year as a modern trading platform for certain agricultural commodities. It is organized around an open 'outcry' auction in Addis Ababa, where buyers and sellers could trade 'lots' of commodities using standardized contracts and grades. The trading platform itself is built on a network of warehouses in nine major coffee-producing areas where primary quality inspection, grading, and warehousing services are provided. Once quality inspection and grading has been carried out, suppliers can deposit their goods against electronically registered warehouse receipts.

The introduction of the ECX into the Ethiopian coffee trading system created significant changes in the local coffee trade. The ECX was, as acknowledged by its founders (Gebre-Madhin 2012), not logistically prepared for handling the nation's coffee, which led to substantial delays in warehousing operations. More damaging, though, were a number of design flaws that made the exchange system ill-suited to trading high-quality coffees. At the ECX coffee is bought anonymously, i.e. based only on the broad locality of origin and the assigned grade—the producer of the coffee is not disclosed to the buyer. The ECX system thereby severed the link between the processing station and the purchaser, undermining the traceability that is an important feature of high-quality coffees, which was particularly damaging to the specialty coffee sector. The lack of traceability removed a key element for determining the value of such coffees in international markets.

In the wake of these reforms, the coffee sector did not perform as anticipated by the government of Ethiopia. In particular exports lagged behind the official high targets as laid out in the ambitious first Growth and Transformation Plan. In response to the perceived failings of the sector, the government eventually embarked on a series of regulatory reforms. It created a single regulatory agency to coordinate coffee production, overhauled the warehousing and grading systems, eased ECX rules to allow easier access for both buyers and sellers, and increased agronomic research efforts. Most importantly, as long as a quality standard for exports was obtained, individual coffee growers and plantations were given the right to directly export coffee from their farm, effectively making the use of the ECX for them voluntary.

29.6 New Forms of Production and Marketing

While coffee production continues to be dominated by smallholder farmers, more production is taking place on large-scale private plantations (see Chapter 30 for details) and smallholders are increasingly joining marketing and production cooperatives. Both of these comparatively new ways of organizing production are important because of their potential to penetrate international niche markets for coffee, where large price premiums can be achieved for coffee that is of particularly high quality or carries sustainability certification. Policymakers have in the past granted marketing privileges to both plantations and cooperatives but have otherwise offered little support for upgrading productivity or quality.

While the share of cooperatives is small, it is increasing over time, albeit from a low base, growing from 4.5 to 6.4 per cent of total exports between 2007 and 2016. The most important cooperative involved in coffee exports is the Oromia Coffee Farmers Cooperative Union, which over this period typically accounted for about 60 per cent of the export transactions made by cooperatives. Other important cooperatives include the Yirgacheffe, Sidama, and Kafa Forest Coffee Cooperatives. It was estimated in 2015 that there were 465 primary cooperatives in Ethiopia (Minten et al. 2015). These primary cooperatives are organized in seven cooperative unions (Table 29.1).

One important new development in international coffee markets is the growing emphasis on voluntary sustainability standards (VSSs) and their certification, seemingly at least in part a response to enhanced global social and environmental pressure (Giovannucci, von Hagen, and Wozniak 2014; Swinnen 2007). International buyers and

Table 29.1 Number of VSS-certified primary cooperatives, 2014

Cooperative unions	Number of primary cooperatives	Number of certified primary cooperatives				
		Any VSS certificate	Type of VSS			
			Organic	Fairtrade	Rainforest Alliance	Utz Certified
Sidama	47	42	39	41	3	5
Yirgacheffe	26	26	26	26	3	2
Oromia	250	41	24	41	3	3
Limmu Inara	27	16	16	5	0	0
Wolaita Damota	42	10	10	0	0	0
Kaffa	34	19	18	15	0	0
Bench Maji	39	3	3	0	0	0
Total	465	157	136	128	9	10

Source: Minten et al. (2015).

consumers are increasingly willing to pay extra for coffee that claims to guarantee the product origin, fairer prices to producers, more ethical standards of production and processing, environmental sustainability, and more stringent safety and quality safeguards. In Ethiopia VSS certification of coffee is a relatively new phenomenon. In 2010 only one certifier in the whole country was accredited to issue these certificates. Since 2006, the country has, however, attracted several international certifiers including for Fairtrade, Organic, Utz Certified, and Rainforest Alliance. While only eighteen cooperatives were Fairtrade certified in 2003, by 2013 a total of 111 cooperatives were certified to export their coffee under Fairtrade. Organic certification is also widely implemented by these cooperatives. However, the adoption of VSS certificates in Ethiopia has been significantly below world averages. It is estimated that VSS-certified exported coffee from Ethiopia made up just 6 per cent in 2015, up from 2 per cent in 2005. Significantly, most of the VSS-certified coffee is exported by cooperatives and VSS-certified coffee accounted for around 75 per cent of all exports by cooperatives over the period 2011–13. While private firms also export VSS-certified coffee, their share of the total exports of certified coffee from Ethiopia is relatively small, just 12 per cent in 2013.

Table 29.1 gives an overview of the different types of VSS certification held by Ethiopian cooperatives. About one-third of the primary coffee cooperatives in Ethiopia have some type of VSS certification. Organic certification is the dominant one, covering 29 per cent of all primary coffee cooperatives. The next most important VSS certification in Ethiopia is Fairtrade. The other two main types of certificates found in Ethiopia, Rainforest Alliance and Utz Certified, are much less widely adopted.[6] Out of all the cooperatives, just 2 per cent are certified with one or the other. An important issue, internationally and locally, is the extent to which producers benefit from this drive

[6] Utz and Rainforest Alliance merged into a single certification system in 2017.

towards certification. Based on large datasets at the producer level, Minten et al. (2018) find that certification has little impact on the welfare of the average coffee farmer. Similarly, a systematic review of the international evidence also cast doubt on the ability of agricultural VSS systems to raise household incomes (Oya et al. 2017), while Cramer et al. (2016) found that Fairtrade certification made no positive difference to wage workers in coffee production in Ethiopia compared to production in non-certified research sites.

29.7 Governance Issues and Prospects for Transformation

The Ethiopian coffee sector faces a series of major challenges, all of which will require concerted policy support to address. These are the threat posed by climate change, the nexus of problems caused by low productivity, and the lack of reliable data on the sector, which serves to greatly impede sector governance.

Arabica coffees, both globally and in Ethiopia, are under severe threat from climate change, which is predicted to reduce the viability of current coffee-growing areas over the coming decades. In Ethiopia hotter and drier conditions are expected to reduce the suitability of many key coffee areas. The loss of suitable coffee land could amount to between 39 per cent and 59 per cent of the currently available area by the end of the twenty-first century (Moat et al. 2017; Davis et al. 2012). At the same time, deforestation as a result of land conversion to agricultural use and land degradation continue to encroach on Ethiopia's coffee forests. While coffee cultivation may perhaps serve to slow deforestation rates, or at least help preserve forest cover, the thinning out of natural forests for coffee cultivation leads to substantial biodiversity losses (Hylander et al. 2013). The silver lining is that climate change will also make parts of the country that are currently not suitable for coffee cultivation viable for commercial coffee production. Moat et al. (2017) estimate that the total coffee-growing area could be increased by up to 400 per cent by the end of the century. However, such a scenario is predicated on a carefully designed and supervised large-scale programme of subsidized migration to new areas, combined with the preservation of core areas of extant wild forests. Such a programme will require long-term commitment by successive Ethiopian governments.

A further challenge is the low average yield in the Ethiopian coffee sector. Relying on a large survey of smallholders, Minten et al. (2017) find self-reported average yields among smallholders of around 375kg/ha per year. The FAO (2015) estimates Ethiopian coffee yields at around 520kg/ha. By contrast, Brazil, where the coffee industry is dominated by large heavily mechanized farms, and most coffee is not grown under shade, average coffee yields were around 1,620kg/ha in 2016/17 (USDA 2016). Even less mechanized producers such as Colombia and Guatemala have average yields of around 850kg/ha and over 1,000kg/ha (FAO 2015). Such differences in yields are not inevitable. Researchers at the Ethiopian Coffee Research Institute, formerly the Jimma Agricultural

Research Institute, have achieved yields similar to those in Brazil in field trials (Kufa et al. 2003). Similarly, self-reported yields on private coffee plantations in Ethiopia appear to average around 1,100kg/ha and can reach over 2,000kg/ha on especially well-run farms (Schäfer 2016). As improving yields is only possible by investing both time and money, low yields can become a trap from which producers find it difficult to extricate themselves. Low yields mean low returns to coffee farming, especially for smallholder producers. In turn, low revenues both limit the incentives to invest and constrain the funds available for investment. Sustainable yield improvements in coffee require access to improved tree varieties and the application of improved agricultural practices, such as pruning, mulching, and regular weeding, which means that producers need access to these inputs, regular training, and reliable sources of agronomic expertise.

Responding to climate change and sustainably improving the productivity of the sector are both areas that will depend on strategic planning and patient intervention. Any such effort will however be hampered by the lack of timely and accurate data on the sector as a whole. Research into the sector in Ethiopia has suffered from a lack of funding and coordination, while official statistics on the coffee sector record only basic data, showing large unexplained swings. In consequence, there is much about the sector we simply do not know with any degree of certainty and we are too often forced to rely on inferences from small and isolated studies.

On the other hand, there are also a number of important opportunities for Ethiopia's coffee sector. Probably the most important of these is the potential to produce world-class coffees much more widely. It has been estimated that between 20 and 30 per cent of Ethiopian coffee could qualify as specialty coffee, further opening up important export opportunities. Much greater efforts to gain increased access for Ethiopian coffee to global specialty coffee markets could be made. Ethiopian producers of all scales could benefit from raising the profile of the Ethiopian coffee brand, increased participation in certification schemes, and emphasizing trade in traceable coffee products. The traceability of Ethiopia's coffee matters for market development and impacts rewards for producers. Minten et al. (2017) showed, for example, that coffee exporters that had the ability to be vertically integrated were able to obtain significantly higher sales prices over time than those that did not. Such efforts are especially important given the growing emphasis of international markets on certifiably sustainable coffee production practices.

The ability of the Ethiopian coffee sector to meet these challenges will depend in large part on the willingness and capacity of the Ethiopian state to put in place effective and well-researched policies to support the productive capabilities of the sector across all scales of production. As we have seen, policy towards the sector was long focused on regulating the market, with much more limited focus on the production side. However, the recent relaxation of rules governing exports through the partial roll-back of the ECX system, the concentration of regulatory functions for the sector in a single agency, and the push to strengthen the national institutions for coffee research all point towards a greater engagement of policymakers with the sector, and help lay the foundations for the strategic interventions the sector will require over the coming decades.

References

Aerts, R., G. Berecha, P. Gijbels, et al. (2013). 'Genetic Variation and Risks of Introgression in the Wild *Coffea Arabica* Gene Pool in South-Western Ethiopian Montane Rainforests', *Evolutionary Applications* 6: 243–52.

Aregay, M. W. (1988). 'The Early History of Ethiopia's Coffee Trade and the Rise of Shawa', *Journal of African History* 29 (1): 19–25.

Berhe, Y. (2010). 'The Legal Regime Regulating Coffee Trade in Ethiopia', MA thesis, Addis Ababa University.

Cramer, C., D. Johnston, C. Oya, and J. Sender (2014). 'Fairtrade, Employment and Poverty Reduction in Ethiopia and Uganda', Final Report to DFID, SOAS, University of London.

Cramer, C., D. Johnston, C. Oya, and J. Sender (2016). 'Fairtrade and Labour Markets in Ethiopia and Uganda', *Journal of Development Studies* 53 (6): 841–56.

CSA (Central Statistical Agency) (2016). 'Agricultural Sample Survey 2014/2015 (2007 E.C.), Vol. I: Report on Area and Production of Major Crops (Private Peasant Holdings, *Meher* Season)', Central Statistical Agency, Addis Ababa.

CTDMA (Coffee and Tea Development and Marketing Agency) (1978). 'The Role of Coffee in the Economy of Ethiopia', Coffee and Tea Development and Marketing Authority, Addis Ababa.

Daviron, B. and S. Ponte (2005). *The Coffee Paradox: Global Markets, Commodity Trade, and the Elusive Promise of Development* (London: Zed Books in association with the CTA).

Davis, A. P., W. Tadesse, S. Baena, and J. Moat (2012). 'The Impact of Climate Change on Indigenous Arabica Coffee (*Coffee Arabica*): Predicting Future Trends and Identifying Priorities', *PLoS ONE*, 7 (11): e4798.

ECEA (Ethiopian Commodity Exchange Authority) (2008). 'Understanding Commodities to Be Traded at the Ethiopian Commodity Exchange, Vol. 1: Analysis of Coffee Supply, Production, Utilization and Marketing Issues and Challenges in Ethiopia', Ethiopian Commodity Exchange Authority, Addis Ababa.

Ellis, G. (1976). 'The Feudal Paradigm as a Hindrance to Understanding Ethiopia', *Journal of Modern African Studies* 14 (2): 275–95.

FAO (Food and Agriculture Organization) (2015). *Statistical Pocket Book: Coffee* (Rome: FAO, United Nations).

Feyera, S. and M. Denich (2006). 'Effects of Wild Coffee Management on Species Diversity in the Afromontane Rainforest of Ethiopia', *Forest Ecology and Management* 232 (1–3): 68–74.

Gebre-Madhin, E. (2012). 'A Market for Abdu: Creating a Commodity Exchange in Ethiopia,' International Food Policy Research Institute, Addis Ababa.

Gebre-Madhin, E. and I. Goggin (2005). 'Does Ethiopia Need a Commodity Exchange? An Integrated Approach to Market Development', EDRI-ESSP Policy Working Paper, International Food Policy Research Institute, Addis Ababa.

Gemech, F. and J. Struthers (2007). 'Coffee Price Volatility in Ethiopia: Effects of Market Reform Programmes', *Journal of International Development* 19 (8): 1131–42.

Gemeda, G. (1994). 'Aspects of Agrarian Change in the Gibe Region: The Rise and Fall of Modern Coffee Farmers, 1948–1976', in *New Trends in Ethiopian Studies, Vol. 1*, ed. H. G. Marcus (East Lansing, MI: Michigan State University): 723–36.

Giovannucci, D., O. von Hagen, and J. Wozniak (2014). 'Corporate Social Responsibility and the Role of Voluntary Sustainability Standards', in *Voluntary Standard Systems: A Contribution to Sustainable Development*, ed. C. Schmitz-Hofman et al. (Berlin: Springer-Verlag): 359–84.

Griffin, K. B. (1992). *The Economy of Ethiopia* (New York: Macmillan).

Hylander, K., S. Nemomissa, J. Delrue, and W. Enkosa (2013). 'Effects of Coffee Management on Deforestation Rates and Forest Integrity', *Conservation Biology* 27: 1031–40.

ICO (International Coffee Organisation) (2000a). 'ICO/CFC Study of Marketing and Trading Policies and Systems in Selected Coffee-Producing Countries. Case Study: Ethiopia', International Coffee Organisation, London.

ICO (International Coffee Organisation) (2000b). 'ICO Country Profile: Ethiopia', International Coffee Organisation, London.

ICO (International Coffee Organisation) (2016). 'The Current State of the Global Coffee Trade'. http://www.ico.org/monthly_coffee_trade_stats.asp (accessed 12 September 2017).

ITC (International Trade Center) (2011). 'The Coffee Exporter's Guide', 3rd edition, International Trade Center, Geneva.

Jena, P. R., B. B. Chichaibelu, T. Stellmacher, and U. Grote (2012). 'The Impact of Coffee Certification on Small-Scale Producers' Livelihoods: A Case Study from the Jimma Zone, Ethiopia', *Agricultural Economics* 43: 429–40.

Kufa, T. (2012). 'Recent Coffee Research Development in Ethiopia', Presentation at the Ethiopian Coffee Export Conference: Strengthening the Legacy of Our Coffee, 8–9 November 2012, Hilton, Addis Ababa.

Kufa, T., A. Yilma, T. Shimber, et al. (2003). 'Yield Performance of Coffee Arabica Cultivars under Different Shade Trees at Jimma Research Center, Southwest Ethiopia', Jimma Agricultural Research Centre, Jimma.

Labouisse, J. P., B. Bellachew, S. Kotecha, and B. Bertrand (2008). 'Current Status of Coffee (*Coffea Arabica L.*) Genetic Resources in Ethiopia: Implications for Conservation', *Genetic Resources and Crop Evolution* 55: 1079.

Love, R. (2001). 'The Ethiopian Coffee Filiere and its Institutions: Cui Bono?', *Review of African Political Economy* 28 (88): 225–40.

McCann, J. (1995). *People of the Plow: An Agricultural History of Ethiopia, 1800–1990* (Madison, WI: University of Wisconsin Press).

McClellan, C. (1986). 'Coffee in Centre–Periphery Relations: Gedeo in the Early Twentieth Century', in *The Southern Marches of Imperial Ethiopia: Essays in History and Social Anthropology*, ed. D. Donham and J. Wendy (Cambridge: Cambridge University Press): 175–95.

Minten, B., M. Dereje, E. Engida, and T. Kuma (forthcoming). 'Coffee Value Chains on the Move: Evidence in Ethiopia', *Food Policy*.

Minten, B., M. Dereje, E. Engida, and S. Tamru (2015). 'Who Benefits from the Rapidly Increasing Voluntary Sustainability Standards? Evidence from Fairtrade and Organic Certified Coffee in Ethiopia', Ethiopian Strategy Support Program Working Paper 71.

Minten, B., M. Dereje, E. Engida, and S. Tamru (2018). 'Tracking the Quality Premium of Certified Coffee: Evidence from Ethiopia', *World Development* 101: 119–32.

Minten, B., T. Seneshaw, T. Kuma, and N. Yaw (2014). 'Structure and Performance of Ethiopia's Coffee Export Sector', Ethiopian Strategy Support Program Working Paper 66.

Moat, J., J. Williams, S. Baena, T. Wilkinson, et al. (2017). 'Resilience Potential of the Ethiopian Coffee Sector under Climate Change', *Nature Plants* 3, Article number: 17081.

NBE (National Bank of Ethiopia) (2018). 'Annual Report FY2016/17', National Bank of Ethiopia, Addis Ababa.

Negash, G. (2017). 'The Rise and Rise of Agricultural Wage Labour: Evidence from Ethiopia's South *c.*1950–2000', *Africa* 87 (1): 36–52.

Nure, D. (2008). 'Mapping Quality Profiles of Ethiopian Coffee by Origin', in *Coffee Diversity and Knowledge*, ed. G. Adugna, B. Bellachew, T. Shimber, et al. (Addis Ababa: Ethiopian Institute of Agricultural Research): 317–27.

Oya, C., F. Schäfer, D. Skalidou, et al. (2017). 'Effects of Certification Schemes for Agricultural Production on Socio-Economic Outcomes in Low- and Middle-Income Countries: A Systematic Review', *Campbell Systematic Reviews* 2017: 3.

Panhuysen, S. and J. Pierrot (2014). 'Coffee Barometer 2014', Tropical Commodity Coalition, The Hague.

Petit, N. (2007). 'Ethiopia's Coffee Sector: A Better or Bitter Future?', *Journal of Agrarian Change* 7 (2): 225–63.

Ponte, S. (2002). 'Standards, Trade and Equity: Lessons from the Specialty Coffee Industry', CDR Working Paper No. 02.13, Centre for Development Research, Copenhagen.

Rhinehart, R. (2017). 'What Is Specialty Coffee?' Specialty Coffee Association of America. http://www.scanews.coffee/2017/03/17/what-is-specialty-coffee/ (accessed 12 April 2017).

Rizzo, M. (2011). 'Rural Wage Employment in Rwanda and Ethiopia: A Review of the Current Policy Neglect and a Framework to Begin Addressing It', ILO Working Paper No. 103, International Labour Organisation, Geneva.

Schäfer, F. T. (2016). 'Revisiting the Agrarian Question: Coffee, Flowers and Ethiopia's New Capitalists', PhD thesis, SOAS, University of London.

Stellmacher, T. (2007). 'The Historical Development of Local Forest Governance in Ethiopia: From Imperial Times to the Military Regime of the Derg', *Africa Spectrum* 42 (3): 519–30.

Swinnen, J. (2007). *Global Supply Chains, Standards and the Poor: How the Globalization of Food Systems and Standards Affects Rural Development and Poverty* (Wallingford: CAB International).

Tröster, B. and C. Staritz (2015). 'Global Commodity Chains, Financial Markets, and Local Market Structures: Price Risks in the Coffee Sector in Ethiopia', Working Paper No. 56, Austrian Foundation for Development Research (ÖFSE), Vienna.

USAID (United States Agency for International Development) (2010). 'Ethiopian Coffee Industry Value Chain Analysis: Profiling the Actors, their Interactions, Costs, Constraints and Opportunities', COMPETE East Africa Trade Hub, United States Agency for International Development, Washington, DC.

USDA (United States Department of Agriculture) (2016). 'Brazil Coffee Annual Report', Foreign Agricultural Service GAIN Report BR16004, United States Department of Agriculture, Washington, DC.

USDA (United States Department of Agriculture) (2017). 'Coffee: World Markets and Trade', World Production, Markets, and Trade Reports, United States Department of Agriculture, Washington, DC.

Wellman, F. L. (1961). *Coffee: Botany, Cultivation and Utilization* (London: Leonard Hill Books).

Worako, T. K., M. Dejene, and B. Minten (2015). 'Coffee Income, Food Security and Diet Diversity of Smallholder Coffee Growers in Ethiopia', EDRI Working Paper No. 15, Ethiopian Development Research Institute, Addis Ababa.

World Bank (2016). 'Commodities Price Data (The Pink Sheet) December 2016'. http://pubdocs.worldbank.org/en/881871516897355563/CMO-Pink-Sheet-December-2016.pdf (accessed 18 February 2018).

Wrighley, G. (1988). *Coffee*. Tropical Agricultural Series. (Harlow: Longman Scientific and Technical).

CHAPTER 30

PRIVATE COFFEE PLANTATIONS IN ETHIOPIA

FLORIAN T. SCHÄFER

30.1 Introduction

Ethiopia has a history of privately organized large-scale coffee farming reaching back to the imperial state of the late nineteenth century (McCann 1995). For most of the last four decades though, the only coffee plantations in the country were gigantic state farms, remnants of the Derg's failed push for collectivized agriculture (Chole 2004). Then, in one of the most striking changes to have occurred in Ethiopia's coffee sector since the end of the civil war in 1991, the turn of the century saw the rapid re-emergence of large-scale plantations financed and run by private capital. Huge new plantations have been established by private investors promising to increase exports and create jobs. The new plantations resulted in land-use changes on a massive scale and necessitated the mobilization of a large—though mostly seasonal—labour force, generating great migratory movements that travel with the coffee harvest. This chapter traces the history of private large-scale coffee farming in Ethiopia across three different political regimes—the imperial state, the military dictatorship of the Derg, and the current EPRDF regime.

The key argument this chapter puts forward is that the latest rise of the Ethiopian private coffee plantations is best understood through an analysis that combines domestic political economy with an examination of the global value chain for coffee. This argument can be broken down into three separate but related aspects. First, the development of the Ethiopian coffee sector must be seen in the context of both current and historical political economy in Ethiopia. The Ethiopian state has long depended on coffee revenues as a core contributor to state finances, and the need to control the sector is a historical constant, irrespective of the regime in power. Coffee is one of the main avenues through which the contemporary Ethiopian state earns the foreign exchange needed for developmental projects, as well as to help finance the trade deficit. As in previous regimes, effective control over income streams from coffee is an important political issue (McClellan 1980).

Second, the incentives and conventions provided by the world market for coffee and the niche markets for high-quality coffees in particular, as well as the response to these parameters by state institutions and private investors, have played a determining role in the growth of private coffee plantations in Ethiopia (Love 2001). Lastly, despite the importance of coffee for state revenues, the emergence of the new private plantations was not primarily the result of strategic and well-planned productive-sector policies by the Ethiopian government. The growth of the new plantations was precipitated by a decisive shift in government strategy away from an exclusive focus on smallholder agriculture, which saw the government open up state land for agricultural investment and facilitate the take-over and consolidation of private land. However, this policy change alone was not sufficient. The government's strategic reorientation coincided with important changes to the regulatory landscape in the Ethiopian coffee sector as well as a period of rising prices for high-quality coffee. Together these three factors provided the circumstances under which private investors found it attractive to put their capital into new coffee plantations.

The resulting new plantations represent one of the most dynamic aspects of the contemporary Ethiopian coffee sector. A subset of these plantations produces world-class coffees and is able to export these at prices far above the average for Ethiopian coffees. As will be shown, this outcome is a direct result of the complex interplay between domestic political economy and international market structures.

Empirically, the chapter draws on a combination of existing research, administrative records, and original primary data. While the history of early coffee plantations can be reconstructed from writings on Ethiopian history, there is no published academic literature on contemporary coffee plantations. The core data on contemporary plantations come from a unique dataset compiled by the author. This dataset comprises both quantitative survey and qualitative interview data and is the result of several months of intensive fieldwork conducted in 2012 and 2013 (see Schäfer 2016 for details).

The chapter is organized as follows. We begin with an overview of the very first plantations in Ethiopian history, and trace the development of the first modern plantations in the twentieth century before discussing the demise of this experiment in agrarian capitalism caused by the anti-imperial revolution and the subsequent formation of state farms. We next consider the interlocking sets of internal and external circumstances enabling the rise of the contemporary plantations before introducing two of the most important types of plantation owners and looking at how regulatory changes and international market opportunities are key to understanding their investment decisions. To illustrate the scale of the new plantations we present the best available evidence on land holdings by plantations. The final sections illustrate the economic dynamism of the best-run plantations and offer some conclusions.

30.2 Coffee Plantations in Imperial Ethiopia

The military conquest of the southern periphery by the Ethiopian state in the late nineteenth century, and the subsequent conversion of quasi-feudal property relations into landlord–tenant relations in the fertile southern provinces, provided the necessary conditions for large-scale private farms to emerge.[1] While the first private coffee plantations probably date back to around the mid-nineteenth century (Gemeda 1994), it was not until the 1920s that private coffee plantations became widely established. Driven by rising prices in the world market, Ethiopia witnessed a coffee boom and exports grew to significant levels for the first time (Berhe 2010). However, these early plantations were generally run by absentee landlords with little interest in agronomy (Gemeda 1994). Nonetheless, they served as important forerunners for the modern plantations that were to follow. The first plantation boom was to prove short-lived, as the depression that gripped consuming countries in the 1930s drove down coffee prices. The invasion by fascist Italy in 1936 finally put an end to the experiment.

The first truly modern coffee plantations, using intensive planting and agronomic techniques, were founded in the 1950s. Slavery had been formally abolished in Ethiopia in 1942 and the new plantation owners found older arrangements such as sharecropping too expensive and relied instead on migrant wage labour (Gemeda 1996; Negash 2017). They actively encouraged migration from the north of the country. Ethiopia's growing integration into international trade flows provided this emergent group of capitalists with access to a reliable market for their produce (Gemeda 1996; Pausewang 1983). Another crucial element, agronomic knowledge, was added when USAID and the World Bank began funding agricultural development programmes in the 1950s (Bekele 1995), which introduced scientific management techniques to commercial farms.

After World War II, Emperor Haile Selassie opened the economy to foreign investment, leading to a modest, but unprecedented, surge in capital inflows. For the first time something resembling a national economy was born, linking the southern periphery ever more closely to the centre, which depended more and more on the surplus produced there for its own survival (Markakis and Ayele 1978). These inflows led to new investments in roads in the southern periphery and brought large numbers of migrant workers to the area (Gemeda 1994).

Initially, these new large-scale farms were hugely successful and expanded rapidly. It is estimated that during the 1960s, 5–10 per cent of Ethiopian coffee was produced by 'modern or quasi-modern coffee plantations owned and managed by private

[1] Markakis (2011) divides Ethiopia up into the highland core, the lowland periphery, and the highland periphery, which includes the most fertile coffee lands.

entrepreneurs' (Rahmato 2009: 47). By the time they were swept away by the revolution and subsequent land reform in 1975, they covered more than 14,000ha (Gemeda 1994).

30.3 Revolution and Nationalization

The imperial regime was broken by the revolution of 1974, which brought the military dictatorship of the Derg to power. The sweeping land reform that followed in 1975 marked the end of the early capitalist plantations. All private plantations were either broken up and the land distributed to peasant associations (*kebeles*) or nationalized and refashioned into gigantic state-owned farms. By pooling the coffee estates of the large capitalists and adding suitable surrounding areas, the revolutionary government created three giant coffee plantations: Limu Kossa near Jimma, Tepi in western Oromia close to the border with Gambella, and Bebeka in Bench Maji zone at the south-western end of SNNPR. By the time the EPRDF began to privatize these in 2008, they had reached 11,000ha, 9,000ha, and 10,000ha in size, respectively. Despite intense efforts to create showcases for the virtues of collectivist agriculture, the Derg's state farms were run very inefficiently, had low levels of productivity, and hence required large subsidies in order to survive (Griffin 1992). In the 1970s, yields on state farms were reportedly no higher than on small-scale farms and state farms produced only a small percentage of the country's coffee output (Abegaz 1982). Despite heavy injections of inputs and funds, most state farms were still loss-making by 1984 (Ghose 1985). However, after the fall of the Derg, the EPRDF government managed to successfully turn them into profitable ventures, while still under government ownership.

The Derg constructed the first truly modern state in Ethiopia and greatly expanded both its administrative and repressive capacities (Markakis 2011; Pausewang 1983). This also extended to the coffee sector, where control of the coffee revenues was a vital strategic aim for the Derg. The military government took direct control of the domestic and export markets for coffee, set artificially low producer prices and instituted a host of taxes on the sector. This transfer of funds was vital to the economic survival of the government. Coffee taxes alone constituted around 30 per cent of all government revenue in 1978 (Griffin 1992).

30.4 The Rebirth of Private Plantations

The state farms survived the Ethiopian civil war and the collapse of the Derg, but private plantations were slow to re-emerge (Keller 1992). The eventual rebirth of private coffee plantations in the twenty-first century is the result of three factors. First, the EPRDF state implemented regulatory innovations, in particular the introduction of the ECX system, which—quite by accident—helped create incentives for investing in large-scale coffee production. Second, international coffee markets at the time were characterized by growing demand for high-quality Arabica coffees and traceable specialty coffees (see Chapter 29). And third, the government of Ethiopia began to open up new land for investment and encouraged regional governments to support applications for land from prospective large-scale farmers. Together these three factors produced a unique situation that favoured the establishment and profitable operation of large-scale private coffee plantations in Ethiopia.

The fall of the Derg in 1991 and the subsequent take-over of the state by the EPRDF completely transformed economic policy in Ethiopia. While the state continued to play a major role in the economy, many markets were liberalized. In coffee, the state marketing board was disbanded and the state eventually completely withdrew from direct involvement in coffee production. However, because of the economic importance of coffee, the sector remained tightly regulated. With the withdrawal of state agencies private capital reasserted itself in coffee processing and the export trade, and by the mid-1990s Ethiopia's coffee auctions were once again dominated by private traders. In 2008 new legislation suddenly forced all coffee trade in the country to go through the recently established Ethiopian Commodity Exchange (ECX) system. What is striking about these reforms is the attention to detail in coffee regulation and its aggressive enforcement, coupled with the absence of a detailed growth policy for the sector.

As explained in Chapter 29, the ECX system severed the link between the processing station and the purchaser, undermining the ability of the purchaser to trace the coffee back either to the station where it was processed or the particular plantation on which it was grown. This was especially damaging to the specialty coffee sector where only traceable coffee can attract the highest prices. It has been estimated that the loss of traceability cost the country around US$280 million between 2008 and 2012 (Leung 2014). After a substantial backlash, the government relented and in 2010 allowed private plantations and the cooperative unions to sell coffee directly to international buyers, but only after having their coffees graded and recorded by the ECX. Further legislation in 2017 allowed all coffee farms to export their coffee directly from the farm.

The introduction of the ECX unwittingly narrowed the supply of traceable specialty-grade coffee in Ethiopia. An unintended side effect of this artificial supply constraint was to strengthen the competitive position of coffee plantations vis-à-vis smallholder farmers in Ethiopia. When in 2010 the government bowed to pressure from the coffee sector, both in Ethiopia and abroad, and lifted the ban on direct coffee exports, it did so only partially. Cooperative unions and plantations became the only entities in Ethiopia able to supply fully traceable coffee to foreign buyers. For many coffee exporters establishing their own coffee plantation was the only way to reliably source the traceable coffee their customers were demanding. Not surprisingly, both cooperatives and private plantations were able to command premiums for their coffee after the introduction of the ECX (Minten et al. 2014). But plantations enjoyed important advantages in terms of access to knowledge, plant varieties, and labour—all of which are necessary for producing

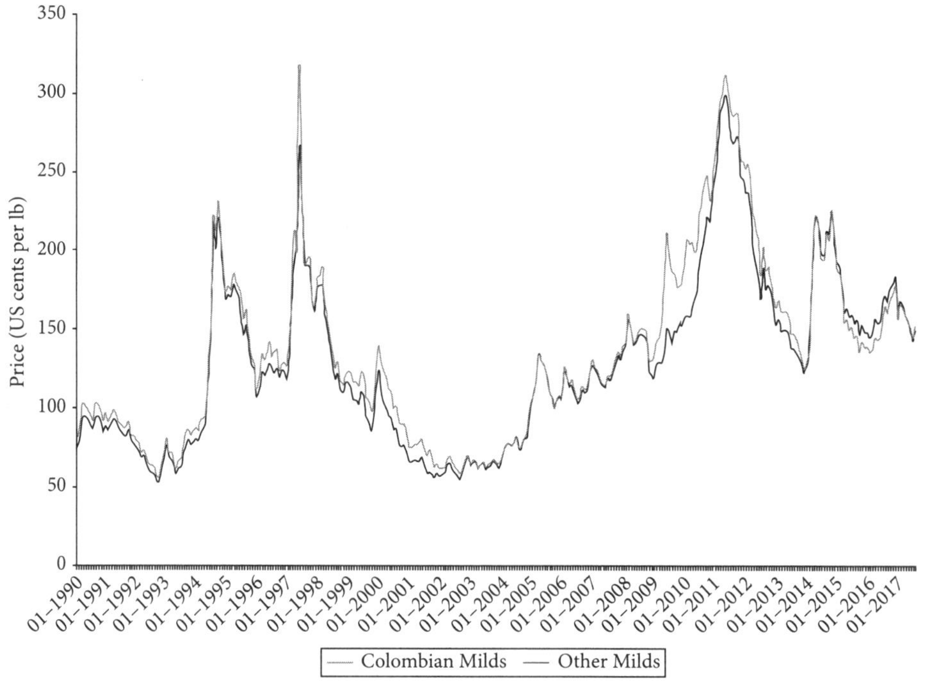

FIGURE 30.1 Arabica coffee price, 1990–2017

Source: Author's elaboration from ICO monthly coffee price data.

high-quality coffee. And plantations, unlike cooperatives, do not have to purchase the coffee they sell, and so are less subject to the cash constraints that can hobble the latter. Finally, while rural poverty is an impediment to the development of cooperatives, plantation owners instead benefit from low reservation wages.

At the same time, rising Arabica prices in international markets provided a favourable environment for the formation of new plantations. Figure 30.1 shows the development of the main International Coffee Organisation (ICO) Arabica price indices between 1990 and 2017. The ICO classifies Arabica coffees as either 'Colombian milds' or 'other milds'. Ethiopian coffees on average trade at a premium compared to these indices. After the prices reached their lowest point at the end of the last coffee crisis in 2002, they began a steady rise that only ended in 2012.[2] The vast majority of plantation investments in Ethiopia fall into this period, that is, a period of high and rising coffee prices. In fact, the price levels attained in 2012 had last been reached in 1987, with a similar, but smaller, peak occurring in 1997. Rising prices pulled investment into the sector and are frequently cited as a motivation by Ethiopian plantation owners.

However, it was only when the Ethiopian government opened up land for investment that private coffee plantations became truly viable. Land ownership has long been a deeply political issue in Ethiopia. The EPRDF government, with its roots in a peasant-based

[2] On the coffee crisis and its consequences, see ICO (2002).

guerrilla army, had long held that a close partnership with, and control over, the smallholder farmers was essential to maintaining political supremacy (Rahmato 2009). A relatively homogeneous mass of smallholders was seen as the backbone of the 'developmental coalition' essential to the maintenance of revolutionary democracy (Weis 2016). The state had therefore put in place a variety of measures to limit capital accumulation and socio-economic differentiation in the countryside, not least by maintaining state ownership of all land.[3] After 2002, however, the government began opening up agricultural land for investment. Where previous agricultural policy had focused mainly on smallholder agriculture, a 2002 poverty reduction strategy paper made clear that the government was no longer relying solely on smallholder farmers to drive agricultural transformation, but would seek and facilitate private investment to establish large-scale farms (MoFED 2002; Berhanu and Poulton 2014).

After the symbolically important Ethiopian millennium in 2007, regional governments were instructed to open additional land to investors, which unleashed a land rush in the country's coffee lands. In 2010 the government's Growth and Transformation Plan (GTP-I) promised that 'in the coming five years efforts will be made to make a meaningful change in terms of the private investment role in agriculture', and that 'efforts will be made to make [sure] the private investor gets government services in an efficient way' (MoFED 2010: 26). Ethiopia's shift towards making room for agrarian capital was prompted by the resource requirements of running its developmental state, especially in terms of foreign exchange (Lavers 2012). The GTP is clear that the output produced by private capitalist farms, both small and large, is not for domestic consumption, but must either be exported or used as inputs to industry (MoFED 2010: 25f). The opening up of land for agricultural investment by private capitalists is thus an integral part of the creation of Ethiopia's developmental state. As the need to generate foreign exchange seems to have overruled all other concerns, huge tracts of land in Ethiopia were cleared for investment (Abbink 2011; Rahmato 2011). This window of opportunity was closed in many areas in 2012, as land outside the lowlands became increasingly scarce and conflicts over land began to mount.

In sum, the current opportunities for investment in coffee plantations came about through the confluence of government action and a favourable external market environment. As part of its drive to establish a development state, the government opened up land for investment and therefore made the emergence of coffee plantations in large numbers possible. Regulatory changes in the coffee sector, which were not aimed at strengthening private capital, had the unintended consequence of strengthening the position of these plantations in the market. These same regulatory changes also encouraged existing actors in the coffee sector, such as large exporters and processors, to invest in plantations. At the same time the long history both of coffee production and of large coffee farms in the country ensured that that there were enough people who had the wish to grow coffee at scale and could access the knowledge necessary to do so.

[3] These measures served only to slow, rather than prevent, differentiation, which is a fact of life in rural Ethiopia (see for instance Petit 2007; Taffesse, Dorosh, and Asrat 2011).

30.5 The New Plantation Owners

So who are the new plantation owners? A full typology is given in Schäfer (2016) but is beyond the confines of this chapter. Instead, we shall limit the discussion to the two types of owner most pertinent to the argument at hand. These are coffee processors, or *akrabe*, and coffee exporters.

Akrabe are large-scale coffee processors and wholesalers who possess their own processing stations. The business model of the *akrabe* is central to understanding why they would seek to invest in plantations. The *akrabe* buy coffee cherries in large quantities from farms within their licence area. Once the coffee is processed, the *akrabe* delivers it to the nearest ECX station for grading and warehousing. The *akrabe* must be sufficiently cash rich not only to purchase large amounts of coffee for processing, but also to pay the sizeable workforces necessary to run large washing stations. A medium-sized processing station will employ upwards of two hundred seasonal workers for three to four months during the processing season, as well as at least a dozen permanent security and administrative staff. But processing coffee takes some time and coffee prices may change while processing is under way. The *akrabe* therefore takes a calculated risk that the revenue achieved from selling the processed coffee is higher than the cost of the cherries plus the cost of processing the coffee. The *akrabe* has a problem if coffee prices decline before the processed coffee can be sold or if the price paid for the cherries was too high. The business is risky—all *akrabe* interviewed in Schäfer (2016) agree that it is possible to lose substantial amounts of money in a single season.

For many *akrabe* the option of investing in coffee plantations arose just as increasing competitive pressures were emerging, endangering the viability of their business model. The profits *akrabe* are able to extract have historically relied on a steady supply of cheap cherries, provided by small-scale farmers with limited outside options. Competition comes not only from the increasing number of *akrabe* in the business, but also from rising numbers of newly founded (or reformed) cooperatives, who often own their own processing equipment. The results have been higher cherry prices and lower profit margins. The danger of narrowing margins is exacerbated by the volatile nature of coffee prices. The same is much less true for coffee farming, where the main cost is labour. In periods of low prices farmers can control costs by scaling back labour input into the farm. While lower labour inputs reduce the quality of the coffee, plantations will generally at least break even. Farming is regarded as a much less risky business, as cheap labour and practically free land have eliminated the downside risks.

Apart from these push factors, *akrabe* also enjoy a number of advantages, making coffee plantations as investment objects particularly interesting to them. First, *akrabe* are already familiar with the complexities of the coffee trade. They are often in close contact with local markets and aware of the differences in coffee type and quality. Before the ECX large *akrabe* often had direct contact with exporters and foreign buyers, giving them insight into the requirements of international markets, including the specialty coffee trade. *Akrabe* are already familiar with the production of high-quality coffee, and are much less likely to have to buy costly expertise. Second, it is relatively easy for large *akrabe* to mobilize the start-up capital necessary for coffee farming, given that they have already accumulated substantial amounts in the past, and frequently have capital assets from other businesses, houses, cars, and, not least, their processing stations to offer as collateral.

A similar move into direct production of coffee is evident among Ethiopia's large coffee exporters. Some of these exporters run gigantic business operations and export thousands of tonnes of coffee annually, generating revenues in the range of millions of US dollars. Prior to the introduction of the ECX, many exporters had also worked as *akrabe*, buying their own coffee from the Addis Ababa auction to secure themselves consistent supplies of high-quality traceable coffee. When, as discussed in Section 30.4, the ECX system removed the possibility of tracing coffee to the precise place it had been processed, these exporters were no longer able to serve the international specialty markets they depend on for part of their profits.

Some of the exporters, in particular those selling high-quality coffees, reacted by moving into large-scale production themselves, where the possibility of direct export restored their access to traceable specialty coffee. Even though specialty coffee may only represent part of their overall sales for exporters, it is an important part that allows them to present a full range of both traceable and non-traceable coffees of various qualities to large buyers, for whom variety is an important consideration in choosing suppliers.

30.6 Land Holdings of Private Plantations

As mentioned in the Introduction, these plantations have brought with them large-scale land-use changes. Exactly how large is, however, a matter of some uncertainty. A lot of the basic data on Ethiopia's coffee plantations is either incomplete or of questionable reliability. Administrative data on large farms is scattered across different regional and *woreda* land offices and a full census of the large-scale coffee sector has never been attempted. Until such a census is undertaken, all data on coffee plantations should be regarded as preliminary. Table 30.1 presents the best available data on land leases for large-scale coffee farms in Ethiopia. It gives the total amount of land leased for coffee plantations for the main coffee-producing zones, as well as the number of plantations in each zone and their mean size. The information presented in Table 30.1 is based on a compilation of data from investment offices at regional, zonal and, in one case, *woreda* levels.

As shown in Table 30.1, around 47,100ha had been leased to active private coffee plantations in Oromia and SNNPR at the time of data collection in 2012/13. Excluded from this estimate are the recently privatized state farms, which collectively control another 30,000ha, as are the lands held by Ethio Agri-CEFT who control over 2,200ha

Table 30.1 Overview of coffee plantations in Ethiopia's main coffee areas in 2013

Zone	Region	Total coffee land leased (ha)	Number of coffee plantations	Mean plantation size (ha)
Kaffa	SNNPR	14,574	82	178
Bench Maji	SNNPR	12,020	20	601
Jimma	Oromia	10,252	69	149
West Wellega	Oromia	2,656	16	166
Kellem Wellega	Oromia	750	4	187.5
Sheka*	SNNPR	2,915	18	161
Illubabor*	Oromia	1,875	10	187
South Omo*	SNNPR	783	2	261
Borena*	Oromia	734	0	122
Konta*	SNNPR	280	1	280
Sidama	SNNPR	250	1	250
West Arsi*	Oromia	120	2	60
Amaro*	SNNPR	122	2	61
Gurage*	SNNPR	42.5	1	42.5
Gedeo*	SNNPR	–	–	–
Awassa*	SNNPR	–	–	–
Konta*	SNNPR	–	–	–
West Haraghe*	Oromia	–	–	–
Arsi*	Oromia	–	–	–
Total Oromia		16,387	101	162.2
Total SNNPR		30,986.5	127	243.8
Grand total		**47,373.5**	**228**	**207.5**

Note: * indicates that the information is based on regional investment lists alone.
Source: Schäfer (2016). NB Excludes former state farms.

in Gemadro, SNNPR. The best estimate for the total size of active capitalist coffee plantations in Oromia and SNNPR in 2013 is, then, around 79,000ha. Ethiopia's Central Statistical Agency (CSA) collects some information on coffee farms as part of a sample survey on large and medium-scale commercial farms. The CSA estimated the total area of commercial farms growing coffee at about 108,000ha in 2014/15 (CSA 2015a). In the same year the CSA estimated the total coffee area on small-scale 'peasant' holdings in Ethiopia at around 561,000ha in 2014 (CSA 2015b), by which measure large-scale private plantations account for around 16 per cent of the total coffee production area. Given that large-scale coffee farms in Ethiopia tend to have higher yields than smallholder farms and bring all of their product to market, their share of marketed coffee is likely to be substantially higher.

As Table 30.1 illustrates, large-scale plantations are concentrated in only a few of Ethiopia's coffee-producing regions, mainly Kaffa, Bench Maji, and Jimma zones, while sizeable portions of land have also been transferred in West Wellega, Sheka, and Illubabor. What is notable is the near-complete absence of large plantations in some of Ethiopia's main coffee-growing areas. A good example is in Sidama zone, historically

Ethiopia's leading coffee-producing area and a global coffee trademark, where there only appears to be a single plantation of 250ha.[4] Similarly, in Gedeo zone, easily the most famous of Ethiopia's coffee regions—though the coffee is better known by the name of its capital, Yirga Cheffe—there are no large coffee plantations at all (McClellan 2002). Both zones have high population densities and there is simply no land available to set up large-scale plantations. Where there are concentrations of plantations, their size differs greatly. The average plantation size ranges from just 149ha in Jimma zone to 601ha in Bench Maji.

A close analysis of the different areas reveals very different patterns of land acquisition. In Jimma, long historical trajectories of rural and agrarian capital accumulation, mostly but not exclusively in coffee, as well as locally based personal networks, help explain current accumulation patterns, which have included systematic land grabbing. In Kaffa, the expansion of coffee plantations has been accompanied by conflicts over the use of forest lands, some of which are now in protected areas. In Bench Maji, the lack of competing 'commercial' land uses and the need for the local government to show investment success has meant that plantations there are much larger than in other parts of the country. In West Wellega, from the limited information available, farms appear to be younger than in the other areas under study, and officials indicated that there is still a lot of land available for investment, marking the area out as a frontier zone for future investment. The area is also quite remote, and a modern road connecting the zone to the rest of Ethiopia's road network was only completed after 2010. Kellem Wellega is even more remote—there was no asphalt road connecting it to West Wellega as late as 2012/13—and land acquisition patterns there have been quite idiosyncratic, in ways that would not have been possible in areas with more developed state control.

30.7 Dynamic Exporters

However, as Ethiopia's coffee sector is highly export oriented, land size is probably a less important consideration than business strategy. Many analyses of agrarian change in low- and middle-income countries are concerned with identifying dynamic capital accumulators in an environment where most producers are not able to accumulate. Such producers will reinvest profits both to grow the scale of their businesses and to increase its efficiency. A fruitful approach in the context of Ethiopian coffee plantations is to ask who has been the most dynamic producer in the sense of serving the highest-value markets. Here we see a clear pattern emerge, with the use of direct export markets also signalling a more successful and sophisticated business model. Direct coffee export markets in Ethiopia are, as explained earlier, almost exclusively used for specialty grades, as non-specialty buyers do not require traceability and can purchase through exporters

[4] This information is taken from ECGPEA. The Sidama zone office refused to provide any data on investments, citing the need for data protection.

who buy coffees from the ECX. Farms that sell via the direct export channel have thus been able to attract foreign buyers, produce the required quality and shown themselves capable of organizing the packaging and transport of their coffees.

This section builds on data collected by the author in 2012/13 as part of a survey of large-scale coffee plantations. At this time many of the newly established plantations had not yet had any sales. To ensure a more meaningful comparison, the following analysis compares only those farms that have had sales. The direct exporters in this sample distinguish themselves by their interest in producing high-quality coffee and by their eagerness to learn about and understand the international coffee trade.

The first thing to note is that farms that serve the direct export market are much larger than farms that do not. On average, they had developed 309ha of coffee land, as opposed to just 131ha on farms that do not export directly, and they had developed a higher share of their overall land holdings. Farms that export directly have developed 78 per cent of their land, while farms that do not export have developed 69 per cent of their land. Direct exporters have also accumulated much more capital. Excluding processing equipment, direct exporters had on average invested over ETB1,300,00 in farm transport equipment and other fixed capital, while farms not exporting directly had invested only around ETB600,000. Direct exporters are also more likely to own processing equipment and are the most likely to own both a dry and a wet mill.

Plantation owners that export directly started their farms at around the same time as non-exporters, so their superior performance is not a question of having been in the market longer. It is rather a result of these owners having had the business acumen to move into an especially challenging but also lucrative market. One of the causes might be the higher than average levels of education that the owners of direct export plantations have enjoyed. While the average non-exporting farmer has completed twelve years of schooling and attended higher education for some time, the average exporting farmer has completed an undergraduate degree—in many cases in either business or agricultural science. There are almost no differences between direct exporters and others in terms of the share of own capital they brought into the plantation and their use of loan finance, meaning that their capital accumulation is driven by sales, rather than credit.

As would be expected, plantations that export directly invest more in the quality of their coffee. They weed on average one more time over the course of the year. To enable them to perform a more intense quality management and maintenance regime, they employ a higher share of permanent workers compared to non-exporters. Direct exporters also seem to treat their workers better. They tend to pay better salaries, though not by much, and around a third of them offer healthcare services of some sort to temporary workers, while only around 12 per cent of non-exporters do. There is, however, no difference in the provision of health care to permanent workers.

In 2013 plantations that exported directly, for all their dynamism, remained a minority. Market discipline in the large-scale coffee sector is not very pronounced and less ambitiously run farms can survive quite easily. Owners all realized that it is relatively simple to avoid losing money while operating a coffee plantation. The reason is that the market, and especially the domestic market, accepts a wide range of quality levels. At the same time, the major costs on a coffee plantation are labour costs. There is a direct connection between labour inputs and coffee quality: a dramatic reduction in labour inputs will lower the quality of the coffee and will probably exclude it from the lucrative speciality market. However, the lower-quality coffee can still be sold into the mid- to low-quality market, allowing the farmer to break even. Coffee plantations do not, apart from labour costs, have many outgoings that are indispensable to the operation of the farm, as almost all other costs can be reduced without seriously impeding yields and quality—at least in the short term. This flexibility means that large-scale coffee farms are quite resilient to price reductions, but also to incompetent management. While a coffee capitalist must combine organizational ability and market knowledge to operate a plantation that produces large profits, a plantation can exist with low or no profits for a considerable length of time. Coffee plantations, at least at small initial scales, have relatively low start-up costs compared to other forms of intensive agriculture, such as floriculture, and are therefore much less dependent on credit. This removes the need to make monthly repayments, further reducing competitive pressure. The combination of opportunities for rapid accumulation provided by the specialty market and the possibility for farms to survive at relatively low levels of productivity while selling only low-quality coffee is likely to bring about substantial differentiation among coffee plantations in the future. If the coffee plantation sector as a whole is to flourish, all plantations must be incentivized to export directly and given the support they require to do so.

30.8 Conclusion

We have seen that the revenues associated with coffee production have been of central importance to the Ethiopian state and its political elites since at least the 1920s. Consequently, the Ethiopian state has always sought to regulate and control the sector, although this control has taken very different forms under successive governments. Haile Selassie's imperial state, despite attempts at modernization, lacked the administrative capacity to control the production stage of coffee to any real degree and satisfied itself with taxation. His regime also witnessed the emergence of the first modern coffee plantations after World War II. Migrations caused by the plantations' demand for workers reshaped the population around the largest concentrations of plantations. After the 1974 revolution the Derg regime wiped out the private plantations. They built a much more centralized and powerful administrative machinery and greatly extended state control over the sector. For the first time, the state directly controlled and immediately involved itself in the production of coffee. The state farms founded to replace some of the plantations of the imperial era, while mismanaged and unproductive under the Derg, preserved knowledge about scientific farming methods and at least some of them later went on to become examples of excellence in production. The next wave of plantation owners was then able to tap into the knowledge and skills thus preserved. The remarkable dynamism witnessed recently has only been possible because the private plantation system had been so long in the making.

The EPRDF substantially liberalized the coffee sector and over time dismantled many of the state institutions used to control it. A shift in economic strategy after 2001 had profound effects on the coffee sector. On the one hand, the government, driven by the need to control the flow of revenues and in particular foreign exchange, moved to re-establish control over the sector. This was attempted through the introduction of a commodity exchange for agricultural produce. On the other hand, the government's new economic strategy drove a change in its agricultural policy. Government at all levels became much more open to and supportive of large-scale private investment in agriculture (Mohammed 1969). When land became available private capital flooded into new plantations. Unwittingly, the introduction of the ECX acted as a catalyst for this process.

The discussion has placed a particular emphasis on the contradictory effects of state action on the accumulation patterns in the sector. It was the Ethiopian state, in pursuit of its own strategic agenda, that created the possibilities for the private coffee plantations to expand to the degree they have done, by opening up land for investment. The rapid capital accumulation processes witnessed in the coffee plantation sector are the direct results of Ethiopia's turn towards a developmental state strategy around the turn of the millennium, which necessitated increased revenues. However, the state has then often had only partial control over the process of plantation development. A similarly contradictory effect results from the rushed introduction of the ECX, and the subsequent re-opening of the direct export route. The fact that large farmers could suddenly sell their coffee directly to overseas buyers opened up new routes of accumulation for the most capable and dynamic plantation owners, who were able to access a premium market segment. The existence of this premium market segment in turn is the result of the way in which the global value chain for coffee, up to the point of retail in rich countries, is organized (Gibbon and Ponte 2005).

Beyond opening up land for investment and making it available at low prices, the state has actually done little to directly support the production of coffee by these enterprises. The plantations therefore have comparatively little technological equipment, and what they do possess they have accumulated in a piecemeal fashion. Nonetheless they have established production systems that set them apart from the norm in Ethiopia's coffee sector. The plantations have survived by pursuing a largely non-mechanized method of production that allows them to scale back the major costs factor—wages. However, growing plantation workforces and increased labour migration are likely to further class conflict; even dispersed labour forces with a high proportion of migrants can sometimes be organized with surprising speed and effectiveness (see for instance Wells 1996; Giel and van Luik 1968; Wood 1983). A failure to correct the harsh and frequently dangerous labour practices prevalent in the sector plants the seeds of future discontent, and prevents the up-skilling necessary to maintain international competitiveness. At the same time, increasing consumer demands for 'sustainable' production systems and the growing sophistication of coffee production in many competitor countries will make a competitive edge built primarily on low wages less and less viable.

References

Abbink, J. (2011). '"Land to the Foreigners": Economic, Legal, and Socio-Cultural Aspects of New Land Acquisition Schemes in Ethiopia', *Journal of Contemporary African Studies* 29 (4): 513–35.

Abegaz, H. Y. (1982). *The Organisation of State Farms in Ethiopia after the Land Reform of 1975: Planning, Realisation, Potential and Problems* (Saarbrücken: Verlag Breitenbach).

Bekele, S. (1995). 'The Evolution of Land Tenure in the Imperial Era', in *An Economic History of Modern Ethiopia*, ed. S. Bekele (Dakar: CODESRIA): 72–142.

Berhanu, K. and C. Poulton (2014). 'The Political Economy of Agricultural Extension Policy in Ethiopia: Economic Growth and Political Control', *Development Policy Review* 32 (2): 197–213.

Berhe, Y. (2010). 'The Legal Regime Regulating Coffee Trade in Ethiopia', MA thesis, Addis Ababa University.

Chole, E. (2004). *Underdevelopment in Ethiopia* (Addis Ababa: Organisation for Social Science Research in Eastern and Southern Africa).

CSA (Central Statistical Agency) (2015a). 'Large- and Medium-Scale Commercial Farms Sample Survey 2014/2015 (2007 E.C.): Statistical Report on Area and Production of Crops, and Farm Management Practices', Central Statistical Agency, Addis Ababa.

CSA (Central Statistical Agency) (2015b). 'Agricultural Sample Survey 2014/2015 (2007 E.C.), Vol. I: Report on Area and Production of Major Crops (Private Peasant Holdings, *Meher* Season)', Central Statistical Agency, Addis Ababa.

Gemeda, G. (1994). 'Aspects of Agrarian Change in the Gibe Region: The Rise and Fall of Modern Coffee Farmers, 1948–1976', in *New Trends in Ethiopian Studies, Vol. 1*, ed. H. G. Marcus (East Lansing, MI: Michigan State University Press).

Gemeda, G. (1996). 'Land, Agriculture and Society in the Gibe Region: Southwestern Ethiopia, *c.*1850–1974', PhD thesis, Michigan State University.

Ghose, A. K. (1985). 'Transforming Feudal Agriculture: Agrarian Change in Ethiopia since 1974', *Journal of Development Studies* 22 (1): 127–49.

Gibbon, P. and S. Ponte (2005). *Trading Down: Africa, Value Chains, and the Global Economy* (Philadelphia, PA: Temple University Press).

Giel, R. and J. N. van Luik (1968). 'Plight of Daily Labourer in a Coffee-Growing Province of Ethiopia', *Psychopathologie Africaine* 4 (3): 451–7.

Griffin, K. B. (1992). *The Economy of Ethiopia* (New York: Macmillan).

ICO (International Coffee Organisation) (2002). 'Global Coffee Crisis: A Threat to Sustainable Development', Submission to the World Summit on Sustainable Development, International Coffee Organisation, Geneva.

Keller, E. J. (1992). 'Drought, War and the Politics of Famine in Ethiopia and Eritrea', *Journal of Modern African Studies* 30 (4): 609–24.

Lavers, Tom (2012). 'Patterns of Agrarian Transformation in Ethiopia: State-Mediated Commercialisation and the "Land Grab"'. https://doi.org/10.1080/03066150.2012.660147 (accessed 25 August 2018).

Leung, L. (2014). 'Eroded Coffee Traceability and its Impact on Export Coffee Prices for Ethiopia', Development Discussion Paper 2014:04, John Deutsch International, Queen's University.

Love, R. (2001). 'The Ethiopian Coffee Filiere and its Institutions: cui bono?', *Review of African Political Economy* 28 (88): 225–40.

Markakis, J. (2011). *Ethiopia: The Last Two Frontiers*, Eastern Africa Series (Rochester, NY: James Currey).

Markakis, J. and N. Ayele (1978). *Class and Revolution in Ethiopia* (Nottingham: Spokesman Books [for the Review of African Political Economy]).

McCann, J. C. (1995). *People of the Plow: An Agricultural History of Ethiopia, 1800–1990* (Madison, WI: University of Wisconsin Press).

McClellan, C. (1980). 'Land, Labor, and Coffee: The South's Role in Ethiopian Self-Reliance, 1889–1935', *African Economic History* 9: 69–83.

McClellan, C. (2002). 'Coffee in Centre-Periphery Relations: Gedeo in the Early Twentieth Century', in *The Southern Marches of Imperial Ethiopia*, ed. D. L. Donham and W. James (Oxford: James Currey): 175–95.

Minten, B., S. Tamru, T. Kuma, and Y. Nyarko (2014). 'Structure and Performance of Ethiopia's Coffee Export Sector', ESSP Working Paper 66, International Food Policy Research Institute, Washington, DC.

MoFED (2002). 'Sustainable Development and Poverty Reduction Program', Ministry of Finance and Economic Development, Addis Ababa.

MoFED (2010). 'Growth and Transformation Plan (GTP) 2010/11–2014/15, Vol. I: main text', Ministry of Finance and Economic Development, Addis Ababa.

Mohammed, D. (1969). 'Private Foreign Investment in Ethiopia (1950–1968)', *Journal of Ethiopian Studies* 7 (2): 53–78.

Negash, G. (2017). 'The Rise and Rise of Agricultural Wage Labour: Evidence from Ethiopia's South *c.*1950–2000', *Africa* 87 (1): 36–52.

Pausewang, S. (1983). *Peasants, Land, and Society: A Social History of Land Reform in Ethiopia* (Munich: Weltforum Verlag).

Petit, N. (2007). 'Ethiopia's Coffee Sector: A Bitter or Better Future?', *Journal of Agrarian Change* 7 (2): 225–63.

Rahmato, D. (2009). *The Peasant and the State: Studies in Agrarian Change in Ethiopia 1950s–2000s* (Addis Ababa: Addis Ababa University Press).

Rahmato, D. (2011). *Land to Investors: Large-Scale Land Transfers in Ethiopia* (Addis Ababa: Forum for Social Studies).

Schäfer, F. T. (2016). 'Revisiting the Agrarian Question: Coffee, Flowers and Ethiopia's New Capitalists', PhD thesis, SOAS, University of London.

Taffesse, Alemayehu Seyoum, Paul Dorosh, and Sinafikeh Asrat (2011). 'Crop Production in Ethiopia: Regional Patterns and Trends', Working Paper No. 0016, Development Strategy and Governance Division, International Food Policy Research Institute, Addis Ababa.

Weis, T. (2016). 'Vanguard Capitalism: Party, State, and Market in the EPRDF's Ethiopia', PhD thesis, University of Oxford.

Wells, M. J. (1996). *Strawberry Fields: Politics, Class, and Work in California Agriculture* (Ithaca, NY: Cornell University Press).

Wood, A. P. (1983). 'The Decline of Seasonal Labor Migration to the Coffee Forests of Southwest Ethiopia', *Geography* 68 (298): 53–6.

CHAPTER 31

CONSTRAINTS ON THE ETHIOPIAN FLORICULTURE INDUSTRY

AYELECH TIRUWHA MELESE

31.1 Introduction

Economic development requires the accumulation of productive capabilities through expanding activities with a greater potential to drive productivity and income growth. Historically, manufacturing has shown a higher tendency to trigger positive 'cumulative causations' through rapid increases in productivity and employment as well as through its effects spreading to other sectors in the national economy. Moreover, since manufacturing requires significant capabilities in production, project execution, and innovation/adaptation, it usually nurtures technical, managerial, and organizational skills as well (Kaldor 1966; UNCTAD 2016; Haraguchi, Cheng, and Smeets 2017). And manufactured exports are particularly important: they are strongly associated with sustained growth in productivity and output, and through their contribution to the balance of payments they facilitate broader development.

However, technologies are not freely accessible nor can they be easily absorbed; rather, it is a costly process that requires deliberate effort (Lall 1992). This process is more challenging for domestic firms in low-income countries as they often lack the necessary experience and support to engage in productive activities or expand their existing businesses. Foreign firms tend to have better capabilities and certain types can help expand productive sectors and be a learning channel for domestic firms (especially with targeted policies), but they may be less likely to drive sustained structural transformation (Amsden 2009; Akyüz 2015; Storm 2015).

At low levels of technology, productive activities require relatively low skills and can have a strong impact on pulling 'surplus' labour away from low-productivity sectors such as under-capitalized small-scale agriculture, absorbing large numbers of unskilled workers and socializing them with industrial discipline (see Chapter 38). This initial start is important for accumulating the manufacturing experience that in turn provides a basis for diversification into intermediate and high technologies in conjunction with improved living standard (Amsden 2001). To this end, it is necessary to ensure labour availability as well as manage wages and/or costs of wage goods. Employment conditions in productive industries need to remain more attractive than in low-productivity sectors and should also be good enough to realize the positive cumulative causation potential of those industries. Unfortunately, these employment effects of productive industries are often neglected (by economists and policymakers alike), which may lead to a failure to develop the foundations of industrialization and poverty reduction. This neglect is what Amsden (2010) calls 'jobs dementia', a sickness that afflicts most development economics and aid agencies.

The first part of this chapter aims to discuss two central issues, linked to expanding productive capabilities, which it is argued pose particular problems for structural transformation in Ethiopia. The first issue is the ability of domestic firms to expand their business into high-productivity sectors such as manufacturing and similar activities; and the second concerns the ability of productive industries to attract adequate labour for their expansion while offering wages that can make a significant difference to workers' well-being. The second part of the chapter shows the significance and the implications of these two issues by drawing on existing literature and recently conducted primary research into the Ethiopian floriculture export sector.[1]

31.2 Capabilities of Domestic Firms and Structural Transformation

Low-income countries like Ethiopia that aspire to promote structural transformation need to expand their productive capabilities, especially in domestic firms, as it is often domestic firms (private and public) that are most important in driving sustained industrialization (Amsden 2009). Moreover, ownership usually determines the strategic location of activities. In contemporary global value chains (GVCs), R&D, technology-intensive inputs, product design, and production processes are often controlled by a few 'lead firms' or global buyers usually situated in their home, advanced countries (UNCTAD 2016). Nonetheless, the phenomenon of GVCs has led to the large-scale

[1] The effect of the sector on environment and workers' health is not covered here due to the limited space but its significance in constraining sustainable development is acknowledged. For more discussion of this issue see Sahle and Potting (2013) and Blattman and Dercon (2016). Also see Chapter 17 in this volume for general discussion of climate-related challenges in Ethiopia's economy.

spread of manufacturing jobs to developing countries (Baldwin, Ito, and Sato 2014). Despite the concentration of some of the higher value activities in advanced economies, thanks to GVCs 'it is now possible for developing countries to participate in the gains from producing the world's most complex and sophisticated products by specializing in tasks' (Ferrantino and Schmidt 2018). Domestic firms can be inserted into GVC nodes where relatively lower capabilities are required and henceforth may continuously upgrade their capabilities to capture higher value in the chains.

However, in such a globalized economy, capabilities are ultimately measured by global standards where huge numbers of firms strive to gain a competitive edge in export markets. This makes improving capabilities more difficult as firms need to be faster and more responsive in the search for 'new' technologies. Yet acquiring, adapting, mastering, and deepening industrial capabilities is often a long and costly process. Doing so is particularly difficult for domestic firms as they are often new to such operations and need more time to learn. This is partly the reason domestic firms in sub-Saharan Africa show limited participation in high-productivity sectors and, when they do, they tend to struggle to expand as they often lack the necessary government and other institutional support (UNCTAD 2013). Historically, domestic firms were able to drive industrialization with targeted assistance and incentives, which were provided through various forms of protectionism, long-term financing, and other forms of industrial policy (Chang 2002). While this is often considered much more difficult for latecomer industrializing economies nowadays, it is arguably still possible to use policy to promote the development of industrial capabilities (UNECA 2016).

31.3 Employment in Productive Industries and its Potential for Structural Transformation

Manufacturing and similar activities have strong potential to trigger positive 'cumulative causation' not only through increases in productivity and capabilities but also via employment and income (Kaldor 1966; Kalecki 1955; UNCTAD 2016). A deliberate focus on the interrelation between productivity, labour earning and employment, and fair distribution of productivity gains between profits and labour, are critical for progressive development (UNCTAD 2010; Wuyts 2011). However, achieving this is a painstaking endeavour requiring capabilities that are beyond the firm, including policy and institutional capacities to deal with factors that arise at global and national levels.

Globally, low-tech productive industries have created widespread employment, especially for women, but 'decent work deficits' have also become widespread in those sectors, partly owing to rising standards of global buyers and intense global competition causing dual pressure on suppliers—cutting production costs while at the same time meeting higher quality requirements (Barrientos et al. 2011). Even when supplying firms achieve technical upgrading, it does not necessarily lead to better employment; rather the outcome can be mixed, contributing positively for some groups of workers while causing wage compression and flexibilization for others. The latter are usually women workers at the bottom of the employment pyramid who also face additional gendered constraints at the workplace and beyond. Therefore, employment effects in female-dominated sectors should be measured not only against economic factors but also against structural ones that perpetuate gender inequality (Barrientos et al. 2011).

At the national level, one of the most common and severe challenges that arise at early stages of development is wage goods inflation, above all rises in the price of food and other basic wage goods that dominate the consumption of workers (Kalecki 1955). This can trouble both capital and labour. If firms have to raise wages to accommodate rising prices of the goods their employees mainly buy, this can easily lead to a squeeze on profits and so reduce investment (especially if they cannot raise prices in highly competitive markets for the firms' output). But if wages do not rise to catch up with wage goods inflation, then there is a risk that workers quit their jobs, that they are under-motivated and less productive, or that there are political protests, all of which also weaken investment dynamics. In the widespread prescription to make labour markets more flexible—which typically means or leads to downward pressure on wages—this fundamental insight of Kalecki's is lost.

The rest of this chapter discusses these two issues in the context of the Ethiopian floriculture export industry after briefly describing the methodology of the primary research underpinning the discussion.

31.4 Methodology

In discussing the first issue (the capabilities of domestic firms), in the national and global context of floriculture, the chapter mainly draws on primary data collected in 2016–17 in four phases in Ethiopia and the Netherlands (the major market) with the aim of measuring and understanding technological capabilities of domestic firms in the sector, their investment in learning and the challenges they experienced in doing so. A firm survey was conducted in all except two of the domestic firms in the sector and firm histories were undertaken for ten of the thirteen firms that participated in the survey. These firm histories involved repeated interviews carried out in three phases with firm owners, management staff, and employees of domestic firms, combined with interviews with relevant institutions—the horticulture producers and exporters association (EHPEA), the Ethiopian Horticulture Development Agency (EHDA),[2] the Development Bank of Ethiopia (DBE), market actors (two unpackers and two traders), a representative of the Royal FloraHolland auction, key informants (5) and foreign firms (3). The technological

[2] EHDA has been undergoing thorough reorganization (including name change) during the fieldwork.

capability approach was combined with the GVC approach to develop a capability matrix that guided the design of the local firm survey (for more detail see Melese 2017a).

The discussion of the second issue (employment) mainly draws on separate primary research conducted in 2014 designed to understand employment in the Ethiopian flower sector and its effect on reducing poverty from asset accumulation and gender perspectives. A survey questionnaire was administered to 147 women workers selected from six farms (three domestic and three foreign owned). Five of the farms were located in peri-urban areas near Holeta and Debre Zeit towns while one was in a rural area of Gurage zone. From the roster of each farm 10 per cent of the workers were randomly selected; each had worked from three months to eight years in the same farm. In addition, twenty-four randomly selected women in each group were interviewed and life histories recorded, including marital status, as well as when possible male members of their household (spouse and/or father), to deepen understanding of gendered constraints at work as well as outside. Semi-structured and informal interviews were conducted with farm management and labour union leaders focusing on employment features, labour management, and labour relations. Labour union representatives at federation level were also interviewed.

31.5 Features of Global Floriculture

Since the emergence of floriculture GVCs, with fragmented functions dispersed across borders and reintegrated through coordination and governance of 'lead firms', export production is increasingly dominated by developing countries. The major markets remain the traditional locations (Western countries), with the Netherlands playing a leading role in the global trade, hosting the largest flower auction worldwide and controlling over 35 per cent of all applications for community plant variety rights.[3] Flowers are globally traded in two major market channels: the auction system and direct sales. The former primarily refers to the Dutch auction, the largest global flower auction owned by Dutch cooperatives, but its standards and operations appear to be influenced by the power of large European wholesalers and retailers. The Dutch auction is a market platform where supply and demand meet to set daily prices through a 'clock system'; this in turn tends to serve as a reference price in the global industry. The auction is open to suppliers with a range of capabilities that meet its minimum quality and safety standards. But successful integration in the system depends on suppliers' abilities to meet rising quality and production standards alongside learning the market culture, and building market relations and reputations by ensuring consistency and reliability, which can also serve as stepping stones to engaging in direct sales.

[3] https://www.hollandtradeandinvest.com/key-sectors/horticulture-and-starting-materials/horticulture-facts-and-figures (accessed on 23 March 2018).

Direct sales, where buyers and suppliers engage in direct trade relations, have been growing in both traditional and emerging markets. In the Western markets, this channel is dominated by a handful of large retailers and, unlike the auction, the direct sales channel usually offers contract-based agreements with fixed prices plus other specifications. But the auction has also accommodated this trend by allowing 'pre-clock' direct deals alongside the traditional system, which creates additional opportunities for smaller supplier firms that specialize in niche markets such as florists. Furthermore, the direct sales channel is prominent in newly emerging markets like the Middle East where import agents play a major role between suppliers and retailers/big buyers.

However, developments in the market have been accompanied by stiff competition and increasing pressure on profit margins. This is partly because the number of flower-exporting countries has increased and year-long demand is now met by abundant supply. More importantly, lead firms that govern and coordinate the GVCs set increasingly stringent standards to differentiate products, also to comply with public and private regulations (including phyto-sanitary standards in international trade, environmental codes of practice, and Fairtrade voluntary standards). These requirements have implications for suppliers' ability to upgrade production processes, managerial and organizational skills, but their impact on labour conditions remains controversial (Cramer et al. 2017).

31.6 The Development of the Flower Sector in Ethiopia

Ethiopia is one of the more recent latecomer suppliers but it has rapidly positioned itself among the top five exporters. The origin of flower export production can be traced back to two state-owned horticulture farms under the Derg regime with their own marketing and distribution centre (Etfruit). Alongside the horticulture crops these farms mainly produced, they also exported summer flowers and briefly experimented with rose production. In the mid-1990s the spillover effect of those state-owned farms attracted small-scale private domestic firms and today's industry is built upon these early experiences. The pioneers had a demonstration effect that attracted a few more investors but the sector failed to achieve meaningful expansion owing largely to the absence of appropriate infrastructure and institutional support. However, since 2002 things have begun to change primarily thanks to targeted industrial policy building on this prior agro-industrial experience.

The government provided generous investment incentives to both domestic and foreign investors, which included cheap land in water-abundant areas in close proximity to Bole international airport, soft loans from the state-owned DBE, income tax holidays, loss rescheduling provision, and removal of tariffs and duties on capital goods, spare parts, and inputs. This led to a large influx of foreign and domestic investors in subsequent years.

Initially promotion and support for the sector were undertaken by a special council under the prime minister's office, but later a lead agency (EHDA) was set up to support the sector under a centralized system. Moreover, the sector received continuous international support especially from Dutch development cooperation which subsidized investors, encouraged institution building, and provided firm-level training. The EHPEA played a prominent role in lobbying government to design incentives, to coordinate and implement all support, and to promote public–private partnership programmes. Altogether these three actors played a prominent role in bringing the sector up to a competitive standard at global level in a relatively short time.

The sector attracted several foreign firms with prior experience in the business including Afriflora (locally Sher Ethiopia), the largest rose farm in the world with over 450 hectares of production in Ethiopia, and others particularly from the Netherlands and Israel. But many more inexperienced domestic and foreign firms also entered the sector without preferential support. Until 2007–8 the sector enjoyed rapid growth with over 70 operational firms cultivating 922 hectares of land, which was more than five-fold growth compared to 2004–5. In the same period, the sector generated an average of US$53 million per year and created direct employment for 34,720 people (Melese 2017a). In 2015, the total cultivated land reached 1,623 hectares and sixty-six firms exported 50 million kilograms of flowers, generating US$225 million in foreign exchange.[4]

The sector also induced more investment and employment in other high- (and low-) productivity activities through backward linkages to the packaging industry and forward linkages to Ethiopian Airlines, which led to a substantial growth in the airline's logistics and perishable cargo lifting capabilities (Oqubay 2015). However, the sector still largely depends on imported inputs (chemicals and fertilizers) and many firms continued importing part of their packaging materials because of quality and cost advantages.

After 2008 the growth of the Ethiopian sector slowed down partly due to the effects of the global financial crisis on the global floriculture trade (Rabobank 2016). The total number of flower firms in Ethiopia peaked (at 86) in 2006–7 but the following years showed a considerable drop and volatility as many domestic and foreign firms began collapsing. The number of domestic firms fell from thirty-eight in 2006–7 to fifteen (including one joint venture) in June 2016, whereas the number of foreign firms increased from twenty-six to sixty-six in the same period.

Apart from the fall in global demand, several other factors help explain this decline in the number of firms, including poor selection of investors which led to abusive and unproductive use of incentives, and lack of a proper 'reciprocal control mechanism' which de-motivated reinvestment and might have diverted the soft finance towards unproductive sectors. In addition, lack of capabilities in institutions to finance and monitor relatively new projects, and to evolve and tailor their support to the development of the sector, played a role.

[4] Based on primary data collected from EHDA.

In addition, several collapsed firms, especially the domestic ones, had joined the sector without knowing what the business requires. Thanks to the investment incentives and the 'government brokers'[5] who provided a ready-made feasibility study, several firms were able to set up operations but failed in their learning efforts or 'learning to learn' (Stiglitz 1987). Yet, there were firms that accumulated significant production capabilities but appeared to fail to build the strong management and market relations that were needed to cope with shocks.

31.7 Characteristics of Domestic Firms and their Capability-Building Problems

In 2016, there were fifteen domestic firms in the sector: five were owned by indigenous private businesses, another five by diaspora, two by party-affiliated endowment companies and the remaining three by Sheik Al-Amoudi, an Ethio-Saudi billionaire who runs various business conglomerates in Ethiopia and elsewhere.[6] The farms in the first two categories were managed by their owners or family members and except for one firm none of the domestic investors had prior experience in floriculture or related businesses. But most of them came from families with a business background and they, especially the diaspora and indigenous investors, were attracted to the sector because of the investment incentives that they came across during their search for profitable business opportunities.

All these firms made progress in developing their technological capabilities beyond the most basic level and faced fewer challenges at the initial stage of their investment as they hired foreign consultants to execute the investment project: choosing equipment, setting up facilities and operations, and training workers. They also hired additional foreign managers for key functions such as production, protection, and irrigation, to oversee the overall production process and facilitate skill formation among local workers. In 2016, except in one firm, all foreign managers were replaced by local experts, and three firms continued intermittently using foreign consultants. But two of the thirteen surveyed firms appeared on the verge of collapse and are not included in Table 31.1.

Although the firms in Table 31.1 continued expanding their business, their productivity (measured by numbers of exported rose stems or export value per worker) and level of land utilization varied significantly, despite applying roughly similar physical technologies

[5] Interviews revealed that individuals who were believed to be government-commissioned brokers were engaged in persuading individuals and businesses (including diaspora) to invest in floriculture by approaching them with ready-made feasibility studies/business plans and explaining government support and incentives.

[6] Domestic firms include businesses owned by those of Ethiopian origin but who officially have another country's nationality.

Table 31.1 Performance of domestic flower firms

Firm	location	Annual average export volume (number of stems) in 000	Annual export value (US$) in 000	Cultivated land (ha)	Share of cultivated land/total land holding	Number of workers	Average annual export/ha	Average annual export/worker	Annual export value/worker
A	D/Zeyit	14,466	1,865	26	0.72	550	556,371	26,301	3,391
B	Sebeta	14,170	2,067	27	0.21	710	524,829	19,958	2,911
C	Holeta	15,183	2,208	16	0.56	400	948,924	37,957	5,521
D	Sebeta	18,769	2,215	20	0.67	520	938,469	36,095	4,260
E	D/Zeyit	28,370	3,947	15	0.75	420	1,891,341	67,548	9,398
F	D/Zeyit	11,628	1,320	10	0.25	260	1,162,773	44,722	5,076
G	Sebeta	7,814	1,144	18	0.9	300	434,114	26,047	3,813
J	Bahir dar	43,939	5,040	38	0.31	955	1,156,294	46,010	5,277
K	Sebeta	29,894	3,921	27	0.5	675	1,107,181	44,287	5,808
L	D/Zeyit	24,254	2,667	17.5	0.56	480	1,385,941	50,529	5,557
M	D/Zeyit	12,890	1,740	12	0.55	400	1,074,174	32,225	4,350
Average		**20,125**	**2,558**	**21**	**0.54**	**515**	**1,016,401**	**39,244**	**5,033**

Source: Adapted from Melese (2017a).

and operating in similar locations. Regardless of these differences, all seemed to struggle to upgrade further as they faced several mutually reinforcing challenges.

31.7.1 Market Diversification

Floriculture GVCs are characterized by trust-based network relations that demand higher marketing skills with particular abilities to keep continued interaction and network building. But this was not a primary concern of domestic firms at the initial stage of their investment since they completely relied on the Dutch auction, which 'freed' them from immediate worries about market search and marketing. This, to a certain extent, influenced their decision to enter the sector and over 60 per cent of most domestic firms' exports are still sold via the Dutch auction.

The firms initially focused only on developing their production capabilities. But as they accumulated export experience and improved product quality, the price fluctuation at the auction alarmed them and provoked some to develop marketing capabilities. While some strategically reacted to this while keeping their position in the auction market, others appeared to take spontaneous measures to diversify markets and sales channels, which in turn affected their performance in the auction market where capturing higher price requires consistency (in quality, volume, presence at the auction) and building market relations. This means successful diversification requires stringent, distinct but also overlapping requirements of various markets to be met, implying the need for more capabilities at production (size and scope) as well as marketing level.

Unlike foreign firms, who often have their own separate marketing subsidiaries in major markets, marketing tasks of domestic firms are typically done by the owner of the farm who tries to handle all market-related issues from market intelligence to promotion in addition to managing the overall business. Yet, most of the owners do not have the marketing know-how and social skills that are expected in global markets. Finding appropriate marketing expertise in the domestic market was reported to be difficult and domestic firms appeared unwilling to invest in on-the-job training in marketing skills because of the costs and other difficulties. For instance, arranging travel to major markets is considered important to develop the necessary skills but is logistically difficult and costly. However, there are relatively easily accessible emerging markets that showed demand growth such as the Middle East. Those and other markets in the Global South can serve as a starting point to build marketing skills while exploiting existing opportunities in the traditional markets. Most domestic firms began diversifying to these markets but their move has not necessarily been accompanied by an upgrade of their marketing and other capabilities.

31.7.2 Management Skills

Flower exporting is a full-time business with significant complexity, requiring fast and smooth flow of decisions and resources. There is a very narrow margin for failure: for example, not only must flowers meet demanding phyto-sanitary, quality, and product specification requirements, but once cut the flowers have to be transported to the airport very fast, efficiently loaded into cold storage facilities, and transported speedily to market. But for owners of domestic firms, often a flower farm is just one of the several businesses they manage. This implies that to expand their flower export business they need to have qualified managers in key positions on the farm, proper delegation of responsibilities, and effective communication. However, many of the firms appear to lack the management skills and long-term vision as well as resources to develop them.

Although having a diversified business seems to support their flower farms by providing finance in bad seasons, it also causes a lack of attention and commitment to further building their capabilities. As the owners usually run businesses in both high- and low-productivity activities (often targeting the domestic market), their time and resource allocation seems to be influenced by the short-term reward in each business. For example, as pressure mounts in their other businesses, owners sometimes delay expansions (replacing old plant) or timely supply of inputs to the flower business, which can have long-term effects on their capabilities.

Furthermore, some firms have a rigid hierarchical management style that hinders learning amongst workers, while a few, particularly party-affiliated endowment firms, have a highly bureaucratic structure without proper management delegation, not to mention lack of commitment, causing delays in important decisions and recurrent failures of production and export. For example, one endowment firm experienced production/export loss several times due to delays in chemical supplies and greenhouse maintenance because the farm management has no authority to supply those inputs; rather it is at the discretion of a management committee at head office that is responsible for diversified businesses. This committee often delayed decisions, providing the inputs after several weeks, when the damage had already been done.

Despite all this, most owners/managers acquired important management and organizational skills because of their participation in the flower sector, which is their largest and the most demanding business. It particularly helped them to gain skills in managing large numbers of workers (160–955 workers), organizing labour, and quickly responding to changes at production and marketing levels. This indicates that if incentivized strategically and selectively, the skills gained can be utilized to expand their existing productive activities and for further technological upgrading.

31.7.3 Investment in R&D

Flower firms invest in testing varieties, and try to improve quality and productivity by using codified technology acquired from breeders and consultants, also using tacit knowledge that is gained from repetitive trials. The same goes for propagation of plants, irrigation technologies and disease prevention techniques where local experts have mastered capabilities embodied in both machines and people. Ethiopians have taken over tasks previously done by foreign experts. But the firms only focus on activities that have an immediate impact on their existing business, for example, never initiating R&D

for developing new varieties or plant propagation techniques, which they regard as beyond their scope. However, in a broader productive capabilities perspective, such R&D can help move into higher technologies both in the specific sector and in other high-value or traditional agriculture businesses. This in turn requires an improvement in Ethiopia's public investment in agricultural R&D, which is one of the lowest in sub-Saharan Africa (IFPRI 2014).[7]

31.7.4 Retaining Labour

Although there is a large and growing labour force in Ethiopia with an estimated 16 per cent unemployment rate and an even higher rate for women (Suzuki, Mano, and Abebe 2017), firms face challenges in attracting and retaining labour. This applies to the entire sector (including foreign firms), which faced a turnover rate of at least 20 per cent in 2013 with several firms indicating a labour turnover rate of 30 to 50 per cent. As EHPEA indicated, the situation has persisted and domestic firms reported an average rate of 30 per cent in 2016, most of them also experiencing labour shortages.

The thirteen domestic firms reported paying a minimum monthly wage of 750–900 ETB including all employment incentives. Although the work is low skilled (at most requiring literacy), it requires delicate handling, dexterity, and speed that can take repetitive practice to master. For example, some firms indicated that a newly recruited packhouse worker usually needs two years to double her speed and three–six months to meet the average numbers of bunches per day per worker. Moreover, as the operation is organized like an assembly line, the loss of one worker affects the performance of the whole team in that specific line, so high turnover means significant loss of productivity for firms.

As redressing measures, firms tend to focus on increasing the productivity of the existing 'stable' labour force by improving labour organization and providing various incentives. But the effectiveness of the incentives tends to be weakened as the workers are aware that the threat of losing their job is low. Lack of labour is another problem especially when firms undertake expansions either replacing old plants or adding new greenhouses. A few firms planned for more ways to attract labour and developed retention strategies such as constructing housing dormitories where there was sufficient land, adopting Fairtrade certificates so they could subsidize food and other in-kind benefits, and so on. However, further increasing basic wages did not seem to appeal to the firms. Nevertheless, a preliminary finding of a study conducted in 2018 shows that there are a few exceptional foreign firms that avoided high labour turnover by significantly increasing their wages and improving non-wage conditions while still enjoying a considerable profit.[8] In those firms, minimum wage is reported to be 1,200 ETB per month plus

[7] https://www.asti.cgiar.org/pdf/factsheets/Ethiopia-Factsheet.pdf (accessed 31 January 2018).

[8] Information obtained during informal discussion with C. Cramer and J. Sender who had just conducted the fieldwork. February 2018, Addis Ababa.

benefits including lunch and medical care. This indicates that market pressure is not the only reason for wage compression, which can also be due to lack of production and market-level capabilities or 'unfair' profit maximizing.

The high labour turnover and firms' inability to find enough labour undermines the common assumption about such industrial activities, their ability to absorb 'surplus' labour from low-productivity sectors and accelerate accumulation of manufacturing experience. It also weakens the potential for rapid increases in productivity, reinvestment, and employment within the sector. Section 31.8 discusses employment in the sector in more detail covering both domestic and foreign firms. It examines the impact of employment on improving the well-being of women workers and its tendency to trigger a virtuous cycle of reducing poverty and challenging gender inequality.

31.8 Employment in the Ethiopian Floriculture Sector and its Impact on Women Workers

The Ethiopian floriculture sector is estimated to directly employ more than 40,000 people, of whom over 70 per cent are women concentrated at the bottom of the employment pyramid (in greenhouse and packhouse work where low-skilled labour is required). Employment and working conditions in the sector have evolved with the sector's development. Initially workers were randomly hired at the farm gate. They were expected to learn by doing with the help of existing workers and supervisors. But as operations expanded, understanding of the business increased, and with the pressures of the global market, farms felt the need to secure a more stable labour force, changing some of their recruitment practices and offering some incentives and benefits.

Employment was commonly on a temporary basis, but since 2011 permanent contracts have become more common owing to the high labour turnover and, to a lesser extent, to the government's tendency to enforce private pension arrangement and the international standards adopted by several farms.

There are labour unions in most farms but they are usually inactive or focus on dispute resolution rather than bargaining with employers for better employment conditions. Employment is officially for six days a week and eight hours a day, but in practice it is extended until the daily work is finished except during peak seasons, when overtime is usually compensated according to the labour law.

Despite some improvements in wage and non-wage working conditions, the sector has continued to face high labour turnover and labour shortages but with the expansion of local and international standards most of the firms have gained insights into labour organization and management, including designing incentive schemes to stabilize labour and improve productivity. More farms have introduced bonus schemes, annual increments, protective clothes (albeit irregularly available), and some subsidized meals, while others have even mobilized labour from relatively remote villages and provided accommodation near the farm site. However, access to most of the incentives is conditional on performance and is used to discipline labour, while the minimum wage is kept between 400 and 600 ETB except in a few large foreign firms, where the minimum wage has reached around 682 ETB (Melese 2017b). Since there is no statutory minimum wage, farms can set wages independently. However, wages in the sector tend to be too low to attract enough labour from informal and less productive sectors or to adjust for the high inflation that has occurred in the last decade (Blattman and Dercon 2016).

Since 2005 annual inflation, mainly driven by cereal prices, has increased rapidly, recording two major spikes in August 2008 and August 2011, reaching 61.6 per cent (food inflation 79.2 per cent) and 40.7 per cent (food inflation 50 per cent) respectively (Geiger and Goh 2012). Although food inflation remained in single digits after 2013, food prices stayed higher than the average price recorded in the five years 2008–12 (WFP and CSA 2014). Inflation continued to rise at unstable rates and the most recent estimate by the CSA (CPI of February 2018)[9] showed a 20.9 per cent increase in food inflation compared to the preceding year. In a situation like this, the poorest members of society such as wage workers are hardest hit, especially if their wages fail to adjust for inflation (Headey et al. 2012; Blattman and Dercon 2016).

In a 2014 survey, basic expenditure data were collected on selected food items, rent, water, and electricity, and on a few consumables (firewood and soap). The result shows an average expenditure of ETB 1,154 per month. But as Table 31.2 shows, only 1 per cent of the workers surveyed could meet these needs from their net wage.[10] This puts the workers in a serious situation, especially the migrant workers who made up 44 per cent of the women surveyed. For migrant workers (who earn below 750 ETB), food expenses were more than 60 per cent of their total expenses and the rest was spent on rent and

Table 31.2 Wage after mandatory deductions and share of workers earning it

Net wage in ETB	Per cent of workers (total = 147)
<=600)	31
601–749	53
750–959	12
960–1153	3
>=1154	1

Source: Author's survey 2014.

[9] http://www.csa.gov.et/index.php (accessed on 26 March 2018).

[10] These women had usually worked above five years in the same farm and raised their wages through annual increments.

basic consumables and sometimes on *iqub*.[11] However, their food usually cannot last till the end of the month so they often cut down food consumption (number of meals per day and variety) and sometimes resort to credit, which can be extended by neighbourhood kiosks based on trust earned after staying in the same rented house for a few months. On top of that, landlords increased their rent once or twice a year on the pretext of rising living costs, which usually eats up any wage increments.

Nonetheless, contrary to the findings of Blattman and Dercon (2016), studies report that workers in the flower sector (in urban and/or peri-urban areas) earn significantly higher wages than workers with similar characteristics in comparable sectors and save more regularly (Suzuki, Mano, and Abebe 2017). But to understand the impact on women's well-being, it is important to examine the saving mechanisms the women use, since the practice of saving alone cannot provide adequate evidence about well-being, especially in this sector where women workers sometimes use destructive saving strategies like cutting meals and increasing their pressure of work through overtime (100 per cent of the surveyed women) as well as spending their day off on an additional day of waged labour in their neighbourhood like washing clothes for better-off families or in rural areas working on household farms when available (41 per cent). Moreover, some women could save because they receive support from their family. For instance, 20 per cent of workers surveyed receive cereal from their family farm in return for their cash support for buying farming inputs, school materials for siblings or for their own child left behind with family members. Similarly, Getahun and Villanger (2017) found that employment in flower farms led to an accumulation of tangible as well as intangible assets, such as improving the bargaining power of women in the intra-household relations of married rural workers. However, the accumulation appeared to reinforce structural gender inequality, as it took the form of reduced leisure time for daughters while increasing that of sons (Getahun and Villanger 2017). This trend is far from exceptional as it was also found that older girls drop out of school and take up domestic work to supplement the income of their mothers, especially in the case of divorced women who were significant in the survey sample (15 per cent).

Apart from that, gender-based structural constraints created greater pressure on women workers including workplace sexual harassment and social stigma in their community. Evidence from life histories suggested that most of the workers had a traumatic background and had experienced sexual abuse and domestic violence (17 women out of 24). This appeared to affect their view of their job on the farm, which they felt rewarded them with dignity and self-sufficiency. But this is not the case for all farms. In four of the six farms workers reported sexual harassment that involved supervisors threatening to fire women workers or bribing them with bonuses or sick leave to get them to sleep with them or to do their domestic work free of charge, such as washing clothes or preparing

[11] *Iqub* is an indigenous form of rotating saving and credit system run by self-selected group members. Workplace *iqub* is prevalent, especially in peak seasons when workers can earn more from overtime. The participants are usually those who stay longer than six months and establish stronger social networks at the workplace.

meals. Furthermore, women workers, especially migrants, face gender-based social stigma unless they returned to their village with a 'visible' better status. As their life histories explained, women migrating to a 'city' are viewed negatively by their community and would not be considered eligible for marriage unless they return with 'better status', which might manifest itself in upgrading the family house, setting up a business, buying/using 'city' consumer goods which even can trigger a new flow of migration.

The women sometimes enter into a relationship with male colleagues in order to protect themselves from workplace sexual harassment and to avoid social stigma ('married' status is socially valued). Although this turned out well for a few, it also led to reproductive health complications for others due to aborting unplanned pregnancies outside clinics.

In general, the evidence shows the complexity of assessing the impact of employment on women workers as any assessment needs to go beyond immediate economic issues to look at shifts in gender relations. However, earning an adequate wage is key in any virtuous cycle of investment, productivity, and employment. In order for employment to have a transformational impact on poverty reduction and gender inequality, wages need to be enough to meet daily necessities without forcing women into destructive accumulations such as skipping meals and girls' withdrawal from school. Unfortunately, the wages in the Ethiopian floriculture sector appear to be very far from that if measured using the Anker methodology (Anker and Anker 2017).[12] In 2015, this methodology was applied to estimate a living wage benchmark in Ziway (Ethiopia) with a focus on foreign-owned flower farms. The prevailing wages on the farms, inclusive of all job benefits and incentives, were found to stand at 1,058 ETB, lower than the wage estimated using the World Bank poverty line of US$1.25PPP, which was ETB 1,206. The living wage excluding mandatory deductions was estimated to be 2,208 ETB (Melese 2017b).

31.9 Conclusion

This chapter discussed two issues that threaten the development of productive industries in Ethiopia. The first is the ability of domestic firms to expand their productive activities and accumulate technological capabilities; the other concerns employment in those industries and firms' ability to attract labour on terms that allow for an improvement in living standards.

[12] In the Anker methodology a living wage estimates the cost of a basic living standard for a worker and his/her family just above the poverty line by considering contextual factors and food commonly consumed by workers. This involves adding up the cost of three expenditure groups, food (for a low-cost nutritious diet), housing (for basic healthy housing), and other essential expenses for a family, and then adding a small margin for sustainability and emergencies. The estimation for Ziway included extensive fieldwork supplemented by various national survey data. A family size of five with 1.653 full-time workers was applied for estimation (for detail see Melese 2017b).

The potential of productive industries like floriculture to contribute to structural transformation lies in both capital and labour dynamics. To unlock this potential it is necessary to address the constraints on both sides. Not doing so might result in a failure to form the solid ground needed for sustained industrialization, in particular allowing poverty to persist. Government policies played a significant role in the early development of Ethiopian floriculture but as the sector developed little was done to select and encourage domestic firms that make technological efforts. Despite this, more than a dozen domestic firms stayed afloat but with varied capabilities. Some are doing very well in a sector that increasingly became dominated by foreign firms, while many failed to adequately expand their production and marketing activities and lacked motivation and/or capabilities in moving up the technology ladder. Industrial policy needed to evolve to support strategically selected domestic (and foreign) firms that make adequate efforts to build their capabilities and improve wages alongside strengthening reciprocal control mechanisms.

Nevertheless, the expansion of these labour-intensive industries, whether by domestic or foreign firms, depends on their ability to attract adequate labour, which is one of the important rationales for expanding productive industries. The Ethiopian flower sector illustrates the challenge well: it has succeeded in creating large numbers of jobs, especially for women, many of whom have migrated long distances and left extremely low-productivity employment; but at the same time, the sector has found it difficult to secure a stable workforce and to pay wages that keep up with the fast rate of increase in prices of food and other basic wage goods. Thus, managing wage levels and the rising cost of wage goods could be one step towards removing constraints on both capital and labour sides to further expansion of investment and employment in productive industries, while at the same time improving living standards for workers.

References

Amsden, A. (2001). *The Rise of 'the Rest': Challenges to the West from Late-Industrialising Countries*, 2nd edition (New York: Oxford University Press).

Amsden, A. (2009). 'Nationality of Firm Ownership in Developing Countries: Who Should "Crowd Out" Whom in Imperfect Markets?' in *Industrial Policy and Development: The Political Economy of Capability Accumulation*, ed. M. Cimoli, G. Dosi, and J. E. Stiglitz (Oxford: Oxford University Press): 409–23.

Amsden, A. (2010). 'Say's Law, Poverty Persistence, and Employment Neglect', *Journal of Human Development and Capabilities* 11 (1): 55–66.

Anker, R. and M. Anker (2017). *Living Wages around the World: Manual for Measurement* (London: Edward Elgar).

Akyüz, Y. (2015). 'Foreign Direct Investment Agreements and Economic Development: Myth and Realities', Research Paper No. 63, South Centre, Geneva.

Baldwin, R., T. Ito, and H. Sato (2014). 'The Smile Curve: Evolving Sources of Value Added in Manufacturing', Joint Research Program Series, IDE-JETRO.

Barrientos, S., F. Mayer, J. Pickles, and A. Posthuma (2011). 'Decent Work in Global Production Networks: Framing the Policy Debate', *International Labour Review* 150 (3/4): 297–317.

Blattman, C. J. and S. Dercon (2016). 'Occupational Choice in Early Industrializing Societies: Experimental Evidence on the Income and Health Effects of Industrial and Entrepreneurial Work', IZA discussion papers No. 10255.

Chang, H. (2002). *Kicking away the Ladder: Development Strategy in Historical Perspective* (London: Anthem Press).

Cramer, C., D. Johnston, B. Mueller, et al. (2017). 'Fairtrade and Labour Markets in Ethiopia and Uganda', *Journal of Development Studies* 53 (6): 841–56.

Ferrantino, M. and G. Schmidt (2018). 'Using Gross Trade Data to Map Archetypal GVCs', Policy Research Working Paper 8296, World Bank, Washington, DC.

Geiger, M. and C. Goh (2012). 'Ethiopia Economic Update: Overcoming Inflation, Raising Competitiveness', World Bank, Washington, DC.

Getahun, T. D. and E. Villanger (2017). 'Labour-Intensive Jobs for Women and Development: Intra-Household Welfare Effects and its Transmission Channels', *Journal of Development Studies* 54 (7): 1232–52.

Haraguchi, N., C. Cheng, and E. Smeets (2017). 'The Importance of Manufacturing in Economic Development: Has This Changed?' *World Development* 93: 293–315.

Headey, D., F. B. Nisrane, I. Worku, et al. (2012). 'Urban Wage Behavior and Food Price Inflation: The Case of Ethiopia', ESSP-II Working Paper No. 41.

IFPRI (2014). 'Taking Stock of National Agricultural R&D Capacity in Africa, South of Sahara', ASTI Synthesis Report, Nienke Beintema Gert-Jan Stads, November.

Kaldor, N. (1966). *Causes of the Slow Rate of Economic Growth of the United Kingdom: An Inaugural Lecture* (Cambridge: Cambridge University Press).

Kalecki, M. (1955). 'The Problem of Financing of Economic Development', *Indian Economic Review* 2 (3): 1–22.

Lall, S. (1992). 'Technological Capabilities and Industrialization', *World Development* 20 (2): 165–86.

Melese, A. T. (2017a). 'Ethiopian-Owned Firms in the Floriculture Global Value Chain: With What Capabilities?' Working Paper No. 2017:2, Centre of African Economies, Roskilde Universitet.

Melese, A. T. (2017b). 'Living Wage Report Non-Metropolitan Urban Ethiopia', Series 1, Report 6, April 2017. Prepared for The Global Living Wage Coalition.

Oqubay, A. (2015). *Made in Africa: Industrial Policy in Ethiopia* (New York: Oxford University Press).

Rabobank (2016). 'World Floriculture Map 2016: Equator Countries Gathering Speed'. https://services.rabobank.com/publicationservice/download/publication/token/bahpNYbxohdtZPhpFMHX (accessed on 25 August 2018).

Sahle, A. and J. Potting (2013). 'Environmental Life-Cycle Assessment of Ethiopian Rose Cultivation', *Science of the Total Environment* 443: 163–72.

Storm, S. (2015). 'Structural Change', *Development and Change* 46 (4): 666–99.

Stiglitz, J. (1987). 'Learning to Learn, Localized Learning and Technological Progress', in *Economic Policy and Technological Performance*, ed. P. Dasgupta and P. Stoneman (Cambridge: Cambridge University Press): 125–53.

Suzuki, A., Y. Mano, and G. Abebe (2017). 'Earnings, Savings, and Job Satisfaction in a Labor-Intensive Export Sector: Evidence from the Cut Flower Industry in Ethiopia', Discussion Paper Series HIAS-E-55, Hitotsubashi Institute for Advanced Study, Hitotsubashi University.

UNCTAD (2010). 'Macroeconomic Aspects of Job Creation and Unemployment', in *Trade and Development Report 2010* (Geneva: UNCTAD) 77–98.

UNCTAD (2013). 'The Private Sector, Enterprises and Productivity', in *Economic Development in Africa Report 2013: Inter-African Trade—Unlocking Private Sector Dynamism* (Geneva: UNCTAD) 63–94.

UNCTAD (2016). *Trade and Development Report 2016: Structural Transformation for Inclusive and Sustained Growth* (New York: UN).

UNECA (2016). *Transformative Industrial Policy for Africa* (Addis Ababa: Economic Commission for Africa).

WFP and CSA (2014). 'Comprehensive Food Security and Vulnerability Analysis (CFSVA)', Ethiopia, World Food Program and Ethiopian Central Statistics Agency.

Wuyts, M. (2011). 'Growth, Employment and the Productivity–Wage Gap: Revisiting the Growth–Poverty Nexus', *Development and Change* 42 (1): 437–47.

CHAPTER 32

AGRICULTURAL MARKETS IN ETHIOPIA

BART MINTEN, SENESHAW TAMRU, AND THOMAS REARDON

32.1 Introduction

When food systems and agricultural markets transform, they tend to go through fairly typical stages (Reardon et al. forthcoming; Reardon and Timmer 2014). In the *traditional* system, farmers are mostly focused on production for own consumption. The urban share of the population is low and supply chains are mainly short and local, serving own consumption, local villages, and nearby towns. In the *transitional* system, markets become more important. Value chains extend spatially because of growing demand from cities and an expansion in the catchment areas for merchants (Braudel 1982). There are emerging public standards of quality, but spot-market relations are still dominant. In the *modern* system, value chains are spatially extensive, but there is disintermediation and consolidation in various segments—such as in retail markets that are characterized by the dominance of supermarkets. Private and safety standards, contracts, and capital intensification are widespread in this stage.

In this chapter, we assess the functioning and the state of transformation of agricultural produce markets in Ethiopia. While Ethiopia has a long history of trade in coffee, spices, and grains, their importance in total agricultural supply has been limited as most of Ethiopia's production has traditionally been geared towards auto-consumption (Rashid and Negassa 2012). However, driven by population growth, improved connectivity, higher incomes, urbanization and consequent diet change, and policy reform, we are seeing a rapid transformation of agricultural supply chains, and we are beginning to see a change from the traditional to a transitional system.

The structure of the chapter is as follows. We first discuss the data used. We then consider contextual changes in Ethiopia. Changes in local and international markets are examined before the conclusions in the final section.

32.2 Data

Diverse datasets are used in this analysis. First, we use data collected by the Central Statistical Agency (CSA) in its annual Agricultural Sample Survey (AgSS) of agricultural households. The data cover the main agricultural season (*meher*) for the period 2004/5 to 2015/16 and pertain to smallholder farmers—those farming less than 25 hectares—who dominate agricultural land use in Ethiopia. During the period covered in this study, the sampling frame of the AgSS included all rural parts of the country except for the non-sedentary population of three zones in Afar and six zones in Somali regions (CSA 2016). We use these data to conduct descriptive analyses of commercial surplus estimates in Ethiopia.[1]

Second, the Ethiopian Grain Trading Enterprise (EGTE), a grain procurement arm of the government, gathers prices of cereals in a number of major wholesale markets in the country. Prices are collected during the early morning, late morning, and afternoon on major market days, with simple averages of these prices over the course of a month being reported as monthly prices. The prices are collected by noting prices from observed transactions. Wholesale prices at twelve selected markets are made available publicly. The use of EGTE prices for our assessment has two advantages: the prices are generally perceived to be of good quality and data have been collected in a similar manner over a long period allowing analysis of trends over time. We rely on the national CPI as constructed by the CSA to deflate these prices.

Third, import data were obtained from the Ethiopian Revenues and Customs Authority or downloaded from the United Nations' Comtrade webpage.[2] We also rely for some data on the National Bank of Ethiopia (NBE 2018), the Ministry of Trade, and the World Bank.

32.3 Contextual Changes

A number of changes that are happening in Ethiopia's economy have important implications for the functioning of agricultural and food markets. We discuss four major factors: infrastructure development, population growth and urbanization, income growth and consequent diet change, and policy reform.

First, Ethiopia has invested heavily in road network development over the last two decades. It is estimated that the length of asphalted roads has expanded four-fold over the last fifteen years from 3,900km in 2000/1 to 15,900 km in 2016/17 (NBE 2018). These investments in roads have led to better connectivity for Ethiopia's population. In 1994 an estimated 29 per cent of the Ethiopian population was located 10 hours or more in travel

[1] Note that output estimates from the AgSS are based on crop-cut methods that might lead to important over-estimations, in the order of 30 per cent (Verma, Marchant, and Scott 1988). Most of our analysis focuses on trends and should therefore be less affected by this caveat but the drawback of this method should be kept in mind during interpretation.

[2] http://comtrade.un.org/.

time from a city of at least 50,000 people. This figure had declined by 2015 to only 5 per cent of the population. Similarly, 23 per cent of the population was within three hours of such a city in 1994, but by 2015 this had improved to 59 per cent of the population (Schmidt et al. 2018). Ethiopia has also benefited from increasing access to mobile phone infrastructure, allowing for overall better communication in the country. It was estimated that tele-density, the number of phone subscribers per 100 inhabitants, increased from 7 per cent in 2008/9 to 63 per cent in 2016/17 (NBE 2018).

Second, the population of Ethiopia is rapidly growing. Since 2000, a population equivalent to that of Canada has been added to the country. The rural population in particular grew by 25 million people between 2000 and 2016. Over the same period, the urban population increased by 10 million. While the rural areas are rapidly growing, cities are growing even more rapidly. It was estimated in 2017 that 22 per cent of the Ethiopian population was living in cities (World Bank 2017a).

Third, Ethiopia has been one of the fastest-growing economies in the world in the last decade, an impressive feat for a low-income African country that exports relatively few natural resources. Average annual GDP growth over the decade 2007/8—2016/17 was 10 per cent (NBE 2018). This growth has been a major contributor to the important reductions in poverty observed in the last decade (World Bank 2014). Because of income growth, important diet change has been noted in recent years. Worku et al. (2017) analysed four rounds of national consumption data between 1996 and 2011 and find that quantities consumed per capita are increasing, that the relative importance of cereals is on the decline, but that cereals—and in particular maize—remain the largest source of calories in the food basket. They also illustrate that there is a relative shift in consumption to more expensive foods and that there are strong differences in food consumption by income level, but that all levels exhibited improvements over time.

Fourth, a number of market reforms have been introduced in recent decades. The government has gradually withdrawn from direct interventions in markets, for example by limiting the roles and responsibilities of the EGTE. However, the EGTE has continued ad hoc market interventions, including domestic and international procurement. The lack of rule-based, transparent, and predictable interventions by EGTE has been identified as a major issue in policy credibility (Rashid and Negassa 2012). An overvalued real exchange rate and elevated inflation are further aspects of policies that have had important impacts on the functioning of agricultural markets (Moller and Wacker 2017).

32.4 Local Markets

32.4.1 Expansion

The quantities traded and the total value of agricultural commercial surpluses are rapidly increasing. To illustrate these changes, we use commercial surplus data from the AgSS, valued at real yearly prices by crop. The left panel of Figure 32.1 shows that the overall

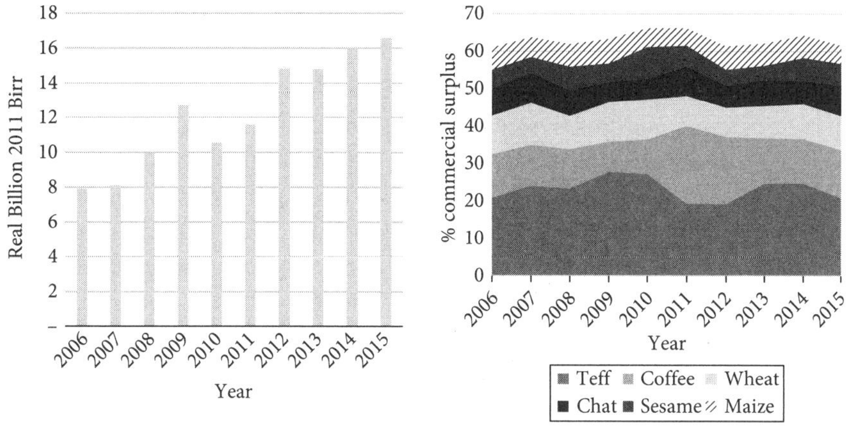

FIGURE 32.1 Real value of commercial agricultural surplus in Ethiopia and composition by commodity, 2006–15

Source: Authors' calculations based on data from CSA (2004–2016).

real value of the commercial surplus in agriculture in Ethiopia has doubled over the last decade, from 8 billion to 16 billion birr. There are also relatively small changes in the composition of this commercial surplus (Figure 32.1, right panel). Teff is by far the most important crop, making up on average 23 per cent of commercial surplus in the country. The other important crops are coffee (13 per cent), wheat (9 per cent), chat (7 per cent), and sesame (6 per cent). Maize—despite being the top crop for quantities produced in the country—is relatively less important as a component of the commercial surplus (at 6 per cent), consistent with consumption patterns in rural areas noted above.

A pattern of increased agricultural commercialization also shows up in the purchase behaviour of households. In the National Consumption Survey of 2011 respondents were asked how they paid for specific food purchases. As expected, there are large differences between rural and urban areas. Consumption of households' own agricultural products accounts for 42 per cent of total food expenditures in rural areas (Worku et al. 2017), but that share is much higher in calorie terms—two-thirds for crop producers—indicating that relatively more expensive foods are acquired through purchase (WFP/CSA 2014). These numbers reflect the high level overall of auto-subsistence of the rural Ethiopian economy (Worku et al. 2017).

However, it is to be noted that the value and share of auto-consumption is considerably lower than is often assumed. Even rural households depend in important ways on commercial food markets. This finding is consistent with other countries in Eastern and Southern Africa. For example, Dolislager, Tschirley, and Reardon (2015) show rural households bought 44 per cent (in value terms) of the food they consume. However, as might be expected, in urban areas in Ethiopia only 3 per cent of food expenditure comes from own production. Towns and cities are therefore important commercial food markets. Despite the low urbanization share in the total population of Ethiopia, urban markets made up about one-third of the total commercial food market in 2011.

32.4.2 Change in the Structure of Supply Chains

In this section we discuss the important growth and transformation in the trading and transport, processing, and food service sectors, and in retailing and distribution. According to Ethiopia's Social Accounting Matrix (SAM), it is estimated that in 2011, 4 per cent of the population was employed in agricultural trade or transport, one of the most important areas of employment in the service sector. This sector has shown rapid change. Minten, Tamiru, and Stifel (2014) reported that the number of trucks in urban agricultural wholesale markets rose by about 75 per cent over a decade. They also illustrate a shift to larger trucks being used for the transportation of agricultural products. Trader focus groups also indicated considerable growth over time in the number of traders in these markets (Minten, Tamiru, and Stifel 2014). With the number of traders perceived to be growing by almost 150 per cent over the past decade, and the number of brokers growing by more than 250 per cent, competition in these markets appears to have become keener and turnover per trader and broker lower. Bachewe et al. (2016) also show that agricultural trade is one of the main non-farm activities in rural areas in Ethiopia, especially so for the relatively rich.

A pattern that is seen globally with increases in income is the increased consumption of processed food. Benfica and Thurlow (2017) estimated the share of the food budget in 2011 in Ethiopia made up by processed food at 17 per cent. We rely on the most up-to-date data from two manufacturing enterprises surveys conducted by CSA to assess the food-processing sector (CSA 2012, 2015). In 2010/11, CSA surveyed large and medium-scale manufacturing firms, defined as those that employ ten or more people and use machinery powered by electricity. Based on this survey, 686 firms were identified as being involved in the manufacturing of food products and beverages, employing more than 67,000 people. The most important sub-sectors for employment in the food-processing sector are firms involved in grain milling, baking, and the production of sugar and sugar confectionery.

In 2013/14, CSA surveyed small-scale manufacturing firms, defined as those that employ less than ten people. Such firms are significantly more important in terms of employment than the larger firms: they employ 1.7 million people nationally, 52 per cent of whom are involved in food processing. Twenty-one per cent of these firms manufacture beverage or food products, with the production of bakery products being particularly important, employing more than 220,000 people. Grain milling accounts for 31 per cent of people employed in small-scale manufacturing industries with more than 540,000 people engaged. Overall, it is estimated that almost one million people are engaged in food processing in Ethiopia, or around 2 per cent of the economically active population of the country, defined as those aged 15–64 years.

Unfortunately, good and consistent time series data for the processing sector as a whole are lacking. However important changes are happening in the sector, as illustrated by two examples. First, in the case of dairy processing plants, there were eight companies active in the country in 2007. By 2017, this had more than tripled to twenty-five.[3] While there now is significant overcapacity in dairy processing, this example illustrates

[3] Data from the Ethiopian Meat and Dairy Industry Development Institute.

significant change in the sub-sector. Second, data were obtained from the Ministry of Trade on the number of licences given out to flour factories in Ethiopia. While in the early 2000s, about fifteen licences were given out annually, this rate had tripled to more than fifty in 2016. Further illustrating large changes in the milling sector, Comtrade data indicate that the three-year moving average of the value of imports of machinery for mills (HS code 8437) quadrupled from 7 million US$ in 2006 to 28 million US$ in 2015. Minten, Tamiru, and Stifel (2014) further provide evidence of the much greater presence of mills in urban areas, their evolving roles in moving towards one-stop retail shops, increasing competition, and lower milling margins over time.

As incomes rise, the share of food eaten away from home is increasing—a development that is seen globally.[4] In Ethiopia in 2011, the share of the urban food budget made up by food eaten away from home was estimated to be 16 per cent, i.e. twice as high as expenditure on fruit and vegetables. Moreover, a strong gradient over income is seen. The poorest quintile spends 6 per cent of its food budget on food eaten away from home, compared to 25 per cent for the richest quintile. Associated with this, we see the increasing emergence of a rapidly growing food service sector. For example, in the case of commercial *enjera*—the local staple pancake—markets, Minten et al. (2016) show how these markets are quickly transforming with a large number of people, especially in urban areas, now buying *enjera* instead of preparing it themselves. They estimate that more than 100,000 people in urban centres in Ethiopia make their living in *enjera*-making enterprises or through the retailing of the *enjera* produced. This sector therefore provides a high level of employment in Ethiopia, comparable to the much-publicized flower export sector (e.g. Oqubay 2015; Schaefer and Abebe 2015).

Modern retail and different food distribution and retail systems are emerging. Assefa et al. (2016) analyse the urban food retail market in Ethiopia and find increasing differentiation in food retail markets in recent years. Despite the prohibition of foreign direct investment in food retail, a domestic modern private retail sector is quickly appearing. However, its share of the total urban food retail market is still very small and, in contrast to roll-outs of modern retail in other countries (e.g. Reardon et al. 2003), it has not yet entered the cereal sector in a big way. The cereal sector remains overwhelmingly in the hands of local flour mills, cereal shops, and cooperative retail outlets. Another example of changes in distribution systems—in input markets—is the 'Ethio-chicken' model, where a private firm has engaged 2,500 agents in the country to distribute its chickens.

32.4.3 Market Performance

We now look at some measures of agricultural market performance. First, the degree to which prices move together across markets, i.e. how well they are integrated, provides a measure of how well these markets function. It has been shown that the absence of market

[4] For example, Smith, Dupriez, and Troubat (2014) note that food eaten away from home increased from 10 to 49 per cent of total food expenditure in the United States between 1900 and 2010 and that similar fast changes are seen in this area in a number of quickly transforming economies such as India, China, and Mauritius.

integration or of the passing on of price changes from one market to the next has important implications for economic welfare. Incomplete price transmission results in a reduction in the price information available to economic agents and consequently may lead to decisions that contribute to inefficient outcomes. Improved price transmission is also linked to encouraging allocative efficiency and long-run growth (Fackler and Goodwin 2001).

Several authors have shown that markets in Ethiopia have become better integrated over time and are more resilient to drought (Minten, Tamiru, and Stifel 2014; Dercon 1995; Hill and Fuje 2017; World Bank 2017b). We update that analysis and assess here the integration of cereal wholesale markets over the period 1999–2016 by studying market integration between various market pairs for each of the major cereals using the methodology developed by Van Campenhout (2007). In particular, we pair Addis Ababa with the most important regional wholesale markets for each of the cereals; thus our analysis reflects the major cereal flows in the country (Table 32.1).

Three important results can be highlighted from this market integration analysis. First, there has been an overall improvement in market integration over the two last decades. While the majority of wholesale markets for white teff, mixed teff, maize, and white wheat were well integrated at the end of 2016, only about half of those markets were integrated in 1999. Fifty per cent of the regional white teff, maize, and white wheat

Table 32.1 Degree of market integration of Addis Ababa with other cereal wholesale markets, 1999–2016

	Year	White teff	Mixed teff	Maize	White wheat	White sorghum
Total market pairs	1999	11	11	8	10	5
	2004	11	11	8	10	5
	2010	11	11	8	10	4
	2016	11	11	8	10	4
Per cent integrated markets	1999	36	27	25	70	60
	2004	38	27	25	80	60
	2010	36	45	50	80	75
	2016	50	45	50	80	50
Half-life of adjustment to price changes, in months	1999	1.2	4.0	2.0	4.3	0.7
	2004	1.0	3.7	1.6	4.0	0.6
	2010	1.0	3.7	0.8	3.6	0.5
	2016	0.8	3.2	0.8	2.2	3.0
Transaction costs, measured as per cent of average cereal prices in that period	1999	16	8	13	10	11
	2004	10	7	13	10	10
	2010	7	6	12	9	5
	2016	6	6	10	8	10

Source: Authors' calculation based on data from Ethiopian Grain Trading Enterprise (EGTE).

markets were integrated with respect to the Addis Ababa market in 2016, compared to 36, 25, and 70 per cent, respectively, in 1999. In contrast, there seems to be no improvement in sorghum market integration over time. Second, the speed of price adjustments has improved. This is illustrated in the average half-life of adjustment to price changes declining from an average of three months in 1999 to a month and a half in 2016. Compared to the case in 1999, it now takes about half the time for prices between wholesale markets to return back to half of the long-run equilibrium after a given price shock. Third, estimated transaction costs between the wholesale markets considered have come down substantially over time (bottom row, Table 32.1). Transaction costs fell by about 50 per cent for all of the cereals examined, except for white sorghum.[5]

Second, the analysis shows that marketing margins between agricultural markets are seemingly decreasing over time. Relying on EGTE price data from a number of wholesale markets in the country, Figure 32.2 shows that the standard deviations between wholesale market prices for cereals have all come down over time, expect for sorghum. Using the trend line for maize, wheat, and teff, standard deviations fell by 100 birr/quintal over the fifteen-year period, indicating that price differences between maize and wheat wholesale markets fell to one-third and half the differences at the beginning of the period. This decrease is probably a reflection of investments in road and communications infrastructure and the more competitive markets that have developed over time (Minten, Tamiru, and Stifel 2014). However, it is to be noted that there is still substantial volatility around this trend. This deviation was especially high in 2008 and 2009 when inflation rates were high in the country.

Third, seasonality is a major characteristic of agricultural markets. We assess with the EGTE wholesale market price data the extent to which seasonal behaviour is present in market prices and how this seasonal behaviour is changing. To do this, we run a simple regression on the logarithm of the wholesale prices with market, year, and monthly dummies on the right-hand side. We then interpret the coefficients for the monthly dummies (Table 32.2). We note that there is significant price seasonality, with prices low immediately after the main harvest and highest at the end of the rainy period before the new harvest starts coming in. Over the period considered, price seasonality was the highest for maize with a price amplitude of 16 per cent, while it was lowest for teff with a price amplitude of 7 per cent. This difference between crops might reflect aptitude for storage as maize is less suited to long storage periods than teff.

Interestingly, comparison of seasonal amplitudes between 2002–8 and 2009–16 shows a significant decline in price seasonality over time. Seasonal price amplitudes were reduced over these two periods by between 8 percentage points for teff and 10 percentage points for wheat. For example, while the price difference for wheat between the highest- and the lowest-priced month in the first period was 17 per cent, this had declined to 7 per cent in the second period. Several explanations could account for this reduction in price seasonality. First, as we have seen, agricultural production

[5] It is to be noted in the latter case that sorghum is not widely consumed in major markets such as in Addis Ababa. As such, the thin sorghum markets with limited flows among them appear to be reflected in these estimation results.

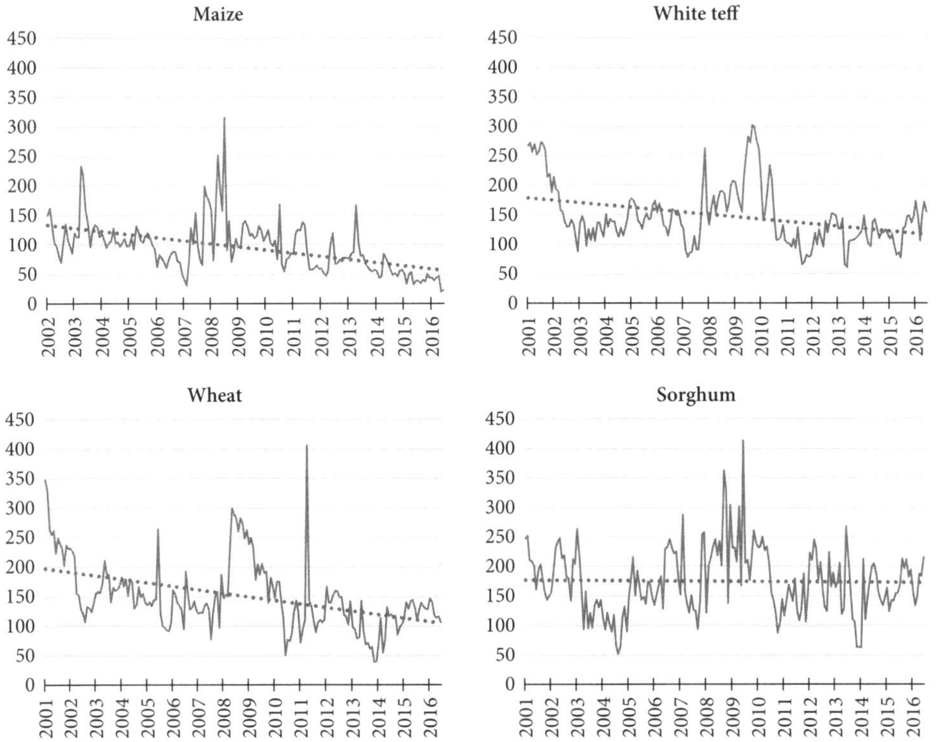

FIGURE 32.2 Standard deviation of real cereal market prices between wholesale markets in Ethiopia, 2001–16, birr/quintal

Note: dotted lines are linear trends in prices over the period considered.

Source: Authors' calculations based on Ethiopian Grain Trading Enterprise (EGTE) price data.

during the main *meher* season has increased rapidly. Thus, there might be more food available for storage and sale later in the year. Second, markets are better integrated and different supply regions can be used to smooth out the lack of seasonal supplies in some areas. Third, farm households are relatively richer now than before and are less cash constrained in the period immediately after the harvest. Consequently, they are not quite so obliged as previously to sell all of their harvest immediately. Fourth, storage conditions have improved due to better access to financial markets, infrastructural improvements, and easier access to agro-chemicals (such as aluminium phosphide) used to reduce storage losses. However, quantifying the impacts of each of these factors is a subject for future research.

Fourth, different food groups have shown different price developments over time. Using a large-scale price dataset collected monthly in 116 urban and rural markets across the country, Bachewe et al. (2017) show that real prices of all nutritionally rich food groups increased between 19 and 62 per cent over the last ten years. This contrasts with staple crops (grains, roots, and tubers), which did not show any real price increase, and with oils, fats, and sugar, the prices of which decreased substantially. Given the great

Table 32.2 Price seasonality in cereals in Ethiopia

	Amplitude				2002-8		2009-16	
	All 2002-16	Period 1 2002-8	Period 2 2009-16	Reduction p1-p2	Lowest price	Highest price	Lowest price	Highest price
All wholesale markets								
Teff	7.34	13.05	5.48	7.57	February	August	December	September
Wheat	8.45	16.81	6.53	10.28	January	August	December	September
Barley	10.84	16.96	8.04	8.92	March	October	December	August
Sorghum	12.89	19.41	11.06	8.35	February	November	April	January
Maize	15.99	25.18	16.58	8.60	January	August	December	August
Addis Ababa								
Teff	9.22	17.17	6.33	10.84	March	August	December	September
Wheat	8.83	17.43	6.84	10.59	January	August	December	June
Barley	12.78	23.04	5.49	17.55	February	August	February	June
Sorghum	12.22	19.52	11.24	8.28	February	November	April	September
Maize	19.33	29.39	19.25	10.14	January	August	December	August

Note: Seasonality calculated as dummies in regression of the form log (real price) = f (city, year, month).

Source: Authors' calculations based on Ethiopian Grain Trading Enterprise (EGTE) data.

influence of prices on consumer choices in countries like Ethiopia, these findings suggest that more investment and attention to the production of nutritious foods—combined with behavioural change messaging—is needed to improve their affordability for consumers.

Finally, cereal price fluctuations (especially price increases) are a major policy concern in Ethiopia. Nominal price increases indeed have been large, particularly in periods of high macro-economic inflation. Movements in real prices (i.e. nominal prices adjusted for overall inflation) have been much smaller though and comparable to other countries in the region such as Kenya and Uganda (Dorosh, Minten, and Stifel 2014). Enhancing price stability for most crops through direct domestic market interventions, however, may be costly in fiscal terms and in terms of discouraging private-sector storage and trade (Dorosh 2009). Dorosh, Minten, and Stifel (2014) show that as Ethiopia imports wheat in most years, liberalization of private-sector imports could often provide a low-cost mechanism for providing a price ceiling at the import parity price.

32.5 International Trade

An important policy consideration in Ethiopia is dependence on international food markets. Ethiopia is a consistent importer of wheat, mostly by the government or international agencies such as the World Food Program (WFP) to be used for distribution in

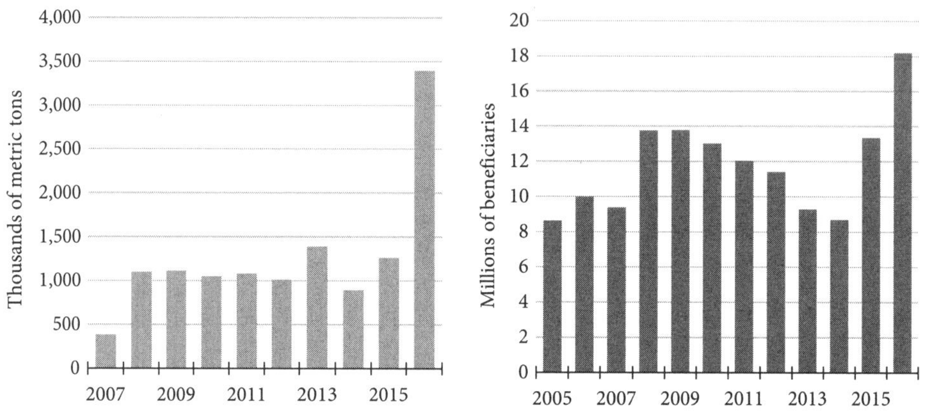

FIGURE 32.3 Wheat imports, 2007–16, and number of aid beneficiaries, 2005–16

Source: COMTRADE webpage, AKLDP (2017), and World Bank (2017b).

humanitarian activities or in its large social safety net, the Productive Safety Net Program (PSNP). The left chart in Figure 32.3 illustrates the quantities of wheat imported into the country over the last decade. Wheat imports were typically about 1 million tons per year (they were much higher in 2016 because of a large El Niño-induced drought in the country) (AKLDP 2017). The chart on the right shows how the overall number of beneficiaries in safety net and aid programmes has changed over the years. It is noteworthy that imported quantities of wheat and the number of aid beneficiaries are, on average, not declining over time.

On the other hand, Ethiopia is also an exporter of a number of agricultural products, particularly coffee, but also oilseeds, chat, flowers, and meat. Figure 32.4 shows to what extent agricultural exports have changed over the last fifteen years. We see an important increase, partly driven by increasing commodity prices in international markets over the last decade for crops such as coffee and sesame, but also by rapidly increasing exported quantities. The overall value of agricultural exports rose six-fold, from 0.4 billion US$ in 2000/1 to 2.5 billion US$ in 2016/17. When we compare the value of these exports with agricultural imports, including those products that are major inputs in the agricultural production process such as chemical fertilizer, we find that both agricultural imports and exports have increased significantly over the last decade.[6] However, Ethiopia in the last decade was a net agricultural exporter in all years except one. The annual value of net agricultural exports hovered around 1 billion US$ over the last five years. This increasing reliance on international trade is noteworthy, especially given the complicated trade regimes in Ethiopia (World Bank 2015).

[6] Relying on the National Bank of Ethiopia classification system, food and live animals, tobacco, fertilizer, and grains are included in agricultural imports. It is to be noted that only data on official imports and exports are included in this analysis. Given lack of data on informal trade, such as that of exports of livestock or imports of rice and pasta, these could not be included.

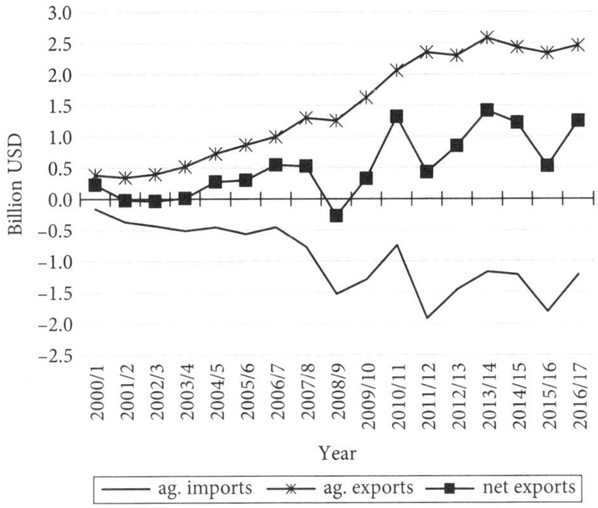

FIGURE 32.4 Ethiopia's agricultural imports and exports, 2000–16

Source: Authors' calculations based on data from the National Bank of Ethiopia.

32.6 Conclusions

In this chapter, we assess the functioning and changes that have happened in Ethiopia's agricultural markets in the last decade. We note that there has been a significant growth in commercial surplus and find evidence of a number of structural changes in supply chains from the trading and transport sector, the food service sector, the processing sector, and urban retail and distribution. We see more reliance on markets by consumers, better integrated markets, and smaller marketing margins and seasonal price variation. However, an increase in prices of non-cereals—especially of those products important to improving dietary diversity and therefore nutritional outcomes—is seen. While food imports are high, and the number of food aid beneficiaries has not reduced over the last decade, Ethiopia also exports significant amounts and in a normal year is a net exporter of food in value terms, illustrating the relative good performance of the agricultural sector and markets over the last decade (Bachewe et al. 2018). Given similar contextual changes—even more pronounced—going forward, it seems future food systems will need to transform even faster, with especially rapid growth in commercial food markets expected. This will have enormous implications for farming, agricultural input supply, logistics, trading, and distribution sectors in the future.

References

AKLDP (2017). 'El Nino in Ethiopia: Bridging the Gap—Cereal Production and Imports: October 2016 to September 2017', Cereal Availability Diagnostic study. Mimeo.

Assefa, T., G. Abebe, I. Lamoot, and B. Minten (2016). 'Urban Food Retailing and Food Prices in Africa: The Case of Addis Ababa (Ethiopia)', *Journal of Agribusiness in Developing and Emerging Economies* 6 (2): 90–109.

Bachewe, F., G. Berhane, B. Minten, and A. S. Taffesse (2016). 'Non-Farm Income and Labor Markets in Rural Ethiopia', Ethiopia Strategy Support Program (ESSP) Working Paper 90, International Food Policy Research Institute (IFPRI) and Ethiopian Development Research Institute (EDRI), Addis Ababa.

Bachewe, F., G. Berhane, B. Minten, and A. S. Taffesse (2018). 'Agricultural Transformation in Africa? Assessing the Evidence in Ethiopia', *World Development* 105: 286–98.

Bachewe, F., K. Hirvonen, B. Minten, and F. Yimer (2017). 'The Rising Costs of Nutritious Foods', ESSP Research Note 67, Addis Ababa.

Benfica, R. and J. Thurlow (2017). 'Identifying Priority Value-Chains in Ethiopia', Ethiopia Strategy Support Program (ESSP) Working Paper 110, International Food Policy Research Institute (IFPRI) and Ethiopian Development Research Institute (EDRI), Addis Ababa.

Braudel, F. (1982). *Civilization and Capitalism, 15th–18th Century: The Wheels of Commerce* (Berkeley, CA: University of California Press).

CSA (2012). 'Report on Large- and Medium-Scale Manufacturing and Electricity Industries Survey, Central Statistical Agency, Addis Ababa.

CSA (2015). 'Report on the Small-Scale Manufacturing Industries Survey', Central Statistical Agency, Addis Ababa.

CSA (2016). 'Agricultural Sample Survey, Vol. 4: Report on Land Utilization (Private Peasant Holdings, *Meher* Season) (2005–2016)', Central Statistical Agency of the Federal Democratic Republic of Ethiopia, Addis Ababa.

Dercon, S. (1995). 'On Market Integration and Liberalization: Method and Application to Ethiopia', *Journal of Development Studies* 32: 112–43.

Dolislager, M. D., D. Tschirley, and T. Reardon (2015). 'Consumption Patterns in Eastern and Southern Africa', Report to USAID by Michigan State University, Innovation Lab for Food Security Policy (May).

Dorosh, P. (2009). 'Price Stabilization, International Trade and National Cereal Stocks: World Price Shocks and Policy Response in South Asia', *Food Security* 1 (2): 137–49.

Dorosh, P., B. Minten, and D. Stifel (2014). 'Cereal Price Stabilization in Ethiopia: Implications of International Experiences', in Proceedings of the conference 'Cereals Price Policy and Analysis for Ethiopia in the Context of Rapid Production Growth', Addis Ababa.

Fackler, P. L. and B. K. Goodwin (2001). 'Spatial Price Analysis', *Handbook of Agricultural Economics* 1: 971–1024.

Hill, R. and H. Fuje (2017). 'What Is the Impact of Drought on Prices? Evidence from Ethiopia', Poverty and Equity Global Practice, Africa Region, World Bank.

Minten, B., T. Assefa, G. Abebe, et al. (2016). 'Food Processing, Transformation and Job Creation: The Case of Commercial *Enjera* Market in Ethiopia', ESSP Working Paper 96, Addis Ababa.

Minten, B., S. Tamiru, and D. Stifel (2014). 'Structural Transformation in Cereal Markets in Ethiopia', *Journal of Development Studies* 50 (5): 611–29.

Moller, L. C. and K. M. Wacker (2017). 'Explaining Ethiopia's Growth Acceleration: The Role of Infrastructure and Macroeconomic Policy', *World Development* 96: 198–215.

National Bank of Ethiopia (NBE) (2018). 'Annual Report 2016/17', Addis Ababa. http://www.nbe.gov.et/pdf/annualbulletin/NBE%20Annual%20report%202016-2017/National%20Bank's%20Annual%20Rep~1.pdf (accessed 2 August 2018).

Oqubay, A. (2015). *Made in Africa: Industrial Policy in Ethiopia* (New York: Oxford University Press).

Rashid, S. and A. Negassa (2012). 'Policies and Performance of Ethiopian Cereal Markets', in *Food and Agriculture in Ethiopia: Progress and Policy Challenges*, ed. P. Dorosh and S. Rashid (Philadelphia, PA: University of Pennsylvania Press): 123–58.

Reardon, T., R. Echeverria, J. Berdegué, et al. (forthcoming). 'Rapid Transformation of Food Systems in Developing Regions: Highlighting the Role of Agricultural Research', *Agricultural Systems*, forthcoming.

Reardon, T. and C. P. Timmer (2014). 'Five Inter-Linked Transformations in the Asian Agri-Food Economy: Food Security Implications', *Global Food Security* 3 (2): 108–17.

Reardon, T., C. P. Timmer, C. B. Barrett, and J. A. Berdegué (2003). 'The Rise of Supermarkets in Africa, Asia, and Latin America', *American Journal of Agricultural Economics* 85 (5): 1140–6.

Schaefer, F. and G. Abebe (2015). 'The Case for Industrial Policy and its Application in the Ethiopian Cut Flower Sector', EDRI Working Paper No. 12, Addis Ababa.

Schmidt, E., P. Dorosh, M. K. Jemal, and J. Smart (2018). 'Ethiopia's Spatial and Structural Transformation: Public Policy and Drivers of Change', Working Paper No. 119, Strategy Support Program, IFPRI, Ethiopia and EDRI.

Smith, L. C., O. Dupriez, and N. Troubat (2014). 'Assessment of the Reliability and Relevance of the Food Data Collected in National Household Consumption and Expenditure Surveys', IHSN Working Paper No. 8, International Household Survey Network.

Van Campenhout, B. (2007). 'Modelling Trends in Food Market Integration: Method and an Application to Tanzanian Maize Markets', *Food Policy* 32 (1): 112–27.

Verma, V., T. Marchant, and C. Scott (1988). *Evaluation of Crop-Cut Methods and Farmer Reports for Estimating Crop Production: Results of a Methodological Study in Five African Countries* (London: Longacre Agricultural Development Centre).

WFP/CSA (2014). 'Comprehensive Food Security and Vulnerability Analysis Ethiopia', WFP, Addis Ababa.

Worku, I., M. Dereje, B. Minten, and K. Hirvonen (2017). 'Diet Transformation in Africa: The Case of Ethiopia', *Agricultural Economics* 48 (supplement): 73–86.

World Bank (2014). 'Ethiopia: Poverty Assessment', Report No. AUS6744, Poverty Global Practice, Africa Region, World Bank, Washington, DC.

World Bank (2015). 'Ethiopia's Great Run: The Growth Acceleration and How to Pace It', Report No. 99399-ET, World Bank, Washington, DC.

World Bank (2017a). 'World Bank Open Data: Population Growth (Annual Percent)'. https://data.worldbank.org/indicator/SP.POP.GROW (accessed 26 November 2017).

World Bank (2017b). 'Quantifying Costs of Drought Risk in Ethiopia: A Technical Note', Disaster Risk Financing and Insurance Program, World Bank, Washington, DC. Mimeo.

CHAPTER 33

LIVESTOCK PRODUCTION IN ETHIOPIA

FANTU BACHEWE AND FANAYE TADESSE

33.1 Introduction

Ethiopia is home to some of the largest stocks of different livestock species in the world.[1] The stock of cattle in Ethiopia, for instance, is the fifth largest in the world and is larger than the stocks in such important beef-producing countries as Argentina and Australia (FAO 2018). The size of animal stocks and the scale of employment suggest livestock is an important subsector in Ethiopia. However, livestock production has contributed little to the rapid economic growth recorded since 2004/5. National official statistics show that livestock output grew at 5.8 per cent per annum during 2004/5–2015/16, when real GDP growth averaged 10.5 per cent. Livestock output not only declined in importance in aggregate GDP but its share in total agricultural output also declined from 23.6 per cent in 2004/5 to 19.5 per cent in 2015/16. Given this relatively slow growth in livestock output, the subsector on average accounted for only 0.5 of the 10.5 per cent growth in GDP recorded during the period. That is, out of every 100 birr added to the economy less than 5 birr came from livestock, while crop output growth contributed about five times as much (24 birr) (National Bank of Ethiopia (NBE) 2017).

Following the rapid growth in income in Ethiopia in the last decade, real expenditure on animal products and its share in total food spending grew during 2000–11 (Tafere and Worku 2012). Moreover, with further increases in income, animal-sourced foods (ASF) are expected to increase in importance, not only given the food preferences of consumers, but also because of their nutritional benefits (Bachewe, Minten, and Yimer 2017). Export of meat, live animals, and animal products increased in importance from 11.4 per cent of the total value of exports in 2004/5 to 13 per cent in 2015 (NBE 2017). Despite these growing

[1] Ethiopia has the largest stock of donkeys in the world in 2016. Moreover, stocks of goats and horses are both eighth largest, and that of mules, camels, and sheep ranked fourth, seventh, and ninth, respectively (FAO 2018).

market opportunities and largely untapped resource potential, livestock production, productivity, and marketed supply remain stagnant.

This chapter uses descriptive analyses to study the dynamics in the stock, average holdings, and composition of live animals during the 2004/5–2015/16 period. It also studies production and productivity of live animals and animal-sourced food, and input use in livestock production. Growth accounting analyses are used to indicate the sources of growth in real livestock output. For this purpose, we use data from the Central Statistical Agency of Ethiopia (CSA) which is representative of mixed crop–livestock farmers in Ethiopia.

The findings of this study indicate that the proportion of farmers owning livestock and average ownership changed little while the number of livestock and the number of livestock farmers were at least 50 per cent higher in 2015/16 than in 2004/5. Milk and egg output increased considerably while productivity of both items stagnated. The proportion of livestock sold for use in meat production was low and changed little during the period. Growth in livestock output came largely from increases in the number of livestock and livestock owners, with modern input use and improvements in production methods contributing little. Although veterinary service provision increased considerably, and livestock death rates slightly declined, the number lost to deaths is still more than twice the number sold for meat production. These findings inform policymaking pertaining to the livestock subsector.

Unlike this study, which provides a broader overview of ASF and live animal production, productivity, and input use, there are a number of studies that investigate a single aspect of the livestock subsector in Ethiopia.[2] These studies indicate weak institutions, markets, and policymaking, particularly the absence of a clear policy framework, as important bottlenecks for the weakly performing livestock subsector. With the recent focus on livestock provided by the Ethiopian government, which has established a livestock sub-ministry within the Ministry of Agriculture, Livestock, and Natural Resources, and if investments envisaged in the livestock sector roadmap are implemented, livestock production and productivity are expected to improve considerably and make significant contributions to reduction of rural poverty (Shapiro et al. 2015).

The remainder of this chapter is organized as follows. Section 33.2 describes the main dataset used in the study. Trends in number and growth rates of livestock are then described, followed by a discussion of livestock output and productivity. Inputs used in livestock production are dealt with and the final section concludes.

33.2 Data Sources and Coverage

The Central Statistical Agency of the Federal Democratic Republic of Ethiopia (CSA) collects agricultural data in its annual Agricultural Sample Survey (AgSS). The AgSS surveys a large number of households. In an average year during the period covered in

[2] For an overview of the research in the area see also Negassa et al. (2017) and Bachewe, Minten, and Yimer (2017).

this study (2004/5–2015/16), 63,000 households were surveyed. Data are collected, among others, on rural households' production of crops and livestock. CSA publishes a summary of these data, which are representative at national, regional, and zonal levels, in its annual statistical reports. The data pertain to smallholder farmers, who dominate Ethiopian agriculture. Our analyses rely on CSA data taken from both household-level (raw) data and the statistical reports, complemented with data from other sources in the discussion of inputs.[3] Unless indicated otherwise, the descriptive analyses presented in the chapter cover the period 2004/5–2015/16.[4]

Households in the Afar and Somali regions as well as in pastoralist (southern) parts of Oromiya rely heavily on livestock production for their livelihood while these areas are also home to a considerable proportion of the country's livestock population. Therefore, a study that investigates livestock production in Ethiopia needs to give due attention to these areas. However, during the period covered in this study, the sampling frame of the AgSS included all rural parts of the country except the non-sedentary areas of three (out of five) zones of Afar and six (out of nine) zones of Somali regions (CSA 2005–16). CSA collected data on livestock production in the two predominantly pastoralist regions in its 2002 Pastoralist Survey. However, we do not use that dataset in our analyses for two reasons. First, the data is too old to provide a timely insight. Second, although the survey covered households in all five zones of Afar, it covered only one zone and left out all six Somali zones not included in the annual AgSS. Therefore, we rely on data from Awsi and Gabi zones in Afar; Siti, Fafan, and Liben zones in Somali; and Borena zone in Oromiya, which are covered in CSA's annual AgSS, for our description of pastoralist areas. Using these data, we characterize the pastoralist areas in terms of average livestock ownership, and importance in nationwide stock of live animals and animal-sourced food production.

33.3 Livestock Size, Composition, and Growth

In this section we describe trends in proportions of households that own livestock, and the number, composition, and growth rates of livestock during the 2004–15 period.

33.3.1 Number, Structure, and Composition of Livestock

CSA data indicate that the cattle stock in Ethiopia stood at 57.8 million at the end of 2015, which is 49 per cent higher than the 38.7 million cattle at the end of 2004. The number of

[3] We compare CSA data on live animal stocks with that of FAO (2018) data. The numbers from the two sources are identical in most cases, particularly those since 2009. In only 11 of the 96 cases compared is the number in one source 1 per cent lower or higher than in the other. We could not do similar comparisons for other variables as equivalently defined data is unavailable.

[4] In the remainder of this chapter 2004/5 is given as 2004, 2015/16 as 2015, and so forth.

sheep in 2015, about 29 million, showed the next lowest growth rate of 60 per cent during the period. The stocks of goats, equines,[5] camels, and poultry were about 100, 80, 168, and 96 per cent higher in 2015 than 2004, in which the stocks were 15, 5.8, 0.5, and 31 million, respectively.

About 92 per cent of farm households surveyed owned at least one type of livestock in 2015 (Table 33.1). Households that owned cattle were the highest followed by those that owned poultry. The trend in the proportion that owned at least one type of livestock remained about the same during the period. However, the (absolute) number of livestock owners increased by about 51 per cent, from 10.3 million in 2004 to 15.5 million in 2015. The trend was also similar for the proportion that owned each livestock species, except for a slight increase in the proportion owning camels and equines, mainly donkeys.

In households that owned livestock, the average number of cattle and chicken owned was the highest at about 4 heads per household in 2015 (Table 33.1). On the other hand, the average number of equines and camels owned was less than one. Except for the slight increase in goats and poultry owned, the trend did not show a notable variation over the years.

Table 33.1 also provides information on livestock composition or the contribution of each livestock type to total tropical livestock units (TLUs) owned by households.[6] An average household owned around 3.7 TLUs in 2015. Cattle and small ruminants (sheep and goats) accounted for around 69 and 14 per cent of the total TLUs, respectively. The composition of TLUs changed little between 2004 and 2015; notable changes include a decline (increase) in the contribution of cattle (equines) to total TLU by 4 (2.4) per cent.

Table 33.1 Livestock ownership and composition by type

	Households that own livestock (%)			Number of livestock owned (head count, among owners)			Livestock composition (% livestock TLU)		
Livestock type	2004	2010	2015	2004	2010	2015	2004	2010	2015
All livestock	92.6	92.9	92.3						
Cattle	82.3	82.1	79.7	4.0	4.0	3.9	73.1	71.7	68.7
Sheep	35.7	36.0	35.2	1.9	1.9	2.0	7.2	7.4	7.6
Goats	27.4	27.5	27.7	1.5	1.7	2.0	5.6	5.7	6.1
Equines	33.9	37.3	41.3	0.6	0.7	0.7	8.3	9.2	10.7
Camels	1.0	1.4	1.7	0.1	0.1	0.1	0.4	0.5	0.6
Poultry	57.2	58.3	58.3	3.2	3.7	4.0	5.5	5.5	6.3

Source: Authors' analyses using CSA holder-level data (CSA 2017).

[5] Equines include horses, mules, and donkeys.

[6] TLU normalizes the number of livestock into camel units. It is computed using the formula: TLU = camels + (0.7*cattle) + (0.8*horses) + (0.5*donkey) + (0.5*mules) + (0.1*sheep) + (0.1*goats) + (0.01*chickens).

We also study the breed composition of cows and chickens, since breed type data is available for these types of livestock. CSA (2017) data indicate that indigenous or local-breed cows and chickens are dominant. Foreign cow breeds are almost non-existent among smallholder farmers' herds, while hybrid cows represented only 1 and 2 per cent of the total number of cows in 2004 and 2015, respectively. A relatively higher percentage of chickens, around 11 per cent, were foreign and hybrid breeds in 2015 compared to just 2 per cent in 2004.

33.3.2 Livestock Size: Pastoralist Areas

CSA (2017) data indicate that the proportion of households in the six pastoralist zones that own any kind of livestock was 96 per cent in 2015. The proportion of pastoralist households that owned cattle was 83.4 per cent in 2004 and it declined to 69 per cent in 2015. The proportion that owned sheep, goats, camels, and poultry in 2015 was 53, 67, 25, and 22 per cent. The data indicate that the proportion of pastoralist area farmers that own cattle and poultry in 2015 was 15 and 18 per cent lower relative to 2004, while the proportion that own sheep, goats, and camels increased by 15, 5, and 6 per cent, respectively. This appears to indicate that pastoralist farmers may be shifting away from cattle and poultry and focusing more on camels and small ruminants.

Cattle ownership averaged 5.4 per household in 2015 and was 1.5 lower than that in 2004. In contrast, sheep, goat, and camel ownership averaged 6, 11.3, and 1.6 in 2015 and was 3, 4.5, and 0.4 higher than average ownership in 2004, which reinforces the observation that pastoralist farmers are shifting towards camels and small ruminants. The six pastoralist zones accounted for 4.7 per cent of the total number of cattle in 2015 while they accounted for nearly 11, 20, and 68 per cent of the total number of sheep, goats, and camels, respectively.

33.3.3 Livestock Technical Performance

This section discusses two important livestock technical performance parameters: annual death rate and annual growth rates. These parameters are measured by looking at a twelve-month recall/retrospective data for each of the years considered in the study.

33.3.3.1 *Annual Death Rate*

The annual death rate of each livestock type is calculated by dividing the total number of deaths by the average stock of that livestock type. CSA (2017) data indicate that livestock death rates generally increased from 2004 until 2008, when there was a spike in death rates of all species, and have generally declined since 2008. Average death rates during 2005–15 for cattle, equines, and camels stood at around 7 per cent while death rates for sheep and goats were 20 per cent. Relative to 2005, death rates in 2014 were about

1 per cent lower in sheep and equines, 2 per cent lower in cattle and goats, and 3 per cent lower in camels.

33.3.3.2 *Annual Growth Rate*

The annual growth rate of each livestock type is calculated by dividing the difference between the ending and beginning stocks by the beginning stock. Growth rates have been positive for all livestock species in most years (CSA 2017). This excludes sheep and camels, in which negative growth rates were observed in four of the eleven years. However, average annual growth rates were positive for all livestock species. The average annual growth rate for cattle was 3.8 per cent while it was 4.6, 6.7, and 6.6 per cent for sheep, goats, and poultry, respectively. The highest average growth was observed in camels (9.4 per cent).

33.4 Livestock and Animal-Sourced Food Production and Productivity

Livestock serve a multitude of purposes. Among others, livestock provide food for farm households and cash income when sold in the market, and are used for ploughing in crop production. Consequently, livestock constitute an important source of income for farm households and ultimately for the national economy. Livestock income accounted for 11 per cent of the total income of households in the Agricultural Growth Programme baseline survey dataset, which included ninety-three *woreda*s in Tigray, Amhara, Oromiya, and Southern Nations, Nationalities, and Peoples (SNNP) regions (Bachewe et al. 2016). The authors further find that the share of livestock income is significantly higher (21 per cent) when the analyses includes households in Afar, Somali, Gambella, and Benishangul-Gumz regions, in all of which livestock production is important.

The livestock subsector has also historically been an important input supplier to the manufacturing sector. Established in the mid-1920s, leather processing and leather products manufacturing firms were among the earliest in Ethiopia (Oqubay 2015), indicating the important contribution of livestock in the industrialization of the country. Despite recent improvements the performance of the leather processing and leather products manufacturing subsector remained poor and thus it was unable to take advantage of the rich primary input endowment from the livestock subsector (Oqubay 2015). However, the contribution of the livestock subsector is expected to grow following recent improvements in the leather processing and manufacturing, meat processing (Addis Ababa Chamber of Commerce and Sectoral Associations (AACCSA) 2015) and dairy processing (AACCSA 2016) subsectors.

The remainder of this section discusses trends in animal-sourced food (milk and egg) production and productivity, and trends in livestock used in meat production (net commercial off-take). The section also discusses trends in real output and productivity.

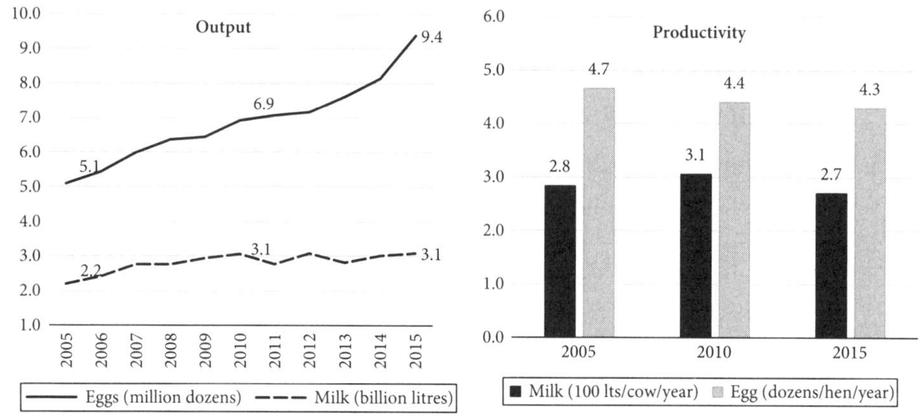

FIGURE 33.1 Milk and egg production and productivity

Source: Authors' analyses using CSA data (CSA 2017).

Finally, results of the growth accounting analyses conducted to indicate the sources of growth in real livestock output are discussed.

33.4.1 Milk and Egg Production and Productivity

Total milk production increased by about 41 per cent between 2005 and 2015 while growth in egg production was 84 per cent (Figure 33.1). Annual growth in milk and egg output averaged about 3.8 and 6.4 per cent, respectively. Despite the significant growth in outputs, milk and egg productivity (output per animal) stagnated during the period. Milk and egg productivity in 2015 were 4.8 and 8 per cent, respectively, lower than 2005. Figure 33.1 also indicates that there were no significant changes in productivity during the period. The stagnant productivity per animal implies that the rapid growth in output is likely to have resulted from the increase in the number of livestock and livestock farmers, a claim which also is corroborated by the growth accounting analyses.

Milk production in the six pastoralist zones accounted for about 12 per cent of national milk production in both 2005 and 2015. The contribution of these zones towards nationwide egg production has been less than 3 per cent in all years studied and has generally declined, which is consistent with the decline in poultry population observed in these areas.

33.4.2 Net Commercial Off-Take

The meat production capacity of the livestock subsector can be directly influenced by the number of live animals produced for such purposes as well as by the quantity of meat per animal produced. This section discusses the net commercial off-take (NCOT) rates of livestock while we discuss productivity in meat per animal in Section 33.4.3.

The NCOT rate is essentially the rate at which livestock leave the farm ultimately for use in meat production or for live exports. While the NCOT rate shows the net market position of households in each livestock type, we also discuss below three related (gross) market participation rates: sales off-take, slaughter off-take, and commercial intake (purchase) rates.

Results of our computations of gross and net commercial market participation rates are presented in Table 33.2. The table indicates that poultry has the highest sales off-take rate followed by sheep, goats, and cattle while camels have the lowest sales off-take rates. The proportion sold increased over the period for all animals except equines although the increase was generally low. The highest increase was observed for cattle and goats (1.7 per cent).

Chicken has the highest slaughter off-take rate at 28.4 per cent in 2015 (Table 33.2). The second and third most slaughtered animals are sheep and goats, respectively. Cattle and camels are the least slaughtered animals. The proportion of slaughtered cattle changed little over the years. The proportion increased by over 4 per cent for chickens, by about 2 per cent for small ruminants, and it declined for camels.

The livestock commercial purchase rate is the highest for chickens (20 per cent) in 2015 followed by sheep (16 per cent) and equines (10.4 per cent) while it is the lowest for camels at 3.7 per cent. The commercial intake rate has shown a slight decline over the period for all livestock types except for cattle and poultry.

The results in Table 33.2 indicate that in 2015 the NCOT rate was only 3.3 per cent for cattle, while it was higher at 7.7, 9.7, and 7 per cent for sheep, goats, and poultry. The net market position in 2015 was one per cent higher than in 2004 for cattle, it increased by nearly 2 per cent for goats, it stagnated in sheep, and declined by about 2 per cent for poultry.

Considering the six pastoralist zones, average NCOT rate of cattle was 5 per cent in 2004 and 7 per cent in 2015. These are higher than twice the corresponding rates in Table 33.2. Similarly, the NCOT rates of sheep and goats were about the same at 17 per cent for pastoralist areas in 2015, which is considerably higher than the nationwide rate.

Table 33.2 Proportion of livestock sold, slaughtered, and purchased

Livestock type	Sales			Slaughters			Purchases			Net commercial off-take*		
	2005	2010	2015	2005	2010	2015	2005	2010	2015	2005	2010	2015
Cattle	9.4	10.6	11.1	0.7	0.8	0.9	7.3	7.9	8.1	2.4	3.0	3.3
Sheep	23.4	22.6	23.5	10.2	12.7	12.2	16.5	15.1	16.1	7.4	8.0	7.7
Goats	16.5	20.6	18.2	6.6	8.8	8.2	9.2	8.6	8.7	8.0	12.6	9.7
Equines	8.0	7.0	6.3	–	–	–	12.0	11.7	10.4	–4.0	–4.7	–4.1
Camels	4.3	6.5	4.9	1.5	0.9	0.3	4.4	4.3	3.7	1.4	3.0	1.5
Poultry	24.0	24.5	25.4	24.1	26.6	28.4	16.6	18.5	20.0	8.7	7.3	6.8

Note: * Gross slaughters used to compute net commercial off-take rates of camels.
Source: Authors' analyses using CSA holder-level data (CSA 2017).

Looking into the numbers that constitute NCOT rate reveals that pastoralist areas have higher NCOT rates due to the relatively lower purchase rates in such areas.

The foregoing discussion indicates that growth in the NCOT rate or the proportion of live animals sold for use in meat production has generally been low. The latter, together with the rapid increase in the real price of meat observed in the country during the period (Bachewe, Minten, and Yimer 2017) imply, among others, that growth in the supply of livestock put to such uses was slower relative to growth in demand. In other words, productivity in livestock produced for meat production has slowed down during the period.

33.4.3 Meat Productivity

We investigate the trends in meat productivity per animal using data from the United Nations Food and Agricultural Organization (FAO) (FAO 2018). The data indicate that meat yield (carcass weight) per animal changed little between 2004 and 2014, the latest year for which data are available. Average meat yields of sheep, goats, poultry, and camels were the same during the entire period at 10, 8.5, 0.8, and about 170 kg per animal, respectively (FAO 2018). There was some variation in the case of cattle but this ranged only between 108 and 109.2 kg per animal during the period.

Although the data needed to triangulate the numbers from FAO are unavailable, we suspect meat productivity per animal may not have remained constant or may even have increased, at least for poultry and cattle. This follows from CSA (2017) data, which show increased adoption of hybrid and foreign poultry by smallholders, from our observation of the increasing number of modern poultry farms producing larger chicken varieties, and from focus-group discussions conducted by the authors that indicate increases in the number of institutions that fatten cattle for live exports and for domestic butcheries that sell premium-quality beef. However, this observation is made with due caution, and we note that whether and by how much these improvements have impacted meat yields needs to be empirically tested.

33.4.4 Real Livestock Output and Productivity

In addition to producing eggs and milk and being used in meat production, livestock provide other services. Most notably, farmers use cattle to plough land used in crop production while livestock also serve as insurance against unexpected cash needs.[7]

[7] CSA (2005–16) data indicate that, of the 3-year-old and older cattle households kept during 2004–15, the highest proportion of 39.5 per cent were meant to provide draft power and the proportion changed little during the period. A considerable and suspiciously high proportion (33 per cent) were intended for breeding. However, CSA survey instruments do not include options such as 'saving' or 'insurance against unexpected cash needs' alongside the question that asks for what purposes livestock are kept. Given this we suspect that some of the households that keep livestock as a means of saving put them in the 'breeding' category.

Production and productivity measures discussed so far ignore these uses of livestock. We provide two additional measures of livestock productivity that account for most outputs/services of livestock. For this purpose, we use data from the National Bank of Ethiopia (NBE) on real value of livestock output. We proxy labour productivity in the livestock subsector by dividing real value of livestock output (NBE 2017) by the total number of livestock farmers (CSA 2017). Similarly, the real productivity of livestock is estimated by dividing real livestock output by the total TLU (CSA 2005–16).

NBE (2017) data indicate that real livestock output in 2015 (53.4 billion birr, at December 2011 prices) was 73 per cent higher than in 2004 (30.9 billion birr) and growth in real output averaged 5.1 per cent per annum. The stock of live animals expressed in TLU terms increased by 56.4 per cent or by an average annual rate of 4.2 per cent during the same period (CSA 2005–16). Real livestock output per TLU was 894 birr in 2004 and 990 birr in 2015, indicating a total growth in livestock output per TLU of 10.7 per cent, or that livestock output per TLU on average grew at 1 per cent per annum. Similarly, real output per livestock farmer grew at an average annual rate of 1.3 per cent (showed a total growth of 15 per cent) from 2,996 birr in 2004 to 3,443 birr in 2015.

33.4.5 Livestock Output Growth Accounting

This section discusses results of the growth accounting analyses we conducted. The analysis, which uses a modified growth accounting model (Solow 1957), decomposes growth in real value of livestock output into changes in input use, exogenous factors that affect output growth, and total factor productivity (TFP). The method starts by assuming that markets are competitive and that there exists a well-behaved aggregate livestock production function that expresses real livestock output as a function of inputs used in production and a variable that represents techniques of production. Starting from such a production function and under the assumptions given, the method expresses growth in real livestock output using the formula:[8]

$$\frac{\Delta Output}{Output} = \Delta TFP + \sum\nolimits_J w_J \frac{\Delta Input_J}{Input_J} + \alpha \Delta Exog$$

where J indexes types of inputs and w_J is the relative share or payment to input J. For instance, if J is labour w_J represents wages paid/imputed for labour used. The equation states that growth in output between two time periods ($\Delta Output\,/\,Output$) is equal to the sum of growths in total payments for all inputs ($\sum_J w_J \, \Delta Input_J\,/\,Input_J$); change in exogenous factors that affect livestock production ($\Delta\, Exog$) times the magnitude of the impact of exogenous factors (α); and change in TFP (ΔTFP), which captures changes in methods of production and effects of other factors not included in the analyses.

[8] Interested readers can also see, among others, Solow (1957) and Carlaw and Lipsey (2003). Bachewe et al. (2018) describe the method in the Ethiopian context and apply it to the crop production subsector.

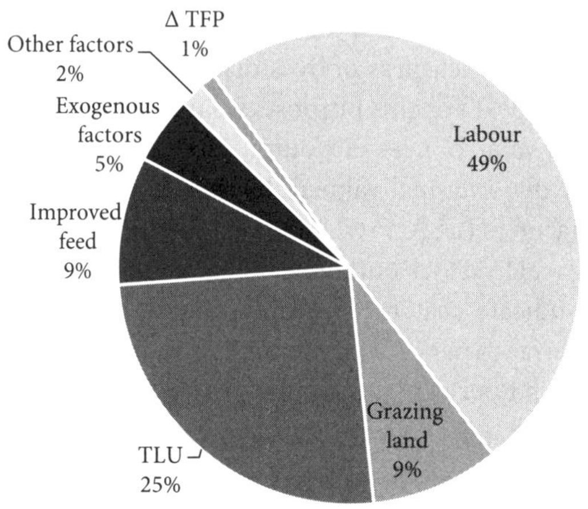

FIGURE 33.2 Average contribution of factors in livestock output growth

Source: Authors' analyses using real livestock output data from NBE (2017) and CSA data (2017, 2005–2016).

We conduct the analyses assuming that real livestock output is a function of labour, which we proxy using total number of livestock farmers; capital, which we proxy using total grazing land; the stock of live animals (TLU); real value of crop output used as livestock feed (used as proxy for intermediate inputs from crop subsector); manufacturing sector by-products used as animal feed (used as proxy for intermediate inputs from manufacturing sector); total number of livestock vaccinated or treated for diseases (used as proxy for intermediate inputs from service sector); and total number of livestock extension users. We provide a summary of the data used in Appendix 1. Furthermore, we derive w_j, payment to factors used in production, from the 2005/6 Social Accounting Matrix of Ethiopia (Ethiopian Development Research Institute 2009) while we follow Bachewe et al. (2018) to approximate the exogenous factors.

We provide results of the growth accounting analysis in Figure 33.2. The figure provides the average contribution of the factors expressed as a percentage of real livestock output growth. During 2004–14, growth in labour used in livestock production accounted for 2.9 per cent of the 5.8 per cent average annual growth in real livestock output. That is, growth in labour accounted for 49 per cent of real livestock output growth. Similarly, growth in TLU contributed 1.5 per cent to the 5.8 per cent growth in livestock output or about a quarter of the output growth came from growth in stock of livestock. Growth in improved feed and grazing land together accounted for 18 per cent growth in real livestock output, extension and veterinary services together accounted for 2 per cent, and exogenous factors for 5 per cent.

The finding that labour and TLU growth accounted for 78 per cent of the growth in real output and that improved feed, veterinary services, and extension services, which can be considered as modern inputs, accounted for only 11 per cent, together indicate that most of the livestock output growth was achieved through increases in the number of livestock and livestock owners (extensive margin) and not through increased use of modern inputs (intensive margin). Furthermore, changes in TFP accounted for only

1 per cent of the growth in output, indicating that almost all the real livestock output growth is accounted for by the factors used in the analyses and that little improvement in methods of livestock production occurred during the period.

33.5 Inputs Used in Livestock Production

In this section we discuss inputs used in livestock production including veterinary and livestock extension services, livestock feed, and employment in livestock production. We also provide a brief description of trends in grazing land as it constitutes the major source of livestock feed.

33.5.1 Animal Feed

Most households use grazing as a source of feed for their livestock followed by crop residue. However, the percentage of farmers using green fodder (grazing) as animal feed is declining, albeit slowly: from 93.3 per cent in 2005 to 90.5 per cent in 2015. The percentage of households that used crop residue remained about the same at 79 per cent while those that used hay slightly increased (by 3 per cent) from 27.5 per cent in 2005. On the other hand, the highest increase of 6.4 per cent occurred in the proportion of households using improved feed (improved pasture and by-products) from 7.2 per cent in 2005 to 13.6 per cent in 2015.

Most farmers use their own property to acquire livestock feed. In 2015 about 62, 11, and 8 per cent of the households used livestock feed obtained from own property, public property, and purchases, respectively. About 16 per cent of the households used feeds acquired from multiple sources. The proportion using purchased feed in 2015 was over 2 per cent higher than that in 2005 or the proportion using purchased animal feed increased by 30 per cent during the period. In contrast, the proportion using public property in 2015 was 37 per cent lower than that in 2005. The trend in feed source observed, which shows a rapid decline in the use of common grazing grounds and an increase in importance of purchased feeds, is consistent with the decline in cultivated area per farmer that occurred during the same period in the country (Minten et al. 2018) and may have resulted from more of the common grazing grounds being brought into cultivation.

33.5.2 Grazing Land

Despite the considerable growth in nationwide agricultural area in the last decade (by 2.9 per cent per annum), landholdings of an average farmer declined by a total of 25 per cent during the period (Minten et al. 2018). A similar pattern was also observed in grazing area. Total grazing area increased from about 1.37 million hectares in 2004 to 1.77 million hectares in 2015. Despite this increase in the aggregate, average grazing area per farmer in 2015 (0.10 hectares) was about 16 per cent lower than the average in 2004 (0.12 hectares).

33.5.3 Veterinary Services

CSA (2017) data indicate that a considerable proportion of cattle, small ruminants, and poultry are afflicted by various diseases. In 2015 one or more diseases affected 16.5 per cent of cattle, 21 per cent of sheep, and 20 per cent of goats. Chickens are the most affected with 57 per cent of the stock diseased while equines (12.5 per cent) and camels (11 per cent) are the least affected. Relative to 2004 the percentage of poultry afflicted with disease increased by 18 per cent in 2015 while the increase ranged between 1 and 5 per cent for other livestock types.

CSA data also indicate that, of animals affected by diseases, the proportion treated (received veterinary services) increased in all livestock types during the period. In 2015, the percentage of affected animals treated was the highest for cattle (68 per cent) followed by equines (60 per cent), sheep (45 per cent), goats (34 per cent), and camels (21 per cent), and it was the lowest for poultry (12 per cent). Relative to 2004 the proportion treated for diseases increased in 2015 by about 34 per cent for cattle and equines, by 31 per cent for sheep, and by 24 per cent for goats. The increase was lower for poultry (10 per cent) and camels (5 per cent). The increase in the proportion of sick animals treated is despite the increase in the proportion afflicted by diseases. This implies that the number of livestock treated increased faster than the number of sick animals. The data also indicate that the number of treated animals grew faster than the total stock of animals.[9]

The proportion of livestock vaccinated (out of total stock) increased considerably for all animal types. About 58, 25.4, 23, and 8 per cent of cattle, sheep, goats, and camels were vaccinated in 2015 and these proportions were about 34, 19, 14, and 4 per cent, respectively, higher than the proportions vaccinated in 2004. The number of cattle vaccinated in 2015 (33.6 million) was over three times the number vaccinated in 2004 (9.2 million). Similarly, the number of sheep, goats, and camels vaccinated in 2004 was over four times the number vaccinated in 2004.

Disease-related animal deaths declined considerably during the period, which may imply a negative relationship between disease-related deaths and the expansion in animal vaccination services (Figure 33.3).[10] The proportion of cattle that died (out of cattle afflicted by diseases) was 28 per cent in 2015. The proportion was higher for other livestock types. Although the proportion of disease-related deaths was considerable in

[9] The proportion treated out of total stock increased by 5–7 per cent in all livestock types except for camels (1 per cent).

[10] Disease-related deaths on average accounted for 76–82 per cent of total deaths during 2005–15 for all livestock types except camels (70 per cent). The share of disease-related deaths remained about the same during the period.

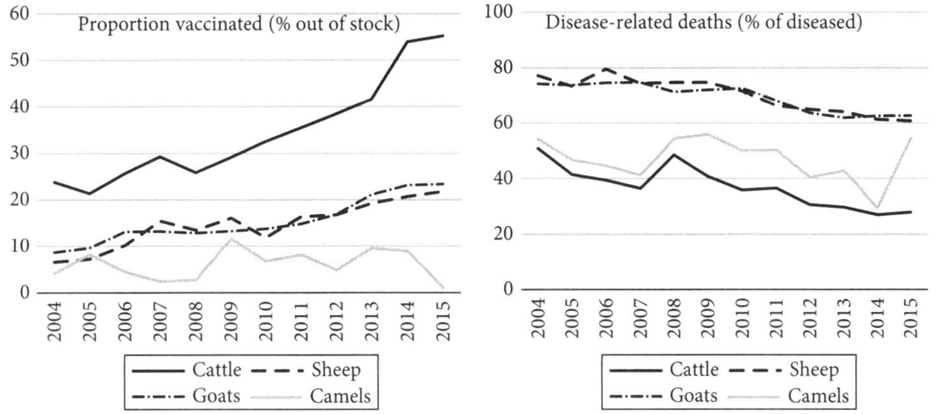

FIGURE 33.3 Proportion of livestock vaccinated and disease-related deaths, 2004/5–2015/16

Source: Authors' computation using CSA data (CSA, 2005–2016).

2015, they were 23, 16.4, 12, and 25 per cent lower relative to 2005 for cattle, sheep, goats, and equines.

33.5.4 Livestock Extension

Extension service provision has expanded rapidly in Ethiopia in the last two decades, particularly in the crop subsector. The promotion and subsequent increase in the use of modern inputs and production methods achieved through the extension system is cited as one of the contributors to the rapid growth in crop production and productivity that has occurred during the last decade (Bachewe et al. 2018). However, the extension system focused only on the crop subsector. Table 33.3 indicates that only 3 and 2 per cent of livestock farmers used extension services in 2005 and 2015, respectively. This contrasts

Table 33.3 Number of farmers using livestock extension services

Extension service type	2005	2010	2015
All livestock extension	227,903	195,251	292,256
Dairy	37,783	48,021	57,801
Meat	29,646	56,700	45,023
Poultry	123,736	41,626	154,967
Honey/Wax	23,172	25,336	13,329
Two or more	13,566	6,338	12,533
Livestock and crop extension users (%)			
Livestock	2.9	1.4	1.9
Crop	27.5	25.5	44.3

Source: Authors' computation using CSA data (CSA 2005–16).

with the higher proportion and steady growth in the proportion using crop extension (Table 33.3). The data further indicate that the proportion of livestock extension users is sporadic, which may have resulted from a campaign-type extension service provided by one programme/project or another.

33.5.5 Labour

Our description of the number of livestock owners indicates only the number of farmers (household heads) that own livestock and does not represent the number of people engaged in such activities as watering, milking, and caring for the animals, which often involve other members of the household in addition to the head. We use CSA's most recent Labour Force Survey (LFS) data to gauge the contribution of the livestock subsector to nationwide employment. The LFS was conducted in 2013. The survey included a sample of 240,660 persons residing in all regions and zones of the country except six zones in Somali region. The sampled persons represented 80.4 million people, which is the country's total population excluding those in the six zones of Somali region.

Using the three-digit employment classification (CSA 2014) we identify nine employment types that involve the production and processing of livestock products. This includes livestock farming, mixed crop–livestock farming, processing of animal-sourced food (ASF), and leather processing and manufacturing of leather products. The number of people employed in these sectors accounted for 54.6 per cent of 47.4 million people employed. The number engaged in mixed crop–livestock production accounted for the largest share (46.9 per cent) followed by those engaged in only livestock production (7.6 per cent). Those engaged in the remaining seven subsectors accounted for less than 0.2 per cent of the nationwide employment in 2013. The latter description provides imprecise information regarding the share of livestock in total employment since a large majority of livestock producers are mixed crop–livestock farmers. Therefore, we can only estimate livestock's contribution to employment. If we assume mixed crop–livestock farmers used 20 or 30 per cent of their time for livestock production, then the share of the livestock subsector in total employment in 2013 is 17 or 22 per cent.

33.6 Conclusions

Ethiopia has recorded rapid economic growth in the last decade. Relative to its size, measured in terms of both the size of employment and stock of live animals, the livestock subsector contributed little to this growth. This low contribution has been attributed mainly to weak institutions and the absence of a clear livestock policy framework. Despite this low contribution to the overall economy, the livestock subsector is an important source of income for farm households, provides employment to many people across the supply chain, and livestock serve as a means of saving and insurance for farm households and as a major source of ploughing power in crop production.

Furthermore, the livestock subsector has historically been an important input supplier to the manufacturing sector, although this has not been sufficiently harnessed. This has begun to change quite recently. With its increasing focus on industrialization and job creation, the government of Ethiopia has prioritized the development of an efficient and competitive leather processing industry capable of providing the necessary inputs to the leather manufacturing sector. With this in mind, equal attention is being given to the development of the livestock sector with forward and backward linkages in the leather value chain. With the introduction of these policies, the livestock subsector is expected to become a significant player in the economic development of the country. Oqubay (2015) indicates that the performance of the leather industry will improve with the implementation of appropriate export and investment promotion and industrial financing policy tools, and with the creation of sufficient implementation capacity and coordination between the policy tools.

APPENDIX

Appendix 33.1A Variables used in livestock growth accounting analyses

Variable	2004	2010	2014
Number of livestock holders (millions)	10.3	13.9	15.0
Grazing area (000 ha)	844.6	1,708.6	1,758.5
TLU (millions)	34.5	48.7	52.4
Value of crop used as animal feed (mill birr)	481.3	740.2	806.5
Veterinary services (millions of livestock)	14.6	33.8	53.7
Number of extension users (000)	302	195	226
Rural roads (000km)[a]	18.4	29.2	32.6
Real livestock (billion birr)[a]	30.9	45.8	54.3

Source: Authors' analyses using CSA data (CSA, 2017; 2005–16) except those with superscript of (a), which are from NBE (2017).

References

Addis Ababa Chamber of Commerce and Sectoral Associations (AACCSA) (2015). 'Value Chain Study on Meat Processing Industry in Ethiopia'. http://addischamber.com/wp-content/uploads/2017/01/Value-Chain-study-on-Meat-Processing.pdf (accessed 15 April 2015).

Addis Ababa Chamber of Commerce and Sectoral Associations (AACCSA) (2016). 'Value Chain Study on Dairy Industry in Ethiopia'. http://addischamber.com/wp-content/uploads/2017/01/Value-chain-study-on-Dairy-industry-in-Ethiopia.pdf (accessed 15 April 2015).

Bachewe, F., G. Berhane, B. Minten, A. S. Taffesse (2018). 'Agricultural Transformation in Africa? Assessing the Evidence in Ethiopia', *World Development* 105: 286–98.
Bachewe, F., G. Berhane, B. Minten, and A. S. Taffesse (2016). 'Non-Farm Income and Labor Markets in Rural Ethiopia', IFPRI-ESSP Working Paper 90, Addis Ababa.
Bachewe, F., B. Minten, and F. Yimer (2017). 'The Rising Costs of Animal-Source Foods in Ethiopia: Evidence and Implications', IFPRI-ESSP Working Paper 108, Addis Ababa.
Carlaw, K. and R. G. Lipsey (2003). 'Productivity, Technology, and Economic Growth: What Is the Relationship?', *Journal of Economic Surveys* 17 (3): 457–95.
CSA (2005–16). 'Agricultural Sample Survey, Vol. 2: Report on Livestock and Livestock Characteristics (Private Peasant Holdings, *Meher* Season)', CSA, Addis Ababa.
CSA (2014). 'Labour Force Survey Data', CSA, Addis Ababa.
CSA (2017). 'Agricultural Sample Survey: Holder Level Data of Livestock and Livestock Characteristics (Private Peasant Holdings, *Meher* Season), CSA, Addis Ababa.
Ethiopian Development Research Institute (EDRI) (2009). 'Ethiopia: Input–Output Tables and Social Accounting Matrix', EDRI, Addis Ababa.
FAO (2018). 'FAOSTAT', United Nations Food and Agriculture Organization, Rome. http://faostat.fao.org/ (accessed 13 January 2018).
Minten, B., F. Bachewe, and M. Dereje, M. (2018). 'Evolving Food Systems in Ethiopia', IFPRI-ESSP Working Paper, Addis Ababa.
National Bank of Ethiopia (NBE) (2017). 'Annual Report 2015/16', Addis Ababa.
Negassa, A., F. Bachewe, A. S. Taffesse, and M. Dereje (2017). 'An Assessment of the Livestock Economy in Mixed Crop–Livestock Production Systems in Ethiopia', IFPRI-ESSP Working Paper 101, Addis Ababa.
Oqubay, A. (2015). *Made in Africa: Industrial Policy in Ethiopia* (New York: Oxford University Press).
Shapiro, B. I., G. Gebru, S. Desta, et al. (2015). 'Ethiopia Livestock Master Plan', International Livestock Research Institute (ILRI) Project Report, ILRI, Nairobi.
Solow, R. M. (1957). 'Technical Change and the Aggregate Production Function', *Review of Economics and Statistics* 39: 312–20.
Tafere, K., and I. Worku (2012). 'Consumption Patterns of Livestock Products in Ethiopia: Elasticity Estimates Using HICES (2004/05) Data', IFPRI-ESSP Working Paper 12, Addis Ababa.

CHAPTER 34

WOMEN'S EMPOWERMENT IN RURAL ETHIOPIA

ANNET A. MULEMA
AND LIKIMYELESH NIGUSSIE

34.1 Background and Context

Agriculture is the mainstay of the Ethiopian economy, contributing up to 41.5 per cent of gross domestic product (GDP) during the five years of the Growth and Transformation Plan (GTP-I) period (National Planning Commission 2016). Smallholder agriculture is the dominant sector in terms of its contribution to GDP, employment, and foreign exchange earnings to Ethiopia. Women, who account for half of the population, contribute significantly to the sector. Studies show that an estimated 46 per cent and 74 per cent of all working women (aged 15–49) and men of the same age are engaged in agricultural occupations (CSA 2011, cited by UN Women 2014). In rural areas these figures increase to 57 per cent and 88 per cent respectively (UN Women 2014). In Ethiopia, the role and participation of women in agriculture varies by region, due to cultural norms and values. Despite this difference in participation, most quantitative studies suggest that the productivity of female farmers is less than that of their male counterparts, which is considered one of the causes of poverty and food insecurity. According to a 2014 World Bank report, in Ethiopia women farmers tend to produce about 23 per cent less per hectare than their male counterparts (Warner, Kieran, and McMullan 2015; UN Women 2014).

Despite the centrality of their contribution to the sector and the economy, women are often disadvantaged, and their contribution is less valued. In terms of larger or commercial farms, the role of women tends to be relegated to that of wage labourer and not that of an international trader or large-scale producer. These positions in the marketing chain are typically dominated by men. With the growing population, the limited availability of land for smallholders, and the increased marketization and development of larger farms, women could be pushed out of smallholder participation into less desirable wage-labour positions, indicating sex-bifurcated economic opportunities (Warner, Kieran, and McMullan 2015; Kostka and Scharrer 2011).

Several authors have argued that empowering women is key in increasing agricultural productivity and food security (FAO 2011; World Bank 2012), and many development interventions have increasingly targeted women as beneficiaries, assuming that they will be in a better position to adopt technologies and practices that increase productivity, food, income, and nutritional security (Malapit et al. 2015). Empowerment is the ability to make decisions about one's own life and act on them to achieve a desired outcome, free from violence, retribution, or fear (Klugman et al. 2014). In recent years, the Ethiopian government and its development partners have been implementing initiatives focusing on women's empowerment and gender equality in the agricultural sector. However, measures of women's empowerment have remained obscure. The Women's Empowerment in Agriculture Index (WEAI), a survey-based tool developed by IFPRI, USAID, and OPHI in 2012 to measure the empowerment, agency, and inclusion of women in the agricultural sector, uses quantitative data collected by interviewing men and women from the same households. There is limited understanding of the local meaning of empowerment and how this is associated with the standardized measures of empowerment. Additionally, most of the measures of empowerment are quantitative and focus on visible forms of agency related to decision-making (O'Hara and Clement 2018), which obscures important qualitative measures.

Because the meaning of empowerment is highly context specific, a survey-based quantitative measurement cannot adequately capture the nuances of the concept and describe complex related aspects such as status, self-esteem, and individuals' perceptions of empowerment. Furthermore, some of the indicators may not be applicable in different contexts. The relationship between the domains and indicators of empowerment at policy, community, and household levels has not been documented, which makes this chapter novel. This chapter interrogates the following research questions: (1) what is the local meaning of empowerment? and (2) what domains and indicators measure women's empowerment both quantitatively and qualitatively at national, community, and household level? This is realized by systematically reviewing policy documents, national survey reports (using data from the Central Statistical Agency), and relevant reports from the Food and Agriculture Organization (FAO). This assessment will provide an understanding of the local meanings of empowerment at household and community levels (drawing from one case study in Ethiopia) and the implications of the current standardized measures of women's empowerment.

34.2 Theoretical and Analytical Perspective

The chapter applies and critiques the recently developed WEAI, examining its effectiveness in measuring the empowerment outcomes of projects that implement empowerment approaches. The WEAI can be used to assess the general state of empowerment and gender parity in agriculture and to identify the empowerment gaps. This chapter focuses on the five-dimension endowment index (5DE), which measures empowerment. The WEAI places a lot of emphasis on quantitative empowerment domains and indicators including: production (women's input to productive decisions, autonomy in production); resources (access to and decisions on credit); income (control over use of income); leadership (group membership and speaking in public); and time (workload and leisure) (Alkire et al. 2013). Empowerment in agriculture is defined as the ability to make decisions on matters related to agriculture as well as access to the materials and social resources needed to carry out those decisions (Alkire et al. 2013). Empowerment is a result of the interaction between three key elements: agency, institutional structures, and resources. Resources are tangible and intangible capital and sources of power that women have, own, or use individually or collectively in the exercise of agency (Eerdewijk et al. 2017). According to Kabeer (1995, 2001), the ability to exercise choice comprises three dimensions: resources (which includes not only access but also claims to material, human, and social resources), agency (including processes of decision-making, negotiation, and manipulation), and achievements (well-being outcomes).

The extent to which an individual is empowered is influenced by her ability to make purposive choices (personal agency) and the institutional context in which choice is made (opportunity structure). Opportunity structure is measured by the presence and operation of formal and informal institutions, including laws, regulatory frameworks,

Table 34.1 Domains, indicators, and weights in the 5DE

Domain	Description	Indicator	Weight*
Production	Decision about agricultural production and sole or joint decision-making about food and cash-crop farming, livestock and fisheries, and autonomy in agricultural production	Input to productive decisions Autonomy in production	1/10
Resources	Ownership of, access to, and decision-making power about productive resources such as land, livestock, agricultural equipment, consumer durables, and credit	Ownership of assets Purchase, sale, or transfer of asset Access to and decision about credit	1/15
Income	Sole or joint control over the use of income and expenditure	Control over use of income	1/5
Leadership	Leadership in the community, measured by membership in economic or social groups and comfort speaking in public	Group membership Speaking in public	1/10
Time	Allocation of time to productive and domestic tasks and satisfaction with the time available for leisure activities	Workload Leisure	1/10

Note: *The weights add up, and the value ranges from 0 to 1, where higher values mean greater empowerment.

Source: Alkire et al. (2013).

and norms governing behaviour (Alsop and Heinsohn 2005). Table 34.1 presents the five domains and indicators of empowerment in the WEAI. We recognize that the WEAI is the first attempt to standardize measures of women's empowerment in the agricultural sector and the results will inform the ongoing improvement of the tool to a project-level WEAI (pro-WEAI).[1]

34.3 Methodology

This chapter analyses various aspects of women's empowerment in the Ethiopian agricultural sector. The analysis focuses on three levels: policy, community, and household. At policy level it analyses the women's empowerment domains of national interest. At community level, it investigates how communities define empowerment. And at household level, it examines the intra-household dynamics of women's empowerment and its manifestation. The authors analysed existing reports that analyse national surveys from the Central Statistical Agency (CSA) to ascertain the data being collected at national level to measure women's empowerment. We reviewed the Ethiopian Constitution and the National Development Policies and Strategies. We also used secondary data from the United Nations Joint Programme on Accelerating Rural Women's Economic Empowerment (UNJP-RWEE) study to provide a case study that analyses the local dimensions of empowerment (Nigussie et al. 2017).[2] We synthesized the findings from the FAO study between July and August 2017. Additionally, we reviewed the quantitative report (Slavchevska and Campos 2017). The analysis is framed by the theoretical and analytical framework.

34.4 A Critical Review of Women's Empowerment in Agriculture at Policy Level

Recognizing the role of women's empowerment in achieving national and international development goals, the government of Ethiopia has instituted various legal and policy reforms. This section discusses various gender-related legal and policy frameworks using the five domains of empowerment lens: production, resources, income, leadership, and time.

[1] http://gaap.ifpri.info/

[2] The UNJP-RWEE is a global initiative of the three Rome-based United Nations Agencies—FAO, WFP, and IFAD—and UN Women to accelerate economic empowerment of rural women.

34.4.1 Production

The Constitution of Ethiopia, Sub-Article 41.2 stipulates the right of every Ethiopian to choose his or her means of livelihood, occupation, and profession (FDRE 1993). To enhance participation of women in economic activities, the Rural Development Policy and Strategy (2003) prescribes due attention to livelihood options which women dominate, including gardening, animal breeding, poultry, bee keeping, and others. It also emphasizes that priority should be given in government employment and in the provision of credit and technical services to women who set up their own ventures. In support of this, the National Employment Policy and Strategy in Ethiopia claims that unemployment and underemployment are more prevalent among women than men. Further, more of the employed women are concentrated in the informal economy which is characterized by low returns and underemployment (MoLSA 2009).

The policy therefore suggests the informal sector should be supported by creating decent jobs and absorbing a large proportion of the labour force (that is, unskilled women and youth). It also emphasizes the importance of interventions focusing on skill development, increasing access to productive resources, and economic protection through institutional support to improve women's labour force participation and their presence in the formal sector. In addition, it proposes rural women should be engaged in productive non-farm activities and rural waged employment to generate income, promote equity, and reduce the rural–urban migration caused by problems of land fragmentation and low agricultural productivity in rural areas (MoLSA 2009). According to the Growth and Transformation Plan II (GTP-II), the indicator used to measure women's gain in production is the number of women in various economic sectors. In addition to this, the Central Statistical Authority, in its Agricultural Sample Survey (AgSS) collects sex-disaggregated data on the number of male and female holders implementing best agronomic practices, as suggested by agronomists (CSA surveys in Kassa, Abate, and Warner 2016). The CSA data collected only from one member of the household—the farm manager or 'head of the household'—provide information on whether they implement a certain agronomic practice or not. Such data hardly indicate the intra-household dynamics. However, adopting a technology or implementing a particular agronomic practice has an effect on labour and time allocation by all members of the household who participate in farming. To measure changes (who benefits or loses), it is useful to collect information regarding who benefited and how from both spouses.

34.4.2 Resources

Several policy documents provide women with equal rights to control resources and decision-making, including land. For example, the Federal Democratic Republic of Ethiopia Constitution, adopted in 1995, acknowledges the equal rights of women in all spheres with their male counterparts. Article 35 of the Constitution explicitly stipulates that: 'Women shall, in the enjoyment of rights and protections provided for by this

Constitution, have equal right with men'. With regard to the right to acquire, administer, control, use, and transfer property, Sub-Article 35.7 states: 'Women have the right to acquire, administer, control, use and transfer property. They have equal rights with men with respect to use, transfer, administration and control of land. They shall also enjoy equal treatment in the inheritance of property.' In addition, Sub-Article 40.7 of the Constitution confirms that every Ethiopian has full rights to the immovable property he/she establishes on their land by personal labour or capital.

To guide enforcement of the Constitution, particularly in relation to land, Federal Land Administration Proclamation No. 89/1997 mandated joint certificates of agricultural holdings between husband and wife. It also provides the legal right for vulnerable groups, including women, to use their holdings by hiring labour, renting, or entering an agreement to share income. To protect women's rights, the proclamation states that the law of a region shall confirm the equal rights of women in respect of the use, administration, and control of land as well as in respect of transferring and bequeathing holding rights (FDRE 1997). The Rural Development Policy and Strategy (MoFED 2003) of the country affirms the same: 'Legally ensuring equal user-rights on the plots of land being farmed by men will automatically affirm women's equality with men in land user-rights guaranteeing the ownership rights of women on their production and development ventures is absolutely necessary.'

In addition, measures to safeguard women's rights to access resources (such as land, credit, and other productive resources) are suggested to protect women from multiple other types of deprivation, such as longer working days, and from the violence and discrimination against women which are still widespread in the country (MoFED 2006). In line with this, in the GTP-II document, the indicators used to measure gains of rural women regarding resources, particularly credit, include the number of women who are organized and benefit from small and micro enterprises, micro finance institutions, or self-help associations, and who have access to credit and saving. Also included is the number of women with access to extension services and access to farm technologies. With regard to land, the indicators used include the number of women with land rights and land-use rights.

34.4.3 Income

There is little mention in the policy documents under review of control over income, one of the domains of empowerment.

34.4.4 Leadership

The government of Ethiopia (GOE) has also instituted legal frameworks to ensure equal participation of women with men in development. For example, Sub-Article 35.6 of the Constitution states: 'Women have the right to full consultation in the formulation of national development policies, the designing and execution of projects, and particularly in the case of projects affecting the interests of women'. GOE also adopted the National Policy on Women (TGE 1993) which aims to provide national direction to advance the equality of women and facilitate participation of women in all political, economic, and social spheres on an equal basis with men. In line with this, the National Action Plan for Gender Equality (NAP-GE 2006–2010), (MWA 2006) is to be used as a tool for promotion of gender-equitable development, aimed at increasing women's access to all levels of decision-making, particularly in political and public affairs. Recognizing the historical legacy of inequality and discrimination, Sub-Article 35.3 of the Constitution prescribes affirmative measures that enable women to compete and participate equally with men in the political, social, and economic sphere of life as well as in public and private institutions. The Rural Development Policy and Strategy (MoFED 2003) document also emphasized the importance of making special efforts targeting women to ensure that they benefit equally from rural development.

To this end, in the first and second Growth and Transformation Plans (GTPs) the GOE adopted a strategy to strengthen women's associations, and organizations for gender equality and women's empowerment. Strengthening these associations is believed to foster women's empowerment and equal participation in the development and governance processes. By the end of GTP-I, the participation of women in economic development and political affairs was deemed to have been strengthened, though there is a difference in strength across associations. The GTP document uses the number of women who are members and in leadership positions of groups such as cooperatives as indicators of achievement in this regard.

34.4.5 Time

The National Policy on Women (TGE 1993, MWA 2006) suggests increasing women's access to different services, facilities, and technologies to reduce their workload, free them from traditional practices that perpetuate their subordination, and decrease their vulnerability to harm. In support of this, the Rural Development Policy and Strategy (2003) stipulates that due attention should be paid to services, facilities, and technologies that reduce women's workload. National development plans such as the Plan for Accelerated and Sustainable Development to End Poverty (2005/6–2009/10) are established as central strategies unleashing the potential of women and liberating them from low-productivity tasks, thereby increasing their participation in the workforce and the social and political processes of the country. This means providing women with access to services (such as education, water and sanitation, and health) and fostering the adaptation of technical and vocational education in agriculture to the needs of women. Providing women with access to services and facilities is assumed to reduce women's workload and the time they spend on unpaid care work, allowing them more time for other productive and leisure activities.

The GOE has conducted a national time-use survey to provide information about the time spent by the population (men, women, and children) on various activities at national, rural, and urban levels. Gains are measured by the number of hours spent on domestic activity, productive activity, and leisure. The survey provides data on women's and children's use of time in order to improve their social welfare; on the distribution of paid and unpaid work among men and women in order to minimize gender inequality; and on the measurement and valuation of the unpaid work of men and women (CSA 2014). The indicators used to measure gains in the GTP document include the number of women with access to services such as an energy-saving stove, safe water, labour-saving devices, extension services, and training.

34.5 A Critical Review of the Local Meaning of Empowerment at Community and Household Level: UNJP-RWEE Case Study

This project (launched in September 2012) has been implemented by UN Women in collaboration with three Rome-based UN agencies—the Food and Agriculture Organization of the United Nations (FAO), the World Food Programme (WFP), and the International Fund for Agricultural Development (IFAD). The United Nations Joint Programme on Rural Women's Economic Empowerment strives to strengthen women's access to financial services in order to accelerate rural women's economic empowerment, coupled with other integrative interventions such as: improving rural women's and their households' food security and nutrition; development of individuals' capabilities and fulfilment of rights; fostering access to markets and agricultural inputs; promoting income-generating activities in agriculture; and strengthening women's participation in and benefit from community and rural institutions such as cooperatives and farmer's associations.

To understand the local meaning of empowerment, from the perspectives of rural women and men, we reviewed secondary data from the qualitative study conducted by the UNJP-RWEE programme in Adami Tulu Jido Kombolcha and Yaya Gulele *woreda*s in Oromia region (Nigussie et al. 2017). About forty group discussions were conducted separately with men and women farmers, and a total of 187 women and 195 men participated. Study participants were purposefully selected based on being a member of the project, level of empowerment (empowered and disempowered), and gender. These data are compared with related results from the quantitative survey conducted at household level by interviewing 750 households (749 women and 630 men) in Adami Tulu Jido Kombolcha and Yaya Gulele *woreda*s in Oromia, and Dodola *woreda* in Afar region. The two types of studies were conducted in action and control sites.

The findings reveal that the term 'empowerment' is subject to local socio-cultural understandings and notions. Communities in these districts associate the concept of empowerment with the ideal characteristics of a woman or man in the local community. The local understanding of empowerment emanates from the society's cultural framework of ideals that make someone strong/able/capable, acceptable, and respectable. The local definition of empowerment for men and women includes the following aspects: ability to meet socially constructed roles, participation in diversified livelihood activities, ability to adopt technology, ability to create wealth by saving and investing, knowledge, good conduct, acceptance in the community, active participation in meetings, planning with spouse, ability to manage time efficiently, and ability to use family planning (only for women). Of these qualities, leadership and mobility are more empowering for women while accumulation of assets, knowledge, and adoption of agricultural technologies is more empowering for men.

The ability to meet social roles is one of the empowerment indicators. Specifically, men that provide for their family by meeting their food, clothing, shoes, educational, and medical needs—thus improving the family's quality of life—are considered empowered. Meanwhile, women that take good care of the family (by feeding the family properly, providing support to their spouses, sending children to school, and maintaining hygiene/cleanliness at home and outside the house) are empowered. Any intervention targeted at men and women that enables them to meet their socially constructed roles is considered a pathway to empowerment by the community. This aspect, important as it is to the community, was not captured in the quantitative study conducted at household level.

Active participation in various income-generating activities is another indicator for empowerment at community level. For men the income-generating activities include crop production, cattle fattening, and waged employment, while for women they include selling drinks, vegetables, handicrafts, eggs and poultry, dairy products, and other petty trade. In this regard, community members appreciate interventions targeted at men and women, such as provision of access to loans, farm inputs, and technical training, as these enhance their participation in income-generating activities. The quantitative results revealed that almost all respondents (99 per cent) are engaged in staple grain farming which is predominantly for food consumption. In both action and control sites, women are significantly more likely to be engaged in non-farm self-employment than men. On the other hand, men are more likely than women to be in waged employment. In the group discussions, men who adopt technologies to enhance production and productivity, such as irrigation, improved seed, compost, fertilizer, hybrid livestock, are considered empowered, while this was not mentioned as characterizing empowered women. One reason for linking the adoption of technology with men could be the attitude that recognizes men as the farmers (i.e. those leading agricultural activities). This indicates that more effort is needed to bring about attitudinal change towards women and farm technologies. This could include sensitization to help communities to value and recognize women's contribution to agriculture.

Men and women who can *create wealth by saving and investing* are considered empowered. In most cases, men that invest in high-value assets, such as renting land for cultivation, buying livestock, and building a property, to increase their wealth, were considered empowered in their society. Women are not expected to be engaged in such high-value investments but those who did accumulate such assets were considered empowered and are mostly female household heads. One reason for this is that savings women have are small compared to spouses' joint savings used to make large investments. Furthermore, investments from joint savings are considered as the man's, as men usually have more decision-making power than women. Targeted interventions to increase the participation of women in income-generating activities will help them to earn income, and to save and invest which is a route to economic empowerment.

Knowledge is the other key indicator for empowered men and women. The women indicated that people who are educated and/or educate their children are empowered because of the knowledge they have compared to illiterate people and/or people who do not send their children to school. These women further indicated that their activities were limited to the home because of their limited awareness of their rights and potential. In this regard, the government's adult literacy programme and other targeted interventions by practitioners are perceived to lead to empowerment. One of the female beneficiaries stated that:

> I am a woman who can explain her ideas clearly. I am not educated but I am knowledgeable. I have a good position in the community because of my knowledge. Empowered woman is she who has good behaviour, uses credit properly, is knowledgeable, shares her knowledge, and contributes to the community. I am also empowered because I am able to participate in farming of crops and vegetables, educate my children, and speak at community meeting, as I am a RWEE beneficiary.
>
> (Abune Germama, a 40-year-old empowered woman from Adami Tulu Jido Kombolcha *woreda*)

Good conduct and acceptance by the community are also considered indicators for an empowered individual. Men and women who do not drink alcohol and chew *khat* are empowered and are liked and trusted by the community. Men that exhibit characteristics like patience, motivation, impartiality/fairness in dealing with community issues, good conduct, and popularity within the family and community were considered empowered. These qualities were believed to be at the root of likelihood to succeed. Fairness/impartiality shown by an empowered man dealing with community issues may indicate a leadership position in community affairs. A woman who is likeable is considered a role model in the community, someone that other women strive to resemble. Thus, investing in such a woman will have a stronger positive ripple effect.

Active participation in collective action is also considered an indicator for an empowered individual. Women particularly underlined that women's participation in community groups is exceptionally empowering because i) it provides them with the opportunity to practice leadership, and ii) it increases their awareness of their rights and potential. The male group participants also described women who speak up and demonstrate community leadership as empowered, while women who do not have the ability to lead the community and are too shy to speak during community meetings are seen as disempowered. Women's participation in collective action provides them with the opportunity to network and learn from each other. Active participation in collective actions such as cooperatives seems to contribute to women's empowerment and improve the community's perception of their empowerment through the activities and education it brings to the local community. Whereas the household survey tool measures membership of groups and ability to speak in public as leadership indicators, the group discussions elicited leadership skills as a primary factor.

Time management is the other indicator for empowerment. A woman who uses her time effectively to carry out domestic, productive, and communal activities is considered empowered, while a man who uses his time effectively for cultivation is considered empowered. This indicates that women have more pressure in terms of time management due to their triple responsibilities, relative to men who are mainly responsible for productive work (where the contribution of women is also significant). This workload negatively affects the time and labour women can invest in targeted income-generating activities. In the WEAI, this indicator has been used, by measuring time allocated to different activities, including leisure, to determine workload levels.

Freedom of mobility is another indicator of empowerment and is determined by sex, age, marital status, headship, and distance. Men of all ages are free to move. However, a woman's mobility depends on: i) age and marital status; ii) cultural norms; iii) distance and time of day; iv) financial status; and v) domestic responsibilities. During childhood, mobility of girls is monitored by adult family members, especially the mother. However, attending school provides freedom of mobility for girls and gives them the opportunity to be aware of their rights. Young unmarried women have relatively more freedom of mobility. After getting married, women's mobility depends on consultation with their husbands. These women are allowed to move only during the daytime, and not at night. They are relatively free to travel to places near their home such as the local market, to visit neighbours, and to attend weddings, *idir*[3] and *iqub*[4] meetings, but they may have to inform their spouses.

Permission must be sought by some women to attend meetings, or to visit relatives and urban markets. Women who fail to do so may face beatings at night and may be considered disempowered by the community. This can even be a source of friction that finally leads to divorce. Separated, widowed, and divorced women have absolute freedom of mobility. A woman who goes wherever she likes is considered by the community as badly behaved, and this amounts to disobeying and challenging the power of a husband. The men opined that they are the main decision-makers regarding women's mobility. Men do not allow their wives to go to distant places or travel unaccompanied at night, for fear of them being hurt or becoming involved in sexual relationships (consensual or otherwise), and for fear of the loss of their power and control over women. These restrictions could arise from the local cultural notion that women's sphere of influence belongs to the home. Older married women have more freedom of mobility than younger married women. On the other hand, necessity rather than choice challenges the community's stance on mobility. Women in remote villages considered mobility for

[3] *Idir* is an association established among neighbours or workers to save funds that can be used during emergencies, such as a death in a family belonging to the group.

[4] *Iqub* is a group savings association established by a small group of people to provide substantial funds to members on a rotational basis.

trading as disempowering as it increases their workload and leaves them little time to take care of their home.

Planning with spouse—in other words, joint decision-making—was another indication of empowerment for both men and women. Joint decision-making mostly occurred with larger assets and larger incomes. Women have autonomy over lower-value assets and low incomes. In the household survey, there was almost a perfect correlation between participating in any of the activities and making a decision (jointly or solely) about that activity. The only exception was poultry rearing, where women involved in poultry farming also made the decisions.

34.6 Connections Between Measures of Empowerment at National, Community, and Household Levels

Discrepancies between national and local levels can be found in the measures of empowerment (Table 34.2). Policy-level indicators tend to measure the 'reach' (in terms of numbers of women reached) as the first stepping stone to empowerment. At local levels, empowerment is understood in terms of access but also capability, in accordance with the values of the community. We also notice some discrepancies in how the indicators of empowerment are measured at household level, with more domains being elicited at community level than are measured in WEAI. From the researcher's perspective, weighting the indicators might not align with the importance of a specific indicator to a given community of both women and men. There could be a mismatch between the perceptions of those whose empowerment is being measured, and the researchers' or development practitioners' perspectives. For example, in the case of land, Adem (see Chapter 4) indicates the significance of addressing structural issues in addition to providing access to resources. Specifically: 'having land titles at hand has not as yet given women new mechanisms for defending their land rights against male-biased cultural expectations especially within their own households and kinship groups'.

There are many emotional and invisible aspects of empowerment that were identified by community members. The measurements at policy and household level (by the WEAI) are all quantifiable, while some of the indicators at community level cannot be easily quantified but are nonetheless important to the communities. Some of the indicators at the root of empowerment are difficult to measure and are thus more likely to be ignored by those charged with implementing projects. This calls for diversification of methods so that non-quantifiable indicators can be captured as well as information that validates the numbers generated by the survey tools. The local understanding of empowerment goes beyond being able to make decisions to being able to realize an ability to engage in decision-making. It includes community values that give meaning to people's actions, such as good conduct. Decision-making is skewed towards joint decision-making

Table 34.2 Measurements of empowerment at national, community, and household levels

Domains of empowerment	Indicators at policy level	Indicators at community and household levels	Household level (WEAI)
Production	Number of women in various economic sectors (National Planning Commission 2016)	Ability to participate in diversified agricultural activities	Input in productive decisions
	Number of female holders implementing best agronomic practices, as suggested by agronomists (Kassa, Abate, and Warner 2016)	Ability to adopt agricultural technologies	Autonomy in production
Resource	Number of female holders who own oxen for ploughing (Kassa, Abate, and Warner 2016)	Access to finance, technology, and technical training	Ownership of assets
	Number of women who are organized and benefit from small and micro enterprises, self-help associations (National Planning Commission 2016)	Ownership of a house	Purchase, sale, or transfer of asset
	Number of women with access to credit and savings (National Planning Commission 2016)		Access to and decision about credit
	Number of women with land rights and land-use rights (National Planning Commission 2016)		
	Number of women with access to financial institutions, extension services, and farm technologies (National Planning Commission 2016)		
Income	–	Ability to earn income from diverse sources, save and invest	Control over use of income
Leadership	Number of women who are in leadership position and are members of various groups or associations (National Planning Commission 2016)	Being member of a group Ability to attend meetings Ability to speak in public Ability to influence others	Group membership Speaking in public
Time	Number of hours spent on domestic and productive activity (CSA 2014) Number of hours for leisure (CSA 2014)	Ability to effectively use time for triple responsibilities (domestic, productive, and community)	Workload Leisure
Other important domains of empowerment	Number of females who attend schoo And have knowledge (awareness of rights) (National Planning Commission 2016)	Freedom of mobility, freedom to use family planning, having knowledge (awareness of rights), having good conduct and acceptance	

Source: National Planning Commission (2016): CSA (2014): Kassa, Abate, and Warner (2016).

(planning with wife and husband) rather than individual autonomy. Women have autonomy over lower-value assets and low incomes which might not be very empowering. Although control over income is pertinent to the community, this dimension has not been explored at policy level. Women perceived participation in making decisions over important resources and participation in the public sphere as empowering. What is more empowering to women is the ability to speak in public and to hold leadership positions. Mobility is empowering but it varies according to the context. Mobility and control over income have not been given attention at policy level.

All in all, policy documents show commitment by the government to addressing gender inequality by creating an enabling environment. However, so far, the reports provided by the government regarding gender show the number of women reached but fail to provide information on impacts of the polices on these women, and specifically on how the policies helped to benefit or empower them. For example, a study by Alsop, Bertelsen, and Holland (2006) indicated that efforts to organize women and continuous participation of women in meetings help them to be more forthcoming when expressing their opinion in public. Qualitative data such as these need to be administered in order to capture the outcomes of attending a meeting.

Given the differences in perceptions of empowerment in different cultures, a universal indicator for measuring empowerment and social change may be challenging (O'Hara and Clement 2018). Thus, quantitative indicators need to be enriched by qualitative data that capture information on who gains and who loses in a given social change, to guide effective project design and to achieve better outcomes in terms of women's empowerment.

34.7 Conclusion and Implications for the Development of Pathways to Empowerment for Women

The WEAI may be an appropriate tool to aggregate measures of empowerment at the national level but is inadequate for measuring community- or project-specific indicators of empowerment at the local level. Data have to be collected on numerous assets and analysed to find out how the flow of assets affects empowerment outcomes and how best to measure empowerment. There is a need to align empowerment measurements at all levels, considering the institutional structures in which women pursue their livelihoods. The current measurements of empowerment have implications for the empowerment approaches employed by different institutions—going beyond 'reach' to 'benefiting' and 'empowering' women, and holistically developing their capabilities to make strategic decisions, using the available resources. The measurements also have implications for framing debates around empowerment as they focus on researcher-driven visible and quantifiable indicators. Using 'numbers of women' and specifying a certain indicator as a universal indicator to measure empowerment in a culturally diverse community could be misleading. Empowerment is also subject to various local meanings and conceptualizations that are difficult to quantify. These are also skewed towards the ideals of feminism and not necessarily to empowerment. Such contextual aspects can help interpret and add meaning to the quantitative findings. Policymakers, development agents, and researchers need to develop holistic empowerment support systems that unleash women's full potential rather than targeting problems, due to the complex relations between the resources that women use to empower themselves, which are also influenced by institutional arrangements. More comprehensive monitoring and evaluation systems to accommodate multiple data collection techniques need to be in place to validate the findings.

References

Alkire, S., R. S. Meinzen-Dick, A. Peterman, et al. (2013). 'The Women's Empowerment in Agriculture Index', *World Development* 52: 71–91.

Alsop, R., M. F. Bertelsen, and J. Holland (2006). *Empowerment in Practice: From Analysis to Implementation* (Washington, DC: World Bank Publications).

Alsop, R. and N. Heinsohn (2005). 'Measuring Empowering in Practice: Structuring Analysis and Framing Indicator', World Bank Policy Research Working Paper 3510, World Bank, Washington, DC.

CSA (2011). 'Ethiopian Demographic Health Survey (EDHS)', Central Statistical Agency, Addis Ababa.

CSA (2014). 'Ethiopia Time Use Survey: How Men and Women Spend their Time', Central Statistical Agency, Addis Ababa.

Eerdewijk, A. V., F. Wong, C. Vaast, et al. (2017). 'White Paper: A Conceptual Model of Women and Girls' Empowerment'. https://2130u636shoptphd141fqei1-wpengine.netdna-ssl.com/gender/wp-content/uploads/sites/3/2017/03/BMGF_KIT_WhitePaper_web-1.pdf.

FAO (Food and Agriculture Organization of the United Nations) (2011). 'Women in Agriculture: Closing the Gender Gap for Development' in *The State of Food and Agriculture 2010–2011* (Rome: Food and Agriculture Organization of the United Nations): 1–62.

FDRE (1995). 'Constitution of the Federal Democratic Republic of Ethiopia', Addis Ababa.

FDRE (1997). 'Federal Rural Land Administration Proclamation', 7 July, Addis Ababa.

Kabeer, N. (1995). 'Resources, Agency, Achievements: Reflections on the Measurement of Women's Empowerment', *Development and Change* 30: 435–64.

Kabeer, N. (2001). 'Reflections on the Measurement of Women's Empowerment', in *Discussing Women's Empowerment: Theory and Practice*, ed. A. Sisask (Stockholm: Swedish International Development Cooperation Agency): 17–57.

Kassa, L., T. G. Abate, and J. Warner (2016). 'Gender Differentials in Ethiopian Agriculture: Results from the CSA-Agricultural Sample Surveys (AgSS)', manuscript.

Klugman, J., L. Hanmer, S. Twigg, et al. (2014). 'Voice and Agency: Empowering Women and Girls for Shared Prosperity', World Bank Publications, Washington, DC.

Kostka, Genia and J. Scharrer (2011). 'Ethiopia's Sesame Sector: The Contribution of Different Farming Models to Poverty Alleviation, Climate Resilience and Women's Empowerment', Oxfam Research Reports, 1–45, Oxford.

Malapit, H. J. L., S. Kadiyala, B. Quisumbing, et al. (2015). 'Women's Empowerment Mitigates the Negative Effects of Low Production Diversity on Maternal and Child Nutrition in Nepal', *Journal of Development Studies* 51 (8): 1097–123.

MoFED (2003). 'Rural Development Policy and Strategies', Economic Policy and Planning Department, Ministry of Finance and Economic Development, Addis Ababa.

MoFED (2006). 'A Plan for Accelerated and Sustained Development to End Poverty (PASDEP)', Ministry of Finance and Economic Development, Addis Ababa.

MoLSA (2009). 'National Employment Policy and Strategy Ethiopia', FDRE, Addis Ababa.

MWA (1993). 'The National Policy on Women', Ministry of Women's Affairs, Addis Ababa.

MWA (2006). 'National Action Plan for Gender Equality (NAP-GE) 2006–2010', Ministry of Women's Affairs, Addis Ababa.

National Planning Commission (2016). 'Growth and Transformation Plan II (2015/16–2019/20)', Addis Ababa.

Nigussie, L., L. Debevec, A. Negera, et al. (2017). 'Economic Empowerment of Rural Women: Qualitative Study for the UNJP in Adami Tulu and Yaya Gulele Woredas', manuscript.

O'Hara, C., and F. Clement (2018). 'Power as Agency: A Critical Reflection on the Measurement of Women's Empowerment in the Development Sector', *World Development* 106: 111–23.

Slavchevska, V. and A. P. Dela O Campos (2017). 'Baseline Report for the Impact Evaluation of the United Nations Joint Program on Accelerating Rural Women's Economic Empowerment (JP RWEE) in Ethiopia', United Nations Addis Ababa.

Transitional Government of Ethiopia, TGE (1993). National Policy on Women.

UN Women (2014). 'Preliminary Gender Profile of Ethiopia', New York.

Warner, J., C. Kieran, and S. McMullan (2015). 'A Review of Selected Topics of Gender and Agricultural Research in Ethiopia over the Last Decades', manuscript.

World Bank (2012). 'World Development Report 2012: Gender Equality and Development', World Bank, Washington, DC.

PART V

INDUSTRIALIZATION AND URBAN DEVELOPMENT

CHAPTER 35

INDUSTRIAL POLICY AND LATE INDUSTRIALIZATION IN ETHIOPIA

ARKEBE OQUBAY

35.1 Industrial Policy in Ethiopia: an Introduction

More than fifteen years into a period of sustained and rapid economic growth, Ethiopia has continued to attract international attention for its achievements and for pursuing a home-grown development strategy, with an active industrial policy at its centre.[1,2] Some have been sceptical about Ethiopia's successful development model. While a 2017 BBC documentary asked: 'Can Ethiopia be Africa's leading manufacturing hub?', the *Financial Times* published a dismissive piece—'Ethiopia's mythical manufacturing boom'—in which the author claimed that the Ethiopian government had waged a successful PR campaign by selling 'a story that does not really exist'.[3]

The Ethiopian People's Revolutionary Democratic Front (EPRDF) had initially targeted agriculture as the key driver of post-war economic take-off (1995–2015) but increasingly pursued the development of the manufacturing sector as the prime driver of sustained economic growth and structural transformation post 2010.[4] Nonetheless by

[1] This chapter provides an account of industrial policy in Ethiopia from the inside, because the author has been closely involved in the design of this policy.

[2] An annual average GDP growth rate of 10 per cent and an increase in the average life expectancy from 45 years in 1991 to 66 in 2016, twice Africa's average.

[3] See BBC (2017) and the *Financial Times* (2017).

[4] See Growth and Transformation Plan I and II (MoFED 2010; NPC 2016). See also Chapter 9.

2018, per capita income remained very low and it was services that had come to dominate the economy, rather than manufacturing. Despite being able to feed its growing population, Ethiopia, Africa's second and the world's twelfth most populous country, faced intense structural constraints.

35.1.1 Industrial Policy and Structural Transformation

An industrial policy is a vehicle for catch-up and structural transformation, and increasingly such a policy must focus on how an economy is integrated into global trade and production networks. Industrial policy may be defined as 'a strategy that includes a range of implicit or explicit policy instruments selectively focused on specific industrial sectors for the purpose of structural change in line with a broader national vision and strategy' (Oqubay 2015: 18).[5] Structural transformation involves the shift (of an irreversible and permanent nature) of people and economic activities between sectors, and from low- to higher-productivity activities. It involves *diversification* (both vertical and horizontal) into new dynamic activities, fostering *domestic linkages* and building *technological capabilities,* and developing the stock of technical knowledge that constitutes wealth (Pasinetti 1981, 1993; Ocampo, Rada, and Taylor 2009).

There continues to be convincing evidence that manufacturing is the engine of structural change and sustained growth.[6] This is because of the greater scope in manufacturing (broadly defined to include high-productivity agricultural production) for economies of scale, learning by doing, technological development, and productivity gains, together with the strong links between manufacturing and other sectors. Manufacturing also has powerful direct and perhaps even more important indirect employment effects (Kaldor 1967; Thirlwall 2013).

Another central—and often neglected—component in structural transformation is the *strategic* role of exports. First, exports drive international learning, and hence catching up (Pasinetti 1981: 271). Second, exports expand demand and increase productivity gains. Third, exports relax the balance of payments constraint, while enhancing the viability of import substitution (Thirlwall 2013). For a late latecomer such as Ethiopia, the key challenge is to be able to catch up by learning from forerunners, and to mobilize abundant, scattered, and underutilized forces for the purpose of development (Hirschman 1958; Gerschenkron 1962; Ohno and Oqubay 2019).

Against this background, this chapter examines the Ethiopian experience of industrialization and industrial policy in the early twenty-first century and is structured as follows. Section 35.2 illustrates the historical evolution and reviews the key features of the Ethiopian manufacturing sector, throughout the Imperial and Derg eras, and into

[5] On the origins and foundations of industrial policy, see Chang (1994, 2003). On the practice of industrial policies in East Asian economies, see also Johnson (1982), Amsden (1989), Wade (2004), and Nolan (2014).

[6] Thirlwall (2013); UNCTAD-UNIDO (2011); UNECA (2016); Szirmai, Naudé, and Alcorta (2013).

the post-1991 EPRDF period. Section 35.3 introduces the policy context, the framework of policy instruments, and relevant institutions. The emphasis is on those policies most clearly expressing the dominant theme of the post-1991 period, i.e. the pursuit of developmental goals through activist industrial policies (some 'facilitative' and some 'getting prices wrong'). Building on this, Section 35.4 assesses the outcomes of industrial policies with a focus on specific archetypical sectors and discusses why and how policy outcomes have been uneven across sectors, despite a single development strategy. Section 35.5 examines the politics and political economy of industrial policies, and the final section highlights the implications of the analysis: that it is imperative that policy focuses on manufacturing and exports to generate structural transformation and accelerate catch-up (Cramer, Oqubay, and Sender forthcoming).[7]

35.2 Industrialization in Twentieth-Century Ethiopia

Despite recent rapid growth, structural transformation of the economy remains Ethiopia's central challenge. The Ethiopian government's efforts to industrialize are not the first and they have evolved after a series of earlier, rather less effective policy campaigns that nonetheless provided a modicum of the prior manufacturing experience that Amsden (2001) identified as important to the success of industrial policy. Ethiopia's manufacturing in the twentieth century was mainly focused on the consumer market and was guided by an import-substitution industrialization (ISI) strategy (see Appendix 2). Despite recent policies that have arguably produced more results, manufacturing continues to play a marginal role in employment creation, output, exports, and in building technological capability, and it is still far from being an engine for growth and economic transformation.

35.2.1 Industrialization in the Imperial Era (1930–74)

Industrialization in Ethiopia is largely a post-World War II phenomenon and underwent evolution throughout the Imperial era, the Derg military regime (1975–91), and the post-1991 period. This does not mean that there were no major events facilitating industrialization prior to the 1950s. For instance, the construction of the Ethio-Djibouti Railway (1897–1917) influenced the pattern of Ethiopia's international trade, the agglomeration of industries, and the growth of new urban centres along the rail corridor. Mussolini's invasion of Ethiopia (1936–41), World War II, and post-war recovery had significant implications for Ethiopia's later economic development (Pankhurst 1968;

[7] See also Lin and Monga (2019).

Zewde 2002). To support its war and its occupying forces, Italy built a 6,000-kilometre road network and dozens of factories aimed at the consumer goods market. After the defeat of Italy in 1941, the British Army dismantled many of these manufacturing facilities, shipping them out to other colonies on the grounds that Ethiopia was 'over-capitalized'.[8]

An ISI strategy and supporting policies were put in place during the Imperial era (1950–1974).[9] These industries were oriented towards the consumer market, dominated by foreign investors, and concentrated in the three cities of Addis Ababa, Asmara, and Dire Dawa. In 1951, the infant manufacturing sector accounted for less than 1 per cent of Ethiopia's GDP, and comprised sixty-three firms, all foreign owned, employing 5,765 persons. Food and beverages and textile industries dominated the sector (World Bank 1967).[10] Between 1953 and 1961, the sector showed modest growth, with total output reaching 81.8 million birr.

Successive medium-term plans were the most important policy instruments for expanding the industrial sector, although the forecasts remained unrealistic and were not strictly adhered to. Investment codes were used to attract foreign capital, but the government lacked a clear policy in the 1950s and the first investment notice in 1950 was ineffective. The 1962 investment decree was the first serious attempt, offering an exemption from profit tax for five years, guaranteed remittances, duty-free machine imports, and equity participation in local firms (World Bank 1967: 13).[11] This decree was not applicable to Ethiopians. The third instrument was related to long-term industrial financing. The government sought to compensate for the weak capacity of the Development Bank of Ethiopia (DBE) by feeding equity into larger industrial firms through the state-owned Ethiopian Investment Corporation (World Bank 1967). As was the order of the day worldwide, protective tariffs were widely used. In view of the weak state of domestic entrepreneurship, the government invested directly in large projects, such as utilities, services, factories, and commercial farms. Savings and gross investment never attained the required levels and external financing filled the gaps.[12]

Manufacturing accounted for 2.6 per cent and 4.4 per cent of GDP in 1964–5 and 1973–4 respectively. In the textile sector, ISI brought benefits in employment creation and foreign exchange savings. Between 1962 and 1969, cotton's share in employment and output reached 40 per cent and 33 per cent respectively, with numbers employed doubling from 10,100 to 21,610.[13] Textile production stimulated backward linkages to

[8] See Pankhurst (1996: 43) '[the British] concluded that the country had been highly, and artificially, industrialised'.

[9] Deguefeė (2006: 153) highlights that Ethiopia's economy 'remained non-monetized' in the 1960s.

[10] The 1951 census of Ministry of Commerce and Industry, MCI. Currency equivalents (US$1: birr 2:50) in 1967.

[11] The State Bank of Ethiopia (founded in 1942 and issuer of the first currency) was restructured into the National Bank of Ethiopia (NBE) and Commercial Bank of Ethiopia (CBE) in 1963 (Deguefeė 2006: 247).

[12] Savings and investment were about 10–11 per cent of GDP in the 1960s (World Bank 1967, 1973).

[13] See Chole's PhD thesis (1973), 'Import-Substitution in Practice: The Case of the Ethiopian Textile Industry'.

cotton production, but its effects on forward linkages (such as stimulating the apparel industry) were weak. In the Awash valley, about 27,000 permanent workers and 60,000 seasonal workers were deployed in cotton plantations (Chole 1973: 142).

The principal weakness of this strategy was structural, in that it was limited to the domestic consumer market, with 'no export horizons for manufactured goods' that could have increased demand and enhanced productivity (Chole 2004: 39). A more fundamental structural problem was the complete neglect of agriculture (the mainstay of 90 per cent of the population, accounting for two-thirds of GDP, and representing the entire source of export earnings), and the lack of land reform, badly needed for the wider transformation of the agriculture sector.[14] The stagnation of agriculture resulted in endemic food shortages and balance of payments issues, and had dramatic political consequences (see Chapters 2, 3, and 4).

35.2.2 Ethiopia's Lost Decades: The Stagnant Derg Era (1975–91)

What followed under the Derg regime was a cocktail of misguided economic policies, the militaristic resolution of national issues, the Eritrean war of independence, and totalitarian political rule that banned any democratic practices. The consequence was economic stagnation and two decades were lost until the early 1990s (see Appendix 1) The Derg's industrialization policies cannot be separated from the government's agricultural and war-economy policies (Deguefeė 2006; Tiruneh 1990).

35.2.2.1 *War Economy and Socialist Industrialization*

The military campaigns and the mobilization of the war economy caused devastating damage. Priority was given to the defence industry and capital investment was geared towards defence needs, which were mostly met by the Soviet Union and its allies (Ottaway 1990). With mass conscription, the human losses on both sides reached hundreds of thousands, if not close to a million. Farms were left without farmers to support their families (Tiruneh 1990); there was virtually no investment in physical infrastructure; and both social and economic infrastructures were destroyed during the war (Clapham 1988). Loans for imported armaments exacerbated the constraints on the balance of payments (Balema 2014; Tekeste 2014).[15] There was also a significant brain drain as many professionals and young students left the country to escape compulsory conscription as well as the Derg's 'Red Terror'. However, some manufacturing capability was stimulated: for example, demand for soldiers' boots kept the leather goods sector going.[16]

[14] The annual rate of growth in agriculture between 1961 and 1965 was only 2–2.5 per cent, and 'modernization of agriculture will be limited without introducing changes in the system of land ownership and tenure' (World Bank 1967: vii).

[15] Balema (2014: 59) highlights 'heavy reliance on foreign aid'. Chole (2004: 109) indicates US$11 billion in military imports between 1978 and 1988.

[16] See Oqubay (2015).

Central planning, social ownership, self-reliance, and import substitution were the key principles behind the Derg's industrial policy. All firms were nationalized in 1975 and public enterprises were established that operated under a centrally planned quota system independent of the rules of the market economy.[17] Sectors such as food and beverages, textiles, leather, cement, and the chemical industry continued as priorities. The food and beverages sectors were relatively competitive, while chemical plants and the defence industry were supported by outdated technology sourced from foreign suppliers (Balema 2014).

Most new firms were larger than those of the Imperial period. The state had a monopoly over imports and exports, and four state-owned banks were the sole players in the financial sector. The key policy objectives were developing the public sector (private-sector participation was not allowed); high protective tariffs; and a continuing anti-export bias that was reinforced by an unchanging and overvalued currency throughout the whole era. In urban areas, all residential property was nationalized, leading to sluggish growth in the construction and electricity sectors. Home ownership froze until after 1991. Towards the end of the Derg regime, a new mixed-economy policy reform was a last remedy but was never implemented (Tekeste 2014; Deguefeė 2006).[18] According to Cheru (1992: 2), this decision was prompted by several factors: 'the government made a partial retreat from socialism in 1987 had to do with the drought of 1986 which came at a time when it was putting up an extravagant 12th anniversary celebration of the Revolution. This was a major embarrassment. In addition, events in Eastern Europe were moving in a different direction. Gorbachev's much publicized economic liberalization had caught up in Eastern Europe like a brush fire. For Mengistu and the Party, it was time to make a strategic move and embrace perestroika in the hope of unfreezing much needed financial assistance from the World Bank and other donors.'

35.2.2.2 *Stagnating Agriculture*

To pre-empt popular demands, in March 1977 the Derg proclaimed a radical land reform, which abolished tenant–landlord ties and broke the power of the landed aristocracy (Rahmato 1984). But this initiative, which simply made the peasants tenants of the regime, failed to transform agriculture. Chole (2004: 2; World Bank 1985) has observed that 'the state replaced the landlord and implemented policies that led to the virtual ruin of the peasantry'. Farmers were reorganized into compulsory peasant associations (Proclamation 1977), a move that led in turn to forced reorganization into producer cooperatives and collectivization; the villagization and forced resettlement of millions of citizens (estimated at about eight million); and a forced procurement and sales system based upon quotas and sales to the Agricultural Marketing Corporation at

[17] In 1984, the Derg endorsed the government's Ten-Year Perspective Plan (1984/5–1993/4).

[18] Economic Policy of Socialist Ethiopia (February 1975) Proclamations No. 3/1975 on rural land, No. 47/1975 on urban land and dwellings, No. 26/1975 on nationalization of factories, No. 76/1975 on restriction of private-sector investment.

fixed prices (Pausewang et al. 1990).[19] According to Cheru (1992: 1): 'The Ethiopian economy has been constrained by a number of factors since the 1974 revolution. While the civil war and successive droughts are partly to blame, the institution of centralized planning, the nationalization of land, the over emphasis on state farms to the neglect of small farmers, forced villagization and resettlement programmes, and excessive taxation of peasants contributed to a decade of economic stagnation.' Under this policy regime, agriculture could neither underpin economic take-off nor support industrialization. This was a major disaster both for the general economy and for the development of the industrial sector—and it also had profound political consequences.[20]

35.3 Developmentalism and Industrial Policy in Ethiopia from the 1990s

When the EPRDF first came to power in 1991, addressing the crisis in agriculture was a fundamental concern, with agricultural recovery also being seen as a spark for renewed commitment to industrialization. In 1994, the government adopted the Agricultural Development-Led Industrialization (ADLI) strategy, to which it adhered for more than two decades (see Chapters 9 and 26).[21] The industrial development strategy (IDS) adopted in 2003 emphasized export-led industrialization, and focused on labour-intensive industries, the development of infrastructure to support rapid economic growth, and the development of small enterprises for massive job creation and poverty reduction (FDRE 2002). The Ethiopian government focused on the transition to market economy and recovery in the 1990s, followed by execution of the industrial development strategies in the 2000s. In the 2010s, the government's five-year plans concentrated on both growth and structural transformation.

35.3.1 Transitional Phase (1991–2000)

The first phase was associated with recovery and the transition from a war to a peacetime economy, and from a centrally planned command economy to a market-led economy. As the World Bank (2002: 5) noted, the government had 'inherited an economy devastated by years of civil war and...a GDP per capita lower than in the 1960s'. Rehabilitation focused primarily on rebuilding war-torn infrastructure, revitalizing

[19] Clapham (1988) and Balema (2014: 64).

[20] The growth of agriculture between 1974 and 1991 was 0.7 per cent (Chole 2004: 99). GDP per capita declined by 1.3 per cent while industry and manufacturing grew 1 per cent respectively (Clapham 1988; Chole 2004: 12). See also Cheru (1992: 1): 'On the whole, the economy has been characterized by low agricultural productivity, a small industrial base, shortages of skilled manpower and weak infrastructure.'

[21] See FDRE (1995, 1996, 2002).

manufacturing enterprises by injecting working capital, and facilitating the imports of parts to increase operating capacity (Cheru and Pausewang 1992).[22] There was also economic liberalization of certain sectors.

Politically, there was a transition from a centralized unitary system to a federal system that encouraged 'unity with diversity', and from a totalitarian military regime to a parliamentary multi-party democracy. A transitional government was instituted in 1991 and comprised a coalition of political forces that backed the economic reforms and the drafting of a new constitution. This came into effect in 1995, and was followed by the first elections at national, regional, and local levels (TGE 1991).[23] The provisions of the new constitution and a referendum in Eritrea ended decades of war there.

Economic liberalization, under the rubric of 'structural adjustment', drew assistance from the IDA, IMF, and other donors (World Bank 2002; ADF 1997). Nonetheless, reforms were not entirely in line with the conventional prescriptions of the Washington Consensus. For instance, the government's approach to privatization was 'gradualist' (in contrast to Eastern European or Mozambican privatization) (Tekeste 2014; Oqubay 2015: 96–9).[24] Nonetheless, the government did privatize more than 300 firms, most of which were acquired by the domestic private sector. Some large firms (such as breweries) were sold to foreign firms to ensure expansion and a foreign currency income. Unlike other sub-Saharan African economies, the government did not privatize utility and other strategic establishments, opting instead to expand and reorganize public enterprises in strategic areas (banking, utilities, air travel, chemicals, and sugar industries). Government also introduced major reforms to improve the corporate governance of state-owned enterprises, and in some cases this initiative has proven effective (Tekeste 2014).

During this period of privatization, government opened the banking sector to domestic investors, while foreign banks were banned.[25] Stiglitz (2002: 32) highlights the disagreements with the IMF: 'Meles was engaged in a heated dispute with the IMF, and the Fund had suspended its lending program... Ethiopia resisted the IMF's demand that it "open" its banking system, for good reason... The IMF was unhappy, simply because it believed interest rates should be freely determined.'

Similar deviations were observed in other areas. Contrary to the Washington prescriptions for full liberalization of the exchange rate, the government adopted a managed floating system, which narrowed the gap between the official and parallel markets. Liberalized market prices were applied, but critical commodities (such as petroleum products and fertilizer) continued to be regulated. A new investment proclamation (Number 15, 1992) was introduced and an investment promotion agency was established (TGE 1992). This was an important step in fostering investment in different sectors.

[22] Emergency Recovery and Reconstruction Program (ERRP) supported by the donor community (Balema 2014).

[23] See FDRE (1995), Balema (2014), Tekeste (2014), and Clapham (2017).

[24] By 1997, the government had privatized the first round of 121 retail stores, twenty-two hotels and restaurants, twenty-five manufacturing plants, and ten agro-industries and state farms (ADF 1997).

[25] In 2017 (NBE), there were seventeen private banks which dominated about 50 per cent of the industry.

But not all sectors were open to foreign investment: retail businesses, domestic freight services, and banking were reserved for Ethiopians (see Chapter 10). Power generation was open to foreign capital, while transmission and distribution remained restricted.

35.3.2 Industrial Policies and the Pursuit of Development Goals

Economic growth accelerated and was sustained after 2004. One outcome of the exclusive pursuit of development goals was that in the post-1991 period, especially after the ruling party's 'renewal movement' of 2001–2, Ethiopia's economic performance significantly improved.[26] This has been attributed to the government's comprehensive economic development strategies and the cohesive development perspectives of the ruling party that had evolved during the earlier seventeen-year liberation struggle.[27] A clear *focus on agriculture* and commitment to rural development were central to Ethiopia's development path. And a deep-rooted belief in and reliance on *long-term investment* in public infrastructure (such as energy, transport, etc.), the development of human capital, and the transformation of vocational, technical, and higher education is evidence of the government's distinctive strategic perspective. About half of the federal government's budget for consecutive five-year programmes was earmarked for pro-poor and high-growth sectors.

Evidence suggests that the government has been keen to both draw inspiration and gain practical experience from mainly East Asian economies.[28] Industrial policy dialogue supported by the Japanese government and scholars has been in place since July 2008. Later developments include the institutionalization of the Japanese Kaizen approach, the transformation of technical and vocational education training (TVET) and university system along German lines, the establishment of sectoral institutes, and science and technology universities in line with the South Korean model, and learning from China's policymaking and industrialization (Oqubay and Lin 2019; see Chapters 41, 46, and 47).[29]

35.3.3 Industrial Policy Instruments

Ethiopia has pursued an active industrial policy since the early 2000s with a large set of carefully designed policy instruments. These include the promotion of exports and

[26] The EPRDF faced a major internal crisis in 2000 that culminated with a victory for the political group that advocated a renewal movement and articulation of development strategies in different sectors.

[27] See De Waal (2012, 2015) and Clapham (2017).

[28] On the developmental state, see Evans (1997) and—on Africa specifically—Zenawi (2012).

[29] Ohno (2013: 268–9) who highlights strong policy ownership, an activist state, and an internationalization of skills and technology as key priorities, and policy learning as key features of the Ethiopian government.

productive investment, industrial financing, and the use of state-owned enterprises (SOEs) to shape strategic sectors. The focus has been on sectors such as leather and leather goods, apparel and textiles, meat processing, food processing and beverages, cement and steel, and horticulture. There has also been recognition of reciprocity and the political economy constraints that hinder productive investment in export-oriented manufacturing, with evidence of learning from the East Asian experience (such as target setting in exports, export coordination councils, sectoral institutes, industrial financing, and the active role of SOEs). Tables 35.1 and 35.2 provide a brief summary of instruments and policy organizations.

Many policy instruments, however, have not been entirely effective. First, most of the export-promotion schemes required effective coordination, automation of the customs system, and qualified professional staff, but these were often lacking. Second, sectoral institutes set up to support priority sectors were unable to attract staff with the professional skills, qualifications, and experience required to support firms. Moreover, the institutes had to assist with administrative requirements, as not all government channels have been streamlined to support exports and industrialization. Some efforts have been made to strengthen the institutes by twinning them with Indian institutes (TIDI and LIDI).

Third, lack of sectoral knowledge and sectoral focus has been a major hindrance. The policy instruments were not entirely based on research and full understanding of the specific industrial structure of each sector. For instance, the development bank lacked experience in financing specific industries such as horticulture. The studies required to monitor and continuously amend policies were not available. Fourth, industry associations have not been equally active in influencing policies, and channels for dialogue between government and private sector were unsatisfactory. Efforts to establish links between universities and vocational centres and industry have been ineffective.

Fifth, the lack of effective vertical and horizontal coordination among and across government agencies (federal, regional, and local) has been a major constraint and has hampered the competitiveness of firms. According to one survey, firm owners and managers find that dealing with government red tape takes up 15–25 per cent of their management time.[30] Sixth, export performance has been sluggish as a result of ineffective policy instruments.

However, despite the rudimentary nature of industrial policies, and their limitations, there has been some learning from the application of the relevant instruments (see Table 35.1). The introduction in 2005 of the National Export Coordinating Council, chaired by the prime minister and inspired by Korean experience, has played a critical role in addressing coordination problems as well as sectoral operational constraints on exports, and in adjusting policy instruments when required. Developing the freight capacity of Ethiopian Airlines, the decision to apply subsidies during the 2008 fuel price increases to support the floriculture sector, and industrial financing for the cement and floriculture industries are examples of successful coordination.

[30] See Oqubay (2015).

Table 35.1 Summary of industrial policy instruments, 2003–18

Policy instruments	'Facilitative'	Getting prices 'wrong'*
Five-year plans	Plan for Accelerated and Sustained Development to End Poverty, 2005/6-9/10 (PASDEP); Growth and Transformation Plan I, 2010/11–14/15 (GTP-I); Growth and Transformation Plan II, 2014/15–19/20 GTP-II)**	
Industrial financing	Critical support in developing priority productive sectors	
Investment financing: Development Bank of Ethiopia (DBE) and Commercial Bank of Ethiopia (CBE) as co-financier)		Targeted at specific sectors, selective allocation, long-term and subsidized loans
Trade financing (CBE, private banks)		CBE: Relaxed terms to exporters and manufacturers
Export promotion	Essential support for export promotion	
Target setting		Exercised on few priority sectors
Retention of forex earnings		Applied to exporters
Voucher, bonded warehouse, duty-drawback		Applied to manufacturing exporters
Exchange rate policy	Aim to support exporters and productive sectors	
Devaluation (jumps: 1992, 2010, 2017)		Aimed at revitalizing and supporting exporters
Managed floating system	Facilitative	
Forex allocation (triggered by scarcity in 2010)		Applied to priority sectors in manufacturing
Investment promotion	Essential support to support productive investment	
Incentive structure		More generous incentives to productive sectors (especially manufacturing)
One-stop service (OSS)	Facilitative for FDI and manufacturers	
Industrial parks (specialized)		Targeted at priority export-oriented manufacturing sub-sectors, subsidized facilities (land, sheds, bank services), one-stop government services, skills development (FDRE 2015)
Trade protection	Essential in protecting domestic manufacturers	
Import tariffs	Tariff protection and harmonization (average 25–35 per cent)	Protective tariffs to support domestic manufacturing (automotive manufacture etc.)
Import ban		Protect the cement industry

(continued)

Table 35.1 Continued

Policy instruments	'Facilitative'	Getting prices 'wrong'*
Export ban (crust and semi-finished)		To promote value addition in leather sector
SOEs investment	Important policy to develop strategic sectors	
Privatization		Gradual process, priority to local firms, selective, to support targeted industries
SOEs in strategic areas		Strategic and targeted to support development goals
Sector-targeted instruments and institutional supports	Targeted support to nurture priority industries	
Cement industry	Expansion of public housing and infrastructure	Targeted: energy, quarry, forex, import ban
Horticulture industry		Targeted: phytosanitary standards, land, airfreight, packaging
Sectoral institutes		Targeted on priority sectors (such as the Textile Industry Development Institute (TIDI), Leather Industry Development Institute-(LIDI) Ethiopian Horticulture Development Agency-EHDA)

Notes: * 'Getting prices wrong' involves being more selective by favouring some sectors or investors over others and possibly defying comparative advantage (see Amsden 1989, 2001; Lin and Chang 2009). 'Facilitative' involves 'levelling the playing field for all actors' and providing conditions for investment, and not defying comparative advantage. ** MoFED (2010) and NECC (2017).
Source: Author's matrix.

In summary, Ethiopian policy in this period combined 'facilitative' policies with those that got prices 'wrong'. It is unlikely that Ethiopia could have built dynamic floriculture or cement industries without active industrial policies. Furthermore, learning by doing and learning from others has increased policy capability and the effectiveness of policy instruments.

35.4 Variations in Industrial Policy Outcome in Ethiopia

Despite Ethiopia's unified industrial development strategy, the outcomes of policy have been *uneven* across sectors, and understanding the key determinants for this is essential (Oqubay 2015, 2019). This section argues that the unique economic and technological

Table 35.2 Industrial policy organizations, 2005–15

Institutions	Mandate	Observations
Regulatory and coordination organs		
Coordination organizations: National Export Coordinating Council (NECC) (2005–)	Chaired by prime minister; focused on export coordinatior	Enhanced focus on exports but with partial outcomes
Ethiopian Investment Board (EIB)	A new approach since 2014; chaired by prime minister; directs investment and industrial policies	Playing critical role in guiding industrial policy
Key regulatory and policy institutions: Ministry of Finance and Economic Development (MoFED), National Bank of Ethiopia (NBE), Ministry of Industry (MOI), Ministry of Public Enterprises (MPE)	Regulating finance and economic development, revenue and customs, central bank, leading industry, and leading SOEs respectively.	Impact gradually improving
Lead and sectoral organs		
Lead agencies: Ethiopian Investment Commission (EIC); Industrial Parks Development Corporation (IPDC)	EIC: Single window for attraction of new investment; supporting investors; proposing and administering incentives IPDC: Development and operation of industrial parks; support for private developers; custodian of land	EIC and IPDC as critical organs in fostering targeted productive investment and agglomeration by industrial parks (2014–)*
Sectoral institutes and agencies (TIDI, LIDI, EHDA, and other institutes for metal, meat and dairy etc.)	Sectoral focal agencies to lead specific priority sectors (textiles, leather, metals, meat and dairy, horticulture, etc.)	Essential; uneven impact due to lower sectoral impact; new institutes being established in pharmaceutical and chemical industries.
Policy banks and SOEs		
Policy banks: DBE; CBE	DBE: Focused on subsidized industrial financing of manufacturing and agriculture (private sector); CBE: Trade finance and working capital co-finances DBE; finances public housing and infrastructure	Outcome improved after reforms to CBE/DBE; lack of sectoral knowledge; lagging international banking service

(continued)

Table 35.2 Continued

Institutions	Mandate	Observations
SOEs (in energy, transport services, production)	Key policy approach to develop SOEs in strategic sectors	Uneven performance; internationally competitive such as Ethiopian Airlines (EAL); weak performance and discipline in some SOEs
Intermediary institutions		
Industrial associations: Ethiopian Horticulture Producers and Exporters Association (EHPEA), Ethiopian Leather Industry Association (ELIA), Ethiopian Textile and Garment Association (ETGA) etc.	Horticulture, leather, and textile sectors	Effective productive partnership in horticulture; lesser impact in others
Dialogue platforms	Chamber of Commerce and specific industries	Uneven outcome; weak sectoral focus

Note: * See Chapter 48.
Source: Author's matrix.

characteristics of specific sectors may lend themselves to (or frustrate) industrial policies, the outcomes of which are shaped by the dynamism of linkage effects. The key insight is that policymakers need to acknowledge not only that linkages may be more prevalent in some sectors than others, but that the unfolding of linkage effects is neither automatic nor static and uniform. It also shows how and why linkage dynamisms have in many instances been frustrated or blocked. Finally, the evidence from specific sectors suggests that policymakers need a better understanding of the interaction and dynamism of industrial structure, linkage effects, and political economy, since policies are designed, monitored, and enforced within a conflictual, interest-ridden context that profoundly affects their outcomes.[31]

The leather and leather products industry and floriculture have been central in the government's efforts to promote export-oriented industries.[32] Leather is a century-old sector, while floriculture is a nascent industry.[33] The leather sector's export, employment creation, labour productivity, output, and value-added performance have been dismal, despite a huge livestock population, the labour intensity of the sector, sustained government attention, and multiple international consultancy studies. For instance, leather's contribution to total merchandise exports fell by half from 8 to 4 per cent between 2004 and 2016 (Oqubay 2019). The leather products sub-industry's relative share in employment and exports has increased to 62 (from 50) and 36 (from 1) per cent respectively in this period, large foreign firms having entered the industry (CSA 1975–2017). But policies have failed to stimulate backward linkages to the livestock sector, once again showing that linkages are not automatic and that comparative advantage does not necessarily produce successful linkage effects (see Chapter 33). The industry's structure provides for a wide 'latitude' for performance, which increases the sector's vulnerability. Export logistics have remained a binding constraint, with heavy reliance on inland road transport. Narrow group interests among tanneries and their dominance of the sector, and fragmentation among the industry's players have hindered the transformation of the sector. Local firms, averse to competition, have resisted the participation of foreign firms.

The floriculture and horticulture sector, meanwhile, has attracted major European investors. Exports reached US$225 million in 2015/16, and the sector's contribution to overall merchandise exports rose from 1 per cent in 2003/4 to 10 per cent in 2015/16. Floriculture employed more than 50,000 people and non-flower horticulture more than 130,000. Linkages to packaging (modest), air freight (strong), and new sub-sectors and corridors have been created (Oqubay 2015). Productivity levels have increased to approach those of Kenya, phytosanitary and cold-chain practices have improved, there are more Ethiopian professionals holding production management positions, and domestic firms have entered the industry (see Chapter 31). Ethiopia has emerged as

[31] See Hall (1986) and Hirschman (1968) on the political economy of industrialization.

[32] Industrial policy is not restricted to manufacturing and may apply to high-productivity agriculture, which exhibits many of the features of manufacturing. See also Cramer, Sender, and Di John (2018).

[33] The first leather factory was established in the 1920s. Ethiopia has the largest livestock population in Africa.

one of the world's top five producers and exporters of roses. Subsidized industrial financing for both foreign and local firms was arranged through the DBE, investment incentives provided, suitable affordable land made available, and air terminals with reliable freight-capable new planes established.[34] A number of technological and economic factors have led to a reciprocal monitoring system (reciprocity principle): these are an exclusively export market; a perishable product; highly intensive management; and the narrow margin for failure. The NECC, chaired by the late prime minister, focused heavily on the sector and a productive dialogue between government and industry was maintained. Firms in the sector organized a cohesive association, and a constructive tripartite relationship between the government, the industry, and Dutch institutions contributed to the industry's rapid growth. Despite this progress, growth has been hampered by the government's failure to enact new policies to boost participation of domestic firms, and to upgrade domestic technological capability (Oqubay 2015, 2019; see also Chapters 31 and 40).

Another key sector is the cement industry, which has played a strategic role in the catch-up of developing countries. Ethiopia had a single state-owned enterprise in the industry in 1991, with an annual installed capacity of 600,000 tons (Oqubay 2015). There was accelerated growth after 2003, mainly due to the remarkable expansion of politically significant government-sponsored housing developments and infrastructure programmes. Both loans and foreign exchange were channelled by government into the industrial financing of large-scale cement projects, and budget and foreign exchange resources were allocated to cement imports. Attractive concessions further encouraged investors to build factories with increased capacity and economies of scale. Mining resources were made available to investors at affordable costs. To improve energy efficiency and support cement producers, the government imported bulk coal. The industry was also given priority allocation during power cuts. On the other hand, the failure margin was narrow not only because of the capital intensity and amount of resources allocated and the technological features of the cement industry (Chandler 2004),[35] but also because of political fragility: the disputed 2005 election, for instance, triggered an 'internal threat' (Doner, Ritchie, and Slater 2005) to the ruling party, especially in urban centres.

In 2017, the seventeen firms in the industry had an installed capacity of more than 16.7 million tons, putting Ethiopia among the top three cement-producing countries in Africa. Four large firms (each with more than 2 million tons annual capacity) account for two-thirds of total installed capacity (Derba, Mugher, Dangote, and Messebo cement factories) in 2017. In contrast to other African countries, where the 'big five' multinational companies dominate, it is domestic cement firms that are dominant in Ethiopia, with 55 per cent of installed capacity, while foreign firms and joint ventures account for 35 and 10 per cent respectively (CSA 2016). The cement industry has stimulated linkages

[34] Development banks serving as 'conduits' are central to a developmental state (Amsden 2001).

[35] Such as large economy of scale, product perishability, and continuous process production.

to transport, building materials, and packaging, and is itself stimulated by the linkage from the construction industry.

The performance of these three sectors and the outcomes of industrial policy across them provide several insights. Sectoral performance was strikingly uneven: sluggish and inconsistent performance in leather and leather goods, and robust growth in both the floriculture and cement industries.[36] Performance was stronger after 2003 than between 1991 and 2002, which may be attributed to the design and implementation of industrial policies (Oqubay 2015: 243). More importantly, research has shown the importance for the evolution and effectiveness of industrial policy of the interaction between *industrial structure* (such as the latitude for performance failure), *linkage dynamics*, and *politics/political economy*.[37] The dynamics of and interrelationships among these variables have 'significant implications for policy design and implementation... for the type of selective intervention chosen to promote industrialization... for how to guide design of reciprocal control mechanisms and assess their viability', all of which are critical in industrial policy (Oqubay 2015: 277; Chang 1994; Amsden 1989).

35.5 Politics and the Political Economy of Industrial Policy

As highlighted earlier, politics and political economy have shaped policy outcomes in Ethiopia (Oqubay 2015). Given the country's long history of political fragility, its ethnic diversity and widespread poverty, a commitment to equitable growth and federalism was essential. Moreover, the ruling party's cohesive political and economic thinking arose not only from its disposition to learn from the rapid industrialization in East Asia, but also from its history as a wartime coalition fighting against the Derg's military totalitarianism (1975–91) (De Waal 2012). Its claim to legitimacy has been based on its support in rural Ethiopia, a legacy of the liberation struggle, and its commitment to rapid economic growth and more inclusive rural transformation. However, this solidarity has been increasingly challenged by various social groups, and EPRDF's internal cohesiveness has not been sustained in recent years. Two major instances of these challenges were after the contentious 2005 national election, and

[36] Unevenness is a more general feature of other priority sectors: there was slow growth in apparel and textiles and pharmaceutical industries (until 2015), but brewing was among the fastest-growing industries, driven by a strong domestic market.

[37] Hirschman (1968, 1958) describes linkages as how one thing leads (or fails to lead) to another, thereby serving as a tool for understanding the process of industrial development.

as recently as 2015–17, where there was continued political discontent in urban, as well as certain rural areas.

Federalism, ethnic diversity, and a commitment to equitable regional growth make concentration of rents, and industrial clustering and agglomeration more challenging in Ethiopia (Oqubay 2019; Oqubay and Lin forthcoming). By contrast, the South Korean political economy allowed for a concentration of 'intermediate assets' among national champions, and agglomeration has been highly concentrated (Amsden 1989). Moreover, the formation of the capitalist class and workforce, which evolved during the Japanese occupation, had significant implications for South Korea's industrialization (Kohli 2004).

Government–industry relations in Ethiopia also differ within industries and have influenced policy outcomes unevenly. In floriculture, the relationship between government and industry was a good fit (picking each other, as it were) and based on building trust and collective learning. Although there were still some tensions observed in the floriculture sector, partly due to the largest firm's logistical privileges, the conflicts were resolved.[38] Experience in the leather sector was different. Path dependency (low value addition and a fixed mindset) and internal fragmentation undermined collective learning in the leather and leather products industry (Oqubay 2015). Domestic floriculture firms viewed FDI firms as sources of technology and market capability, while mutual distrust permeated the leather sector.

Whether a sector is dominated by larger firms or cohesive associations of industrialists, or by dispersed smallholders, has a substantial impact on the kind and intensity of political pressure that can be brought to bear on government and policymaking. Political pressure by social groups depends on their visible presence, strength, and cohesiveness (Hall 1986; Hirschman 1968).[39] The existing political economy in Ethiopia has favoured speculative activities rather than productive investments in export-oriented manufacturing (Oqubay 2015). The government–business dialogue has not been strong and productive, and an opportunity for collective learning was lost. This was primarily because of the problem of 'mutual suspicion' on the part of the government and the private sector, and a lack of strong commitment and an inconsistent approach by government. This was exacerbated by the lack of dynamism of industrial associations and a pervasive culture of 'short-termism' and quick gains by the private sector. Ethiopia could learn from experiences in Mauritius, where a dynamic state–industry developmental coalition was forged and sustained (Brautigam 2009). Moreover, the increased importance of political and economic inclusiveness, young people's rising

[38] There is also clearly a local political economy whereby, for example, large floriculture firms can do deals with local officials to ensure smooth operations. There have also been conflicts of interest over, for example, levels of compensation and the accuracy of compensation targeting, so that despite the many 'winners' (investors, the balance of payments, indirect beneficiaries such as service suppliers, and employees) there are also losers, including people who may have lost access to land or water, or who may not get cheap credit for other purposes because it is directed to floriculture, etc.

[39] For instance, as observed in East Asian and Latin American contrasts, and in early eighteenth-century US reforms.

expectations, and tensions within ethnic-based federalism remain significant challenges for the government.[40]

35.6 Conclusion: Late Development and Learning to Catch Up

Critics have suggested that there is no such thing as Ethiopian industrialization. This chapter has acknowledged the profound shortcomings of the industrial policy and its outcomes thus far. But it has also shown that there have been clearly designed policy interventions, which have had non-negligible effects. Industrial policy in Ethiopia is not a mirage. It draws on a longer-term historical experience of policy experiments and manufacturing activity since the time of the Italian occupation in the 1930s. It has since the 1990s and especially after 2003 achieved more than was achieved in the past. Policymakers have engaged with the shifting pressures of the global economy to produce some remarkable results, though overall the strategy remains a work in progress and the jury is still out on outcomes.

The chapter also presents an alternative to the dominant perspective in mainstream development economics, which often denies sectoral considerations and suggests that industrial ambitions are beyond the reach of African countries. Instead, mainstream development economists argue that African countries should limit themselves to existing 'latent comparative advantages', and that the state should be 'facilitative' and confine itself to periodically addressing 'market failures', rather than playing an active developmental role to create and shape markets.[41]

Finally, much of the literature on industrial policy fails to link it with the learning that is central to late industrialization.[42] The evidence in this chapter shows how policy learning has evolved in Ethiopia, reinforced not only by policy independence, but also by learning by doing and emulation (Oqubay 2015; Ohno and Oqubay 2019; see also Chapter 36).

Acknowledgements

The author thanks Christopher Cramer, Peter Lawrence, John Sender, and Fantu Cheru for insightful and useful comments, Yohannes Gebru and Meron Tilahun for data collection, and Deborah M. Kefale and Binyam Arkebe for their continued support and inputs to improve the draft.

[40] The expansion and transformation of university education and technical schools has given rise to the challenge of creating hundreds of thousands of professional and technical jobs for graduates.

[41] See Lin and Chang (2009) for debates on comparative advantage and the role of the state.

[42] Amsden (1989) highlights that 'all late industrializers have in common industrialisation on the basis of learning'.

Appendix 1

Economic Growth and Sectoral Composition (1975–91)

35.1 (a) Economic growth trends (1975–91)

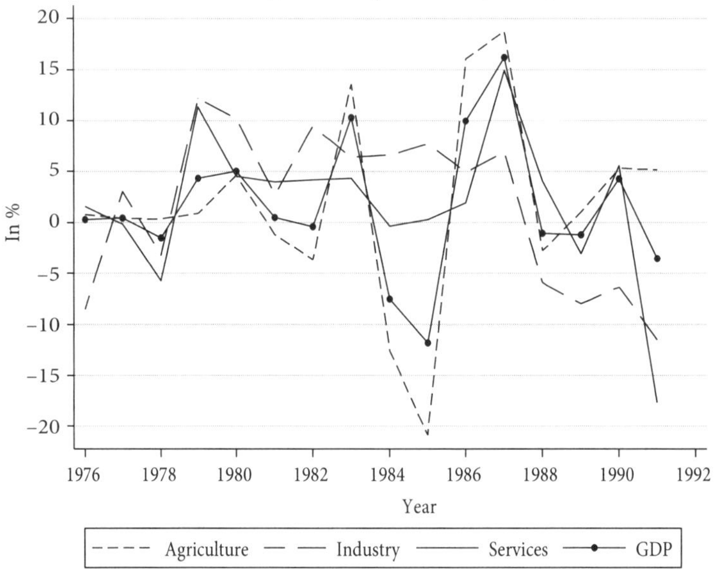

35.1 (b) Sectoral composition

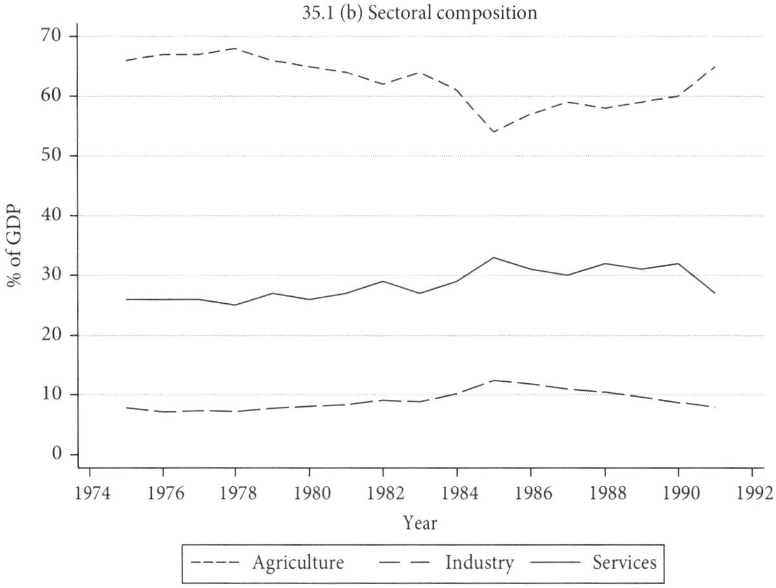

Source: CSA (1975–92)

Appendix 2

Industrial Composition: Firms and Employment

35.2 (a) Firms in dominant sectors (1975–91)

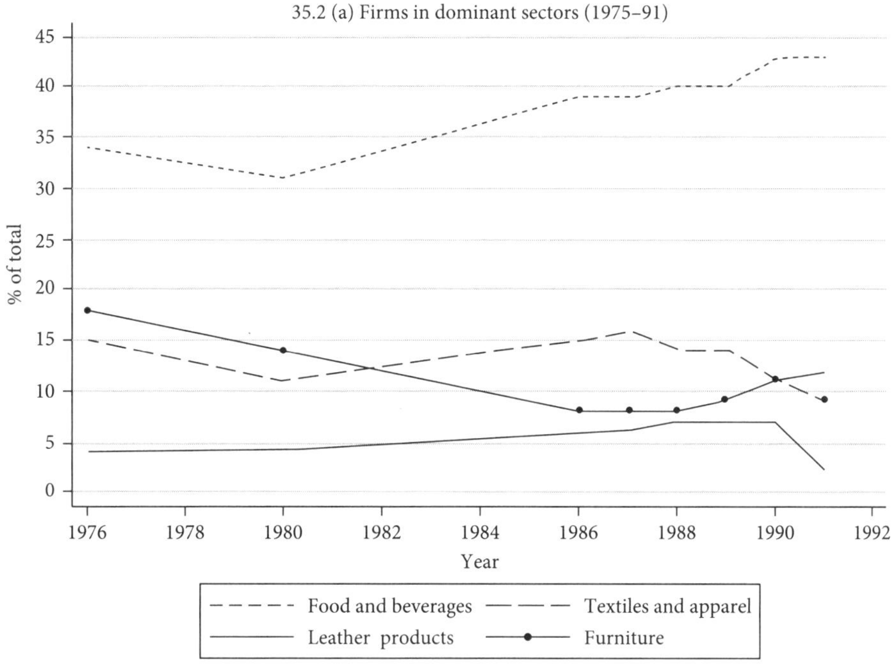

35.2 (b) Employment in dominant manufacturing (1976–91)

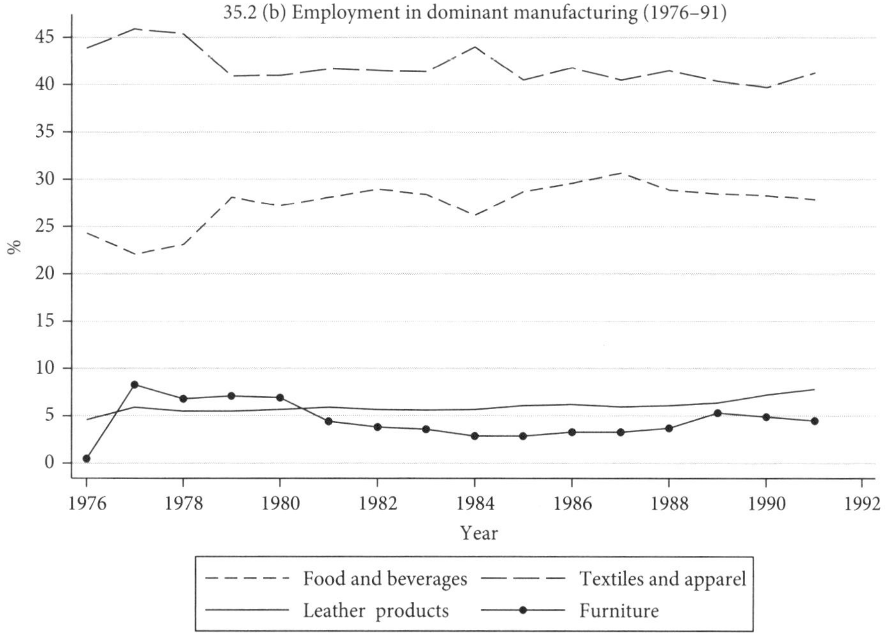

Source: CSA (1975–92)

References

ADF (1997). 'Structural Adjustment Program: Project Completion Report', Africa Development Fund, Washington, DC.

Amsden, Alice H. (1989). *Asia's Next Giant: South Korea and Late Industrialization* (Oxford: Oxford University Press).

Amsden, Alice H. (2001). *The Rise of 'The Rest': Challenges to the West from Late-Industrializing Economies* (Oxford: Oxford University Press).

Balema, Addisalem (2014). *Democracy and Economic Development in Ethiopia* (Trenton, NJ: Red Sea Press).

BBC (2017). 'Can Ethiopia Be Africa's Leading Manufacturing Hub? Ethiopia's "Industrial Revolution": How Ethiopia Is Dealing with Population Growth', Alastair Leithead, 24 August 2017. http://www.bbc.co.uk/news/world-africa-41035141; http://www.bbc.co.uk/news/av/world-africa-41028096/can-ethiopia-create-enough-jobs-for-its-growing-population

Brautigam, Deborah (2009). 'Coalitions, Capitalists and Credibility: Overcoming the Crises of Confidence at Independence in Mauritius', with Tania Diolle, Research Paper No. 4, Developmental Leadership Program.

Chandler, Alfred (2004). *Scale and Scope: The Development of Industrial Capitalism* (Cambridge, MA: Harvard University Press).

Chang, Ha-Joon (1994). *The Political Economy of Industrial Policy* (London: Macmillan).

Chang, Ha-Joon (2003). *Kicking Away the Ladder: Development Strategy in Historical Perspective* (London: Anthem Press).

Cheru, Fantu (1992). 'Designing a Structural Adjustment Program for Ethiopia: Reconstruction, Rehabilitation and Long-Term Transformation' Development Research and Action Programme, *DERAP, D 1992,* 3 May: pp. 1–23.

Cheru, Fantu and S. Pausewang (1992). 'Economic Reconstruction and the Peasants in Ethiopia', Two papers presented at the Symposium on the Ethiopian Economy, with a post-script, Bergen: Chr. Michelsen Institute (DERAP Working Paper D 1992).

Chole, Eshetu (1973). 'Import Substitution in Practice: The Case of the Ethiopian Textile Industry', PhD thesis, Syracuse University.

Chole, Eshetu (2004). *Underdevelopment in Ethiopia* (Addis Ababa: Organisation for Social Research in Eastern and Southern Africa (OSSREA)).

Clapham, Christopher (1988). *Transformation and Continuity in Revolutionary Ethiopia* (Cambridge: Cambridge University Press).

Clapham, Christopher (2017). *The Horn of Africa: State Formation and Decay* (London: Hurst).

Cramer, Chris, Arkebe Oqubay, and John Sender (forthcoming). *African Economic Development: Evidence, Theory, and Policy* (Oxford: Oxford University Press).

Cramer, Christopher, John Sender, and Jonathan Di John (2018). 'Poinsettia Assembly and Selling Emotion: High Value Agricultural Exports in Ethiopia', SOAS/EDRI/AFD, Report for the Agence Francáis du Développement (AFD), Paris.

CSA (1975–2017). 'Manufacturing Survey of Medium and Large Enterprises', Central Statistical Agency, Addis Ababa.

CSA (2016). 'Report on Small-Scale Manufacturing Industries Survey', Addis Ababa.

De Waal, Alex (2012). 'The Theory and Practice of Meles Zenawi', *African Affairs* 112 (446): 148–55.

De Waal, Alex (2015). *The Real Politics of the Horn of Africa: Money, War and the Business of Power* (Cambridge: Polity Press).

Deguefeè, Taffara (2006). *Minutes of an Ethiopian Century* (Addis Ababa, Shama Books).

Doner, Richard, Bryan Ritchie, and Dan Slater (2005). 'Systemic Vulnerability and the Origins of Developmental States: Northeast and Southeast Asia in Comparative Perspective', *International Organization* 59 (2):327–61.

Evans, Peter (1997). *Embedded Autonomy: States and Industrial Transformation* (Princeton, NJ: Princeton University Press).

FDRE (1995). *Constitution of the Federal Democratic Republic of Ethiopia*. House of Representatives, Addis Ababa, Ethiopia.

FDRE (1996). 'Ethiopia's Development Strategy (ADLI)', Information Ministry, Federal Democratic Republic of Ethiopia, Addis Ababa.

FDRE (2002). 'The Industrial Development Strategy of Ethiopia', Information Ministry, Federal Democratic Republic of Ethiopia, Addis Ababa.

FDRE (2015). 'Proclamation on Industrial Parks', Information Ministry, Federal Democratic Republic of Ethiopia, Addis Ababa.

Financial Times (2017). 'Ethiopia's Mythical Manufacturing Boom', Steve Johnson, 15 June 2017. https://www.ft.com/content/76968dc4-445f-11e7-8d27-59b4dd6296b8.

Gerschenkron, Alexander (1962). *Economic Backwardness in Historical Perspective* (Cambridge, MA: Harvard University Press).

Hall, Peter (1986). *Governing the Economy: The Politics of State Intervention in Britain and France* (Cambridge: Polity Press).

Hirschman, Albert (1958). *Strategy of Economic Development* (New Haven, CT: Yale University Press).

Hirschman, Albert. (1968). *Development Projects Observed* (Washington, DC: The Brookings Institution).

Johnson, Chalmers (1982). *MITI and the Japanese Miracle: The Growth of Industrial Policy, 1925–1975* (Stanford, CA: Stanford University Press).

Kaldor, Nicholas (1967). *Strategic Factors in Economic Development* (Ithaca, NY: Cornell University Press).

Kohli, Atul (2004). *State-Directed Development: Political Power and Industrialization in the Global Periphery* (Cambridge: Cambridge University Press).

Lin, Justin, and Ha-Joon Chang (2009). 'Should Industrial Policy in Developing Countries Confirm to Comparative Advantage or Defy it? A Debate between Justin Lin and Ha-Joon Chang', *Development Policy Review* 27 (5): 483–502.

Lin, Justin, and Celestin Monga (2019). *Oxford Handbook of Structural Transformation* (Oxford: Oxford University Press).

MoFED (2010). 'Growth and Transformation Plan 2010/11–2014/15 (GTP I)', Ministry of Finance and Economic Development, Addis Ababa.

NECC (2017). 'Export Review of Manufacturing and Agricultural Goods', unpublished, National Export Coordinating Council.

Nolan, Peter (2014). *Chinese Firms, Global Firms: Industrial Policy in the Era of Globalization* (New York: Routledge).

NPC (2016). 'Growth and Transformation Plan 2015/16–2019/20 (GTP II)', National Plan Commission, Addis Ababa.

Ocampo, José A., Codrina Rada, and Lance Taylor (2009). *Growth and Policy in Developing Countries: A Structuralist Approach* (New York: Columbia University Press).

Ohno, Kenichi (2013). *Learning to Industrialize: From Given Growth to Policy-Aided Value Creation* (New York: Routledge).

Oqubay, Arkebe (2015). *Made in Africa: Industrial Policy in Ethiopia* (Oxford: Oxford University Press).
Oqubay, Arkebe (2019). 'Ethiopia: Lessons from an Experiment', in *The Oxford Handbook of Structural Transformation* (Oxford: Oxford University Press): 591–618.
Oqubay, Arkebe, and Justin Lin (2019). *China-Africa and an Economic Transformation* (Oxford: Oxford University Press).
Oqubay, Arkebe, and Justin Lin (forthcoming). *The Oxford Handbook of Industrial Hubs and Economic Development.* (Oxford: Oxford University Press).
Oqubay, Arkebe, and Kenichi Ohno (2019). *How Nations Learn: Technological Learning, Industrial Policy, and Catch Up* (Oxford: Oxford University Press).
Ottaway, Marina (ed.) (1990). *The Political Economy of Ethiopia* (New York: Praeger Publishers).
Pankhurst, Richard (1968). *Economic History of Ethiopia (1800–1935)* (Addis Ababa: Haile Selassie University Press).
Pankhurst, Richard (1996). 'Post-World War II Ethiopia: British Military Policy and Action for the Dismantling and Acquisition of Italian Factories and Other Assets 1941–2', *Journal of Ethiopian Studies* 29 (1): 35–77.
Pasinetti, Luigi (1981). *Structural Change and Economic Growth: A Theoretical Essay on the Dynamics of the Wealth of Nations* (Cambridge: Cambridge University Press).
Pasinetti, Luigi (1993). *Structural Economic Dynamics: A Theory of the Economic Consequences of Human Learning* (Cambridge: Cambridge University Press).
Pausewang, Sigfried, Fantu Cheru, Eshetu Chole, and S. Brunen (eds) (1990). *Ethiopia: Rural Development Options* (London: ZED Books).
Rahmato, Dessalegn (1984). *Agrarian Reform in Ethiopia* (Uppsala: Scandinavian Institute of African Studies).
Stiglitz, Joseph E. (2002). *Globalization and its Discontents* (London: Penguin).
Szirmai, Adam, Wim Naudé, and Ludovico Alcorta (2013). *Pathways to Industrialization in the 21st Century: New Challenges and Emerging Paradigms* (Oxford: Oxford University Press).
Tekeste, Abraham (2014). *Trade Policy and Performance of Manufacturing Firms in Ethiopia* (Saarbrücken: Scholars' Press).
TGE (1991). 'Ethiopia's Economic Policy during the Transitional Period', Transitional Government of Ethiopia, Addis Ababa.
TGE (1992). 'The Encouragement, Expansion and Coordination of Investment Proclamation No. 15/1992 (as Amended)', Negarit Gazeta of the Transitional Government of Ethiopia, Addis Ababa.
Thirlwall, Anthony (2013). *Economic Growth in an Open Developing Economy: The Role of Structure and Demand* (Cheltenham: Edward Elgar).
Tiruneh, Andargachew (1990). 'The Ethiopian Revolution 1974–1987', PhD thesis, London School of Economics.
UNCTAD-UNIDO (2011). 'Fostering Industrial Development in Africa in the New Global Environment', Economic Development in Africa Report 2011, UNCTAD-UNIDO, Geneva.
UNECA (2016a). *Transformative Industrial Policy* (Addis Ababa: UNECA).
Wade, Robert (2004). *Governing the Market: Economic Theory and the Role of the Government in East Asian Industrialization* (Princeton, NJ: Princeton University Press).
World Bank (1967). 'The Economy of Ethiopia, Vol. I: Main Report', Report No. AF-601, 31 August, World Bank, Washington, DC.
World Bank (1973). 'Recent Economic Performance and Future Prospects in Ethiopia, Vol. I: Main Report', Report No. 9a-ET, World Bank, Washington, DC.

World Bank (1985). 'Ethiopia: Industrial Sector Review', Report No. 5301-ET, 16 December World Bank, Washington, DC.

World Bank (2002). 'IDA's Ethiopia Structural Credit', Report No. 7521 ET', 15 May, World Bank, Washington, DC.

Zenawi, Meles (2012). 'States and Markets: Neoliberal Limitations and the Case for Developmental State', in *Good Growth and Governance in Africa: Rethinking Development Strategies*, ed. Akbar Noman, Kwesi Botchwey, Howard Stein, and Joseph E. Stiglitz (Oxford: Oxford University Press): 140–74.

Zewde, Bahru (2002). *A History of Modern Ethiopia 1855–1974* (Athens, OH: Ohio University Press).

CHAPTER 36

THE STRUCTURE AND PERFORMANCE OF THE ETHIOPIAN MANUFACTURING SECTOR

ARKEBE OQUBAY

36.1 The Ethiopian Manufacturing Sector: Introduction

SINCE the 2000s, Ethiopia has emerged as one of the fastest-growing economies in Africa. Nevertheless, Ethiopia's manufacturing sector is still far from being the engine of growth and structural change. The manufacturing sector plays a marginal role in employment generation, exports, output, and inter-sectoral linkages. In some ways, the structure and performance of the Ethiopian manufacturing sector mirrors the wider sub-Saharan African experience (Lawrence 2005). The Ethiopian manufacturing sector has had two distinct features: first, 'a low level of industrialization in terms of the sector's share in GDP, export earnings, industrial intensity, and competitiveness. Second, the industrial structure is dominated by small firms and resource-based industries (in particular the food industry), and concentrated around the capital city' (Oqubay 2015: 66; see also Chapters 35, 37, and 39).[1]

[1] Africa's share of global manufacturing was below 1 per cent, while Asia and other developing economies accounted for 25 per cent and 23.7 per cent respectively in 2008 (UNCTAD-UNIDO 2011: 15). Africa's manufacturing value added (MVA) share of GDP was only 14 per cent in 2003, with a decrease of 2 per cent from 1965, the result of almost four decades of sluggish growth (Lawrence 2005, 2015). Moreover, the

Based on data and evidence from the past twenty-five years, the chapter provides an in-depth analysis of the structure and performance of the Ethiopian manufacturing sector and further explores the reasons behind the 'paradox' of the slow growth of manufacturing outputs (especially manufactured exports) despite determined efforts through industrial policy. Although the performance of manufacturing has been unimpressive, the evidence does suggest that there may have been a turning point in the mid-2010s. There are some promising signals that the manufacturing sector might have begun to emerge from the doldrums. The chapter presents this evidence, identifying signs of positive dynamics but also emphasizing the enduring weaknesses of the sector. In particular, the chapter highlights the difficulties of building an industrial workforce, the weaknesses in domestic productive capability, and the very limited manufacturing export capacity. Nonetheless, I argue that there is evidence of nascent structural change. This chapter complements but differs from Chapter 35, in that its focus is on the structure and performance of the manufacturing sector, while Chapter 35 outlines the origin of Ethiopia's industrialization and discusses industrial policies in detail. This chapter also complements and again differs from Chapter 37, in that it focuses on explaining poor manufacturing performance and covers the last twenty-five years.

This chapter is organized in five sections. Section 36.2 reviews the slow manufacturing growth and patterns of industrial development in Ethiopia. Section 36.3 examines the structure of the Ethiopian manufacturing sector with a particular focus on firms' dynamics (growth of firms, firm size and ownership, agglomeration patterns, linkages, and manufactured value added and output). Section 36.4 explores the 'paradox' of slow industrial development, the intensifying structural constraints on Ethiopia's structural transformation in recent years, and the key global structural pressures. Section 36.5 highlights the government's recent policy responses to improve the performance of the manufacturing sector. There are now clear signs of dynamism in the manufacturing sector, which gives hope for the possibility of late industrialization in the early twenty-first-century Ethiopia. Section 36.6 summarizes some of the key challenges and their policy implications.

36.2 Patterns of Industrial Development: Acceleration but Limited Scale

The wider industrial sector, and manufacturing within it, grew much faster after 2005. Thus, the annual rate of growth of industrial output doubled to nearly 20 per cent by 2015–17, while manufacturing output grew by 10 per cent a year from 2005 to 2010 and by

sector has been dominated by low-value, labour-intensive, resource-based activities and by small firms and the informal sector (Dinh et al. 2012).

17.9 per cent in 2015–17.[2] Despite this acceleration, however, the level of industrialization remained low. Value added in manufacturing had only reached 6.4 per cent of GDP by 2017, though value added in the wider industrial sector was by then up to more than 25 per cent (NPC 2018: 8; NBE 2018a, 2018b: 6).[3] During the same period, the annual growth rate of the industrial sector almost doubled from 10.1 to 19.8 between PASDEP and GTP-I period.

Nonetheless, in 2016/17 the net contribution of the manufacturing and industrial sectors to the 10.9 per cent annual GDP growth rate rose to 1.1 and 4.4 per cent respectively (see Table 36.1). This is much higher than the 0.4 and 1.1 per cent that these sectors had respectively contributed to overall growth during the PASDEP period (2005/6–2009/10). By contrast, the net contribution of agriculture remained the same (at 2.5 per cent), while that of the service sector dropped from 5.6 per cent in 2006–10 to 4 per cent of the GDP in 2016/17 (NPC 2018; NBE 2018a, 2018b). This suggests that the industrial sector may be evolving to become the primary driver of the economy for the first time in Ethiopia. However, further observation of this trend is necessary. Furthermore, this trend needs to be sustained for a longer period of time to have a greater impact.

Despite the increase in manufacturing output, there has been no comparable growth in manufactured exports and employment. The share of manufactured exports in total exports remained less than 13 per cent while total exports decreased from 12.7 to 7.7 per cent of GDP during 2001 and 2016/17 (see Figure 36.1). Manufactured exports were characterized by low-value products, which were generated in the leather and leather goods, textiles and apparel, and meat industries, and which generally went to other low/middle-income markets. This may be compared to the traditional coffee and the new cut-flower exports, which accounted for 25 and 7.5 per cent of total merchandise exports respectively in 2014–17, and a greater share of these exports were destined for higher income markets. The failure to increase manufactured exports as a share of total exports suggests limited structural transformation and the significance of the balance of payments constraint on growth through industrialization (Thirlwall 2013; Cramer, Oqubay, and Sender forthcoming; Lin and Monga 2019).[4]

Manufacturing employed 4.5 per cent of the total workforce in 2013. Employment by the sector grew at an annual rate of 4.8 per cent (similar to the 4.7 per cent growth for total employment) between 2005 and 2013 (NPC 2018).[5] Jobs in the construction industry tripled from 229,000 to 825,000. This has doubled the construction industry's share of total employment from 0.9 to 1.9 per cent. Meanwhile, stimulated by expansion of

[2] This acceleration reflected the greater emphasis on industrialization in the government's five-year plans, PASDEP (2005–10), GTP-I (2011–14), and GTP-II (2015–19).

[3] Agriculture and services accounted for 36.3 and 39.3 per cent respectively in 2016/17 (CSA 2018).

[4] Arguably, this intensifies the need to pursue structural change by raising productivity and export output in high-value agriculture and through the 'industrialization of freshness' (Cramer, Sender, and Di John 2018).

[5] The total active workforce increased from 24.9 million to 42.4 million between 2005 and 2013. The share of agriculture decreased from 79.8 to 72.7 per cent, while construction doubled from 0.9 to 1.9 per cent, and the service sector increased from 14.8 to 20.4 per cent. The share of manufacturing employment remained the same, 4.5 per cent, during this period.

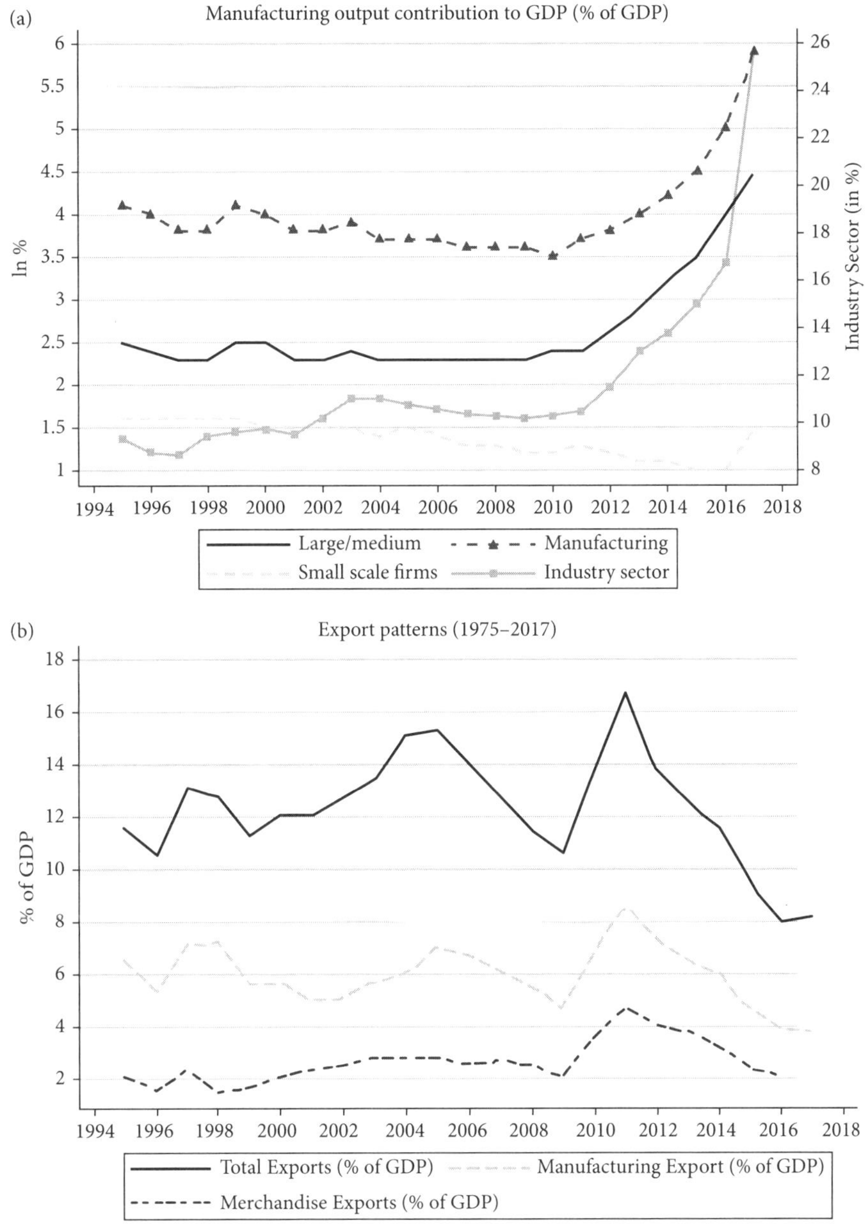

FIGURE 36.1 Growth patterns of manufacturing output and exports

Source: Author's computation based on CSA 1994–2017; ERCA 2018; NBE 2018b; NPC 2018.

public infrastructure and favourable policies, value added in the construction industry increased from 11.1 to 27.7 per cent between 2010/11 and 2014/15 and then slightly dipped to 22.85 per cent in 2015/16–2016/17.[6] Manufacturing industries related to the construction sector (such as the cement industry and other building materials) have also shown rapid growth and shifts in industrial structure (Oqubay 2015; CSA 1975-2017; see also Chapter 35).

36.3 The State and Structure of Manufacturing

36.3.1 Growth of Firms and Employment

Drawing on the CSA's annual manufacturing surveys as well as on data from the National Planning Commission (NPC), ERCA, and the EIB, we review experiences in medium and large firms between 1995/6 and 2016/17. According to the CSA's classification, such firms are enterprises that employ ten persons or more.[7] During this period, the number of such firms increased more than five-fold from 642 to 3,594. Likewise, total employment in these firms increased three-fold, with the biggest increase recorded between 2005/6 and 2015/16, while the average employment per firm nearly halved from 142 to 77 persons (see Figure 36.2). This last change in employment may be associated with the increased capital intensity of firms, intense pressure to improve productivity, and the shrinking of public enterprises that used to be overstaffed. Food products and beverages, other non-metallic mineral products, and apparel and textiles accounted for about 50 per cent of these firms.

Manufacturing of other non-metallic mineral products grew fast between 2005 and 2010, while apparel and textile firms experienced rapid growth between 2011 and 2016, which arguably mirrors the government's sectoral focus.[8] These three industries together accounted for 55.2 per cent of total registered manufacturing employment in 2016, down from 68.4 per cent in 1996, suggesting some diversification across manufacturing industries, though primarily among those producing for the consumer market. For instance, employment in food products and beverages declined from 26 to 21.7 per cent, while apparel and textiles declined from 35.7 to 15.1 per cent (see Figure 36.2). Employment in the manufacturing of other non-metallic mineral products tripled from

[6] This may be linked to the scaling down of the housing development programme and the foreign exchange shortage that hampered imports of some building materials.

[7] The CSA's firm classification has not changed despite the shifts in manufacturing activities. The definition raises methodological questions and limits the analytical depth, as all medium and large firms employing above 50 persons fall under the same category.

[8] This trend has continued in 2018, and the workforce in the apparel and textile sector increased to more than 100,000, mostly in new industrial parks (TIDI 2018). Other non-metallic mineral products include the manufacture of cement and lime, glass and glass products, lime, and concrete, cement, and plaster articles (CSA 2017 based on ISIC Revision 3.1).

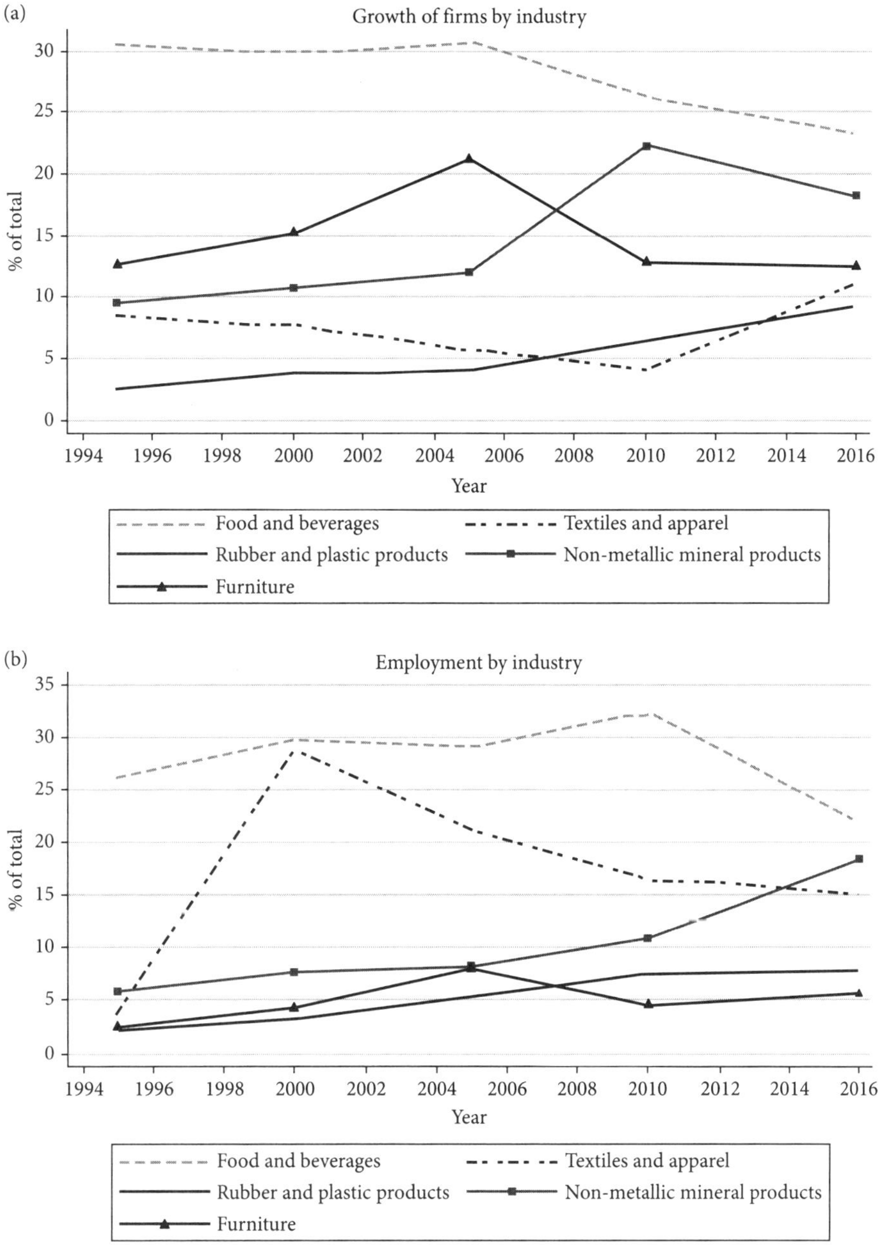

FIGURE 36.2 Industrial structure: firms and dominant industries, 1995–2017

Source: Own computation based on CSA (1994–2017).

6.7 to 18.4 per cent, consistent with the expanding construction sector. There was also employment growth in production for new consumer markets (such as furniture, chemical and plastic products). This suggests that growth in income and private consumption were key demand drivers. Overall, 80 per cent of enumerated wage employment in manufacturing was in food products and beverages, other non-metallic mineral products, textiles and apparel, rubber and plastic products, wood and wood products, furniture, and chemicals and chemical products.

36.3.2 Firm Size

In 2014/15, 29 per cent of medium and large manufacturing firms accounted for more than 90 per cent of employment in manufacturing (computation based on CSA data). Moreover, these medium and large firms accounted for 75 per cent of manufactured value-added output (NPC 2018). The economic history of advanced economies and East Asian latecomers confirms the prominent role of internationally competitive large firms and the significance of policies that focus on developing 'national champions' (Chandler 2004; Penrose [1959]2013; Amsden 1989, 2001). China is also following a similar industrial policy by building globally competitive firms (Nolan 2014). Larger firms play a pivotal role because of their typically higher productivity and exploitation of economies of scale, their tendency to create high-paying stable jobs, their technological capability, and their ability to compete in the export sector.

However, one of the key characteristics of the Ethiopian manufacturing sector remains the numerical dominance of small firms (Dinh et al. 2012; Lawrence 2005). This is in part the result of the conventional policy prescription that African countries should focus on the 'dynamism' of micro and small enterprises and the informal sector. This approach is reinforced by a 'small is beautiful' romanticization and the inflated valuation of the role of 'individual entrepreneurship' and self-employment in economic development (Cramer, Oqubay, and Sender 2019).[9] Another aspect of this confusion is the ill-defined concept of 'the missing middle', which is supported by neither theoretical nor empirical evidence (Hsieh and Olken 2014; Söderbom 2011).[10] Ethiopian medium and large firms accounted for three-quarters of manufacturing output. The lesson is that Ethiopia needs to develop larger firms and national champions that reinforce and complement the development of vibrant smaller enterprises, which are linked to large firms and global markets through sub-contracting and spin-offs, thereby harnessing inter-firm learning.[11]

[9] On entrepreneurship promotion in Africa, see Poole (2016); on the limited extent to which micro-enterprises 'scale up' successfully, see White, Larquemin, and Steel (2017).

[10] Hsieh and Olken (2014: 89) highlight that 'middle-sized firms are missing, but large firms are missing too...although a large literature seeks to explain the "missing middle" of mid-sized firms in developing countries, there is surprisingly little empirical backing for existence of the missing middle'. Söderbom (2011) highlights that there is a significant gap between firms employing above 50 and those below ten workers.

[11] Gebreeyesus et al. (2019) show that from a survey of 8,174 firms (in Addis Ababa and other major cities) 6 per cent were linked to large domestic firms and 3.5 per cent to FDI firms through sub-contracting. Moreover, about 77 per cent of jobs were temporary.

36.3.3 Firm Ownership

There have been shifts in corporate ownership as public enterprises were privatized and the government limited its participation to a few strategic areas. In 2014/15, the 141 public enterprises accounted for 4.5 per cent of all firms but for 12.9 per cent of employment and 28.6 per cent of value added in manufacturing output. The number of public enterprises is expected to shrink further.[12] Participation by foreign firms increased after 2011 and was estimated to account for 54 per cent of capital outlay and employment (EIC 2018). The stock of manufacturing FDI between 2007/8 and 2016/17 rose to US$14 billion (83 per cent of the total FDI inflow), with more than 73 per cent of this generated after 2011/12. The flow of domestic private investment into manufacturing has been slow, and especially marginal in export-oriented manufacturing (see Chapter 39).

36.3.4 Agglomeration Patterns

Agglomeration and clustering enhance specialization, inter-firm linkages, learning and innovation, and function on the basis of a combination of cooperation and competition (Marshall 1920; Jacobs 1969; Porter 1998; Oqubay and Lin forthcoming). Agglomeration patterns exhibit both continuation and new trends: more than 64 per cent of firms are concentrated around the capital, yet Addis Ababa has witnessed a sharp decline in the share of firms from 68 to 36 per cent between 1995/6 and 2015/16. The highest increase in concentration of firms (from 11 to 28 per cent) is in the Oromia region (primarily Addis Ababa–Adama corridor). A major increase from 15 to 31 per cent was also observed in the Southern Nations, Nationalities, Peoples' Region (SNNPR), Amhara, and Tigray regions (see Figure 36.3). This spread may be linked to the expansion of infrastructure and universities, increased urbanization, and the emergence of hubs around the regional capital cities. The strategic location of industrial parks, and proximity to ports and railway networks are also likely to shape future patterns of agglomeration (Oqubay and Lin forthcoming).

36.3.5 Imported-Input Dependency

The ratio of imported inputs to total raw materials for the overall manufacturing sector has been 0.50, mostly uniform during the period of 1995/6–2015/16, underscoring the weak backward linkages in Ethiopia's manufacturing sector, despite the unevenness across industries (Chapter 35). Imported-input dependency ratio increased by 75 per cent in the leather and leather goods industry; by 57 per cent in the manufacturing of food products and beverages; and by 38.5 per cent in textiles and apparel production, suggesting weak backward linkages with agriculture and the weaknesses of existing

[12] In 1989, public enterprises accounted for 50 per cent of firms and 93 per cent of total employment in the manufacturing sector.

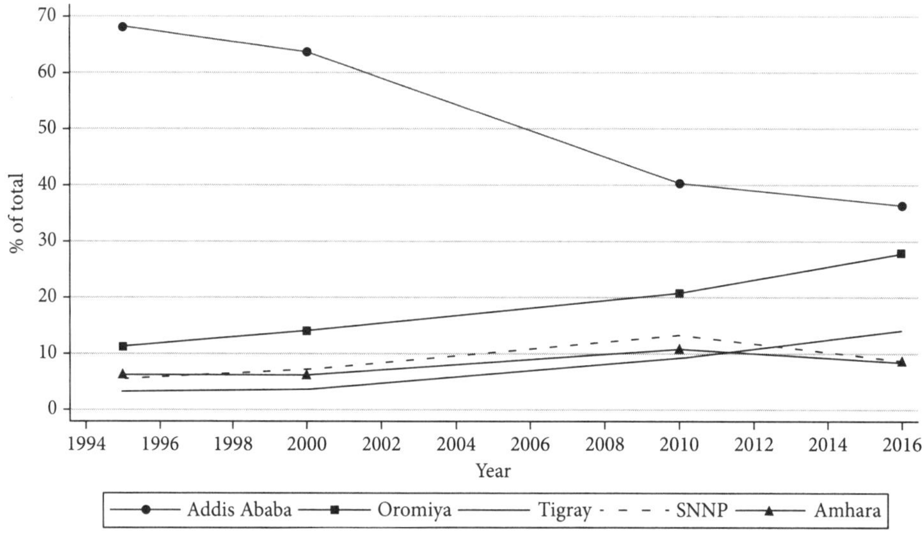

FIGURE 36.3 Geographic concentration of firms, 1994–2017

Source: CSA (1994–2018).

industrial policy in developing verticality in these sectors (CSA 1994–2017). Nevertheless, the manufacturing of other non-metallic products enjoyed a 55 per cent decline in the imported-input dependency, suggesting some improved domestic linkages. The imported-input dependency ratio also fell in fabricated metal products (a reduction of 53 per cent), and more modestly in rubber and plastic products and basic iron and steel.

36.3.6 Manufactured Value Added (MVA) and Gross Value of Production (GVP)

Food products and beverages, non-metallic mineral products, and apparel and textiles accounted for about 61 per cent of manufacturing value added throughout 1995–2016, with no fundamental shift, although there were uneven shifts across specific sectors. Of particular importance, manufacturing value added in export-oriented industries (such as leather and leather goods, and textiles and apparel) has remained very low (see Figure 36.4).

Four sub-sectors drove the growth in the gross value of production in manufacturing after 2005: food products and beverages, other non-metallic mineral products, chemicals and chemical products, and textiles and apparel. There was, nonetheless, some diversification, with other non-metallic mineral products, chemicals and chemical products, and rubber and plastic products rising from 15.9 to 28.4 per cent of manufacturing production. Textiles and apparel production, together with leather and leather products, shrank from 24.2 to 8 per cent (CSA 1994–2017).

Manufacturing activities more associated with exporting—like textiles and apparel and leather and leather goods—have declined in significance within the manufacturing

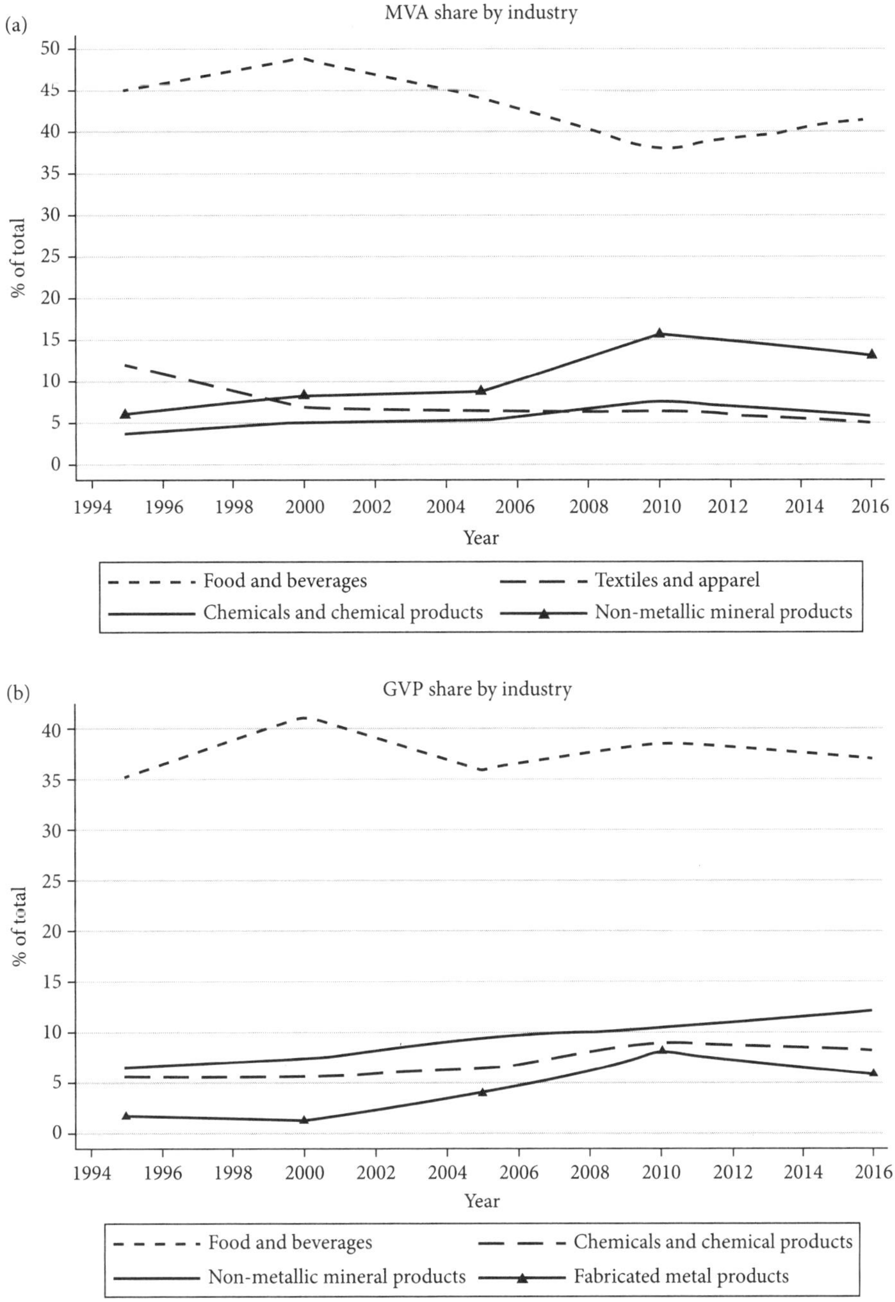

FIGURE 36.4 Sectoral share of MVA and GVP, 1995–2017

Source: Own computation based on CSA (1994–2017).

sector in terms of employment share, share of gross value of production, and share of manufacturing value added. At the same time, domestically oriented activities—above all, cement and related products—have increased their contribution to output, value added, and employment. This emphasizes the weakness of industrial policy in generating dynamic growth in export-oriented industries.

In sum, the industrial structure of Ethiopian manufacturing has not changed dramatically. This may appear disappointing given the commitment by the Ethiopian government to an active industrial policy (Chapter 35). Nonetheless, there are important departures and emerging shifts in terms of the contribution of the manufacturing and industrial sector. For instance, in the apparel and textiles industry the economic drivers (for instance, the role of FDI), and employment (with very fast growth since 2015) have been changing. The cement industry has undergone fundamental shifts during 2005–15. Driven by a strong domestic market, the brewery industry has also undergone considerable expansion.

36.4 Explaining the Performance of Ethiopian Manufacturing: A Paradox?

A quandary for policymakers and researchers is the weak performance of the Ethiopian (and sub-Saharan African) manufacturing sector, which has been slow to transform and become an engine of structural change, in spite of Ethiopia's active industrial policy.[13] There have been three common arguments to explain the weak performance of manufacturing throughout sub-Saharan Africa in recent decades, none of them wholly satisfactory (Lawrence 2005). One—the 'dependency' argument—implies that resources flow from poor to rich economies at the expense of the former and that developing countries cannot industrialize in the new global economic order. The main dependency is on advanced or even intermediate technology, under the domination of global corporates which determine where investment goes. This view suggests that international capital in advanced economies is tightly controlled by global value chains, run in the interests of 'systems integrator' producer or buyer firms in advanced economies.

This perspective rejects the importance of attracting FDI and is wary of integration into the global economy, anticipating at best that African economies are consigned to a restricted, dependent position in international production and that a weak domestic bureaucratic bourgeoisie, in the absence of a strong domestic capitalist class, will merely kowtow to the interests of foreign capital.[14] On the other hand, this perspective generalizes that protection and import substitution are required. Such a view rejects the possibility

[13] On manufacturing as engine of structural change, see also Kaldor (1967), Thirlwall (2013), Pasinetti (1981, 1993).

[14] See Hymer (1976: 212) on hostility to direct investments in 'underdeveloped' countries.

Table 36.1 Summary of key indicators on manufacturing growth, 2005–17

1) Annual growth rate of output (%)			
	2005/6–09/10 PASDEP	2010/11–14/15 GTP-I	2015/16–16/17 *GTP-II*
Manufacturing	10.0	15.1	17.9
Construction	11.1	27.7	22.85
Industry	10.1	19.8	19.65
GDP	11	10.1	9.45
2) Contribution to annual GDP growth rate (% of total)*			
Manufacturing	0.4	0.6	1
Industry	1.1	2.3	3.1
GDP	11	10.1	9.45
3) Exports, capital formation (% of GDP)			
Exports total (% of GDP)	12.5	12.8	7.85
Imports total	32.5	30.3	25.75
Capital formation	25.6	36.1	38.75
Domestic saving	9.8	19.3	23.5
Private consumption	79.5	71.5	65.75
Government consumption	10.7	9.2	11
	2014/15	**2015/16**	**2016/17**
Manufacturing exports (of GDP)	**0.6**	**0.5**	**0.5**
Merchandise exports (of GDP)	**4.7**	**4**	**3.6**
4) Employment annual growth rate (%)			
	1998–2005	2005–13	1998–2013
Manufacturing	5.4	3.0	4.8
Mining	58.9	14.9	68.3
Construction	13.5	10.6	17.4
Industry total	8.68	5.2	8.2
Total	3.8	4.4	4.7
5) Sectoral employment (% of total)			
	1998	2005	2013
Manufacturing	4.4	4.9	4.5
Mining	0.1	0.3	0.4
Construction	0.9	1.4	1.9
Industry	4.5	6.6	6.8

Note: * The manufacturing and industry sectors contributed 1.1 per cent and 4.4 per cent respectively. Services and agriculture contributed 4 and 2.5 per cent.

Source: Compilation based on ERCA (2018); CSA (1975–2017); NBE (2018b); NPC (2016, 2018); and national accounts (NPC and MoFED 2017).

(and evidence) that latecomers can catch up on the basis of latecomer advantage, as suggested by the economic history of late industrializers. Empirical evidence from the late twentieth and early twenty-first centuries, above all from East Asian (including China) and increasingly South-east Asian economies, shows that developing countries can succeed in industrial catch-up. China has successfully inserted itself into the global production and market network, and is upgrading its position through global exports, FDI inflows, and technological knowhow (UNCTAD 2013; Rodrik 2012; Dickens 2015; Nolan 2014; Lin 2015; Oqubay and Lin 2019).

Another view that gained currency in the 1990s (backed by international donors) was the neopatrimonialism perspective, which argues that African countries cannot industrialize or industrial policy cannot succeed because of inherent backwardness, bad governance, and patronage. This pessimistic view portrays lack of rapid industrialization as an 'African problem'.[15] This argument lacks a theoretical basis, while empirical evidence from Ethiopia and elsewhere prove the opposite (UNECA 2016).

A more dominant conventional explanation championed by the IFIs and many neoclassical economists identifies an excess of state interventions, 'policy syndromes', and price distortions as the culprit for slow growth and lack of structural change. Proponents of this view have seen the answer to Africa's industrialization and export promotion as economic liberalization, minimal role of the state, and dismantling of the state apparatus and industrial policy. In the 2000s and 2010s, supporters of this argument promoted privatization of SOEs, liberalization of the banking sector, and reduction of public expenditure (said to 'crowd out' the private sector: IMF 2015) in Ethiopia. But as observed in many African countries and elsewhere, the promise of unbridled liberalization failed to materialize. Instead, unbridled liberalization has often led to 'premature' deindustrialization and difficulties in sustaining rapid growth.

A more convincing explanation, at least for the recent Ethiopian experience, has to begin from the specifics of the country's context. Any realistic explanation has to take into account the long civil war that devastated an already frail economy and derailed economic development, especially when combined with the neglect of agriculture under the Derg (see Chapters 2, 3, and 35). The manufacturing sector in Ethiopia accounted for less than 5 per cent of GDP while Africa's average level was above 10 per cent in the 1960s (UNCTAD-UNIDO 2011; Lawrence 2005; Dinh et al. 2012). The volatile geopolitics of the Horn of Africa had continued to impose constraints on Ethiopia's economic development and war with Eritrea in the late 1990s further complicated the geopolitical reality. These constraints—a weak starting point even by comparison with much of the rest of Africa and a difficult regional political environment—are significant; and undoubtedly mean that the challenges of industrial policy in the twenty-first century are particularly acute. But they are insufficient as an explanation for the disappointingly slow industrialization of recent years.

Unlike in many countries, Ethiopia's industrial policy has been relatively coherent rather than unplanned (see Chapters 46, 47, and 49). An initial focus on rapid growth

[15] See Oqubay (2015: 249–52).

through agricultural revival and expansion ought to have been conducive to the subsequent growth of manufacturing. Gross fixed capital formation increased from 26.6 to 39 per cent, while gross domestic savings rose from 9.3 to 24.1 per cent between 2001/2 and 2016/17. The focus on infrastructure development and education (especially the expansion and reform of vocational and technical education schools and universities) was vital for the expansion of manufacturing (see Chapters 12 and 25). The industrial development strategy and successive post-2005 five-year plans focused on specific priorities. For instance, the expansion of productive capacity through expansion of small enterprises in combination with medium and large firms, and active promotion of FDI and the Ethiopian state's investment in strategic industries to deepen structural transformation were among these priorities. But still the performance has been underwhelming.

Despite what is arguably an unusual degree of coherence in industrial policy, the design and execution of this policy has continued to exhibit many weaknesses (see Chapter 35). There was inadequate application of reciprocal control mechanisms to enhance performance and change the behaviour of industrialists across sectors. Incentives had been partially misused with little monitoring or discipline, especially in the services sector, such as the hotel industry (see Chapter 35). Weak capabilities in project design and implementation, as well as misguided procurement practices, have hobbled some strategic large-scale projects, such as sugar and fertilizer production, and this in turn has made it more difficult to achieve import substitution and export earnings targets in GTP-I and II.[16] Furthermore, industrial policies have been uneven across selected key sectors and often not wholly based on well-researched industry-specific studies.

Much research remains to be done fully to understand what has gone wrong with industrial policy in Ethiopia. In addition to these factors, it is worth highlighting a few other key issues, beyond the scope of this chapter, that appear relevant. First, it may be that there is too little shared appreciation among officials of the scale of the challenge of catching up with advanced industrialized economies: beyond cutting red tape here or tweaking incentives there. The challenge of building a capitalist society was a fundamental one, which required productive capabilities to be generated among enterprises, stimulating development of an industrial or capitalist wage labour force, and inculcating an understanding of the dynamics of the global economy among policymakers. Second, the reforms undertaken during the initial phases after the end of the Derg rule in 1991, were relatively 'soft', i.e. the measures taken to revive agriculture, to develop a more sustainable approach to macroeconomic balances, and so on were not sufficient. However, subsequent policy efforts focusing on structural change have pitched officials into more difficult policy territory, and at a time when there has been a greater proliferation of contending interest groups. Third, the fundamental significance of generating foreign exchange, as part of broader structural change, employment creation, and poverty reduction, was not necessarily something equally appreciated at all levels of government. There was evidence of tension between this objective and other ideas and interests at

[16] NPC (2016) and UNDP (2017).

regional levels and within parts of the federal government. Fourth, the government made a string of policy experiments, some more successful than others, but it had not yet distilled these further, in order to work out how best to overcome the tilt of incentives which still favoured domestic investment in relatively low-productivity commerce and services sectors. This requires the selection and enforcement of specific policy interventions, which depends on monitoring capacity, on the focus on generation of foreign exchange, linkage stimulation, and employment-generating capacity. As suggested earlier in this chapter, part of the explanation for the relatively disproportionate outcomes thus far of Ethiopia's industrial policy in some export-oriented sectors may lie in the very small number of large-scale, export-oriented Ethiopian firms.

36.5 A Bias for Hope: Late Industrialization in the Early Twenty-First Century

Achieving Vision 2025, a vision to make Ethiopia the leading manufacturing hub in Africa, requires an annual manufacturing growth rate of 25 per cent and an increase in manufacturing's share of GDP to 20 per cent by 2025.[17] The evidence above suggests the economy may fall short of this ambitious target. And as discussed, there are plenty of reasons to be sceptical about the prospects for success. Nonetheless, the evidence also suggests that Ethiopia's commitment to structural transformation in recent years may actually be starting to bear fruit. The government has also developed the beginnings of a sharper policy focus. First, it encouraged investment in new productive capacity, especially in priority manufacturing activities (in light manufacturing, basic wage goods and import substitution, and strategic new industries such as new energy). Light manufacturing industries are acknowledged to be export oriented, labour intensive, linked to agriculture, and involve tradable goods.[18]

Second, a new approach to hub development, agglomeration, and clustering was deemed essential, with the focus on building sustainable, specialized parks that apply a plug-and-play model.[19] The major departure occurred during GTP-II when the government decided on a comprehensive industrial hubs strategy, with the aim of developing 25 industrial parks, of which some were operational by December 2018.[20] Ethiopia's

[17] See the industrial development plan of GTP-II (Ministry of Industry 2016, unpublished).

[18] See Dinh et al. (2012).

[19] Green industrialization and climate change, understanding and insertion into the global value chain, and accelerated technological advances and increased servicification are important international trends that should be incorporated into the design of industrial polices. See also UNCTAD (2013); Schmitz (2007); Rodrik (2012); World Bank (2018); and ADB (2017).

[20] More than 50,000 direct manufacturing jobs were created by 2018. The list of industrial parks includes fifteen federal-level export-oriented specialized parks that aim to attract high-quality productive

unique model of hub development and industrial parks has been based on systematic learning (from South Korea, Singapore, China, Vietnam, Mauritius, Nigeria, and a review of the brief experience in Ethiopia) (Oqubay and Lin forthcoming). Learning by doing was supported through piloting and experimenting at Hawassa Industrial Park (FDRE 2015; Llobet and Mihretu 2017; Oqubay and Lin forthcoming).

There are positive indications of the effect of this new strategic approach. The quality and volume of FDI inflow has shown very rapid growth and change. FDI almost quadrupled to US$4.2 billion in 2016/17 from US$1.1 billion in 2011/12. Manufacturing drew in more than 80 per cent of FDI during this period (see Figure 36.5). McKinsey's survey (2017) shows that about two-thirds of all Chinese firms in Ethiopia were engaged in the manufacturing sector, which is twice the average of Chinese firms' engagement in Africa.[21] In the export-oriented apparel and textiles sector, the contribution of FDI firms has grown in recent years and accounts for about 70 and 60 per cent of exports and employment respectively (TIDI 2018).

36.6 Conclusion: Enduring Constraints

By early 2018, there was inadequate evidence to fully assess the effectiveness of these policy responses. The three strategic issues below required comprehensive and long-term attention.

First, as Ethiopia embarks on late industrialization, building an industrial workforce has become a strategic issue of concern (EIC and IPDC 2017; Enterprise Partners 2017, 2018; see Chapter 38). Firms and industrial associations have developed joint initiatives to develop and upgrade workers' skills in collaboration with government agencies and development partners, which has led to some positive results. High absenteeism and labour turnover eroded attempts to develop labour force skills in order to increase productivity (Gebrechristos 2018). Labour sourcing and supply has been constrained by lack of well-developed labour market institutions to recruit and train workers, low wages, weak industrial relations, rapidly increasing living costs, and lack of affordable housing in host cities. Moreover, human resource issues related to personnel management and communication have also been cited as potential constraints in firms observed (Enterprise Partners 2017, 2018; World Bank 2015; see also Chapters 31, 38, and 40). Oya highlights that building an industrial workforce is uneven, protracted, and requires wider state intervention (see Chapter 38). Based on historical accounts of the United Kingdom and continental Europe, Thompson (1967: 90) underlines that it may take several generations to perpetuate and 'institutionalize' industrial work discipline.

investment, four regional agro-industrial parks that focus on fostering linkages between agriculture and manufacturing, and six private industrial parks.

[21] See also World Bank (2012); Oqubay and Lin (forthcoming).

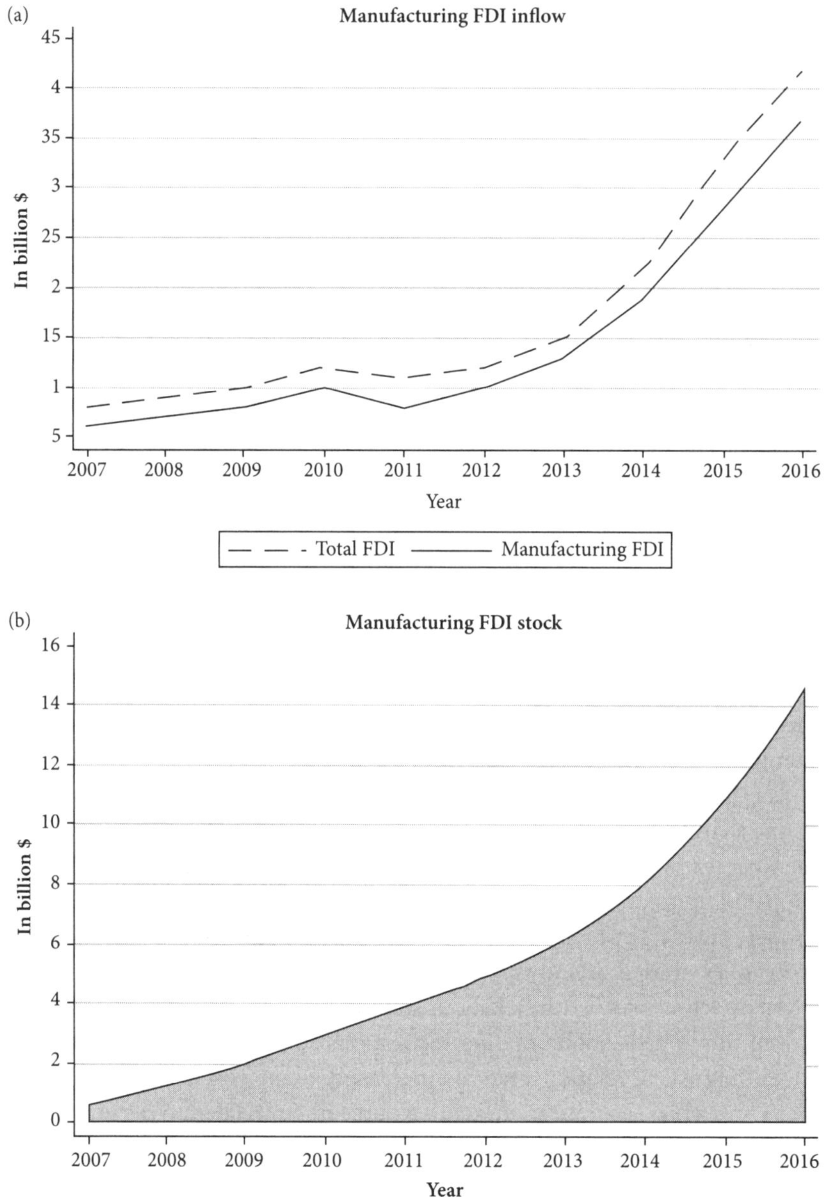

FIGURE 36.5 FDI and manufacturing FDI inflow, 2007–17 (in US$)

Source: NBE and EIC (2018a).

Second, an equally important strategic issue for Ethiopia's industrialization is the development of domestic industrialists and linkages (Hirschman 1958; Rweyemamu 1973; Iliffe 1983). There has been little participation by domestic firms in highly competitive export-oriented manufacturing for a number of reasons. There has also been a lack of access to long-term industrial financing for domestic firms, due to the limited capacity of public banks and the lack of interest by private banks in such financing. The political economy constraints favoured investment in more profitable sectors and speculative activities rather than in export-oriented manufacturing (see Chapter 35). Despite an industrial policy that has in some respects been prepared to 'get prices wrong' in order to encourage accelerated manufacturing activity, relative prices in the Ethiopian economy clearly still deflect investors away from manufacturing.

Accelerating learning within the global economy is as critical as relaxing constraints on the balance of payments. The hope was that industrial parks would facilitate this, by promoting production linkages and learning from the interaction between domestic and foreign firms. But these learning outcomes did not instantly materialize (UNCTAD 2013; Rodrik 2012; Ohno and Oqubay 2019). Moreover, additional support schemes and incentives (such as government cost sharing and loans) designed to promote skills and productivity were not entirely translated into action.[22]

Third, Ethiopian manufacturing needed a breakthrough in export performance.[23] Export-led industrialization and import substitution should be seen as complementary (Amsden 1989; Ocampo, Rada, and Taylor 2009) rather than mutually exclusive.[24] In addition to an overvalued exchange rate and inadequate institutional support for exporters, the lack of internationally competitive export logistics and trade facilitation, especially important given that Ethiopia is landlocked, became key binding constraints on export-led industrialization. The construction and operationalization of the new national railway network and construction of the Grand Ethiopian Renaissance Dam are part of the strategic responses that will ultimately determine the success of Ethiopia's late industrialization. So too are the recent investments by Ethiopian Airlines to expand its freight terminal and to foster integration into global logistics networks.

Finally, industrial policies needed to go beyond the obvious manufacturing sector, since their key aim is to promote a faster shift of people and resources into high-productivity economic activity, which increasingly also involves some services and some agriculture (Cramer, Sender, and Di John 2018; see also Chapter 35).

Acknowledgement

The author thanks Christopher Cramer, Peter Lawrence, John Sender, and Fantu Cheru for insightful and useful comments; Yohannes Gebru and Meron Tilahun for data collection; and Deborah M. Kefale and Binyam Arkebe for their continued support and inputs to improve the draft.

[22] Various studies highlight industrial finance, access to land and electricity, supply of inputs and raw materials, business climate, shortages of foreign exchange, and trade logistics as binding constraints, as well as entrepreneurial skills and worker skills (World Bank 2015; CSA surveys 2017).

[23] Economic history and the structuralist development perspective suggests manufacturing as engine of structural change and the strategic role of exports in international learning and constraints on balance of payments (Kaldor 1967; Thirlwall 2013; Pasinetti 1981, 1993).

[24] In addition to export expansion, the opportunities for import substitution are substantial considering that 87 per cent of imported goods were raw materials and semi-finished inputs (17 per cent), consumer goods (30 per cent), and capital goods (40 per cent) (NBE 2018b).

References

ADB (2017). 'African Economic Outlook 2017: Entrepreneurship and Industrialization', Africa Development Bank, Abidjan.

Amsden, Alice H. (1989). *Asia's Next Giant: South Korea and Late Industrialization* (Oxford: Oxford University Press).

Amsden, Alice H. (2001). *The Rise of 'The Rest': Challenges to the West from Late-Industrializing Economies* (Oxford: Oxford University Press).

Chandler, Alfred (2004). *Scale and Scope: The Dynamics of Industrial Capitalism* (Cambridge: Cambridge University Press).

Cramer, Chris, Arkebe Oqubay, and John Sender (forthcoming). *African Economic Development: Evidence, Theory, and Policy* (Oxford: Oxford University Press).

Cramer, Christopher, John Sender, and Jonathan Di John (2018). 'Poinsettia Assembly and Selling Emotion: High Value Agricultural Exports in Ethiopia', SOAS/EDRI/AFD, Report for the Agence Franćais du Développement (AFD), Paris.

CSA (1975–2017). 'Manufacturing Survey of Medium and Large Enterprises', Central Statistical Agency, Addis Ababa.

CSA (2018). 'Report on Small-Scale Manufacturing Industries Survey', Addis Ababa.

Dickens, Peter (2015). *Global Shift: Mapping the Changing Contours of the World Economy (2015)*, 7th edition (London: SAGE Publication Ltd).

Dinh, Hinh, Vicent Palade, Vandana Chandra, and Francis Cossar (2012). 'Light Manufacturing in Africa: Targeted Policies to Enhance Private Investment and Create Jobs', World Bank, Washington, DC.

EIC (2018). 'The 2017 Ethiopian Investment Report'. http://www.investethiopia.gov.et Series1/18, Addis Ababa.

EIC and IPDC (2017). 'Data on Investment and Industrial Parks', manuscript, Ethiopia Investment Commission and Industrial Parks Development Corporation, Addis Ababa.

Enterprise Partners (2017, 2018). 'Industrial Workforce Development', unpublished surveys and reviews on Hawassa Industrial Park.

ERCA (2018). 'Ethiopian Export Performance 1998–2018', unpublished, Ethiopian Revenue and Customs Authority, November 2016. Addis Ababa.

FDRE (2015). 'Proclamation on Industrial Parks', Federal Democratic Republic of Ethiopia, Addis Ababa.

Gebrechristos, Nigisty (2018). 'Labour Retention in the Ethiopian Apparel Industry: The Case of Hawassa Industrial Park', unpublished.

Gebreeyesus, Mulu, A. Ambachew, T. Getahun, et al. (2019). 'Main Features of the Manufacturing MSEs in Ethiopia: Baseline Survey Report', Ethiopia Development Research Institute (EDRI), Addis Ababa, Ethiopia.

Hirschman, Albert (1958). *Strategy of Economic Development* (New Haven, CT: Yale University Press).

Hsieh, Chang-Tai, and Benjamin Olken (2014). 'The Missing "Missing Middle"', *Journal of Economic Perspectives*, American Economic Association, 28 (3): 89–108.

Hymer, Stephen (1976). *The International Operations of National Firms: A Study of Direct Foreign Investment* (Cambridge, MA: MIT Press).

Iliffe, John (1983). *The Emergence of African Capitalism* (Basingstoke: Macmillan).

IMF (2015). 'The Federal Democratic Republic of Ethiopia: Selected Issues', IMF Country Report No. 15/326, 4 September. https://www.imf.org/external/pubs/ft/scr/2015/cr15326.pdf

Jacobs, Jane (1969). *The Economy of Cities* (New York: Vintage Books).

Kaldor, Nicholas (1967). *Strategic Factors in Economic Development* (Ithaca, NY: Cornell University Press).

Lawrence, Peter (2005). 'Explaining Sub-Saharan Africa's Manufacturing Performance', *Development and Change* 36 (6): 1121–45.

Lawrence, Peter (2015). 'Is There an Africa Problem?' in *Handbook of Industry and Development*, ed. J. Weiss and M. Tribe (London: Routledge): 350–81.

Lin, Justin (2015). 'China's Rise and Structural Transformation in Africa: Ideas and Opportunities' in *The Oxford Handbook of Africa and Economics, Vol. 2: Policies and Practices*, ed. Celestin Monga and Justin Yifu Lin (Oxford: Oxford University Press): 792–814.

Lin, Justin and Celestin Monga (2019). *Oxford Handbook of Structural Transformation* (Oxford: Oxford University Press).

Llobet, Gabriela and Mamo Mihretu (2017). *Beyond the Horizon: A Case Study of PVH's Commitment to Ethiopia's Hawassa Industrial Park.* (Washington, DC: World Bank Group). https://openknowledge.worldbank.org/bitstream/handle/10986/28334/117230-REVISED-PVH-Case-Study-13th-July-HR-singles.pdf?sequence=1&isAllowed=y

Marshall, Alfred (1920). *Principles of Economics* (London: Palgrave Macmillan).

McKinsey (2017). 'Dance of the Lions and Dragons: How Are Africa and China Engaging and How Will the Partnership Evolve?' McKinsey & Company, New York.

MoI (2016). 'The Industrial Development Plan of GTP II', unpublished, Ministry of Industry, Addis Ababa.

NBE (2018a). 'FDI Inflow to Ethiopia', unpublished, National Bank of Ethiopia, Addis Ababa.

NBE (2018b). 'The 2016/17 Annual Report', Domestic Economic Analysis and Publication Directorate, Addis Ababa. http://www.nbe.gov.et

Nolan, Peter (2014). *Chinese Firms, Global Firms: Industrial Policy in the Era of Globalization* (New York: Routledge).

NPC (2016). 'Growth and Transformation Plan 2015/16–2019/20 (GTP II)', National Planning Commission, Addis Ababa.

NPC (2018). 'Mid-Term Review of GTP II', unpublished, April, Addis Ababa.

NPC and MoFED (2017). 'National Accounts Data of Ethiopia', unpublished.

Ocampo, José A., Codrina Rada, and Lance Taylor (2009). *Growth and Policy in Developing Countries: A Structuralist Approach* (New York: Columbia University Press).

Oqubay, Arkebe (2015). *Made in Africa: Industrial Policy in Ethiopia* (Oxford: Oxford University Press).

Oqubay, Arkebe (2019). 'Ethiopia: Lessons from an Experiment', in *The Oxford Handbook of Structural Transformation* (Oxford: Oxford University Press).

Oqubay, Arkebe, and Justin, Lin (2019). *China-Africa and an Economic Transformation* (Oxford: Oxford University Press).

Oqubay, Arkebe, and Justin Lin (forthcoming). *The Oxford Handbook of Industrial Hubs and Economic Development* (Oxford: Oxford University Press).

Oqubay, Arkebe, and Kenichi Ohno (2019). *How Nations Learn: Technological Learning, Industrial Policy, and Catch Up* (Oxford: Oxford University Press).

Pasinetti, Luigi (1981). *Structural Change and Economic Growth: A Theoretical Essay on the Dynamics of the Wealth of Nations* (Cambridge: Cambridge University Press).

Pasinetti, Luigi (1993). *Structural Economic Dynamics: A Theory of the Economic Consequences of Human Learning* (Cambridge: Cambridge University Press).

Penrose, Edith ([1959] 2013). *The Theory of Growth of the Firm* (Oxford: Oxford University Press).

Poole, David Leonard (2016). 'Entrepreneurship and SME Sector Development in Post-Genocide Rwanda: A Search for the "Missing Middle"', PhD thesis, SOAS, University of London.

Porter, Michael (1998). *The Competitive Advantage of Nations* (Basingstoke: Palgrave Macmillan).
Rodrik, Dani (2012). *The Globalization Paradox: Why Global Markets, States, and Democracy Can't Coexist* (Oxford: Oxford University Press).
Rweyemamu, Justinian (1973). *Underdevelopment and Industrialization in Tanzania: A Study of Perverse Capitalist Industrial Development* (London: Oxford University Press).
Schmitz, Hubert (2007). 'Reducing Complexity in the Industrial Policy Debate', *Development Policy Review* 25 (4): 417–28.
Söderbom, Mans (2011). 'Firm Size and Structural Change: A Case Study of Ethiopia', *Journal of African Economies* 21 (2): 126–51.
Thirlwall, Anthony (2013). *Economic Growth in an Open Developing Economy: The Role of Structure and Demand* (Cheltenham: Edward Elgar).
Thompson, E. P. (1967). 'Time, Work-Discipline, and Industrial Capitalism', *Past and Present* 38: 56–97.
TIDI (2018). 'Firm-Level Data in Textile and Apparel Sector', unpublished.
UNCTAD (2013). 'Global Value Chains: Investment and Trade for Development', World Investment Report 2013, UNCTAD, Geneva.
UNCTAD-UNIDO (2011). 'Fostering Industrial Development in Africa in the New Global Environment', Economic Development in Africa Report 2011, UNCTAD-UNIDO, Geneva.
UNDP (2017). *A case study of growing manufacturing industry in Ethiopia.*
UNECA (2016). *Transformative Industrial Policy* (Addis Ababa: UNECA).
White, Simon, Aurelie Larquemin, and William Steel (2017). 'Rapid Evidence Assessment: Financial Services and Small and Medium-Sized Enterprise Growth and Development', DfID, London.
World Bank (2012). 'Chinese FDI in Ethiopia: A World Bank Survey', Addis Ababa.
World Bank (2015). 'Overcoming Constraints in the Manufacturing Sector', 4th Ethiopia Economic Update, 8 July, World Bank, Washington, DC.
World Bank (2018). 'The Inescapable Manufacturing–Services Nexus', Ethiopia Economic Update, World Bank, Washington, DC.

CHAPTER 37

THE ETHIOPIAN MANUFACTURING SECTOR

Productivity, Export, and Competitiveness

ADMASU SHIFERAW AND MÅNS SÖDERBOM

37.1 Introduction

Ethiopia's agricultural sector has developed favourably over the past decade, but rapid population growth, limited access to fertile land, and volatile agricultural outcomes pose problems for the agricultural sector regarding its ability to deliver new jobs and sustained per capita income growth in the medium term. Land is less of a constraint for growth in the non-farm sector, such as manufacturing, services, and trading, and non-farm production is typically associated with higher labour productivity and tends to be less exposed to severe shocks. For these reasons, diversification is often argued to be the way forward for Ethiopia and other countries in sub-Saharan Africa.

Ethiopia's manufacturing sector is small, even by African standards. For over 20 years, the share of manufacturing value added in total value added in Ethiopia has varied between 4 and 5 per cent. Compared to other countries in sub-Saharan Africa (SSA), this is a very modest contribution (see Figure 37.1). Like many other African countries, the industrial sector in Ethiopia is characterized by a large number of very small, typically informal, enterprises and a small number of large firms that account for the bulk of manufacturing output and employment. Micro and small firms tend to record low value added, low wages, virtually no exports, and little technological progress. Moreover, it is uncommon for small firms to transform themselves into large firms that invest, export, offer skilled jobs, and pay high wages (Shiferaw and Bedi 2013).

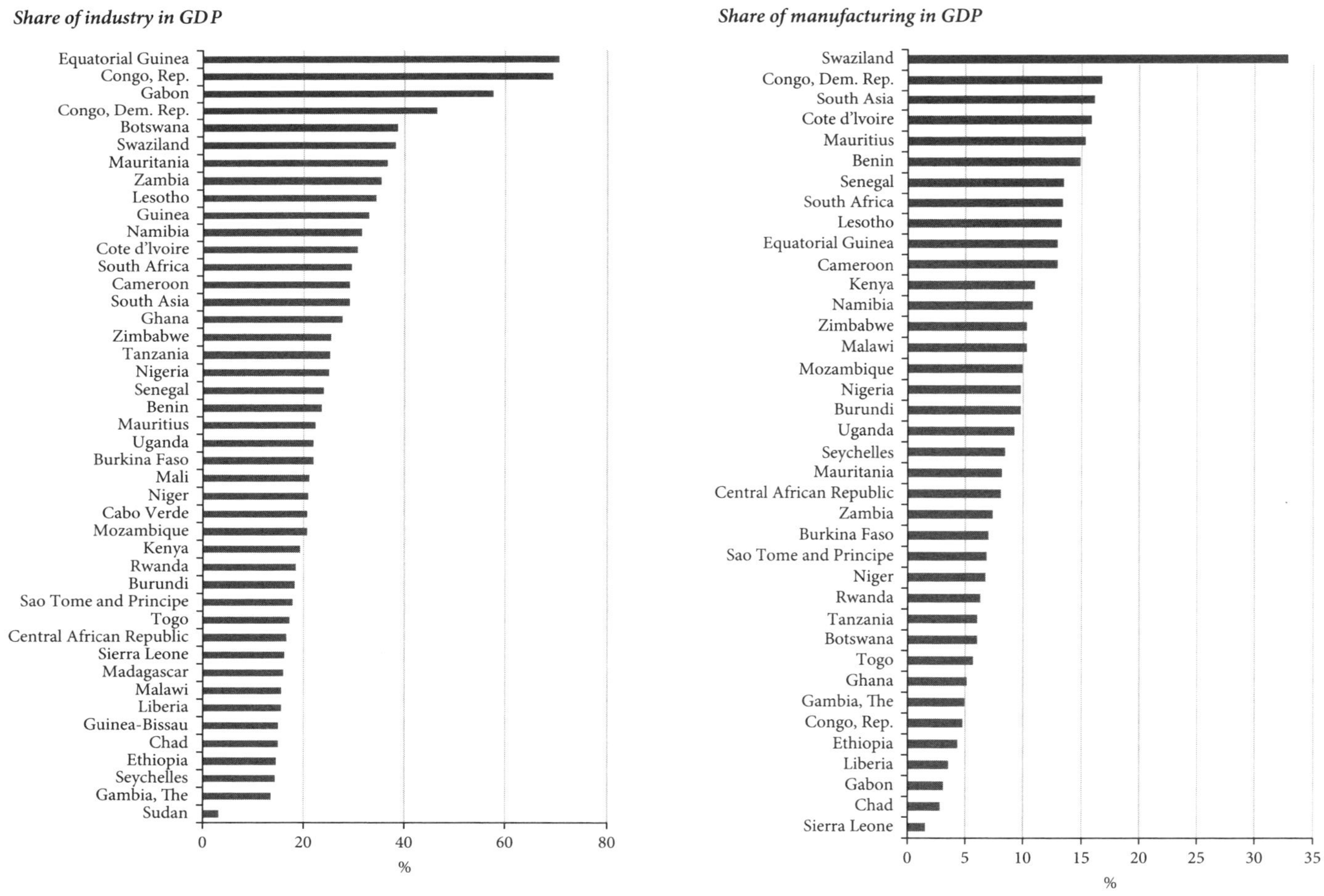

FIGURE 37.1 Industry and manufacturing in sub-Saharan Africa

Source: World Development Indicators.

The structure of the manufacturing sector, in particular the concentration of activity in very small firms and the small number of large firms, is an important reason for the modest contribution of manufacturing to Ethiopia's economy (see also Chapters 35, 36, and 39).

In this chapter we analyse productivity, exports, and competitiveness in Ethiopia's manufacturing sector. We will pay special attention to the structure of the sector, especially firm size distribution, and to dynamic patterns—in particular firm turnover (entry and exit) and productivity growth—and show that such dynamics can be important sources of aggregate growth. As we shall see, there exist rich firm-level data for Ethiopia and a relatively large number of studies have been produced accordingly.[1] We will not be able to survey the entire literature on Ethiopia's manufacturing sector in this chapter. Instead, our goal is to highlight the most salient features of the sector associated with firm growth and job creation. Our approach is entirely descriptive. We begin Section 37.2 by reviewing aggregate data on Ethiopia's manufacturing and industrial sector, with sub-Saharan Africa as a benchmark. We go on to describe the firm-level data, which while not public is reasonably accessible for researchers, and focus on differences in performance and productivity across firms of differing size. We then use the firm-level data to study firm dynamics and productivity dynamics, again with some emphasis on firms of differing size. A discussion of the main development issues facing Ethiopia's manufacturing sector follows. We deliberately do not devote a lot of space to discussing industrial policy in this chapter. As already noted, our narrative throughout is primarily descriptive, and we are therefore not in a strong position to identify policy options. Readers interested in Ethiopia's industrial policies are referred to the excellent review by Gebreeyesus (2016).

37.2 Ethiopia's Manufacturing Sector: the Aggregate View

Table 37.1 summarizes key indicators of economic and industrial performance in 1993–2016 for Ethiopia and, for reference, SSA. Even though Ethiopia has recorded impressive growth in per capita income since 2005 (column 1), the share of industry in total value added (GDP) has increased from 0.08 in 1993 to 0.16 in 2016. Manufacturing value added relative to GDP, however, has been between 4 and 5 per cent throughout the period (column 2), showing no signs of an increase despite rapid overall growth. While

[1] For example, Bigsten and Gebreeyesus (2007) examine the relationship between firm-level productivity and firm growth; Shiferaw (2007, 2009) analyses the relationship between firm survival and productivity; Söderbom (2012) analyses the role of product choice for value added; Shiferaw and Bedi (2013) investigate the relationship between firm size and gross job flows; Shiferaw et al. (2015) analyse the effects of road infrastructure on firm entry, location choice and growth; Bigsten, Gebreeyesus, and Söderbom (2016) examine the links between trade liberalization and firm performance; Gebreeyesus and Siba (2017) study the causal links between exporting and productivity; and Shiferaw (2016) examines investment behaviour.

Table 37.1 Industrial performance in Ethiopia and sub-Saharan Africa

	(1) GDP per capita		(2) Share of manufacturing value added in GDP		(3) Share of industry value added in GDP		(4) Manufactured exports per capita	
Year	ETH	SSA	ETH	SSA	ETH	SSA	ETH	SSA
1993	179	1134	0.04	0.12	0.08	0.38	0.0	
1994	178	1125	0.04	0.11	0.09	0.37		
1995	183	1130	0.05	0.12	0.09	0.37	0.8	
1996	199	1158	0.04	0.11	0.08	0.36		34.9
1997	199	1169	0.04	0.11	0.08	0.36	0.9	37.4
1998	187	1167	0.04	0.11	0.09	0.35	0.6	29.4
1999	191	1162	0.04	0.11	0.09	0.34	0.5	31.4
2000	197	1172	0.04	0.11	0.09	0.35	0.7	37.0
2001	207	1187	0.04	0.11	0.09	0.35	0.9	34.4
2002	204	1190	0.04	0.11	0.09	0.35	1.0	43.4
2003	194	1216	0.04	0.10	0.10	0.36	0.8	47.1
2004	214	1322	0.04	0.10	0.10	0.34	0.3	
2005	233	1358	0.04	0.10	0.10	0.33	0.5	
2006	251	1415	0.04	0.10	0.10	0.31	0.7	78.4
2007	272	1474	0.04	0.10	0.10	0.31	2.2	78.5
2008	294	1512	0.04	0.10	0.10	0.29	1.7	115.6
2009	311	1513	0.04	0.09	0.10	0.28	1.6	66.8
2010	341	1552	0.04	0.09	0.09	0.28	2.4	93.8
2011	370	1576	0.04	0.09	0.10	0.28	3.3	103.5
2012	391	1591	0.04	0.10	0.11	0.28	2.7	103.4
2013	421	1622	0.04	0.10	0.12	0.28	3.7	99.8
2014	453	1652	0.04	0.10	0.13	0.28	3.9	101.2
2015	487	1656	0.05	0.10	0.14	0.27	3.7	
2016	511	1632	0.05	0.09	0.16	0.26		
Growth*								
95–02	1.6%	0.7%	-0.7%	-1.0%	0.7%	-0.7%	2.4%	
02–09	6.0%	3.4%	-0.7%	-2.4%	0.3%	-3.0%	7.4%	6.2%
09–16	7.1%	1.1%	3.7%	0.5%	6.9%	-1.0%	13.5%	

Note: * Average annual growth rates.
Source: World Development Indicators.

these figures imply that manufacturing output per capita has grown in *absolute* terms, had manufacturing actually *led* economic growth one would expect the sector to have become relatively larger over time. Hence, the period of rapid growth has not been accompanied by a 'take-off' in manufactured output in Ethiopia. Column 4 shows data on manufactured exports expressed in current US$ per capita. While there has been some growth over the past decade, the volume of exports from Ethiopia has been strikingly low throughout the period. By 2014, manufactured exports per capita reached a mere US$3.9 in Ethiopia, far behind the average for SSA (US$101). Gebreeyesus and

Siba (2017) use firm-level data and confirm that the proportion of firms that do any exporting is very low: between 4 and 6 per cent during the 1995–2009 period, and even lower than that for small firms. The authors point to very high entry and exit costs in the export market as an important explanation.

This pattern for Ethiopia of fairly strong economic performance combined with moderate progress in the industrial sector appears to be at odds with one of the most influential ideas in development economics, namely that the manufacturing sector will be the 'engine of growth' for low-income countries. However, the conventional notion has been disputed. Adrian Wood and collaborators have long argued that since Africa is abundant in natural resources and short on skills, and since manufacturing is intensive in the use of skills but not natural resources, Africa does not have a comparative advantage in manufacturing (Wood 1994). This argument, which is consistent with the fact that Africa tends to export mostly resource-intensive goods and imports skill-intensive ones, suggests that countries like Ethiopia should not design policies to prioritize industrial development. On the other hand, comparative advantages are not static. Relative prices change continuously; in agriculture, for example, increasing pressure on land makes manufacturing production more attractive, shifting resources towards industry. Moreover, policy can affect comparative advantages. For example, as noted by Collier (2000), poor institutions and poor infrastructure hurt manufacturers disproportionally since they are intensive users of these services. General improvements in the investment climate, therefore, can be expected to change relative prices in favour of manufacturing production. Krugman (1980, 1981) shows how comparative advantages in trade can arise as a result of exploiting economies of scale, clustering of production, learning, network effects, and spillovers.

Numerous surveys of the investment climate have been fielded, both of enterprises and industry analysts, generating data that enable us to assess Ethiopia's performance relative to other countries. These indicators suggest that, compared to other less developed countries, Ethiopia's business environment is in fact reasonably good. Table 37.2 shows how Ethiopia ranks in terms of ease of doing business and per capita income among all countries in the world (column 1) and among sub-Saharan African countries (column 2).[2] With regard to per capita income, Ethiopia is ranked 162 out of the 167 countries in the world for which we have data. In contrast, for the same group of 167 countries, Ethiopia ranks 97 in terms of overall ease of doing business. Focusing on sub-Saharan Africa only, Ethiopia ranks 37 out of a total of 42 countries with regard to per capita income. The country is doing well particularly in the ease of starting a business. For example, the required procedure and time to start a business in Ethiopia is less than the sub-Saharan African average and almost equal to the average of OECD countries. With regard to ease of doing business, only eight sub-Saharan African countries are higher ranked than Ethiopia.

[2] The data on per capita income were obtained from the World Development Indicators. The 'doing business' rankings were downloaded from www.doingbusiness.org. The data are for 2010.

Table 37.2 Ease of doing business in Ethiopia

	All countries (N = 167)	Sub-Saharan Africa (N = 42)
Rank: Overall ease of doing business	97	9
Rank: Per capita GDP	162	37
Rank: Per capita GDP (PPP adjusted)	155	31
Rank: Doing business topics		
Starting a business	85	9
Dealing with construction permits	56	7
Employing workers	87	15
Registering property	99	13
Getting credit	118	17
Protecting investors	115	18
Paying taxes	37	8
Trading across borders	146	30
Enforcing contracts	56	7
Closing a business	68	9

Source: Data obtained from www.doingbusiness.org.

Thus, the manufacturing landscape of Ethiopia is somewhat unusual, compared to most other African countries. The business environment is reasonably favourable, but the sector is extremely small and, in relation to other sectors of the economy, not growing. In Section 37.3 we describe the data available on Ethiopia's manufacturing firms and show some descriptive statistics by firm size category.

37.3 Ethiopia's Manufacturing Firms

Research on the constraints, characteristics, and performance of the enterprise sector in low-income countries is often constrained by scarcity of data. In Ethiopia, the data on the formal manufacturing sector is unusually rich, compared to other African countries. Most of the existing data derive from surveys conducted by the Central Statistical Agency (henceforth CSA) of Ethiopia. The most comprehensive survey is the Large and Medium Manufacturing Industries Survey, which attempts to cover all manufacturing establishments in the country that employ ten persons or more and use power-driven machinery. The survey covers both public and private industries in all regions, and is often referred to as a census of manufacturing firms, because of its universal coverage. There is information in the data on output, inputs (local and imported), sales (local and export), employment, location, ownership type, costs, etc. The survey is fielded every year, and the different waves of data can be combined into a panel dataset. The data are not in the public domain, but the CSA has generously been granting access to the data for researchers who want to use it to study the Ethiopian economy. The most recent survey for which detailed data are available on the website of Ethiopia's Central Statistical Agency (CSA), http://www.csa.gov.et, covers 2010/11. In that year, the sector consisted of 2,170 firms and employed 175,698 workers. Average value added per worker was approximately 70,000 birr (US$ 4,100).

As noted, the Large and Medium Manufacturing Industries Survey only covers manufacturing firms with at least ten employees. Manufacturing enterprises (including grain mills) that use power-driven machinery and that engage less than ten people, including owners and family workers, are covered in the Small-Scale Manufacturing Industries Survey. Reports from five survey rounds are currently available: 2001/2, 2005/6, 2007/8, 2009/10, and 2013/14. This sector consisted of 116,606 enterprises in 2013/14, and employed a total of 1.7 million workers. Annual value added per worker was 6,240 birr (US$ 328), which is less than 10 per cent of the value added per worker in the sector of larger firms and considerably lower than Ethiopia's GDP per capita. There is not enough information in these data to enable researchers to construct a panel dataset; however the repeated cross-sections can be used to study some dynamic aspects of the sector, e.g. growth of employment and output, and investment. More details about these data, and survey reports, can be obtained at the CSA's website.

The two surveys described above cover Ethiopia's power-driven manufacturing industry.[3] Next, we combine the data from the surveys to show how value added per worker and average wage vary across the enterprise size range, for the year 2007/8.[4] The data indicate very large productivity differences across firms of differing size. In the category of micro firms, total value added per person engaged is 8,200 birr (US$854). This is more than twice as high—17,400 birr—for the category of firms with 10–19 employees. Among firms with 20–49 employees, value added per worker is 27,200 birr, while for the group of firms with more than 50 employees it reaches 79,400 birr (US$8,271). The magnitude of these differences is quite striking: a worker in a firm with 50 or more employees produces as much value added in an hour as does a worker in a micro enterprise in a day, on average. Wages exhibit a similar pattern, although the rate of increase with firm size is much more modest than for value added. The average wage in small firms with 10–19 workers is fairly similar to that in micro firms. In the group of firms with 50 or more employees, the annual average wage is 11,700 birr across all workers. Important reasons for these large differences between firms of differing size are that larger firms have better technology (capital–labour ratios in the group of firms with 50 or more employees are about ten times higher than that of the micro sector; see Table 37.3), more skilled workers, and better management.

How do wages in the manufacturing sector compare with other sectors? Table 37.3 shows that the annual average labour cost per paid employee in the micro enterprise sector is 3,144 birr (US$328). Consistent with this, Rijkers, Söderbom, and Loening (2010) report survey data indicating that the going daily wage rate for a casual agricultural worker in Ethiopia

[3] In addition, there exist enterprises that do not use power to produce output. This class of enterprise, known as the cottage and handicraft sector, is the technologically least sophisticated segment of manufacturing and engages substantially more people than manufacturing firms with power-based production. We abstract from this sector in the current chapter.

[4] This is the most recent year for which it is possible to obtain comparable data.

Table 37.3 Value added per worker, capital intensity, and average wage by firm size, 2007/8

Size range (number of workers)	Less than 10	10–19	20–49	50+
Survey	Small-scale mfg		Formal mfg	
Value added per worker in birr (US$)	8,200 (854)	17,400 (1,813)	27,200 (2,833)	79,400 (8,271)
Capital installed per worker in birr (US$)	7,269 (757)	22,872 (2,382)	47,611 (4,960)	70,039 (7,296)
Average wage in birr (US$)	3,144 (328)	3,590 (374)	5,750 (599)	11,700 (1,219)

Note: The official exchange rate birr/US$ was 9.6 for 2008 (World Development Indicators).
Source: CSA (2009, 2010) and own calculations.

was then around 9 birr. This suggests that, whether you are a casual worker in a micro enterprise being paid piece rates or a casual agricultural worker, your earnings are similar. It would thus appear unlikely that a transfer of workers from agriculture into the micro enterprise manufacturing sector (in its current form) can generate jobs that result in economic growth. Self-employment in the manufacturing micro enterprise sector offers somewhat better prospects, in terms of earnings. If we subtract labour costs from value added we obtain a basic measure of the surplus that accrues to owners—let us refer to this quantity simply as profits. The data from the small-scale manufacturing industry survey indicate that the total profit divided by the number of owners and unpaid workers (the latter are typically family workers) is equal to about 14,000 birr, which is 4.5 times higher than the average earnings for paid casual workers in this sector. This suggests that individuals equipped with the human and physical capital necessary to run a micro manufacturing enterprise can generate levels of income significantly higher than what casual workers get. However, the available data suggest the amount of installed physical capital is not negligible in the micro manufacturing enterprise sector, averaging 23,300 birr per firm. Few unskilled people can access that sum of money, pointing to the importance of financing for enterprise start-up.

37.4 The Dynamics of Firms and Productivity

In this section we use data from the Large and Medium Manufacturing Industries Survey to document dynamic patterns of firm turnover, productivity levels, and growth rates during the period 1999–2007. The aggregate data discussed above suggest that manufacturing is a small, stable, and slow-changing sector. However, to a considerable extent, the aggregate data mask dynamics and heterogeneity across firms. Table 37.4 shows a breakdown of the number of firms, distinguishing surviving, entering, and

Table 37.4 Number of firms in 1999 and 2007

	Year	
	1999	2007
All firms	587	1141
Surviving firms	251	251
Entering firms		890
Exiting firms	336	

Source: CSA data and own calculations.

Table 37.5 Descriptive statistics for Ethiopian manufacturing firms in 1999 and 2007

	ln value added per employee	Number of employees	
	Mean	Mean	Median
All firms, both periods	7.178	58.7	20
Surviving firms, 1999	7.422	72.6	27
Surviving firms, 2007	7.743	94.2	39
Entering firms	7.049	55.8	18
Exiting firms	6.878	29.3	13.7

Source: CSA data and own calculations.

exiting firms. In the first year of the sampling period there were 587 firms. Of these, 251 firms (43 per cent) survived throughout the entire sampling period and were thus operative in 2007, while 336 firms (57 per cent) exited from the market at some point between 1999 and 2007. In 2007 there were 1,141 firms in total, of which 890 had entered the market at some point after 1999. Hence 78 per cent of the firms in the 2007 cross-section had a firm age of less than eight years. These figures suggest that entry barriers to Ethiopian manufacturing are not very high, while surviving in the market is quite challenging.

Table 37.5 shows descriptive statistics for the different types of firms.[5] The first column shows unweighted mean values of log (real) value added per worker, a standard measure of labour productivity. For the group of firms that survived throughout the sample period (1999–2007), average labour productivity grew from 7.42 (which corresponds to US$1,312) to 7.743 (US$2,305). The group of entering firms had considerably lower average labour productivity than surviving firms, but somewhat higher than exiting firms. Similarly, surviving firms are generally larger than entering firms, and entering firms tend to be larger than exiting firms. There is a strong positive relationship between employment and capital intensity (capital per worker) in the data, and labour productivity differentials across firms of differing size are to a substantial extent due to differences in capital intensity.

[5] For this analysis, all financial values are expressed in constant US$ with base year 2006.

In the remainder of this section we discuss in more detail the broad patterns of firm turnover (exit and entry) and productivity dynamics that can be observed in the data.

37.4.1 Firm Exit and Firm Size

Table 37.4 documents significant entry and exit rates in Ethiopia's manufacturing sector. Exit rates are especially high among small firms. To illustrate the importance of firm size for firm survival, we use probit to model exit as a function of log employment, firm age, and total factor productivity (more details about the latter variable will be provided below). The only statistically significant variable in these models is firm size, which has a negative and quantitatively large effect on the probability of exit. We omit the probit results to conserve space (they are available on request). Instead, based on the probit estimates, we compute predicted exit probabilities for two hypothetical firms: one with ten employees and one with 100 employees. These probabilities are shown in Table 37.6. The likelihood that a firm with 100 employees exits from the market one year after it has been surveyed as part of a baseline (in 1999) is just 0.03. For the firm with ten employees, the exit probability is 0.35. Hence, one out of three small firms in the cross-section will exit over the next year, and one out of thirty large firms. Eight years after the baseline year, the exit probability is 0.72 for the small firm and 0.33 for the large firm. It should be noted that productivity is controlled for in the probit regressions and held constant across the predictions. Hence, productivity differentials are not the reason for the much higher risk of exit among small than among large firms. There is some other factor at play in this context.

It is reasonable to suppose that small firms are more vulnerable to adverse shocks than large firms. Using the Ethiopian firm-level data, Page and Söderbom (2015) highlight that the exit risk for small firms is especially high in the first three years after start-up. Using a subsample of new entrants in Ethiopian manufacturing over the period 1995/6–2005/6, Page and Söderbom model firm exit as a function of size at start-up, firm age, and an interaction term between initial employment and firm age. They find that the interaction term is positive and highly significant, indicating that the adverse effect of small size is particularly pronounced for young firms. Figure 37.2, which reproduces Chart 9 in the study by Page and Söderbom, shows predicted exit rates based on the probit results. It shows that young small firms have very high exit rates. Conditional on surviving, the exit rates are becoming gradually less dependent on start-up size. Thus, there is a class of young, small firms—and some of these are highly productive—that are at high risk of exit.

37.4.2 Productivity Dynamics

In general, aggregate productivity changes because of productivity improvements within surviving firms and as a result of a reallocation of inputs and outputs between surviving, entering, and exiting firms. In order to distinguish between the contributions of these

Table 37.6 Predicted probability of exit before year *t* for a firm in the 1999 cross-section

	Employment at baseline year (1999)	
Year *t*	$EMP_{1999} = 10$	$EMP_{1999} = 100$
2000	0.35	0.03
2001	0.44	0.12
2002	0.48	0.16
2003	0.53	0.19
2004	0.57	0.21
2005	0.62	0.23
2006	0.65	0.26
2007	0.72	0.33

Note: The table shows predicted exit probabilities based on probit specifications of the form $Pr(exit_{it}=1)=\Phi(\beta_0+\beta_1 \ln(EMP_i)+\beta_2 ln(AGE_i+1)+\beta_3 TFP_i)$ where *exit* is a dummy variable for firm exit; EMP_i, *AGEi*, and TFP_i denote number of employees, firm age and total factor productivity for firm *i* in the base year 1999; Φ denotes the cumulative density function; and the *βj* are parameters. The predicted probabilities are evaluated at probit estimates and sample means of the age and tfp variables.

Source: CSA data and own calculations.

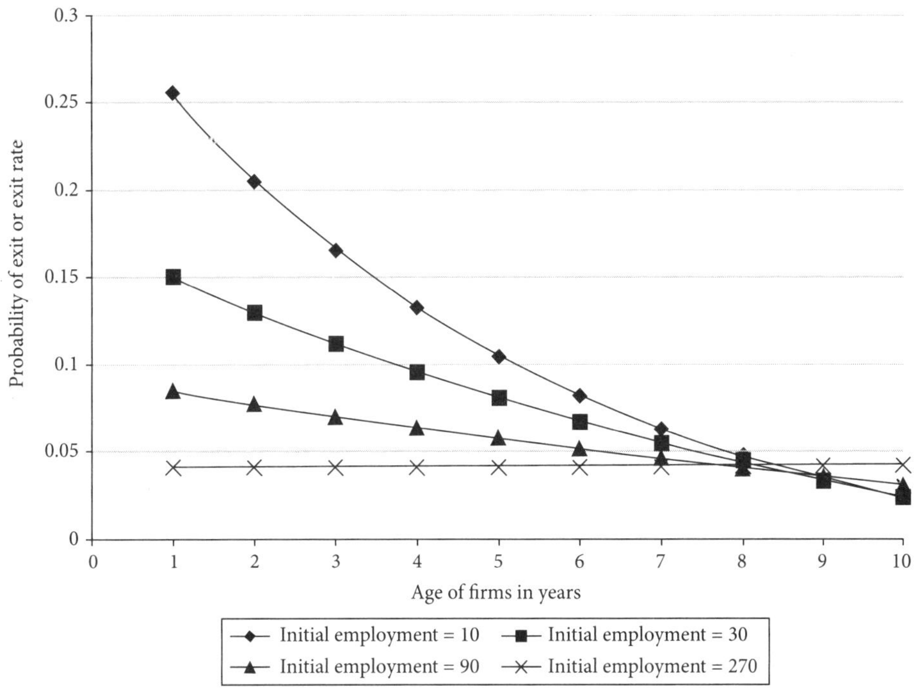

FIGURE 37.2 Firm size, age, and the probability of exit in Ethiopian manufacturing

Source: Adapted from Page and Söderbom (2012).

processes, we now conduct a decomposition of productivity (growth) distinguishing among surviving, entering, and exiting firms. We adopt the approach proposed by Melitz and Polanec (2015), which is a generalization of the method proposed by Olley and Pakes (1996) that accounts for the contributions of surviving, entering, and exiting firms to aggregate productivity levels and changes. Aggregate productivity at time *t* is denoted Φ_t and defined as a share-weighted average of firm productivity φ_{it}:

$$\Phi_t = \sum_i s_{it} \varphi_{it}$$

where the market shares $s_{it} \geq 0$ sum to 1. The underlying productivity measure φ_{it} is in logs, which implies that aggregate productivity growth between periods 1 and 2, denoted $\Delta\Phi_t = \Phi_2 - \Phi_1$, represents a percentage change. Next, decompose aggregate productivity growth into three sets of surviving (*S*), entering (*E*) and exiting (*X*) firms:

$$\Delta\Phi = \sum_{i \in S} \left(s_{i2} \varphi_{i2} - s_{i1} \varphi_{i1} \right) + \sum_{i \in E} s_{i2} \varphi_{i2} - \sum_{i \in X} s_{i1} \varphi_{i1}$$

The first term on the right-hand side, i.e. the contribution of surviving firms, can be further decomposed into one part representing productivity growth *within* firms with shares kept constant, and one part representing changes in market shares *between* firms with productivity levels kept constant:

$$\sum_{i \in S} \left(S_{i2} \varphi_{i2} - S_{i1} \varphi_{i1} \right) = \sum_{i \in S} S_{i1} \left(\varphi_{i2} - \varphi_{i1} \right) + \sum_{i \in S} \left(S_{i2} - S_{i1} \right) \varphi_{i2},$$

Abstracting from entering and exiting firms, Olley and Pakes (1996) rewrite aggregate productivity Φ_t as:

$$\Phi_t = \overline{\varphi_t} + \sum_i \left(s_{it} - \overline{s_t} \right) \left(\varphi_{it} - \overline{\varphi_t} \right) = \overline{\varphi_t} + \operatorname{cov}\left(s_{it}, \varphi_{it} \right)$$

where $\overline{\varphi_t} = n^{-1} \sum_i \varphi_{it}$ is the unweighted firm productivity mean. Aggregate productivity growth over two periods is thus equal to the change in the unweighted mean $\overline{\Delta\varphi_t}$ and change in the covariance between market shares and firm-level productivity. This decomposition highlights the fact that a positive correlation between market shares and productivity is a driver of aggregate productivity. It follows that changes in the correlation between market shares and productivity affect aggregate productivity growth. That is, if the most productive firms tend to increase their market shares, aggregate productivity grows, all else equal.

The main contribution of Melitz and Polanec (2015) was to extend the Olley-Pakes approach to account for entering and exiting firms. Melitz and Polanec thus write aggregate productivity growth as:

$$\Delta\Phi = \Delta\overline{\varphi_s} + \Delta \operatorname{cov}_S + S_{E2}\left(\Phi_{E2} - \Phi_{S2} \right) + S_{X1}\left(\Phi_{X1} - \Phi_{S1} \right),$$

where

$\Delta\overline{\varphi_s}$: Unweighted mean change in the productivity of surviving firms

Δcov_S: Contribution of market share reallocations between surviving firms

$S_{E2}\left(\Phi_{E2}-\Phi_{S2}\right)$: Productivity contribution of entrants, with surviving firms as benchmark

$S_{X1}\left(\Phi_{X1}-\Phi_{S1}\right)$: Productivity contribution of exiting firms, with surviving firms as benchmark

Table 37.7 shows aggregate (average) labour productivity, defined as log value added per worker, and share data for the three types of firms—survivors, entrants, and exiting firms—across all timespans. The average labour productivity for all firms in the first period observed in the data (1999) is 7.80, which corresponds to US$ 2,334 per worker. The firms that survived between 1999 and 2000 accounted for 92 per cent of total

Table 37.7 Aggregate labour productivity and employment shares

		In $t=1$				
Year		Surviving firms		Exiting firms		All firms
$t=1$	$t=2$	Φ_{S1}	S_{S1}	Φ_{X1}	S_{X1}	Φ_1
1999	2000	7.871	0.917	6.984	0.083	7.797
1999	2001	7.979	0.821	6.967	0.179	7.797
1999	2002	8.027	0.786	6.957	0.214	7.797
1999	2003	8.062	0.754	6.987	0.246	7.797
1999	2004	8.066	0.731	7.068	0.269	7.797
1999	2005	8.078	0.714	7.095	0.286	7.797
1999	2006	8.094	0.690	7.136	0.310	7.797
1999	2007	8.135	0.627	7.230	0.373	7.797
		In $t=2$				
Year		Surviving firms		Entering firms		All firms
$t=1$	$t=2$	Φ_{S2}	S_{S2}	Φ_{E2}	S_{E2}	Φ_2
1999	2000	7.903	0.708	7.154	0.292	7.684
1999	2001	7.937	0.673	7.703	0.327	7.860
1999	2002	8.072	0.569	7.495	0.431	7.823
1999	2003	8.112	0.570	7.451	0.430	7.828
1999	2004	8.065	0.530	7.717	0.470	7.901
1999	2005	8.040	0.484	7.697	0.516	7.863
1999	2006	8.051	0.411	7.767	0.589	7.884
1999	2007	8.179	0.316	7.627	0.684	7.802

Source: CSA data and own calculations.

employment, while the firms that exited during this period accounted for 8 per cent of total employment. The average of the labour productivity measure among the firms that survived at least until 2000 was 7.87, which corresponds to US$ 2,620 per worker, while the average of the labour productivity measure among the firms that exited after 1999 was 6.98 (US$ 1,078 per worker). Hence, the firms that exited had considerably lower initial labour productivity than the surviving firms, implying that the group of exiting firms lowered aggregate labour productivity in 1999. This pattern is qualitatively the same for all timespans. Average labour productivity during 1999 for the group of firms that survived at least until 2007 was 8.14 (US$ 3,412 per worker), and 7.23 (US$ 1,380) for the group of firms that exited during the 1999–2007 period.

The lower panel of Table 37.7 shows data on the productivity contributions of new entrants. The average labour productivity for all firms in the second period observed in the data (2000) is 7.68, which corresponds to US$ 2,174 per worker. The firms that had survived until 2000 accounted for 71 per cent of total employment in 2000, while new entrants accounted for 29 per cent of total employment in that year. The average of the labour productivity measure in 2000 among the surviving firms was 7.90 (US$ 2,706 per worker), while the average of the labour productivity measure among entering firms was 7.15 (US$ 1,279). Hence, the entering firms had considerably lower average labour productivity than the surviving firms, implying that the group of new entrants contributed negatively to aggregate labour productivity in 2000. This pattern holds qualitatively for all time spans. Average labour productivity during 2007 for the group of firms that had existed at least since 1999 was 8.18 (US$ 3,565), and 7.63 (US$ 2,054) for the group of firms that had entered after 1999.

One reason for the higher labour productivity among surviving firms, compared to firms that (are about to) exit and new entrants, is selection and 'survival of the fittest'. That is, productive firms may simply last longer. The link between productivity and enterprise longevity has been studied quite extensively in the literature on firms in Africa (e.g. Frazer 2005; Söderbom, Teal, and Harding 2006; Shiferaw 2007, 2009; Bigsten and Gebreeyesus 2007). Several of these have analysed the Ethiopian data. Shiferaw (2007), for example, tracks Ethiopian firms over seven years (1996–2002) and shows that relatively efficient firms are more likely to survive and stay at the top of the productivity distribution while the exit hazard is substantially higher among inefficient firms. Hence, this literature indeed suggests a positive relationship between underlying total factor productivity and firm survival. Ethiopian firms, just like firms in other parts of the world, are subject to market selection.

An additional possible explanation for the higher labour productivity among surviving firms is that firms learn to grow their underlying total factor productivity over time. To shed some light on whether such learning is taking place, we now study TFP growth within and between firms. For this analysis we calculate TFP as a residual from a production function:

$$\ln TFP_{it} = \ln VAD_{it} - \hat{\beta}_0 - \hat{\beta}_K \ln K_{it} - \hat{\beta}_L \ln L_{it}$$

where VAD_{it}, K_{it}, and L_{it} denote real value added, real capital, and employment, respectively, of firm i in year t, and $\hat{\beta}_0, \hat{\beta}_K, \hat{\beta}_L$, are OLS estimates. We estimate the production function separately for each industrial subsector, hence $\hat{\beta}_0, \hat{\beta}_K, \hat{\beta}_L$, vary across subsectors. For the decomposition of TFP growth, we use value-added shares as weights. Table 37.8 shows the contributions to TFP growth of surviving, entering, and exiting firms, with 1999 as the base year. Column 6 shows total TFP growth, and the decomposition is shown in columns 1–5.

Over the entire sampling period, 1999–2007, average ln TFP grew by 0.61, which corresponds to 83 per cent growth or about 8 per cent growth per year. The surviving firms contributed 0.34 in total. The contribution of changes in the covariance between market shares and productivity was very small, implying that the contribution of surviving firms was driven almost entirely by within-firm growth—which may be due to learning. New entrants contribute 0.37, i.e. approximately as much as surviving firms, to aggregate productivity growth. The contribution of exiting firms is qualitatively as expected (i.e. negative) but quantitatively modest (−0.10). Hence, long-run growth in manufacturing is primarily sourced from intra-firm productivity growth and from the process by which new entrants replace failing firms, thus making better use of fixed resources. Shiferaw (2007) makes a similar point based on his analysis of data from an earlier period.

While we do not address in detail the drivers of intra-firm productivity growth in this chapter, there are a number of plausible contenders. Chapter 9 shows very high import intensity of intermediate inputs in Ethiopian manufacturing. Given the critical shortage of foreign exchange in Ethiopia in recent years, this is very likely to undermine capacity utilization and productivity growth. Some authors argue that the labour cost advantages

Table 37.8 Melitz-Polanec decomposition of TFP growth

	Surviving firms			Entering firms	Exiting firms	All firms
	(1) Total	(2) Unweighted mean change	(3) Contribution of market share reallocations	(4) Total	(5) Total	(6) Total
Year		$\Delta\overline{\varphi_s}$	Δcov_s	$S_{E2}(\Phi_{E2}-\Phi_{S2})$	$S_{X1}(\Phi_{X1}-\Phi_{S1})$	$\Phi_2-\Phi_1$
2000	0.010	0.021	−0.010	0.016	0.005	0.031
2001	0.194	0.036	0.158	0.021	−0.086	0.129
2002	0.069	0.184	−0.116	0.019	−0.077	0.010
2003	−0.034	0.108	−0.143	0.223	−0.076	0.113
2004	0.088	0.171	−0.083	0.150	−0.076	0.162
2005	0.042	0.251	−0.209	0.247	−0.082	0.208
2006	0.223	0.231	−0.008	0.305	−0.081	0.446
2007	0.342	0.339	0.004	0.367	−0.103	0.606

Source: CSA data and own calculations.

of African countries relative to East Asian countries may actually be offset by high input costs (Abegaz 2018). Shiferaw (2016) also shows lacklustre investment in Ethiopian manufacturing particularly among firms that do not have relationships with banks. Given the strong link between investment in modern machinery and technology transfer in low-income countries, weak investment may contribute to slow productivity growth in addition to constraining capacity expansion. On the up side, continued public investment in infrastructure, education, and skill development are expected to help manufacturers improve their productivity.

37.5 Conclusions

It is often argued that a poor investment climate is an important reason why growth in most of Africa's industrial sector has been weak. Firms producing tradeables, particularly manufacturers, are extensive users of investment climate services, and a poor investment climate thus hampers such firms disproportionally (Collier 2000). In recent years, while recognizing that the investment climate has an important role to play, some commentators have argued for the need to go beyond a focus on regulation in order to understand more fully the constraints on growth. It has been argued that a policy agenda aimed at facilitating for manufacturing development should acknowledge the important roles of infrastructure, post-primary education, and regional integration, for example (Page 2012). Ethiopia provides a very good case study for researchers who wish to document the importance of factors that are not strongly associated with the investment climate. We began this study by showing that Ethiopia's manufacturing sector is underdeveloped compared with the sub-Saharan benchmark, both in terms of its relative size and its international competitiveness (gauged by its weak presence in export markets), despite the fact that the business environment is reasonable. It has been beyond the scope of this chapter to identify what other factors could be constraining manufacturing in Ethiopia. We have, however, documented some striking differences in firm performance, especially across firms of differing size, and we have identified some areas that deserve closer attention by researchers and policymakers. Our analysis of firm survival suggests that small firms are particularly vulnerable to shocks in the first four years of operation. During this phase, we observe high exit rates among small firms, some of which have a high underlying productivity. A better understanding of the reasons for these patterns could help in the formulation of policies that help young, small, and productive firms to survive. Our analysis of productivity growth shows that aggregate TFP growth is driven, in roughly equal measures, by growth among existing firms and by new entrants. This suggests that potential entrants constitute an untapped potential for further growth. It would appear that a better understanding of the barriers to entry into the sector could be helpful in order to design policies that facilitate entry for more firms and thus the creation of more jobs. Manufacturers are expected to play a central role in the Growth and Transformation Plan of the Ethiopian government that aims, among other things, to make Ethiopia a lower middle-income country by 2025 (see Chapter 5). There is considerable potential for growth and development of the sector, and it is hoped that this chapter has identified some areas in which obstacles need to be better understood and subsequently removed in order for the sector to take off.

Acknowledgements

We are grateful to Christopher Cramer for insightful comments on draft versions of this paper. All errors are our own. Söderbom would like to dedicate this chapter to the memory of his friend Krister Backlund who passed away in May 2018.

References

Abegaz, B. (2018). *Industrial Development in Africa: Mapping Industrial Pathways for a Leaping Leopard* (London: Routledge).

Bigsten, Arne and Mulu Gebreeyesus (2007). 'The Small, the Young, and the Productive: Determinants of Manufacturing Firm Growth in Ethiopia', *Economic Development and Cultural Change* 55: 813–40.

Bigsten, Arne, Mulu Gebreeyesus, and Måns Söderbom (2016). 'Tariffs and Firm Performance in Ethiopia', *Journal of Development Studies* 52 (7): 986–1001.

Collier, Paul. (2000). 'Africa's Comparative Advantage', in *Industrial Development and Policy in Africa*, ed. H. Jalilian, M. Tribe, and J. Weiss (Cheltenham: Edward Elgar): 151–69.

Frazer, Garth (2005). 'Which Firms Die? A Look at Exit from Manufacturing in Ghana', *Economic Development and Cultural Change* 53 (3): 585–617.

Gebreeyesus, Mulu (2016). 'Industrial Policy and Development in Ethiopia', in *Manufacturing Transformation: Comparative Studies of Industrial Development in Africa and Emerging Asia*, ed. Carol Newman, John Page, John Rand, et al. (Oxford: Oxford University Press): 27–49.

Gebreeyesus, Mulu and Eyerusalem Siba (2017). 'Learning to Export and Learning by Exporting: The Case of Ethiopian Manufacturing', *Journal of African Economies* 26 (1): 1–23.

Krugman, Paul (1980). 'Scale Economies, Product Differentiation, and the Pattern of Trade', *American Economic Review* 70 (5): 950–9.

Krugman, Paul (1981). 'Intraindustry Specialization and the Gains from Trade', *Journal of Political Economy* 89 (5): 959–73.

Melitz, Marc J. and Saso Polanec (2015). 'Dynamic Olley-Pakes Productivity Decomposition with Entry and Exit', *RAND Journal of Economics* 46 (2): 362–75.

Olley, G. Steven and Ariel Pakes (1996). 'The Dynamics of Productivity in the Telecommunications Equipment Industry', *Econometrica* 64 (6): 1263–97.

Page, John (2012). 'Can Africa Industrialize?' *Journal of African Economies* 21 (AERC Supplement 2): ii86–ii125.

Page, John and Māns Söderbom (2015). 'Is Small Beautiful? Small Enterprise, Aid and Employment in Africa', African Development Review 27(S1): 44–55.

Rijkers, Bob, Måns Söderbom, and Josef Loening (2010). 'A Rural Urban Comparison of Manufacturing Enterprise Performance in Ethiopia', *World Development* 38 (9): 1278–96.

Shiferaw, Admasu (2007). 'Firm Heterogeneity and Market Selection in Sub-Saharan Africa: Does It Spur Industrial Progress?' *Economic Development and Cultural Change* 55 (2): 393–423.

Shiferaw, Admasu (2009). 'Survival of Private Sector Manufacturing Establishments in Africa: The Role of Productivity and Ownership', *World Development* 37 (3): 572–84.

Shiferaw, Admasu (2016). 'Constraints to Private Investment in a High-growth Environment: Firm-level Evidence from Ethiopia', Working Paper No. 168, The College of William and Mary, Department of Economics.

Shiferaw, Admasu and Arjun S. Bedi (2013). 'The Dynamics of Job Creation and Job Destruction in an African Economy: Evidence from Ethiopia', *Journal of African Economies* 22 (5): 651–92.

Shiferaw, Admasu, Måns Söderbom, Eyerusalem Siba, and Getnet Alemu (2015). 'Road Infrastructure and Enterprise Dynamics in Ethiopia', *Journal of Development Studies* 51 (11): 1541–58.

Söderbom, Måns (2012). 'Firm Size and Structural Change: A Case Study of Ethiopia', *Journal of African Economies* (AERC Supplement 2) (21): ii126–ii151.

Söderbom, Måns, Francis Teal, and Alan Harding (2006). 'The Determinants of Survival among African Manufacturing Firms', *Economic Development and Cultural Change* 54 (3): 533–55.

Wood, Adrian (1994). *North-South Trade, Employment and Inequality: Changing Fortunes in a Skill-Driven World* (Oxford: Clarendon Press).

CHAPTER 38

BUILDING AN INDUSTRIAL WORKFORCE IN ETHIOPIA

CARLOS OYA

> There is no such thing as economic growth which is not, at the same time, growth or change of a culture; and the growth of social consciousness, like the growth of a poet's mind, can never, in the last analysis, be planned.
>
> (E. P. Thompson 1967: 97)

38.1 Introduction

BUILDING on years of rapid economic growth to generate a sustained process of structural change and high-quality employment growth is a major challenge. Ethiopia, like many other African countries, is experiencing a youth bulge in a context in which a demographic transition in Africa is not evident yet (Meagher 2016). The lack of higher-productivity jobs until only recently means that a very large proportion of the population is still employed in very low-productivity agricultural and 'informal' service activities, and unemployment rates in large urban centres remain high despite steady decline since the 1990s (Meagher, Mann, and Bolt 2016; World Bank 2016; Martins 2016). As Oqubay (Chapter 35) warns, the Ethiopian economy has thus far made limited progress in providing decent permanent jobs for the rapidly expanding young labour force and better-educated population, thus threatening economic and political stability.

To be sure, there are signs of positive trends. Unemployment and underemployment rates have declined in both urban and rural areas since the 1990s (World Bank 2016: 33); labour participation rates have increased with dependency ratios declining (EEA 2016; CSA 2014); and some structural change has taken place in the past ten years. However, much of this is not of the 'classic' type associated with rapid industrialization

(Martins 2016). The acceleration in manufacturing development in recent years is yet to be reflected in up-to-date statistics on employment shares, as Section 38.2 will show.

Therefore labour surplus transfer from agriculture to more productive activities will represent one of the biggest challenges that the Ethiopian economy, society, and state will face in the medium to long run. As Amsden (2001) puts it, poverty reduction will not be possible with only supply-side measures without attention to 'jobs', i.e. by forgetting about the demand side of the employment equation. However, we also know from history that building an industrial labour force is a lengthy and uneven process that has taken generations in many of today's industrialized countries. Moreover, the rise of automation in manufacturing also means that less employment per capital invested can be created so the contribution of other sectors remains critical.

This chapter will provide an overview of the factors and dynamics involved in the creation and formation of an industrial workforce in an agrarian-based economy. This is a long-standing issue that has been a theme in much of classic political economy as well as in the 'old' development economics tradition. The topic is relevant for contemporary Ethiopia if the current take-off of industrial development is followed by sustained growth and consolidation of manufacturing activities as sources of employment and linkages with the rest of the economy. The main argument is that the process of building an industrial working class is uneven, protracted, and requires interventions and a range of important economic and social shifts over a sustained period. Having a large pool of young labour and potentially competitive labour costs is no guarantee that industrial investors will not find significant obstacles in the labour market. Historical lessons of early and late industrializers are highly relevant for contemporary Ethiopia as it seems that history does repeat itself in some ways.

The chapter will be organized as follows. The first section will provide basic analytical and conceptual pointers on the dynamics of labour surplus transfer, and the realities of such employment shifts in the Ethiopian context. This will be followed by a brief analysis of key social and cultural barriers to the formation of an industrial working class and how the current obstacles referred to by emerging industrial investors in Ethiopia have a long history in previous experiences of rapid industrialization. This point connects with the problematic of finding and retaining workers, managing migrant labour, and especially the role of housing, an issue often repeated in current debates on industrial parks in Ethiopia. The following section documents the current skill gaps and historical lessons on the process of skill development and industrial working-class formation in other successful cases of industrialization in relevant sectors. Finally, a discussion of clashes of expectations and how they can affect the early stages of industrial development will be necessary to understand worker retention problems, and instances of conflict that many firms face in these initial phases. These sections also show that varieties of industrial capitalism (and of 'capital') observed in contemporary developing countries in the past thirty years are relevant to understand the challenges and options facing Ethiopia today. The concluding section will summarize some of the key challenges Ethiopia faces in making sure that current industrialization efforts respond to the employment challenge of creating mass jobs in more productive activities, at the same time ensuring that labour-related constraints do not slow down the acceleration of manufacturing development.

38.2 Building an Industrial Workforce in Contemporary Ethiopia

The aim of this core section is to consider key medium and long-run challenges for Ethiopia's process of building an industrial workforce. This analysis is based on an understanding of relevant historical experiences and the particular situation of Ethiopia's economy and labour markets as of 2018. The chapter draws on a selective review of key studies on other experiences of industrialization, relevant secondary sources on labour structures and shifts in Ethiopia, as well as some material from qualitative research and fieldwork conducted in Hawassa Industrial Park and other industrial areas in Addis Ababa and surroundings in 2017 and 2018.

38.2.1 Structural Change and Labour Surplus Transfer

The dominant narrative suggests that Ethiopia has a very large pool of labour still employed in low-productivity activities or simply unemployed, which can be the basis for a dynamic labour surplus transfer. Does Ethiopia conform to the classic Lewis context of labour surplus transfer with 'unlimited supplies of labour' (Lewis 1957)? In some ways it does, insofar as the contemporary emergence of a modern capitalist sector (often equated with industrial activities but not necessarily so) can create conditions for both static and dynamic labour surplus transfers. However, even in a scenario with unlimited supplies of labour, labour surplus transfer from low-productivity subsistence activities is neither automatic nor inevitable (Thirlwall 2011). Furthermore, labour surplus transfer can also happen towards other equally low-productivity activities in non-farm sectors, as is the case in Ethiopia and many African countries.

What is the evidence of labour transfer dynamics in contemporary Ethiopia? For static and dynamic labour surplus transfer to happen, and to eventually accelerate, the supply side of the story is not enough. On the supply side, some research suggests there is a demographic dividend in Ethiopia. Martins (2016) argues that since 2005 there are signs of demographic transition (falling fertility rates) and a potential demographic dividend demonstrated by a sharp increase in the proportion of the working-age population and the employment rate.[1] On the demand side, however, there is still scant evidence that sectoral employment shares are changing rapidly, at least until 2014 for which we have

[1] This is in contrast with evidence of a stalled demographic transition in many other parts of Africa, where dependency ratios remain stubbornly high, also because a sharp decline in the proportion of youth leaving the parental household by the age of 25, as documented by Meagher (2016: 489).

published statistics. According to the EEA 2016 report on the Ethiopian economy and with data from the latest labour force survey (2013/14), the Ethiopian labour force is still predominantly rural and agrarian-based, and it keeps growing. Despite ongoing urbanization, the rural population grew by 23 million between 2001 and 2014, of whom 13.1 million are of working age. Most rural employment is officially recorded as unpaid family workers (55 per cent). Given increasing land fragmentation and less viable land-based livelihoods, alternative employment options will be imperative in order to absorb all the additional labour force in the coming fifty years. Additional employment for the growing mass of rural labour may be created via structural change and industrialization as well as through the transformation of the agricultural sector, in the form of the rise of technologically dynamic export agriculture as argued by Melese (see Chapter 31). Martins (2016) shows that the structure of *production* has changed considerably, reflected in faster decline of agriculture in total GDP, but the composition of *employment* has been slow since the 1990s, and basically reflects the expansion of services, in activities like trade, transport, and other services, mostly as low-productivity 'informal' jobs.[2] In sum, the picture that emerges from available official data is one of (a) continuous growth in the rural labour force with a large proportion of labour market entrants who are under 25; (b) significant unemployment in large urban centres, disproportionately affecting more educated youth, especially those with secondary and post-secondary education; and (c) a high degree of informality and uncertainty in employment, with a large pool of labour stuck in low-productivity activities in micro-scale services and agriculture. This evidence suggests that there is not only substantial potential rural–urban migration but also that mass job creation is also needed in rural areas.

Three important caveats need to be understood when considering labour surplus dynamics and the role of industrialization in Ethiopia. First, the 'modern' sector does not need to be in manufacturing strictly speaking, as other sub-sectors can also generate high-productivity jobs and job linkages with industry-related activities are equally important. Second, the process is likely to be a long and probably uneven one, as in previous historical experiences. Third, there may be current obstacles to a more rapid transition that will need to be managed. Let us discuss these issue in turn.

First, the Lewis model of labour surplus transfer is based on a dual economy with two fundamentally different sectors, the modern-capitalist and the traditional-non capitalist, separated by a gulf in productivity levels. However, in reality economic structures even in poor countries are far more differentiated. The agricultural sector contains a range of types of farms along a productivity continuum, rather than simply 'subsistence'

[2] This evidence is based on the CSA labour force surveys of 1999, 2005, and 2013, which do not capture the impressive growth in manufacturing employment since 2014. Manufacturing employment also grew rapidly between 2002 and 2014 from less than 40,000 workers to over 200,000 (Ansu et al. 2016). Still, even with this recent impressive growth, employment structures have not substantially changed. Similar patterns of employment shares have been observed in much of Africa in the past twenty-five years (Diao, Harttgen, and McMillan 2017). Jayne, Chamberlin, and Benfica (2018) show that much of the employment shifts observed in dynamic African countries have been between agriculture and employment expansion in informal rural off-farm activities.

farming, but households may still make the maintenance of own farm a priority (Thirlwall 2011). The agricultural sector also includes sub-sectors that look more like industrial fields and absorb part of the labour surplus. Floriculture is an example of this in Ethiopia. The development of this sector has not only created thousands of direct jobs (over 40,000, mostly for unskilled women) but also generated even more indirect jobs, as in the production of cardboard packaging, logistical services, cold storage, and additional jobs via *induced* demand for services arising in the areas receiving flower investments: bars, hotels, construction, motorized rickshaw transport, etc. (Oqubay 2015: 49).[3] Thus labour surplus transfer can happen in stages and between sectors that blur the boundaries between agriculture and industry.[4]

Second, the process of building an industrial and non-agricultural labour force is uneven, protracted, and often slowed down by multiple obstacles. Historically the formation of an industrial labour force in Europe took a long time, gradually building from the 'industrious revolution' preceding the industrial revolution as far back as the early eighteenth century (De Vries 1994). It took over five hundred years for France to see a reduction in the share of agriculture in its labour force from over 70 per cent to about 40 per cent (Broadberry and Gardner 2016: 32). Yet, evidence from Asia since the 1960s and the recent experience from Ethiopia and other African countries (Newman et al. 2016) suggest that three factors produce a different set of conditions that allow a speeding up of the labour transfer dynamics for industrialization: (a) new international division of labour and the rapid transition from old to new sources of manufacturing production, making it possible for low-income countries to industrialize despite low income per capita; (b) the dynamics of global production networks and flexible sourcing, which permit an expansion in the centres of production on a flexible basis over short periods of time; and (c) technological change affecting production processes in different manufacturing sectors and in different countries, which opens up possibilities for 'trade in tasks'. So, Ethiopia will potentially not need to wait so long to substantially increase the proportion of jobs in dynamic high-productivity capitalist sectors.

Third, low productivity in 'subsistence' sectors is not enough to push a transfer towards new capitalist sectors. Thirlwall (2011: 216) notes that the wage differential between the new industrial (capitalist) sectors and 'subsistence' agriculture should at least offset the higher living costs in an urban or new environment, compensate for the 'forfeit of non-monetary benefits of rural life', and possibly compensate for more uncertainty in industrial employment if workers are not given permanent positions and turnover is high. This is highly relevant to Ethiopia as there is much debate around the adequacy of the level of wages initially offered by new industrial investors, as well as the living

[3] Oqubay (2015): 'evidence suggests that one job created in manufacturing will create a larger number of jobs in other sectors than one job in any other part of the economy.'

[4] Recent research from the World Bank also suggests that economic migration from rural areas to nearby towns rather than big cities holds substantial potential in terms of poverty reduction (Christiaensen et al. 2018).

conditions around the industrial workplace.[5] There are other potential hurdles for a more successful labour surplus transfer, which are analysed in more detail in the following sections: addressing socio-cultural barriers and the problem of 'work cultures' and work ethic; sourcing workers and managing migrant labour; scarcity of employable skills (including soft skills); and the mismatch in expectations between employers and workers.[6]

These potential obstacles are all inter-related. The development of skills and adaptation to industrial work environments depends on the process of change in social norms, i.e. on the social construction of a work ethic for industrial capital; managing expectations also depends on how quickly such adaptation takes place; likewise finding and retaining workers depends on successful management of different expectations, developing the required skills, paying fair wages and creating the infrastructure that makes the transition easier to bear.

38.2.2 Industrialization, Social Change, and Work Cultures

Historical analysis has shed light on how the process of building an industrial workforce is as much about social and cultural change as it is about economic.[7] There are multiple aspects to this process but for the purposes of this analysis it is worth focusing on the issues of time management and work discipline (or 'work ethic' as it is frequently called) as well as gender norms. Work ethic is a recurrent theme in conversations with foreign managers about their encounters with workers in new manufacturing destinations. In Ethiopia, the perceived lack of work ethic and discipline is a major complaint among newly arrived factory managers, especially those from Asia, who invest in developing 'social skills' among new workers, i.e. precisely timekeeping, understanding incentives, and reactive speed to boost productivity.[8] However, culturalist explanations are unconvincing as such complaints are historically recurrent. Kohli (2004: 370) convincingly argues that the issue of work ethic and productivity is socially constructed 'either by corporations or by state structures and policies'. In other words, work cultures evolve and are shaped by broader economic and political changes.

Thompson (1967), in his analysis of early capitalist transitions, contrasts the task orientation of economic and social life in agrarian-based societies and their seasonal and irregular rhythms with the precise time focus and discipline of industrial capitalism. The introduction of new work habits did not just take the form of workplace timesheets, timekeeping, and sticks and carrots on time management. It was a complex and

[5] Interviews with trade union representatives (CETU) and firm managers (August 2017 and March 2018).

[6] These issues have also been selected in light of the most common challenges mentioned by new industrial investors, trade union leaders, government officials, and new manufacturing workers in interviews conducted in 2017 and 2018.

[7] E. P. Thompson (1963) is a classic example of such analysis in his *Making of the English Working Class*.

[8] Interviews in Hawassa and Bole Lemi industrial parks, August 2017.

all-encompassing process spanning factory relations, ideology, schooling, and cultural habits. New labour habits were thus formed over several generations through various interlinked mechanisms, e.g. division of labour, specialization, labour supervision fines, clocks, bells, financial incentives, lectures, and the suppression or marginalization of manifestation of tradition, in order to progressively improve the 'commitment to the industrial way of life' (Thompson 1967: 90–3). Many of these discourses and processes are reproduced in contemporary experiences of structural change; as Thompson (1967: 91) puts it: 'what was said by the mercantilist moralists as to the failures of the eighteenth-century English poor to respond to incentives and disciplines is often repeated, by observers and by theorists of economic growth, of the peoples of developing countries today'.[9] Resistance to socio-cultural change and specifically to proletarianization is indeed a recurrent theme in the political economy of development, especially when there is no complete divorce from the land.

Recent episodes of labour-intensive industrialization in Asia present similar obstacles. The fear of losing workers after some time when migrants do not fully commit to the factory way of life, as explained by various factory managers in Ethiopian industrial parks, is documented by authors researching new industrial working classes in Southeast Asia, for example, how young rural–urban migrants in Cambodia or Vietnam still perceive themselves as 'rural people' and see factory employment as a stepping stone to a return to the village in better conditions or to other less demanding but equally remunerative activities (Peou 2016; Tran 2013). Whether this aspiration is fulfilled or the one-way migration is consolidated is an empirical question (Carswell and De Neve 2013).

The issue is not simply the transition to industrial factory jobs, but rather the penetration of capitalist relations of production driven by productivity imperatives. In fact, there is a well-established 'work ethic' discourse that has been historically found in most instances of capitalist penetration, also in plantation agriculture (see Alatas 1977; O'Laughlin 2016). As argued by O'Laughlin (2016) we all have socially constructed 'work cultures', but dominant discourses focus on the individual when work cultures are collective in nature and are shaped by labour relations and different production processes. Indeed sustained productivity increases are the result of complex structural forces that transcend individual performance as understood by managers, and require the deployment of investment, infrastructure, and state-mediated systems of labour control, as Kohli (2004) and Amsden (2001) explain in their studies of industrialization in developing countries.

Finally, social norms and cultural adaptation are also critical for the incorporation of women in factory work. Emerging labour-intensive factories in Ethiopia employ a large proportion of women, and gendered socio-cultural 'clashes' are worth considering. Evidence of such encounters abounds in the literature on industrialization in Asia.

[9] See also O'Laughlin (2016) on the 'cultures of work' and how patronizing discourses of 'lack of work culture' mask the variety of reasons underpinning low productivity and apparent lack of effort, which reflect conflictive perspectives from managers and employees. Behind a particular 'culture of work' often lie disaffection, class struggle, and thus conflict over effort.

For example, Ong (1987) argues that for Malaysian women factory workers the move from task-based village activities interwoven 'into the flow of social life' (p. 111) to the regimented patterns of industrial work was 'traumatic' (p. 168). Kabeer (1991) and Kibria (1998) both note how censure from home communities could inhibit workforce participation in Bangladesh, but such constraints seem negotiable given the large numbers of rural women in garment clusters all over Asia. In Bangladesh, Feldman (2009) notes that the state and NGOs enacted a process of acculturation to women's participation in paid work before the garment sector took off, and factories had to de-sexualize the factory environment in order to project an image of factories as consonant with the local moral expectations (Kabeer 1991). Once taboos were broken, migrant networks were established and earlier migrants facilitated access to employment in factories for new migrant women (Kibria 1998). In short, as with problems of 'work ethic', social change happens and norms are negotiated and reframed.

38.2.3 Finding and Accommodating Workers

The previous two sections have documented some of the obstacles affecting a smooth and rapid labour surplus transfer and the building of an industrial workforce. Despite the expected pool of available labour in Ethiopia, there are still questions of how to source workers, especially considering that the use of migrant labour in factories is a well-established fact in early industrializers and especially in the Asian context. Thus, many industrial investors ask whether workers will be available in the vicinity of factories and industrial parks or whether they will need to look for 'labour reservoirs' elsewhere.[10] Meanwhile, the question that the Ethiopian federal and regional governments ask is how to make job creation as inclusive as possible and give opportunities to young people, especially women, from different areas of the country. In short, having millions of potential workers scattered across parts of a large country with difficult terrain is no guarantee that factories will find workers easily.

The policy of development of industrial parks has generated opportunities to attract thousands of migrant workers from rural areas or nearby towns. More than 40,000 jobs have been generated in recent years by industrial parks, especially government ones (see Chapter 35). Most of these jobs are for unskilled or semi-skilled workers with limited educational background and often from rural areas, according to most factory managers interviewed. In the course of research conducted in some of these parks it soon became apparent that managing the move of thousands of people from rural areas to industrial clusters, and the infrastructure needed to accommodate this labour transfer, requires careful planning and potentially large investments. Both investors

[10] There is evidence that the proportion of migrant population within different areas of the country is high. Abebe et al. (2016) report 36 per cent of migrants mostly from Amhara and Oromo in a large sample of job seekers in Addis. Labour force statistics also report proportions of migrants between 45 and 55 per cent in most urban areas (CSA 2014). Rural-rural migration also represents one-third of total recorded migration in 2013.

and government may contribute to create the infrastructure needed to absorb large inflows of people in unprepared towns or areas surrounding the parks. But this process is resource intensive and takes time. Thus frictions and obstacles in the early stages of operation of parks may be common in areas around the newly built parks.

The recent Asian industrialization record shows that attracting and housing migrant workers is a critical aspect of the labour-sourcing problem. In Cambodia, as in Ethiopia, a steady stream of rural migrants move to factory sites in search of more regular cash, generating substantial competition for jobs, and therefore low wages (Derks 2008). However, when migrants arrive, they face living costs they did not anticipate and struggle to make ends meet in the initial stages, adding to potential high turnover in newly established factories. In some cases migrant workers depend on their rural households supplementing their low factory wages with resources such as rice (Kibria 1998). Alternatively firms or the state have to supplement wages with provisions that add to the social wage.

Housing is a key need. As evidence shows in Asia, the requirements of a 'migrant labour regime' in terms of housing and other social reproduction needs, are significant. Migrant labour regimes in Asia often come with the expansion of dormitory labour where companies are forced to invest in workers' housing to ensure an adequate supply of cheap labour from poorer regions of the country, as the case of China's export-oriented industrial zones of Guangdong, Zhejiang, and Shanghai demonstrates (Pun and Smith 2007). Although this may also help factories enhance labour control, a dormitory regime may be resisted by firms that are not prepared to allocate resources to workers' accommodation with the added risk of having to meet highly demanding standards required by their buyers, as reported by a number of reluctant companies in Hawassa Industrial Park. According to our own interviews and information from the ILO Addis Ababa office, the proportion of T&G firms providing housing or housing allowances is still very low, although most provide workers with transport.

In Ethiopia, in the absence of large company-owned workers' dormitories or workers' 'towns' as in some Chinese and other Asian cities, the government must balance the options of extending public housing for migrant workers arriving in Hawassa, Mekelle, Dukem, or Dire Dawa against incentivizing the private sector and domestic residents to contribute to the expansion of the rental market. The first option requires large-scale investment that may not be immediately affordable in the absence of adequate finance. The latter option is subject to the uncertainty of take-up from local residents and real estate entrepreneurs, credit market constraints, and indeed the moral hazard of potentially high rents for workers who earn low wages.[11] Perhaps a three-pronged approach of combining public housing with (non-company-linked) industrial park dormitories and local rental accommodation may provide a good mix of incentives for workers with different preferences and constraints and make the 'eco-systems' surrounding the parks more enticing for rural-based workers who may otherwise be put off by a harsh working

[11] In various interviews with factory managers and trade union leaders the private housing option in Hawassa was questioned in terms of its potential scalability.

environment in terms of accommodation and local services. Much depends on how expectations are managed and the tolerance that migrant workers display in each context (see Section 38.2.5).

An alternative option, if labour supply is constrained by conditions in urban centres, is to locate factories in rural areas, i.e. to move where the sources of cheaper labour are. Reasons for this vary. Tran (2013) notes that in Vietnam there is a national wage zoning system and investors have relocated to rural areas to take advantage of the fact they are in low minimum wage zones. In other contexts such as South India (Carswell and De Neve 2013) and Cambodia (Derks 2008) factories have relocated to villages in order to access labour that would otherwise not be willing to enter factory work or migrate. Whether this is an option for Ethiopia in the future remains to be seen but clearly not in the current context given existing infrastructure gaps.

38.2.4 Developing Skills

Finding and housing workers coming from different parts of the country is challenging enough, but making sure they are employable and potentially productive so as to sustain the expansion of a globally competitive industry in Ethiopia is demanding too.

Evidence suggests that Ethiopia's skills gap remains substantial considering the needs of a fast-expanding industrial sector. Comparatively, the quality of Ethiopia's labour supply on average appears lower than many other African countries both in terms of nutrition indicators and in terms of education levels, despite vast improvements in the last twenty years (Sender, Oya, and Cramer 2005). By 2011 the mean number of years of schooling for adults over 25 was only 2.41 (3.58 for male adults), suggesting that a large proportion of the adult population are still functionally illiterate and innumerate.[12] Adult literacy rates have improved substantially in the past ten years from 30 per cent to nearly 50 per cent but there is still progress to be made. Youth literacy rates are higher but there are still 30 per cent of youth, many women, who are not literate according to official statistics (this does not necessarily mean functionally illiterate as rates for this may be higher). Primary completion rates have very substantially increased from only 14 per cent in 1994 to 54 per cent in 2015, whereas lower secondary completion rates have also increased, albeit less rapidly, from 12 per cent to 30 per cent over the same period (see Figure 38.1). Despite rapid improvements in the last twenty-five years, more than half of the urban labour force has primary or no education, which contrasts with much higher levels of education for unskilled workers in industrializing economies in Southeast Asia, such as Cambodia or Vietnam where the median education of an urban worker is higher secondary education (World Bank 2016: 30, quoting data from the UEUS 2014 survey).

It is important to consider the educational attainment in rural areas and especially for women, since emerging industrial parks are focusing on the recruitment of young

[12] Data quoted in this paragraph have been largely estimated from the online UNESCO datasets accessed at http://data.uis.unesco.org/#

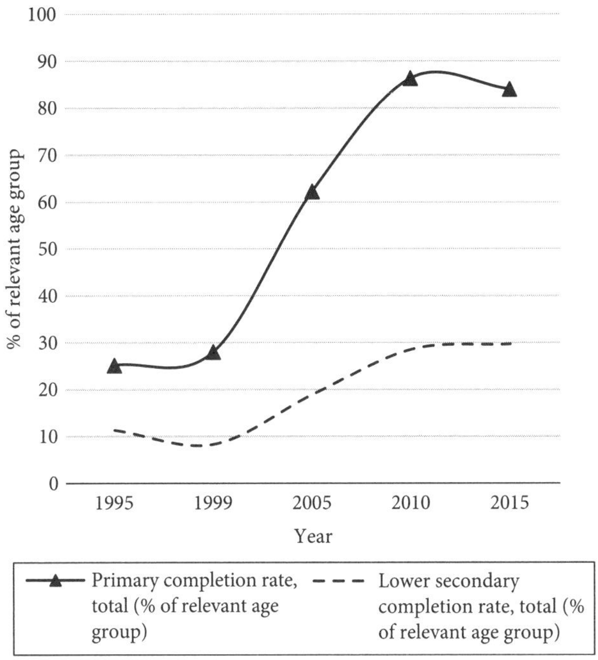

FIGURE 38.1 Completion rates for basic education, 1995–2015
Source: Author's elaboration from UNESCO database.

women from rural areas. According to the latest labour force survey with data from June 2013, 58 per cent of rural women never attended school and only 1.4 per cent had reached secondary school without completing it, meaning that most of the roughly 40 per cent having attended school only completed a grade within the 1–8 basic education level (CSA 2014: 43).[13] Vast inequalities in education provision are present, and the literature on Africa has shown that the inadequate quantity and quality of provision in rural schooling systems are an outcome of the high degree of bias towards expenditures on students in the upper levels of education provision and training systems designed to quell the potentially restive educated urban male entrants in the labour market (Sender, Oya, and Cramer 2005).

In Ethiopia, in fact, at the other extreme of the education levels, substantial improvements have been achieved in the expansion of higher and post-secondary education with the number of graduates in key fields for industrial development increasing since the 1990s, but gaps both in quantity and quality of employable graduates persist. According to the NLFS 2013, out of about 3.4 million trained Ethiopians with a certificate/diploma/degree, almost half studied social sciences, only 209,000 did engineering and allied services and just over 60,000 focused on production operations (CSA 2014: 46). Data for Addis Ababa University in 2011 confirm this distribution: the

[13] This dataset includes population aged 10 and above. Therefore some figures are lower than the usual attainment indicators that only include population aged 15 and above.

Institute of Technology produced 542 graduates (half for civil engineering) out of a total of nearly 10,000 graduates, i.e. just about 5 per cent (calculated from FDRE-MoE 2011). The balance is not skewed towards the kinds of fields that are most relevant to industrial operations. The practice in Sri Lanka is informative and points to possible directions that Ethiopia could take. The development of the textile and garment (T&G) industry and the rapid expansion of the domestic network of second- and third-tier suppliers was facilitated by and generated pressure for the creation of specialized training institutions to serve the sector. Thus the Textile Training and Services Centre (TTSC) and the Clothing Industry Training Institute (CITI) were established in 1984, remaining under the responsibility of the Ministry of Industry and eventually merged under Parliament Act No.12 in 2009 to create the Sri Lanka Institute of Textile and Apparel (SLITA) (Kelegama 2009). These institutes received substantial external support from Japanese aid and UN agencies and established collaborations with top global institutions in the field of textile technology.

Ethiopia therefore faces a double test that must be tackled in tandem. First is transforming an overwhelmingly rural workforce with little education and no relevant experience in time-driven jobs into a factory-type disciplined and highly productive labour force. Second is producing the required talent and experience for middle management and technical/skilled workers for much-needed positions in emerging factories across the country. This means that existing training programmes must be connected on a systematic basis with the growing manufacturing sector, by making sure, for example, that all graduates in relevant occupations require 6–12 months on-the-job training/modules in real factories, or by linking TVET (technical and vocational education and training) programmes with industrial parks and areas where industrial clusters develop.

Vocational and technical training is usually reported to be critical in this regard. Progress has indeed been made in the past ten to fifteen years but a large proportion of pupils going through the schooling system still do not benefit from TVET. Since 2001 the growth in absolute numbers has been remarkable though: from less than 9,000 vocational pupils in the secondary system (less than 1 per cent of total in secondary) to more than 350,000 enrolled in 2015, i.e. about 8 per cent of the total.[14] It is not clear, however, how many of these young people acquire enough *relevant* skills for industrial occupations. Analysis of TVET data from 2011 (FDRE-MoE 2011) suggests that only 15 per cent of all graduates acquire skills directly relevant to factory work.[15]

The building of industrial work skills is also achieved through decades of manufacturing experience and on-the-job training. Prior manufacturing experience contributes to further industrialization, a point long emphasized by Amsden (2001) in her analysis of the industrialization prospects for developing countries. Amsden concluded that the period under Japanese occupation was critical in the building of an industrial workforce

[14] A recent randomized control trial on job seekers in Addis Ababa reported that 43 per cent from a sample of over 4,000 people had finished a course or vocational training at an official vocational college or TVET, suggesting that in large urban pools of unemployed youth access to TVET is not negligible (Abebe et al. 2016).

[15] See also Sender, Oya, and Cramer (2005) for critical appraisal of the effectiveness of TVET programmes elsewhere in Africa.

as 'Korea had...accumulated by the (WWII) war's end considerable manufacturing experience in the form of a *workforce accustomed to paid labor (under very disciplined conditions)*, a managerial elite with production capabilities in a wide range of industries and government bureaucracies, as well as a small cadre of entrepreneurs with project execution skills, both in private and public enterprise' (Amsden 2001: 104, emphasis mine).[16] Ethiopia does not currently enjoy this prior manufacturing experience, despite the usefulness of the recent growth in floriculture (see Chapter 31), but this historical lesson underscores the importance of current dynamics of investment in light industries for the future expansion of the manufacturing sector and the critical role that factories will play in contributing to develop industrial work skills.

The combination of decent basic education and factory-level training seems the way forward in early stages of industrialization. As suggested by many industrial employers interviewed in 2017–18, more than the scarcity of TVET graduates, the problem for unskilled workers is that lack of schooling and low quality of education have implications for the adaptation of workers to a factory environment and the quality and time-efficiency demands that a global production network expects to meet. Basic literacy and numeracy are essential but also the social skills needed to be productive in highly demanding working environments. Social skills such as time management, work discipline, and speed of reaction may or may not be acquired in schools but workers with more schooling are more likely to develop them more quickly if on-the-job training is adequate.[17] Indeed, a key issue is that workers come with enough basic education of decent quality to become 'trainable'.[18]

Direct and indirect employment is therefore likely to become a crucial source of skill development given the context of education provision. Evidence suggests that firms/investors are particularly likely to contribute to sustainable skill development through 'tacit knowledge' related to production, especially organizational and management capabilities that are likely to be transmitted through two main channels (Calabrese 2017): (a) by employing middle-level Ethiopian managers and factory-floor supervisors, whose job experience will be crucial to disseminate to other companies as the number of domestic firms expands; and (b) through sub-contracting schemes that will connect domestic companies and their employees with lead firms in their clusters. The state has a coordinating role to play to make sure these mechanisms are activated and sustained.

38.2.5 Managing Expectations

If finding enough workers with the skills needed is a challenge, retaining the emerging industrial workforce may also prove difficult in early stages of industrial development.

[16] The early stages of industrial working-class formation in Korea had been achieved during Japanese occupation, as described in detail by Kohli (2004: 58–60).

[17] This was perhaps one of the most often repeated points by factory managers and floor supervisors.

[18] T&G factory managers report that hired workers should have a minimum of grade 8, although this requirement may not be systematically enforced (interviews with factory managers in March 2018).

Wage determination, workers' expectations, and reservation wages in the early stages of mass job creation in factories can lead to high turnover, an unstable labour force, and the negative effects on productivity that so many firms fear when setting up operations in a new country with little prior manufacturing experience.

There is a potential contradiction between the expectations of some investors of finding low-cost (and initially unproductive) labour and the expectations of potential workers of finding decent jobs with levels of remuneration that should substantially exceed wage levels in other low-productivity sectors in the economy. In the Ethiopian context, given the absence of a national or sector minimum wage there is a risk of a process of wage setting that is not sufficiently incentivizing even for poor rural migrants as demonstrated in the case of floriculture (see Chapter 31). Wages may be set too low, as emerging evidence from some industrial parks seems to suggest.[19] At the same time, the performance of the industry may not really depend on marginal increases in wages even when profit margins are low. For example, Oqubay (2015: 168) reports that the share of operating costs for one of the most labour-intensive industries in the country, floriculture, was only 10.4 per cent in 2012. Air freight represented over 55 per cent of costs. Similar figures apply to light manufacturing sectors. Employers may have different reasons to resist wage increases in these situations, especially when initial productivity levels are very low (and therefore unit labour costs not low enough), and are wary of generating expectations that may lead to unsustainable wage increases, as various managers reported in our interviews. However, the survival of these firms will not be affected by reasonable increases in nominal wages from a low base, especially in a context of rising living costs.

Another unsurprising source of contrasting expectations, which can hinder a smooth development of the industrial workforce, is the potential clash of work cultures that arises in initial encounters between rural-based workers and factory managers. As discussed above, there is plenty of historical literature and studies of contemporary processes of industrialization in Asia that document these clashes and the mechanisms and processes of resistance, negotiation, and adaptation that accompany the building of an industrial workforce. The practical question for Ethiopia is how the process of adaptation and change can be accelerated through a careful combination of state interventions at level of sourcing and grading of workers, and clear guidelines for processes of induction of new workers in factory environments, a remit of human resource departments that are often too focused on hiring and firing matters. The critical issue, therefore, is the process of convergence of different work cultures and the endogenous mechanisms of adaptation of both workers and management to generate both competitiveness and adequate labour conditions, even if the process may sometimes entail conflict over 'effort'.

For Ethiopian policymakers a key issue will be to consider what is the *minimum* that employers should offer even in a context where 'cheap labour' is a key attracting point.

[19] Especially the case in Hawassa, according to interviews in August 2017. A recent diagnostic survey conducted by the ILO in 46 T&G factories confirms the excessively low wages especially for low-skilled workers (interview at ILO, Addis Ababa, March 2018).

A statutory minimum wage or sectoral collective bargaining would definitely contribute in this direction. Considering that labour costs may not be the leading cost component in most industries, there is margin for improvement in basic wages and also for expansion in the social wage, especially in the form of accommodation and food provision. Meeting basic expectations on those fronts will not only generate the incentives for more youth from rural and urban areas to join the ranks of more productive industrial workers, but will also generate conditions for a faster rate of catching up in productivity by having a better selection of workers, lower turnover, and also better conditions for learning on the job. Leaving the bar too low in the short term may mean higher long-term costs for industrial investors as progress towards higher productivity and better product quality is slowed down, as lessons from the experience in floriculture suggest (see Chapter 31).

There is another consideration that should inform interventions to manage conflict of expectations in early stages of industrialization. Cramer (2011), in his study of youth unemployment and violence, suggests that a key source of conflict lies in disaffection from those with poor-quality jobs rather than those without jobs. While emphasis on mass job creation and 'quantity' of employment is pertinent and understandably seems to dominate existing policy discourses, demeaning and exploitative working conditions or unmet expectations may fuel violence as much as or more than the absence of jobs. Indeed, those with jobs are also more likely to be able to mobilize whether through trade unions or not. There is already some evidence of mobilization and strikes in factories and industrial parks in recent years despite a very weak level of unionization across sectors.[20]

This is particularly relevant in the current scenario where instances of social unrest may threaten the stability of the country and the viability of accelerated industrialization. An additional argument is that a successful and sustained industrialization process is also conditional on broad acceptance and support from the working class. In contemporary Ethiopia, a backlash against industrialization derived from perceptions of harsh working conditions can make the task of sourcing and retaining workers even more difficult.

38.3 Conclusions

This chapter has offered a selective overview of the obstacles to and dynamics of the process of creation and formation of an industrial workforce in an agrarian-based economy. The overview combines evidence on the current situation in Ethiopia with historical lessons from the *longue durée* of structural transformations in early industrializers and in recent experiences of industrial workforce formation in Asian contexts. A key lesson

[20] According to interviews with trade union leaders in the relevant industrial federation union density in the T&G sector does not exceed 20 per cent yet. Interviews in Addis Ababa, March 2018.

from history, this chapter argues, is that the process of building an industrial working class is uneven, protracted and requires interventions and important economic and social shifts across a wide range of aspects over long periods of time.

Historically, the process of building an industrial and more productive workforce has encountered different kinds of obstacles that must be addressed to avoid premature de-industrialization (Rodrik 2015). Some are structural obstacles derived from the demographic, social, and economic constraints common to many developing countries yet to achieve structural transformation. Some are related to the dynamics of emerging industrial relations in predominantly agrarian-based settings. The historical literature teaches us that even with potentially unlimited supplies of labour the process of labour surplus transfer is neither automatic nor always equally dynamic. Much depends on the interaction between local, national, and global contexts and how such interactions shape the potential incorporation of countries into dynamic global production networks in manufacturing. State policy certainly matters in terms of making the formation of an industrial workforce more rapid and sustainable but ultimately the political economy of accumulation and of the encounters between foreign or national industrial employers and the emerging working classes originating from low-productivity agricultural or informal activities determines the path towards a more stable and productive industrial workforce. For Ethiopia key challenges include (a) the process of smoothly managing labour transfer from agrarian-based settings to clusters of industrial production, especially industrial parks, and the resource costs and frictions of such transfers, especially housing provision; (b) strengthening and shaping the processes of skill development (both schooling and on-the-job training) to speed up the transition to a more productive industrial labour force; and (c) dealing with contrasting expectations from employers and new industrial workers and the inevitable conflicts that such encounters often generate, particularly when wages are too low and wage good inflation too high.

Acknowledgements

The research informing this chapter was funded by the ESRC-DFID grant ES/M004228/1. This chapter has benefited from excellent research assistance by James Brown and owes improvements to an anonymous reviewer and the three editors of the book. All errors and omissions are my sole responsibility.

References

Abebe, G., S. Caria, M. Fafchamps, P. Falco, et al. (2016). 'Curse of Anonymity or Tyranny of Distance? The Impacts of Job-Search Support in Urban Ethiopia', NBER Working Paper No. w22409, National Bureau of Economic Research.

Alatas, H. (1977). *The Myth of the Lazy Native: A Study of the Image of the Malays, Filipinos and Javanese from the 16th to the 20th Century and its Function in the Ideology of Colonial Capitalism* (London: Frank Cass).

Amsden, A. H. (2001). *The Rise of 'the Rest': Challenges to the West from Late-Industrializing Economies* (New York: Oxford University Press).

Ansu, Y., M. McMillan, J. Page, and D. Willem te Velde (2016). *Promoting Manufacturing in Africa* (London: ODI-SET).

Broadberry, S. and L. A. Gardner (2016). 'Economic Development in Africa and Europe: Reciprocal Comparisons', *Revista de Historia Económica/Journal of Iberian and Latin American Economic History* 34 (1): 11–37.

Calabrese, L. (2017). 'Chinese Investment and Knowledge Transfer in Africa', Growth Research Programme, http://www.degrp.sqsp.com.

Carswell, G. and G. De Neve (2013). 'Labouring for Global Markets: Conceptualising Labour Agency in Global Production Networks', *Geoforum* 44: 62–70.

Central Statistical Agency (Ethiopia) (CSA) (2014). 'Analytical Report on the 2013 National Labour Force Survey', Addis Ababa.

Christiaensen, L., J. De Weerdt, B. L. M. Ingelaere, et al. (2018). 'Migrants, Towns, Poverty and Jobs: Insights from Tanzania (English)', Policy Research Working Paper No. WPS 8340, World Bank, Washington, DCroup.

Cramer, C. (2011). 'Unemployment and Participation in Violence', WDR Background Report, World Bank, Washington, DC.

De Vries, J. (1994). 'The Industrial Revolution and the Industrious Revolution,' Journal of Economic History 54(2): 249–70.

Derks, A. (2008). *Khmer Women on the Move: Exploring Work and Life in Urban Cambodia* (Honolulu: University of Hawaii Press).

Diao, X., K. Harttgen, and M. McMillan (2017). 'The Changing Structure of Africa's Economies', *The World Bank Economic Review* 31 (2): 412–33.

Ethiopian Economics Association (2016). 'Report on the Ethiopian Economy 2016', Addis Ababa.

FDRE-Ministry of Education (2011). 'Education Statistics Annual Abstract 2003 E.C.-2010/2011 G.C', Addis Ababa.

Feldman, S. (2009). 'Historicizing Garment Manufacturing in Bangladesh: Gender, Generation, and New Regulatory Regimes', *Journal of International Women's Studies* 11 (1): 268–88.

Jayne, T. S., J. Chamberlin, and R. Benfica (2018). 'Africa's Unfolding Economic Transformation', *Journal of Development Studies* 54: 777–87.

Kabeer, N. (1991). 'Cultural Dopes or Rational Fools? Women and Labour Supply in the Bangladesh Garments Industry', *European Journal of Development Research* 3 (1): 133–60.

Kelegama, Saman (2009). 'Ready-Made Garment Exports from Sri Lanka', *Journal of Contemporary Asia* 39 (4): 579–96.

Kibria, N. (1998). 'Becoming a Garments Worker: The Mobilization of Women into the Garments Factories of Bangladesh', UNRISD Occasional Paper No. 9, United Nations Research Institute for Social Development, Geneva.

Kohli, A. (2004). *State-Directed Development: Political Power and Industrialization in the Global Periphery* (Cambridge: Cambridge University Press).

Lewis, W. A. (1957). 'International Competition in Manufacturers', *The American Economic Review* 47 (2): 578–87.

Martins, P. (2016). 'Structural Change in Ethiopia', UN Economic Commission for Africa, Kigali.

Meagher, K. (2016). 'The Scramble for Africans: Demography, Globalisation and Africa's Informal Labour Markets,' The Journal of Development Studies 52(4): 483–97.

Meagher, K., L. Mann, and M. Bolt (2016). 'Introduction: Global Economic Inclusion and African Workers', *Journal of Development Studies* 52 (4): 471–82.

Newman, C., J. Page, J. Rand, et al. (2016). *Made in Africa: Learning to Compete in Industry* (Washington, DC: Brookings Institution Press).

O'Laughlin, B. (2016). 'Produtividade agrícola, planeamento e a "cultura do trabalho" em Moçambique', *Desafios para Moçambique 2016*. IESE, Maputo.

Ong, Aihwa (1987). *Spirits of Resistance and Capitalist Discipline: Factory Women in Malaysia* (Albany: State University of New York Press).

Oqubay, A. (2015). *Made in Africa: Industrial Policy in Ethiopia* (Oxford: Oxford University Press).

Peou, C. (2016). 'Negotiating Rural–Urban Transformation and Life Course Fluidity: Rural Young People and Urban Sojourn in Contemporary Cambodia', *Journal of Rural Studies* 44: 177–86.

Pun, N. and C. Smith (2007). 'Putting Transnational Labour Process in its Place: The Dormitory Labour Regime in Post-Socialist China', *Work, Employment and Society* 21 (1): 27–45.

Rodrik, D. (2015). 'Premature Deindustrialization', NBER Working Paper No. 20935, National Bureau of Economic Research.

Sender, J., C. Oya, and C. Cramer (2005). 'Unequal Prospects: Disparities in the Quantity and Quality of Labour Supply in sub-Saharan Africa', Social Protection Discussion Paper No. 0525, World Bank, Washington, DC.

Thirlwall, A. P. (2011). *Economics of Devleopment*. (Basingstoke: Palgrave Macmillan).

Thompson, E. P. (1963). The Making of the British Working Class (New York: Pantheon).

Thompson, E. P. (1967). 'Time, Work-Discipline, and Industrial Capitalism', *Past & Present* 38: 56–97.

Tran, N. A. (2013). *Ties that Bind: Cultural Identity, Class, and Law in Vietnam's Labor Resistance* (Ithaca, NY: Cornell Southeast Asia Program).

World Bank (2016). 'Why so Idle? Wages and Employment in a Crowded Labor Market. Ethiopia 5th Economic Update', World Bank, Washington, DC.

CHAPTER 39

THE PRIVATE SECTOR IN ETHIOPIA'S TRANSFORMATION

MULU GEBREEYESUS

39.1 Introduction

This chapter examines the development and role of the private sector[1] in the economic structural transformation of Ethiopia. Since the incumbent government took power in 1991, private-sector development has become an integral part of Ethiopia's economic development strategy. The approach to private-sector development in Ethiopia during this period can be divided into two phases: the reform phase (1991–2001) and the post-2001 period.[2] At the heart of the differences in policy approaches between these two phases is the relationship between state and business and their respective roles. In the reform phase, the private sector was seen as ensuring economic growth and poverty reduction while the state provided the enabling environment. Many market-economy oriented policy reforms were introduced revitalizing the reentry of the private sector but at a slow pace (see Chapter 35).

In 2002–3, the government adopted industrial development strategy (IDS) and introduced the language of 'developmental state' as its policy principle regarding the state-business relationship. The government has made extensive efforts to support the private sector and implement its vision through a series of consecutive five-year development plans. The country has seen an ever-increasing number of domestic private businesses, particularly in the last decade. It has also become one of the preferred destinations of foreign direct investment (FDI) in Africa.[3]

[1] The private sector can simply be defined as non-state business activity seeking profit whether by production of goods or services and/or commercialization. However, smallholder farmers are not considered here due to the scope of this study.

[2] Gebreeyesus (2013) gives an extensive review of the history of Ethiopian industrial policy.

[3] According to a recent UNCTAD (2017) report, Ethiopia was the largest recipient in Africa of FDI amounting to US$3.2 billion in 2016, which is a rise of about 46 per cent in comparison to the previous year.

Despite these developments, the private sector has not yet made strong inroads into the manufacturing sector and export market, which are perceived by the government as crucial for industrialization and structural transformation. The private sector instead focuses on the service sector and domestic market where returns are high and quick. As a result, the pace of structural transformation has been slow. For example, manufacturing's contribution to GDP and to merchandise exports has remained at only 5 per cent and 10 per cent respectively over the last two decades.

The successful industrial transition in Asia (notably in South Korea and Taiwan) in which the private sector has played a prominent role, however, tells us that the manufacturing sector not only grew faster but also more than doubled its share in GDP in about twenty years, accounting for about 30 per cent. Similarly, exports have exhibited rapid growth, reaching 40–50 per cent of GDP. This success was a result of the respective governments' pursuing selective policies favoring certain sectors that are more productive and offer higher learning possibilities and externalities, which Amsden (1989) branded as 'getting prices wrong' and Wade (1990) 'governing the market to over-ride market allocation of resources'.

In light of this, the chapter examines the effectiveness of the policies and instruments instituted by the Ethiopian government to promote the private sector and improve its contribution towards economic structural transformation. It specifically tries to identify key weaknesses and constraints impeding private-sector participation in manufacturing and exports.

In exploring these issues, this chapter relies on different sources. Primary written sources include academic journals and books, newspaper articles, annual reports, policy papers, and other documents from both private and public organizations involved in promoting the private sector. In addition, secondary data sources from Central Statistical Agency (CSA), National Bank of Ethiopia (NBE), World Development Indicators, and others are used to specifically measure performance.

The remainder of the chapter is organized as follows. Section 39.2 reviews policies and programmes promoting the private sector in Ethiopia. We then examine the performance of the private sector and identify key challenges impeding it from unleashing its potential in Section 39.3. The final section, Section 39.4, concludes and draws some useful lessons.

39.2 Review of Policies and Programmes Promoting the Private Sector

39.2.1 The Reform Period Transition to Market Economy (1991–2001)

The incumbent government of the Ethiopian People's Revolutionary Democratic Front (EPRDF) overthrew the Derg regime in 1991 and has since instituted wide reforms towards a market-oriented economy which envisage a leading role for the private sector.

Over the 1990s, the government implemented three phases of IMF/WB-sponsored reform programmes, including liberalization of the trade and foreign exchange regimes, deregulation of prices, and privatization of state owned enterprises. It also enacted a new investment code in 1992 allowing the private sector to invest in all but a few strategic sectors retained by the government such as utilities and the military. The investment code has been amended several times since then to further liberalize the investment regime. In the early 1990s, the nine state corporations that dominated industry were dissolved to stimulate private investment. Concomitantly, in 1994 the government established the Ethiopian Privatization Agency to facilitate and administer the privatization of publicly owned enterprise.

In 2001, Ethiopia launched its Sustainable Development and Poverty Reduction Programme (SDPRP) covering the period 2000/1 to 2002/3, and poverty reduction became the core development agenda. The focus of SDPRP was on agriculture development and largely concerned smallholder famers, while industry and urban development was underemphasized.

39.2.2 Nurturing the Private Sector under the Developmental State (2002–Present)

39.2.2.1 *The Industrial Development Strategy (IDS) and Private-Sector Development*

In a clear departure from the neoliberal paradigm, in 2002 Ethiopia launched a comprehensive industrial development strategy (IDS) (FDRE 2002). This strategy recognizes the role of the private sector as an engine for the industrialization and structural transformation process. The policy made a distinction between the 'developmental' and 'rent-seeking' private sectors and the need to support the former while curtailing the latter. It identified two important mechanisms under which the government could engage and promote the private sector: (i) creating a conducive business environment for all; and (ii) providing direct support to strategically selected sectors that include textile and apparel, meat, leather and leather products, other agro-processing industries, construction, and micro and small enterprises (MSEs). Extensive support programmes ranging from economic incentives and capacity building to cluster development and direct public investment were identified to support firms operating in the priority sectors.

The support programmes were further refined and extended to a large number of firms and a wider context with follow-up five-year development plans: the Plan for Accelerated and Sustained Development to End Poverty (PASDEP) (2005/6–2009/10) and subsequent Growth and Transformation Plans (GTP-I and GTP-II).

39.2.2.2 *Private-Sector Development Initiatives in the PASDEP Period*

The PASDEP builds on the initiatives introduced in the IDS and SDPRP to accelerate the development of the private sector. It gave due emphasis to the improvement of the business environment by way of institutional and regulatory reforms. It also aimed at financial sector reform to increase the availability of capital; progressive withdrawal of state entities from areas that can be efficiently provided by the private sector; continued reforms to establish land tenure security; intensification of infrastructure development; and upgrade of the skills of the workforce through expanded education and technical and vocational programmes. Maintaining macroeconomic stability, a stable exchange rate, and low inflation were all integral parts of the PASDEP plan to accelerate private-sector development (FDRE: MoFED 2006). Various institutional reforms have been implemented during this period as a result.

In the PASDEP period, the export-oriented manufacturing sectors continued to receive special attention and support. Moreover, the government promoted private-sector investments to develop commercial agriculture in two directions: (i) private commercial investment in the Highlands with a focus on high-value horticulture products that can be produced on limited land, using abundant labour; and (ii) large-scale commercial investment in areas where there is extensive land but labour scarcity prevails (mainly in the Lowlands).

39.2.2.3 *Private-Sector Development Initiatives under the Growth and Transformation Plan (GTP-I and GTP-II)*

In 2010, the government launched a new series of growth and transformation plans called GTP. GTP-I (2010/11–2014/15) undertook to continue ensuring macroeconomic stability, improve the business environment, and provide direct support to the private sector willing to invest in priority sectors. In this period, additional support programmes such as twinning, benchmarking, Kaizen, industrial input supply, and skill development programmes were introduced to enhance the international competitiveness of private manufacturing industry. Several sector-based development institutes were set up to strengthen support for the private sector. Currently, there are seven sectoral institutes under the Ministry of Industry (MoI).

In order to institutionalize state–business relations by way of continuous dialogue, in 2010 the government established the Ethiopian Public Private Consultative Forum (EPPCF) by signing a MoU between the then Ministry of Trade and Industry and the Ethiopian Chamber of Commerce and Sectoral Association (ECCSA). This national forum was to be supported by sector sub-committees for those industries identified as priority industries. As a result, several sub-committees representing specific sectors were established.

Private investment in large commercial farming was also emphasized and a major increase in the scale of investment during this plan period was anticipated. Land transferred to large-scale commercial agricultural investors through the federal land bank was expected to increase from 0.5 million hectares in 2011 to 2.8 million in 2013 and 3.3 million in 2015 (FDRE; MoFED 2010).

A significant departure of GTP-I from earlier plans was the need to boost investment in state enterprises jointly with the private sector or alone. Despite increasingly privatizing several public enterprises, the government enhanced its engagement through direct investment including in new and expansionary investment projects, which are currently in various phases of implementation. Moreover, two state corporations (Mctal and Engineering Corporation and Sugar Corporation), each consisting of a substantial number of existing and newly established public enterprises, were reorganized.

The ongoing GTP-II (2015/16–2019/20) carries further ambitious plans for the development of the economy. A new vision to make the country a leader in light manufacturing in Africa has also been laid out. The plan envisages the private sector playing a key role in achieving its goals. Cognizant of the weak performance of the domestic private sector, on the one hand, the plan proposes a multi-track approach to transform the domestic private sector, in particular redirecting investment from the service and construction sectors towards manufacturing and supporting transition of small manufacturing enterprises to medium and large scale. On the other hand, the plan gives special emphasis to attracting foreign direct investment (FDI) in the manufacturing sector (FDRE: NPC 2016).

The most important initiatives undertaken in the GTP-II period to attract investment and improve industrial performance are the aggressive expansion and development of industrial parks and agro-processing zones. The development of industrial parks is seen as crucial to address the production and logistics constraints that impede productivity and competitiveness for both domestic and foreign investors (see Chapter 36). To this end, new investment regulations were endorsed in 2012 by Parliament and the Council of Ministers.

39.3 Performance and Key Challenges for the Private Sector

39.3.1 Employment and Output Contribution of the Non-Farm Private Sector

39.3.1.1 *Employment*

CSA has so far conducted three rounds (1999, 2005, and most recently 2013) of the Labour Force Survey (LFS). According to the CSA 2013 LFS survey report, about 42.4 million people aged 10 and above were employed in Ethiopia. The majority (72.7 per cent) were absorbed by the agriculture sector. This survey report also provides some estimates of the private sector's contribution to employment. Of the total 6.38 million people employed in urban areas in 2013, about 42.4 per cent were self-employed, 20.5 per cent employed by private business organizations, 18.4 per cent by government (general and SOEs), and 14 per cent were unpaid family workers. This shows that the majority of people in urban areas are in an informal sector, by and large self-employment, while the formal private-sector contribution to salaried employment remains low.

When looking at the manufacturing sector, the 2015 CSA survey estimates the number of manufacturing enterprises that use power-driven machines and tools to be about 124,150, of which 3,150 are large and medium-scale manufacturing (LMSM) establishments that employ ten or more people, while the rest are small-scale manufacturing (SSM). In terms of employment, in 2014–15 the LMSM sector generated about 333,084 jobs, of which the private sector accounted for about 87 per cent. SSM, which is wholly owned by the private sector, is the largest employment generator in manufacturing. According to the CSA 2015 survey report, SSM generated over 660,000 permanent jobs with as many as 1.7 million people employed.

39.3.1.2 *Gross Domestic Output*

The official data on national accounts from the MoFED and NBE do not distinguish shares of national output by actor, such as public, private-sector, and household. A study (Kolli 2010) commissioned by Addis Ababa Chamber of Commerce and Sectoral Associations estimated that in 2008/9 the private-sector share in non-agriculture GDP was 40.1 per cent.

According to various years' CSA survey reports on LMSM, Ethiopia's manufacturing gross output (at constant price) grew by an annual average of about 12.7 per cent over the 15 years from 2000/1 to 2014/15, with the private sector contributing hugely towards this. For example, the private-sector share in the LMSM value added increased from 27.7 per cent in 1999/2000 to 71 per cent in 2014/15.[4] The growth in manufacturing output, however, did not keep pace with the growth in other sectors such as services. As a result manufacturing's share of GDP remained constant at around 5 per cent for an extended period.

39.3.2 Capital Formation: Macro Perspective

39.3.2.1 *Gross Capital Formation*

Ethiopia has exhibited double-digit economic growth, accompanied by a remarkable growth in capital formation, over the last decade. As can be seen from Figure 39.1, Ethiopia's gross fixed capital formation (GFCF)-to-GDP ratio increased from 24 per cent in 2007 to about 39 per cent in 2015, much higher than the average ratio in regions such as sub-Saharan Africa (20.2 per cent) and least developed countries (23.5 per cent).[5] Ethiopia's capital formation is, rather, comparable to that of the East Asian Tigers, such as South Korea and Taiwan, at their take-off stage. For example, the GFCF-to-GDP ratio of Taiwan increased steadily from about 11 per cent in the 1952 to 30 per cent in 1980 (Taiwan 2006). Similarly Korea's GFCF to GDP ratio about doubled between the 1960s and the 1980s, rising even higher to reach about 35 per cent in the mid-1990s (Korea Development Institute 1997).

[4] Table not reported to save space.

[5] The source of data for Ethiopia as well as the other regions is World Bank, World Development Indicators database.

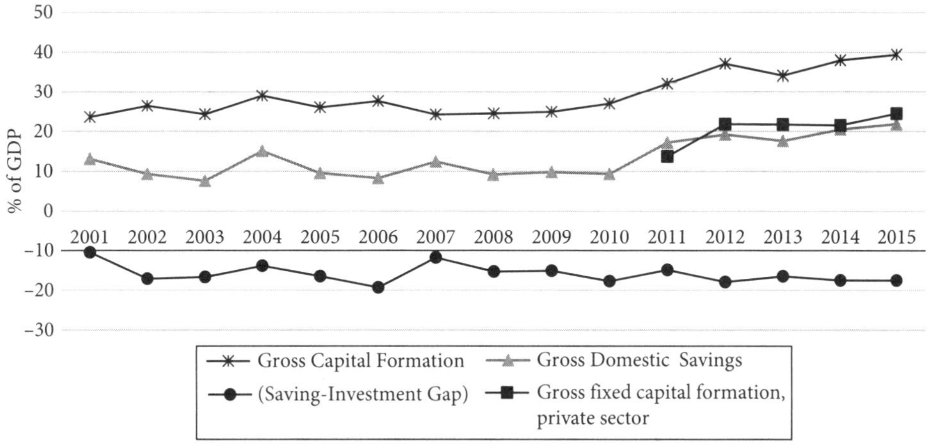

FIGURE 39.1 Ethiopia: Gross fixed capital formation and saving

Source: WDI for the trade data and NBE for the investment saving data.

39.3.2.2 *Public versus Private Capital Formation*

Gross fixed capital formation by the private sector in Ethiopia has also increased in recent years, reaching about 25.4 per cent of GDP in 2015. Despite improvements private-sector investment, crowded out by the public sector, remained low, accounting for about half of the gross capital formation. Ethiopia has the third-highest public investment in the world, but the sixth-lowest private investment (World Bank 2016). The private-sector and donor community often complain that credit is not made sufficiently available to the private sector partly due to priorities given to public investment. According to World Bank (2015), SOEs are estimated to account for about 62 per cent of credit stock. Private-sector credit to GDP is only about 9 per cent of GDP, compared to more than 20 per cent in sub-Saharan Africa. Crowding out is also an issue in relation to foreign exchange allocation, again due to the priority given to public projects as well as a general national shortage of foreign exchange.

The government and others counter-argue (i) that the private sector is not even coming forward to use the available credit, and (ii) that public investment is largely on infrastructure and human capital development to address the historic infrastructure deficit in the country. Ethiopia has achieved substantial expansion in energy, road, railway, and telecommunications infrastructure, which is a prerequisite for private-sector development.

In principle, public infrastructure investment can augment private capital formation (crowd-in). But this assumes efficient allocation of resources. The literature on the impact of public investment in developing economies including Ethiopia gives mixed results on whether it complements or crowds out private investment. According to the governments' own admission, many large public investment projects suffer from poor project planning and management as well as inadequate monitoring and evaluation. As a result, the costs of many projects have been reported as substantially escalating through time.

39.3.2.3 *Investment–Saving Nexus*

Figure 39.1 also shows that Ethiopia's gross domestic saving-to-GDP ratio has sharply increased since 2010 and reached about 21 per cent in 2015. But it has not grown with the pace of investment. As a result the saving–investment gap not only remained large but also increased slightly from 11.8 per cent in 2007 to about 17.5 per cent in 2015. Ethiopia's savings pattern contrasts with the successful experiences of Korea and Taiwan where rapid investment was accompanied by higher growth in domestic savings. Both countries achieved above 30 per cent of saving-to-GDP ratio in the 1960s, 1970s, and 1980s (Taiwan 2006; Korea Development Institute 1997).

The low level of domestic saving in Ethiopia means a significant proportion of the investment has been financed through foreign savings. A high dependence on foreign saving raises issues not only of access to finance but also of sustainability. The 2015 IMF report on debt sustainability analysis (DSA) raised Ethiopia's risk of external debt distress from 'low' to 'moderate' following a surge in debt-to-GDP ratio from 42 per cent of GDP in 2014 to an estimated 54.2 per cent in 2015/16. The debt-to-GDP ratio was only 18 per cent of the GDP in mid-2012. High debt-to-GDP ratio can lead to higher uncertainty and low private-sector investment.

39.3.3 Private Investment Flows: Low Conversion Rate from Investment Licence to Operations

This sub-section examines in detail Ethiopia's private investment flow patterns over the last twenty-five years (1992 to 2016) using the Ethiopian Investment Commission (EIC) database. Table 39.1 reports investment flow by project status and ownership type. In the last twenty-five years, about 85,603 private investment project requests were approved, of which the majority (94 per cent) were submitted by domestic private investors. Recent years have seen a surge of both domestic and foreign investment. For example, nearly 50 per cent of investment projects licences were issued in 2011–16 alone.

Despite the large number of investment project approvals, the implementation rate has been very low. Out of the 85,603 investment projects approved in the last twenty-five years, only 10,269 projects (12 per cent) have become operational, which have injected about 166 billion birr and generated permanent employment for nearly half a million people. The implementation rate of domestic approved projects has been far too low (9.5 per cent) when compared to foreign projects (51.3 per cent). This means about 90 per cent and 49 per cent of, respectively, registered domestic and foreign private investment projects has not yet translated into actual investments on the ground.

Next we try to highlight the likely cause of the alarmingly low level of investment license conversion into operation among domestic investors. We start by examining the broader business environment, which is one key ingredient for successful participation of the private sector. According to the World Bank's index reports on the ease of doing business, Ethiopia's rank deteriorated from 101st out of 155 countries in 2006 to 159th

Table 39.1 Investment projects by ownership and status, 1992–2016

Year	Number of approved projects	Number of operational projects	Share (%) operational projects	Generated capital and employment by operational projects		
				Capital, million birr	Permanent employment	Temporary employment
All investments						
1992–2001	5,489	2,434	44.3	20,715.2	108,410	296,977
2002–10	38,728	5,183	13.4	70,761.2	296,045	501,856
2011–16	41,269	2,651	6.4	74,432.4	71,373	78,119
Total (1992–2016)	85,603	10,269	12.0	165,913.2	475,837	876,952
Investment by ownership (domestic versus foreign)						
Domestic						
1992–2001	5,334	2,317	43.4	14,490.7	87,214	288,679
2002–10	36,274	3484	9.6	18,870.0	93,850	244,347
2011–16	38,738	1809	4.7	33,246.6	22,354	50,254
Total (1992–2016)	80,419	7610	9.5	66,607.3	203,418	583,280
FDI						
1992–2001	155	117	75.5	6,224.5	21,196	8298
2002–10	2,454	1,699	69.2	51,891.2	202,195	257,509
2011–16	2,531	842	33.3	41,185.8	49,019	27,865
Total (1992–2016)	5,184	2,659	51.3	99,305.9	272,419	293,672

Source: Ethiopia Investment Commission (EIC) database and own calculations.

out of 190 countries in 2017. A closer look at the reports shows that Ethiopia had the worst score (above 159) in some critical elements, such as starting a business (179), dealing with construction permits (176), protecting minority investors (175), getting credit (170), and trading across borders (167).

A recent EDRI study (Gebrehiwot, Gebreeyesus, and Woldeyes 2017) examines why the prevailing investment conversion rate is so low and what major constraints to proceeding beyond the licensing stage to start production are faced by domestic private investors. Unlike previous studies which rely on existing firms, this study gathered information on the major constraints not only from successful investors but also from those who were discouraged. The qualitative survey looked at forty-two firms (investors) in Addis Ababa, mostly in manufacturing. The main finding is that the key barriers to investment relate to land, finance, regulatory and institutional inefficiency, poor infrastructure, particularly power, and lack of skills. These are basically consistent with World Bank reports and other previous studies and suggests that the poor business environment is not only undermining exiting firms but also discouraging new investments and transition from project to operations.

39.3.4 The Bulk of Private Domestic Investment Is Outside the Productive Sector

Table 39.2 reports the sectoral breakdown of operational investment projects in the last twenty-five years, again based on the EIC database. In terms of the number of operational projects, agriculture, manufacturing, and the service sector respectively account for about 20 per cent, 30 per cent, and 43 per cent. In terms of capital investment, however, out of the nearly 165.9 billion birr investment made over the last twenty-five years, about 50 per cent was invested in the manufacturing sector, while agriculture and the service sector respectively accounted for 22 per cent and 18 per cent.[6]

Table 39.2 further shows a big difference between domestic and foreign investors in terms of sector focus. FDI's focus has been on manufacturing, accounting for 52 per cent and 81 per cent of respectively operational projects and capital investment for foreign firms. The restriction by the government on FDI in many of the service sub-sectors might have helped to channel most of the FDI towards manufacturing. Unlike foreign investors, the focus for domestic private investment has been largely on the service sector. Over the last twenty-five years, only 25 per cent of the total number of operational projects and 21 per cent of capital investment by domestic investors was channelled to the manufacturing sector. In contrast, nearly 45 per cent of the operational projects and 30 per cent of capital from domestic investors was invested in the service sector.

Above we have pointed out GTP-II put certain strategies in place to redirect domestic investors from the construction and service sector towards manufacturing. To examine

[6] The fact that the share of manufacturing in the number of projects is low but in terms of capital is high suggests high capital intensity of manufacturing in comparison to other sectors.

Table 39.2 Sectoral breakdown of operationalized investment projects

	Operational number of projects			Capital invested (in billion birr)			Operational domestic investment projects (Comparing 2 years pre-GTP-II and the first 2 years of GTP-II)	
	Domestic	FDI	Total	Domestic	FDI	Total	2013 and 2014	2015 and 2016
All sectors total (in number)	**7,610**	**2,658**	**10,268**	**66.6**	**99.3**	**165.9**	**325**	**1295**
Sectoral share (in %)								
Agriculture, hunting, and forestry	**23.5**	**10.8**	**20.2**	**42.6**	**8.9**	**22.4**	**17.5**	**9.5**
Manufacturing	24.9	45.1	30.1	21.2	69.5	50.1	10.8	9.6
Mining and quarrying	0.6	0.6	0.6	0.4	0.5	0.5	1.2	0.6
Construction	5.8	6.5	6.0	5.7	11.1	9.0	24.6	18.0
Industry total	**31.3**	**52.1**	**36.7**	**27.4**	**81.1**	**59.5**	**36.6**	**28.2**
Education	5.4	2.2	4.6	4.5	0.4	2.0	1.5	0.2
Health and social work	1.6	2.1	1.7	2.1	0.5	1.1	1.2	0.2
Hotels and restaurants	5.7	5.3	5.6	4.1	1.8	2.7	6.2	0.2
Tour operation, transport, and communications	4.3	2.5	3.8	3.1	0.2	1.4	4.9	0.6
Real estate, machinery and equipment, rental and consultancy services	26.5	22.8	25.5	14.9	6.4	9.8	31.1	60.5
Other community, social, and personal service activities	0.4	2.2	0.9	0.1	0.7	0.5	0.6	0.5
Wholesale, retail trade, and repair services	1.3	0.0	1.0	1.2	0.0	0.5	0.3	0.0
Service total	**45.3**	**37.0**	**43.1**	**30.0**	**10.0**	**18.0**	**45.8**	**62.3**

Source: Ethiopia Investment Commission (EIC) database and own calculations.

whether this strategy has brought the expected result in the domestic sectoral investment allocation, we compared the two years prior to GTP-II and the first two GTP-II years. As can be seen in the last two columns of Table 39.2, in terms of number of operational projects the agriculture and manufacturing sectors' shares show a declining rather than rising trend. In contrast, the service sector share increased from 45.8 per cent in the two years prior to GTP-II to more than 62.3 per cent in the first two GTP-II years. Surprisingly, the majority of investment within the service sector comes from the real-estate and rental activities sub-sectors, where the share of investment in operational projects in all sectors increased from 31 per cent to nearly 60.5 per cent. This suggests that the service and particularly the real-estate sector remained attractive for domestic investment despite the government's plan to redirect investment towards productive sectors such as manufacturing.

There are various explanations as to why the incentives designed to redirect investment towards the productive sectors are not producing the expected outcomes. First and foremost is that the system creates larger rents in the service sector (for example, the real-estate and rental, construction, trading, and banking sectors), leading to very high and quick profits in these sectors. For example, the profitability of banking remains very high, with returns on equity (ROE) at about 44.6 per cent by the end of March 2014, which is more than double than the SSA average (17 per cent) at the end of 2013 (World Bank 2015). Although there are no exact figures, the profitability of the real-estate sector and of wholesale and retail trade are among the highest. In contrast, the profit margin in the productive sectors such as manufacturing and agriculture, particularly in the export market, remained very low. The service and non-traded sectors in Ethiopia are highly protected from international competition, while manufacturing and agriculture operate in a more competitive environment. As a result, private investors, particularly domestic ones, are not interested in investing in less profitable sectors, such as manufacturing, and in the export market. This implies that the government has either not been able to limit the excessive rents created in unproductive sectors largely emanating from the non-competitive environment and/or has not provided sufficient incentives for the productive sectors.

Second, the effectiveness of the incentives is substantially constrained by the lack of efficient bureaucracy and a coordination problem among different public institutions. This has made it difficult to ensure investors in priority sectors have proper access even to the limited level of existing incentives. This is largely due to low capability and motivation as well as increasing rent-seeking practices by civil servants.

Third, limited monitoring by the civil service has further encouraged rent seeking and the diversion of incentives by the private sector to other uses. Many investors take out investment licences in the productive sectors (manufacturing and large-scale manufacturing) with no intention of investing and abuse the incentives or divert the resources to other sectors. Gebrehiwot, Gebreeyesus, and Woldeyes (2017) show that several so-called investors that received land for manufacturing activity misused the land by using it for warehouses, renting (transfer) to other actors (or activities), or leaving it idle over a long period.

The dismal performance of the large-scale commercial farming sector, despite high expectations, is another example of rent-seeking behaviour by private investors. UNDP (2013) shows that out of the total 440,163 hectares of land transferred from the federal land bank by the end of GTP-I, only 42 per cent was converted to production. It further argues that the sector's poor performance is partly caused by deliberate abuse of land investment licences or land lease agreements. With very low land lease rates, in some cases land has been taken for speculative purposes or to take advantage of tax and financial privileges.

Notwithstanding the dismal performance of the large-scale farm in general, Ethiopia has achieved remarkable success in the flower industry. The major success factor for the emergence of the floriculture industry is the shared vision for the sector's development and strong collaboration between government and the private sector (Gebreeyesus and Iizuka 2012).

39.3.5 Poor Export Performance and Underlying Causes

Ethiopia has long recognized the role of exports in economic growth and development. Ethiopia's exports have been dominated by the private sector since the government's withdrawal from the trading sector in the command economy regime of the early 1990s. Various export incentives and capacity-building programmes have been devised and implemented to encourage the private sector into exports. Exports have grown moderately over the last two decades but have not kept pace with the growth in imports. For example, Ethiopia's exports grew around tenfold between 1995 and 2015, reaching US$3.8 billion. However, merchandise imports grew even faster (nineteen-fold) in the same period, widening the trade deficit to over US$11.4 billion. This has resulted in a critical shortage and rationing of foreign exchange (Gebreeyesus and Kebede 2017a).

A related concern is that Ethiopia still relies heavily on primary and agricultural exports. In 2015/16, for instance, the five major export items (coffee, oilseed, gold, chat, and pulses) accounted for nearly 70 per cent of total export values. In contrast, manufacturing's share in total merchandise exports remained very low (below 10 per cent), with no sign of improvement (NBE 2016). The majority of firms in manufacturing sector have focused on the domestic market. According to the 2015 CSA LMSM survey report, only 5 per cent of manufacturing firms participated in exports and the share of exports in total sales of the sector was only 4 per cent.

Gebreeyesus and Kebede (2017a) examined the factors behind the poor export performance, particularly in the manufacturing sector, in the face of extensive efforts to promote exports. They specifically look at the relative attractiveness of the domestic market versus export markets and seek to measure the anti-export bias arising from tariffs and overvaluation of the exchange rate. In their disaggregated industry-level anti-export bias estimates, they found a wide difference among industries in the manufacturing sector. With about 35 per cent nominal duty rate, the export-oriented sectors such as textiles, apparel, leather, and footwear are the most protected within the manufacturing sector. The anti-export bias estimates suggest that the value added obtainable in the domestic market vis-à-vis exporting is 150 per cent greater for leather and footwear and more than 70 per cent for textiles and apparel. This study also shows that the overvaluation of the exchange rate further aggravated the disincentive to export. The implication is that tariff and exchange rate policies are not consistent with the export promotion of the country.

According to the 2015 World Bank 'Doing Business' report, Ethiopia stands at 168 out of 189 countries in terms of ease of trading across borders. Exporting a standard container of goods in Ethiopia takes on average about 44 days and costs US$2,380. Gebreeyesus and Kebede (2017b), on the other hand, revealed that the anti-export bias arising from non-tariff trade barriers (trading costs) such as time delay caused by logistics inefficiency and customs procedures has been greater than the anti-export bias from tariffs.

The low level of productivity is another factor in poor export performance (see Chapters 36, 37). Ethiopia lags in terms of total factor productivity behind its peer countries in Africa such as Côte d'Ivoire, Nigeria, Zambia, Kenya, Tanzania, and South Africa (World Bank 2015). Low productivity in turn is caused by a multitude of factors—among others low labour productivity and skill shortage, lack of supply of inputs, and poor business environment and infrastructure service. For example, the CSA (2015) survey of MLSM enterprises revealed that more than half are working below capacity mainly due to shortage of raw materials, lack of demand, and power shortages.

Gebreeyesus and Demile (2017) examined the effectiveness of existing export incentives in reducing the anti-export bias. They found that the mediocre additional incentives provided for exporters are insufficient motivation for the private sector, taking into account not only the anti-export bias created by the existing policies but also the investment incentives available to all investors including firms producing for the domestic market. More importantly, the study found that the effectiveness of the export incentives is substantially constrained by the lack of efficient export bureaucracy and coordination problems. This has made it difficult to ensure exporters have access even to limited export incentives, which has encouraged diversion and rent seeking by the private sector.

39.4 Concluding Remarks

The aim of this chapter was to examine the development of the private sector in Ethiopia and identify the key challenges hindering it from unleashing its potential to realize economic structural transformation in the country. Ethiopia has seen a surge of private investment (both domestic and foreign), particularly in recent years. Once associated with famine and war, Ethiopia's image is changing and the country is portrayed as the future hub of manufacturing investment in Africa.

This study shows that despite these developments, Ethiopia's domestic private sector has not yet vigorously entered the productive sectors (e.g. manufacturing and agriculture) and the export market, which are perceived as critical pathways towards industrialization and structural transformation. Instead most domestic private investors are increasingly concentrated in the service sector or/and domestic market where returns on investment are large and rapid. This study highlighted the following key weaknesses and constraints hindering the domestic private sector from robustly entering the productive sectors and export market.

First, several studies, including the present one, have pointed to the poor and deteriorating business environment as one cause for the underperformance of the private sector. The attention of the government in this regard seems currently to be focused on improving the business environment within the industrial parks. It is true that the industrial park scheme is one critical route toward industrialization, and improving the business environment in these parks would greatly help attract investment. It is also relatively easier and more manageable to provide efficient services to firms in the parks than those outside parks. But unfortunately, not all manufacturing firms, let alone other businesses, are going to be located in the parks. Improving the business environment in the industrial parks cannot, thus, be a substitute for improving the overall national business environment. The implication is that government needs to also quickly address the deteriorating overall national business environment.

Second, the most important policy issue concerns rent creation and management, which is the hallmark of industrial policy (Khan and Blankenburg 2009). Although the government would like to see investment flow to the productive sectors, the large rents are created in other sectors, notably in the service sector which includes real estate and rental, construction, trading, banking, etc. With substantial and rapid returns from these sectors, private investors are not interested in investing in less profitable sectors such as manufacturing and in the export market.

Government can address this problem at least with the following complementary mechanisms. First, closing or narrowing down the routes through which large rents are created in the non-productive sectors. This is because the large rents in these sectors are not created in a competitive market environment but by and large are due to distortions, inefficiency, and the protection of the domestic market. Second, using different innovative instruments to transfer sufficient rents from the less preferred to the favoured industries in order to make the latter financially attractive for the private sector. Third, managing such rents, however, requires a capable and efficient civil service. This chapter highlights that one of the main reasons why the various government incentives are not producing the expected results is bureaucratic red tape and the incompetence of the civil service. Moreover, with weak monitoring systems, the rent-seeking behaviour of the private sector is increasingly unchecked. Hence, building a civil service that will shoulder its responsibilities is of paramount importance for the proper implementation of policies and incentives, and hence the enhancement of the transformative role of the private sector. Fourth, Ethiopia's economy is currently suffering from two imbalances: an export–import gap and a savings–investment gap, both of which are adversely affecting private-sector development. Ethiopia's fast economic growth has been accompanied by an increasing trade deficit. As a result, private businesses are increasingly constrained by the shortage of credit and foreign exchange, both of which are crucial for investment, production, and sustained growth. This chapter also shows that poor export performance is caused by the misalignment of certain macro policies (for example tariffs and exchange rates) with the export promotion currently pursued by the country. Moreover, the low real interest rate is thought to contribute to the low level of domestic savings, hence to credit rationing. Integrating macro and trade policies with sectoral policies is, thus, critical for the way forward.

Successful East Asian countries provide great lessons in all the above respects: creating and managing rent, building a capable and disciplined civil service, and the alignment of macro and industrial policies.

References

Amsden, Alice (1989). *Asia's Next Giant: South Korea and Late Industrialization* (Oxford: Oxford University Press).

Central Statistics Agency (CSA) (2013). 'National Labor Force Survey 2014/15', Addis Ababa, March 2016.

Central Statistics Agency (CSA) (various years). 'Report on Large and Medium Manufacturing and Electricity Industries Survey', Addis Ababa.

Ethiopia Investment Commission (EIC) (2017). 'Investment Flow Data (1992–2015)', unpublished.

Federal Democratic Republic of Ethiopia (FDRE) (2002). 'Ethiopian Industrial Development Strategy', Addis Ababa (Amharic version).

Federal Democratic Republic of Ethiopia; Ministry of Finance and Economic Development (2006). 'Ethiopia: Building on Progress: A Plan for Accelerated and Sustained Development to End Poverty (PASDEP) (2005/6–2009/10)', Addis Ababa.

Federal Democratic Republic of Ethiopia; Ministry of Finance and Economic Development (2010). 'Growth and Transformation Plan (2010/2011–2014/15) (GTP-I)', Addis Ababa.

Federal Democratic Republic of Ethiopia; National Planning Commission (2016). 'Growth and Transformation Plan II (2015/16–2019/20)', Addis Ababa.

Gebreeyesus, M. (2013). 'Industrial Policy and Development in Ethiopia: Evolution and Present Experimentation', WIDER Working Paper 2013/125, UNU-WIDER, Helsinki.

Gebreeyesus, Mulu and Ashagrie Demile (2017). 'Why Export Promotion Efforts Failed to Deliver? Assesssment of the Export Incentives and their Implementation in Ethiopia', EDRI Working Paper No. 17, Ethiopian Development Research Institute, Addis Ababa.

Gebreeyesus, Mulu and Michiko Iizuka (2012). 'Discovery of Flower Industry in Ethiopia: Experimentation and Coordination', *Journal of Globalization and Development* 2 (2): 1–25.

Gebreeyesus, Mulu and Alekaw Kebede (2017a). 'Ethiopia's Export Promotion and the Misalignment of the Tariff and Exchange Rate Regimes', EDRI Working Paper No. 19, Ethiopian Development Research Institute, Addis Ababa.

Gebreeyesus, Mulu and Alekaw Kebede (2017b). 'Tariff Equivalents for Time in Ethiopian's Merchandise Trade', (mimeo), Ethiopian Development Research Institute, Addis Ababa.

Gebrehiwot, B., M. Gebreeyesus, and F. Woldeyes (2017). 'Alleviating the Barriers to Domestic Investment in Addis Ababa: Underlying Causes and Proposed Solutions', EDRI, unpublished research report.

IMF (2015). 'The Federal Democratic Republic of Ethiopia'. Staff Report for the 2015 Article IV Consultation—Debt Sustainability Analysis. https://www.imf.org/external/pubs/ft/dsa/pdf/2015/dsacr15300.pdf (accessed January 2018).

Khan, Mushtaq and Stephanie Blankenburg (2009). 'The Political Economy of Industrial Policy in Asia and Latin America', in *Industrial Policy and Development: The Political Economy of Capabilities Accumulation*, ed. Giovanni Dosi, Mario Cimoli and Joseph E. Stiglitz (Oxford: Oxford University Press): 336–77.

Kolli R. (2010). 'A Study on the Determination of the Share of the Private Sector in Ethiopian Gross Domestic Product', Ababa Chamber of Commerce and Sectoral Associations.

Korea Development Institute (KDI) (1997). 'The Korean Economy 1945–1995: Performance and Vision for the 21st Century', Seoul, Korea.

National Bank of Ethiopia (various years). 'Annual Reports'. http://www.nbe.gov.et/publications/annualreport.html

Taiwan (2006). 'Taiwan Statistical Data Book', Council for Economic Planning and Development. https://www.ndc.gov.tw/en/News_Content.aspx?n=607ED34345641980&sms=B8A915763E3684AC&s=33CEAC7C9171C880.

UNDP (United Nations Development Program) (2013). 'An Assessment of Operation and Performance of Commercial Farmers in Ethiopia: Summary of Commissioned Studies', UNDP Ethiopia, Addis Ababa.

United Nations Conference on Trade and Development (UNCTAD) (2017). 'World Investment Report 2017: Investment and the Digital Economy', United Nations, Geneva.

Wade, Robert (1990). *Governing the Market: Economic Theory and the Role of Government in East Asian Industrialization* (Princeton, NJ: Princeton University Press).

World Bank (2015). '4th Ethiopia Economic Update: Overcoming Constraints in the Manufacturing Sector', World Bank Group, Washington, DC, 8 July.

World Bank (2016). 'Ethiopia: Priorities for Ending Extreme Poverty and Promoting Shared Prosperity: Systematic Country Diagnostic', Report No: 100592-ET, World Bank, Washington, DC.

World Bank (various years). 'Doing Business Report', World Bank, Washington, DC. http://www.doingbusiness.org/rankings.

World Bank (various years). 'World Development Indicators', World Bank, Washington, DC. http://databank.worldbank.org/ddp/home.do.

CHAPTER 40

LIGHT MANUFACTURING IN ETHIOPIA

The Apparel Export Industry

CORNELIA STARITZ AND LINDSAY WHITFIELD

40.1 Introduction

THE apparel export industry in Ethiopia began modestly in the 2000s, increased significantly by the mid-2010s and will continue to do so as firms in and around the industrial parks become fully operational. Ethiopia is positioned to become an important supplier country in the globalized apparel industry. Apparel exports emerged in Ethiopia as a result of a combination of factors, including comparatively low labour, electricity, and water costs as well as duty-free access to the EU market under 'Everything but Arms' (EBA) and to the US market under the African Growth and Opportunities Act (AGOA) combined with liberal rules of origin.[1] Yet, all sub-Saharan African countries have these trade preferences. The factors that set Ethiopia apart are the government's proactive industrial policy targeting the apparel and textile sectors and attracting some EU and US global buyers and core suppliers to invest in, or source from, Ethiopia. Ethiopia is also different to most other sub-Saharan African apparel exporter countries, given the existence of diverse ownership structures, including locally owned export firms, as well as the foundation of a national supply chain from cotton to textile to apparel that can be built upon to make production vertically integrated in Ethiopia (Staritz, Plank, and Morris 2016).[2]

[1] Under AGOA and more recently under EBA, Ethiopia and other sub-Saharan African countries enjoy 'single-transformation' rules of origin, which means that only sewing has to take place in the beneficiary country, allowing all inputs (including textile) to be imported globally.

[2] For a discussion of the limited local investment in the apparel export sectors in Kenya, Lesotho, and Swaziland (see Staritz and Frederick 2016). Madagascar has a larger share of and more developed locally owned apparel export firms, and in Mauritius the apparel export sector largely consists of locally owned firms (see Morris, Plank, and Staritz 2016).

This chapter provides an overview of the emergence and evolution of the apparel export sector in Ethiopia. It focuses on the importance of locally owned firms in economic transformation, and how they have (or have not) learned and built their technological capabilities in order to become internationally competitive on quality, productivity, delivery time, and compliance standards; sustained relations with global buyers; and moved into more complex processes, products, and/or functions in order to increase value added and unit prices. In doing so, it considers the different roles of industrial policy, foreign direct investment linkages, and global value chain integration in supporting and incentivizing local firms to learn.

The chapter starts by discussing the opportunities and challenges of apparel sector-led industrialization, and providing an overview of the apparel export industry in Ethiopia. The following section identifies and discusses three different phases of industrial policy supporting the development of the industry and related challenges, with a focus on the situation of locally owned firms. The final section draws conclusions related to the successes and failures of industrial policy, the level of learning among local firms, and the potential role of foreign direct investment in catalysing local firm learning.[3]

40.2 Opportunities and Challenges of Apparel Sector-Led Industrialization

The apparel sector is regarded as a first step for low-income countries embarking on an export-oriented industrialization process. Given its low fixed costs, relatively simple technology, and labour-intensive nature, the apparel sector employs large numbers of unskilled workers (mostly women) and provides upgrading opportunities into higher value-added activities within and across sectors. Hence, apparel sector development can have important short-term effects by providing employment, income, and foreign exchange, and longer-term effects through the development of local firms with higher technological and organizational capabilities; the making of a working class with an industrial culture and a cadre of managers; linkages to other sectors, most importantly textiles; and the development of government institutions that can be employed to support other industrial sectors (Amsden 1994, 2001).

[3] This chapter is based on data collected during five research trips to Ethiopia in November 2015, June 2016, November/December 2016, June 2017, and January 2018. The first research trip was for a project funded by the International Centre for Trade and Sustainable Development together with Mike Morris. We interviewed 47 local and foreign textile and apparel firms (out of 99), including 23 locally owned firms (out of 49 in total, and all of those exporting) and 24 foreign firms. Interviews were also conducted with staff in government agencies including the Ethiopian Textile Industry Development Institute, Industrial Parks Development Corporation, Ethiopia Investment Commission, and Development Bank of Ethiopia; with the Secretary of the Ethiopian Textile and Garment Manufacturers Association; and with staff at Enterprise Partners.

But developing an apparel export sector in late-late industrializing countries such as Ethiopia is not easy. The global apparel market is organized in buyer-driven global value chains, meaning that it is characterized by decentralized, globally dispersed production networks coordinated by lead firms or global buyers that control high value-added activities (design, branding, retail) and outsource the manufacturing process and increasingly also non-manufacturing activities to a global network of suppliers. Requirements of global buyers in terms of quality, delivery and lead time, flexibility, and standard compliance, including safety, labour, and environmental standards, are high. Furthermore, lead firms expect supplier firms to acquire non-manufacturing capabilities such as skills in input sourcing, product development, inventory management, and stock holding, and organizing logistics as well as financing with which to do all of these things. But competition is also fierce, driving down unit prices, and production and trade patterns can be adjusted rather quickly to changing market conditions (Abernathy et al. 1999; Gereffi 1999; Gibbon and Ponte 2005; Palpacuer, Gibbon, and Thomsen 2005; Staritz 2011).

Locally owned firms in new supplier countries usually start with assembly. An assembly or cut-make-trim (CMT) manufacturer is responsible for sewing apparel and may be responsible for cutting the fabric and providing simple trim (buttons, zippers, etc.). The buyer provides product specifications and the fabric. The apparel factory is paid a processing fee. But lead firms increasingly demand broader functions from their suppliers. A full package (or FOB) supplier purchases the textile and accessory inputs and provides all production services, finishing, and packaging for delivery to the retail outlet. The customer provides the design and often nominates the textile suppliers that manufacturers must use. An FOB-textile supplier is a firm that also produces the fabric in-house. An original design manufacturer (ODM) is involved in the design and product development process. The last role in this trajectory is original brand manufacturing (OBM) where supplier firms develop their own brands and are thus also in charge of branding and marketing (Gereffi 1999). Taking over these functions means firms are paid higher prices but it also involves higher costs and risks that are challenging for local firms as they depend on intra-firm capabilities but also on factors outside the firm such as training institutes, transport infrastructure, logistics services, customs procedures, and access to finance and the creation of new financial instruments by local banks.

Historically, preferential trade agreements and foreign direct investment combined with supportive government industrial policies have been central to the development of apparel export sectors in new supplier countries. Trade agreements create the motivation for foreign direct investments, and in turn, foreign firms bring access to global sourcing and merchandising networks as well as tacit knowledge, providing the opportunity for local firms to learn the manufacturing and non-manufacturing capabilities required to be internationally competitive. However, such linkages and learning between foreign and local firms does not take place automatically. On the contrary, foreign firms may only focus on rather simple assembly activities in host countries, use their globalized input supplier networks, and be located in export processing or other industrial zones with limited contact and learning opportunities for local firms. This is particularly the case for many Asia-based transnational producers that organize global production and sourcing networks, while higher value-added functions and decision-making are located in their head offices in Asia. More embedded foreign investors with more local decision-making power may provide greater learning potential (Morris, Plank, and Staritz 2016).

40.3 State of the Apparel Export Sector in Ethiopia

Ethiopia's apparel exports were modest and remained largely flat at around US$1 million until the mid-2000s, climbing to around US$12 million by 2010. Since then, they have continued to rise substantially, accounting for US$82 million in 2016, as shown in Figure 40.1. The major end markets for apparel exports were the EU-15 (48 per cent) and the US (42 per cent). Textile exports accounted for US$26 million in 2016 and went primarily to Turkey (44 per cent) and the EU-15 (32 per cent). The decline in textile exports after 2013 is explained by the closure of several Turkish textile firms, for reasons explained later. In 2016, the textile and apparel export sector together accounted for 19 per cent of total manufacturing exports and 4 per cent of total exports, and employed around 55,000 people.[4] These figures are set to increase significantly, as firms in new apparel-specific industrial parks become fully operational. For example, the first phase of the Hawassa industrial park has the potential to employ 30,000 workers and even 60,000 workers if firms adopt two shifts.

The apparel export sector began with the establishment of locally owned firms in the mid-2000s, but exports only took off due to several waves of foreign direct investment (Staritz, Plank, and Morris 2016). The first was Turkish investment from around 2008/9 as a result of close diplomatic relations between the two governments and of Turkish firms' search for new low-cost locations as an alternative to North Africa in the context of the Arab Spring. Investment was largely in textile mills producing yarn and fabric, with the exception of Ayka Addis, which also produced apparel and became the largest apparel exporter, accounting for 43 per cent of total apparel exports in mid-2016. However, by 2017, four Turkish textile and apparel firms had defaulted on their loans to the Development Bank of Ethiopia (DBE) and were taken over by DBE, which continued to keep them operational while searching for buyers. The government strategy in the short term was to showcase Ethiopia as a country that could become a new global apparel supplier.

This strategy seems to have worked, particularly with the arrival of Ayka Addis, which put Ethiopia on the global apparel-sourcing map. This helped the government to convince a second group of foreign investors—Asian transnational apparel producers—to

[4] UN COMTRADE 2017; Ethiopian Textile Sector Profile 2016 from TIDI. Data from the Ethiopian Revenue and Custom Authority show similar but slightly different export developments. Differences are due to different reporting periods and reporting measures (imports reported in partner country versus exports reported by Ethiopia).

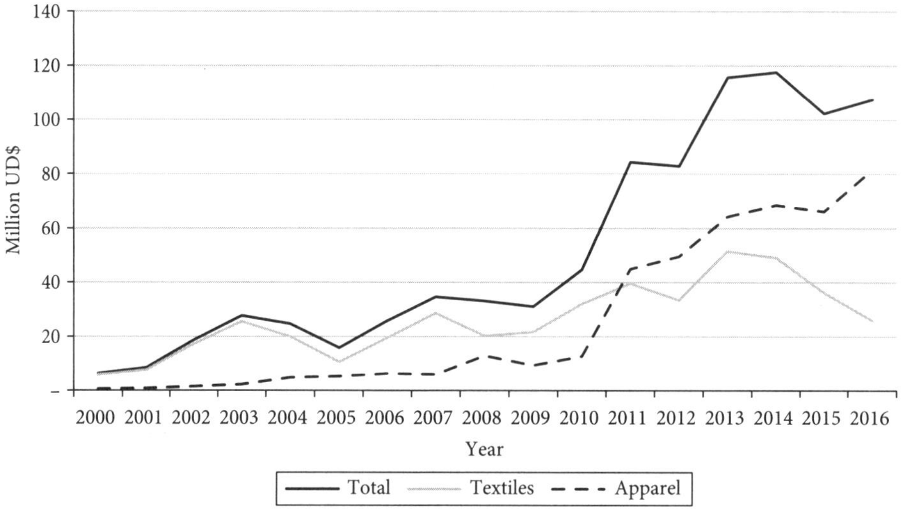

FIGURE 40.1 Ethiopia's apparel and textile exports, 2000–16

Note: Apparel represents HS92 61+62; textile represents HS92 50, 60+63; exports represent partners' imports.

Source: UN COMTRADE https://comtrade.un.org accessed (2017).

invest in Ethiopia. These firms and their global buyers sought out new low-cost countries as an alternative to Asian suppliers, also in response to compliance issues in major Asian producer countries. Ten foreign apparel firms opened factories in Bole Lemi Industrial Park in 2016, some of which were large first-tier supplier firms. The Eastern Industrial Park, a private park developed by Chinese investors, contains four smaller Chinese apparel and textile export firms.[5]

A third wave of foreign investments occurred in and around the industrial parks financed and operated by the government (see Figure 40.2). Hawassa Industrial Park was the flagship park with fifty-two sheds dedicated solely to the apparel export industry. By the end of 2017, nineteen foreign firms had taken almost all the sheds in Hawassa. They included one woven textile mill and two accessory firms supplying inputs to apparel firms in the park. Eleven firms had started exporting, although not at full capacity. The Mekele and Kombolcha parks were constructed by 2017, but investors had not yet moved in. These parks are on a smaller scale, with Kombolcha park having nine sheds and Mekele having fifteen sheds, but almost all sheds were taken by foreign investors. In 2018, industrial parks under construction in Adama and Dire Dawa already have some investors secured in textile and apparel manufacturing, and parks in Jimma and Bahir Dar are also planned. A planned railway under construction will link these parks to the Djibouti port. In Mekele, the government granted licenses and land for private industrial parks constructed by Vogue International from Dubai and DBL from

[5] For background information on Chinese special economic zones in Africa, see Brautigam and Xiaoyang (2011).

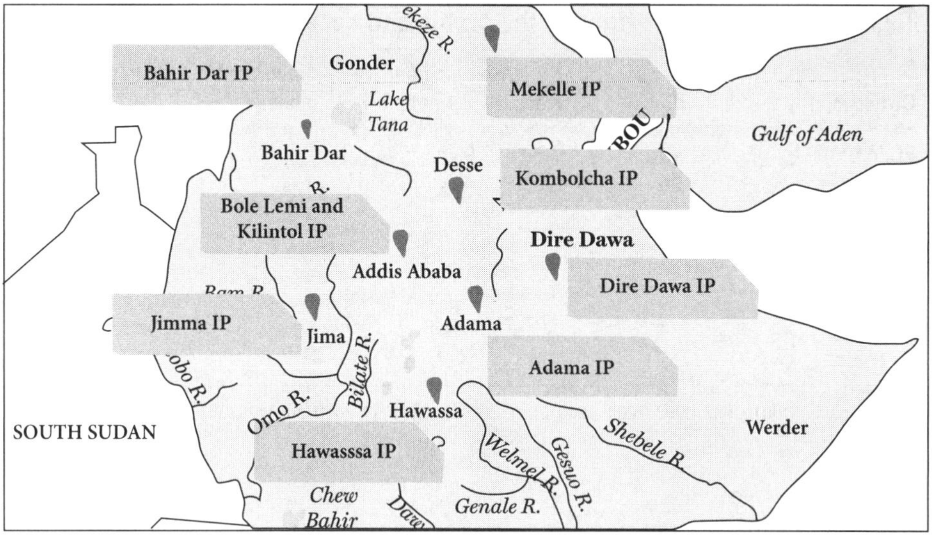

FIGURE 40.2 Industrial parks in Ethiopia constructed between 2015 and 2018

Source: IPDC 2016.

Bangladesh, which will probably not be completed until 2019. Velocity, the factory established by Vogue, started exporting on a small scale in 2017.

In sum, the textile and apparel sector includes twenty-three spinning and weaving/knitting mills, fourteen vertically integrated textile and apparel firms, and sixty-two apparel firms, making a total of ninety-nine firms, with seventy-six firms involved in apparel production, as shown in Table 40.1.[6] These figures include all the firms that had set up operations in the industrial parks by the end of 2017, even if they were not yet exporting. Notably, not all of the firms in Table 40.1 export. Some of the foreign firms located outside the industrial parks produce solely or partly for the domestic market, despite pressure from the government to export. In addition, most local firms produce solely for the domestic market. Of the forty Ethiopian-owned apparel and textile firms, only fourteen firms were exporting in 2017, twelve of which exported apparel and the other two made-up textiles (e.g. bed linen, towels). The share of local firms in exports declined continuously, from around 50 per cent of total textile and apparel exports between 2004/5 and 2007/8, to only 20 per cent in 2016/17 (see Figure 40.3).

The EPRDF government privatized state-owned textile and apparel firms.[7] They were sold largely to local private investors, but there were a few foreign investors or joint ventures. Two textile mills in Kombolcha and Bahir Dar could not be sold initially and thus the government invested in partial rehabilitation and encouraged the firms to export made-up textiles. They were eventually sold in 2017 to the Tiret Corporation, the

[6] Handwoven or cultural clothing firms are not included in these statistics.

[7] Ethiopia had several state-owned textile and apparel firms as a result of foreign direct investment in this sector encouraged during the Imperial era, which the Derg military government nationalized in addition to creating new state-owned enterprises.

Table 40.1 Overview of firms in the textile and apparel sector in 2017

Ownership	Total	Textile (spinning and weaving/knitting)	Integrated (textile and apparel)	Apparel
Ethiopia*	**49**	**9**	**10**	**30**
Foreign	**50**	**14**	**4**	**32**
China	18	11		7
India	6	2		4
Turkey	4	1	2	1
Korea	4			4
Sri Lanka*	4			4
European*	3			3
Pakistan	2		2	
Taiwan	2			2
UAE	2			2
Hong Kong	2			2
US	1			1
Indonesia	1			1
Israel	1			1
Total	**99**	**23**	**14**	**62**

Note: * The European firms include one joint venture with an Ethiopian partner, where the foreign partner seems to be dominant in business decisions. The Sri Lankan firms include one joint venture with a Chinese firm. One Ethiopian integrated firm is a joint venture with a Chinese firm but the local partner seems to be dominant. Two Ethiopian textile firms used to be Turkish, but they were taken over by DBE.

Source: Based on data from TIDI (2017) Data on Textile Industry. Addis Ababa, Unpublished. The data were confirmed by fieldwork information from firms. The number of total firms is an estimate, as not all firms producing for the domestic market may be captured.

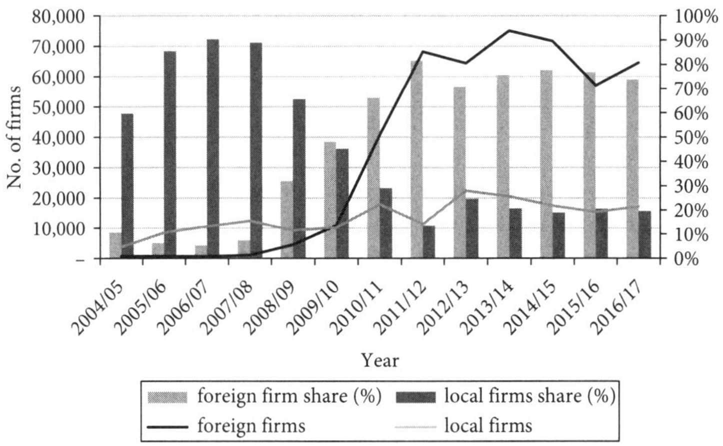

FIGURE 40.3 Apparel exports by local and foreign firms, 2004/5–2016/17

Source: TIDI, January 2017.

endowment-owned firm linked to the ANDM party. The privatized state-owned enterprises did not contribute to the sector's export growth and their performance was mixed: some eventually went bankrupt, some stopped exporting, and others only exported marginally. The outdated technology in the textile firms caused low efficiency and required significant investments, which local private entrepreneurs rarely had available, and loans from DBE for refurbishment were slow.

The eleven locally owned exporting firms that did not have a state-owned history had diverse ownership. Two of them were large vertically integrated firms located in the Tigray region, with one established by EFFORT, the endowment-owned firm linked to the TPLF party, and the other a sister company of the MIDROC diversified business group owned by Al-Amoudi. The remaining nine apparel-exporting firms were quite small in size.

40.4 Three Phases of Industrial Policy to Support Apparel Exports

This first industrial development strategy in 2002/3 was part of a general shift that recognized the need for active industrial policy and selected a number of priority sectors for targeted government support. The late Prime Minister, Meles Zenawi, was not only the intellectual driver behind this approach, he was also instrumental in choosing textile and apparel as a priority, because he knew that the sector historically had been a first step in the economic transformation of almost every now industrialized country (de Waal 2012). Industrial policy targeting the sector can be divided into three phases: first, incentivizing local investment in apparel production for export by providing access to land and credit; second, shifting to addressing key constraints of local export firms as well as attracting foreign direct investment; and third, prioritizing specialized industrial parks and attracting global buyers and their transnational producers. There were successes and failures with these industrial policies (see also chapters 35 and 36). In many ways, government policymakers and institutions learned from their failures with policy design and implementation, which was reflected in new approaches in subsequent policies.

40.4.1 Industrial Policy Phase One

The first phase of industrial policy included preferential credit and land schemes. The Development Bank of Ethiopia (DBE) provided local investors with a loan covering 70 per cent of the investment, with the investors providing the remaining 30 per cent in cash or in kind. The loan was provided at a 7.5 per cent interest rate for eight years with a two-year grace period. Firms also received income tax exemption for two years, which was later extended to five years. The government also provided access to land at favourable lease rates, or access to factory sheds in industrial villages at low rents.

Top EPRDF officials personally contacted people and encouraged them to invest. Several of these people were Ethiopian diaspora who had returned to Ethiopia and had close relations with the TPLF. From the mid-to-late 2000s, fifteen local investors took advantage of the government incentives and established small factories. These local investors came from various occupations and none of them had previous experience in textile and apparel production. Most of them did not succeed. Only six of the initial investors were actually exporting some proportion of their production in mid-2016, and only two of these firms were exporting 100 per cent.

Local investors jumped into the apparel export business without knowing what was required, but they were also encouraged by government officials who at that time also did not understand what was required to become competitive in the globalized apparel industry. The Ministry of Industry required local investors to have a feasibility study approved before giving them a business licence and DBE financing, but directed them to a local consultancy firm that produced the same feasibility study for every firm, which was not tailored to the global apparel industry. The investment plans did not build in enough working capital, and most firm owners did not hire foreign experts to assist them in learning apparel production and marketing.

All local firms struggled in the early years and were not really exporting. The government and local investors thought that locally available textile could be used for apparel export production, but most of the inputs had to be imported because many buyers nominated textile mills for their apparel suppliers to use in order to ensure conformity of products and because the existing textile mills in Ethiopia did not produce the kinds of fabric or the quality level required. Furthermore, there were no local accessory supplier firms. In response, the government set up a voucher system to facilitate the import of fabric and accessories tax free, but it was quite elaborate to ensure that local firms did not divert the imports to the domestic market and local firms had to learn how to use the system. Furthermore, the customs authorities were slow to clear imports and strictly administered the voucher system, which caused firms to miss delivery deadlines.

Firms were able to get buyers but not to keep them, because they could not meet delivery deadlines or product quality. Additionally, firms generally operated at low productivity, and their small factory size meant that they could only handle small orders. The only firms that managed to create stable relations with buyers were those producing for the same small set of US workwear and sportswear buyers, which were sourcing standard products with longer lead times. There was a lot of learning by mistakes with buyers, which was very costly, and thus many local firms exited exporting. They either sold their factories or shifted to producing mainly or only for the domestic market. In the domestic market, many firms produced uniforms for the government through tenders or for large corporations, using woven fabric that could be sourced locally. Most of them were not able to produce fashion products for the domestic market, because it required higher-quality fabric imports and priority access to foreign exchange, which firms that were not exporting did not have.

For all of these reasons, most (if not all) local firms operated at a loss, which meant that they could not pay off their DBE loans and accumulated debt. Thus, DBE had many non-performing loans to local apparel export firms, which in turn affected the general ability of all apparel firms to access finance. Shifting to the domestic market was also one strategy used by firms to pay back their loans.

40.4.2 Industrial Policy Phase Two

As a result of these challenges, the government pursued new industrial policies that were intended to resolve some of the constraints. It created the Ethiopian Textile Industry Development Institute (TIDI), a specialized agency that would be in charge of supporting local apparel and textile firms. TIDI offered free benchmarking studies; salary contribution when hiring foreign experts; free training for sewing machine operators, supervisors, and managers; and support in export marketing through sharing the cost of participating in trade shows abroad and sending prospective buyers to local firms. The government also put considerable effort into expanding universities to build local knowledge and to create vocational schools specializing in apparel. While this was important, the curricula were often outdated and graduates had no practical experience, and thus they were of little use to local firms that were trying to learn international standards. Of these policies, the most important for the immediate capability building of local firms was access to foreign experts who could bring into the firm the tacit knowledge that the owners and local management staff lacked.

The staff at TIDI had no practical experience in the apparel export business, and thus they hired consultancy firms to find foreign experts and place them with firms. However, the programme was still a failure, because the experts chosen were not very good and did not transfer knowledge. TIDI recognized not only this failure, but also that it had been unable to judge the quality of the experts and that their staff needed to gain knowledge before they could support local firms. Therefore, TIDI initiated its own learning process, and sent sixteen staff members to the National Institute of Fashion Technology in India to obtain master's degrees in technical and management aspects of apparel production. In addition, Indian experts came to TIDI to teach on the training programmes provided to local firms, undertake benchmarking studies for selected local firms, and design solutions to address their problems. However, TIDI's focus, using the Indian expert support, was on its own staff building capacity and not on directly solving local firms' problems. Thus the impact of these activities on local firms' performance was not monitored and there were few incentives for local firms to put effort into learning.[8]

TIDI's focus on its own capability building left local firms in the meantime without much support and under pressure to invest in learning. Donor-funded projects tried to fill this gap, but they were only marginally successful. The World Bank created the

[8] It is necessary for government institutions to learn before they can implement industrial policies that effectively catalyse local firms' learning, an issue that emerged not only at TIDI. DBE also had little expertise with which to judge the performance of the local firms and their constraints and thus how to deal with these non-performing loans.

Ethiopia Competitiveness Facility (2008–12), which aimed to help apparel export firms to build their export capabilities through knowledge transfer from foreign experts. The Facility covered the majority of the costs of hiring experts, and most of the local apparel-exporting firms benefited from the scheme. It was continued after 2012 with financing from the UK aid agency DFID, which along with co-financing experts also provided co-financing for some equipment. The UK aid agency created another scheme in 2015 to support local exporting firms, which covered all expert costs and participation in international trade fairs. However, these schemes were not working. Knowledge transfer between experts and local firm managers was either not taking place or only very slowly. Many firm owners were not taking an active role in monitoring experts and ensuring knowledge transfer, and some of them just used the experts to do daily tasks rather than to learn from them. The local firms that have performed the best are those that sourced and financed foreign experts themselves and devised ways to encourage knowledge transfer.

Other donor agencies tried to help local firms by bringing buyers to Ethiopia to visit local firms, but making contact with buyers was not the main constraint; it was supplying them on time and with the required quality. Delivery time was a particular problem with European buyers that wanted to source on an FOB basis. Some challenges were internal to the firm, where firms had weak merchandising and planning capabilities and lacked experience with global input sourcing, as well as low labour productivity due to weak monitoring schemes and high labour turnover. Firms reacted differently to labour turnover with some offering free services and installing incentive schemes to retain workers. Other challenges were external to the firm, such as access to working capital with which to finance fabric imports, a long wait for foreign exchange, and slow customs clearance. While the DBE and customs worked to improve their services, constraints remained. Apparel firms that moved into production on an FOB basis only did so because their buyers demanded it, but the buyers provided support in negotiating the price and quality of fabric through their nominated suppliers, and thus shouldered the input sourcing risk. The main problem, however, was still meeting delivery times due to the slow purchase and receipt of inputs. Integrated textile firms that produce export-quality knit fabric were better able to deliver on time because they produced their own fabric. They were able to source 100 per cent cotton yarn locally, capitalizing on the existence of and improving quality of cotton production and spinning mills in Ethiopia.

The local firms that continued with CMT apparel exports often managed to secure one or two stable buyers. But such a small number of buyers left the firms vulnerable to external factors, such as the Eurozone crisis causing buyers to withdraw orders. With small factories, firms could often, however, not produce for more than one or two buyers. In response, the firms that continued to export had to expand their factory, which they did through DBE expansion loans. Some firms that continued to export on a CMT basis also developed new strategies for domestic market production in basic and fashion products, because they had access to foreign exchange.

More local apparel firms emerged in the 2000s and early 2010s, but only produced for the protected domestic market where profits are higher. Only a few of these firms tried to export. They primarily did so in order to have their own foreign exchange with which to buy imports for their domestic market business, but also to learn about productivity, quality, and design, often also for their domestic business. The latter aspect is particularly important as some of these local firms began CMT production for exports while they produced on an ODM basis, including their own designs and even brands for the domestic market.

Local apparel-exporting firms struggled to develop the required manufacturing and non-manufacturing capabilities to be internationally competitive despite these support programmes. As a result, the technological capabilities of locally owned firms in 2016 were generally low, despite some diversity. This assessment is based on a survey that we carried out with all of the local apparel export firms active at that time.

In this phase of industrial policy, the government also placed more emphasis on attracting foreign firms (Staritz, Plank, and Morris 2016). It initiated marketing visits to leading apparel buying and producing countries and built the Bole Lemi Industrial Park for apparel and footwear exports with World Bank financing. The park provided factory sheds with low rents, and supplied electricity, water, an effluent water treatment plant, and communication services. While many of the foreign firms that invested in Bole Lemi were large transnational suppliers, they produced on a CMT basis, having higher value functions in their headquarters and importing all inputs using their own textile producers or global supplier networks. It became clear to the government that the foreign exchange benefits derived from exporting apparel if all the inputs are imported is not large. The single focus on foreign direct investment meant that the park had few benefits for local firms, either directly through profiting from services offered in the park or indirectly through linking with and learning from the foreign firms in the park.

40.4.3 Industrial Policy Phase Three

A government white paper in 2015 set out the concept of the industrial parks targeting specific sectors and the proactive policy of seeking certain kinds of foreign direct investment. This white paper was based on a study by government officials of the experiences of other developing countries with export processing zones, particularly South Korea, Singapore, and China, as well as what had gone wrong with these zones in some African countries. Some key ideas from these experiences that influenced how the industrial parks in Ethiopia were set up include the following. First was the need to make industrial parks sector specific in order to promote cluster and agglomeration benefits. A second key idea was that the parks should create something more than CMT in order to avoid the risk of foreign firms being footloose and leaving when labour costs rose. Thus, the parks should have textile and accessories production, with the broader aim of developing complete vertical integration within the country from cotton fibre to apparel. A third key idea was to make the parks environmentally sustainable by having zero-liquid discharge facilities and making factory sheds in the parks compliant with international standards, in order to market Ethiopia as a sustainable sourcing country.[9] Lastly, the industrial parks were seen as providing a solution to the challenges that had emerged for existing local and foreign investors. The parks would reduce delivery time and production costs by providing all necessary facilities within the parks, improving customs clearance speed, and investing in an electric railway system connecting the parks to the Djibouti port.

The new parks were financed solely by the government so that they could lead the process, and implemented by the Ethiopian Investment Commission (EIC) and the Industrial Park Development Corporation (IPDC). Hawassa Industrial Park was the government's flagship textile and apparel industrial park. The US company Phillips-Van Heusen (PVH), a major global apparel buyer, became the 'anchor' for the park and instrumental in its design and realization of the park by encouraging some of its own preferred apparel suppliers and one of its nominated woven fabric supplier firms to open factories. Other Asian transnational producers invested in the Hawassa park because their US buyers encouraged them to set up factories in Ethiopia. The Mekelle and Kombolcha industrial parks do not have a leading buyer as an 'anchor' to the same extent as Hawassa yet, but several big buyers such as H&M are looking to source from those parks, which have attracted large and small foreign firms as well as investment in spinning and textile facilities.

Despite its impressive status as Africa's largest industrial park and an environmentally sustainable one, many challenges were encountered at Hawassa as the foreign firms began operations. Many of the initial bottlenecks inside the park related to government and utility services were resolved quickly, and ongoing transport logistics issues related to speed and cost may be addressed relatively quickly as the railway becomes operational. However, constraints facing foreign firms related to labour sourcing, retention, and productivity as well as housing, transport, and food prices in Hawassa town (which drive up the cost of labour) will take some time to resolve. Many of these issues have to do with factors outside the park and thus involve the regional government and the Hawassa municipal government. High labour turnover and low labour productivity within the park is also a challenge that relates to the making of an industrial working class, as operators learn industrial culture and supervisors perceive career opportunities. The EIC, IPDC, Investors Association, labour unions in the park, regional governments, and other actors have to work together to come up with and implement solutions.

In contrast to Bole Lemi, the new industrial parks are supposed to include local investors. The industrial policy includes support for local firms to take sheds in the parks through DBE investment loans where local firms only put up 15 per cent of the investment as well as co-financing for the hire of expatriate experts and support with buying machines. The strategy also entails direct efforts to link local firms with buyers and as sub-contractors and input suppliers to foreign firms operating in the parks. However, there was limited progress on this aspect of the industrial policy by the

[9] Tragedies in Asian supplier countries highlight the problematic labour and environmental conditions that have prevailed in the global apparel industry.

beginning of 2018, as government efforts were focused on solving the challenges facing foreign firms described above.

40.5 Conclusions

Despite the comparatively low costs of labour, trade preferences, the interest of EU and US buyers in sourcing from Ethiopia, and proactive industrial policies, it was difficult for Ethiopian-owned firms to take advantage of the possibilities to enter and remain in the apparel export sector (see also Chapters 35, 36, and 39). The entry costs into apparel global value chains were high. Firms have to acquire technological, managerial, and organizational knowledge, forge relations with input suppliers across the globe, create trust with buyers where constant and fast communication is key, build a compliant factory, and perhaps most importantly in a labour-intensive activity, have a managerial team that can motivate workers using incentives and monitoring to achieve a high level of productivity. At the same time, unit prices for apparel are low due to high competition, resulting in low profit margins for CMT and FOB production and a steep learning curve, as buyers are not very patient when they can easily switch to new suppliers.

Some buyers seem to make some concessions in Ethiopia and are trying to help local firms, or at least put up with a greater number of mistakes, because they see Ethiopia as a strategic supplier country in their longer-term sourcing strategies. This has allowed local firms more scope for learning, but only with a particular set of buyers in basic products with long lead times, which is also where unit prices tend to be the lowest. Locally owned firms have established stable relationships with these buyers, but struggled to do so with other types of buyers, which limits the learning possibilities of buyer–supplier relationships. As to local firms that do have stable relationships, buyers tend to help them by giving feedback during their quality control checks and selectively on switching to FOB; however, buyers generally do not support firms further.

Therefore, local firms have struggled to learn and develop the requisite manufacturing and non-manufacturing capabilities to be internationally competitive in CMT and FOB production. The crucial question is how to support and finance the period of learning for local firms and ensure that local firms put investment and effort into learning. Learning is a costly process and takes time, and thus many local firms are experiencing losses in their export business due to their low productivity combined with low prices set by buyers. The Ethiopian government sees this and has offered loans through DBE that allow for grace periods and for debt to be rescheduled.

To remain operational, firms need a source of further capital including working capital without taking out more loans. This working capital comes, at least partly, from producing for the domestic market or from other business activities in the case of owners having diversified businesses or other business lines. Many of the local firms produce apparel for the domestic market as a strategy to ensure profits while learning how to meet the cost, quality, and delivery standards and investing in their physical facilities in order to meet the productivity and quality as well as social and environmental standards of their export markets. Firms that have other businesses also seem to fund losses in apparel exporting through their other business activities.

Hence, the government's dual policy that combines export focus with import substitution through a protected domestic market has helped the development of apparel exports by local firms by subsidizing their cost of learning to become competitive.[10] But it has also reduced the incentives for them to undertake the hard process of developing the capabilities required to compete, creating a wide 'latitude for performance standards' (Oqubay 2015). The dangers are: never moving from the comfort of the domestic market to the rigours of the export market; and not using the buffer of the domestic market and related profits for investment in learning and capability building.

Of crucial importance are the reciprocal control mechanisms that ensure that industrial policy catalyses local firms to invest in learning and is linked to performance improvements (Amsden 2001). The schemes TIDI provided did not monitor the impacts on local firms' performance, and no mechanisms were put in place whereby local firms were expected to increase their performance in return for subsidized support. Hence, firm owners got used to receiving free or subsidized support. DBE tried to link investment and expansion financing to export performance but was limited in its own knowledge of the sector and in the need to help firms become profitable rather than shut down non-performing firms. It seems that reciprocal control mechanisms of the kind that Alice Amsden discusses with respect to Asian countries worked because local firms already had some experience in manufacturing and managing complex firms, which is not the case in Ethiopia. Thus, Ethiopian entrepreneurs need more than enforcement of learning, they need direct support for learning, which cannot be provided by government institutions whose staff have an equivalent or even more limited understanding of the sector.

For late-late export-oriented industrialization, but particularly for African countries where there is much less experience with manufacturing than in other developing-country regions, foreign firms that have the knowledge to compete successfully in apparel global value chains may provide a necessary source from which local firms can learn the capabilities required in the sector. Historically this has been the case, as learning from foreign firms was crucial in the emergence of the Mauritian, Bangladeshi, and Sri Lankan apparel export industries (see for example Lamusse 1989; Quddus and Rashid 2000; Kelegama 2009).

The foreign firms operating in industrial parks offer an important opportunity for locally owned firms to build their capabilities indirectly through closer contact with and observation of state-of-the-art factories and best practices, and through the circulation of workers and managers trained at foreign firms. More importantly, local firms can also learn directly by providing inputs or services and sub-contracting to foreign firms.

[10] The government continues to protect the domestic market with a 35 per cent tariff on imported fabric and apparel, and a further 10 per cent surcharge and 10 per cent excise tax. Import substitution is also an important means of saving foreign exchange and creating jobs, and can create backward and forward linkages in the economy.

But the outcomes will still have to be seen in terms of existing or new local firms being able to use linkages with foreign firms in the new industrial parks to increase exports and capabilities. Outside the parks there are minimal linkages between foreign and local firms in the export business.

These limited linkages result from the low capabilities of locally owned apparel and textile firms but also foreign firms' and their buyers' globalized sourcing strategies and restrictions on sub-contracting that limit any linkages with local firms from the outset. Foreign firms in the industrial parks may support eventual subcontracting to local firms in the parks, because their factory sheds meet compliance standards, or buyers sourcing from foreign firms in the parks may try sourcing from local firms located there as well. However, industrial policy will have an important role in supporting local apparel firms in the parks (and outside) and their learning through linkages with foreign firms. Learning from foreign investments also involves targeting selected foreign investors that are more embedded in the host country and hence are willing to operate differently from the usual transnational producers rather than being dependent on CMT production and global sourcing networks. For the apparel sector to have broader industrialization and economic transformation effects it will be crucial to retain a focus on local firms and incentivize local firms' capability building.

Labour turnover and low labour productivity is a general issue affecting the profitability of local and foreign firms. It is not just an issue for firms located in and near Addis Ababa, where there are broader employment opportunities, but also for firms in Hawassa and most likely in the other parks as they start operations. There was high labour turnover in Hawassa not only among machine operators, but also among middle managers, some of whom undertook training in Asian countries paid for by the foreign investor. The issue is a structural one. Workers migrating from rural areas, as well as workers who had jobs in other sectors in towns and cities, are not used to the discipline, pace, and culture of working in an apparel export factory. Middle managers, finding the job demanding, sought easier employment elsewhere. There is no immediate solution, and it will be several years before an industrial working class emerges. Some foreign firms understood this and built it into their expectations of starting operations in a new supplier country, estimating that it would take five years to achieve a stable workforce, but local firms were less able to absorb the costs of low labour productivity and high turnover (see also Chapter 31 and 38).

To ensure competitiveness, higher value added, and broader learning, and to avoid the traditional footloose nature of the global apparel industry, it is also crucial to remain focused on the whole national supply chain. The government's efforts to do that involve improving the domestic production and quality of cotton and encouraging foreign and local textile and accessories firms to invest in the country. The outcomes remain to be seen.

References

Abernathy, Frederick H., John T. Dunlop, Janice H. Hammond, and David Weil (1999). *A Stitch in Time: Lean Retailing and the Transformation of Manufacturing—Lessons from the Apparel and Textile Industries* (New York: Oxford University Press).

Amsden, Alice (1994). 'The Textile Industry in Asian Industrialization: A Leading Sector Institutionally?' *Journal of Asian Economics* 5 (4): 573–84.

Amsden, Alice (2001). *The Rise of 'The Rest': Challenges to the West from Late-Industrializing Economies* (Oxford: Oxford University Press).

Brautigam, Deborah and Tang Xiaoyang (2011). 'African Shenzhen: China's Special Economic Zones in Africa', *Journal of Modern African Studies* 49 (1): 27–54.

de Waal, Alex (2012). 'The Theory and Practice of Meles Zenawi', *African Affairs* 112 (446): 148–55.

Gereffi, Gary (1999). 'International Trade and Industrial Upgrading in the Apparel Commodity Chain', *Journal of International Economics* 48: 37–70.

Gibbon, Peter and Stefano Ponte. (2005). *Trading Down: Africa, Value Chains, and the Global Economy* (Philadelphia, PA: Temple University Press).

Kelegama, Saman (2009). 'Ready-Made Garment Exports from Sri Lanka', *Journal of Contemporary Asia* 39 (4): 579–96.

Lamusse, Roland (1989). 'Adjustment to Structural Change in Manufacturing in a North–South Perspective: The Case of the Clothing Export Sector in Mauritius', World Employment Programme Working Paper No. 27, International Labour Organization, Geneva.

Morris, Mike, Leonhard Plank, and Cornelia Staritz (2016). 'Regionalism, End Markets and Ownership Matter: Shifting Dynamics in the Apparel Export Industry in Sub-Saharan Africa', *Environment and Planning A* 48 (7): 1244–65.

Oqubay, Arkebe (2015). *Made in Africa: Industrial Policy in Ethiopia* (Oxford: Oxford University Press).

Palpacuer, Florence, Peter Gibbon, and Lotte Thomsen (2005). 'New Challenges for Developing Country Suppliers in Global Clothing Chains: A Comparative European Perspective', *World Development* 33 (3): 409–30.

Quddus, Munir, and Salim Rashid (2000). *Entrepreneurs and Economic Development: The Remarkable Story of Garment Exports from Bangladesh* (Dhaka: The University Press).

Staritz, Cornelia (2011). 'Making the Cut? Low-Income Countries and the Global Clothing Value Chain in a Post-Quota and Post-Crisis World', World Bank Study, World Bank. https://openknowledge.worldbank.org/handle/10986/2547.

Staritz, Cornelia, and Stacey Frederick (2016). 'Harnessing Foreign Direct Investment for Local Development? Spillovers in Apparel Global Value Chains in Sub-Saharan Africa', ÖFSE Working Paper No. 59, Austrian Foundation for Development Research, Vienna. http://www.oefse.at.

Staritz, Cornelia, Leonhard Plank, and Mike Morris (2016). 'Global Value Chains, Industrial Policy, and Sustainable Development: Ethiopia's Apparel Export Sector', Country Case Study, International Centre for Trade and Sustainable Development, September, Geneva. 2016. https://www.ictsd.org/sites/default/files/research/global_value_chains_industrial_policy_and_sustainable_development.pdf (accessed on 1 September 2018)

CHAPTER 41

TECHNOLOGICAL LEARNING AND INDUSTRIALIZATION IN ETHIOPIA

TAFFERE TESFACHEW

41.1 Introduction

Ethiopia has been among the fastest-growing economies globally since 2003, with growth consistently well above the African and global averages, and extreme poverty was halved between 2003 and 2014. Building on these initial successes, Ethiopia has embarked on the next stage of the catch-up process, adopting an export-led and private sector-driven industrialization strategy anchored in the manufacturing sector, focused on medium-term development goals for 2025. The key objectives of Vision 2025 include: attaining middle-income status; increasing the share of manufacturing in GDP from 5 per cent to 17 per cent; achieving and sustaining double-digit growth; and becoming a leading manufacturing hub in Africa. As the country pursues these ambitious and demanding goals, however, it may prove increasingly difficult to rely on the same public investment-led and service sector-driven growth trajectory. In addition to overcoming existing trade, investment, and logistics-related constraints, achieving Vision 2025 will require the technological and innovative capabilities needed to manufacture and export higher-value, higher-quality, and more sophisticated products. Technological progress and innovation are fundamental drivers of industrialization and competitiveness, and their absence is a key factor underlying both the limited progression of low-income countries to middle-income status and the middle-income trap (Lundvall 2016; Lin 2017). Ethiopia's ability to achieve its middle-income and manufacturing goals will thus depend heavily on its success in building local technological and innovation capability (Lall 1992).

This chapter examines the level of technological development and the pattern of technological learning and upgrading in Ethiopia in the light of these goals, and assesses the country's potential to build the technological, innovation, and organizational capabilities needed to catch up with middle-income countries and develop an internationally competitive manufacturing capable of sustaining development beyond the middle-income trap. The chapter is organized as follows. We begin with a comparative analysis of Ethiopia's technological capability, based on indices commonly used for international comparisons. Next a conceptual framework is presented that describes the main channels of technology transfer and technological learning in the early stages of industrialization. This framework is then applied to assess the pattern of technological learning in Ethiopia and its congruence with the goals of Vision 2025. The final section draws conclusions.

41.2 Benchmarking Ethiopia's Technological and Innovation Capabilities

This chapter provides a snapshot of Ethiopia's technological development based on three sets of indirect measures of technological and innovation capabilities reflecting:[1]

- a macro perspective based on five directly relevant pillars of the Global Competitiveness Index (GCI) (infrastructure, higher education and training, technological readiness, business sophistication, and innovation);[2]
- the relative importance of technology in manufacturing;[3] and
- the technological content of total exports based on the export shares of high- and medium-technology products.

Ethiopia's relative position is assessed by benchmarking against Kenya and Bangladesh, with which Ethiopia hopes to catch up in the next decade; and Vietnam and the Republic of Korea, as countries with which Ethiopia ultimately hopes to converge (Table 41.1). The overall conclusion is that Ethiopia lags behind in global benchmarking on key indicators of technological development and innovation.

[1] While firm-level evidence typically presents a more accurate and reliable measurement of a country's technological development than international indices, which are prone to data gaps and unreliability, careful and selective use of the latter can be useful in gauging relative performance and technological or development gaps between countries.

[2] The GCI, published annually by the World Economic Forum as part of the Global Competitiveness Report, ranks 137 countries in terms of international competitiveness based on twelve pillars (policy domains), each being a weighted average of a set of relevant indicators. This study considers five pillars relevant to technological development: *infrastructure* (quality of electricity supply, roads, fixed-telephone lines, mobile telephone subscriptions, etc); *higher education and training* (tertiary education enrolment, quality of education systems, particularly maths and science, schools' internet access, specialized technical training, etc); *technological readiness* (availability of latest technologies, firm-level technology absorption, percentage of internet users, FDI technology transfer, broadband internet subscriptions, etc); *business sophistication* (local supply quantity and quality, cluster development, value-chain breadth, production process sophistication, etc); and *innovation* (quality of scientific research institutions, R&D expenditure, university–industry collaboration, availability of scientists and engineers, etc.).

[3] Data on manufacturing are from UNIDO's Competitive Industrial Performance Index 2016.

Table 41.1 Selected indicators of competitiveness and level of technological development

The Macro Perspective					
Competitiveness score 2017	Bangladesh	Ethiopia	Kenya	Korea, Rep.	Vietnam
Infrastructure	2.9 (111)	2.7 (115)	3.5 (96)	6.1 (8)	3.9 (79)
Higher education and training	3.1 (117)	2.8 (125)	3.9 (97)	5.3 (25)	4.1 (84)
Technology readiness	2.8 (120)	2.4 (130)	3.7 (88)	5.6 (29)	4 (79)
Business sophistication	3.7 (91)	3.5 (112)	4.3 (47)	4.9 (26)	3.7 (100)
Innovation	2.8 (114)	3.2 (86)	3.8 (37)	-	3.3 (71)
The sectoral perspective					
Manufacturing sector 2016	Bangladesh	Ethiopia	Kenya	Korea, Rep.	Vietnam
Share of MVA in total GDP	12%	4%	10%	29%	20%
Med-high tech VA share in total MVA	24%	16%	13%	64%	40%
Med-high tech ME share in total ME	49%	33%	22%	76%	49%
Industrialization Intensity Index	32	15	22	80	53
At product level by technological classification					
% of total exports	Bangladesh	Ethiopia	Kenya	Korea, Rep.	Vietnam
2015					
High tech	0%	1%	2%	42%	40%
Low tech	94%	10%	17%	10%	35%
Medium tech	1%	5%	5%	32%	9%
Primary products	3%	65%	59%	3%	12%
Resources-based	1%	20%	17%	13%	5%
2005					
High tech	0%	0%	1%	45%	5%
Low tech	88%	8%	16%	12%	42%
Medium tech	2%	1%	5%	30%	7%
Primary products	6%	80%	52%	2%	40%
Resources-based	3%	10%	26%	10%	6%

Notes: Numbers in brackets represent competitiveness ranking out of 137 countries. MVA = Manufacturing Value Added; ME = Manufacturing Exports.

Source: WEF; UNIDO; World Bank, WITS.

Ethiopia is in the bottom quintile globally for four of the five technology-related GCI pillars, remaining behind Bangladesh, Kenya, Vietnam, and Korea in infrastructure, technological readiness (ranking 130th of 137 countries), business sophistication (112th), and higher education (125th). However, its ranking on innovation (86th) is comparable with Vietnam and ahead of Bangladesh, due largely to a major recent increase in public expenditure on R&D, motivated by the African Union target of 1 per cent of GDP.

UNIDO's Industrialization Intensity Index measures the technological complexity of production structures, technological capabilities, and knowledge intensity of production systems. Ethiopia scores significantly lower than the comparators, especially Vietnam and Korea (Table 41.1), suggesting that its manufacturing sector remains at an early technological catch-up phase of development. Despite sustained rapid growth since 2002, its manufacturing share in GDP remains significantly below both the comparators and the low-income country average (12.9 per cent) (UNIDO 2017).

Limited manufacturing-sector development also explains Ethiopia's poor performance in medium- and high-tech exports.[4] Between 2005 and 2015, high-tech exports only rose from zero to 1 per cent, while primary and resource-based products (such as coffee, oil seeds, live animals) fell only from 90 per cent to 85 per cent. Over the same period, increasing technological capabilities and diversification of production capacity allowed Vietnam to increase high-tech exports from 5 per cent to 40 per cent, while its primary and resource-based exports fell from 46 per cent to 17 per cent. In Bangladesh, continuing consolidation of textile production and exports led to continued dominance of low-tech exports (rising from 88 per cent to 94 per cent), despite more than thirty years of successful diversification into the manufacturing sector. This may reflect limited technological learning and upgrading in manufacturing, locking the country into a low-productivity and low-technology production trap. Moving forward, Ethiopia must decide which of these paths—Bangladesh's or Vietnam's—to follow.

41.3 Technological Learning During Early Catch-Up Stages of Industrialization: an Analytical Framework

Reflecting space constraints, this chapter focuses on three elements widely acknowledged as critical to technological learning in the early stages of development: technology transfer; local absorptive capacity development; and the industrial policy framework, technology policy.[5] Successful technological learning and capability building depends on the interaction of these three closely connected elements, focused on absorptive capacity building.

41.3.1 Technology Transfer

Technology transfer is the diffusion of technology and knowledge across national boundaries, through formal commercial transactions or informal channels.[6] In the

[4] UNIDO's technological classification of exports of manufactures is based on Lall's classification of export products by technology content; see Lall (2000).

[5] A more comprehensive coverage of the issues is available elsewhere (Lall 1992; Bell and Pavitt 1992)

[6] See Wahab, Rose, and Osman (2012) for a review of the literature on technology transfer. As shown from the East Asian experience, the most effective technology policies were those that were formulated as an integral part of industrial policy and complementary to investment, production, trade, skills, and other policies

absence of local technology generation capacity, technology transfer remains an important source of technological learning and innovation for latecomers to industrialization such as Ethiopia, particularly through trade, foreign direct investment (FDI), and movement of skilled persons, highlighting the importance of policies in these areas.[7]

41.3.2 International Trade

In the early catch-up stages of development, innovation and technological learning generally occur mainly through importation of machinery and equipment, which allows application, adaptation, and assimilation of the technologies they embody, and ultimately mastery of the capabilities needed to replicate and improve on them. Technological learning and upgrading and trade are thus closely linked. However, the link is neither automatic nor simple, rather depends on the types of goods imported, their compatibility with local factors of production, domestic absorptive capacity, and the intensity of policy efforts.

Trade policies, trading costs, and market access also have implications for technology transfer. Indeed, advocacy of trade liberalization is motivated partly by its potential to facilitate technology transfer by reducing legal, regulatory, and political barriers to trade in goods with a high technology content, and thus to increase access to imported capital goods and reduce the cost of technology adaptation (Wahab, Rose, and Osman 2012). However, the presumption of such a trade–technology nexus may be over-optimistic.[8] Trade openness rather needs to be accompanied by industrial and technology policies that improve capacity to identify and absorb technology.

41.3.3 Foreign Direct Investment (FDI)

Investment in new production capacity by foreign firms can bring with it technological, managerial, and marketing capabilities, and firm-specific competencies and assets that distinguish it from competitor firms, making FDI a potentially important source of technology. Knowledge and skills may spread to local firms through spillovers, demonstration effects, supplier linkages, FDI-driven competition (forcing local firms to upgrade), and training of workers who subsequently move to domestic firms (Saggi 2002). Efficiency-seeking FDI also creates opportunities for host countries' participation in global value chains (GVCs).

essential for growth and structural transformation. While recognizing the role of industrial policy, for lack of space, this chapter will focus on technology policy.

[7] Other channels of technology and knowledge transfer include licensing, interaction with suppliers or customers; and purchase of technology property rights.

[8] The declining shares of manufacturing in GDP that accompanied trade liberalization in in Ethiopia and other African countries in the 1980s, for example, are suggestive of 'premature deindustrialization'. See Tregenna (2015).

However, the impact of FDI on technological learning in the host economy is neither straightforward nor 'always benign' (Akyuz 2017: 198), but depends, inter alia, on the structure of the host economy, the policy environment, the learning capacity of local firms and the nature and sectoral focus of FDI. In principle, FDI in sectors with greater potential for local sourcing, such as agro-processing, generates more spillovers than in sectors such as mining, where enclave operations are common. Equally, green-field investment establishing new production capacity generates greater productivity gains and technology sharing, as do joint ventures between FDI and local firms (Harrison and Rodriguez-Clare 2009). Thus, a sectoral focus and emphasis on green-field investments and joint ventures may be more beneficial than blanket incentives and subsidies for FDI.

Increasing the share of trade and investment flows among developing countries (South–South cooperation) has opened an alternative route for technological learning and capability building in early stages of the catch-up process. Over half of Africa's imports originate from other developing countries, mainly in East Asia. Similarly, half the top ten investors in Africa during 2016 were developing economies, and China's FDI stock in Africa increased almost three-fold between 2010 and 2015 (UNCTAD 2017). While the evidence is limited, trade and FDI flows between countries with narrower technological gaps may have qualitatively different impacts on technological learning and capability building. This issue deserves closer attention, considering the growing importance of South–South trade and investment.

41.3.4 Movement of Skilled Persons

Technological learning depends critically on the mobility of skilled and experienced workers, managers, and technicians, particularly from technologically better endowed firms (notably foreign-owned corporations) to other firms. This type of movement can determine firms' learning efficiency and rate of technological capability building (Kim 1999; Lee 2013).

This is of particular importance for technological understanding (the ability to utilize technology efficiently and adapt it to local needs and conditions), as opposed to technological means (machinery and equipment) and technological information (instructions and blueprints). An important component of virtually all technologies and technological understanding is tacit or non-codified knowledge, which is difficult to transmit or transfer (Wahab, Rose, and Osman 2012). It is acquired primarily through training and time-consuming processes of interactive learning, and learning by doing, using, and observing (Nelson and Winter 1982), making continuous interaction the key channel for technology transfer. Thus 'the mobility of experienced technical people was one of the most effective ways for late-entrants to acquire the necessary tacit knowledge base' (Kim 1999: 20). In the early catch-up stage, deficiencies in tacit knowledge could be compensated by encouraging cross-border movement of highly skilled and experienced persons to work as expatriates and transfer knowledge through interactive engagement with local workers.

While temporary movements of skilled workers may increase a country's overall skill endowment, permanent outward migration of educated and skilled professionals will almost certainly reduce its stock of tacit knowledge and human capital, and thus its capacity to learn from imported technology (UNCTAD 2013). In the newly industrialized East Asian economies, reversing the 'brain drain' by encouraging skilled and experienced members of the diaspora to return was an important part of the policy effort to promote technological learning and upgrading (Kim 1997).[9]

41.3.5 Absorptive Capacity Building

Ultimately, the ability of countries and firms to apply, assimilate, adapt, and learn from imported technologies depends on the 'existing knowledge base' (Kim 1999: 8) and the capacity of the domestic economy to expand and broaden that base through investment and policies that support continuous learning and accumulation of tacit knowledge. This is the core of a country's 'absorptive capacity' and the enabling environment for technological learning and capability building. Strengthening absorptive capacity necessarily requires policy interventions across a wide range of areas directly or indirectly affecting the ability of individuals, firms, and organizations to learn and increase their knowledge base (Kim 1995).

Two policy areas are particularly important in this context: human capital development and building R&D capacity.

41.3.6 Human Capital Development

Human capital is a fundamental determinant of absorptive capacity and the ability to benefit from technology transfer and technological learning. East Asian experiences highlight the importance of optimizing the use of human capital, especially when skills are limited. Lee, for example, concludes that 'only those countries that have invested heavily in the formation of skills and R&D ability seem to be capable of catching up, and those that have not made such investment are falling further behind' (Lee 2013: 25).

While investment is essential, more important is the quality of education and strengthening the essential basic technical skills needed for the operation and maintenance of technology and for business management. This requires a three-pronged approach: an inclusive national education system offering learning opportunities; building the

[9] The policies used to attract members of the diaspora included direct engagement with highly skilled individuals and creating attractive working conditions (higher salaries, better accommodation) for them to return and contribute to home-country development.

capacity for technical and vocational education and training (TVET); and prioritizing advanced human capital development at the tertiary level, with the emphasis on science- and engineering-related skills.

41.3.7 R&D Capacity Building

During the early catch-up stage of development, technological learning and upgrading occurs through acquisition of new technologies and knowledge from elsewhere rather than local R&D and innovation. The R&D capabilities of low-income countries, both at firm level and in R&D-focused centres, are generally limited. Of 3.1 million patent applications filed worldwide during 2016, fewer than 10,000 (0.4 per cent) were from the 31 low-income countries (WIPO 2017: 45).

However, R&D activities in firms and specialized institutions are by no means unimportant. Expanding R&D capacity is an integral part of domestic absorptive capacity building, playing an essential role in reinforcing technological learning by generating new products and processes that can improve productivity, both by increasing firms' capacities to absorb transferred technologies and through direct effects on innovation (Kinoshita 2000). This requires close interaction between specialized R&D centres and local firms, which tends to be limited at early stages of development. Institutions dedicated to promoting such linkages may thus be beneficial.

41.3.8 National Technology Policy

Views on policies to support technological learning and capability building in early catch-up countries are divergent. The neoliberal view sees access to foreign technology as the critical factor, often equating this with its effective use and dissemination in the domestic economy and technological capability building as depending primarily on technology transfer and economic openness.[10] This implies an emphasis on open trade and investment policies to encourage technology transfer, increased investment in education to boost local absorptive capacity, and fewer regulations to create a competitive market environment.

The heterodox view, by contrast, distinguishes between technology transfer and local technological learning and capability building, seeing the latter as resulting from deliberate and strategic policy intervention across sectors, particularly at the firm level, rather than automatically from technology transfer. This chapter takes the view that the changing dynamics in international production systems dominated by global value chains (GVCs) leave latecomers with no choice but to pursue a heterodox approach in formulating policies towards technological development.

[10] For analysis and literature review of neoliberal verses heterodox approaches to technology development, see Deraniyagala (2006).

41.4 The Dynamics of Technological Learning and Capability Building in Ethiopia

This section examines the opportunities for technological learning and innovation in Ethiopia, reviewing the evidence on the relative importance of the channels for technology transfer discussed above and progress in strengthening domestic absorptive capacity over the last two decades. It begins by presenting the key findings of a recent innovation survey conducted by the Ethiopian Ministry of Science and Technology, which shed some light on the potential for technological learning and local firms' perceptions of technological innovation,[11] also highlighting relevant findings from recent sectoral and firm-level studies of innovation.

41.4.1 Technological Innovation: Key Findings from a Survey

Following OECD principles, the survey defines innovation broadly as 'the implementation of a new or significantly improved product (good and service), a new marketing method, or a new organizational method in business practices, workplace organization or external relations' (OECD/Eurostat 2005: 46). Innovative enterprises are those that 'introduced at least one type of innovation' in 'product, process, marketing and organizational efficiency',[12] while 'innovation active' enterprises are those in the process of introducing such new technologies during the survey period (2012–14). The national survey, the first of its kind in Ethiopia, provides unprecedented insights into the transmission mechanisms for technological learning, the barriers to technological diffusion, and the space for innovation policy—although it does not allow assessment of trends.

Key findings include the following:[13]

- Nearly 93 per cent of manufacturing enterprises gave their main source of technological innovation as acquisition of machinery, equipment, and know-how from abroad, highlighting the critical role of this channel in Ethiopia. Only 15 per cent, all

[11] The National Innovation Survey covered more than 1,200 locally owned enterprises with ten or more employees, in manufacturing (40 per cent), construction, services, and mining, including large-scale (250+ employees), medium (50–249) and small (10–49) firms. The survey was based on the 2005 Oslo Manual guidelines developed by the Organisation for Economic Cooperation and Development (OECD) (Ministry of Science and Technology 2015a).

[12] See Ministry of Science and Technology (2015a: xviii). Technological innovation affecting products and processes is distinguished from non-technological innovation aimed at improvements in marketing and organizational efficiency.

[13] For details, see Ministry of Science and Technology (2015a).

large manufacturing firms, reported using in-house R&D to enhance their innovative capacity. In fact, private sector R&D spending has declined and accounted for only 1.2 per cent of total R&D spending in 2013 (Kuriakose , Tsuzaki, and Aga 2016).

- While 59.6 per cent of firms had introduced new technologies impacting on products, processes, marketing, and/or organization, only 8.2 per cent had introduced technologies affecting all four. Product and process innovations appear most difficult, with only 0.7 per cent of firms introducing new or significantly modified products, and only 1 per cent introducing new technologies that significantly changed production methods. Only 15 per cent of product innovations introduced products new to the market, the remainder being new only to the firm concerned. These results are validated by a firm-level study of innovation in the cement, textile, and leather sectors in Ethiopia (Wakeford 2017). While focusing on 'green innovation', the study confirms that the 'extent of product and process innovation is generally low, and green innovation is even less common' (p. 1). Among the firms surveyed, less than 20 per cent reported undertaking product and process innovation. Although the percentage for product innovation in the leather sector is higher (65 per cent) because of the variety of finished leather goods produced, the rate of process innovation is lower (28 per cent) (Wakeford 2017). Both the innovation survey and the sectoral studies reveal that firms that introduced product and process innovations showed higher sales growth than those that had not, underlining the importance of product and process innovations for growth and competitiveness.
- By contrast, non-technology innovation was widespread, 49.5 per cent of firms engaging in innovative activities that improved their marketing capabilities, and 34 per cent in 'organizational innovation'. While this is likely to have a positive impact on the country's trading capacity, the competitiveness dividend will not be realized if the slow progress in product and process innovation continues.
- Technological innovation was greatest among manufacturing enterprises (68 per cent), and non-technological (particularly marketing) innovation in the services sector (54.4 per cent). This suggests that manufacturing firms may be responding to the recent shift towards a manufacturing-driven and export-led industrialization strategy by acquiring new technologies to improve product quality, production processes, marketing, and organizational efficiency. Services have been the fastest-growing sector in the last two decades, now accounting for 47 per cent of GDP. Since both these sectors tend to be knowledge intensive, their engagement in innovative activities is a positive trend.
- Only 3 per cent of innovative enterprises were able to sell goods to African and European markets, suggesting weaknesses in competitiveness and technological competence. Patent registrations by local enterprises were also disappointing, only 4 per cent of innovative manufacturing enterprises filing patent rights within Ethiopia, and less than 0.5 per cent outside Ethiopia. While the innovative activities observed may have increased opportunities for technological learning, they thus do not yet appear to have transformed firms' technological capabilities.

- The survey also highlighted weak interaction among firms and between firms and R&D centres and support institutions,[14] even where firms were engaged in product modification. Normally, firms engaging in product and/or process innovation seek technical inputs or advice from other firms, R&D centres or specialized technology support institutions, and such interactions are considered critical to technical innovation, through exchange of ideas and experiences. However, the survey reveals collaborative partnerships only with machinery, equipment, and software suppliers abroad and other firms within enterprise groups, and not with domestic firms or R&D institutions. Similar findings emerged from a study of innovation in a cluster of foot-ware manufacturerers in Addis Ababa, Ethiopia (Gebreeyesus and Mohnen 2011). In contrast to the widely held view that clustering strengthens inter-firm linkages and knowledge flows within the cluster, 'interactions with buyers, suppliers and other producers (i.e. *outside the cluster*) were the major channels through which firms acquire knowledge' (p. 24). While this may reflect weak domestic absorptive capacity and the informal nature of the cluster, such under-developed inter-firm linkages could be a major impediment to Ethiopia's vision of becoming a leading manufacturing hub in Africa.
- The most widely cited constraint on innovation among both innovative and 'innovation active' enterprises was the cost of acquiring new technologies, closely followed by lack of qualified workers, particularly technically competent personnel. Predictably, the cost of new technologies and access to credit were particular concerns for small and medium enterprises. Lack of information on technology within the country was also a critical constraint, highlighting the early stage of development of the technology support system and the lack of relevant knowledge and skills within firms.
- Additional constraints revealed by various sectoral and firm-level studies may also help to explain why Ethiopia lags behind comparable countries. A study of innovation barriers in small and medium enterprises (SMEs) in Addis Ababa, for example, reveals as barriers to innovation 'unfavourable government policy and regulation', such as the tax system and lack of patent protection, and 'organizational culture', particularly 'low employee empowerment, low synergies of resources, insignificant role of managers and/or owner to promote innovation' (Talegeta 2014: 98).

In summary, both the innovation survey and sectoral and firm-level studies highlight the key role of imported capital goods as the principal channel of technology transfer, while exposing the weakness of domestic absorptive capacity, especially in terms of skilled personnel, technology support services, and the limited capacity of specialized

[14] The Ethiopian government has established a number of specialized intermediary institutions to support the development of priority sub-sectors, including through technology transfer and technological learning. It is envisaged that these institutions will play a critical role in technological upgrading of domestic enterprises in priority sectors. Most of these institutions are recent creations and, unfortunately, no systematic evaluation of their effectiveness exists.

R&D institutions. They also signal the need for policy efforts to increase local firms' capabilities to undertake product and process innovation, and to create an environment conducive to accelerated technological learning and innovation.

41.4.2 Technology Transfer

41.4.2.1 *International Trade: Imports of Capital Goods*

Table 41.2 presents indicators of the importance to the economy of imported technology and the intensity of efforts in technological capability building, comparing Ethiopia with five current and potential competitors between 2000 and 2015. Bangladesh, Cambodia, and Tanzania, like Ethiopia, are least developed countries that aspire to reach middle-income level through manufacture-driven and export-led industrialization, while Kenya and Vietnam have already reached this level.

Capital goods imports as a proportion of GDP indicate the share of domestic resources devoted to importing products that embody technology. In Ethiopia, this increased sharply from 5.1 per cent in 2000 to 13.3 per cent in 2005, possibly reflecting the adoption of the Export Promotion Strategy in 1998 and the Industrial Development Strategy in 2002 (Gebreeyesus 2013). Despite a slight decline since 2005, the figure has remained above 10 per cent, higher than in Kenya, Tanzania, and Bangladesh.

A greater share of capital goods imports in gross fixed capital formation (GFCF) is associated with greater opportunities for technological upgrading and a greater knowledge content of fixed investment, as technological catch-up economies typically devote a greater proportion of fixed investment to importing technologies. While time series data for Ethiopia are unavailable, the ratio in 2015 was only 25 per cent, significantly less than in competitor countries, particularly Vietnam (151.8 per cent) and Cambodia (61.9 per cent).

The share of capital goods in total imports indicates the prioritization of technological learning and innovation relative to consumption goods. In Ethiopia, this share has remained consistently high, particularly relative to competitor countries, at 40 per cent in 2005 and 38.8 per cent in 2015. This indicates both the continuing demand for imports of capital goods and the importance that the government attaches to technology transfer. Importers of capital goods are exempted from customs duties and other import taxes. Such incentives effectively represent public investment in technological learning and the accumulation of knowledge and technological capabilities in the economy.

Capital goods imports relative to total exports indicate how much of a country's foreign exchange earnings are used to pay for imports of capital goods. Unlike any of the competitor countries, Ethiopia spends more on capital goods than it earns from merchandise exports, indicating that foreign exchange earnings have been used in full, and foreign debt incurred, to build technological capabilities. Again, this may be interpreted as public investment in technological learning.

A large proportion of Ethiopia's capital goods imports consist of machinery and equipment, rising from 57.7 per cent in 2000 to 67.2 per cent in 2015, of which transport-related

Table 41.2 Indicators of capital goods imports in selected countries

	Capital goods imports as a share of GDP, %				Capital goods imports as a share of GFKF, %				Capital goods imports as a share of total imports, %				Capital goods imports as a Share of total exports, %			
	2000	2005	2010	2015	2000	2005	2010	2015	2000	2005	2010	2015	2000	2005	2010	2015
Bangladesh	3.7	4.5	5.9	4.6	15.4	17.4	22.4	15.9	22.0	24.7	22.2	21.3	30.6	33.4	35.2	28.2
Cambodia	8.3	10.5	10.3	13.3	45.2	55.7	63.7	61.9	15.6	16.8	17.1	22.5	21.8	21.9	20.8	28.1
Ethiopia	5.1	13.3	10.8	10.2	n/a	n/a	n/a	25.0	33.6	40.2	37.6	38.8	87.8	177.9	138.8	215.1
Kenya	6.7	9.6	9.0	8.2	40.0	51.4	44.1	37.6	29.4	30.8	29.6	32.3	54.0	52.7	69.3	93.3
Tanzania	5.1	5.8	7.4	5.8	31.4	23.1	26.0	17.0	33.0	30.2	29.2	24.6	79.8	58.7	57.7	53.8
Vietnam	15.4	16.6	22.2	37.4	55.8	53.0	67.9	151.8	30.7	26.0	30.3	43.6	33.2	29.4	35.6	44.6

Source: WDI, UNCTADStat.

equipment accounted for 29.4 per cent. The origin of these imports has changed over the last fifteen years, with potential implications for technological learning and capability building. Between 2000 and 2015, the proportion of Ethiopia's capital goods imports originating from developed countries halved from 76 per cent to 39.1 per cent, while the proportion originating from developing countries tripled from 18.6 per cent to 60.6 per cent. This reflects the increasing technological capabilities of some developing countries as well as the growing importance of South–South trade and investment to Ethiopia, notably from China, India, and Turkey. Only time will tell, however, whether technology transfer from other developing countries will have qualitatively different impacts on technological learning and technological catch-up efforts.

41.4.2.2 *FDI as a Channel of Technology Transfer*

To the extent that Ethiopia's capital goods imports are associated with inward FDI, their impact on technological learning and capability depends in part on the technology-diffusing role of FDI. As we have seen, however, this role is by no means guaranteed. For many years, Ethiopia attracted much less FDI than might be expected for a large and fast-growing economy with diverse investment opportunities in various sectors. Notwithstanding rapid growth in capital goods imports (Table 41.2), FDI inflows in 2000–5 were less than 2 per cent of GDP. The peak was 11.8 per cent of GDP in 2016/17 when announced FDI exceeded US$3 billion. The contribution of FDI to national fixed investment also remained low until 2012/13, rising thereafter as FDI aimed at export-oriented activities in the industrial parks increased (Figure 41.1). Since 2012, FDI inflows into Ethiopia have grown by 50 per cent per year on average, reaching US$3.2 billion in 2016; much of this investment has occurred in export-oriented manufacturing activities (UNCTAD 2017).

Assessment of the impact of FDI on local technological learning and diffusion is difficult without detailed firm-level information on linkages and the interactions between foreign and local firms. However, the National Innovation Survey results suggest that such interactions may be limited.

Experience elsewhere shows that the contribution of FDI to technological learning and capability building through spillovers and demonstration effects is greatest where skill-intensive jobs are created and labour turnover between foreign and domestic firms is high (Görg and Strobl 2005). While FDI in industrial parks in Ethiopia has created thousands of jobs, with the expectation that more than 1 million manufacturing jobs will be created within a decade,[15] the jobs created to date have not been skill intensive and do not require high-level qualifications. Neither has Ethiopia yet developed an industrial workforce with the discipline and culture needed for learning by doing, interacting and engaging in a dynamic and modern knowledge system (see Chapters 35 and 38). Successful learning and knowledge diffusion from FDI may thus take longer than is currently assumed. Foreign investors, especially large corporations with wider global networks and reach, are also reluctant to engage with local firms. The

[15] Discussion with officials at the Ethiopian Investment Commission.

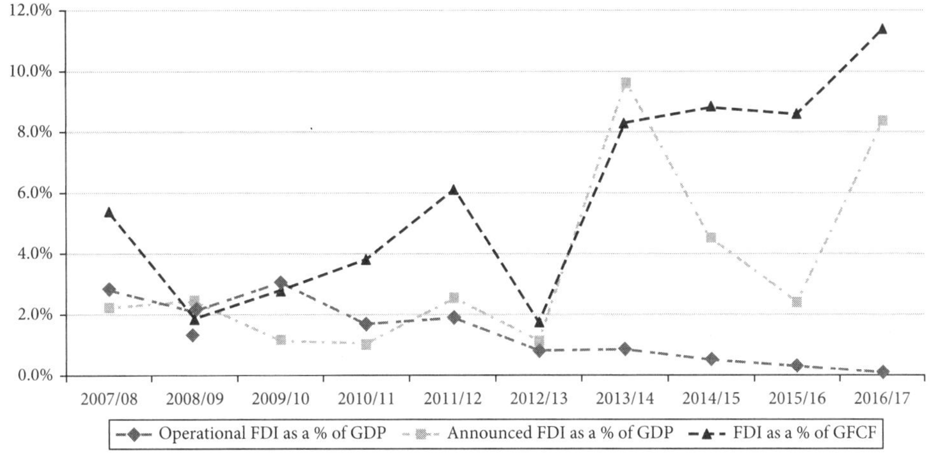

FIGURE 41.1 FDI as a share of GDP and GFCF

Source: EIC, UNCTAD.

private sector in Ethiopia will not benefit from opportunities for technological learning arising from the presence of foreign firms if the latter make a policy decision not to engage before even exploring the potential.[16] Generally, as Akyuz (2017) rightly points out, successful examples of FDI-driven linkages are 'found not necessarily among developing countries that attracted more FDI, but among those which used it in the context of national industrial policy designed to shape the evolution of specific industries through intervention so as to accelerate industrialization and growth. In fact, extensive presence of foreign firms could well be a sign of weakness of indigenous capabilities.'

41.4.3 Movement of Skilled Persons

As the findings of the innovation survey show, Ethiopia suffers from skill shortages, particularly of technical skills and know-how. Recognizing this constraint, the government has prioritized education and technical training, while facilitating recruitment of skilled expatriate personnel, especially by foreign companies investing in priority sectors and industrial parks. However, high outward migration rates of skilled Ethiopians make the country a net exporter of skills, which is problematic in light of its limited human capital.[17]

[16] See, for example, the response of the representative of PVH, a major foreign investor in Hawassa Industrial Park, to a question regarding the potential for supplier linkages with local firms: 'we want to work with a few people, and we want them to be global. We are asking our approved-level suppliers to come and open in East Africa. We are asking our trade suppliers to come and open in East Africa. So we don't want to buy locally produced. We want to encourage our global supply chain people to come here' (Mihretu and Llobet 2017).

[17] There are a number of reasons for the large number of educated Ethiopians in the diaspora but the most important is lack of employment opportunities in the local economy compatible with high-level skills.

Between 1990 and 2000, the emigration rate of Ethiopians with tertiary education averaged around 20 per cent, high for a skills-deficit country, with a direct impact on absorptive capacity and technological catch-up (Docquier and Marfouk 2006). Outward migration tends to be particularly high in skill-intensive professions where skills are relatively uniform internationally, such as academia, medicine, and engineering. In 2011, for example, there were more Ethiopian academics teaching at universities in the United States than in Ethiopia itself, despite Ethiopian universities' desperate need for highly qualified lecturers (UNCTAD 2013). The question is how to tap into this reservoir of talent and experience. There are valuable lessons from countries such as China, Korea, Taiwan, and India, which have successfully engaged their diasporas and treated them as a 'brain trust' or 'brain bank' (Kim 1999).

41.4.4 Building Absorptive Capacity

41.4.4.1 *Human Capital Development*

Ethiopia's recent efforts to build its human capital give out mixed signals. Despite huge strides in expanding the skills base and educational system in recent years, including tertiary education and TVET, there are signs that the system is being stretched to its limit, with adverse effects on quality and sustainability. In moving forward, therefore, there is a need for education, training, and science and technology policies to be better aligned with industrial policy and skills requirements.

The number of public universities has increased from four to thirty-four in the last two decades, while enrolments in higher education have grown by 25 per cent per year since 2003/4, taking undergraduate-level enrolments to 750,000 in 2015/16 (Ministry of Education 2015/16). Progress in narrowing the gender gap has been equally impressive, female students accounting for 35 per cent of tertiary enrolment in 2015/16. Twenty-three per cent of the 51,521 students on postgraduate programmes were female, compared with 13 per cent in 2010/11 (Ministry of Education 2015/16). Around 70 per cent of undergraduate students are reading science- and technology-related subjects. While the commitment to expanding higher education is laudable and will doubtless contribute to technological learning, there are concerns that the expansion has been achieved at the expense of quality and standards.

The government has also launched a massive TVET programme, based on the German dual-corporative (or apprenticeship) model, and aimed at providing the technical skills that young people need to work in productive sectors or start their own businesses. The programme provides TVET in diverse areas, involving one to three years' study to provide students with the vocational skills and qualifications needed to build a career in their chosen field. TVETs are also expected to play a critical role in technology accumulation and transfer, which is one of the important pillars of the Industry Extension Service (IES) (Assefa, Zerfu, and Biruk 2014). Since the launch of a TVET strategy in 2003, the programme has expanded rapidly in terms of both enrolment (which tripled from 106,336 to 352,144 between 2004/5 and 2014/15) and the number of entities providing training (Ministry of Education 2015/16). As a public-sector-led and supply-driven programme (though with the involvement of private TVET providers and in collaboration with the Kaizen Institute), the scheme is designed to enable the government to plan skill formation in accordance with national development priorities.

However, recent trends suggest that the TVET programme may have fallen victim to its own success. In 2015/16, TVET enrolment fell 13 per cent to 304,139, and the number of TVETs from 919 to 583 (Ministry of Education 2015/16). A key constraint is the lack of highly skilled trainers, whose role in passing on best-practice skills is at the heart of the programme: graduates are apparently discouraged from teaching at TVET institutions by the lack of prestige attached to this role (Krishnan and Shaorshadze 2013).

41.4.4.2 *R&D Capacity Building*

R&D activities in specialized and publicly funded centres has been part of Ethiopia's science and technology development programme since the early 1950s, especially in agriculture (Ministry of Science and Technology 2015b). On the advice of international organizations such as UNESCO, Ethiopia and other African countries established these centres to conduct mainly scientific research but without linkages with firms or farms. This tradition has been maintained, and R&D, particularly in agriculture, has intensified since the fall of the Derg regime in 1991, in line with the Agricultural Development-Led Industrialization strategy (ADLI) (Bechere 2007).

Despite an increase in R&D spending from 0.24 per cent of GDP in 2010 to 0.61 per cent in 2014, and of R&D personnel from 13,095 to 14,200, most R&D centres in Ethiopia are not even fully functional as research institutions, still less able to generate new technologies. Most of the additional public spending was used to acquire scientific equipment, but 'There is poor cooperation and absence of R&D resource sharing among R&D units which result in duplication of expensive scientific equipment purchase' (Ministry of Science and Technology 2015b: 3), and there are limited local technical capabilities for equipment repairs. Consequently, capacity utilization and effectiveness in most R&D institutions is undermined by faulty or 'malfunctioning' scientific equipment (Ministry of Science and Technology 2015b). According to a survey of R&D institutions conducted by the Ministry of Science and Technology in 2015, 83 per cent of agricultural research institutes, 76 per cent of research centres in higher education and 77 per cent of government research agencies are operating at less than 50 per cent capacity because of 'malfunctioning' instruments and equipment (Ministry of Science and Technology 2015b).

41.4.4.3 *National Technology Policy*

Ethiopia's current science, technology, and innovation (STI) policy, launched in 2012, contains an eclectic mix of the two approaches discussed above. Its primary objective is to create a less cumbersome policy and regulatory environment for technology transfer (Ministry of Science and Technology 2012). To move forward, however, greater clarity is needed on the purpose and long-term objectives of STI policy in light of the country's development goals. The revision of the policy framework planned for 2018 provides an opportunity to rethink the principles guiding the next-generation technology policy framework.

As well as taking account of the time, costs, and risks involved in technological learning and the adoption and assimilation of foreign technology, the design of a new-generation STI policy needs to recognize the dependence of success on the 'intensity of effort' of the government and support institutions (Kim 1999; Lundvall 2016). While not explicit in Ethiopia's STI policy, the importance of these efforts is recognized by the government, as demonstrated by the establishment of specialized support institutions and ongoing efforts to upgrade local technological capability through public sector-driven import substitution, particularly in metalworking and engineering.

The priority of the current technology policy is to facilitate access to foreign technology, with less attention to what happens once technology has been transferred, beyond generic statements on the need to build local technological capability. Essential as it is, technology transfer is only the first phase of a complex process of local technological learning and capability building.

A key focus of technology policy, especially in countries where economic growth and transformation are dependent on export-oriented industrialization, is firm-level technological learning and innovation capability building (Mytelka and Tesfachew 1998). The historical distinction between traditional (low-tech and labour-intensive) industries which did not need knowledge inputs, and knowledge-intensive and high-tech industries which did, has largely broken down. Knowledge intensity is no longer confined to specific firms or activities, but cuts across multiple fields, including product design, marketing, quality control, management, and maintenance. In the twenty-first century, competitiveness in an open market (whether domestically or internationally) requires technology/knowledge-intensive production processes, whether in shoe manufacturing in Ethiopia or Italy, fish production in Mozambique or Japan, or the production of bicycles in Sri Lanka or Korea. Regardless of firm size, location, and sector, sustaining competitiveness thus depends on a process of continuous learning, innovation, product improvement, marketing, customer services, management routines, and effective use of ICT.

In revising its technology policy, Ethiopia thus needs to shift from the current predominant focus on technology transfer to a greater emphasis on what happens after technology is transferred, and on its integration into the local economy through technological learning and upgrading, particularly at the firm level. This would mean designing incentives for local firms to develop a culture of learning and an awareness of the importance of acquiring innovative capability for competitiveness.

41.5 Conclusions

After more than a decade of successful economic growth driven mainly by public-sector investment, Ethiopia embarked on an ambitious economic diversification programme driven by a manufacturing sector-based and export-led industrialization strategy. A key requirement for successful export-led industrialization is technological and innovation capability, which determines a country's ability to improve productivity and produce higher-value and increasingly sophisticated manufactured products that the country can sell competitively in international markets. No country has ever achieved sustained growth and development through industrialization without successful technological catch-up and innovation capability building. This chapter has therefore assessed Ethiopia's technological development and examined the main sources of technological learning and technological capability building.

The analysis points to four broad conclusions. First, the available macro, sectoral, and product-level indicators confirm that Ethiopia is at an early catch-up stage of technological development. Available indices indicate a major technological gap between Ethiopia and its current and potential competitors. Ethiopia's declared vision is to become a middle-income economy and a leading manufacturing hub in Africa by 2025. The fact that only 1 per cent of Ethiopia's total exports in 2015 were of high-tech products and 85 per cent were primary and resource-based gives a strong sense that without a major acceleration of technological learning and upgrading, it is highly likely to be caught in the 'middle-income trap'.

Second, the good news is that the recent surge in growth has created momentum for rapid transfer of technology. By far the most important source of technology transfer is imports of capital goods, followed by FDI. However, while FDI can be an important channel of technology transfer, the link between FDI-related technology transfer and technological learning and upgrading in the domestic economy is not as automatic as is often assumed. Caution is, therefore, necessary when designing incentives to attract FDI. The expatriate workers that accompany foreign investment, however, can be an important source of skills and knowledge transfer, especially the 'tacit knowledge' that is essential for learning through interaction and observing. The chapter has also highlighted Ethiopia's dilemma as a net exporter of highly qualified workers through emigration, despite their skills being in short supply. Reversing this 'brain drain' by learning from East Asian experiences will go a long way towards easing the skill constraints.

Third, concerted efforts are underway to improve domestic absorptive capacity, which is an essential requirement for technological learning and upgrading. Despite resource constraints, strides have been made within a limited period on two important drivers of absorptive capacity: human capital development and the development of R&D capacity. While current efforts to expand and diversify the skills base, including through TVET, are consistent with the country's manufacturing-based and export-led industrialization strategy, there are however signs that the system is stretched by the speed of development and there is a potential trade-off between quantity and quality. The fact that about 70 per cent of R&D centres and institutions operate at less than 50 per cent capacity because of 'malfunctioning' scientific machines and equipment and shortage of technical skills is another graphic indicator of the country's low level of technological capability.

Finally, on technology policy, the chapter argues that enhancing technological learning and capability building would require Ethiopia to rethink its current policy approach, which is focused primarily on transfer of technology rather than what happens to the technology once it has been transferred. As the knowledge intensity of production increases across sectors, it is only through technological learning and upgrading at the firm level that countries like Ethiopia can develop a dynamic and competitive private sector.

References

Akyuz, Y. (2017). *Playing with Fire: Deepened Financial Integration and Changing Vulnerabilities of the Global South* (Oxford: Oxford University Press).

Assefa, B., A. Zerfu, and Tekle Biruk (2014). 'Identifying Key Success Factors and Constraints in Ethiopia's MSE Development: An Exploratory Research', Research Report No. 18, Ethiopian Development Research Institute, Addis Ababa.

Bechere, E. (2007). 'Agricultural Research and Development in Ethiopia', Centre for African Development Policy Research, Western Michigan University.

Bell, M. and K. Pavitt (1992). 'Accumulating Technological Capability in Developing Countries', *The World Bank Economic Review* 6, (1): 257–81.

Deraniyagala, S. (2006). 'Analysis of Technology and Development: A Critical Review', in *The New Development Economics after the Washington Consensus*, ed. K. Jomo and B. Fine (London: Zed Books): 123–44.

Docquier, F. and A. Marfouk (2006). 'International Migration by Education Attainment, 1900–2000', in *International Migration, Remittances and Brain Drain*, ed. C. Özden and M. Schiff (World Bank and Palgrave Macmillan: Washington, DC): 151–200.

Gebreeyesus, M. (2013). 'Industrial Policy and Development in Ethiopia: Evolution and Present Experimentation', Working Paper No.6. UNU-WIDER, AfDB, Brookings Institute.

Gebreeyesus, M. and P. Mohnen (2011). 'Innovation Performance and Embeddedness in Networks: Evidence from the Ethiopian Footwear Cluster', Working Paper Series No. 43, UNU-MERIT.

Görg, H. and E. Strobl (2005). 'Foreign Direct Investment and Local Economic Development: Beyond Productivity Spillovers', in *Does Foreign Direct Investment Promote Development?*, ed. T. Moran E. Graham, and M. Blomstrom (Washington, DC: Institute for International Economics, Centre for Global Development): 137–58.

Harrison, A. and A. Rodriguez-Clare (2009). 'Trade, Foreign Investment and Industrial Policy for Developing Countries', Working Paper No. 15261, National Bureau of Economic Research, Cambridge, MA.

Kim, L. (1995). 'Absorptive Capacity and Industrial Growth: A Conceptual Framework and Korea's Experience', in *Social Capability and Long-Term Economic Growth*, ed. K. Bon and D. Perkins (Basingstoke: Macmillan Press for Korean Development Institute): 266–87.

Kim, L. (1997). *Imitation to Innovation: The Dynamics of Korea's Technological Learning* (Cambridge, MA: Harvard Business School Press).

Kim, L. (1999). 'Building Technological Capability for Industrialization: Analytical Frameworks and Korea's Experience', *Industrial and Corporate Change* 8 (1): 111–36.

Kinoshita, Y. (2000). 'R&D and Technology Spillovers Via FDI: Innovation and Absorptive Capacity', SSRN Scholarly Paper No. ID258194, Social Science Research Network, Rochester, New York.

Krishnan, P. and I. Shaorshadze (2013). 'Technical and Vocational Education and Training in Ethiopia', Working Paper, IGE.

Kuriakose, S., H. Tsuzaki, and G. Aga (2016). 'Unlocking Firm-Level Productivity and Promoting More Inclusive Growth: The Role of Innovation in Ethiopia', World Bank Group, Washington, DC.

Lall, S. (1992). 'Technological Capabilities and Industrialization', *World Development* 20 (2): 165–86.

Lall, S. (2000). 'The Technological Structure and Performance of Developing Country Manufactured Exports, 1985–1998', QEH Working Paper Series No. 44, Oxford.

Lee, Keun (2013). *Schumpeterian Analysis of Economic Catch-Up* (Cambridge; Cambridge University Press).

Lin, J. (2017). 'Industrial Policies for Avoiding the Middle-Income Trap: A New Structural Economic Perspective', *Journal of Chinese Economic and Business Studies* 15 (1): 5–18.

Lundvall, B.-A. (2016). *The Learning Economy and the Economics of Hope* (London: Anthem Press).

Mihretu, M. and G. Llobet (2017). 'Looking beyond the Horizon: A Case Study of PVH's Commitment to Ethiopia's Hawassa Industrial Park', World Bank Group, Washington, DC.

Ministry of Education (2015/16). 'Education Abstract, 2015/16', FDRE, Addis Ababa.

Ministry of Science and Technology (2012). 'Science, Technology and Innovation Policy', FDRE, Addis Ababa.

Ministry of Science and Technology (2015a). 'Ethiopian Innovation Survey', FDRE, Addis Ababa.

Ministry of Science and Technology (2015b). 'Research & Development Infrastructure in Ethiopia: A Cross-Sectional Survey', FDRE, Addis Ababa.

Mytelka, L. and T. Tesfachew (1998). 'The Role of Policy in Promoting Enterprise Learning during Early Industrialization: Lessons for African Countries', UNCTAD/GDS/MDPB/Misc.7. UNCTAD, Geneva.

Nelson, Richard and Sidney Winter (1982). *An Evolutionary Theory of Economic Change* (Cambridge, MA: The Belknap Press of Harvard University Press).

OECD/Eurostat (2005). *Oslo Manual: Guidelines for Collecting and Interpreting Innovation Data*, 3rd edition (Paris: OECD).

Saggi, K. (2002). 'Trade, Foreign Direct Investment, and International Technology Transfer: A Survey', *The World Bank Research Observer* 17 (2): 191–235.

Talegeta, S. (2014). 'Innovation and Barriers to Innovation: Small and Medium Enterprises in Addis Ababa', *Journal of Small Business and Entrepreneurship and Development* 2 (1): 83–106.

Tregenna. F. (2015). 'Deindustrialization, Structural Change and Sustainable Economic Growth', MERIT Working Paper 032, UNU-MERIT, Maastricht.

UNIDO (2017). Competitive Industrial Performance Report 2016. UNIDO, Vienna.

UNCTAD (2013). 'The Least Developed Report 2013', United Nations, Geneva.

UNCTAD (2017). 'World Investment Review 2017', United Nations, Geneva.

Wahab, S., R. Rose, and S. Osman (2012). 'Defining the Concepts of Technology and Technology Transfer: A Literature Analysis', *International Business Research* 5 (1): 61–71.

Wakeford, J. (2017). 'Innovation for Green Industrialization: An Empirical Assessment of Innovation in Ethiopia's Cement, Leather and Textile Sectors', QGRL Working Paper 1.

WIPO (2017). 'World Intellectual Property Report 2017', World Intellectual Property Organization, Geneva.

CHAPTER 42

THE LEGAL FRAMEWORK FOR THE PROTECTION OF FOREIGN DIRECT INVESTMENT IN ETHIOPIA

WON L. KIDANE

42.1 Introduction

No economy palpably thrives in a legal vacuum. The allocation of risks and benefits inherent in economic interactions of any kind appreciates the predictability that comes along with the normative universe delineated by the legal system. Historically, Ethiopia's near-perpetual independent existence has uniquely permitted it significant latitude in shaping its own legal framework and policy for the admission, protection, and management of foreign direct investment (FDI). The contemporary legal framework is nonetheless a function of a multitude of internal and external influences.

International investment law principles have been a part of Ethiopia's investment law at least as far back as 1903,[1] the year Ethiopia signed what was then called the Treaty of Amity and Commerce with the United States. This treaty contained modicums of modern notions of international law such as the most favoured nation treatment.[2]

[1] 1903 was the year that Ethiopia formally established diplomatic relations with the United States. See Department of State Bureau of African Affairs, 'US Ethiopia Relations, Fact Sheet' (10 May 2017). available at https://www.state.gov/r/pa/ei/bgn/2859.htm

[2] According to official Ethiopian government sources, 'The US–Ethiopian relationship was formally established in December 1903 following nine days of meetings in Ethiopia between Emperor Menelik

Following an era of military rule from 1974 to 1991, during which any semblance of domestic and international principles of fairness and equity were purposefully abrogated, Ethiopia attempted to build a new legal framework for the ordering of FDI. The existing framework is comprised of a complex web of evolving domestic legislation[3] and an increasing number of international bilateral and regional investment treaties.[4] This corpus of law appears to also be equipped with some essential institutional mechanisms of enforcement. This chapter provides a brief overview and critique of the existing rules and institutions.

Any analysis of the existing framework will be incomplete without a historical perspective. The chapter therefore begins with a section on the historical evolution of Ethiopian investment law. It will then focus on the two ostensibly distinct but virtually inseparable sources of law: domestic and international. The domestic sources of law include a whole host of state and federal proclamations, regulations, directives, and agency rulings. The international sources of law include *inter alia* treaties, customs, general principles as well as some 'precedents'. These sources of law collectively define the contours of Ethiopia's legal framework for the protection and management of foreign direct investment. The framework is growing in complexity largely because of the growth in the scale and intricacy of the economic relations that it seeks to govern. The advent of industrial parks and special economic zones has also added an entirely fresh dimension. This chapter will finally situate the rules and regulations pertaining to these parks and zones within the general legal framework.

and the government of Ethiopia and Robert P. Skinner, an emissary of President Theodore Roosevelt. Ethiopia appreciated America's commercial interest in Ethiopia, and that the United States did not possess colonial designs similar to those that were currently being pursued throughout Africa by European powers.

The talks between Ethiopia and the United States yielded a jointly signed document known as the Treaty of Amity and Commerce. This agreement accorded Ethiopia Most Favoured Nation status and eventually led to full diplomatic relations between the two countries.' http://www.ethiopianembassy.org/AboutEthiopia/AboutEthiopia.php?Page=EthiopiaUS.htm

[3] The principal current domestic legal instrument is Investment Proclamation No. 769/2012. The text is available at www.hopr.gov.et

[4] These comprise bilateral investment treaties (BITs) and investment chapters contained in Free Trade Areas (FTAs). Ethiopia currently has BITs in force with Algeria, Austria, China, Denmark, Egypt, Germany, Finland, France, Iran, Israel, Italy, Kuwait, Libya, Malaysia, the Netherlands, Russia, Sudan, Sweden, Switzerland, Tunisia, Turkey, and Yemen. Ethiopia has also signed BITs with the following countries that have not yet come into effect: Belgium/Luxembourg, Equatorial Guinea, India, Nigeria, South Africa, Spain, United Kingdom, United Arab Emirates, South Sudan, and Morocco. The texts of most of Ethiopia's treaties are available on UNCTAD's Investment Hub website at http://investmentpolicyhub.unctad.org/IIA/CountryBits/67#iiaInnerMenu and http://investmentpolicyhub.unctad.org/IIA/CountryOtherIias/67#iiaInnerMenu. It shows 33 Bilateral Investment Treaties and six Treaties with Investment Provisions.

42.2 Historical Background

The history of codification of laws in Ethiopia is long and complicated but in the most contemporary sense, its origin could comfortably be traced to the Imperial Constitution of 1931,[5] revised in 1955.[6] The Constitution of 1955 defined the rights and responsibilities of the three branches of government.[7]

The bicameral parliament established under the 1955 constitution took one of the most important steps in the codification of laws in the history of the country. The adopted codes included the Penal Code of 1957, the Civil Code of 1960, the Commercial Code of 1960, the Maritime Code of 1960, the Criminal Procedure Code of 1961, and the Civil Procedure Code of 1965. These Codes, collectively, established the essential foundation of the Ethiopian legal system and shaped the direction of its development.

Legislative activity in the area of foreign investment was a significant part of this modern legal development in the 1950s and 1960s. The most notable piece of legislation was the Investment Code of 1963.[8] Possessing all the indicia of a modern investment code, this relatively brief Code aimed at encouraging foreign capital investment primarily through tax incentives[9] and waiving restrictions on foreign ownership of real property.[10]

The Investment Code was also supplemented by some international treaties, most notably the 1953 Ethiopia–United States Treaty of Amity and Economic Relations.[11] This treaty, still theoretically in effect,[12] is notable for its inclusion of

[5] Ethiopian Constitution of 1931 (16 July 1931). Text available at https://archive.org/stream/TheEthiopianConstitution/EC_djvu.txt Article 5 states: 'By virtue of his imperial blood, as well as by the anointing which he has received, the person of the Emperor is sacred, his dignity is inviolable and his power indisputable.'

[6] Ethiopian Constitution of 1955 (Revised). Text available at https://archive.org/stream/TheEthiopianConstitution/EC_djvu.txt

[7] Ethiopian Revised Constitution of 1955. Article 88 states: 'All laws duly approved by both Chambers of Parliament shall be forwarded to the Emperor through the Prime Minister by the Presidents of the Chamber of Deputies or the Senate. In the event that such law shall receive the approval or signature of the Emperor, it shall be published by the Minister of the Pen in the Negarit Gazeta, with recital of the affixing of the Signature and the Great Seal of the Emperor. All Imperial decrees and all ministerial decrees and orders shall be published in the Negarit Gazeta.'

[8] Decree No. 51 of 1963. Decree to Provide for the Encouragement of Capital Investment in Ethiopia. *International Legal Materials* 3 (1) (January 1964): 41–4.

[9] See Investment Code 1963, Article 5 (income tax exemption for five years with the notable exception of investment in production of alcoholic beverages or liquor); Article 6 (Import Duty Exemption); Article 7 (Export Duty Exemption), Article 8 (Remittance of Foreign Currency).

[10] See Investment Code 1963, Article 10 (Ownership of Immovable Property).

[11] Text of the Treaty is available at http://tcc.export.gov/Trade_Agreements/All_Trade_Agreements/exp_002815.asp

[12] See Department of State Bureau of Economic and Business Affairs, Investment Climate Statement for 2017, part 2. Available at https://www.state.gov/e/eb/rls/othr/ics/investmentclimatestatements/index.htm#wrapper ('A Treaty of Amity and Economic Relations, which entered into force in 1953, governs economic and consular relations with the United States.')

modern principles of international investment law such as the principle of non-discrimination.[13]

The overthrow of the monarchy by the military in 1974 was followed by unprecedented legislative activity that severely and systematically curtailed foreign investment.[14] The era of open hostility towards foreign capital investment and ideologically induced isolation was replaced by a policy of openness and cautious optimism when the Ethiopian People's Revolutionary Democratic Front (EPRDF) assumed government power in 1991. The EPRDF government undertook gradual but intrinsically radical legislative steps to open up the economy to foreign investment (see Chapter 35 and 36). Although one of the first legislative efforts of the transitional government was an investment proclamation (Investment Proclamation No. 15/1992),[15] the laws of most current importance in the area of foreign investment were enacted after the adoption of the Constitution of the Federal Democratic Republic of Ethiopia (FDRE) in 1995 (see Chapter 7).[16] The existing corpus of law is thus essentially a function of post-1991 legislative effort.

42.3 Contemporary Sources of Investment Law

Under the constitutional order established by the FDRE Constitution of 1995, the first major investment law was Investment Proclamation No. 37 of 1996.[17] This Proclamation was later replaced by Investment Proclamation No. 280/2002.[18] Following some legislative

[13] See e.g. United States–Ethiopia Treaty of Amity and Commerce, supra note 11 at Article VIII:

1. Each High Contracting Party shall at all times accord fair and equitable treatment to nationals and companies of the other High Contracting Party, and to their property and enterprises; shall refrain from applying unreasonable or discriminatory measures that would impair their legally acquired rights and interests; and shall assure that their lawful contractual rights are afforded effective means of enforcement, in conformity with the applicable laws.
2. Property of nationals and companies of either High Contracting' Party, including interests in property, shall receive the most constant protection and security within the territories of the other High Contracting Party. Such property shall not be taken except for a public purpose, nor shall it be taken without the prompt payment of just and effective compensation.

A related notable feature is MFN in the area of admission of each other's citizens: Article VI:

1. Nationals of either High Contracting Party shall be permitted, subject to immigration laws and regulations, to enter the territories of the other High Contracting Party and to reside therein for the purpose of engaging in industry, carrying on international trade, or pursuing studies, upon terms no less favorable than those accorded to nationals of any third country.

[14] For a discussion of the major legislative activities during the military rule between 1974 and 1991, see Library of Congress, *Ethiopia: A Country Study* (1991), pp. 187–90.

[15] Proclamation No. 15,/1992 (July 1992–June 1996). Text available at www.hopr.gov.et

[16] Proclamation of the Constitution of the Federal Democratic Republic of Ethiopia (Federal Negarit Gazeta, 1st Year, No. 1, 21 August 1995).

[17] Investment Proclamation No. 37/1996. Text available on the official website of the Ethiopian House of Peoples' Representatives at www.hopr.gov.et

[18] Investment Proclamation No. 280/2002. Text available at www.hopr.gov.et

activity, mainly in the form of amendments to the existing laws,[19] Ethiopia's investment law continued its maturation through the enactment of Proclamation No. 769/2012[20] and accompanying implementing Council of Ministers Regulations No. 270/2012 (hereinafter 'Current Investment Law' or 'Current Law').[21]

The recently enacted Industrial Park Proclamation[22] not only introduced a relatively new normative milieu but also added an appreciable degree of complexity to the existing legal framework for the management and protection of foreign investment. The following section will first explore the features of these domestic laws salient to the protection of foreign investment, and then provide commentary on their interaction with the external standards that Ethiopia has adopted on account of its bilateral and regional investment treaties.

42.4 Domestic

Although Ethiopia's existing domestic investment law is basic and transactional in nature,[23] it contains important substantive rules on the protection of foreign investment, and provides corresponding procedural remedies.

42.5 Substantive Norms

The most notable substantive rule for the protection of any investment (foreign as well as domestic) is the rule against expropriation. Under the existing Ethiopian constitutional system,[24] in the realm of investment law, this principle made its first notable

[19] Examples of these amendments include: Proclamation No. 116/1998; Proclamation No. 168/1999; Proclamation No. 375/2003. Some additions and amendments were very specific. Examples include Proclamation No. 103/1998 (Capital Goods Leasing Business Proclamation) and Proclamation No. 543/2007 (The Revised Export Trade Duty Incentive Scheme Establishing Proclamation.) The text of each of these proclamations is available at www.hopr.gov.et

[20] Investment Proclamation No. 769/2012. Text available at www.hopr.gov.et

[21] Investment Regulation No. 270/2012. Text available at www.hopr.gov.et It is important to note here that some sector-specific pieces of legislation also make a part of the domestic legal framework. These include the Mining Proclamation No. 678/2010, and Petroleum Operations Proclamation No. 295/1986. Texts of these are also available at www.hopr.gov.et

[22] Industrial Parks Proclamation No. 886/2015. Text available at www.hopr.gov.et

[23] See e.g. Investment Proclamation No. 769/2012 Part Three (areas of investment), Part Four (permits), Part Six (incentives).

[24] The Constitution of 1995 itself contains a rule on expropriation. The relevant part states: 'Without prejudice to the right to private property, the government may expropriate private property for public purposes subject to payment in advance of compensation commensurate to the value of the property.' FDRE Const. Article 40(8).

appearance in Investment Proclamation No. 37/1996.[25] It remained a part of Ethiopian law after the enactment of the Current Investment Law, i.e. Investment Proclamation No. 769/2012, although curiously the formulation varied in some material respects.[26]

In its 1996 formulation, the principle of non-expropriation contained the following details:

> Investment Guarantee and Settlement of Disputes
> 21. Investment Guarantee and Protection
> (1) No investment may be expropriated or nationalized except when required by the public interest and then, only in compliance with the requirements of the law.
> (2) *Adequate* compensation, corresponding to the prevailing market value, shall be paid *without delay* in case of expropriation or nationalization of an investment for public interest.
> (3) Any foreign investor may remit compensation paid to him pursuant to this Article out of Ethiopia in coverable currency. [27]

Under international investment law, few, if any, principles have attracted more acrimony and vigorous debate than the principle against exploration and the remedies thereof. An oft-cited 1938 exchange of letters between US Secretary of State Cordell Hull and his Mexican counterpart pertaining to Mexico's expropriation of agricultural property belonging to citizens of the United States puts matters into perspective here. Secretary of State Hull, after whom the Hull Rule or Formula is named, wrote: 'We cannot question the right of a foreign government to treat its own nationals in this fashion [expropriation] if it so desires. This is a matter of domestic concern. But we cannot admit that a foreign government may take the property of American nationals in disregard of the rule of compensation under international law.'[28] The Foreign Minister of Mexico responded: 'there does not exist in international law any principle universally accepted by countries, not by the writers of treatises on this subject, that would render obligatory the giving of adequate compensation for expropriations of a general and impersonal character.'[29] Although the extent of compensation continues to be debated, the rule seems to be currently settled that some form of compensation needs to be offered. Most investment treaties now enshrine what is known as the Hull Rule of prompt, effective, and adequate compensation. The version of this rule contained in Article 21 of the 1996 Ethiopian Investment Proclamation appears to be a close approximation of the Hull Rule, which states in its classic formulation 'prompt, effective, and adequate compensation'.

[25] Investment Proclamation No. 37/1996, Article 21.

[26] Investment Proclamation No. No. 769/2012, Article 25.

[27] Investment Proclamation No. 37/1996, Article 21 (1–3).

[28] Letter from US Secretary of State to Mexican Minister of Foreign Affairs (July 1938), *excerpted* in Lowenfeld (2008: 474–5).

[29] Letter from the Foreign Minister of Mexico, quoted in Lowenfeld (2008: 477).

Curiously, Ethiopia's current investment law introduced some variation in the taxonomy of the non-expropriation rule. The relevant part reads:

> Article 25: Investment Guarantees and Protection
> (1) No property may be expropriated or nationalized except for public interest—and then, only in conformity with the requirements of the law.
> (2) *Adequate* compensation, corresponding to the prevailing market value, shall be paid *in advance* in case of expropriation or nationalization of an investment for public purpose.
> (3) For the purpose of this article, the word 'nationalization' shall be used interchangeably with the world 'expropriation' and results in the payment of appropriate or adequate compensation.[30]

The new law changed 'without delay' to 'in advance' and replaced the remittance sub-provision with a rather superfluous definitional provision. It is fair to assume that the changes were purposeful but the objectives are not readily discernible from the text itself. In any case, one rule now appears clear: before expropriation for public purpose is effected, the investor must be offered adequate compensation '*in advance*'. Adequate compensation is defined as 'corresponding to the prevailing market value'—presumably of the expropriated investment.[31]

The assessment of the prevailing market value is often a very contentious matter because of the inherent clash of interests between the offeror of the compensation and offeree. Unfortunately, international jurisprudence pertaining to the law of expropriation does not necessarily provide the required degree of clarity.[32] In terms of the substantive rules of protection of investment contained in the Current Investment Law, the rule against expropriation appears to be the principal protection expressly guaranteed.

The current Investment Law promises many incentives and benefits to qualifying investors. Although there are no express provisions guaranteeing a non-discriminatory and judicious allocation of these benefits, the complaints procedures set up under the law suggest that aggrieved investors may be able to seek remedy for discriminatory or arbitrary exercise of administrative power or unlawful denial of benefits. The lack of express substantive provisions in that regard appears to be a function of legislative

[30] Investment Proclamation No. 769 (2012), Article 25(1–3).

[31] The Investment Proclamation defines investment in Article 2(1) as: 'expenditure of capital in cash of in kind or in both by an investor to establish a new enterprise or to expand or upgrade one that already exists.'

[32] The founding arbitral cases in this area are considered to be the three Libya Oil cases. These cases have added as much clarity as they have confusion. The three cases are: British Petroleum Exploration Co. (Libya) v. Libyan Arab Republic, 53 *International Law Report* 297 (Lagergren, sole arb., 1973); Texaco Overseas Petroleum Co. v. Libyan Arab Republic, 55 *International Law Report* 354 (consolidated with the case of California Asiatic Oil Company (CALASIATIC) (René-Jean Dupuy, sole arb., 1975); and Libya American Oil Co. (LIAMCO) v. Libyan Arab Republic, 62 *International Law Report*, 140; 20 ILM 1 (1981) (Mahamassani, sole arb., 1977). For a discussion of these cases, see von Mehren and Kourides (1981).

oversight rather than a purposeful omission. The complaints procedures are discussed in the next section.

42.6 Procedural Guarantees

The 1996 Investment Proclamation contained a separate provision on dispute settlement. It stated in particular:

> (1) Where any dispute arises between a foreign investor and the Government in respect of an investment, all effort shall be made to reach an amicable settlement through mutual discussions.
> (2) A dispute not amicably settled may be submitted to the competent court of the country or to international arbitration within the framework of any bilateral or multilateral agreement to which the Government and the country of which the foreign investor is a national are contracting parties.[33]

The Current Investment Law completely omits this rule and introduces an administrative complaints procedure:

> Article 32: Lodging of Complaint
> (1) Any investor shall have the right to lodge complaints related to his investment with the appropriate investment organ.
> (2) An investor who has a grievance against the decision of the appropriate investment organ may, within 30 days, from receipt of the decision, appeal to the Investment Board or to the concerned regional organ, as maybc appropriate.

By definition, the 'appropriate investment organ' is either the 'Agency or the executive organ of a region empowered to issue permits'.[34] The 'Agency' is re-established by Council of Minister's Regulation No. 269/2012.[35] In defining the powers and duties of the agency, Article 5 of this Regulation incorporates the powers and duties of the agency set forth under Article 28 of the Current Investment Law, i.e. Proclamation No. 769/2012. Although Article 28 provides a list of the powers and duties of the agency, it fails to clearly delineate the agency's complaint or dispute settlement functions. This appears to be a very significant prescriptive gap, particularly in view of Article 32 reproduced above, which clearly anticipates a robust administrative dispute settlement role with an accompanying appellate mechanism.

As a matter of fact, the definitions of powers and duties of the agency under Article 28 (of the Current Investment Law) and of the Board under Article 29 need to be reconciled with the dispute settlement role that Article 32 seems to envision.

[33] Investment Proclamation No. 37/1996, Article 22.
[34] See Investment Proclamation No. 769/2012, Article 2(14) & (16).
[35] Ethiopian Investment Agency Re-establishment Council of Ministers Regulation No. 269/2012.

Consider, for example, Article 28(8). This provision grants the agency the authority to 'issue, renew and cancel permits'. Cancellation of permits carries dramatic consequences. It is not inconceivable that the affected investor may claim direct or indirect expropriation if the cancellation is allegedly capricious and in violation of law. In theory, the investor may avail herself of the complaints procedure contemplated under Article 32. In practice, however, she will fear that the kind of justice that she will get may not be independent or impartial. The guarantees of impartiality and independence could to a certain extent be built into the system by detailed rules providing for separate roles for separate departments, just like many administrative agencies that combine legislative, executive, and quasi-judicial functions.

In any case, in this particular setting, there appears to be a severe regulatory gap that needs to be filled without delay. The quickest remedial measure could come from the Board. Under Article 29(4) of the Current Investment Law, the Board has the authority to 'issue directives necessary for the implementation of this Proclamation and Regulations issued hereunder'. Such directives, if formulated properly and imbued with guarantees of due process, could potentially streamline the complaints management process and help avoid escalation of complaints into court cases or even international arbitration under Ethiopia's investment treaties.

42.7 The Law of Industrial Parks

Economic policy objectives and designs can be properly effected only through legislative enactments. By no means unique to Ethiopia, Industrial Parks and/or Special Economic Zones,[36] wherever they exist, are creations of the law.[37] While their objectives, successes,

[36] Although the terms 'industrial parks' and 'economic zones' are often used interchangeably, the term 'industrial park; is defined under Section 2(1) of the Industrial Parks Proclamation No. 886/2015. As an economic phenomenon, however, one of the world's exhilarating success stories is Shenzhen, China. A recent *Forbes* article aptly described it as follows:

> Forty years ago, Shenzhen, China, was a sleepy fishing village of 30,000. But in 1980, then-Communist Party leader Deng Xiaoping designated the southern town as one of four special economic zones (SEZs), thereby giving it special tax benefits and preferential treatment to foreign investment. In the years that followed, Shenzhen expanded at an alarming pace. Its GDP per capita grew a jaw-dropping 24,569 per cent between 1978 and 2014, and by 2016 its population stood at nearly 12 million.
>
> Today Shenzhen is universally held up as one of capitalism's great success stories. Because of Deng's willingness to liberate its economy and open Shenzhen up to foreign investment, the once-poor, now-thriving megacity is known as a world-class tech hub, home to the Shenzhen Stock Exchange and one of the busiest financial centers in the world.' Franck Holmes, 'China's New Special Economic Zone Evokes Memories of Shenzhen', 21 April 2017. Available at https://www.forbes.com/sites/greatspeculations/2017/04/21/chinas-new-special-economic-zone-evokes-memories-of-shenzhen/#4c0b55b676f2

[37] One of the earliest and by now the evidently successful legislative measure is the Regulation passed by the Chinese National People's Congress in August 1980 entitled 'The Regulation on Special Economic

and failures continue to be debated among economists and policymakers,[38] they are invariably operationalized through their own legal frameworks. The Ethiopian Law of Industrial Parks is scant but presumably growing along with the parks. The principal legislation in this regard is Industrial Parks Proclamation No. 886/2015 supplemented by Industrial Parks Development Corporation Establishment Council of Ministers Regulation No. 326/2014[39] (collectively hereinafter Industrial Parks Law.) This section focuses on the salient features of this body of law.

The law's definition of 'Industrial Park' is not merely definitional; it also states the objectives in the following terms:

> 'Industrial Park' means an area with distinct boundary designated by the appropriate organ to develop comprehensive, integrated, multiple or selected functions of industries, based on a planned fulfillment of infrastructure and various services such as road, electric power and water, one stop shop and have special incentive schemes, with a broad view to achieving planned and systematic, development of industries, mitigation of impacts of pollution on environment and human being and development of urban centers, and includes special economic zones, technology parks, export processing zones, agro-processing zone, free trade zones and the like designated by the Investment Board.[40]

In carving out certain geographic units for a particularly favourable treatment, as economic zones are known to do, the law essentially divides Ethiopia into 'customs territory'[41] and 'industrial park customs controlled area'.[42] The law creates smaller territorial areas subject to federal jurisdiction[43] and specific industrial park norms. Although most of the provisions of the Industrial Parks Law are transactional, mainly focusing on who may benefit from what incentives, the Law contains important provisions that establish the territorial units as special legal domains. For

Zone in Guangdong Province'. For the history and the impressions that it created relatively shortly after it was passed in 1980, see Fenwick (1984). Since then, the city of Shenzhen alone has issued thousands of rules and regulations. Recent Regulations are available at http://www.szqh.com.cn/Home/LAW_AND_REGULATIONS/

[38] See, e.g. Farole (2006: 1) Available at http://siteresources.worldbank.org/INTRANETTRADE/Resources/Pubs/SpecialEconomicZones_Sep2010.pdf ('Orthodox economic perspectives view zones as "second best", preferring instead economy-wide liberalization of trade and investment. But other researchers and policymakers point to potential of economic zones to overcome market and coordination failures and to act as catalysts, both of market forces and of political-economic reforms.')

[39] These legislations are available at www.hopr.gov.et

[40] Industrial Parks Proclamation No. 886/2015, at Article 2(1).

[41] Industrial Parks Proclamation No. 886/2015, at Article 2(21) '"customs territory" means the territory of Ethiopia in which the conventional customs laws relevant to the Industry Park of the country are applicable.'

[42] Industrial Parks Proclamation No. 886/2015, at Article 2(22) '"industrial park customs controlled area" means an area that is part of the industrial park where customs has the power to control but deemed to fall outside the customs territory.'

[43] Federal jurisdiction is expressly stated in Investment Proclamation No. 769/2012, Articles 33–5.

example, industrial parks may have their own 'legal residents' with special rights and responsibilities.[44]

In terms of investment protection, two important provisions are worth highlighting. These are the ones pertaining to national treatment and expropriation. The general investment law does not contain the principle of national treatment. The Industrial Parks Law states, under the heading National Treatment: 'Without prejudice to the provisions of other applicable laws of the country with respect to a foreign investor, any foreign investor individually or jointly with Ethiopian may participate as Industrial Park Developer, Industrial Park Operator or Industrial Park Enterprise.'[45]

Although it suggests that foreign investors would be entitled to national treatment, the 'without prejudice' clause makes it unremarkable. The same cannot, however, be said about the non-expropriation provision. This offers some level of clarity and promises better protection than the provisions of the Current Investment Law. It reads in full:

> Guarantee and Protection:
> 1. No Industrial Park investments may be expropriated unless otherwise required for public purpose, and subject to prompt payment of adequate compensation.
> 2. The compensation shall be paid in any convertible currency in the international financial markets if the investor is foreign investor.
> 3. Any unlawful expropriation shall entitle the Industrial Park Developer, Industrial Park Operator or Industrial Park Enterprise to the restitution of its assets or investment together with reasonable interest rate calculated as of the time the unlawful expropriation until restitution of such property.
> 4. The provisions of appropriate law shall be applicable with respect to manner of expropriation and what constitutes unlawful expropriation, compensation and restitution.

Although its modification of the key taxonomy with respect to the prohibition against expropriation and the promise of providing prompt and adequate compensation is rather unremarkable, this provision introduces a few new concepts that appear on balance more beneficial to the investor than not. These concepts are restitution, interests, and unlawful expropriation. To begin with, this provision contains a 'choice of law' segment for the determination of the lawfulness or unlawfulness of expropriation and the computation of the quantum of restitution. That choice of law is 'the provision of appropriate law'. The Industrial Parks Law itself does not define 'appropriate law' but instead

[44] See Industrial Park Proclamation, No. 886/2015, Articles 14 and 15. In terms of benefits, although the said Regulation could elaborate, the importation of 'personal effects' duty free seems to be the only notable benefit. It might have been intended to accommodate low-skilled foreign workers who do not qualify for hire under Article 13 as technically skilled or for top managerial positions. Even in that context, it is unclear, on the face of the provision itself, what kinds of mobility or residency restrictions are anticipated and what purpose they serve. Article 13(1) states: 'Any industrial park developer, industrial park operator or industrial park enterprise may hire expatriate personnel for its top management, supervisory, training or other technical functions.'

[45] Industrial Park Proclamation No. 886/2015, Article 19.

defines 'applicable law' as 'any proclamation, regulations or directives applicable within Industrial Park supplementing or being interpreted in light of this Proclamation and the Industrial Park Regulation'.[46] Because the definition of 'applicable law' is narrow in scope, the 'appropriate law' would have to have a meaning broader than the Industrial Parks Law. In that regard, the legal concepts used in the industrial park investment protection provisions such as the legality of expropriation, restitution, interests, and compensation seem to trigger the application of general laws of obligation or even, where there is a treaty, perhaps also international investment law principles, which will be discussed in the next section.

More significantly, however, while the Industrial Parks Law offers numerous benefits and exemptions to foreign investors,[47] it does not suspend or modify the application of federal and regional laws in two very important areas: labour and the environment. The Industrial Parks Law unambiguously states the unmodified applicability of the general labour and environmental laws of the country in the industrial parks. In regard to labour, it states: 'Labor Proclamation No 377/2003 (as amended) shall be applicable in any industrial park.'[48] With respect to the environment, it states categorically: 'The federal and regional environmental legislations shall apply within industrial parks.'[49] Because, in modern times, claims of indirect expropriation often pertain to these kinds of regulations, mostly environmental regulations, the non-waiver is a profound policy choice.

The Industrial Parks Law has its own limited dispute settlement rules pertaining mainly to rights and benefits within the industrial parks. The pertinent part reads: 'Any industrial park developer, industrial park operator, industrial park enterprise or industrial park resident shall have the right to lodge complaints to the Commission against *measures taken by any competent authority*.'[50] The term 'competent authority' is defined as 'any federal, regional or city administration government organ having regulatory powers and duties over particular subject matters or geographic areas in respect of Industrial Parks'.[51]

The complaints procedure is multi-tiered: it begins with the Investment Commission, continues with the Investment Board, both institutions established by the Current Investment Law, and escalates into the court system for judicial review.[52] Although this complaints procedure is clearly intended for the resolution of disputes pertaining to the

[46] Industrial Park Proclamation No. 886/2015, Article 2(23).

[47] See, e.g. Industrial Park Proclamation No. 886/2015, Article 21 (foreign exchange rules), and Article 22 (acquisition of law and other forms of property.)

[48] Industrial Park Law Park Proclamation, No. 886/2015, Article 28(1). It does, however, seem to anticipate that some of the concerns of both sides (employer and labour) could be addressed through contractual means. See Article 28 (2): 'Without prejudice to sub-article (1) of this Article labor contract may be negotiated between the employer and employee taking into account the Industrial Park's peculiar feature.'

[49] Industrial Park Proclamation, No. 886/2015, Article 24(1).

[50] Industrial Park Proclamation, No. 886/2015, Article 31(1). Emphasis added.

[51] Industrial Park Proclamation No. 88/2015, Article 2(19).

[52] See Industrial Park Proclamation No. 886/2015, Article 31(2–5).

management of rights and benefits accorded to investors under the Industrial Parks Law within the industrial parks, such as the issuance and revocation of permits,[53] the language of Article 31(1) appears broad enough to encompass complaints relating to labour and environmental regulations. 'Measures taken by any competent authority' by definition include labour and environmental laws or regulations that may be enacted by 'any federal, regional or city administration' because the Industrial Parks Law does not exempt industrial parks from the operation of these laws of general applicability. That would make it not entirely inconceivable that claims of expropriation and other violations of law may be submitted to the designated administrative agencies, namely, the Commission and the Board, for adjudication followed by judicial review. Notwithstanding this interpretation of the breadth of the Commission and Board's dispute settlement jurisdiction, the Industrial Parks Law clearly anticipates that they would have a robust dispute settlement role. It is thus fair to expect that they would develop the administrative apparatus and expertise in due course.

An appreciable percentage of foreign investors in Ethiopia enjoy the added protection of investment treaties. The following section briefly describes the substantive norms and procedural guarantees under Ethiopia's international investment treaties.

42.8 International Standards

As far back as 1758, Vattel, in *The Law of Nations*, advocated the application of external standards for the protection of 'alien' property for fear that the level of protection provided under domestic laws and legal processes may be inadequate or parochial.[54] Although colonial imposition and the resulting economic and other forms of hierarchy had deprived the basic principles of the protection of 'alien' property of their innocence in the eyes of those who had endured a subordinate position,[55] their importance has not been lost forever. The basic principles of non-discrimination and fair treatment continue to underpin modern reciprocal investment treaties.

This section briefly outlines the important substantive protections and procedural guarantees that foreign investors covered under Ethiopia's investment treaties may

[53] See, e.g. Industrial Park Proclamation No. 886/, Article 30 (Issuance of Reprimand, Suspension and Revocation of Permit.)

[54] Vattel, *The Law of Nations* (1758) Vol. II, 8, 104. Cited in Sornarajah, (2010: 19).

[55] See Miles (2013: 1) citing Lipson (1985:11–12); Neufeld (1971: 6); Dawson and Head (1970: 5). ('[i]t is a matter of historical fact that the international rules on the protection of foreign-owned property originated in the reciprocal arrangements of European nations.') The principles that were originally designed to be applied on a reciprocal basis lost their innocence through the 'process of applying these [the Eurocentric] standards to non-European states that became inextricably linked with colonialism, oppressive protection of commercial interests, and military intervention' (Miles 2013: 21).

enjoy. Ethiopia has signed at least thirty-three bilateral investment treaties (BITs) and is a party to at least six additional international regional instruments with investment chapters.[56] Ethiopia is also a member of the Multilateral Investment Guarantee Agency (MIGA) of the World Bank.[57] The brevity of this chapter permits a focus only on one set of instruments. This section focuses on the BITs because they show all the basic substantive principles of protection and procedural guarantees in their various permutations.

42.9 Substantive Norms of Investment Protection Under Ethiopia's Bilateral Investment Treaties

Most capital-exporting countries such as the United States,[58] Canada,[59] and more recently, China[60] negotiate bilateral investment treaties based on their own models. Many capital-importing developing countries often accept the terms of whatever model they are presented with and sign them not only because they are anxious to attract foreign investment and lack the negotiating power but also just because of the allure of convenience. As a developing country, the making of Ethiopia's investment treaties has all the hallmarks of the latter category. Evidence of that is found in the variability of the taxonomy. Notwithstanding the variations in formulation, foreign investors covered in Ethiopia can expect to benefit from the fundamental principles of international investment law such as full protection and security, fair and equitable treatment, national treatment and/or most favoured nation treatment, non-expropriation, prompt, effective, and adequate compensation for expropriation, and procedural due process including access to ISDS. This section highlights some of the most common provisions in Ethiopia's BITs.

[56] The texts of most of these treaties are available at http://investmentpolicyhub.unctad.org/IIA/CountryBits/67#iiaInnerMenu

[57] See https://www.miga.org/who-we-are/member-countries Comprehensive information on the mandates of MIGA and the benefits of its members is available on its official website at https://www.miga.org/investment-guarantees

[58] The most recent US BIT model (2012) is available from official US sources at https://ustr.gov/sites/default/files/BIT%20text%20for%20ACIEP%20Meeting.pdf

[59] Canadian BITs are available from official Canadian sources at http://www.treaty-accord.gc.ca/index.aspx

[60] China's BITs are available from Chinese official sources at http://english.mofcom.gov.cn/article/bilateralchanges/201603/20160301287079.shtml China's use of its own model is somewhat complicated because of its dual capital-importing and capital-exporting position. For a discussion, see, generally, Kidane (2016).

42.10 Treatment

Any random look at Ethiopia's BITs suggests that almost all BITs contain national treatment (NT) and/or most favoured nation treatment (MFN). An example of this is Article 3 of Ethiopia's BIT with the United Kingdom signed on 19 November 2009:

> Neither Contracting Party shall in its territory subject investments or returns of nationals or companies of the other Contracting Party to treatment less favourable than that which it accords to investments or returns of its own nationals or companies or to investments or returns of nationals or companies of any third State.[61]

Ethiopia's BIT with China, which is a decade older, contains a different formulation merging MFN with fair and equitable treatment (FET):

> 1. Investments and activities associated with investments of investors of either Contracting Party shall be accorded fair and equitable treatment and shall enjoy protection in the territory of the other Contracting Party.
> 2. The treatment and protection referred to in Paragraph 1 of this Article shall not be less favorable than that accorded to investments and activities associated with such investments of investors of any third State.

Juxtaposing the above two quoted provisions, it appears that while UK investors benefit from NT, Chinese investors do not. This appears to be not so much a function of disparate treatment as of the fragmentation of the treaty-making process.

42.11 Non-Expropriation

All of Ethiopia's BITs prohibit expropriation unless it is for public purpose and pursued in compliance with law. Although the formulations differ, this rule is entrenched in Ethiopian BITs. The differences in formulation are, however, not insignificant. A closer look at the formulation in Ethiopia–China and Ethiopia–United Kingdom offers a good demonstration.

Article 4 of the Ethiopia–China BIT reads:

> 1. Neither Contracting Party shall expropriate, nationalize or take similar measures (hereinafter referred to as "expropriation") against investments of investors of the other Contracting Party in its territory, unless the following conditions are met: (a) for the public interests; (b) under domestic legal procedure; (c) without discrimination; (d) against compensation.

[61] Ethiopia–United Kingdom BIT, Article 3(1). The text of the BIT is available at http://investmentpolicyhub.unctad.org/Download/TreatyFile/1180 This treaty has not come into effect as of this writing.

2. The compensation mentioned in Paragraph 1, (d) of this Article shall be equivalent to the value of the expropriated investments at the time when expropriation is proclaimed, be convertible and freely transferable. The compensation shall be paid without unreasonable delay.

Two notions are worth noting: 'for public interests' and 'without unreasonable delay'. These notions appear to be more permissive to the state than the following formulation contained in Article 5 of the Ethiopia–United Kingdom BIT:

1. Investments of nationals or companies of either Contracting Party shall not be nationalized, expropriated or subjected to measures having effect equivalent to nationalisation or expropriation (hereinafter referred to as 'expropriation') in the territory of the other Contracting Party except for a public purpose related to the internal needs of that Party on a non-discriminatory basis and against prompt, adequate and effective compensation. Such compensation shall amount to the market value of the investment expropriated immediately before the expropriation or before the impending expropriation became public knowledge, whichever is the earlier, shall include interest at a normal commercial rate until the date of payment, shall be made without delay, be effectively realizable and be freely transferable. The national or company affected shall have a right, under the law of the Contracting Party making the expropriation, to prompt review, by a judicial or other independent authority of that Party, of his or its case and of the valuation of his or its investment in accordance with the principles set out in this paragraph.[62]

The differences in the formulation of what is supposed to be the same principle of non-expropriation and the offering of compensation when and if it occurs, tells a story more interesting than the variability of legal norms or the differing experiences of the negotiators. The interesting story relates to China's economic transformation from being the largest recipient of FDI to one of the largest senders of FDI faster than it could update its BITs. China's second-generation BITs,[63] of which the Ethiopia–China BIT is one, were designed to impose the least possible restrictions on the host state. It was clearly a function of China's position as a receiver not a sender of FDI. It is quite remarkable to observe that because China's BIT policy was largely temporal or generational (not varied according to the economic standing of the partner), BITs designed to preserve host-country decisional autonomy (including the lawfulness of expropriation) were signed with least developed countries such as Ethiopia.

The United Kingdom's BITs on the other hand are non-dilemmatic. They are designed to maximize protection and constrain host-state autonomy in significant ways. For

[62] Ethiopia–United Kingdom BIT, Article 5(1).

[63] China has had at least three generations of BITs. Those signed in the 1990s would fall under the second generation. Each generation had its own defining characteristics. The most notable progress in the third generation is the permission of the arbitrability of liability, a departure from the previous two generations, which limited access to ISDS to the arbitration only of the amount of compensation. For a detailed discussion of China's BITs, see generally, Gallaher and Shan (2009). For a discussion of Chinese Africa-specific BITs, see generally, Kidane (2016).

example, while the Chinese BIT limits access to ISDS to the quantum of damages, the UK BIT contains no such restriction. The UK BIT also contains clearer and investor-friendly rules on the offering of compensation and the computation of damages. The grounds on which expropriation is permitted are 'for a public purpose related to the internal needs of that Party on a non-discriminatory basis and against prompt, adequate and effective compensation'. The Chinese BIT does not contain this kind of clarity. Investor property maybe expropriated 'for the public interest,' which is clearly broader than 'for public purpose related to the internal needs.' The rule on compensation also appears more accommodating to the host state: 'without unreasonable delay' instead of 'effective, prompt and adequate'.

These are some examples of the variations in Ethiopia's BITs. It is evident from the above examples that Ethiopia signed the Chinese model with China and the UK model with the United Kingdom, and that pattern is clear with all the other partners. Ethiopia's BITs with other developing countries appear to have relied on models of the more developed countries such as the United Kingdom.[64] In any case, it is important to note that while all foreign investors are treated equally under Ethiopia's domestic laws, the entitlements and benefits that derive from international investment treaties contain significant variations. It remains unclear how much of the variations in benefits and access to ISDS could be equalized through the MFN clause, a principle all of Ethiopia's BITs contain.

42.12 Procedural Guarantees under Ethiopia's Bilateral Investment Treaties and ISDS

Ethiopia's BITs offer procedural due process to foreign investors in the form of domestic remedies, including judicial remedy, that come after the exhaustion of the administrative remedies discussed in Section 42.6. Moreover, presumably due to fear of the possible inadequacy and even the potential parochialism of domestic legal processes, all of Ethiopia's BITs, like most in the rest of the world, offer an alternative to domestic legal remedy in the form of ISDS.[65]

Many of the ISDS provisions in Ethiopia's BITs have some common defining characteristics. They permit the investor to choose between a domestic court remedy and ISDS; sometimes this choice is final, as in the Ethiopia–China BIT,[66] at other times it is not final

[64] See e.g. Ethiopia–Algeria BIT, at http://investmentpolicyhub.unctad.org/Download/TreatyFile/44

[65] It is important to note from the outset that Ethiopia is a party to neither the New York Convention (Convention for the Recognition and Enforcement of Foreign Arbitral Awards (1958), details at http://www.newyorkconvention.org/) nor the ICSID Convention (The International Convention for the Settlement of Investment Disputes (1965), details at https://icsid.worldbank.org/en/Pages/icsiddocs/ICSID-Convention.aspx).

[66] See Ethiopia–China BIT, Article 9(3). Under this provision, even for quantum, once the investor resorts to the courts, it cannot later invoke ISDS.

as in the Ethiopia–United Kingdom BIT.[67] The ISDS provisions often offer the investor the option of either ICSID or UNCITRAL or ad hoc arbitration under other rules chosen by the arbitrators. Most notably, however, almost all of Ethiopia's BITs give the default appointing authority to either the Secretary General of ICSID or Secretary General of the Permanent Court of Arbitration (PCA). Because Ethiopia is currently not a member of ICSID, ad hoc arbitration under UNCITRAL or other rules would apply.

Ethiopia's BIT with the United Kingdom provides a good example. The relevant part reads:

> Where the dispute is referred to international arbitration, the national or company and the Contracting Party concerned in the dispute may agree to refer the dispute either to: a. The International Centre for the Settlement of Investment Disputes (having regard to the provisions, where applicable, of the Convention on the Settlement of Investment Disputes between States and Nationals of other States, opened for signature at Washington DC on 18 March 1965 and the Additional Facility for the Administration of Conciliation, Arbitration and Fact-Finding Proceedings); or
> b. The Court of Arbitration of the International Chamber of Commerce; or
> c. An international arbitrator or ad hoc arbitration tribunal to be appointed by a special agreement or established under the Arbitration Rules of the United Nations Commission on International Trade Law.[68]

With few exceptions this is the predominant formulation in Ethiopia's BITs regarding ISDS. Ethiopia's BIT with China contains a notable departure in at least one respect. As indicated above, China's BIT does not permit the submission of the merits of the claim to ISDS limiting the ISDS option to the determination of the quantum of compensation only.[69] China has since updated its BIT model allowing the arbitrability of the merits of the claim[70] but its BIT with Ethiopia remains unchanged as of this writing.

[67] See Ethiopia–United Kingdom BIT, Article 8(2). Under this provision, even after the investor has availed itself of the jurisdiction of the domestic courts, it could still resort to ISDS.

[68] Ethiopia–United Kingdom, BIT, Article 8(3).

[69] Ethiopia–China BIT, Article (8):

> 3. If a dispute involving the amount of compensation for expropriation cannot be settled within six months after resort to negotiations as specified in Paragraph I of this Article, it may be submitted at the request of either party to an ad hoc arbitral tribunal or arbitration under the auspices of the International Center for Settlement of Investment Disputes (ICSID) established by the Convention on the Settlement of Investments Disputes between States and Nationals of Other States opened for signature in Washington on March 18, 1965 once both Contracting Parties become member States thereof. The provisions of this Paragraph shall not apply if the investor concerned has resorted to the procedure specified in the Paragraph 2 of this Article.
> [...]
> 6. The tribunal shall reach its decision by a majority of votes. Such decision shall be formal and binding upon both parties to the dispute. Both Contracting Parties shall commit themselves to the enforcement of the decision in accordance with their respective domestic law.

[70] See Kidane (2016: 159–63 ('The Salient Features of the Contemporary Chinese BITs')).

42.13 Conclusion

Ethiopia currently has a maturing legal framework for the protection of foreign direct investment. The domestic legal regime is a patchwork of principal and subsidiary legislation which collectively defines the parameters of a fairly predictable and modern normative universe. The gaps in this universe cannot be overstated, however. The most significant pertains to the institutional mechanisms of enforcement including complaints handling and dispute settlement.

Ethiopia's dozens of investment treaties complement the domestic legal regime. Lacking its own BIT model, Ethiopia has essentially readapted the existing models of its economic partners. That has had adverse effects on the harmonization of rules. Nonetheless, many of these treaties, although with considerable variation in taxonomy, offer foreign investors in Ethiopia protection under external substantive standards such as national treatment and/or most favoured nation treatment, full protection and security, fair and equitable treatment, non-expropriation and prompt, effective, and adequate compensation whenever expropriation occurs. The treaties also offer procedural guarantees in the form of access to the domestic courts as well as to ISDS alternatively or sequentially as the case may be.

Although, arguably, the MFN clause contained in almost all of these treaties could help harmonize some of the rules, jurisprudential harmonization is a very slow and unpredictable process. More importantly, at the most general level, almost all of these treaties appear outdated. In recent times, some of the basic assumptions of the older BITs are being questioned, including the wisdom of the ISDS system itself.[71] To remedy the existing problems of incoherence, and benefit from the most contemporary legal thoughts, Ethiopia must take a closer and systematic look at its existing BITs, renegotiate each one and even develop more, as needed, on the basis of a model that accounts not only for its own specific needs but the needs of its economic partners.

In recent decades, the legal framework has been steadily growing in volume and complexity along with the rapid growth and sophistication of the economy. Experience from other countries that have rapidly transformed their economies (such as China) suggests that the maturation and adaptability of the legal framework is an indispensable precondition for sustaining economic transformation and avoidance of debilitating obstacles. Ethiopia appears to be improving its investment laws and institutions but perhaps not as fast as the demands of the rapidly growing economy. The improvement of the law seems to require more attention than it has so far received.

[71] See, e.g. European Union Commission (2015: 1) Available at http://trade.ec.europa.eu/doclib/docs/2015/may/tradoc_153408.PDF ('In the past, investment agreements have often been drafted more with the protection of investments in mind than the state's right to regulate. Certain investment agreements have even explicitly included a reference to the rights of investors to a "stable business environment".')

Appendix: List of most pertinent investment law-related domestic legislation

1. Petroleum Operations Proclamation No. 295/1986.
2. Proclamation No. 15/1992 (July 1992–June 1996).
3. Investment Proclamation No. 37/1996.
4. Proclamation No. 103/1998
5. Proclamation No. 116/1998.
6. Proclamation No. 168/1999.
7. Investment Proclamation No. 280/2002.
8. Proclamation No. 375/2003.
9. Proclamation No. 543/2007.
10. Mining Proclamation No. 678/2010.
11. Investment Proclamation No. 769/2012.
12. Investment Regulation No. 270/2012.
13. Industrial Parks Proclamation No. 886/2015.

References

Dawson, F. and I. Head (1971). *International Law, National Tribunals and the Rights of Aliens* (New York: Syracuse University Press).

European Union Commission (2015). 'Investment in TTIP and beyond—the Path for Reform, Enhancing the Right to Regulate and Moving from Current ad hoc Arbitration towards an Investment Court', Concept Paper, European Union Commission, Brussels.

Fenwick, A. (1984). 'Evaluating China's Special Economic Zones', *Berkeley Journal of International Law* 2: 376.

Farole, T. (2006). *Special Economic Zones: Performance, Policy, and Practice with a Focus on Sub-Saharan Africa* (Washington, DC: World Bank).

Gallagher, N. and W. Shan (2009). *Chinese Investment Treaties* (Oxford: Oxford University Press).

Kidane, W. (2016). 'China's Bilateral Investment Treaties', *Cornell International Law Journal* 49: 141.

Lipson, C. (1985). *Standing Guard: Protecting Foreign Capital in the Nineteenth and Twentieth Centuries* (Berkeley, CA: University of California Press).

Lowenfeld, A. (2008). *International Economic Law*, 2nd edition (Oxford: Oxford University Press).

Miles, K. (2013). *The Origins of International Investment Law: Empire, Environment and the Safeguards of Capital* (Cambridge: Cambridge University Press).

Neufeld, H. (1971). *The International Protection of Private Creditors from the Treaties of Westphalia to the Congress of Vienna (1648–1815)* (Leyden: A. W. Sijthoff).

Sornarajah, M. (2010). *The International Law on Foreign Investment*, 3rd edition (Cambridge: Cambridge University Press).

von Mehren, R. and N. Kourides (1981). 'International Arbitration between States and Private Parties: The Libyan Nationalization Cases', *American Journal of International Law* 75: 476.

Key Web Resources

https://www.state.gov/r/pa/ei/bgn/2859.htm
www.hopr.gov.et
http://investmentpolicyhub.unctad.org/
http://tcc.export.gov/Trade_Agreements/All_Trade_Agreements/exp_002815.asp

CHAPTER 43

RURAL–URBAN LINKAGES IN ETHIOPIA

TADELE FEREDE AND BELAY FILE

43.1 INTRODUCTION

43.1.1 The Context

THE government of Ethiopia has adopted an overall development strategy known as agricultural development-led industrialization (ADLI) to stimulate farm output and rural incomes, laying the foundation for broad-based growth, poverty reduction, and industrialization. Since 2010 the government has taken a holistic and visionary approach with a focus on growth and transformation, explicitly recognizing the role of industrial development in triggering structural transformation to achieve lower middle-income status by 2025 in a carbon-neutral development pathway (MoFED 2010; NPC 2016). This has been articulated in the first (2010/11–2014/15) and second (2015/16–2019/20) Growth and Transformation Plans (GTPs). These development plans focus on greater commercialization of agriculture and development of the private sector, as well as growth and transformation of rural and urban areas, with an emphasis on rural development and industrialization. Overall, three phases can be distinguished in the development efforts of Ethiopia (Figure 43.1). While the first phase (1992–9) focused on recovery and adjustment, the second (2000–9) aimed at growth and poverty reduction including urban development. Urbanization as a development agenda has been given an explicit focus since 2005 with the launch of a national urban development policy (see Chapter 44). In the third phase (2010 onwards), the government focuses on growth and transformation, with significant emphasis on commercialization of agriculture, industrialization, and urban development. These interventions and urbanization are expected to shape rural–urban interactions to come.

The linkage between rural activities and urban enterprises has been central in structural transformation literature (Lewis 1954; Johnston and Mellor 1961). Structural

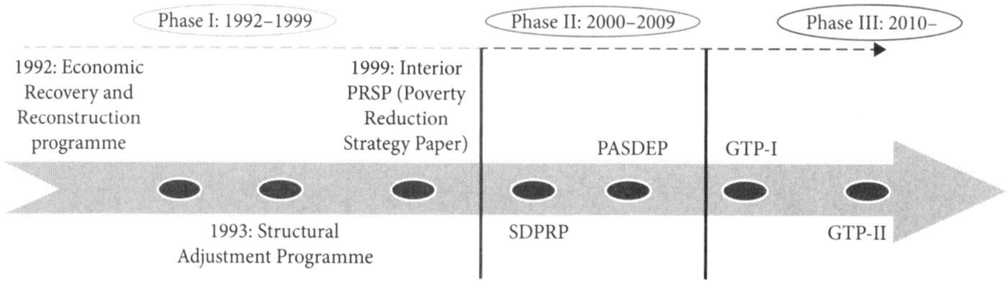

FIGURE 43.1 Timelines of development plans

Source: Authors' computations based on development plans.

transformation has been accompanied by improved inter-sectoral linkages which enhance sectoral performance and productivity in both rural- and urban-based activities. Inter-sectoral linkages matter for both structural transformation and rural–urban interactions which can be influenced by changes in factor markets, demand patterns due to changes in income levels, and flow of goods and services. The sustainability and pace of structural transformation heavily depend on the extent of economic integration, especially within the domestic economy which is linked to urbanization. Evidence shows that no country has achieved middle-income status without significant urbanization (UNECA 2017), which is an important force for accelerating structural transformation. The link between urban and rural economies is manifested not only through increased consumption in cities and rural areas but also through changes in the pattern of consumption. Given that urban areas or cities vary by function, diversity of economic activities, and geography, their roles in strengthening rural–urban linkages could also vary (Duranton 2015). The spatial dimension is an important aspect that influences not only urban economic growth but also the degree to which urban areas are linked to the rural hinterlands.

Two needs are highlighted. First, it is necessary to assess, in a comprehensive manner, the extent to which the various interventions have shaped the nature of rural and urban economies. Second, it is useful to examine the extent of inter-sectoral linkages as well as the nature of rural–urban interactions. Broadly, rural–urban linkages refer to the social, economic, cultural, and political relationships maintained between individuals and groups in the urban environment and those in rural areas (Lesetedi 2003). The focus of this chapter is limited to sectoral flows of agricultural products to urban areas, and goods from urban manufacturing areas to rural areas (Tacoli 1998).

43.1.2 Objective and Research Questions

The main objective of this study is to investigate the extent to which the rural–urban linkage in Ethiopia forms a virtuous circle whereby growth in income in the rural economy boosts consumption of rural households, thereby creating a strong demand for urban products and a reciprocal demand for agricultural produce.

Although the various reforms and development interventions undertaken in Ethiopia since 1992 are expected to influence rural–urban interactions, the extent of such linkage has yet to be assessed. Specifically, how do consumption patterns in rural and urban areas change over time?

43.1.3 Approach and Methodology

43.1.3.1 *Conceptualizing Rural–Urban Linkages*

Rural–urban linkages exist on a continuum of various types and can be seen as two ends of a spatial continuum. Proximity to the town or city means that rural farmers located closer to cities/towns can exploit their proximity to urban markets, and hence exhibit stronger linkages, while those far from cities/towns tend to have weak linkages (Figure 43.2). Urban areas depend on rural areas for food production and other services, while urban areas provide markets for rural goods and services, indicating bidirectional linkage between rural and urban areas. Increased agricultural production stimulates forward production linkages by providing raw materials to further value-adding activities. Agriculture in turn generates backward linkages as it uses inputs such as fertilizers, improved seeds, veterinary services, sprayers, equipment, and repair services which are produced and distributed by enterprises located in urban areas (Pundir and Singh 2001).

43.1.3.2 *Analytical Framework and Data Sources*

In the literature of rural–urban interdependencies, three types of linkage can be identified (Roberts 1998): inter-industry linkages, links between production and institutions (through factor inputs), and household spending on goods and services. A two-level approach has been followed. First, an analysis of demand structure in terms of changes in consumption patterns in both rural and urban areas. Households are grouped into expenditure quintiles to understand the extent of their contribution to rural–urban

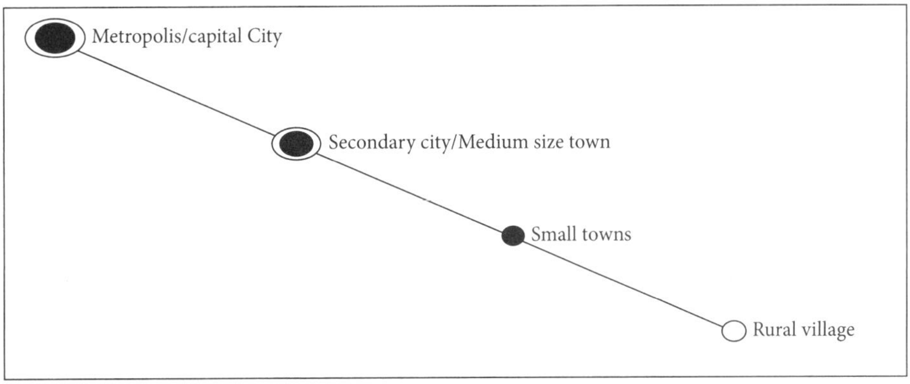

FIGURE 43.2 Conceptualizing rural–urban linkages

Source: UN (2005).

linkages. The relevant data for such type of analysis are contained in the Household Income and Consumption Expenditure Survey (HICES) collected by the Central Statistical Agency (CSA) of Ethiopia. Three rounds of HICES are used: 2004–5, 2010–11, and 2015–15.

Second, the study also looks at production linkages in terms of inter-industry and factor income linkages using a social accounting matrix (SAM) framework. The SAM approach measures the size of linkages across sectors at a point in time. SAMs are designed as a means of characterizing and understanding the structure of the economy in terms of input use (technology coefficients), sources and distribution of income, location of economic activities, saving and investment, and trade structure. In particular, three types of linkages can be identified (Roberts 1998): inter-industry linkages, links between production and institutions (through factor inputs), and household spending on goods and services. Using the SAM framework, detailed characterization of the three types of linkages can be made in terms of the importance of each and the significance of interdependencies between rural and urban dimensions.

The 2010 SAM for Ethiopia consists of fifty-four activities (eighteen agriculture, twenty-six industry, and ten services activities), ten factors of production (five labour types and five different forms of capital), and six household groups distinguished by poverty (poor and non-poor) and location (rural and urban). It also contains other institutions including government, enterprises, and rest of the world.[1]

43.2 Production Linkages

43.2.1 Inter-Industry Linkage

The SAM provides pertinent information regarding the nature and magnitude of inter-industry demand across sectors. Rural–urban linkages involve the flow of agricultural commodities from rural-based activities (mainly agriculture) to urban-based consumers and producers (mainly manufacturing industries and urban-based services) and international markets (e.g. exports). There is also a flow of manufactured and imported goods from urban areas to rural-based activities and consumers (Tacoli 2003). For the sake of analysis and brevity, activities are classified into major groups to help quantify the extent of interdependencies between rural and urban areas. Cereals, which account for the bulk of agricultural output, depend largely on other industries, mainly on chemical fertilizers and pesticides, accounting for 53 per cent of cereal intermediate demand in 2010. Pulses and oilseeds also depend on other industries, but less so than cereals. Contrary to expectation, agro-processing manufacturing industries' linkage with cereals is somewhat limited, accounting for about 12 per cent of the industry's total intermediate demand. Spending by agro-processing industries on overall agricultural

[1] The SAM is constructed by the Ethiopian Development Research Institute (EDRI).

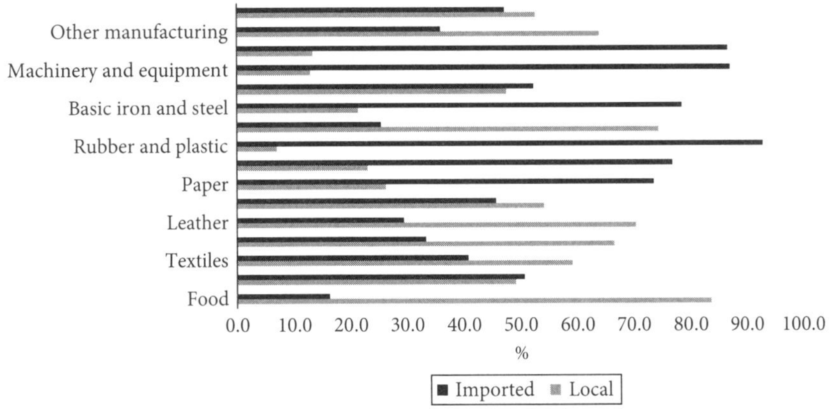

FIGURE 43.3 Share of local and imported raw materials in total raw materials in large and medium manufacturing

Source: CSA (2012).

commodities was about 31 per cent, indicating that a substantial proportion of intermediate inputs for agro-processing industries are sourced from the rest of the world. This seems to suggest weak linkage between the rural (agriculture)—and urban (industries)-based activities. This could be related to limited supply and poor quality of agricultural inputs for the agro-processing industries. In 2013–14, about 36 per cent of large and medium manufacturing establishments reported shortage of raw materials as the primary reason for not operating at full capacity (CSA 2012). For these establishments, imported inputs accounted for about 47 per cent of total raw materials consumed over the same period. As expected, agro-processing manufacturing industries (e.g. food, beverages, textiles, leather, and wood) depend on local raw materials more than other manufacturing industries (Figure 43.3). The share of local raw materials in total raw materials ranges from 54 per cent in wood to 86 per cent in food manufacturing industries. The import intensity of non-agro-processing manufacturing industries appears to be very high. Increasing dependence on imported inputs weakens the domestic linkage between agriculture and manufacturing industry.

What is striking is that intra-industry (linkage between agro-processing and other industries) appears to be rather strong. For instance, close to 57 per cent of the agro-processing industry sourced inputs either from itself or other industries in 2010 (Table 43.1). The services sector depended mainly on agro-processing and other industries, which together accounted for about 60 per cent of intermediate demand by the sector; strikingly, the services sector has negligible linkage with the agricultural sector; cereals accounted for only 2.9 per cent of the services sector's total intermediate demand. These results suggest that enhancing inter-sectoral linkage through improving the supply and quality of agricultural output needs to be part of the overall development strategy to support sustainable industrialization in the country.

Table 43.1 Inter-industry demand linkage

	Cereals	Pulses	Oilseeds	Fruit and vegetables	Other agriculture	Flowers	Livestock	Forestry	Agro-processing	Other industry	Minerals	Services
Cereals	46.16	0.00	0.00	0.00	0.00	0.00	0.00	0.00	11.59	0.00	0.00	2.86
Pulses	0.00	80.63	0.00	0.00	0.00	0.00	0.00	0.00	0.15	0.00	0.00	0.73
Oilseeds	0.00	0.00	62.21	0.00	0.00	0.00	0.00	0.00	0.70	0.00	0.00	0.00
Fruit and vegetables	0.00	0.00	0.00	28.43	0.00	0.00	0.00	0.00	0.85	0.00	0.00	0.85
Other agriculture	0.00	0.00	0.00	0.00	73.35	0.00	99.13	0.00	10.00	0.04	0.00	0.86
Flowers	0.00	0.00	0.00	0.00	0.00	6.95	0.00	0.00	0.00	0.00	0.00	0.09
Livestock	0.00	0.00	0.00	0.00	0.00	0.00	0.00	0.00	6.67	0.00	0.00	3.19
Forestry	0.00	0.00	0.00	0.00	0.00	0.00	0.00	0.00	0.54	0.49	0.00	1.67
Agro-processing	0.00	0.00	0.00	0.00	0.93	0.00	0.00	0.00	27.50	1.04	0.00	27.19
Other industry	53.84	19.37	37.79	71.57	23.00	84.10	0.00	0.00	30.21	67.97	89.99	35.50
Minerals	0.00	0.00	0.00	0.00	0.00	0.00	0.00	0.00	0.52	12.78	0.00	0.00
Services	0.00	0.00	0.00	0.00	2.73	8.95	0.87	100.00	11.27	17.68	10.01	27.06
Total	**100.00**	**100.00**	**100.00**	**100.00**	**100.00**	**100.00**	**100.00**	**100.00**	**100.00**	**100.00**	**100.00**	**100.00**

Source: Based on the 2010 Ethiopian SAM.

43.2.2 Factor Income Linkage

The 2010 SAM for Ethiopia consists of five types of labour: agricultural labour, administrative workers, professional workers, skilled workers, and unskilled workers. It also includes five groups of household: poor rural household, non-poor rural household, poor household in small urban, non-poor household in small urban, poor and non-poor household in big urban.[2]

As expected, rural poor households generate most (about 61 per cent) of their income from agricultural labour, while rural non-poor households have relatively diversified sources of income; they rely on capital income from enterprises (42 per cent), land (29.1 per cent) and agricultural labour (17.5 per cent) (Table 43.2). It appears that agriculture serves as the main source of income for a large segment of rural population in the early periods of structural transformation as about 70 per cent of the labour force is engaged in the sector. Poor households in small urban areas depend on skilled labour (39 per cent) in the form of wage income, unskilled labour (22 per cent), transfers from enterprises (13.8 per cent), and remittances from the rest of the world (RoW) (10 per cent). Non-poor households in small urban areas depend on skilled labour (39 per cent), professional labour (21.2 per cent), and remittances from RoW (25 per cent). Poor and non-poor households in big urban areas generate their income from enterprises, unskilled and skilled labour and transfers from RoW. Interestingly, non-poor households in urban areas generate a significant share of their income from remittances, compared to poor households that have very limited income linkage with the rest of the world. The share of transfers from the rest of the world in total household incomes accounted for 31.3 per cent for non-poor households in big urban areas, indicating the importance of linkages with the rest of the world. Facilitating and strengthening such linkages could thus lead to welfare gains in the short run, by increasing household consumption, and in the long run, by raising household investment (Taffesse and Ferede 2004).

43.2.3 Demand Linkage: Household Consumption-Based Analysis

The literature on rural–urban linkage has to a great extent depended on the virtuous circle of growth model, whereby growth can be propagated from sector to sector through linkages and interdependencies (Evans 1992; Douglass 1998). For Evans (1992), the entry point for the linkage is agriculture, in that rising agricultural income spurs demand for food and other consumer goods (consumption linkage) leading to diversification of urban activities that meets the rising rural demand. Urban-based industries tend to absorb the rural surplus labour, once again boosting agricultural productivity

[2] Urban areas are classified based on population size: urban areas with population less than 50,000 are considered as small, with those above 50,000 as big urban towns.

Table 43.2 Sources of income

		Household group					
Sources of income	Factor input type	Rural poor	Rural non-poor	Small urban poor	Small urban non-poor	Big urban poor	Big urban non-poor
Income from labour	Agricultural labour (both skilled and unskilled labour)	61.91	17.53	7.43	3.22	0.30	0.29
	Administrative workers	1.19	0.89	0.67	5.08	0.48	2.56
	Professional workers	0.43	0.91	5.49	21.20	3.14	4.06
	Skilled workers	3.27	1.29	39.41	34.92	8.43	8.04
	Unskilled workers	2.58	1.47	22.86	9.34	8.54	6.62
Capital income	Land rural poor	5.59	0.00	0.00	0.00	0.00	0.00
	Land rural non-poor	0.00	29.11	0.00	0.00	0.00	0.00
	Livestock rural poor	4.71	0.00	0.00	0.00	0.00	0.00
	Livestock rural non-poor	0.00	5.04	0.00	0.00	0.00	0.00
	Non-agricultural capital	0.00	0.00	0.00	0.00	0.00	0.00
Transfers	Enterprises	18.07	41.90	13.84	0.71	71.04	47.13
	Government	0.08	0.04	0.04	0.02	0.01	0.01
	Rest of the world	2.16	1.83	10.27	25.51	8.05	31.29
	Total	100.00	100.00	100.00	100.00	100.00	100.00

Source: Based on the 2010 Ethiopian SAM.

and income. However, according to Irz et al. (2001), certain conditions must be met for agriculture to serve as an entry point for the virtuous circle: access to farm land, sustaining output prices, and the creation of jobs upstream and downstream. The virtuous circle of growth model seems to have emphasized consumption linkages more than production linkages.

This part of the analysis focuses on assessing consumption linkages between rural and urban households. An implicit assumption here is that most unprocessed products are largely based in rural areas while cities provide semi-processed or fully processed goods. The assessment is based on the CSA's Household Income and Consumption Expenditure Surveys (HICES) which were collected in 2004–5, 2010–11, and 2015–16. Household consumption expenditures were deflated using the relevant consumer price index (CPI) to account for price changes.

43.2.4 Structure of Household Final Demand

In low-income countries such as Ethiopia where a large proportion of population resides in rural areas with agriculture as the main livelihood, rural demand is the dominant factor stimulating expansion of urban-based activities (Diao et al. 2007). This works through providing market opportunities for both industrial products and services produced in the economy. The commodity composition of private consumption demand in Ethiopia reveals a pattern characteristic of economies at the early stages of modern development (Syrquin 1989).

Given the low level of average incomes, poor rural households spend a large proportion of their income on agricultural products (19.4 per cent), agro-processing (13.5 per cent), and services (13 per cent), while rural non-poor households spend mainly on services (18.7 per cent), agro-processing (16.6 per cent), and agricultural products (15.6 per cent) (Figure 43.4). Note that the majority of the poor live in rural areas and work in agriculture, while food comprises the bulk of their expenditures.

Households in small urban areas consume largely agricultural commodities, agro-processing products, and services. In particular, poor households in small and big urban areas spend a significant share of their income on agricultural commodities compared to non-poor households. On the other hand, non-poor households in big urban areas spend a large share of their income on services (28.6 per cent), followed by agricultural products (15.4 per cent and agro-processing products (14.3 per cent), suggesting that rural non-poor households have limited linkages with rural-based activities.

The commodity composition of household expenditure indicates that flows of goods and services exist between urban and rural areas. For instance, expenditure by non-poor rural households on industrial products accounted for a quarter of their income. For poor rural households, this leaves slightly less than a quarter of total consumption expenditure. On the other hand, urban households spend a relatively large proportion (27 per cent) of their income on services. Overall, this seems to suggest that increasing the income of rural households could generate strong demand for manufactured products.

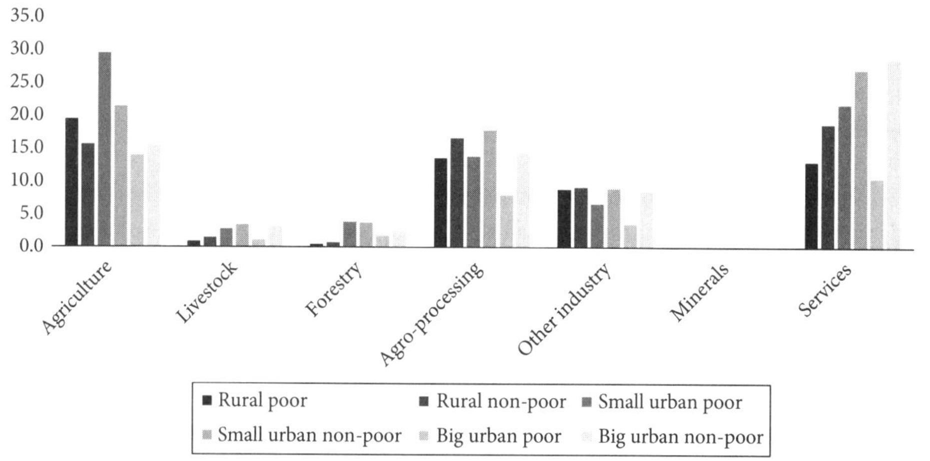

FIGURE 43.4 Average spending by household group and commodity type

Source: Based on the 2010 Ethiopian SAM.

Contrary to the 'trickle down' theory, low-income households have higher income-generating potential than high-income household groups (Mellor and Lele 1973). For poor households, disproportionately more income will be spent on urban-based non-agricultural commodities. Studies indicate that rural households would spend about 0.60 birr for each additional birr of income on non-agricultural commodities and low-income rural households have a higher marginal budget share (MBS) of non-agricultural spending compared with higher-income groups (Diao et al. 2007). In rural areas, for example, the MBS of non-agricultural products and services for lowest income quintiles is about 0.74 compared to 0.47 for the top income quintile, indicating that additional income for the lowest income groups will stimulate demand for urban-based products and hence spur higher economy-wide growth.

43.2.5 Trends in Rural Household Consumption Expenditure

Rural household consumption expenditure increased in real terms, growing by about 6.9 per cent per year between 2005 and 2015. Food consumption expenditure grew by 3 per cent, driven largely by increased consumption of processed food (by 3.8 per cent) compared with non-processed food of 1.6 per cent (Table 43.3). Likewise, household expenditure on beverages grew by about 12.4 per cent, with expenditure on manufactured beverages registering high growth (29.7 per cent) compared with a 10.4 per cent rate for locally processed beverages (e.g. local liquor). Expenditure on non-food items also grew significantly. These include, for instance, expenditure on housing, electricity, water, gas, and other fuel (11.4 per cent), furnishing and household equipment and maintenance (7.7 per cent), transport (25 per cent), unincorporated household enterprise

Table 43.3 Rural real consumption growth rate of selected commodity items

Commodity type	Growth rate (2005–15) (per cent)
Food	3.0
Processed food	3.8
Non-processed food	1.6
Beverages	12.4
Locally processed beverages	10.4
Manufactured beverages	29.7
Clothing and footwear	1.0
Housing, water, gas, electricity, and other fuels	11.4
Furnishing and household equipment maintenance	7.7
Health	125.5
Transport	25.6
Communications	0.0
Recreation and culture	0.8
Education	-2.9
Restaurants and hotels	5.4
Miscellaneous goods and services	16.7
Unincorporated household enterprise expenditure	46.3

Source: Based on Household Consumption and Expenditure Surveys (2004–5, 2010–11, and 2015–16).

expenditures (e.g. farm inputs and operational costs) (46 per cent), and personal care, social protection, insurance, and financial services (16.9 per cent). Rural household consumption expenditure on manufactured products grew between 2005 and 2015, indicating strong linkages with urban-based activities as rural incomes grow.

As expected, expenditures on food items form a major part of rural household consumption expenditure, but declining over time as a share of total consumption expenditure (Figure 43.5). The share of food expenditure in real terms in total consumption expenditure fell from 65 per cent in 2005 to 45 per cent in 2015, a 20 percentage point decline. Both processed and non-processed food expenditure as a share of total consumption expenditure declined, while the share of beverages (both locally produced and manufactured) increased between 2005 and 2015. In particular, rural household consumption expenditure on processed food items accounted for a large share of total rural household consumption expenditure, indicating strong demand stimulus for the manufacturing sector. Rural household expenditure on non-food items, such as housing, water, electricity and gas, transport, communications, and inputs increased, suggesting expenditure diversification towards urban-based non-food items. The share of non-food expenditure in real terms increased from 29 per cent in 2005 to 46 per cent in 2015. It appears that the share of expenditure on manufactured goods and services has greatly increased in rural Ethiopia, indicating the existence of a virtuous rural–urban linkage.

Although aggregate consumption expenditure by rural households in real terms has increased recently, not all rural households were able to enjoy higher consumption of food and non-food items. To account for heterogeneity, rural households are classified into expenditure quintiles which help assess the evolution of their consumption expenditure.

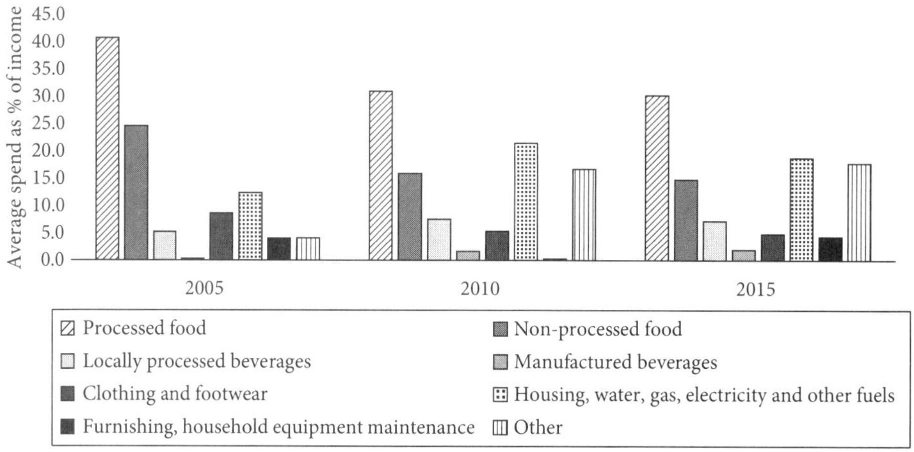

FIGURE 43.5 Trends in real consumption expenditure by rural households for selected commodity groups

Source: Based on Household Consumption and Expenditure Surveys (2004–5, 2010–11, and 2015–16).

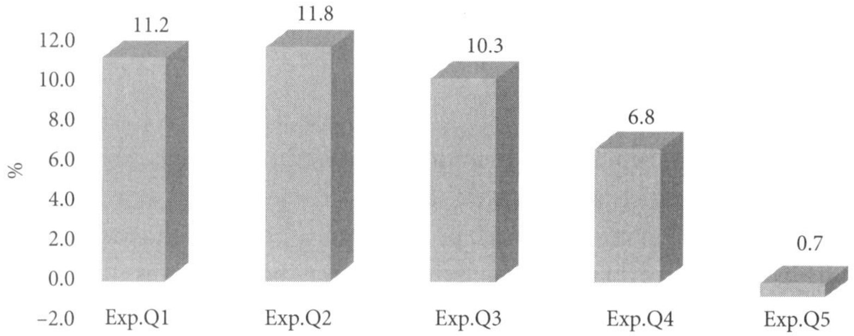

FIGURE 43.6 Rural consumption expenditure growth rate by quintile

Source: Based on Household Consumption and Expenditure Surveys (2004–5, 2010–11, and 2015–16).

Expenditure quintiles reveal changes in consumption pattern by income/consumption group. Households in the bottom three expenditure quintiles (1st, 2nd, and 3rd) experienced robust growth in real consumption expenditure, with each registering a growth rate of 11.2, 11.8, and 10.3 per cent, respectively, between 2005 and 2015 (Figure 43.6). Real consumption expenditure declined for the fifth quintile. This could be due to the top-quintile households allocating more of their income to investment activities than low-income households. Specifically, the growth rate of expenditure on processed[3] and unprocessed food, clothing and footwear, and furnishing and household equipment maintenance declined over the same period for the top quintiles.

[3] For the top quintile, expenditure on processed food items and clothing and footwear declined by about 5.8 and 9.4 per cent, respectively, while expenditure on locally processed beverages increased by 2.1 per cent.

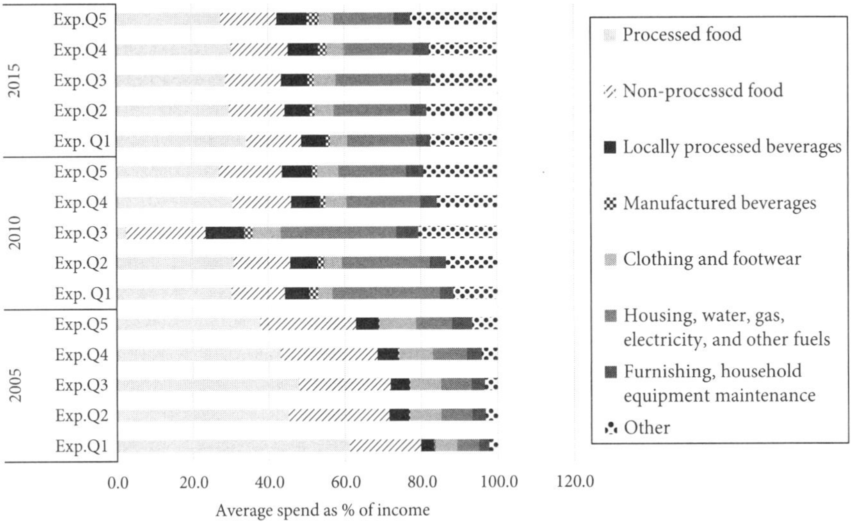

FIGURE 43.7 Expenditure share by quintile for selected commodity groups

Source: Based on Household Consumption and Expenditure Surveys (2004–5, 2010–11, and 2015–16).

The share of food expenditure declined for all expenditure quintiles; the decline is high for the first quintile, followed by the second and third quintiles (Figure 43.7). Between 2005 and 2015, households in all quintiles experienced consumption expenditure diversification towards urban-based non-food items, a sign of demand shift among rural households.

43.2.6 Trends in Urban Household Consumption

Similar to rural households, consumption expenditure by urban households increased in real terms, growing by about 15.1 per cent per year between 2005 and 2015. Food consumption expenditure grew by 10.8 per cent, driven largely by increased consumption of both processed (10.7 per cent) and non-processed (11 per cent) food items (Table 43.4). Urban household expenditure on beverages grew by about 17.9 per cent, with expenditure on manufactured beverages registering high growth (28.6 per cent) compared to a 13.6 per cent growth rate of locally processed beverages (e.g. local liquor). There was also significant growth in expenditure by urban households on non-food items such as housing, electricity, water, gas and other fuel (19.3 per cent), furnishing and household equipment and maintenance (7.7 per cent), transport (22.4 per cent), clothing and footwear (5.8 per cent), communications (348 per cent), and transport (24.1 per cent). Similar to rural households, there is significant consumption expenditure diversification, with increased consumption of manufactured products, indicating the prospect of stronger demand-induced urban-based industrial products.

Table 43.4 Urban real consumption growth rate for selected commodity items

Commodity type	Growth rate (2005–15) (%)
Food	10.8
Processed food	10.7
Non-processed food	11.0
Beverages	17.9
Locally processed beverages	13.6
Manufactured beverages	28.6
Clothing and footwear	5.8
Housing, water, gas, electricity, and other fuels	19.3
Furnishing, household equipment maintenance	22.4
Health	130.37
Transport	24.08
Communications	348.65
Recreation and culture	6.53
Education	16.83
Restaurants and hotels	9.75
Miscellaneous goods and services	36.56
Unincorporated household enterprise expenditure	11.70

Source: Based on Household Consumption and Expenditure Surveys (2004–5, 2010–11, and 2015–16).

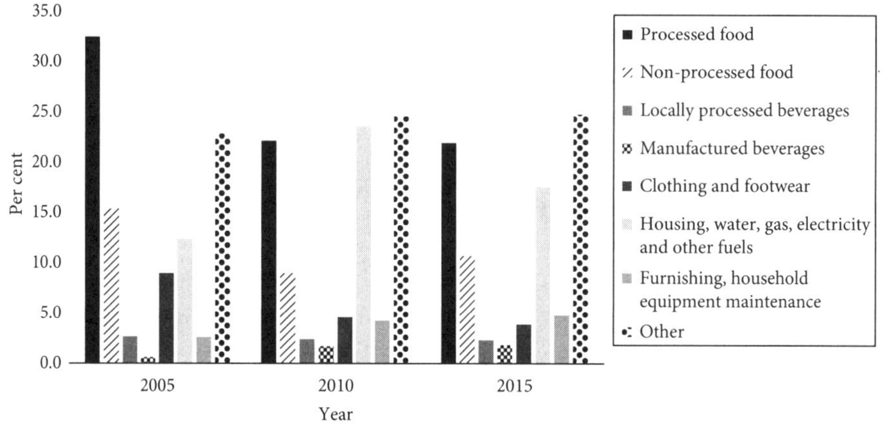

FIGURE 43.8 Trends in real consumption expenditure by urban households for selected commodity groups

Source: Based on Household Consumption and Expenditure Surveys (2004–5, 2010–11, and 2015–16).

The share of processed and non-processed food expenditure in real terms declined from 32.4 and 15.4 per cent in 2005 to 21.9 and 10.7 per cent over the same period (Figure 43.8). Expenditure by urban households on clothing and footwear also declined, while expenditure on manufactured beverages increased threefold though from a low base: from 0.6 per cent to 1.8 per cent. The share of expenditure on other non-food items

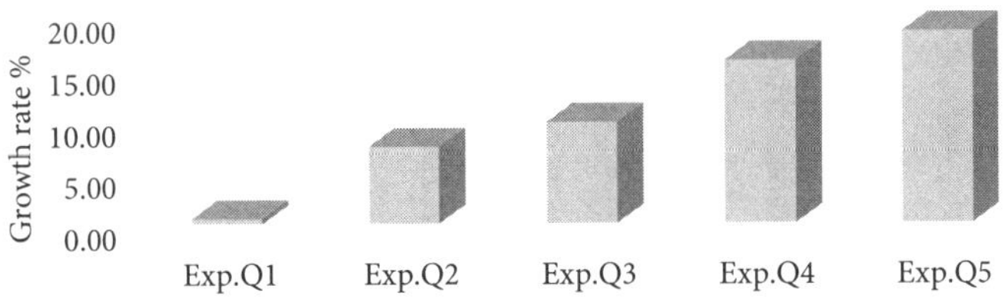

FIGURE 43.9 Growth rate of urban consumption expenditure by quintile, 2005–15

Source: Based on Household Consumption and Expenditure Surveys (2004–5, 2010–11, and 2015–16).

such as furnishing and household equipment maintenance, housing, electricity, water, and fuels also increased over the same period. Overall, urban households have limited consumption linkages with rural-based activities.

The average consumption expenditure masks changes in the structure of consumption among different household groups. Unlike rural households, urban households in the top two (4th and 5th) expenditure quintiles registered very high consumption growth rates of 18.4 and 15.8 per cent, respectively, between 2005 and 2015 (Figure 43.9). Households in the bottom (1st) quintile experienced a negligible (0.40 per cent) growth rate of real consumption expenditure, indicating that the bottom 20 per cent of urban households, who are considered to be poor, have not significantly benefited from the overall growth dividend. Consumption expenditure on unprocessed food grew for all quintiles, and the growth rate is higher for households in the top (4th and 5th) quintiles than in lower quintiles between 2005 and 2015, suggesting increased consumption inequality among urban households despite the economic burst that the last couple of decades have registered. For instance, consumption expenditure on unprocessed food grew by 11.5 and 13 per cent in the top two quintiles, respectively. It appears that urban households in the lower quintiles have limited demand linkage with rural-based activities.

With the exception of the first quintile, the share of food expenditure declined for other expenditure quintiles; the decline is higher for the top quintile (Figure 43.10). The share of expenditure on rural-based non-processed food by the first quintile increased from 10.9 to 12.7 per cent. This suggests that urban households, especially the top quintiles, consume processed items, with little linkages with rural-based activities. Urban households experienced consumption expenditure diversification within urban-based non-food items.

43.3 Quantifying Rural–Urban Linkages: an SAM Multiplier Analysis

Further insights into the strength, structure, and distribution of linkages between rural and urban areas can be obtained by imposing some assumptions on selected accounts of the SAM. Additional information on the extent of rural–urban interdependencies can be generated, assuming fixed prices and Leontief-type technology (Pyatt and

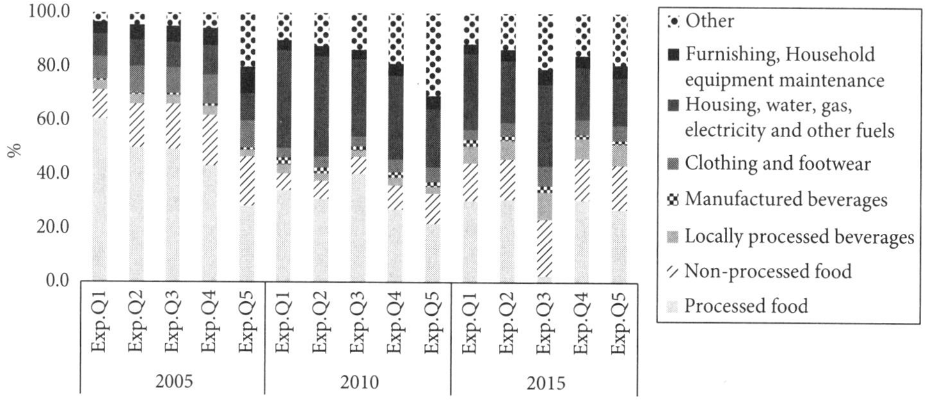

FIGURE 43.10 Share of urban consumption expenditure by quintile

Source: Based on Household Consumption and Expenditure Surveys (2004–5, 2010–11, and 2015–16).

Round 1979). Following the SAM multiplier model, accounts such as activity, commodity, factor, and household accounts are endogenously determined, with government, capital, and rest of the world as exogenous.

The basic row accounting balances implied in the SAM can be written as $y = By + x$ where y is a column vector of endogenous account totals, B refers to a coefficients matrix obtained by dividing the elements in the SAM by the corresponding column total, and x *is* a column vector showing flows from the endogenous accounts to the combined exogenous account (Roberts 1998). The aggregate multipliers can be expressed as $y = (I—B)^{-1}x = Mx$. Note that the multiplier matrix (M) captures both direct and indirect relationships in the entire economic system.

Box 43.1 Some concepts

Output multipliers: an increase in an industry's output when the final demand for goods produced by another (or the same) industry increases by one birr. Total output multiplier is the sum of output multipliers across industries for a change in final demand of a given industry.

GDP multipliers: refers to an increase in an industry's value added when final demand for goods produced by an industry increases by one birr. It is the sum of factor multipliers (e.g. labour and capital multipliers).

Household income multiplier: describes an increase in households' earnings for a one birr increase in the final demand of an industry's output.

Backward linkage: refers to how a given sector depends on other economic sectors for input supply.

Forward linkage: describes how a sector supplies its output to other sectors to be used as intermediate inputs of production.

Source: Pyatt and Roe (1977); Stewart (1976).

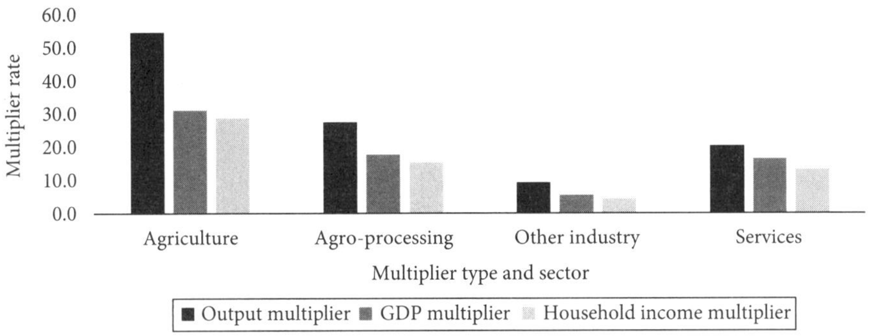

FIGURE 43.11 Aggregate multipliers

Source: Based on the 2010 Ethiopian SAM.

At aggregate level, agriculture has large output, GDP, and household income multipliers compared to urban-based agro-processing and other industries (Figure 43.11). Output multipliers are larger than other types of multiplier due to production activities facing the dual impulse from final and intermediate demands. Note that output and GDP multipliers for agro-processing industries are lower than for agriculture, indicating weak linkage of the latter with the rest of the economy. Low output multipliers for manufacturing industries is due to, among other things, their dependence on imported inputs that tend to weaken domestic linkages, and this is not desirable from the point of view of enhancing demand-driven industrialization.

Backward and forward linkages exist between sectors, mainly between agriculture and urban-based manufacturing and services, such as production of inputs and the processing of agricultural raw materials. For instance, small and medium urban centres rely on surrounding economic activities for broad-based demand for basic goods and services that help develop secondary and tertiary sectors in these centres. Table 43.5 presents output multipliers for selected activities, focusing on the impact on the industry accounts of a unit change in the demand for activity output. Note that activities with large multipliers can be considered as strategic, where investment would introduce, through the various linkages in the system, the greatest benefit for the whole economy.

Similar to the aggregate multipliers, agricultural activities tend to have larger linkage effects than urban-based activities. However, rural-based agricultural activities have large own multipliers, indicating limited linkage with other activities of the economy, especially with that of the manufacturing industries (Table 43.6). For instance, a positive demand increase for the output of wheat leads to ETB 0.73 million increase in its own output and food-processing activity of ETB 22,000. With the exception of food processing, beverages, and textiles, agro-processing industries have very limited linkages in terms of stimulating other activities. For instance, an exogenous increase in the demand for beverages will result in an increase in barley activity of ETB 13,700. Overall, given the current economic structure, output multipliers indicate weak economic linkages (both backward and forward) between urban-based industries and the rural economy, reflecting the high import intensity of urban-based manufacturing industries as noted above.

Table 43.5 Output multiplier matrix for selected activities

	Teff	Barley	Wheat	Maize	Sorghum	Pulses	Vegetables	Oilseeds	Fruits	Cattle	Milk	Food	Dairy	Beverages	Textiles	Wearing apparel	Leather	Wood	Paper
Teff	0.98	0.08	0.06	0.07	0.08	0.08	0.06	0.10	0.06	0.08	0.10	0.08	0.00	0.04	0.05	0.02	0.03	0.03	0.02
Barley	0.04	0.97	0.03	0.03	0.04	0.04	0.03	0.04	0.03	0.04	0.04	0.03	0.00	0.01	0.02	0.01	0.01	0.01	0.00
Wheat	0.07	0.07	0.73	0.06	0.07	0.07	0.05	0.08	0.05	0.07	0.08	0.05	0.00	0.07	0.04	0.02	0.02	0.02	0.01
Maize	0.08	0.08	0.05	0.85	0.08	0.07	0.05	0.08	0.05	0.08	0.09	0.05	0.00	0.03	0.04	0.01	0.02	0.02	0.01
Sorghum	0.08	0.08	0.05	0.06	0.87	0.07	0.05	0.08	0.05	0.08	0.09	0.05	0.00	0.03	0.04	0.02	0.02	0.02	0.01
Pulses	0.05	0.05	0.04	0.04	0.05	0.87	0.04	0.06	0.03	0.05	0.06	0.04	0.00	0.02	0.03	0.01	0.02	0.02	0.01
Vegetables	0.02	0.03	0.02	0.02	0.03	0.02	0.57	0.03	0.02	0.03	0.03	0.02	0.00	0.01	0.01	0.01	0.01	0.01	0.00
Fruit	0.01	0.01	0.00	0.01	0.01	0.01	0.00	0.01	0.54	0.01	0.01	0.01	0.00	0.01	0.00	0.00	0.00	0.00	0.00
Oilseeds	0.00	0.00	0.00	0.00	0.00	0.00	0.00	0.89	0.00	0.00	0.00	0.00	0.00	0.01	0.00	0.00	0.00	0.00	0.00
Livestock	0.17	0.17	0.12	0.14	0.17	0.17	0.12	0.20	0.13	0.99	1.16	0.12	0.59	0.06	0.05	0.03	0.18	0.03	0.03
Processed food	0.03	0.03	0.02	0.03	0.03	0.03	0.02	0.04	0.02	0.03	0.04	0.66	0.03	0.05	0.01	0.01	0.01	0.01	0.01
Dairy	0.00	0.00	0.00	0.00	0.00	0.00	0.00	0.00	0.00	0.00	0.00	0.04	0.09	0.00	0.00	0.00	0.00	0.00	0.00
Beverages	0.04	0.04	0.03	0.03	0.04	0.04	0.03	0.04	0.02	0.04	0.04	0.02	0.02	0.66	0.01	0.01	0.01	0.01	0.01
Textiles	0.03	0.03	0.02	0.03	0.03	0.03	0.02	0.04	1.00	0.03	0.04	0.02	0.02	0.01	0.35	0.05	0.08	0.01	0.05
Wearing apparel	0.00	0.00	0.00	0.00	0.00	0.00	0.00	0.00	0.00	0.00	0.00	0.00	0.00	0.00	0.01	0.00	0.03	0.00	0.00
Leather	0.02	0.02	0.01	0.01	0.02	0.02	0.01	0.02	0.01	0.02	0.02	0.01	0.01	0.01	0.00	0.01	0.69	0.01	0.01
Wood	0.00	0.00	0.00	0.00	0.00	0.00	0.00	0.00	0.00	0.00	0.00	0.00	0.00	0.00	0.00	0.01	0.00	0.32	0.01
Paper	0.01	0.01	0.01	0.01	0.01	0.01	0.01	0.01	0.01	0.01	0.01	0.01	0.01	0.00	0.00	0.59	0.00	0.00	0.59
Total	**1.63**	**1.67**	**1.19**	**1.39**	**1.52**	**1.53**	**1.06**	**1.70**	**2.02**	**1.56**	**1.82**	**1.17**	**0.77**	**1.02**	**0.65**	**0.20**	**1.14**	**0.51**	**0.17**

Source: Based on the 2010 Ethiopian SAM.

Table 43.6 Income multiplier matrix for selected activities

Household group	Teff	Barley	Wheat	Maize	Sorghum	Pulses	Vegetables	Oilseeds	Fruits	Cattle	Milk	Food	Dairy	Beverages	Textiles	Wearing apparel	Leather	Wood	Paper
Rural poor	0.65	0.75	0.46	0.61	0.74	0.64	0.50	0.54	0.44	0.74	0.84	0.34	0.01	0.21	0.28	0.11	0.16	0.20	0.06
Rural non-poor	0.90	0.78	0.60	0.64	0.77	0.86	0.55	1.18	0.58	0.80	0.91	0.66	0.01	0.34	0.48	0.20	0.28	0.29	0.11
Small urban poor	0.02	0.02	0.01	0.02	0.02	0.02	0.01	0.02	0.01	0.02	0.02	0.02	0.00	0.01	0.01	0.01	0.01	0.01	0.01
Small urban non-poor	0.13	0.15	0.09	0.12	0.14	0.13	0.10	0.13	0.09	0.14	0.16	0.18	0.00	0.06	0.11	0.04	0.07	0.06	0.05
Big urban poor	0.01	0.01	0.01	0.01	0.01	0.01	0.01	0.01	0.01	0.01	0.01	0.03	0.00	0.01	0.01	0.01	0.01	0.01	0.00
Big urban non-poor	0.11	0.12	0.08	0.10	0.12	0.11	0.08	0.12	0.07	0.12	0.13	0.23	0.00	0.08	0.13	0.05	0.08	0.07	0.04

Source: Based on the 2010 Ethiopian SAM.

Table 43.7 Aggregate household multiplier matrix

	Rural poor	Rural non-poor	Small urban poor	Small urban non-poor	Big urban poor	Big urban non-poor
Rural poor	1.46	0.44	0.39	0.36	0.16	0.28
Rural non-poor	0.63	1.60	0.58	0.53	0.24	0.44
Small urban poor	0.01	0.01	1.01	0.01	0.01	0.01
Small urban non-poor	0.13	0.13	0.11	1.10	0.05	0.08
Big urban poor	0.01	0.01	0.01	0.01	1.01	0.01
Big urban non-poor	0.13	0.12	0.13	0.12	0.05	1.11

Source: Based on the 2010 Ethiopian SAM.

This seems to suggest there is large latitude for harnessing and exploiting rural and urban economic linkages for sustained growth and industrialization.

On the income linkage, both poor and non-poor rural households benefit more than other household groups from the increase in both rural- and urban-based activities, but non-poor rural household groups gain more from the economic expansion. The aggregate household income multipliers indicate that the rural household groups (both poor and non-poor) have far greater income-generating potential than urban households (Table 43.7). The indirect effect of an increase in the income of poor rural households would benefit rural non-poor households followed by non-poor urban households in small and big urban areas. For instance, a one million birr increase in the income of poor households would result in an increase in the income of non-poor rural households of 0.63 million birr. This can be compared with the same amount of injection into urban households. Interestingly, household groups in small urban areas (both poor and non-poor alike) tend to have a greater rural income-stimulating effect than households in big urban areas. Contrary to 'trickle down' theory, low-income households in rural areas have higher income-generating potential than high-income groups in urban areas. These results suggest that investments in rural and urban-based agro-processing industries could have the potential to generate significant welfare gains in terms of income growth and poverty reduction. In particular, the future of rural transformation can be shaped by targeted investments in small urban areas and this has the potential to speed up rural transformation as there are strong economic leakages from small urban areas to rural areas.

43.4 Concluding Remarks

Rural and urban areas are linked by the reciprocal exchange of unprocessed and processed products and services. Rural–urban linkages are stepping stones toward rural transformation and industrial growth.

The scale of linkage between agriculture and non-agricultural activities, especially manufacturing, appears to be slight, with the latter depending on imported inputs with significant leakages. This suggests that the magnitude of inter-sectoral linkages between agriculture and other sectors has remained weak despite the rapid economic growth of the last couple of decades.

Contrary to 'trickle down' theory, low-income households in rural areas have higher income-generating potential than high income groups in urban areas. These results suggest that investments in rural and urban-based agro-processing industries could have the potential to generate significant welfare gains in terms of income growth and transformation. In particular, the future of rural transformation can be shaped by targeted investments in small urban areas and this has the potential to speed up rural transformation because of the strong economic leakages from small urban areas to rural areas (see Chapter 44).

Strengthening the rural–urban linkage requires accelerated urbanization through the promotion of small towns and medium-sized cities which would improve accessibility of key non-agricultural goods and services such as agricultural inputs for rural producers, while at the same time providing the necessary marketing infrastructure for rural-based activities. Investments in infrastructure is equally critical for improving rural–urban linkages since improved access to modern infrastructure (e.g. roads) and services (e.g. finance) would help rural households meet their economic and social needs.

The key message is that exploiting potential rural–urban linkages to enhance structural transformation and induce endogenous industrial growth requires a balanced growth strategy that consists of targeting rural-based agricultural activities and urban-based activities, thereby achieving a 'win–win' outcome. For successful rural transformation to occur, urban-based activities, especially processing and other manufacturing sectors, need to grow to absorb the growing supply of agricultural products and satisfy the increasing demand for non-agricultural products. The best route out of subsistence rural-based agricultural activity is the development of the non-agricultural sector, especially the manufacturing sector.

References

CSA (2015). 'Household Consumption and Expenditure (HCEE) Survey 2015/16', Central Statistical Agency, Addis Ababa.

CSA (2012). 'Report on Large and Medium-Scale Manufacturing and Electricity Industries Survey', *Statistical Bulletin* 531, Addis Ababa.

CSA (2007). 'Household Income, Consumption and Expenditure (HICE) Survey 2004/05, Vol. 1: Analytical Report', *Statistical Bulletin* 394, Addis Ababa.

Diao, X., B. Fekadu, S. Haggblade, et al. (2007). 'Agricultural Growth Linkages in Ethiopia: Estimates Using Fixed and Flexible Price Models', IFPRI Discussion Paper No. 695, International Food Policy Research Institute (IFPRI), Washington, DC.

Douglass, M. (1998). 'A Regional Network Strategy for Reciprocal Rural–Urban Linkages: An Agenda for Policy Research with Reference to Indonesia', *Third World Planning Review* 20 (1).

Duranton, G. (2015). 'Growing through Cities in Developing Countries', *The World Bank Research Observer* 30 (1): 39–73.
Evans, E. (1992). 'A Virtuous Circle Model of Rural–Urban Development: Evidence from a Kenyan Small Town and its Hinterland', *Journal of Development Studies* 28 (4): 640–67.
Irz, X., L. Lin, C. Thirtle, and S. Wiggins (2001). 'Agricultural Productivity Growth and Poverty Alleviation', *Development Policy Review* 19 (4): 449–66.
Johnston, B. and J. Mellor (1961). 'The Role of Agriculture in Economic Development', *The American Economic Review* 51 (4): 566–93.
Lesetedi, G. (2003). 'Urban–Rural Linkages as an Urban Survival Strategy among Urban Dwellers in Botswana: The Case of Broadhurst Residents', *Journal of Political Ecology* 10: 37–44.
Lewis, A. (1954). 'Economic Development with Unlimited Supplies of Labour', *Manchester School* 22 (1954): 139–91.
Mellor, J. and U. Lele (1973). 'A Labor Supply Theory of Economic Development', Occasional Paper No. 43, Department of Agricultural Economics, Cornell University, Ithaca, NY.
MoFED (2010). 'Growth and Transformation Plan 2010/11–2014/15, Vol. I (main text)', Addis Ababa.
NPC (2016). 'Growth and Transformation Plan II (GTP II) (2015/16–2019/20), Vol. I (main text)', Addis Ababa.
Pundir, S. and K. Singh (2001). 'Rural–Urban Linkages and Socio-Economic Development: A Case Study of Two Villages in Gujarat', Institute for Rural Management, Anand, India.
Pyatt, G. and N. Roe (1977). *Social Accounting for Development Planning with Special Reference to Sri Lanka* (Cambridge: Cambridge University Press).
Pyatt, G. and J. Round (1979). 'Accounting and Fixed Price Multipliers in a Social Accounting Matrix Framework', *The Economic Journal* 89 (356): 850–73.
Roberts, D. (1998). 'Rural–Urban Interdependencies: Analysis Using an Inter-Regional SAM Model', *European Review of Agricultural Economics* 25 (1998): 506–27.
Stewart, J. (1976). 'Linkages and Foreign Direct Investment', *Regional Studies* 10: 245–58.
Syrquin, M. (1989). 'Patterns of Structural Change', in *Handbook of Development Economics, Vol. I*, ed. Hollis Chenery and T. N. Srinivasan (Amsterdam: Elsevier Science): Chapter 7.
Tacoli, N. (2003). 'The Links between Urban and Rural Development', *Environment & Urbanization* 15 (1): 3–12.
Tacoli, C. (1998). 'Bridging the Divide: Rural–Urban Interactions and Livelihood Strategies', International Institute for Environment and Development, London.
Taffesse, A. and T. Ferede (2004). 'The Structure of the Ethiopian Economy: A SAM-based Characterisation'. https://pdfs.semanticscholar.org/54c9/9f3d9b59f4c8bdc67961e479730898 265bab.pdf
United Nations (2005). 'Rural–Urban Linkages for Poverty Reduction: A Review of Selected Approaches from Asia and the Pacific', Bangkok, ESCAP, ETF (European Training Fund).
UNECA (2017). 'Economic Report on Africa 2017: Urbanization and Industrialization for Africa's Transformation', Addis Ababa.

CHAPTER 44

URBANIZATION AND INDUSTRIAL DEVELOPMENT IN ETHIOPIA

TEGEGNE GEBRE-EGZIABHER AND
EDLAM ABERA YEMERU

44.1 Introduction

Urbanization is closely associated with industrialization and structural transformation of national economies (Jedwab 2013; Gollin, Jedwab, and Vollrath 2016). However, the link between urbanization and economic growth largely depends on a number of factors. Countries that have successfully made the transition from agriculture- to manufacturing-based economy are those that have efficient, competitive, and 'productive' cities that serve as nodes of innovation, production, and accumulation (Jedwab 2013; Freire, Lall, and Leipziger 2014). In many developing countries such as Ethiopia, however, rapid urbanization has occurred without industrialization and structural transformation (Jedwab 2013; Gollin, Jedwab, and Vollrath 2016). This process is often referred to as 'urbanization without development' (Fay and Opal 2000), whereby consumption in the cities is financed by surpluses extracted from the agricultural sector (Jedwab 2013). Consumption cities are less likely to exhibit agglomeration effects and provide incentives for capital accumulation and therefore have lower positive impact on long-term growth, job creation, and the revenues needed by the state to invest more in productive activities (Jedwab 2013).

By contrast, efficient and productive cities can contribute to the structural change of economies as they generate agglomeration effects, which refer to the benefits firms reap from proximity to other firms. These benefits include labour pooling, lower input costs, knowledge spillover, and the lower costs of transportation and other services due to the greater density and scale of activity (Randolph and Jain 2016). Well-managed urbanization is thus a necessary condition for economic growth since long-run growth requires efficient cities which can produce industrial goods and high-value services (Freire, Lall, and Leipziger 2014).

Ethiopia is one of the least urbanized countries in Africa, with only 20 per cent of the population living in urban centres. This puts Ethiopia in a unique position to promote and guide its urbanization process in the right direction before it is too late. The country is also entering a demographic transition, significantly increasing the youth population and thus the labour force (Hailemariam and Gurmu 2017). The working-age population (age group 15–64) is projected to rise to 65.7 per cent by 2037 (CSA 2013). Ethiopia thus needs to strengthen the productive and job-creation capacities of its urban centres to accommodate this enormous demand for employment.

While the agricultural sector has historically been the main driver of economic growth (Pickett 1991), the next growth trajectory requires industry and manufacturing to drive growth tied to an improved performance by agriculture. Since 1991, the EPRDF government has pursued a growth strategy known as Agricultural Development-Led Industrialization (ADLI). It was implemented in successive five-year development plans: the Sustainable Development and Poverty Reduction Plan (SDPRP) and the Plan for Accelerated and Sustained Development to End Poverty (PASDEP), 2005/6–2009/10. ADLI is an evolving strategy which can respond to changing circumstances and ideas.

Drawing on the lessons learned from implementing the ADLI programme, the government embarked in 2010 on a more ambitious industrialization strategy with the adoption of the first Growth and Transformation Plan (GTP-I). The GTP envisioned transforming Ethiopia into a major manufacturing hub in East Africa (MoFED 2010). While GTP-I was vague on the contribution of urbanization to industrialization, GTP-II explicitly recognized the important role that urbanization can play in enhancing economic productivity across sectors and unlocking the country's potential to become a manufacturing hub in Africa (MoFED 2016). The plan states that 'the envisaged expansion of manufacturing and industrial development could not be thought of without sustainable development of urban centres. Hence, utmost emphasis will be given to the urban development process' (MoFED 2016).

The aim of this chapter is, therefore, to critically examine the process of urbanization in Ethiopia and its potential contribution to the industrial development of the country. The chapter also examines potential barriers to achieving the industrialization goals and possible pathways for transforming Ethiopian cities to become centres of innovation, economic productivity, and accumulation. We begin by examining trends and drivers of Ethiopia's urbanization. Next is an overview of the policy environment for urbanization and industrialization in Ethiopia, followed by consideration of urban cluster-based industrial development along the agricultural value chains. Finally we look at the urban challenges of industrialization before offering some concluding remarks.

44.2 Urbanization in Ethiopia: Trends, Drivers, and Patterns

At 20 per cent urbanization level in 2017, Ethiopia remains one of the least urbanized countries in the world (Table 44.1).[1] The country, however, has a fast rate of urban growth and the urban population nearly tripled from 4.7 million to 11.8 million between 1984 and 2007, a 150 per cent increase. In the same period, the rural population grew from 37.2 million to 61.8 million, an increase of only 66 per cent. The rates of urban growth during the periods 1984–94 and 1994–2007 were 4.43 per cent and 3.78 per cent, respectively. These urban growth rates are higher than the average for Africa (3.4 per cent) and the world (2 per cent).The high urban growth rates in Ethiopia are reflected in a high growth of the urban share of population over time. In a little over two decades (1984–2007), the urban share grew from 11.3 per cent to 16.1 per cent, a difference of 4.8 per cent. In the last decade alone (2007–17), however, the urban share grew from 16.1 per cent to 20.2 per cent, an increase of 4.1 per cent. The total urban population will more than double over the next twenty years to reach 42.4 million in 2037 (CSA 2013). The country will also have a higher proportion of its population living in cities, with the share of urban population expected to reach 29.4 per cent by 2035 (UNDESA 2014).

Natural growth is a key driver of Ethiopia's urban growth. Between 2008 and 2017, it contributed 35–42 per cent of urban growth, and will continue contributing a little more than one-third up to 2037 (World Bank 2015). With regard to migration, in 2013, 12.1 million people or 15.1 per cent migrated or moved from place to place, a reduction from 17.8 per cent in 2005 (Table 44.2). However, the proportion of migrants in urban areas is

Table 44.1 Total population, rural population, urban population, and urban population share

Year	Total population	Rural population	Urban population	Urban share (%)
1967	23,667,400	21,742,000	1,925,400	8.0
1972	24,068,800	21,730,900	2,337,900	9.7
1984	42,019,418	37,276,563	4,742,855	11.3
1994	53,477,265	46,154,058	7,323,207	13.7
2007	73,750,932	61,888,111	11,862,821	16.1
2017	94,351,001	75,265,001	19,087,000	20.2

Source: Compiled from various Central Statistical Authority (CSA) surveys, census.

[1] Ethiopia has a lower level of urbanization compared with countries that have similar levels of income.

Table 44.2 Mobility in Ethiopia, 2005 and 2013

	2005			2013		
	All persons	All migrants	% migrants	All persons	Migrants	% migrants
Urban+rural	63,228,600	11,268,457	17.8	80,444,148	12,115,263	15.1
Urban	8,974,598	4,436,478	49.4	14,726,933	6,537,455	44.4
Rural	54,254,002	6,831,979	12.6	65,717,215	5,577,808	8.5

Source: Various labour force surveys.

high, about 44.4 per cent. In specific cities, it is even higher as in the case of Semera-Logia (71.6 per cent), Assosa (68.1 per cent), Adama (59.2 per cent), Gambella (58.8 per cent), Bahir Dar (55.6 per cent), and Addis Ababa (47.6 per cent) (CSA 2008). Employment remains the top reason for urban migrants (28.6 per cent) followed by the desire to live with family (25.7 per cent), marriage arrangements (9 per cent), and education (8.4 per cent) (CSA 2013). Increased migration to mega project sites such as sugar plantations and irrigation projects is also taking place, potentially driving further urban growth. Reclassification is a further factor behind urban growth in Ethiopia, accounting for an estimated 14–31 per cent of growth from 2008 to 2017, with upgrading of rural centres taking the highest share (World Bank 2015). In addition, the federal structure of the country, the massive infrastructural push, and private-sector development provide an enabling environment for continued rapid urban growth in Ethiopia (Gebre-Egziabher 2012).

The spatial distribution of the urban population in Ethiopia is highly skewed (Table 44.3). Between 1984 and 2015, the majority of urban centres in Ethiopia had a population of between 2,000 and 20,000. There is, however, a shift in population distribution, with the share of population in small towns declining from 38 per cent in 1984 to 33 per cent in 2015. There is also a parallel shift in population share as those residing in cities with populations between 20,000 and 100,000 grew from 25 per cent in 1984 to 29 per cent in 2015. In addition, the number of cities with populations between 100,000 and 500,000 grew from only three in 1994 to eighteen in 2015, and the share of total urban population in such cities rose from 6 per cent to 20 per cent during the same period. The primacy of Addis Ababa has also been on the decline. In 2015, the population in Addis Ababa formed 18 per cent of the total urban population, a decline from 36 per cent in 1984, 30 per cent in 1994, and 23 per cent in 2007.

Despite the declining primacy, Ethiopia has a top-heavy urban system. The principal city, Addis Ababa, being ten times bigger than the next largest city,[2] stands in isolation from other cities and towns. The numerous small cities—those with a population of less than 20,000—are less competitive in terms of their functionality. The country has no cities with a population of 500,000–1,000,000, indicating a size gap in the urban

[2] Adama with a population of 323,999 is the second largest city in 2015.

Table 44.3 Urban population distribution by size class

	2,000–20,000	20,000–100,000	100,000–500,000	500,000–1,000,000	>1,000,000	Total
Total urban population (2015)	5,876,368	5,191,568	3,488,279	-	3,273,000	17,829,215
Share (%)	32.9	29.1	19.6		18.4	100
Number of cities	757	120	18		1	896
Average city size (thousand)	7,763	43,263	193,793		3,273,000	19,899
Total urban population (2007)	4,511,399	2,880,001	1,672,852	0	2,739,551	11,803,803
Share (%)	38.2	24.4	14.2	0	23.2	100
Number of cities	708	75	10	0	1	794
Average city size	6,372	38,400	167,285	0	2,739,551	13,429
Total urban population (1994)	2,667,242	1,775,236	404,942	0	2,084,588	6,932,008
Share (%)	38.5	25.6	5.8	0	30.1	100
Number of cities	483	47	3	0	1	534
Average city size	5,522	37,771	134,981	0	2,084,588	12,981
Total urban population (1984)	1,539,829	1,008,947	0	0	1,412,575	3,961,351
Share (%)	38.9	25.5	0	0	35.6	100
Number of cities	289	22	0	0	1	312
Average city size	5,328	45,861	0	0	1,412,575	12,697
Share change	−6.0	+3.6	19.6		−17.2	-
(1984–2017)	468	98	18	-	-	
City count change						

Source: Computation based on CSA (1991), CSA (1998), CSA (2008), and CSA (2015).

hierarchy. In terms of linkages, there are gaps in the connectivity between urban centres and rural areas and among urban centres. The weak rural–urban linkage is manifested, among others, by the poor trade linkage due to the numerous constraints of the trade value chain (Gebre-Egziabher 2017). An imbalanced national urban system limits the options available for industrial firms which have differing locational preferences based on the requirements for specific types of industry.

The regional distribution of cities shows significant variation (Table 44.4). While some regions (Gambela, Afar, and Benishangul Gumuz) have only a few small urban centres, other regions (Amhara, Oromia) have many urban centres and intermediate towns.

Regarding the structure of the economy in Ethiopian cities, wholesale and retail trade and other services constitute the major sectors of employment while manufacturing accounts for a limited share (Table 44.5). Among those employed, the informal sector remains a significant sector which, while vibrant, falls short of generating the higher-productivity employment needed for productive structural change. According to CSA (2016), employment in the informal sector was 38 per cent in Shashemene and

Table 44.4 Regional distribution of towns by size class, 2015

	2,000–20,000		20,000–100,000		100,000–500,000			>1,000,000	
Region	No. of towns	Pop	No. of towns	Pop	No. of towns	Pop	500,000–1,000,000	No. of towns	Pop
Tigray	44	397,890	11	516,869	1	323,700	–	–	–
Afar	32	244,357	4	99,167	–	–	–	–	–
Amhara	165	1,357,090	28	1,081,254	4	857,168	–	–	–
Oromia	294	2,143,506	47	1,799,547	5	907,420	–	–	–
Somali	59	438,059	4	162,915	1	159,252	–	–	–
Benishangul Gumuz	19	151,386	1	46171	–	–	–	–	–
SNNP	136	1,082,129	24	1,419,550	5	834,739	–	–	–
Gambela	8	61,951	1	66,095	–	–	–	–	–
Harar	–	–	–	–	1	129,000	–	–	–
Addis Ababa	–	–	–	–	–	–	–	1	3,273,300
Dire Dawa	–	–	–	–	1	277,000	–	–	–
Total	757	5,876,368	120	5,191,568	18	3,488,279	–	1	3,273,300

Source: CSA Statistical Abstract (2015).

Table 44.5 Share of employment by major industries in some regional cities, 2016

	Mekele	Bahirdar	Adama	Jijiga	Assosa	Hawassa	Gambela	Harar	DD	AA
Agriculture, forestry, and fishing	2.40	5.59	2.70	1.63	1.92	1.33	3.06	1.10	1.09	0.46
Mining and quarrying	1.04	0.28	0.20	0.00	1.14	0.18	1.44	0.28	0.13	0.37
Manufacturing	19.01	13.93	16.64	4.38	5.49	11.94	6.06	9.83	12.54	14.06
Electricity, gas, steam and air conditioning supply	0.42	0.09	0.79	0.42	0.48	0.53	0.27	0.08	2.01	0.49
Water supply; sewerage, waste management, and remediation activities	1.88	2.11	0.82	0.41	0.16	0.71	1.48	1.25	1.10	0.68
Construction	8.13	9.86	7.36	10.91	11.75	9.75	8.32	7.55	8.67	6.39
Wholesale and retail trade; repair of motor vehicles and motorcycles	16.71	15.77	25.59	25.35	14.15	17.05	15.38	25.89	28.36	19.63
Transportation and storage	4.18	6.57	10.58	8.61	4.91	4.14	3.76	5.14	9.60	8.53
Accommodation and food service activities	9.35	10.00	8.46	4.41	5.92	10.68	4.79	6.37	5.13	5.57
Information and communications	1.46	2.20	0.90	0.96	1.59	1.15	0.91	1.73	1.03	2.19

Source: CSA, 'Statistical report on the 2016 urban employment unemployment survey', *Statistical Bulletin* 581: 127–8.

Gonder, 31 per cent in Harar, and 28 per cent in Jijiga. Unemployment also remains high, with Addis Ababa registering 21 per cent (CSA 2016), suggesting the limited ability of the urban economy to respond to the massive demand for jobs.

In terms of their functionality, Ethiopian cities continue to face considerable constraints compromising their productivity and competitiveness. Major gaps in services and infrastructure serve as barriers to economic performance, while also negatively impacting the social and economic well-being of urban residents. Even though the proportion of households connected to mains water and to sewerage did increase between 2000 and 2010, 51.6 per cent remain without mains water and only 2.4 per cent were connected to sewerage by 2010 (UN-Habitat 2016). While the proportion of urban residents living in slums declined from 88.6 per cent in 2000 to 73.9 per cent in 2014, the absolute number of slum dwellers increased from 8.6 million to 13.5 million during the same period (UN-Habitat 2016). Capacity for urban planning is weak across the board and given the low level of development in the cities, municipal revenues remain too small to finance even the most basic services (Jamal and Weeks 1988; Turok and McGranahan 2013).

Despite major gaps in infrastructure and basic services, Ethiopia's cities continue to serve as engines of growth with urban-based sectors making significant contributions to GDP and rising relative to the contribution of agriculture (MoUDHCo 2014). In 2012/13, the country's urban centres generated an estimated aggregate output worth ETB 227.3 billion or 39.8 per cent of the national GDP (MoUDHCo and ECSU 2015). This clearly points to the as yet untapped potential of Ethiopian cities that can be unleashed through deliberate planning, design, and management to enhance performance across the national urban system.

44.3 The Policy Environment for Urbanization and Industrialization in Ethiopia

Ethiopia's National Urban Policy, issued in 2005, was the first government initiative to recognize the role of urban development in the national development agenda. The policy aims to make cities and towns serve as centres of development that can foster national and rural development. A set of principles were outlined in the policy document: strengthening of urban–rural and urban–urban linkages; ensuring balanced development of urban centres; attaining decentralized urbanization; poverty reduction; increasing participation of the community in urban development; forming partnerships with the private sector; and creating more decentralized urban governance (FDRE 2005).

In terms of institutional structures, cities derive their legal entity from the 1995 Ethiopian Constitution (see Chapter 7). Article 50 (1) of the Constitution empowers state governments to establish lower administration levels and provide them with adequate power and responsibility to mobilize citizens for regional and local development

(FDRE 1995). In this regard, the urban development policy states that 'It is especially imperative that their right [city residents] to self-rule is expressly confirmed by the Regional Constitution' (FDRE, 2005). Many regions, however, enacted the Urban Local Government Proclamations to provide a legal basis for cities and improve their functions (Gebre-Egziabher and Alemayehu 2014).

The five-year national plans issued in different years—PASDEP(2005/6–2009/10), GTP-I (2010/11–2014/15), and GTP-II (2015/16–2019/20)—had urban dimensions that illustrate the different focus areas. These areas, among others, were: supporting MSEs to reduce urban unemployment; integrated housing programmes to reduce slums; improved access to land infrastructure and services; promoting urban–rural and urban–urban linkages; reducing urban poverty; encouraging the urban population to participate in development; ensuring good governance; forming partnerships with investors; and establishing decentralized systems (MoFED 2005, 2010, 2016; see also chapter 44).

The Ministry of Urban Development, Housing and Construction (MoUDHCo) also prepared sector plans that include the urban PASDEP to align with the PASDEP strategy, and the Ethiopian Resilient Cities, Green Growth and Governance Programs and Packages (ECR-3G2P) to align with GTP-I (MoUDHCo 2013). The ECR-3G2P had ten pillars, each of which specified objectives, sub-programmes (projects), and implementing partners. It contains numerous programmes and sub-programmes but does not focus on building competitive, productive, and resilient cities. There should instead be a focus on cost-effective and sharply focused initiatives aimed at enhancing the capacity of cities (UN-Habitat 2015).

GTP-II reaffirmed that sustainable urban development is the basis for the envisaged expansion of manufacturing and industrial development. Cities will be required to prepare urban plans to be integrated with regional and national development plans and spatial plans. Some of the strategic directions include balanced settlement, ensuring equity for farmers and pastoralists in the process of urban programmes and urban expansion, efficient land use, creating conducive conditions for financing, integrating, and providing quality urban infrastructure, strengthening the ongoing integrated housing programme, and pursuing green urban development.

With regard to industrialization, the key policy thrust is the main national development strategy of ADLI, which focuses on improving the productivity of smallholder farmers by providing them with technological inputs such as fertilizers and improved seeds. The growth in agricultural productivity is expected to create a high demand for manufactured goods. ADLI thus views industrialization along with urbanization as a derivative process that naturally accompanies the rapid development of the agricultural sector (Nega 2003). Within the broader policy of ADLI, the 2002 Industrial Development Strategy of Ethiopia (IDSE) is intended as the basis of the country's industrial policy (see also Chapter 35, 36, 39). The main thrust of IDSE is to promote industrial development that is export led, agriculture led, and focused on employment generation through labour-intensive industries (Oqubay 2015). The focus areas of the strategy are development of MSE, and priority-sector medium and large-scale industries such as textiles, meat processing, leather and leather products, agro-processing, and construction (Ministry of Information 2002).

The industrial road map issued in 2012 recognizes a strategic objective of bringing about structural change in the economy through industrial development by improving the contribution of the industry and manufacturing sector to GDP (Ministry of Industry 2012). The road map has five strategic objectives: expanding and developing the existing priority manufacturing sectors; diversifying manufacturing into new sectors; enhancing enterprise cultivation and entrepreneurship; increasing public, local, and foreign investment; and developing and operationalizing industrial zones and cities. While the road map is sectoral in nature and shows not only how productivity and capacity can be increased but also the shift in the composition of manufacturing, the strategic objective of developing industrial parks or zones has implications for urbanization and industrial transformation. The industrial zones are envisaged as equipped with essential infrastructure and social services to attract investment and eventually grow into industrial cities.

The institutional arrangements for managing the industrial parks involve the establishment of an Industrial Park Development Corporation that will oversee operations and ensure the timely provision of basic services such as utilities, banks, customs clearance, and transport and logistics. The corporation is chaired by a minister in the Prime Minister's office. The Industrial Parks Development Corporation operates as a 'one stop shop' providing a streamlined business environment, institutional support (e.g. customs clearance, secure land for development), and enhanced delivery of public services, such as electricity, water, and infrastructure. This institutional arrangement is designed to significantly shorten the length of time required to start up production and export to world markets (see Chapter 36).

The government has also initiated a cluster-based industrial development programme focusing on small and medium industries. In this programme, numerous towns were selected to develop industrial clusters at different levels: first-level towns with 250 hectares of land, second-level towns with 100 hectares of land, and third-level towns with 50 hectares of land. The latter include all *woreda* centres not selected as first- and second-level towns. The cluster-based industry development is expected to achieve regional industrialization and to help with both exports and poverty reduction (Ministry of Industry 2017).

44.4 Urban Cluster-Based Industrial Development Along Agricultural Value Chains

Ethiopia is one country that is experimenting with cluster-based industrial development to achieve high levels of economic growth and structural transformation. A cluster-based approach brings together transacting firms in a single location to reduce transaction costs and provide a platform for learning from each other. The key to the success of cluster-based industrial development has been found to be multi-faceted product quality, marketing, and enterprise management innovations, as well as learning from abroad (Sonobe and Otsuka 2006; Oqubay 2015).

In 2014, the Ministry of Urban Development, Housing and Construction (MoUDHCo) commissioned two diagnostic studies on how to mainstream urbanization in the national development strategy. The two studies came up with almost identical recommendations on the way forward. The National Urbanization Review, jointly undertaken by the government and the World Bank (2015), recommended ten specialized urban clusters within a polycentric urban pattern and ensuring that these clusters drive development in their respective rural hinterlands. The study organized the identified clusters into three urban hierarchies—metropolitan, secondary, and tertiary clusters—and went on to describe the current and future economic functions of each cluster (World Bank 2015) (see Table 44.6). The second diagnostic study, undertaken by EDRI and the Global Green Grown Initiative (GGGI), identified six clusters as growth poles or industrial zones: Addis Ababa, Dire Dawa, Mekele, Kombolcha, Bahir Dar, and Hawassa (EDRI 2014). Although the findings of the diagnostic studies were never officially adopted by the very ministry that commissioned them, these studies nevertheless had an indirect influence on the formulation of the second Growth and Transformation Plan (GTP-II) and the policy on industrial parks.

The overall conclusion that emerged from the two benchmarking studies is that spatial planning and urban cluster zone development are critical for economic growth and accelerated industrialization in Ethiopia. The growth poles concept emphasizes an integrated approach (across sectors, space, and time) focused on delivery of basic services in areas with actual or demonstrated growth potential. Moreover, the design of a growth pole strategy covers spatially targeted interventions and focused investments in strategic locations within a country for accelerating economic growth. It must be noted at the outset, however, that the concentration of economic activity in a given location does not necessarily produce agglomeration effects and productivity gains in the absence of effective coordination between different tiers of government institutions and private economic agents. Coordination failures may prevent strategic complementarities between agents due to information asymmetries or sometimes bureaucratic foot-dragging (Farole 2011).

Informed by the two diagnostic studies, the government prepared the second Growth and Transformation Plan (GTP-II) in 2015. GTP-II envisages the development of twelve major industrial parks (IPs) in three different development corridors: the Addis-Djibouti Development Corridor, North-East Development Corridor, and South-West Development Corridor (MoFED 2016). The government plans to invest US$1 billion annually for the next ten years in growth poles and industrial parks to boost exports and transform Ethiopia into Africa's top manufacturing destination in textiles, leather, agro-processing, and other labour-intensive manufactures. The purpose of the IPs is to enhance economic transformation by attracting investment, promoting technological learning, upgrading and innovation, and generating stable and decent employment (Oqubay 2015). The establishment of IPs signifies the close relationship between

Table 44.6 Current and anticipated functions of the key urban centres of Ethiopia

Hierarchy of urban centres	Cluster	Current economic functions	Future dominant urban and economic functions
Metropolitan cluster	Addis Ababa	International affairs Industry and extractives Trade and logistics Tourism and leisure Education Administrative and political	Financial, business and professional services Trade, industry, and logistics International affairs Administrative and political Research and education
Secondary clusters	Bahir Dar Urban Cluster	Agriculture Tourism and leisure Education Services	Agro-processing Tourism and leisure Education International conferences R&D Centre—textiles and agriculture Services
	Gonder-Metema	Agriculture Tourism and leisure Education Services	Trade and logistics Tourism and leisure International conferences Industry and extractives Agro-processing
	Eastern Urban Cluster (Dire Dawa-Harar-Jijiga)	Industry and extractives Tourism and leisure	Industry and extractives Trade and logistics Tourism and leisure
	South Rift Valley Urban Cluster	Agro-processing Extractives Trade Tourism and leisure Education	Agro-processing Industry and extractives Trade and logistics Tourism and leisure Education
	Mekele Urban Cluster	Industry and extractives Tourism and leisure	Industry and extractives Tourism and leisure
	Dessie-Kombolcha-Woldya Urban Cluster	Services Industry	Industry Services Trade and logistics

	Jimma Urban Cluster	Agriculture	Agro-processing R&D centre for agriculture
	Nekemte Urban Cluster	Agriculture	Agro-processing Some mining potential
Tertiary clusters	Semera-Assaita Oasis City	Administrative Trade and logistics	Trade and logistics Extractive industries Agro-processing
	Gode-Kebri Dehar Oasis Cluster	Agriculture and livestock	Extractive activities Agro-processing Livestock

Source: World Bank (2015), 'Ethiopia Urbanization Scheme Study'.

urbanization and industrialization through urban plans, infrastructure development, regional service centres, housing, and so on, to support industrial growth. GTP-II anticipates the manufacturing sector expanding by 25 per cent and creating employment for 200,000 Ethiopians per year (MoFED 2016).

The industrial parks are not self-contained enclaves like export-processing zones (EPZs); rather, they are in a geographical/spatial landscape consisting of both urban and rural settlements and are designed to stimulate economic activities in the surrounding regions and beyond in the context of regional spatial planning (or city cluster development), further strengthening rural–urban linkages (World Bank 2015). The selected cities are to be linked together functionally, structurally, and spatially to small towns and their surrounding rural hinterland to form an integrated urban region. Cluster-based industrial development considers the provision of infrastructure and services in relation to the 'park' economic growth potential and dispenses with the rural–urban dichotomy of traditional development planning, recognizing that urban centres are not only hubs of economic growth but also service centres for surrounding areas.

There will be a phased approach to the implementation of the industrial park strategy, since simultaneous growth of the clusters identified is not possible due to lack of infrastructure, availability of economic opportunities, and budgetary constraints. The study recommended that Phase I should concentrate on the Addis Ababa Capital Area and the Dire Dawa-Jijjiga Economic Cluster through the promotion of the Dire Dawa Special Economic Zone, strengthening inter-city transport infrastructure and offering planning and tax incentives along the growth axis. Phase II may include driving the development of growth corridors to the north and/or south of the country, followed by action to develop growth clusters in the west and south-west (EDRI 2014).

In addition to the seven cities mentioned, four agro-industry parks with the potential to become agro-processing centres will be established. With technical assistance from UNIDO and financing from other development partners, the parks will be built in Western Tigray, South Western Amhara, Central-Eastern Oromia, and SNNP regions. The four proposed parks will be supported by 50 rural transformation centres (RTCs) that will serve as aggregation points with modern warehousing and market facilities, connecting the parks with the surrounding rural community. The parks are expected to host large foreign and domestic companies, create more jobs, and link smallholder farmers to food industries (UNIDO 2016).

The selected cities where industrial parks are to be established are expected to prepare urban master plans, detailed plans, urban designs, architectural designs, and so on. They are also required to delineate, develop, and transfer land for industrial park use. The area of land to be developed for the thirteen industrial parks that are envisaged until 2020 totals about 13,000 hectares in different cities (Ethiopian Investment Commission 2017). In 2013 Addis Ababa delineated 924 hectares and developed 990 hectares, while Adama delineated 870.36 ha and developed 321.73 (MoUDHCo and ECSU 2015). Industrial development also requires the provision of major infrastructure and coordination with the infrastructural projects, such as universities, hospitals, airports, telecoms, and logistics.

44.5 Harnessing Urbanization for Ethiopia's Industrialization: Key Challenges

Managing urbanization for structural transformation involves more than investing in hard infrastructure. The policy and institutional dimensions necessary for steering urbanization in the right direction must be carefully analysed, and policies and strategies developed and sequenced accordingly (Kassahun and Tiwari 2012: 59–72). An efficient institutional and leadership system must be in place to create the right conditions for Ethiopian cities to act as centres of innovation diffusion and socio-economic transformation (World Bank 2009, 2011; OECD 2008). Among the key constraints that must be tackled in Ethiopian cities are the following.

Poor urban planning capacity and land-use policy: Urban planning remains poor and inadequate particularly at the lower levels of local government. Land development and management remain inefficient and are complicated by the absence of clear and transparent laws and regulations. The horizontal expansion of cities and low-density development has undercut economic efficiency and firm productivity. Most Ethiopian cities experience low-density development and urban sprawl while at the same time possessing unused vacant land in the interior. The way land-use policy is applied has a direct impact upon a city's competitiveness. Critically, land-use policy plays a key role in determining the levels of mobility within cities and the costs of residential and business properties (World Bank 2013: 24). With improved planning, most of these problems can be solved to lead Ethiopian cities and towns in a prosperous and productive direction.

Prioritizing investment in critical infrastructure to enhance connectivity: Connectivity is one of the key factors determining whether a country or a city becomes a favourite investment destination and an important 'engine of growth', stimulating production and exchange in a wider geographical location. External connections, such as airports, seaports, and rail networks are critical for improving the competitiveness of cities and countries. Over the years, infrastructure has become a significant constraint on growth in many countries, including Ethiopia. Without improved infrastructure, it is hard to imagine that Ethiopia's productive potential can be realized (World Bank 2013). Investment in these essential components of the urban 'economic engine' requires a long lead time for planning and execution. How easily these essential ingredients can be brought together depends on the capacity of the national government and municipalities to engage in disciplined planning and in the efficient execution of the various investment plans.

Improving the business environment: The World Bank's 2018 Doing Business report ranks Ethiopia 161 out of 190 countries for 'ease of doing business'. The ease with which entrepreneurs can access credit, land, and basic services is an important determining factor for city competitiveness (World Bank 2009). Bureaucratic red tape and gridlocks are known to increase the costs of doing business. The successful harnessing of potential for urbanization requires a strong business–government–community strategic alliance. Without regular dialogue between planning officials and the private sector, limitations on the productivity and competitiveness of the private sector in Ethiopia cannot be identified.

Strengthening data-collection, research, and policy analysis capacity: Cities are complex enterprises and their effective management requires a huge amount of knowledge and information for evidence-based policymaking. At present, however, empirical knowledge on urbanization trends and on the economic functions of cities in Ethiopia is inadequate or partial. Given the cross-cutting nature of the urbanization phenomenon, capacity building in data collection, research, and analysis should be prioritized by the authorities. In the absence of up-to-date and reliable data on different dimensions of urbanization, it is not possible to properly identify binding sector-specific constraints, nor to make informed decisions on investment choices and the sequencing of policy actions to achieve maximum results (Ministry of Science and Technology 2015b).

Investing in knowledge and innovation systems: Ethiopia's ability to take advantage of the opportunities available in the global economy depends very much on reversing the poor state of higher education, particularly in the areas of science and technology research, and analytical skills. Productivity is a function of the quality of skills and adequacy of research and development (R&D) capacity to support innovation, and the capacity to assimilate new technologies. Innovation is the foundation of competitiveness and improved productivity (Ministry of Science and Technology 2015a). A concerted effort is required to reverse the poor state of education in Ethiopia. Investment in education should emphasize climbing the technological ladder and tapping into global information and knowledge systems (see also Chapter 41).

In summary, harnessing the potential of urbanization for Ethiopia's industrialization and structural transformation requires planning innovation to support urban-led national development and will ultimately depend on the effectiveness of policies and institutions. The quality of governance, the business environment, and the efficiency and responsiveness of government institutions must be improved significantly. Innovation strategies must address services and technology as well as organizational, institutional, and social issues, with new forms of governance required to tackle the complexity of the challenges ahead.

44.6 Conclusion

At present, Ethiopian cities face many challenges: bottlenecks in infrastructure; skill shortages; inefficient trade logistics; poor internal connectivity; inefficient distribution systems; and severe shortage of domestic credit. Despite these problems, Ethiopia's early stage of urbanization, with only 20 per cent of the population residing in urban centres, presents the country with a unique opportunity to ensure that the urban development trajectory is managed strategically before it is too late, and to enable its urban centres to play a catalytic role in the country's industrialization and long-term structural transformation.

Historical evidence shows that urbanization has been an essential part of most nations' development towards a stronger and more stable economy. Cities provide economies of scale, agglomeration, and location; they provide efficient infrastructure and services by concentrating in one place investments in transportation, communication, and power networks; and they become centres of financial capital, hubs of information and talent (Hamer 1994; World Bank 2009). Cities also attract a pool of labour that makes specialization in knowledge, skills, and management capabilities possible. These are important attributes that make cities competitive, productive, and attractive. Ethiopia's quest for structural transformation will be difficult to realize without harnessing the development potential of its urban centres.

References

CSA (1991). 'The 1984 Population and Housing Census: Analytical Report at National Level', Addis Ababa.

CSA (1998). 'The 1994 Population and Housing Census: Analytical Report at National Level', Addis Ababa.

CSA (2008). 'The 2007 Population and Housing Census: Preliminary Report at National Level', Addis Ababa.

CSA (2013). 'Population Projections for Ethiopia 2007–37', Addis Ababa.

CSA (2015). 'Statistical Abstract', Addis Ababa.

CSA (2016). 'Statistical Report on the 2016 Urban Employment Unemployment Survey', *Statistical Bulletin 581*, Addis Ababa.

EDRI (2014). 'Catalyzing Efficient and Effective Urbanization in Ethiopia', Ethiopian Development Research Institute, Addis Ababa.

Ethiopian Investment Commission (2017). Data on Investment and Industrial Parks. Unpublished.

Farole, T. (2011). *Special Economic Zones in Africa: Comparing Performance and Learning from Global Experience* (Washington, DC: World Bank).

Fay, Marianne and Charlotte Opal (2000). 'Urbanization without Growth—a: A Not So Uncommon Phenomenon', World Bank: Washington, DC (unpublished).

FDRE (1995). 'The Constitution of Ethiopia', Addis Ababa.

FDRE (2005). 'National Urban Development Policy, Approved by the Council of Ministers', Addis Ababa.

Freire, M. E., S. Lall, and D. Leipziger (2014). 'Africa's Urbanization: Challenges and Opportunities', Working Paper No. 7. The Growth Dialogue. http://www.dannyleipziger.com/documents/GD_WP7.pdf

Gebre-Egziabher, Tegegne (2012). 'Urbanization and Economic Growth in Ethiopia with a Focus on Growth and Transformation (GTP)', Unpublished paper presented for a workshop on urbanization in Ethiopia, organized by Town Planners Association of Ethiopia.

Gebre-Egziabher, Tegegne (2017). 'Urbanization and Linkages with Rural Economies', Paper presented at the national conference on rethinking development in Ethiopia, organized by Forum for Social Studies (FSS), Addis Ababa.

Gebre-Egziabher, Tegegne and Abebaw Alemayehu (2014). 'Urban Governance and Institutional Setting', A background paper for the World Bank, Urbanization Review document (unpublished).

Gollin, D., R. Jedwab, and D. Vollrath (2016). 'Urbanization with and without Industrialization', *Journal of Economic Growth* 21 (1): 35–70.

Hailemariam, Assefa, and Eshetu Gurmu (2017). 'Demographic Dividend in Ethiopia: Reality and Possibility', Discussion Paper, Ethiopian Academy of Sciences, Addis Ababa.

Hamer, Andre (1994). 'Economic Impacts of Third World Mega-Cities: Is Size the Issue?' in *Mega-City Growth and the Future* ed. Roland Fuchs, Ellen Brennan, Joseph Chame, et al. (Tokyo: United Nations University): 172–91.

Jamal, V. and Weeks, J. (1988). 'The Vanishing Rural–Urban Divide in Sub Saharan Africa', *International Labour Review* 127 (3): 271–92.

Jedwab, R. (2013). 'Urbanization *without* Structural Transformation: Evidence from Consumption Cities in Africa'. http://ibread.org/bread/sites/default/files/0313conf/Jedwab_1.pdf

Kassahun, S. and Alok Tiwari (2012). 'Urban Development in Ethiopia: Challenges and Policy Responses', *The IUP Journal of Governance and Public Policy* 7 (1): 59–72.

Ministry of Industry (2012). 'Industrial Development Road Map of Ethiopia 2012–2025' (in Amharic), Addis Ababa.

Ministry of Industry (2017). 'Presentation on Site Assessment and Product Validation for Small and Medium Enterprises Cluster Development Plan Ethiopia', (unpublished), Addis Ababa.

Ministry of Information (2002). 'Industrial Development Strategy of Ethiopia', Federal Democratic Republic of Ethiopia, Addis Ababa (Amharic version).

Ministry of Science and Technology (2015a). 'Ethiopian Innovation Survey', Federal Democratic Republic of Ethiopia, Addis Ababa.

Ministry of Science and Technology (2015b). 'Research & Development Infrastructure in Ethiopia: A Cross-Sectional Survey', Federal Democratic Republic of Ethiopia, Addis Ababa.

MoFED (2005). 'A Plan for Accelerated and Sustained Development to End Poverty (PASDEP), 2005/6–2009/10', Federal Democratic Republic of Ethiopia, Addis Ababa.

MoFED (2010). 'Growth and Transformation Plan (GTP) (2010/11–2014/15)', Federal Democratic Republic of Ethiopia, Addis Ababa.

MoFED (2016). 'Growth and Transformation Plan II (GTP II) (2015/16–2019/20)', Federal Democratic Republic of Ethiopia, Addis Ababa.

MoUDHCo (2013). 'Ethiopian Cities Resilient and Green Growth and Governance Program (ECR-3G2P)', Federal Democratic Republic of Ethiopia, Addis Ababa.

MoUDHCo (2014). 'National Report on Housing and Sustainable Urban Development', Ministry of Housing and Urban Development, Addis Ababa.

MoUDHCo and ECSU (2015). 'The State of Ethiopian Cities Report', Ministry of Urban Development, Housing and Construction and Ethiopian Civil Service University, June, Addis Ababa.

Nega, Berhanu (2003). 'Introduction: Development Options for Ethiopia, Rural, Urban or balanced', in *The Role of Urbanization in the Socio-Economic Development Process*, ed. Berhanu Nega and Befkadu Degefe (Addis Ababa: Ethiopian Economic Policy Research Institute): 5–19.

OECD (2008). *Competitive Cities in a Global Economy* (Paris: OECD).

Oqubay, Arkebe (2015). *Made in Africa: Industrial policy in Ethiopia* (Oxford: Oxford University Press).
Pickett, J. (1991). *Economic Development in Ethiopia: Agriculture, the Market and the State*, OECD Development Center (Paris: OECD).
Randolph, G. and D. Jain (2016). 'Promoting Job-Rich Urbanisation in Zambia', ZIPAR 'More and Better Jobs' Policy Paper No. 2, ZIPAR, Lusaka. https://opendocs.ids.ac.uk/opendocs/handle/123456789/12034
Sonobe, T. and K. Otsuka (2006). *Cluster-Based Industrial Development: An East Asia Model* (Basingstoke: Palgrave Macmillan).
Turok, Ivan, and Gordon McGranahan (2013). 'Urbanization and Economic Growth: The Arguments and Evidence from Africa and Asia', *Environment and Urbanization* 25: 465–82.
UNDESA (2014). 'World Urbanization Prospects: The 2014 Revision', New York. https://esa.un.org/unpd/wup/publications/files/wup2014-highlights.pdf
UN-Habitat (2015). *Structural Transformation in Ethiopia: The Urban Dimension* (Nairobi: UN-Habitat).
UN-Habitat (2016). *World Cities Report* (Nairobi: UN-Habitat).
UNIDO (2016). 'Integrated Agro-Industrial Parks in Ethiopia.' UNIDO and PCP Ethiopia, Addis Ababa.
World Bank (2009). 'Ethiopia: Towards the Competitive Frontier—Strategies to improve Ethiopia's Investment Climate', Finance and Private Sector Development, Washington, DC.
World Bank (2011). *Light Manufacturing in Africa: Targeted Policies to Enhance Private Investment and Create Jobs, with a Case Study of Ethiopia* (Washington, DC: World Bank).
World Bank (2013). 'Ethiopia's Economic Update II: Laying the Foundation for Achieving Middle Income Status', Report No. 78501, World Bank, Washington, DC.
World Bank (2015). *Ethiopia Urbanization Scheme Review: Urban Institutions for a Middle-Income Country* (Washington, DC: World Bank).

PART VI

STRUCTURAL TRANSFORMATION AND THE AFRICAN CONTEXT

CHAPTER 45

SPECIAL ECONOMIC ZONES AND STRUCTURAL TRANSFORMATION IN ETHIOPIA

A New Structural Economics Perspective

JUSTIN YIFU LIN, JIAJUN XU, AND SARAH HAGER

Special Economic Zones (SEZs)[1] have been used by a number of countries, most notably China and other rapidly growing countries in Asia such as Korea, Singapore, Thailand, and Vietnam, to catalyse growth in the early stages of development.[2] This historical success has led to a wave of SEZs being created across developing countries. Unfortunately, many of these failed to realize the benefits of foreign direct investment, job creation, and technology transfer that typified the Asian experience (Farole 2011). Despite this uneven performance record for SEZs, Ethiopia has directed substantial resources towards their development. This chapter argues that there are reasons to be cautiously optimistic about the potential for success of the Ethiopian SEZ programme in contributing to structural transformation, based on a New Structural Economics (NSE) analysis and examples of historical SEZs in China.

This chapter draws on ongoing qualitative research in both China and Ethiopia carried out by the Institute of New Structural Economics. The field studies contributing

[1] In this chapter, 'special economic zones' (SEZs) is used as an umbrella term for all geographically delineated areas deliberately set up as part of the country's industrial policy strategy with special incentives offered to firms within the zones. When referring to these policy areas in general the chapter uses the term SEZ; however, when a specific zone is mentioned the original name of that zone is maintained.

[2] The first modern zone is said to be have been established in Brooklyn, New York's Navy Yard in 1937 to promote exports. The first European zone, the Shannon Free Zone in Ireland, was established in 1959. SEZs have been widely used by both developed economies and developing ones (CIIP 2017).

to this chapter were conducted in Ethiopia in 2016 and 2017 and in China in 2017. The approach in these studies has been semi-structured interviews. While conversations with respondents have been thematically similar, no common questionnaire was applied across these field research engagements. In total, fifty-two entities were interviewed across seventy-one interviews, 90 per cent of which were conducted in Ethiopia. Interviews were conducted with firms, zone developers/managers,[3] and government.[4]

The chapter proceeds as follows. First, it looks at how SEZs have been established in Ethiopia; second, it examines the key ingredients for China's success in leveraging SEZs for structural transformation in order to better evaluate the prospects of the Ethiopian SEZ programme; third, it draws insights from NSE to better understand why and how SEZs can help a developing country such as Ethiopia to turn latent comparative advantage into a competitive edge in global markets; and finally, it sets out key findings and directions for future research.

45.1 The Ethiopian SEZ Programme

The first SEZ, Eastern Industrial Park, was planned and constructed from 2007 and hosted its first firm, the Zhongshun Cement Company, in 2010 (Gakunu et al. 2015). Since then, the government has made substantial investments in improving both the infrastructure and institutional frameworks required to develop a national SEZ programme.[5]

In Ethiopia, SEZs are regulated by the Ethiopian Investment Commission (EIC). The Industrial Parks Development Corporation (IPDC) acts as developer, manager, and landbank[6] for maintaining and allocating the land that can be transferred for the development of SEZs. There are two types of SEZs in Ethiopia: public zones owned by IPDC and zones established by private capital. In 2017, a total of five zones were operational and exporting. Of these, two are government-run zones—Hawassa Industrial Park (HIP) and Bole Lemi. The remaining three—Eastern Industrial Park (EIP), George Shoe Industrial Park, and Vouge Industrial Park (VIP)—are privately owned. To date, all private zones have been financed by foreign capital.

This section examines the evolution of Ethiopia's sector-specific policies with a focus on the key sectors for structural transformation. It investigates government problem solving and the demonstration effect by leading firms, and analyses how firms within

[3] 'Developer' refers to any entity responsible for an SEZ, either as owner or manager. This follows convention in Ethiopia but may be confused by some readers with the use of 'developer' to mean the company that builds an SEZ. Due to Ethiopia having private zone developers, a developer may also be counted as a firm.

[4] Government refers to any agency or person representing any government or quasi-government institution.

[5] Zone-level export data in this section are supplied by EIC and refer to the second half of 2017. When not otherwise citied, they are based on qualitative interviews as described in the introduction.

[6] This is the term used in Ethiopia for the IPDC's role maintaining a store of land which can be allocated for development of industrial parks.

SEZs foster technology transfer. Finally it explores how Ethiopia has taken advantage of China's state-owned capacity to embark on a learning-by-doing process.

45.1.1 Sector-Specific Focus Drives Ethiopia's SEZ Policy

The facilitation activities of the government and the types of investment are guided by a national industrial strategy. Ethiopia has consistently selected two broad sectors, agriculture and light manufacturing, as priority sectors for government facilitation. As discussed elsewhere in this *Handbook*, agricultural upgrading is one of the most pressing needs for the Ethiopian economy and a key sector for providing inputs to the manufacturing sector. Manufacturing is particularly prized due to its high employment multiplier (Lavopa and Szirmai 2012) and its historical concurrence with development in high-growth countries both in Asia (including Japan, Singapore, Korea, China, and Taiwan China) and in Africa (such as Mauritius). An 18 per cent share of manufacturing in output and employment for a sustained period is important for industrialization and that, with few exceptions, countries have not obtained high-income status without manufacturing at or above this level (Rhee 2013: 71). Currently, Ethiopia is developing from a low base with a target to reach an 8 per cent share of manufacturing in total GDP by 2019/20 and 18 per cent of GDP by 2025.

In order to understand the way that the government of Ethiopia has emphasized key sectors, it is useful to briefly review the development of Ethiopian five-year plans as they relate to sector-specific targets. While all the plans featured targets for both agriculture and manufacturing, the balance of these shifted over time towards manufacturing. In addition, all the economic plans except PASDEP demonstrated consideration of and research towards the development of the SEZ programme in Ethiopia. The themes of job creation, export promotion, productivity increases, and technological and skill upgrading dominate the sector-specific targets.

The first of the Ethiopian five-year plans was the Sustainable Development and Poverty Reduction Programme (SDRP), which covered 2002–7. The importance of manufacturing exports was acknowledged in this plan and the leather goods and textile and garment sectors were specifically named, but greater emphasis was placed on agriculture. At this stage SEZs had been studied with a view to supporting the manufacturing sector to upgrade to modern technology to compete in global markets. Institutions designed to service manufacturing were also strengthened in this period, including the Ethiopian Leather and Leather Products Technology Institute, the Ethiopian Textile and Garment Industry Institute, and the Ethiopian Export Promotion Agency.

The Plan for Accelerated and Sustained Development to End Poverty (PASDEP) for 2007–12 built on the SDRP and began to put in place specific targets for a few key manufacturing industries, including again leather and garment, as well as identifying a range of potential export products. In both SDRP and PASDEP, however, limited emphasis was placed on foreign direct investment (FDI) as a means to stimulate the manufacturing sector and in PASDEP there is no mention of SEZs.

In the Growth and Transformation Plan (GTP-I), covering 2010/11–2014/15, the focus shifted to FDI and manufacturing exports in order to build up foreign exchange and accelerate technology transfer. At this stage SEZs were still envisioned as privately owned with the government pursuing four strategies to support their development (MoFED 2010): promptly solve problems encountered by developers in basic infrastructure such as land, power, roads, and customs; expand and strengthen training centres giving developers access to skilled labour; assist developers to attract FDI; and cover 30 per cent of the cost of the provision of basic infrastructure in the park.

At the start of the GTP-II (2015/16–2019/20), the plan's authors acknowledged that previous plans had failed to deliver intended results, and export earnings from manufacturing were estimated at only 22.5 per cent of the intended US$1.82 billion target for 2014/15 (National Planning Commission 2016). However, in response to this GTP-II solidified the focus on SEZs and sector-specific targets, with the aim of Ethiopia becoming a leader in light manufacturing globally, and production targets were set for a greater number of industry sectors. Nevertheless GTP-II continues to encourage those industries that are labour intensive and to maximize linkages with the agricultural sector.

GTP-II (National Planning Commission 2016) recognized the potential of SEZs to contribute to the technological and skill upgrading that supports structural transformation's goal to 'create jobs and improve income, promote export development, and improve the competitiveness of the economy, as well as enhance technological capability and skills development'. This is reinforced by an Ethiopian government official who described the four major objectives for the SEZs as technology transfer, job creation, export promotion, and foreign exchange earnings.

45.1.2 Government Problem-Solving and the Demonstration Effect of Leading Firms

Although the current level of industrial development is low and the concentration of exports with a few large firms creates potential vulnerability, we argue that government problem solving and the demonstration effect created by having already attracted internationally recognized brands should be regarded as creating favourable conditions for the future development of the SEZ programme.

As Ethiopia has just started to develop export-oriented manufacturing, large firms are better positioned to export in terms of management, technology, and buyer trust. At EIP, with a total of six exporting firms, 88 per cent of exports are produced by the shoe factory of leading firm Huajian. At Bole Lemi, there are nine exporting firms; the top three firms by export value, Shints, Jay Jay, and George Shoe, account for a combined total of 70 per cent of exports. The concentration of exports within a few large firms creates potential vulnerability. Under the influence of these three firms, export performance across the five parks dropped in November 2017 from an average of US$6.9 million across the six-month window to around US$5.3 million. However, it had recovered to around US$7.4 million in December 2017. Despite the potential vulnerability at this early stage of development, the example of leading firms such as these can attract more FDI and helps Ethiopia by jump-starting domestic firms into developing export manufacturing, mitigating the vulnerability in the medium term as the number of firms and the diversity of exports increase.

The potential for future success is high because the Ethiopian government has actively supported industry and solved problems for investors at a micro level. Challenges in both infrastructure and labour relations resulted in the drop in export performance in November 2017. In response to these challenges, EIC reports that the infrastructure issue relating to electricity transmission had been fixed within ten days, and claims that government mediated effectively between labour and producers were substantiated by multiple firms and interviews. Although concerns over absenteeism and productivity are also consistently reported by firms, the Ethiopian Textile Development Institute (ETIDI) has made substantial efforts to provide worker screening, training, and tracking to try to coordinate labour issues amongst the firms. Thus, the government's commitment to direct involvement in attracting major investors and its reputation for solving their problems is an intangible but highly influential factor in the success potential of Ethiopia's SEZ programme.[7]

Another reason for optimism is that leading firms have been generating a demonstration effect. It is noteworthy that Ethiopia has been able to attract major global players in the light manufacturing industry (Mihretu and Llobet 2017). International buyers decide on what orders to place with which suppliers based on country-specific conditions rather than simply based on the suppliers' capabilities. These buyers analyse a country in detail and decide what kind of products they would expect from which production locations based on an assessment of the country's labour skills, natural resources, infrastructure development, environmental standards, and governance. This means that once they have decided that a given country is not able to produce high-end products, they will not give high-end orders to the producers based in that country. For example, HIP contains a concentrated value chain in textiles and garments led by strong anchor firms including the American Phillips-Van Heusen Corporation (PVH), the Chinese Wu Xi Jinmao (locally JP Textile), and Indian company Arvid. HIP has provided a powerful demonstration effect despite not yet being at full production, and subsequent government zones such as Mekelle are also heavily subscribed with textile and garment producers.

45.1.3 Firms within SEZs Are Showing a Willingness to Transfer Technology and Skills

Technology is not an intangible and fungible property of a modern economy, but real machines in real factories used by workers with specific skills. Even within Ethiopian SEZs at this early stage, there exists a wide range of different productive technologies

[7] For a detailed discussion of these results see Xu, Hager, and Prasad (2017).

that have been chosen by producers within the same narrow sector—such as upstream textile production or garment assembly. Despite reports of firms' difficulty implementing their technology strategy or accessing advanced production capabilities in Ethiopia,[8] there is evidence that firms within the SEZs in Ethiopia are willing to contribute to technology transfer through both training and the introduction of more advanced production methods than previously existed in the country.

As an illustration, a leading FDI-backed firm in an SEZ expressed a willingness to sell any materials or production equipment at any technology level to both domestic and international firms operating in Ethiopia. In interviews, the manager explained that this approach is a way of stimulating growth of the sector and that the firm is willing to allow local firms to use its more capital- and technology-intensive processes. For instance, mould making is a highly technological process in which the design for a new product is fed into a computer and an automated process is used to turn this into a steel mould. This firm claims to offer local firms the capability of producing original designs without the need for the capital expenditure on the high-end moulding machines by enabling them to commission moulds to their own designs. It is not known if any local firms have benefited from this opportunity; however, the firm's manager believes that this is a key to stimulating the growth of a productive cluster which would support the interests of the leading firm as well.

Another channel of potential technology and skills transfer is staff training. All the firms interviewed in Ethiopia provided in-house training for their employees, which ranged from a few weeks to several months of training in the company's home country, despite high turnover rates.[9] In one case, a firm claimed to have trained more than 1,000 employees in their home country.[10] The company maintains two training centres in the home market—one for computer and managerial skills and the other focusing on manufacturing skills. A representative of the Ethiopian Ministry of Industry (MOI) claimed that least two firms located within SEZs have reported success in employee training. Huajian took employees to China for training in both language skills and the culture of productivity. This training has focused on demonstrating what is expected of a worker and how this expectation is driven by the buyers' demands for quality goods produced on time (on the development of an industrial working class see Chapter 38). Both Huajian and George Shoes are reported by MOI to have transitioned to make use of more Ethiopian supervisors and middle management—a move which also supports their business competitiveness as locals are much more cost effective than expatriate workers.

[8] Giannecchini and Taylor (2018) strike a sceptical note about the potential of EIP to catalyse development due to what they see as weak technology transfer opportunities and backward linkages, which they attribute to the concentration of Chinese investment in the SEZ.

[9] For a evidence of employee turnover, preferences, and outcomes in Ethiopia see Blattman and Dercon (2016).

[10] As of August 2017.

45.1.4 Ethiopia Is Taking Advantage of China's State-Owned Capacity to Direct Learning by Doing

Ethiopia has learned from the development process in other countries, including fostering cooperation between India and the ETIDI, adopting kaizen practices from Japan, and cooperating with the Danish International Development Agency on strengthening the private sector (Amsden 2001). In regard to China, Ethiopia has sought to learn from both positive and cautionary experiences. As a positive example, China has demonstrated the potential of SEZs to promote structural transformation and to teach management practices relating to the administration of these zones. On the cautionary side, Ethiopia has sought to avoid the environmental challenges and land-grabbing behaviour that accompanied China's economic development. This strategy of adapting the successful cases from other countries was deliberately undertaken by the Ethiopian government and described in GTP-II: 'The development of large industrial parks will be informed by the experiences of developed countries that have successfully used this strategy for their development.' (National Planning Commission 2016: 144). This section examines the partnerships between EIC, IPDC, and Chinese state-owned enterprises (SOEs).

Chinese experience has had an impact on the development of the SEZ programme in Ethiopia in a process that has been increasingly owned and directed by the Ethiopian government. EIP had its genesis as an overseas development cooperation zone supported by the Chinese Ministry of Commerce (MOFCOM).[11] Following this, the Ethiopian government entered directly into the administration of SEZs with Chinese SOEs as partners, first in construction and later supporting management practice as well. The first of these zones, Bole Lemi, was built by Chinese contractors and took more than three years to complete, with the management of the zone and one-stop shop (OSS) conducted by the Ethiopian government. Following this, the HIP saw Chinese firms as both construction and management partners. The partnership with the SOEs enabled the HIP to be envisioned, completed, and fully subscribed in nine months. The Chinese SOE that constructed the park, CCECC, is also a member of the management team, which includes expertise from China's Kunshan Industrial Park (KIP) and leading Indian company Arvind (Walta 2016). This partnership with CCECC and KIP has enabled the adaptation of management practices, provided HIP with experts to diagnose potential problems, and has arranged for members of the Ethiopian management team to be sent to the SEZ in China to directly experience the process and procedures involved in the management of a world-class SEZ.

The Ethiopian-Chinese partnership has been based on a spirit of mutual cooperation. While companies bring benefits to the Ethiopian economy, they are commercial operations that enjoy support and incentives from the Ethiopian government to increase

[11] See the list of confirmation checked China Overseas Economic and Trade Cooperation Zones (in Chinese). Available at: http://hzs.mofcom.gov.cn/article/ac/g/

their corporate profits. While overwhelmingly industrial transfer to Ethiopia has taken place through Chinese private-sector firms, including the Huajian shoe factory and the investment group that runs EIP,[12] a substantial amount of knowledge and skills transfer is being sought through partnership between Chinese SOEs and the Ethiopian government.

The existence of SOEs in China not only facilitated China's transition to a private sector-led economy while maintaining economic stability in the process, but also enabled the creation of world-leading institutions that are capable of taking on long-term strategic investments (Lin 2007). Having participated in and learned from the development of China, these companies are becoming significant actors in Africa's industrialization. At least three Chinese contractors related to SOEs have repeatedly worked with the Ethiopian government—CGCOC Group (CGCOC), Chinese Civil Engineering Construction Corporation (CCECC), and China Communications Construction Company (CCCC). Contrary to the prevailing narrative of Chinese SOEs as extractive, the pattern of their involvement in Ethiopia is one of long-term mutual cooperation. The special characteristics of these firms, including their ability to access state-backed finance at preferential rates, expansive scale, and accumulation of capital-intensive equipment in East Africa, enable them to provide services to the Ethiopian government that are beyond the capacity of most private-sector companies. Notably, this includes the ability to agree to zero-variation contracts with a fixed price for construction projects within the SEZs. A zero-variation contract means that the government agrees to pay a fixed amount for the construction of the SEZ with agreed quality standards and timeline. The construction firm then bears the risk of any changes in its costs, as no set of circumstances or delays will lead to an increase in the amount paid to the contractor. This means the government can predict the cost of construction projects and helps to mitigate, although it does not alleviate, capital constraints for Ethiopia.

45.2 China's Historical Experience with SEZs: Ingredients for Success

It is useful to consider how China's experience with SEZs may reflect on the potential for success in the Ethiopian SEZ programme, despite the nearly forty-year gap between their respective beginnings. China introduced SEZs as part of its experimentation towards economic liberalization and the creation of a private sector. This contrasts with Ethiopia, whose transition from a command economy focused on privatization and the domestic market (Oqubay 2015) before later accepting SEZs principally for their role in

[12] Primary shareholders include Jiangsu Qiyuan Group, Jiangsu Yonggang Group Co. Ltd., Zhangjiagang Yangyang Pipe-Making Company, and the Zhangjiagang Free Trade Zone Jianglian International Trading Co. Ltd. Eastern Industry Zone (2018).

attracting manufacturing foreign direct investment and their potential for export earnings. These differences in approach reflect both the specific country contexts and the different times at which these transitions are taking place. However, the experience of China remains relevant for understanding what can be achieved with SEZs. This section briefly reviews some of the secondary literature on the role of SEZs in China's development, provides insight both into the Chinese zones' contributions to structural changes in the economy and into the evolution of the zones in response to these changes, and synthesizes the key ingredients for success.

SEZs have contributed to China's structural transformation. In their analysis of China's economic transition Storesletten and Zilibotti (2014) cited a number of changes in the structure of the Chinese economy: increasing employment in private enterprises from 10 per cent in 1994 to 50 per cent in 2007 (Song, Storesletten, and Zilibotti 2011), substantial increases in real wages in the urban manufacturing sector and urban GDP per capita averaging 7.6 per cent and 10 per cent annually in the period 1992–2007 (Ge and Yang 2014), and a fall in labour's contribution to output from 50 per cent in 1992 to 41 per cent in 2005 (Hsieh, Bai, and Qian 2006). Zeng argues that 'special economic zones (SEZs) and industrial clusters that emerged after the country's reforms were without doubt two important engines of China's remarkable development' (Zeng 2010: xiii). That these zones attracted FDI is undisputed—due to China's low base, the four zones at Shenzhen, Zhuhai, Shantou, and Xiamen accounted for 59.8 per cent of total FDI in China in 1981 (Zeng 2010). Subsequent efforts by the government to create additional zones through the 1980s and 1990s also produced strong economic performance. In 2006, the four original SEZs accounted for a full 2 per cent (15 million) of Chinese jobs, which then numbered 758 million, and the fifty-four national-level Economic and Technical Development Zones (ETDZs) accounted for 0.5 per cent (4 million) of total employment (Zeng 2010). Interestingly, these ETDZs attracted more investment in total despite their lesser employment generation, reflecting the structural transformation taking place in the wider economy.[13]

An illustrative case of the top-ranking zones is at Tianjin (TEDA). TEDA was founded in 1984 as part of the second wave of SEZ development and the introduction of ETDZs. Officials familiar with TEDA describe two phases of production. In the 1990s, TEDA was predominantly home to low-skilled, labour-intensive production. Later, after 2006, the firms in the zones were increasingly attracted to China's large market size and preferential policies on VAT. China initially maintained strong export orientation in the zones and only later allowed progressively more access to the domestic market. In this way, TEDA may offer an important lesson for policymakers and international organizations who often argue that either the labour-intensive phase or the export-oriented phase of industrial development can be bypassed in favour of more advanced industries. In addition to the many individual benefits of wage-earning jobs in factories, the learning that

[13] The four original SEZs attracted US$0.55 bn of utilized investment vs. US$1.3 bn in the ETDZs (Zeng 2010).

employees get in these factories can be valuable, both for the individuals and for the development of domestic firms in the medium term. Such was the case at TEDA, where many of the management staff of internationally recognized Huawei were previously employees of Motorola, a leading firm in the 1990s with a production base in TEDA.

The functions of SEZs have evolved with the structural change that has taken place in China. The SEZs of the 1980s had been successful contributors to economic liberalization and capital accumulation. Rising wages created pressure on firms to move into higher value-added segments of manufacturing. Yet initially the skills and raw materials needed for these more advanced industries did not exist abundantly in China. The result was the creation of a new type of zone that both encouraged and regulated the processing trade by focusing incentives on 'import for export' while also increasing the government's regulatory oversight of these industries. The next major wave of SEZ development was in the early 1990s, with the expansion to fifty-eight export-processing zones (EPZs), called development zones in China, by the end of 1992 (Fu and Gao 2007). Amiti and Freund (2010) find that the structure of Chinese exports changed from 1992, with declines in agriculture, textiles, and apparel in favour of consumer electronics, particularly those based on the processing trade. Initially these EPZs were well subscribed; however, there has been a substantial change in the behaviour of firms in response to structural changes in the economy. First, changes in the backward linkages have undermined the logic of the EPZs, which used to be primarily focused on import-for-export trade. Today, raw materials are abundant domestically and importing most components no longer makes sense. Second, increasing costs of factors including labour and land have reduced the incentives for processing trade. Officials indicated that 2014 was an inflection point—prior to this firms had mostly engaged in moving up the product value chain—for example, moving from assembling TVs to smartphones as described above. However, according to officials at one EPZ, after 2014 more firms began to look for opportunities abroad, including in Africa.

China's experience cannot be directly replicated elsewhere; however, it does provide insights into the ingredients for success. First, strong commitment by high-level leadership is the key to unleashing the potential of SEZs. Second, taking an experimentation approach and learning from mistakes provides a crucial feedback loop. Third, it is essential to target the right sectors in line with latent comparative advantages in the given region and to adjust the sectoral focus dynamically. Fourth, capable and dedicated public administration is key to leading the investment promotion and building the confidence of potential investors.

It comes with the caveat that not all SEZs are successful in China. Empirical studies show that some SEZs in mainland China have undermined firm productivity, in contrast to the productivity-enhancing SEZs in the coastal region (Xiang and Lu 2015). What is even worse, SEZs were once manipulated to grab land as the number of SEZs proliferated in the 1990s (Zhang and Li 2007). One cause of failure is that some local governments provide subsidies to unviable sectors against their comparative advantages in order to attract firms into the zone.

45.3 The Prospects of Ethiopian SEZs: A New Structural Economics Perspective

This chapter opened with the claim that despite its early stage of development, there are reasons to be optimistic about the potential of SEZs in Ethiopia. This section provides a theoretical grounding to explain why Ethiopia may succeed where others have failed.

SEZs are one of the six steps of the NSE practical policy tool, the Growth Identification and Facilitation Framework (GIFF) (Lin 2012). In order to understand why these zones are an important part of the policy toolkit in developing countries, it is important to understand what industrial policy should be seeking to influence if it is aiming to create rapid and sustained economic growth. According to NSE, industrial policy should be targeted towards creating and maintaining dynamic upgrading in a country's industrial structure. This upgrading is achieved by facilitating the transformation of latent comparative advantage into competitive advantage and rapid upgrading of factor endowment structure through accumulation of physical and human capital for subsequent upgrading of endowment structure, comparative advantage, and industrial structure.[14]

Factor endowments are the starting point of the NSE analysis. A country's factor endowments at any given time are the total amount and skill of labour, capital, and natural resources in that country. At different stages of development, these factors exist in differing relative abundances. The relative abundances of these endowments, taken as a whole, constitute the country's endowment structure. The endowment structure of a country, by determining relative factor prices in the economy, determines what can be produced in that country at a lower opportunity cost than in other potential production locations. This familiar, but contested,[15] concept is known as comparative advantage (Ricardo 1821).

Participation in global trade produces changes in factor costs, as firms accumulate capital and wages rise. Profit-maximizing firms then respond to these changing relative factor costs by changing their production patterns—diversifying products or upgrading production. This upgrading occurs in a distributed, but systematic way. It is distributed because most of the decisions are taken by individual firms, but the overall pattern is systematic because the decisions are being taken in response to incentives—incentives given by the relative factor prices determined by the endowment structure. Thus, NSE describes rapid and sustained economic growth as a process of

[14] For a deeper discussion of the core ideas of New Structural Economics, see Lin (2013).

[15] The role of comparative advantage in pursuing development strategies is contested and readers may wish to familiarize themselves with the views of Ha-Joon Chang and Arkebe Oqubay. For a general discussion, see Lin and Chang (2009). For a discussion of comparative advantage in the context of Ethiopia, see Oqubay (2015).

sustained upgrading in the technology and industries driven by the change in a country's endowment structure.[16]

45.3.1 Why Doesn't Comparative Advantage Automatically Lead to Productive Participation in Global Trade?

The preceding section described how comparative advantages can lead to industrial upgrading. However, developing countries have *latent* comparative advantages. This is because high transaction costs and global perceptions of product quality and timely delivery hinder the ability of firms in the country to convert the comparative advantage implied by factor costs into actual competitive advantage in the global marketplace (Porter 1990).

The inability to invariably identify industries that will develop into competitive advantage based on their comparative advantage, as demonstrated by the historical failure to 'pick winners', has led to some economists dismissing the idea of comparative advantage as pragmatic post-hoc justification. However, the test of a comparative advantage is systematic utilization of the endowment structure by firms at a given stage of development. Returning to the example of China, it was not the case that one or two firms used the low factor price of labour to produce exports for the international market but that a substantial and increasing amount of the productive capacity was devoted to labour-intensive production until the price of labour and land began to rise. These increased costs pushed firms to relocate or substitute more capital-intensive production methods. Successful SEZs with devolved policy oversight independently developed labour-intensive industrial clusters. However, the endowment structure alone did not spontaneously produce these clusters. The policy conditions created by SEZs in China removed binding constraints in the infrastructure and business environment and catalysed productive FDI to bring in capital, technology, management expertise, and access to global markets.

45.3.2 How SEZs Convert Latent Comparative Advantages into Competitive Advantages and Why Some Fail

Developing countries face many simultaneous challenges including large infrastructure deficits, low levels of skill, weak institutions, poor business environments, and governance challenges. Given the capital scarcity and limited implementation capacity that define these economies, the challenges can seem overwhelming and intractable. However, SEZs enable improvements and investments to be made on a manageable scale. While it is somewhat straightforward to measure the amount of FDI, for instance,

[16] For an alternative perspective, readers may wish to consider the balanced growth theory of Ragnar Nurkse, the unbalanced growth theory of Albert Hirschman, and the institutional theories of Acemoglu.

digging deeper into the reasons why that particular amount or type of FDI became located in a particular area quickly becomes quite complex.

There are at least two issues at play in the challenge of understanding the drivers of FDI. First, the criteria that firms use for investment decisions are influenced by the dynamic and changing global trade system, trends and competition within each industry, and the information that they have about potential production locations. Second, the government's active investment promotion and facilitation are crucial to a foreign investor's confidence in their investment decision. Comparative advantage is proven in the marketplace through trial, iteration, and in some cases failure. A first mover is essential in the process. Once a firm enters a new sector and is successful, it creates information for other entrepreneurs who will quickly enter that sector, resulting in competition and reducing the profit value for the first mover. Conversely, if that firm is unsuccessful it will bear the cost of its failure alone and discourage other firms from entering. Therefore, one of the important roles of government facilitation is to provide incentives to attract and compensate first movers for the information externality they generate.

SEZs require substantial investment, but the amount is far less than the cost of trying to improve the infrastructure and business environments for the entire country simultaneously. Within the geographically demarcated area of the zone, the government is able to improve the infrastructure on a sector-specific basis to meet the needs of the industries that it is targeting based on its factor endowments. For instance, an agri-processing zone that works with dairy production will require cold-chain facilities and a modern textile zone will require some form of effluent treatment. Thus, it is important that a government has a clear idea of what kinds of firms it is hoping to attract into its SEZs prior to the planning phase.

One cause of SEZ failure in developing countries has been the haphazard creation of 'general' SEZs open to any form of production to capture any kind or amount of investment. This may lead to tensions in the production base, rather than the formation of a dynamic and mutually reinforcing cluster. Here the accomplishment of the Ethiopian government in the creation of the Hawassa Industrial Park is particularly promising—by working closely with private-sector partners the SEZ was planned and infrastructure developed to support a primary industry value chain. Following this seminal experience, all government SEZs in Ethiopia are expected to be sectorally differentiated. This contrasts with the private Eastern Industrial Park, which due to its position as first in market had developed in a more ad hoc manner. In less than ten years since it became operational, this lack of sectoral focus and early permissive access to the domestic market has hampered the viability of firms in the zone, with at least one firm having fully suspended production.

Another benefit arising from SEZs is their potential to stimulate changes in the local and regional economies where they are located. Early indications at HIP point to substantial increases in local tax revenues and increasing investment in the local economy beyond the zone. Furthermore, the increasing number of jobs and mobility towards the area of the zone may stimulate infrastructure development outside it. In the short term, the demands on water, transportation, and housing created by the zone may prove challenging, but if these problems are solved they will boost local economic development.

A similar pattern was seen at China's first economic zone, Shekou, where the zone developer took on a number of local socio-economic challenges including the development of schools and hospitals in the areas surrounding the zone.

In order to realize these benefits, however, effective SEZ parameters must be put in place. As mentioned at the beginning of the chapter, SEZs, particularly in developing countries, have frequently failed to meet expectations. There are many reasons for this, including lack of appropriate infrastructure and politically rather than economically motivated choice of location. In particular, however, there are two reasons for SEZ failure that are directly related to comparative advantage. The first is that the SEZs may either target sectors without latent comparative advantages, such as those that are too capital intensive for the level of development or that fail to target any sectors at all, thereby weakening the potential of the SEZ to form productive agglomerations. The second is that the government, in an effort to attract investment, may allow firms located in the zones to produce for the domestic market. In such a case, the logic of SEZs as a place enabling a country with a lower level of development to participate productively in global trade, and thus actually benefit from its factor endowments, is severely curtailed. In order to convert a latent comparative advantage possessed by a country into a competitive advantage enjoyed by a firm, that country must actually be trading the goods for which it has a lower opportunity cost on the international market.

From the perspective of NSE, there are grounds for optimism for the development of Ethiopia's SEZ programme if the right ingredients are in place. Firms in Ethiopia are showing signs of the systematic exploitation of factor endowments after the initial pilot success of pioneering zones and firms. This is producing changes, albeit on a small and tentative scale, in the level of technology and worker skills. Insofar as this theoretical foundation is taken as explaining the success and evolution of the Chinese SEZs from the initial use of labour-intensive production methods to increasingly capital-intensive production, then it may be hoped that the early success of Ethiopia's SEZs is similarly creating the conditions for structural transformation. In this effort, Ethiopia is making full use of China's experience and the productive partnership, with both Chinese firms and SOEs seeking to benefit from the conditions created by Ethiopia's endowment structure.

45.4 Conclusion and Directions for Future Research

This chapter has argued that despite the early stage of Ethiopia's SEZ programme there is reason for optimism that it will become a successful example of SEZ development. The SEZ programme in Ethiopia has a number of strengths that are supported by examples from history and consistent with the theoretical analysis of NSE.

The SEZ programme in Ethiopia demonstrates the key ingredients for success emerging from the Chinese historical experience. The government has demonstrated commitment in its active approach to solving problems and creating institutions to support development. While the political issues relating to public administration in Ethiopia are handled in other chapters, it is clear that the government has continued to build on the commitment of former Prime Minister Meles Zenawi in seeking to build the confidence of investors. These efforts have been recognized by international manufacturers and buyers such as Phillips-Van Heusen Corporation (PVH) at the HIP. Experimentation and learning from mistakes is evident in the progression from EIP to Bole Lemi, and into the model for HIP as well as the progressive adjustment of sectors and strategies throughout the development of the five-year economic plans. Furthermore, this learning has been deliberately cultivated by the Ethiopian government in its search for wide-ranging international partnerships and best practices. In the case of SEZs, this has meant partnering with Chinese SOEs who are capable of both applying the lessons of Chinese developmental history and structuring projects in a way that helps to maintain budgetary discipline and Ethiopian government control. Creating the regulatory space for both private and public SEZs in Ethiopia supports experimentation. However, to date the Ethiopian model has diverged from the Chinese experience in that SEZ policy in public zones is centrally controlled and individual SEZ leadership has not been given substantial agency for the adaptation of industrial policy to zone-level conditions.

Having the benefit of China's experience has helped to shape the SEZ programme in Ethiopia. Ethiopia has learned from the environmental impacts of development in China and other countries and has sought to establish high-quality waste treatment facilities in public parks and raise standards in private parks. As a leader in producing hydro-electric power in Africa, the government has promoted Ethiopia as a destination for firms seeking to use greener energy resources and has used these renewable resources to provide low-cost electricity for producers—sharpening its advantages to offset high transaction costs.

Despite the optimism for the future of SEZs in Ethiopia, it behoves us to end on a cautionary note. While we have identified historical and theoretical support for the current direction of the Ethiopian SEZ programme, much remains unknown about the determinants of success and failure in SEZs. Current studies have made efforts to document and analyse the development of SEZs but quality data remains scare, not only in Ethiopia, but also in the majority of countries where SEZs are being developed. One reason for this is the difficulty of untangling the complex interplay between global markets, industrial policies, geography, management, and political leadership. Another is that data creation is often seen as a luxury in the early stages of development when a country is fighting for its first steps onto the industrialization ladder. Hence, rigorous SEZ research programmes are essential for a better understanding of the enabling conditions for successful SEZs on the path to structural transformation in Ethiopia and beyond.

Acknowledgements

For work in Ethiopia, the authors would like to acknowledge the support of the Ethiopian Development Research Institute (EDRI).

References

Amiti, M. and C. Freund (2010). 'The Anatomy of China's Export Growth', in *China's Growing Role in World Trade*, ed. Robert C. Feenstra and Shang-Jin Wang (Chicago, IL: University of Chicago Press): 35–56.

Amsden, A. H. (2001). *The Rise of 'The Rest': Challenges to the West from Late-Industrializing Economies* (Oxford: Oxford University Press).

Blattman, C. and S. Dercon (2016). 'Occupational Choice in Early Industrializing Societies: Experimental Evidence on the Income and Health Effects of Industrial and Entrepreneurial Work', NBER Working Paper No. w22683, Cambridge, MA.

Competitive Industries and Innovation Programme (2017). *Special Economic Zones: An Operational Review of their Impacts* (Washington, DC: World Bank Publications).

Eastern Industry Zone (2018). Shareholder [online]. http://e-eiz.com/about.asp?id=14&pagetitle=Shareholder&language=en (accessed 18 January 2018).

Farole, T. (2011). 'Special Economic Zones in Africa: Comparing Performance and Learning from Global Experiences', World Bank Publications (Directions in Development), Washington, DC. https://openknowledge.worldbank.org/handle/10986/2268.

Fu, X. and Y. Gao (2007). 'Export Processing Zones in China: A Survey', International Labour Organization, Geneva.

Gakunu, P. et al. (2015). 'Comparative Study on Special Economic Zones in Africa and China', Working Paper No. 06/2015, United Nations Development Programme and the International Poverty Reduction Center in China.

Ge, S. and D. T. Yang (2014). 'Changes in China's Wage Structure', *Journal of the European Economic Association*, 12 (2): 300–36.

Giannecchini, P. and I. Taylor (2018). 'The Eastern Industrial Zone in Ethiopia: Catalyst for Development?', *Geoforum* 88: 28–35.

Hsieh, C.-T., C.-E. Bai, and Y. Qian (2006). 'The Return to Capital in China', *Brookings Papers on Economic Activity* 2: 61–88.

Lavopa, A. and A. Szirmai (2012). 'Industrialization, Employment and Poverty', International Finance Corporation (World Bank Group). https://www.merit.unu.edu/publications/working-papers/abstract/?id=4831

Lin, J. and H.-J. Chang (2009). 'Should Industrial Policy in Developing Countries Conform to Comparative Advantage or Defy It? A Debate between Justin Lin and Ha-Joon Chang', *Development Policy Review* 27 (5): 483–502.

Lin, J. Y. (2007). 'Development and Transition: Idea, Strategy, and Viability', Development Economics Working Paper No. 22709, East Asian Bureau of Economic Research. https://ideas.repec.org/p/eab/develo/22709.html

Lin, J. Y. (2012). *New Structural Economics: A Framework for Rethinking Development and Policy* (Washington, DC: The World Bank).

Lin, J. Y. (2013). 'New Structural Economics: The Third Wave of Development Thinking: The 12th Heinz W. Arndt Memorial Lecture, The Australian National University, Canberra, 6 June 2012', *Asian-Pacific Economic Literature* 27 (2): 1–13.

Mihretu, Mamo and Llobet, Gabriela (2017). *Looking Beyond the Horizon: A Case Study of PVH's Commitment in Ethiopia's Hawassa Industrial Park* (Washington, DC: The World Bank).

Ministry of Finance and Economic Development (2010). 'Growth and Transformation Plan, GTP I', Addis Ababa.

National Planning Commission (2016). 'Growth and Transformation Plan II (GTP II)', Addis Ababa.

Oqubay, A. (2015). *Made in Africa: Industrial Policy in Ethiopia* (New York: Oxford University Press).

Porter, M. E. (1990). *The Competitive Advantage of Nations* (New York: Free Press).

Rhee, J. (2013). 'Asia's Economic Transformation Where to, How, and How Fast?' in *Key Indicators for Asia and the Pacific 2013* (Manila: Asian Development Bank). https://www.adb.org/sites/default/files/publication/30358/ki2013-special-chapter.pdf (accessed 28 August 2018).

Ricardo, D. (1821). *On the Principles of Political Economy and Taxation*. Library of Economics and Liberty. http://www.econlib.org/library/Ricardo/ricP.html (accessed 10 April 2018).

Song, Z., K. Storesletten, and F. Zilibotti (2011). 'Growing Like China', *American Economic Review* 101 (1): 196–233.

Storesletten, K. and F. Zilibotti (2014). 'China's Great Convergence and Beyond', *Annual Review of Economics* 6 (1): 333–62.

Walta (2016). 'IPDC Outsources Management Operation of HIP'. http://www.waltainfo.com/news/detail/16177&locale=en (accessed 30 August 2018).

Xiang, K. and M. Lu (2015). 'Speed versus Quality: Why Regional Dispersion Tendency of Development Zone Policy Is Not Sustainable?', *Journal of Finance and Economics* 41 (4): 4–17.

Xu, J., S. Hager, and R. Prasad (2017). 'Key Success Factors in Ethiopia's Early-Stage Industrialization', Gates Foundation.

Zeng, D. Z. (2010). 'Building Engines for Growth and Competitiveness in China: Experience with Special Economic Zones and Industrial Clusters', World Bank Publications (Directions in Development; countries and regions). https://openknowledge.worldbank.org/handle/10986/2501.

Zhang, P. and X. Li (2007). 'New Thoughts on Preventing the Illegal Enclosure of the Development Zone' (in Chinese), *China Land* 2: 15–19.

CHAPTER 46

THE CONCEPT OF A 'DEVELOPMENTAL STATE' IN ETHIOPIA

JOSTEIN HAUGE AND HA-JOON CHANG

46.1 Introduction

Characterizations of Ethiopia as a developmental state (DS) have started to become commonplace in recent years. Clapham (2017: 1) writes that 'Ethiopia provides the most significant attempt to implement the idea of a "developmental state" in sub-Saharan Africa'. Oqubay (2015: 74) describes Ethiopia as an aspiring developmental state. Meles Zenawi (Ethiopia's strongman from 1991 until his death in 2012), the one person who most clearly embodied Ethiopia's vision of development, made a thorough case in an academic book chapter for 'implementing' a developmental state in Ethiopia—a book chapter entitled 'States and Markets: Neoliberal Limitations and the Case for a Developmental State' (Zenawi 2012).

Given Ethiopia's rapid economic growth, the high degree of state intervention in the economy, and the state's focus on industrialization—somewhat in the image of Japan and the 'Asian tiger' economies[1] from which the DS concept emerged—these characterizations of Ethiopia as a DS come as little surprise. The inspiration that the Ethiopian state explicitly draws from the East Asian development experiences is perhaps the most notable manifestation of the implementation of the DS model in Ethiopia. In July 2017, the *Financial Times* published a Big Read on Ethiopia's development model, focusing on its low-tech manufacturing boom and emphasizing how the country is 'trying to ape the centrepiece of Asia-style industrialization' (Aglionby 2017: 3).

[1] The 'Asian tigers' is a reference to Hong Kong, Singapore, South Korea, and Taiwan. South Korea and Taiwan are more frequently studied in the DS literature, as Singapore and Hong Kong are considered more 'special cases'.

Zemedeneh Negatu, a prominent Ethiopian businessman, is quoted in the article as saying that the Ethiopian government is 'piggybacking on the best elements of China and South Korea, and perhaps, some aspects of Singapore, with an Ethiopian flavour. And if they get it right, they have a high probability of creating an Asian Tiger-like economy in Africa' (Aglionby 2017: 9).

This chapter discusses the concept of a DS in Ethiopia. However, it does not do so by trying to answer explicitly whether or not the Ethiopian state *is* a DS. The concept of the DS emerged from the development experiences of countries in a particular place (East Asia) at a particular point in time (1950s to 1980s, with the exception of Japan, whose rapid economic development started in the 1920s). Ethiopia is clearly not Hong Kong, Japan, Singapore, South Korea, or Taiwan. However, this does not mean that Ethiopia cannot draw inspiration from the development experiences of these countries, or that it is not interesting to see if and how Ethiopia is doing so.

That is why our chapter focuses on questions such as: how has the Ethiopian state been drawing inspiration from the East Asian DS model? How is the Ethiopian development model different from the East Asian DS model? And how does this translate in terms of economic development in Ethiopia (and *not* in terms of 'becoming' a DS)? This is done by analysing the ideas that have influenced the political leadership and bureaucracy in Ethiopia; the degree of state intervention in the economy; the country's industrialization trajectory and the centrality of industrial policy in it; the sources of the state's legitimacy; the degree of state autonomy (in particular the autonomy of the bureaucracy); and the state's relationship with the private sector. But before addressing these questions, it would be useful to first discuss at some length the foundations of the concept of the DS.

46.2 The Concept of the Developmental State: Foundations

As mentioned, the concept of the DS emerged from the development experiences of Japan and the Asian tiger economies in the post-World-War-II era. So, the first thing we should note when talking about the concept is that it is a concept that emerged from a particular context/contexts at a particular point/points in time. The second thing to note is that the foundations of the DS literature are well defined, so analysing this literature will help us understand the concept clearly. The concept was introduced by Chalmers Johnson in his book *MITI and the Japanese Miracle: The Growth of Industrial Policy, 1925–1975*, published in 1982. In the late 1980s and early 1990s, a stream of literature followed that studied other East Asian development experiences, most notably South Korea and Taiwan, using the theoretical framework, if not necessarily the concept of the DS. The works in this tradition that have come to be considered most seminal in a 'DS' sense include Alice Amsden's *Asia's Next Giant* (1989), Robert Wade's *Governing the*

Market (1990), Ha-Joon Chang's *The Political Economy of Industrial Policy* (1994), and Peter Evans' *Embedded Autonomy* (1995).[2]

Chalmers Johnson explains that 'one of my main purposes in introducing the idea of the "capitalist developmental state" into a history of modern Japanese industrial policy was to go beyond the contrast between the American and Soviet economies' (Johnson 1999: 32). Johnson was trying to describe something that did not fit into the dichotomy of the socialist state and the free-market state that was dominant at the time—let us not forget that he was writing during the Cold War—to a description of a state that was conjoining private ownership with state guidance. The influential works listed above also emphasize the 'third way' nature of the East Asian states. The DS concept is therefore a concept of a state that allows for the operation of a private market economy but which is highly interventionist and certainly not conforming to the principles of neoliberalism or laissez-faire. It is a state that 'governs the market', to paraphrase the title of Wade (1990).

The DS literature is also consistent in its view of the orientation of the DS: a DS is a state that first and foremost is developmental. That is, the East Asian DS model gives its first priority to development and treats as secondary other goals, like regulation, social welfare, or equality. More specifically, it gives its first priority to *economic* development through the process of industrialization.

This is why the DS literature puts so much emphasis on industrial policy. According to Chang, Hauge, and Irfan (2016: 26), industrial policy can be understood as a policy that 'deliberately favours particular industries—or even firms—over others, against market signals, usually to enhance efficiency and to promote productivity growth for the targeted industries as well as for the whole economy, but also to manage the industries' decline smoothly'. This is a refined definition of the one set out in Chang (1994) and does not differ in any significant way from the understanding of industrial policy by the other seminal works in the DS literature. Apart from the focus on industrialization as the main ingredient in the process of development, we should stress that the concept of industrial policy in the DS literature emphasizes the role of the state as one that, again, is *not* laissez-faire.

Moreover, the DS literature views the legitimacy of the state as derived from its record in economic development. In the words of Johnson (1999: 52), 'the successful capitalist developmental states have been quasi-revolutionary regimes, in which whatever legitimacy their rulers possessed did not come from external sanctification or some formal rules whereby they gained office but from the overarching social projects their societies endorsed and carried out'. Legitimation occurs from the state's achievements, not from the way it came to power. This has fuelled some debate over whether a DS can avoid being authoritarian.

[2] Additionally, Meredith Woo-Cumings' *The Development State* (an edited book), published in 1999, is a supremely important contribution to understanding the concept of the DS, alongside many papers (too numerous to mention) that have been published in the aftermath of the introduction of the concept. We acknowledge that the finite list of seminal works that we have proposed is certainly debatable.

We want to make two points with respect to this debate. First, it is important to highlight that while aspects of the DS literature recognize elements of authoritarianism in the DS model, it does not accept a necessary connection between authoritarianism and development. To the authors advocating the concept of the DS, the real issue is not really authoritarianism but the nature of the political system—there are authoritarian states that are predatory, rather than developmental. According to Evans (1995: 12), predatory authoritarian states, as opposed to developmental authoritarian states, extract resources from the economy (without giving back), lack the ability to prevent individual incumbents from pursuing their own goals, and create a polity in which personal ties are the only sources of cohesion, and in which individual maximization takes precedence over pursuit of collective goals. The second point we want to make is that the concept of democracy that is usually used to judge the DS is one that is an idealized version of the Anglo-American state structures, which is uncritically assumed to be the 'gold standard' that every country should aspire to emulate. As Johnson (1999: 52) succinctly put it, the legitimacy of developmental states cannot be explained using the usual state–society categories of 'Anglo-American civics'.

The last point of emphasis we should make about the DS literature is that it looks deeply into the functioning of state institutions, particularly into the role of the state bureaucracy and how it interacts with the private sector for the purpose of development. Johnson (1982) describes a DS bureaucracy as one that is highly capable and committed, usually headed by a pilot agency of elite civil servants, which is given the freedom to implement measures as it sees fit, unencumbered by the constraints of everyday politics. Evans (1995) emphasizes that, additionally, it is important that the bureaucracy understands the needs of the private sector but at the same time is sufficiently detached from private-sector interests to avoid having its independence compromised (a characteristic he famously named 'embedded autonomy'). Putting these together, Woo-Cumings (1999) proposes that a core feature of the East Asian DS model is a professional bureaucracy that keeps its distance from everyday politics and from the lure of the private sector but at the same time is a partner with the private sector, sharing the goal of industrial transformation and having mechanisms to mediate relationships between key interest groups.

The DS literature emphasizes a variety of tools that the state utilizes to 'steer' the private sector towards industrial transformation. For example, Amsden (1989, 2001) highlights the state's use of reciprocal control mechanisms (RCMs) in Taiwan and South Korea: the state would give special favours and assistance to firms in exchange for meeting certain performance targets (such as exporting, local contents, or product specifications). Wade (1990, 2012) writes how East Asian developmental states were in some instances leading the market—when the state made investment decisions that private firms were hesitant to make—and in other instances following the market—when the state supported some of the bets of private firms. Evans (1995) uses the terms 'midwifery' and 'husbandry' to describe the relations between state agencies and private entrepreneurial groups. He argues that in South Korea, the state was able to build on a base of firms with a broad range of related industrial skills, fostered by prior midwifery.

This allowed the state to shift easily to the combination of prodding and supporting, which he calls husbandry.

While we acknowledge that there is no universally agreed upon definition of a DS and that each state that could plausibly be characterized as a DS has unique features, this section has attempted to highlight some core characteristics of the DS that will serve as a useful basis for discussions in subsequent sections of this chapter. In summary, we argue that the DS is a state that (i) emerged from—but is not necessarily confined to—the development experience of Japan and the Asian tiger economies; (ii) conjoins private ownership with heavy state intervention; (iii) gives priority to economic development, which is to be achieved through industrialization; (iv) is legitimized from its record in economic development; and (v) has a professional bureaucracy that keeps its distance from everyday politics and from the lure of the private sector but at the same time is a partner with the private sector, sharing the goal of industrial transformation.

46.3 How has the Ethiopian State Drawn Inspiration from the East Asian DS Model?

46.3.1 Intellectual Channels and Collaborations

The influence of the East Asian DS model in Ethiopia goes all the way back to the intellectual roots of the Tigrayan People's Liberation Front (TPLF)—the branch of today's ruling party (the Ethiopian People's Revolutionary Democratic Front, commonly referred to as the EPRDF) that has held a majority of influential cabinet positions since 1995. The TPLF is known to have had a strong intellectual bent: a fascinating aspect of the party's intellectual drive was the establishment of a business college in Hagereselam towards the end of the insurgency against the Derg, a socialist military junta, in the late 1980s. At the business college, considerable resources were put into translating the works of Lenin, writing studies on Albania's socialist revolution and, not least, studying South Korean industrial policy (Weis 2016).

The intellectual influence of the state-led industrialization experiences of South Korea and other countries in East Asia, such as Japan, Taiwan, and later China on the TPLF cannot be understated. A long-time TPLF member and special adviser to the current Prime Minister recounted his experience of studying for a distance-taught MBA programme in 1991 at the Open University in the United Kingdom, together with Meles Zenawi and several other high-ranking TPLF officials, 'where we studied in particular the East Asian experience' (Hauge 2018: 144). Clapham (2017) argues that it is clear that Ethiopia draws explicitly on the East Asian development models, with China as the single most important inspiration, but seeking to learn from other cases as well, including South Korea, Taiwan, and Japan.

According to De Waal (2012), South Korea and Taiwan were Meles' favourite examples of developmental states. In an interview with the *New African* in 2011, Meles summarized Ethiopia's development model in the following way:

> Essentially, the concept hangs on the prudent combination of market forces and state intervention, where the state plays a leading role not only in providing infrastructure and basic services, but also in providing the right conducive environment for the development of productive and manufacturing capacities. For sure, the experience of a number of East Asian countries supports the validity of our approach. (*New African* 2011: 2)

The influence of the East Asian DS model has not happened purely through 'intellectual' channels but also more directly through development assistance. Around the time when the Ethiopian government was formulating a development strategy for 2010–15, it began regular, high-level consultations on industrial policy with a delegation of Japanese experts from the Tokyo-based National Graduate Institute for Policy Studies (GRIPS). Meles had approached GRIPS at a workshop hosted by the economist Joseph Stiglitz, and between 2009 and 2011, a delegation from GRIPS conducted quarterly seminars for the Prime Minster and his economic advisers (Weis 2016).[3]

The dialogue focused largely on drafting an economic master plan and turned out to be integral to the formulation of the five-year national development plan for the period 2010–15 (the Growth and Transformation Plan), published by the Ethiopian Ministry of Finance and Economic Development. At the core of the plan was an industrialization programme, similar to the development plans formulated by the East Asian developmental states. The plan set a growth target for the industrial sector at 21.4 per cent per year in the five-year period, significantly higher than that of both the agricultural sector (14.9 per cent) and the services sector (12.8 per cent). It also emphasized how efforts to develop skills and infrastructure should be focused to meet the demands of the growing manufacturing industry (MoFED 2010). We discuss the centrality of industrialization in Ethiopia's development model in more detail later in the chapter.

46.3.2 The Rejection of Neoliberalism and the Heavy Hand of the State

As we have seen, one of the core elements of the East Asian DS model is the conjoining of private ownership with heavy state intervention and state ownership in key sectors of the economy. Naturally, all DS scholars are highly critical of free-market explanations of the East Asian development experiences and, more broadly, neoliberalism.

This rejection of neoliberalism among policy practitioners in the East Asian developmental states (and in the DS literature) is also a core feature of the Ethiopian development

[3] Chapter 47 provides detailed information about development cooperation between Japan and Ethiopia.

model and TPLF ideology. After all, the TPLF grew out of a Marxist student movement in the 1970s. It would not be an exaggeration to call the EPRDF, and in particular the TPLF branch of the EPRDF, anti-neoliberal. The EPRDF has consistently been insistent on being autonomous from the ideological demands of Western donors, in particular Washington Consensus-based institutions. This makes Ethiopia unique in the context of Africa—a continent where the World Bank and the IMF have had immense influence ever since the 1980s. In his book, *Globalization and its Discontents*, Joseph Stiglitz recounts details of his conversations with Meles Zenawi in 1997, Stiglitz's first year as chief economist at the World Bank. At the time, the IMF had suspended its lending programme to Ethiopia due to the country's 'unstable' fiscal revenue generation. The IMF demanded structural reforms, most importantly liberalization of the financial sector, but Zenawi staunchly refused them. Stiglitz, according to his own account, managed to lobby the World Bank and, eventually, the IMF to restore development assistance to the country (Stiglitz 2002).

The continued unwillingness to liberalize the financial sector is one of Ethiopia's strongest manifestations of the rejection of neoliberalism. The understanding is that foreign banks will only be allowed to operate in Ethiopia when domestic banks have developed the financial, managerial, and technological capacities to compete against them. For now, most medium- to long-term loans for investment projects are provided by the Development Bank of Ethiopia (DBE), a state-owned bank. The importance of state-owned banks for funding industrial development and long-term investment projects is another similarity that Ethiopia shares with the East Asian DS model. For example, in South Korea in 1957, the Korea Development Bank (KDB) accounted for 45 per cent of total bank lending to all industries in the country (Amsden 2001). More importantly, all banks were nationalized in South Korea between 1961 and 1983—the height of the country's developmentalism. Many of them remained state owned until the mid-1990s (Chang 1993).

The Ethiopian state not only has a heavy hand in the financial sector but also in practically every other aspect of the economy. The state-owned Metals and Engineering Corporation (METEC) managed by the military stands out as the clearest example. Established in 2010 and now the largest industrial complex in Ethiopia with a capital of over US$1 billion, it has played a key role in the country's infrastructural and industrial mega-projects—acting as the primary contractor for engineering works on the Grand Renaissance Dam),[4] leading the establishment of sugar and fertilizer factories, and assembling carriages for the expanding national railway system. It has also been a key player in Ethiopia's import substitution strategy, with its subsidiaries manufacturing everything from AK-47s to household furniture, from duffel bags to city buses, and from solar panels to light aircraft (Weis 2016). Export-oriented manufacturing industries are also dominated by the state, at least among those firms that are domestically owned. For example, three of the four largest vertically integrated domestic textile firms

[4] A hydropower dam on the Nile that will be one of the ten largest hydropower dams in the world when it is finished in 2018–19.

are either state owned (Bahir Dar Textile and Kombolcha Textile) or affiliated to the TPLF's endowment fund EFFORT[5] (Almeda Textile) (Hauge 2018).

Again, we have a feature shared with the East Asian DS model—the importance of state-owned enterprises (SOEs).[6] South Korea's steel-maker POSCO, currently the fourth-largest steel maker in the world, was established as an SOE in the late 1960s. But Taiwan is the country among the Asian tigers in the post-World-War-II era best known for hosting a huge SOE sector. In 1952, the SOE sector in Taiwan accounted for 57 per cent of industrial production (Amsden 1985). It gradually declined in importance, but still played an important role for a long time. Between 1950 and 1980, the average investment share of SOEs in gross fixed capital formation in Taiwan was 32 per cent, higher than that of other countries with sizeable SOE sectors in this time period, such as Singapore, South Korea, and Brazil (Short 1983).[7]

Such heavy state intervention and scepticism about leaving things to the free market begs the question of how much space there really is for the private sector in Ethiopia.

46.3.3 A Developmental Orientation to be Achieved through Industrialization

Establishing first and foremost whether the Ethiopian state has a developmental orientation is not straightforward. As already evidenced at some length in this chapter, the Ethiopian government certainly likes to use the phrase 'developmental state' with a positive connotation to describe the development model of the country (Clapham 2017; Hauge 2018; Oqubay 2015). But does the developmental orientation rank as more important than other types of state orientation in Ethiopia? It clearly ranks highly but any prominent political figure or bureaucrat in Ethiopia would obviously not declare that it ranks higher than an 'equality' orientation or a 'welfare' orientation.

The centrality of national development plans to the political agenda of the Ethiopian state can help us understand this though. Since 2005, it appears that five-year national development plans have become a staple of the state's development agenda, starting with the Plan for Accelerated and Sustained Development to End Poverty (PASDEP), followed by the Growth and Transformation Plan (GTP), covering 2010 to 2015, and the Growth and Transformation Plan II (GTP-II), covering 2015 to 2020. According to Weis (2016: 90), these development plans have become the cornerstone of economic policy in Ethiopia, serving as a focal point for coordinating and evaluating the efforts of different ministries and government agencies.

[5] EFFORT is the acronym for the Endowment Fund for the Rehabilitation of Tigray. It was established and is still controlled (though no longer formally owned) by the TPLF. Its current CEO is Azeb Mesfin, the widow of former Prime Minister Meles Zenawi. Its total assets exceed half a billion dollars (Weis 2016).

[6] Japan is somewhat of an exception in this respect, as it did not have many SOEs after World War II.

[7] However, we should note that today, SOEs play a larger role in Singapore than in any of the other Asian tigers—SOEs make up 22 per cent of GDP in Singapore, against Taiwan's 16 per cent (Chang 2014).

In line with the East Asian DS model, the growth of industry, and the manufacturing sector in particular, is a principal feature of these development plans. In the GTP-II, for example, the annual growth rate target for the manufacturing sector is 22 per cent, the highest growth rate target of any sector of the economy (NPC 2016).

It is therefore not surprising to see that, alongside these ambitious targets for manufacturing development, industrial policy measures have also become more visible, particularly since 2005 when the first five-year national development plan was launched. Such measures include clear sectoral targeting in national development plans, an expansion of the 'industrial bureaucracy', state-led credit allocation to prioritized industries, export promotion measures, import substitution in certain industries, attraction of FDI, infrastructure investments, and the construction of industrial parks (see Table 46.1 for details. Chapter 35 in this book also presents a comprehensive taxonomy of Ethiopia's industrial policy measures). This reinforces the belief that what we are seeing in Ethiopia right now are the beginnings of rapid industrialization. It also explains why people, in particular those interested in industrial policy in Africa, associate Ethiopia with industrial development (see Hauge and Irfan 2016).

So, while we cannot assert with certainty that the developmental orientation of the Ethiopian state ranks more highly than other types of state orientation, it is clearly of central importance. Moreover, in line with the East Asian DS model, industrialization is a core feature of the Ethiopian development model, as evidenced by ambitious growth targets for the manufacturing sector and the prominence of industrial policy.

There is, thus, strong evidence indicating many parallels between Ethiopia's development model and the East Asian DS model. This is evident from both the Ethiopian state's ideological orientation and its economic policies—the state has strong ownership in the economy, it is highly critical of neoliberalism, and industrialization is the core feature of its development agenda. Some high-ranking politicians of the ruling party (in particular the TPLF branch of the party) even explicitly cite the East Asian DS model as an inspiration for Ethiopia's development model. Next, we turn to differences between the Ethiopian development model and the East Asian DS model.

46.4 How is the Ethiopian Development Model Different from the Core Features of the East Asian DS Model?

46.4.1 Legitimized from a Record in Economic Development?

The EPRDF is widely perceived as being controlled by people from the Tigray region (from which its initial leadership derived), a small and unrepresentative region in

Table 46.1 Taxonomy of Ethiopia's industrial policy measures

Sectoral targeting	Prioritized industries are clearly articulated in national development plans, based on a range of criteria, including productive potential, labour intensity, linkages to the agricultural sector, technological entry barriers, and export potential. These include: leather, textiles, metals, agro-processing, chemicals, construction inputs, and pharmaceuticals.
Expansion of 'industrial bureaucracy'	Several new government agencies have been set up to more effectively provide state support to prioritized industries. Examples of such institutions would be the sectoral development institutes, the Industrial Parks Development Corporation, and the Ethiopian Industrial Inputs Development Enterprise.
Credit allocation: Development Bank of Ethiopia (DBE) and Commercial Bank of Ethiopia (CBE)	These are state-owned banks that provide subsidized credit to prioritized industries. The DBE provides investment capital, whereas the CBE provides working capital.
Export promotion	Several incentives are put in place to encourage exports in prioritized industries. These incentives are targeted at export-oriented firms and include: reduced interest rate on loans from DBE and CBE; subsidized leasing of land; subsidized salaries for foreign experts hired; and tax exemptions. Policies geared to keeping the currency under-valued can also be seen as an export promotion instrument.
Import substitution	High tariffs are applied to industries which the Ethiopian government wants to 'nurture'. Tariffs are also in place to limit growth of the current account deficit and to raise tax revenues. High tariffs are common in the heavy manufacturing industries, but also for finished products in the light manufacturing industries, such as apparel.
FDI attraction	Several measures have been put in place to attract FDI in prioritized industries, in order to create employment, generate export earnings, and acquire technology. Such measures include favourable access to infrastructure (e.g. industrial parks and rail transport), tax exemptions, and subsidized land leases (in some cases, free land).
Infrastructure investments	Infrastructure investments especially in power generation and transport are geared towards industrial development.
Industrial park development	The Ethiopian government has undertaken a massive commitment to build several industrial parks, in large part to cater to foreign investments, but also more generally to ease the logistics constraints of exporting.

Source: Hauge (2018).

Northern Ethiopia. The party's ascent to power in the early 1990s through an armed struggle bestowed no entitlement to rule the country as a whole. According to Clapham (2017), this has imposed a need to seek 'performance legitimacy' through economic development. In this sense, the EPRDF undoubtedly sees itself mirroring aspects of the East Asian DS model—legitimation arising from the state's achievements, not from the way it came to power.

Can the Ethiopian state show such economic development achievements though? To some extent, yes. While real GDP per capita in Ethiopia in 2016 was only US$511 (in 2010 US$)—indicating a low level of economic development—GDP growth and investment rates have been high, industrial policy is becoming more pronounced, and the manufacturing sector is growing.

There is also evidence of legitimation arising from public endorsement of high-profile development projects. The construction of the Grand Renaissance Dam, the hallmark infrastructure project in Ethiopia, serves as a good example. With a budget of close to US$6bn, it is the single largest project ever to have been undertaken by an Ethiopian government. The dam is financed almost purely domestically, as the World Bank and even the Chinese government have been hesitant to fund it because of 'hydro-political' sensitivities with Egypt. Seeing the unwillingness of international creditors to become involved in the project, the government has encouraged public-sector workers and other salaried employees to pledge a month's salary to the project. This has been done by issuing a special Renaissance Dam bond that is within the means of domestic savers. The government has also enabled the diaspora community to invest in the project by issuing a version of the bond denominated in foreign currencies (Berhane 2013). This domestic financing scheme has largely worked, as purchasing the bond is seen as a civic duty (Weis 2016).

Aside from this example, election outcomes in 2010 and 2015 suggest that the EPRDF enjoys strong public support. But the legitimacy of this support is controversial as the party has systematically closed down space for political dissent, especially since 2005, when the EPRDF almost lost the general election. In recent years, public discontent has become more visible. Mosley (2016) rightly points out that the state has hyped up expectations for economic development to an unrealistic level, which is now producing disillusionment and anger, especially among young people. This anger is intensified because of the widespread perception that a disproportionate share of the growing economy has gone to ethnic Tigrayans, whose TPLF forms the core of the EPRDF. Cracks are appearing in the system of ethnic federalism—people belonging to the two major ethnic groups, Oromo and Amhara (who together represent approximately 61 per cent of the country's population), have been staging anti-government protests because of corruption in the political system and lack of equal economic benefits. The conclusion is, therefore, that while public support for the state's high-profile development projects exists, it is highly ethnically fragmented.

46.4.2 The Independence and Power of the Bureaucracy and the State's Relationship with the Private Sector

We highlighted in the introduction that a core feature of the East Asian DS model is a professional bureaucracy that keeps its distance from everyday politics and from the lure of the private sector, but at the same time is a partner with the private sector, sharing the goal of industrial transformation, and has mechanisms to mediate relationships between key interest groups. While in many ways the industrial policy apparatus of Ethiopia is impressive, as already evidenced, it deviates somewhat from this model.

The size of the bureaucracy concerned with industrial policy in Ethiopia has certainly expanded, as seen from Table 46.1, but many of these new institutions either report directly to the Prime Minister's Office (PMO), which micro-manages their operations, or are dwarfed in power by the PMO and, more generally, the EPRDF. Oqubay (2015: 76) acknowledges that the power and strong organizational capabilities of the EPRDF are used to compensate for deficiencies of the bureaucracy.

The concentration of 'industrial policy power' in the ruling party, rather than the professional bureaucracy, suggests that the Ethiopian industrial policy regime is rather different from the East Asian one. However, if Ethiopia gets it right, does it matter which branch of the state is pulling the load? In fact, the characterization of the East Asian DS model as one managed by a professional bureaucracy that keeps its distance from everyday politics is not completely uniform. For example, in Taiwan, a lot of industrial policy was formulated by the ruling party, Kuomingtang (KMT). And many important state-affiliated enterprises were owned by the KMT, rather than being directly state owned.

Another distinctive feature of the Ethiopian development model is the small size of the domestic private sector in manufacturing industry and the consequent reliance on foreign investors. While the domestic private sector in Ethiopia has increased considerably in size since the early 2000s, as measured by investment rates, this growth has mostly happened in the domestic-oriented service sector (see Chapter 39 for a detailed account of private-sector development in Ethiopia). There is simply not much basis for an 'alliance' or 'symbiotic' relationship between the bureaucracy and the domestic private sector (at least that which is focused on manufacturing) to exist. The East Asian DS model did to some extent rely on FDI though, as Ethiopia is doing now. The most prominent example is Singapore, whose net FDI inflows as a proportion of gross fixed capital formation between 1971 and 1995 was 22.9 per cent, the highest in the world in this period (Chang 2006). South Korea and Taiwan had more restrictive attitudes to FDI (South Korea more so than Taiwan) but it was definitely not absent from their development strategies. For example, FDI in South Korea's textile sector in 1974 amounted to 20 per cent of total foreign capital in the country (Chibber 1999). In Taiwan, 20–25 per cent of manufactured exports came from foreign firms in the 1970s (Wade 1990).

The type of policies on which the FDI strategy in the East Asian DS model relied are very much in line with Alice Amsden's framework of RCMs. Financial incentives and indirect subsidies were handed out to foreign firms on condition of, most commonly, export orientation, sourcing inputs from domestic firms, and engaging in joint ventures with domestic firms (Chang, Hauge, and Irfan 2016).

The Ethiopian government is handing out financial incentives to foreign investors in a similar fashion. In the manufacturing sector, these incentives include exemption from income tax for up to ten years, subsidized land lease, and exemption from duties and taxes on imported raw material and capital equipment. The degree of generosity of these incentives depends on the share of export in output, in line with the East Asian DS model. However, apart from that, the attitude to FDI in Ethiopia seems relatively lax, and the Ethiopian government has so far not been doing much to 'nudge'—still less to 'force', as the East Asian governments did—foreign investors to source locally or to transfer technology to existing domestic firms. Formulating such policies would be an important part of trying to build up a domestic private sector.

46.5 How has the Attempt to Emulate the East Asian DS Model Worked in Terms of Economic Development in Ethiopia (and *not* in Terms of 'Becoming' a DS)?

Japan and the Asian tigers have arguably been the most successful examples of 'catch-up' development throughout the history of capitalism. Thus, any catch-up economy today that draws the 'right' lessons from the East Asian DS model and adapts the model successfully to its own circumstances will have good prospects for developing economically. In Ethiopia, is there any evidence that the implementation of aspects of the East Asian DS model is successfully contributing to economic development? If not (yet), are there prospects of this happening?

First, let us look at what has been achieved so far. In terms of economic growth, the Ethiopian development push has been impressive. Since 2004, Ethiopia's economy has been booming. Real GDP per capita increased from US$214 in 2004 to US$511 in 2016 (WDI 2017).[8] While acknowledging that this growth has started from a low base, an annual real GDP per capita growth rate of 7.5 per cent over a twelve-year timespan is impressive. The growth performance comes across as even more impressive when considering that, except for Rwanda, Ethiopia is the only country in Africa whose GDP

[8] As measured by constant 2010 US$, meaning that the growth is measured in real terms, not nominal terms.

growth has been consistently high for over a decade without relying on a natural resource boom (Chang, Hauge, and Irfan 2016).

Part of the growth can be attributed to the growth of the manufacturing sector. Exports of manufactured goods grew 21-fold from 2004 to 2015 (from US$21m to US$436m), largely thanks to the increasing earnings of the textile and leather industries. This represents more than a doubling of manufactured goods' share in total merchandise exports, which itself grew from US$503m to US$3,819m over this period (WTO 2017). However, manufacturing value added as a share of GDP in Ethiopia remains 4.8 per cent (WDI 2017), well below the African average of 10 per cent (Chang, Hauge, and Irfan 2016).

Seeing that the manufacturing sector is growing but is still not at a point where it is contributing significantly to the economy, what other factors then underpin this impressive economic boom? Massive federal spending on infrastructure and construction, which has in part boosted growth of especially the services sector, has been the most important factor (Hauge 2018). More than 40 per cent of the federal budget is spent on infrastructure projects, primarily transport and power generation (Oqubay 2015). These infrastructure investments are incredibly important for future growth of the manufacturing sector. Without stable electricity supply and developed road and rail networks, there is little hope of developing an internationally competitive manufacturing sector.

Additionally, Ethiopia has made impressive strides in the areas of education and health under the current regime. Net enrolment in primary schools reached 79 per cent in 2014, up from only 19 per cent in 1994; and the average life expectancy has hit 64 years, an impressive increase of 12 years since 2000 (Oqubay 2015).

So we can conclude that the numbers indicate a positive trajectory but that it is premature to claim success in terms of industrialization and economic development. What about future prospects for economic development? It goes without saying that predicting the future is a thankless task, but let us try to highlight some important points.

First, the range of industrial policy measures highlighted in Table 46.1—many of which are deliberately modelled on the industrial policies of the East Asian DS model—is a positive sign. These measures largely explain the growing anticipation of rapid industrialization in Ethiopia. If any African country will become an industrial powerhouse, it is likely to be Ethiopia.

Second, one could legitimately debate the extent to which Ethiopia's development model is endorsed by the public. It is certainly endorsed by many, but the system of ethnic federalism and the perception of policies disproportionately marginalizing the Oromo and Amhara people means that the development model, as it is structured now, is somewhat fragile. However, problems of ethnic strife and, more generally, protests against the national government are not unique to Ethiopia—the East Asian countries also had high levels of conflict during their developmental periods: Japan lost more working days per worker in industrial strikes than did Britain or France (not to speak of West Germany or Sweden) in the second half of the 1950s and the first half of the 1960s; the pitched battles that pro-democracy student demonstrators fought with riot police on the streets of South Korea in the 1970s and the 1980s are world famous; and Taiwan was ruled under martial law until the late 1980s. The general manager of a foreign footwear company in Ethiopia likened the protests right before the declaration of the state of emergency in Ethiopia in October 2016 to those of Tiananmen Square in 1989, saying that 'you can't have smooth sailing when you're investing in emerging markets' (Hauge 2018: 169).

Third, there is an over-reliance on SOEs and foreign firms as actors in the market. The East Asian DS model endorses state ownership in the economy but also emphasizes the importance of an internationally competitive domestic private sector. A domestic private sector is virtually non-existent in Ethiopia at this point, at least in manufacturing industry, particularly that which is export oriented. This needs to change if economic growth is to be sustained and translate into economic development.

46.6 Conclusion

Ethiopia's rapid economic growth over the past decade, the high degree of state intervention in the economy, and the state's focus on industrialization—somewhat in the image of the East Asian DS model—are prompting characterizations of Ethiopia as a DS. In this chapter we discussed the concept of a DS in relation to Ethiopia. However, we did not do so by trying to answer explicitly whether or not the Ethiopian state is a DS. We rather focused on the following questions: how has Ethiopia been drawing inspiration from the East Asian DS model? How is the Ethiopian development model different from the East Asian DS model? And how does this work in terms of economic development in Ethiopia (and *not* in terms of becoming a DS)?

We used the theory of the DS as a framework to answer these questions. We argued that the DS is a state that (i) emerged from—but is not necessarily confined to—the development experience of Japan and the Asian tiger economies; (ii) conjoins private ownership with heavy state intervention; (iii) gives priority to economic development, which is to be achieved through industrialization; (iv) is legitimized from its record in economic development; and (v) has a professional bureaucracy that keeps its distance from everyday politics and from the lure of the private sector but at the same time is a partner with the private sector, sharing the goal of industrial transformation.

Based on this understanding of a DS, it is evident that the Ethiopian state draws inspiration from the East Asian DS model in many ways. First, there has been a strong 'East Asian' intellectual influence on prominent political figures of the ruling party, dating all the way back to the 1980s. Second, the Ethiopian state strongly rejects the ideological tenets of neoliberalism and has a heavy hand in the economy, manifested especially (albeit not exclusively) in state ownership in the economy. Third, the Ethiopian state has a strong developmental vision to be achieved through industrialization, evidenced by five-year development plans with ambitious growth targets for the manufacturing sector and a range of industrial policy measures.

However, the Ethiopian development model differs from the East Asian DS model in other ways. While the EPRDF sees itself deriving legitimacy from a record in economic development, including high-profile development projects, rather than procedural sanctification—in line with the East Asian DS model—the public support for the state's development projects is ethnically fragmented. Most importantly, there is anger among the Oromo and Amhara because of the widespread perception that a disproportionate share of the growing economy has gone to ethnic Tigrayans, whose TPLF forms the core of the EPRDF.

Another deviation from the East Asian DS model is the lack of power and independence of the bureaucracy, and the small size of the domestic private sector in manufacturing industry. Most 'industrial policy power' in Ethiopia lies in the hands of the ruling party, the EPRDF. The dominant actors in the Ethiopian economy are SOEs and foreign firms. There is therefore not much of a basis for the existence of an 'alliance' or a 'symbiotic' relationship between the bureaucracy and the 'productive' domestic private sector, which characterized the East Asian DS model.

Ultimately though, the Ethiopian 'developmental state', with its many similarities and some differences with the East Asian DS model, is leading a positive economic development trajectory. Ethiopia has been Africa's fastest-growing economy for over a decade, impressively so without being dependent on a natural resource boom. Most of the growth can be attributed to public investments in infrastructure and construction, investments that are important for developing an internationally competitive manufacturing sector. The manufacturing sector still makes up a small share of the economy in Ethiopia, but the fast growth of the sector and all the industrial policy measures formulated in recent years gives hope for future success in industrialization. If there is one African country that is likely to achieve success in economic development through industrialization under the tutelage of a 'developmental state', similarly to the East Asian developmental states, it is Ethiopia.

References

Aglionby, J. (2017). 'Ethiopia Bids to Become the Last Development Frontier', *Financial Times*, 3 July.

Amsden, A. (1985). 'The State and Taiwan's Economic Development', in *Bringing the State Back In*, ed. P. Evans, D. Ruschemeyer, and T. Skocpol (Cambridge: Cambridge University Press): 78–106.

Amsden, A. (1989). *Asia's Next Giant: South Korea and Late Industrialization* (Oxford: Oxford University Press).

Amsden, A. (2001). *The Rise of 'The Rest': Challenges to the West from Late-Industrializing Economies* (Oxford: Oxford University Press).

Berhane, D. (2013). 'Nile: Ethiopians Raise Billions, Despite Foreign-Backed Saboteurs', *Horn Affairs English*, 29 April.

Chang, H.-J. (1993). 'The political economy of industrial policy Korea', *Cambridge Journal of Economics*, 17: 131–57.

Chang, H.-J. (1994). *The Political Economy of Industrial Policy* (Basingstoke: Macmillan Press).
Chang, H.-J. (2006). *The East Asian Development Experience: The Miracle, the Crisis and the Future* (London: Zed Books).
Chang, H.-J. (2014). *Economics: The User's Guide* (London: Penguin Books).
Chang, H.-J., J. Hauge, and M. Irfan (2016). *Transformative Industrial Policy for Africa* (Addis Ababa: UNECA).
Chibber, V. (1999). 'Building a Developmental State: The Korean Case Reconsidered', *Politics and Society* 27 (3): 309–46.
Clapham, C. (2017). 'The Ethiopian Developmental State', *Third World Quarterly*. DOI: 10.1080/01436597.2017.1328982.
De Waal, A. (2012). 'The Theory and Practice of Meles Zenawi', *African Affairs* 112 (446): 148–55.
Evans, P. (1995). *Embedded Autonomy: States and Industrial Transformation* (Princeton, NJ: Princeton University Press).
Hauge, J. (2018). 'African Industrial Policy in an Era of Expanding Global Value Chains: The Case of Ethiopia's Textile and Leather Industries', PhD thesis, Cambridge University. https://doi.org/10.17863/CAM.20781.
Hauge, J. and M. Irfan (2016). 'Why Ethiopia Is on Track to Become Africa's Industrial Powerhouse', *The Conversation*, 22 June.
Johnson, C. (1982). *MITI and the Japanese Miracle: The Growth of Industrial Policy, 1925–1975* (Stanford, CA: Stanford University Press).
Johnson, C. (1999). 'The Developmental State: Odyssey of a Concept', in *The Developmental State*, ed. M. Woo-Cumings (Ithaca, NY: Cornell University Press): 32–59.
MoFED (2010). 'Growth and Transformation Plan 2010/11–2014/15' Ministry of Finance and Economic Development, Addis Ababa.
Mosley, J. (2016). 'Ethiopian Politics beyond the Vanguard?' *Chatham House Expert Comment*, 18 October.
New African (2011). 'Zenawi: "We're on the Right Track"', *New African Magazine* 10 December. https://newafricanmagazine.com/news-analysis/long-reads/zenawi-were-on-the-right-track/.
NPC (2016). 'Growth and Transformation Plan II 2015/16–2019/20', National Planning Commission, Addis Ababa.
Oqubay, A. (2015). *Made in Africa: Industrial Policy in Ethiopia* (Oxford: Oxford University Press).
Short, R. (1983). 'The Role of Public Enterprises: An International Statistical Comparison', Department Memorandum Series 83/84, International Monetary Fund, Washington, DC.
Stiglitz, J. (2002). *Globalization and its Discontents* (London: Penguin).
Wade, R. (1990). *Governing the Market: Economic Theory and the Role of Government in East Asian Industrialization* (Princeton, NJ: Princeton University Press).
Wade, R. (2012). 'How Can Low-Income Countries Accelerate their Catch-Up with High-Income Countries? The Case for Open-Economy Industrial Policy', in *Good Growth and Governance in Africa: Rethinking Development Strategies*, ed. A. Noman, K. Botchwey, H. Stein, and J. Stiglitz (Oxford: Oxford University Press): 246–72.
WDI (2017). World Development Indicators online database, World Bank, Washington, DC. Accessed December 2017.
Weis, T. (2016). 'Vanguard Capitalism: Party, State and Market in the EPRDF's Ethiopia', D.Phil dissertation, University of Oxford.

Woo-Cumings, M. (ed.) (1999). *The Developmental State* (Ithaca, NY: Cornell University Press).

WTO (2017). World Trade Organisation trade statistics online database. Accessed December 2017.

Zenawi, M. (2012). 'States and Markets: Neoliberal Limitations and the Case for a Developmental State', in *Good Growth and Governance in Africa: Rethinking Development Strategies*, ed. A. Noman, K. Botchwey, H. Stein, and J. Stiglitz (Oxford: Oxford University Press): 140–73.

CHAPTER 47

A JAPANESE PERSPECTIVE ON ETHIOPIA'S TRANSFORMATION

KENICHI OHNO AND IZUMI OHNO

47.1 Introduction

Ethiopia aims to industrialize by adopting a developmental state model that actively guides and harnesses private actors (see Chapters 46 and 49). For this reason, Ethiopian industrial policy is naturally influenced by the experiences of other countries that have adopted such a regime as well as policy advice given in that spirit by international experts. The Ethiopian government has vigorously sought such lessons rather than passively waiting for their arrival. Relevant experiences and advice mostly—though not exclusively—originate in East Asia where developmental states actually existed and in some cases even succeeded brilliantly in achieving fast growth and high technology levels.

Ethiopia's industrial policy exhibits strong East Asian qualities in four related aspects: (i) policy orientation; (ii) vigorous learning from East Asian mentors; (iii) selective adoption of concrete East Asian policy measures with local modification; and (iv) a large inflow of light manufacturing foreign direct investment (FDI) as a driving force of early industrialization, which was a typical developmental pattern observed in East Asia. As a result, despite its still low income and poor investment climate, Ethiopia has emerged as a unique and dynamic country featuring economic philosophy, policy capability, and growth performance which are more akin to those of East Asia's past and currently industrializing economies than of its African peers.

This chapter reviews and evaluates Ethiopia's policy learning from the East with particular attention to the industrial policy dialogue with Japan which started in 2008, with the National Graduate Institute for Policy Studies (GRIPS) Development Forum and the Japan International Cooperation Agency (JICA) as joint partners on the Japanese side. It also discusses remaining difficulties and differences between Ethiopian and East Asian industrial experiences.

47.2 The Meaning of Learning from Others

Learning from the East should not mean copying policies adopted in an East Asian country in the past or at present—be it Meiji Japan's engineering education, South Korea's comprehensive export drive, or Malaysia's one-stop service for investors—to the home country without due regard to the latter's local context. The same can be said about learning from the West or any other advanced region or country. Blind acceptance of others' methods does not produce results because policies work only when they fit political, social, and economic readiness on the receiving side, which differs from one country to another. At the same time, a potential learner should not reject foreign models as irrelevant simply because 'our country is unique and times have also changed'. Such a claim is universally heard from the governments of latecomer countries. While recognition of the uniqueness of each nation and age is important, it should not be used as an excuse for not absorbing precious lessons from others.

Careless copying and flat rejection are two extreme attitudes that shut out the possibility of dynamic and intelligent policy improvement. What is needed for latecomer countries is systematic and pragmatic learning of alternative international best practices (and even failures) in order to strengthen the capacity to create their own policy package. A large number of country studies must be viewed as potential building blocks of home policy. Selecting, modifying, and combining them is a delicate task which can be done effectively only by policymakers equipped with humility, patience, great imagination, and a deep knowledge of how things are in the domestic society. A learner must also distinguish common factors from local peculiarities that lead to successful development, a capability which can be gained by examining many cases from a comparative perspective. Such learning is not easy and cannot be achieved by random reading or discussion. Nations must first learn how to learn policy methods.

Besides this, successful policy learning requires three more conditions (Ohno 2013: 55–7). First, it must be backed by strong political ownership. It is the national leader(s) of a developing country, not foreign consultants or international organizations, who must set priorities, decide policy content, create necessary conditions, and be responsible for implementing and monitoring projects. The proper role of foreign experts is to support a national development strategy from the sidelines. In turn, the challenge for a developing country is to prepare a development strategy worthy of such support, and this may require initial tutoring by well-informed foreigners. Moreover, strong national ownership must be accompanied by a desire for national pride and global excellence along with a sense of humiliation over the current inability to compete effectively. Such national aspiration was clearly visible in Meiji Japan as well as Singapore, South Korea, and Taiwan in the post-World-War-II period. It is also detected in the current Ethiopian government.

Second, policy must be learned on the ground by executing concrete industrial projects rather than abstractly or aimlessly in classrooms or conference halls. Policy learning is an ongoing process that must coincide with the process of industrialization, not a precondition for industrial take-off. Many of the high-performing East Asian economies built policy capability through trial and error and hands-on struggles to attain specific targets rather than to raise their positions in investment climate contests or fulfill externally imposed conditionalities or governance criteria. Training was conducted, institutions were created, funds were raised, and officials and experts were mobilized to execute particular projects stipulated in five-year development plans or sectoral master plans. This pragmatic approach has several advantages, including concentration of limited human and financial resources on the areas where they are truly needed, clear criteria by which to assess performance, flexible shifting of resources and organizations to where they are needed, and the sense of pride and achievement that emerges as concrete projects are accomplished one by one.

Third, policy scope and instruments must be expanded as learning progresses. As with any learning, a novice must start with basics and climb the ladder in orderly steps. Skipping lessons, which many countries try to do after hearing East Asian miracle stories, is not advisable. South Korea's wide-ranging export policy is too difficult to emulate for governments that have little practical experience of promoting exports, and Japan's highly complex system of small business support is not a good model for recent starters. Mastery of front-line technology such as bio-tech, nano-tech and Industry 4.0 is often targeted in plan documents of developing countries, but there may be other elementary things—such as ensuring road connectivity and stable power supply, introducing kaizen or improving technical education programmes—that need to be done before aiming at high industrial goals.

In learning how to learn, industrial policy dialogue with experienced officials and experts from advanced economies may prove useful. Among the various forms of international assistance to improve policy quality are lectures and seminars, expert dispatches, training at home and abroad, tours and visits, policy reports, and help with drafting industrial plans. These can amply provide fragmentary ideas and cases, but industrialization is an effort that requires the ability to integrate individual policy components into a coherent whole. A good teacher can show how to do this. Meanwhile, the teacher must also know deeply about the current mindset, capabilities, and constraints of the learning country before giving advice. Academics who give the same one-sizes-fits-all advice to every country must be avoided. These principles and objectives govern the Ethiopia–Japan Industrial Policy Dialogue which is explained in detail below.

47.3 Industrial Policy Dialogue with Japan

By the authors' definition, policy dialogue is intellectual cooperation between a developing country and an advanced country held regularly over a few to several years with an open, evolving, and action-oriented agenda for promoting economic development. It is a flexible consultative mechanism Japan employs routinely in East Asia and elsewhere. Since the 1980s, Japan has conducted policy dialogue with around a dozen partner countries,[1] and Ethiopia is the first African country in which Japan has applied this kind of consultative mechanism.

Japan's policy dialogue is unique in several ways. First, it aims to directly strengthen the state's role and capacity in industrialization rather than reduce the scope of government intervention. Second, there is no pre-determined agenda or formula. Policy consultation and knowledge sharing are tailor-made to each country conducted through a highly interactive process. Japan's policy dialogue usually starts with a national leader of a developing country asking Japan to discuss developmental strategies generally or to teach and transfer East Asian development experience. This certainly differs from normal technical assistance with its narrowly prescribed terms of reference. Third, while intellectual cooperation takes place in a bilateral context, concrete cases from all around the world are cited. Unlike seminars organized by some industrial countries, we do not publicize or boast about Japanese past achievements as models to emulate. This is because Japanese experiences are usually too hard for beginners to digest.

Western donors and international organizations also conduct 'policy dialogue', but their topics tend to be less industrial and more oriented towards macroeconomic, legal, social, or governance aspects. Where industrial issues are taken up, they usually cover cross-sectoral problems such as ICT, globalization, green growth, and enterprise reform rather than sector-specific targeting and support. South Korea also offers large-scale policy cooperation to developing countries, called the Knowledge Sharing Programme (KSP), but its approach is less interactive and far more standardized than Japan's.

As of 2008, when policy dialogue with Japan was requested, the development partners having visible industrial support projects in Ethiopia were the United Nations Industrial Development Organization (UNIDO), the United Nations Development Programme (UNDP), Germany, Italy, and the United States Agency for International Development (USAID). Most other donors, including Japan, were assisting poverty reduction and hunger elimination. However, two events in that year caught the attention of Prime Minister Meles Zenawi who decided to accelerate Ethiopia's learning from the East.

[1] Starting with Argentina in 1985, Japan has formally conducted policy dialogue (according to our definition) on around twelve occasions (there are overlapping countries) using various modalities regarding purpose, scale, participants, duration, and frequency. In countries such as Vietnam, Indonesia, Laos, and more recently Myanmar, the Japanese government has mobilized a large number of academics, businesses, and aid consultants to identify and analyse key issues and offer policy advice.

In May 2008, in Yokohama, Japan hosted the Fourth Tokyo International Conference on African Development (TICAD IV) attended by forty African heads of state, including Prime Minister Meles Zenawi. The key feature of TICAD IV was expansion of the scope of bilateral cooperation from official support to private business partnership. Separately, on 10–11 July 2008, Professor Joseph Stiglitz hosted the third Africa Task Force meeting of the Initiative for Policy Dialogue at Sheraton Addis, supported by JICA. Meles was present at most sessions and the present authors discussed the concept of Dynamic Capacity Development (Ohno and Ohno 2012). We also offered our edited book to the Prime Minister which he began to read during the conference sessions.[2] The following week, Meles requested from the Japanese government two-part bilateral industrial cooperation consisting of a quality and productivity (kaizen) project (just as JICA did in Tunisia) and regular policy discussion with GRIPS. Meles later explained that TICAD IV and discussion with GRIPS researchers had convinced him that the time was ripe for direct intellectual exchange with Japan, the first country to initiate the East Asian miracle (policy dialogue, 14 October 2008).

Later in 2008, two (unofficial) policy dialogue sessions were held with Meles, while JICA prepared kaizen support. Bilateral industrial policy dialogue and the kaizen project were both officially launched in May 2009. The former was led by GRIPS but also involved not only JICA but other Japanese—and even international—organizations such as the Ministry of Foreign Affairs, the Ministry of Economy, Trade and Industry (METI), the Japan External Trade Organization (JETRO), the Japan Bank for International Cooperation (JBIC) and the UNIDO Tokyo as well as Japanese private firms interested in Ethiopia. On the Ethiopian side, the Prime Minister, relevant ministers and state ministers, and officials and experts at the operational level were involved. These three levels of participants met with the Japanese team in separate sessions. Policy dialogue sessions were held four times a year during Phase 1 and twice a year during Phases 2 and 3. Although the frequency was reduced in later phases, the workload was the same or even greater because of increased research, additional reciprocal visits, exchange of policy letters, and policy missions to third countries in Asia and Africa. After Prime Minister Meles passed away in 2012, bilateral dialogue was continued by Prime Minister Hailemariam Desalegn with equal commitment and enthusiasm.

Between 2008 and 2017, eighteen policy discussion sessions lasting one to two hours were held with the Prime Minister,[3] nineteen high-level forum sessions at minister and state minister level were conducted in Addis Ababa, and sixteen policy research visits to third countries in Asia and Africa were organized (not counting mutual visits between Ethiopia and Japan). In addition, there were numerous visits to offices, factories, and

[2] GRIPS Development Forum (2008), which was a collection of ten papers by development economists and officials in Japan, UK, Malaysia, and Uganda. Chapter 7 of the book compares how Japan and EU approached the problem of quality and productivity in Tunisia and explains how JICA implemented kaizen in that country. This book was later re-issued commercially as Ohno and Ohno (2013) with additions and updating.

[3] There were eight face-to-face meetings with Meles Zenawi and twelve such sessions with Hailemariam Desalegn (two of which were conducted when he was deputy prime minister).

project sites, discussions with international organizations and other donors, regional trips inside Ethiopia and Japan, and invited lectures (JICA and GRIPS 2011 and 2016). Table 47.1 illustrates the topics deliberated at High Level Forums. These Forums were used not only to disseminate desired ideas and experiences to Ethiopian policymakers but also to test and propose new policy directions that were missing but considered necessary in the context of Ethiopian policy evolution. As this table makes clear, sharing of policy knowledge was mutual rather than unilateral from Japan to Ethiopia. Moreover, discussions were not confined to the experiences of Japan or countries that Japan had assisted to develop. A large number of concrete cases were drawn from Asia and Africa, and non-Japanese industrial officials and experts from Malaysia, Thailand, and Vietnam were invited to present their practices and research.

Table 47.1 Topics discussed at high-level forums (ministerial level)

	Presentations by Japan or third country	Presentations by Ethiopian government
<PHASE 1> Session 1 June 2009 Session 2 Sep. 2009	JICA's plan for policy dialogue ADLI and future directions for industrial development Cross-cutting issues on industrial policy and East Asian policy menu Organizational arrangements for industrial policy formulation SME policies in Japan	Evaluation of current PASDEP focusing on industrial development and related sectors Comments and feedback by the Policy Dialogue Steering Committee on Japanese presentations
Session 3 Nov. 2009	Designing industrial master plans: international comparison Industrial policy direction of Ethiopia: suggestions for PASDEP II	Concept for the industrial chapter of PASDEP II and the formulation plan
Session 4 Mar. 2010	Basic metals and engineering industries: international comparison of policy framework and Ethiopia's case	Draft of industry sector for PASDEP II Overview, contents of PASDEP II draft of chemicals sub-sector
Session 5 July 2010	Result of basic metal and engineering industries firm-level study—parts conducted by MPDC and JICA	Report of kaizen training in Osaka Report of kaizen training in Chubu Current status of kaizen project and institutionalization of kaizen
Session 6 Oct. 2010	(1) Singapore's experience with productivity development: internalization, scaling-up, and international cooperation	Contents of industry sector in GTP Singapore's productivity movement and lessons learned
Session 7 Jan. 2011	(1) The making of high-priority development strategies: international comparison	Organizational structure of MoI and linkage with other ministries
Session 8 May 2011	Ethiopia's industrialization under GTP Achievements of Kaizen Project Kaizen movement in Asia and Africa Taiwan: policy drive for innovation	MSE development strategy of Ethiopia Kaizen dissemination plan Botswana's productivity movement and its implications for Ethiopia

(*continued*)

	Presentations by Japan or third country	Presentations by Ethiopian government
<PHASE 2> Session 1 Jan. 2012	Export orientation: three policy directions Export promotion: JICA's experience Export promotion centre in Egypt	Export promotion of Ethiopia Assessing Ethiopian investment and export policies
Session 2 Aug. 2012	Results of champion product seminar Export promotion of Malaysia Economic diplomacy in Thailand	Performance of export promotion in Ethiopia Export promotion by foreign mission
Session 3 Jan. 2013	Proactive FDI policy FDI policy experience of Malaysia JICA's assistance in Zambia etc.	FDI inflow into Ethiopia
Session 4 Jul. 2013	JICA's PSD assistance in Indonesia FDI-linked technology transfer	Malaysia's strategic FDI policy Revision of Investment Proclamation
Session 5 Feb. 2014	International comparison of manufacturing performance Handholding programmes	Sectoral institutes: roles and performance Kaizen in GTP-II and long-term vision
Session 6 Aug. 2014	FDI-led industrialization in East Asia FDI inflow into latecomer Asia	Proposal for key ideas in GTP-II Current status of Ethiopian FDI
Session 7 Jan. 2015	Modality and key points of Japanese-run industrial zones in Vietnam and Thailand Industrial zones and foreign currency issues in Myanmar and India	Productivity and competitiveness chapter, industry chapter, and kaizen in GTP-II
Session 8 Oct. 2015	Remaining industrial issues ahead Industrial zone experience in Cambodia	Discussion on GTP-II draft Ethiopian wage and labour productivity survey
<INTERIM> Jul. 2016	(1) Japan's alignment to Industrial objectives of GTP-II	(1) Macro issues related to GTP-II (2) Industrial policy of GTP-II (3) Hawassa Industrial Park
<PHASE 3> Session 1 Feb. 2017	(1) Japan's industrial cooperation for GTP-II (2) Asian experience of high growth and income polarization/equalization	(1) Anti-export bias and effects of export incentives (2) Youth Revolving Fund (3) Impact of urban job application assistance
Session 2 Nov. 2017	(1) Productivity in Ethiopia and Sri Lanka (2) Productivity issues in Vietnam	(1) Productivity of garment and metals sectors (2) Mini review of productivity studies and data

Source: prepared by the authors based on JICA and GRIPS Development Forum (2016).

The most prominent features of Ethiopia–Japan Industrial Policy Dialogue have been as follows. First, many of the proposed actions were actually adopted by the Ethiopian government either partially or fully. Second, Ethiopian leaders asked Japan to be direct and frank rather than polite and diplomatic, and discussion has always been held in this spirit. Third, the Japanese often stressed quality over speed in policymaking, an idea which Ethiopians did not accept. The difference in policy stance between the two nations is a permanent trait of this dialogue, and this is now accepted as given. Fourth, topics were selected carefully and at the last minute to cover the burning issues of the day rather than set a few years in advance. Fifth, Japanese resources and concrete industrial projects were mobilized to realize some—if not all—of the proposals made during the dialogue sessions so that talk actually led to action instead of remaining just talk. Sixth, past East Asian experiences have increasingly become pertinent to Ethiopia as it focuses on skills, productivity, value creation, and attracting high-quality manufacturing FDI. Seventh, Japanese policy support in Ethiopia is conducted within the network of various private and public actors from Japan as well as other advanced or emerging economies because, unlike in Southeast Asia, Japan is a small player in Africa and cannot achieve its purposes through bilateral official efforts alone.

47.4 Evolving Policy Issues

As noted above, the Ethiopia–Japan Industrial Policy Dialogue has been conducted jointly by the GRIPS Development Forum and JICA at three levels: prime minister, ministers and state ministers, and officials and experts at the operational level. It has covered broad subjects. In sessions with these three different levels of dialogue partners, topics often overlapped but were not exactly the same. As circumstances surrounding Ethiopia and attention of policymakers shifted, topics also evolved from basic learning to implementation of new tools such as kaizen, champion exports, productivity movement, industrial park design, handholding,[4] and the like. Once debated, policy ideas were followed up by concrete industrial projects. Naturally, one cannot expect all suggestions to be accepted by the Ethiopian government, but many points raised in the bilateral policy dialogue were seriously considered by Ethiopian authorities and shaped their policies. The ratio of such effective policy advice was surprisingly high—about half or more—whereas in most other countries policy proposals are heard only to be ignored.

In the first phase of the Industrial Policy Dialogue (2009–11), both sides deepened knowledge of each other. Ethiopians explained existing policies such as Agricultural Development-Led Industrialization (ADLI) and A Plan for Accelerated and Sustained Development to End Poverty (PASDEP) while the Japanese side explained how East Asia and the rest of Africa designed and implemented policies and how they made the necessary institutional arrangements for policy coordination. Facilitation of such mutual understanding was key to ensuring the quality of policy dialogue that followed. Separately, Meles requested information packages on many issues he personally wanted

[4] Handholding (also called hands-on or *yorisoi* support) is an intensive SME promotion method practised in East Asia including Japan, South Korea, Taiwan, and Malaysia. It selects a small number of firms that show an appropriate attitude and potential, sets a single business goal (export, product development, etc.) and a customized support menu for each firm, and implements the support needed for two to three years until the firm succeeds. It is an invitation-only programme, not one to which any firm can apply.

to investigate, and they were compiled and sent to him.[5] Since Ethiopia–Japan industrial cooperation started with kaizen, much time was spent on how it should be localized and enhanced in Ethiopia. Much advice was also given to the next five-year development plan under preparation which was initially called PASDEP II and later renamed the Growth and Transformation Plan (GTP). Many ideas were offered, including incorporation of concrete quality and productivity targets, but the final version of GTP did not contain much of these. This was questioned by the Japanese side, and Ethiopian leaders promised that this would not happen again.[6] In April 2013, they officially asked the GRIPS team to assist with formulation of GTP-II (FDRE 2010, 2016).

The second phase of policy dialogue (2012–15) began with a proposal to enhance export promotion, with a particular focus on the creation of narrowly selected, culture-laden, high-quality champion products with national branding rather than general export promotion. Ethiopian private firms enthusiastically supported this idea, and JICA's champion product approach project was launched. Japan's intention was to add customer orientation to Ethiopian policymaking. Kaizen had become popular by then but it only dealt with supply-side efficiency at production sites while demand-side consideration was missing. Another important theme in the second phase was improving FDI policy because manufacturing FDI inflow was accelerating. Other countries' experiences were reviewed along with JICA's cooperation with FDI agencies in latecomer countries. In this connection, in 2013 a large Ethiopian delegation headed by a Ministry of Industry state minister was dispatched to Malaysia to learn from its FDI and export promotion agencies, and related issues such as one-stop investor services, handholding support, and industrial park management were also discussed. As requested by the national leaders, the policy dialogue also advised on the content of the upcoming GTP-II. Unlike the previous GTP, many of the recommendations actually made it to the final document, including the light manufacturing vision, kaizen philosophy and targets, and extensive use of the phrase 'quality, productivity, and competitiveness' throughout GTP-II.[7] A paper summarizing remaining industrial policy issues, as seen from the Japanese side, was drafted at the end of the second phase (JICA and GRIPS Development Forum 2016). Many policy actions that started in the second phase continued to be implemented in the following phase (GRIPS 2016).

[5] The information packages included topics such as Japanese technical education, rural life improvement movements in East Asia, steel industry, chemical industry, international comparison of industrial policy formulation methods, and how Japan and South Korea absorbed technology through foreign-aided industrial projects. Additionally, *Introducing Kaizen to Africa* (2009) and *Kaizen National Movement* (2011) were provided in book form.

[6] The word 'kaizen'—and other productivity tools such as benchmarking and twinning—were not even mentioned in the GTP. There were objections from the Japanese team because this was contrary to the ongoing kaizen fever as well as the great importance the Ethiopian government attached to the upgrading of human capital and technology.

[7] Even though quality, productivity, and competitiveness (QPC) were highlighted, the government admitted that it was not sure exactly what these meant or what additional policies were needed to achieve them. Japan was thus asked by the Ministry of Industry to become a lead donor on QPC promotion.

The third phase starting in 2017 turned to productivity as the core issue for Ethiopia in the years to come. In fact the wage–productivity nexus and related Asian experiences of managing—or failing to manage—this delicate balance had already been discussed towards the end of the second phase. A mini-survey on Ethiopia's past productivity tools (kaizen, benchmarking, and twinning) was conducted, and existing Ethiopian studies and data were reviewed in anticipation of a new report on productivity. Annual manufacturing data collected by the Central Statistical Agency was targeted for cleaning and panel data construction. An in-depth firm survey to identify the cause(s) of success and failure in labour management and incentivization is planned. Besides these, a Japanese private developer is about to create a rental factory zone dedicated to Japanese investors inside Bole Lemi II Industrial Park, while JICA experts are assisting IPDC and EIC in hard and soft aspects of attracting FDI. The Japan External Trade Organization (JETRO) explained its experience of combined export and FDI promotion. Support for manufacturing SMEs is also being initiated, and will be strengthened and integrated in the future. In particular, handholding support in metals and engineering, a sector that Ethiopian leaders regard as critical but where international cooperation has so far been thin, has begun. Mobilization of selected Ethiopian researchers for substantive preparation and discussion of the Industrial Policy Dialogue is another goal to be pursued in the third phase.

Kaizen itself warrants some further remarks. Japanese industrial cooperation in Ethiopia began with kaizen, and policy dialogue initially discussed the various practical aspects of kaizen to support JICA's project. Common questions about introducing kaizen were also discussed.[8] But as experience and knowledge were gained, day-to-day management and troubleshooting were delegated first to JICA experts, then to the Ethiopian Kaizen Institute (EKI). Ethiopians can now teach kaizen to other Africans bilaterally and through the New Partnership for Africa's Development (NEPAD),[9] a great achievement of which Japan is very proud. Even so, policy concern on kaizen of both Mr Meles and Mr Hailemariam remained considerable, and kaizen continued to be deliberated at almost each dialogue session with the Prime Minister. Among many issues, the most crucial is how kaizen can be transformed from a fashionable but superficial tool to be abandoned shortly, to the deeply ingrained national philosophy so that it will be practised willingly and forever without external coercion or instruction. This we

[8] In most countries, introduction of kaizen raises two questions. The first is the effectiveness of kaizen in a country where a different mindset and culture from Japan's prevail. However, the fact is that peoples very different from Japanese, such as Indians and Latin Americans, produce similar gains with kaizen as there is no place on earth where conscious *muda* elimination fails to boost productivity. The second is whether kaizen is compatible with other methods such as benchmarking, business process re-engineering, and balanced score cards. The answer is that they are mutually consistent, at least in theory, but we need to pay attention to the pressure imposed on enterprise managers and workers who are asked to use many productivity tools at the same time.

[9] NEPAD is the socio-economic development flagship programme of the African Union (AU), with a vision and framework that facilitates and coordinates the development of continent-wide programmes and projects, mobilizes resources, and engages the global community, Regional Economic Communities, and AU member states in the implementation of these programmes and projects.

call the 'mindset problem'. A national productivity movement is a partial answer to this. Kaizen Month was one proposal accepted by Prime Minister Hailemariam, and September was designated Ethiopia's Kaizen Month (in Japan or Singapore November is Kaizen Month). City kaizen movement, as well as coaching of sectoral institutes so they can teach basic kaizen to firms under their responsibility, are other important drives by EKI through purely Ethiopian initiative. But more needs to be done to solidify kaizen in the minds of all Ethiopians.

Thus, within several years, Ethiopia–Japan Industrial Policy Dialogue has grown to cover much ground, combining talk with many actions in industrial cooperation. It is the broadest industrial cooperation menu for Japan in Africa, and its content is essentially the same as Japanese industrial cooperation in latecomer economies in Southeast Asia.

It is important to recognize that Ethiopia is learning from many others, not only from Japan or East Asia. Officials, businesses, and experts from the West and emerging economies are also mobilized for Ethiopian industrial learning. Germany can teach many topics including technical and vocational education and training (TVET) and business associations, Italy teaches leather and fashion, France brought wine to the Rift Valley, the Netherlands leads on floriculture, USAID can help Ethiopia to reach the US market, and both the United Kingdom and the European Union have large budgets for industry-related projects. India helps the Leather Industry Development Institute (LIDI), the Ethiopian Textile Industry Development Institute (TIDI), and the Metals Industry Development Institute (MIDI) with twinning arrangements. The World Bank, which previously promoted private-sector capacity building through a matching fund, now offers a broader range of support to Ethiopia including industrial parks, women entrepreneurs, and job creation for refugees (together with the UK and the EU). The International Labor Organization (ILO) is actively developing 'decent work'-related projects, in partnership with European donors and FDI firms. UNIDO has designated Ethiopia a model partner country for inclusive and sustainable industrial development.

Three things can be said about this situation. First, while virtually all bilateral donors now engage in industrial support—unlike the past—most newcomers have little concrete knowledge of industrial project implementation and rely heavily on NPOs, businesses, and the matching fund method. This is not the case with JICA or German development cooperation (such as GIZ) which have extensive industrial experience on the ground. Second, Japanese advice is often unique and different as it stresses (some say excessively) quality, productivity, and on-time delivery, while European buyers are more worried about labour and environmental conditions at the factory than perfect stitching and packaging of the product. Ethiopia needs to understand this difference, and hopefully to learn from both. Third, industrial strategies in East Asia are not all the same; policies across countries and over time have both commonalities and differences. Japan does not represent all of East Asia, and it only practises and teaches one particular model derived from its own history and social structure. Even then, it is hoped that the Japanese model, especially its spiritual and methodological aspects, is instructive in realizing Ethiopia's economic aspirations. Japan can also talk about how other economies in East Asia are catching up due to its long experience of assisting them.

47.5 Ethiopia and the 'Flying Geese' Pattern of East Asia

East Asia is unique because it has attained economic development through the very existence of the East Asian region as a powerful arena for policy learning, production cooperation, and business competition among its member countries, and not by the effort of each country alone. One by one, countries in different development stages have participated in the dynamic production network created by private multinational corporations. Linked by trade and investment and assisted by economic cooperation, a regional division of labour with a clear order and structure emerged. Industrialization proceeded through geographic widening on the one hand and structural deepening within each country on the other. This supply-side phenomenon is called the Flying Geese pattern, through which East Asia has become the global factory of manufactured goods. No other developing region has such a collective growth mechanism.

For any economy in East Asia, development means jumping into this arena and becoming one crucial link in it, being on the receiving end of competitive pressure as well as cooperation from neighbouring economies, and upgrading industrial capabilities along the technological ladder. Over time, industries are passed from advanced economies to less advanced ones through FDI, so all latecomers seek to absorb as much manufacturing FDI as possible. What drives these countries is not conditionalities or policy matrices imposed by international organizations, but a nationalistic urge to achieve industrial excellence by copying the good practices of others.

Figure 47.1 illustrates industry passing among 'Flying Geese'. Taking a country (say, Japan), we can observe the transition of main activities along the time axis (direction 1).

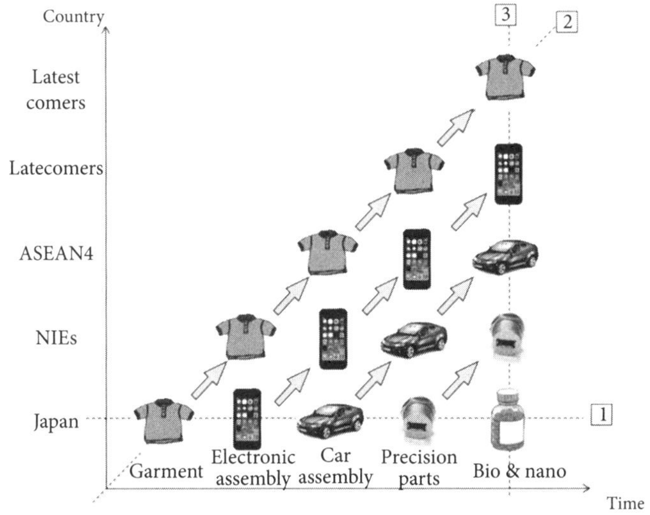

FIGURE 47.1 Structural transformation in East Asia

Source: prepared by the authors based on JICA & GRIPS Development Forum (2016).

Looking at a product (say, garment), we can diagonally trace shifting production sites across countries (direction 2). Taking a time (say, now), geographic distribution of activities within East Asia can be explained (direction 3). While reality is a little more complex than this, the picture illustrates, to a first approximation, the story of how order and structure are created in the regional production network.

For a long time Japan was the leading bird in this configuration, but late starters such as South Korea, Taiwan, and China are now ahead of Japan in certain high-tech and electronics sectors. In view of this, some observers say that the Flying Geese are now dead, and that what we see is random acrobatic flight. Even with some shifting players, however, order and structure are still clearly visible in East Asia—except that they are not exactly the same as before. If we allow the possibilities of overtaking and leapfrogging, we can confirm that the Flying Geese are still alive and well.

An accelerating inflow of labour-intensive light manufacturing FDI from emerging economies, including China, into Ethiopia implies that Ethiopia has just joined the Flying Geese formation of East Asia at its tail. FDI is also arriving from non-East Asian regions—India, Turkey, the European Union, the United States, and so on. This means that Ethiopia has entered an era in which past and current growth experiences of East Asia—both successes to emulate and failures to avoid—are directly relevant to its policy formulation. There is no other country on the African continent to which this statement applies more aptly. The policies needed to propel Ethiopia's industrialization forward must be forged carefully, and East Asia can offer many concrete suggestions.

47.6 Remaining Differences and Difficulties

East Asia exhibits a mixture of diverse developmental performance. Not all economies show miraculous growth. Some have already finished climbing to high income but others are trapped in upper- or lower-middle income, and still others have not even attained early industrialization. Colonialism, wars, and late start certainly mattered in the past, but the cause of diverse performance today essentially boils down to the presence or absence of two fundamental factors—private dynamism and policy competence. Japan, Singapore, Taiwan, and South Korea, which possessed vibrant private and public players, did not stop on the way to high income even though political and/or military shocks sometimes intervened temporarily. Meanwhile, the economies of Malaysia, Thailand, the Philippines, Indonesia, and Vietnam are slowing down at the middle-income stage due to various internal weaknesses. Cambodia, Laos, and Myanmar are at a very early stage of FDI-led growth with low industrial skills and technology. China, a huge country with many positive and negative aspects, is a special case for which simple assessment seems hardly possible.

Until recently Ethiopia resembled the third group of poor countries but it has made a big leap in the last fifteen years or so. The immediate national goal should be to catch up with East Asia's second group, namely, attaining middle income by 2025. Beyond that, the country has to avoid a middle-income trap, and this requires enhancement of private dynamism and policy competence for which effort must start now, not after 2025, to avoid slowdown at that time (see Chapter 41). Given this perspective, four final remarks are in order.

First, Ethiopia began from a very low point socially and economically and, despite recent high growth, it still stands at a low level on the long journey to industrialization. The private sector is very weak (see Chapter 39) and industrial policy remains primitive by East Asian standards even though national leaders are very active, manufacturing FDI is pouring in, and new buildings and infrastructure are being erected. Weaknesses are visible in the lack of elementary skill and discipline in workers, low productivity, slow growth, and the stagnant output and export of manufactured products (see Chapters 35 and 37). The business climate is unfavourable, Ethiopia ranking 161st among 190 entities in the World Bank's Doing Business assessment in 2018. National aspiration is high but current achievement is low. This hard fact must be admitted, and policy must be drafted in a pragmatic way to reflect this reality.

Second, the lack of competent technocrats prevents policy ideas being put into practice. Policy is often made hastily at high level without consideration of the applicability of the detailed design to Ethiopian reality. Speed is prioritized over quality. Top leaders are very busy but the rest of the administrative machinery seems inactive or incompetent—or both. In high-performing East Asian governments, policy decisions are made interactively in both top-down and bottom-up directions. A vision is first handed down from the top, then details are researched and decided by competent mid-level officials. Ministers are briefed on the essence and approve the final document. In Ethiopia, where such interactive decision-making does not occur, all substantive negotiation must be done with ministers or state ministers. This situation is surely not unique to Ethiopia; many developing countries face the problem of weak bureaucratic machinery. Analysts in East Asian studies conclude that a thick layer of professional and politically insulated technocrats have contributed greatly to high growth in such countries as Japan, Singapore, South Korea, and Taiwan (World Bank 1993; Campos and Root 1996), whereas countries without them are unable to rise beyond middle income. Ethiopia needs dramatic administrative reform that significantly boosts the capacity of bureaucrats while reducing their number.

Third, Ethiopia's industrial growth is taking place in Africa where conditions are quite different from East Asia. As noted above, the principal difference is the absence of the 'Flying Geese' pattern featuring a leading nation and structured layers of follower nations, and the resulting lack of strong trade, FDI, and aid linkages and technology transfer within the region. East Asia as a region provided a dynamic ground for each country to grow in mutual competition and cooperation, letting latecomers emulate the good practices of advanced teachers. But no such regional production network exists in

Africa. The relatively low income and small market size of Africa is another negative factor, which prompts most exporters to target EU or US markets using trade access privileges such as 'Everything but Arms' (EBA) and the African Growth and Opportunity Act (AGOA). This means that Ethiopia must industrialize as a solitary bird. It must directly face the global economy and work with any partner companies or countries from any region that offer business or cooperation opportunities because Africa as a region does not function as a collective factory or mentor. This requires certain adjustments when adopting East Asian lessons, especially regarding the formation of foreign partnership in marketing and knowledge transfer.

Finally, in today's world, there are newly emerging opportunities which Ethiopia should capture. In the twenty-first century, accelerated globalization and advances in ICT are changing the path of economic development. Due to technological progress and the reduced costs of transport and telecommunications, production of goods and services is becoming increasingly fragmented and is taking place in global networks spanning many countries. Global value chains are usually driven by lead firms which coordinate design, logistics, component supply, assembly, marketing, and branding in multiple locations around the globe to optimize their sourcing strategy (Bernhardt 2013). In this age, the absence of the 'Flying Geese' pattern around Ethiopia may no longer pose serious disadvantages because Ethiopia can participate in global value chains by becoming part of a particular chain where the country has comparative advantages—without necessarily having linkages at or near home (AfDB, OECD, and UNDP 2014). Yet, this requires vigorous efforts by the public and private sectors to enhance their policy, human, and enterprise capabilities so that the country can satisfy the international standards required by lead firms and keep upgrading its position in global value chains. This is a tall order for a latecomer. Geography and distance have certainly become less important than in previous centuries, but whether they have become irrelevant for economic development is an open question.

References

African Development Bank, Organisation for Economic Co-operation and Development, and United Nations Development Programme (2014). *African Economic Outlook 2014: Global Value Chain and Africa's Industrialization.*

Bernhardt, Thomas (2013). 'Developing Countries in the Global Apparel Value Chain: A Tale of Upgrading and Downgrading Experiences', Capturing the Gains Working Paper 22, University of Manchester.

Campos, Jose Edgardo and Hilton L. Root (1996). *The Key to the Asian Miracle: Making Shared Growth Credible* (Washington, DC: The Brookings Institution).

FDRE (2010). 'Growth and Transformation Plan (GTP) 2010/11–2014/15, Vol. I: Main Text', Ministry of Finance and Economic Development (English Translation), Addis Ababa.

FDRE (2016). 'Growth and Transformation Plan II (GTP II) 2015/16–2019/20, Vol. I: Main Text', National Planning Commission (English Translation), Addis Ababa.

GRIPS Development Forum (ed.) (2008). 'Diversity and Complementarity in Development Aid: East Asian Lessons for African Growth', National Graduate Institute for Policy Studies (GRIPS) Development Forum Report, Tokyo.

GRIPS Development Forum (2016). 'Records of Ethiopia-Japan Industrial Policy Dialogue Vol. I: Policy Dialogue and Research in Ethiopia', National Graduate Institute for Policy Studies (in Japanese), Tokyo.

JICA and GRIPS Development Forum (2011). 'Kaizen National Movement: A Study of Quality and Productivity Improvement in Asia and Africa', GRIPS Development Forum, Tokyo.

JICA and GRIPS Development Forum (2016). 'Assisting Industrial Transformation in Africa: Japan-Ethiopia Industrial Policy Dialogue Phase II', GRIPS Development Forum, Tokyo.

Ohno, Izumi and Kenichi Ohno (2012). 'Dynamic Capacity Development: What Africa Can Learn from Industrial Policy Formulation in East Asia', in *Good Growth and Governance in Africa: Rethinking Development Strategies*, ed. A. Norman, K. Botchwey, H. Stein, and J. E. Stiglitz (New York: Oxford University Press): 221–45.

Ohno, Kenichi (2013). *Learning to Industrialize: From Given Growth to Policy-Aided Value Creation* (New York: Routledge).

Ohno, Kenichi and Izumi Ohno (eds) (2013). *Eastern and Western Ideas for African Growth: Diversity and Complementarity in Development Aid*. Routledge-GRIPS Development Forum Studies (London: Routledge).

World Bank (1993). *The East Asian Miracle: Economic Growth and Public Policy* (Oxford: Oxford University Press).

CHAPTER 48

INSTITUTION BUILDING FOR INDUSTRIALIZATION

The Case of the Ethiopian Investment Commission

JOHN SUTTON

48.1 Introduction

Foreign Direct Investment has played a central role in Ethiopia's push for industrialization, and developing the appropriate institutional structures to support the attraction, retention, and expansion of FDI projects has been an important focus of policy over the past decade (see Chapter 35).

A key role in any such effort is played by the host country's investment agency, and the academic literature points to the value for developing countries of having a well-functioning agency (Harding and Javorcik 2011). The literature also points to the importance of placing the control of the agency at the highest levels of government, with the head of the agency reporting directly to the prime minister or president (Morisset 2003). As to the scope of the agency's activities, it is well understood from international experience that a narrow focus on attracting investors ('investment promotion') is not enough; rather, the agency's remit needs to have at its core the duty of helping incoming companies remove unnecessary and inappropriate obstacles that prevent them from becoming operational. Once the firms begin operating, the work of the agency continues; ongoing liaison can lead to the early identification of both problems and opportunities. The value of such 'aftercare' in generating additional jobs through expansion projects has been demonstrated in the literature (Miskinis and Byrka 2014). In Ireland, for example, half the jobs created by foreign firms are generated through the expansion of firms already operating in the country; indeed, it is regularly emphasized by practitioners that it is far easier to encourage and support expansion by existing investors than to identify and cultivate new leads.

This process of relationship building by way of continued contact with incoming firms through both the pre-operational stage and the early years of operation lies at the heart of international best practice for investment agencies. Pioneered in the 1970s by Finland, Singapore, and Ireland, its central aim is to shift the culture of the agency away from 'putting out fires', in favour of a carefully managed programme of regular contact with firms that are significant employment creators. This allows issues to be dealt with before they turn into crises.

Establishing such a programme at an investment agency involves a major effort, the focus of which is to change the day-to-day practices of professional staff, through establishing routines and procedures built around a series of regular meetings at which firms and issues are reviewed in a standard and systematic way, and actions are agreed that will be implemented before the next meeting of the group.

While it requires considerable time to establish the new practices and procedures, the benefits that flow from the programme are considerable and far-reaching. The new way of working allows the agency to offer a hugely improved level of service to foreign companies arriving in the country, and to foreign companies wishing to expand their activities and create further employment.

Further benefits also follow. A central part of the programme lies in the creation of a systematic and regularly updated database of those foreign companies that create significant numbers of jobs, and these companies are typically major exporters. The systematic tracking of all issues that hold back their success in creating jobs and generating exports not only allows the agency to focus its priorities on removing critical obstacles, but also provides the agency with a wealth of information that it needs in liaising with other ministries and with the Office of the Prime Minister.

In what follows, we begin with the story of how a relationship-building programme was established at the (then) Ethiopian Investment Agency, and how the programme evolved over time under the leadership of commissioner Fitsum Arega and (later) deputy commissioner Teka Gebreyesus.[1] We then evaluate the performance of the programme and describe the wider benefits that have flowed from it in recent years, both in respect of the management of relations in industrial parks, and in establishing better ways of tracking firms' export performance within the Office of the Prime Minister.

48.2 Establishing the Relationship-Building Programme

Early in 2013, Fitsum Arega took up his position as Director General. Building on a report delivered in 2012 by the International Growth Centre at the London School of Economics, he began to put in place the structures and procedures that underpin

[1] In April 2018 Fitsum Arega was reassigned to the Office of the Prime Minister, as chief of staff of the new prime minister. Dr Belachew Mekuria Frkre was appointed the new commissioner of the EIC.

the relationship-building programme. He also initiated the setting up of a 'one stop shop' system, which was almost fully implemented within eight months. All documentation requirements were brought in house, with twenty-seven of the twenty-nine documents administered directly at the agency, while the remaining two were dealt with for the licence seeker by agency personnel. But one-stop-shop arrangements, valuable as they are, constitute only a first step in bringing an investment agency up to global best practice standards. Much more central, and much more challenging, is the establishment of a full-blown relationship-building programme, and it is this that lay at the heart of the agency's endeavours during 2014 and 2015.

48.3 Selecting the Firms

The relationship-building programme requires, to begin with, the appointment of a single named contact person for each firm; an initial visit to establish relations; and subsequent regular visits or phone conversations (by the contact person or their regional counterpart).

The benefits of maintaining regular contact with companies both in their pre-operational phase, and after they begin operations, are enormous. In the pre-operational phase, good contacts between the agency and the company maximize the probability that the company will become operational. Once the company has become operational, the continued support of the agency through regular contacts will enhance the likelihood of its successful future expansion, and its creation of new activities that generate further jobs. Above all, these regular contacts allow the agency to anticipate problems on which it can be helpful to the company, and avoid these problems becoming critical. Efforts by the agency to tackle a problem at an early stage involve much less energy than 'putting out fires' once the problem has become critical.

This kind of programme rests on the establishment of new practices and procedures within the agency. Putting these new practices and procedures in place, and working within them over a sustained period so that they become the normal method of working within the agency, is the central task in establishing the programme.

Within the (then) EIA, these new routines began with the setting up of five groups of professional staff to deal with the five main sectors: agro-processing, chemicals and pharmaceuticals, leather and textiles, metals, and other manufacturing. Each group was charged with identifying, and agreeing with the Director, a preliminary list of firms to include in the programme. A rule of thumb in selecting this group of (pre-operational or operational) firms was that they should employ, or aim to employ, over fifty people; but this rule of thumb was supplemented by other sector-specific criteria in selecting the initial group to be incorporated. The key idea motivating a 'minimum size' criterion is that the agency's time and effort should be focused on job creation: the vast majority of new jobs come from a small fraction of medium-sized and larger companies, and scarce time and resources must be focused on these firms.

Starting with an initial set of some two hundred firms, new systems were put in place, and as these became well established, the coverage of the programme was extended to the point where it now covers over four hundred companies.

48.4 Establishing the Practices

When the system was first put in place, between 2013 and 2015, each of the five groups met weekly, usually on Mondays, to review all company visits and contacts made in the preceding week, and to update the information on each company. Each visit or phone call to a company was recorded in a computer-based company folder. These folders were set up as an electronic file, which became part of the shared database of the relationship-building team.

At the weekly meetings, group members reviewed progress, and updated information on each company's status on a standard form. A report was then prepared and sent by email to the director general, so that he obtained a weekly update of the work of each industry group. At the end of each month, a review meeting was held at which each of the group leaders presented an update on their companies to the director general in the presence of their professional colleagues. A uniform PowerPoint presentation format was used across all groups to set out the present status of contacts with companies, and news relating to changed circumstances at any company.

A standard form was used to summarize the state of company contacts. The time that had elapsed since the last visit or contact with each company was recorded, and the state of the company's details as recorded in its folder was summarized.

Each company's folder was designed to contain scanned documents previously kept in paper form in the archive of the agency. All this information was uploaded as a single file within the new computer-based system. This allowed the director general and team members unprecedented easy access to all relevant information on a company, prior to discussions with them about any new issues that arose.

By June 2014, all these arrangements were in place, and the benefits of the scheme were becoming apparent through the positive feedback the agency was receiving from firms. These benefits were quite tangible and specific. One example will serve to illustrate the value of the high level of information that was now reaching the director general: one of the points flagged by the textiles group in a weekly report related to a company that had tax problems that threatened its survival. An immediate investigation by the director general led to his advising the owner of some crucial details of her obligations and entitlements under Ethiopian tax law. She had been unaware of some key aspects of the relevant laws and regulations, and the problem was essentially solved, assuring the firm's survival.

The central achievement of the programme in this initial phase of its operation, up to mid-2014, lay in carrying through the tedious but essential work of embedding new practices and procedures, and insisting that these be followed rigorously on a week-to-week basis, while providing group leaders with constant support from day to day so that their work was focused on being fully prepared for all forthcoming weekly and monthly meetings, and on ensuring that all firm folders were complete and up to date. By this point, in mid-2014, the number of firms in the programme had reached 250, and the regularity of contacts had reached a very satisfactory level.

48.5 A New Beginning: The Designation of the EIA as a Commission

In June 2014, a proclamation of the Ethiopian parliament established the status of the agency as a Commission responsible to the prime minister, and governed by a body comprising nine members of whom seven are government ministers concerned with economic affairs. The proclamation also extended the remit of the agency to cover investment promotion, industrial parks, and export promotion.

As these new arrangements came into force, a new organizational structure was designed, within which commissioner Fitsum Arega would henceforward be supported by three deputy commissioners, one of whom, Ato Teka Gebreyesus, was assigned to lead the relationship-building programme. Under his leadership the programme has developed in new and important directions. Its scale increased to include over four hundred companies by early 2015, and procedures and practices have evolved in a highly fruitful manner, as the commissioner, the deputy commissioner and the team of professional colleagues have explored new ways of organizing their work, and new ways of handling those types of problem that crop up on a regular basis. This is the story we turn to in Section 48.6.

48.6 How the Programme Evolved (2015–17)

The acid test for the successful establishment of a relationship-building programme is that it should take on a life of its own. Ownership of the programme should be taken by the people who run it, and their efforts to develop and improve its operation should lead to major qualitative changes in practices and procedures. As the team's experience in running the system, and their constant experimentation with new ways of tackling recurring problems, lead them to develop new methods that reflect local circumstances, opportunities, and constraints, they arrive at more efficient and effective ways of getting results.

This key transition to an evolving system was achieved under the leadership of commissioner Fitsum Arega and deputy commissioner Teka Gebreyesus during the period 2015–17. The two key strands in the evolution of the system were the establishment of practices and procedures, and the development of new ways of handling recurring issues.

In March 2015, the commissioner initiated a reorganization of the agenda for monthly meetings. The business of the meeting was organized, not by going sequentially through the full list of firms, but by reference to a list of currently live issues that had been designated as such at some previous meeting of the group ('tabled issues'). This streamlined the working of the group and has since become standard practice.

A second key innovation was to designate a single colleague to become the lead person for problems of a specific type. Thus, for example, EIC now has a single Point Person for power issues, a single Point Person for land issues, and a single Point Person for liaison with Ethiopian Shipping Lines. This led to a mode of operation in which it is understood that certain kinds of issues are dealt with at different levels/through different channels.

The key levels/channels now used are: (a) the firm's contact person ('expert') at EIC; (b) the Point Person for the type of issue; and (c) commissioner or deputy commissioner level.

The single biggest advantage of this is that problems of a given type are 'bundled', so they can be dealt with as a group, saving time not only for EIC personnel but also for their counterparts in other ministries or organizations. A second advantage is that the internal management of issues is smoother and more efficient, since new issues are immediately channelled in a standard manner.

It is worth looking at some examples of this process within particular categories of issue.

48.6.1 Power

The Ethiopian Electric Power Corporation (EEPCo) was divided into two separate entities, Ethiopian Electric Power and Ethiopian Electric Service (EES). EES, tasked with electricity delivery service, is the entity the EIC works with to enable investors to meet their electricity demands.

Power issues are among the most commonly occurring, and various experts and team leaders had in the past been contacting EEPCO individually. It was decided at a monthly meeting that a Point Person would be designated to communicate all issues arising in operational firms to EEPCO. This resulted in EIC having more formal communication pathways and thus receiving better and more timely information from EEPCO. This also allowed the EIC to 'bundle' certain issues that have a common solution (as, for example, with power relays that may be affecting multiple companies).

48.6.2 Land

An application for land acquisition is sometimes made during an early field visit by an investor, but is often made after the firm has acquired an investment licence. The EIC has a mandate to facilitate the allocation of land for FDI projects throughout the country. Urban land for use by investors is available on an auction basis. The auction prices vary, depending on demand. The cost of the lease of urban and rural land varies according to location, the type of investment, and the characteristics of the land. The leased land cannot be mortgaged or sold.

Some sectors have been affected by recent changes in legal rules. Under the Urban Land Proclamation 721/2011, the right to acquire land by bidding in auctions announced in public advertisements was extended to investors in the service sector (e.g. hotels, schools, hospitals). Experts at the EIC assist investors by seeking opportunities to bid following public advertisements, and they actively seek out opportunities and encourage investors to bid. With these considerations in mind, a single Point Person was appointed to handle all land-related issues tabled.

48.6.3 Business Licences

Most business licence-related issues can be solved by the firm's EIC contact person. However, this is an area where occasional problems require action by the commissioner. For example, in one case, the firm in question became operational (selling products) without taking out a business licence from the EIC. The EIC contact person ('expert') repeatedly contacted the company and urged them to take out a business licence. The company refused, as they believed that they did not need a licence by virtue of the fact that they are a constituent company of a parent company that already had a licence. Finally, the company met with the commissioner, who discussed the issue at the relevant government department. New regulations were implemented, and the company will not now need to take out a licence from the EIC.

Another such case involved a firm that expanded into a new area of business and became operational (started selling) using their old business licence. The EIC contact person ('expert') repeatedly advised the firm that an additional (expansion) licence was needed, but the firm declined to accept this advice. Only with the intervention of the commissioner was the issue resolved.

48.6.4 Liaison with Other Ministries

Most problems falling under this heading relate to logistics, and many of these require liaison with the Customs Ministry; the record of success in resolving these issues is high. There are, however, other kinds of logistics issues, the most notable being those related to shipping services. Many companies across all sectors import resources via Ethiopian Shipping Lines and face various logistical issues. A Point Person was therefore designated to handle all such issues. This colleague now meets regularly with Ethiopian Shipping Lines representatives.

48.6.5 Summing Up

During the past year, the commissioner, the deputy commissioner, and the group leaders have developed new and more effective ways of handling recurring problems. This is important for two reasons. First, it has raised the effectiveness of the EIC. Second, it has shown that the relationship-building programme is now fully internalized at the Commission, and its custom and practice has been designed by the team itself, on the basis of the system originally introduced in 2013, but fine-tuned under the leadership of deputy commissioner Ato Teka to the particular circumstances of the Ethiopian Ministries and the Commission.

48.7 Evaluating the Programme

The many ways in which the performance of an investment agency can be evaluated were set out in detail in a United Nations report of 2008, which discusses, for example, the solicitation of feedback from firms on their dealings with the agency (UNCTAD 2008: 41). In what follows, we are concerned with the separate issue of internal assessment, i.e. the monitoring by the team of its own record in dealing with issues.

Perhaps the best way to evaluate the programme as it now operates is to examine the number and proportion of tabled issues that are resolved, and the time taken to resolve them, by type of issue and sector. While this seems easy in principle, it is fraught with complications that make it necessary to treat any results in a very cautious way. Nonetheless, it is the best available metric, and the aim of this section is to set out a snapshot of the rates of resolution now being achieved as compiled for the relationship-building team to allow it to monitor its own future performance.

48.7.1 The Caveats

We begin by noting the complications that must be borne in mind when using the data presented below. The most important caveat lies in the fact that the system is evolving over time in ways that change the mix of issues tabled. For example, some types of issue will come to be handled 'out of committee' through direct action by one designated expert from the group. This means that such issues are no longer tabled. But if the rate of resolution of these issues were higher, or lower, than the average rate for all other tabled issues, then the figure for the rate of resolution of issues in the future would be biased downwards, or upwards, making a comparison with the figure for an earlier period invalid.

It might seem at first glance that figures could easily be corrected to allow for this. Suppose, for example, that we knew in advance that some set of issues would be taken 'off committee'. Then, with sufficient time, we might define the relevant 'class of issues', and calculate a separate figure for the rate of resolution of issues of this class. Armed with that figure, we could correct the new, or the old, figure for rates of resolution, and eliminate the problematic bias. But the whole point of the present arrangement is to allow the group's growing experience in dealing with different problems to shape its deliberations as to how it can more efficiently handle different types of issue. Classifications of problems are themselves shifting over time as the group learns from dealing with specific issues, initially in ad hoc ways, and only over time comes to a neat solution.

With that caveat in mind, we cautiously present one key measure of progress. During May–October 2015, we tracked a large cohort of 'all issues tabled'. There were sixty-nine issues tabled, and 51 per cent of them were resolved within six months. By way of comparison, for the most recent period on which we have data (all 82 issues tabled during June 2016 to December 2016), the six-month resolution rate was 71 per cent. Thus the rate of resolution has increased substantially. Now this comparison is, as we have just noted, fraught with difficulties, and if the change were more modest, we might question whether it was driven by biases of measurement. But the rate of improvement, over the critical year that began as the present operating practices of the group took shape, is large enough to suggest that a real improvement in the effectiveness of the programme has been achieved.

It is interesting to dig deeper, and to ask where the improved performance occurred in terms of types of issue, and so on. But as we noted earlier, the mix of issues being tabled has evolved over time, and so any comparison must be treated with caution.

48.7.2 Resolution Rates by Type of Issue

Tables 48.1 and 48.2 provide a summary of issues tabled, rates of resolution, and the number of days (average and median) it took the teams to resolve these problems. In aggregate, 71 per cent of the issues tabled during the recent period were resolved within six months. For those issues that were resolved, it took an average of eighty-eight days to reach resolution. The median period for resolution is fifty-eight days. The difference between the mean and the median indicates that there are a small number of issues that require a relatively long time to resolve.

Table 48.1 Issues tabled and proportion resolved, May to October 2015

Issues tabled and proportion resolved				Total days to resolve	
Types of issues	Number of issues tabled	Issues resolved	Per cent resolved	Mean	Median
Customs	4	4	100	32	33
Land	25	11	44	51	38
Licensing	14	11	79	80	68
Others	13	2	15	42	45
Power	13	7	54	87	38
Grand total	**69**	**35**	**51**	**64**	**38**

Source: EIC database 2017

Table 48.2 Issues tabled and proportion resolved, June to December 2016

Issues tabled and proportion resolved				Total days to resolve	
Types of issues	Number of issues tabled	Issues resolved	Per cent resolved	Mean	Median
Customs	20	16	80	86	180
Land	10	5	50	161	188
Licensing	10	9	90	51	32
Others	21	14	67	67	45
Power	21	14	67	111	91
Grand Total	**82**	**58**	**71**	**88**	**58**

Source: EIC database 2017

Licensing and customs issues have the highest rates of resolution. In the more recent period, all but one of the ten tabled licensing issues were resolved, with the median time to resolution being a month and the mean below two months. This strong and timely resolution is indicative of the fact that the EIC has substantial oversight over licensing and is not dependent on other institutions to help resolve these issues.

For customs issues, there are three reasons why a relatively high proportion of issues are resolved. First, unlike some of the other issues listed (e.g. land and power), the Customs Authority has an office at EIC with authority to make investment-related decisions on site. The power authorities do not have a representative office at EIC, while land issues are dealt with at regional level.

Second, in the past, customs issues were handled in an ad hoc manner, and recurring issues were not dealt with in a standard way. The new operating processes put in place by deputy commissioner Ato Teka meant that recurring customs issues were now handled in a uniform way. Many of these issues involve questions of interpretation of existing customs rules; such issues now came to be dealt with in a smooth and effective manner.

The third factor relates to requests for exemptions from customs restrictions or duties. These requests tended to involve disproportionate effort by senior management and group members, usually leading to a negative outcome. The Commission decided in mid-2016 that it would no longer entertain requests for exemptions, subject to occasional exceptions. This provided clarity to investors and reduced the number of requests coming forward.

Land and power issues are relatively difficult to resolve, and are the most time consuming. Together, they constitute a third of all issues tabled, and those that are resolved take an average of 161 and 111 days respectively to resolution. Some recent instances of national unrest were linked to land issues and there is a careful deliberative process for allocating land, which is generally carried out at regional level.

Power issues are of two kinds: the first relates to the absence of the power grid in areas where certain investors locate. The second relates to the availability of industrial power capacity in some areas. Infrastructure building and planning issues impose delays in resolving these issues.

48.7.3 Resolution Rates by Sector

Tables 48.3 and 48.4 provide summary data for issues classified by sector.

In agriculture, half of the issues were about land and power (as against 42 per cent for our sample as a whole), and the time to resolution is particularly long. The agriculture sector was particularly affected by political unrest in July–November 2016, and the team leader was heavily engaged in a committee dealing with compensation claims. The team was also affected by the transfer of other members to new duties.

The leather group is a new one, spun off from the former textiles and leather group, and is staffed by new members of the team. Issues in the sector were heavily biased towards customs and licensing. While the median time to resolve is sixty-two days, the average rate is quite high, reflecting the fact that there are a small number of issues that are relatively difficult to resolve. In the chemicals sector, two-thirds of issues related to land and power. The team has been relatively successful in dealing with these, with 82 per cent of issues resolved, though the average time to resolution was relatively long, reflecting the difficulty of these issues. In the 'other manufacturing' sector, two-thirds of issues relate to the relatively tractable areas of licensing and customs, and this is reflected in the team's high rate of resolution.

The agro-processing sector has the lowest rate of resolution. This partly reflects two factors. First, companies in this sector face damage and theft issues associated with recent political unrest. Second, there are some unusual and difficult legal issues that remain unresolved.

Table 48.3 Issues resolved by sector, May to October 2015

Issues resolved by sector				Total days to resolve	
Sector	Number of issues tabled	Issues resolved	Per cent resolved	Mean	Median
Agriculture	7	4	57	98	82
Agro-processing	8	6	75	57	42
Chemicals	12	7	58	95	38
Leather and textile	17	7	41	73	35
Metals	8	3	38	16	5
Other manufacturing	14	5	36	28	38
Services	3	3	100	52	48
Grand total	**69**	**35**	**51**	**64**	**38**

Source: EIC database 2017

Table 48.4 Issues resolved by sector, June to December 2016

Issues resolved by sector				Total days to resolve	
Sector	Number of issues tabled	Issues resolved	Per cent resolved	Mean	Median
Agriculture	5	3	60	173	210
Agro-processing	16	9	56	97	80
Chemicals	11	9	82	99	97
Leather	17	13	76	100	62
Metals	14	9	64	109	87
Other manufacturing	11	8	73	26	20
Textile and garment	8	7	88	49	32
Grand Total	**82**	**58**	**71**	**88**	**58**

Source: EIC database 2017

48.7.4 Unresolved Issues

Of the 82 issues tabled in the recent period, 24 remained unresolved after six months. Of these, four related to customs, five to land, one to licensing and seven to power. The remaining seven issues fell into three areas: (a) damage and theft; (b) community disputes; and (c) loan requests.

These are somewhat intractable issues that may remain unresolved for some time. Power issues constitute almost one-third of unresolved issues (seven of twenty-four). The team is currently examining this area by mapping out grid expansion in collaboration with Ethiopia Electric Utility (EEU), in order to see how new investments in power supply can be aligned with investors' needs. Land issues tend to be particularly sensitive, and some will always be long-lived.

Outstanding customs issues are mostly historical, in the sense that they relate to requests for exemptions that pre-date the Commission's new, restrictive, policy in this area. These requests still need to be considered, and can prove slow to resolve.

48.7.5 Pitfalls with Metrics

While the metrics described above offer a very valuable way for the Commission to monitor its own performance, it is important that these metrics are not used by any outside group to assess the performance of the relationship-building team. The reasons for this are familiar, and important: if metrics of this kind were used by an outside body to monitor the progress of the Commission, it would distort decision-making within the group, to the detriment of performance. This is because we are dealing with a system that is not static, but which is being constantly improved by changing the ways in which issues are addressed. If the Commission's attention became focused on achieving certain targets in relation to the above metrics, then it would become less attractive to move issues that had become easier to deal with 'off committee'. Yet the movement of such issues 'off committee' is one of the best ways to enhance effectiveness, and is in fact a measure of the group's success.

This pitfall in the use of performance metrics, often referred to in the literature as Goodhart's Law (Goodhart 1975), forms the starting point for the recent critique of the misuse of metrics, which has been most fully developed by Muller (2018). External monitoring of the relationship-building team's performance by reference to the above metrics would actually cause that performance as measured externally to appear to improve more slowly: monitoring of this kind should be an in-house activity carried out by and for the team members, who make the decisions as to what issues get tabled, and can themselves best interpret changes in measured resolution rates.

48.8 The Wider Pay-offs

Two recent developments have been set in motion as a result of the work of the relationship-building programme: use of the group's database to strengthen the tracking of export performance; and an extension of the EIC's role to industrial parks.

48.8.1 Tracking Export Performance

This work relates to the prime minister's monthly Export Report meeting which is attended by various government agencies. The EIC has for some time been providing support for these meetings. In order to strengthen the quality of information provided, the EIC undertook, as of November 2016, the preparation of a detailed analysis of the performance of key exporting firms.

The first stage of this work built directly on the database developed as part of the relationship-building programme, which by that time had come to cover over 400 companies. The relationship-building team has detailed and up-to-date information on these firms, of a kind that allows them to show what kinds of obstacles might stand in the way of the achievement of target levels of exports in the coming months. This lies at the heart of the agenda of these meetings: the goal is to provide early warnings of obstacles to exporting, and thereby trigger early intervention. This demands a deep familiarity with current developments at the company, of the kind that the relationship-building process generates.

In a recent extension of this work, the Commission secured from the Ethiopian Revenue and Customs Authority data on all export transactions from 2015/16 and

2016/17, which included, for each exporter, its identity and location, and the value, weight, and destination of each of its consignments.

This analysis proved extremely enlightening in showing that the data and information provided by some companies was very unreliable and potentially misleading, and the EIC now plans to extend and strengthen this strand of its work.

48.8.2 Industrial Parks

A major initiative began in 2015 to establish a new generation of industrial parks. A successful carryover of the relationship-building model will be an important ingredient in the success of these parks. There are many differences in the operating environment of firms in industrial parks, as against firms operating outside the parks. The main difference is that two of the leading problem areas discussed in Section 48.6—land and power—are largely resolved by the existence of industrial parks. A third area, liaison with the Customs Ministry, takes on a different form in this environment, in that each park has an on-site customs team. But new problems arise in industrial parks that reflect the fact that firms are operating in a newly constructed physical environment with a unique set of problems impinging on all firms in each park.

Notwithstanding the difference in the menu of issues, what continues to be valid is the use of a structured approach that aims to avoid a culture of 'putting out fires'. As the parks filled with investors, the EIC had to address the challenge of designing a suitably modified reporting and monitoring structure that could carry through these objectives to this new environment.

48.9 Conclusions

When the relationship-building programme was established at the then EIA in 2013, the aim was to transform the culture of the agency by establishing new practices and procedures to support a programme of the kind pioneered fifty years ago by Finland, Ireland, and Singapore, and which now constitutes international best practice in the running of investment agencies. This goal has been achieved, and the Ethiopian Investment Commission now operates a programme that is fully in the hands of a team that consists wholly of EIC personnel.

The most striking measure of success lies in the fact that, over the course of 2016 and 2017, the team itself, led by commissioner Fitsum Arega and deputy commissioner Ato Teka Gebreyesus, took over the reshaping of practices and procedures, and introduced new and better ways of handling recurring problems, which involved taking many types of issue off the table to be dealt with by individual team members following new and standardized procedures. In other words, the in-house team took ownership of this programme and shaped it in a way that is optimal for the environment in which the Commission operates.

Developing an effective investment agency is a slow process that requires dedicated leadership exercised in a consistent way over a lengthy period. Best practice in this area is well understood, and easily communicated. It is the implementation of this practice that is the challenge: changing habits, establishing procedures, and painstakingly following new routines until a different way of working becomes the norm.

References

Goodhart, C. A. E. (1975). *Monetary Theory and Practice: The UK Experience* (London: Macmillan).

Harding, Torfinn and Beata Javorcik (2011). 'Roll out the Red Carpet and They Will Come: Investment Promotion and FDI Inflows', *Economic Journal* 121 (557): 1445–76.

Miskinis, Algirdas and Mariya Byrka (2014). 'The Role of Investment Promotion Agencies in Attracting Foreign Direct Investment', *Ekonomika* 93 (4): 41–57.

Morisset, Jacques (2003). 'Does a Country Need a Promotion Agency to Attract Foreign Direct Investment? A Small Analytical Model Applied to 58 Countries', World Bank Policy Research Working Paper No. 3028, Washington, DC.

Muller, Jerry Z. (2018). *The Tyranny of Metrics* (Princeton, NJ: Princeton University Press).

UNCTAD (2008). 'Evaluating Investment Promotion Agencies', Investment Advisory Series, Series A, No. 3, United Nations, New York and Geneva.

CHAPTER 49

THREE SECTORAL POLICIES IN ETHIOPIA'S STRUCTURAL TRANSFORMATION

CARLOS LOPES

49.1 Introduction

The debate on African development policymaking has shifted from externally crafted projects such as the ill-fated Structural Adjustment Programmes (SAPs) to a new Africa narrative championing human capital development, technology adoption, industrialization, and export-led manufacturing. These sweeping political and economic changes have been heralded by reformed global power structures, realigned international relations, and the loosening of old hegemonies and assessment of existing development paradigms. Now, these changes present a huge opportunity for Africa to emerge as a global economic player but not without serious challenges that leaders must navigate. These development challenges require African countries to embark on bold and wide-ranging structural economic transformation and massive industrialization to realize their development objectives (Lopes et al. 2017; Soludo et al. 2004; Monga and Lin 2015).

In retrospect, Africans perceive Ethiopia as the ultimate manifestation of this structural transformation-cum-industrialization promise, with sustained economic growth above that of the continent and the world average achieved during the last two decades. The government has pursued broad-based pro-poor policies with, on average, about 70 per cent of the national budget allocated to social development and poverty reduction (in education, health, agriculture, access to clean drinking water and sanitation, and roads). The decline in poverty is the result of the successful implementation of the Productive Safety Net Programme (PSNP) as well as systematic tracking of food insecurity dimensions for appropriate social targeting in the form of distribution of household necessities such as wheat, sugar, and cooking oil (AfDB, OECD, and UNDP 2017), leading to absolute poverty decreasing more than food poverty (IMF 2015). Furthermore, income inequality has remained extremely low as measured by the Gini coefficient, 0.298 in 2010/11 from 0.3 in 2004/5, making it one the most egalitarian countries in the world. In urban areas it has declined to 0.37 from 0.44 over the same period (AfDB, OECD, and UNDP 2017; IMF 2015).

Likewise, Ethiopia has managed to maintain a robust fiscal policy with a positive distributional impact on income inequality, despite increasing tax collection and rising fiscal pressure, standing at 12.8 per cent in 2015. Ethiopia, like most countries in Africa, has a low tax-to-GDP ratio and disproportionate addiction to trade taxes (IMF 2015). Performing tax administration and enforcement capacity kept the deficits within acceptable thresholds—2 per cent in 2014/15—with the real amount of collected revenue growing at an average of 30 per cent annually for the last ten years (NPC 2016).

Concomitantly, Ethiopia has managed to keep its urban population at around 20 per cent (out of 100 million), making it one of the least urbanized countries in the world. Likewise, it has demonstrated the role played by the emerging planning capacity in limiting urban expansion, promoting impressive housing schemes, and infrastructure investments as well as a decentralized higher education system.[1] These impressive social indicators were obtained through national strategies embodied in the Growth and Transformation Plans (GTP) I and II. These elements of Ethiopia's post-1991 development are elaborated and assessed in other chapters of this *Handbook*.[2]

The main objective of GTP-I and GTP-II was to promote growth with structural transformation. Economic growth has exceeded 10 per cent in the period between 2004 and 2013, outperforming the country's peers and commanding world attention. World Bank PPP comparisons show Ethiopia following China in a tight twenty-five-year gap growth trajectory, which is a better performance than countries such as India or Bangladesh.

In short, Ethiopia's stellar growth performance, guided by amicable development planning, has created a common and shared agenda for economic transformation that has fostered better social outcomes in poverty, universal education, child health, and combating AIDS.[3] The following sections introduce three sectors (or case studies on industrialization, Ethiopian Airlines, and food security), to demonstrate how Ethiopia has been able to couple economic growth and social development on the road to structural transformation.

[1] For more details on Ethiopia's structural transformation policies, see Chapter 9.

[2] For example, Chapters 5 and 11 ably demonstrate this point.

[3] See, for example, Chapter 19.

49.2 Ethiopia's Industrialization Experiment

In 1994, Ethiopia adopted the Agricultural Development-Led Industrialization (ADLI) strategy, and in 2015 the leadership decided to proceed to the next stage of the industrialization ladder. Manufacturing was anticipated as the future propeller of economic growth, as captured in GTP-II:

> The Ethiopian experience shows that development policy is complex and highly contested, and that industrial policy is no different. Carefully thought-through policies are necessary but not sufficient to produce desired results. Policies often yield intended outcomes only when driven by 'transformative' institutions, and where there is strong state capacity (and adaptive capacity) to pursue goals and enough flexibility to allow for course changes when things go wrong. These attributes have to become embedded in institutionalized policy learning.
>
> (Oqubay 2015: 296)

Admittedly, the early years of implementation of the new industrial strategy faced a depressed global demand for commodities, contributing to low prices, accompanied by severe drought and social and political unrest and the declaration of a state of emergency (Delte Gardner 2018). However, the Ethiopian economy was able to shrug off these external and internal constraints. Economic growth decreased from an average of 10 per cent to the new normal of 7 to 8 per cent, while manufacturing's contribution to GDP stagnated at below 5 per cent (Gebreeyesus 2013).

The adoption of the strategy came at a time when technological developments caused China, one of Ethiopia's key partners, to start questioning its strategy of delocalizing industries from China towards other destinations such as those in Africa (Sun 2017). Artificial intelligence and machine efficiency could replace traditional tasks on a much larger scale than previously anticipated, leading to doubts about potential investments based on labour costs.

49.3 How Did the Debate on Industrial Policy Evolve?

Oqubay (2015) remained engaged in the topic both from a scholarly and policy practice perspective, expanding his network of like-minded Africa specialists. In an effort to overcome the pessimism blown in by persistent headwinds, he sought to persuade key policymakers in Ethiopia of the need to rather accelerate what had been agreed.

The building of industrial parks planned for various locations in the country, as a trigger for an export-led strategy, was by far the biggest bet.

GTP-I had plans to build five industrial parks but in fact none was completed during the period of the plan. The first attempt, Bole Lemi Industrial Park, took five years to be completed and created only 3,000 jobs.[4]

The experience of Mauritius was particularly relevant. After experiencing rapid growth through well-sequenced reforms and an active industrial policy, the limitations of the model were becoming apparent when the 2008–9 global financial crisis made the case more urgent. The country realized that in order to sustain its value-added economic trajectory it needed to improve its productivity performance through two key instruments: trade policy and labour policy (World Bank 2010). On trade it needed to go beyond reducing tariffs and visible non-tariff barriers, through improvements in the policy and regulatory environment to increase competitiveness. It had to explore further measures to reduce exporters' costs while stimulating spillovers from exporting to domestic firms.

On labour, unskilled workers needed to be moved to the transformations in course (low end of the market) and there needed to be capacity to generate and absorb high-skilled workers in the high-end segment. The balance between the competitiveness and social agendas is a challenge in itself, but placing Mauritius in a position to jump ahead of the technological impact on labour costs made the task urgent and more complex (World Bank 2010).

Hawassa Industrial Park, located in the southern part of Ethiopia, became the model park to test new institutional arrangements and mobilize anchor investors, the so-called 'queen bees'. The 130-hectare-park was built by a Chinese engineering company in a year, at a cost of US$250 million, with 150km of integrated pipelines and roads and a Zero Liquid Discharge system.[5] It is located next to a new university that specializes in disciplines of interest to textile production, the sole focus of the park. This is a single-focus park and arguably the largest investment of this kind for a dedicated textile production centre in Africa. It began production for exports in 2017. Unsurprisingly, the park generated immense interest among investors, despite its remote location and complex transport logistics, with the whole park leased even before completion of construction. With a one-stop administrative window and other logistical incentives, the park has proven to be an early success, attracting some of the most prestigious global brands.[6]

Prospects for accelerated industrialization through manufacturing in Ethiopia remain good, nevertheless. The combination of the three factors of coherence, ambition,

[4] Arkebe Oqubay led a team that spent a year studying industrial parks in countries such as Vietnam, Singapore, South Korea, and China. Countries like Nigeria and Mauritius were also visited to compare how they assimilated or otherwise exceptional Asian experiences. From the assessments made during the visits and lessons learned from errors made by others in the recent past a white paper was tabled for government to decide on a strategy. Once the strategy was adopted the focus shifted quickly to deal with swift implementation.

[5] Data collected during field visit to China Civil Engineering Corporation (CCECC).

[6] The Hawassa Industrial Park experiment is assessed in Chapters 35 and 37, and by Oqubay (2015).

and innovation position the country among a few that can benefit from the delocalization of manufacturing from Asia and can integrate value chains in time, before the windows close. A few countries can imitate this path, but the opportunities are becoming slimmer and the windows are closing fast. Important lessons from the Ethiopian experience are, nevertheless, relevant for a wider number of African economies.

The immense possibilities for agribusiness or agro-processing as well as for commodity-based industrialization are a much easier way for African countries to industrialize. Immense regional, and some national, agribusiness value chains can be constructed or scaled up. African regional markets offer substantial numbers of consumers and are expanding. The signing of a Continental Free Trade Area in March 2018 will create an integrated market of over US\$3 trillion and 1.2 billion consumers largely disconnected from the sophisticated value chains (ECA/AU and AfDB 2017).

Commodity-based industrialization is also an important avenue to pursue. It reduces exposure to commodity price volatility and retains employment opportunities in the countries of origin. Traditional national content policies have not produced the desired effects in terms of employment creation partly because they were not based on sophisticated industrial policy. Ethiopia's floriculture example shows how this can be achieved.

Ethiopia's entry into floriculture production and exports started slowly until the government became involved in 2003. In just one year production doubled from US\$5 million to US\$10 million. In 2012 exports attained a quarter of a billion dollars, second only to Kenya in the African market. Employment exceeds 50,000 workers, 70 per cent of whom are women (Gebreeyesus 2014). This extraordinary success was due to a policy focus on private-sector leadership with strong government support. One by one the difficulties exposed by the entrepreneurs, mostly Ethiopian nationals—such as access to credit, cold warehousing, air cargo and transport routes, shortage of skilled personnel, access to land, or excessive red tape—were addressed by relevant government agencies (Gebreeyesus 2014; Oqubay 2015). Ethiopian producers started by emulating Kenya and eventually became more self-confident because of strong state support and good logistical coordination. The lesson here is about the need for strong business–government dialogue and for each prioritized value chain to be nurtured and to expand.

Coffee exports is another example of successful commodity-based industrialization in Ethiopia. The government has been able to increase the value of exported coffee through repatriation of the purchase mechanisms. Ethiopia has become more independent in establishing prices and controlling flows through the establishment of a commodity exchange. Labelling and marketing have also played a big part in reinvigorating the value of Ethiopian coffee exports. Kenya has replicated the model and other African countries have requested Ethiopian assistance in this field. The African Union included a commodities strategy, inspired by this Ethiopian case, among its flagship projects for the implementation of its Agenda 2063.

Another important lesson for other African countries is the way Ethiopia has embraced the principles of a green economy and adjusted its industrial policy by adopting the concept of green industrialization. The opportunities for leapfrogging, by adopting the cleanest manufacturing technologies and sustainable infrastructure investments, coupled with a heavy use of renewable energy in the energy mix, position the country as an environmental and climate leader. This is happening while industrialized countries are busy retrofitting their industrial capacity—but at a much higher cost.

49.4 Food Security

The share of agriculture in GDP of African countries ranges from the highest—Liberia at 72 per cent—to the lowest—Equatorial Guinea at 1.9 per cent. Ethiopia has a share of around 38 per cent, in good company with countries that usually have a rather small extractive industries sector, either because of limited natural resources endowment, or for other reasons (Admassie 2013). While for some of these countries, agricultural products are their main exports (Ethiopia, Comoros), some others, such as Niger, have their exports almost entirely concentrated in extractive industries. About ten African countries have more than 30 per cent of their GDP coming from the primary sector, but in all of them, apart from DRC, the tertiary or, less commonly, the secondary sector are larger than the primary sector.[7]

From a long-term historical perspective, food prices have suffered a downward trend since the 1930s, going through several cycles and reaching their lowest levels in the 1990s. Terms of trade for tropical agricultural products deteriorated more than those for temperate crops. There is much discussion as to whether food prices will go up or down in the long run. This will depend on numerous factors, including consumption patterns, agricultural production, and the impact of biofuels production, distribution systems, speculation, and other factors on the functioning of food markets.

Ethiopia suffers from two trends that cannot be predicted or controlled: the volatility of food prices and weather patterns. Exposure to international markets is relatively high for countries with large food deficits and a tradition of food insecurity. Prices are often decided far away even for products to be sourced locally. Low productivity in the primary sector translates quite simply in an agricultural production dependent on weather more than technologically necessary. The absence of vast irrigation and other modern production capabilities limits resilience to adverse weather.

Drought is a regular if not frequent visitor to Ethiopia. This prompted the government to put in place a reliable risk reduction system to tackle food insecurity. Agriculture sustains 85 per cent of the population and generates 90 per cent of the export earnings (Gebreeyesus 2013). Twenty-one per cent of the national budget is linked to agriculture, against an African average of 4 per cent. Over 60,000 agriculture support workers and 9,000 farming training centres guarantee improved access to quality information.

However, the fact that Ethiopia exports coffee, oilseed, or livestock and has increased its agricultural productivity at an astonishing rate masks massive food imports, which increase when there is a drought as domestic production struggles to meet demand. Despite this supply volatility Ethiopia has maintained low inflation, including in food

[7] NEPAD (2016).

prices (Gebreeyesus 2013). This is partly due to better supply predictability and rapid government intervention when scarcity is on the horizon. Better-quality market information, infrastructures, and storage, and improved trade practices have all contributed towards a much safer environment. Remittances also play a supportive role. Ethiopia receives more from remittances than it exports, and a great deal of these funds are channelled to families under economic stress in rural areas.

However, good agricultural policies are not sufficient to address the risks posed by the severe droughts Ethiopia is familiar with. There is a need for a more proactive stance. In 2000 Ethiopia re-established the Emergency Food Security Reserve Administration with wide-ranging preparation and risk reduction powers. According to FAO (2011), Ethiopia regularly releases food grain reserves in addition to the relief food aid delivered by international partners such as the World Food Programme (WFP). These stocks are sold at subsidized prices through consumer associations, cooperatives or *kebele* community representatives (Gebreeyesus 2013; FAO 2011).

A complementary policy followed a more structured food security and relief administration system: moving from safety nets into production by introducing a more robust system of cash transfer for public works (for example, feeder roads, forestation, and soil conservation) to chronically food-insecure households (Gebreeyesus 2013). Buffer stocks and emergency aid are, therefore, used strategically to move households towards better and more reliable income-earning activities. Such approaches constitute the essence of a protection floor for some of the most vulnerable Ethiopians—but one that actively tries to address future resilience and enhance capabilities.

Environmental stress in arid lands is a pervasive problem across the Sudan-Sahelian band which stretches from Mauritania and Senegal in the west to the Horn in East Africa, south of the Sahara. It is inhabited by pastoralists and communities dependent on traditional agriculture, struggling to survive against the backdrop of climate change and isolation from modern economic trends. Lessons from Ethiopia on how to deal with food insecurity while addressing a wider range of concerns can be extremely valuable for many countries with similar challenges, particularly countries with similar large populations dispersed in arid lands, such as Sudan, Eritrea, Niger, Nigeria, or Mali.

49.5 Ethiopian Airlines' Ambitious Goals

Ethiopian is one of the oldest airlines operating in Africa, having started its operations in 1945 with initial support from TWA. It has always been a source of pride for the country given its superior performance over the decades, including during periods of war and crisis. The current leadership of the airline has been involved in two strategic plans. The ambitious plans of Vision 2010 having been achieved ahead of schedule, under Vision 2025, Ethiopian was projected to lead the African aviation market as largest cargo operator and cost leader, to possess the most aircraft and serve the most destinations, and to attain 10 per cent of the inter-continental market share (currently all airlines in the continent have 20 per cent) (Ethiopian 2009).

Seven years later Ethiopian had tripled its size in terms of passenger numbers (from 3.5 million in 2010 to over 9 million in 2016/17), international destinations (from 65 to more than 100), fleet size (from 46 to 95), available seat kilometre(ASK) (from 18 billion to 45 billion) and revenue passenger kilometre (RPK) (from 13 billion to 31.5 billion). It increased its domestic destinations to twenty and reached forty-four cargo destinations compared to the single-digit numbers of its closest African cargo competitors, Egypt Air and South Africa Airways. Ethiopian established a US$100 million Aviation Academy with an annual intake capacity of 4,000 trainees and built a catering facility that produces 100,000 meals a day. Ethiopian is now the African leader in all these domains and has recently added the Administration of the Airports to its group (Ethiopian 2018).

How was this possible? One can argue it was due to Ethiopian Airlines' management's sophisticated understanding of the value chain, the granular management of all aspects that allow this competitive industry to deliver high productivity rates. From the way Ethiopian Airlines manages its connection waves in Bole Airport to the financial engineering it employs to secure the best deals for its fleet and facilities, few doubt the planning and strategic capacity of Ethiopian. Its ambitions are so vast that it has ordered an additional fifty aircraft and expects to reach its target of 186 international destinations by 2030.

Ethiopian is the envy of many African countries. The consistency of its performance is linked to discipline, heavy investment in capacity and training, superior IT and technological preparedness, and an obsession with cutting costs. Ethiopian knows that its immediate competition is shifting from African to Middle Eastern carriers and Turkish Airlines. The way to beat them is to cut costs, modernize its fleet, and rapidly expand its network.

Building a regional champion of this calibre would not have been possible without backward and forward linkages, as in any industrialization process. For example, the success of the flower and coffee exports is due to the unique cargo capacity of Ethiopian. The operations of Ethiopian generate 12,000 direct jobs and many more indirect ones in areas that are modernizing the entire economy. Ethiopian is arguably the largest exporter in the country.

Ethiopian has enormous lessons for other parastatals across the continent, not least national airlines. First, it has neither survived on subsidies, nor made any special concessions to its state clients. Second, it has established its own credit rating history independent of the state, avoiding being shielded from competition through state intervention in the market. Third, it has operated both continentally and globally, looking to Africa as a whole rather than just Ethiopia or the neighbouring countries. Ethiopian Airlines' hallmark policy of 'open-skies' competition could be adopted by other African airlines. Fourth, it took productivity measurement as its survival tool, obsessively outperforming its competitors as well as its own ambitious targets.

The rest of this chapter grapples with the characteristics and policy values which propelled Ethiopia's food security policy, industrialization and Ethiopian Airlines to their prominence in the annals of African policy metaphors as an experiment worth critically replicating. These characteristics do not discount subjectivity because in the domain of policymaking and implementation, leadership (a combination of objectivity, subjectivity, and intuition) is as important as hard-nosed management principles. (Lopes and Theisohn 2003).This following section aims to reconcile the objective and subjective as complementary rather than contradictory policy narratives.

49.6 An Ensemble of Sectoral Structural Transformation: Ambition, Coherence, and Innovation

Since the early 1990s, Ethiopia has heralded a return to more comprehensive development plans going beyond narrowly focused PRSPs. GTP-I was a manifestation of a profound shift in the level of ambition and an affirmation of autonomous thinking (MoFED 2002, 2010). Indeed, many African countries have started to adopt long-term development visions and planning frameworks with far more ambitious growth and social development objectives, some inspired by the fact that Ethiopia's daring attitude was not causing a diminution of support from aid donors. Teshome (2012) synthesizes the moment effectively. According to Meles (quoted in Teshome 2012: 11):

> It is possible to achieve economic development with a range of policy instruments that include command-and-control approaches, market-based tools, information, cooperation, education and research. That is why he encouraged market for the goods and services that can be provided by market outcomes. The state should not follow the market, rather the state must lead the market. Since free market forces will not drive economic transformation on their own, the developmental state must play a central role in resource allocation and in efficient coordination of crucial economic activities.

National Development Strategies (NDSs) have since gone beyond the narrow goal of poverty reduction to encompass objectives such as accelerated growth, employment creation, structural transformation, and sustainable development. Unlike the plans of the 1960s, they employ a mix of state- and market-based approaches and appreciate the critical role of both the public and the private sector in the development process.

What distinguishes Ethiopia from other less high-performing African countries in this regard?

First, being able to translate development aspirations and priorities into concrete results. Coordination between the ministry in charge of finance and the ministries or entities in charge of development planning, among others, has improved the links between the planning and budget cycles, ensuring effective implementation of most of the GTP targets. This has probably been enabled by autocratic traits. But there is no doubt that it has proved effective. Some African leaders believe this demonstrates the need for development to be prioritized over democracy.

Second, another lesson from Ethiopia concerns the role of institutions as critical prerequisites for successful implementation of development plans. While the construction of developmental states is driven by visionary leadership, they are sustained through transformative institutions buttressed by a competent and professional bureaucracy. Although Ethiopia's administration is notoriously conservative, weak, and unimaginative, its spread and coverage are considerable.

Third, institutions that facilitate transformation and sustainable development are inclusive and not clientelist. Clientelist economic institutions do not create the incentives needed for people to save, invest, and innovate. On the contrary, such institutions are captured by elite groups which seek to exploit the resources of the country for their own use, leaving little for the citizens at large. Meles Zenawi and the Ethiopian leaders' obsessive war on rent seeking has helped counter such tendencies, although that may have been at the expense of keeping overall control of political activities (Gardner 2018).

Fourth, stability is critical for planning. Discontinuities, including those caused by constitutional and unconstitutional regime change, have contributed to implementation failures across Africa. Planners have also been distracted by continual requests to align development plans with an ever-growing list of priorities and agendas, temptations Ethiopians are good at resisting. Predictability has become the number one comparative advantage for countries: it is better than having oil or diamonds. Ethiopia's credibility is based on predictability and that has become a unique asset.

Fifth, political commitment and deliberative leadership are vital for nurturing a strong central planning body. In the initial stages of the planning process, the effectiveness of the central planning body depended on the political commitment to nurture and sustain it. A high-level body of ministers/advisers to the Prime Minister focus on policy formulation and strategic thinking as well as monitoring implementation, leaving to the ministries the day-to-day running of the bureaucracy.

Sixth, the National Planning Commission is an ensemble of power (or legitimate authority) coordinating a central planning authority, and even has a legal mandate to address the pressing coordination challenges that such an entity is likely to face vis-à-vis other ministries. A case in point is the Finance Ministry. The issue is more about the power and support that the central planning agency receives and less about its location. Concomitantly, decentralized approaches boost planning efficiency. Given the federal nature of the Ethiopian state, decentralized approaches should have contributed to greater local support and ownership of development plans but also exposed weaknesses in sub-national capacities for public financial organization, service delivery, and political management. Recent developments where ethnic clashes exacerbated the questioning of central authority call for a mixed review of the Ethiopian experience.

Essentially, there are common threads in the way the notion of state-centred development is being implemented in Ethiopia.[8] GTPs have instilled a high degree of coherence, better demonstrated by the profound sense of ownership of defined national priorities, particularly within the state apparatus and major economic agents. Sectoral policies are subordinated to these priorities and the key goals of the GTPs in turn influence political discourse, administrative mobilization, and resource allocation. Here Ethiopia is learning from the very cohesive practices of countries such as Mauritius, Cape Verde, Namibia, and at times Zimbabwe and Ghana. However, the challenge of achieving the same in a country with such a large population is of a different magnitude. Coherence and ambition are good demonstrations of determination but what really inspires policymakers across Africa most is the innovation that Ethiopia has demonstrated in implementing its key national development priorities in the pursuit of structural economic transformation.

49.7 Conclusions

The three sectoral experiences delineated in this chapter attempt to demonstrate the seriousness of Ethiopia's attempt to pursue a nationally crafted developmental approach. The lessons accumulated so far in each of the sectors (food security, industrialization, and Ethiopian Airlines), is that beyond the state's centrality in development, there is a decentralized federal system, which is meant to bring development closer to where it happens. The curiosity about the Ethiopian experiment can probably be explained against this dialectic and its capacity to deliver results.

Current African debate on developing industrial policy pathways, both at national and continental levels, can no longer be pursued without invoking the benefits and achievements, but equally importantly the challenges Ethiopia has experienced on its road to development. Likewise, food security and the 'open-skies' policy embedded in continental free trade have taken commendable strides, with Ethiopian Airlines leading the way in this respect.[9]

Ethiopia's development path affirms that rapid transformation depends on a strong state and leaders committed to prioritizing and provisioning public goods to foster social development. It is as if the legitimacy of such leaders becomes a hostage to effective delivery of development outcomes, as a way for them to perpetuate themselves either through legitimate power (authority) or legacy. The more the state delivers, the greater the anguish and expectations of more.

[8] For more on the developmental state in Ethiopia see Chapter 46.

[9] For example, AU 2018. The African Continental Free Trade Area. https://au.int/sites/default/files/documents/33984-doc-qa_cfta_en_rev15march.pdf (accessed 15 May 2018).

References

Admassie, A. (2013). 'The Political Economy of Food Price: The Case of Ethiopia', WIDER Working Paper No. 2013/001, Helsinki.

AfDB, OECD, UNDP (2017). *Ethiopia 2017*. www.africaneconomicoutlook.org.

AU (2018). 'The African Continental Free Trade Area'. https://au.int/sites/default/files/documents/33984-doc-qa_cfta_en_rev15march.pdf (accessed 15 May 2018).

ECA/AU (2014). 'Economic Report on Africa: Dynamic Industrial Policy in Africa', Addis Ababa.

ECA/AU and AfDB (2017). 'Assessing Regional Integration in Africa VIII', Addis Ababa.

Ethiopian (2009). 'Vision 2025 and Strategic Road Map (Scaling up of ET's Growth Strategy)', Ethiopian Airlines, Addis Ababa.

Ethiopian (2018). 'Ethiopian Airlines Group and Other Airlines Seven Years Statistics Comparison', Ethiopian, Addis Ababa.

FAO (2011). *Undernourishment Around the World: Impact of the 2006–08 Price Shock* (Rome: FAO).

Gardner, T. (2018). 'Ethiopia's Great Rift', *Foreign Policy*. http://foreignpolicy.com/2018/02/20/ethiopias-great-rift/

Gebreeyesus, M. (2013). 'Industrial Policy and Development in Ethiopia: Evolution and Present Experimentation', WIDER Working Paper No. 2013/125, Helsinki.

Gebreeyesus, M. (2014). 'A Natural Experiment of Industrial Policy: Floriculture and the Metal and Engineering Industries in Ethiopia', WIDER Working Paper No. 2014/163, Helsinki.

IMF (2015). 'The Federal Democratic Republic of Ethiopia, selected issues', IMF Country Report 15/326, Washington, DC.

Lopes, C. and T. Theisohn (2003). *Ownership, Leadership and Transformation: Can We Do Better for Capacity Development?* (London: Earthscan).

Lopes, C. et al. (2017). *Macroeconomic Policy Framework for Africa's Structural Transformation* (London: Palgrave Macmillan).

MoFED (2002). 'Ethiopia: Sustainable Development and Poverty Reduction Program', Addis Ababa.

MoFED (2010). 'Growth and Transformation Plan (GTP) 2010/11–2014/15,', Addis Ababa.

Monga, C. and J. Y. Lin (2015). *The Oxford Handbook of Africa and Economics*, 2 vols (Oxford: Oxford University Press).

National Planning Commission (2016). 'Growth and Transformation Plan II', 2 vols, Addis Ababa.

NEPAD (2016). 'A New Emerging Rural World', NEPAD. http://www.nepad.org/resource/new-emerging-rural-world-overview-rural-change-africa (accessed 15 May 2018).

Oqubay, A. (2015). *Made in Africa: Industrial Policy in Ethiopia* (Oxford: Oxford University Press).

Soludo, C. et al. (eds) (2004). *The Politics of Trade and Industrial Policy in Africa: A Forced Consensus?* (Trenton, NJ: Africa World Press).

Sun, I. Y. (2017). *The Next Factory of the World: How Chinese Investment is Reshaping Africa.* (Cambridge, MA: Harvard Business Review Press).

Teshome, A. (2012). 'Meles's Development Paradigm and its Impacts on Economic Transformation in Ethiopia'. http://aigaforum.com/articles/meles-development-paradigm.pdf

World Bank (2010). 'Mauritius Enhancing and Sustaining Competitiveness: Policy Notes on Trade and Labor', Report No: 53322-MU, Washington, DC.

CHAPTER 50

GROWING WITH DEPTH

What African Countries can Learn from the Ethiopian Experience

K. Y. AMOAKO

50.1 Introduction

The United Nations Economic Commission for Africa (UNECA) convened the first African Development Forum (ADF) in Addis Ababa over five days in October 1999. The event attracted almost 1,000 participants from African governments, the private sector, civil society, and bilateral and multilateral organizations—a cross-section of stakeholders ranging from community activists and entrepreneurs to global policymakers and heads of state and government. The forum sprang from the idea that Africa would never achieve sustainable development unless African countries began to design and implement their own development policies, strategies, and actions.

The timing for such an event seemed right. By 1999 there were strong tailwinds for change in Africa. Refreshing new leaders had emerged—Nelson Mandela, of course, but also Paul Kagame, Thabo Mbeki, and Meles Zenawi, among others. Daunting economic challenges persisted across the continent, but these leaders and their counterparts increasingly called for a new approach to development policies that broke with the past. It was an exciting time in Africa—and Ethiopia was leading the way in many respects.

Meles, Ethiopia's prime minister, was an obvious choice as the ADF's opening speaker. The forum used globalization as a loose organizing theme, and Meles offered two preconditions that would enable Africa to benefit long term from the increasingly globalized economy.

First, African countries had to develop a vibrant domestic private sector. 'Unless the domestic private sector leads the way with enthusiasm and confidence,' Meles said, 'it is unlikely for foreign investment to take part in our economies with any degree of effectiveness.' But in order to attract both domestic and foreign resources, African countries had to be politically stable, with effective institutions and a commitment to the rule of law. The only way to ensure such stability was Meles' second precondition: a strong, capable state with an indisputable authority over its own agenda. A radical change in Africa's development paradigm was needed, Meles argued. He called it 'an overhaul of relations'. Meles referred not only to Africa and its development partners but also African policymakers and their constituents—meaning the need to fulfill expectations that the state would craft and implement reasonable, progressive, and transformational policies that create jobs, spur development, and raise the overall quality of life.

At the heart of what Meles proposed was a mutually beneficial relationship between the public and private sectors, a move away from the statism of the Marxist Derg regime. The quest for such a relationship, fraught but evolving, has been central to the pattern of Ethiopia's growth in the early twenty-first century. It is also one of the fundamental tenets of economic transformation, which the government of Ethiopia embraced well before it became the leading paradigm for Africa's sustainable development. Ethiopia's boldness in trying to transform its economy is among the primary reasons for the country's economic turnaround. Starting in 1992, the year after the Derg's overthrow, the new transitional government embarked on an economic reform programme to liberalize the economy. Over time, those efforts paid major dividends.

Between 2004 and 2014 (a period beyond Meles' time in office, which ended with his death in 2012), per capita growth in Ethiopia was the highest on the continent. Many other African countries looked to be turning the corner during this period, only to see their economies suddenly stall or even contract, particularly due to the 2008 global financial crisis. Ethiopia avoided the pattern, despite facing many of the same pressures: drought, falling commodity prices, more restrictive global markets, and the global economic downturn. By 2016, Ethiopia had become one of the fastest-growing economies in the world, averaging 10.9 per cent growth over the previous decade.

When Meles spoke at the ADF of the need to overhaul development approaches, he conveyed what Ethiopia already knew to be true for developing countries: that economic growth alone is not enough to sustain development; rather, the structure of economies must change. That's where economic transformation comes in. Ethiopia's understanding of what is required to carry out a successful transformation strategy—and the lessons the country's success so far can offer the rest of Africa—is the subject of this chapter.

50.2 The ACET 'DEPTH' Framework and Ethiopia's Progress to Date

Even as many African countries have shown steady economic gains in the new millennium, most are not positioned to sustain their progress. Instead, they continue to rely excessively on traditional, low value-added commodity export markets that are unpredictable and are not linked to the broader national economy. Or they still rely on low-productivity, and in turn low-wage, traditional agriculture to drive employment, even as urban centres are growing dramatically across the continent. The result is what can be called 'shallow' growth, which is not doing enough to permanently improve the African condition. As is increasingly recognized, this exposes economies to the risk of episodic, rather than sustained, growth and to debilitating growth reversals or collapses (Pritchett et al. 2016).

For instance, while poverty rates have decreased, the number of people who are poor continues to rise. The African Development Bank reports that although the proportion of poor people in Africa declined from 56 per cent in 1990 to 43 per cent in 2012, the actual number of poor people increased over that same period. Population growth is outpacing poverty reduction. It is also outpacing job creation. Between 2000 and 2008, employment in Africa grew at an annual average of 2.8 per cent, roughly half the rate of economic growth and between 2009 and 2014 annual employment growth increased to an average of 3.1 per cent (AfDB 2018). Only five countries—Algeria, Burundi, Botswana, Cameroon, and Morocco—experienced annual employment growth of more than 4 per cent. This problem is especially pronounced among the next generation of African workers. Real output growth is estimated to have increased 3.6 per cent in 2017 but has not translated into jobs for Africa's teeming youth, an untapped—and increasingly restless—labour force.

These unimpressive indicators are partly the result of stagnating economic structures that have not changed in most countries since the 1960s. Across Africa, strong manufacturing sectors remain undeveloped and complex bureaucracies stifle the rise of a vibrant private sector, particularly for sectors such as manufacturing, including agro-processing, and infrastructure, which is critical to sustainable development but remains limited, or poor at best.[1]

Shallow growth based primarily on commodity prices or a global economic surge is something Africa has experienced before. In the years after independence, quite a few newly formed governments received a boost from the booming demand for commodities—but they failed to take the right steps to withstand future external shocks and internal stresses. The result, of course, was a disastrous downturn for the entire continent from the late 1970s into the mid-1990s; a lost period exacerbated by political strife and instability as well as ineffective development strategies that drove up debt and inflation without tackling long-term challenges.

The African Center for Economic Transformation (ACET) was formed in 2008 to help Africa avoid repeating its past mistakes by supporting the design and implementation of transformational economic reforms that went beyond 'growth' as a measure of success. Increasingly, global economists and thought leaders talked about transformation as the key to sustaining growth in Africa, but at the country level not much was happening.

[1] New findings reveal that Africa's infrastructure requirements have ballooned to US$130–170 billion annually, instead of the earlier accepted figure of US$93 billion a year (AfDB 2018).

In 2014, ACET released the first 'African Transformation Report', which drew on extensive research across numerous sub-Saharan African countries to make an empirical case for economic transformation as the only way for Africa to pursue sustainable growth.[2] The report compared major aspects of African economies, such as their production efficiency and diversification, with that of eight earlier transforming countries: Brazil, Chile, Indonesia, Malaysia, Singapore, South Korea, Thailand, and Vietnam. Forty or so years ago, their economies had several features that today characterize many African countries—widespread poverty, low productivity, low technology, and limited exports, among others. But those countries ignited and sustained long periods of high GDP and export growth, economic diversification, technology upgrading, and productivity increases that greatly improved the lives of their people and the opportunities available to future generations. They transformed from developing countries into middle-income or even, in some cases, high-income countries. Comparing their growth experiences to that of Africa's, ACET laid out the first quantifiable definition of the multidimensional process that is economic transformation—in other words, what transformation actually means for countries in practical terms. It means economic growth with depth—not the shallow growth driven by high commodity prices but transformational growth based on a common set of attributes. Those attributes make up the DEPTH framework:

> D stands for *diversified production*. While pursuing further improvements in the macroeconomic and business environments, countries must acquire the capability to produce a broad array of goods and services. In this way, countries can draw upon a stratified labour force from low-skill wage labour to highly skilled workers, while also deepening value addition through manufacturing and processing. At the same time, diversified production will allow firms to respond to different market segments, both for domestic consumption and for exports, which can have a positive long-term impact on domestic resource mobilization through corporate taxes.
>
> E is for *export competitiveness*. African countries need to be bigger players in global markets. Robust export strategies provide the opportunity to increase production, reduce unit costs, boost employment, and raise incomes, and to overcome the pressing balance of payments constraint on sustained growth and development.
>
> P is for *productivity increases*. African countries must get more out of all resource inputs, especially in farming and manufacturing. Around 60 to 70 per cent of the population in Africa lives in rural areas. Increasing and modernizing agricultural productivity would be a powerful way to raise incomes. Productivity growth in any sector defines the process of structural transformation (Lewis 1954).

[2] The countries studied were Senegal, Burkina Faso, Ghana, and Nigeria in West Africa; Ethiopia, Kenya, Uganda, Tanzania, and Rwanda in East Africa; Cameroon in Central Africa; and Zambia, Botswana, South Africa, Mozambique, and Mauritius in Southern Africa.

T represents *technology upgrades*. Productivity gains can begin with greater efficiencies, but they can only be sustained through new and improved technologies and through the use of those technologies to master more sophisticated economic activities.

And H stands for *human well-being*. An improved quality of life for citizens involves many essentials, including health, education, peace, and security. But the two most directly related to economic transformation are GDP per capita and employment. Simply put, successful transformation should lead to higher wages and more productive jobs—a building block for improved livelihoods.

When it comes to economic transformation, one size does not fit all. Each country must adapt its strategy to its own circumstances. But the DEPTH framework is comprehensive enough to provide a baseline for forming policies and measuring success. A country that embarks on a development strategy built around the DEPTH attributes and objectives will position itself to grow its economy, and transform its economy through fundamental change.

Ethiopia offers a good example of how the framework translates. A centralized economic system that discouraged private-sector growth and a prolonged civil war were the main causes of Ethiopia's dismal growth in the 1980s and 1990s. But growth has been impressive since 2000, powered not by the extraction of natural resources and higher commodity prices, but largely by the government's sustained pursuit of economic transformation, a change in policy direction towards welcoming the private sector, support to agriculture and export promotion, rapid expansion in public investment that attracted private investment and capital inflows, and debt relief (see Chapter 9).

As a result, Ethiopia's performance within the DEPTH framework shows an increasing trend. In 2000, the country ranked 18 of 21 among the countries ACET measured against the various DEPTH attributes for a composite index ranking. By 2015, it had improved to eighth. The main driver for Ethiopia's improved DEPTH performance over that time was export competitiveness, although there were many factors that contributed to its strong improvement. When ACET compared Ethiopia's export competitiveness against twenty other countries it was particularly steady from 2000 to 2010 and generally out-ranked all but four other countries in the cohort. Through 2010, technology was Ethiopia's second-best performing attribute on the DEPTH index, though improvements in that area began to wane considerably afterwards (see Chapter 41). Productivity gains then took over as the second primary driver of transformation gains.

To be more specific, a number of critical advances in certain sectors have helped propel Ethiopia forward within the DEPTH framework. Though Ethiopia has little agricultural commercialization, it has seen a surge in agricultural production. Since 2000, productivity improvement has been the dominant source of growth, stemming from improved uses of technology and farm inputs. During the mid-2000s, Ethiopia's agricultural production grew annually at more than 9 per cent, and cultivated area expanded at more than 4.5 per cent. The productivity increases have been consistent with the government's massive push to promote and deliver technology packages to farmers, dating back to the mid-1990s. Nonetheless, productivity gains were mainly concentrated in maize production; and agricultural productivity, despite strong growth, remains very low by international standards (see Chapters 9 and 27).

Manufacturing in Ethiopia grew at 11 per cent between 2004 and 2014, while industry's share of GDP increased from 16.7 per cent in 2015/16 to 25.6 per cent in 2016/17. Export-led manufacturing alone accounted for 20 per cent of total exports in 2016 (AfDB 2018). On the surface, these are strong numbers. But Ethiopia's manufacturing sector, long dominated by resource-based processing activities, has failed to live up to its potential even amid strong growth. For example, manufacturing export revenue in the 2016/17 fiscal year met less than 50 per cent of the government's target. Here again, though, the government has been extremely aggressive, offering favourable benefits packages to attract clothing and textile companies in an attempt to turn Ethiopia into a light manufacturing hub for global markets.

Ethiopia has also worked to increase the efficiency of its urban labour markets and turn them into centres of innovation and industrial development—a key approach to improving human well-being since unemployment in Ethiopia is primarily an urban phenomenon. Contributing factors to this trend have been increasing university enrolment rates, increased participation of women in the workforce (Seid, Taffesse, and Ali 2016) and a growing innovation culture as evidenced by the work of institutions such as the Science and Technology Information Centre and the Ethiopian Climate Innovation Centre. Still, the country's growth has brought with it positive trends in poverty reduction in both urban and rural areas. While 55 per cent of Ethiopians lived in extreme poverty in 2000, according to the World Bank, by 2011 this figure was reduced to 33.5 per cent.

The government has devoted a substantial share of its budget to pro-poor programmes and social and physical infrastructure investments, and it has managed to keep inflation in check at the same time, though food inflation has at times been extremely high. These are all critical elements of a successful transformation strategy. Of course, any country starting from a point as low as Ethiopia cannot transform itself completely in such a short time frame. According to the World Bank's 5th Ethiopia Economic Update from 2016, labour productivity for low-skilled workers remains low, and the performance of the export sector and current account balance is weak. An overvalued currency limits the country's export competitiveness, and was one contributing factor as exports fell three years in a row from 2013 through 2016.

There are ample other constraints to address, as there are with any economy trying to emerge from among the world's lowest income countries. The point here is not to focus on what Ethiopia still must do but on what it has done right.

50.3 Lessons in Transformation

The 2014 'African Transformation Report' assessed the successes and challenges in transforming Africa and drew heavily on the experience and performance of the early transformers. But there is no single formula for economic transformation; what works in one country might not work as well in another. Still there are standard requirements at the country level to transform economies, regardless of country circumstances. Among some of the most critical, Ethiopia has excelled, or at the very least exhibited sound decision-making that other countries could emulate. In this way, the Ethiopian experience offers useful lessons for African countries on how to grow with depth and, ultimately, transform their economies. Five such lessons are explored here in greater detail.

50.3.1 Lesson 1: Countries Must Have a Plan

There is a broad consensus among economists that planning is a critical component of economic transformation and good governance. To realize transformation prospects, a crucial first step is to develop a national vision and strategy—preferably through broad consultations, such as regional forums, with the private sector, civil society organizations, think tanks, and other stakeholder groups. The next step, of course, is to stick with it over time. One defining feature of the rapid transformers in East and South-east Asia in the second half of the twentieth century was their capacity to prepare—and rigidly implement—long-term development plans spanning decades. One of the first acts of the new Singapore Government when it attained self-rule in 1959 was to develop an economic plan for Singapore. Likewise, strategic planning and coordination at the national, regional and local levels has been one of China's core strengths during its transition into a global economic powerhouse in the new century (Warwick 2017).

Sub-Saharan African countries periodically produce national economic plans, but rarely have these plans focused specifically on transformation objectives. And they have often put their name to 'plans' or 'visions' (e.g. Poverty Reduction Strategy Papers) that have essentially been externally drafted and conformed to global projections of change rather than being driven by specifically domestic designs. This must change given the centrality of economic transformation to the global post-2015 development agenda. Some countries are ahead of the curve, having first already placed strong emphasis on planning and second, incorporated transformation as an integral element of that planning. Ethiopia is one of those countries.

Since 2005, Ethiopia has had three five-year national development plans. The first, the Plan for Accelerated and Sustained Development to End Poverty (PASDEP), was implemented through 2010. For its follow-up, Ethiopia targeted transformation more directly. The 2011–15 Growth and Transformation Plan (GTP-I) aimed to foster broad-based, sustainable development in part by building stronger implementation capacity. A civil service reform programme, for example, was one of the plan's pillars. In 2015, the government moved into a second phase (GTP-II) of the same underlying plan, to run through to 2020 and, theoretically, to guide the country towards its ultimate goal of achieving middle-income status and boasting a climate-resilient, green economy by 2025. To get there, GTP-II focuses on core transformation components: continuing improvements in physical infrastructure through public investment, and positioning the country as a global manufacturing hub.

Ethiopia's process in creating these plans is instructive. After spending five years implementing PASDEP, the government still faced major challenges, including high inflationary pressures, inadequate capacity, low levels of domestic revenue, and inadequate irrigation. So when it came to designing GTP-I, the government took a different approach. It kicked things off by convening a high-powered macroeconomic team to guide the overall preparatory process, something that was not done for PASDEP. It also involved the implementing departments and agencies throughout the government, including at the regional and district level, in the initial planning process. Then it began a public consultation process that was quite thorough, engaging all the key stakeholders in the private sector and civil society, as well as development partners. The consultations did what they were intended to do: raised public awareness so that the plan reflected the direct interests of the citizenry and the demands of the constitution.

The plan focused on fiscal and monetary policies geared towards growth sustainability and macroeconomic stability. The driving objective was to maintain an average real GDP growth rate of 11 per cent to achieve the Millennium Development Goals, but other objectives were more expansive, such as ensuring quality of health and education and establishing favourable conditions to create a stable democratic, developmental state. On a more direct level, Ethiopia aimed to build an economy with modern, productive, and technologically enhanced agricultural and industrial sectors that would expand employment and incomes by taking direct aim at certain transformational goals: enhancing infrastructure, attracting industry, building capacity, and creating equitable and inclusive growth, including a commitment to create better opportunities for women and youth.

Another effective step the government took involved measuring results—an aspect of long-term planning that countries are often eager to diminish because of cost, complexity, or simple disregard. Ethiopia put in place a policy matrix to integrate the GTP and track the progress of key indicators across several sectors of the economy. The system provided the government with mechanisms to measure the efficiency of government actions and the effectiveness of public policies in achieving plan objectives.

According to Ethiopia's National Planning Commission, during the five-year GTP-I, real GDP growth averaged 10.1 per cent. Real GDP growth could primarily be attributed to agriculture, industry, and services, which on average grew at 6.6 per cent, 20.2 per cent, and 10.8 per cent, respectively, during the same period. More importantly, the growth helped generate expanded investments and employment, both vital building blocks for successful transformation.

The government maintained the vision of GTP-I after the five-year implementation period by continuing on the same course with GTP-II, albeit with additional specific objectives, such as the development of engineering and fabrication capacity to further boost agriculture and manufacturing. Even though the plan was seen as a 'Phase 2' continuation, GTP-II went through another stakeholder consultation process at the regional and federal levels to once again establish a sense of national ownership.

Given the time it takes to realize tangible results from long-term plans, a national vision—and a demonstrated commitment to it—can inspire citizens and mobilize support for a lengthy process that often requires sacrifice in the early stages. Also, a well-developed strategy with broad inputs can clarify the roles of government and the private sector, so that each side is working in tandem, towards the same goals. Ethiopia seems to have taken the right steps—and so far seen positive results. This is one reason the 'African Transformation Report' described GTP-I as a 'next-generation transformation plan'.

50.3.2 Lesson 2: Institutional Capacity Matters

Ethiopia's experience shows that if adequate and appropriate attention is focused on building capacity in key institutions, reform agendas are more likely to be maintained or even accelerated. However, most African countries face significant capacity constraints, and as a result many of the most important state functions are not performed well. These include core activities such as sound macroeconomic management, basic infrastructure investments, sensible regulatory policies, an exchange rate that keeps exports competitive, and a system for developing skills to match labour demands. Of course, countries face a myriad of challenges not only in building strong skills but retaining them in the public sector. Over the past seventy-five years, governments, development partners, and educational systems have often failed to produce institutions that are well staffed, sustainable, effectively managed, and capable of delivering high-quality services to citizens. Ethiopia, by contrast, addressed some of those challenges in unique and even groundbreaking ways.

In 1998, recognizing the country's serious deficiencies in human and institutional capacity, the government issued a national capacity-building strategy. The strategy was unique in that it was framed within the country's overall development policy—neither as a response to donor demands nor as a little-known effort by a weak ministry. Leaders designed the strategy to address sustainable development and poverty alleviation and tailored it to the circumstances of the country. It contained goals and strategic objectives for enhancing education, training, and learning, transforming the public sector, strengthening the private sector, giving a voice to civil society, and promoting capacity building through sectoral programmes. An early seed of this approach was the highly unusual experience of the EPRDF leadership in the immediate aftermath of taking power in 1991, when, within months, more than twenty senior officials, Meles included, were enrolled on an Open University management course (which the great majority completed successfully).

In 2001 and 2003, the government buttressed its original strategy with even more comprehensive and ambitious efforts. The first of these, the National Capacity Building Programme, was a multi-sectoral, intergovernmental effort to institutionalize capacity building to meet the demands of rapid transformation. Again, Ethiopia linked the effort directly to achieving its overall, long-term development policy. Two years later, the government created the Public Sector Capacity Building Programme, in which it consolidated six core public-sector reform programmes under a single five-year initiative. The individual programmes were not necessarily unique in themselves as they focused on common areas such as civil service reform, tax reform, and urban management. But the consolidated programme stood out for its efficiency in focusing limited resources on what was most beneficial: clarity, accountability, and a participatory approach to building capacity in support of long-term development. But the government went much farther than a series of programmes.

In most countries (developed or developing), there is no single institution with a capacity-building portfolio. Capacity agendas are split between ministries, sometimes with a Ministry of Education trying to play a coordinating role. But capacity-building plans are not usually aligned with higher education and vocational training, so they are not necessarily linked to donor-funded training or regional efforts. Ethiopia found a different way by establishing a wholly separate ministry within the government. The Ministry of Capacity Building (MCB) became the first of its kind, as it was not part of human resources or national development ministries which many other countries have—and where capacity building programmes or directorates often reside.

Ethiopia's MCB serves as the focal point for supervising and coordinating a broad range of national initiatives to strengthen institutional capacity and human resources, while also maintaining the donor-country dialogue. At its inception, the MCB was intended to establish mechanisms to open up greater channels of communication between the government and the private sector and civil society. In reality, relations between the state and these actors have sometimes remained strained (see Chapter 39). Nevertheless, Ethiopia's approach, while not always fully inclusive, recognizes the interdependence of many complex factors involved in capacity building.

Together, these innovative strategies demonstrated the Ethiopian commitment to improving core state functions. They strengthened institutional capacity and improved human resource capability. In fact, the establishment of the MCB, created to address technical capacity constraints that may hinder the decentralization process, has resulted in a dramatic increase in capacity at regional and district level, with many local administrative personnel now holding a civil service college degree or diploma. Many people still experience state institutions as slow, heavily bureaucratic, and stifling and it is not clear that credentials have fully translated into widespread organizational change. Nonetheless, if unevenly, there have been clear shifts in some institutions (see Chapter 48 on the evolution of the Ethiopian Investment Commission).

50.3.3 Lesson 3: Governments Must Coordinate their Actions and be Accountable

Most transformation initiatives cut across several ministries and agencies. Therefore, it is imperative that various arms and agencies of government stay in close contact and work towards shared goals, rather than operate as individual units. The MCB is one example of Ethiopia harnessing the benefits of intergovernmental coordination. Another is the Agricultural Transformation Agency (ATA), established in 2010 to accelerate sustainable development in Ethiopia's most dominant sector.

Agriculture sits at the centre of Ethiopia's economy—and its transformation efforts. According to World Bank estimates, in 2014 agriculture accounted for almost half of Ethiopia's GDP, 84 per cent of exports, and 80 per cent of total employment. The government has been aggressive in supporting agricultural development by setting aside significant resources, approximately 17 per cent of its 2015 national budget, per the UN (Tafirenyika 2015). But it has done more than throw money at the problem, since money alone will not transform a sector. First, it identified the most critical agricultural bottlenecks to address—such as training, resources, and access to inputs—then it created a new body, the ATA, to coordinate efforts to remove those bottlenecks.

The ATA is a semi-autonomous agency charged with developing, supporting, tracking, and monitoring Ethiopia's agricultural transformation agenda, including an annual progress report. It also provides policy and strategy advice to government counterparts and implements 'deliverables'—dozens of projects and initiatives intended to increase agricultural knowledge, boost productivity, and modernize processes. One of the most successful, producing digital soil maps for every region in the country, was the first of its kind in Africa. It led to the creation of twelve new types of fertilizer, each with a different composition to better match specific farmer soil (Tafirenyika 2015). As with any public agency, the ATA is capable of performing at higher capacity; Ethiopia's overall investment in public agricultural research could be stronger, for instance. But the existence of the agency itself should not be undersold as a good example of public commitment.

As with its national development plans, Ethiopia utilized a multi-stakeholder, consultative process to form the ATA, which is governed by an intergovernmental council, chaired by the Prime Minister. Council members include the Ministers of Finance and Economic Development, Water and Energy, and Cabinet Affairs, as well as regional agricultural bureau heads from across the state. The Director General of the Ethiopian Institute of Agricultural Research also sits on the Council and serves as its secretary (Berhanu 2013). The Council governs the ATA, but nongovernmental agencies and the private sector also contribute, either directly in implementation of the deliverables or by providing feedback and expertise where they have relevant experience.

The Agricultural Commercialization Clusters (ACC) initiative is another example of coordinated action by the government. The ACC initiative emerged from a request made by Prime Minister Hailemariam Dessalegn, who succeeded Meles in 2012 (until 2018), to make better use of geographically focused strategies. It contains twenty-four clearly defined geographic clusters specializing in twelve priority commodities across the four major agricultural regions of the country (ATA 2017). Governance and coordination is decentralized, with regional transformation councils and regional presidents guiding work at the local level, and a project management office at the national level to oversee successful implementation of priority work. Additionally, the government established eighteen value chain alliances across the clusters to create platforms at the local level for peer learning and joint problem solving.

The importance of coordination among implementing agencies to ensure common goals and accountability during the lengthy transformation process cannot be overstated. The unique and original institutional arrangements for Ethiopia's agricultural sector stand out as examples worth further study and, where possible, emulation.

50.3.4 Lesson 4: The Public and Private Sectors Must Work Together

Successful economic transformation is wholly dependent on a productive working relationship between government and business, which means getting the balance right between the state and private enterprise. Each side has a role to play, and each is dependent on the other holding up its end of the bargain. Government must steer the long-term strategy through supportive policies and actions that enable businesses to thrive—such as regulations that encourage innovation and the elimination of unnecessary red tape. The private sector, in turn, should spearhead job creation, utilize local resources as much as possible, and lead the way for upgraded technologies and processes.

In other words, the government sets the agenda and provides underlying infrastructure and enabling environment while the private sector drives the agenda through investment and job creation. In 2010, the government formed the Ethiopian Public Private Consultative Forum (EPPCF) as a central platform to shape and strengthen that relationship. The government is represented by the Ministry of Trade, with the Ethiopian Chamber of Commerce and Sectoral Associations representing the private sector.[3] The EPPCF is ambitious, covering the federal, state, and district levels, and it has a secretariat, hosted by the Chamber, to promote dialogue between the two sides at each level. It receives both financial and technical assistance from the World Bank (on the enduring constraints on private sector development, see Chapter 39).

Since its establishment, the EPPCF has successfully organized more than sixteen dialogue forums focusing on issues such as taxation, trade and customs procedures, government procurement, company registration, finance constraints, and property rights, among others. It has also organized two national business conferences with the prime minister. Ethiopia still ranks in the bottom half of sub-Saharan African countries in the World Bank's *Doing Business 2018* rankings,[4] but the investment climate has improved considerably due to reforms that have emerged from the public–private dialogues. Some examples include restructuring customs procedures to meet international standards and practice; streamlining the licencing, registration, and costs associated with starting a new business; and making the public procurement process more transparent and fair (Mihretu and Tolina 2015; World Bank 2018).

Government reform over the years has led to a surge in foreign direct investment (FDI)—more than US$4 billion in 2017—which is now a significant factor in the nation's GDP. According to the Ethiopian Investment Commission (see Chapter 48), which the government established in 1992 to promote private investment opportunities, particularly

[3] The ECCSA is an apex organisation consisting of eighteen members, which includes nine regional chambers of commerce and sectoral associations, two city chambers of commerce and sectoral associations, one national chamber of sectoral associations and six sectoral associations organized at national level. It has represented the private sector on issues addressing tax laws, trade logistics, commercial registration, business licencing, government procurement, and tourism.

[4] Ethiopia's overall rank among sub-Saharan African countries was 31 of 48.

FDI, the bulk of the inflows have come from China, Sudan, and the United States, although significant sources of FDI projects have come from European countries and other developing countries in the Middle East, Asia, and other parts of Africa (EIC 2017).

Opening an economy for the aggressive pursuit of FDI creates its own difficulties: a well-run and rigorous regulatory regime is critical, for instance (Teka 2014). But if a country is able to find the right balance, it will reap significant benefits and build a more stable foundation for growing with depth. Consider the Huajian Group, a large-scale Chinese shoe manufacturer that established a factory in 2012 in one of Ethiopia's booming industrial zones. Within five years, this US$700 million investment employed over 4,000 workers, more than 90 per cent of whom were local Ethiopians. The factory has been so successful in exporting leather shoes to the United States and China that investors are planning a US$2 billion manufacturing expansion over the next decade. Meanwhile, the success has translated into broader skills development for Ethiopian workers. In cooperation with a local institute, Huajian intends to initiate a shoemaking diploma course that will be open to all Ethiopian nationals regardless of whether they work for Huajian.

In Ethiopia, the Ethiopian Chamber of Commerce and Sectoral Associations, the Ministry of Trade, and the Ethiopian Investment Commission each have their own agendas and activities to foster public–private collaboration. The dialogues produced have not only raised optimism but also uncovered concerns. To continue with the example of shoe production, manufacturers have expressed concern about the weak links in the value chain between leather and shoe manufacturing, while local tanneries have historically preferred to sell semi-processed leather in export markets rather than sell leather to local shoemakers (Brautigam, McMillan, and Tang 2013). These hurdles are not unique to one industry or one country. But they do show the need for the public and private sector to engage regularly, and in a mutually beneficial way. A big reason other countries could look to Ethiopia as an example is the government's acknowledgement—and its supporting actions—that the full participation of the private sector is critical for efficient and sustained economic and social development.

50.3.5 Lesson 5: Political Leaders Must be Committed and Engaged

Transformation is an ongoing process spanning twenty or thirty years—a length of time that is often at odds with transfers of power from one set of leaders to the next. A transformation vision, therefore, must be long term, and the support for it must be consistent over time. Political will is paramount. Leaders must be willing to stay the course over the long haul rather than going for a quick fix. Meles recognized this. While his years in office were not without opposition, Ethiopia would not have its sights set on achieving middle-income status without hands-on leadership from the very top. The Huajian shoe factory succeeded in part because Meles was directly involved, including travelling to China to make the initial sales pitch to investors. Leading foreign investors in horticulture and floriculture have also noted the importance of Meles playing a direct role in supporting nascent investments and helping to resolve constraints.

Meles fully committed Ethiopia to transformation because he saw it as the only viable path to sustainability and economic self-sufficiency (De Waal 2012). He argued that Africa needed to discard the predatory state and neoliberal paradigm that had long defined unsuccessful development and move instead towards a more progressive, democratic developmental state. Meles favoured the Asian Tigers, especially South Korea and Taiwan, as examples of developmental states with strong leaders that succeeded by subverting neoliberal orthodoxy. Indeed, it is not uncommon to find many African intellectuals, ordinary citizens, and for that matter international development specialists who compare the divergence in growth and transformation between Africa and the Asian countries since the 1950s and identify the leadership factor as the key explanatory variable. So far, history has shown that many of the most successful transforming, or transformed, countries—whether in Asia, Latin America, or Africa—have been ruled by leaders with lengthy, uninterrupted tenures, strong-arm or authoritarian tendencies, and track records that are more favourable on economic outcomes than civil rights.

Under Meles, the Ethiopian model of the developmental state aimed to balance aggressive economic growth with heavy social development within a centralized, top-down political apparatus. On the economic side, the model de-emphasized commodity export dependence while focusing heavily on capital investment and productivity growth in agriculture and manufacturing. On the political side, Meles' hardline approach to governance drew both criticism and praise: the former from political opponents, ethnic groups, and human rights activists who decried his tactics and grip on power; the latter from fellow policymakers, world leaders, and development economists who were impressed by his country's turnaround. Nonetheless, after Meles' death, it proved more difficult to hold together the delicate balance of centralized developmental state and broader political legitimacy, and the EPRDF faced rising challenges to the model.

Ultimately, this is another discussion with many complex variables, but it is worth mentioning in the context of political leadership and transformation, especially in relation to the Ethiopian experience. There is a fairly broad consensus that developing countries are best served by a strong, capable state that provides visionary leadership, manages resources, and directs development. However, such a country does not have to be ruled by a single leader for decades, provided transfers of power do not undermine the features of a capable state.

Most African countries are still trying to figure out the right mix of governance that yields the most democratic and economic returns. Regardless of where a country settles, the main point for transformation is that it requires discipline and the implementation of a consistent vision by policymakers committed to achieving that vision. The gains are not linear, and the political will must be strong enough to weather the ups and downs. Under Meles, Ethiopia's particular system proved effective, but that does not mean it is right in every circumstance—a point Meles also believed.

In his unpublished thesis, 'African Development: Dead Ends and New Beginnings', he said that every country was unique and needed to shape its own model, arguing for 'more political space for experimentation in development policy than has been the case so far in Africa' (Meles Zenawi in De Waal 2012). In his view, African countries could create such space through good leadership, strong and coordinated institutions, and adherence to a consistent vision—the process by which they do so being less important than the commitment to see it through.

50.4 Conclusion

The opening of this chapter noted that in 1999 there were strong tailwinds for new approaches to development in Africa, with Ethiopia already out in front. That is the case again. Economic transformation is now the leading paradigm for development, while the shift that Meles advocated—away from donor-driven strategies in favour of local ownership and more equitable development partnerships—has increasingly come to pass. However, the composition of development partners—which now includes emerging economies such as China, Brazil, South Korea, and other East Asian countries, among others—and the source of development financing to drive economic transformation have undergone a radical change amid an uncertain global political landscape. Perhaps the most lasting change is a shift towards the private sector. This is where the Ethiopian experience once more proves instructive.

Nearly all development stakeholders agree that the private sector must jointly drive economic development in Africa, a position that Ethiopia took early on and even more aggressively with its first Growth and Transformation Plan in 2011. In the years since, the global community has rallied behind private sector-led development, with the United Nations, World Bank, and many bilateral development agencies putting private finance front and centre. Global initiatives such as Finance for Development, an outcome of the July 2015 Third International Conference on Financing for Development in Addis Ababa, support a range of programmes to enhance investment flows into developing countries. However, the scope of Ethiopia's commitment to promote private-sector solutions—and its ability to create the environment for successful external investment—provides many lessons for financing transformation.

FDI to Ethiopia increased from US$135 million at the beginning of the century to nearly US$4 billion in 2016, according to the World Bank's World Development Indicators.[5] FDI reached US$4.17 billion in 2017, the highest for a low-income country in Africa, creating approximately 16,000 jobs, according to the Ethiopian Investment Commission.[6] Investors from China, India, and the Netherlands are at the forefront of the government's engagement in textiles, manufacturing, and horticulture, while

[5] Retrieved 22 December 2017.

[6] This is according to the Ethiopia Investment Commission's investment guide to Ethiopia in 2017.

Ethiopia's booming industrial parks are attracting more and more FDI and establishing Ethiopia as the manufacturing hub its development plans and political leaders have envisioned (Tiwari 2015).

Investors targeting Ethiopia have praised its stability, a macroeconomic environment conducive to business, and well-developed infrastructure—an emerging comparative advantage, given the infrastructure gap that threatens the continent's future growth, not to mention transformation. Across Africa, modern rail transport is almost non-existent, few ports have been built in the past fifty years, and unpaved highways are still dotted across much of Africa. Yet a modern rail service does exist in Ethiopia, including the 656km Addis Ababa–Djibouti electric railway, which began commercial operations in 2018. Ethiopia prioritized manufacturing-related transport to ensure goods get to market—at home and abroad. Ethiopia placed infrastructure investment at the core of its development paradigm, and its ripple effect across the economy is undeniable.

The uniqueness of the Ethiopian model is that natural resources extraction or raw commodities do not drive its economic growth. In fact, its largest export product has decreased from 53 per cent of total exports in 1995 to 43 per cent in 2005 to only 17 per cent in 2015 (Observatory of Economic Complexity, MIT Media Lab). On the contrary, the rise of Ethiopian GDP over the last decade results from public capital investment (including roads, dams, power plants, and housing) and from productivity growth in key economic sectors, particularly agriculture and manufacturing (Moller and Wacker 2017; Fantini 2013). Additionally, Ethiopia has attracted firms that have improved trade logistics and increased knowledge and skills—in turn, making the firms more competitive and allowing them to move into regional and global value chains.

African countries are gradually buying into the idea of carving their own development path towards sustained economic growth, just as Ethiopia did. They must begin, of course, by crafting and implementing a robust strategy to drive economic transformation. There is also a growing belief among African leaders, the private sector, and government agencies that together they can speed up the economic transformation process, and some are taking leading roles here.

While Ethiopia continues to face significant challenges, there are real lessons to be learned from the Ethiopian experience. Whether they relate to effective strategy development, dedicated capacity development or political leadership, they all are ingredients for growth and transformation. African countries are gradually buying into the idea of carving out their own development path towards sustained economic growth, just as Ethiopia did. As they do, each nation will need to adapt Ethiopia's lessons to their own circumstances—economic, social, and political. If they do, transformation can become an even more immediate possibility.

References

African Center for Economic Transformation (2014). 'African Transformation Report 2014: Growth with Depth', New York.

African Development Bank (2018). 'African Economic Outlook 2018', Abidjan.

ATA (2017). 'Agricultural Transformation Agenda: Annual Report 2016–2017', Agricultural Transformation Agency, Ethiopia.

Berhanu, Kassahun (2013). 'CAADP Ethiopia: A New Start?' *Futures Agricultures* 60: 1–28.

Brautigam, Deborah, Margaret McMillan, and Xiaoyang Tang (2013). PEDL Research Note: 'The Role of Foreign Investment in Ethiopia's Leather Value Chain.' Centre for Economic Policy Research (CEPR). https://www.gov.uk/dfid-research-outputs/pedl-research-note-the-role-of-foreign-investment-in-ethiopia-s-leather-value-chain

De Waal, Alex (2012). 'The Theory and Practice of Meles Zenawi', *African Affairs* 112 (446): 148–55.

EIC (2017). 'Ethiopia—A Preferred Investment Destination in Africa', Ethiopia Investment Commission. http://www.investethiopia.gov.et/images/pdf/An%20Investment%20Guide%20to%20Ethiopia,%202017.pdf

Ethiopia Ministry of Finance and Economic Development (2010). 'Growth and Transformation Plan (GTP) 2010/11–2014/15', Addis Ababa.

Ethiopia National Planning Commission (2016). 'Growth and Transformation Plan II', Addis Ababa.

Fantini, Emanuele (2013). 'Developmental State, Economic Transformation and Social Diversification in Ethiopia'. https://www.ispionline.it/it/pubblicazione/developmental-state-economic-transformation-and-social-diversification-ethiopia-7650

Lewis, W. Arthur (1954). 'Economic Development with Unlimited Supplies of Labor', *The Manchester School* 22 (2): 139–91.

Mihretu, Mamo and Eyob Tekalign Tolina (2015). 'ETHIOPIA: Ethiopian Public Private Consultative Forum (EPPCF).' Presented at the Public-Private Dialogue 2015 Workshop, Copenhagen, 10–13 March 2015. http://www.publicprivatedialogue.org/workshop%202015/2015%20-%20Public%20Private%20Dialogue%20in%20Ethiopia.pdf

Moller, Lars Christian and Konstantin M. Wacker (2017). 'Explaining Ethiopia's Growth Acceleration: The Role of Infrastructure and Macroeconomic Policy', *World Development* 96: 198–215.

Pritchett, Lant, Kunal Sen, Sabyasachi Kar, and Selim Raihan (2016). 'Trillions Gained and Lost: Estimating the Magnitude of Growth Episodes', *Economic Modelling* 55: 275–91.

Seid, Yared, Alemayehu Seyoum Taffesse, and Seid Nuru Ali (2016). Ethiopia: An Agrarian Economy in Transition', WIDER Working Paper No. 2015/154, Helsinki.

Tafirenyika, Masimba (2015). 'Ethiopia: Fixing Agriculture', *Africa Renewal*, United Nations Department of Public Information, New York.

Teka, Henok Gebremedhin (2014). 'Determinants and Impediments of FDI Inflows in Ethiopia: A Firm-Level Investigation', MPRA Paper No. 55955, Munich Personal RePEc Archive, Catholic University of the Sacred Heart, posted 20 May 2014. http://mpra.ub.uni-muenchen.de/55955/

Tiwari, Prateeksha (2015). 'Indian and Chinese FDI in Ethiopia: Nature, Impact, and Challenges', *Delhi University Journal of Undergraduate Research and Innovation* 1 (3): 124–43.

Warwick, Mara K. (2017). 'Philippines 2021: Steering towards the Golden Age of Infrastructure', *Manila Times* Sixth Business Forum.

World Bank (2018). *Doing Business 2018: Reforming to Create Jobs* (Washington, DC: World Bank).

Index